Russell G. Schuh
UCLA
Dept of Linguistics

Yale Language Series

# Editorial Staff

*Editor in Chief*
Roxana Ma Newman

*Editor for Hausa Grammatical Analysis*
Paul Newman

*Assistant Editors*
Abdullahi Bature
Abdoulaye Idi
Ismail Junaidu
Sammani Sani

*Computerization*
Daya Atapattu
Emma Pease

# An English-Hausa Dictionary

Roxana Ma Newman

Yale University Press   New Haven & London

Printed in the United States of America by
Hamilton Printing Co., Castleton, New York.

Library of Congress catalog card number: 89–51452
International standard book number: 0–300–04702–9

The paper in this book meets the guidelines for permanence and
durability of the Committee on Production Guidelines for Book
Longevity of the Council on Library Resources.

10 9 8 7 6 5 4 3 2 1

# Contents

# ACKNOWLEDGMENTS

This dictionary was begun in 1985 as a research project of Indiana University's African Studies Program under a grant from the U.S. Department of Education, Grant No. G0085-40637, whose support is gratefully acknowledged. The project was completed at Stanford University, where the compiler was a National Science Foundation visiting professor in the Department of Linguistics.

The preparation of this dictionary has involved the combined interests and efforts of many individuals. I am most especially indebted to Ismail Junaidu and Sammani Sani, whose unfailing patience and dedication in elucidating the complexities of Hausa lexicon and discourse have contributed to the richness of the dictionary. I am equally grateful to Abdullahi Bature and Abdoulaye Idi, whose critical insights and knowledge helped greatly to improve the final version of the dictionary. My appreciation extends to colleagues who were consulted at various stages of the project, in particular Neil Skinner, Russell Schuh, Philip Jaggar, Edward Gates, and Roger Blench. I am also grateful to Connie Stephens of the Voice of America and to Barry Burgess of the BBC for their help in providing Hausa technical terminology. All these people are of course blameless for any errors which may remain in the final version.

I would like to thank the many people whose enthusiasm, friendship, and hospitality during a field trip to Nigeria and Niger were so vital to the success of the project. In Kano, Nigeria, I express my gratitude to the Vice-Chancellor of Bayero University, Professor Dandatti Abdulkadir, who provided generous logistic support, and to Dr. Abba Rufa'i, Director of the Centre for the Study of Nigerian Languages, for use of the Centre's facilities and staff. I also thank Mustapha Ahmad, Dan Lami Bala, and Abdullahi Fagge, as well as Mohammed Sarki, for valuable assistance and materials. In Niamey, Niger, thanks are due to Dr. Bachir Attouman of the University of Niamey and Abdou Mijinguini of INDRAP for their participation and interest, and to Ekkehard Wolff, visiting professor at the university, whose hospitality and advice on practical and linguistic matters were greatly appreciated.

At Indiana University, I am extremely grateful to Patrick O'Meara, Director of the African Studies Program, whose friendship and encouragement throughout have been so important, and to the program administrator, Jude Wilkinson, for her help and good cheer. I also thank the Department of Linguistics for providing office space, and Robert Port for his time and interest in getting the dictionary computerized. I especially acknowledge my debt to the Department of Computer Science for the use of their VAX computer, and to Daya Atapattu for designing innovative programs to manipulate the files. Technical assistance was also provided by Aaron Shryock, Kemp Williams, Frank Wright, and particularly William Anderson.

At Stanford University, I am grateful to the Department of Linguistics, especially its chairman, William Leben, and the Center for the Study of Language and Information for providing such a stimulating and supportive environment in which to work. I am also indebted to Emma Pease of CSLI, whose expertise in the T$_{\mathrm{E}}$X typesetting system has made possible the final production of the dictionary. Finally, I thank Ellen Graham of Yale University Press for her assistance in seeing this book into press.

R. M. N.

## ABBREVIATIONS and SYMBOLS

| | | | |
|---|---|---|---|
| *abbr* | abbreviation | *interrog* | interrogative |
| *abstr.* | abstract | *Law* | Law |
| *adj* | adjective | *lit.* | literal |
| *addr.* | address, addressing | *Lit.* | Literature |
| *admin.* | administration, administrative | *L* | low tone |
| *adv* | adverb | *m* | masculine |
| *affirm.* | affirmative | *Med.* | Medicine |
| *Agri.* | Agriculture | *Mil.* | Military |
| *ano.* | another | *misc* | miscellaneous |
| *approx.* | approximate(ly) | *Mus.* | Music |
| *art* | article | *n* | noun |
| *attrib.* | attributive | *neg.* | negative |
| *aux* | auxiliary | *obj* | object |
| *Br.* | British English | *oft.* | often |
| *ca.* | circa | *p, pl* | plural |
| *cf.* | compare | *partic.* | particular |
| *cl.* | clause | *pejor.* | pejorative |
| *compar.* | comparative | *phr.* | phrase |
| *complet.* | completive | *plurac.* | pluractional |
| *conj* | conjunction | *Pol.* | Politics |
| *constr.* | construction | *poss.* | possessive |
| *contin.* | continuous | *prec.* | preceding |
| *def* | definite | *pred.* | predicate, predicative |
| *det* | determiner | *prep* | preposition |
| *dimin.* | diminutive | *prev.* | previous(ly) |
| *dir obj* | direct object | *pro* | pronoun |
| *Econ.* | Economics | *psn.* | person |
| *Educ.* | Education | *qnt* | quantifier |
| *e.g.* | for example | *re.* | regarding |
| *emphat.* | emphatic | *ref.* | reference, referring |
| *esp.* | especially | *rel.* | relative |
| *etc.* | et cetera | *Relig.* | Religion |
| *euphem.* | euphemism | *sent.* | sentence |
| *expr.* | express, expressed, expression | *so.* | someone |
| | | *Sport* | Sports |
| *explet.* | expletive | *sth.* | something |
| *f* | feminine | *subj* | subject |
| *F* | falling tone | *subjunct.* | subjunctive |
| *fig.* | figurative | *subord.* | subordinate |
| *fml.* | formal | *syll.* | syllable |
| *fut.* | future | *tradit.* | traditional |
| *gen'l* | general | *usu.* | usually |
| *Gram.* | Grammar | *v* | verb |
| *habit.* | habitual | *var.* | various, variety |
| *H* | high tone | *vbl.* | verbal |
| *hon.* | honorific | *vi* | intransitive verb |
| *idph* | ideophone | *viz.* | namely |
| *i.e.* | that is | *vt* | transitive verb |
| *impers.* | impersonal | *vulg.* | vulgar |
| *incl.* | including | ʍ. | ʍani (someone) |
| *indir obj* | indirect object | ʍ.a. | ʍani àbù (something) |
| | | *West.* | Western |

| | |
|---|---|
| ~ | replaces headword in examples and idioms |
| = | links alternative and equivalent Hausa translations in examples |
| X,Y | indicates formulae which stand for anything in subentries or examples |
| [F] | indicates that the following word is used in francophone Hausaland |

# User's Guide to the Dictionary

## 1 Introduction

This is a practical dictionary designed for the English-speaking user who wishes to acquire an active control of the modern vocabulary and structure of the Hausa language.[1] The vocabulary covers English words which the average user is likely to want to express in speaking or writing Hausa. Many of the entries are accompanied by natural, conversational phrases and sentences considered useful in everyday communicative situations. The translations are stylistically matched as far as possible. While the dictionary entries are fairly well differentiated with regard to meaning and grammatical usage, it is assumed that the user already has a grasp of the fundamentals of Hausa grammar.[2] Dictionary appendices include pronoun paradigms, a guide to the pronunciation of Hausa personal names, a pronouncing gazetteer, an index of Nigerian and international organizations, and a description of the currencies of Nigeria and Niger.

The principles and conventions adopted in compiling the dictionary are explained below. Remarks relevant to the English side of the dictionary are presented in §2, followed by those relevant to the Hausa side in §3.

## 2 Head Entries

### 2.1 Alphabetization and Cross References

All English headwords, single words as well as hyphenated and non-hyphenated compounds, are printed in **boldface** type. Compounds are alphabetized as if they were one word, e.g. **air terminal** comes between **airs** and **aisle**. Words that are spelled alike but are unrelated in meaning are entered as separate headwords marked by superscript numbers, e.g. **defect**[1] (blemish) and **defect**[2] (to flee). Common abbreviations, like **etc.**, are found in normal alphabetical order. Spelling variants are listed as separate entries and cross-referenced to the main entry with the notation *see* in italic typeface. Cross references are sometimes used to refer to a fuller account under another headword.

---

[1] For a practical Hausa to English dictionary, see P. Newman and R. M. Newman, *Modern Hausa-English Dictionary*. Ibadan & Zaria: University Press Nigeria, 1977.

[2] A generally available introduction to Hausa grammar is C. H. Kraft and A. H. M. Kirk-Greene, *Hausa*, Teach Yourself Books. London: The English Universities Press, 1973.

## 2.2   Vocabulary Selection and Field Labels

The English headwords cover basic vocabulary as well as common technical terms drawn from subject fields such as medicine, politics, and religion. Extensive treatment has been given to basic words (especially verbs and function words) which are important in everyday language use. Some common English words do not have true lexical equivalents in Hausa; such words are illustrated for a few likely contexts, followed by functionally equivalent translations in Hausa. To save space and reduce redundancy, many productively formed word classes have not been included, such as abstract nouns (e.g. **heaviness**) and adverbs derived regularly from adjectives (e.g. **angrily**). Similarly, certain nouns related to verbs (e.g. **hypothesis** and **hypothesize**) are not given as separate headwords when it is clear that the Hausa translation of the verb consists of the general verb "do" plus that noun.

Field labels, e.g. *Mil., Relig.*, are used to identify those senses of a word which are specifically restricted in meaning to particular subject fields. Field labels begin with a capital letter and are indicated in *italic* typeface in parentheses (see *Abbreviations*).

## 2.3   Grammatical Categories

All English headwords are identified by traditional part-of-speech labels in *italic* type (see *Abbreviations*). Many English words belong to more than one part of speech or word class without any change in spelling; each such word class is treated separately as a numbered subentry within the main entry. For example, the headword **call** has two subentries, marked **1.** *v*, where it is treated as a verb, followed by **2.** *n*, where it is treated as a noun.

Most English verbs are identified simply as *v*. When it is necessary to separate the transitive from the intransitive uses of a verb, they are presented as separate subentries marked by **1.** *vt* and **2.** *vi* respectively. Passive/stative forms of verbs, i.e. those formed with **be** + a past participle, e.g. **bloated, be** *v* or **entangled, be(come)** *v*, are entered as main entries when they are the most commonly used forms of those verbs.

## 2.4   Differences in Meaning and Order of Presentation

When the English headword has more than one distinct meaning, each meaning is separated from the others and identified within the entry as a lettered subdivision marked by **boldface** letters **a, b, c**.... Meaning indicators or explanations are noted in *italic* type enclosed in parentheses. For example, **hard** as an adjective has two distinct senses, **a.** *(not soft)* and **b.** *(difficult)*. Meaning indicators are of various kinds. Many are synonymous with the headword. Some describe a typical subject or object that a verb may take. Others provide grammatical information such as *used only in the negative*.

In addition to divisions based on differences in meaning, some divisions are necessary because a single English headword will have several equivalents in Hausa. Divisions are also used to organize the entry by grammatical or syntactic features. For example, many English verbs combine with various adverbs or prepositions to form what are known as "phrasal verbs". Such verb combinations are generally grouped together as a separate division labelled *various v + adv/prep uses* and alphabetized according to the second element of the phrase. Thus the entry for the verb **take** includes a subsection where "take apart, take back, take over...take up" can be found.

In general within the entry, the order of presentation of the divisions and their accompanying examples proceeds from the more general meanings and uses to the more specific, ending with idiomatic or figurative expressions.

## 2.5  Examples of Use

The dictionary contains numerous examples in the form of phrases and full sentences to illustrate the meanings and use of the Hausa equivalents. Examples are preceded by a colon. In the examples, the headword is represented by the swung dash ~. If, however, a differently spelled inflected form of the headword is used, it is written out in full. When the headword is a phrasal verb, the dash only represents the verb itself. When the headword is any other kind of compound, the dash stands for the entire compound.

Examples in English are followed directly by their corresponding Hausa translations. The Hausa examples are intended to illustrate natural ways of expressing the Hausa equivalents of the English examples; they are not meant to be direct, literal translations. In cases where a range of words can combine with the headword in both English and Hausa, they may be listed as a sequence separated by commas. To illustrate, "seek advice, office, the truth" is followed by parallel translations in Hausa, nềmi shāwarằ, zầɓē, gàskiyā.

Sometimes several translations are offered for one English phrase to illustrate differences in Hausa phraseology; these alternatives are linked by the = sign, e.g. "I have a headache" inằ cĪwòn kāi = cĪwòn kāi yanằ dāmŭnā. Alternative phrases are generally provided in cases where Hausa synonyms for the English headword require different structural patterns, e.g. **sad** *adj:* (mài) baƙin cikĪ, (mài) ɓàcìn râi: he is sad yanằ baƙin cikĪ = rânsà yā ɓàcì.

## 2.6  Usage Labels

The style of language aimed at in this dictionary is "conversational", i.e. language considered appropriate for normal everyday use. A few usage labels, however, are employed in order to alert the reader that certain Hausa words or phrases may be restricted to certain social contexts or situations. These are indicated in *italics*.

> *(euphem.)* shows that the following word or phrase is a euphemism and considered the polite way to refer to the concept in question;
> *(fml.)* shows that the following word is a formal term or used in a formal context;
> *(pejor.)* shows that the following word or phrase has pejorative connotations;
> *(vulg.)* shows that the following word or phrase is considered vulgar and should not be used in normal "polite" society.

## 2.7 Idiomatic Expressions

The examples include many idiomatic expressions in English (such as "throw light on sth.," "have a narrow escape," "take to one's heels") with their Hausa counterparts. Where the idiomatic expressions are particularly figurative or metaphorical, they are marked by *(fig.)* in parentheses. Sometimes a non-idiomatic English expression is matched by an idiomatic Hausa one, in which case the notation *(fig.)* is placed between the English and the Hausa, e.g. "it was not worth the effort" *(fig.)* kwalliyā bà tà biyā kuɗin sàbulū ba.

# 3   Hausa Entries

This section describes the various conventions and features used in the dictionary to represent the phonological, lexical, and syntactic structures of Hausa.

## 3.1   Transcription

All Hausa words in the dictionary are printed in a distinct `courier` typeface, e.g. dōkì "horse". The transcription system is standard Hausa orthography with the addition of diacritics for the rolled ř and for tone and vowel length.

### 3.1.1   Alphabet

The Hausa alphabet consists of the following letters: ', a, b, ɓ, c, d, ɗ, e, f, g, h, i, j, k, ƙ, l, m, n, o, (p), r, ř, s, t, ts, u, w, y, 'y, z. The letter ' represents the glottal stop. The letters ɓ, ɗ, ƙ, known as "hooked" letters, are glottalized consonants that are distinct from normal b, d, k. The digraphs ts and 'y represent glottalized s and y respectively. The two r consonants in Hausa are distinguished as follows: the unmarked r is the flap and ř with a tilde over it is the roll or trill. Capital R in proper names is always a roll and therefore not marked with the tilde. The orthographic letter f has a wide range of pronunciations ([f], [p], [h], [hw]), depending on dialect and its position in the word. The (p), as distinct from f, is found in many recent loanwords from English and French (see §3.2.2 for discussion).

### 3.1.2   Consonant Changes

A number of Hausa consonants regularly undergo changes when they precede certain vowels. Thus words with t, d, s, z, w, for instance, may have inflected or derived forms with c, j, sh, j, y, respectively, when these precede the vowels i/ī or e/ē. For example, the verb sātā "steal" has the following forms:

| | |
|---|---|
| he stole | yā yi sātà |
| he stole a goat | yā sàci àkuyà |
| he stole it | yā sācē tà |
| he stole a goat from me | yā sācè minì àkuyà |

Similarly, the noun cìyāwà "grass" has a plural form cìyàyī, which results from the addition of the plural suffix -ī. It is particularly important to keep such consonant changes in mind when inflecting verb stems, forming noun plurals or feminines of nouns and adjectives, or deriving adjectival past participles and stative adverbs from verb stems.

### 3.1.3   Tone and Vowel Length

All Hausa words are marked for tone (H(igh), L(ow), and F(alling)) and vowel length (short vs. long). These features are marked by the following diacritics appearing above the vowels:

- A grave accent over a vowel indicates that it has L tone, e.g. àbù "thing". A circumflex accent over a vowel indicates that it has F tone, e.g. yâmma "west". H tone is not marked, e.g. maza "quickly".

- A long vowel with L or H tone is marked by a macron over the vowel, e.g. dōkì "horse". Long vowels never occur in syllables ending in a consonant. Vowels in open syllables which have F tone are all long; they are marked by the circumflex, e.g. yârā "children". Short vowels are unmarked.

## 3.2   Translation Equivalents

Hausa synonyms presented as equivalents of an English headword are separated by a comma; near synonyms, those requiring meaning indicators, are either separated by a semicolon or have their own subdivisions. When a polysemous English word does not have a Hausa equivalent for all of its distinct meanings, the meaning indicator shows which sense of the English word is being translated.

Sometimes an English headword has no matching lexical equivalent in Hausa. In such cases, only examples of use are given directly after the colon, e.g. **armed** *adj:* "he is armed" yanà rìƙe dà màkàmai; "commit armed robbery" yi fashì dà màkàmai.

### 3.2.1   Variant Forms

Some Hausa words have commonly used contractions, variants, or alternative pronunciations. These variants are separated by a slash, e.g. lassàftā / lissàfā "count up". Tonal variants are generally not given except with a very few common, high frequency words e.g. gàskiyā / gaskiyā ([LHH/HHH]) "truth".

### 3.2.2   Hausa in Niger

The dictionary is based on the Standard Hausa dialect of Nigeria. In order to make this book more accessible to users in Niger, however, regional differences between Nigeria and Niger with respect to loanwords are indicated. Where Nigerian Hausa has a loanword from English, Niger Hausa will often use a French loanword or a native Hausa word or phrase. These distinctively Niger usages are marked with [F] preceding them, e.g. fākitì, cf. [F] fàkê "pack, packet", or sêf, cf. [F] asūsù "safe (for valuables)". Some of these recent [F] words are spelled with p, e.g. yi fāsìn, cf. [F] yi pàsê "pass (an examination)" since they are not pronounced with h or hw, the normal Niger variant of standard Hausa f. The user is cautioned, however, that the acceptability and pronunciation of French loanwords in Hausaland is subject to fluctuation, given their relatively recent introduction into the language. This variability exists to a much lesser extent with older English loanwords in Nigeria.

## 3.3  Grammatical Classes

Hausa translation equivalents are generally followed by their part of speech code in *italics* (see *Abbreviations*).

### 3.3.1  Nouns

GRAMMATICAL GENDER. Nouns with intrinsic gender are marked $m$ for masculine or $f$ for feminine. There is no gender distinction in the plural. Some nouns, particularly animate nouns, have common gender, i.e. can be either masculine or feminine without any change in form. This includes noun compounds formed with the particle mài "one who". All these are marked simply as $n$, e.g. kằkā $n$ "grandparent", likità $n$ "doctor", mài īkɔ̀ $n$ "ruler". A few nouns may be either masculine or feminine, depending on the dialect; these are marked $m/f$, e.g. sàndā $m/f$ "stick".

Most animate nouns have distinct masculine and feminine forms. When the feminine form is derived in a fully regular manner from the masculine, only the masculine is given as the Hausa headword equivalent. The regular feminine formations include the following:

a. feminines formed by changing the final vowel to -ā, e.g. "student" ɗālībā $f$, cf. ɗālībī $m$

b. feminines formed by the addition of a suffix -iyā, e.g. "deaf-mute" bēbiyā $f$, cf. bēbē $m$

c. feminines of ma- agentive nouns, e.g. "farmer" manɔ̄mìyā $f$, cf. manɔ̀mī $m$

d. feminines of bà- ethnonymics, e.g. "Arab" bàlār̃abìyā $f$, cf. bàlār̃abè $m$

e. feminines of phrasal agentive nouns formed by substituting 'yar̃ for ɗan, e.g. "genius" 'yar̃ baiwā $f$, cf. ɗan baiwā $m$

Other feminine forms are spelled out in full, e.g. "leper" kuturwā $f$, cf. kuturū $m$, "blind woman" màkauniyā $f$, cf. màkāhɔ̀ $m$.

PLURALITY. Nouns which are intrinsically plural are marked $p$. Elsewhere, plurals of nouns (and adjectives) are organized into regular plural classes whose codes are enclosed in angle brackets <> immediately following the gender code of the noun, e.g. gidā $m$ <aCe> "house". These codes are explained below. Although Hausa nouns often have many plural forms, only one widely used form is given in the dictionary. In a few cases, very common alternative forms may be indicated, e.g. kwānɔ̀ $m$ <uka, oCi> "enamelware". Irregular or infrequent plural types are spelled out in full, e.g. yārɔ̀ $m$ <yārā> "boy", gàr̃mā $f$ <gar̃ɛ̀manī> "hoe". Regular plural formations consist of an affix and/or reduplication, indicated by a superscript number [2], plus an associated tone pattern, indicated here by capital letters H, L, F enclosed in square brackets [ ]. The following two rules apply when inflecting nouns for plurality:

- The final vowel of the singular stem is dropped when a suffix is added;

- The tones of the plural tone pattern replace the singular tone pattern and are distributed over the plural form from right to left.

The plural codes below are grouped together in roughly alphabetical order and illustrated with a typical singular/plural noun of that class.

<aye> = -āyē [HLH], e.g. "hare" zōmō/zōmằyē

<aCe> = ā + C (= a copy of the preceding consonant) + ē [HLH], e.g. "place" wurī/wurằrē

<a-e> = ā + 3rd consonant of the stem + ē [HLH], e.g. "stream" gulbī/gulằbē

<a-a> = ā + 3rd consonant of the stem + ā [HLH], e.g. "saddle" sir̃dì/sir̃ằdā

<a-u> = ā + 3rd consonant of the stem + ū [HLH], e.g. "grove" kurmì/kurằmū

<ai> = -ai [LH], e.g. "teacher" mālàm/mằlàmai (In northwest dialects, the final consonant is often doubled, e.g. mằlàmmai.)

<Cai> = -ai with doubling of the stem-final consonant [LH], e.g. "high ground" tudũ/tùddai

<a..ai> = stem + ā + stem + ai [LH], e.g. "wing" fiffikḕ/fìkằfìkai

<aki> = -akī [LH], e.g. "farm" gōnā/gònàkī

<aki²> = -akī with partial reduplication [HLHH], e.g. "load" kāyā/kāyàyyakī

<anni> = -annī [LH], e.g. "month" watằ/wàtànnī

<awa> = -āwā [H or LH] plural suffix on ethnonymics, e.g. "Yoruba person" Bàyar̃abḕ/Yar̃abāwā

<Ca> = stem + C (= a copy of the preceding consonant) + ā [FH], e.g. "stain" tabǒ/tábbā; if the stem vowel is either ē or ō, it changes to a in the plural, e.g. "ring" zōbḕ/zábbā

<e²> = -e with full reduplication [LH-LH], e.g. "beating" bùge-bùge

<i> = -ī [LH], e.g. "star" tàurārǒ/tàurằrī

<oCi> = ō + C (= a copy of the preceding consonant) + ī [H], e.g. "window" tāgằ/tāgōgī

<u> = -ū [LH], e.g. "chair" kujḕrā/kùjḕrū

<u²> = -ū with partial reduplication [LH], e.g. "talk" màganằ/màgàngànū

<uka> = -ukā [HL], e.g. "lane" lāyì/lāyukằ

<uka²> = -ukā with partial reduplication [HL], e.g. "fault" lâifī/laifuffukằ

&lt;una&gt; = -unā [HL], e.g. "gown" rỉgā/rīgunầ

&lt;Cuna&gt; = -unā with doubling of the stem-final consonant [HL], e.g. "belly" cikỉ/cikkunầ

&lt;una$^2$&gt; = -unā with partial reduplication [HL], e.g. "bow" bàkā/bakunkunầ

&lt;uwa&gt; = -uwā [HL], e.g. "ear" kûnnē/kunnuwầ

&lt;uwa$^2$&gt; = -uwā with partial reduplication [HL], e.g. "town" gàrī/garūruwầ

&lt;u-a&gt; = u + 3rd consonant of the stem + ā [HL], e.g. "spoon" cōkàlī/cōkulầ; the 3rd consonant of the stem is doubled when the initial syllable of the stem contains a short vowel, e.g. "sword" takồbī/takubbầ

&lt;u-a$^2$&gt; = u + 3rd consonant of the stem + ā with partial reduplication [HL], e.g. "remedy" māgànī/māgungunầ

&lt;x$^2$&gt; = full reduplication, e.g. "clerk" àkầwu/àkầwu-àkầwu

The plurals of nouns belonging to regular derivational classes are not indicated. These classes include:

a. plurals of ma- instrumental nouns formed with the plural suffix &lt;ai&gt;, e.g. "brushes" màgồgai, cf. magồgī *m*

b. plurals of ma- agentive nouns formed with the plural suffix -ā [HLH], e.g. "farmers" manồmā, cf. manồmī *m*

c. plurals of bà- ethnonymics formed with the ethnonymic plural suffix &lt;awa&gt;, e.g. "Arabs" lāřabāwā, cf. bàlāřabề *m*

d. plurals of ɗan phrasal agentive nouns formed by substituting 'yan for ɗan, e.g. "geniuses" 'yan baiwā, cf. ɗan baiwā *m*

e. plurals of mài expressions formed by substituting the corresponding plural particle mằsu, e.g. "rulers" mằsu īkồ, cf. mài īkồ *n*

f. plurals of maràs expressions formed by substituting the corresponding plural particle maràsā, e.g. "the unemployed" maràsā aikỉ, cf. maràs aikỉ *m*

Most mass nouns as well as many count nouns do not have a plural form distinct from the singular. Compound nouns are not generally marked for plurality. Many recent English and French loanwords do not have corresponding plural forms.

## 3.3.2  Adjectives

Hausa has only a small number of "true" adjectives; thus English adjectives are translated by a variety of Hausa constructions. Certain English adjectives used predicatively are best translated by Hausa intransitive verbs, as in "be confident" haƙī̀ƙàncē *v*, "be content" gàmsu *v*, "be bloated" kùmburà *v*. The various adjectival constructions are as follows.

a.  a small basic set of simple adjectives, e.g. "small" ƙàramī *m*, ƙàramā *f* <ƙanānà̰>; "blue" shūɗḭ̀ *m*, shūɗìyā *f* <Ca>

b.  derived agential adjectives with ma-, e.g. "cruel" maƙḕtàcī *m* maƙḕtacìyā *f* <maƙḕtàtā>

c.  derived ethnonymic adjectives with bà-, e.g. "left-handed" bàhagò̰ *m*, bàhagùwā *f* <ai>

d.  derived adjectival past participles, e.g. "cooked" dàfaffē *m*, dàfaffiyā *f* <u>; "skilled" gò̰gaggē *m*, gò̰gaggiyā *f* <u>

e.  ideophonic adjectives with -ēCḛ̀, e.g. "huge" mākēkḛ̀ *m*, mākēkìyā *f* <mākā-màkà̰>

f.  phrasal adjectives formed with mài, e.g. "hot" (mài) zāfī <mà̰su zāfī>; "reliable" mài amincḭ̀ <mà̰su amincḭ̀>

g.  phrasal adjectives formed with maràs, e.g. "unpleasant" maràs dāɗī <maràsā dāɗī>; "aimless" maràs būrḭ̀ <maràsā būrḭ̀>

h.  derived intensive adjectives of sensory quality, e.g. "very hot" zàzzāfā <zāfāfā>

i.  phrasal adjectives formed with the genitive markers na *m/p*, ta *f* (or their reduced forms n/ř), e.g. "true" na/ta gàskiyā <na gàskiyā>; "forced" na/ta dōlè <na dōlè>

GENDER AGREEMENT. All adjectives except types [f, g, h, i] have corresponding feminines whose forms are derived from the masculine in the same way as feminine nouns. In providing the Hausa equivalents of adjectives, only the masculine form is given and it is coded simply as *adj*. Irregular feminine forms are given in full. In the illustrative phrases and examples, the appropriately inflected feminine forms of adjectives are always provided.

PLURALITY. Plurals of adjectives use the same plural classes as nouns. Type [a] adjective plurals are marked individually in the dictionary, either by a plural class code or, in the case of irregular plurals, by writing them out in full. The remaining types have predictable plurals and are therefore not marked. In the illustrative examples, the appropriately inflected plural forms of adjectives are always provided.

PHRASAL ADJECTIVES WITH mài, maràs, AND na/ta. A great many English adjectives are translated by a Hausa phrase formed with mài, which means "having *x*" where *x* is usually an abstract noun, e.g. "deep" (mài) zurfī (cf. "depth" zurfī). In the Hausa translation of the English headwords, the gender of the abstract noun is always marked, e.g. "creative" mài hikimà̰ *f*, "useless" maràs àmfānī *m*. Phrasal adjectives with mài are given with mài in parentheses to show that it is used in some but not all contexts, e.g. "the well is deep" rījìyā tanà̰ dà zurfī, cf. "a deep well" rījìyā mài zurfī. The negative counterpart of mài is maràs³ "not having *x*", e.g. "shallow" maràs zurfī, as in "a shallow hole" rāmḭ̀ maràs zurfī. In some contexts, an English adjective might not be translated with a maràs phrase but by a negative sentence instead, e.g. "the hole is shallow" rāmḭ̀ bā shi dà zurfī.

---

³This is always transcribed maràs but it is commonly pronounced marà̰ř or marà̰.

Some English adjectives are translated by Hausa phrasal adjectives formed with the genitive markers **na** *m/p* and **ta** *f* (or their reduced forms n/r̃) followed by an abstract noun marked for gender, e.g. "true, real" **na gàskiyā** *f*, "modern" **na zāmànī** *m*. Such Hausa adjectives are only given with the masculine genitive **na**. Whether **na** or **ta** is used will depend on the gender and number of the noun being modified, e.g. "a true story" **làbār̃in gàskiyā**, "a true statement" **màganàr̃ gàskiyā**, "true reports" **r̃àhòtànnin gàskiyā**.

### 3.3.3  Pronouns

Hausa personal pronouns fall into a number of distinct sets depending on their grammatical function. Complete sets of Hausa pronouns are presented in APPENDIX A.

### 3.3.4  Determiners

English determiners (demonstratives, interrogative pronouns, quantifiers) are expressed in Hausa sometimes by separate words and sometimes by suffixes. Whenever the forms are inflected for gender and/or plurality, they are so marked.

### 3.3.5  Verbs

VERB GRADES. Hausa verbs are classified into different classes known as "grades", some of which are basic and some of which are derived (i.e. they add a semantic nuance to the core meaning of the verb). The dictionary form chosen for a Hausa verb is the most neutral grade for that verb, but the examples employ whatever grade is most suitable for the sentence under consideration. These verb grades are coded according to the numerical system listed below. The verb code immediately follows the verb plus any associated prepositional element, e.g. "increase" **ƙār̃à** *v1*, "meet" **hàɗu** *v7*, "abstain" **ƙauràcē wà** *v4*, "send" **aikà dà** *v1*, "sell" **sayar̃ (dà)** *v5*.

> *v0* Grade zero = H tone monosyllabic verbs plus a few HH disyllabic verbs, e.g. "eat" **ci**, "drink" **shā**, "call" **kirā**

> *v1* Grade 1 = HL(H) verbs ending in -ā, e.g. "cook" **dafà**, "frighten" **tsōràtā**

> *v2* Grade 2 = LH(L) verbs ending in -ā, e.g. "buy" **sàyā**, "help" **tàimakà**

> *v3* Grade 3 = basic intransitive verbs with a short final vowel, of which there are three subclasses:

>> *v3* = LH(L) verbs ending in -a, e.g. "enter" **shìga**, "flow into" **màlālà**

>> *v3a* = HH verbs ending in -a, e.g. "faint" **sūma**

>> *v3b* = HL verbs ending in -i, -u, or (in one case) -a, e.g. "get up" **tāshì**, "die" **mutù**, "get lost" **ɓatà**

> *v4* Grade 4 (the "totality" grade) = HL(H) verbs ending in -ē, e.g. "close" **rufè**, "investigate" **bincìkē**

*v5*  Grade 5 (the "efferential/causative" grade) = verbs with all H tone ending in
-ař. These occur with the preposition dà when followed by an expressed direct
object, e.g. "teach" kōyař (dà), "confirm" tabbatař (dà). Some Grade 5
verbs also have a commonly used short form with which the dà is obligatory,
e.g. "pour out" zub dà, cf. zubař (dà). (In northwest dialects, the dà is fused
to the verb as a suffix.) These short variants are indicated along with the long
form, e.g. "pour out" zub dà / zubař (dà)

*v6*  Grade 6 (the "ventive" grade) = verbs with all H tone ending in -ō, e.g. "bring"
kāwō, "come out" fitō

*v7*  Grade 7 (the "sustentative/medio-passive" grade) = (L)LH verbs ending in -u,
e.g. "happen" fằru, "become rich" wàdằtu

*v\** = irregular verbs whose primary form is outside the grade system

*vdat* = verbs that have a special form before the indirect object marker e.g. "accomplish (goal)" cim mà, "pounce on" dirař wà, "give to" bai wà

SYNTACTIC CONTEXTS. Within each grade, transitive verbs have three variant forms
depending on the syntactic context. The differences between the forms are mainly in
the final vowel and the tone pattern. Form A is used when the verb is not followed
by a direct object. Form B is used when there is a personal pronoun direct object.
Form C is used when there is a noun direct object. In the Hausa translation equivalents, verbs are given in Form A, the conventional citation form. In the examples
themselves, the verb appears in whatever form is required by the context being illustrated. The general outline of the syntactically determined grade forms of transitive
verbs is summarized in the chart below, where the verbs given are representative of
their class.

|  |  | A | B | C |
|---|---|---|---|---|
| *v0* | "eat" | ci | cī | ci |
|  | "drink" | shā | shā | shā |
| *v1* | "cook" | dafằ | dafằ | dafà |
|  | "frighten" | tsōràtā | tsōràtā | tsōràtà |
| *v2* | "buy" | sàyā | sàyē | sàyi |
|  | "ask" | tàmbayằ | tàmbàyē | tàmbàyi |
| *v4* | "close" | rufè | rufè | rufè, rufè |
|  | "investigate" | bincìkē | bincìkē | bincìkè, bincìkē |
| *v5* | "pour out" | zubař | zubař dà, zubshē | zubař dà |
|  | "confirm" | tabbatař | tabbatař dà | tabbatař dà |
| *v6* | "discover" | gānō | gānō | gānō |

IRREGULAR VERBS. A few high frequency verbs are irregular and cannot be cate-
gorized within the grade sytem. These are noted as *v\**, e.g. zama *v\** "become". The
complete list of these verbs is given below. The irregular transitive verbs have the

three A/B/C forms (separated by slashes) discussed above. A few Grade 2 verbs
marked *v2** have irregular A forms and are included on this list in their A/B/C
forms.

> *v** "give to" bā/bā/bā; "know" sanī/san/san; "let, allow"barī/bař/bař; "see"
> ganī/gan/ga; "become" zama; "carry, take" kai; "draw near" kusa; "ride,
> mount" hau; "say" cê

> *v2** "dip, scoop" ɗībā̀/ɗēbē̄/ɗèbi; "get" sāmū̀/sāmē̄/sāmi; "release, let go of"
> sakī̀/sàkē/sàki; "take" ɗaukā̀/ɗàukē/ɗàuki; "tell" faɗī̀/fàɗē/fàɗi

PHRASAL VERBS. Hausa has two types of phrasal verbs, those formed with wà
and those formed with dà. The verbs with wà take an indirect object in Hausa
although they may correspond to a direct object in English, e.g. "avoid (someone or
something)" ƙauràcē wà *v4*, "excuse (someone)" gāfàřtā wà *v1*. When the indirect
object is a pronoun, the indirect object pronoun set consisting of ma- plus a pronoun
is used (see APPENDIX A), e.g. "he excused them" yā gāfàřtā musù, cf. "he excused
Ladi" yā gāfàřtā wà Lādì. Examples of phrasal verbs with dà are "remember" tunà
dà *v1*, "notice" lūř̀a dà *v3*.

COMPOUND VERBS. A number of English verbs have Hausa equivalents which are
compound expressions generally consisting of a verb plus a noun direct object, e.g.
"cooperate" haɗà kâi, "telephone" bugà wayā̀. For such compounds, no verb code
is provided. The most common verbal compound consists of the verb yi "do/make"
plus a noun denoting an action or activity, e.g. "speak" yi màganā̀, "promise" yi
àlkawàřī. In such compounds, the gender of the noun is given, e.g. "sing" yi wāƙā̀
*f*.

   When an English transitive verb is translated by a Hausa compound verb, the
English direct object is frequently expressed by an indirect object in Hausa, e.g.
"telephone someone" bugà wà wani wayā̀, "promise someone" yi wà wani àlkawàřī.
To economize on space, the wà wani in such compounds has been simplified to wà
with the indirect object being understood, e.g. "annoy (someone)" ɓātà wà râi, cf.
"she annoyed her husband" tā ɓātà wà màigidā râi.

VERBAL NOUNS. Many verbs, especially Grade 2 verbs, require a participial or
gerundive form when used in the continuous tenses. These verbal nouns are indicated
in <> after the verb code. Masculine verbal nouns are not marked for gender, e.g.
"listen to" sàurārā̀ *v2* <sàurārō>. Feminine verbal nouns are marked *f*, e.g. "fall"
fāɗì *v3b* <fāɗùwā> *f*.

### 3.3.6  Adverbs

Hausa adverbs include a number of different construction types ranging from simple
adverbs to derived adverbs to compound expressions formed in various ways. There
is one specific type that needs to be mentioned. Many body-part nouns have related
locative adverbs formed by shortening the final vowel, e.g. "on the back" à bāya
(cf. bāyā "back"), "up to one's knees" iyā gwīwà (cf. gwīwā̀ "knee"). Some of these
adverbs also involve a tonal change, e.g. "in the eye" à ido (cf. idò "eye"). In a
few cases, the derivation also involves other changes, e.g. "in the mouth" à bakà (cf.
bàkī "mouth").

### 3.3.7   Ideophones

The label *idph* identifies a large class of phonologically distinctive phonaesthetic words that intensify notions of sound, color, shape, manner, etc. Some ideophones are closely associated with specific verbs, adjectives, or nouns, and serve to translate closely bound English expressions such as "snow-white" farī fat, "stand stock-still" tsayà ƙiƙàm, "refuse point-blank" ƙi sam-sam.

### 3.3.8   Prepositions

Hausa has a few "true" prepositions, e.g. à "at", dab dà "near", dàgà "from". Spatially related prepositions tend to be derived from nouns indicating parts of the body, e.g. kân "on, on top of" (from kâi "head"), bāyan "behind" (from bāyā "back").

An English-Hausa Dictionary

# A

a, an *art* a. (*not translated; its mean-ing is implied in the noun*): I bought ~ hat nā sàyi hūlā; he has ~ watch yanà dà àgōgo; ~ few people mutānē kàɗan; ~ dozen eggs ƙwai dōzìn. b. (*a certain*) wani *m*, wata *f*, waɗansu/wasu *p*: ~ tall man came to see you wani mùtûm dōgō yā zō nēmankà; ~ friend of mine is in the hospital wata ƙawātā tanà asìbitì. c. (*each, every*) kōwànè *m*, kōwàcè *f*, kōwàɗànnè *p*: twice ~ day sàu biyu kōwàcè rānā; ₦100 ~ month naiɍā ɗàrī kōwànè watā.

abandon *v* a. (*leave*) barì *v**: ~ a project barì aikì; an ~ed site kufai *m*. b. (*cast aside*) wātsaɍ (dà) *v5*: ~ one's family wātsaɍ dà ìyālì.

abate *v* (*of fire, wind*) lafà *v1*; (*of anger*) hūcè *v4*.

abattoir *n* mahautā *f*, mayankā *f*.

abbreviation *n* gàjàrtacciyaɍ kalmà *f*.

abdicate *v* yi mùɍābùs *m*.

abdomen *n* cikì *m* ⟨Cuna⟩; (*esp. organ it-self*) tùmbī *m*; (*lower part*) mārà *f*; the bullet entered the ~ hàɍsāshì yā shiga tùmbī; abdominal pains cīwòn cikì = muɍɗàwaɍ cikì = cīwòn mārà.

abhor *v* yi ƙyāmā *f*: they ~ all forms of vi-olence sunà ƙyāmaɍ kōwànè irìn tāshìn hankàlì.

abide by *v* yàɍda dà *v3*.

ability *n* iyāwā *f*: she has more ~ than he tā fī shì iyāwā; to the best of their ~ haɍ iyàkaɍ iyāwaɍsù.

able *adj* a. be ~ to iyà *v1*: will you be ~ to finish it by tomorrow? zā kà iyà gamàwā gòbe? all the children are ~ to read yârā duk sun iyà kàɍàtū. b. (*capable*) (mài) ƙōƙarī *m*, ƙwàrarrē *adj*.

ablutions *n* (*Relig., prior to saying prayers*) àlwàlā *f*.

abolish *v* kashè *v4*: when was the slave trade ~ed? yàushè akà kashè cìnikin bāyī?

abortion *n* zub dà cikì *m*; she had an ~ tā zub dà cikìntà.

abortive *adj*: an ~ coup jūyìn mulkìn dà bài yi nasaɍà ba.

about 1. *adv* (*approx.*) wajen, kàmaɍ, mìsālìn: come ~ 2 o'clock kà zō wa-jen ƙarfè biyu; ~ how much will it cost? kàmaɍ nawà nē kuɗinsà? the work will take ~ 3 hours aikìn zâi ɗau wa-jen awà ukù; take out ~ 2 dozen dē6i mìsālìn dōzìn biyu; (*esp. re. size or quantity*) kìmānìn: it is ~ this size gir-mansà kìmānìn wannàn; it weighs ~ 10 pounds nauyinsà kìmānìn wayà gōmà = ƙīmaɍ nauyinsà wayà gōmà.
2. *prep* a. (*concerning*) gàme dà *prep*: I don't know anything ~ that bàn san kōmē gàme dà wannàn ba; the rumors ~ her jìta-jìta gàme dà ita; this folktale is ~ Gizo and Ƙoki wannàn tàtsūnìyaɍ Gizò dà Ƙōƙì cē. b. (*with verbs of talking, say-ing*) (à) kân *prep*: let's talk to him ~ our plans bàri mù yi masà màganà kân shirìnmù; they agreed ~ one thing only sun yàɍda à kân àbù ɗaya tak; what is this poem ~? à kân mè wannàn wāƙàr takè zàncē? c. be ~ to (*on the point of*) nà haɍamà *f*, dab dà *prep*: we are ~ to say our prayers munà haɍamaɍ sallà; they were ~ to leave when we arrived sunà dab dà tàfiyà sai mukà isō; (*esp. sponta-neous*) nà shirì *m*: he is ~ to cry yanà shirìn kūkā; that's just what I was ~ to say to you! àbìn dà nakè shirì ìn gayà makà kè nan! d. what ~, how ~ X? X fà: if he is getting some, how ~ us? ìdan shī zâi sāmū, mū fà? I want a mango, what ~ you? inà sôn mangwàɍò, kē fà?

above 1. *adv* a. (*overhead*) samà *adv*: it is up ~ yanà samà; from ~ dàgà samà; ~ and below samà dà ƙasà; see ~ for an ex-planation dùbi samà kà sàmi bàyānì. b. (*beyond*) bisà *adv*: it got lodged ~ those branches yā maƙàlē bisà ràssân nan.
2. *prep* samà dà *prep*: he is ~ me in rank yanà samà dà nī à mùƙāmì; the plane flew up ~ the clouds jirgī yā tāshì haɍ samà dà gìzàgìzai; ~ all (*more than anything else*) fìye dà kōmē.

abrade *v* kūjè / ƙūjè *v4*, sālè *v4*.

abrasion *n* kūjèwā / ƙūjèwā *f*.

abroad *adv* à ƙasàshen wàje: live ~ yi zamā à ƙasàshen wàje; go ~ for further study jē ƙasàshen wàje don ƙàrà ilìmī.

abruptly *adv* kwatsàm *idph*: they got up ~ sai kwatsàm sukà tāshì.

abscess *n* gyàmbō *m* ⟨una⟩.

absence *n* (*from work, school*) fāshì *m*; in my ~ à bāyānā.

absent *adj*: he is ~ bā yà nân.

absent-minded *adj* shàgàlallè *adj*.

**absolute** *adj* a. (*esp. emphasizing neg. qualities of psn.*) na innānàhā *f*, na ƙīn ƙārāwā: an ~ idiot wāwā nè na innānàhā; an ~ miser maròwàcī na ƙīn ƙārāwā. b. (*Pol.*): ~ rule baƙin mulkī *m*.

**absolutely** *adv* (*emphat.*) kwata-kwata *idph*: I agree ~ with what you say nā yàrdā kwata-kwata dà àbīn dà ka cè; you're ~ right! gaskiyarƙà! (*emphat., with neg. sent. or v*) sam-sam *idph*: ~ not sam-sam; I ~ refuse to do it nā ƙi sam-sam ìn yī shì.

**absolution** *n* gāfarā *f*: God alone grants ~ Allàh nē kawài mài yîn gāfarā.

**absolve** *v* yāfā wà lâifī.

**absorb** *v* a. shā *v0*: plastic doesn't ~ water ƙōbā bā tà shân ruwā. b. (*preoccupied*): be ~ed with nìtsu dà *v7*, shàgàltu dà *v7*: I'm deeply ~ed in my work nā nìtsu dà aikìnā.

**abstain** *v* ƙauràcē wà *v4*: ~ from smoking ƙauràcē wà shân tābà.

**abundance** *n* yawà *m*; (*esp. re. food, crops*) yàlwā *f*: there was an ~ of food last year àkwai yàlwar àbinci bàra; in great ~ dà dimbin yawà, jìngim *idph*.

**abundant** *adj* (*esp. re. food, crops*) (mài) àlbarƙà *f*: the harvest was ~ this year girbì yā yi àlbarƙà bana.

**abuse** 1. *v* a. (*insult*) zàgā *v2* ⟨zāgì⟩; (*by using vulgar language*) yi àshārā *m*, yi àshāriyà *f*: whenever they did sth. wrong, he would ~ them kōyàushè sukà yi lâifī, yā fàdà su dà àshār̃. b. (*treat cruelly*) azàbtā *v1*, yi wà ƙètā *f*, (*sexually*) lālàtā *v1*. c. (*misuse*) wulāƙàntā *v1*, wulāƙantar̃ (dà) *v5*, yi àmfānī *m*: ~ one's position wulāƙantar̃ dà mùƙāmì = yi àmfānī dà mùƙāmì.
2. *n* (*cruelty*) àzābà *f*, ƙètā *f*.

**abusive** *adj*: ~ language (*sexually explicit*) bātsa *f*, mūgùn bàƙī *m*, ɗanyen bàƙī *m*.

**acacia** *n* (*arabica*) bàgàruwā / gàbàruwā *f*; (*albida*) gàwō *m*.

**academic** *adj*: ~ gown rìgar̃ jāmi'à; the ~ year shēkar̃ar̃ kàr̃ātū.

**accelerate** *v*: the train ~d jirgin ƙasà yā ƙārà wutā; ~ and pass that car! kà ƙārà mâi kà wucè mōtar̃ cân! he ~d up to 80 yā kai mōtà tàmānin.

**accelerator** *n* (*of car*) tōtùr̃ *m*, [F] àskìlàtar̃ *m*.

**accent** *n* a. (*partic. way of speaking*) karìn harshè *m*: I don't recognize his English ~ bàn gānè karìn Tūr̃ancinsà ba; he has a British ~ Tūr̃ancinsà na Ingìlà nē. b.

(*pronunciation*) lafàzī *m*, nuɗùƙī *m*; ~ mark àlāmàr̃ nuɗùƙī.

**accept** *v* a. (*receive*) kàrɓā *v2*, àmsā *v2*: ~ a bribe, an invitation kàrɓi cîn hancì, gàyyatà; ~ a trophy àmshi kwâf; ~ advice ɗauki shāwar̃à. b. (*agree to*) yàrda dà *v3*, yi na'àm dà: I don't ~ your reasons bàn yàrdà dà dàlìlankà ba.

**acceptable** *adj*: it is not ~ bà zâi ɗauku ba.

**accident** *n* haɗàrī *m* ⟨uka²⟩: there was a serious ~ at the factory an yi mùmmūnan haɗàrī à ma'aikatàr̃; there have been a lot of ~s lately anà haɗàrī da yawà kwānan nàn.

**accidentally** *adv* bà dà gàngan ba: he was ~ shot an har̃bē shi bà dà gàngan ba.

**accommodate** *v* saukar̃ (dà) *v5*: he can ~ 3 guests in his house zâi iyà saukar̃ dà bàƙī ukù à gidansà.

**accommodations** masaukī *m*.

**accompany** *v* rakà *v1*, yi wà rakiyà *f*: he accompanied me all the way home yā yi minì rakiyà har̃ zuwà gidā.

**accomplish** *v* a. (*one's goal, objective*) cim mà *vdat*: I've ~ed my goal nā cim mà būrìnā. b. (*a duty, task*) kammàlā *v1*, kàmmalà *v3*: the mission has been ~ed aikìn yā kàmmalà.

**accomplished** *adj* (*psn.*) gwànī *adj* ⟨aye⟩: he is an ~ musician shī gwànin makàɗī nè.

**accord** *n* yàr̃dā *f*, àlkawàrī *m*; mutual ~ yàr̃jējēnìyā *f*; come to an ~ daidàita *v1*.

**accordingly** *adv* gwar̃gwadō: you will be paid ~ zā à biyā kù gwar̃gwadō.

**according** *prep* a. (*in proportion to*) gwar̃gwadon *prep*: everyone will get paid ~ to his abilities kōwā zâi sāmù gwar̃gwadon iyàwar̃sà. b. (*as said by*) in ji: ~ to a top official, there's been a coup wai an yi jūyìn mulkì, in ji wani bàbban jāmì'ī. c. (*concerning*) danganè / dàngàne dà: ~ to what he told me danganè dà àbîn dà ya gayà minì.

**account**¹ *n* a. (*of finances*) lìssāfìn kuɗī *m*: keep ~s yi lìssāfìn kuɗī. b. (*in bank*) àjiyar̃ bankì *f*: open, close an ~ būdè, rufè àjiyà. c. (*report*) làbār̃ī *m* ⟨u, ai⟩, bàyānì *m*: give an ~ of sth. bā dà bàyānì.

**account**² 1. *n* (*consideration*): take sth. into ~ yi nazàrin w.a.; on ~ of sabòdà *prep*, sàbìlì dà *conj*, à sanàdin *prep*: the meeting was cancelled on ~ of the rain an sōkè tàrôn sabòdà ruwā.
2. *v*: ~ for sth. bayyànā *v1*, yi bàyānì *m*:

everyone has to ~ for his own actions kōwā sai yā bayyànā àbîn dà ya aikàtā.

**accountant** n àkàntā n ⟨oCi⟩, [F] kwàntābìl n, [F] mùshen kuɗī m.

**accounting** n ilìmin àkàntā m.

**accumulate** v tārà v1.

**accurately** adv daidai adv: this watch keeps time ~ àgōgon nàn yanà nūnà lōkàcī daidai; very ~ daidai wà daidà adv: explain it as ~ as you can kà yi bāyānìnkà daidai wà daidà.

**accusation** n (Law) tùhumà f; false ~ ƙāge m, jàmhūřù m.

**accuse** v (Law) tùhumà v2, càjā v2: he has been ~d of theft anà tùhumàřsà dà lâifin sātā = an càjē shi dà lâifin sātā; (falsely) ɗafà wà v1, maƙàlā wà v1, yi wà ƙāge m, yi wà jàmhūřù m, jèfi w. dà v2: he ~d me of stealing his watch yā ɗafà minì sātāř àgōgonsà = yā jèfē nì dà sātāř àgōgonsà.

**accused** n (Law): the ~ wāndà akè tùhumà.

**accustomed, be** v sābà dà v1: we've become ~ to the cold mun sābà dà sanyìn.

**ace** n (in cards) sarkī m.

**ache** 1. n cīwò m; (esp. muscular) tsāmī m, zōgī m.
2. v yi wà cīwò m, yi wà tsāmī m: my body ~s all over duk jìkīnā nà minì tsāmī.

**achieve** v a. (obtain) sāmù v2*: he ~d success in a short time yā sāmi nasařà bằ da daɗēwā ba. b. (accomplish) cim mà vdat: he ~d his goal of becoming president yā cim mà būřinsà na zamā shùgàbā.

**Achilles heel** n lagò m.

**Achilles tendon** n agàrā f ⟨ai⟩.

**acid** n (e.g. in battery) ruwan bātîř m: ~ corrodes ruwan bātîř yanà cî.

**acidic** adj (in taste) (mài) tsāmī m.

**acknowledge** v a. (recognize) yàřda dà v3, shâidā v1: he ~d his error yā yàřda dà kuskurènsà. b. (confirm) amsà v1: he ~d receipt of the letter yā amsà sāmùn wàsīƙàř; he ~d his guilt yā amsà lâifinsà.

**acknowledgement** n a. (reply) amsà f: I've had no ~ of my request bàn sàmi amsàř rōƙōnā ba. b. (in book) gōdiyā f.

**acme** n gāniyà f.

**acne** n bàř-ni-dà-mūgù m: ~ has broken out all over his face bàř-ni-dà-mūgù yā fiřfitō masà à fuskà.

**acquaintance** n (friend) idòn sanì n: please say hello to all my ~s kà gayař mini dà duk idòn sanì; superficial ~ sanìn shānū: he's just an ~ of theirs

sun san shì àmmā sanìn shānū; (mutual) sànayyà f.

**acquaint** v: be ~ed ɗan sanì v*: I'm ~ed with Ladi nā ɗan san Lādì; I'm very slightly ~ed with her nā san tà àmmā sanìn shānū.

**acquire** v sāmù v2*: words continually ~ new meanings kalmōmī nà ta sāmùn sàbàbbin ma'anōnī; (Gram.): ~ a language tāshì dà harshè.

**acquit** v sàkā v2 ⟨sakì⟩, sàllamà v2: was he convicted or ~ted? an kāmà shi dà lâifin kō an sàkē shì?

**acquittal** n sakì m.

**acre** n ēkà f, see hectare.

**across** 1. prep a. (on other side) (à) ƙètarèn: the bank is ~ the street bankì yanà ƙètarèn hanyà. b. (facing) fùskantàř, kallon: the bank is ~ from the post office bankìn nà fùskantàř gidan wayà. c. (over) à kân prep: there isn't a bridge ~ the river bābù gadà à kân kōgī.
2. adv: lay sth. ~ gittà v1, gilmà v1.

**act** 1. v a. (do sth.) yi àbù m: now is the time to ~ yànzu nè yā kàmātà à yi wani àbù; he was ~ing like a madman yanà àbû kàmař mahàukàcī. b. (take, perform an action) aikàtā v1: ~ in consultation with so. aikàtā tàre dà shāwařàř w.; he ~ed wickedly yā aikàtà shařřì.
2. n a. (law of parliament) dōkà f ⟨oCi⟩. b. (action) aikì m ⟨ayyukà⟩: a useless ~ aikìn banzā. c. (of a play) kashì m.

**action** n: take ~ aikàtā v1; they were condemned for their ~s an yi tiř dà àbîn dà sukà aikàtā.

**active** adj (energetic) (mài) kùzārī m, (mài) ƙōƙarī m, (mài) kàzàř-kazař idph: she is very ~ tanà dà kàzàř-kazař.

**activity** n a. àbin yî m: there isn't much ~ now bâ wani àbin yî mài yawà yànzu. b. (business, social) sha'ànī m ⟨oCi⟩: there's a lot of ~ in town today yau anà sha'ànī dà yawà cikin gàrī.

**actor** n ɗan wàsā m.

**actress** n 'yař wàsā f.

**actual** adj ainihin, hàƙīƙànin: that's the ~ truth wannàn shī nè hàƙīƙànin gàskiyā; the ~ fact is that... ainihin màganà ita cè....

**actually** 1. adv dà gàske: I ~ mean it, I'm not joking dà gàske nakè yî, bằ dà wàsā ba.
2. conj à gàskiyā: ~, I forgot à gàskiyā, nā yi mantuwā.

acute *adj* (mài) tsananī *m*: poverty is an ~ problem everywhere talaucì màtsalà cē mài tsananī kō'ìnā.

adapt *v* (*adjust sth.*) daidàitā *v1*; (*adjust oneself to*) sājè dà *v4*: at first it is difficult to ~ to a new environment dà farkō dai, dà wùyā à sājè dà sābon màhâllī.

add *v* a. (*increase*) daɗà *v1*, ƙārà *v1*: ~ some more water kì daɗà ruwā. b. (*make a total*) yi jimlà *f*: please ~ these figures up for me don Allàh kà yi minì jimlàr̃ wannàn lìssāfìn; the figures ~ up to 100 lìssāfìn yā kai har̃ ɗàrī. c. (*do addition*) tārà *v1*, *see* plus: 3 ~ed to 4 equals 7 ukù à tārà dà huɗu bakwài kè nan = in an tārà ukù dà huɗu bakwài kè nan.

addict *n* (*drugs*) ɗan ƙwàyā *m*.

addicted, be *v* kàmu *v7*, ƙwāyàncē *v4*: he is ~ to drugs yā kàmu dà ƙwàyā = ƙwàyā tā zamè masà jàr̃abà.

addiction *n* jàr̃abà *f*: ~ to drugs, alcohol jàr̃abàr̃ shân ƙwàyā, shân giyà.

adding machine *n* nā'ūrar̃ lìssāfì *f*.

addition *n* a. (*in mathematics*) tārầwā *f*: our lesson today is on ~ dar̃àsinmù na yâu à kân tārầwā nè; ~ sign àlāmàr̃ tārầwā. b. (*increase, esp. sth. concrete*) ƙārì *m*. c. (*esp. re. family*) ƙàruwā *f*: there's been an ~ to our family mun sằmi ƙàruwā. d. in ~ (*furthermore*) har̃ ìlā yâu, daɗìn daɗầwā, bugù dà ƙārì: in ~ he went on to say... daɗìn daɗầwā yā ci gàba dà cêwā...; in ~ to bāyan *prep*, ban dà *conj*: he wants fame in ~ to money bāyan kuɗī yanà nēman sūnā; in ~ to a fine, he was imprisoned ban dà tàrā mā an ɗaurè shi.

additional *adj* ƙārìn: an ~ explanation ƙārìn bàyānì.

address[1] *n* (*of a place*) àdìrēshì *m*: what is your ~? mềnē nề àdìrēshìnkà?

address[2] *n* (*speech*) jàwābì *m* ⟨ai⟩: deliver an ~ to so. yi wà jàwābì = yi jàwābì gà w.

adequate *adj* mayàlwàcī *adj*, ìsasshē *adj*, wàdằtaccē *adj*: he has ~ funds yanà dà kuɗī mayàlwàtā = yanà dà wàdằtàttun kuɗī.

adhere to *v* a. (*stick to*) mannè wà *v4*: the stamp didn't ~ to the envelope kân sarkī bài mannè wà ambùlàn ba. b. (*have faith in*) bi r̃a'àyin w.a.

adherent *n* mabìyī *m*.

adhesive tape *n* filastà *f*, [F] ìspàr̃àdàr̃à *f*.

adjacent *adv* dab dà *prep*: the stores are ~ to each other kantunà sunà dab dà jūnā.

adjective *n* siffà / sifà *f* ⟨oCi⟩.

adjourn *v* dākatar̃ (dà) *v5*.

adjournment *n* dākatâr̃wā *f*: motion of ~ bàtun dākatâr̃wā.

adjust *v* daidàitā *v1*: ~ a watch, work schedule daidàità àgōgo, tsārìn aikì; ~ to (*a situation*) sābà dà *v1*, sājè dà *v4*: ~ to one's circumstances sābà dà hālin dà akè ciki; be ~ed dàidàitu *v7*.

adjustable *adj* (mài) dàidàituwā.

administer *v* tafiyar̃ (dà) *v5*, gudānar̃ (dà) *v5*: ~ the affairs of the foundation gudānar̃ dà har̃kōkin gìdauniyā; ~ a test to yi wà jar̃r̃àbâwā.

administration *n* (*governing body*) hùkūmà *f* ⟨oCi⟩: local ~ ƙàramar̃ hùkūmà.

administrative officer *n* ma'àikàcī *m*, jāmì'ī *m* ⟨ai⟩; (*esp. agricultural*) bàtūr̃è *m*.

administrator *n* ma'àikàcī *m*, jāmì'ī *m* ⟨ai⟩.

admiration *n* shà'awà *f*.

admire *v* yi shà'awà *f*: I ~ his work inà shà'awàr̃ aikìnsà = aikìnsà yā bā nì shà'awà = aikìnsà yā bur̃gè ni.

admission *n* shìgā *f*; ~ fee kuɗin shìgā.

admit *v* a. (*agree*) yàr̃da *v3*: he ~ted committing the crime yā yàr̃da yā yi lâifìn. b. (*to hospital*) kwantar̃ (dà) *v5*: she has been ~ted to the hospital an kwantar̃ dà ita à asìbitì; be ~ted (*e.g. to school*) sằmi shìgā.

admittance *n* shìgā *f*: no ~ without permission bâ shìgā sai dà izìnī.

admonish *v* gàr̃gaɗà *v2*.

admonition *n* gàr̃gàɗī *m*; (*preaching*) wa'àzī *m*.

adolescence *n* bàlagà *f*, ƙùrūciyā *f*.

adolescent *n* matàshī *m*, (*boy*) sauràyī *m* ⟨sàmằrī⟩, (*girl*) bùdurwā *f* ⟨oCi⟩; become an ~ bàlagà *v3*.

adopt *v* ɗàuki riƙòn w., ɗàuki rènon w.: they ~ed an orphan sun ɗaukō riƙòn màrāyà; an ~ed child ɗan riƙò.

adoption *n* ɗaukàr̃ riƙò *f*, ɗaukàr̃ rènō *f*.

adore *n* yi ƙàunā *f*.

adornment *n* adō *m*, kwalliyā *f*.

adult *n* mùtûm *m* ⟨mutằnē⟩, bàbba *adj* ⟨mânyā⟩: everyone should come, children and ~s yā kàmātà kōwā yà zō mânyā dà yârā; become an ~ (*reach legal status*) bàlagà *v3*, (*reach grown-up status*) ìsa mùtûm.

adult education *n* ilìmin mânyā *m*, [F] kur̃dầdī *m*.

adulterer *n* kwar̃tō *m* ⟨aye⟩, mazìnằcī *m*.

adultery *n* kwar̃tancì *m*, (*esp. Law*) zìnā *f*: commit ~ yi zìnā = yi kwar̃tancì.

**advance**[1] **1.** *v* a. (*make progress*) ci gàba: the work is advancing well aikìn nā cî gàba sôsai. b. (*move*) ~ on, toward tùnkārā *v2*: they ~d toward the enemy sun tunkārō àbôkan gābařsù. **2.** *n* a. (*progress*) cî-gàba *m.* b. (*beforehand*) in ~ à gàba = kằfìn lōkàcîn.

**advance**[2] **1.** *v* (*give money from wages*): I ~d you ₦20 from your wages last month, don't you remember? nā bā kà bāshìn naiřā àshìřin dàgà cikin àlbāshì watàn jiyà, kō kā mântā? **2.** *n* a. (*from wages*) bāshì *m.* b. (*money for services, down payment*) àdìbâs *m*, [F] àbâns *f*: I paid ₦20 in ~ for the car repairs nā bā dà àdìbâs na naiřā àshìřin don gyāran mōtà; he gave the mālàm an ~ of ₦10 (to make the charm work) yā bā mālàm kafìn àlƙalàmī na naiřā gōmà.

**advancement** *n* cî-gàba *m.*

**advantage** *n* a. (*use, usefulness*) àmfānī *m*, fā'idā *f* ⟨oCi⟩: what is the ~ of doing that? mēnē nè àmfānin yîn hakà? this method has an ~ over the other one wannàn hanyà tā fi wàccan àmfānì; take ~ of one's position to become wealthy yi àmfānī dà mùƙāmì don ařzùtà kâi; take unfair ~ of so. yi wà zàmba cikin amincì = ci āmānař w. b. (*esp. Econ.*) řībà *f* ⟨oCi⟩; enjoy the ~s of sth. ci řībōbin w.a.

**adverb** *n* bàyànau *m.*

**advertise** *v* yi tàllà *m.*

**advertisement, advertising** *n* tàllà *m* ⟨tàllàce-tàllàce⟩: there are a lot of ~s on television anā tàllàce-tàllace dà yawā à talàbijìn.

**advice** *n* shāwařā *f* ⟨shāwářwařī⟩: good ~ shāwařā tagàri; accept so.'s ~ kàrɓař shāwařař w. = rùngùmi shāwařař w.; give ~ bā dà shāwařā, bā dà màganà; give ~ to so. shāwařtā *v2*, shāwàřtā wà *v1*; seek so.'s ~ tùntuɓā *v2*, shāwařtà *v2*: I sought Musa's ~ about the matter nā tùntùɓi Mūsā gàme dà àl'amàřìn.

**advise** *v* bā w. shāwařā, shāwàřtā *v2*, shāwàřtā wà *v1*: I ~d him to do that nā bā shì shāwařā dà yà yi hakà = nā shāwàřcē shìi dà yà yi hakà.

**adviser** *n* mashāwàřcī *m.*

**advocate** *n* a. (*for a cause*) ɗan yāƙìn X *m*: she is an ~ of women's rights ita 'yař yāƙìn hakkìn mātā. b. (*lawyer*) lauyà *n* ⟨oCi⟩, [F] àbōkà *n.*

**adze** *n* gìzāgō *m*, masassaƙī *m*; (*large*) dundùřūsù *m.*

**aerial** *n* (*of radio*) eřiyà *f*, [F] àntân *f.*

**aeroplane** *n, see* **airplane.**

**afar** *adv*: from ~ dàgà nēsà: I caught a glimpse of him from ~ nā hàngē shì dàgà nēsà.

**affair** *n* a. (*matter*) àl'amàřī / lamàřī *m* ⟨u-a⟩, màganā *f* ⟨u²⟩: it is none of my ~ bā ni dà hannū cikin màganà. b. (*Pol., Econ.*) hařkā *f* ⟨oCi⟩: they've been banned from political ~s an hanà su harkàř sìyāsà; ~s of state hařkōkin ƙasà; external ~s hařkōkin wàje; internal ~s hařkōkin cikin gidā; international ~s hařkōkin dūniyā. c. (*esp. business*) sha'ànī *m* ⟨oCi⟩: a business ~ sha'ànin cìnikī.

**affect** *v* shāfā *v2*: this doesn't ~ our plans wannàn bài shāfi shirìnmù ba.

**affirmative** *adj* (*Gram.*) tàbbàtau *m*: an ~ sentence jimlā tàbbàtau.

**afford** *v*: I can't ~ a Mercedes, only a Volkswagen bâ ni dà ƙarfin màllakàř Mařsandî sai dai Bōsùwājà.

**afraid** *adj* a. (*fear*): be ~ yi tsòrō *m*, ji tsòrō, tsòratà *v3*; be ~ of yi tsòron, ji tsòron: children are ~ of lightning yârā nā tsòron àřàdù; she is ~ of his criticism tanà jîn tsòron sūkàřsà; I'm ~ something bad has happened to her inā tsòron wani àbù maràs kyâu yā sàmē tà; be ~ that (*lest*) yi tsòrō kadà: he is ~ that a wild animal will eat him yanā tsòrō kadà nāmàn dājì yà cînyē shi. b. (*doubt*) yi shakkà *f*: I'm ~ I won't be able to come inā shakkà kō zân iyà zuwà; I'm ~ he's become confused gà àlāmà yā rūɗè nè.

**Africa** *n* Afiřkà *f.*

**African** *adj* (*psn.*) ɗan Afiřkà *m*, mùtumìn Afiřkà *m*; (*sth.*) na Afiřkà.

**after** *prep & conj* bāyan *prep*: ~ class, I went to the library bāyan ajì, nā jē lābùřāřè; ~ they left, we went to bed bāyan sun tàfi, mun kwântā; ~ all... àlhālī kùwa...; it was only ~ X that Y sai dà X (tùkùn) Y: it was only ~ they finished up the work that we paid them sai dà sukà ƙāràsà aikìn tùkùn mukà biyā sù.

**afterbirth** *n* mahaifā *f*, mabiyìyā *f*; uwař cìbìyā *f.*

**afternoon** *n* (*early*) rānā *f*, (*late*) yâmmā *f*: good ~! bàřkà dà rānā! = bàřkà dà yâmmā! (*from ca. 2-4 pm*) àzahàř *f*; (*just before sunset*) màràicè *m*; in the early ~ dà rana *adv*; in the late ~ dà yâmma *adv.*

**afterwards** *adv* dàgà bāya, dàgà bìsānī.

**again** *adv* a. do ~ sākè *v4*, ƙārà *v1*, kumà *v1*: I saw him ~ on Monday nā sākè ganinsà ran Lìttìnîn; he did it ~ yā sākè = yā kumā; please say that ~ don Allàh kà sākè màganà; don't do that ~! kadà kà kumā! b. do sth. ~ and ~ shā (+ action n): I've asked him ~ and ~ for the information nā shā tùntuɓàr̃sà; (use plurac. v): he hit him ~ and ~ yā dàddàkè shì; she asked them ~ and ~ tā tàntàmbàyē sù.

**against** prep a. (direction): lean ~ a wall jìnginà dà bangō; lean a ladder ~ the wall jìnginà tsānì gà bangō; it is leaning ~ the door yanà jìnginè dà ƙōfà; push sth. ~ the wall tūrà w.a. à bangō. b. (not agreeing with) bà (tàre) dà...ba: he did it ~ my wishes yā yī shì bà tàre dà sônā ba; I was ~ the decision bàn gòyi bāyan shāwar̃ar̃ dà akà yankè ba; fight ~ yi yāƙì dà; medicine ~ malaria māgànin zàzzàɓin cīzòn saurō.

**age** 1. n a. (in years) shèkàrà f ⟨u⟩, shèkàrū dà haihùwā: what is the child's ~? shèkàrun yārò nawà dà haihùwā? = shèkàrar̃ yārò nawà nē? be, come of ~ (legal) bàlagà v3; person of legal ~ bālìgī m ⟨ai⟩. b. (era) zāmānī m. 2. v tsūfa v3a: she ~d quickly tā tsūfa dà saurī; women ~ faster than men mātā sun fi mazā saurin tsūfā.

**age-mate** n tsārā n ⟨aki²⟩, sa'à n ⟨oCi⟩.

**agency** n a. (branch office) rēshè m ⟨Ca⟩: there's a postal ~ at the airport àkwai rēshèn gidan wayà à fīlin jirgin samà. b. (admin.) hùkūmà f ⟨oCi⟩: A. for Mass Education Hùkūmàr̃ Yàdà Ilìmin Mânyā.

**agenda** n àjandà f.

**agent** n a. (representative) wàkīlì m ⟨ai⟩; (e.g. insurance, travel) ējà m. b. (secret) ɗan lèƙen àsīr̃in ƙasā m, sī'aidî n, [F] àjân n.

**aggravate** v (make worse) dāgùlā v1, tsanàntā v1: the scarcity of rain ~d the problem rashìn sāmùn ruwā yā dāgùlà màtsalar̃; become ~d tsànàntà v3, dàgulà v3.

**aggravating** adj (serious) (mài) tsananī m, dàgùlallē adj.

**aggravation** n (annoyance) àbin fìtinà m, àbin dàmuwā m.

**aggressive** adj (mài) cîn zālī m, mamùgùncī adj.

**agility** n (physical) zāfin nāmà m; (mental) kaifin bàsīr̃à m.

**agitate** v a. (shake, stir) kaɗà v1. b. (bother) dāmā v2 ⟨dāmù⟩. c. (arouse interest): ~ for nèmā v2 ⟨nēmā⟩: they are agi-

tating for statehood sunà nēman à bā sù jihàr̃sù.

**ago** adv: 2 weeks ~ mākò biyu dà sukà wucè; how long ~? tun yàushè? I left Kano 3 months ~ nā barò Kanò tun watà ukù; long ~ (some time ~) tun tùni = tun tuntùni = tun dà dadèwā; not long ~ ban dà dadèwā; long long ~ (in olden times) dâ dâ, can dâ; many many years ~ shèkarà dà shèkàrū.

**agonizing** adj a. (painful) (mài) r̃àɗàɗī m. b. (difficult) (mài) wùyā f.

**agony** n r̃àɗàɗī m: he's suffering in ~ from the illness yanà fāmā dà r̃àɗàdin cīwò.

**agree** v a. yàr̃da v3: I ~ with you, your plan nā yàr̃da dà kai, shirìnkà; ~ for so. to do sth. yar̃dar̃ wà vdat: he ~d for me to drive his car yā yar̃dam minì ìn tùƙi mōtàr̃sà; ~ on sth. shiryà à kân; ~ on a price (by seller) sallàmā v1. b. (suit, go well with) yi shirì dà m, jìtu v7: chocolate doesn't ~ with me bà nà shirì dà cākùlàn.

**agreeable** adj (psn.) (mài) dādin kâi m, (mài) sauƙin kâi m, (mài) fàr̃a'à f.

**agreement** n a. yàr̃dā f, àlkawàr̃ī m: be in ~ jìtu v7; come to, reach an ~ daidàità v1, yankè shāwar̃à, tsai dà màganà: their inability to reach an ~ is causing delays rashìn daidàitâwar̃sù yanà haddàsà jìnkirī. b. (formal agreement) yàr̃jējènìyā f, àlkawàr̃ī m: enter into an ~ with ƙullà àlkawàr̃ī dà; break an ~ karyà yàr̃jējènìyā; they reached a mutual ~ sun cim mà yàr̃jējènìyā. c. (for repayment of sth.) jìnginà f. d. (Gram.) jìtuwā f.

**agricultural** adj na gōnā f: ~ officer bàtūr̃èn gōnā.

**agriculture** n ilìmin aikìn gōnā m; a country which depends on ~ ƙasar̃ dà kè dògarà dà aikìn nōmā.

**ahead** adv à gàba adv: there is a lot of work ~ of us àkwai aikì dà yawà à gàbanmù; go ~ ci gàba: go ~ with the work kù ci gàba dà aikìn; get ~ of so. (in progress, distance) wucè v4; be ~ of so. (in shared activity) bā dà rātà: he's ~ of me in reading the book yā bā nì rātà wajen karàntà littāfìn.

**aid** 1. n a. (help) tàimakō m: first ~ tàimakon farkō; relief ~ tàimakon àgàjī. b. (tool) jà-gōrà m: a dictionary is an important ~ in language learning ƙāmùs bàbban jà-gōrà nē gà kòyon harshè. 2. v tàimakà v2.

**aide** *n* matàimàkī *m*, mài tàimakō *m*.

**aide-de-camp** *n* ēdīsî *m*, ōdàlè *m*.

**AIDS** *n* cũtā mài karyà gàrkuwař jìkī *f*.

**aim 1.** *n* būrī / gūrī *m*, màƙàsūdî *m*: his ~ was to become famous in sports būrìnsà yà shàhařà cikin hařkàř wàsànnī. **2.** *v a.* (*a weapon*) yi saitìn *m*: ~ your gun carefully before shooting kà yi saitìn bindigā sōsai kāfìn kà hařbà; ~ at (*a target*) yi bārā *f*: they are ~ing at the tree sunā bāřař bishiyà; ~ for sth., so. (*lunge at*) kai wà bārā: I ~ed straight for the rooster but I missed nā kai wà zàkarā bārā àmmā bàn sāmē shì ba; they ~ed but missed sun yi bārā àmmā bà sù sāmù ba; ~ sth. at so. aunà *v1* ⟨awò⟩: he ~ed the gun at me yā aunà ni dà bindigā. **b.** ~ for: (*a place*) dōsā *v2*: they ~ed straight for Kano sun dōshi Kanò sak.

**aimless** *adj a.* (*psn. who wanders from place to place*) gàntàlallē *adj*, (mài) wàlàgīgī *m*. **b.** (*without a goal*) maràs būrī *m*.

**aimlessly** *adv a.* wander ~ yi gàntàlī *m*, yi gàràrī *m*, yi gīlò *m*, yi ràgaitā *f*: I met him in town wandering ~ nā hàɗu dà shī cikin gàrī yanà gàntàlī. **b.** (*incoherently*) bâ ƙai bâ gìndī: talk ~ yi màganā bâ ƙai bâi gìndī.

**air 1.** *n* iskà *f*: cold ~ iskà mài sanyī; put ~ in a tire yi wà tayà gējī. **2.** *v* shānyā *v1*: put these clothes out to ~ kì shānyà tufāfìn nân.

**air conditioner** *n* iyàkwàndishàn *m*, [F] kìlìmàtìzâř *m*.

**airfield** *n*, *see* airport.

**air force** *n* sōjōjin mayāƙan samà *p*.

**airmail** *adj*: an ~ letter wàsīƙā ta jirgin samà.

**airplane** *n* jirgin samà *m* ⟨a-e⟩, [F] àbìyô *m*.

**airport** *n* fīlin jirgin samà *m* ⟨aye⟩, [F] àbìyàsô *m*.

**airs** *n*: put on ~ hūrà hancī, yi jī-jī da ƙai, yi ɗagāwā *f*: put on ~s about clothes yi ɗagāwā sabòdà tufāfī; (*esp. by women in manner, dress*) yi fēlēƙē *m*, yi yàngà *f*, yi gwallī *m*.

**air terminal** *n* tashàř jirgin samà *f*.

**aisle** *n* lāyī *m* ⟨uka⟩.

**ajar** *adv* à būɗe *adv*.

**alarm**[1] *n a.* (*of clock, school*) ƙàrarrawā *f*: the ~ rang ƙàrarrawā tā yi ƙārā; turn off an ~ tsai dà ƙàrarrawā = kashè ƙàrarrawā; set the ~ (*of clock*) yi saitìn ƙàrarrawā = sâ ƙàrarrawā. **b.** (*for fire*) ōdàř 'yan kwāna-kwāna *f*; sound an ~ kaɗà ōdā = kaɗà ƙàrarrawā.

**alarm**[2] *v a.* (*worry*) tā dà hankàlī *m*: his behavior ~ed them hālinsà yā tā dà hankàlinsù. **a.** (*make so. take notice, for a purpose*) tunzùrā *v1*: politicians are always trying to ~ people about their situation kullum 'yan sìyāsā nā sô sù tunzùrà mutānē gàme dà hālīn dà sukè ciki.

**alarm-clock** *n* àgōgo mài ƙàrarrawā *m*.

**alas** *excl* (*for sorrow, regret*) àsshā! *excl*.

**albino** *n* (*psn. or animal*) zàbìyā *n* ⟨oCi⟩.

**alcohol** *n* (*for medical use*) sìfiřìt *m*, [F] àlkwâl *m*; (*any ~ic beverage*) bāřàsā *f*: Islam prohibits the drinking of ~ and its like àddīnìn Musuluncī yā hařàmtà shân bāřàsā dà makàmàntantà.

**alcoholic** *n* ɗan giyà *m*, mashāyī *m*; be an ~ shāyu *v7*.

**alcoholism** *m* shân giyà *m*.

**alert 1.** *v* faɗakař (dà) *v5*; (*the public of danger, emergency*) yi gangamī *m*: the village was ~ed about the flood an yi gangamī à ƙauyèn sabòdà ambàliyàř ruwā. **2.** *adj* (*esp. quick*) (mài) hanzarī *m*: an ~ worker ma'àikàcī mài hanzarī; be ~ (*to danger*) yi hattàřā *f*.

**algae** *n* (*e.g. in borrow-pit*) gànsàkūkà *f*.

**algebra** *n* àljabářā *f*.

**alias** *n* laƙàbī *m*, *see* nickname.

**alien** *n* (*psn.*) bāƙō *m* ⟨i⟩; illegal ~ bāƙon hàurē; the problem of illegal ~s màtsalàř 'yan bāƙin hàurē.

**align** *v* (*adjust*) daidàitā *v1*: ~ a wheel daidàitā wīlìn dà ya kařkàcē; non-~ed nations ƙasàshen 'yan-bâ-ruwanmù.

**alignment** *n*: be out of ~ kařkàcē *v4*.

**alight**[1] *adv* (*lit up*) à hàskàke *adv*.

**alight**[2] from *v* sàuka dàgà *v3*.

**alike** *adv*: be, come out ~ tāshì bâi ɗaya: their colors came out ~ launìnsù yā tāshì bâi ɗaya; look ~ yi daidai, yi kàmā: Kande and Ladi look ~ dà Kànde dà Lādì sun yi kàmā; be exactly ~ yi daidai dà jūnā; (*fig.*) as ~ as two peas in a pod kàmař an tsagà kwabò.

**alive** *adj* à ràye *adv*: they were found ~ an sāmē sù à ràye; is he still ~? yanà nan dà râi? my father is no longer ~ mahàifīnā yā ràsu tun tùni.

**all 1.** *quant & pro a.* dukà/duk *det & pro*: ~ of them came dukànsù sun zō; I like them ~ inà sônsù dukà; this is ~ that is left shī nè duk àbin dà ya ragè; ~ the same duk ɗaya: it's ~ the same to me duk

ɗaya gàrē nì.
2. *adv* a. (*entire, entirely*) gàbā ɗaya: I'll
be here ~ day long yâu inā nân rānā gàbā
ɗayantà; ~ at once gàbā ɗaya: they arrived ~ at once dukànsù sun isō gàbā
ɗaya; ~ together, ~ at the same time
(gà) bàkī ɗaya: take them away ~ together kà kwāshè su gà bàkī ɗaya; mix
it up ~ at the same time kì gauràyā gà
bàkī ɗaya; they migrated ~ together sun
tāshì (gà) bàkī ɗaya. b. (*in neg.*) not at
~ kō kàɗan, kwata-kwata *idph*, sam-sam
*idph*: I don't know him at ~ bàn san shì
ba kō kàɗan; we didn't find them at ~ bà
mù sàmē sù ba kwata-kwata; he didn't
understand it at ~ bài gānè ba kō kusa.
c. ~ the same (*even so*) duk dà hakà: ~
the same, I prefer this one duk dà hakà nā
fi sôn wannàn; ~ in ~ dukà-dukà *adv*: ~
in ~ we enjoyed our visit dukà-dukà mun
ji dāɗin zìyàràrmù; ~ of a sudden faɽat
ɗaya, nan dà nan.

**allegation** *n* zàrgī *m,* (*false*) ƙāge *m.*

**allege** *v* zàrgā *v2*: he is ~d to have committed the crime an zàrgē shì dà lâifîn.

**allegiance** *n* bìyayyà *f*: pledge one's ~ to
the emir yi bìyayyà gà sarkī.

**alley** *n* (*narrow path*) ɓàraunìyaɽ hanyà *f;*
(*narrow, dark street*) lungū *m.*

**alliance** *n* ƙàwàncē *m;* form an ~ yi ƙàwàncē
= ƙullà àbōtà = ƙullà àmānà; (*esp. Pol.*)
gamà kâi *m,* haɗìn kâi *m.*

**alliteration** *n* ƙàràngiyā *f.*

**allocate** *v* kasàftā *v1*: ~ funds kasàftà
kuɗī.

**allocation** *n* kasàfī *m.*

**allow** *v* a. (*permit*) yàrda *v3*: I didn't ~ him
to stay bàn yàrda yà zaunā ba; no smok-
ing ~ed bā à shân tābà. b. (*let*) barì *v\**:
why did you ~ them to do this damage? mè
ya sâ ka baɽ sù sukà yi wànnan ɓàrnā?

**allowance** *n* a. (*school*) àlāwùs *m,* [F] bûɽs
*f.* b. (*in garment for expansion*) àlāwùs *m.*

**alloy** *n* gamī *m.*

**all right 1.** *adv* a. (*safe*): are you ~? kōmē
lāfiyà? b. (*correct*) daidai *adv.*
2. *excl* (*okay*) tô *excl;* that's ~ (*that's fine*)
shī kè nan = bâ kōmē.

**ally** *v* àbōkī *m* (ai), ƙawā *f* (aye).

**almanac** *n* kàlandà *f.*

**almighty** *adj*: God A. Allàh Maɗàukàkin
Sarkī.

**almost** *adv* a. (*on the point of*) gab dà *prep,*
bàkin *prep*: she's ~ asleep tanà gab dà
yîn barcī = tanà bàkin yîn barcī. b.
(*nearly*) kusan *prep*: ~ every year kusan kōwàcè shèkarà; ~ all of them kusan

dukànsù; ~ always kusan kōyàushè; be
~ (*be approaching*) kusa *v\**: it's ~ noon
tsakaɽ rānā tā kusa; the bananas are
~ ripe àyàbà tā kusa nūnā; I have ~
finished nā kusa gamāwā. c. (*for quantity*) kìmānìn: he gave me ~ ₦5 yā bā nì
kìmānìn naiɽà bìyaɽ. d. (*for past unre-
alized event*) saurā kàɗan, saurā ƙiris
(+ *subjunct.*): we ~ collided saurā ƙiris
mù yi karō dà jūnā; the plane ~ left us
behind saurā kàɗan jirgîn yà baɽ mù.

**alms** *n* sadakà *f* (oCi): give ~ bā dà sadakà
= yi sadakà; beg for ~ yi baɽà *f.*

**aloe** *n* kabàɽ gīwā *f.*

**alone** *adv* a. (*only*) kaɗai *adv*: he ~ did it
correctly shī kaɗai yā yī shì daidai;
I did it all ~ nā yī shì nī kaɗai; she
lives ~ tanà zàune ita kaɗai; the house
stands ~ on the hill gidân shī kaɗai nè
kân tudùn; only we and we ~ can do
this wannàn sai mū. b. (*by oneself*) à
kàɗàice *adv*: she sat there ~ tā zaunà
cân à kàɗàice.

**along** *prep* à bàkin *prep*: trees grow ~ the
road àkwai itātuwà à bàkin hanyà; ~
with tàre dà: he came ~ with 2 friends
yā zō tàre dà àbōkī biyu.

**alongside** *prep* dab dà *prep*: we were riding our horses ~ each other munà hàye dà
dawākī dab dà jūnā.

**aloof** *adj*: be ~ (*hang, stand back*) tōgè *v4*,
yi tōgiyā *f,* rābē *v4.*

**aloud** *adv*: read ~ kaɽàntā à fīlī.

**alphabet** *n* a. abjàdī / àbjàdī *m*: Arabic,
Roman ~ abjàdin Làɽabcī, Tūɽancī;
alphabetical order tsàrìn abjàdī: put
them in ~ical order in Hausa kà tsàrà
su cikin abjàdin Hausa. b. (*ABC's*)
àbàcàdà *m*: he doesn't know the ~ yet bài
iyà àbàcàdà ba tùkùna.

**already** *adv*: ~ do sth. rigā *v0* (+ *complet.*): this chair is ~ coming apart
kujèraɽ nàn tā rigā tā fàrà ɓallèwā;
he has ~ left yā rigā yā tāshì.

**also** *adv* a. (*too*) mā *adv*: I ~ saw him nī mā
nā gan shì. b. (*and*) kuma *adv*: he went
to Kano and ~ to Sokoto yā jē Kanò yā
kuma jē Sakkwato.

**alter** *v* a. (*change*) sākè *v4,* canzà / canjà
*v1*: the plane ~ed its course jirgìn samà
yā sàkè hanyàrsà; he ~ed his passport
illegally yā canjà fàsfô ɗinsà bà bisà
ƙā'idà ba. b. (*clothing*) gyārà *v1*: the
tailor ~ed my pants tēlà yā gyārà minì
wàndō.

**alteration** *n* canjī *m* (e²).

**alternate 1.** *v* sauyà *v1*: they ~ planting

maize and guinea corn anā sauyà shūkàȓ masāȓā dà dāwā.

2. *n* (*admin.*) na ᴡucìn gādì *m*: I've been appointed as an ~ an sâ ni à matsayin ᴡucìn gādì.

**alternation** *n* jūyì *m*: the ~ of wet and dry seasons jūyìn rānī dà dāminā.

**alternative** *n*: there's no ~ bābù ᴡata hanyà dàbam.

**although** *conj* kō dà yakè...(àmmā), duk dà yakè, duk dà cêᴡā *conj*: ~ I was sick I went to the meeting kō dà yakè inā rashìn lāfiyà, àmmā nā jē tàrôn; = duk dà bā nī dà lāfiyà, nā jē tàrôn; ~ it may seem strange to you, it is true duk dà cêᴡā zā kà yi màmākìnsà, gaskiyā nè.

**altitude** *n* tsawō *m*: the mountain has an ~ of 1800 meters dūtsèn yanà dà tsawon mītà dubū dà dàrī takwàs; the plane gained ~ jirgîn yā yi samà sòsai.

**alum** *n* (*crystal form*) alàm / alùm *m*: they soak ~ in water and then rinse their mouths with it anà jiƙà alàm à ruwa à kurkùrè bàkī.

**aluminum, aluminium** *n* gòran ruwā *m*, sànhōlò *m*.

**always** *adv* a. kōyàushè, kullum, dàɗai *adv*: that's how it is ~ done hakà akè yî kōyàushè; it's ~ like that kullum hakà = dàɗai hakà. b. (*to express customary action, use habit. tense*): we ~ eat dinner at 6 mukàn ci tuᴡō dà ƙarfè shidà.

**amateur** *n* a. (*non-professional*): an ~ sportsman matàshin ɗan ᴡàsā. b. (*beginner*) ɗan kòyō *m*, sābon kòyō *m*: he is an ~ ɗan kòyō nè = bài ƙwarè ba = (*pejor.*) ɗan dāgajī nè.

**amaze** *v* bā dà màmākì, buȓgè *v4*: his strength ~d us ƙarfinsà yā bā mù màmākì; be ~d ji màmākì, yi màmākì: we were ~d at his strength mun ji màmākìn ƙarfinsà = ƙarfinsà yā buȓgè mu; amazing! àbin màmākì! = bâ dāmā! = dà buȓgēᴡā!

**ambassador** *n* jàkādà *m*, jàkādìyā *f* ⟨u⟩, [F] àmbàsàdàȓ *n*.

**ambiguity** *n* ninkìn mà'ànā *m*.

**ambition** *n* (*positive*) kīshìn zūci *m*, būrì / gūrì *m*: his ~ is to become a minister būrìnsà yà zama ministà.

**ambitious** *adj*: he is ~ (*greedy*) zàrā nè; he is (too) ~ (*pejor.*) yanà dà sôn īkò = yā cikà būrì.

**ambulance** *n* mōtàȓ asìbiti *f*, àmbùlàn / àmbùlàs *f*, [F] àmbùlâns *f*.

**ambush** 1. *n* (*lying in wait*) fàkō *m*, kwantō *m*; (*trap*) haƙò *m*.

2. *v* fàkā *v2*, yi fàkon ᴡ. *m*, yi ᴡà kwantō *m*, yi haƙòn ᴡ. *m*; (*Mil.*) yi kwanton-ɓaunā *m*: they were ~ed and killed an yi musù kwanton-ɓaunā an kashè su.

**amen** *excl* āmin *excl* (*used whenever Allàh is invoked in greetings or wishes*).

**amends** *n*: make ~ to so. yi ᴡà gyāran fuskà.

**America** *n* Amìȓkà *f*, Àmēȓikà *f*, [F] Àmìȓîk *f*.

**American** 1. *n* (*psn.*) bà'àmiȓkè *m*, [F] àmìȓkân *m*.

2. *adj* na Amìȓkà.

**amicably** *adv* cikin girmā dà aȓzìkī.

**ammunition** *n* hàȓsāshì *m*, [F] kàȓtūshì *m*: ~ belt dàmaràȓ hàȓsāshì = jìgìdaȓ hàȓsāshì.

**amnesia** *n* mantuᴡā *f*.

**amnesty** *n* ahuᴡà *f*: grant so. ~ yi ᴡà ahuᴡà.

**among, amongst** *prep* a. cikin *prep*: it is ~ the world's largest cities tanà cikin mànyan garūruᴡàn dūniyà. b. (*out of*) à cikin, dàgà ciki: ~ my relatives, I like Sule best à cikin 'yan'uᴡānā dukà, nā fi sôn Sulè. c. (*between*) tsàkānin *prep*: divide it ~ yourselves kù rabà tsàkāninkù; he lived ~ them yā zaunà tsàkāninsù.

**amount** *n* a. (*quantity*) yawà *m*: the ~ of rain was insufficient yawàn ruwā bài isa ba; a huge ~ mài ɗimbin yawà, hamì *adv*: a huge ~ of goods kāyā mài ɗimbin yawà = kāyā hamì; a moderate ~ kīmà *adv*, (mài) ɗan dāmā: give me a small ~ of peanuts ɗebō minì gyàɗā 'yaȓ kīmà; there's a moderate ~ of water in the tank ruwan tankì dà ɗan dāmā. b. (*estimated* ~) kìmānì *m*: the approximate ~ to be spent kìmānìn kuɗī dà zā à kashè. c. (*total*) jimlà *f* ⟨oCi⟩: what is the ~ of the bill? mènē nè jimlàȓ kuɗîn?

**amount to** *v* kai *v\**: it didn't ~ to ₦5 bài kai naiȓà bìyaȓ ba; the matter doesn't ~ to anything màganàȓ bà tà kai kōmē ba = màganàȓ bà à bàkin kōmē takè ba.

**amphetamine** *n* à-ji-garau *m*, kafsò *m*.

**amplify** *v* (*sound*) ƙārà ƙarfin sautì.

**amputate** *v* yankè *v4*: they ~d his leg sun yankè masà ƙafà.

**amulet** *n* (*with writing*) lāyà *f* ⟨lāyū⟩, *see* charm.

**amuse** *v* bā ᴡ. dàriyā, sâ ᴡ. dàriyā.

**amusing** *adj* (mài) ban dàriyā.

**an** *art*, *see* a.

**anaemia**, *n*, *see* anemia.

**anaesthesia**, *n*, *see* anesthesia.

analogy n ƙìyāsì m: make an ~ with yi ƙìyāsì dà.

analysis n nazàřī m, lìssāfì m.

analyst n mài nazàřī m.

analyze v a. yi nazàřī m, yi lìssāfì m, lissāfā v1. b. (in Lit.) fēɗè v4; ~ poetic meter yankà karìn wāƙà.

anarchy n mulkìn rūɗū m, mulkìn ìnā-ruwānā m.

anatomy n ilìmin hàlittàř jìkī m.

ancestors n (predecessors) mutànen dàurī p, (one's own kin) kàkànnin-kàkànnī p.

ancestral adj ~ home asalī m.

ancestry n jinī m: they have the same ~ jininsù ɗaya; of mixed ~ nā dà gamì: she is of mixed ~ tanā da gamì.

anchor n ƙūgìyā f (oCi): lower the ship's ~ ɗaurà wà jirgī ƙūgìyā.

ancient adj na dâ, na dàurī: in ~ times à zāmànin dâ; ~ history tāřīhìn mutànen dâ.

and conj a. (between nouns) dà conj: women ~ children dà mātā dà yârā; Kande ~ Ladi dà Kànde dà Lādì. b. (for sequential action) sai conj (with rel. complet): they chatted awhile ~ then went on their own way sun yi 'yař hīřa sai sukà kāmà hanyàřsù dàbam. c. (between full clauses, not usu. translated): I went ~ told them nā jē nā gayà musù; he didn't go out ~ look bài fìta yā dūbà ba; d. (also, in addition, used between clauses) kuma adv: they went to Zaria ~ to Kaduna sun jē Zāriyà kuma sun jē Kàdūna; take this to him ~ wait for his reply kà kai wannàn wurinsà kà kuma jirā amsàřsà. e. (contrastively): ~ as for X X mā: she went to market ~ as for me, I stayed home tā tàfi kàsuwā nī mā nā zaunà gidā.

anemia n fara f, ƙarancin jinī m: he became anemic fara tā kāmà shi.

anesthesia n māgànin sâ barcī m; give so. ~ yi wà àllūřař barcī.

angel n màlā'ikà m (u).

anger 1. n fushī m, hàsalà f.
2. v sâ w. fushì, fusātā v1: his behavior ~ed me hālinsà yā sâ ni fushì; (infuriate) tunzùrā v1.

angle n kusùrwā f (oCi).

anglophone adj: ~ countries ƙasàshē rènon Ingìlà.

angry adj (mài) fushī m; be, get ~ fùsātà v3, (infuriated) hàřzuƙà v3, hàsalà v3; be ~ with yi fushī dà: don't be ~ with me kadà kì yi fushī dà nī = kadà kì yi minì fushì; make so. ~ sâ w. fushì:

she made the other women ~ tā sâ sauran mātā sun yi fushì.

anguish n (esp. physical) àzābà f; (esp. mental) ùƙūbà f, tàgàyyařà f; cause so. ~ tagayyàřā v1.

animal n (esp. domesticated) dabbà f (oCi), (wild) nāmàn dājì m (nāmun dājì).

animal husbandry n kīwòn dabbōbī m.

animate 1. adj (mài) râi m.
2. v rāyař (dà) v5.

animism n tsāfì m; (~ combined with Islam) tsubbù m.

animosity n ƙìyayyà f.

ankle, anklebone n idòn ƙafà m, idòn sau/sāwu m: she hurt her ~ tā ji cīwò à santà; on the ~ à sau/sāwu adv.

anklet n (of heavy brass) munduwā f (mundàyē).

annihilate v (a group) rūshè v4.

anniversary n bìkin tunāwā m.

announce v bā dà sanâřwā, shēlàntā v1: they ~d the arrival of the train an bā dà sanâřwař isôwař jirgin ƙasà; (by town crier) yi shèlà f, yi yēkùwā f: the town crier went around town announcing that a child was lost mài shèlà yā yi shèlà cêwā wani yārò yā ɓacè.

announcement n sanâřwā f; (done by town crier) shèlà f, yēkùwā f; public ~ (of trouble, emergency) gangamī m: make a public ~ bugà gangamī.

announcer n mài shèlà n, mài yēkùwā n; (on radio, television) mài bā dà làbàřai n.

annoy v a. (bother, disturb) bâ w. haushī, ɓātà wà râi: he ~ed me yā bā nì haushī = nā ji haushinsà = yā ɓātà minì râi; why were you so ~ed? mè ya ɓātà makà râi hakà? I was ~ed that you didn't come rashìn zuwànkà yā ɓātà minì râi; nothing ~s me more than gossip bâ àbîn dà ya sâ ni haushī sai tsēgùmī; be ~ed ji haushī m, ɓācì v3b: I was ~ed nā ji haushī = râinā yā ɓācì; we were ~ed at the delay mun ji haushin jìnkirī; I was ~ed that he got angry with the children nā ji haushī dà ya yi fushī dà yârā; look ~ed sākè fuskà, ɓātà fuskà. b. (pester) fìtinà v2, kāwō fìtinà.

annoyance n haushī m, ɓācìn râi m, tsāmin râi m.

annoying adj a. (mài) ban haushī, (mài) kāwō fìtinà: a very ~ thing àbin gwànin ban haushī. b. (frustrating) (mài) tàkâicī m: the ~ thing is that... àbîn tàkâicī shī nè....

annually adv shèkarà-shèkarà adv.

**annul** v (a marriage) kashè v4; (a law) sōkè v4, ɗanyàtā v1; (a treaty, agreement) warwàrē v4.

**another** det & adj a. (of the same kind) wani m, wata f: I want ~ one inà sôn wani. b. (of a different kind) wani dàbam, wata dàbam: they moved to ~ town sun ƙaura zuwà wani gàrī dàbam.

**answer** v a. (respond to so.) amsà wà v1: she didn't ~ him at all bà tà amsà masà dà kōmē ba. b. (a question, request) bā dà amsà, mai dà amsà / mayar̃ (dà) amsà: she wasn't able to ~ all the questions bà tà iyà mai dà amsà gà duk tambayōyîn ba = bà tà iyà bā dà amsōshin duk tambayōyîn ba.

**ant(s)** n (no gener. term): (very small) kiyāshī m; (small black biting ~) cìnnākà m; (with wings) tùmà-dà-gayyà m; (large black, driver ~) tùr̃ùruwà f; (very tiny, in masses) kwar̃kwàsà f; (large stink ~) gwānō m; sugar ~ shā-zumāmì m.

**antagonist** n àbōkin gàbā m, àbōkin hàmayyà m.

**antagonistic** adj (psn.) mài faɗà n, (mài) jìdālì m.

**anteater** n dâbgī m ⟨ai⟩.

**antelope** n (diff. types): (bushbuck) màzō m, r̃àgon ruwa m; (roan) gwankī m ⟨aye⟩; (cob) mār̃àyā f ⟨oCi⟩; (western hartebeest) kankì m; (Senegal hartebeest) darī m; (klipspringer) gàdar̃ dūtsè f; (reedbuck) kwàntà-r̃àfi m.

**antenna** n ēr̃iyà f.

**anthem** n: the Nigerian national ~ tāken Nìjēr̃iyà.

**anthill** n (small) jiɓà f, (large) sūrì / shūrì m.

**anthology** n dīwānì m ⟨ai⟩.

**anthrax** n cīwòn saifà m, har̃bìn dājì m.

**anthropology** n (social) ilìmin hàlayyà dà àl'àdun ɗan Adàm m.

**anticipate** v a. (reckon on) ƙaddàr̃à v1: they ~ having a good harvest this year sun ƙaddàr̃à sāmùn àmfànin gōnā bana. b. (expect) zàtā v2 ⟨zàtō⟩, yi tsàmmānì m: I'm anticipating his arrival inà tsàmmānin zuwànsà.

**antidote** n makarī m: an ~ to venom makarin dafì; there are some poisons for which no ~ exists àkwai wasu gubà waɗàndà bābù makarinsù.

**antimony** n kwàllī m, tōzàlī m: she applied ~ to her eyes tā shāfà kwàllī = tā sā tōzàlī.

**anti-Semitism** n ƙyàmar̃ Yahūdāwā f.

**anus** n (euphem.) dubùr̃ā f, (pejor.) takāshi f, tsūlìyā f.

**anvil** n uwar̃ maƙērā f.

**anxiety** n jŭyàyī m, fādùwar̃ gàbā f.

**anxious** adj a. (worried): be ~ yi jŭyàyī m, dàmu v7: his failure to return made her ~ rashìn dāwôwar̃sà yā sâ ta dàmuwā. b. (impatient): be ~ ƙàgarà (dà) v3: we're ~ to leave before it rains mun ƙàgarà mù tāshì kàfìn à yi ruwā. c. (eager, hopeful): be ~ yi allà-allà f: the children are ~ to please the teacher yârā nà allà-allà sù kyâutā wà mālàmī.

**any** quant & pro a. wani m, wata f, waɗansu/wasu p: do you want ~? kanà sôn wata? I haven't seen ~ around here bàn ga wani à nân ba; are there ~ children there? àkwai wasu yârā can? ~ at all kō ɗaya: I haven't seen ~ at all around here bàn ga kō ɗaya à nân ba. b. (in neg. sent. or questions, usu. not overtly translated) he didn't give me ~ bread bài bā nì bur̃ōdì ba; do you have ~ money? kanà dà kudī? he doesn't have ~ work bâ shi dà aikì; is there ~ water here? àkwai ruwā à nân? = dà ruwā à nân? no, there isn't ~ ā'à, bābù (shī); is there ~? are there ~? àkwai shi? àkwai su? c. (whatever) kōwànè m, kōwàcè f, kōwàɗannè p: I'll settle for ~ bicycle that you can give me zân dànganà dà kōwànè irìn kèkèn dà zā à bā nì.

**anybody** pro, see anyone.

**anyhow** adv, see anyway.

**anyone** pro a. (in neg. sent.) kōwā pro: we didn't meet ~ on the road bà mù hàɗu dà kōwā à hanyà ba; there isn't ~ here bâ kōwā à nân. b. (as subj of interrog. sent.) wani m, wata f, waɗansu/wasu p; (or use àkwai + wândà m, wâddà f, waɗàndà p): has ~ come? wani yā zō? = àkwai wândà ya zō? is ~ outside? àkwai wâddà kè wàje? = kā ga wata à wàje? is there ~ here? dà mùtûm nân? c. (~ at all, everyone) kōwā m: ~ can learn a language kōwā nà iyà kòyon harshè; he knows her better than ~ else yā san tà fìye dà kōwā. d. ~ who (whoever) duk wândà m, duk wâddà f, duk waɗàndà p; kōwànnē m, kōwàccè f, kōwàɗannè p: ~ who wants to leave may do so duk wândà yakè sô yà tāshì sai yà tāshì = kōwànnē yakè sô yà tāshì sai yà tāshì.

**anything** pro a. (whatever) duk àbîn dà m, kōmēnē nè m: I'll do ~ that needs to be done zân yi duk àbîn dà akè bùkātà; ~ that you find is yours kōmēnē nè ka sāmù, nākà nē; ~ you need, just ask kōmē kakè bùkātā kà yi tàmbayā; I don't want ~ to do with him bā nà sôn wata mà'āmalā dà shī. b. (~ at all, everything) kōmē m: more than ~, they want to live in peace fìye dà kōmē, sunā nēman zaman lùmānā. c. (in neg. sent.) kōmē m: I don't know ~ about that bàn san kōmē ba gàme dà wannàn; there isn't ~ in it bā kōmē à ciki. d. (esp. in interrog. sent.) wani àbù, àbîn dà: has ~ happened to him? wani àbù yā sàmē shì? = àkwai àbîn dà ya sàmē shì? is there ~ that you need? kanā bùkātàr̃ wani àbù nē? = àkwai àbîn dà kakè bùkātā? ~ else wani àbù dàbam.

anyway adv a. (in whatever way) (ta) kōyàyā adv, kō ta yàyā: do it ~ you like kà yī shì kōyàyā. b. (nevertheless) duk dà hakà: he didn't want to go but he went ~ bā yà sô yà tàfi àmmā duk dà hakà yā tàfi.

anywhere adv a. (~ at all, everywhere) kō'ìnā, duk indà: you can get it ~ anā sàmùnsà kō'ìnā; sit ~ you like kà zaunà duk indà kakè sô. b. (in neg. sent.) kō'ìnā adv: we didn't go ~ bà mù jē kō'ìnā ba = bà indà mukà jē. c. (in interrog. sent.) wani wurī: did you go ~ yesterday? kun tàfi wani wurī jiyà?

apart adv a. keep ~ from k̃auràcè wà v4, kaucè wà v4: the women keep ~ from the men mātā sunā kaucè wà mazā. b. ~ from ban dà: ~ from that, what else did you buy? ban dà wannàn, sauran mè ka sàyā?

apartheid n wāriyar̃ launìn fātā f.

apartment n gidā m ⟨aCe⟩; ~ building (with upper storey) bēnē m ⟨aye⟩.

apathy (lack of energy) kàsālà f.

ape n, see monkey.

apex n (tip of hat, roof) k̃ōk̃uwā f.

aphrodisiac n (for men) gagài m.

apologetic adj (mài) nēman gāfar̃ā m.

apologize v tūba v3a; ~ to so. nèmi gāfar̃ar̃ w.

apostate n wàndà ya yi r̃iddā.

apostasy n r̃iddā f.

apostrophe n bak̃in 6òye m.

apparatus n (tools) kāyan aikì m; (piece of equipment) nā'ūr̃ā f ⟨oCi⟩.

apparently adv gà àlāmā f: ~ there's been a mistake gà àlāmā an yi kuskurè.

appeal 1. n a. (request) r̃ōk̃ō n. b. (Law) k̃ārā f, àfîl m.
2. v yi àfîl, ɗaukàkà k̃ārā.

appear v a. (come out) fìta v3: the newspaper ~s 3 times a week jàr̃īdā tanā fitôwā sàu ukù à sātī; ~ on so. (e.g.

of rash on body) fitō wà v6: some pimples ~ed on his cheek k̃urājē sun fitō masà à kuncì. b. (unexpectedly) 6ullō v6: they were going along when a goat suddenly ~ed anā tàfiyà sai wata àkuyà ta 6ullō. c. (be apparent): it ~s that gà àlāmà: it ~s that he is sick gà àlāmā bā shi dà lāfiyà. d. (Relig., be revealed) bàyyanà v3: it is believed that the Mahdi will ~ first in the east an yi īmānì Màhàdì zâi bàyyanà dàgà gabàs.

appearance n a. (of thing, psn.) sūr̃ā f: she has a nice ~ tanā dà kyàkkyāwar̃ sūr̃ā. b. (the look of) kàmā f, shìge m: he has changed his ~ yā sākè kàmā; the skink has the ~ of a snake jìkin kul6à shìge na macìjī nē = jìkin kul6à kàmar̃sà ta macìjī nè. c. (in terms of dress, clothing) shìgā f: he has the ~ of a European yā yi shìgar̃ Tùr̃àwā; don't judge people by their ~ kadà kà yankè hukuncìn mutànē ta hanyàr̃ shìgar̃sù.

appease v làllāsà/r̃àrrāsà v2 ⟨lallāshī⟩: she always tries to ~ her husband kullum tanā ta lallāshin màigidantà; he was not ~d by the gift that they gave him kyàutar̃ dà akà bā shi bài làllāshē shì ba.

append v mak̃àlā v1.

appendicitis n tsirò à uwar̃ hanjī m.

appendix n (of book) r̃àtàyē m.

appetite n cî m: he has a big ~ cî gàrē shì; (yen for delicacies) marmarī m: he has an ~ for sweet things yanà marmarin kāyan zākì.

applaud v tāfà hannū m, yi tàfī m.

applause n ban tàfī m.

apple n tùffā f.

application form n (for work) takàr̃dar̃ nēman aikì f.

apply v a. (e.g. for work) nēmā v2 ⟨nēmā⟩: ~ for entrance to university nèmi shìgā jāmi'à. b. (concern) shāfà v2: the rule doesn't ~ here dòkā̃r̃ bà tà shāfi wannàn ba. c. ~ oneself (work hard) mai dà himmà, mai dà k̃ōk̃arī: you should ~ yourself to your work kù mai dà himmà gà aikìnkù.

appoint v (for official position) naɗà v1: he has been ~ed chairman an naɗà shi shùgàbā.

appointment n a. àlkawàr̃ī m; make an ~ (for a certain time) yi àlkawàr̃ī, sâ rānā: we made an ~ for next Wednesday mun yi àlkawàr̃ī à ran Làr̃abà mài zuwà = mun sâ rānar̃ Làr̃abà mài zuwà; fail to make an ~, break an ~ karyà àlkawàr̃ī.

b. (*rendezvous*) magamā *f*: we made an ~ at a certain place mun yi magamā à wurī kàzā. c. (*to a position*) nadĩ *m*: everyone was pleased with his ~ as president kōwā yā ji dādin nadìnsà shũgàbā.

appraisal *n* (*by judge for settlement of debt*) kīmā / ƙīmā *f*: they have made an ~ of his goods an yi wà kāyansà kīmā.

appreciate *v* yabā dà *v1*: we ~ his help mun yabā dà tàimakonsà.

apprehend *v* (*catch*) kāmā *v1*.

apprehension a. (*anxiety*) jũyàyī *m*, fādũwaɍ gàbā *f*. b. (*arrest*) kāmũ *m*.

apprehensive *adj*: be ~ (*anxious*) yi jũyàyī *m*: I was ~ about seeing him inà jũyàyin ganinsà; be ~ (*alarmed, fearful*): on hearing the noise, she became ~ dà jîn ƙārāɍ sai gàbantà yā fādì.

apprentice *n* ɗan kõyō *m*; (*of a truck driver*) kàren mōtā *m*.

approach 1. *vt* (*come close*) rà6ā *v2*, kùsātā / kùsantā *v2*.
2. *vi* ƙarātō *v6*, kusātō *v6*, gabātō *v6*: Sallah is ~ing sallā tā kusātō.

appropriate¹ *adj* a. (*suitable, of sth.*): be ~ dācè *v4*: the way he was dressed was perfectly ~ shìgāɍ dà ya yi tā dācè sôsai; this would be an ~ gift to give her wannàn zâi dācè à bā tà kyàutā. b. (*fitting, of an action*): be ~ càncantà *v3*, kyàutu *v7* (+ *impers. 3rd pers. subj pro*): it would be ~ for us to visit him next week yā càncantà mù zìyàrcē shì māƙò mài zuwà; it would not be ~ for us to tell him bài kyàutu mù gayà masà ba.

appropriate² *v* yi kasāfī *m*.

appropriation *n* kasāfī *m*: ~ of funds kasàfin kudī.

approval *n* yàɍdā *f*, izìnī *m*: without ~ bā tàre dà an bā dà izìnī ba.

approve *v* a. (*consider favorably*) amìncē wà *v4*, yàɍda dà *v3*, yi na'àm dà: they ~d the bill sun amìncē wà shirìn dōkā; he ~s of my work yā yàɍda dà aikìnā they ~d of our going sun yi na'àm dà tàfiyàɍmù; ~ of so. yi wà yàbō *m*: I ~ of her nā yi matà yàbō; ~ of so. doing sth. yaɍjè wà *v4*, yàɍdaɍ wà *vdat*: I ~ of Audu buying a car nā yaɍjè wà Audù yà sàyi mōtā; not ~ ƙi jinin w.a.: I don't ~ of smoking nā ƙi jinin shân tābà. b. (*affirm*) tabbataɍ (dà) *v5*.

approximate *adj* kīmāɍ, kìmānìn: what is its ~ weight? mēnē nè kīmāɍ nauyinsà? the ~ amount to be spent kìmānìn kudī dà zā à kashè.

approximately *adv* mìsālìn, kàmaɍ, wajen, kìmānìn: there were ~ 200 people there àkwai mìsālìn mùtûm dàrī biyu à càn.

approximation *n* kīmā / ƙīmā *f*.

April *n* Àfìɍīlù *m*.

Arab *n* bàlāɍabè *m*.

Arabic *n* Lāɍabcī *m*.

arbitrate *v* sulhùntā *v1*.

arbitration *n* sulhũ *m*.

arch 1. *n* bàka *m* 〈una²〉.
2. *v* (*stretch backwards*) yi mīƙā *f*; (*of cat*) yi dōrō *m*.

archer *n* mahàɍbī *m*, mài bàkā *n*.

area *n* a. (*geographical, directional*) sāshè / sāshì *m* 〈Ca〉, yankì *m* 〈una〉: in the ~ of Kano à yankìn Kanò; Tasawa is an ~ within Maradi Tāsāwā wani yankìn ƙasaɍ Marādi. b. (*part of, portion of*) ɓangarè *m*: a large ~ of the country is in the desert bàbban ɓangarèn ƙasāɍ nā cikin hàmādà. c. (*open ~, space*) fīlī *m* 〈aye〉. d. (*dimensions*) yawàn fīlī *m* 〈aye〉: what is the ~ of this room? nawà nē yawàn fīlin dākin nân? e. (*grounds of partic. place*) hàɍābà *f*: the university ~ (*campus*) hàɍābàɍ jāmi'à.

arena *n* fagē *m* 〈aCe〉: in the political ~ à fagen sìyāsà.

argot *n* zàuràncē *m*.

argue *v* yi gaɍdamā *f*, yi jàyayyà *f*, yi fadà *m*: ~ about politics yi gaɍdamā à kân sìyāsà; (*back & forth without resolution*) yi cācaɍ bàkī.

argument *n* a. fadà *m* 〈fàdàce-fàdàce〉, gaɍdamā / gaddamā *f* 〈gaɍdàndamī〉: what brought about this ~? mè ya kāwō wannàn fadà? I don't want any ~s bā nà son gaɍdamā; a heated ~ ƙàzāmaɍ gaɍdamā. b. (*debate, discussion*) mùhāwaɍā *f*.

argumentative *adj* (mài) gaɍdamā *f*, (mài) jìdālì *m*: don't be so ~ kadà kà cikà gaɍdamā.

arise *v* tāshì *v3b*.

aristocracy *n* sàrākai *p*.

arithmetic *n* lìssāfì *m*.

arm *n* hannū *m* 〈uwa, aye〉; ~ in ~ ƙàme dà hannū; upper ~ damtsè *m* 〈a-a〉.

armed *adj*: he is ~ yanā rìƙe dà makāmī; they were ~ with spears and swords màkàmansù māsu dà takubbà; commit ~ robbery yi fashì dà màkàmai.

armistice *n* yàɍjējēnìyaɍ tsai dà yāƙī *f*.

armlet *n* (*with charms sewn in*) kàmbū *m* 〈una〉, dāgùmī *m* 〈u-a〉; *see* charm.

armor *n* (*of chain mail*) sùlkè *m*.

armpit *n* hamàtā *f* 〈u〉.

arms n (Mil.) màkǎmai p: the ~ race gàsař ƙīràř màkǎmai; ~ control agreement yàřjējēnìyař ƙayyàdè màkǎman nūkìlìyà.

army n (rùndunař) sōjà f, [F] sōjì f, [F] lařmē f, (esp. in tales) yāƙì m; join, leave the ~ shìga, bař sōjà.

around 1. adv a. (approximately) wajen, mìsālìn, kàmař, see about. b. (included in the meaning of var. verbs): go, turn ~ (rotate in a circle) jūyà v1: the wheel is going ~ and ~ wīlì nà ta jūyàwā; go ~ (circumnavigate) kēwàyà v1, zāgà v1, zāgàyē v4: they went for a ride ~ town sun zāgà gàrī à mōtà; go all ~ the country zazzàgà duk ƙasář; the earth goes ~ the sun dūniyà tanà zāgàyà rānā; show so. ~ zāgà dà w.; look ~ waigà v1: he looked ~ and stared at us yā waigō yā zubà manà idò; come ~ (wake up from coma) fařfadō v6.
2. prep wajen prep: she lives somewhere ~ Gwale gidantà wajen Gwàlè nē.

arouse v tā dà / tāyař (dà) v5, fařkař (dà) v5.

arrange v a. (prepare) shiryà v1: we've ~d to meet at the station mun shiryà zā mù hàɗu à tashàř; ~ for so. to do sth. yi wà hanyà f: can you ~ for me to meet the village head? zā kà yi minì hanyàř ganin hākìmī? b. (put in order) tsārà v1, yi fasàlī m; the new city is well ~d sābon birnîn yanà dà kyân fasàlī.

arrangement n a. (preparation) shirì m: they made ~s to leave early in the morning sun yi shirìn yîn sàmmakō. b. (orderliness) fasàlī m, tsārì m.

arrears n tsōhon bāshì m: he is in ~ yanà ɗauke dà tsōhon bāshì.

arrest 1. v a. (seize) kāmà v1: he was ~ed by the police 'yan sàndá sun kāmà shi. b. (stop) tsai dà / tsayař (dà) v5: the spread of the disease has been ~ed an tsai dà yàɗuwař cùtař.
2. n kāmù m: many ~s were made an yi kāmù dà yawà; house ~ ɗaurìn tālālà m: some politicians have been placed under house ~ an yi wà wasu 'yan sìyāsà ɗaurìn tālālà.

arrival n isôwā f, ìsā f, zuwà m, sàuka f: on his ~ dà isōwařsà = dà zuwànsà.

arrive v (esp. of plane) sàuka v3; ~ at kai v*, ìsa v3: they ~d at Kano at 6 o'clock sun ìsa Kanò dà ƙarfè shidà.

arrogance n (of character) girman kâi m, fādin râi m, dàgawà f, jī-jī dà kâi m. b. (in dress or manner) tàƙamā f.

arrogant adj (mài) girman kâi, (mài) fādin râi, (mài) jī-jī dà kâi: he is really ~ girman kâi gàrē shì; behave ~ly to so. yi wà girman kâi.

arrow n kibiyà f ⟨oCi⟩: set an ~ in the bow haƙà kibiyà à bàkā; shoot an ~ hařbà kibiyà; bow and ~ kwàrī dà bàkā.

arrowhead n tsìnin kibiyà m.

arsenal n (Mil.) gidan màkǎmai m.

art n (artistry) fàsāhà f.

artery n jījìyā f ⟨oCi⟩, bà-jìki m.

arthritis n amōsànin gàɓɓai m, sanyin ƙashī m.

article n a. (any thing) àbù m (in the genitive, use àbin), àbā f ⟨uwa²⟩. b. (in newspaper) làbārì m ⟨u⟩. c. (essay) maƙàlà f.

artillery n ìgwā f ⟨oCi⟩: long-range ~ ìgwā mài dōgon zangò.

artisan n ɗan sànā'à m.

artistic adj (mài) fàsāhà f.

artistry n fàsāhà f.

as 1. conj & prep a. (in compar. constr., use kai v* + abstr. n): he is ~ tall ~ I yā kai nì tsawō = tsawonmù ɗaya; he is ~ strong ~ a lion mài ƙarfī sai kà cê zākì; today is not ~ cold ~ yesterday yâu bài kai sanyin jiyà ba. b. (like) kàmař: I consider him ~ a friend nā ɗauke shì kàmař àbōkī; do just ~ I tell you to kù yi kàmař yàddà na gayà mukù; leave it ~ it is bàř shi yàddà yakè. ~ you all know... kàmař yàddà kukà sanī dai.... c. ~ if kàmař: he treated me ~ if he didn't know me yā ɗaukē nì kàmař bài san nì ba; I felt ~ if I would faint jī nakè kàmař zân yi sūmā; ~ if (simile) sai kà cê: he's dressed ~ if he were the chief yanà sànye dà kāyā sai kà cê shī sarkī nè. d. (other uses): ~ far ~ (up to) hař prep: they went ~ far ~ Katsina sun yi tàfiyà hař Kàtsinà; ~ far ~ (up to a limit) hař iyākař/iyākacin: ~ far ~ we could see hař iyākacin ganinmù; ~ long ~ I live hař iyākař rāinā; ~ for X X kàm = X kùwa: ~ for politics, I have nothing to do with it sìyāsà kàm, bâ ruwānā dà ita; ~ well ~ duk dà: I want this one ~ well ~ that one inà sôn wannàn duk dà wancàn.
2. conj a. (while, in rel. cl.) lōkàcîn dà, sā'àn dà / sā'àd dà, yàyîn dà: ~ we were preparing to leave, it began to rain sā'àn dà mukè shirìn tàfiyà, an yi ta ruwā. b. (since, because) tun dà: ~ I didn't hear from you, I continued on tun dà bàn ji làbārìnkà ba, nā ci gàba. c. (other uses): ~ soon ~ nan dà nan: ~ soon ~ you see him tell me nan dà nan

ascetic 15 assure

dà ka gan shì kà gayà minì; ~ long ~ muddìn / muddàř *conj*: ~ long ~ you don't inform him, I will agree muddìn bà kà shâidā masà ba, zân yàřda.

**ascetic** *n* mài zuhudù *n*, (*esp. in Islam*) sūfī *m* ⟨aye⟩.

**asceticism** *n* zuhudù *m*, halwà *f*.

**ashamed** *adj*: be ~ ji kunyà *f*, kùnyatà *v3*: aren't you ~ of yourself? bā kyà jîn kunyà? I am ~ of him inà jîn kunyàřsà = yā bā nì kunyà; make so. ~ bâ w. kunyà, sâ w. kunyà: the boy's behavior made his father ~ hālin yāròn yā bâ ùbansà kunyà.

**ashes** *n* tòkà *f*.

**aside** *adv*: put, set ~ ajìyē w.a. wajē ɗaya; step ~ for so. kaucè wà *v4*, bâ w. hanyà: I stepped ~ for the soldier nā kaucè wà sōjà = nā bâ sōjà hanyà.

**ask** *v* (*so.*) tàmbayà *v2*, yi wà tàmbayà *f*; I ~ed him for news of the war nā tàmbàyē shì làbāřìn yāƙìn = nā yi masà tàmbayà gàme dà làbāřìn yāƙìn; he ~ed Ladi what she wanted yā tàmbàyi Lādì àbîn dà takè sô; ~ a question yi tàmbayà *f*; ~ around for sth. needed yi cigiyàř w.a.: he's ~ing around for a cook yanà cigiyàř kūkù; ~ for (*request*) ròƙā *v2* ⟨ròƙō⟩, nèmā *v2* ⟨nēmā⟩: he is ~ing for money yanà ròƙon kudī; ~ somewhere for information tùntuɓà *v2*: I ~ed at the police station for information nā tùntùɓi ōfìshin 'yan sàndā.

**askew** *adv* à kàřkàce *adv*: he wore his cap ~ yā sâ hùlařsà à kàřkàce.

**asleep** *adv*: she's ~ tanà barcī; he has fallen ~ barcī yā kwāshè shi; he is still fast ~ hař yànzu yanà shārè barcī.

**aspect** *n* a. (*appearance*) kàmā *f*. b. (*Gram.*) hàngē *m*.

**asphalt** *n* kwàltā *f*.

**aspiration** *n* (*desire*) kīshìn zūci *m*, bùrī *m*.

**aspirin** *n* asfìřìn *m*, [F] àsfìřìn *m*: take an ~ shā asfìřìn.

**ass** *n* a. (*donkey*) jàkī *m* ⟨ai, una⟩. b. (*fool*) wāwā *n* ⟨aye⟩, shāshàshā *n*: what an ~ he is! wannàn àkwai wāwā!

**assassinate** *v* kashè *v4*.

**assassination** *n* kisàn gillà *m*.

**assault** *n* fàřmakī *m*, harì *m*: make an ~ on so. kai wà fàřmakī; make an all-out ~ on (*fig.*) yi kūkan kūrā à kân.

**assemble** *v* a. (*gather*) tārà *v1*. b. (~ *equipment*) haɗà *v1*, hařhàdà *v1*.

**assembly** *n* a. (*gathering*) tàrō *m* ⟨uka²⟩; House of A. Màjàlisàř Wàkìlai *f*, [F] Gi-

dan Shāwařà *m*. b. (*at school*) àsambùlè *m*.

**assembly plant** *n* ma'aikatař hařhàdà w.a. *f*: Peugeot car ~ plant ma'aikatař hařhàdà mōtōcī Fìjô.

**assert** *v* (*state*) fuřtà *v1*: he ~ed that... yā fuřtà cêwā....

**assertive** *adj* (*esp. of children*) (mài) iyà yî *m*; be ~ yi gîggīwà *f*, nūnà iyà yî *m*.

**assess** *v* kīmàntā / ƙīmàntā *v1*, ƙiyàstā *v1*: the assessor ~ed the amount of the fine to be paid muhùtī yā kīmàntà tàřâř dà zā à biyā; ~ damages ƙiyàstà ɓařnā; ~ so.'s taxes yankè wà hàřājì.

**assessment** *n* kīmà / ƙīmà *f*.

**assessor** *n* (*Law*) muhùtī *m*.

**assets** *n* (*property*) kadařà *f*; (*money*) kudī *m/p*.

**assign** *v* rabà aikì, bā dà aikì.

**assignment** *n* aikì *m*.

**assist** *v* tayà *v1*, tàimakà *v2*: children ~ their parents with housework yârā nà tayà iyàyensù aikìn gidā.

**assistance** *n* tàimakō *n*: this may be of some ~ to you wannàn zâi zama àbin tàimakō gàrē kù.

**assistant** *n* mài tàimakō *n*, matàimàkī *m*: research ~ matàimàkin bìncìkē.

**associate** *v* a. (*connect*) dangàntà *v1*: money is usually ~ed with power anà dangàntà kudī dà īkô. b. (*mix*) haɗà *v1*: don't ~ me with him kadà kà haɗà ni dà shī.

**association** *n* a. (*organization*) ƙungìyà *f* ⟨oCi⟩. b. in ~ with tàre dà.

**assorted** *adj* irì-irì *adv*, dàbam-dàbam *adv*; (*esp. of colored things*) kalà-kalà *adv*: ~ clothing tufāfì kalà-kalà.

**assume** *v* a. (*suppose*) ƙaddàřà *v1*, daukà cêwā: he ~d he would get the position yā ƙaddàřà zā à bā shì mùƙāmìn; I ~ you have permission to do this nā daukà cêwā an bā kà izìnin yîn wannàn. b. (*an office, position*) hau *v**: he ~d the presidency, the throne yā hau kujèrař shùgàbā, gadon sàrautà; ~ responsibility for sth. dàuki nauyin w.a.

**assurance** *n* a. (*certainty*) tabbàcī *m*, àlkawàřī *m*: you have my ~ that it will be finished today nā bā kà tabbàcin zā à gamà yâu. b. (*insurance*) ìnshōřà *f*.

**assure** *v* tabbatař wà (dà) *v5*, tabbàtā wà *v1*: he ~d me that he would send it today yā tabbàtā minì cêwā zâi aikà dà shī yâu; let me ~ you that you won't have any regrets bàri ìn tabbatař makà dà cêwā bà zā kà yi dà-nā-sanì ba.

asthma *n* fùkā *f*, asmā̀ *f*.

astonish *v* bā dà màmākì, buřgè *v4*; something ∼ing àbù mài ban màmākì = àbin buřgèwā.

astray *adv*: go ∼ (*get lost*) ɓatà *v3b*; go ∼ (*in morals*) baudè̃ *v4*, fanɗàrē *v4*: since living in Europe, he has gone ∼ tun zamansà à Tūřai yā fanɗàrē.

astringent *adj* (*esp. of unripe fruit*) (mài) baurī *m*, (mài) bařcī *m*.

astrology *n* hìsābì *m*.

astronaut *n* ɗan samà jànnàtì *m*.

astronomy *n* ilìmin taùřārī *m*.

asylum *n*: insane ∼ gidan mahàukàtā; political ∼ mafakař sìyāsà; seek political ∼ nèmi mafakař sìyāsà; take ∼ in another country yi gudùn hijiřā.

at *prep* a. (*location*) à *prep* (*often omitted before a locative n or after a motion verb; not used after* nà̀): I saw her ∼ school nā gan tà (à) makařantā; she is ∼ school tanà makařantā; when does the train arrive ∼ the station? yàushè jirgîn zâi ìsa (à) tashàř? ∼ so.'s place (à) wurin *prep*: they are ∼ Audu's sunà wurin Audù. b. (*temporal*) à *prep*, dà *prep*: ∼ that time à lōkàcîn nan; the meeting will take place ∼ 6 o'clock zā à yi tàrō à ƙařfè shidà; ∼ 3 o'clock dà ƙařfè ukù; ∼ midnight dà tsakař darē; ∼ first dà farkō; ∼ once nan dà nan; ∼ various times lōkàcī-lōkàcī *adv*, sā'ì-sā'ì *adv*.

atheism *n* mulhidancì *m*.

atheist *n* mulhìdī *m* ⟨ai⟩.

athlete *n* ɗan wàsa *m*.

athletics *n* wàsànnī *p*.

atmosphere *n* (*physical or fig.*) yanàyī *m*: protect the earth's ∼ kiyàyè yanàyin dūniyà̃; the ∼ of the meeting was good yanàyin tàrôn yanà dà kyâu.

atom *n* ƙwàyař zařřà *f*.

atom bomb *n* atàm bâm *m*, [F] bâm *m*.

atonement *n* (*Relig.*) kàfāřā *f*: fast for 3 days as ∼ (*for breaking a law*) yi azùmin kàfāřà kwānā ukù.

atrocity *n* aikìn māshā'à *m*.

attach *v* haɗà *v1*.

attack 1. *v* fàɗà/fař wà *v1*, kai wà harì *m*, kai wà fàřmakì *m*; (*by surprise*) màmayà *v2*; be ready to ∼ tāsam mà *vdat*: when I saw he was ready to ∼ me and beat me up, I took to my heels dà na ga yā tāsam minì zâi dàkē nì, sai nā shēƙà dà gudù; they started ∼ing him verbally sun tāsam masà dà faɗà; ∼ unawares màmayà *v2*: the robbers ∼ed the villagers unawares 'yan fashì sun màmàyi ƙauyàwā.

2. *n* a. (*assault*) harì *m*, fàřmakì *m*. b. (*of epilepsy*) fařfāɗiyā *f*.

attempt 1. *n* ƙòƙarī *m*: we failed in our ∼ ƙòƙarinmù yā kāsà.

2. *v* a. (*try*) yi ƙòƙarī *m*, tāɓùkā *v1*: he didn't ∼ anything bài tāɓùkà kōmē ba. b. (*an act involving great strain*) yunƙùrā *v1*, yi yùnƙurī *m*: an ∼ed coup yùnƙurin jūyìn mulkì.

attend *v* a. (*a particular event*) hàllařtà *v3*, hàlařtà *v2*: I didn't ∼ bàn hàllařà ba; all the students ∼ed the lecture ɗàlìbai dukà sun hàlařci laccà. b. (*on continual basis*): ∼ school yi makařantā = zō makařantā.

attendance *n* zuwà *m*: ∼ at the lectures is required zuwà laccōcîn yā zama tīlàs.

attention *n*: draw so.'s ∼ jāwō hankàlin w., faɗakař dà w.; pay ∼ mai dà hankàlī, lùřa *v3*, kùla *v3*; pay ∼ to so., sth. (*notice*) kulà (dà) *v1*, kùla dà *v3*, lùřa dà *v3*: she doesn't pay any ∼ to him bā tà kùla dà shī = bā tà kulàwā dà shī; they didn't pay ∼ to what he was saying bà sù kulà dà àbin dà yakè màganà à kâi ba; pay ∼ to so., sth. (*listen to*) sàurārà *v2* ⟨sàurārō, sàurārē⟩, kasà kûnnē: some students don't pay ∼ to their teacher wasu ɗàlìbai bā sà̀ sàurāron màlàminsù; stand at ∼ (*Mil.*) yi tanshà *f*, tsayà ƙìƙàm.

attentiveness *n* kùlā *f*, lùřā *f*, hattařā *f*.

attitude *n* (*opinion*) řa'àyī *m*; an I-don't-care ∼ řa'àyin kō ŏho.

attorney *n* lauyà *n* ⟨oCi⟩, [F] àbòkâ *n*; ∼-general bàbban lauyàn gwamnatì *n*.

attract *v* a. (*turn toward*) jāwō / janyō *v6*: ∼ so.'s attention jāwō hankàlin w.; candy ∼s flies àlēwà nà janyō ƙuɗàjē. b. (*be pleasing to*) shērè *v4*: that man always ∼s women mùtumîn nan yakàn shērè mātā.

attractive *adj* (*pretty*) kyàkkyāwā *adj*.

aubergine *n*, see eggplant.

auction *n* gwànjō *m*: there's an ∼ today anà bugà gwànjō yâu.

audience *n* (*of listeners*) màsu sàurārō *p*; (*of spectators*) 'yan kallō *p*.

auditor *n* mài bìncìken kuɗī *n*, ōdità *n* ⟨oCi⟩.

auditorium *n* bàbban dākìn tàrō *m*.

August *n* Àgustà *m*.

aunt *n* (*paternal*) gwaggò *f*, (*term of addr.*) bābà *f*, (*maternal, term of addr. or ref.*) innà *f*.

austerity *n*: ∼ measures shirìn tsūkè bàkin àljīhun gwamnatì.

authentic *adj* a. (*genuine*) na gàske, na
ainihī: is this an ~ Timex watch? wannàn
àgōgon 'Timex' na gàske nḕ? = àgōgon
nàn ainihin Timex nē? b. (*verifiable*)
(mài) ingancī *m*, ìngàntaccē *adj*.

author *n* mawàllàfī *m*, maṛùbùcī *m*.

authority *n* a. (*power*) īkò *m*, ìsā *f*; show
~ nūnà ìsā; have ~ over màllakà *v2*;
government authorities màsu mulkì. b.
(*admin. body*) hùkūmā *f* ⟨oCi⟩: local ~
ḳàramaṛ hùkūmā.

authorization *n* izìnī *m*: I was given ~ to
do so an bā nì izìnī ìn yi hakà.

autobiography *n* tārīhìn kâi *m*.

automobile *n* mōtà *f* ⟨oCi⟩: drive an ~ tūḳà
mōtà.

autonomy *n* (*Pol.*) gashìn kâi *m*, zaman
kâi *m*: be autonomous ci gashìn kâi;
become autonomous sàmi gashìn kâi.

autumn *n*, *see* season.

available *adj* (*accessible*) nan *adv*: are there
any left? yes, there are still some ~ àkwai
saurā? ī, sunà nan haṛ yànzu.

avenge *v* rāmà *v1*: Kano ~d itself for last
year's defeat Kanò tā rāmà cîn dà akà yi
matà bàra; (*esp. by invoking God*) sākà
wà *v1*: if I have cheated you, may God
~ you ìdan nā cùcē kà, Allàh yà sākà
makà; God will ~ us (for the evil done)
Allàh yà sākà manà.

average *adj* a. (*statistically*) matsàkàicī
*m*, madàidàicī *m*: an ~ salary, height
matsàkàicin àlbâshī, tsawō; on ~ à
ḳàddàṛance; be ~ (*neither too much
nor too little*) yi kadàṛan-kadàhan: it
is an ~ price kuɗinsà yā yi kadàṛan-
kadàhan. b. (*ordinary*): his teaching is ~
kōyâṛwaṛsà bâ lâifī; he is a student of
~ ability ɗālìbī nḕ wàndà yakè tsàkà-
tsakī.

aversion *n* ḳyàmà *f*: I have an ~ to flies inà
ḳyàmaṛ ḳudā.

avert *v* a. (*turn away*) kau dà / kawaṛ (dà)
*v5*: she ~ed her eyes tā kau dà kâi. b.
(*ward off, prevent*) kārè *v4*: ~ a disaster
kārè rìkicī.

avoid *v* a. (*esp. physically*) kaucè wà *v4*:
~ him by any means possible ta kōwànè
hālī kà kaucè masà; she ~ed my question tā kaucè wà tàmbayàtā. b. (*shirk*):
there is no ~ing it bâ makawà sai an yī
shì. c. (*prevent from doing*) in order to ~
don gudùn (+ *n*), don (gudùn) kadà: we
took provisions to ~ stopping along the
way mun yi gùzurī don gudùn tsayàwā à
hanyà = ...don kadà mù tsayà à hanyà;
I kept quiet to ~ a quarrel nā yi shirū

don gudùn faɗà.

avoidance *n* (*shirking doing sth.*) makawā *f*;
the Hausa custom of name ~ (*ref. to or
addr. so. indirectly to avoid using his real
name*) àlkunyà *f*.

await *v* jirā *v0*: we are ~ing his arrival munà jiràn zuwànsà; (*eagerly or pa-
tiently*) zubà idò gà, yi dòkī *m*: he
is ~ing her return yanà zubà idò gà
dāwôwaṛtà.

awake *adj* à fàṛke *adv*: are you ~? à fàṛke
kakè? = idònkà biyu? the children are ~
yârā idònsù biyu.

awaken *v* tàsā *v2*, tā dà / tāyaṛ (dà) *v5*,
faṛkaṛ (dà) *v5*: the noise ~ed them ḳāràṛ
tā tā dà sū; be ~ed faṛkà *v1*, tāshì *v3b*.

award 1. *n* lambà *f* ⟨oCi⟩.
2. *v* bā dà lambà.

aware *adj* à sànè *adv*: we are ~ of the
facts munà sànè dà làbàrì = mun san dà
làbàrì; I am fully ~ of his deceit inà dà
matuḳaṛ masanìyā gàme dà yàudaràṛsà;
make so. ~ faɗakaṛ (dà) *v5*; be ~ of oneself, have self-~ness (*fig.*) san cìwòn kâi:
he has no self-~ness bài san cìwòn kânsà
ba = bài san indà kânsà kḕ masà cīwò
ba.

away *adv* a. (*for use as a particle with
verbs, see relevant verb entries; v4 and v5
verbs often include the meaning of 'away'*);
tow a car ~ jànyè mōtà; take ~ his license ḳwācè masà lāsìn; this medicine
will take ~ the pain māganìn nàn zâi
kau dà cīwòn; throw the water ~ zubaṛ
dà ruwā. b. (*var. uses*): he ran ~ from
home yā gudù dàgà gidā; 10 kilometers
~ kilòmītà gōmà dàgà nân; far ~ from
here dà nīsā dàgà nân; do it right ~! kà
yī shì kâi tsàye!

awe *n* a. (*wonder*) àbin àl'ajàbī *m*; be
in ~ of, be ~d by yi àl'ajàbin w.a.
*m*: the children were ~d by the sight of
it yârā sun yi àl'ajàbin ganinsà. b.
(*fear*) àbin tsòrō *m*.

awful *adj*: the weather is ~ yanàyîn bâ
dāɗī; he was ~ to us bài kyâutā manà
ba; how ~! àyyâ!

awhile *adv*: please wait ~ dàkàtā kàɗan =
kà ɗan dākàtā.

awkward *adj* (*clumsy*) maràs kintsì *m*.

awl *n* mahūjī *m*, tsinkē *m* ⟨aye⟩.

axe *n* gàtarī *m* ⟨u-a⟩; (*small*) kuràdā *f*;
(*fig.*) he has an ~ to grind in the matter
yanà dà sôn râi à wannàn màganà.

# B

babbling n (*silly talk*) ɓaɓātū m.

baboon n gwaggòn birì m, bìkā m ⟨aCe⟩.

baby n jằrīrì m ⟨ai⟩, jinjìrī m ⟨jìrằjìrai⟩; (*esp. one carried on one's back*) gōyō m: she has a ~ tanằ dà gōyō; she's expecting a ~ tanằ dà jūnā biyu.

babysit v yi rènō m.

babysitter n mài rènō n, 'yař rènō f.

bachelor n (*never married*) tùzūrū m ⟨ai⟩; (*previously married*) gwaurō m ⟨aye⟩; *see* unmarried.

Bachelor of Arts n dìgìřì na farkō.

back 1. n a. bāyā m, (*lower* ~, *lumbar*) kwànkwasò m: my ~ hurts bāyā nằ minì cìwò; in the ~ of the book à bāyan littāfì; carry baby on one's ~ yi gōyō; fall on one's ~ fādì dà bāya; lie on one's ~ yi řigìngìne; talk about so. behind his ~ ci bāyan w., ci nāmàn w., yī dà w.; turn one's ~ on so. jūyằ wà bāyā; (*fig.*) behind one's ~ bằ dà sanìn w. ba. b. (*adverbial uses*): in ~, at the ~ (à) bāya *adv*: they sat in the ~ sun zaunằ à bāya; fall on one's ~ fādì dà bāya; front and ~ cikì dà bâi; the ~ door ƙōfằ ta bāya; go ~ and forth yi kai-dà-kằwō m, yi zìřgằ-zìřgā f: I always see them going ~ and forth kullum inằ ganinsù sunằ kai-dà-kằwō; the plane goes ~ and forth from here to Lagos jirgī nằ zìřgằ-zìřgā tsàkānin nân dà Lēgàs. c. (*for use as a particle with verbs, see relevant verb entries*): take ~ mai dà / mayař (dà) v5; go ~ kōmằ v1.

2. v a. (*support*) gòyi bāyan w. ⟨gōyō⟩: they ~ the party on this issue sunằ gòyon bāyan jàm'iyyằř gàme dà wannàn màganằ. b. (*support sth. dubious, a bad cause*) ɗaurè wà gìndī: ~ a totalitarian regime ɗaurè wà gwamnàtin kằmā-kàryā gìndī. c. (*reverse a vehicle*) yi řìbâs m, [F] yi bāya-bāya: he ~ed the car into the street yā yi řìbâs dà mōtà yā hau hanyằ.

backache n cìwòn bāyā m.

backbite v yī dà w. v0, ci nāmàn w.

backbone n ƙàshin bāya m.

backing n (*help, support*) gōyon bāyā m: he has our ~ yanằ dà gōyon bāyanmù.

backwards *adv* dà bāya: the child fell over ~ yārò yā fādì dà bāya; they are not progressing but going ~ bā sằ cî gàba sunằ kōmằwā bāya; count ~ řidằyā ta bāya-bāya.

bad *adj* a. (*not good*) maràs kyâu m: his work is ~ aikinsà bā kyâu; be ~ for ɓātà v1: smoking is ~ for one's health shân tābà zâi ɓātà lāfiyàř jìkī; bring sth. ~ on oneself jāwō wà kâi wàhalà; give so. a ~ time bâ w. wàhalà; he's in a ~ mood bā yằ cikin nìshāɗì; I'm on ~ terms with him bā nằ shirì dà shī; what ~ luck! ayyằ! *excl;* too ~! kaico! *excl.* b. (*serious*) mùmmūnā *adj*, ƙàzāmī *adj* ⟨ai⟩, mūgù *adj* ⟨miyằgū⟩: ~ news mūgùn làbằřì; a ~ accident ƙàzāmin haɗàřī; a ~ wound mūgùn ràunī; a ~ mistake bàbban kuskurè. c. (*rotten*): go ~ (*of food*) rùɓa v3, ruɓè v4, lālằcē v4: the meat has gone ~ nāmằ yā ruɓè; go ~ (*of person, situation*) lālằcē v4, ɓàcì v3b. d. (*immoral*) mūgù *adj* ⟨miyằgū⟩, mùmmūnā *adj*: ~ advice mùmmūnař shāwařằ; it is ~ to tell lies yîn ƙaryā mūgùn àbù nē; use ~ language yi mūgùn bằkī = yi mūgùwař màganằ; do so. a ~ turn yi wà shařřì m.

badge n bājò m, [F] gàlô m.

badger v ƙuntàtā wà v1: they ~ed him with questions sun ƙuntàtā masà dà tambayōyī.

badly *adv* a. (*in neg. constr. or with neg. v*) sòsai *adv*: he speaks Hausa ~ bài iyà Hausa sòsai ba = Hausařsà ɗanyā cè; he failed the examination ~ yā fādì à jařřàbâwā sòsai. b. (*seriously, excessively*) (*use specialized v + n constr.*): he was ~ beaten yā shā dūkằ = an ƙwàlằ masà dūkằ; they whipped him ~ sun zabgằ masà būlālằ.

badminton n ƙwallon gāshì m.

bad-tempered *adj* (mài) saurin fushī m, (mài) baƙin râi m, tsagèrā n ⟨u⟩.

baft n àkōko m, nàmūzù m.

bag n jàkā f, [F] jìkā ⟨una²⟩; (*of plastic*) lēɗà f ⟨oCi⟩; (*of goatskin, sheepskin*) burgāmì m ⟨ai⟩; (*handbag*) jàkā / jìkā f ⟨una²⟩; (*with handles & zipper*) [F] sằkwât f.

baggage n kāyā p : they've lost my ~ sun ɓatař minì dà kāyā.

bail 1. n bēlì m : they set his bail at ₦1000 an bā dà bēlìnsà naiřằ dubū.

2. v ~ so. out yi bēlìn w., tsayà wà v1.

bake v gasà v1; ~ bread yi burōdì.

baker *n* mài yîn burõdì *m*.

baking powder *n* baƙin hōdà *m*.

balance 1. *n* a. (*an amount outstanding*) cikõ *m*: I'll pay you ₦10 today and the ~ next week zân biyā kà naiŕà gōmà yâu in yi makà cikòn mākõ mài zuwà. b. (*of accounts*) balàs *m*. c. (*surplus*) rārā *f*: a favorable ~ of payments rārar̃ cìnikī. d. (*a scale*) ma'aunī *m*, sìkēlì *m* ⟨oCi⟩. e. (*equilibrium*): lose one's ~ zāmè *v4*, yi tàngadī *m*. 2. *v*: ~ sth. on the head yi dìgìrgìre *m*: she ~d the calabash of milk on her head tā yi dìgìrgìre dà ƙwaryar̃ nōnõ; I can't ~ a ball on my head bàn iyà dìgìrgìre dà ƙwallō ba.

balcony *n* bàr̃andà *f*, fàfàr̃andà *f*.

bald *adj* a. (*psn.*) (mài) sanƙō *m*: he is ~ yanà dà sanƙō. b. (*smooth, of tire*): the tires are ~ tāyōyī sun sudè.

bale *n* àdīlà / dīlà *f* ⟨oCi⟩.

baling wire *n* làngà-làngà *m*.

ball *n* a. bâl *f* ⟨a..ai⟩, tamaula *f*, [F] bālô *f* ⟨una⟩; (*esp. Sport*) ƙwallō *f* ⟨aye⟩: a foot~ (*soccer*) ƙwallon ƙafà; what kind of ~ is this? it's a foot~ wàcè irin ƙwallo cè wannàn? ƙwallon ƙafà cē; a tennis ~ bâl din ƙwallon tanìs; a pingpong ~ bâl din ƙwallon tēbùr̃; a basket~ bâl din ƙwallon kwàndō. b. (*of kneaded food*) cūrì *m*; (*the size of a fist*) dunƙulè *m*; make, mold into a ~ (*food*) cūrà *v1*, mulmùlā *v1*, dunƙùlā *v1*. c. ~ of string tārìn zàrē.

ball bearings *n* 'yā'yan bōr̃ìs *p*.

balloon *n* r̃ōbà *f*, bàlàn-balan *m*, [F] bàtâ *f*: blow up a ~ hūrà r̃ōbà.

ballot *n* ƙur̃i'à *f* ⟨oCi⟩: secret ~ ƙur̃i'àr̃ àsīr̃ī; cast a ~ jēfà ƙur̃i'à.

ballpoint pen *n* bīr̃õ *m*, [F] bîk *m*.

bamboo *n* gōrà *f* ⟨oCi⟩.

ban 1. *v* hanà *v1*: journalists have been ~ned from the courtroom an hanà 'yan jàr̃īdà dàgà dākin kōtù. 2. *n* hanì *m*; (*censhorship*) tàkunkùmī *m*.

banana(s) *n* àyàbà *f*: a bunch of ~ nōnòn àyàbà.

band¹ *n* (*for fastening sth.*) madaurī *m*.

band² *n* (*of musicians*) màsu bùshe-bùshe dà kàde-kàde; (*small group of people*) gungù *m*: a ~ of robbers gungùn 'yan fashì.

bandage *n* & *v* bandējì *m*: the nurse ~d my arm nâs tā daurà mini bandējì à hannu.

bandaid *n* filastà *f*, [F] ìspàr̃àdàr̃â *f*.

bandicoot *n*, *see* rat.

bandit *n* ɗan fashì *m*.

bang 1. *v* bugè *v4*, bankè *v4*: he fell and ~ed his knee yā fādì yā bugè gwìwà; the wind ~ed the door shut iskà tā bankō ƙōfà har̃ tā rufè; it ~ed into him yā kai masà kar̃õ r̃îm; ~ on bugà *v1*: he ~ed on the table yā bugà tēbùr̃ dà hannū. 2. *n* (*noise*) ƙārā *f*: the gun went off with a loud ~ har̃bìn bindigà yā yi ƙārā.

bangle *n* (*of gold, silver*) warwarō *m*.

banish *v* kōrà *v2*.

banjo *n* (*approx. Hausa equivalents*): (*round, 2-stringed*) gàrāyā *f* ⟨u⟩, (*larger*) kōmō *m*, (*smaller*) gurmī *m*; (*oval, 2-stringed*) mōlō *m* ⟨aye⟩; pluck the ~ kaɗà gàrāyā, kaɗà mōlō.

bank¹ *n* bankì *m* ⟨una⟩: ~ account àjiyàr̃ bankì; Federal Reserve B. Bankin Àjiyà na Tàrayyà; World B. Bankin Dūniyà.

bank² *n* (*of body of water*) bàkī *m*; (*opposite side of river, lake*) gāɓà *f*, gacì *m*, hayì *m*: he reached the other ~ yā kai gacì.

banker *n* ma'àikàcin bankì *m*.

banknote *n* takàr̃daŕ kudī *f*, takàr̃daŕ bankì *m*, [F] bìyê *f*.

bankrupt *adj*: go ~ tsiyàcē *v4*; (*of institution, economy*) karyè *v4*, yi kàrayàr̃ ar̃zìkī: the company has gone ~ ar̃zìkin kamfànī yā karyè.

bankruptcy *n* kàrayàr̃ ar̃zìkī *f*.

bank up *v* (*ridges of farm*) hūɗà *v1*, yi hùɗā *f*.

banner *n* tūtà *f* ⟨oCi⟩.

banquet *n* wàlīmà *f* ⟨oCi⟩, lìyàfà *f*.

baobab *n* (*tree*) kūkà *f*: ~ leaves are ground up for seasoning in stews anà niƙà ganyen kūkà don à yi kāyan miyà dà shi.

baptism *n* bàftizmà *f*.

bar¹ *n* a. (*crossbeam of door*) sàkatà *f* ⟨u⟩. b. (*long stick*) sàndā *m/f* ⟨una⟩. c. a ~ of (*laundry*) soap sàndar̃ sàbulù, (*cut into pieces*) sàbulùn yankan ƙūsà; a ~ of (*bath*) soap (*usu. wrapped*) ƙwàyar̃ sàbulù.

bar² *n* (*drinking place*) mashāyā *f*, hòtâl *m*, [F] bâr̃ *m*.

bar³ *v* a. (*prevent*) hanà *v1*: they have been ~red from entering politics an hanà su shìgā sìyāsà. b. (*forbid, esp. in Islam*) har̃àmtā wà *v1*.

barb *n* ƙayà *f* ⟨oCi⟩, ~ed wire wayà (mài ƙayà); (*esp. tip of arrow, spear*) kûnnē *m* ⟨uwa⟩.

Barbary sheep *n* r̃àgon dūtsè *m*.

barbecue *v* gasà *v1*: skewered meat is ~d over a fire mound anà gasà tsìrē à tukùbā; ~d meat (*gen'l term*) sūyà *m*;

(*skewered & grilled*)) tsìrē *m;* (*set on wire rack over hot coals*) balangù *m.*

**barber** *n* (*tradit.*) mài askì *m,* wànzāmì *m* ⟨ai⟩; (*modern*) mài askìn bābà *m:* ~ shop shāgòn mài askìn bābà = [F] shāgòn kwāf̃ẽr̃.

**bare** 1. *adj & adv:* make ~ (*a place*) tsìràitā *v1:* the building was completely ~ an tsìràitā ginìn; strip ~ (*esp. by robbers*) wāshḕ *v4:* the robbers stripped my house ~ ɓàrāyī sun wāshḕ gidānā; the cupboard was ~ bā kōmē cikin kabàd. 2. *v:* ~ one's teeth yāƙè haƙòrā.

**barefoot** *adj:* walk ~ yi tàfiyà̀ bā tàkàlmī.

**barely** *adv* (*with effort*) dà ƙyar̃/ƙyar̃ (+ *rel. complet.*): I ~ managed to lift it up dà ƙyar̃ na ɗaukō shì; I ~ know him (*fig.*) nā san shì sanìn shānū.

**bargain** 1. *n* (*sth. inexpensive*) àr̃àhā *f:* this coat was a real ~ kwāt ɗin nàn tā yi àr̃àhā ƙwar̃ai; (*sth. extremely reduced in price*) gàrāɓàsà *f:* today I got a real ~ on meat yâu nā kwàshi gàrāɓàsar̃ nāmà. 2. *v* (*offer to buy*) yi cìnikī *m:* she really knows how to ~ tā iyà cìnikī ƙwar̃ai; whatever you want to buy, you must ~ for it first kōmē kakè sôn sàyē, sai kā yi cìnikinsà tùkùna.

**barge** *n* bājì *m.*

**barge in** *v* kūtsà kâi *v1,* cūsà kâi *v1:* they came barging into the room sun cūsà kâi sun shigō dākì.

**bark**[1] *v* (*of animal*) yi haushì *m.*

**bark**[2] *n* a. (*of tree*) ɓāwō *m:* strip ~ off tree sassàƙè ɓāwon itàcē. b. (*for medicinal use*) sassàƙè *m.*

**barley** *n* shà'ìr̃ *m.*

**barracks** *n* bār̃ikì *f,* gidan sōjà *m.*

**barrel** *n* a. (*container*) gàngā *f* ⟨una⟩, (*for crude oil*) tànô *m.* b. (*of gun*) hancìn bindigà̀ *m.*

**barren** *adj* a. (*woman*) jūyà̀ *f:* she's ~ ita jūyà̀ cē. b. (*ground*) faƙò *m:* this is ~ ground ƙasar̃ nàn faƙò cē.

**barter** *v* fur̃fùrā *v1,* yi fùr̃fùrē *m:* they ~ed food for clothing sun yi fùr̃fùren àbinci sù sàmi tufāf̃ì.

**base** 1. *n* a. (*bottom*) gìndī *m:* the ~ of the pot gìndin tukunyà̀; at the ~ of the mountain à gìndin dūtsè. b. (*Mil.*) sànsanī *m* ⟨ai⟩: an air ~ sànsanin mayàƙan jirāgen samà. 2. *v* dōgarà *v3:* on what evidence is your story ~d? dà wàcè hujjà làɓār̃ìnkà ya dōgarà? the accusation must be ~d on

facts yā kàmātà tùhumàr̃ tà sàmi tūshḕ; ~d on what I know, it isn't so gà yâddà na sanī, bà hakà ba nè.

**bashful** *adj* (mài) jîn kunyà̀ *f.*

**basin** *n* (*of metal*) kwānò *m* ⟨uka⟩, [F] bàsân *m;* (*large, with handles for heavy loads*) kwānòn sarkī *m.*

**basis** *n* a. (*foundation*) tūshḕ *m:* what is the ~ of their complaint? mènē nè tūshèn ƙār̃ar̃sù? the accusation has no ~ in fact tùhumàr̃ bā ta dà tūshḕ. b. (*support*) madōgarà *f,* makāmà *f:* the ~ for his opinion madōgaràr̃ r̃a'àyinsà; that story has no ~ zàncēn nan bā shi dà makāmà.

**basket** *n* (*wicker*) kwàndō *m* ⟨una⟩: the ~ has come apart kwàndôn yā ɓarkè; (*var. types*): (*of palm fronds, with 2 handles*) sanhò *m* ⟨una⟩; (*usu. large, coiled, with lid*) àdùdù *m* ⟨ai⟩; (*flat & round, like a tray*) lêfē *m* ⟨una⟩.

**basketball** *n* (*game*) wàsan ƙwallon kwàndō *m,* [F] bàskêt *m;* (*ball*) ƙwallon kwàndō *f.*

**bastard** *n* shēgḕ *m* ⟨u⟩, ɗan zìnā *m.*

**bat**[1] *n* jēmāgḕ *m* ⟨u⟩, (*small*) yàbirbìrā *f.*

**bat**[2] *n* (*thick stick*) kulkī *m* ⟨a-e⟩.

**bath** *n* wankā *m:* take a ~ yi wankā.

**bathe** *v* yi wankā *m,* yi wà wankā: ~ a baby in warm water yi wà jàrīrì wankā dà ruwā mài ɗùmī.

**bathroom** *n,* see toilet.

**bathtub** *n* (*modern*) bāhò *m,* (*metal tub for bathing children*) kwānòn wankā *m.*

**battalion** *n* bàtāliyà̀ *f* ⟨oCi⟩, [F] bàtàliyà̀ *f.*

**batter** *n* (*of certain foods*) ƙullū *m.*

**battery** *n* (*of car*) bātìr̃ *m* ⟨u-a⟩; (*e.g. for flashlight*) bātìr̃ *m* ⟨u-a⟩, [F] pîl *f:* the ~ is weak bātìr̃ bā yà dà wutā sòsai; the ~ is dead bātìr̃ yā mutù; ~-powered mài aikì dà bātìr̃.

**battle** 1. *n* yāƙì *m* ⟨e[2]⟩, dāgà *f:* a great ~ ƙàsàitaccen yāƙì; the front line of ~ bàkin dāgà. 2. *v* shā dāgà.

**battlefield** *n* fagen yāƙì *m,* fagen fāmā *m,* fīlin dāgà *m.*

**bayonet** *n* banatì *f,* [F] bànatì *m.*

**bazaar** *n* 'yar̃ kàsuwā *f.*

**be** *v* a. (*use stabilizers* nē *m/p,* cē *f in most equational sent.; the tone of the stabilizer is opposite to the immediately prec. tone*): he is a farmer manòmī nè; it is a new pot sābuwar̃ tukunyà̀ cē; this bag isn't mine jàkar̃ nàn bà tàwa ba cè; (*in certain sent., the stabilizer is omitted*): his name is Garba sūnansà Gar̃bà; tomorrow is market day gòbe ran kàsuwā. b. (*in*

*pred. adj constr. or other non-verbal sent.,*
*use contin. aspect pro, or use stabilizers* nē
*m/p,* cē *f:* she is beautiful tanā dà kyâu
= kyàkkyāwā cè; he is sick yanā cīwò;
the bicycle is new kèkè sābō nē. c. (*in
certain adj constr.*) yi *v0* (+ *abstr. adj
or n*): the robe is beautiful rìgā tā yi
kyâu; it is correct yā yi daidai. d. there
is, there are, *see* there. e. (*in progressive
verbal constr., use contin. aspect pro, see
Appendix A*): they are building a school
sunā ginà makařantā. f. (*exist, come to
~*) kasàncē *v4:* they were here even before the Europeans came sun kasàncē à
nân tun mā kàfin zuwàn Tūřāwā. g. (*happen to ~*) kasàncē *v4:* when will you ~
in your office tomorrow? yàushè zā kà
kasàncē à ōfìs gòbe? she happened to ~
at the market yesterday yā kasàncē tanā
kàsuwā jiyà.

**beach** *n* bàkin tèku *m,* bàkin kògī *m.*

**bead(s)** *n* (*ornamental*) dūtsèn adō *m:* a
~ed necklace dūtsèn wuyà; prayer ~s
càřbī / càzbī *m* (una), (*esp. black
wooden ones*) kàřambā *f.*

**beak** *n* bàkin tsuntsū *m.*

**beam** *n* (*vertical*) gìnshiƙì *m* (ai); (*horizontal support for ceiling*) azāřā *f* (u); (*of
cement*) bîm *m.*

**beancake** *n* (*fried patty from ground black-
eyed peas*) ƙōsai *m.*

**bean(s)** *n* (*black-eyed peas*) wākē *m;* green
~s wāken Tūřāwā = danyen wākē.

**bear** *v* a. (*give birth*) hàifā *v2:* she bore 6
children tā hàifi 'yā'yā shidà. b. (*endure*) daurè *v4,* jūrè *v4,* yi jìmirī *m:* ~
pain daurè cīwò = yi jìmirin cīwò; I
can't ~ him any longer bà zân iyà daurè
shi ba = yā shā minì kâi; ~ a grudge
ƙùllatā *v2:* he bore a grudge against me
for what I did to him ya ƙùllàcē nì dà
àbîn dà na yi masà. c. ~ a relation
to shāfā *v2:* this ~s no relation to that
wannàn bài shāfi wancàn ba.

**beard** *n* gēmū / gēmè *m:* a tall ~ed man
wani mùtûm dōgō mài gēmù; he has a full
~ yanā dà sājē dà gēmù.

**bearing** *v* (*force of personality*) kwàrjinī *m.*

**bearings** *n:* lose one's ~ (*sense of direction*)
yi dīmuwā *f,* yi ɓatàn kâi *m.*

**beast** *n* dabbā *f* (oCi); wild ~ dabbàř dawà,
nāmàn dājì.

**beat** 1. *vt* a. (*a psn., animal*) dàkā *v2,* bùgā
*v2* (bugù), dòkā *v2* (dūkà): he's ~ing the
donkey with a cane yanā dūkàn jàkī dà
tsabgà; the donkey was severely ~en an
ƙwālā wà jàkī dūkà; I'm going to really

~ you up! zân yi makà dūkàn tsìyā! the
rain ~ down on us ruwā yā dàkè mù = (*fig.*)
ruwā yā bā mù kāshī. b. (*sth. with re-
peated action*) kadā *v1:* ~ an egg, a drum
kadā ƙwai, gàngā. c. (*by blacksmith*)
lallàsā *v1.* d. (*in competition*) lāshè *v4,*
kā dà / kāyař (dà) *v5:* our team ~ theirs
by a score of 4 to 1 ƙunglyařmù tā lāshè
tāsù huɗu dà ɗaya.
2. *vi* (*of thing*) bugā *v1:* his heart was
~ing fast zūcìyařsà nā bugāwā dà saurī;
(*fig.*) ~ around the bush yi kèwàye-
kèwàye, yi ƙùmbìyā-ƙumbiyā, yi gôce-
gôce.

**beating** *n* a. (*physical*) dūkā *m,* bugù *m,*
(*fig.*) kāshī *m:* he got a good ~ yā shā
dūkā = an bā shi kāshī; a hell of a ~
dūkàn kàwō-wuƙā; he took a ~ in the election yā shā kāshī wajen zàɓen. b. (*of
drum*) kidā *m* (e²).

**beautiful** *adj* a. (*psn.*) (mài) kyâu *m,*
kyàkkyāwā *adj;* (*emphat.*) tùbařkallā
*excl:* what a ~ day yâu gàrī yā yi kyâu
ƙwařai; what a ~ girl she is! yārinyàř
nan kyàkkyāwā dà ita! = yārinyàř nan
tùbařkallā! make sth. ~ kyautàtā *v1.* b.
(*artistic, well crafted*) (mài) fàsāhā *f:* a ~
poem wāƙā mài fàsāhà.

**beauty** *n* kyâu *m.*

**because** *prep & conj* sabōdà *prep & conj,*
sàbīlì dà *prep & conj,* dòmin / don *conj,*
à sanàdin *prep:* I am angry ~ you are
late nā yi fushì sabōdà kā màkarà; I
don't trust him ~ I know what he is like
bàn amìncē dà shī ba dòmin kùwa nā san
hālinsà.

**beckon** *v* (*with hand*) yāfutā *v2:* she ~ed
to me to come tā yāfutō nì.

**become** *v* a. (*come to be*) zama *v\*:* pound it
until it ~s flour sai kì dakà ta tà zama
gàrī; he became rich yā zama mài kudī;
my hands became black from the ink
hannūnā yā kōmā baƙī sabōdà tàwadà.
b. (*happen to*): ~ of sāmù *v2\*:* what has
~ of my keys? mè ya sāmi makullīnā?
what finally became of him? dàgà ƙàrshē,
mè ya sāmē shì? c. (*suit*) dācè *v4:* that
dress is very becoming on you wannàn rìgā
tā dācè dà kē sòsai.

**bed**[1] *n* gadō *m* (aCe), (*modern, iron frame*)
gadon ƙarfè; (*low, made of cornstalk*)
karan gadō *m;* (*made of bamboo, sticks*)
kàragā *f;* change the ~ (*bedding*) sākè
shìmfidàř gadō; go to ~ kwàntā *v1,* yi
barcī *m:* go to ~! jè ka kà kwàntā!
make so. go to ~ sâ w. yà kwàntā; in
~ à kwànce: she is still in ~ hař yànzu

tanằ kwằnce; ~ and board makwancī dằ àbinci.

bed[2] n a. (of river) ƙwaryař kồgī f. b. (of irrigated farm) fangalī m ⟨u-a⟩; (for flowers) bēdì m.

bedbug n kuɗin cīzồ m.

bedding n zanèn gadō m, kāyan shìmfiɗàř gadō m, [F] dằřằ f.

bedroom n ɗākì m ⟨una⟩.

bedspread n shìmfiɗằ f.

bee n ƙudan zumằ m, zumằ f: the ~ stung him zumằ tā hàřbē shì.

beef n nāmàn shānū m; shredded ~ (cooked) dambun nāmằ.

beehive n amyằ f ⟨oCi⟩.

beer n (gener.) giyằ f, (from millet, sorghum) bùřƙùtù m, fìtō m.

beeswax n kākìn zumằ m.

beetle n: dung ~ bùzūzừ m ⟨ai⟩; blister ~ (cantharides) hàngarằ f; (type which 'plays dead') ƙùngurgùmằ f; (small ~ which bores holes in wood) kìcciyằ f.

befit v dācē dằ v4, kàmātằ v2, see fit[1].

before 1. prep a. (re. time) kằfìn / kằfin prep: he arrived ~ noon yā isō kằfìn àzahàř; long ~, even ~ tun kằfìn: even ~ the rains begin tun kằfìn ruwā yà sàuka; just ~ gab dà prep, dab dà prep, à gòshin: just ~ my trip dab dà tằfiyằtā = à gòshin tằfiyằtā; do sth. ~ so. else (in time) rìga v0: he came ~ I did yā rìgā nì zuwằ; he was the principal ~ me yā rìgā nì shūgabancìn makařantā. b. (re. location) gàban prep: I was in line ~ her inằ gàbantà à lāyì; everyone must appear ~ the judge kōwā yà bàyyanà à gàban àlƙālī. 2. conj a. kằfìn / kằfin conj (+ subjunct.): will you be able to finish up ~ you leave? zā kà iyà ƙàràsâwā kằfìn kà tāshì? b. (in case that) kadà conj (+ subjunct.): ~ I forget, here's your money gà kuɗinkà kadà ìn mântā.

beforehand adv a. (in advance) kằfìn lōkàcī adv: let me know ~ kà sanař dà nī kằfìn lōkàcîn. b. (before sth. happened) tun tùni adv: I knew it ~ nā sanì tun tùni.

beg v a. (ask for) nèmā v2: they ~ged us to help them sun nèmi mù tàimàkē sù; ~ for mercy, pardon nèmi gāfařằ = nèmi ahuwằ; I ~ your pardon! (to one's superior) à gằfàřcē nì! (to one's equal) don Allàh, kà yi hàƙurī! I ~ your pardon? (request for repetition): mè akà cê? b. (beseech) rồƙā v2 ⟨rồƙō⟩: the woman ~ged for a little money màcèn tā rồƙi

wasu 'yan kuɗī; the thief ~ged for forgiveness ɓàrāwòn yā rồƙi gāfařằ. c. (for alms) yi bařằ f: the students are ~ging for alms àlmàjìřân sunằ bařằ.

beget v hàifā v2: Usman dan Fodio begat Abdullahi Shēhù yā hàifi Abdullāhì.

beggar n àlmàjìřī m ⟨ai⟩, mabàřàcī m; (attached to praise-singers) bàbambaɗē m.

begging n bařằ f.

begin v fārà v1, sōmà v1: it's begun to rain an fārà ruwā; he is ~ning to understand yā fārà gānêwà; to ~ with dà farkō dai.

beginner n ɗan kồyō m, sābon kồyō m; (pejor.) ɗan dāgàjī m.

beginning n farkō m: in the ~ dà farkō; start from the very ~ fārà dà farkon fārằwā = fārà dà fārìn fārằwā; from ~ to end dàga farkō hař ƙàrshē.

behalf n a. on ~ of so., on so.'s ~ (in so.'s place) à madàɗin, à màimakon: I've come on his ~ nā zō à madàɗinsà. b. on so.'s ~ (for so.'s sake) (use ind obj, see Appendix A): she asked for the news on our ~ tā tambàyā manà làbāřìn; he sold the horse on Audu's ~ yā sayař wà Audù dōkì.

behave v a. (act) nūnà hālī: he ~d properly yā nūnà hālin yâddà ya kàmātà; he ~d strangely yā nūnà wani irìn hālī dàbam; that's the way he ~s hālinsà kề nan; don't ~ like a child kâř kà yi (hālin) yàrìntā. b. (show good upbringing) yi ladàbī m: ~ yourself in front of the judge kà yi wà àlƙālī ladàbī; he is well ~d yanằ dà ladàbī = yā nūnà hālī mài kyâu; ~ yourself! (esp. admonishing a child) bàri!

behavior n a. (action, character) hālī / halī m ⟨aye⟩: he was released for good ~ an sàkē shì sabồdà kyân hālinsà. b. (good upbringing) ladàbī m. c. (habit, way) ɗàbī'ằ f: his ~ disgraced his family ɗàbī'àřsà tā zub dà mutuncìn dangìnsà; animal-like ~ dàbbàntakằ f; childish ~ yàràntakằ f.

behead v fillè kâi v4.

behind 1. prep (à) bāyan prep: he hid ~ the door yā ɓūya à bāyan ƙồfằ; they are ~ us sunà bāyanmù. 2. adv a. (à) bāya adv: they were attacked from ~ an màmàyē sù ta bāya; leave sth. ~ bař w.a. à bāya. b. (late, delayed): my watch is 5 minutes ~ àgōgōnā yanà lattìn mintì bìyař; I'm ~ in my work inằ màkarằ dà aikìnā.

being n a. (creature) tālìkī m ⟨ai⟩, hàlittằ f ⟨e[2]⟩. b. come into ~ kasàncē *v4.*

**belch** *v* yi gyàtsā *f.*

**belching** *n* gyàtsā *f:* ~ is a sign of satisfaction gyàtsā àlāmà cē ta k̃oshī.

**belief** *n* a. (*ideology*) àk̃īdà *m.* b. (*religious faith, personal conviction*) īmānì *m:* it is my ~ that he will do it nā yi īmānìn cêwā zâi yī shì; be beyond ~ wucè hankàlī, wucè mìsālì.

**believe** *v* a. (*agree with*) yàr̃da dà *v3:* I ~ what you say nā yàr̃da dà abîn dà ka cê. b. (*have religious, personal conviction*) yi īmānì *m,* amìncē *v4:* ~ in God yi īmānì dà Allàh; it is ~d that the Mahdi will appear first in the east an yi īmānì Màhàdī zâi bàyyanà dàgà gabàs; we truly ~ it can be done mun amìncē àbîn zài yìwu. c. (*assume*) ji *v0:* is he coming? I ~ so kō yanà zuwà? hakà nakè jî.

**belittle** *v* (*a psn.*) k̃askantar̃ (dà) *v5,* k̃ank̃antar̃ (dà) *v5,* cī wà zar̃āfī *m,* ci zar̃āfin w.: they ~d me sun k̃ank̃antar̃ dà nī = nā shā k̃ank̃ancì à hannunsù; (*a psn., action*) rainà / rēnà *v1:* they ~d his efforts sun rainà k̃ok̃arinsà.

**bell** *n* k̃àrarrawā *f:* ring a ~ kaɗà k̃àrarrawā; the ~ rang k̃àrarrawā tā yi k̃ārà; (*worn by donkey, bull*) gwàrjē *m.*

**bellow** *v* yi rūrī *m.*

**bellows** *n* zugàzugī *m* ⟨ai⟩: blow up a fire with ~ zugà wutā dà zugàzugī.

**belly** *n* cikī *m* ⟨Cuna⟩, tùmbī *m:* he has a big ~ yanà dà tùmbī.

**belong** *v* (*expressed by genitive constr. with* na *m,* ta *f* na *p, or possessive prounouns, see Appendix A*): to whom does this book ~? wannàn littāfì na wànē nè? does this robe ~ to you? wannàn rīgā tākà cē?

**belongings** *n* kāyā *p.*

**beloved** *n* àbin k̃àunā *m:* she is my ~ ita àbar̃ k̃àunātà cē.

**below** 1. *adv* (à) k̃asà *adv:* above and ~ samà dà k̃asà.
2. *prep* k̃asà dà *prep,* à k̃asàn *prep:* children ~ the age of 7 yârā k̃asà dà shèkarà bakwài; he has a wound ~ the knee yanà da ràunī à k̃asàn gwīwà.

**belt** *n* (*West. style*) bêl *m,* [F] sàntīr̃ *f;* (*fig.*) tighten one's ~ tsūkè àljīhū; (*tradit. with charms sewn in*) gūr̃ū *m* ⟨aye⟩.

**bench** *n* bencì *m* ⟨una⟩.

**bend** 1. *vt* a. (*sth. made of metal, wood*) lank̃wàsā *v1,* tank̃wàrā *v1;* (*sth. into a curve*) gàntsarà *v2;* (*sth. out of shape*) mur̃dè *v4,* mur̃gùdē *v4.* b. (*fig., so.'s will*) tank̃wàsā *v1.*
2. *vi* a. (*of road*) kar̃kàcē *v4:* the road

~s to the south hanyà tā kar̃kàcē tā yi kudù. b. ~ down, over sunkùyā *v1,* sùnkuyà *v3,* dūk̃ā *v1:* ~ down and pick the child up! dūk̃ā kì ɗaukō yārò! ~ down in prayer (*in Islam*) yi r̃aka'à *f* ⟨oCi⟩;
3. *n* (*in road*) kwanà *f* ⟨x²⟩.

**beneath** *prep* a. (*underneath*) (à) k̃àr̃k̃ashin *prep:* there is room for the box ~ the table àkwai fīlī à k̃àr̃k̃ashin tēbùr̃ don ajìyè àkwàtì. b. (*at base of*) (à) gìndin *prep:* sit ~ a tree zaunà à gìndin itàcē. c. (*in inferior, lower position*) k̃asà dà *prep:* he is ~ me in rank yanà k̃asà dà nī à mùk̃āmī.

**beneficial** *adj* (mài) àmfànī *m,* (mài) fā'idà *f.*

**benefit** 1. *n* a. (*usefulness*) àmfànī *m,* fā'idà *f:* of what ~ is it? ìnā àmfāninsà? be of ~ to àmfānà *v2,* ci mòriyar̃: it is of ~ to everyone yā àmfāni kōwā = yanà dà àmfànī gà kōwā = kōwā zâi ci mòriyar̃sà; get some ~ from sàmi fā'idà dàgà. b. (*enjoyment*) mòriyà *f:* I did it for his ~ nā yi shì sabòdà mòriyar̃sà = nā yī shì dòminsà = nā yi shì sabòdà àmfānin kânsà; enjoy the ~s of science ci mòriyar̃ kìmiyyà.
2. *v* àmfānà *v3,* k̃āru *v7:* when I read the book, I ~ted (from it) dà na kar̃àntà littāfìn, nā àmfānà; ~ from ci àmfānin, ci mòriyar̃, àmfānà dàgà: we ~ed from the lecture mun ci àmfānin laccàr̃ = mun àmfānà dàgà laccàr̃; we ~ from his prosperity munà cîn mòriyar̃ ar̃zìkinsà.

**beniseed** *n* rīɗī *m,* (*with red flowers*) nōmè *m.*

**bent, be** *v* a. (*buckled outward*) lank̃wàshē *v4,* lauyè *v4:* the key is ~ out of shape makullī yā lank̃wàshē; be ~ over (*of psn.*) yi dōrō *m,* yi k̃ōbōbō *m,* r̃ank̃wàfā *v1:* he is ~ over with age yā r̃ank̃wàfā sabòdà tsūfā. b. (*buckled inward*) kōmàɗē / mōkàɗē *v4,* lōtsè *v4:* the car fender is ~ mutàgàdī yā lōtsè.

**bequeath** *v* bar̃ wà gādòn w.a.

**beret** *n* [F] bēr̃ē *f.*

**berries** *n* 'yā'yā *p.*

**beside** *prep* (à) gēfèn *prep:* the chair is ~ the table kujèrā nà gēfèn tēbùr̃; he sat ~ me yā zaunà à gēfènā.

**besides** 1. *prep* ban dà *prep:* ~ the humidity, there is also no breeze ban dà gùmī, gà rashìn iskà kuma.
2. *adv* bugù dà k̃ārì, daɗìn daɗàwā: ~, I don't have any more money bugù dà k̃ārì, kudīnā sun k̃arè.

**best** *adj* a. mafī̀ kyâu: the ~ thing for him is to stay àbù mafī̀ kyâu gàrē shì shī nè̃ yà zaunā̀; that's the ~ thing for you shī nè̃ abîn dà ya fī makà kyâu; the very ~ thing is... àbù mafī̀ kyâu dukà shī nè̃...; this is the ~ of the bunch wannàn shī nè̃ gwaṙzonsù dukà; do one's ~ yi iyā ƙòƙarī: I did my very ~ but failed nā yi haṙ iyā ƙòƙarīnā àmmā nā kāsā̀; let's make the ~ of a bad situation (*fig.*) à ci bà̃ don dādī ba. b. it would be ~ to gāra, gwàmmà (+ *subjunct.*): it would be ~ to leave him alone gwàmmà mù baṙ shi shī kaɗai. c. the ~ man (*at a wedding*) àbōkin angò̃ *m*.

**bet** *v* yi faṙe *m*: I bet ₦20 on that horse nā yi faṙen naiṙā̀ àshìṙin à kân dōkìn nan; how much will you ~? faṙen nawà zā kà yi? = nawà zā kà sâ?

**betray** *v* (*a trust*) ci àmānā̀: he ~ed his country yā ci àmānàṙ ƙasaṙsù; ~ so.'s confidence tōnā̀ wà àsīṙī.

**betrothal** *m*, *see* engagement.

**better** *adj & adv* a. be ~ fi kyâu: it will be ~ to work together zâi fi kyâu mù yi aikī̀ tāre; the place is ~ now than before yànzu wurîn yā fi dâ kyâu; be somewhat ~ yi dāma-dāma: how's business? it's a bit ~ yàyā̀ cìnikī? tô, dà dāma-dāma. b. feel ~ (*in health*) ji saukī̀ *m*: I feel ~ today yâu nā ji saukī̀; I hope you feel ~ soon Allàh yà sawwàƙē. c. (*in compar. constr., use verb* fi *v0*): Musa is a ~ runner than Audu Mūsā yā fi Audù gudù; he is a ~ driver than you yā fī kà iyà mōtà̃; they can explain it to you ~ than I zā sù fī nì bā kà cìkakken bàyānī; she can do it ~ now tā fi dâ iyāwā̀. d. had ~ do (*ref. to fut. event*) gāra, gwàmmà (+ *subjunct.*): we had ~ hurry up gwàmmà mù yi saurī; we'd ~ not go there gāra kadà mù jē cân; ~ you than he gwàmmà kai dà shī; ~ late than never gāra màkarà dà ƙin zuwà̃. e. would have been ~ had (*ref. to past event*) dà̃ (+ *complet.*) ...dà̃ yā fi: it would have been ~ had we gone together dà̃ mun tàfi tāre dà̃ yā fi; for ~ or worse dà dādī kō dà bâ dādī; the sooner the ~ (*fig.*) dà zāfi-zāfi kàn bugè ƙarfè.

**between** *prep* tsàkānin *prep*: Zaria is ~ Kaduna and Kano Zāriyà tanà tsàkānin Kàdūna dà Kanò; in ~ tsàkà-tsakī *adv*: he went and sat in ~ yā shìga tsàkà-tsakī yā zaunā̀; (*fig.*) ~ the devil and the deep blue sea gàba kūrā̀, bāya sìyākī̀.

**beware** *v* yi hankàlī *m*, yi hattaṙà̃ *f*: ~

of the dog! yi hankàlī dà kàrē!

**bewitch** *v* (*put spell on*) yi wà sammù *m*, sammàcē *v4*.

**beyond** *prep* gàban *prep*: the village is ~ that mountain ƙauyèn yanà gàban dūtsèn cân; be ~ wucè *v4*: it is ~ belief, description, comparison àbîn yā wucè hankàlī, màganà̀, mìsālī̀; be ~ one's power gàgarà *v2*, bùywāyà *v2*, fi ƙarfin w.: this work is ~ me aikìn nân yā gàgàrē nì = aikìn nân yā fi ƙarfīnā̀; this bicycle is ~ repair kèkèn nân bà zâi gyàru ba; go ~ (*a place, time*) wucè *v4*, zaṙcè *v4*: we've gone 10 minutes ~ our time mun zaṙcè lōkàcī dà mintì̃ gōmà; go ~ (*a limit, law*) ƙētàrē *v4*, kētà *v4*.

**Bible** *n* Lìnjīlā *f*, Littāfī̀ Mài Tsarkī *m*, [F] Littāfìn Àlmàsīhù *m*.

**bibliography** *n* jērìn lìttàttàfai *m*.

**biceps** *n* ƙwànjī *m*.

**bickering** *n* ka-cè-na-cè *m*: I saw them ~ nā gan sù sunà ka-cè-na-cè.

**bicycle** *n* kèkē / kèkē *m* ⟨una⟩, bāsukùṙ *m* ⟨oci⟩, lâulāwā̀ *f*, [F] bèlô *m*: know how to ride a ~ iyà (hawan) kèkè; rent, hire a ~ yi hayàṙ kèkè.

**bicycle rack** *n* kàṙiyà *f*.

**bid** *v* (*in gambling*) sâ kuɗī *m*.

**bier** *n* màkàrā *f*.

**big** *adj* a. (*large*) bàbba *adj* ⟨mànyā⟩: a ~ rock bàbban dūtsè̃; (*esp. of girth, volume*) (mài) girmā *m*: the horse is ~ dōkì̃ nā̀ dà girmā; this is ~ger than that wannàn yā fi wancàn girmā; how ~ is it? yàyā̀ girmansà yakè? become, get ~ girma *v3a*: they have become very ~ sun girma sòsai; be slightly ~ger than ɗarà *v1*: this is slightly ~ger than that wannàn yā ɗarà wancàn. b. (*important*) bàbba *adj* ⟨mànyā⟩, mùhimmī̀ *adj* ⟨ai⟩, (mài) muhimmancī̀ *m*.

**big shot** *n* (*usu. used in pl*) mànyan ƙūsōshī *p*: he is a ~ yanà̀ dàgà cikin mânyan ƙūsōshī.

**bike** *n* (*motorized*), *see* motorbike.

**bilharzia** *n* tsagiyā *f*.

**bilingual** *n* mài iyà harshè biyu *n*, mài maganà̀ dà harshè biyu *n*.

**bill**[1] *n* a. lìssāfī̀ *m*: where is the ~? ìnā lìssāfī̀? pay a ~ biyà kuɗī. b. (*of currency*) takàṙdaṙ kuɗī *f*: a ₦5 ~ takàṙdaṙ naiṙā̀ bìyaṙ.

**bill**[2] *n* (*Pol.*) shirìn dòkā *m*.

**bill**[3] *n* (*of bird*) bàkin tsuntsū *m*.

**billboard** *n* àllon tàllà *m*.

**billfold** *n* wālèt *m*.

**billion** *quant* miliyàn dubū *f*.

billy-goat *n* bùnsurū *m* ⟨ai⟩.

bin *n* (*for grain storage*) rùmbū *m* ⟨una⟩.

bind *v* ɗaurè *v4*: they bound the grain with rope an ɗaurè damī dà igiyà; (*the edge of a mat, cloth*) dājè *v4; ~* a book yi wà littāfī bangō.

binding[1] *n* (*of book*) bangō *m* ⟨aye⟩.

binding[2] *adj*: be *~* wàjabà *v3, see* incumbent, obligatory.

binoculars *n* tàbàran hàngen nēsà *m*.

biography *n* tārīhìn mùtūm *m*.

biology *n* ilìmin hàlìttū *m*.

bird *n* tsuntsū *m* ⟨aye⟩.

birth *n* haihùwā *f;* give *~* haihù *v3b*, sàuka *v3;* when will she give *~*? yàushè zā tà haihù? she is giving *~* tanā kân gwīwā; give *~* to hàifā *v2*: she gave *~* to a boy tā hàifi ɗā; *~* control yāƙìn ragè yawàn haihùwā; *~* pains nāƙudā *f.*

birthday *n* rānař tunà haihùwā *f;* I wished him a happy *~* nā yi masà 'Allàh yà maimàità'; *~* of the Prophet Mohammed Màulūdì *m.*

birthmark *n* rōwā *f.*

birthplace *n* wurin haihùwā *m.*

biscuit *n* (*sweet cookie*) bìskît *m.*

bit[1] *n* a. (*small quantity*) kàɗan *adv*: he gave me a *~* yā bā nì kàɗan; a little *~* kàɗan-kàɗan; not one *~* (*fig.*) kō ƙwařzanè: she is not to blame one *~* bā ta dà lâifī kō ƙwařzanè. b. (*small piece*) guntū *m* ⟨aye⟩: a *~* of paper guntuwař takàřdā. c. (*as dimin. modifying v or pred.*) ɗan *adv*: I read the newspaper a *~* nā ɗan kařàntà jàrīdā; it is a *~* cold today yâu anā ɗan sanyī.

bit[2] *n* (*of bridle*) lìnzāmì *m* ⟨ai⟩.

bitch *n* kàryā *f;* (*fig.*) shēgìyā *f,* 'yař iskà *f;* you son-of-a-*~*! (*vulg. explet.*) uwākà! = ùbākà! son-of-a-*~*! (*excl. of surprise*) ɗan fářkà! = ɗan kàrē! = shēgè!

bite 1. *v* cìzā *v2* ⟨cīzò⟩, cījè *v4;* (*by snake*) sārā *v2* ⟨sārā⟩; (*by scorpion, spider*) hàřbā *v2* ⟨hařbì⟩; *~* one's fingernails ci yātsū; *~* a piece off gàtsā *v2*: she bit off a piece of sugar cane tā gàtsi ràkē. 2. *n* a. (*by animal, insect*): mosquito *~* cīzòn saurō; snake *~* sāran macìjī; spider *~* hařbìn gizò-gizò. b. (*mouthful of food, esp. tuwō or rice*) lōmā *f* ⟨oCi⟩.

bitter *adj* (mài) dācī *m*: it has a *~* taste yanā dà dācin ɗanɗanō; the truth is *~* gàskiyā dācī gàrē tà; *~* cold (*weather*) sanyī mài sūkà.

bitterleaf *n* shìwākā *f.*

bitterly *adv*: cry *~* yi kūkan wuřjànjàn.

bitterness *n* dācī *m.*

blab *v* (*tell so.'s secret*) kwarmàtā wà *v1*, yi wà kwàrmatò *m.*

black 1. *adj* baƙī *adj* ⟨aCe⟩: jet-*~* baƙī ƙirin = baƙī wuluk; *~* and white farī dà baƙī. 2. *n* (*dark-skinned psn.*) baƙař fātā *n/p.*

blackboard *n* àllō *m* ⟨una⟩.

blacken *v* baƙàntā *v1.*

black-eyed peas *n* wākē *m.*

blackish *adv* baƙi-baƙi *adv.*

blackmail *v* yi wà shařřī *m.*

black market *n* kàsuwař shunkù *f.*

blackquarter disease *n* (*of cattle*) hàřbau *m.*

blacksmith *n* maƙērī *m.*

bladder *n* (*of body*) mafitsārā *f;* (*of football*) bìlādā *f.*

blade *n* a. (*of knife, weapon*) ruwā *m*: *~* of sword ruwan takòbī; razor *~* řēzā *f.* b. shoulder *~* àllon kàfadā *m.*

blame 1. *v* a. (*hold so. at fault*) ɗōrā wà lâifī: he *~*d his goat's death on me yā ɗōrā minì lâifin mutuwař àkuyàřsà; he is to *~*, not me shī yakè dà lâifī, bā nī ba; everyone is to *~* kōwā dà nāsà lâifìn. b. (*falsely*) dafā wà lâifī, yi wà ƙage *m.* c. (*reproach*) zàrgā *v2*: don't *~* me for what happened kadà kà zàrgē nì dà àbîn dà ya fàru. 2. *n* a. (*fault*) lâifī *m* ⟨uka[2]⟩; put the *~* on ɗōrā wà lâifī; take the *~* for sth. ɗàuki nauyin w.a. b. (*reproach*) zàrgī *m.*

bland *adj* (*esp. of sauce, soup*) (mài) lāmī *m.*

blanket *n* bàřgō *m* ⟨una⟩; (*small, handwoven cotton, used by men as garment*) gwàdò *m* ⟨Cuna⟩; (*large, of brightly colored handwoven cotton strips*) lūřū *m* ⟨aye⟩, sàkàlā *f.*

blasphemy *n* sàɓō *m.*

blaze *v* ci *v0*, ƙūna *v3a*: the fire is blazing away wutā tanā ƙūnā sòsai.

bleach 1. *n* bìlîc *m*: put *~* in, on sâ bìlîc. 2. *v* kōɗař (dà) *v5*: the sun has *~*ed the (color of the) curtain rānā tā kōɗař dà lābulē.

bleat *v* yi kūkā *m.*

bleed *v* yi jinī *m*, (*esp. internally*) zub dà jinī: his hand was *~*ing from the cut hannunsà nā jinī sabòdà sārā; it has stopped *~*ing jinī yā tsayà; (*from nose*) yi haɓò *m*: my nose is *~*ing inā haɓò; (*fig.*) he bled me dry yā tātsè ni kakaf.

blemish *n* illà *f* ⟨oCi⟩, lâifī *m* ⟨uka[2]⟩, lahànī *m.*

*blatent* [margin note]

blend v garwàyā / gauràyā v1; ~ in, into
sājè dà v4: this color ~s in with that
one wannàn launī yā sājè dà wancàn;
he ~ed into the crowd yā sājè cikin
jàma'à.

blender n injìn màrkàdē m.

bless v àlbàr̃katà v2: God has ~ed them
Allàh yā àlbàr̃kàcē sù; God has ~ed
him with many children Allàh yā ar̃zùtā
shi dà 'yā'yā màsu yawà; God ~ you!
Allàh yà yi makà àlbar̃kà! = Allàh yà
bā dà àlhēr̃ì!

blessing n àlbar̃kà f.

blind 1. adj (psn.) màkāhò m, màkaunìyā f
⟨màkàfī⟩; become, go ~ makàncē v4.
2. v makantar̃ (dà) v5; the light ~ded us
haskē yā kashè manà idò.

blindman's bluff n màdindimī / màd́ind́imī
m.

blindness n makantà f; night ~ dìndimī m.

blink v a. r̃iftà idò v1, yi r̃ìfcē m; (fig.)
in the ~ of an eye kàfìn r̃iftàwā dà
bìsmillà = kàfìn r̃iftàwar̃ idò. b. ~
one's lights (car headlights) yi dîm m, sâ
dîm m: I ~ed my lights at him nā yi masà
dîm.

blister n bòr̃ōr̃ò m: I have a ~ on my hand
hannūnā yā yi bòr̃ōr̃ò; the beetle bite
has given me ~s cīzòn hàngarā tā sâ ni
bòr̃ōr̃ò.

blister beetle n hàngarā f.

bloated, be v (from illness) kùmburà v3.

block[1] n a. (for construction) bùlô m, [F]
bìr̃gī m: a cement ~ bùlôn sìmintì. b.
(of salt, sugar) kantù m. c. (of streets in
city) lāyì m ⟨uka⟩.

block[2] 1. v a. (close off a passage) rufè v4,
dàtsā v2, datsè v4: the road is ~ed off
an dàtsi hanyàr̃. b. (intercept) tarè wà
v4: the police ~ed our way 'yan sàndā
sun tarè manà hanyà. c. (clog an opening, hole) tōshè v4: the trash is ~ing the
flow of water shàrā tanà tōshè hanyar̃
ruwā. d. (obstruct an area) tsarè v4: a
truck was ~ing the road wata bàbbar̃ mōtà
nà tsarè hanyàr̃.
2. n: road ~ àlāmàr̃ rufè hanyà.

blockade n: economic ~ tàkunkùmin tattalin ar̃zìkī m.

blood n jinī m: a ~ stain tabòn jinī; be
stained with ~ ɓàcè dà jinī; ~ types
ìre-ìren jinī; give so. a ~ transfusion
d́ūrà wà r̃arìn jinī; take ~ from so. d́ībà
wà jinī; test so.'s ~ aunà jinin w.

blood bank n ma'ajiyar̃ jinī f.

blood pressure n r̃arfin jinī m: high
~ hàuhawàr̃ jinī; take one's ~ pressure

aunà hàuhawàr̃ jinī.

bloodshot adj: my eyes are ~ idònā yā yi
jā.

blood vessels n hanyōyin jinī p, jījiyō-
yin jinī p.

bloody adj jinā-jìnā idph: he was ~ after
the fight yā yi jinā-jìnà bāyan fad́à; it
was a ~ battle an zub dà jinī dà yawà
à yār̃ìn.

bloom v yi hùdā f, fid dà fùrē m; (fig., of
girl) nùna v3.

blossom n fùrē m ⟨anni⟩, hùdā f, fulāwà f.

blot v shānyē v4.

blotter n bùlōtà f ⟨oCi⟩.

blouse n rìgā f ⟨una⟩; (West African
style) bùbā f; (West. style) 'yar̃ kàntī f,
bùlāwùs f, [F] kòr̃sājì f.

blow[1] 1. vi a. (of mild wind) kad́à v1, (of
strong or sudden wind) tāshì v3b, tāsō
v6: a gentle wind was ~ing iskà mài dād́ī
nà kad́àwā; a storm blew in from the south
iskà tā tāsō dàgà kudù. b. (of tire) yi
fancà f, yi fācì m. c. (of fuse) mutù v3b:
the fuse has ~n fìs dîn yā mutù.
2. vt a. (a musical instrument) būsà v1
⟨būsà⟩ f: he is ~ing a flute, horn yanà
būsàr̃ sàrēwā, r̃ahò; (fig.) ~ one's own
horn yàbi kâi, wāsà kâi, kōd́à kâi. b.
~ one's nose fyàcè/fācè màjinà. c. (var.
v + adv/prep uses): ~ down a tree kà
dà itàcē; ~ on a fire hūrà wutā; ~ on
food (to cool it off) būsà àbinci; ~ out
a candle, match hūrè kyandìr̃, àshānā;
~ up (get angry) hàsalà v3, kùfulà 3; ~
up a balloon hūrà bàlàn-balan; ~ up a
fire (with fan, bellows) zugà wutā; ~ up
a bridge (with explosives) karyà gadà dà
nàkiyà; ~ up a mountain fasà dūtsè dà
nàkiyà.

blow[2] n dūkà m, bugù m: he received several
~s yā shā dūkà; deliver a ~ to so. kai
wà dūkà; their argument resulted in ~s
fad́ànsù yā kai gà dūkà.

blow-out n (of tire) bindigà f, fancà f, fācì
m: he had a ~ on the road tāyàr̃sà tā yi
bindigà kân hanyà.

blue adj shūd́ì adj ⟨Ca⟩: a ~ gown shūd́ìyar̃
rìgā; deep ~ shūd́ì shar̃; bright ~ shūd́ì
bàu; indigo ~ dye shūnī m; deep indigo
~ shùnayyà f, bar̃ī adj; (fig.) I'm feeling
~ today yâu bā nà jìn dād́ī.

blueing n zàr̃gīnà f, bulà f.

bluejeans n jîn m.

blunder n kuskurè m ⟨kùràkùrai⟩; (verbal) kàtōɓarā f: his ~ caused us a lot of
trouble kàtōɓaràr̃ dà ya yi tā jāwō manà
màtsalà.

**blunt** *adj* a. (*of an edge*): be ~ dāsàshē *v4*: the knife is ~ wuƙā tā dāsàshē. b. (*tactless, in speech*): be ~ yi kàtōɓarā *f*.

**bluntly** *adv* ɓarō-ɓàrò *idph*: he spoke ~ to us yā yi manà màganà ɓarō-ɓàrò.

**blurt out** *v* yi sùɓutař̃ bàkī *f*, yi ɓàrin bàkī *m*.

**bluster** *v* yi wà kūrī *m*; (*esp. with children to quiet them*) yi wà dōdōr̃idò *m*.

**boar** *n*, see warthog.

**board**[1] *n* a. (*of wood*) kātākō *m*. b. (*for writing*) àllō *m* ⟨una⟩. c. (*committee*) hùkūmà *f* ⟨oCi⟩, kwàmìtî *m*, [F] kwàmìtê *m* ⟨oCi⟩.

**board**[2] *v* (*a bus, airplane*) shìga *v3*.

**boarder** *n* ɗan hayà *n*.

**boast** *v* cikà bàkī, kambàmà kâi, yi bùr̃gà *f*, yi hōmà *f*: pay no attention to him, he's just ~ing kyàlē shi, cikà bàkī kawài yakè; he's ~ing about his new car yanà hōmà dà sābuwar̃ mōtàr̃sà.

**boat** *n* jirgin ruwa *m; see* canoe.

**bob** *v* (*up & down*) yi rawà *m*: the boat is ~bing in the water jirgī nà rawā cikin ruwa.

**bobbin** *n* (*for weaving*) kwarkwarō *m*; (*for weaving or sewing machine*) tāriyā *f*; ~ holder ƙùndū *m*.

**body** *n* a. (*of psn., animal*) jìkī *m* ⟨una⟩; on the ~ à jìkà *adv*: he was shot in the ~ an hàr̃bē shì à jìkà. b. (*corpse*) gāwā *f* ⟨aki[2]⟩: where did they bury the ~? ìnā akà binnè gāwar̃? c. (*main part of sth.*) uwā *f*: ~ of the pot uwar̃ tukunyā. d. (*of car, truck*) bōdì *m*.

**bodyguard** *n* mài kārè lāfiyar̃ w.

**bog** *n* ɗàmbà *f*.

**boil**[1] *v* a. (*water*) tafàsā *v1*, tàfasà *v3*: one must ~ the water for at least 10 minutes dōlè à tafàsà ruwā àƙallà mintì gōmà; the water is ~ing rapidly ruwā nà ta tàfasà; ~ away (*& burn food*) ƙōnè *v4*; ~ over yi bòrī *m*: the pot is ~ing over tukunyā tanà bòrī. b. (*cook by ~ing*) dafà *v1;* hard-~ed egg dàfaffen ƙwai.

**boil**[2] *n* (*Med.*) màrūrù *m*; (*on knee*) fitsārin gwaurō *m*.

**boiler** *n* hītā *f*, [F] shàpâj *m*.

**bold** *adj* a. (*brave*) (mài) ƙarfin zūcìyā *m*; make so. become ~ zugà *v1*, tunzùrà *v1*, har̃zùƙā *v1*. b. (*impressive*) gàgārùmī *adj* ⟨ai⟩: a ~ plan gàgārùmin shirì.

**boll** *n* (*of cotton*) gùlūlū *m*.

**bolt**[1] 1. *n* a. (*for fastening door*) sàkatà *f* ⟨u⟩. b. (*used with nut*) ƙūsà *f* ⟨oCi⟩, [F] bìs *m*.

2. *v*: ~ a door sâ sàkatà, kullè dà sàkatà.

**bolt**[2] a. (*of printed cloth*) sàndā *f* ⟨una⟩, bandìr̃ *m*. b. (*of lightning*) ar̃ādù *f*.

**bomb** *n* bâm *m*: atom ~ atàm bâm; drop a ~ jēfà bâm; the ~ has exploded bâm yā fashè.

**bombardment** *n* ruwan bâm *m*, lùgùden bâm *m*.

**bone** *n* a. ƙashī *m* ⟨uwa[2]⟩: I'm chilled to the ~ inà jîn sanyī kàmar̃ ƙashīnā yā tsāgè; set a ~ dōrà kàrayà; (*fig.*) ~ of contention àbin gàr̃damà. b. (*of fish*) ƙayā *f* ⟨oCi⟩.

**bone marrow** *n* ɓargō *m*.

**bonus** *n* bōnàs *m*, [F] pìr̃îm *f*.

**boo** *v* yi ȉhù *m*.

**book** *n* littāfì *m* ⟨lìttàttàfai, lìttàfai⟩ a history ~ littāfin tār̃īhì; a ~ about birds littāfì kàn tsuntsàyē.

**book cover** *n* bangon littāfì *m*.

**bookcase** *n* kantà *f*, [F] kwabà *f*.

**bookkeeper** *n* àkantà *n* ⟨oCi⟩, [F] kwàntābìl *n*.

**booklet** *n* ƙàsīdà *f* ⟨u⟩.

**bookstore** *n* kàntin lìttàttàfai *m*.

**boot** *n* (*of car*), see trunk[2].

**booth** *n* (*at market*) rùmfā *f* ⟨una⟩.

**boots** *n* bût *m*, [F] bōtì *m*; (*for rain*) tàkàlman ruwā *m*.

**booty** *n* (*from war*) gànīmà *f*: make off with the ~ ɗèbi gànīmà.

**border** *n* a. (*of nation*) iyàkā *f* ⟨oCi⟩: Nigeria has a ~ with Cameroon Nìjēr̃iyà tanà iyàkā dà Kàmar̃u. b. (*edge*) bàkī *m*: ~ of a mat bàkin tàbarmā.

**bore**[1] *v* (*hole in wall or handle of tool*) ɓusà *v1;* (*make very small hole*) hūɗà *v1*.

**bore**[2] *v* gùndurà *v2*, cī wà râi: this work ~s me aikìn nân yā gùndùrè nì = aikìn nân yanà cī minì râi.

**borehole** *n* r̃ījìyar̃ bùr̃tsàtsē *f*.

**boring** *adj* (mài) cîn râi *m*, (mài) gùndurà *f*: this book is ~ wannàn littāfì àkwai cîn râi.

**born, be** *v* hàifā *v2*: where were you ~? ìnā akà hàifē kà? she was ~ in March an hàifē tà cikin watàn Mār̃ìs.

**borrow** *v* a. àrā *v2*, yi arō *m, see* lend: Hausa has ~ed many words from Arabic Hausa tā àri kalmōmī dà yawà dàgà Lār̃abcī; may I ~ your book? kō zā kà bā nì aron littāfìnkà? b. (*esp. money*) r̃àntā *v2*, yi ràncē *m, see* lend: he ~ed ₦10 from me yā rànci nair̃ā gōmà dàgà gàrē nì = yā yi ràncen nair̃ā gōmà à wurīnā. c. (*food*) kàr̃ɓā *v2*: she came to

~ some salt from us tā zo kàrɓaɽ gishirī
à wurinmù.

**borrower** n mài arō m, (esp. of money) mài
ràncē m.

**borrow-pit** n kùduddufī m ⟨ai⟩.

**bosom** n (chest) k̃ìrjī m; (of women) nōnò
m.

**boss** 1. n shũgàbā n ⟨anni⟩; (term. of addr.)
màigidā m.
2. v (dominate) gājè v4: he ~es the other
workers yanà gājè sauran ma'àikàtā; ~
so. around yi wà mulkī m: stop ~ing me
around kà dainà yi minì mulkī.

**bossy** adj (mài) mulkī m: so-and-so is very
~ wānè yā cikà mulkī.

**botany** n ilìmin tsìrrai m.

**botch** v jagwalgwàlā v1.

**both** quant duk biyu: she gave me ~ tā
bā ni duk biyu; I saw ~ of them nā ga
duk biyunsù; she has ~ beauty and brains
kyàkkyāwā cè gà kuma k̃wak̃walwà.

**bother** 1. v a. (disturb) dāmā v2 ⟨dāmù⟩,
dāmu v7: what's ~ing you? mè ya dāmē kì?
what is ~ing us is... àbîn dà kè dāmùnmù
shī nè...; don't ~, don't be ~ed kadà kà
dāmu; I'm ~ed about his rudeness nā dāmu
dà rashìn kunyàr̃sà. b. (annoy) bā w.
haushī, ɓātà wà r̃ai. c. (take trouble to
do sth.): she didn't ~ to notify us bà tà
yi k̃ôk̃arī tà sanasshē mù ba;
2. n àbin dāmuwā m: it's really no ~ bà
àbin dāmuwā ba nè.
3. excl (mild) kash! excl; (strong) tir̃!
excl.

**bothersome** adj (mài) ban haushī m, (mài)
kāwō fìtinà.

**bottle** n a. (of glass, plastic) kwalabā f ⟨a-
e⟩, [F] būtàlī m: baby, nursing ~ kwal-
abar̃ jàr̃ìrai; thermos ~ filàs m, [F]
tàr̃mās m. b. (var. tradit. types): (small,
for perfume) wàkiyyà f; (of hide for storing oil, honey) tandū m ⟨aye⟩; (small,
for snuff, tobacco) battà f; (of clay or
from gourd, for water) būtà f ⟨oCi⟩; (from
gourd, for water) gōrā m ⟨una⟩.

**bottom** n a. (base) gìndī m: at the ~ of the
hill à gìndin tsaunî; (fig.) get to the ~
of a matter bi diddigin màganà. b. (underside) k̃àr̃k̃ashī m: the ~ of it is rough
k̃àr̃k̃ashinsà nā dà kaushī; it was on the
~ of the pile yanà k̃àr̃k̃ashin tārìn; at
the ~ of à k̃asàn prep: it's at the ~ of the
page yanà k̃asàn shāfì; he was at the ~
of his class yā yi na k̃àr̃shē cikin ajì.
c. (buttocks) ɗuwāwū m ⟨ɗuwàiwai⟩, (euphem.) gìndī m.

**bouillon cube** n māgī m, [F] dunk̃ulèn màjī
m.

**boulder** n bàbban dūtsè m.

**bounce** v a. (a ball) bugā v1, tambàrā v1:
~ against bùgā v2 ⟨bugù⟩; the ball ~d
against the wall bāl tā bùgi bangō. b.
(so. up and down) jijjìgā v1: she ~d the
baby on her lap tā jijjìgà dā à cinyà.

**bound** adj a. (fastened) à ɗaure adv. b.
(inevitable): it is ~ to happen lallē zâi
àuku. c. be ~ for (a place) nùfā v2: the
ship is ~ for Port Harcourt jirgîn yā
nùfi Fàtākwàl.

**boundary** n (border, frontier) iyàkā f
⟨oCi⟩.

**bourgeoisie** n māsu hannū dà shūnī p.

**bow**[1] 1. n a. (of archer) bàkā f ⟨una[2]⟩: ~
and arrow kwàrī dà bàkā. b. (for playing
stringed instrument) izgā f.
2. v (a stringed instrument) gōgà v1.

**bow**[2] v (to so. in greeting) rusùnā wà v1: the
people ~ed to the emir jàma'à sun rusùnā
wà sarkī; ~ down low sunkùyā v1; ~
one's head sunkuyar̃ dà kâi v5: Muslims ~ down during prayer while Christians ~ their heads in prayer Mùsùlmī nà
sunkùyāwā wajen sallà, Kir̃istōcī kuma
nà sunkuyar̃ dà kâi wajen àddu'àr̃sù.

**bowels** n hanjī m.

**bowl** n (metal) kwānò m ⟨uka⟩; (earthenware) kaskō m ⟨a-e⟩; (ornamental brass)
tāsà f ⟨oCi⟩; (of wood, for eating) akùshī
m ⟨u-a⟩.

**bow-legged** adj (mài) câssā f: he is ~ yanà
dà câssā = câssā gàrē shì.

**bowstring** n tsarkìyā / tsirkìyā f.

**box**[1] n àkwàtì m ⟨una⟩, sàndūk̃ī m ⟨ai⟩;
(of cardboard) kwàlī m ⟨aye⟩, [F] kàr̃tô
m; (esp. of wood, metal) àdakà f ⟨oCi⟩, [F]
kyâs f.

**box**[2] v yi dambe m.

**boxer** n ɗan dambe m, madàmbàcī m.

**boxing** n (tradit.) dambe m.

**boy** n yārò m ⟨yārā⟩; baby-~ dā namijì;
it's a ~! namijì ta hàifā! ~s and girls
yârā mazā dà mātā; he has 3 children, 2
~s and one girl yanà dà 'yā'yā ukù, mazā
biyu dà màcè ɗaya; (teenager) sauràyī
m ⟨sàmàrī⟩.

**boycott** v k̃auràcè wà v4: they called for a ~
against classes an yi kirā dà à k̃auràcè
wà azùzuwà.

**boyfriend** n (of girl) sauràyī m ⟨sàmàrī⟩;
(of boy) àbōkī m ⟨ai⟩, (close) àmīnì m
⟨ai⟩, see friend.

**boyhood** n k̃ùr̃ùciyā f.

**bra** n, see brassiere.

**braces, brackets** n (*parentheses*) bàkā-biyu p.

**brackish** adj (mài) zařtsī m.

**bracelet** n àbin hannu m, (*usu. of gold, silver*) warwarō m, (*of heavy brass*) munduwā f ⟨aye⟩.

**brag** v cikà bàkī, yi hōmā f, yi bùřgā f: stop ~ging about yourself kà dainà cikà bàkī.

**braid** 1. v (*so.'s hair*) yi wà kitsò m, kitsā v1; (*a rope*) tufkà v1.
2. n a. (*small ~s at temple*) taurā f ⟨aye⟩.
b. (*trimming on robes*) sàfīfà f.

**brain** n ƙwaƙwalwā f, kwanyā f; (*fig.*) he's got ~s yanā dà ƙwaƙwalwā.

**brake** n biřkī m ⟨oCi⟩; pull the ~ jā biřkì; step on the ~ tākà biřkì = dannà biřkì; step off the ~ ɗagà biřkì; hand-~ biřkìn hannu: release the hand-~ sakař dà biřkì.

**bran** n dùsā f.

**branch** n a. (*of tree, company*) rēshè m ⟨Ca⟩: there's a ~ office in Kano àkwai rēshèn kamfànîn à Kanò. b. (*of knowledge*) fannì m ⟨oCi⟩: different ~es of knowledge fannōnin ilìmī irì-irì.

**brand**[1] n (*for identifying animals*) wutā f, lambà f ⟨oCi⟩: the cattle have been ~ed an yi wà shānū wutā.

**brand**[2] n (*of goods*) àlāmā f ⟨oCi⟩: Elephant ~ of soap sàbulù mài àlāmàř Gīwā.

**brand-new** adj sābō ful idph.

**brass** n farin ƙarfè m.

**brassiere** n rìgař nōnò f, rìgař màma f.

**brave** adj jàřùmī m ⟨ai⟩, namijì m; be ~ yi ta-mazā, daurè v4.

**bravery** n jàřùntakā f, màzàkutā f, jař zūcìyā f.

**bray** v yi kūkā m.

**breach** 1. v: ~ a contract sā6à yàřjējēnì-yā; ~ so.'s trust yi zàmba cikin amincì = ci àmānàř w.
2. n (*in wall*) tsāgà f.

**bread** n buřōdì m.

**breadth** n fādī m, see width.

**break** 1. v a. (*sth. brittle*) fasà v1, fashè v4, rōtsà v1: ~ an egg, glass fasà ƙwai, tambùlàn; the mirror broke madūbī yā fashè; (*sth. which snaps*) karyà v1, karyè v4: ~ a leg, stick karyà ƙafà, sàndā. b. (*cease functioning*) lālàcē v4, tsayà v1: my watch is broken àgōgōnā yā lālàcē. c. (*Law*) karyà v1, kētā v1, ƙētàrē v4: ~ a law, fast, promise karyà dòkà, azùmī, àlkawàřī. d. the dawn broke gàrī yā wāyè. e. (*var. v + adv/prep uses*): ~ away from (*secede*) 6allè dàgà; ~ down

(*deteriorate*) lālàcē v4; ~ off a piece of kàryā v2, gùtsurā v2: please ~ off a piece of kolanut for me don Allàh kà gut-surō minì gōřò; ~ off a large chunk of sth. 6àntarā v2; ~ in (*discipline*) hòrā v2 ⟨hòrō⟩: he's ~ing a horse in yanā hòron dōkì; ~ into (*rob*) fasà v1; ~ off (*of button, rope*) 6allà v1, 6allè v4; ~ off (*official relations*) yankè huldā; (*personal relations*) 6a6è v4: Audu and Ladi have broken off their relationship dà Audù dà Lādì sun 6a6è; ~ out (*of war, quarrel, disease*) 6arkè v4, tāshì v3b; ~ out (*of rash, pimples*) fiřfitō v6, hàifu v7: acne has broken out all over his face bàř-ni-dà-mūgù yā fiřfitō masà à fuskà; ~ out laughing, crying fashè dà dàriyā, kūkā; ~ through (*pierce*) hūdà v1; ~ up a crowd fasà tàřō.
2. n a. (*pause to rest*) ɗan hūtū m; let's take a ~ mù ɗan hūtà = mù ɗan shāƙàtā; (*fig.*) give me a ~! don Allàh kà ƙyālè ni! b. (*school holiday*) hūtū m. c. (*rupture*) 6àrakà f: after an earthquake, there are many ~s in the ground bāyan an yi gìřgizář ƙasā, àkwai 6àrakà dà yawà. d. the ~ of day wāyèwař gàrī.

**breakdown** n (*of car*) lālàcēwař mōtà f, fancà f, [F] àmpàn m: have a ~ yi fancà.

**breakfast** n karìn kùmallō m: eat, have ~ karyà kùmallō = sàmi àbin karìn kùmallō.

**break-in** n fashì m.

**breast** n a. nōnò m ⟨Ca⟩, màma f; small-~ed ƙunƙumā f; large-~ed mài nōnò tantsā-tàntsā. b. (*chest*) ƙìrjī m.

**breastbone** n murfin ƙìrjī m.

**breast-feed** v shā dà / shāyař (dà) v5: she is ~-feeding tanà shāyářwā.

**breath** n numfāshī m: hold one's ~ (*from fear*) ɗaukè numfāshī, (*from bad smell*) riƙè hancì; take a deep ~ yi dōgon numfāshī = yi gwauron numfāshī; he has bad ~ yanà dà wārin bàkī.

**breathe** v yi numfāshī m; he is breathing with difficulty numfāshī yā yi masà wùyā; ~ heavily (*as from pain*) yi nīshì m.

**breed** v a. haifař (dà) v5, hàyàyyafà v2: uncleanliness ~s germs rashìn tsabtà nà haifař dà ƙwāyōyin cùtā. b. (*animals*) yi kīwò m.

**breeze** n iskà mài dādī f.

**brew** 1. v (*e.g. roots for medicinal use*) tsimà v1; (*beer*) dafà v1.
2. n (*of herbs*) tsimì m, jiƙò m.

**bribe** n hancì m, řashawā f, tōshiyař bàkī f: give a ~ bā dà hancì = bā dà řashawā;

accept a ~ ci hancì = kàrɓi hancì =
kàrɓi tōshiyař bâkī.

bribery n cîn hancì m: ~ and corruption
řashawā dà cîn hancì; ~ is prevalent cîn
hancì yā zaunā dà gìndinsà.

brick n (of dried mud) tūbàlī m ⟨u-a⟩,
(modern) [F] bìřgī m.

bricklayer n magìnī m, bìřkìlà m ⟨oCi⟩,
[F] mâsô m.

bride n amaryā f ⟨amārē⟩.

bridegroom n angò m ⟨aye⟩.

bride-wealth n (given by groom) sàdâkī m.

bridge n a. gadā f ⟨oCi⟩, (small) kàdarkò
m ⟨ai⟩. b. ~ of nose karan hancì m.

bridle n kāyan lìnzāmì m.

brief adj tàkàitaccē adj: a ~ speech
tàkàitaccen jàwābì; a ~ letter 'yař
wàsīkā; in ~, ~ly à tàkàice.

briefcase n jàkař hannu f.

brigadier n bìřgēdiyà m, [F] bùřgàji m.

bright adj (of light, color) (mài) haskē m,
bàu idph: ~ blue shūdì mài haskē =
shūdì bàu.

brightly adv (use specific ideophones with
verbs): the fire is burning ~ wutā tā yi
bàl = wutā tanā cî bàlbàl; it is shining
~ yanà kyàllī wàl; the sun is shining ~
rānā tā yi haskē bàu.

brilliant adj a. (of light) (mài) haskē bàu.
b. (of intelligence) (mài) hàzākā f.

brim n bàkī m; be full to the ~ bàtsē v4,
cìka fal, cìka mâkil.

bring v a. kāwō v6: she brought us some
water tā kāwō manà ruwā; ~ trouble
upon jàwō, janyō wà rìkicì. b. (var. v
+ adv/prep uses): ~ about sâ v1, jàwō
v6: reckless spending brought about his
bankruptcy yawàn kashè kuɗinsà nē yā
jàwō kàrayař ařzìkinsà; ~ about many
changes sâ cànje-cànje dà yawà; ~
about peace wanzařtař dà zaman lāfiyà;
~ back dāwō dà: she brought back some
bananas tā dāwō dà àyàbà; ~ out, ~
to light fitō à fīlī: the investigation
brought to light the true facts of the case
bìncìkên yā fitō dà gàskiyař lamàřîn
à fīlī; ~ up (a matter) tā dà / tāyař
(dà) v5; ~ up (a child) rēnā v2 ⟨rainō⟩.

bristle n gāshì m.

British adj na Ingìlà: he speaks ~ English
Tūřancinsà na Ingìlà nē.

brittle adj (mài) gautsī m.

broad adj (mài) fādī m, fàffāɗà adj: ~
shoulders fàffāɗař kàfaɗà; a ~ river
kògī mài fādī; extremely ~ fankamēmè
adj, fankamī adj: a ~ expanse of river
fankamēmèn kògī = kògī fankamī; in ~

daylight dà rāna tsakà = dà rāna kirī-
kìrì; ~-minded (mài) saukin kâi.

broadcast v (by radio, television) wàtsà làbàřai v1, yāɗà làbàřai; radio, television ~ing station gidan řēdiyò, talàbijìn; British ~ing Corp. gidan řēdiyò
na Bībīsî; Kano ~ing Corp. ma'aikatař
sādàřwā ta Kanò.

brocade n (cotton) shaddā f.

brochure n kàsīdà f ⟨u⟩.

broil v gasā v1.

broker n dìllālì m ⟨ai⟩.

bronchitis n màshàkò m.

bronze n tagùllā f, jan kařfē m: they won
a ~ medal sun ci lambař tagùllā.

brood v a. (sulk) yi zùgum / jùgum idph.
b. (sit on eggs) yi kwàncī m.

broom n tsintsìyā f ⟨oCi⟩.

broth n rōmō m.

brothel n gidan kàřùwai m, gidan magā-
jiyā m.

brother n ɗan'uwā m ⟨'yan'uwā⟩; full ~
shàkīkì m ⟨ai⟩; older ~ wā m, yâyā
m ⟨yayyē, yāyū⟩; younger ~ kanè m
⟨kannē⟩.

brother-in-law n (younger brother of wife
or husband, younger sister's husband)
kanè m ⟨kannē⟩; (older brother of wife
or husband, older sister's husband) wā m,
yâyā m ⟨yayyē, yāyū⟩.

brotherhood n (Relig., esp. Sufi) dàřīkà f.

brow n gòshī m.

brown adj kasa-kasa adj, (reddish-~, maroon) ruwan màkubā m, (light orange-~)
ruwan kōyà m.

bruise 1. v kūjè / kūjè v4.
2. n kūjèwā / kūjèwā f, jè-ka-hūdà m.

brush[1] 1. n bùřōshì m magōgī m; (for teeth)
magōgin hakōrī m.
2. v a. (teeth, clothes) gōgè v4: he ~es his
teeth twice a day yanà gōgè hakòransà
sàu biyu à rānā. b. (hair) shařcè v4.

brush[2] n (the 'bush') dājì m ⟨uka[2]⟩, jèjì
m; wild, uninhabited ~ kungurmin dājì
= dòkař dājì; thick ~, undergrowth
sàřkakkiyā f.

brutal adj maràs īmānì m, mamùgùncī adj,
makètàcī adj, kàzāmī adj ⟨ai⟩: a ~ war
kàzāmin yākì.

brutality n rashìn īmānì m, kètā f.

bubble forth v (of water out of ground)
6ù66ugà v3.

bubbles n (of soap) kumfā m.

buck v (of animal) yi tūtsū m.

bucket n bōkitì m ⟨ai⟩, [F] sô m; (of
leather, for drawing water from well) gùgā
f ⟨una⟩.

**buckle** 1. *n* bōkùl *m*, maɓallī *m*.
  2. *vt* (*e.g. a belt*) jā bōkùl, ɓallà *v1*.
  3. *vi* (*inward*) kōmàɗē / mōkàɗē *v4*, lōtsè *v4*; (*outward*) lanƙwàshē *v4*, lauyè *v4*.
**bud** 1. *n* tòhō *m*, hùdā *f*: the trees are putting out new ~s itātuwà nà sābon tòhō.
  2. *v* tōhō *v6*, yi tòhō *m*, yi hùdā *f*.
**budge** *v* mōtsà *v1*: I couldn't ~ it an inch nā kàsà mōtsà shi kō kàɗan.
**budget** *n* kasàfin kuɗī *m*: supplementary ~ ƙàramin kasàfin kuɗī.
**buffalo** *n* ɓaunā *f* (ɓakànē, aye), (*bull*) tōron ɓaunā *m*.
**bug** *n* (*any kind*) ƙwàrō *m* (i).
**bugle** *n* bēgìlà *m* (oCi), [F] kàlàlô *m*.
**build**[1] *v* a. (*a structure*) ginà *v1* (ginì); be built up (*developed*) ƙàsaità *v3*, bùnƙàsà *v3*: Kano has been built up within the last few years Kanò tā ƙàsaità cikin 'yan shèkàrun nàn. b. (*found*) kafà *v1*: where are they going to ~ the factory? ìnā zā sù kafà ma'aikatàr̃?
**build**[2] *n* (*of body*) ƙīr̃ā *f*: she is well built kyân ƙīr̃ā gàrē tà.
**building** *n* ginì *m* (e[2]); (*with upper stories*) bēnē *m* (aye); (*flat-roofed*) sōrō *m* (aye).
**bulb** *n*, *see* lightbulb.
**bulge** *v* tūrō *v6*, tàsō *v6*: he ate so much his stomach was bulging yā ci har̃ cikìnsà yā tàsō.
**bull** *n* sâ *m* (shānū), bìjimī *m* (ai); ~ elephant, buffalo tòron gīwā, ɓaunā.
**bullet** *n* hàr̃sāshì *m* (ai), [F] kàr̃tūshì *m*: a hail of ~s ruwan hàr̃sāshì.
**bull-headed** *adj* (mài) taurin kâi.
**bullock** *n* fur̃tùmī *m* (u-a), dakè *m* (Ca).
**bully** *v* ci zālin w., (*by bluster*) yi wà kūrī *m*: she's always ~ing her younger brother tā cikà cîn zālin ƙanèntà.
**bulrush-millet** *n*, *see* millet.
**bum** 1. *n* (*unemployed*) zàunà-gàrī-banzā *n*.
  2. *v* (*cadge*) hàgā *v2*: I ~med a cigarette, kolanut from Mudi nā hàgi sìgār̃ì, gòr̃ò wajen Mūdì.
**bump**[1] 1. *v* (*collide*) yi karò *m;* ~ into so. (*unexpectedly*) ci karò dà, yi kìcìɓìs dà: I ~ed into my former teacher nā yi kìcìɓìs dà tsōhon mālàmīnā; ~ oneself on head bugè kâi *v4*, ƙumè kâi *v4*: watch out so you don't ~ your head yi hankàlī kadà kà ƙumè kânkà.
**bump**[2] (*in road*) galàn *m*.
**bumper** *n* (*of car*) bamfà *f*, [F] pàr̃shâk *m*.

**bumpy** *adj* (*of road*) (mài) gar̃gadà *f*, (mài) galàn *m*: the road is very ~ hanyà tā cikà gar̃gadà.
**bunch** *n* a. (*of bananas, dates, grapes*) nōnò *m* (Ca). b. (*group of people*) gungù *m*.
**bundle** 1. *n* a. (*esp. of harvested grain*) damì *m* (Cai): a ~ of millet damìn gērō. b. (*tied*) ɗaurì *m*: a ~ of wood ɗaurìn itàcē. c. (*wrapped*) ƙunshì *m*: a ~ of clothes ƙunshìn kāyā.
  2. *v* ƙunshè *v4*: he ~d the clothes into a plastic bag yā ƙunshè tufāfì à lēdà.
**burden** *n* (*responsibility*) nauyī *m*, ɗàwàiniyā *f*: he took on the ~ of looking after them yā ɗauki ɗàwàiniyar̃ kùlā dà sū; put a ~ on so. ɗōrà wà nauyī; the ~ of proof is on you nauyin wankè kânkà yanà wajenkà.
**bureau** *n* (*office*) ōfìs *m* (oCi), [F] bùr̃ò *m*: B. of Motor Vehicles ōfìshin lāsīsì.
**bureaucrat** *n* ma'àikàcin gwamnatì *m*, [F] ɗan sàr̃ushì *m*.
**burglar** *n* ɓàrāwò *m* (i).
**burglary** *n* sātà *f*.
**burial** *n* binnèwā *f*.
**burial grounds** *n* makabàr̃tā *f*, màkwàntai *p*.
**burlap** *n* àlgàr̃àr̃à *f*: ~ is made from hemp anà yîn àlgàr̃àr̃à dà ramà.
**burly** *adj* mur̃ɗēɗè *adj*: a big, ~ man mur̃ɗēɗèn ƙātò.
**burn** 1. *v* a. ƙōnà *v1*: she ~ed the food tā ƙōnà àbinci; the food is hot, it will ~ your tongue àbinci nà dà zāfī, yanà ƙōnà harshè; be careful, fire ~s yi hankàlī wutā tanà ƙōnàwā; ~ sth. up ƙōnè *v4*: take out the trash and ~ it up kà kwāshè shàrā kà ƙōnè. b. (*oneself*) ƙōnè *v4*: she ~ed herself while cooking tā ƙōnè wajen girkì; she ~ed her hand tā ƙōnè à hannu. c. ~ uncultivated land tōyà *v1*, yi tòyī *m*. d. (*of any fire*) ci *v0*, (*esp. intensely*) ƙuna *v3a*: the fire is ~ing brightly wutā tanà cî bàlbàl = wutā tanà ƙūnā sòsai; the lamp is ~ing well fìtilà tanà cî; don't leave a fire ~ing in the room kadà à bar̃ wutā tanà cî cikin dākì; start to ~ (*of a fire*) kāmà cî; ~ up completely ƙōnè ƙùr̃mus.
  2. *n* (~ *mark on body*) ƙūnā *m*.
**burnous** *n* àlkyabbà *f* (u).
**burp** *v* yi gyàtsā *f*.
**burrow** *n* rāmì *m* (uka).
**burrs** *n* ƙàràngiyā *f*.
**bursar** *n* bāsà *n*.
**bursary** *n* ōfìshin bāsà *m*.

**burst** *v* a. (*of balloon, pipe*) ɗashè *v4;* (*of boiler, dam*) ɓarkè *v4.* b. (*do suddenly*): ~ into (*a place*) kūtsà *v1;* ~ into laughter ɓarkè = kècè = ƙyalƙyàlē = būshè dà dàriyā; ~ into tears ɗashè dà kūkā. c. (*overflow*) bàtsè *v4:* the market is ~ing with people kàsuwā tā bàtsè dà mutànē.

**bury** *v* (*a psn.*) binnè *v4,* rufè *v4,* (*euphem.*) sutùr̃tā *v1;* (*in soft earth, ashes*) turbùɗē *v4.*

**bus** *n* sàfā *f,* bàs *f,* [F] kàr̃ *f;* mini~ hayìs *f,* [F] hiyâs *f,* kiyā-kiyā *f* catch a ~ shìga bàs.

**bush** *n* a. (*plant*) ɗan itàcē *m,* shūkā *f* ⟨e²⟩; (*fig.*) beat around the ~ yi kèwàye-kèwàye *m,* yi ƙumbìyà-ƙumbiyā *idph.* b. (*wilderness*) dājì *m* ⟨uka²⟩, jējì *m;* uninhabited ~ ƙungurmin dājì *m,* dòkar̃ dājì *f;* dense ~ (*area where so. can hide out*) sùnƙūrù *m;* there is a ~ fire jējì yā ɗauki wutā; in, to the ~ (à) dawà *adv:* look for firewood in the ~ nèmi itàcē à dawà.

**bushbuck** *n* màzō *m,* r̃àgon ruwa *m.*

**bush-cow** *n* ɓaunā *f* ⟨ɓakànē, aye⟩.

**bush-fowl** *n* makwarwā *f* ⟨makwàr̃ē⟩.

**business** *n* a. (*commercial activity*) cìnikī *m,* kàsuwancì *m,* hulɗàr̃ cìnikī *f,* sha'ànin cìnikī *m:* we do ~ with him munà kàsuwancì dà shī = munà sha'ànin cìnikī dà shī; he started ~ as a dealer yā shìga kàsuwancì dà dillàncì; have ~ ties with yi hulɗàr̃ cìnikī dà; he's in the ~ of selling cars yanà hulɗàr̃ sai dà mōtōcī; he runs a ~ yanà da kàntī; he's on a ~ trip yanà safar̃à; be in private ~ ci gashìn kâi, yi zaman kâi: he is in ~ for himself yanà cîn gashìn kânsà = yanà zaman kânsà = yanà dà hulɗàr̃ cìnikinsà. b. (*quantity of trading*) kàsuwā *f:* ~ was good today yâu kàsuwā tā yi kyâu; there's no ~ today yâu bâ kàsuwā. c. (*gen'l activity*) har̃kà *f* ⟨oCi⟩, hidimā *f* ⟨oCi⟩, zar̃àfī *m:* I have a lot of ~ to do today yâu inà dà har̃kōkī dà yawà; I'm not going because I have no ~ to do there bà zân jē ba sabòdà bâ nī dà wani zar̃àfī à can; this is none of your ~! bâ àbîn dà ya shā makà kâi dà wannàn! (*fig., rude*) none of your ~! bâ ruwankà! what ~ is it of ours? ìnā ruwanmù fa?

**businessman** *n* ɗan kàsuwā *m,* (*prominent, wealthy*) àttàjìrī *m* ⟨ai⟩.

**bust** *n* (*chest*) ƙìrjī *m;* (*bosom, of women*) nōnò *m.*

**bustle about** *v* yi hàyà-hàyà *f,* yi hàdà-hadā *f.*

**busy** *adj* a. (*with activity*): we're very ~ today yâu munà har̃kōkī; are you very ~? kanà aikì dà yawà? he is ~ writing yanà tsakiyàr̃ r̃ùbùtū; be ~ with (*preoccupied*) shàgalà dà *v3,* shàgàltu dà *v7:* everyone was ~ studying kōwā yā shàgalà dà kàr̃àtū. b. (*esp. with chores, errands*) yi dàwàiniyā *f,* yi hidimā *f* ⟨oCi⟩: she is ~ with housework tanà hidimōmin gidā; today I was very ~ yâu inà dà hidimā dà yawà. c. (*of telephone*): the line is ~ anà wayà = wani nà wayà = wani yanà bugàwā.

**busybody** *n* kar̃ambànā *n.*

**but** *conj* a. àmmā *conj:* she came ~ didn't stay long tā zō àmmā dai bà tà daɗè ba. b. (*except*) ban dà, sai (dai): he doesn't do anything ~ play bā yà yîn kōmē ban dà wàsā; she told everyone ~ me tā gayà wà kōwā sai nī; she gives me nothing ~ trouble bā tà janyō minì kōmē sai r̃ìkicī.

**butcher** 1. *n* mahàucī *m;* head ~ sarkin fàwā.
2. *v* yankà *v1.*

**butchering** *n* fàwā *f.*

**butt**[1] *v* (*by animal*) tunkùɗā *v1;* ~ in (*on conversation*) sâ bàkī, tsōmà bàkī, kūtsà kâi.

**butt**[2] *n* a. (*of cigarette*) guntuwar̃ tābà *f.* b. (*of rifle*) gìndin bindigà *m.*

**butter** *n* mân shànū *m,* dunƙulèn mâi *m.*

**butterfly** *n* mālàm-bùɗā-manà-littàfì *m.*

**buttocks** *n* ɗuwàwū *m* ⟨ɗuwàiwai⟩, (*euphem.*) gìndī *m.*

**button** 1. *n* maɓallī *m,* ànīnī *m,* bōtìn / bōtìr̃ *m* ⟨u-a⟩, [F] bùtò *m:* the ~ has come off maɓallī yā cirè = maɓallī yā ɓallè; sew a ~ on sâ maɓallī.
2. *v* ɓallà *v1:* he ~ed his coat yā ɓallà maɓallin kwât ɗinsà.

**buttonhole** *n* ƙōfar̃ maɓallī *f.*

**buxom** *adj* shamɓar̃ēr̃ìyā *adj,* mài nōnò tantsà-tàntsà.

**buy** *v* a. sàyā *v2* ⟨sàyē⟩; ~ for so. sai wà / sayà wà *v1:* I want her to ~ me some soap inà sô tà sayà minì sàbulù; ~ a car on credit, on time sàyi mōtà bāshì; ~ing and selling sàyē dà sayàr̃wā. b. (*small items on credit, often without paying*) hàgā *v2:* I bought some kolanuts from him nā hàgi gōr̃o à wajensà. c. (*esp. tickets*) yànkā *v2* ⟨yankà⟩: I bought a train ~ nā yànki tikitìn jirgī.

**buyer** *n* mài sàyē *n.*

**buzz** *v* (*of bees*) yi zīzà *f,* yi ƙugì *m.*

**by** *prep* a. (*in*) à *prep:* ~ car, air à mōtà, jirgin samà. b. (*via*) ta *prep:* he sent it ~ air yā aikō ta jirgin samà; we came ~ the dry season road mun zō ta hanyàr̃ rānī. c. (*with*) dà *prep*: he explained it to me ~ giving an example yā bayyànā minì dà wani mìsālì; it is made ~ hand an yī shì dà hannu; he swore ~ God yā rantsè dà Allàh; ~ and ~ in an jimà, jimàwā kàɗan. d. (*for passive constr., may use corresponding active sent.*): I was examined ~ the doctor likità yā ɗùbē nì. e. (*for "middle" passive constr.*) wàjen *prep*: the car can be fixed ~ a good mechanic mōtà zā tà iyà gyàruwā wajen ƙwàrarren bàkànikè; this can't be lifted ~ one person wannàn bà zâi ɗàuku wajen mùtûm ɗaya ba.

bye-bye *excl, see* goodbye.

# C

cab *n* a. (*taxi*) tằsî *m*, [F] tàkàsî *f*: ~ driver ɗan tằsî; catch a ~ tsai dà tằsî. b. (*of truck*) kân tantēbùr̃ *m*, [F] kàbîn *m*.

cabbage *n* kābējì *m*, [F] shû *m*.

cabinet *n* a. (*for storage*) kabàd *m*, [F] kwabằ *f*. b. (*Pol.*) màjàlisằ ta gudānằr̃wā *f*.

cable *n* wayằ *f* ⟨oCi⟩; (*of clutch, brake*) kēbùr̃ *m*, [F] kābìl *m*.

cackling *n* (*of hen*) kyar̃kyar̃ā *f*.

caftan *n* kàftānî *f*.

cage *n* (*for birds*) kējì *m*, gidan tsuntsằyē *m*.

cake *n* a. (*var. types*): (*sweet, baked*) kyât *m*, [F] gằtô *m*; (*fried, from cereals*) wàinā *f*, māsā *f*; (*fried, from beans*) ƙōsai *m*; (*fried, from wheat, eaten with sauce*) fùnkằsō *m*; (*fried, from millet*) gūr̃un hatsī *m*; (*sweet, fried, from refined white flour*) fànkē *m*. b. a ~ of soap ƙwằyar̃ sàbulû *f*.

calabash *n* a. (*gen'l term*) dumā *m* ⟨aCe⟩, see gourd. b. (*var. types*): (*medium size, for food*) ƙwaryā *f* ⟨ƙōrē⟩; (*large, for bathing, feeding animals*) masakī *m* ⟨ai⟩, gìdaunìyā *f*; (*shallow fragment shaped for dipping out food*) mārā *f* ⟨oCi⟩; (*any ~ fragment*) sàkainā *f* ⟨u⟩; ~ mender gyar̃tai *m*.

calamity *n* màsīfằ *f* ⟨oCi⟩, bàlā'ì *m* ⟨oCi⟩, jàr̃abằ *f*.

calcium *n* âllī *m* .

calculate *v* lāsằftā / lissằfā *v1*.

calculation *n* lìssāfî *m*: according to my ~s à lìssāfînā.

calculator *n* nā'ūr̃ar̃ lìssāfî *f*, kalkùlētā *f*.

calendar *n* kàlandằ *f*, [F] kằlàndìr̃ê *m*.

calf[1] *n* (*of cow*) màraƙī *m* ⟨u-a⟩.

calf[2] *n* (*of leg*) shằ-rā6ā *f*, dâmbūbù *m*.

calico *n* (*off-white color*) alawayyò *m*, far̃ar̃ sàndā *f*: shrouds are made of ~ anằ lìkkafànī dà alawayyò.

call 1. *v* a. kirā *v0*: so-and-so is ~ing you wằnè nằ kìrànkà; we were about to leave when he ~ed us back zā mù tàfi

kề nan sai ya sākề kirànmù; ~ sth. to so.'s attention janyō hankàlin w. à kân, faɗakar̃ (dà) *v5;* ~ so. to a meeting kirā w. tằrō; ~ so. loudly ƙwālā wà kirā. b. (*name sth.*) kirā *v0*, cê dà: what do you ~ this kind of pot? yằyằ akề kiràn irìn wannàn tukunyā? he ~ed me a coward yā cê dà nī matsòràcī; he is ~ed Audu anằ cê dà shī Audù = anằ kirànsà Audù; a man ~ed Musa wani mài sūnā Mūsā; ~ so. names zằgā *v2* ⟨zāgì⟩, zàzzāgā *v2*. c. (*so. on telephone*) bugā wà wayằ, kirā à wayằ: I'll ~ you tomorrow zân bugā makà wayằ gòbe. d. (*var. v + adv/prep uses*): ~ for yi kirā dà: the opposition ~ed for an investigation àbōkan hàmayyằ sun yi kirā dà à yi bìncìkē; ~ off (*an event*) fāsằ *v1;* ~ on so. (*pay a visit*) kai wà zìyār̃ằ. 2. *n* a. kirā *m*; (*loud ~ for help*) kùrūruwằ *f*; (*fig.*) have a close ~ aunà ar̃zìkī. b. (*on telephone*) wayằ *f*: there is a ~ for you anằ bugō makà wayằ; ask him to return my ~ à cê masà yà yiwō minì wayằ. c. (*visit*) zìyār̃ằ *f*: they paid a ~ on us sun kai manà zìyār̃ằ. d. (*of bird*) kūkā *m* ⟨kòke-kòke⟩.

callus *n* (*on hands, feet*) kantā *f*.

calm 1. *adj* (*psn.*) (mài) nìtsuwā *f*; be ~, collected nìtsu *v7*, kìntsu *v7*; become ~ hùcề *v4*: after I comforted him, he became ~ bāyan nā bā shì hàƙurī yā hùcề. 2. *v* làllāsā *v2* ⟨lallāshī⟩, kwantar̃ dà hankàlin w., sanyàyā wà zūcìyā: I ~ed the child down nā sanyàyā wà yāròn zūcìyā; ~ down hùcề *v4*.

calmly *adv* dà nìtsuwā, cikin nìtsuwā.

camaraderie *n* ƙàwàncē *m*.

camel *n* rằƙumī *m* ⟨u-a⟩, (*female*) rằƙumā *f*, tằguwằ *f*; (*male*) amālè *m*.

camera *n* àbin ɗaukàr̃ hòtō *m*, kyamar̃ằ *f*; (*esp. for TV, movies*) [F] kàmàr̃ā *f*.

camp 1. *n* a. (*transitory, during a trip*) zangò *m* ⟨una⟩: break, set up ~ yā dà zangò; (*Fulani type*) rugā *f* ⟨oCi⟩. b. (*Mil.*) sànsanī *m* ⟨ai⟩.

campaign *n* (*political*) kàmfên *m*; (*political, social*) yāƙì *m*: election ~ yāƙìn nēman zàɓē; literacy ~ yāƙì dà jāhilcì.

campground *n* zangò *m* ⟨una⟩.

camphor *n* kāfùr̃ *m*.

campus *n* (*of university*) hàr̃ābar̃ jāmi'ằ *f*.

can[1] *v aux* a. (*be able*) iyā *v1*: ~ the child walk? yārò yā iyà tàfiyằ? ~ you speak English? kā iyà Tūr̃ancī? = kanà jîn Tūr̃ancī? b. (*permit*) (*use subjunct. in interrog.*): ~ I go? ìn tàfi? ~ I give you

sth. cold to drink? ìn bā kà àbin shâ mài
sanyī?

can² n a. (for food) gwangwanī m ⟨aye⟩,
[F] kwankwanī / kwankô m ⟨aye⟩: ~ned
food àbincin gwangwanī. b. (of motor
oil) galàn m, [F] bìdô m; watering ~
būtūtun gādìnà m.

canal n (for irrigation) dōkìn ruwa m.

canary n kànàŕī m.

cancel v a. (a meeting, order, decision) sōkè
v4: the game was ~led because of the rain
an sōkè wàsân sabôdà ruwā. b. (a debt)
yāfè wà bāshì v4, sōkè bāshì.

cancellation n sūkā f.

cancer n kansā f, cīwòn kansā m, cùtaŕ
dājì f; malignant ~ cīwòn kansā mài
yàɗuwā.

candidate n ɗan tākaŕā m.

candle n kyandìŕ m, [F] bùjî f.

candy n àlēwā / àlāwā f, [F] bàmbô m: but-
terscotch, mint ~ àlēwàŕ madaŕā, mintì;
eat ~ shā àlēwā.

cane 1. n (of bamboo) gōrā f ⟨oCi⟩; (of
cornstalk, sugar ~) karā m ⟨aCe⟩; (flexible stick) tsabgā f ⟨oCi⟩, tsumāgìyā /
tsumangìyā f ⟨oCi⟩.
2. v diŕkà wà sàndā v1.

canine n a. (tooth) fīkā f ⟨oCi⟩. b. (ref. to
dogs) na kàrē.

cannabis n, see marijuana.

cannibal n mài cîn mùtûm n.

cannon n ìgwā f ⟨oCi⟩.

canoe n jirgī m ⟨a-e⟩; (wooden) kwàlekwàle m, (for fishing) kōmī m ⟨aye⟩.

can opener n mabūɗin gwangwanī m, ôfanā
f, [F] ūbìŕbwât m.

cantankerous adj (psn.) hūtsū n ⟨aye⟩,
tsagèrā n ⟨u⟩.

canteen n (for carrying water) būtā f ⟨oCi⟩:
an aluminum ~ būtàŕ gòran ruwā.

canter v yi rīshī m, yi zagaŕaftū m.

canvas n tàmfâl m.

cap n a. hùlā f ⟨una⟩, tàgiyà f ⟨u⟩; (var.
types): (fez) (hùlaŕ) dàŕā f; (beret) bèŕê
f; (tall, hand-embroidered) Zannà Bukàŕ
f, ƙùbè f; (soft Fulani cap covering ears)
habàŕ kadà f; (with bill) hànà-sallà f. b.
(for bottle, gas tank) murfī m ⟨ai⟩.

capability n iyàwā f.

capable adj (psn.) n gwànī m ⟨aye⟩.

cape n àlkyabbà f.

capital¹ n (Econ.) jāŕī hujjà m, uwaŕ kuɗī
f.

capital² n (city) bàbban biŕnī m, hêdkwatà
/ hêlkwatà f: Abuja is the ~ of Nigeria
Àbūjā ita cè bàbban biŕnin Nìjēŕiyà.

capital³ adj: ~ punishment hukuncìn kisà
m.

capitalism n ŕa'àyin jāŕī hujjà m.

capitalist n ɗan jāŕī hujjà m.

capitol (government house) fādàŕ gwamnatì
f.

capsize v kifè v4: the boat ~d with 50
people aboard jirgin ruwa yā kifè dà
mutānē hàmsin.

captain n kyaftìn n, [F] kàftân n: he
has been made a ~ an bā shì mùƙāmìn
kyaftìn; Capt. Sule kyàftìn Sulè.

captive n kàmammē m, fuŕsùnà m ⟨oCi⟩.

capture v (a psn.) kāmā v1; (a town) ci v0,
danƙè v4.

car n a. mōtā f ⟨oCi⟩: a rented ~ mōtàŕ
hayà; by ~ à mōtà; drive a ~ yi tūƙìn
mōtā = tūƙà mōtā; know how to drive a
~ iyà mōtā; park a ~ ajìyè mōtā; start
a ~ tā dà mōtā. b. (of railroad) tàŕagù
m ⟨ai⟩, wāgùnù m ⟨oCi⟩.

caravan n (of camels, vehicles) āyàŕī m
⟨oCi⟩.

carbon n gawàyī m.

carbon paper n baƙaŕ takàŕdā ta tāfìŕē-
tā f.

carburetor n kàfìŕētô m, [F] kàŕbìŕàtâŕ
m.

carcass n ƙwàŕàngwal m.

card n kātì m ⟨una⟩, see cards; mem-
bership ~ kātìn ƙunglìyā m; greeting ~
kātìn gaisuwā = kātìn muŕnà; identification ~ kātìn shaidà, [F] kaŕtìdàndìtê
f.

cardboard n kwālī m; ~ box kwālī m
⟨aye⟩, [F] kàŕtô m.

cardinal adj: ~ numbers alƙalumā p.

cards n (game of ~) kaŕtā f: play ~ yi
kaŕtā; shuffle ~ lālè kātì.

care 1. v a. (mind) dàmu v7, kùla v3: they
don't ~ if you are late bā sà dàmuwā ìdan
kā màkarà; I don't ~, it's all the same
to me bàn kùla ba, duk ɗaya nè = bàn
dàmu ba, duk ɗaya nè; why should I ~
(about it)? ìnā kùlātà? b. (be concerned
about so.) ji v0: you really do ~ about
Audu lallē kanà jîn Audù; ~ for (have
compassion for) ji tàusàyin w.; I could
~ less! (fig.) kō bìŕis kō ôho! c. ~ for
(look after so.) kulā dà v1, kùla dà v3:
she ~d for us when we were sick tā kulā
dà mū lōkàcîn dà bā mà dà lāfiyà. d. ~
for (rear a child) rènā / ràina v2 ⟨rènō /
ràinō⟩: the grandmother is caring for the
children kàkā tanà rènon 'yā'yā. e. ~
for (like) sô v0: I don't ~ for desserts bā
nà sôn kāyan zāƙī.

**2.** *n* a. (*attention*) hankàlī *m*, kùlā *f*, lùr̃ā *f*: take ~! kù mai dà hankàlī! you should take better ~ of yourself kì r̃àr̃à kùlā dà kânkì; take good ~ of sth. ādànā *v1*, kùla dà *v3*: she takes good ~ of her clothes tanā ādànà kāyantà. b. (*custody*) hannū *m*: she's under the doctor's ~ tanā hannun likità; you can write to me in ~ of our department kā iyà r̃ubūtō minì ta hannun sāshènmù. c. (*burden, duty*) dàwàiniyā *f*, hidimā *f* (oCi): my friends took ~ of all my needs àbōkainā sun dàuki duk dàwàiniyātā = sun yi minì hidimā mài yawā. d. (*deliberation*) tsànākī *m*: his work shows great ~ aikìnsà cikin tsànākī yakè.

**careful** *adj* a. (*cautious*) (mài) hankàlī *m*, (mài) lùr̃ā *f*, (mài) kùlā *f*: a ~ child yārò mài hankàlī; be ~! yi hankàlī! = kà lùr̃a! = kà kùla! = yi sànnu dai! b. (*with deliberation*) (mài) tsànākī *m*: do ~ work yi aikì cikin tsànākī.

**carefully** *adv* à hankàlī, cikin tsànākī, à tsànàke.

**careless** *adj* (*not caring*): he is ~ bā yà kùlā; (*through haste*): don't be ~ with your work kadà kà yi gàr̃àjē dà aikìnkà = kadà kà yi aikì cikin gàr̃àjē.

**carelessness** *n* rashìn kùlā *m*, rashìn lùr̃ā *m*, (*esp. negligence*) sakacī *m*: his ~ was the cause of the trouble rashìn kùlar̃sà yā haddàsà fìtinā.

**cargo** *n* kāyā *m* ⟨aki²⟩.

**caricature** *n* mūzàntâwā *f*.

**caries** *n*, *see* cavity.

**carp** *n* (*fish*) karfasā *f*.

**carpenter** *n* mài kātākō *m*, kāfintà *m* ⟨oCi⟩, [F] mìnìzē *m*.

**carpentry** *n* sàssar̃ā *f*; do ~ yi aikìn kāfintà.

**carpet** *n* kāfèt *m*, dàr̃dūmā *f*, [F] tàpî *m*.

**carrier** *n* a. (*porter*) ɗan dakō *m*, ɗan alār̃ò *m*, ɗan lōdì *m*. b. (*bicycle rack*) kàr̃iyà *f*.

**carrion** *n* mūshè *m*.

**carrots** *n* kar̃às *m*, [F] kàr̃ōtì *m*.

**carry** *v* a. (*take*) kai *v\**, ɗaukà *v2\**: who will ~ this package for me? wā zâi kai minì r̃unshìn nân? goods are carried by rail anā ɗaukàr̃ kāyā ta jirgin r̃asà; ~ goods on the head ɗauki kāyā à ka; they are ~ing things back and forth sunā kâiwā sunā kāwôwā; ~ so. on the back gōyà *v1*, yi gōyō *m*: she's ~ing the baby on her back tanā gōyon ɗantà = tanā gòye dà ɗantà; he carried his friend on the back of his bicycle yā gōyà àbōkinsà à kèkè; ~

off a prize kwāshè lambā. b. (*hold*) rìr̃à *v1*; he is ~ing a spear in his hand yanā rìr̃e dà māshì à hannunsà. c. (*reach*) kai *v\**: the sound carried a long distance amōn yā kai nēsà r̃war̃ai. d. ~ out (*implement*) zar̃taf (dà) *v5*, aikataf (dà) *v5* aiwataf (dà) *v5*, aikàtā *v1*: I carried out his instructions nā zar̃taf dà ùmàr̃ninsà. e. ~ on with one's work ci gàba dà aikì = mai dà hankàlī gà aikì.

**cart** *n* (*4-wheeled*) kūrā *m* ⟨aye⟩; (*2-wheeled*) amālanke *m*; (*pulled by oxen*) kèken shānū *m*, amālanke *m*.

**cartilage** *n* gurunguntsī *m*.

**carton** *n* kwālī *m* ⟨aye⟩, kātàn *m*, [F] kàr̃tô *m*; ~ of cigarettes zîn tābā *m*, r̃unshìn tābā *m*, [F] kàr̃tūshìn sìgārì *m*; empty ~ fànkō *m*, emtì *m*.

**cartridge** *n* (*for bullet*) har̃sāshì *m* ⟨ai⟩.

**carve** *v* a. (*make a product*) sassàr̃à *v1*: he is carving a mortar yanā sassàr̃à turmī. b. (*wood, stone*) sàssar̃à *v2*: he ~d a saddle from the wood yā sàssàr̃i itàcē yà mai dà shī sir̃dì. c. (*meat*) yankè *v4*.

**carver** *n* (*of wood*) masàssàr̃ī *m*.

**carving** *n* (*image used in worship*) gumkì *m* ⟨a-a⟩.

**case**[1] *n* a. (*matter*) màganà *f* ⟨u²⟩, màtsalà *f* ⟨oCi⟩: regarding the boy's ~ game dà màganàr̃ yāròn; your ~ is problematic màtsalàr̃ tākà àkwai rìkicì. b. (*circumstance*) hālī / hālì *m* ⟨aye⟩: in any ~ kō dà wànè hālī = kō ta yàyà = kōmē akè ciki; in that ~ tun dà hakà nē; if that's the ~, why did you do it? in dai hakà nē don mè ka yī shì? in ~ kō dà: in ~ you come and I'm not here... kō dà kakà zō, bà nā nân... = ìdan kā zō bā nā nân... = kō dà zā kà zō bā nā nân.... c. (*Law*) r̃ārā *f*: his ~ is before the judge r̃ārar̃sà tanā hannun àlr̃ālì; hear a ~ sàuràri r̃ārā; dismiss a ~ kòri r̃ārā.

**case**[2] *n* a. (*of wood or metal with hinged cover*) àdakà *f* ⟨u⟩, [F] kyâs *m*. b. (*container for small things*) gidā *m*: cigarette ~ gidan sìgārì.

**cash** *n* kuɗī *p*; ~ payment kuɗī hannu *m*: I'll pay you in ~ zân biyā kà kuɗī hannu.

**cashew** *n* kanjū *m*, yàzāwā *f*.

**cashier** *n* kàshiyà *n*, [F] kyàsiyè *n*.

**cassava** *n* rōgò *m*; ~ flour kwākī *m*, gàrin rōgò *m*.

**cassette** *n* (*tape*) kàsât / kāsàt *m*.

**cassette recorder** *n* r̃àkōdā *f*, [F] mànyètô *m*.

**cassia** *n* (*tree*) runhū *m*.

cast v: ~ a ballot jēfà ƙùƙi'à; ~ a fishing line zurà fatsa = jēfà fatsa; ~ a spell over so. yi wà sammù.

castor oil n mân gēlŏ m.

castrate v yi wà dàndaƙằ f, fidìyē v4: ~ a ram yi wà rằgŏ dàndaƙằ.

cat n kyânwā f ⟨oCi⟩, mằge f ⟨una⟩, mussằ f, kulè f; (male) mùzūrū m ⟨ai⟩; wild ~ mùzūrun dājì m, kyânwaƙ dājì f; see civet, serval, genet; (fig.) let the ~ out of the bag fīgè gāshìn kằzā.

catapult n gwàfaƙ danƙŏ f, [F] kàushû m: he shot the bird with a ~ yā hàƙbi tsuntsū da gwàfā.

cataract n (on eye) yānaƙ idŏ f, àlgaƙwài m.

catastrophe n màsīfà f ⟨u⟩, bàlā'ì m: there was a catastrophic earthquake an yi wani bàlā'ìn gìƙgizàƙ ƙasà.

catch v a. (get, get hold of) kāmằ v1: they didn't ~ the thief bà sù kāmà 6àrāwòn ba; I've caught a cold muƙà tā kāmằ ni = nā kằmu dà muƙà; I ~ colds easily inằ kằmuwā dà muƙà; the house caught on fire gidân yā kāmằ dà wutā. b. (sth. thrown) cafè v4: he still doesn't know how to ~ a ball bài iyà cafè ƙwallŏ ba haƙ yànzu. c. (other uses): ~ a bus, train sằmi bâs, jirgī; ~ sight of hàngā v2; ~ up with so. taƙ dà / taraƙ (dà) v5: we caught up with our friends at the market mun taƙ dà àbòkanmù à kằsuwà; (fig.) the times have caught up with us zāmànī yā rìskē mù.

categorize v rabà v1, kasà v1.

category n a. (type) nau'ì m ⟨oCi⟩, jinsì m. b. (division) ràbŏ m, kashì m: it can be divided into 3 categories anà iyà kasà shi kashì ukù.

caterpillar n a. (hairy) gìzākā f. b. (tractor) kàtàfīlà f, [F] kàtàƙpìlà f.

catfish n (spotted, big headed) ƙùrungù m, (electric, small) minjiryā f; (mudfish resembling a ~) taƙwadā f ⟨taƙēwaɗī⟩.

Catholic n kàtōlìkà m.

cattle n shānū m: herd of ~ garkèn shānū.

cattle egret n bâlbēlà f.

Caucasian n bàtūƙè m, bànasāƙè m, nàsāƙa n ⟨u⟩, jaƙ fātằ n/p, faraƙ fātằ n/p.

cause 1. n a. (reason) sanàdī m ⟨ai⟩, dàlīlì m ⟨ai⟩: no one knows the ~ of the disease bà à san sanàdin cùtàƙ ba. b. (origin) mafārī m, tūshè m, asalī m: what is the ~ of the trouble? mènē nè asalin rìgimaƙ? poverty is one of the ~s of crime talaucì shì nè ɗaya dàga cikin mafārin aikàtà laifuffukằ nē.

2. v a. (make so. do sth.) sâ v1*: he ~d me to make a mistake yā sâ nà yi kurè. b. (bring about sth. bad) jāwŏ v6, kāwŏ v6, yi sanàdī m, haddàsà v1: his carelessness ~d the fire rashìn kùlaƙsà shī yā jāwŏ gŏbaràƙ; don't ~ us any trouble around here! kadà kà kāwŏ manà rìkicī à nân! what ~d the delay? mề ya haddàsà jìnkirìn?

caution 1. n tsànākī m, tằkā-tsantsan m: proceed with ~ yi tằkā-tsantsan = yi à tsànàke; you should proceed with ~ in life kà yi tằkā-tsantsan à dūniyằ.

2. v gàƙgaɗà v2: let me ~ you that... bàri ìn gàƙgàdē kà cêwā....

cautious adj (mài) hankàlī m, (mài) tsànākī m.

cavalry n baƙàden yāƙī p.

cave n kŏgon dūtsè m, kùrfī m ⟨a-u⟩.

cave in v (from above, e.g. roof) 6urmā v1; (inwardly, e.g. sides) fādà v1, 6urmè v4, rūshè v4.

cavity n a. (natural formation) kŏgŏ m ⟨anni⟩. b. (in tooth) rāmìn haƙōrī m: I have a ~ haƙōrīnā yā hūjè = inà dà rāmì à haƙōri; fill a ~ for so. cikè wà rāmì.

cayenne pepper n (ground) gàrin bàƙkŏnŏ m.

cease v tsayà v1: ~ completely tsayà cak.

ceasefire n shirìn dākataƙ dà yāƙī m; declare a ~ bā dà ùmàƙnin tsai dà yāƙì.

ceiling n a. (of room) rufī m, sīlìn m. b. (fig., limit) iyàkằ f.

celebration n shagàlin bìkī m: have a ~ yi shagàlin bìkī; enjoy a ~ shā bìkī; Independence Day ~ shagàlin bìkin mulkìn kâi.

cell n a. (of prison) dākìn kûƙkukù m, [F] sullūƙù m. b. (of living organism) ƙwằyā f ⟨oCi⟩.

cement 1. n sìmintì / sùmuntì m; a ~ block bùlŏ m, [F] bìƙgin sìmintì m; (made from dye-pit sediment) lāsŏ m.

2. v sâ sìmintì; (fig.) ~ a friendship ƙārà danƙòn zùmùntā.

cemetery n makabaƙtā f, huƙùmì m ⟨ai⟩.

censor v yi wà tằkunkùmī m.

censorship n tằkunkùmī m: impose ~ on yi tằkunkùmī wajen: the government has imposed ~ on the publication of newspapers gwamnatì tā yi tằkunkùmī wajen tsārìn bugà jàƙīdū; lift ~ ɗagà tằkunkùmī.

censure v yi wà zàrgī m.

census n ƙìdāyaƙ mutằnen ƙasā f.

center n a. (location) tsakiyằ f: the school is in the ~ of town makaɍantā tanằ tsakiyāɍ gàrîn; in the ~ à tsakà = à tsakiyằ. b. (institution) cībìyā f ⟨oCi⟩: a ~ of learning cībìyaɍ ilìmī. c. (hub) cībìyā f ⟨oCi⟩: it is a great ~ of trade bàbbaɍ cībìyaɍ cìnikī cḕ.

centimeter n sàntìmētằ m, [F] sàntìmētîɍ m.

centipede n shànshànī m.

central adj a. (of location) na tsakiyằ. b. (important) bàbba adj ⟨mânyā⟩: Kurmi market is the ~ market of Kano kàsuwaɍ Kurmī ita cḕ bàbbaɍ kàsuwaɍ Kanò.

century n kàɍnì m ⟨uka⟩: the 20th ~ kàɍnì na àshìɍin.

cereal n (millet & sorghum) hatsī m.

ceremony n bìkī m ⟨uwa²⟩: marriage ~ bìkin aurē; inaugural ~ bìkin naɗìn sàrautằ.

certain¹ det a. (some) wani m, wata f, waɗansu, wasu p: ~ people like it but others don't wasu sunā sô, wasu kuma bā sằ sô. b. (special) na mùsammàn: there is a ~ reason for doing it this way àkwai wani dàlīlìn mùsammàn na yîn hakà.

certain² adj tabbàs adv, hakkàn adv: it is not ~ he will come zuwànsà bằ tabbàs ba nḕ; be ~ of, about sth. tabbàtā v1, hakīkàncē v4: we are ~ about this mun tabbàtā dà wannàn; I'm ~ that she can do it nā hakīkàncē zā tà iyằ; make ~ tabbataɍ (dà) v5: make ~ that you arrive on time kà tabbataɍ dà kā isō daidai lōkàcîn; it is almost ~ that he will win the election kusan an tabbataɍ dà zâi cînyḕ zàɓên; be absolutely ~ yi yàkīnì m: it's only if I am absolutely ~ about it that I'll agree sai nā ga yàkīnì zân yàɍda.

certainly 1. adv a. (indeed) lallē adv: he is ~ late lallē yā màkarà. b. (undoubtedly) à hakīkằ, tabbàs adv, bâ shakkằ: it is ~ not true à hakīkằ bằ gaskiyā ba nḕ; he will ~ come bâ shakkằ zâi zō. 2. excl a. (indeed) kwaɍai kùwa! sòsai! ~ not! kō kusa! kō àlāmằ! kō kàɗan! b. (undoubtedly, esp. assenting in conversation) bâ/bābù shakkằ! hakkàn! hàkīkằ!

certainty n a. (reality) hàkīkànī m. b. (assurance, confirmation) tabbàcī m: I can't say with ~ whether he will do it or not bâ ni dà tabbàcī kō zâi yi kō bà zâi yi ba.

certificate n takàɍdaɍ shaidằ f; (school) sàtifikàt m, [F] sàɍtìpìkà f.

certification n tabbatāɍwā f.

certify v tabbataɍ (dà) v5, hakīkàntā v1.

cesspit n masai m, kwàtamī m.

chaff n (of sorghum, millet) kàikàyī m; (of rice, wheat) ɓuntū m.

chain n a. sarkằ f ⟨oCi⟩: put a prisoner in ~s ɗaurè fuɍsùnà dà sarkằ; she wore a beautiful ~ (around her neck) tā yi adō dà sarkằ mài kyâu. b. (of bicycle) kacằ f, cên m.

chain case n (of bicycle) kùnkurun kèkè m.

chain mail n sùlkē m.

chain wheel n (of bicycle) ɍankì m.

chair 1. n kujḕrā f ⟨u⟩. 2. v shùgàbantā v2: he ~ed the meeting yā shùgàbànci tàrôn.

chairman shùgàbā n ⟨anni⟩; ~ of the board ciyàmân m.

chalk n âllī m: a piece of ~ guntun âllī.

challenge 1. n kàlūbàlē m: his speech was a ~ to everyone jàwābìnsà kàlūbàlē nḕ gà kōwā dà kōwā; it was a bold ~ kàlūbàlē nḕ ɓarō-ɓàrò. 2. v kàlùbàlantā v2, tàɍā v2: he ~d me to show him yā kàlùbàlàncē nì ìn nūnà masà; I ~d him to wrestle nā tàrē shì kòkawằ.

chamber of commerce n jàm'iyyàɍ kāsuwancī f.

chameleon n hàwainìyā f, hànwāwằ f.

champion n zàkarà m ⟨u⟩: world boxing ~ zàkaràn damben dūniyằ.

chance 1. n a. (opportunity, means) dāmā f, hālī m ⟨aye⟩; (free time) sùkūnì m: I won't have a ~ to come tomorrow bâ ni dà hālin zuwằ gòbe; we missed our ~ to see him bà mù sàmi dāmaɍ ganinsà ba; we didn't get a ~ to go bà mù sàmi sùkūnì ba; please give me another ~ don Allàh kà sākè bā nì wata dāmā dai. b. (fate) kàddaɍằ f: it was pure ~ that we met kàddaɍằ cḕ ta sâ mukà hàɗu dà shī. c. (risk) kàsadà f: take a ~ yi kàsadằ. d. (odds): the ~s of his winning are small dà kyaɍ zâi ci nasaɍằ. 2. v: ~ upon v tsìntā v2: he ~d upon ₦10 on the road yā tsìnci naiɍằ gōmà à hanyằ.

chancellor n (Educ.) shùgàban jāmi'ằ m; vice ~ matàlmàkin shùgàban jāmi'ằ; (Pol.) wàzīɍì m ⟨ai⟩.

change 1. v a. (do over) sākè v4: the name of the road has been ~d an sākè wà hanyàɍ sūnā; ~ one's mind, one's clothes sākè shāwaɍằ, kāyan jìki. b. (exchange) mùsāyằ / mùsanyằ v2, canjằ / canzằ v1: I want to ~ this for that inà sôn ìn mùsāyi wannàn dà wancàn; we want to ~ dollars for nairas munā sô mù canjà dalā zuwā naiřā; ~ this ₦20 for me kà canjā minì naiřā àshìřin nàn; ~ trains canjà jirgī. c. *(make, become different)* canjā / canzā *v1*, jūyā *v1*, sauyā *v1*, sākè *v4*, jūyè *v4*: Kano has ~d these past few years Kanò tā sauyā à cikin 'yan shèkàrun nàn; the wind ~d from east to west iskā tā jūyā dàgà gabàs zuwā yâmma; the weather, his appearance has ~d yanàyī, kàmařsà yā sākè; since his return, he has ~d tun dāwôwařsà, kânsà yā jūyè; he ~d his voice to sound like a woman yā canjà muryàřsà (zuwā) tamàta; ~ oil *(of motor)* yi jùyen baƙin mâi. d. *(transform)* rìkiɗà *v3*: he ~d into a monkey yā rìkiɗà zuwā birì. 2. *n* a. canjì *m*, jūyì *m*. b. *(esp. money)* canjì *m* ⟨e²⟩: do you have ~ for ₦5? kō kanā dà canjìn naiřā bìyař? give so. correct ~ cikō wà kuɗī daidai.

**channel** *n* a. *(for liquids to flow)* magudānā *f* ⟨ai⟩, mazurārī *m*; *(deep ~ cut by water)* kwàzazzabô *m*. b. *(television)* tashā *f* ⟨oCi⟩: get, receive a ~ kāmà tashā. c. *(ways, means)* hanyā *f* ⟨oCi⟩: you should go through the proper ~s sai kà bi hanyōyìn dà sukà kàmàtà.

**chant** *v* rērà wāƙā *v1*.

**chaos** *n* hàrgàgī *m*, hàrgitsī *m*.

**chaotic** *adj*: be ~ *(of a situation)* hargìtsē *v4*, yāmùtsē *v4*; *(esp. of a place)* cākùɗē *v4*: this room is ~ dākìn nân yā cākùɗē.

**chapped skin** *n* *(on feet)* fàsō *m*.

**chapter** *n* a. *(of book)* bābì *m*, fasàlī *m*; *(of Koran)* sūřā *f*. b. *(of organization)* rēshè *m* ⟨Ca⟩.

**char** *v* babbàkē *v4*.

**character**[1] *n* a. *(personality, so.'s nature)* hālī / halī *m* ⟨aye⟩: he is a man of good ~ yanā dà hālī nagàri = mùtumìn kiřkì ne; exemplary ~ hālin à-zō-à-ganī; he ~ is bad halinsà bâ kyâu = halin banzā gàrē shì = bâ shi dà kiřkì; it's in his ~ to ask so many questions yā fayè yîn tambayōyī. b. *(Lit.)* tàurāròn làbāřì *m*, a favorite ~ gōgà *m*.

**character**[2] *n* *(in system of writing)* baƙī *m* ⟨aCe⟩.

**characteristic** *n* *(habit)* hālī / halī *m* ⟨aye⟩: some ~s are shared by all animals àkwai wasu hālāyè waɗàndà duk dabbōbī sunā dà sū.

**charcoal** *n* gawàyī *m*.

**charge**[1] 1. *n* a. *(Law)* cājì *m*, tùhumā *f*: a ~ of murder cājìn kisàn kâi. 2. *v* *(Law)* cājā *v2*, yi cājì *m*, tùhumā

*v2*: he's been ~d with stealing ₦1000 an cājē shì dà sātāř naiřā dubū.

**charge**[2] 1. *n* a. *(costs)* kuɗī *m*: freight ~s kudin jigilař kāyā. b. *(of a battery)* cājì *m*, [F] shařjì *m*: the battery needs a ~ bātìř ɗin mōtā nā bùkātāř cājì. 2. *v* a. *(a sum of money)* cājā *v2*: how much will you ~ me? nawà zā kà cājē nì? b. *(a battery)* yi cājì *m*, [F] yi shařjì *m*.

**charge**[3] *n* *(control)* shūgabancì *m*: he was put in ~ of the work an bā shì shūgubancìn aikì; he is in ~ shī nè shūgàbā.

**charisma** *n*: he has ~ yanā dà girmā à idòn mutānē; a ~tic personality kwàrjinī *m*: a ~tic person mùtûm mài kwàrjinī.

**charitable** *adj* *(psn.)* kařīmì *m* ⟨ai⟩, (mài) kyàutā *f*; a ~ organization ƙungìyař tàimakō.

**charity** *n* sadakā *f* ⟨oCi⟩; give, contribute to ~ bā dà sadakā.

**charm**[1] 1. *n* *(any magic spell)* àsīřī *m*, māgànī *m*; *(esp. written, to ward off evil)* lāyā *f* ⟨uka⟩; *(for invincibility)* lāyàř zānā *f*; *(to avoid being wounded)* kàu-dà-bāřa *m;* his ~ worked lāyàřsà tā ci; she used a ~ on her husband so she could manipulate him tā yi wà mijìntà māgànī don tà màllàkē shì. b. *(var. types)*: *(wrapped in blue cloth, worn on arm)* dāgùmì *m* ⟨u-a⟩; *(wrapped in leather, worn on arm)* kàmbū *m* ⟨una⟩; *(belt worn around waist as preventative)* gūřū *m* ⟨aye⟩. 2. *v* yi wà māgànī *m*; *(bewitch, for neg. results)* yi wà sammù *m*, sammàcē *v4*.

**charm**[2] *n* *(personality)* fàřa'ā *f*.

**chart** *n* jadawàlī *m* ⟨ai⟩.

**charter**[1] *n* *(Pol.)* usūlā *f* ⟨oCi⟩.

**charter**[2] *v* *(hire transport)* yi shatā *f*: he ~ed a car to Sokoto yā yi shatàř mōtā zuwā Sakkwato.

**chase** *v*: ~ after so. bi w. dà gudù: they ~d after the thief but he got away sun bi ɓàrāwòn dà gudù àmmā yā tsērè; ~ so. away kōrā *v2*; ~ so. off *(by threatening)* fàfarā *v2;* ~ so. to *(a place)* kōrā *v1*: they ~d the animal way out to the bush sun kōrā dabbā can dawà.

**chassis** *n* fìřâm *m*, [F] shàsî *m*.

**chaste** *adj* (mài) tsarkī *m*.

**chastize** *v* hòrà *v2*.

**chat** *v* yi tàɗì *m*, tàɗà *v1*; *(esp. night-time)* yi hīřa *f*; ~ privately with so. gānà dà *v1*.

**chatter** *v* yi sùřūtù *m*: the girls were ~ing away 'yan màtā sunā ta sùřūtù.

**chatterbox** *n* càkwaikwaiwā *f*.

chattering *n* (*shivering*) kyàkkyàɓī *m*, kařkařwà *f*.

chauffeur *n* difēbà *m* ⟨oCi⟩, matūƙin mōtà *m*.

cheap *adj* (mài) àřàhā *f*, (mài) řàhūsā *f*: it is ~ yanà dà àřàhā = yā yi àřàhā = mài àřàhā nè; ~ and useless dà àřàhař banzà; extremely ~ goods kāyan gàřaɓàsà: at a sale, one can get very ~ goods wajen gwànjō anà sāmùn kāyan gàřaɓàsà.

cheaply *adv* à banzà *f*, dà àřàhā *f*, dà řàhūsā *f*, à ɓagas *idph*.

cheat *v* a. cūtā *v2*, yi wà cūtā *f*, kasà w. dà cūtā: he ~ed me out of ₦5 yā cùcē nì naiřà bìyař. b. (*esp. breach so.'s trust*): ~ on yi màgudī *m*, yi àlgùs/àlgushù *m*: ~ on an examination, on weighing grain yi àlgushù wajen jařřabāwā, wajen awòn hatsī; (*in marriage*) ci àmānàř w.: she's ~ing on her husband tanà cîn àmānàř màigidantà. c. (*by adulteration, overcharging, underpaying*) ƙwàrā *v2*: if you see that you're being ~ed, then don't take it ìdan kā ganī dà ƙwàrā sai kà barī. d. (*Law*) zàmbatà *v2*, yi zàmba *f*.

check[1] *n* (*for money*) câk / cakī *m*, [F] shêk *m*: pay by ~ biyà dà câk; ~ stub gìndin câk *m*.

check[2] *v* a. (*look at*) dūbà / [F] dībà *v1* ⟨dūbā⟩: the doctor ~ed her blood pressure likità yā dūbà awòn ƙarfin jinintà; go to the hospital to get the wound ~ed kì jē asìbitì don à dūbà mikì ràunī; please ~ this list of figures for me don Allàh kà duddùbā minì adàdin nàn. b. ~ out a book from the library àri littāfì dàgà lābùřāřè.

checkers *n* darà *f*.

checking account *n* àjiyàř bankì *f*.

cheek *n* kuncì *m* ⟨kumàtū⟩; on the ~ à kunci.

cheer 1. *n* yi shēwà/sōwà *f*; (*ululate, by women*) yi gūdà *f*.
2. *n* fàřa'à *f*.

cheerful *adj* (mài) fàřa'à *f*.

cheese *n* cukū / cukwī *m*.

chemical *adj*: ~ warfare yāƙìn àmfànī dà gubà; ~ weapons màkàman màsu gubà.

chemist *n*, *see* pharmacist.

chemistry *n* kìmiyyàř hařhàɗà māgungunà *f*, [F] shìmî *f*.

cherish *v* yi ƙaunā *f*.

chest[1] *n* (*of body*) ƙìrjī *m* ⟨a-a⟩.

chest[2] *n* (*box*) bàbban àkwàtì *m*.

chevron *n* (*Mil.*) igiyà *f* ⟨oCi⟩.

chew *v* taunà *v1*; ~ sugarcane shā ràkē; ~ kolanut ci gōřò; (*fig.*) bite off more than you can ~ shāwō àbîn dà ya fi ƙarfinkà.

chewing gum *n* cìngâm *m*, [F] shìngwâm *m*.

chewing tobacco *n* tābà gàrī *f*.

chewstick *n* a. (*tree*) markē *m*, farin gamjì *m*, (*bittterleaf shrub*) shìwākā *f*. b. (*for cleaning teeth*) asawàkī *m*.

chick *n* ɗan tsākō *m* ⟨'yan tsākī⟩, ɗan shilà *m* ⟨'yan shilōlī⟩.

chicken *n* kàzā *f* ⟨i⟩, (*pullet*) sàgarā *f*.

chicken pox *n* ƙàràmbau *m*; ~ spots zanzanā *f*.

chief 1. *n* a. (*tradit. Hausa leader*) sarkī *m* ⟨sarākunà⟩; (*non-Hausa*) cîf *m* ⟨x²⟩, [F] shâf *m*. b. (*of admin. unit*) shùgàbā *n* ⟨anni⟩; ~ of police (*divisional*) dīpī'ô *m*. c. (*Mil.*): ~ of staff bàbban hafsàn hafsōshī *m*; ~ of the army bàbban hafsàn sōjà *m*.
2. *adj* bàbba *adj* ⟨mānyā⟩: ~ agricultural officer bàbban bàtūřèn gōnā.

chiefly *adv* mùsammàn *adv*.

chigger *n* jìgā *f*.

child *n* a. yārò *m*, yārinyà *f* ⟨yārā⟩; (*any male ~*) dā namijì *m*, (*any female ~*) 'yā màcè *f*; eldest, first-born ~ ɗan fārī *m*; youngest ~ aùtā *n*. b. (*infant*) jàrīrī *m* ⟨ai⟩, jinjìrī *m* ⟨jìràjìrai⟩; act like a ~ (*inappropriately*) yi yàrantakà *f*.

childbirth *n* haihùwà *f*; pains of ~ nāƙudà *f*: she's in ~ tanà nāƙudà = tanà kân gwīwà.

childhood *n* (*early*) yàrìntā *f*; (*youth*) ƙùřùciyā *f*.

childish *adj*: be ~ (*befitting a child*) yi yàrìntā *f*; be ~, act ~ly (*inappropriately, like a child*) yi yàrantakà *f*.

children *n* yârā *p*; (*one's offspring*) 'yā'yā *p*: he has 4 ~, 3 boys and one girl 'yā'yansà huɗu, mazā ukù dà màcè ɗaya.

chili *n*, *see* chillies.

chill 1. *n* sanyī *m*, dārī *m*: he caught a ~ sanyī yā kāmà shi; she is suffering from a fever and the ~s tanà fāmā dà zàzzàɓī dà rawař dārī.
2. *v* sanyàyà *v1*: he ~ed the water yā sanyàyà ruwā.

chillies *n* (*gener.*) bàřkònō *m*, [F] tonkà *f*; (*large, long*) tàttàsai *m/p*; (*green, milder*) kōřèn tàttàsai, ɗanyen tàttàsai; (*long, thin*) tùgandè *m*; (*small, very hot*) tsīduhū *m*; (*small, round, very hot*) àttàřugu *m*; (*Ethiopian*) kimbā *f*.

chilly *adj* (mài) sanyī *m*.

**chimney** *n* a. (*of factory*) būtūtun hayāƙī *m.* b. (*of glass, for kerosene lamp*) ƙwan fītilā *m.*

**chimpanzee** *n* , *see* monkey.

**chin** *n* haɓā *f* ⟨oCi⟩.

**chinaware** *n* tangaƙan *m* ⟨tangaƙāyē⟩, fāɗi-kà-mutù *m.*

**chip** 1. *v* a. (*a pot, enamelware*) ɓalgàtā *v1*, ɓalgàcē *v4*, ɓantàrē *v4*, ɓangàrē *v4*: the plate is ~ped fàƙantì yā ɓangàrē. b. (*wood*) sassàƙā *v1.*
2. *n* ɓagurē *m*, (*of wood*) sassaƙē *m.*

**chips** *n* (*potato*) sòyayyen dànkalì *m.*

**chisel** *n* cīsùƙ *m*, maƙanƙarī *m.*

**chloroform** *n* iskàƙ làmbàwân *f.*

**chloroquine** *n* nībàkwîn *m*, [F] nìbàkîn *m.*

**chocolate** *n* cākùlàn / cākùleetì *f*, [F] shàkwàlâ *f;* eat ~ shā cākùlàn.

**choice** *n* zàɓì *m:* you have no ~ in the matter bâ ka dà zàɓì cikin màganàƙ; tell me what your ~ is fàdā minì zàɓìnkà; make a ~ yi zàɓē *m;* make a good ~ daƙjē *v4;* make the wrong ~ (*fig.*) yi zàɓen tumùn dare; a large ~ of goods kāyā irì-irì.

**choke** *v* a. (*on food*) ƙwàrā *v2*, ƙwàru *v7:* he ~d on a bone ƙashī yā ƙwàrē shì. b. (*so.*) shàƙē *v4*, màƙùrē *v4:* the killer ~d him to death mài kisà yā shàƙē shi haƙ lāhiƙā. c. (*be dense with*) sarƙē *v4:* the farm is ~d with weeds gōnā tā sarƙē dà cìyāwà. d. (*fig.*) siƙē *v4:* his lack of shame made me ~ with rage rashìn kunyàƙsà yā siƙē ni.

**cholera** *n* mài baushè *m*, kwalaƙā *f*, [F] kwàlàƙâ *f.*

**choose** *v* zàɓā *v2*, yi zàɓē *m:* you may ~ any one you want kà zàɓi duk wândà kakè sô.

**chop** *v* a. dàtsà *v1:* ~ it into two kà dàtsà shi biyu; ~ down, off (*a tree, branch*) sārē *v4* (sārā); ~ up (*a log, wood into pieces*) faskàrā *v1*, daddàtsā *v1*, sassàrā *v1*, sārā gunduwā-gunduwā. b. (*food into pieces*) yayyànkà *v1:* she ~ped up the okra tā yayyànkà kuɓēwā.

**chore** *n* hidimā *f* ⟨oCi⟩.

**chorus** *n* (*Lit., Mus.*) 'yan amshì *p*, 'yan karɓì *p.*

**Christian** *n* Kiƙistā *m* ⟨oCi⟩, nàsāƙa *n* ⟨u⟩, [F] ɗan àlmàsīhù *m;* ~ name sūnan yankā *m.*

**Christmas** *n* Kiƙsìmatì *m.*

**chuckle** *n* 'yaƙ dàriyā *f.*

**chunk** *n* (*broken off*) ɓantarē *m;* break off a ~ ɓantàrā *v2.*

**church** *n* cōcì *m* ⟨x²⟩, [F] gidan àlmàsīhù *m;* (*term used by Christians*) màjàmi'à *f.*

**churn** *v* (*milk for making butter*) buƙgà *v1;* (*mix by beating*) kadā *v1.*

**cicada** *n* gyàrē *m.*

**cicatrization** *n* shàsshāwà *f.*

**cigarette** *n* tābà *f*, sìgāƙì *f:* ~ tobacco tābà sìgāƙì; one ~ karan tābà = karan sìgāƙì; how many ~s a day do you smoke? karā nawà kakè shā à rānā gùdà? smoke ~ shā tābà = shā sìgāƙì; pack(et) of ~s fākitìn sìgāƙì = kwàlin sìgāƙì; carton of ~s ƙunshìn sìgāƙì.

**cinders** *n* tòkā *f.*

**cinema** *n* (*movie*) fîm *m*, sìlimà *m;* (*esp. theater*) (gidan) sìlimà *m;* (*outdoor movie, slide show*) màjìgī *m;* mobile ~ van mōtàƙ màjìgī.

**cinnamon** *n* kirfà *f.*

**circle** 1. *n* dā'iƙā *f* ⟨oCi⟩, ƙawanyà *f* ⟨u⟩: in the shape of a ~ à siffàƙ dā'iƙà; in a ~ à kèwàye: they sat in a ~ around him sun zaunà à kèwàye dà shī.
2. *v* zàgā *v1*, zàgàyē *v4:* the moon ~s around the earth watà yanà zàgà ƙasā; ~ the best answer kù zàgàyè amsàƙ da ta fi dācèwā.

**circular** *adj* zàgàyayyē *adj*, kèwàyayyē *adj*, (mài) siffàƙ dā'iƙà.

**circulate** *v* a. (*spread*) bazà *v1:* rumors are circulating that... anà bazà jìta-jìtaƙ cêwà.... b. (*move around*) zàgàyà *v1.*

**circumcision** *n* kàciyà *f*, shàyī *m.*

**circumcize** *v* yi wà kàciyà *f;* be ~d shā kàciyà.

**circumference** *n* kēwàyè *m*, zàgayè *m.*

**circumlocution** *n* kèwàye-kèwàye *m.*

**circumstances** *n* a. hālī / hālì *m* ⟨aye⟩: under the present ~ à hālin/hālìn dà akè ciki yànzu; under any ~ kō ta wànè hālī = à kōwànè hālī; that all depends on the ~ wannàn sai àbin dà hālī ya yi; the ~ have changed sha'ànîn yā sauyà = abūbuwà sun canzà; ~ beyond our control abūbuwàn dà sukà fi ƙarfinmù. b. (*unforeseeable, unavoidable*) làƙūƙā *f:* an unforeseen ~ delayed the plane wata làƙūƙā tā jinkirtaƙ dà jirgîn.

**cite** *v* (*esp. from Koran*) jā nassì *m.*

**citizen** *n* ɗan ƙasā *m:* become a ~ zama ɗan ƙasā; a Nigerian ~ ɗan Nìjēƙiyà.

**citizenry** *n* jàma'à *f.*

**city** *n* (*incl. tradit. walled* ~) biƙnī *m* ⟨a-e⟩; (*smaller*) gàrī *m* ⟨uwa²⟩; ~ dweller ɗan biƙnī.

**civet** *n* màgen jūdà *m*, mùzūrun jūdà *m*, màgen tantàl *m*, tùnkun jūdà *m.*

**civic** *adj:* ~ duty kīshìn gàrī *m.*

civil *adj:* ~ defense tsàron gidā *m;* ~ duty hakkīn ɗan ƙasā; ~ servant ma'àikàcin gwamnatì *m,* [F] ɗan sàrūshì *m;* ~ service aikìn gwamnatì, [F] sàrūshì *m;* ~ war yāƙin bāsāsā *m.*

civilian *n* farar̃-hūlā *n:* ~ rule mulkìn farar̃-hūlā.

civilization *n* wāyèwar̃-kâi *m.*

claim 1. *n* a. (*esp. doubtful* ~) dà'àwā *f:* state one's ~ mai dà dà'àwā. b. (*right*) hakkī *m:* make a ~ nèmi hakkī. c. (*compensation for damages*) diyyà *f:* make a ~ for damages nèmi diyyà.
2. *v* a. yi dà'àwā *f:* he ~s to be a descendant of Usman Dan Fodio yanà dà'àwar̃ wai shī jinin Shēhù Ɗan Hōdiyò nē. b. ~ one's rights nèmi hakkī.

claimant *n* mài dà'àwā *n.*

clamor *n* (*noisy*) hàyàniyā *f,* r̃ūr̃ūmā *f;* (*angry*) hàrgōwā *f,* hàrgāgī *m.*

clan *n:* they don't belong to the same ~ tsatsònsù bà ɗaya ba nè.

clap 1. *v* tāfà hannū *v1,* yi tàfī *m.*
2. *n.* a. (*of hand*) tàfī *m.* b. (*of thunder*) àr̃ādù *f.*

clapping *n* ban tàfī *m.*

clarification *n* bàyānì *m.*

clarify *v* bayyànā *v1.*

clash 1. *v* karā *v1,* yi karò *m:* the demonstrators ~ed with the police màsu zàngàzangà sun karā dà 'yan sàndā.
2. *n* (*physical, verbal*) karò *m;* (*Mil.*) aràngamā *f.*

class *n* a. (*in school*) ajì *m* ⟨uwa²⟩. b. (*social* ~es): ruling ~ màsu mulkì, (*tradit.*) sarākunā *p;* upper middle ~ (*bourgeoisie*) màsu hannū dà shūnì; middle class màsu sùkūnì; working ~ ma'àikàtā *p;* lower ~ talakāwā *p,* (*esp. peasants, craftsmen*) màsu ƙaramin ƙarfī. c. (*type*) ràbō *m,* ajì *m* ⟨uwa²⟩. d. (*level, rank*) ƙarfī *m:* he's not in the same ~ as Audu bà ƙarfinsà ɗaya dà Audù ba. e. (*quality*): first-~ na gangàriyā, na làmbàwàn: he is a first-~ athlete gangàriyàn ɗan wàsā nē; this is a first-~ job wannàn aikìn làmbàwàn nē. f. (*of fares, tickets*): first-~ faskìlà; second-~ sikinkìlà = na gàmà-gàri; third -~ tākìlà.

classified *adj* (*restricted*) kèɓaɓɓē *adj:* ~ information kèɓaɓɓen làbārì.

classify *v* kar̃kàsā *v1,* rarràbā *v1:* ~ sth. into different types kar̃kàsà w.a. kashì-kashì; be classified kàsu *v7,* kàr̃kàsu *v7,* ràbu *v7,* ràrràbu *v7:* musicians are classified into different types makàɗā sun ràrràbu kashì-kashì.

classroom *n* ɗākìn ajì *m,* [F] kàlâs *f.*

clause *n* a. (*of an agreement*) shar̃àɗī *m* ⟨ua⟩. b. (*Law*) kashì *m* ⟨uwa²⟩. c. (*Gram.*) sāshèn jimlà *f,* gàngā *f:* a conditional ~ gàngā maràs tabbàs.

clavicle *n* ƙashin wuyà *m.*

claw 1. *n* ƙàmbòrī *m* ⟨ai⟩, akaifā *f* ⟨u⟩.
2. *v* yàkusā *v2,* yàgā *v2.*

clay *n* (*for building*) lākā *f;* (*for pottery*) yumɓū *m.*

clean 1. *adj* (mài) tsabtà *f,* tsàbtàtaccē *adj;* (*pure*) (mài) tsarkī *m;* spanking ~ fes *idph,* sumul *idph,* tas *idph:* it's been washed spanking ~ yā wànku fes; (*fig.*) my hands are ~ in the matter bā hannūnā à cikin màganàr̃.
2. *v* tsabtàcē *v4,* wankè *v4:* ~ this place today kà tsabtàcè wurîn yâu; ~ a blackboard gōgè àllō; ~ a floor gōgè dàɓē; ~ a room shārè ɗākì; ~ out (*by removing sediment, residue*) yāshè *v1:* ~ out a latrine, well yāshè salgā, rījìyā; (*fig.*) the robbers ~ed us out ɓàrāyī sun wāshè gidanmù = sun yi manà kakaf.

cleanliness *n* tsabtà *f,* (*Relig., ritual*) tsarkī *m.*

clear¹ *adj* a. (*evident*) zāhìr̃ī *m:* it is ~ that our team will win zāhìr̃ī nè ƙungìyar̃mù zā tà ci; a ~ explanation bàyānì mài saukin gānèwā; is that ~? an fàhimtà kō? b. (*unequivocal*) ɓarō-ɓàrō *idph:* he made it ~ to us that he didn't like it yā fitō manà ɓarō-ɓàrō cêwā bà yà sò. c. (*free of*): the streets were ~ tītunā wayam; the weather is ~ gàrī yā yi garau; the water is ~ baƙin ruwā nè.

clear² 1. *vt:* ~ away the dishes kwāshè kwānukà; ~ goods through customs bi ta 'yan kwastàn; ~ the land sassàbè gōnā, yi sāran gōnā; ~ one's name wankè kâi; ~ one's throat gyārà muryà; ~ up a matter kashè màganà; ~ an obstruction (*without touching*) yi kìliyà *f:* the car barely ~ed the doorway dà ƙyar̃ mōtàr̃ tā yi wà ƙōfà kìliyà.
2. *vi:* (*fig.*) let's ~ out of here! mù yi ta kânmù! ~ up (*of weather*) wāshè *v4:* the weather has ~ed up gàrī yā wāshè.

clearly *adv* a. (*completely*) sar̃ai *idph,* garau *idph:* he understood ~ yā gānè sar̃ai. b. (*in a distinct manner*) à fīlī: he spoke ~ so that everyone could hear him yā yi màganà à fīlī don kōwā yà ji shì. c. (*in detail*) dakì-dakì *adv,* fillà-fillà *idph,* dallà-dallà *idph:* he explained the situation to us ~ yā bayyànà manà àl'amàr̃īn dallà-dallà. d. (*un-*

equivocally, *bluntly*) ɓarō-ɓàrò *idph*: he
indicated very ~ that he wouldn't give us
a thing yā fitō manà ɓarō-ɓàrò bà zâi
bā mù kōmē ba.

**clemency** *n* ahuwā *f*, rangwamè *m*: grant so.
~ yi wà ahuwā; (*esp. Relig.*) r̃ahamā *f*.

**clench** *v* (*fist*) dunƙùlā *v1*; (*teeth*) datsè *v4*.

**clerk** *n* (*office*) àkàwu *m* ⟨x²⟩; (*store*) mài
jiràn kàntī *n*, [F] kwàmî *m*, [F] mûshe *m*,
[F] màdân *f*; (*government*) ma'àikàcī *m*.

**clever** *adj* a. (*resourceful*) (mài) azancī *m*,
(mài) dàbār̃ā *f*. b. (*skillful*) (mài) fàsāhà
*f*. c. (*crafty*) (mài) wàyō *m*.

**climate** *n* yanàyī *m*: I'm not yet accustomed to the ~ here har̃ yànzu bàn sābà
dà yanàyin nàn ba.

**climb** *v* hau *v\**; ~ down from sàuka *v3*; ~ on
top of hayè *v4*; ~ over (*e.g. a wall*) haur̃à
*v1*.

**cling to** *v* ɗafè wà *v4*, maƙàlè wà *v4*: the
baby clung to her jàrīrī yā ɗafè matà.

**clinic** *n* asìbitì *m* ⟨oCi⟩, kililìn *m*;
(*urban, private*) [F] kìlînîk *f*; maternity ~ asìbitìn haihùwā; veterinary ~
asìbitìn dabbōbī, [F] èlìbājì *m*.

**clip**¹ *n* (*for paper*) kìlîf *m*, [F] tàr̃àmbân *m*.

**clip**² *v* (*cut hair, grass*) dātsè *v4*.

**clipping** *n* (*newspaper*) ɗan yankìn jàr̃īdà
*m*.

**clitoris** *n* ɗan tsakà *m*.

**cloak** *n* (*men's long ~ of thick material*)
àlkyabbà *f*, (*lightweight*) àbāyà *f*.

**clock** *n* àgōgo *m* ⟨ai, una⟩: alarm ~ àgōgo
mài ƙàrarrawā; set a ~ yi saitìn àgōgo.

**clockwise** *adv*: turn ~ jūyà ta hannun
dāma; turn counter-~ jūyà ta hannun
hagu = mai dà hannun àgōgo bāya.

**clod** *n* (*of earth*) hōgè *m* ⟨Ca⟩.

**clog** *v* tōshè *v4*: the pipe is ~ged up famfò
yā tōshè.

**clogs** *n* ɗàngàr̃àfai *p*.

**close**¹ 1. *adv* kusa *adv*, gab dà *prep*, (*very
~ to*) dab dà *prep*: their houses are ~
together gidàjensù nà gab dà jūnā; ~
at hand kusa-kusa, bàkī dà hancì: the
stores are ~ at hand gà kantunà bàkī dà
hancì; stay ~ to r̃àɓa *v2*: he was walking ~ to the wall yā r̃àɓi katangà; (*fig.*)
have a ~ call aunà ar̃zìkī.
2. *adj* (*intimate*): he is a ~ friend àbōkī
nè na ƙwar̃ai = àmīnī nè.

**close**² *v* a. rufè *v4*: ~ a book, a business rufè littāfì, kàntī; the road is
~d to traffic an rufè hanyà = an datsè
hanyà; ~ eyes tightly rintsè idò; b.
(*conclude*) kammàlā *v1*: ~ a speech by saying... kammàlà jàwàbì dà cêwā....

**closely** *adv* dà hankàlī; examine sth. ~
duddùbā *v1*.

**closeness** *n* (*esp. of family, friends*) zumuncī
*m*, zùmùntā *f*.

**closet** *n* ɗan kabàd *m*, [F] almuwâr̃ *f*.

**cloth** *n* (*yardage*) yādì *m*, zanè *m* ⟨Cuwa⟩,
[F] tîsì *m*; (*printed yardage*) àtàmfā *f*
⟨oCi⟩; (*shirting*) zàwwàtī *m*; a piece of ~
ƙyallè *m*; a length of printed ~ turmì *m*.

**clothe** *v* tufantar̃ (dà) *v5*; feed and ~ one's
family ciyar̃ dà ìyālì.

**clothes** *n* tufāfì *p*, (*clothing*) kāyan jìki
*p*, sùtur̃ā *f*; ready-made ~ kāyan kàntī;
change one's ~ sākè kāyan jìki; put ~
on sâ tufāfì; take ~ off tūɓè tufāfì.

**clothesline** *n* igiyar̃ shānyā *f*.

**clothing** *n* sùtur̃ā *f*, kāyan jìki *m*.

**cloud** 1. *n* (*white, fleecy*) gàjìmàrē *m*; (*rain*)
gir̃gijè *m* ⟨a..ai⟩; storm ~s hadarī *m*.
2. *v*: ~ over, become ~y lumshè *v4*: the
sky is ~ing over gàrī nà lumshèwā.

**cloves** *n* kànumfàr̃ī *m*.

**clown** *n* càli-càli *m*.

**club**¹ *n* (*stick*) kulkī *m* ⟨a-e⟩; the police
used ~s to disperse the crowd 'yan sàndā
sun wàtsà tàron dà kulàkè.

**club**² *n* (*esp. Sport*) ƙungiyā *f* ⟨oCi⟩, kùlâb
/ kwàlâb *f* ⟨x²⟩: ~ member ɗan ƙungìyā.

**clubs** *n* (*in cards*) caka *f*, kùrî *f*.

**clucking** *n* (*of hens*) kyar̃kyar̃ā *f*.

**clumsy** *adj* maràs kintsì *m*, maràs tsārì
*m*: he is ~ bâ shi dà kintsì.

**clutch**¹ *v* dàmuƙà *v2*, dàdumà *v2*: he ~ed at
his mother's dress yā dàmùƙi rìgar̃ ma-
haifìyar̃sà.

**clutch**² *n* (*of car*) kulōcì *m*, [F] àmbìr̃ìyājì
*m*.

**coach**¹ *n* (*bus*) sàfā *f*, bâs *f*, [F] kâr̃ *f*; (*of
train, for passengers*) wāgùnù *m*.

**coach**² 1. *n* (*Sport*) kōciyà *n*, mài kōyar̃ dà
'yan wàsā *n*, [F] àntìr̃ènâr̃ *n*.
2. *v* kōyà wà *v1*.

**coagulate** *v* daskàrē *v4*, sandàrē *v4*.

**coagulation** *n* daskàrêwā *f*.

**coal** *n* kwâl *m*, gawàyī *m*: mine ~ haƙà
kwâl; a ~ mine mahaƙar̃ kwâl.

**coalition** *n*: ~ government gwamnatìn
haɗìn gwìwā *f*, gwamnatìn kàr̃ō-kàr̃ō *f*:
the 3 parties formed a ~ government
jàm'iyyà ukù sun haɗà gwìwā sun kafà
gwamnatì.

**coarse** *adj* (*of bark, skin*) (mài) kaushī *m*;
~ flour tsàkī *m*; ~ sugar tsàkin sukàr̃ī.

**coast** *n* gāɓar̃ tèku *f*, gàɓar̃ bahàr̃ *f*.

**coat** *n* a. (*clothing*) kwât *f*, [F] màntô *m*; (*of
animal*) fātà *f*. b. (*of paint*) shàfē *m*.

**coax** v làllāsà / ràrrāsà v2 ⟨lallāshī⟩: they kept on ~ing him to write the story sunà ta lallāshinsà yà r̃ubùtà làbār̃ìn.

**cob** n (of maize) tōtòn masàr̃à m.

**cobra** n (black-hooded) gàmshèk̃à f.

**cobweb** n : sāk̃àr̃ gizò-gizò f, yānā f, yānar̃ gizò-gizò f, gidan tautàu m.

**cocaine** n hōdàr̃ ìbìlîs f, k̃òkên f; sniff ~ shàk̃i k̃òkên.

**coccyx** n dàndarì m.

**cock**[1] n zàkarà m ⟨u⟩.

**cock**[2] v (a gun) danà v1.

**cockroach** n kyànkyasò m ⟨ai⟩.

**cocoa** n (tree or fruit) k̃òkō m.

**coconut** n (tree or fruit) kwākwà f; ~ oil mân kwākwà.

**coco-yam** n gwāzā f.

**coddle** v yi wà lēlē m.

**code** n tsārì m: legal ~ tsārìn dōkōkī; penal ~ tsārìn laifuffukà; highway ~ dòkar̃ hanyà f.

**codeine** n k̃òdîn m.

**coerce** v tīlàstà wà v1, tur̃sàsà v1: he was ~d into carrying out their orders an tīlàstà masà bîn ùmàr̃ninsù.

**coercion** n tur̃sàsàwā f.

**coexistence** n zaman tàre m.

**coffee** n k̃òfî m, [F] kàppê m, (esp. Turkish) gahawā f.

**coffin** n àkwàtìn gāwā m.

**coiffure** n (of woman) kitsò m.

**coil** 1. n hanjī m: watch ~ hanjin àgōgo m; mosquito ~ māgànin saurō m, [F] igiyàr̃ lēgàs f.
2. v nadà v1: he ~ed the turban around his head yā nadà rawànī; ~ sth. up nannàdà v1.

**coin** v k̃āgà v1: they've ~ed a name for that an k̃āgà wà wannàn sūnā.

**coin(s)** n (loose change) tsābàr̃ kudī f, kwàbbai p, [F] cìngarangaran m; flip a ~ yi kân sarkī kō dàmarà; ~ purse cìkàkà-yar̃ f.

**coincide** v zō daya dà: his arrival ~d with ours isòwar̃sà tā zō daya dà tāmù; make sth. ~ with dàidaità v2: make your arrival ~ with mine kà dàidàici lōkàcin zuwānā.

**coincidence** n a. (lucky) mùwāfakà f, yi gàm-dà-k̃atar̃ m, yi kàtar̃ì m, yi dàcē m: it was a happy ~ that we met in Kaduna hàduwar̃mù à Kàduna gàm-dà-k̃àtar̃ cē = mun yi kàtar̃in hàduwā dà shī à Kàduna; by sheer ~ bisà k̃àddar̃à. b. (unlucky, unfortunate) tsàutsàyī m.

**colanut** n, see kolanut.

**cold**[1] 1. adj (mài) sanyī m, (esp. dry ~ of winter season) (mài) dārī m; ~ water ruwā mài sanyī = ruwan sanyī; it isn't very ~ bài cikà sanyī ba = bài yi sanyī ba sòsai; it's ~ today yâu gàrī yā yi sanyī = yâu anà sanyī; feel ~ ji sanyī; very ~ sanyī k̃alau; (fig.) give so. the ~ shoulder yi bìr̃is dà w. = yi banzā dà w.; (fig.) get ~ feet yi dàri-dàri.
2. n (weather) sanyī m, (esp. of winter season) dārī m; they made me wait outside in the ~ sun sâ ni jirà à wàje cikin sanyī; severe ~ sanyī mài sūkà.

**cold**[2] n mur̃à f, sanyī m: he has a ~ yanà mur̃à = yanà sanyī; he's caught a ~ mur̃à tā kāmà shi; he's suffering from a bad ~ yanà fāmà dà mūgùwar̃ mur̃à; we did that to avoid catching a ~ mun yi hakà don gudùn kàmuwā dà mur̃à.

**cold-blooded** adj na k̃ètà f, mak̃ètàcī adj, na bak̃in cikì m: a ~ murder mak̃ètàcin kisàn kâi.

**cold season** n hùntūr̃ù m, lōkàcin dārī m.

**cold war** n yāk̃in cācar̃ bàkī m.

**colic** n tsânkī m.

**collapse** v a. (partially) gabcè v4: the river bank ~d gā6à tā gabcè; (totally) rūshè v4: the bridge has ~d gadà tā rūshè; (inwardly) 6urmè v4, fādà v1: the house ~d dākì yā 6urmè; the well ~d rījìyā tā fādà. b. (fall apart, scatter) war̃gàjē v4, r̃agar̃gàjē v4, r̃ugùjē v4: the peace negotiations have ~d shāwàr̃war̃in lùmānàr̃ dà akà yi sun r̃ugùjē. c. (physically from exhaustion) sārè v4: he ~d and couldn't continue yā sārè yā kāsà cî gàba.

**collar** n a. (any kind) wuyà f; (West. style) kwalà f, [F] kwâl m. b. (for animal) madaurin wuyà m, [F] shên m.

**collar bone** n k̃àshin wuyà m.

**colleague** n àbōkin aikì m.

**collect** v a. tārà v1; ~ one's thoughts tārà hankàlī wurī daya = yi nìtsuwā. b. (~ and remove) kwāsà v2: they ~ garbage on Tuesdays anà kwāsar̃ shàrà ran Tàlātà. c. (money, wages) kàr6à v2. d. (junk, odds & ends) tarkàtà v1.

**collection** n a. (of things) tārì m. b. (of money for charity) k̃àr̃ō-k̃àr̃ō m.

**collective** adj na gamà kâi.

**college** n (post-secondary) kwalējì f; (university) jāmi'à f; teachers' training ~ makar̃antar̃ hòron màlàmai, [F] kur̃ nòmâl f; go to ~ shìga jāmi'à.

**collide** v yi karò m, karà v1.

**collision** n karò m: head-on ~ karò gàbā dà gàbā.

collusion *n* gamà bàkī *m*.

colon[1] *n* mazàwarì *m*.

colon[2] *n* (*Gram.*) ruwā biyu *f*.

colonel *n* kanàř *m*, [F] kwàlànâl *m*.

colonialism *n* mulkìn màllakà *m*: neo-~ mulkìn màllakà sābon salō.

colony *n* màllakà *f*: Nigeria is a former British ~ Nìjēřiyà màllakàř Ingìlà ta dà cē.

color 1. *n* launī *m* ⟨uka⟩, ruwā *m*; (*esp. of yardage*) kalà *f*: what ~ is this? wànè launī nē wannàn? its ~ is like this ruwansà irìn na wannàn nē; a cloth with many ~s zanè mài kalà irì-irì; pink-~ed mài kalà ruwan hōdà; brightly ~ed řàmbàtsàu *idph*.

2. *v*: ~ a picture yi wà hōtò kalà.

color-blind *adj*: he is ~ bài iyà bambàntà launì ba.

colt *n* dùkushī *m* ⟨ai⟩.

column *n* a. (*in building*) gìnshiƙī *m* ⟨ai⟩. b. (*in newspaper*) sāshì *m* ⟨Ca⟩. c. (*tabular*) lāyì *m* ⟨uka⟩.

coma *n*: he is in a ~ and near death yā fìta dàgà hayyàcinsà, ajàlinsà yā kusa.

comb 1. *n* a. matsēfī *m*, mashařcī *m*; (*West. style*) kûm *m*, [F] fanyì *m*; (*Afro-style*) ùřyà *f* ⟨oCi⟩. b. (*of cock*) zankō *m* ⟨aye⟩, tukkū *m* ⟨aye⟩.

2. *v* (*hair*) shařcè *v4*, tsēfè *v4*, tājè *v4*.

combat *n* dāgà *f*, jìdālì *m*, gwagwàřmayà *f*.

combative *adj* (*psn.*) (mài) jìdālì *m*.

combination *n* gàmuwā *f*, hàɗuwā *f*.

combine *v* a. (*unite*) gamà *v1*, haɗà *v1*: ~ resources haɗà gwīwà. b. (*mix*) haɗà *v1*, garwàyā / gauràyā *v1*: ~ the flour and salt garwàyà fulāwā dà gishirī.

come *v* a. zō *v0* ⟨zuwà⟩, tahō *v6*; he ~s everyday yanà zuwà kōwàcè rānā. b. (*in commands*): ~ here! (*m/f/p*) yā kì/kà/kù! = kì/kà/kù zō nân! c. (*var. v + adv/prep uses*): ~ across, upon tař dà / tarař (dà) *v5*, ci karō dà: you'll ~ across them at the market zā kà tař dà sū à kàsuwā; ~ apart ɓallè *v4*, ɓarkè *v4*: this chair is beginning to ~ apart wannàn kujèrà tā fàrà ɓallèwā; the basket has ~ apart kwàndôn yā ɓarkè; ~ back dāwō *v6*, kōmō *v6*; ~ down sàuka *v3*: he came down from upstairs yā saukō dàgà bēnè; the prices have started to ~ down fàřāshì yā fàrà sàukā; ~ into (*a place*) shigō *v6*; ~ off ɓallè *v4*: the handle of the drawer has ~ off mariƙin àljīhun tēbùř yā ɓallè; ~ out fìta *v3*, fitō *v6*: he came out of the store yā fitō dàgà kàntîn; the dirt won't ~ out daudàř bà zā tà fìta

ba; ~ to a place isō *v6*; ~ to an end ƙārè *v4*; ~ up (*of plants*) tsirō *v6*; ~ upon tař dà / tarař (dà) *v5*. d. (*become, ~ into being*): ~ true zama gàskiyā; ~ about, up (*happen*) àuku *v7*, fàru *v7*: unforeseen circumstances are always coming up kullum lalūřōřī sunà àukuwā. e. (*in exclamations*): ~, ~! (don't be so foolish!) habà! *excl*; ~ on, who would believe that? habà! wà zâi yàrda dà wànnan?

comedian *n*, see comic.

comedy *n* wàsan ban dàriyā *m*.

comet *n* tàurārùwā mài wutsiyà *f*.

comfort *v* bâ w. hàƙurī, sanyàyà wà zūcìyā, kwantař dà hankàlin w., làllāsà *v2* ⟨lallāshī⟩: she ~ed me tā bā nì hàƙurī = tā làllàshē nì.

comfortable *adj* a. (*at ease*) (mài) dāɗī *m*: do you feel ~? kanà jîn dāɗī dai? he made us feel ~ yā sâ mun ji dāɗī. b. (*of furniture*) (mài) dāɗin zamā.

comic *n* mài ban dàriyā *n*; (*who uses obscenity for humorous effect*) shàƙiyyī *m* ⟨ai⟩; (*tradit. professional*) ɗan kāmà *m*, ɗan gàmbarà *m*; (*modern, e.g. in cinema, TV*) càli-càli *m*.

coming *adj* mài zuwà, na gàba: the ~ months wàtànnī màsu zuwà = wàtànnin gàba.

comma *n* waƙàfī *m*.

command 1. *n* a. (*order*) ùmàřnī / ùmùřnī *m*. b. (*control*) shūgabancì *m*: who is in ~ here? wà kè shūgabancîn wurin nàn = wànē nè shūgàbà à nân? ~ of a language iyà sarràfà harshè.

2. *v* a. ùmàřtà *v2*, bā dà ùmàřnī. b. (*lead*) shūgàbantà *v2*.

commander *n* kwàmandà *m* ⟨oCi⟩, shūgàban sōjà *m*, [F] kùmàndân *m*; ~-in-chief bàbban kwàmandà.

commando(s) *n* sōjàn ƙundùmbālā *p*.

commemoration *n* bìkin tunàwā *m*.

commend *v* yabà *v1*: they ~ed his bravery an yabà masà jàřuntakàřsà.

commensurate *adj*: be ~ with dàcē dà *v4*.

commentary *n* (*literary critique*) shařhì *m*; (*on Koranic texts*) tàfsīřì *m* ⟨ai⟩.

commerce *n* kāsuwancì *m*, cìnikì *m*.

commercial 1. *adj* na cìnikī: ~ affairs sha'ànin cìnikī.

2. *n* (*advertisement*) tàllà *f* ⟨tàllàce-tàllàce⟩.

commiserate *v* yi jùyàyī *m*: I ~d with her nā yi jùyàyintà; (*over sth. lost*) yi jàjē *m*: he ~d with me over my loss and said, 'may God let it be found' yā yi minì jàjē ya cè, 'Allàh yà bayyànā'.

commission 1. *n* a. (*fee*) là'adā *f*, kàmashò *m*: contractors get a big ~ 'yan kwangilā nā sāmùn kàmashò mài yawà; it cost ₦200 plus ~ kuɗinsà naiřā ɗarī biyu là'adà wàje. b. (*admin. body*) hùkūmā *f* ⟨oCi⟩: ~ of inquiry hùkūmāř bìncìkē.
2. *v* (*so. travelling to buy & bring back*) yi wà sautù *m*: I ~ed him to buy me some cloth from Egypt nā yi masà sautù yà sayō minì atamfòfī dàgà Masář.

commissioner *n* kwàmishinā *n*, [F] kwamsāř *n*.

commit *v* (*enact*) yi *v0*, aikàtā *v1*: ~ a crime, an offense yi lâifī; ~ suicide yi kìsàn kâi; ~ an evil act aikàtà shařřì = yi shařřì.

commitment *n* àlkawàřī *m* ⟨u-a⟩.

committee *n* kwàmìtî *m* ⟨oCi⟩, [F] kwàmìtê *m*: steering ~ kwàmìtîn shiryà aikì; the ~ will meet from time to time kwàmìtî zâi yi zaman tàrō lōkàcī-lōkàcī.

commodities *n*: the basic ~ of life kāyan màsàřūfî *p*; sugar and salt are basic ~ dà sukàřī dà gishirī duk kāyan màsàřūfî nē.

common *adj* a. (*ordinary, of things*) gàmà-gàri *adv*: this plant is very ~ wannàn shūkā gàmà-gàri cè; Audu is a ~ name Audù sūnā nề gàmà-gàri; it is ~ly found in the market anā sāmunsà gàmà-gàri à kàsuwà; be ~ly done fayè / fiyè *v4*: that word is not ~ly used bā à fayè àmfānī dà kalmàř nan; a ~ noun (*Gram.*) sūnan gàmà-gàri. b. (*everday, of events, phenomena*) na yâu dà kullum: accidents are a ~ occurrence on this road haɗàřī àbù nē na yâu dà kullum à hanyàř nân; the ~ people talakāwā *p*. c. (*well-known*) sànannē *adj*: a ~ mistake sànannen kuskurè. d. (*belonging to all*) na kōwā ~ knowledge sanìn kōwā; the ~ good àmfànin kōwā, jîn dāɗin kōwā.

commoner *n* talàkà *n* ⟨talakāwā⟩, yākūbāyì *n/p*.

commonplace *adj* yâu dà kullum: accidents on that road are ~ haɗàřī yā zama yâu dà kullum à hanyàř nan.

common sense *n* hankàlī *m*, tùnànī *m*; (*resourcefulness*) dàbàřā *f*, wàyō *m*, (mài) kàn gadō *m*.

Commonwealth *adj*: the British ~ kasā-shē màsu rènon Ingìlà.

commotion *n* hàyàniyā *f*, hàdā-hadā *f*: on market day, there is always a lot of ~ duk rānař kàsuwà, àkwai hàdā-hadā dà yawā.

communal *adj* na jàma'à; ~ work gàyyā *f*, aikìn tàimakon kâi dà kâi; ~ organization (*for self-help projects*) kungìyař tàimakon kâi dà kâi.

communicate *v* sādař (dà) *v5*.

communication *n* sādàřwā *f*: ~s network hanyōyin sādàřwā; ~s satellite kumbòn sākò *m*.

communiqué *n* jàwābìn bāyan tàrō *m*: a ~ has been distributed to the reporters an rarràbà jàwābìn bāyan tàrō gà 'yan jàřīdā.

communism *n* guřguzancì *m*, kwaminisancì *m*.

communist *n* ɗan guřguzū *m*, ɗan kwamìnìs *m*; ~-bloc countries kasàshen kungìyař 'yan guřguzū.

community *n* àl'ummā *f* ⟨oCi⟩, jàma'à *f/p* ⟨oCi, u⟩.

commute *v* (*Law*): ~ a sentence kā dà hukuncì.

companion *n* àbōkī *m* ⟨ai⟩.

company *n* a. (*commercial*) kamfànī *m* ⟨oCi⟩; (*association*) kungìyā *f* ⟨oCi⟩. b. (*Mil.*) kamfànī *m*, [F] kwampanyè *m*. c. (*guest*) bākò *m* ⟨i⟩: we had ~ last night mun yi bākò jiyà dà dare.

comparatively *adv* a. (*in comparison to*) à kwàtànce: this was ~ easier than that à kwàtànce, wannàn yā fi wancàn saukī. b. (*relatively, proportionately*) daidai gwàřgwadō: he speaks Hausa ~ well yanā jîn Hausa daidai gwàřgwadō.

compare *v* a. (*judge differences*) kwàtàntā *v1*, gwadā *v1*: ~ this to that kà kwàtàntà wannàn dà wancàn. b. (*model, liken sth. to sth.*) misàltā *v1*: the heart can be ~d to a pump anā iyā misàltà zūcìyā dà famfò.

comparison *n* kwatancì *m*: the ~ doesn't hold kwatancìn bài dācè ba; in ~ to idan an kwàtàntā: in ~ to you he is tall yanā dà tsawō idan an kwàtàntà shi dà kai; by, in ~ à kwàtànce.

compass *n* a. (*for direction*) kamfàs *m*. b. (*for drafting*) bùkàřī *m*.

compassion *n* a. (*sympathy*) tàusàyī *m*, jùyàyī *m*, īmānì *m*: see how he is beating that donkey, he has no ~ gà yàddà yakè dūkàn jàkīn, bâ shi dà īmānì; have ~ for ji tàusàyin w. b. (*mercy, esp. on occasion of death*) řahamā *f*, jîn kai *m*; have ~ řahamař (dà) *v5*, ji kai *m*: may God have ~ on him Allàh yà řahamshē shì = Allàh yà ji kànsà.

compel *v* tīlàstā wà *v1*: he ~led us to leave the meeting yā tīlàstā manà barìn tàrôn.

compensation *n* (*for injury, damages*) diyyà *f*.

compensate *v* a. (*pay compensation*) biyā diyyà: the government will ~ the farmers for their land gwamnatī zā tà biyā manōmā diyyàr ƙasàr̃sù. b. (*give money for services*) biyā *v0*. c. (*reciprocate*) sākà wà *v1*.

compete *v* yi gàsā *f*: they are competing for the job sunà gàsar̃ sāmùn aikìn; ~ for so.'s favors yi ɗan'ubancì *m*.

competence *n* gwànintà *f*.

competent *adj* gwànī *adj* ⟨aye⟩; he is a ~ tailor gwànī nè wajen ɗinkì; he is a ~ worker shī ma'àikàcī nè dà ya dācè.

competition *n* a. (*contest*) gàsā *f*: economic ~ gàsar̃ cìnikī. b. (*usu. betw. 2 people or opposing groups*) tākar̃ā *f*.

competitive *adj* (*psn.*) (mài) gàsā *f*.

competitor *n* ɗan gàsā *m*, àbōkin tākar̃ā *m*.

compile *v*: ~ a list of complaints lāsàftà kōke-kōke; ~ a dictionary tsārā ƙāmùs.

complacent *adj*: be ~ yi yàkànā *f*.

complain *v* a. yi kūkā *m*: ~ about the weather yi kūkan yanàyī; ~ to so. kai wà kūkā: we ~ed to the manager mun kai wà manajà kūkā; stop ~ing so much! kà dainà yawàn kūkankà! ~ about so. sàr̃ā *v2*. b. (*grumble, ~ about trivial matters*) yi mītà *f*, yi gùngùnī / gunàgunī *m*: his wife ~s constantly to him màtar̃sà tā cikà (yi) masà mītà.

complaint *n* a. kūkā *m* ⟨kōke-kōke⟩: what is your ~ about? don mè kakè kūkā? make a ~ about so. kai kūkan w.: why are you making a ~? mènē nè dàlīlìn kai kūkankà? b. (*Law*) ƙār̃ā *f* ⟨aki²⟩: lodge a ~ with the court kai ƙār̃ā gàban àlƙālī; he is lodging a ~ against his neighbor yanà ƙarar̃ maƙwàbcinsà.

complement *n* (*Gram.*) cìkàmakō *m*.

complete *v* a. (*finish*) gamà *v1*: ~ one's schooling gamà makar̃antā = saukè ƙàr̃ātū; (*finish up*) ƙàràsā *v1*, (*esp. successfully*) kammàlā *v1*: ~ the project on time kammàlā aikìn cikin lōkàcī; ~ the period of fasting kammàlā azùmī. b. (*a set amount of sth.*) cikàsā *v1*: he has ~d one year of study ya cikàsà shèkar̃à ɗaya ta ƙàr̃ātū; I've ~d payment of the loan nà cikàsà kuɗin dà akè bìnā bāshī; be ~ cìka *v3*: the collection is ~ tàr̃ī yā cìka.
2. *adj* cìkakkē *adj*: I want a ~ explanation of what happened inà sôn cìkakken bàyānìn àbîn dà ya far̃u.

completely *adv* sar̃ai *adv*: he understood ~ what our problem was yā gānè àbîn dà kè dāmùnmù sar̃ai; (*may be expr. by ideophones which go with specific verbs*): I paid him ~ nā biyā shì cif; you did it ~ wrong! bà kà yī shì daidai ba kwata-kwata! it has stopped raining ~ ruwā yā ɗaukè cak; it is ~ finished yā ƙàr̃è kakaf; the crowd was ~ assembled jàma'à tā tàr̃u kaf; it is ~ chopped up yā fàskàru cif; it is ~ washed yā wànku tas.

complex *adj* a. (*difficult*) (mài) wùyā *m*. b. (*complicated*) rìkìtaccē *adj*.

complicate *v* rikìtā *v1*: this has ~d matters for me wannàn yā rikìtā minì sha'ànī; be(come) ~d rikìcē *v4*, cūɗè *v4*: the matter has become ~d màganà tā cūɗè.

compliment 1. *v* yàbā *v2*, yabā wà *v1*: I ~ed him for doing a good job nā yabā masà aikìn dà ya yi.
2. *n* yàbō *m*: deserve a ~ ìsa yàbō.

comply *v* bi *v0*: you must ~ with the rules dōlè kà bi dōkà; I cannot ~ with your request bà zân iyà biyā makà bùkātar̃kà.

compose *v* (*a story*) ƙāgà *v1*; (*a poem, song*) shiryà *v1*, tsārā *v1*.

composition *n* (*Lit.*) tālīfì *m* ⟨ai⟩.

compound *n* a. (*residence*) gidā *m* ⟨aCe⟩. b. (*Mil., police*) gidan sōjà *m*, bàr̃ikì *f*.

comprehend *v* fàhimtà *v3*, (*sth.*) fàhimtā *v2*.

compress¹ *v* danƙàrā *v1*; (*by squeezing*) mātsà *v1*.

compress² *n* (*hot, for medicinal use*) gashì *m*.

compromise 1. *v* daidàitā *v1*, shiryà *v1*: at first they disagreed, but later on they ~d dà farkō sunà musù, sā'àn nan sukà daidàitā dàgà bāya.
2. *n* shirì *m*, sulhù *m*; make so. (*2 parties*) reach a ~ sulhùntā *v1*.

compulsory *adj* na tīlàs, na dōlè: ~ duty aikìn dōlè; schooling is ~ zuwà makar̃antā tīlàs nè; it is ~ wājìbī nè = yā zama tīlàs nè; it is ~ for everyone to pay taxes wājìbī nè gà kōwā yà biyā hàr̃ājì.

compute *v* lāsàftā / lissàfā *v1*: I ~d how much tax I had to pay nā lissàfā kō nawà zân biyā hàr̃ājì.

computer *n* nā'ūr̃à mài ƙwaƙwalwā *f*, injì mài ƙwaƙwalwā *m*.

comrade *n* àbōkī *m* ⟨ai⟩.

concave *adj* kòmàɗaɗɗē *adj*.

**conceal** v a. (*hide*) ɓōyè v4, ɓūya v3a; (*one-self*) laɓè v4: he ~ed himself behind the wall yā laɓè dà bangō. b. (*sth. held in one's hand*) sunnè v4: he ~ed the knife in his pocket yā sunnè wuƙā à àljīhunsà. c. (*suppress*) dannè v4: he ~ed the truth yā dannè gàskiyā.

**conceit** n fāɗin râi m, jī-jī dà kâi m, ɗagāwā f; be ~ed dagà hancì.

**conceive** v a. (*become pregnant*) ɗau cikì. b. (*an idea*) tunō v6: I've ~d a plan of escape nā tunō dàbaɽàɽ gudù.

**concentrate** v mai dà hankàlī, tattàrà hankàlī, nitsè v4: she ~d on her work completely tā mai dà hankàlintà wurī ɗaya gà aikìntà; you are not concentrating kā rabà hankàlinkà.

**concentration camp** n sànsanin gwālè-gwālè m.

**concept** n tùnànī m.

**concern** 1. v a. (*involve*) shāfā v2, dàngantā v2: the strike ~s everyone in the country yājìn aikìn yā shāfi kōwā dà kōwā à ƙasàɽ; it's a matter that ~s money wata màganà cē dà ta dàngànci kuɗī. b. (*preoccupy*): be ~ with dâukē wà hankàlī: he is more ~ed with his work than with his family aikìnsà yā fi dâukē masà hankàlī dà ìyālìnsà. c. (*worry*): be ~ed about dàmu dà v7, yi jùyàyin w.a.
2. n a. (*worry*) àbin dàmuwā m. b. (*sth. important to so.*) kùlā f: it's no ~ of ours! ìnā kùlaɽmù! = bâ ruwanmù!

**concerning** prep a. (*about*) à kân, gàme dà, bisà gà: it is a matter ~ a loan màganà cē à kân bāshì; ~ his wishes bisà gà àbin dà yakè sô; what has been done ~ the problem? mè akà yi gàme dà màtsalàɽ? b. (*in relation to*) danganè/dàngàne dà: ~ this matter danganè dà zàncen nàn; this is ~ our conversation of yesterday wannàn yanà dàngàne dà màganàɽmù ta jiyà.

**concession** n a. (*sth. yielded*) sassaucì m; make a ~ to so. sassàutā wà v1, (*esp. in bargaining*) yi wà rangwamè m: I'll make you a ~ since you are such a good customer inà mikì rangwamè sabòdà kē àbōkìyaɽ cìnikì cè ta ƙwarai. b. (*commercial right*) hakkì m ⟨oCi⟩: oil ~s hakkìn màllakàɽ hàƙar mân fètùɽ.

**concise** adj taƙaitaccē adj.

**conclude** v a. (*complete*) kammàlā v1, ƙarè v4: he ~d his speech by saying that... yā kammàlà jàwābìnsà dà cêwā.... b. (*decide*) yankè hukuncì.

**conclusion** n a. (*end*) ƙarshē m: in ~ dàgà ƙarshē. b. (*opinion, decision*) hukuncì m: they came to the same ~ sun yankè hukuncì irì ɗaya. c. (*last chapter of book*) kammàlāwā f, rufèwā f, nadèwā f.

**concord** n (*Gram.*) jìtuwā f.

**concrete**[1] n (*cement*) kankare m, [F] bètân m.

**concrete**[2] adj (*definite*) ìngàntaccē adj: a ~ example ìngàntaccen misàlì.

**concubine** n ƙwaɽƙwaɽā f, sà-dakà f.

**condemn** v a. (*criticize*) yi tiɽ dà, yi Allàh wadai dà: we ~ed their position on the matter mun yi tiɽ dà matsayinsù gàme dà haɽkàɽ. b. (*Law*) yankè wà hukuncì m: he was ~ed to death an yankè masà hukuncìn kisà.

**condescension** n rainì / rēnì m.

**condiments** n kāyan yājì m.

**condition** n a. (*state*) hālī / hālì m ⟨aye⟩: it is in the same ~ as I left it yanà nân a hālinsà yâddà na baɽ shì; the human ~ hālìn ràyuwaɽ bìl Adamà; the house is in bad ~ gidân bâ kyân zamā. b. (*stipulation*) shaɽàdī m ⟨u-a⟩: lay down ~s on azà shaɽuɗɗà.

**conditional** adj (*Gram.*): a ~ clause gàngā maràs tabbàs.

**condolences** n tà'àziyyà f, gaisuwaɽ mutuwā f: we extended our ~ to them mun yi musù tà'àziyyà = mun yi musù gaisuwā.

**condone** v daurè wà gìndī.

**conduct**[1] n (*behavior*) hālī / halī m ⟨aye⟩, dàbī'à f ⟨u⟩: his ~ was disgraceful hālinsà àbin kunyà nē.

**conduct**[2] v a. (*lead*) jā wà gōrà: he ~ed them on a tour of England yā jā musù gōràɽ zìyāɽàɽ Ingìlà. b. (*manage*) shùgàbantā v2.

**conductor** n (*of bus, train*) kwàndastā m, [F] ɗan kàmashò m.

**confederation** n tàrayyà f, gwamnatìn ƙawàncē f.

**conference** n (*bàbban*) tārō m; an international ~ (*esp. academic*) tàron ƙārā wà jūnā ilìmī na dūniyà; the ~ is in session anà zaman tàrôn.

**confess** v amsà lâifī, yi ìƙìɽāɽì dà lâifī.

**confession** n ìƙìɽāɽì dà lâifī m.

**confidant** n àmīnì m, àmīnìyā f ⟨ai⟩: she is my ~ àmīnìyātā cè = munà siɽɽì dà ita.

**confide** v yi siɽɽì dà m, asìɽtā wà v1: I want to ~ in you inà sô mù yi siɽɽì dà kai.

confidence *n* a. (*certainty*) tabbàcī *m*: they have ~ that they will win the game sunã dà tabbàcin zā sù ci wàsân. b. (*trust, confidentiality*): have ~ in so. amìncē dà w. *v4*, yàr̃da dà *v3*, bâ w. àmānã: I have lost ~ in his ability to function bàn amìncē dà zâi iyà aikì ba; self-~ yàr̃dā dà kâi *f*, jî dà kâi *m*: he has self-~ yanã jî dà kânsà = yanã jîn kânsà. betray so.'s ~ tōnã wà àsīr̃ī, ci àmānàr̃ w.

confident *adj*: be ~ (*certain*) hak̃īk̃àncē *v4;* (*of oneself*) yàr̃da dà kâi, jî dà kâi.

confidential *adj* àsìr̃taccē *adj*.

confine *v* tsarè *v4*: he was ~d to his house an tsarè shi à gidā.

confirm *v* tabbatar̃ (dà) *v5*, hak̃īk̃àntā *v1*: have the rumors been ~ed? an tabbatar̃ dà jìta-jìtar̃? be ~ed tàbbatà *v3*: the matter has been ~ed zàncên yā tàbbatà.

confirmation *n* tabbàcī *m*: I don't have any ~ of that bâ ni dà tabbàcinsà.

confiscate *v* k̃wācè *v1*, kāmè *v1*, yi wà kāmuwā *f*: the police have ~d the drugs 'yan sàndā sun k̃wācè k̃wàyā.

conflagration *n* gòbar̃ā *f*.

conflict 1. *n* a. (*quarrel*) rìgimã *f;* (*strong* ~) hùsūmã *f*, rìkicī *m*: they are constantly in ~ with each other kōyàushè sunã rìkicī dà jūnā. b. (*lack of agreement*) sàɓānī *m*.
2. *v* sāɓã *v1*: these two reports ~ with each other àkwai sàɓānī tsàkānin r̃àhòtànnin nàn biyu; the story which you told me ~s with his làbār̃ìn dà ka gayà minì yā sāɓã dà nāsà.

confront *v* yi fìtō-nā-fitō, yi tàhō-mù-gamã, yi jā-ìn-jā: the rioters ~ed the police 'yan bòr̃ē sun yi fìtō-nā-fitō dà 'yan sàndā.

confrontation *n* tàhō-mù-gamã *m*, fìtō-nā-fitō *m*, jā-ìn-jā *m*.

confuse *v* a. rikìtā *v1*, rūdã *v1*, dābùr̃tā *v1*: the commotion ~d me hàyàniyā tā rikìtā ni; I ~ you with your brother nā rikìcē tsàkānin kai dà yàynakà; make so. ~d rikitar̃ (dà) *v5*, rūdar̃ (dà) *v5*: I told him that in order to ~ him nā gayà masà hakà don ìn rikitar̃ dà shī. be, get ~d rūdè *v4*, rikìcē *v4*: I am always ~d about those words kullum inà rūdèwā dà kalmōmin nàn. b. (*be disoriented, flustered*) gīgìcē *v4*, kidìmē *v4*, rikìcē *v4*: when I heard the noise, I became ~d dà jîn hàyàniyā sai na rikìcē. c. (*of things, places*) yāmùtsē *v4*, cākùɗē *v4*: things are all ~d abūbuwàn duk sun yāmùtsē.

confusing *adj* mài rikitàr̃wā, mài rūdàr̃wā.

confusion *n* a. rìkicī *m*, yàmutsī *m;* (*esp. due to quarreling*) hàrgitsī *m*, hàtsàniyā *f*: that will cause a lot of ~ zâi kāwō rìkicī. b. (*din, hubbub*) hàyã-hàyã *f*, hàyàniyā *f*, hàdã-hadā *f*.

congeal *v* daskàrē *v4*, sandàrē *v4*.

congenial *adj* (mài) fàr̃a'à *f*.

congested, be *v* màtsu *v7*, yi cùnkōsō / cìnkōsō *m*, yi cìkōwã *f*, yi tìnjim *idph*: the roads were ~ with cars hanyōyī sun yi tìnjim dà mōtōcī = an sàmi cùnkōson mōtōcī.

congratulate *v* tayã wà mur̃nã, yi wà bar̃kà *f*: we ~d them on the birth of their child mun yi musù bar̃kàr̃ haihùwar̃sù; we ~ you on getting your degree mun tayã makà mur̃nàr̃ sāmùn dìgìr̃ī.

congratulations 1. *n* mur̃nã *f*: a letter of ~ takàr̃dar̃ mur̃nã; we offer our heartiest ~ munã mur̃nã k̃war̃ai.
2. *excl* bar̃kà! = à gaishē kà! ~ on your success! bar̃kà dà ar̃zìkī!

congregation *n* (*Relig.*) masàllàtā *p*.

congress *n* a. (*large meeting*) bàbban tàr̃ō *m*. b. (*governing body*) màjàlisã *f* ⟨u⟩: C. of the United States Màjàlìsun Wàkìlai na Amìr̃kà. c. (*official organization*) jàm'iyyã *f* ⟨oCi⟩; Northern Women's C. Jàm'iyyàr̃ Mātan Arèwa; Labor C. Jàm'iyyàr̃ K̃wādago.

conjunction *n* (*Gram.*) hadì *m*, haràfin hàɗau *m;* subordinate ~ dòrì *m*.

conjunctivitis *n* jan idò *m*.

conjure *v* yi dabò *m*.

connect *v* hàɗã *v1*: ~ the electricity sâ wutā; ~ a phone hàɗà wayàr̃ tàr̃hō.

connection *n* hadì *m*.

connotation *n* nūnī *m*.

conquer *v* ci *v0*: ~ a town, the enemy ci gàrī, àbòkan gàɓā.

conquest *n* nasar̃ã *f*, cî *m*.

conscience *n* zūcìyã *f*, r̃ai *m*: your ~ will tell you (what is the right thing to do) zūcìyar̃kà zā tà bā kà.

conscientious *adj* (mài) k̃òk̃arī *m*: you are more ~ than Sule kā fī Sulè k̃òk̃arī.

conscious *adj* a. (*aware*) à sàne *adv*. b. (*awake*) à fàr̃ke *adv*.

consciousness *n*: lose ~ (*faint*) sūma *v3a*, yi sūmā *f;* (be in a coma) fìta dàgà hayyàcī; make so. lose ~ sōmar̃/sūmar̃ (dà) *v5;* regain ~ far̃faɗō *v6*.

consecutively *adv* bî dà bî, ɗai-ɗai dà ɗai-ɗai.

consent 1. *n* a. (*permission*) yàr̃dā *f*, izìnī *m*, (*esp. one's own*) sôn râi *m*: they sold it without my ~ an sayar̃ dà shī bã dà nā bā sù izìnī ba = an sayar̃ dà shī bã tãre dà sôn râinā ba. b. (*formal agreement*) yàr̃jējēnìyā *f*.
2. *v* yàr̃da *v3*, amsā *v1*.

consequence *n* a. (*result*) sàkàmakō *m*, sànàdiyyà *f*: as a ~ of this à sàkàmakon wannàn = sabõdà wannàn; as a ~ of his rude behavior, he was punished à sànàdiyyar̃ rashìn kunyàr̃ dà ya yi an hõrē shì. b. (*import, meaning*) mà'ànā *f*: what he said is of no ~ màganàr̃sà bâ ta dà mà'ànā.

conservation *n* kiyàyêwar̃ àlbar̃kàr̃ k̃asā *f*; ~ group k̃ungìyar̃ yàk̃ì dà màsu gur̃6àtà dūnìyà.

conservative *n & adj* (*Pol.*) (mài) r̃a'àyin mazan-jiyà *m*, ɗan mazan-jiyà *m*.

conserve *v* a. (*preserve*) kiyàyē *v4*. b. (*be sparing of what is available*) yi tattalī *m*, yi tsimī *m*: during the dry season, everyone ~s water lõkàcin rānī, kõwa nà tattalin ruwā. c. (*reserve, save for future use*) yi tānàdī *m*: ~ energy, natural resources yi tānàdin makàmashī, tattalin ar̃zìkin k̃asā.

consider *v* a. (*take into account*) yi là'akàr̃ī *m*, bi *v0*, dūbà *v1*: ~ the matter yi là'akàr̃ī dà màganàr̃ = bi màganàr̃. b. (*weigh so.'s advice, think about*) jinjìnā *v1*: you should ~ carefully what I'm about to say to you yā kàmātà kù jinjìnà àbin dà zân cê mukù. c. (*think about doing*) yi shāwar̃ā *f*: I am ~ing getting married inà shāwar̃ar̃ yîn aurē. d. (*regard*) ɗaukà (cêwā) *v2\**: I ~ that an insult nā ɗauki wànnan kàmar̃ zāgì; I ~ him a fool nā ɗaukē shì (à) wāwā; baobab trees are ~ed to be haunted an ɗaukà cêwā àkwai àljànu à kūkà.

considerable *adj* (mài) yawà *m*.

considerate *adj* (mài) sanìn yā kàmātà *m*, (*esp. of ano.'s feelings*) (mài) kàrā *f*: she is very ~ of others tanà dà sanìn yā kàmātà gà mutànē; he was ~ of my feelings yā yi minì kàrā; he is not ~ of anyone bã yà yi wà kõwā kàrā =bã yà dà lìssāfì gà kõwā; treat so. ~ly mutùntà *v1*.

consideration *n* a. (*sth. being considered*) là'akàr̃ī *m*: you should take into ~ what happened kù yi là'akàr̃ī dà àbin dà ya fàru; the matter is under ~ anà dūbà màganàr̃; after careful ~ of the matter bāyan zurfin tùnànī à kân bàtūn. b.

(*being considerate of others*) sanìn yā kàmātà *m*, kàrā *f*.

consist of *v* k̃ùnsā *v2*: the story ~s of questions and answers làbārìn yā k̃ùnshi tambayõyī dà amsōshī; the house ~s of 3 rooms, a kitchen, and a bathroom gidân yanà k̃ùnshe dà dākunà ukù dà madafī dà makēwayī.

consonant *n* (*Gram.*) bak̃ī *m* ⟨babbak̃ū⟩.

conspiracy *n* k̃ùllalliyā *f*, mak̃ar̃k̃ashìyā *f*, mākìr̃cì *m*, jàmhūr̃ù *m*, [F] kwàmbîn *m*; (*esp. Pol.*) hadìn bàk̃ī *m*, gamà bàk̃ī *m*.

conspire *v* k̃ullà *v1*, yi k̃ullì *m*, (*Pol.*) haɗà bàk̃ī, gamà bàk̃ī: ~ to cheat a company yi k̃ullì don à yi wà kamfànī zàmba; ~ to overthrow a government haɗà bàk̃ī don à yi jūyìn mulkì; ~ against so. k̃ullà wà munāfuncì, yi wà mākìr̃cì, yi wà jàmhūr̃ù, gamè wà k̃ai.

constantly *adv* kullum *adv*, kõyàushè *adv*: they quarrel ~ kullum à cikin faɗà sukè; (*without interruption*) bâ jî bâ ganì: he studies ~ yanà kàr̃àtū bâ jî bâ ganì.

constipation *n* kùmburin cikì *m*, ɗaurèwar̃ cikì *f*: he is constipated cikìnsà yā ɗaurè = cikìnsà yā kùmburà = cikìnsà yā sank̃amē.

constituency *n* mazā6ā *f*.

constituent *n* a. (*Pol.*) ɗan mazā6ā *m*. b. (*Gram.*) tūbàlī *m* ⟨tūbalà⟩.

constitution *n* a. (*Pol.*) tsārìn mulkì *m*. b. (*state of health*) hālin jìkī *m*.

constrain *v* tauyè *v4*.

constrict *v* (*press together*) matsè *v4*; be ~ed (*be narrow*) yi k̃uncī *m*.

construct *v* a. (*a building*) ginà *v1*. b. (*an argument, line of reasoning*) shiryà *v1*.

construction *n* a. (*building*) ginì *m* ⟨e²⟩: ~ work aikìn ginì. b. (*Gram.*) ginì *m*, jimlà *f* ⟨oCi⟩.

constructive *adj* (*useful*) (mài) àmfànī *m*, ìngàntaccē *adj*.

consul *n* ɗan k̃àramin jàkādà *m*.

consulate *n* ōfìshin jakādancì *m*.

consult *v* a. (*ask for advice*) shāwar̃tà *v2*, nèmi shāwar̃ā dà: they always ~ each other sukàn shāwàr̃ci jūnansù. b. (*ask somewhere for information*) tùntu6à *v2*: you should ~ the police station to find out what to do kà tùntù6i ōfìshin 'yan sàndā don kà san àbin yî.

consultation *n* shāwar̃ā *f* ⟨shāwàr̃war̃ī⟩.

consume *v* cînyē *v4*; (*by a fire*) lāshè *v4*: the fire ~d the building within half an hour wutā tā lāshè ginìn cikin rabìn awà;

(*time*) ci *v0*: time-consuming work aikī̀
mài cîn lōkàcī̀.

contact 1. *n* huldā̀ *f*, mà'āmalā̀ *f*: are you in
~ with him? kanā̀ huldā̀ dà shī? I have
lost ~ with him nā dainà mà'āmalā̀ dà
shī.
2. *v* (*inquire about information, opinion*)
tùntuɓā̀ *v2*.

contagious *adj* (*disease*) (mài) yā̀ɗuwā *f*,
(mài) wàtsuwā *f*.

contain *v* ƙùnsā *v2*: the box ~ed some
money and papers àkwātìn yā ƙùnshi
kuɗī dà tàkàrɗū.

container *n* àbin zubà kāyā *m;* cardboard
~ kwālī *m* ⟨aye⟩.

contaminate *v* gurɓātā *v1*, gurɓàce *v4*: the
water is ~d ruwā yā gurɓàce.

contemplate *v* (*consider*) yi shāwarā̀ *f*:
he's contemplating writing a book yanà
shāwaràr wallàfà littāfī.

contemporary 1. *adj* (*modern*) na yâu dà
kullum, na zāmànī/zàmānī *m*.
2. *n* (*mate in age*) sa'ā̀ *n* ⟨oCi⟩, tsārā *n*
⟨aki[2]⟩.

contempt *n* rainī̀ / rēnī̀ *m*, wulā̀ƙancī̀ *m*:
I have nothing but ~ for him tsàkānīnā dà
shī sai rainī̀; be in ~ of court rainà
kōtù; have ~ for so. rainà *v1*, nūnā̀ wà
rainī̀, tōzàrtā *v1*, wulā̀ƙàntā *v1*.

contemptuous *adj* na rainī̀/rēnī̀ *m*, na
wulā̀ƙancī̀ *m*: what he did was really ~
àbîn dà ya yi àbin rainī̀ nē sòsai; a
~ look kallon rainī̀, kallon wulā̀ƙancī̀;
he looked at us ~ly yā dūɓē mù à
wùlā̀ƙàncè; a ~ noise (*sucking in with
pursed lips*) tsā̀kī *m*.

contend *v* a. (*vie*) yi hàmayyà̀ *m*. b. (*dispute, assert*) yi jìdālī̀ *m*.

content(ed) *adj* a. (*satisfied*): be ~ gàmsu
*v7*, wàdātu *v7*: he's not ~ with his job bài
gàmsu dà aikìnsà ba. b. (*resigned*): be
~ with one's lot yi yàkànā *f*, hàƙurà *v3*,
nūnà dànganā̀.

contentious *adj* (mài) jìdālī̀ *m*, (mài)
màsīfā *f*, màsīfaffē *adj*: he is very ~ yā
cikà jìdālī̀ = yanā̀ dà màsīfā̀.

contents *n* kāyan ciki/cikī̀ *p;* table of ~
àbūbuwàn dà kḕ ciki.

contest *n* gā̀sā *f;* (*usu. between 2 people or
opposing groups*) tākarā̀ *f*.

contestant *n* ɗan gā̀sā *m*, ɗan tākarā̀ *m*.

context *n* màhàllī / mùhàllī *m*, yanàyī *m*:
this word is just right for this ~ kalmàr
nân tā dācḕ dà wannàn màhàllī sòsai.

continent *n* ɓangarèn dūniyā̀ *m*, nāhiyā̀ *f*
⟨oCi⟩: the African ~ ɓangarèn Afìrkà
= nāhiyàr Afìrkà; there are 7 ~s in

the world àkwai mânyan nāhiyōyī gùdā
bakwài à dūniyā̀.

continual *adj* na kullum.

continually *adv* a. (*all the time*) kullum
*adv*, kōyàushè / kō dà yàushè: he's ~
getting into trouble kullum yanā̀ shìgā
cikin rìkicī̀. b. (*of uninterrupted action*) bâ jî bâ ganī, bâ katsḕwā, bâ
tsayā̀wā, bâ darē bâ rānā: the machine
works ~ injìn yanā̀ aikī̀ bâ darē bâ
rānā.

continue *v* a. (*go ahead*) ci gàba: ~ with
your work kù ci gàba dà aikìn. b. (*keep
on doing*) dingā̀ / ringā̀ *v1*, riƙā̀ *v1*, yi
ta: he ~d walking yā yi ta tàfiyā̀; they
~d pounding the corn sun dingà dakà
hatsī. c. (*keep going, last*) dōrḕ *v4*: will
this noise ~ for long? ƙārar̃ nan zā tà
dōrḕ? the work cannot ~ if the machine
stops aikìn bà zâi dōrḕ ba in nā'ūr̃ā
tā tsayā̀.

continuously *adv* bâ tsayā̀wā, bâ jî bâ
ganī.

contraceptive *n* māgànin hanà haihùwā *m*,
māgànin yîn cikī̀ *m*.

contract[1] *n* a. (*e.g. construction, supplies*)
kwangilā *f*, kwantàr̃āgī *m*, [F] kwàntàr̃ā̀
*m*: get a ~ kàrɓi kwangilā; breach a
~ karyà ƙa'idàr̃ kwangilā. b. (*sth. entrusted*) āmānā̀ *f*.

contract[2] *v* a. (*a disease*) kàmu dà *v7*: he
~ed malaria yā kàmu dà zàzzàɓin cīzòn
saurō. b. (*shrink*) ƙanƙànce *v4*: heat ex-
pands, cold ~s zāfī nà fāɗàɗàwā, sanyī
nà ƙanƙàncèwā. c. (*reduce*) ragḕ *v4*.

contraction *n* a. (*abdominal, prior to vom-
iting*) tūƙā *f;* ~s (*birth pains*) nāƙudā *f*. b.
(*Gram.*) ragḕwā *f*, ɗagḕwā *f*.

contractor *n* ɗan kwangilā *m*.

contradict *v* a. (*express opposite*) ƙaryàtā
*v1*: your story ~s his lābār̃inkà yā
ƙaryàtà nāsà. b. (*deny statement*) yi
musù *m*: if you're going ~ what I said, then
ask someone else in zā kà yi minì musù
sai kà tàmbàyi wani. ~ oneself ƙaryàtà
kâi, yi bàƙī biyu.

contradiction *n* bàƙī biyu *m*, màganà̀ biyu
*f*.

contrary *adj* a. (*divergent*) (mài) sā̀ɓānī *m;*
be ~ to sā̀ɓā wà *v1;* that is ~ to our agreement wannàn yā sā̀ɓā wà yàr̃jējēnìyar̃
dà mukà yi kḕ nan. b. (*difficult, of psn.*)
miskìlī *m* ⟨ai⟩.

contrast 1. *n* bambam *m*, bambancī̀ *m*:
there's a big ~ between the two parties
jàm'ìyyū biyu sun shā bambam dà jūnā;
there is no ~ between them bâ bambancī̀

tsàkāninsù.

2. *v* bàmbantà *v2*, shā bambam.

**contrastive** *adj*: be ~ bambàntā *v1*: these two words are ~ in meaning kalmōmin nàn biyu sunà bambàntā mà'ànā = kalmōmin nàn biyu sunà dà bambancìn mà'ànā.

**contribute** *v* a. (*add to*) ƙārā *v1*: it was his personality which ~ed to his success kwàrjininsà nē ya ƙàrà masà nasaŕā; education ~s to one's worldly experience ilìmī nà ƙārà dàbàɍun zaman dūniyà. b. (*make contribution, esp. money*) yi kàɍō-kàɍō *m*: we all ~d to buy him a gown mun yi kàɍō-kàɍō mun sayà masà rìgā.

**contribution** *n* (*esp. of money*) kàɍō-kàɍō *m*: make a ~ of ₦10 bā dà kàɍō-kàɍon naiɍà gōmà; receive a ~ àmshi kàɍō-kàɍō; ~ for relief kàɍō-kàɍō don gudùmmawā.

**control** 1. *n* a. (*power*) īkò *m*; (*Pol.*) ragàmaɍ mulkì *m*: they are in ~ of the government sunà rìƙe dà ragàmaɍ mulkì. b. (*ability to* ~): self-~ màllakàɍ kâi *f*; he lost ~ of the wheel and crashed into a tree sìtīɍìn yā kubcè masà sai ya yi karò dà bishiyà; be out of ~ (*of thing, situation*) ƙi *v0* (+ *vbl. n*): the fire is out of ~ gòbaɍā tā ƙi kàsuwā; the demonstration got out of ~ zàngà-zangà tā ƙi kwàntàwā; be beyond so.'s ~ gàgarà *v2*, fàskarà *v2*, bijìre wà *v4*, fi ƙarfin w.: Musa has gotten beyond his family's ~ Mūsā yā bijìre wà iyàyensà = yā gàgàri iyàyensà.

2. *v* a. (*manage*) saɍɍàfā *v1*, (*esp. people*) yi wà mulkì *m*: he knows how to ~ a car yā iyà saɍɍàfà mōtà; he ~s his wife yanà wà màtaɍsà mulkì; he ~led himself yā kāmà kânsà. b. (*Pol.*) rìƙe ragàmaɍ mulkì: which party ~s the government? wàcè jàm'iyyà kè rìƙe dà ragàmaɍ mulkì? c. (*restrict*) ƙayyàdē *v4*: ~ the price of basic commodities ƙayyàdè kuɗin kāyan màsàɍūfì.

**controversial** *adj* (*of a matter*) (mài) kāwō rìgimà; (*of psn.*) mawùyàcin hālī *m*.

**controversy** *n* jàyayyà *f*, àbin zàrgī *m*: ~ over election results jàyayyà à kân sàƙàmakon zàɓen.

**convalesce** *v* ji saukī *m*.

**convene** *v* ƙaddamaɍ dà tàrō.

**convenience** *n*: at your ~ lōkàcìn dà ka ga dāmā = lōkàcìn dà ya dācè makà = lōkàcìn dà ya fī makà saukī.

**convenient** *adj* a. (*suitable*): be ~ dācè *v4*: he came at a ~ time yā zō à lōkàcìn

dà ya dācè. b. (*easy*) (mài) saukī *m*: 2 o'clock will be more ~ for me dà ƙarfè biyu zâi fī nì saukī.

**convention** *n* (*meeting*) bàbban tàrō *m*.

**conventional** *adj* (*of a psn.*) mùtumìn kōwā, nagàri na kōwā.

**conversation** *n* màganà *f* ⟨u²⟩, zàncē *m* ⟨uka⟩; (*friendly, among equals*) tàdì *m*; (*esp. night-time*) hīɍa *f*: we had a serious ~ about politics mun yi dōguwaɍ màganà à kân sìyāsà; our ~ centered around Kande's wedding hīɍaɍmù tā tsayà kân bìkin auren Kànde; the ~ became animated hīɍa tā kauɍè.

**converse** *v* yi zàncē *m*, yi tàdì *m*, yi hīɍa *f*.

**convert** *v* a. (*change into*) mai dà / mayaɍ (dà) *v5*: I ~ed the box into a table nā mai dà àkwàtìn tēbùɍ. b. (*currency*) mùsāyà *v2*. c. (*to Islam*) musuluntaɍ (dà) *v5*: he ~ed the unbelievers yā musuluntaɍ dà kāfìɍàn. d. (*to Christianity*) nasàɍantaɍ (dà) *v5*.

**convex** *adj* lànƙwàsasshē *adj*.

**convey** *v* a. (*carry*) kai *v***: the oil is ~ed by pipes anà kai mân ta būtūtū. b. (*deliver*) isaɍ (dà) *v5*, mīƙà *v1*: ~ my greetings to your wife kà mīƙà mini dà gaisuwātā gà uwaɍgidā; the message was ~ed to the chief an isaɍ dà sàƙôn wurin sarkī.

**convict** 1. *v* sàmi w. dà lâifī, tabbataɍ dà lâifin w.

2. *n* fuɍsùnà *m* ⟨oCi⟩, [F] ɗan kasò *m*.

**convince** *v* a. (*persuade*) shāwō kân w.: I ~d him to go nā shāwō kânsà yà jē; I've done everything in the world possible to ~ her bâ irìn jūyìn dūniyàɍ dà bàn yi ba ìn shāwō kântà. b. (*satisfy, assure*) gamsaɍ (dà) *v5*: he ~d me of his honesty yā gamsaɍ dà nī gàme dà gàskiyaɍsà; be ~d tabbàtā *v1*: I am ~d that... nā tabbàtā cêwā... = bâ ni dà shakkà cêwā....

**convincing** *adj*: ~ evidence shaidà mài gamsaɍwā.

**convocation** *n* (*academic*) bìkin sàukaɍ kàɍātū *m*, [F] faɗìn kwànkûɍ *m*.

**convulsions** *n* (*epileptic*) faɍfāɗiyā *f*; (*of infants*) bòrin jàkī *m*, tàfiyaɍ ruwā *f*.

**cook** 1. *v* a. (*activity of cooking*) girkà *v1*, yi girkì *m*: she doesn't know how to ~ bà tà iyà girkì ba; she ~ed some spinach stew tā girkà miyaɍ àlayyàhō = tā dafà miyaɍ àlayyàhō. b. (*food*) dafà *v1*; be ~ed dàfu *v7*: they (foods) are ~ing together on the fire sunà ta dàfuwā bàkī ɗaya à kân wutā.

2. n (incl. ~-steward) kūkù m, [F] kùzìnyê m.

**cooker** n, see hotplate, stove.

**cookie** n (hard, crunchy) bìskît m; (soft, crumbly) kyât m.

**cooking** n a. (act, way of ~) girkì m ⟨e²⟩; I don't like her ~ bā nà sôn girkìntà; ~ area murhù m ⟨a-u⟩. 2. (cuisine) àbinci m: Hausa ~ àbincin Hàusàwā.

**cool** 1. adj a. (to the senses) (mài) ɗan sanyī m, (mài) sanyi-sanyi adj: keep this in a ~ place kì sâ shi à wani wurī mài ɗan sanyī; it is a bit ~ today yâu dà sanyi-sanyi. b. (~ and moist, of a place) (mài) ni'imà f: Kaduna has a ~ climate Kàdūna gàrī nè mài ni'imà. c. (of temper) (mài) sanyin zūcìyā, (mài) sanyin râi.

2. v: ~ down (of metal, food, temper) hūcè v4; ~ down (of angry psn.) kwantař dà hankàlī; ~ sth. hot (by diluting) surkà v1; ~ sth. off sanyàyā v1; ~ off (of food) shā iskà.

**coop** n (for fowl) akurkī m ⟨ai⟩.

**cooperate** v haɗà kâi, haɗà gwīwà, gamà kâi: let's ~ to resolve the problem mù haɗà kâi don shāwô kân màtsalà.

**cooperation** n gamà kâi m, haɗìn kâi m: she won't give me her ~ bā tà bā nì haɗìn kâi; afterwards, there was greater ~ between them dàgà bāya an sàmi ƙarìn haɗìn kâi tsàkāninsù.

**cooperative** n & adj: farmers' ~ ƙungìyař (haɗà kân) manòmā; ~ society ƙungìyař gamà kâi = ƙungìyař haɗà kâi; ~ project gàyyā f, aikìn tàimakon kâi dà kâi m.

**cope** v: she can't ~ with the children yârā sun gàgàrē tà = yârân sun fi ƙarfintà; he can ~ with anything bâ àbîn dà zâi gàgàrē shi; unable to ~ gàji v3*.

**copper** n tagùllā f, jan ƙarfè m.

**copulate** v yi jìmā'ì m, tārā dà v1, (pejor.) ci v0; (by animals) yi barbarā f.

**copy** 1. n (photocopy) hôtō m ⟨una⟩, kwafî m, [F] kôpî f.

2. v a. jùyā v2 ⟨jūyì⟩: the scribe copied it out mařùbùcī yā jùyē shi; (esp. photocopy) kwàfā v2, yi kwafî m. b. (imitate) kwàikwayà v2, maimàitā v1.

**copyright** n hakkìn màllakà m: the material herein is protected by ~ an kàrē abûbuwàn dà kè ciki dà hakkìn màllakà.

**coral** n (red) mùřjānì / mùřzānì m.

**cord** n a. (for trousers) mazāgī m, zārìyā f, làwùřjē m. b. (thick) igiyà f ⟨oCi⟩: electric ~ igiyař làntařkì = wayář làntařkì.

**cordial** adj na ƙàwàncē m: there are ~ relations between them àkwai dàngàntakàř ƙàwàncē tsàkāninsù.

**core** n (middle) tsakiyà f.

**corkscrew** m bàřīmà f ⟨u⟩.

**corn** n a. (grain) hatsī m, dāwà f. b. (maize) masàřā f: ~ silk gēmùn masàřā; ~ husk ɓāwon masàřā.

**cornelian** n (esp. necklace of ~ beads) tsàkiyà f.

**corner** 1. n a. (of street, building) kwanà f. b. (of a room) kusùrwā f ⟨oCi⟩; at the innermost ~ (of a room) à ƙuryà f. c. (dark, out of the way area) lungù m ⟨una⟩, sāƙò m.

2. v a. (surround & confine) ritsà v1: the soldiers ~ed them in the town sōjōjī sun ritsà su cikin gàrī. b. (put so. into difficult position) ƙurè v4: during our discussion, I managed to ~ him à cikin gařdamàřmù, nā sàmi yàddà na ƙurè shi; he's been ~ed an ƙurè masà wurī; (fig.) he has painted himself into a ~ wurī yā ƙurè masà.

**cornmeal** n gàrin masàřā m.

**corn silk** n gēmùn masàřā m.

**cornstalk** n karà m ⟨aCe⟩; (crushed ~ used for animal bedding) tattakà f; ~ bundles (in field) būshiyā f, bāgà f.

**corona** n (of moon, sun) sànsanī m.

**coronation** n naɗin sarkī m.

**corporal** n kôfùř m, [F] kàfàřân m.

**corporation** n a. (government) hùkūmà f ⟨oCi⟩, ma'aikatā f ⟨u⟩. b. (business) kamfànī mài řajistà m.

**corps** n: (Mil.) ƙungìyař sōjà f; National Youth Service C. Ƙungìyař 'Yan Bâutā wà Ƙasā.

**corpse** n gāwā f ⟨aki²⟩, mamàcī m: wrap a ~ in a shroud sutùřcè gāwā.

**corral** n kēwayè m, shingè m ⟨aye⟩.

**correct** 1. adj & adv madàidàicī adj, daidai adv: this is the ~ pot for cooking rice wannàn tukunyā madaidaicìyā cè wajen dafà shìnkāfā; that's ~ daidai nè = hakà nè.

2. v (so.) gyārā wà v1; (esp. by teacher, parent) ci gyārā m: the teacher ~ed my pronunciation mālàmā tā ci gyāran lafàzīnā; (homework) gyārā v1 ⟨gyārà⟩: I spent all night ~ing the students' homework nā kwāna inà gyāran aikìn dàlìbai.

correction *n* gyārā *m* ⟨e²⟩.

correctly *adv* daidai *adv*, sòsai *adv*.

correspond to *v* dācè dà *v4*, yi daidai dà: the translation doesn't ~ to the original speech fassafāř bà tà dācè dà jàwābì na ainihī ba.

correspondent *n* (*of news media*) wàkīlī *m* ⟨ai⟩, mài bā dà řàhōtò *n*; (*of newspaper*) ɗan jàřīdà *m*.

corrode *v*: the acid has ~d the metal ruwan bātīř yā lālàtā ƙarfèn; the knife was ~d and rusty tsātsà tā ci wuƙā.

corrugated iron *n* kwānòn rufī *m*; ~ roof rufìn kwānò.

corrupt *v* ɓātà *v1*: he was ~ed by money kuɗī sun ɓātà shi.

corruption *n* řashawà *f*, ɓācì *m*: bribery and ~ are universal cîn hancì dà řashawà sun zama ruwan dare.

cost 1. *n* a. (*price*) kuɗī *m/p*; (*esp. fixed price*) fàřāshì *m*; production ~s kuɗin yī; the ~ of living keeps rising sha'ànin zaman jàma'à sai hàuhawà yakè yī. b. (*difficulty*) wàhalà *f*: whatever its ~ kōmē wàhalàřsà; we must avoid war at all ~s kōmē wàhalà lallē nè mù kaucè wà yāƙī. 2. *v*: it ~ a lot of money yā ci kuɗī dà yawà; how much will it ~ me? nawà nē zān biyā? it will ~ you ₦100 total naiřà ɗarī zā kà biyā dukà; what does it ~ to fly to Jos? nawà nē kuɗin zuwà Jàs ta jirgin samà? that mistake ~ him his life kuskurèn nan yā janyō masà hàsāràř rânsà.

costly *adj* (mài) tsàɗā *f*.

cotton *n* audùgā *f*: pick ~ cirè audùgā; tease ~ shiɓà audùgā; ~ boll gùlūlù *m*; ~ merchandise hājà *f*; ~ mill ma'aikatař gyārà audùgā *f*.

cottonseed *n* angùryā *f*.

couch *n* kujèrā *f* ⟨u⟩.

cough 1. *n* tàrī *m*: she had a bad ~ tā yi mūgùn tàrī; whooping ~ tàrin shìƙà. 2. *v* yi tàrī *m*.

could *v* a. (*be able*) iyà *v1*: he ~ not understand the speech bài iyà gānè jàwābìn ba. b. (*to indicate possibility, use fut. tense*): I didn't think he ~ do it bàn yi tsàmmānī zâi iyà ba; ~ you bring me a glass of water? kō zā kà bā nì ruwan shâ?

council *n* màjàlisà *f* ⟨u⟩, hùkūmà *f* ⟨oCi⟩.

councillor *n* ɗan màjàlisà *m*; (*esp. local government*) kansilà *n*, [F] kwànsàyyê *m*.

counsel *n* (*advice*) shāwařà *f*.

count 1. *v* a. ƙidàyā *v1*, yi ƙìdāyā *f*, ƙirgà *v1*: I ~ed 50 cows nā ƙidàyà shānū hàmsin; can you ~ from 1 to 10? kun iyà ƙirgàwā dàgà ɗaya hař zuwà gōma? ~ up lāsàftā / lissàfā *v1*: they ~ed up all the money they had received sun lāsàftà duk kuɗin dà sukà kàrɓā. b. (*rely*): ~ on dògarà dà/gà *v1*: I'm ~ing on your support inà dògarà dà gōyon bāyankù. 2. *n* adàdī *m*: I lost ~ of the score adàdin cî yā kubcè minì.

counter *n* kantà *f* ⟨una⟩.

counter-attack *v* mai dà harì.

counter-clockwise *adv*: turn ~ jūyà ta hannun hagu = mai dà hannun àgōgo bāya.

counterfeit *adj* na jàbu *m*: it is not genuine but ~ bà na gàske ba nè jàbu nè; ~ goods kāyan jàbu; ~ money kuɗin jàbu, [F] kuɗin ganyē *m*.

counterfoil *n*, *see* check¹.

counterpart *n* ɗan'uwā *m*, makàmàncī *m*; (*esp. at work*) àbōkin aikì *m*, tàkwàřā *n* ⟨oCi⟩.

countless *adj* màsu ɗimbin yawà, ninkìn bà ninkìn: I saw ~ cattle nā ga shānū ninkìn bà ninkìn.

country *n* a. (*nation*) ƙasā *f* ⟨aCe⟩: Nigeria is one of the largest countries in Africa Nìjēřiyà nà ɗaya dàgà cikin mânyan ƙasāshen Afiřkà; he was forced to leave the ~ an tīlàstā masà barin ƙasāř. b. (*as opposed to town*) ƙauyè *m*: I prefer living in the ~ nā fi sôn zaman ƙauyè dà na biřnī.

country bumpkin *n*, *see* simpleton.

countryside *n* (*open farmland*) kàřkařā *f*.

county *n* ƙaramař hùkūmà *f* ⟨oCi⟩.

coup (d'état) *n* jūyìn mulkì *m*: a ~ has taken place an yi jūyìn mulkì; an attempted ~ yunƙurin jūyìn mulkì.

couple 1. *n*: a married ~ mùtûm dà màtařsà = màtā dà mijì; a newlywed ~ angò dà amaryā. 2. *det*: a ~ of days 'yan kwànakī kàɗan; a ~ of books wasu littàttàfai.

courage *n* a. (*bravery*) jàřùntakà *f*, bàjintà *f*: show ~ nūnà jàřùntakà; his ~ failed him gàbansà yā fàɗì; reckless ~ ƙùru *m*, (*fig.*) ƙūnař baƙin wàkē *f*. b. (*of character*) ƙarfin zūcìyā *m*, ƙarfin râi *m*, jan halī *m*, ƙarfin halī *m*: his ~ inspired me ƙarfin zūcìyařsà yā tsimà ni.

courageous *adj* (*brave psn.*) jàřùmī *m* ⟨ai⟩; (*of character*) (mài) ƙarfin zūcìyā *m*; be ~ nūnà bàjintà = yi ta-maza.

course 1. *n* a. (*of study*) kwâs *m* $\langle x^2 \rangle$, [F]
kûř *m;* in-training ~ bītā̀ *f,* [F] ìstājī *m.*
b. (*direction*) hanyā̀ *f* $\langle$oCi$\rangle$. c. (*time*): in
due ~ nân bằ dà dàɗềwā ba; in the ~ of
our conversation à cikin tādìnmù.
2. *excl* of ~! ƙwařai kùwa! = ī mànà!

court[1] *n* a. (*of chief*) fādà *f.* b. (*Law,
tradit.*) shāřì'ā̀ *f;* (*modern*) kōtù *f,* [F]
gidan jūjù *m,* [F] jàstîs *f;* ~ of ap-
peals kōtùn ɗaukàkà ƙārā; high ~ bàbbař
kōtù; supreme ~ kōtùn ƙòli; go to ~
tàfi gàban àlƙālī = tàfi lāyī̀; take
so. to ~ kai ƙarař w. = kai w. gàban
àlƙālī = kai w. lāyī̀.

court[2] *v* (*a woman*) nềmi w. dà aurē.

courteous *adj* (mài) ladàbī *m,* (mài)
bìyayyà̀ *f.*

courteousness *n* ladàbī *m,* bìyayyà̀ *f.*

courtesy *n* sanìn yā kàmātā *m.*

courtier *n* bàfādề *m;* (*of low rank*) dògarī
*m* $\langle$ai$\rangle$.

courtship *n* nềman aurē *m.*

courtyard *n* (*inner*) cikin gidā *m,*
tsakař gidā *f;* (*outer, in front of house*)
fàřfàjìyā *f.*

couscous *n* dàshīshī *m,* kuskùs *m.*

cousin *n* (*var. terms*) ɗan'uwā *m,* 'yař'uwā
*f,* àbōkin wàsā *m,* taubàshī *m;* they are
~s (*from fathers who are brothers*) 'yan
mazā biyu, (*from mothers who are sis-
ters*) 'yan mātā biyu.

cover 1. *v* a. rufề *v4:* she ~ed the pan tā
rufề kwānò; he was ~ed with dust ƙùrā
tā rufề shi; ~ oneself (*with outer gar-
ment*) lùllù6à *v3,* lullù6ā *v1* $\langle$lullù6ī$\rangle$:
she ~ed the child with a cloth tā lullù6ā
wà yārò zanề; they ~ themselves against
the cold sunā̀ lullù6ề kânsù sabòdà
sanyī = sunā̀ lullù6ī sabòdà sanyī; ~
sth. lightly (*with a thin layer or cloth*)
yānề *v4:* he ~ed the kolanuts with a piece
of sacking yā yānề gòřò dà àshāsha. b.
(*conceal*): ~ up (*hide*) 6ōyề *v4,* tōgề *v4,*
rufề àsīřī; ~ up (*not be frank*) yi rufā-
rùfā *f:* stop trying to ~ up and come
out in the open kà dainà rufā-rùfā kà
fitō à fīlī. c. (*go some distance*) ci
*v0:* we ~ed 40 miles in an hour mun ci
mîl àřbà'in cikin awà ɗaya.
2. *n* a. (*lid*) murfī *m* $\langle$ai$\rangle$; book ~ bangon
littāfī *m.* b. (*shelter*) mafakā *f;* take ~
fakề *v4.*

covert *adj* (à) 6ōye *adv,* à àsīřce *adv:* a ~
operation shirìn 6ōye.

cover-up *n* rufìn àsīřī *m,* rufā-rùfā *f.*

covet *v* kwàɗaità *v2.*

covetousness *n* ƙyàshī *m.*

cow *n* sānìyā *f* $\langle$shānū$\rangle$; (*heifer*) kàřsanā
*f* $\langle$u$\rangle$; (*old* ~) guzumā *f;* bush-~ 6aunā *f*
$\langle$6akằnē, aye$\rangle$.

coward *n* mài rākì *n,* matsòràcī *m.*

cowardice *n* rākì *m.*

cowboy *n* kābòyī *m,* [F] kwàbâi *m.*

cowhide *n* (*untanned*) ƙirgì *m* $\langle$a-a$\rangle$.

cowpeas *n* wākē *m.*

cowries *n* wurī *m* $\langle$kudī$\rangle$.

crab *n* ƙaguwā *f* $\langle$oCi$\rangle$.

crab lice *n* dànkà-ɗafi *m.*

crack 1. *v* a. (*sth. brittle, hard*) fasā̀ *v1,*
fashề *v4:* she ~ed the egg tā fasā̀ ƙwai;
the mirror is ~ed madūbin nàn yā fashề;
~ so. on the head rōtsā̀ *v1,* yi wà rōtsī
*m:* he ~ed me on the head with a stone
yā rōtsā̀ ni dà dūtsề. b. (*wood, a wall*)
tsāgā̀ *v1,* tsāgề *v4:* this table is ~ed
tēbùř din nàn yā tsāgề.
2. *n* a. (*in wood, a wall*) tsāgā̀ *f.* b. ~ of
a rifle amon bindigā̀.

craft *n* (*occupation*) sānā̀'ā̀ *f* $\langle$oCi$\rangle$.

craftsmanship *n* fàsāhā̀ *f:* this ring shows
great ~ zōbèn nàn yā nūnà fàsāhā̀.

crafty *adj* (*shrewd*) (mài) wằyō *m;* (*deceptive*) (mài) girì *m;* (*cunning*) (mài)
mākiřcī *m.*

cram *v* a. (*stuff*) shāƙề *v4:* he ~med the
suitcase full with his clothes yā shāƙề
jàkâř dà kāyansà. b. (*for exams*) yi
haddā̀ *f.*

cramps *n* (*abdominal, in women*) cīwòn
mārā̀ *m,* mùřdā *f.*

crane *n,* see crownbird.

cranium *n* ƙwalluwař kâi *f.*

crank *n* (*psn.*) tsagềrā *n* $\langle$u$\rangle$.

crankshaft *n* kařanshâf *m,* [F] ařbîř *m.*

cranny *n:* in every nook and ~ sāƙò-sāƙò
*adv,* lungū̀-lungū̀ *adv.*

crash 1. *v* fāɗì *v3b:* the car ~ed mōtā̀ tā
fāɗì; ~ into (*a place*) fāɗà *v1:* the plane
~ed into the ocean jirgin samà yā fāɗà
tēku; ~ into sth. yi karò dà: the car ~ed
into a tree mōtā̀ tā yi karò dà bishiyā̀.
2. *n* a. karò *m,* fāɗùwā *f;* (*accident*)
hadàřī *m* $\langle$uka$^2\rangle$.

crave *v* yi kwàɗayī *m,* yi ƙāwā/ƙwāwā *f;* (*pejor.*) yi mâita *f:* he's craving a cigarette
yanà ƙāwàř tābà; (*esp. delicacies*) marmarī *m:* children often ~ sweets yārā
sunà yawàn marmarin kāyan zāƙī.

crawl *v* (*by psn.*) rarràfā *v1,* yi ràrràfē
*m;* (*by snake*) jā cikì; ~ through, under
kuřɗà *v1:* he ~ed out from under the door
yā kuřɗà ta ƙōfà ya fìta.

crayfish *n* jàtan landề *m.*

crazy *adj* a. (*mad*) mahàukàcī *adj;* go ~
yi hàukā *m,* haukàcē *v4:* drive so. ~ sâ
w. hàukā; do you think I'm ~ enough to
lend you money! hàukā nakè dà zân bā
kà ràncen kuɗī! b. (*foolish psn.*) wāwā
*n:* we thought he was ~ mun ɗàukē shì
wāwā. c. (*enthusiastic*): be ~ about nā
mūgùn sô, nā (dà) màsīfàř sô: he's ~
about her yanā màsīfàř sôntà.

cream *n* mâi *m:* butter ~ mân shānū; skin
~ mân shāfàwā; hair ~ mân gāshī.

crease *n* a. (*fold*) karī *m:* ~ in trousers
karìn wàndō = karìn gūgà. b. (*wrinkle*)
yàmutsā *f.*

create *v* a. (*by God only*) hàlittā *v2:* God
~d the earth Allàh yā hàlìcci dūniyà.
b. (*by man*) ƙirƙirà *v2:* several new
states were ~d an ƙirƙirō wasu sàbàbbin
jihōhī.

creation *n* a. (*by God, esp. animate*)
hàlittā *f,* (*incl. inanimate*) màhàlūkì *m*
⟨ai⟩; the C. farkon dūniyà *m.* b. (*by
man*) ƙīrà *f.*

creative *n* (*artistic*) (mài) fàsāhà *f;* (*talented*) (mài) hikimà *f;* (*skillful*) (mài)
azancī *m:* he is a ~ builder yanā dà
azancī gà ginì.

creator *n* mahàlìccī *m.*

creature *n* hàlittā *f* ⟨e²⟩, tālìkī *m* ⟨ai⟩:
yesterday I saw the most beautiful ~ (girl)
jiyà nā ga wata hàlittā kyàkkyāwà;
we are all God's ~s mū dukà hàlìcce-
hàlìccen Allàh nē; (*animals only*) dabbà
*f* ⟨oCi⟩.

credit *n* a. (*Econ.*) bāshī *m* ⟨uka²⟩ ⟨uwa²⟩:
buy sth. on ~ ɗaukō w.a. bāshī, ci
bāshìn w.a.: buy a car on ~ sàyi mōtà
bāshī = ɗau mōtà bāshī = ci bāshìn
mōtà; extend so. ~ lāmuntà *v2,* bā dà
bāshī, bā dà ràncē: they extended me
~ of ₦500 sun lāmùncē nì naiřà ɗarī
bìyař; extension of ~ lāmùnī *m.* b.
(*praise*) yàbō *m:* deserve ~ for ìsa yàbō
gà; I give him ~ for his bravery inà yàbon
jàřùntakàřsà.

credit card *n* kātìn bāshī *m.*

creditor *n* mài bīn bāshī *m,* mài bā dà
bāshī *m.*

creep *v* yi sanɗa *f:* the cat crept towards
the mouse to catch it kyânwā tā yi sanɗa
tà cafkè ɓērā.

crescent *n* (*of moon*) hìlālì *m.*

cress *n* làfsûř *m.*

crest *n* a. (*of bird*) zankō *m* ⟨aye⟩, tukkū
*m* ⟨aye⟩. b. (*of hill*) kân tudù *m.*

crevice *n* sāƙō *m:* the money was hidden
in a ~ in the wall an ɓōyè kuɗîn cikin

sāƙòn bangō.

crew *n* (*of ship, plane*) ƙungìyař ma'àikàtan jirgī.

cricket¹ *n* (*large*) gyàrē *m;* (*small*) tsanyà
*f* ⟨oCi⟩.

cricket² *n* (*Sport*) wàsan kuřkèt *m.*

crime *n* lâifī *m* ⟨uka²⟩: commit a ~ yi
lâifī; he was cleared of the ~ bà à kāmà
shi dà lâifin ba; ~ has increased in
many cities laifuffukà sun yàwaità à
bìřànē dà dāmā.

criminal *n* mài lâifī *m.*

cringe *v* tàkurà *v3.*

cripple 1. *n* gurgù *m* ⟨a-u⟩, nàƙàsasshē
*adj.*
2. *v* gurgùntā *v1,* naƙasà *v1:* leprosy has
~ed him kuturtà tā naƙàsā shi; (*fig.*) ~
the economy gurgùntà tattalin ařzìkī.

crisis *n* (*political, social*) hàrgitsī *m,*
rìkicī *m:* Middle East ~ rìkicin
Gabàs ta Tsakiyà; (*due to deteriorat-
ing conditions*) tàɓařɓarà *f:* economic ~
tàɓařɓařař tattalin ařzìkī.

critic *n* mài sūƙà *n,* (*esp. Lit.*) mài tàřkē *n.*

critical *adj:* the matter has become ~
màtsalàř tā yi tsāmārī; he is in ~ condition (*of health*) rânsà nā hannun Allàh.

criticism *n* a. (*constructive*) cîn gyārà *m;*
(*neg.*) sūƙà *m.* b. (*Lit.*) tařkē *m.*

criticize *v* a. (*constructively*) ci gyārà *m;*
(*neg.*) sòkā *v2* ⟨sūƙà⟩: he is always criti-
cizing us about everything we do kullum
yanā sūƙànmù kân duk àbîn dà mukè yî.
b. (*give opinion*) bā dà řa'àyī. c. (*Lit.*)
yi shařhì *m,* fèdè *v4.*

critique *n* shařhì *m.*

croak *v* (*e.g. of frogs*) yi ƙūgī *m.*

crocheting, crochet needle *n* tsinken
sāƙā *m,* kwàřashì *m,* [F] kwàřàshē *m.*

crockery *n, see* chinaware.

crocodile *n* kadà / kadò *m* ⟨anni, oCi⟩.

crook *n, see* robber.

crooked, be *v* (*bent*) lanƙwàshē *v4,* kantàrē
*v4:* the branch is ~ rēshè yā kantàrē;
(*askew*) kařkàcē *v4:* the doorway is ~
ƙōfà tā kařkàcē; his teeth are all ~
haƙòransà duk à sàrkè sukè.

crop *n* (*of bird*) màƙōƙò *m.*

crops *n* a. (*plants*) shùke-shùke *p;* root
~ mabùnƙùsà ƙasà *m/p.* b. (*produce*)
àmfànin gōnā *m:* the ~ were good this
year bana àmfànin gōnā yā yi àlbařkà
= bana an sàmi àlbařkàř àmfànin gōnā.

cross¹ *n* (*shape*) kùřōs *m.*

cross² *v* a. (*a road, river*) ƙètàrē *v4:* he
~ed the river and reached the other side

yā ƙetàrè kògī yā kai gãɓã; ~ unexpectedly in front of giftã (ta) v1, gilmã
(ta) v1: beware of wild animals ~ing
yi hankàlī, nāmun dājì nã giftãwā; ~
over (a boundary) hayã v1: we ~ed over
the Cameroonian border mun hayà iyãkaŕ
Kàmãŕu; ~ through (a place) rātsã ta
v1: we ~ed through his farm to reach the
river mun rātsã ta gōnaŕsà don mù kai
kògī. b. (make a mark) sâ àlāmã; ~ out
kashè v4, sōkè v4: ~ out a name from a
list kashè sūnā dàgà jērin sūnãyē; the
teacher ~ed out his first 2 (incrorectly answered) questions mālàmī yā sōkè masà
tàmbayã ta ɗaya dà ta biyu.

cross³ adj (angry) (mài) fushī m: she was
~ with the children tā yi fushī dà yârā.

cross-examination n tà'annàtī m.

cross-eyed adj (& considered frightening)
dūban-rūduwā m, dūbà-rūdũ m: he is ~
yanã dà dūban-rūduwā.

crossing n mararrabā f, maƙetarā f.

cross-legged adj: sit ~ haŕdè v4, yi hàŕdē
m.

crossroads n mararrabā f.

crotch n (of trousers) hantsã f.

crouch v (in concealed positon) laɓè v4.

crow¹ n hànkākã m ⟨i⟩.

crow² v (by cock) yi cāŕā f.

crowd 1. n a. tãrō m, jàma'ã f/p: he
was lost in the ~ yā ɓacè cikin tãron
mutãnē. b. (multitude): a ~ of people
mutãnē tulì = mutãnē tìnjim = ɗimbin
mutãnē.
2. v: ~ together matsã v1, yi matsì m:
the people ~ed around the radio to hear
the news mutãnē sun yi matsì don sù shā
làbãŕì à ŕēdiyò; be ~ed (overflowing)
cunkùshē v4, yi cìkōwã f, cìka cùnkus:
the room was very ~ed dākìn yā cunkùshē
dà mutãnē = dākìn yā yi cìkōwã dà
mutãnē.

crown 1. n kambī m.
2. v (so. as king) naɗã wà sàrautã, naɗã
w. sarkī.

crownbird n gàurākã m, gàurākìyā f ⟨i⟩,
kùmãrē m.

crude adj (rough) ɗanyē adj ⟨u⟩: ~ language
ɗanyen bãkī.

crude oil n ɗanyen mâi m.

cruel adj àzzālùmī m ⟨ai⟩, mamùgùncī m,
maƙetàcī m; be ~ to so. yi wà àzābā f, yi
wà ƙetā f, wulãƙàntā v1: people shouldn't
be ~ to animals bài kàmatà mutãnē sù yi
wà dabbōbī ƙetā ba; (fig.) a ~ blow àbin
baƙin cikī.

cruelty n àzābã f, ƙetā f.

crumb n ɓaŕɓashī m, bùŕbùdī m, màŕmashī
m: bread ~s ɓaŕɓashin buŕōdì; he didn't
leave even a ~ of bread for us kō
ɓaŕɓashin buŕōdì bài baŕ manà ba.

crumble v maŕmashē v4; (of cooked food)
zāgè v4.

crumple v yāmùtsā v1, (sth. in a ball)
dunƙùlē v4, muŕtsùkē v4: I ~d the
letter and threw it in the wastebasket
nā dunƙùlè wàsīƙã nā jēfã à kwàndon
shãrã; be ~ed yāmùtsē v4, cukwīkwìyē
v4: his clothes were all ~ed duk kāyan
jìkinsà sun yāmùtsē.

crusade n (Relig.) jìhādì m.

crush                                                    v
(sth. brittle) ŕagaŕgàjē / ŕuguŕgùjē v4;
(pulverize) niƙè v4, murƙushē v4; (make
crumpled) yāmùtsā v1; (squeeze) mâtsè v4;
(press, squash) lātsè v4: the truck ~ed
them to death bàbbaŕ mōtã tā lātsè su
haŕ lāhiŕã; (fig.) murƙushē v4: the enemy was ~ed an murƙùshè àbòkan gàbā.

crust n ɓāwon buŕōdì m.

crutch n sàndā f ⟨una⟩.

cry 1. n ƙārā f, īhū m, kirā m, (of bird, animal) kūkā m ⟨kòke-kòke⟩.
2. v a. (tears) yi kūkā m, yi hawãyē p:
~ bitterly yi kūkā wuŕjànjàn; make so.
~ sã w. hawãyē: the smoke, story made
me ~ hayāƙī, làbãŕì yā sâ ni hawãyē.
b. (shout) ƙwālā īhū, ƙwālà kūkā, yi
kùrūruwã f: ~ for help ƙwālà īhū don à
yiwō gudùmmawā. c. (by bird) yi kūkā m.

crying n kūkā m: ~ will get you nowhere
bā indà kūkā zâi kai kì; burst out ~
fashè, ɓarkè dà kūkā.

cub n (of lion, hyena) kwīkwiyò m.

cube n: bouillon ~ dunƙulèn mâgī; ~ of
sugar ƙwàyaŕ sukāŕī.

cucumber n (small, native) gùrjī m; (European) kòkwambã f.

cud n: chew the ~ yi tùƙā f.

cudgel n kulkī m ⟨a-e⟩, kōkarā f.

cue n matashìyā f: I gave him a ~ nā yi
masà matashìyā.

cuisine n àbinci m: Hausa ~ àbincin
Hàusãwā.

cul-de-sac n sãƙò m, lungũ m.

cult n (of spirit possession) bòrī m: ~ member ɗan bòrī m.

cultivate v yi nōmā m.

cultivator n (tractor) kaltìbētã f ⟨oCi⟩,
[F] injìn nōmā m.

culture n àl'àdun gaŕgàjiyā p: cultural
exchange mùsāyaŕ àl'àdū.

culvert n kwalbatì m ⟨oCi⟩.

**cunning** n (shrewd) wằyō m; (deceptive) (mài) girì m, (mài) mākiř̃cì m.

**cup** n a. (for drinking) kōfì m, [F] kwâf m, [F] bwâl m. b. (trophy) kwâf m, [F] kûf m: win a ~ ci kwâf, lāshè kwâf.

**cupboard** n kabàd m, [F] kwabằ f.

**curdle** v yi bař̃cì m, daskàrē v4.

**cure**[1] 1. n (medicine) māgànī m ⟨u-a²⟩: find a ~ for nèmi māgànin w.a.; there is no ~ for that disease wànnan cīwŏ bàbù māgàninsà; prevention is the best ~ rìgằkafì yā fi māgànī.
2. v warkař̃ (dà) v5.

**cure**[2] v (leather) shānyā v1.

**curfew** n dòkař̃ hanà fìtař̃ dare f, [F] kūbìř̃ fê m: a ~ was imposed an kafà wata dòkař̃ hanà fìtař̃ dare.

**curiosity** n (inquisitiveness) ƙwằ ƙwā f, ganin ƙwaf m; (eager ~) ƙàgarā f, ɗòkī f.

**curl** v nannàɗē v4; lie ~ed up kanannàɗē v4, ƙudundùnē v4.

**curly** adj (of hair) nànnàɗaɗɗē adj.

**currency** n kuɗī p: (national) kuɗin ƙasā m, see Appendix F; (foreign) kuɗin ƙasàshen wàje. ~ note takàř̃dař̃ kuɗī.

**current**[1] n a. (of water) igiyàř̃ ruwā f: she was carried along by the ~ igiyàř̃ ruwā tā kāmằ ta. b. (of electricity) ƙarfin làntař̃kì m, [F] kùř̃ân m.

**current**[2] adj: ~ affairs harkōkin yâu dà kullum; the ~ chief sarkī mài cî yànzu = sarkī mài cîn gadō; it's not the ~ fashion bā à yầyinsà yànzu.

**curry** n (powder) kōř̃ì m.

**curse** 1. v (mildly) yi tiř̃ idph; ~ so. zằgā v2, yi wà zāgì m, yi tiř̃ dà; (strongly) là'antā v2: he ~d me by saying, 'God damn you!' yā là'àncē nì dà cêwā, 'Allàh yà tsīnè makà!' ~ you! Allàh wadankà! = Allàh wadař̃ankà!
2. excl ~s! Allàh wadai!
3. n là'anà f.

**cursing** n (bad language) àshâř̃ m, àshāř̃iyà f.

**cursive** adj: ~ script ř̃ùbùtun tàfiyàř̃ tsūtsằ m.

**curtain** n lābulē m, zanè m, [F] ř̃ìdô m.

**curvature** n (of back) gàntsarằ f.

**curve** 1. v (outward, esp. of one's back) gantsàrē v4; (of road) kař̃kàcē v4: the road ~s to the right hanyằ tā kař̃kàcē dāma.
2. n a. (of a line) lāyì mài lànƙwasà m, lànƙwàsasshen lāyì m. b. (of road) kwanà f ⟨e²⟩: the road has a lot of ~s hanyằ tā cikà kwàne-kwàne.

**cushion** n matāshī m; (leather pouf) tìntìn / tùntùn m; (esp. on furniture) kushìn m, [F] kùsân m.

**custody** n: the police have taken the thief into ~ 'yan sàndā sun sâ ɓàrāwòn à bāyan kantằ; remand so. to ~ sâ w. à gidan waƙàfī.

**custom** n a. (specific ~) àl'ādằ f ⟨u⟩: our ~s are different from yours àl'àdunmù sun bambàntā dà nākù; it is our ~ to do that àl'àdař̃mù cē mù yi hakà. b. (gen'l behavior) ɗàbī'ằ f ⟨u⟩: that is his ~ ɗàbī'ař̃sà kè nan.

**customer** n ɗan cìnikī m: a regular ~ àbōkin cìnikī; the ~ is always right bā à fushī dà àbōkin cìnikī.

**customs** n (immigration) kwastàn m, [F] dùwân m: upon arrival, everyone has to go through ~ dà isôwař̃sà, kōwā sai yà bi ta 'yan kwastàn; ~ duty kuɗin kwastàn; ~ office gidan kwastàn; ~ officer ɗan kwastàn = jàmì'in kwastàn, [F] dùwànyê = sōjàn dùwân.

**cut** 1. v a. (sth. up, off) yankằ v1 ⟨yankā⟩: ~ meat, cloth yankà nāmằ, yādì; ~ meat into long strips yanyànā v1; this knife doesn't ~ well wuƙâř̃ nan bā tằ yankā sòsai; ~ up a lot of, ~ into bits yayyànkā / yanyànkā v1. b. (oneself or sth.) yankè v4: I ~ myself with a knife nā yankè dà wuƙā; I stepped on a piece of glass and ~ my foot nā tākà guntun kwalabà nā yankè ƙafà. c. (reduce) ragè v4, dàtsè v4, yankè v4: ~ salaries ragè àlbâshī; ~ short a visit ragè lōkàcin zìyārằ; ~ hair dàtsè gāshì = ragè gāshì; ~ fingernails, grass yankè farcè, cìyāwằ. d. (var. v + adv/prep uses): ~ across, through (a place) kētà (ta) v1, rātsà v1: if you go to my farm, you must ~ through the bush in zā kà jē gōnātā, sai kà rātsà dājì; ~ down (a tree) sārè v4, sassàrē v4; ~ off electricity (due to technical failure) ɗaukè wutā; ~ off electricity (due to non-payment) yankè wutā; ~ so. off (interrupt) tàrbi numfāshin w., katsè wà zàncē; ~ so. off (block passage) tarè wà v4.
2. n a. (wound) yankà m; (slash) sārā m. b. (reduction) ragì m: a ~ in salary ragìn àlbâshī.

**cute** adj a. (small, attractive) dàɓař̃ɓàshī adj ⟨ai⟩: she's a ~ girl yārinyằ cē dàɓař̃ɓàsā = yārinyằ cē ɗagwas dà ita. b. (clever) (mài) wằyō m.

**cutlass** n (locally made from baling wire to cut grass) làngà-làngà m.

cycle[1] 1. *n* kèkè *m, see* bicycle.
  2. *v* (*go by bicycle*) hau kèkè.
cycle[2] *n*: go in ~s zāgayō *v6.*
cylinder *n* (*car*) sìlindã *f,* [F] sìlandìr̃ *m.*
cyst *n* ƙarì *m.*

# D

dab *v* yāɓà *v1*: he ~bed some paint on the wall yā yāɓà wà bangō fentì.

dacron *n* dākàřàn *m*.

dad *n* (*term of addr.*) bàba *m*; (*for term of ref., see* father).

dagger *n* wuƙā *f* ⟨aCe⟩.

daily *adv* kōwàcè rānā, kullum *adv*.

dais *n* (*esp. in mosque*) mumbàřī *m*.

dam 1. *n* madatsař ruwā *f*.
2. *v* datsè *v4*: they are ~ming the river to catch fish sunà datsè kōgī don sù kāmà kīfī.

damage 1. *v* a. ɓātā *v1*, lālàtā *v1*; (*esp. extensive ~*) ɓařnatař (dà) *v5*, yi tà'adī *m*: the flood ~ed 20 houses ambàliyà tā ɓātà gidàjē àshìřin; it was monkeys that ~d the crops birai nè sukà ɓařnatař dà shùke-shùke. b. be(come) ~d ɓācì *v3b*, lālàcē *v4*; ~d goods kāyā dāmējì *m*. c. (*harm*) raunànā *v1*, yi wà ràunī *m*: alcohol can ~ the liver bàřàsā nà iyà raunànà hantà.
2. *n* a. ɓàřnā *f*, tà'adī *m*: the cattle did a lot of ~ to the farm ɓàřnař shānū tā yi yawà à gōnàř. b. (*Law*) lahànī *m*.

damages *n* (*Law*) diyyà *f*: he is claiming ~ on his car yanà nēmà à biyā shì diyyàř mōtàřsà.

damask *n* (*cotton*) shaddà *f*.

damn 1. *v* (*by God*) tsīnè wà *v4*: God ~ you! (*strong explet.*) Allàh yà tsīnè makà! the ~ed 'yan wuta *p*.
2. *excl*: ~ it! (*strong explet.*) Allàh wadai! (*mild explet.*) tiř! = ař! ~ you! (*strong explet.*) Allàh wadankà! = Allàh wadařankà! (*mild explet.*) kaiconkà! = tiř dà kai!

damp *adj* (mài) laimà *f*, (mài) danshī *m*: lately it has been cold and ~ kwànan nàn an yi sanyī mài laimà; (*seeping through a surface*) (mài) yîn nàsō *m*: this wall is ~ bangon nàn yanà nàsō = bangon nàn dà laimà.

dampness *n* laimà *f*, (*of ground, in house*) danshī *m*, (*seeping through a surface*) nàsō *m*; (*from morning dew*) rāɓā *f*.

dance 1. *n* rawā *m* ⟨e²⟩: the ~ became very lively an cāshè dà rawā = rawā tā yi rawā.
2. *v* yi rawā *m*: there was drumming and dancing anà kiɗà anà rawā.

dancer *n* mài rawā *n*.

dandruff *n* amōsànī / amōsànin ka *m*, [F] amōdàřī *m*.

danger *n* haɗàřī / hatsàřī *m* ⟨uka²⟩, danjà *f* ⟨oCi⟩: ~ lies ahead àkwai haɗàřī à gàba; bring ~ upon oneself jāwō haɗàřī; his life is in ~ rànsà nà cikin haɗàřī; confront, expose oneself to ~ head-on (*fig.*) tàri àřàdù dà ka.

dangerous *adj* a. (*risky*) (mài) haɗàřī *m*: ~ work aikì mài haɗàřī; get into ~ situation shìga haɗàřī; driving fast is ~ yawàn gudù kàn jāwō haɗàřī; the bridge is in a ~ condition wannàn gadà bà àmìntacciyā ba cè. b. (*bad*) mūgù *adj* ⟨miyāgū⟩: he's a ~ man shī mūgùn mùtûm nē; a ~ curve wata mūgùwař kwanà.

dangle *v* yi rētō *m*: a chain was dangling from his neck sarƙà nà rētō à wuyàřsà.

dare *v* (*challenge*) ƙàlùɓàlantà *v2*.

daring *n & adj* ƙarfin zūcìyā *m*; take a ~ risk yi ƙùru *v*.

dark 1. *adj & adv* a. (*dim*) (mài) duhù *m*: a ~ place wurī mài duhù; it is ~ (*nighttime*) darē yā yi = àlmūřù tā yi; get ~ (*lose brightness*) dākùshē *v4*. b. (*of colors*) (mài) baƙi-baƙi; this is the ~est one wannàn yā fi saurân baƙī.
2. *n* a. duhù *m*: children are usually afraid of the ~ yârā nà tsòron duhù; (*fig.*) I was kept in the ~ about the matter an bar nì cikin duhù gàme dà màganàř. b. (*dusk*) màgàřibà / màngàřibà *f*, àlmūřù *f*: don't go out after ~ kâř kù fìta bāyan àlmūřù.

darken *v* (*of sky*) rinè *v4*: the sky is ~ing gàrī yā rinè = gàrī yā yi baƙī.

darn *v* (*mend*) daddàgē *v4* ⟨dàddagà⟩ *f*: ~ socks daddàgē hūdàř sàfā.

dash¹ *v* zàɓuřà *v3*; in a ~ à zàɓùře, à gùje: he ~ed out of the house yā fìta dàgà gidā à zàɓùře = yā zàɓuřà yā fìta dàgà gidā; make a ~ for safety yi ta kânsà; ~ off to (*a place*) gařzàyā *v1*: she ~ed off to the store before it closed tā gařzàyā kàntì kàfìn à rufè.

dash² *n* (*Gram.*) àlāmàř fid dà mà'ànā *f*.

dash³ *n* (*small gift, tip*) dāshì *m*, [F] kàdô *m*.

data *n* bàyànai *p*.

date *n* a. (*time*) kwānan watà *m*, rānā *f*: the letter has no ~ on it wàsīƙàř bâ ta dà kwānan watà; set a ~ sâ rānā; what is the ~ today? yâu nawà gà watà? ~ of

birth rānař haihùwā *f;* out-of-~ na dâ;
up-to-~ na yànzu ; to ~ hař yànzu = hař
yà zuwā̀ yâu. b. (*meeting between man &*
*woman*) zàncē *m*, hīřa *f*, [F] řàndêbû *m:*
I have a ~ tonight zā ni zàncē yâu dà
dare.

date *n* (*fruit or palm*) dàbīnồ *m* ⟨ai⟩:
~s are a staple food for desert dwellers
dàbīnồ bàbban àbincin mazàunā hàmādā̀
nē; desert ~ (*fruit or tree*) aduwā̀ *f* ⟨oCi⟩.

daub *v, see* dab.

daughter *n* a. (*a female child*) 'yā̀ màcè *f,*
dìyā *f* ⟨'yammātā⟩: she gave birth to a ~
tā hàifi 'yā màcè; all his ~s go to school
duk 'yā̀'yānsà mātā sunā̀ makařantā. b.
(*one's own*) 'yā *f* ⟨'yā̀'yā⟩: his ~ is
named Ladi sūnan 'yařsà Lādì; his ~ is
in school 'yařsà tanā̀ makařantā; step~
agōlìyā *m* ⟨ai⟩.

daughter-in-law *n* sàràkuwā *f* ⟨sùrùkai⟩,
(*term of addr.*) 'yā *f.*

dawdle *v* shantàkē *v4,* yi jìnkirī *m.*

dawn 1. *n* àssàlātù *m,* wāyèwař gàrī *f,*
àlfijìř *m,* àsùbâ *f;* they get up at ~ sunā̀
tashì dà àsùbâ.
2. *v:* the day has ~ed gàrī yā wāyè.

day *n* a. rānā *f* ⟨rānàikū⟩ (*in the geni-*
*tive,* rānař *often contracts to* ran): market ~ rānař kàsuwā = ran kàsuwā; ~ before yesterday shēkaranjiyà *f;* 2 ~s hence
jībi *f;* 3 ~s hence gātā *f;* 4 ~s hence
città *f;* the next, following ~ kàshêgàrī
/ wàshêgàrī *f;* ~ before an Islamic holiday
jàjibêřè *m;* every ~ kōwàcè rānā = kullum; twice a ~ sàu biyu à rānā; all ~
long gàbā̀ ɗayan rānā̀ř; ~ and night darē
dà rānā: they are as different as ~ and
night bambancìnsù kàmař darē dà rānā;
on that ~ ràn nan; some ~, one ~, one
of these ~s wata rānā; in the olden ~s à
(zāmànin) dâ. b. (*adverbial uses*): during
the ~ dà rāna *adv:* I can't come during
the ~ bà zân iyà zuwā̀ dà rāna ba; ~
and night (*without interruption*) bâ darē
bâ rānā: the machines work ~ and night
injunā̀ nā̀ aikì bâ darē bâ rānā; ~ by ~
rānā-rānā *adv.* c. (*12-hour period*) yinī /
wunī *m:* they were studying all ~ long sun
yinì sunā̀ kā̀řātū. d. (*24-hour period*)
kwānā *m* ⟨aki⟩: how many ~s did you
spend in Jos? kwānā nawà ka yi à Jàs?
how many ~s will you be there? kwānankà
nawà à can? ~ after ~ kwānā dà kwànàkī;
the other ~ (*past*) kwānan bāya; a few
~s ago kwànàkin bāya; 4 ~s ago kwānā
huɗu dà sukà wucè. e. (*periods of the*
~ *corresponding to prayer times*): (*dawn*)

àsùbā *f;* (*ca. 2 pm*) àzahàř *f;* (*ca. 4-5 pm*)
là'asàř *f;* (*dusk*) màgàřibā / màngàřibā̀
*f,* àlmūřû *f;* (*nightfall*) lìshā *f.*

daybreak *n* wāyèwař gàrī *f.*

daydream *n* mafařkī *m* ⟨ai⟩.

daylight *n:* let's work while there is still ~
mù yi aikì tun gàrī yanā̀ ganī; in broad
~ dà rāna ƙirī-ƙirì.

daytime *adv:* in the ~ dà rāna *adv.*

dazed, be *v* (*confused*) yi dīmuwā *f,* kiɗìmē
*v4.*

dazzle *v* kashè wà idò, ɗaukà wà idò: I
was ~d by the sunlight hasken rānā yā
kashè minì idò; something dazzling àbù
mài ɗaukàř idò.

DDT *n* hōdàř ƙwàrī *m,* [F] gàrin ayyā *m.*

dead 1. *adj* à màce *adv,* màtaccē *adj;* a ~
person mamàcī *m,* (*corpse*) gāwā *f* ⟨aki²⟩;
be ~ (*of people*) ràsu *v7, see* die; his wife
is ~ màtařsà tā ràsu; be ~ (*of things*)
mutù *v3b:* the tree is ~ bishiyà̀ tā mutù;
(*fig.*) over my ~ body! sai bāyan râinā!
2. *adv:* stop ~ tsayà̀ cik; be ~ tired gàji
tiƙis = gàji tilis; be ~ set against sth.
ƙi w.a. sam-sam: I'm ~ set against going
there nā̀ ƙi sam-sam ìn jē can.
3. *n:* in the ~ of the night dà tsakař darē
= dà dàddare.

dead-end *n* (*street*) bâ mafitā *m.*

deadline *n* wa'àdī *m:* give so. a ~ bâ
w. wa'àdī = ƙayyàdè wà lōkàcī; the ~
given us has passed lōkàcìn dà akà bā mù
yā cìka.

deadly *adj* (*mài*) kisà *m:* a ~ disease cùtā
mài kisà.

deaf *adj* (*psn.*) kurmā *n* ⟨a-e⟩: he is quite ~
kurmā nḕ sōsai; become ~ kurùmcē *v4;*
make so. ~ kurùmtā *v1,* mai dà w. kurmā;
(*fig.*) turn a ~ ear on so. yi wà kûnnen
uwař shègū = yi bîřis dà w. = yi banzā
dà w.

deafen *v* (*temporarily*) kashè wà kûnnē: a
~ing noise ƙārā mài kashè kûnnē.

deaf-mute *n* bēbē *m* ⟨aye⟩, summùn-
bukumùn *n:* the child has been a ~ since
birth tun haihùwā yārồn bēbē nè̀.

deal 1. *v* a. (*relate to*) yi huldà̀ *f,* yi
mà'āmalà̀ *f:* we ~ only with him and no
one else bà mā̀ huldà̀ dà kōwā sai shī
kaɗai; he doesn't know how to ~ with
the problem bài san yàddà zâi yi dà
màtsalàř ba. b. (*trade*) yi cìnikī *m:* he
~s in hides and skins yanā̀ cìnikin ƙirgì
dà fātā̀. c. (*cards*) rabà kātì.
2. *n* a. (*esp. business*) huldà̀ *f,* mà'āmalà̀ *f.*
b. (*agreement*) yàřjējēnìyā *f.* c. (*buying*

& *selling*) cìnikī *m;* a good ~ (*bargain*) gàrā6āsā *f.*

dealer *n* dìllālī *m* ⟨ai⟩, dīlā *m:* a car ~ dìllālìn mōtōcī.

dealership *n* dillancī *m:* he has a ~ to sell sugar yā sāmi dillancìn sai dà sukàrī.

dealings *n* huldā *f,* mà'āmalā *f.*

dear 1. *adj* a. (*close, intimate*) na ƙwařai: he is a ~ friend shī àbōkī nē na ƙwařai. b. (*in letters*): D. Sir rànkà-yà-dadē; D. Musa zuwā gà Mūsā. c. (*costly*) (mài) tsādā *f.*
2. *excl:* oh ~! (*slight regret*) kâi! = wàyyō! = àyyā! = wàyyō Allàh! = kash! oh ~, I don't have any time right now kash, ai kō bâ ni dà lōkàcī yànzu.

death *n* a. mutuwā *f;* (*euphem.*) ràsuwā *f,* rashī *m,* ajàlī *m:* there's been a ~ in his family an yi masà ràsuwā = an yi rashī à gidansà; he is near ~ ajàlinsà yā kusa matsōwā; she preceded him in ~ tā rigā shì gidan gàskiyā; a sudden ~ mutuwāř fuji'à; unto ~ hař lāhiřà; we had a narrow escape from ~ saurā kàɗan mù mutù. b. (*killing*) kisā *m:* ~ penalty hukuncìn kisā; he was sentenced to ~ an yankè masà hukuncìn kisā; a ~ threat bàràzanař kisàn kâi.

death rattle *n* kākārìn mutuwā *m.*

death'shead *n* ƙwàřàngwal *m.*

debate 1. *n* (*formal*) mùhāwařā / màhāwařā *f;* (*back & forth without resolution*) yi cācař bàkī.
2. *v* a. (*argue formally*) yi mùhāwařā *f.* b. (*be indecisive*) yi wàswāsī *m:* I'm debating whether to go or not inā wàswāsìn kō ìn tàfi kō ìn zaunā.

debit *n* 1. bāshī *m* ⟨uka²⟩.
2. *v:* please ~ my account sai à dībā dàgà cikin kuɗīnā.

debt *n* (*of money*) bāshī *m* ⟨uka²⟩: be in ~ ci bāshī; incur a ~ kàr6i bāshī = ɗauki bāshī; be deep in ~ nā cikin ɗimbin bāshī = ci bāshī hař yà wuyà; the national ~ bāshìn ƙasā; write off a ~ sōkè bāshī.

debtor *n* mài cîn bāshī (à ka) *m.*

decadence *n* lālātā *f,* lālācêwā *f.*

decapitate *v* fillè kâi *v4.*

decay *v* a. (*of teeth, building, food*) ru6è *v4;* it is in a ~ed state à rù6e yakè. b. (*usu. moral, cultural*) lālācè *v4.*

deceased *n* mamàcī *m;* the recently ~ chief sarkī marìgàyī.

deceit *n* a. rūdī *m,* cūtā *f.* b. (*fraudulent means*) zàmba *f,* yàudarā *f.* c. (*hoax*) girī *m.*

deceitful *adj* (*full of deceit*) mài rūdī *m,* mài yàudarā *f;* (*being evasive, indirect*) mài wùnī-wunī *idph.* mài ƙùmbìyà-ƙumbiyā *idph.*

deceive *v* a. (*mislead*) rūɗā *v2,* cūtā *v2:* she ~d her husband tā rūɗi màigidantà. b. (*Law, by fraudulent means*) yàudarā *v2,* zàmbatā *v2.*

December *n* Dìsambā *m.*

decency *n* nàgàřtā *f,* hālī nagàri *m,* mutuncī *m,* kàmālā *f.*

decent *adj* nagàri *m,* tagàri *f* ⟨nagàrgàrū⟩, (mài) kàmālā *f:* he is a ~ person nagàri nē = mài nàgàřtā nē = mùtûm nē mài kàmālā.

deception *n,* see deceit.

deceptive *adj* mài rūdī *m,* mài yàudarā *f.*

decide *v* yankè shāwařā, shāwàřtā *v1,* tsai dà màganà: they have ~d to go sun yankè shāwařař tàfiyà = sun shāwàřtā zā sù tàfi; you yourself must ~ kai dà kânkà sai kà yankè shāwařā; it's up to you to ~ sai àbìn dà ka cē.

decision *n* shāwařā *f* ⟨shāwàřwařī⟩: the ~ is up to you shāwařā tanà gàre kà; come to a mutual ~ daidàità shāwařā; make, reach a definite ~ yankè shāwařā = tsai dà shāwařā = tsayà kân shāwařā.

declaration *n* bayyànāwā *f.*

declare *v:* ~ assets fàdi àbìn dà akē màllakā; ~ goods at customs nūnā wà 'yan kwastàn kāyā; ~ independence bayyànà 'yancìn kâi; ~ a state of emergency kafà dōkā-tà-6àcì; ~ war yankè shāwařař yāƙī.

decline 1. *v* a. (*weaken*) ràunanà *v3:* his health ~d rapidly yā ràunanà sōsai. b. (*refuse*): he ~d the invitation to the party bài amsà gayyař lìyāfàř ba.
2. *n* ràunanā *f:* the ~ of the Roman empire ràunanař daulàř Rûm.

decode *v* warwàrē *v4.*

decorate *v* yi wà adō *m.*

decoration *n* kāyan adō *m;* (*esp. interior*) kāyan ālātù *m.*

decrease 1. *v* a. (*lessen*) ragè *v4,* ràgu *v7:* ~ wages, the volume on the radio ragè àlbâshī, ƙarař řēdiyò; the price of oil has ~d in the last few years fàřāshìn màn fētùř yā ràgu cikin 'yan shèkàrun nàn. b. (*diminish*) tsagàità *v1.*
2. *n* ragī *m.*

decree 1. *n* (*Mil.*) dōkā *f* ⟨oCi⟩.
2. *v* kafà dōkā.

decrepit *adj* kwàràrrà6a66ē *adj:* a ~ old car kwàràrrà6a66iyař mōtā = garwař mōtā.

dedicate v sadaukař (dà) v5: I ~ this book
to... nā sadaukař dà wannàn littāfī
gà....

dedication n (in book) sadaukářwā f.

deduct v zāmē v4, cirè v4, dībầ v2*: I will
~ ₦10 from your salary zân dèbi naiřā
gōmà dàgà cikin àlbâshinkà.

deduction n (from wages of money owed)
zāmiyā f, (from wages by government)
dèbe-dèbe p.

deed n aikì m ⟨ayyukầ⟩: a good ~ aikìn
kiřkì = àbin kiřkì; you've done him a
good ~ kā yi masà aikìn kiřkì; a bad,
evil ~ mūgùn àbù.

deep adj a. (of dimension) (mài) zurfī m:
dig a ~ pit hakầ rāmì mài zurfī; how
~ is the pit? zurfin rāmì kafà nawà nē?
which is the ~est ocean in the world? wàcè
tèku cè mafì zurfī cikin dūniyầ? very
~ zùzzurfā adj. b. (fig. uses): a ~ breath
dōgon numfāshī = gwauron numfāshī; a
~ sigh àjiyầř zūcìyà; ~ sleep barcī
mài nauyī = dōgòn barcī; a ~ thinker
mài zurfin tùnầnī; a ~ voice bàbbař
muryầ; be ~ in thought yi zùgum idph; ~
in debt cikin ɗimbin bāshì. c. (of colors) (mài) cīzầwā: ~ red jā jầ-wuř = jā
mài cīzầwā; ~ blue, green shūdì, kōřè
shař.

deepen v zurfàfā v1.

deer n, see gazelle.

defame v 6ātà sūnan w., yi wà jàmhūřù
m, shāfā wà kāshin kầjī.

defeat 1. v (any opponent) kā dà / kāyař
(dà) v5; (Sports) ci v0: they ~ed our team
3-1 sun ci tìm ɗinmù ukù dà ɗaya; (in
games) kasầ v1: they ~ed us by cheating
dà cūtà sukà kasầ mu.
 2. n kāyářwā f; suffer a ~ (fig.) shā kāshī.

defect[1] n a. lahànī m, lâifī m ⟨uka[2]⟩,
illầ f ⟨oCi⟩; speech ~ tsāmin bằkī m.
b. (of character) aibù / aibì m ⟨oCi⟩.

defect[2] v yi gudùn hijiřā m.

defective adj: ~ goods kāyā dāmējì m,
kāyan 6āřnā: this watch is ~ because
it has no mainspring àgōgon nàn nằ dà
dāmējì don bâ shi dà hanjī.

defend v (town, home) tsarè v4; (self) kārè
kâi v4.

defendant n (Law) wândà akè kārā: the ~
has not been found guilty bà à sàmi wândà
akè kārařsà dà lâifī ba.

defender n (Sport) mài tsàron gidā m.

defense n a. tsārō m, kāriyā f: national ~
tsàron kasā; self-~ tsàron kâi = kārè
kâi. b. (Sport) tsàron gidā m.

deference n (esp. name avoidance) àlkunyà
f: Hausa women do not utter their hus-
bands' names out of ~ to them mātan
Hàusầwā bā sầ ambaton sūnan màigidā
sabòdà àlkunyà; he didn't show any ~
at all to me kō àlkunyà bài yi minì ba.

defiance n kàngarầ f.

defiant adj kàngàrarrē adj; be ~ kàngarà
v3.

deficient adj: mentally ~ person (retarded)
gaulā n ⟨aye⟩.

deficiency n a. (lack) karancī m. b. (shortcoming) cīkàs m.

deficit n kāsầwař kuɗī f; trade ~ gī6ìn
cìnikī m.

defile v kazantař (dà) v5, (with excrement)
kāsàyē v4.

define v bayyànà mà'ànā, bā dà mà'ànā:
please ~ this word for me don Allàh
bàyyànà mîn mà'ànař wannàn kalmầ.

definitely adv lallē, bâ shakkầ, tabbàs,
hầkīkầ / hàkīkầ, lâbuddà adv: we ~
saw him on the road hầkīkầ mun gan shì
à hanyầ; it is ~ a mistake bâ shakkầ
kuskurè nē.

definition n mà'ànā f ⟨oCi⟩.

deflate v (a tire, balloon) sacè v4.

deflect v kārè v4: they ~ed the shots aimed
at the president sun kārè hařbìn dà akà
yi wà shùgàban kasā.

deform v nakàsā v1: the blow has ~ed his
foot bugùn yā nakàsā masà kafầ.

deformed adj nakàsasshē adj; (psn.)
mùsākī m ⟨ai⟩.

deformity n nàkasầ f, (esp. resulting from
illness) tàwayầ f.

defraud v yi wà zàmba f, zàmbatầ v2,
hằ'intà v2: he was jailed for ~ing the
bank an ɗaurè shi sabòdà hằ'intař
bankìn dà ya yi.

defy v a. (so.) kangàrē wà v4: the students
defied the police dàlìbai sun kangàrē wà
'yan sàndā. b. (orders) ki bî: they defied the orders given them sun ki bîn
ùmàřnîn dà akà bā sù.
 2. v (challenge) kàlùbàlantầ v2: I ~ you
to do better nā kầlùbàlàncē kà dà kà yi
àbîn dà ya fi hakà.

degenerate v 6albàlcē v4, lālàcē v4: his
daughter has ~d 'yařsà tā 6al6àlcē.

degrade v yi wà kankancì m, wulàkantař
(dà) v5, kankantař (dà) v5, kaskantař
(dà) v5: ~ onself kankàntà kâi =
kaskàntà kâi.

degree[1] n (academic) dìgìřī m, [F]
dìfìlâm m: Bachelor's ~ dìgìřī na

farkō; Master's ~ dìgìřî na biyu; honors ~ dìgìřîn yàbō; his ~ is from Oxford dìgìřînsà na Oxford nē.

degree² n (of temperature): it is 100 ~s today yâu zāfî yā kai dàrī.

dejection n baṛin cikî m, sanyin jìkī m.

delay 1. v jinkìrtā v1, jinkirtař (dà) v5, shirīrītař (dà) v5, dākatař (dà) v5: we will ~ the meeting until he comes zā mù jinkìrtà tằrôn sai yā zō; they ~ed the train at the station an jinkirtar dà jirgîn à tashàř.
2. n jìnkirī m, màkarà f: a 2-hour ~ jìnkirin awà biyu; without ~ bâ jìnkirī = kâi tsàye.

deleb-palm n giginyà f (u); frond of ~ karî m; ~ shoots mùrūcī m.

delegate n wàkìlî m (ai).

delegation n wàkìlai p.

delete v (sth. written) gōgè v4, shāfè v4: several words were ~d from the paragraph an gōgè wasu kalmōmī dàgà cikin sakìn lāyì.

deliberate 1. v yi shāwařà f: they ~d all through the night sun kwàna sunà ta shāwařà.
2. adj a. (intentional) dà niyyà, dà gàngan: tell a ~ lie yi ḳaryā dà gàngan. b. (with deliberateness) dà tsànākī, à tsànàke adv: speak in a ~ manner yi màganà dà tsànākī.

deliberately adv dà niyyà: I said what I did ~ dà niyyà na fàɗi màganà; (with neg. purpose) dà gàngan adv: they insulted me ~ dà gàngan sukà zằge nì; he ~ disobeyed the law yā kḕtà dōkà dà gàngan; I ~ made it look like a mistake dà gàngan na mai dà shī yà zama kàmař kuskurè.

deliberation n (care) tsànākī m.

delicacy n kāyan marmarī m, lāsà f.

delicious adj (mài) dāɗī m.

delight n muřnà f: I was ~ed by his coming nā yi muřnà dà zuwànsà.

delinquent n, see juvenile.

delirious adj: be ~ (talk incoherently) yi sàmbàtū m; (be dazed, half-conscious) yi màgàgī m.

deliver v a. (a package, message) kai v*, isař (dà) v5. b. (a speech) yi v0, gabātař (dà) v5; (a public lecture) ḳaddamař (dà) v5. c. (a baby by its mother) sàuka v3; she is due to ~ this month watàntà nē. d. (a baby from its mother) saukař (dà) v5: who ~ed this baby? wà ya saukař dà uwař jàrīrìn?

deliverance n (Relig.) cḕtō m.

delivery room n (in hospital) ɗākìn haihùwā m.

demand 1. v a. (require) bùkātà v2: this work ~s great skill aikìn nân nà bùkātař ḳwarèwā. b. (ask for) nēmà v2 (nēmā): ~ one's rights nēmi hakkî.
2. n (need) bùkātà f (u): there is a great ~ for teachers in Nigeria àkwai tsananin bùkātař màlàmai à Nìjḕřiyà.

demean v wulàḳàntā v1, mūzàntā v1.

democracy n dìmòkùřàɗiyyà f.

demolish v rūsà v1, rūshḕ v4: the rebels ~ed the bridge 'yan tāwāyè sun rūshè gadà.

demon n (devil) shàiɗân m, ìbìlîs m; (evil spirit) àljàn m (u), iskà f (oCi).

demonstrate v a. (show) gwadà v1, nūnà v1, yi nūnî m. b. (Pol., protest) yi zàngà-zangà f: they ~d because of inadequate housing sun yi zàngà-zangà sabòdà ḳarancin wuràren kwānā.

demonstration n a. (show) nūnî m, gwajî m. b. (esp. Pol.) zàngà-zangà f, tằřzōmā f; (violent) tāshìn hankàlī m; a peaceful ~ tằřzōmā cikin lùmānà.

demonstrative n (Gram.) manùnî m.

demonstrator n mài zàngà-zangà n.

demoralize v a. (ruin one's character) sangařtař (dà) v5. b. be ~d (discouraged): the army was ~d gwìwař sōjà tā yi sanyī.

demote v ragè wà mùḳāmî, karyà wà mùḳāmî.

den n (lair) kōgō m, kùřfī m.

denial n a. musù m, ìnkārî m. b. (asceticism) zuhudù m.

denounce v yi tiř dà, yi Allàh-wadai dà.

dense adj a. (thick): ~ smoke hayāḳī mài yawà; a ~ forest kurmì mài duhù. ~ undergrowth sàrḳaḳḳiyà f. b. (not smart), see stupid.

dent 1. v kōmàdā / mōkàdā v1: ~ a fender kōmàdà mutàgadî; be ~ed kōmàdḕ v4, lōtsè v4.
2. n kōmàdà f: fix a ~ tā dà kōmàdā.

dental adj na haḳōrī m.

dentist n likitàn haḳōrā n.

deny v musà / musàntā v1, yi ìnkārî m: he will ~ whatever you say zâi musà duk àbîn da ka cễ; he denied the allegations made against him yā musàntà zàrgîn dà akà yi masà.

depart v tāshì v3b: the train ~s in 10 minutes jirgîn zâi tāshì bāyan mintì gōmà.

**department** n a. (admin.) ma'aikatā f. b. (at university) sāshè / sāshì m ⟨Ca⟩: D. of African Languages Sāshèn Harsunàn Afiřkà.

**departure** n tāshì m.

**dependable** adj àmìntaccē adj.

**dependence** n (Econ.) dồgarā f, dồgarō m, tà'àllakā f: economic ~ tà'àllakàř tattalin ařzìkī.

**dependent** 1. n (esp. one's family) ìyālì m.
2. adj (mài) dồgarā f; she is ~ on her children tanā dồgarā dà 'yā'yantà = 'yā'yantà sū nè gātantà.

**depend on** v dồgarā dà v3, dàngantà dà v3, tà'àllakà dà v3: I'm ~ing on you inā dồgarā dà kai; don't ~ on anyone else except him kadà kà dànganà dà kōwā sai shī; the country's progress ~s on oil ràyuwař ƙasâř tā tà'àllakà dà mâi; that all ~s on the circumstances wannàn sai àbîn dà hālī ya yi = wannàn yā dàngantà dà hālìn dà akè ciki.

**deport** v kōrè dàgà ƙasā.

**depose** v tūɓè v4, tumɓùkē v4, hamɓàrē v4, fid dà / fitař (dà) v5.

**deposit** 1. v (money in bank) zubà v1.
2. n (for services in advance) àdìbâs m, [F] àbàns f: I gave him a ~ of ₦100 nā bā shì àdìbâs na naiřà ɗàrī.

**depot** n daffồ m, [F] dìpô m.

**depress** v (press down) dannè v4.

**depressed** adj (emotional): I am feeling ~ râinā à ɓàce yakè; I'm feeling ~ about my situation inā baƙin cikìn hālin dà nakè ciki; look ~ yi jàgàlam idph.

**depression** n a. (in ground) kwarì m ⟨uka²⟩. b. (emotional) baƙin cikî m. c. (Econ.) tàwayař tattalin ařzìkī f.

**deprivation** n tàgàyyařà f.

**deprive** v hanà v1: they ~d him of food and water sun hanà shi ruwā dà àbinci; ~ so. of his rights tauyè hakkìn w.

**depth** n zurfī m.

**deputy** n a. wàkīlì m ⟨ai⟩; make so. a ~ yi wà wakilcì m; ~ police officer (divisional) dīpì'ồ m. b. (Relig.) nā'ìbì m ⟨ai⟩.

**derail** v gōcè v4: the train ~ed jirgī yā gōcè dàgà kân dōgō.

**deride** v yi wà ba'à f, ba'àntā v1, yi wà jàfā'ì m.

**derision** n ba'à f, jàfā'ì m.

**derive** v (Gram.) ƙirƙirō v6.

**descend** v a. (slope downward) gangàrā v1 ⟨gangarè⟩: the road ~s from this point hanyàř nà gangarè à nân; the cattle ~ed into the stream to drink shānū sun

gangàrā ràfī sù shā ruwā. b. (from above) sàuka v3: he ~d the stairs yā sàuka ta matākalā.

**descendants** n zùřiyà f.

**descent** n a. (of slope) gangarè m. b. (common) jinī m, tsatsồ m: they are of the same ~ jininsù ɗaya = tsatsònsù ɗaya; ~ group zùřiyà f.

**describe** v a. (explain) bayyànā v1: she ~d what her trip was like tā bayyànà yâddà tàfiyàřtà ta kasàncē. b. (tell about appearance of so., sth.) siffàntā v1: he ~d the criminal as having a long beard yā siffàntà mài lâifîn dà dōgon gēmù. c. (give directions or illustration) kwàtàntā v1, yi wà kwàtàncē m: I ~d the way to get there to him nā yi masà kwàtàncen hanyàř zuwā cân.

**description** n siffà / sifà f⟨oCi⟩: he gave them a ~ of her yā bā sù siffàřtà; (esp. directions to a place) kwàtàncē m; (fig.) be beyond ~ wucè mìsālì, wucè kīmà.

**desert**[1] n hàmādā f: most of Mauritania is ~ yawancin Mòřîtāniyà hàmādà cē; cross the ~ by camel rātsà hàmādà dà ràƙumī; encroachment of the ~ kwarārồwař hàmādà.

**desert**[2] v a. (abandon so.) yā dà / yař (dà) v5: all his friends ~ed him àbồkansà duk sun yāshē shì. b. (from authority) gudù dàgà v3b: ~ the army gudù dàgà sōjà.

**deserted** adj a. (structure, building) kangō m ⟨aye⟩: this building is ~ ginìn nân kangō nè. b. (settlement, area) kufai m: a ~ village kufan ƙauyè; the village is ~ ƙauyèn bâ kōwā.

**deserve** v càncantà v2: they ~ praise sun càncànci yàbō = yā càncantà à yàbē sù; ~ to be ci v0, càncantà v3 (+ impers. 3rd pers. subj pro): they ~ to be praised yā ci à yàbē sù = yā càncantà à yi musù yàbō.

**desiccated, be(come)** v ƙèƙasà v3, ƙèƙashē v4: the land became ~ hundreds of years ago ƙasâř tā ƙèƙasà tun shèkarà àřu-àřu.

**design** 1. v a. (plan) tsārā v1, shiryà v1 ⟨shirì⟩: this dictionary is ~ed especially for beginners an shiryà wannàn ƙāmùs mùsammàn don 'yan kồyō. b. (make orderly): a well-~ed building ginì mài fasàlī; it is well ~ed yanā dà kyân fasàlī. c. (a building, clothing) zānà v1.
2. n (drawing, pattern) zànè m ⟨e²⟩: interesting ~s zànè-zànè màsu ƙàwatàřwā; a flower ~ mài fùrē; by ~ (on purpose) à sàne adv, dà gàngan adv: it was done by

designer 66 develop

~ an yī shì à sàne.

**designer** n mài zānē m.

**desire** 1. v sō v0, yi shà'awã f; (strongly) yi ƙwàdàyī m: we got what we most ~d mun sàmi àbīn dà mukà fi sō dukà.
2. n a. sô m, shà'awã f; a keen ~ kāfīɍin sō; I have no ~ to travel any more bā nà shà'awàɍ sākè tàfiyà; (strong) kwàdàyī m, ƙāwã / ƙwāwã f; (esp. for delicacies) marmarī m; (sexual) sôn mātà m, jàɍabã f ⟨u⟩. b. (goal) mùɍādì m, bùkātã f ⟨u⟩.

**desist** v dainà v1.

**desk** n (office) tēbùɍ m ⟨oCi⟩, [F] bùɍô m: school ~ tēbùɍin ɍùbùtū.

**despair** 1. v fid dà râi, fid dà tsàmmānì, yankè ƙàunā: he ~ed of getting the position yā fid dà râi dàgà sāmùn mùƙāmìn.
2. n: he was in ~ yā rasà àbīn dà zâi yi = bài san indà zâi sâ kânsà ba.

**desperate** adj: he is in a ~ situation bā shi dà ta yî; look for sth. ~ly nēmi w.a. idò rûfe = nēmi w.a. ruwā à jàllō.

**despise** v rainà / rēnã v1: they ~ him because of his cowardice sunà rainà shi sabôdà dà rākìnsà.

**despite** conj duk dà conj: ~ the rain, we arrived on time duk dà ruwā, mun isō cikin lōkàcī.

**despondent** adj: she is ~ rântà à ɓàce yakè.

**dessert** n kāyan zāƙī m.

**destination** n: what is your ~? ìnā zâ ka?

**destined, be** v ƙaddàɍā wà v1: he was ~ to die abroad an ƙaddàɍā masà cikàwā à ƙasàshen wàje.

**destiny** n a. (fate) ƙaddàɍã f, ràbō m: he accepts his ~ yā yàɍda dà ƙaddàɍàɍsà. b. (ultimate end, position) makōmā f: each country is free to decide its own ~ kōwàcè ƙasā tanà dà 'yancìn yankè shāwaɍàɍ makōmàɍtà.

**destitute** adj (penniless) mìskīnì m ⟨ai⟩, fàƙīrì m ⟨ai⟩; (pejor.) matsìyàcī m, tàntīɍì m ⟨ai⟩; (~ & disabled) gàjìyayyē adj; become ~ tsìyàcē v4.

**destroy** v a. (esp. people, population) halàkā v1, halakàɍ (dà) v5: he gave orders to ~ the entire town yā bā dà ùmàɍnī à halàkà gàrīn dukà; ~ the human race halakàɍ dà bìl Adamà; be ~ed halàkà v3. b. (sth.) ɓatà v1, lālàtà v1; (make disintegrate) rūsà v1, rūsàɍ (dà) v5, ɍagaɍgàzā / ɍuguɍgùzā v1: the rain ~ed the wall ruwā yā rūsàɍ dà gānuwā; the town was totally ~ed an ruguɍgùzà gàrin gàbā ɗaya.

**destruction** n hàlakã f: the ~ of the crops was a serious loss hàlakàɍ àmfànin gōnā bàbbaɍ hàsāɍã cē.

**detach** v ɓallè v4; ~ sth. from kwancè v4.

**detail** n: in great ~ fillā-fillā idph, dallā-dallā idph: they give the news in great ~ sunà bā dà làbàɍū fillā-fillā; report sth. in great ~ bā dà cìkakken bàyānì.

**detailed** adj cìkakkē adj: he gave the police a ~ report of the accident yā bā 'yan sàndā cìkakken ɍàhōtòn hadàɍī.

**detain** v a. (delay) tsai dà / tsayaɍ (dà) v5: I won't ~ you any longer bà zân ƙārà tsai dà kai ba. b. (put in detention) tsarè v4: he has been ~ed by the police 'yan sàndā sun tsarè shi = yanà (tsàre à) hannun 'yan sàndā.

**detective** n ɗan sàndan ciki m.

**detention** n a. (Pol.) tsarì m; in ~ à tsàre adv. b. (Law, awaiting trial) gidan waƙàfī m: he has been put in ~ an sâ shi à gidan waƙàfī.

**detergent** n ōmō m.

**deteriorate** v taɓarɓàrē v4, lālàcē v4: the economy has ~d aɍzìkin ƙasā yā taɓarɓàrē.

**determination** n a. (perseverance) àniyã / niyyã f, ƙwàzō m, himmã f: he shows great ~ in his studies yanà mai dà himmã wajen kàɍàtunsà. b. (resolve, courage) ƙarfin zūcìyã m.

**determined, be** v ƙùdùri àniyã / niyyã, tsayà tsayìn dakà, (fig.) làshi takòbī: he was ~ to stop smoking yā ƙùdùri àniyàɍ dainà shân tābà; the government is ~ to combat unemployment gwamnatì tā làshi takòbin yà̀ƙaɍ rashìn aikìn yî; in a ~ way à tsàitsàye adv.

**detest** v tsànā v2, yi ƙyàmā f: I ~ cockroaches nā tsàni kyànkyasò = inà ƙyàmaɍ kyànkyasò.

**detonate** v fasà v1, sàkā v2: ~ explosives a bomb fasà nàkiyã, sàki bâm.

**detour** n ràtsē m ⟨e²⟩, kèwàyē m: there are ~s because of road repairs àkwai ràtse-ràtse à hanyà sabôdà gyārà; make a ~ ràtsè hanyà = kēwàyè hanyà.

**devalue** v (currency) ragè daɍajàɍ kuɗī: the naira has been ~d an ragè daɍajàɍ naiɍã; (goods) karyà kadàɍī.

**develop** 1. vt a. (Econ.) rāyà v1, ciyaɍ dà w.a. gàba, bunƙàsā v1: we want to ~ our town munà sô mù ciyaɍ dà gàrinmù gàba; the government is determined to ~ the rural areas gwamnatìn tā làshi takòbī sai tā rāyà kàrkarā. b. (increase) ƙārà

*v1:* ~ one's mind ƙàrà zurfin tùnằnī.
c. (*film*) wankè hồtō.
2. *vi* bùnƙàsà *v3,* hàɓakà *v3;* (*grow fully*) gằwùr̃tà *v3,* ƙằsaità *v3.*

**developing** *adj* (mài) tāsôwā: ~ countries ƙasằshē màsu tāsôwā.

**development** *n* a. (*Econ.*) rāyà ƙasā *m,* cî-gàba *m:* ~ projects ayyukàn rāyà ƙasà; rural, urban ~ rāyà kàrkarā, bir̃ằnē. b. (*progress*) cî-gàba *m:* there has been a lot of ~ in some countries an sằmi cî-gàba mài yawầ à waɗansu ƙasằshē. c. (*Lit.*): ~ of a theme wàr̃war̃ằr̃ jīgồ.

**deviate** *v* (*differ from*) sāɓằ dà *v1;* (*esp. Relig.*) fanɗàr̃ē *v4,* yi bidi'ằ *f:* ~ from the path of religion fanɗàr̃ē dàgà tafarkìn àddīnì.

**Devil** *n* Shàiɗān *m,* Ìbìlîs *m;* (*fig.*) between the ~ and the deep blue sea gàba kūrā, bāya sìyākī.

**devilishly** *adv* (mài) kāfìr̃in X: ~ difficult, clever mài kāfìr̃in wùyā, wằyō.

**devious** *adj* na cùƙù-cuƙū: he is a ~ person ɗan cùƙù-cuƙū nề; he got his job through ~ means yā sằmi mùƙāmìnsà ta hanyàr̃ cùƙù-cuƙū.

**devise** *v:* ~ a plan gānō hanyầ.

**devour** *v* (*eat voraciously*) lāmùshē *v4,* lanƙwàmē *v4.*

**devote** *v:* ~one's energy to dùƙufà *v3,* dàgè *v4:* we ~d all our time to our studies mun dùƙufà à kân kàr̃ằtunmù.

**devotion** *n* sô *m.*

**devotions** *n* (*obligatory daily prayers*) sallằ *f* ⟨oCi⟩; (*invocations*) àddu'ằ *f* ⟨oCi⟩.

**dew** *n* rāɓā *f:* the grass was covered with ~ rāɓā tā yi yawầ à cìyāwầ.

**diabetes** *n* cīwòn sukàr̃ī *m.*

**diabetic** *n* mài cīwòn sukàr̃ī *n.*

**diagnose** *v* gānō *v6:* they have ~d his illness as hepatitis an gānō cêwā cùtar̃sà cīwòn shāwar̃ằ cē.

**diagonally** *adv* à gìccìye *adv.*

**diagram** *n* zằnē *m* ⟨e²⟩, sūr̃ằ *f* ⟨oCi⟩.

**dial** 1. *v* (*a telephone number*) bugà lambầ *f:* please ~ this number for me don Allàh kà bugồ minì wannàn lambầ.
2. *n* (*of telephone*) fuskằ *f.*

**dialect** *n* a. (*accent, pronunciation*) karìn harshē *m.* b. (*esp. vernacular of an ethnic minority*) yâr̃ē *m,* lahajằ *f* ⟨oCi⟩: he speaks one of the southern ~s yanà màganầ dà ɗaya dàgà cikin lahajōjin mutằnen kudù. c. (*for major Hausa ~ areas, use name of town or area* + *suffix* -~ncī):

Sokoto ~ Sakkwatancī; Damagaram ~ Damagarancī.

**dialogue** *n* zàncē *m* ⟨uka⟩, tāɗî *m.*

**diamond** *n* lu'ùlu'ù *m,* daimùn *m,* [F] dēmàn *m.*

**diamonds** *n* (*in cards*) zî *m,* kằlâu *m.*

**diaphragm** *n* (*membrane*) tantānī *m.*

**diarrhea** *n* zāwồ / zāwàyī *m;* (*euphem.*) gudằwā *f.*

**dice** *n* ɗan lìdô *m,* (ɗan) dāyìs *m,* [F] (ɗan) lìdô *m:* roll the ~ kaɗè ɗan dāyìs.

**dictation** *n* shif̃tằ *f:* give, take, have a ~ bā dà, ɗauki, yi shif̃tằ.

**dictator** *n* mài mulkìn kằmā-kàryā *m.*

**dictatorship** *n* mulkìn kằmā-kàryā *m.*

**dictionary** *n* ƙāmùs *m* ⟨oCi⟩: compile a ~ tsārà ƙāmùs.

**didactic** *adj* na wa'àzī *m.*

**die** *v* a. mutù *v3b* ⟨mutuwằ⟩ *f;* (*euphem., of people*) ràsu *v7,* cikà *v1:* he ~d (*most euphem.*): yā kwàntā dāma = yā rigā mù gidan gàskiyằ = wa'àdinsà yā cìka = yā cikà kwằnàkinsà = yā tar̃af̃ dà shêkar̃ằ; ~ instantly, on the spot ràsu nan tằke; (*of an infant*) kōmằ *v1;* (*of chiefs*) ràsu *v7,* fāɗì *v3b;* (*of saints, prophets*) ƙaura *v3a,* fàku *v7.* b. ~ of kashè *v4:* they are dying of hunger (*lit.*) yunwằ zā tà kashè su, (*fig.*) sunà jîn yunwằ kàmar̃ zā tà kashè su. c. (*of plants*) būshè *v4,* shūr̃ằ *v1.* d. (*of animals*) mutù *v3b,* yi bungầ *f.* e. ~ down (*of fire, wind, dispute*) lafằ *v1,* hūcè *v4.* f. ~ out (*of customs*) shūɗè *v4:* many traditional customs are dying out àl'ằdun gar̃gājiyā dà dāmā sunà shūɗèwā.

**diesel** *n* a. (*fuel*) gâs *m,* [F] gàzwâl *m.* b. (*vehicle*) dīzàl *f,* [F] dìzâl *f.*

**differ** *v* a. (*be different*) shā bambam, bàmbantà *v1:* the words ~ in meaning kalmōmîn sun shā bambam à mà'ànā = mà'ànar̃sù tā bàmbantà = sunà dà bambancìn mà'ànā. b. (*deviate*) ~ from sāɓằ dà *v1,* yi dàbam dà: his story today ~s completely from yesterday's màganar̃sà ta yâu tā sāɓằ dà ta jiyà.

**difference** *n* a. bambancì *m* ⟨e²⟩: there's no ~ between them bâ bambancì tsà-kāninsù; understand clearly the ~ between X and Y mayyàzē tsàkānin X dà Y; it makes no ~ to me duk ɗaya gàrē nì. b. (*due to divergence*) sāɓānī *m:* even the best of friends have their ~s (*fig.*) harshè dà haƙōr̃ī sū mā sunà sāɓānī; settle one's ~s shiryà *v1:* earlier they were disagreeing but now they've settled their ~s dâ sunà sāɓānī àmmā yànzu sun shiryà.

**different** *adj* dàbam *adv*: this book is ~ from that one wannàn littāfī dàbam dà wancàn; well, that is an entirely ~ matter ai wannàn wata màtsalà cē dàbam; everyone is ~ kōwā dà hanyàřsà; (*of several things*) dàbam-dàbam, irì-irì: many ~ kinds of fish kīfāyē irì dàbam-dàbam; be ~ yi dàbam, shā bambam: this one is ~ from mine wannàn yā shā bamban dà nàwa = wannàn dàbam yakè dà nàwa.

**differential** *n* (*of car*) gìndin mōtà *m*.

**differentiate** *v* bambàntā *v1*, bambàncē *v4*, rabā *v1*, rarràbē *v4*: what ~s them? mè ya rabā su? = yàyà sukè bambàntāwā?

**difficult** *adj* a. (*of thing, situation*) (mài) wùyā *f*, (mài) wàhalà *f*, mawùyàcī *m*: this work is very ~ aikìn nân nà dà wùyā sòsai; we don't think it is so ~ bā mà ganin wùyařsà; he was put into a ~ situation an sâ shi cikin mawùyàcin hālī; be too ~ for yi wà wùyā: the test was too ~ for me jařřàbāwā tā yi minì wùyā. b. be ~ (+ *infinitive*): it is ~ to know how to deal with this dà wùyā à san yàddà zā à yi dà wannàn; it would be ~ for it to happen dà wùyā yà fàru; the ~ thing is to write all of it down àbîn dà kè dà wùyā shī nè à řubùtā dukà; the horse is ~ to catch dōkì nà dà wùyař kāmàwà; his handwriting is ~ to read řubùtunsà nà dà wùyař kařàntāwā = řubùtunsà bā yà kàřàntuwā. c. make sth. ~ wuyàtā *v1*, wahalař (dà) *v5*: lack of water makes construction ~ rashìn ruwā nà wahalař dà aikìn ginì. d. (*esp. of psn.*) (mài) wùyař halī, (mài) mawùyàcin halī: she is ~ (to get along with) tanà dà wùyař halī.

**difficulty** *n* a. wùyā *f*, wàhalà *f*: I have ~ remembering his name nakàn shā wùyař tunàwā dà sūnansà = yanà dà wàhalà ìn tunà dà sūnansà; he has ~ earning a living àbinci yā yi masà wùyā; it was only with ~ that we climbed the hill dà řyař mukà hayè tsaunìn; without ~ cikin saukī. b. (*problem*) wàhalà *f* ⟨oCi⟩, màtsalà *f* ⟨oCi⟩: the ~ is... màtsalàř ita cè...; be in extreme ~ nà cikin ùřūbař wàhalà; get out of a ~ kuɓùcē wà wàhalà = kaucè wà wàhalà; overcome a ~ shāwō kàn màtsalà: we were forced to overcome our difficulties tīlàs cē ta sâ mukà shāwō kàn matsalōlī. c. (*financial*) matsì *m*: he's having difficulties because of lack of money yanà cikin matsì sabōdà řarancin kuɗī.

**dig** *v* a. (*a hole, well*) haƙà *v1* ⟨haƙà⟩: ~ging a well is hard work haƙàn rījìyā jan aikì

nè. b. (*ground*): ~ up ground for planting yi kàřtū *m*. c. (*in farming & harvesting, use specific verbs for specific plants*): ~ up (*weeds*) nōmè *v4*; (*low-lying crops, beans, groundnuts*) rōrā *v2* ⟨rōrō⟩; (*groundnuts*) fàřtā *v2* ⟨fařtā⟩ *f*; (*tubers, root crops*) tōnā *v2* ⟨tōnō⟩; (*fig.*) they dug up the truth about his past an tōnà masà àsīřin ainihin asalinsà.

**digit** *n* a. (*number*) lambà *f* ⟨oCi⟩. b. (*finger, toe*) yātsà *m* ⟨yātsū⟩.

**dignified** *adj* a. (*having respect, dignity*) (mài) kàmālà *f*. b. (*having rank, prestige*) (mài) dařajà *f*, (mài) mařtabà *f*, (mài) mùřāmì *m*.

**dignitary** *n, see* functionary.

**dignity** *n* a. (*respect, humanity*) mutuncì *m*: strip so. of his ~ cī dà mutuncìn w.; lose one's ~ zub dà mutuncì; (*decency*) kàmālà *f*: he has ~ yanà dà kàmālà. b. (*prestige, rank*) mařtabà *f*.

**digress** *v* shìga dājì.

**dilapidated** *adj* zàizàyayyē *adj*: a ~ cornstalk fence zàizàyayyen dàřnī.

**dilemma** *n* hālin řàřà-nikà-yi *m*, shìga ukù *m*: I was in a ~ nà shìga hālin řàřà-nikà-yi = nā shìga ukù; a ~ tale làbāřìn wāsà řwařwalwā.

**diligence** *n* himmà *f*, řwàzō *m*.

**diligent** *adj* (mài) himmà *f*, (mài) řwàzō *m*: he is a ~ worker ma'àikàcī nè mài řwàzō; be ~ in mai dà himmà gà.

**dilly-dally** *v* shantàkè *v4*, yi nàwā *m*.

**dilute** *v* surkà *v1*, tsarmà *v1*: you should ~ the medicine with a little water kì surkà māgànîn dà ɗan ruwā.

**dim** 1. *adj*: be ~ dushè *v4*: the light, his sight was ~ haskên, ganinsà yā dushè. 2. *v* (*headlights of car*) yi dîm *m*: I ~med my lights nā yi masà dîm.

**dimension** *n* (*size*) girmà *m*: what are the ~s of the box? mēnē nè girman àkwàtìn?

**diminish** *v* ràgu *v7*: each year the amount of rainfall ~es kōwàcè shèkarà yawàn ruwan samà nà ràguwā; my funds are ~ing rapidly kuɗīnā sunà ta tàfiyà nan dà nan.

**diminutive** 1. *adj* ɗan řaramì *adj*; (*psn.*) mìtsītsì *adj* ⟨mitsī-mitsī⟩, tsigil *idph* ⟨tsigil-tsigil⟩: a ~ girl wata yàrinyà tsigil dà ita = wata 'yař řàramař yàrinyà. 2. *n* (*Gram.*) tsìgìlau *m*.

**dimwit** *n* dàřīřì *m* ⟨ai⟩.

**din** *n* hàyà-hàyà *f*, hàyàniyà *f*, řuřumà *f*.

**dinner** *n* cîn tuwō *m*, àbincin dare *m*: we eat ~ at 6 o'clock mukàn ci tuwō dà řarfè shidà; I've been invited for ~ an gàyyàcē nì cîn àbincin darē; ~ party dinà̰ f.

dip v: ~ in, into tsōmà̰ v1: she ~ped her fingers into the sauce tā tsōmà̰ yātsà̰ cikin miyà̰; ~ out (liquids, grain) dība̰ v2*.

diphtheria n mà̰ka̰rau m.

diphthong n tagwan wasàlī m.

diploma n sà̰tifikàt m, [F] dìfìlâm m.

diplomacy n dìflōmàdiyyà̰ f.

diplomat n ma'àikàcin huldâr jakādancḭ̀ m.

diplomatic adj a. (Pol.): ~ affairs har̃kàr̃ jakādancḭ̀; ~ relations huldâr̃ jakādancḭ̀. b. (tactful) (mài) sìyāsà̰ f: he was ~ in telling us the news dà sìyāsà̰ ya gayà̰ manà làbār̃in; by ~ means ta hanyàr̃ sìyāsà̰; treat so. ~ally yi wà sìyāsà̰.

dipper n (mug-like vessel) mōdā f ⟨aye⟩; (ladle) lūdàyī m ⟨luwà̰dū⟩.

direct[1] v a. (give directions to a place) yi wà kwàtàncē m: can you ~ us to the station? zā kà iyà yi manà kwàtàncen tashà̰r̃? (by guiding) nūsar̃ (dà) v5. b. (order) ùmàr̃tà̰ v2: I've been ~ed to inform you that... an ùmàr̃cē nì ìn shaidà̰ makà cêwā.... c. (manage, control) gudānar̃ (dà) v5, tafiyar̃ (dà) v5; ~ traffic bā dà hannū.

direct[2] adj (straight) mīk̃ak̃k̃ē adj, k̃ai tsàye: a ~ route hanyà̰ mīk̃ak̃k̃iyā = hanyà̰ k̃ai tsàye.

direction n a. (geographical) shiyyà̰ f: in an easterly ~ ta shiyyà̰r̃ gabàs; in which ~ did they go? ta ìnā sukà bi? go in the ~ of (a specific place) dōsà̰ v2, nùfā v2: he went in the ~ of the farm yā dōshi gōnā; lose one's sense of ~, bearings yi dīmuwā f, yi ɓatàn k̃ai m; he has a good a sense of ~ yā san hanyà̰. b. (goal, aim in life) àlk̃iblà̰ f, manufà̰ f: he has no ~ in life bâ shi dà àlk̃iblà̰.

directional signal n sìgìnà̰ f, [F] kìlìyò̰tân m: turn on the ~ yi sìgìnà̰.

directions n a. (to a place) kwàtàncē m: I gave him ~ to the hospital nā yi masà kwàtàncen asìbitì. b. (instructions for using sth.) bàyānì m: read the ~ written on the box kà dūbà bàyānìn dà akà r̃ubùtà kân àkwàtì.

directly adv (immediately) k̃ai tsàye adv: they went ~ to the chairman sun tāshì k̃ai tsàye wajen shùgàbā.

director n shùgàbā n ⟨anni⟩, dà̰r̃aktà n ⟨oCi⟩, [F] dìr̃kìtâr̃ / dìr̃àktâr̃ n; managing ~ manajàn dà̰r̃aktà.

dirt n a. daudà̰ f, dàtti m, k̃àzântā f, [F] saltē m: wash the ~ off your hands

wànkè daudâr̃ hannuwànkà. b. (sweepings) shàr̃ā f: sweep up the ~ yi shàr̃ā.

dirty 1. adj a. (mài) daudà̰ f, (mài) dàtti m: the floor is ~ dàɓên yā yi daudà̰; your hands are very ~ hannunkà yā cikà daudà̰; the room is ~ àkwai dàtti à dākḭ̀; make sth. ~ lālàtā v1, sâ w.a. daudà̰, ɓātà̰ (dà daudà̰), dāgùlā v1: who made the water ~? wà̰ ya ɓātà ruwân? b. (esp. of psn.) k̃àzāmī adj ⟨ai⟩: she is a ~ messy person ita k̃àzamā cḕ. c. (fig. uses): give a ~ look yi kallon banzà; play a ~ trick on so. yàudarà̰ v2, yi wà zàmba f.

2. v ɓātà̰ (dà daudà̰), dāgùlā v1: those children were the ones who dirtied his gown yârân nan nḕ sukà ɓātà masà r̃īgā dà daudà̰.

dis- neg. prefix a. (for attrib. adj, use maràs (+ n) or mài (+ n of neg. quality); for predic. adj, use neg. sent.): a dishonest man mùtûm maràs gàskiyā; a disagreeable man mùtûm mài tsāmin râi; he is dishonest bâ shi dà gàskiyā. b. (for verbs, use neg. sent. or affirm. sent. with neg. v): he disapproved of her behavior bài yàr̃da dà hālintà ba = yā k̃i jinin hālintà. c. (for nouns, use rashìn + n): discontent rashìn zaman lāfiyà̰.

disabled adj nàk̃àsasshē adj, gàjìyayyē adj.

disadvantage n k̃wàr̃ā f, illà̰ f; put so. at a ~ (esp. dishonestly) k̃wàr̃ā v2.

disagree v a. sàɓà̰ dà v1, yi jàyayyà̰ f, yi gàr̃damà̰ / gaddamà̰ f: he ~s with her yā sàɓà̰ dà ita; they are ~ing over money sunà jàyayyà̰ à kân kud̃ī; he is always ~ing yā cikà gàr̃damà̰; totally ~ with so. (fig.) yi hannun rīgā dà w. b. (be incompatible): chocolate ~s with me bā nà̰ shirḭ̄ dà cākùlàn.

disagreeable adj (psn.) (mài) wùyar̃ hālī, (mài) gàr̃damà̰, (mài) d̃aur̃à fuskà̰, (mài) tsāmin râi, (mài) rìkicī.

disagreement n gàr̃damà̰ / gaddamà̰ f ⟨gàr̃dàndamḭ̄⟩, jā-ìn-jā f, jàyayyà̰ f, sà̰ɓānḭ̄ m; (formal) tak̃àddamà̰ f.

disappear v ɓacḕ v4: my ring has ~ed zōɓè yā ɓacḕ minì; he ~ed into the crowd yā ɓacḕ cikin tàrō; the moon ~ed behind the clouds watà yā lumḕ cikin gìzàgìzai; (fig.) ~ into thin air yi lāyà̰r̃ zānā = yi lāyà̰.

disappearance n ɓacēwā f.

disappoint v a. (fail to satisfy one's hopes) bā dà / bāyar̃ (dà) v5: I was really ~ed that you couldn't come kā bāshē nì dà

bà kà zō ba wàllāhì; the results really
~ed us sàkàmakôn yā bā dà mū wàllahì.
b. (*frustrate, annoy*) ɓātà wà râi: I was
~d râinā yā ɓācì.
disappointment *n* ɓācìn râi *m*, tàkâicī
*m*.
disapproval *n* rashìn yàr̃dā *m*.
disapprove *v* ƙi jinin w., yàr̃da dà *v1* (*+
neg.*): they ~ of smoking, lazy people sun
ƙi jinin shân tābà, malàlàtā = bā sà
yàr̃dā dà shân tābà, malàlàtā.
disarm *v* a. (*take arms away*) ƙwācè
màkàmai: the police ~ed the robbbers
'yan sàndā sun ƙwācè màkàman 'yan
fashì. b. (*put down arms*) ajè màkàmai.
disarmament *n*: nuclear ~ treaty yàr̃jē-
jēnìyar̃ ƙayyàdè màkàman nūkìlliyà.
disaster *n* a. (*from natural causes*) màsīfà
*f* ⟨u⟩, bàlā'ì *m*: a terrible ~ mūgùwar̃
màsīfà. b. (*from human error*) haɗàr̃ī
*m* ⟨uka²⟩: the spaceship ~ took 7 lives
haɗàr̃in kumbò yā halakar̃ dà mutànē
bakwài.
disastrous *adj* (mài) màsīfà *f*: a ~ famine
has occurred wata màsīfàr̃ farì tā
sàuka.
disc *n, see* disk.
discard *v* wātsar̃ (dà) *v5*, yi wàtsī dà *m*,
yā dà / yar̃ (dà) *v5*.
discharge¹ 1. *v* a. (*so. from job, institution*)
sàllamà *v2*: he was ~d from the army an
sàllàmē shì dàgà sōjà. b. (*a weapon*)
bugà *v1*, har̃bà *v1*.
2. *n* kòrā *f*: he was given a dishonorable
~ an yi masà kòrar̃ kàrē.
discharge² *n* (*pus*) mūgunyà *f*; (*from eye*)
kwantsà *f*.
disciple *n* (*Koranic*) àlmājìr̃ī *m* ⟨ai⟩.
discipline 1. *n* (*training*) hòrō *m*; self-~
dā'à *f*, kāmà kâi *n*; (*moral, esp. for children*) tàr̃biyyà *f*.
2. *v* (*train or punish*) hòrā *v2* ⟨hòrō⟩,
ladàbtā *v1*: she ~d the children for teasing the old man tā hòri yârân sabòdà
tsòkanàr̃ tsōhòn dà sukà yi.
disclose *v* (*sth. shameful*) fallàsā *v1*;
~ so.'s secret tōnà àsīr̃in w., yi wà
kwàrmatò *m*.
discolored, be(come) *v* kōɗè *v4*, dìnānà *v3*.
discomfort *n* rashìn jîn dādī *m*: the patient was in ~ the whole night maràs
lāfiyà bài ji dādī gàbā ɗayan darên
ba.
disconnect *v* a. (*separate*) rabà *v1*. b. (*by
pulling apart*) cirè *v4*: ~ an electric cord
cirè igiyàr̃ wutā. c. (*any public utility*) yankè *v4*: ~ the electricity, telephone

yankè wutar̃ làntar̃kì, wayàr̃ tàr̃hō.
discontent *n* rashìn zaman lāfiyà *m*: people are ~ed jàma'à tanà cikin rashìn
zaman lāfiyà.
discontinue *v* dainà *v1*, barì *v**: that
model has been ~d an dainà irìn wannàn
yāyìn.
discount *n* rangwamèn kuɗī *m*: he gave me
a ~ on this cloth yā yi minì rangwamèn
kuɗin yàdìn nân.
discourage *v* a. kashè wà zūcìyā, sagè
wà gwīwà, sacè wà iskà: he did everything he could to ~ me yā yi iyā
ƙòƙar̃insà yà yankè minì ƙaunà. b. be,
feel ~d: yi sanyī *m*, kàrayà *v3*: he feels
~d jìkinsà yā yi sanyī = gwīwàr̃sà tā
yi sanyī; I am ~d about getting the position nā kàrayà gà sāmùn mùkāmìn; I'm
~d about my situation jìkīnā yā mutù
sabòdà hālin dà nakè ciki.
discover *v* gānō *v6*: a new comet was ~ed
recently an gānō wata sābuwar̃ tàurārùwā
kwānan nàn.
discovery *n* gānôwā *f*.
discrepancy *n* bambancì *m*, hìlāfà *f*.
discretion *n* hankàlī *m*.
discriminate *v* nūnà bambancì *m*, tsàr̃gā
*v2*: this organization ~s against women
wannàn ƙungìyā nà nūnà bambancì gà
mātā =wannàn ƙungìyā takàn tsàrgi
mātā; (*by race*) nūnà wāriyar̃ àl'ummà.
discrimination *n* wāriyā *f*, bambancì
*m*; racial ~ wāriyar̃ àl'ummà, *see*
apartheid; sexual ~ wāriyar̃ jinsì;
ethnic ~ kabīlancī *m*.
discuss *v* tattàunā *v1*, yi shāwar̃à *f*,
shāwàr̃tā *v1*: I have an important matter to ~ with you inà dà wata bàbbar̃
shāwar̃à; they are ~ing it but they
still haven't come to a decision sunà
shāwàr̃warī àmmā har̃ yànzu bà sù tsai
dà màganà ba; ~ something down to the
last detail (*fig.*) fēɗè birì har̃ wutsi.
discussion *n* (*gen'l*) tattàunâwā *f*, shāwar̃à *f*
⟨shāwàr̃warī⟩, màganà *f* ⟨u²⟩: there's been
a lot of ~ about that an shā màganà kân
wannàn; (*formal debate*) mùhāwar̃à *f*.
disdain 1. *v* rainà / rēnà *v1*.
2. *n* rainì / rēnī *m*.
disease *n* cùtā *f* ⟨uka²⟩: carry, transmit a ~
kāwō cùtā; catch, contract a ~ kàmu dà
cùtā = ɗauki cùtā dàgà w.; what is the
cause of the ~? mè kè kāwō cùtàr̃? what
kind of ~ is he suffering from? wàcè irìn
cùtā yakè fāmā dà ita?
disentangle *v* warwàrē *v4*.

disgrace 1. *v* kunyàtā *v1*, wulāƙàntā *v1*, zub dà mutuncî: she ~d her family tā kunyàtà iyâyentà = tā zub dà mutuncîn iyâyentà; ~ oneself wulāƙantař dà kâi. 2. *n* àbin kunyà *f*: he was a ~ to his family yā zama àbin kunyà gà ìyālìnsà = ya kunyàtā ìyālìnsà.

disguise *v* a. (*oneself*) yi shìgā *f*, yi shìgař buřtū, sākè kàmā, ɓad dà kàmā: he ~d himself as a beggar yā yi shìgā irìn ta àlmājìřī. b. (*one's feelings*) ɓōyè *v4*, tōgè *v4*, yi tōgiyā *f*: he ~d his feelings for her yā ɓōyè matà àbîn dà kè zūcìyařsà.

disgust *n* ƙyāmā *f*.

disgusting *adj* (*abhorrent*) (mài) ƙyāmā *f*; (*dirty, immoral*) ƙàzāmī *adj* ⟨ai⟩: a ~ movie ƙàzāmin fîm.

dish *n* a. (*of enamelware*) tāsà *f* ⟨oCi⟩, (*bowl-shaped*) kwānò *m* ⟨uka⟩: clear away the ~es kwāshè kwānukà; (*of porcelain*) tangařan *m* ⟨tangařâyē⟩: break a ~ fasà tangařan; (*wooden eating bowl*) akùshī *m* ⟨u-a⟩. b. (*food*) àbinci *m*, cìmā *f*: everyone should bring a ~ and then we can eat together kōwā yà zō dà cìmařsà à hadà à ci.

disheartened *adj*: on hearing the news, he was ~ dà jîn làbārìn sai gàbansà ya fādì.

dishonest *adj* maràs kiřkì *m*, maràs gàskiyā *f*, (mài) māgudī *m*, macì àmānà *m*: he is ~ bâ shi dà gàskiyā = mài māgudī nè.

dishonesty *n* hā'incì *m*, rashìn gàskiyā *m*, cûtā *f*; (*esp. breach of trust*) māgudī *m*, mākiřcì *m*.

dishonor *v* ci mutuncìn w., kā dà mutuncìn w., kunyàtā *v1*.

dishonorable *adj* (mài) ban kunyà; a ~ discharge kòřař kàrē *f*.

disintegrate *v* řagařgàjē / řuguřgùjē *v4*, (*esp. of foods in liquid*) rōgàjē *v4*: the wall has ~d because of the rains gānuwā tā řagařgàjē sabòdà ruwā = ruwā yā rūsař dà gānuwā; it has ~ed completely an yi matà řugu-řugu.

disk *n* (*phonograph record*) faifai *m* ⟨a..ai⟩, [F] dîs *m* ⟨oCi⟩.

dislike *v* wàsā *v2*, sō *v0* (+ *neg.*): she ~s spinach tā wàshi àlayyàhō = bā tà sôn àlāyyàhō.

dislocate *v* guřdè *v4*, gōcè *v4*: I've ~d my knee ƙashin gwīwàtā yā guřdè.

dislocation *n* (*of a bone*) gōcèwā *f*.

dislodge *v* sàkatā *v2*.

dismantle *v* wařgàzā *v1*; become ~d wařgàjē *v4*; a ~d car wàřgàzajjiyař mōtà.

dismay *n* fādùwař gàbā *f*.

dismiss *v* a. (*fire so. from work*) sàllamà *v2*, fid dà / fitař (dà) *v5*, kōrè *v4*: he was ~ed from his job an fisshē shì dàgà mùƙāmìnsà. b. (*a group, meeting*) tàsā *v2*: he ~ed the students yā tàshi dàlìbai. c. (*Law, ignore sth. as invalid*) kōrà *v2*: the court ~ed the case for lack of witnesses kōtù tā kòri ƙāřař sabòdà rashìn shàidū.

dismissal *n* sàllamà *f*, kōrā *f*.

dismount *v* sàuka *v3*.

disobedience *n* ƙîn bî *m*, ƙîn ùmařnī *m*, rashìn bìyayyà *m*.

disobey a. (*so.*) sāɓà wà *v1*, bijìrē wà *v4*: he ~ed his father yā sāɓà wà mahàifinsà; (*sth.*) ƙi bî *v0*: he ~ed his father's orders yā ƙi bîn ùmařnin mahàifinsà. b. (*violate*) kētà *v1*: ~ a regulation, law kētà ƙā'idà, dōkà.

disorder *n* a. (*uproar*) hàrgitsī *m*; be in a state of ~ hargìtsē *v4*: the country was thrown into a state of ~ ƙasař tā hargìtsē; in ~ à hàrgìtse *adv*. b. (*of a place*) à bàřkàtai *idph*, biji-biji *idph*: the room was in complete ~ dākìn à bàřkàtai yakè.

disorganized *adj* à bìrkìce *adv*, maràs tsārì *m*: his work is terribly ~ aikìnsà à bìrkìce yakè = aikìnsà bâ shi dà tsārì kō kàɗan; his work is completely ~ (*fig.*) yā yi sallař kūrā à aikìnsà.

disparage *v* yi wà ƙanƙancì *m*.

dispel *v*: ~ any doubts about sth. kōrè duk wata tābābà.

dispensary *n* dìsfansàřè *m*, dākìn māgànī *m*, [F] gidan likità *m*.

dispenser *n* (*of medicine*) mài bā dà māgànī *n*, likità *n* ⟨oCi⟩.

disperse *v* wàtsā *v1*, tařwàtsā *v1*, wàtsè *v4*, fasà *v1*: they ~d the crowd with tear gas an wàtsà tàron mutànē dà bàřkònon tsōhuwā.

displace *v* kau dà / kawař (dà) *v5*.

display *v* a. nūnà *v1*: he ~ed great courage yā nūnà bàjintà. b. (*items for sale*) bařbàzā *v1*: the traders ~ their wares on the ground 'yan tiřēdà sunà bařbàzà kōlìnsù à ƙasà.

displease *v* ɓātà wà râi.

displeasure *n* ɓācìn rai *m*.

dispose of *v* zub dà / zubař (dà) *v5*, yā dà / yař (dà) *v5*.

**dispute** 1. *n* a. (*esp. social, political*) rìkicī *m*, jàyayyà *f*: they are having a ~ over national boundaries sunā rìkicī à kân iyākōkin k̄asàshensù. b. (*argument*) gar̃damà / gaddamà *f* ⟨gar̃dàndamī⟩. c. (*denial*) musù *m*.
2. *v* a. (*argue*) yi wà gar̃damà / gaddamà *f*. b. (*deny, contradict*) musà *v1*, yi musù *m*: they ~d the report sun musà r̃ahōtòn.

**disregard** *v* k̄yālè *v4*, yi bìr̃is dà, r̃àbu dà *v7*.

**disrespect** *n* (*impoliteness*) rashìn ladàbī *m*; (*rudeness*) rashìn kunyà *m*; (*esp. toward husband*) tsīwà *f*: she was ~ful to her husband tā yi wà mijìntà tsīwà; ~ful speech gautsī / gantsī *m*.

**disrespectfully** *adv*: he stood there ~ yā tsayà k̄èr̃èr̃è; he stared ~ at her yā yi matà kallon mùzùr̃ài.

**disrupt** *v* katsè *v4*.

**dissatisfaction** *n* rashìn gàmsuwā *m*.

**disseminate** *v* (*information*) yādà *v1*, wātsà *v1*.

**dissension** *n* (*disagreement*) jàyayyà *f*; (*violent*) hàrgitsī *m*, rìkicī *m*, tāshìn hankàlī *m*.

**dissertation** *n* kundī *m* ⟨aye⟩.

**dissident** *n* ɗan bōr̃ē *m*, ɗan tāwāyè *m*.

**dissimilar** *adj* dàbam *adv*.

**dissipate** *v* wātsè *v4*.

**dissipated** *adj* fāsìk̄ī *m* ⟨u⟩: he is ~ fāsìk̄ī nè; he leads a ~ life yanà ɓātà r̃àyuwar̃sà à banza.

**dissipation** *n* fāsik̄ancì *m*.

**dissolute** *adj* (*psn.*) fāsìk̄ī *m* ⟨u⟩.

**dissolve** 1. *vt* a. nark̄ar̃ (dà) *v5*: ~ the pill in water and then drink it kà nar̃k̄ar̃ dà k̄wàyā cikin ruwa sā'àn nan kà shā. b. (*a committee*) rūshè *v4*.
2. *vi* narkè *v4*.

**distance** *n* nīsā *m*, tazarā *f*: the village is a short ~ from town k̄auyèn nà dà ɗan nīsā dàgà gàrī; I let him get some ~ ahead of me nā bā shì tazarā; from a ~ dàgà nēsà; see sth. from a ~ hàngā *v2* ⟨hàngē⟩: I saw him from a great ~ nā hàngē shì dàgà can nēsà; can you see the river in the ~? kanà iyà hàngen kògīn?

**distant** *adj* (mài) nīsā *m*, (mài) tazarā *f*, na nēsà *adv*: he is a ~ relative of the president ɗan'uwan shūgàban k̄asā nè na nēsà.

**distended, be** *v* kùmburà *v3*.

**distilled water** *n* ruwan bātìr̃ *m*.

**distinct** *adj* (*clear, unambiguous*): there is a ~ difference between them àkwai cìkakken bambancī tsàkāninsù.

**distinctly** *adv* (*certainly*) tabbàs *adv*, à hàk̄īk̄à: I ~ remember that occasion à hàk̄īk̄à nā tunà dà wànnan karòn.

**distinction** *n* a. (*difference*) bambancī *m*. b. (*superior quality*) fīfīk̄ò *m*, dar̃ajà *f*: a man of ~ mùtûm mài fīfīk̄ò = mùtûm mài dar̃ajà.

**distinguish** *v* bambàntā *v1*, rabà *v1*: what ~es the two candidates? mè ya bambàntā 'yan tàkar̃ā biyu? ~ between rar̃ràbē *v4*, tantàncē *v4*: I can't ~ between the twins bàn iyà rar̃ràbè tagwàyên ba.

**distinguished** *adj* (*psn.*) màshàhūr̃ì *adj* ⟨ai⟩.

**distort** *v* a. (*twist out of shape*) mur̃dè *v4*, mur̃gùdē *v4*: ~ the truth, one's mouth mur̃dè gàskiyā, bàkī. b. (*by exaggeration*) k̄ārà wà gishirī: he ~ed the story yā k̄ārà wà làbār̃ì gishirī.

**distortion** *n* mur̃diyā *f*.

**distract** *v* ɗaukè hankàlin w.

**distress** 1. *n* a. (*anxiety*) fāɗuwar̃ gàbā *f*. b. (*sorrow*) ɓacìn r̃ai *m*.
2. *v* a. (*worry*): he is ~ed gàbansà yā fāɗì. b. (*sadden*) ɓātà wà r̃ai: the news ~ed her làbār̃in yā ɓātà matà r̃ai.

**distribute** *v* rar̃ràbā *v1*: kolanuts are ~d during the ceremony to everyone à bìkîn anà rar̃ràbā wà kōwā dà kōwā gōr̃ò.

**distribution** *n* (*sharing out*) rabàwā *f*.

**distributor** *n* a. (*sales representative*) ējàn *n*. b. (*of car engine*) dìsfētò *m*, [F] dàlkô *m*.

**district** *n* (*admin.*) gùndumà *f* ⟨oCi⟩, [F] sar̃kè *m*; (*area*) sāshè / sāshì *m* ⟨Ca⟩, shiyyà *f* ⟨oCi⟩.

**district head** *n* hākìmī *m* ⟨ai⟩.

**district officer** *n* dī'ò *m* ⟨x²⟩.

**distrust** 1. *v* amìncē dà *v4* (+ *neg.*): I ~ people like him bàn amìncē dà mutànē irìnsà ba.
2. *n* rashìn àmānà *m*.

**disturb** *v* a. (*worry*) tā dà hankàlī: the news ~ed us deeply làbār̃in yā tā dà hankàlinmù sòsai; don't ~ her kadà hankàlintà yà tàshì. b. (*bother*) dàmā *v2* ⟨dāmù⟩, dàmu *v7*: keep quiet, you are ~ing the others kù yi shirū kunà dāmùn saurân; the thing that really ~s me is... bàbban àbin dàmuwātā shī nè.... c. (*shock emotionally*) dàgùlà wà r̃ai: what he said really ~ed me àbîn dà ya cè yā dàgùlà minì r̃ai; mentally ~ed tàɓaɓɓē *adj*.

**disturbance** *n* (*dissension, trouble*) hàrgitsī *m*, rìkicī *m*, tāshìn hankàlī *m*:

cause a ~ tā dà rìkicī = tā dà han-kàlī.

**ditch** *n* a. kwalbatì *m*, gatà̃ *f*, [F] gwalalō *m*, [F] gadà̃ *f*: the car got stuck in the ~ mōtàř tā kafē à kwalbatì. b. (*esp. open sewer*) làmbàtū *m*.

**dive** *v* tsindùmà *v1*, yi àlkāhùřā *f*, yi dàkē *m*: they ~d into the water sun yi àlkāhùřā cikin ruwa.

**diverge** *v* a. (*go in ano. direction*) rātsē *v4*, ràbu *v7*: the road ~s near the market-place hanyàř tā rātsē à bàkin kàsuwà. b. (*differ*) bàmbantà *v3*: their opinions ~ on the matter řa'àyinsù yā bàmbantà à kân màganàř.

**divide** *v* a. rabà *v1*: he ~d the bread into 4 pieces yā rabà buřōdì huɗu; they ~d the food equally among the children an rabà wà yârân àbinci daidai wà daidà; he ~s his time between teaching and writing yā rabà lōkàcinsà rabì wajen kōyàřwā rabì wajen řùbùtū; they are ~d into three types sun ràbu ir'i ukù. b. (*in mathematics*): 80 ~d by 5 is 16 bìyař cikin tàmànin shà shidà kè nan; how much is 10 ~d by 2? biyu tā shìga gōmà sàu nawà?

**divination** *n* dūbà *m*.

**divine** *adj*: ~ knowledge baiwā *f*.

**diving** *n* àlkāhùřā *f*.

**division** *n* a. (*in mathmetics*) rabà̃wā *f*: ~ sign àlāmàř rabà̃wā. b. (*within an organization*) ɓangarē *m*: the army's artillery ~ ɓangarèn ìgwā na sōjà.

**divorce** 1. *n* sakì *m*, (*euphem.*) ràbuwā *f*; the judge granted her a ~ àlkàlī yā sawwàkè matà aurên. 2. *v* sàkā *v2*: he ~d his wife yā sàki màtařsà; (*euphem.*) ràbu dà *v7*: he ~d his wife sun ràbu dà màtařsà; they are ~d an kashè musù aurē = aurensù yā mutù.

**divorcee** *n* bàzawàrā / zawàrā *f* ⟨zawarāwā⟩.

**divulge** *v* tōnà *v1*: he ~d my secret to the boss yā tōnà minì àsīřī wajen shùgàbân.

**dizzy** *adj*: feel ~ yi jùwā *f*, yi jìrī *m*: the medicine has made me ~ māgànīn yā sâ ni jùwā; (*from turning round & round*) yi hàjījiyà *f*: the girls got ~ from the game 'yammàtā sun yi hàjījiyà sabòdà wàsân.

**do** *v* a. yi *v0*: what is to be done about it? mè zā à yi? don't ~ that again kâř kà sākè yîn hakà; you should always ~ just as you are told kullum sai kà yi daidai yàddà akà gayà makà; ~ completely yînyē / wànyē *v4*: he's done all the work completely yā yînyè aikìn; ~ one's best yi iyā kòřarī; ~ sth. all by oneself (*without help*) yi dà kàshin kâi: they did it all by themselves sun yī shì dà kàshin kânsù; I have nothing to ~ with it bài shàfē nì ba = bâ ruwānā; there's nothing I can ~ about it bâ ni dà màgàninsà. b. (*act*) aikàtà *v1*: don't ~ anything in anger kadà kà aikàtà kōmē cikin fushī; we had no choice but to ~ what we did bâ mu dà wani zàɓì à kân àbîn dà mukà yi. c. (*be ready*) gamà *v1*: is the food done? an gamà àbinci? d. (*in emphasizing a request*): ~ try harder! don Allàh don Ànnabì kù řàrà yîn kòřarī!

**dock** 1. *n* matsayař jirgī *m*. 2. *v*: where does the boat ~? ìnā jirgin ruwa kè tsayàwā?

**doctor** *n* a. (*modern*) likità *n* ⟨oCi⟩, [F] làkwàtařò *n*. b. (*native herbalist*) bōkā *n* ⟨aye⟩. c. (*academic or medical*) daktà *n*, [F] dàktâř *n*.

**doctorate** *n*: he has a ~ in history likità nē à fannìn tāřīhì.

**doctrine** *n*: ~ of the unity of God tàuhīdì *m*.

**doctrinaire** *adj* (mài) řa'àyin rìřau *m*, (mài) tsàttsauran řa'àyī *m*.

**document** *n* (*Law*) takàřdā *f* ⟨u⟩: she lost all her important ~s tā zub dà mùhìmman tàkàřduntà.

**dodge** *v* a. (*avoid sth. by swerving*) kaucè wà *v4*, baudè wà *v4*: if I hadn't ~d the arrow it would have pierced my hand dà bàn kaucè wà kibiyà ba dà tā sōkè minì hannū. b. (*be evasive*) zūřè wà *v4*, yi wà zūře-zūře: he kept dodging the questions yā yi ta zūřè wà tambayōyîn dà akà yi masà.

**dog** *n* kàrē *m*, kàryā *f* ⟨kařnukà⟩; wild ~ kyarkècī *m* ⟨ai⟩; set a ~ on so. cūnà wà kàrē *v1*.

**doll** *n* 'yař tsana *f*.

**dollar** *n* dalàř Amìřkà *f*: the ~ is weakening against the pound dalàř Amìřkà nà̃ ràununà̃ à an kwatàntà ta dà fâm ɗin Ingìlà; Maria Theresa ~ lìyàřì *m*.

**dome** *n* kubbà̃ *f* ⟨oCi⟩: ~ of the mosque kubbàř masallàcī.

**domestic** *n* yārò *m* ⟨yārā⟩, bòyi *m* ⟨$x^2$⟩, [F] bōyì *m*.

**domesticated** *adj*: ~ animal dabbàř gidā.

**dominant** *adj* (*bossy*) (mài) mulkì *m*; be ~ rìnjāyà *v3*.

dominate *v* a. (*exert control over*) shā
kân w., jūyà *v1*: the senior wife ~s the
other wives uwařgidā ta shā kân sauran
kishiyōyī; she is trying to ~ her husband
tanà ƙōƙarin shân kân mijìntà. b. (*occupy most important place*) māmàyē *v4*: he
~d the conversation, his political party yā
māmàyè hīřařsù, ƙungìyařsà ta sìyāsà.

donate *v* taimàkā *v1*, bāyař dà gudùmmawā:
they ~ to Amnesty International sunà bā
dà gudùmmawā wajen Ƙungìyař Ahuwà ta
Dūniyà.

donation *n* àbin tàimakō *m*, gudùmmawā *f*.

donkey *n* jàkī *m*, jàkā *f* ⟨una⟩.

don't *v aux* a. (*used as neg. command*) kadà
/ kâř *conj* (+ *subjunct*.): ~ forget about
the meeting kadà kà mântā dà tàrôn; ~
let it get wet kâř kì bař shì yà jìƙa.
b. (*used as gen'l admonition*) ban dà (+
*action n*): ~ play with fire ban dà wàsā
dà wutā; ~ quarrel with friends ban dà
faɗà dà àbòkai.

doom *n* ƙàddařà *f*.

door *n* ƙyaurē *m* ⟨ƙyamàre⟩; (*made of grass
mats*) tufānìyā *f*; (*door, doorway*) ƙōfà
*f* ⟨oCi⟩: front, back ~ ƙōfà ta gàba,
bāya; don't leave the ~ open kadà kà bař
ƙōfà à bùɗe; knock on a ~ ƙwanƙwàsà
ƙōfà; someone is at the ~ anà sallamà;
leave a ~ ajar sâyè ƙōfà; shut ~ tightly
ƙullè ƙōfà kankan; live next ~ to yi
màƙwàbtakà dà.

doorbell *n* ƙàrarrawař ƙōfà *f*: ring a ~
dannà ƙàrarrawař ƙōfà.

doorknob *n* mariƙin ƙōfà *m*.

doorstep *n* dōkìn ƙōfà *m*, (*stoop*) dandamàlī *m*.

dormitory *n* mazaunin ɗàlìbai *m*.

dose *n* awòn māgànī *m*.

dossier *n* fāyìl *m* ⟨oCi⟩, [F] dòsê *m*.

dot *n* ɗigò *m* ⟨e²⟩: they are indicated by ~s
on the map an nūnà su dà ɗìge-ɗìge à
tàswīřà.

double 1. *adj* biyu *f*, dōbùl *m*, [F] dūbùl
*m*: I want ~ the amount inà sôn dōbùl
ɗinsà; this one is ~ the size of that one
wannàn biyun wancàn nē.
2. *v* riɓà sàu biyu *v1*: its cost has ~d in
5 years kuɗinsà yā riɓà sàu biyu cikin
shèkarà bìyař.

double-talk *n* bàkī biyu *m*.

doubt 1. *v* a. (*find questionable*) yi shakkà
*f*, yi kòkwantō *m*: I ~ whether I can do
it inà shakkà kō zân iyà yīnsà; no one
~s his honesty bā mài shakkàř cêwà shī
mài gàskiyā nè. b. (*deny*) yi musù *m*:
I don't ~ your word for a minute bàn yi

makà musù ba kō kàɗan.
2. *n* shakkà *f*, shakkū *m*, tābābà *f*,
kòkwantō *m*; (*lingering reservation*) tantamà *f*: I have no ~ of his guilt bā
nà shakkàř làifinsà; we have some ~s
about that munà tantamař hakà; without a ~ lābuddà *adv*, bâ shakkà *f*, bābù
tābābà: without a ~ that is the truth
lābuddà wannàn gaskiyā nè; I'm certain
beyond a shadow of a ~ nā yi yàƙīnì.

doubtful *adj* (*questionable*): his story is ~
anà shakkàř làbāřìnsà; the outcome is
~ màganàř bâ tabbàs.

dough *n* kwàbabben fulāwà *m*.

dove *n* kurciyā *f* ⟨oCi⟩.

down *adv* a. (*on the ground*) à ƙasà / ƙas
*adv*: he put it ~ yā sâ shi ƙasà. b.
(*for use as particles with verbs, see relevant verb entries*): the sun went ~ rānā
tā fāɗì; knock ~ a goat bankè àkuyà;
put a calabash upside ~ birkìcè ƙwaryā;
the tire is worn ~ tāyà tā suɗè; put the
loads ~ saukè kāyā; the car broke ~ mōtà
tā lālàcē; get ~ sàuka *v3*; go ~ (*descend
an incline*) gangàrā *v1*; lie ~ kwântā *v1*;
upside ~ à kìfe = à bìrkìce.

downhill *adv* ta gàngarà *f*: the road went
~ hanyàř tā bi gàngarà.

down payment *n* àdìbâs *m*, [F] àbâns *f*.

downpour *n*: there was a tremendous ~ of
rain an shêƙà ruwā = an gabcè dà ruwā =
(*fig.*) an yi ruwā kàmař dà bàkin ƙwaryā.

downstairs *adv* à ƙasà / ƙas *adv*, dàgà
ƙasà.

downtown *n* gàrī *m*: I'm going ~ zâ ni
gàrī.

downtrodden *adj* zàlùntaccē *adj*.

downward *adj* zuwà ƙasà.

doze off *v* yi rùrùmì *m*, yi gyàngyaɗì *m*.

dozen *n* dōzìn *m*: these are ₦10 per ~
kuɗin waɗànnân naiřà gōmà nē dōzìn-
dōzìn.

drag *v* jā *v0*: don't let your robe ~ on
the ground kadà rìgařkà tà jā ƙasà; ~
away jânyē *v4*; ~ out jāwō *v6*: he ~ged
the animal out of the forest yā jāwō dabbà
dàgà cikin dājì; (*fig.*) time ~s when you
are idle lōkàcîn bā yà tàfiyà in anà zaman kashè wàndō.

dragonfly *n* ɗan mazarin-iyà *m*.

drain 1. *n* a. (*inside house*) magudānā *f*:
the ~ is all stopped up magudānā tā
tōshè; (*from house out to street*) rāriyā
*f*; (*sewage ~ from house to cesspit*) kwatà
*f*. b. (*gutter on rooftop*) ìndařařò *m* ⟨ai⟩.
2. *v* a. (*flow out*) malàlē *v4*; ~ off (*become*

*partially dry*) tsanè *v4*. b. (*oil from engine*) jûyè *v4*, yi jûyè *m*: they ~ed the oil out of my engine an yi minì jûyen baƙin mâi.

**drainage ditch** *n, see* ditch.

**drainage hole** *n* (*in wall*) rāriyā *f.*

**drainpipe** *n* (*on roof*) ìndaɍaɍō *m* ⟨ai⟩.

**drake** *n* tǒɍon àgwàgwā *m.*

**drama** *n* wàsan kwaikwayō *m.*

**drastic** *adj* mūgù *adj* ⟨miyàgū⟩, tsàttsaurā *adj*: there's been a ~ cut in salary an yi mūgùn ragìn àlbâshī; ~ measures are being followed to stop smuggling anā bîn tsauràran màtàkai don hanà fàsàƙwàuri.

**draughts** *n* (*tradit. game like checkers*) darà *f.*

**draw**[1] *v* a. (*pull sth.*) jā *v0*: ~ a plow, a bow jā gàɍmā, bàkā; ~ sth. out (*from narrow opening*) zārè *v4*: I drew out the drawstring from my pants nā zārè mazāgin wàndō; he drew out his sword yā zārō takòbinsà; ~ together (*pursestrings, lips*) tsūkè *v4*. b. (*liquid from*) dībā *v2\**: ~ water from a well ɗebi ruwā dàgà rījìyā; ~ blood from so. ɗebi jinin w. c. (*var. v + adv/prep uses*): ~ back jā dà bāya, nōƙè *v4*: the children were shy and drew back yârā sun ji kunyà sun jā dà bāya; (*withdraw into a place*) kuɗè *v4*: the tortoise drew back into its shell kân kùnkurū yā kuɗè; ~ near (*in time*) kusa *v\**, ƙarātō *v6*: the end of the month is ~ing near ƙàrshen watā yā kusa; ~ near (*in space*) matsà *v1*: they drew near to hear the news sun matsà don sù ji làbàrī; ~ up (*a plan*) shiryà *v1*, tsārà *v1*.

**draw**[2] *v*: ~ a picture zānà *v1*, yi zànè *m*, (*with decoration, color*) zayyànā *v1*; ~ a line under a word jā lāyì ƙàɍƙashin kalmà; ~ up a treaty tsārà yàɍjējènìyā.

**draw**[3] *n* (*a tie*) dùɍô *m*: end in a ~ yi dùɍô = yi kûnnen dōkì = yi canjàɍas.

**drawback** *n* cīkàs *m.*

**drawer** *n* àljīhun tēbùɍ *m.*

**drawers** *n* (*men's underwear*) dùɍôs *m*, [F] kàlìsô *m.*

**drawing** *n* zānè *m*, hòtō *m.*

**drawstring** *n* mazāgī *m*: draw out the ~ from the waistband zārè mazāgī dàgà ƙūbakà.

**dread** 1. *n* fàɍgàbā *f.*
2. *v* yi fàɍgàbā *f*: I ~ appearing before the judge inā fàɍgàbaɍ zuwā gàban àlƙālī.

**dreadful** *adj* mùmmūnā *adj.*

**dream** 1. *n* mafaɍkī *m*: what is the meaning of that ~? mènē nè manufin mafaɍkîn nan? it was only a ~ àshē mafaɍkī nè kawài.
2. *v* yi mafaɍkī *m*: he would never ~ of doing that kō dà mafaɍkī bà zâi yi tùnànin yîn haƙà ba.

**dregs** *n* dìddigā *f.*

**drench** *v*: the rain ~ed him ruwā yā bā shì kāshī; be ~ed jiƙè shaɍaf = jiƙè shàɍkaf.

**dress** 1. *n* (*esp. modern style*) rìgaɍ mātā *f*, [F] ɍôb *f*; (*esp. worn in villages*) [F] kamsàl *f.*
2. *v* a. sâ tufāfì, sanyà tufāfì, sâ kāyā; ~ up (*in best clothes*) yi adō *m*, yi kwalliyā *f*; (*fig.*) she was ~ed to kill tā shā kwalliyā = tā ƙurè àdakà = tā cāɓà adō; be ~ed like yi shìgaɍ w.: he is ~ed like a European yā yi shìgaɍ Tùɍàwā = yā zanzàrè. b. (*a wound*) ɗaurè ràunī.

**dressmaker** *n* mài ɗinkà kāyan mātā *m.*

**dried** *adj* bùsasshē *adj*, ƙèƙàsasshē *adj*; ~ fish bùsasshen kīfī; ~ dates ƙèƙàsasshen dàbīnō; ~ meat kilìshī *m*; ~ foods (*esp. tomatoes, chillies, squash*) kaudà *f.*

**drill**[1] *n* (*Mil.*) rawaɍ sōjà *f.*

**drill**[2] 1. *v* (*a hole*) hūɗà *v1*, yi hūɗà *f*, yi hūjì *m*, haƙà *v1*: he ~ed 3 holes in the wall yā yi hūɗà ukù à bangō; ~ for (*oil, water*) haƙō *v6* ⟨hàƙā⟩ *f*: it's oil they are ~ing for mâi sukè haƙā.
2. *n* mahūjì *m.*

**drilling** *n* (*a hole, well*) haƙà *m*; (*for oil, water, minerals*) hàƙā *f.*

**drink** 1. *v* shā *v0*: what would you like to ~? mè zā kà shā? ~ up shânyè *v4*.
2. *n* àbin shā *m*: we want a ~ munà sôn àbin shā; is this ~ing water? wannàn ruwan shā nē? soft ~ lèmō *m*; (*alcoholic ~*) bàɍàsā *f*, giyà *f.*

**drinker** *n* mài shân giyà *n.*

**drip** *v* ɗiga *v3*, tàrārà *v3*: the tap is ~ping kân famfò nà ɗìga.

**drive** *v* a. (*a vehicle*) tūƙà *v1*, yi tūƙì *m*; it is easy to ~ tanà dà saukin tūƙàwā; know how to ~ iyà mōtà; he drove me to the station yā kai nì tashà à mōtà. b. (*cattle*) kōrà *v2*; ~ so. away fàfarà *v2*, kōrà *v2*: the soldiers succeeded in driving the enemy away sōjōjîn sun yi nasaɍaɍ fàfaràɍ àbōkan gàbā; (*fig.*) ~ so. crazy sâ w. hàukà. c. (*a nail*) kafà *v1*: ~ a nail in with a hammer kafà ƙūsā dà hamā.

**driver** *n* diɍēbà *m* ⟨oCi⟩, matūƙì *m*; he is not a careful ~ bà yā tūƙì à hankàlī;

a reckless ~ dir̃ēbà mài gangancī; ~'s
mate kàren mōtã m.

driver ants n tùrūruwā f.

drizzle v yi yayyafī m, yi tsattsafī
m: it's been drizzling since morning anã
yayyafī tun sāfe.

dromedary n rãƙumī m ⟨u-a⟩.

droop v (of head, plant) langàɓē v4, (of
plant) yi yaushī m, yàusasà v3: the
plants are ~ing due to lack of water shǔke-
shǔke sunã yaushī sabõdà rashìn ruwā.

drop 1. v a. (let fall) yā dà / yar̃ (dà) v5:
she ~ped the basket and broke the eggs
tā yā dà kwàndôn tā far̃fàsà ƙwân; (let
fall & spill) ɓar̃ dà / ɓarar̃ (dà) v5: she
~ped the water jug tā ɓar̃ dà gõrân; ~ a
bomb sakà bâm; ~ medicine into ɗigà wà
māgànī; ~ down fāɗì v3b; ~ out fāɗō v6:
the key ~ped out of his pocket makullī
yā fāɗō dàgà cikin àljīhunsà. b. (of
prices) saukō v6, fāɗì v3b. c. (of temperature) sàuka v3. d. (leave alone) barĩ v*:
let's ~ the subject! mù bar̃ zàncên!
2. n (lowering) fāɗùwā f: a ~ in price
fāɗùwar̃ fàr̃āshì.
3. n (e.g. of water) ɗigõ m ⟨e²⟩; there is
not a single ~ of water left bābù ruwā kō
ɗis; the water fell in huge round ~s ruwā
yā saukō danƙwal-dànƙwàl; pour out in
~s ɗigà v1, ɗarsà v1, ɗisà v1.

drought n farī m: a ~-stricken area
shiyyàr̃ dà akè farī; if we don't get
more rain soon, there will be a ~ in bà
à sàmi ƙārìn ruwā nân gàba ba, zā à
yi farī.

drown v ci v0: he ~ed ruwā yā cī shi; we
nearly ~ed saurā kàɗan ruwā yà cînyē
mu; children can ~ in this pond wannàn
kùduddufī yanã cîn yârã; (sink into)
nitsè v4: he saved her from ~ing yā cēcē
tā dàgà hàlakàr̃ nitsēwā.

drowsy adj: feel ~ ji mutuwàr̃ jìkī, yi
gyàngyaɗī m.

drug n a. (medicine) māgànī m ⟨u-a²⟩. b.
(illicit) ƙwãyā f ⟨oCi⟩.

drugs n ƙwãyā f, miyàgun ƙwãyōyī p; halluci-
natory ~s ƙwãyōyī màsu sanyà māyè; do,
take ~ shā ƙwãyā; be high on ~ ƙwãyàntu
v7; deal in ~ yi fataucìn ƙwãyōyī.

drugstore n, see pharmacy.

drum n a. (gen'l term) gàngā f ⟨una⟩:
we heard the noise of ~s from afar mun
ji amon gangunã dàgà nēsà = mun ji
kìɗe-kìɗe dàgà nēsà. b. (var. types):
(long, set on ground, beaten with sticks)
dùndufã f; (hour-glass shape, 2 mem-
branes) kàlàngū m ⟨una⟩; (small hour-

glass shape) jaujē m; (hour-glass shape,
1 membrane) kõtsō m; (large ceremonial)
tambàrī m ⟨u-a⟩; (small, worn around
neck, beaten with cloth mallet) kazagī m;
(small, worn around neck) kuntukurū /
kur̃tukū m; (bowl shape, beaten with fingers) taushī m, bàngā f, ⟨una⟩. c. (storage) tànô m, dùr̃ô m: ~ of oil, water dùr̃ô
ɗin mâi, ruwā; (for crude oil) gàngā f,
⟨una⟩.

drummer n makàɗī m, mài kiɗī m; (of var.
drums) mài kàlàngū , mài tambàrī, mài
taushī n.

drumming n kiɗã f, kiɗì m ⟨kìɗe-kìɗe
/ kàɗe-kàɗe⟩: during Sallah, there is ~
throughout the day anã ta kàɗe-kàɗe à
rānar̃ Sallã gàbā ɗayantà.

drumstick n makaɗī m.

drunk adj bùgaggē adj, à bùge adv; be, get
~ bùgu v7: he is ~ yā bùgu = à bùge yakè
= [F] yā yi sû.

drunkard n mashàyī m, ɗan giyã m.

dry 1. vi a. būshè v4: the paint has dried
fentì yā būshè; she put it in the sun
to ~ tā sā shi à rānā yà būshè; be
dried stiff būshè cir̃; ~ off tsanè v4,
ƙyāfè v4: come out and ~ off fìtō kà
tsanè; come closer to the fire and you'll
~ off màtsā kusa dà wutā kō kà ƙyāfè; ~
up (of stream, lake) jânyē v4; ~ up completely (esp. of well) ƙafè ƙaf v4. b. (by
spreading under sun) shānyā v1: spread
the clothes out to ~ kì shānyà tufāfì. c.
(become desiccated, e.g. earth, tree) ƙēƙasà
v3, ƙēƙàshē v4: the earth dried up ƙasā
tā ƙēƙasà.
2. vt a. (by wind, sun) būsar̃ (dà) v5: the
sun has dried the clothes rānā tā būsar̃
dà tufāfìn. b. (preserve food, spices)
būsar̃ (dà) v5. c. (by mopping, wiping)
tsanè v4, ƙyāfè v5.
3. adj: the well has run ~ rījìyā tā
ƙafè; it is one of the driest places in
the whole world tanã dàgà cikin wurār̃ē
maflyā rashìn ruwā à dūniyà.

dry season n rānī m, see season.

dubious adj (questionable): his motives are
~ anã shakkàr̃ dàlīlansà.

duck n àgwàgwā f ⟨i⟩, (drake) tõr̃on
àgwàgwā m.

due¹ adj & adv: go ~ north yi arèwa
sòsai; in ~ course nân gàba = nân bã dà
daɗèwā ba; the payment is ~ next week
anã bùkātàr̃ biyàn mākõ mài zuwã; ~ to
sabõdà conj.

due² 1. n (one's right) hakkì m ⟨oCi⟩.
2. adj: he treated them with ~ respect yā

bā sù dařajà yàddà ya kàmātà.

duiker n (crested) gàdā f; (red-flanked) màƙwařnā f.

dull adj a. (of sharp edge, point) dàkùsasshē adj, maràs kaifī m: the knife is ~ wuƙàř bā ta dà kaifī; become ~ (of knife, intelligence) dākùshē v4. b. (of psn.) dàƙī-ƙī adj ⟨ai⟩. c. (uninteresting) maràs ban shà'awà: the book was ~ littāfìn bâ shi dà ban shà'awà = littāfìn bâ shi dà dādī. d. (of color) yi duhù m.

dumb adj a. (foolish), see stupid. b. (mute): deaf and ~ person bēbē m ⟨aye⟩.

dumbfound v dābùřcē v4: the story so ~ed them that they had nothing to say làbāřìn yā dābùřcē su hař sun rasà ta cêwā.

dummy n a. (fool) wāwā n ⟨aye⟩. b. (mannequin) mùtum-mùtumī m.

dump 1. v jagwàɓē v4, jagwaɓař (dà) v5: he ~ed his goods right in the middle of the room yā jagwaɓař dà kāyansà à tsakiyàř dākì.
2. n (for rubbish) jūjī m, bōlà f.

dum-palm n gòrubà f ⟨ai⟩; frond of ~ kabà f ⟨oCi⟩.

dumpster n bōlà f ⟨oCi⟩.

dun¹ adj: a ~ horse gunyà f.

dun² v càccakà v2: I ~ned him for the money he owed me nā càccàkē shì yà biyā nì kuɗin dà nakè bînsà.

dung n tàrōsō m, tākī m.

dung beetle n bùzūzù m.

dupe v yi wà girì m, yàudarà v2.

duplicate 1. n kwafì m, [F] kòpî m: type it in ~ kà bugà shi kwafì biyu.
2. v yi kwafì m; (by mimeograph-type machine) gùřzà v1: type this and then ~ it for me kà bugà wannàn sā'àn nan kà gùřzà minì.

durability n ƙwārī m, ƙarkō m, ingancì m.

durable adj (mài) ƙwārī m, (mài) ƙarkō m, ingàntaccē adj: this is a ~ chair wannàn kujèrā nā dà ƙwārī; make sth. ~ ingàntā v1.

duration n tsawō m: for the ~ of the war gàbā ɗayan lōkàcin yāƙìn.

durbar n dābà f, (during Islamic holidays) hawan Sallà m.

during prep lōkàcin prep, dà prep (+ time expres.): ~ the war, rainy season lōkàcin yāƙì, dàminā; come to see me ~ office hours kà zō wurīnā lōkàcin aikì; ~ the dry season dà rānī; ~ the morning, afternoon dà sāfe, yâmma.

dusk n màgàřibà / màngàřibà f, àlmūřù f.

dust 1. n ƙùrā f, tùrɓāyā f: the ~ has covered everything ƙùrā tā rufè kōmē dà

kōmē.
2. v kaɗè ƙùrā: the table is ~y, please ~ it tēbùř nā dà ƙùrā, don Allàh kì kaɗè.

duster n dastà f, [F] shìfân m.

dust storm n (esp. before harvest) hadarìn kàkā m.

duty¹ n a. (at work) aikì m ⟨ayyukà⟩: he evaded his duties yā gujè wà aikìnsà; one of my duties is to answer letters amsà wàsīƙū yanà ɗaya dàgà cikin ayyukànā; be, go off ~ tāshì dàgà aikì. b. (obligation) wàjìbī m: it is everyone's ~ to do it wàjìbī nē gà kōwā yà yi hakà = yā wàjabà gà kōwā yà yi hakà. c. (moral obligation) àlhakī m: it is his ~ to feed his family àlhakinsà nē yà ciyař dà ìyālìnsà. d. (Relig.) fàrillà f ⟨oCi⟩. e. (esp. household chores) hidimà f ⟨oCi⟩: the women's duties are to cook and care for children hidimōmin mātā sù dafà àbinci sù kulà dà yârā.

duty² n (tax) hàřajì m; customs ~ kuɗin kwastàn m.

dwarf n wàdā n; (euphem. and term of addr.) màlàm dōgo.

dwell v zaunà v1.

dwelling n (housing) màhàllī m; (residential) mazaunī m.

dye 1. v rinà v1, turà v1; (with blue) shūɗà v; ~ hands, feet with henna yi ƙunshì dà lallè.
2. n (any color) rinì m; (var. types): indigo ~ bābā m: the indigo ~ has taken well bābā yā ci dà kyâu; dark blue ~ (from indigo) shūnī m; magenta ~ (from crystals) gàřūřà f; red ~ (from cornstalk) karan dafì m; yellow ~ (from root of shrub) ràwayà f, zàbībì m.

dyeing n rinì m: ~ is one of the most important Hausa crafts rinì ɗaya dàgà cikin mùhimman sanā'ō'in Hàusàwā.

dyeing area n marinā f.

dye-pit, dye-vat n (for indigo only) karōfī m ⟨ai⟩.

dyer n marìnī m.

dynamite n nàkiyà f.

dynasty n daulà f ⟨oCi⟩.

dysentery n atùnī m.

# E

**each 1.** *det* kōwànè *m*, kōwàcè *f*: ~ child brought a pencil kōwànè yārȍ yā zȍ dà fensìr̃; I gave ~ man ₦2 nā bā kōwànè mùtûm naira̓ biyu; ~ one of them has a pencil kōwàd̃ànnensù nȁ dà fensir̃.
**2.** *pro* kōwànnē *m*, kōwàccē *f*: ~ one has to help yā kàmātà kōwànnē yà bā dà gudùmmawar̃sà; ~ and every one kōwā dà kōwā; ~ other jūnā *m*: they know ~ other sun san jūnā.
**3.** *adv* (*to express notion of 'X each', repeat the final numeral*): 3 pencils ~ fensìr̃ ukù ukù; 15k ~ kwabȍ gōmà shā bìyar̃ bìyar̃.

**eager** *adj*: be ~ yi allà-allà *f*, yi ɗȍkī *m*: we are ~ to meet the visitors munā allà-allà mù hàɗu dà bȁk̃īn; I am ~ for that day to come inȁ ɗȍkin rānar̃ tà zȍ.

**eagerness** *n* ɗȍkī *m*, zàgwàdī *m*.

**eagle** *n* (*bateleur*) gaggāfà *f*, (*martial*) juhùr̃mà *f* ⟨oCi⟩.

**ear** *n* **a.** kûnnē *m* ⟨uwa⟩: my ~ hurts kûnnē nȁ minì cīwȍ; turn a deaf ~ (*fig.*) yi kûnnen uwar̃ shȅgū; pierced ~s hūjìn kûnnē. **b.** (*adverbial uses*): in, on the ~ à kunne/kûnnē *adv*: he got cut on the ~ yā yankè à kunne. **c.** (*of corn, millet*) zangar̃nìyā *f*.

**eardrum** *n* ɗȍdon-kunne *m*.

**earlier** *adv*: that is what he said ~ dâ hakà ya fàdā; don't come ~ than 9 o'clock kadà kà zō kȁfìn k̃arfè tar̃à; he arrived ~ than expected yā isȍ dà wuri fìye dà yȁddà akȅ zàtō.

**earlobe** *n* fātàr̃ kûnnē *f*.

**early** *adv* **a.** (*not late*) dà wuri *adv*: they left ~ sun tāshì dà wuri; very ~, as ~ as possible dà wurwuri; get an ~ start (*esp. in morning*) yi sàmmakō *m*. **b.** (*before expected time*) kàfìn lōkàcī: they arrived ~ sun isō kàfìn lōkàcī.

**earn** *v* **a.** (*wage, salary*) sȁmi lādā, sȁmi àlbâshī: he ~s ₦600 a month yanà sāmùn àlbâshin naira̓ ɗàrī shidà à watà; ~ a living nȅmi àbinci: he ~s his living as a leatherworker yanà nȅman àbincinsà ta dūkancì; he ~s an honest living dà gùminsà yakȅ cî; ~ a degree sȁmi dìgìr̃î. **b.** (*deserve*) càncantà *v2*: his efforts ~ed him praise k̃wȁzonsà yā càncànci yàbō.

**earnings** *n* àlbâshī *m*, lādā *m*; gross ~ àlbâshī kàfìn d̃ȅbe-d̃ȅbe.

**earrings** *n* 'yan kunne *p*: wear ~ sâ 'yan kunne.

**earth** *n* **a.** (*ground, dirt*) k̃asā *f*: fill the hole first with ~ kà cikè rāmìn dà k̃asā tùkùna. **b.** (*the planet*) dūniyà *f*: the ~ is round like a ball dūniyà zȁgàyayyā cè kàmar̃ k̃wallō; (*fig.*) to the ends of the ~ har̃ bangon dūniyà.

**earthenware** *n* kāyan yumɓū *m*.

**earthquake** *n* gìr̃gizàr̃ k̃asā *f*: a terrible ~ mūgùwar̃ gìr̃gizàr̃ k̃asā.

**earthworm** *n* tānā *f*.

**earwig** *n* tsātsȍ *m*.

**ease 1.** *n* sauk̃ī *m*: he did it with ~ yā yi shì cikin sauk̃ī; I am at ~ hankàlīnā à kwànce yakȅ; I am ill at ~ hankàlīnā à tàshe yakȅ.
**2.** *v* sauk̃àk̃à / sawwàk̃à *v1*: the medicine ~d his pain māgànîn yā sauk̃àk̃à masà cīwȍ.

**easily** *adv* **a.** (*without effort*) dà sauk̃ī, cikin sauk̃ī, bâ wùyā, bâ wàhalà: I found it ~ nā sàmē shì dà sauk̃ī; this cloth tears ~ yādìn nân nȁ dà saurin yȁgàwā. **b.** (*quickly*) dà wuri, dà saurī: he gets angry ~ yanà dà saurin fushì; he forgave me ~ yā yāfè minì dà wuri; sugar melts ~ suk̃àr̃ī saurin narkȅwā gàrē shì.

**east** *n & adv* gabàs *m*: the Middle E. k̃asàshen Gabàs ta Tsakiyà; the Far E. k̃asàshen Gabàs mài Nīsā; E. Africa Afir̃kà ta Gabàs; it is ~ of town yanà gabashin gàrī = yanà gabàs dà gàrī.

**eastern** *adj* na gabàs, gabashin *prep*: the ~ states jīhōhin gabàs; ~ Nigeria Nìjēr̃iyà ta gabàs; ~ European countries k̃asàshen gabashin Tūr̃ai.

**easterner** *n* bàgabâshī *m*.

**easy** *adj* (*mài*) sauk̃ī *m*, maràs wùyā *f*, maràs wàhalà *f*: that's ~ yanà dà sauk̃ī = bâ wùyā; knowledge is not ~ to get ilìmī nȁ dà wùyar̃ sāmù; this car is ~ to drive mōtàr̃ nân tanà dà saurin tūk̃àwā = mōtàr̃ nân tanà dà dāɗin tūk̃àwā; make sth. ~ for so. sauk̃àk̃à wà *v1*, sassàutà wà *v1*: he made it ~ for us yā sauk̃àk̃à manà; you should take it ~ kà kwantar̃ dà hankàlī; live an ~ life zaunà cikin dāɗin râi; that's real ~! kàmar̃ cîn tuwȍ nȅ!

**easy-going** *adj* (*mài*) sauk̃in k̃âi *m*, (*mài*)

lāfiyà *f*: he's an ∼ person yanà dà sauƙin kâi.

**eat** *v* a. ci (àbinci) *v0*, (*have a meal*) yi kàlàcī *m*: we've already ∼en mun rigā mun ci àbinci; we're sitting down to ∼ munā ƙwaryā; let's ∼! bìsìmillà! *excl*; ∼ heartily nàɗi àbinci; ∼ up completely cînyē kaf, lāshè *v4*; ∼ voraciously lāmùshē *v4*, lanƙwàmē *v4*. b. (*fruits or sth. juicy*) shā *v0*: ∼ an orange, mango, pineapple shā lēmō, mangwàɍò, àbàɍbā.

**eaves** *n* zankō *m*.

**eavesdrop** *v* yi sātàɍ jî: he's ∼ping on them yanà sātàɍ jînsù = yanà làɓe yanà sàuràrensù.

**ebony** *n* kanyà *f*.

**echo** 1. *v* amsà *v1*: the cave ∼ed his shout kōgō yā amsà kuwwàɍsà.
2. *n* àmsà-kuwwà *f*.

**eclipse** *n* hùsūfî *m* ⟨ai⟩: solar ∼ hùsūfìn rānā; there is a solar ∼ watà yā kāmà rānā; lunar ∼ hùsūfìn watà = (*fig.*) zàzzàɓin watà; there is a lunar ∼ rānā tā kāmà watà = (*fig.*) watà yā yi zàzzàɓī.

**ecology** *n* nazàɍin lāfiyàɍ yanàyin ƙasā *m*.

**economic** *adj* na tattalin aɍzìkī *m*: ∼ boom, growth bùnƙàsàɍ tattalin aɍzìkī; ∼ crisis taɓarɓàrêwaɍ tattalin aɍzìkī; ∼ depression tàwayàɍ tattalin aɍzìkī.

**economical** *adj* (mài) tattalī *m*, (mài) tsimī *m*: she is ∼ about spending money tanà dà tattalī wajen kashè kuɗintà.

**economics** *n* ilìmin tattalin aɍzìkī *m*.

**economize** *v* tattàlā *v1*, yi tānàdī *m*.

**economy** *n* a. (*thriftiness*) tattalī *m*, tsimī *m*. b. (∼ *of a country*) tattalin aɍzìkin ƙasā *m*.

**ecstasy** (*Relig.*) shauƙì *m*.

**eczema** *n* kircī *m*.

**edge** *n* a. (*flat side*) gēfè *m* ⟨gyàffā⟩: move the glass away from the ∼ of the table kà kau dà tambùlàn dàgà gēfèn tēbùɍ. b. (*of a vessel*) bàkī *m*; the ∼ of the plate, calabash is chipped bàkin fàɍantì, ƙwaryā ya ɓagurà. c. (*sharp ∼ of knife, sword*) kaifī *m*: a double-∼d knife wuƙā mài kaifī biyu. d. (*proximity*) bàkī *m*: his house is at the ∼ of town gidansà à bàkin gàrī yakè.

**edible** *adj* (mài) cîwuwā: the food was not ∼ àbincîn bā yà cîwuwā.

**edit** *v* shiryà *v1*, tācè *v4*: ∼ poems for publication tācè wāƙōƙī don à bugà.

**edition** *n* bugù *m*: first ∼ bugù na farkō.

**editor** *n* ēdità *n* ⟨oCi⟩, [F] èdìtâɍ *n*.

**editorial** *n* ɍa'àyī *m*: ∼ page shāfìn ɍa'àyī.

**educate** *v* a. (*provide formal schooling*) ilmantaɍ (dà) *v5*, bā dà ilìmī, kaɍantaɍ (dà) *v5*: the goverment's goal is to ∼ every citizen būrìn gwamnatì shī nè ilmantaɍ dà kōwànè ɗan ƙasā; he was ∼d in England yā yi kàɍātū à Ingìlà. b. (*enlighten*) wāyaɍ dà kân w., wāyè wà kâi, būɗè idòn w.

**educated** *adj* (mài) ilìmī *m*, wàyayyē *adj*.

**education** *n* a. (*formal*) ilìmī *m*, kàɍātū *m*; complete one's ∼ saukè kàɍātū; agency for mass ∼ hùkūmàɍ yàɗà ilìmin mânyā. b. (*enlightenment*) wāyèwaɍ kâi *f*: they've had a broad ∼ kânsù yā wāyè. c. (*academic subject*) ilìmin aikìn kōyàɍwā *m*; college of ∼ kwalējìn kōyaɍ dà aikìn kōyàɍwā; adult ∼ ilìmin mânyā; higher ∼ ilìmī mài zurfī; Western ∼ ilìmin bōkō; Islamic ∼ Mùhàmmàdiyyà *f*.

**educator** *n* mài aikìn kōyàɍwā *n*, mài aikìn màlàntā *n*.

**effect** *n* a. be in ∼ yi aikì *m*: the law is no longer in ∼ dōkàɍ bā tà aikì yànzu; put into ∼ zaɍtaɍ (dà) *v5*, aiwataɍ (dà) *v5*; take ∼ ci *v0*: the medicine is beginning to take ∼ māgànîn yā fārà cî. b. in ∼ à tàƙaice *adv*: in ∼, you've suffered a loss à tàƙaice kā yi hàsāɍà kè nan.

**effective** *adj* a. (*beneficial*) (mài) àmfànī *m*, (mài) fā'idà *f*; an ∼ medicine māgànī mài àmfànī; aspirin is ∼ for headaches asfìrìn yanà māgànin cīwòn kâi. b. (*taking effect, working*) (mài) cî *m*: this medicine is not ∼ māgànin nàn bài ci ba.

**effigy** *n* mùtum-mùtumī *m*.

**effort** *n* a. ƙōƙarī *m*, iyàwā *f*, ƙwàzō *m*: he appealed to the people to increase their ∼s yā yi kirà gà mutànē dà sù ƙārà ƙwàzō; combine ∼s haɗà ƙarfī: the countries are combining ∼s to combat drugs ƙasàshên nà haɗà ƙarfī wajen yāƙì dà haɍkàɍ ƙwàyā; make an ∼ yi ƙōƙarī, ƙōƙàrtā *v1*, tāɓùkā *v1*; exert great ∼ yunƙùrā *v1*, jà ƙōƙarī, yi namijìn ƙōƙarī. b. (*involving difficulty*) wàhalà *f*: their ∼s paid off wàhalàɍsù tā biyā = (*fig.*) kwalliyā tā biyā kuɗin sàbulù; it was not worth the ∼ (*fig.*) kwalliyā bà tà biyā kuɗin sàbulù ba.

**e.g.** *abbr* mìsālìn, alal mìsālì.

**egg** *n* ƙwai *m*: how much is a dozen ∼s? ƙwai nawà dōzìn? hard-boiled ∼ dàfaffen ƙwai; crack open an ∼ fasà ƙwai; hatch an ∼ ƙyanƙyàsà ƙwai; the ∼ has hatched ƙwai yā ƙyanƙyàshē; lay an

~ nasà ƙwai = sakà ƙwai; a new-laid ~ ƙwai sābon nashī; sit on an ~ yi kwàncī *m*: the hen is sitting on her ~s kàzā tanà kwàncī.

**egg beater** *n* maburgī *m*.

**egg on** *v* zugà *v1*, tunzùrā *v1*, hařzùƙā *v1*: he ~ed me on to insult the trader yā zugà ni ìn zàgi ɗan kàsuwā.

**eggplant** *n* (*local var.*) ɗātā *f*, gautā *m*; (*European var.*) [F] òbàřjî *m*.

**eggshell** *n* kwàfsař / kwàsfař ƙwai *f*, ɓāwon ƙwai *m*.

**egg yolk** *n* ƙwandùwā *f*, gwaidùwā *f*.

**egotism** *n* sôn kâi *m*.

**egret** *n* (*cattle*) bâlbēlà *f* ⟨u⟩.

**Eid** *n, see* Id.

**eight** *quant* takwàs *f*.

**eighteen** *quant* (gōmà) shà takwàs, àshiřin biyu bābù, àshiřin bâ biyu.

**eighth** *quant* na takwàs; one-~ sumùnī *m*.

**eighty** *quant* tàmànin *f*.

**either 1.** *conj*: ~...or kō...kō: I leave ~ tomorrow or the next day zân tāshì kō gòbe kō jībi; ~ keep it or throw it away kō kà ajìyē shī kō kà yař; ~ you or he has taken my bag tsàkānin kai kō shī, wani yā ɗaùki jàkātā. **2.** *pro*: ~ one kōwànnē *m*, kōwàccē *f*: ~ (one) of them will do kōwànnensù zâi yi; ~ one (*in neg.*) kō ɗaya: I don't want ~ one of them bā nà sôn kō ɗayansù = bā nà sôn kōwànnensù.

**eject** *v* fid dà / fitař (dà) *v5*.

**elastic** *n* řōbà *f*, [F] kàushû *m*.

**elbow** *n* gwīwàř hannu *f*; recline on one's ~ kìshìngiɗà *v3*, yi kìshìngiɗe *m*.

**elder** *n* dattījò *m*, dattījùwā *f* ⟨dàttàwā⟩ ⟨ai⟩; tsōhō *m*, tsōhuwā *f* ⟨tsòfàffī⟩; ~ brother wâ *m*, yàya *m* ⟨yayyē, yāyū⟩; ~ sister yâ *f*, yàya *f* ⟨yayyē, yāyū⟩; one's ~s magàbàtā *p*; the village ~s tsòfàffin ƙauyèn = magàbàtan ƙauyèn.

**eldest child** *n* bàbban ɗā *m*, ɗan fārì *m*.

**elect** *v* zàɓā *v2*: he was ~ed president an zàɓē shì shùgàban ƙasā.

**election** *n* zàɓē *m*: ~ campaign yàƙin nēman zàɓē; bye-~ zàɓen cikà gurbì; general ~ bàbban zàɓē; primary ~ ƙàramin zàɓē = zàɓen shìgā tākarā.

**electoral** *adj* na zàɓē *m*.

**electric, electrical** *adj* na làntařkì: an ~ iron dūtsèn gūgà na làntařkì; ~ company hùkūmàř làntařkì *f*, Nēpà *f*, [F] Nìjèlâk *m*.

**electrician** *n* mài aikìn làntařkì *n*.

**electricity** *n* wutā *f*, làntařkì *m*, [F] làtìřîk *m*: the machine is driven by ~

injì ɗîn nà aikì dà làntařkì; connect the ~ sâ wutā; cut off the ~ (*due to power failure*) ɗaukè wutā; cut off the ~ (*due to non-payment*) yankè wutā.

**element** *n* (*small amount*): an ~ of truth ƙanshin gàskiyā.

**elementary** *adj* a. (*easy*) (mài) sauƙī *m*. b. (*beginning*) na farkō: an ~ course kwàs na farkō.

**elementary school** *n, see* school.

**elephant** *n* gīwā *f* ⟨aye⟩; (*bull*) tòřon gīwā *m*.

**elephantiasis** *n* tundurmī *m*.

**elevate** *v* ɗagà *v1*: keep your leg ~d so it can heal kà bař ƙafàřkà à ɗage don tà warkè.

**elevation** *n* hawan tudù *m*, tsayì *m*: the mountain has an ~ of 1500 meters tsayìn tudùn mītā dubū dà ɗarī bìyař.

**elevator** *n* lîf *m*.

**eleven** *quant* (gōmà) shà ɗaya *f*.

**eleventh** *adj* na shà ɗaya.

**eliminate** *v* a. (*get rid of*) kashè *v4*: this formula will ~ all cockroaches māgànin nàn zâi kashè duk wani kyànkyasò. b. (*Sport*) fid dà / fitař (dà) *v5*: our team was ~d in the 3rd match an fid dà tîm ɗinmù à karàwā ta ukù.

**elliptical** *adj* (mài) siffàř ƙwai.

**eloquence** *n* fàsāhàř màganà *f*: he speaks with ~ yanà dà fàsāhàř màganà.

**else** *adv* a. (*also*) kuma *adv*: who ~ is coming? wà kuma kè zuwà? she also bought something ~ tā kuma sàyi wani àbù. b. (*different*) dàbam *adv*: someone ~ wani dàbam. c. (*remaining*) saurā *m*: who ~ saw the accident? sauran wà ya ga haɗàřīn? no one ~ has come bâ sauran wàndà ya zō; there's nothing ~ to do but wait bâ wani àbin dà zā à yi sai à dākàtā; apart from that what ~ did you buy? ban dà wannàn, sauran mè ka sàyā?

**elsewhere** *adv* à wani wurî dàbam.

**elude** *v* ɓacè wà *v4*: he ~d them yā ɓacè musù = yā ƙi kàmuwā.

**emaciated, be(come)** *v* ƙanjàmē *v4*, tsōtsè *v4*, yanƙwànē *v4*.

**emancipate** *v* 'yàntā *v1*: the emir ~d the slaves sarkī yā 'yàntā bāyîn.

**embargo** *n* tàkunkùmī *m*: an arms, oil ~ tàkunkùmin sai dà màkàmai, mân fētùř; impose an ~ yi wà tàkunkùmī.

**embarrass** *v* a. (*make so. ashamed*) bâ w. kunyà, yi wà àbin kunyà, kunyàtā *v1*: the child's disobedience ~ed his mother rashìn ladàbin yāròn yā bâ mahaifìyařsà kunyà; be ~ed ji kunyà *f*,

kùnyatà *v3*: I was too ~ed to ask him
nā ji kunyằr̃ tằmbayằr̃sà; I am ~ed
to admit that that is true nā ji zāfin
cêwā wannàn àbù gàskiyà nề. b. (*humiliate*) ci fuskằr̃ w., ci mutuncìn w.,
wulākàntā *v1*. c. (*by interrupting or snub-
bing so.*) gwalề *v4*.

embarrassment *n* kunyằ *f*: what you have
done has caused us ~ àbîn dà kikà yi yā
sâ mu kunyằ.

embassy *n* ōfìshin jakādancì *m*, [F]
àmbàsâd *f.*

embellish *v* ƙārā wà gishirī, sâ gishirī:
she knows how to ~ a folktale tā iyà
ƙārā wà tàtsūnìyā gishirī = tā iyà sâ
gishirī à tàtsūnìyā.

embers *n* garwashì / garwāshī *m*,
ɓàr̃ɓàshin wutā *m*.

embezzle *v* yi wà zàmba *f*, zàmbatà *v2*,
hằ'intà *v2*: he ~d thousands of nairas
from the bank yā yi wà bankì zàmbar̃
naïr̃à dùbbai; ~ public funds zàmbàci
gwamnatì = ci kuɗin jàma'à.

embezzlement *n* zàmba *f*, hằ'incì *m.*

emblem *n* tambàrī *m* ⟨u-a⟩, lambằ *f* ⟨oCi⟩;
(*heraldic, e.g. Northern knot*) dằgī *m*
⟨una⟩.

embrace *v* rùngumà *v2*; ~ Islam rùngùmi
Musuluncì, mùsùluntà *v3*.

embroider *v* yi wà aikì, yi wà adō: the
robe was ~ed with gold thread an yi wà
rìgā adō dà zàren zīnàr̃ì; an ~ed robe
rìgā mài aikì = rìgā mài adō; it is
beautifully ~ed tā àikàtu dà kyâu.

embroidery *n* aikì *m*, adō *m*; (*open-stitch
type*) sùr̃fànì *m*; hand ~ aikìn hannu;
machine ~ aikìn kèkè.

embryo *n* tằyī *m.*

emergency *n* gaggàwā *f*: ~ exit mafitar̃
gaggàwā; ~ landing sàukar̃ ƙùndùmbālā;
~ relief tàimakon gaggàwā; ~ room (*of
hospital*) dākìn hadàr̃ī = dākìn tàimakō;
~ session (*of legislature*) tàron gaggàwā;
in an ~ in tīlàs tā kāmà = in dai dà
làr̃ūr̃à; declare a state of ~ kafà dōkar̃-
tā-ɓàcì.

emigrate *v* yi ƙaurā *f*, ƙaura *v3a*: they ~d
from their country to a new one sun yi
ƙaurā dàgà ƙasar̃sù zuwà ƙasàshē wàje.

emigré *n* ɗan gudùn hijìr̃à *m.*

eminent *adj* màshàhūr̃ì *adj*, shàhàr̃ar̃r̃ē
*adj.*

emir *n* sarkī *m* ⟨sarākunà⟩.

emissary *n* ɗan àikè *m.*

emotion *n* mòtsin râi *m*, sōsùwar̃ râi *f*,
jîn zūcìyā *m.*

emotional *adj* (mài) mōtsà râi, (mài) sōsà
râi.  —— *empathy*

empire *n* daulà *f* ⟨oCi⟩: the British ~
daulàr̃ Ingìlà.

emphasis *n* ƙarfàfàwā *f.*

emphasize *v* ƙarfàfā *v1*: he ~d the importance of getting an education yā ƙarfàfà
muhimmancìn sāmùn ilìmī.

emphatic *adj* ƙaƙƙarfā *adj*: speak ~ally yi
màganà dà ƙaƙƙarfar̃ muryằ = yi màganà
dà bàbbar̃ muryằ.

employ *v* ɗau/ɗàuki w. aikì *v1*: this factory ~s 100 workers an ɗau mùtûm ɗàrī
aikì à ma'aikatar̃ nàn.

employee *n* ma'àikàcī *m.*

employer *n* màigidà *m*, shùgàbà *m*; (*corpo-
rate*) ma'aikatā *f*, kamfànī *m.*

employment *n* aikìn yî *m*: provide ~
sāmar̃ dà aikìn yî.

empty 1. *adj* emtì *m*: an ~ bottle kwalabā
emtì; (*esp. box, container*) fànkō *m*; this
box is ~ àkwàtìn nân fànkō nề; it is ~
bâ kōmē à cikinsà.
2. *v* (*take out*) fid dà / fitar̃ (dà) *v5*,
zub dà / zubar̃ (dà) *v5*: please ~ the
trash outside kà zub dà shàrā wàje.

empty-handed *adj* hannū banzā.

empty-headed *adj* wòfī *n* ⟨aye⟩.

enable *v*: the money he earned ~d him to
go on with his studies kuɗin dà ya sāmù
sun bā shì ƙarfin cî gàba dà kàr̃àtū.

enact *v* (*a bill*) kafà *v1.*

enamelware *n* kwanō *m* ⟨uka, oCi⟩.

encampment *n* (*Mil.*) sànsanī *m* ⟨ai⟩;
(*transitory*) zangò *m* ⟨una⟩.

enchant *v* a. (*cast spell*) sammàcē *v4*. b.
(*please*) bā dà shà'awà.

encircle *v* kēwàyē *v4*, zāgàyē *v4*: the police ~d the house 'yan sàndā sun kēwàyè
gidā; a town ~d by hills gàrī mài kèwàye
dà tsaunukà.

enclose *v* a. (*surround*) kēwayar̃ (dà) *v5*.
b. (*insert into*) sakà *v1*: he ~d a self-
addressed envelope yā sakō ambùlàn mài
àdìr̃ēshìnsà à kâi.

enclosure *n* kēwayè *m*: the goats are kept
in an ~ anà tsarè awākī à kēwàyè.

encounter *v* ci karò dà; (*unexpectedly or
to one's dismay*) yi kìciɓìs dà: the dog
unexpectedly ~ed a hyena kàre yā yi
kìciɓìs dà kūrā.

encourage *v* ƙarfàfā wà (gwīwằ) *v1*,
ƙarfàfā wà zūcìyā, bā dà ƙarfī: he
didn't ~ me bài ƙarfàfā minì gwīwằ ba =
bài bā nì ƙarfī ba; be, feel ~d ƙàrfafà
*v3*: I felt ~d zūcìyātā tā ƙàrfafà.

encouragement n: children really need lots of ~ yârā nā bùkātāɍ à ɓarfàfā musù gwīwā ɓwaɍai.

encroach v (of desert) kwarārō v6; ~ment of the desert kwarārôwaɍ hàmādā.

end 1. n a. ɓàɍshē m: the ~ of the book, month ɓàɍshen littāfī, watā; in the ~ dàgà ɓàɍshē; all good things must come to an ~ kōmē na dūniyā mài ɓārèwā nē; 'the ~' (in a book) tàmat. b. (endpoint) maɓurā f: I rode the bus until the ~ of the line nā shìga bâs haɍ maɓuraɍ hanyàɍtà. c. (fate) makōmā f: he came to a bad ~ yā yi mùmmūnaɍ makōmā. d. (death) ajàlī m: his ~ was near ajàlinsà yā kusa.
2. v a. (finish) ɓārè v4: the month has ~ed watàn yā ɓārè = watàn yā mutù; how does the folktale ~? yàyā tàtsūnìyā ta ɓārè? how did he ~ up? yàyā akà ɓārè dà shī? = yàyā ya ɓārè? b. (conclude) kammàlā v1: he ~d his speech by saying... yā ɓārè jàwābìnsà dà cêwā....

endeavor v yi ɓôɓarī m.

endorse v gòyi bāyan: the party did not ~ the candidate jàm'iyyàɍ bà tà gòyi bāyan ɗan tākaràɍ ba.

endurance n daurèwā f, jūriyā f, jìmirī m: his ~ failed yā kàsà daurèwā = jìmirinsà yā kàsà.

endure v a. (bear pain, trouble) daurè v4, jūrè v4, yi jìmirī m: the pain is hard to ~ ɍàɗàɗin cīwòn yanā dà wùyaɍ daurèwā. b. (tolerate) yi hàɓurī dà, jūrè dà v1: although we hated him, we ~d his abuse duk dà cêwā mun tsànē shì mun jūrè dà cîn mutuncìnsà. c. (last) ɗōrè v4: their friendship will not ~ àbòtaɍsù bà zā tà ɗōrè ba.

enema n gūgūtū m.

enemy n àbōkin gàbā m, magàbcī m, maɓìyī m: his worst ~ àbōkin gàbaɍsà na ɓîn ɓāràwā.

energetic adj mùzakkàɍī m ⟨ai⟩, (mài) kùzārī m, (mài) zāfin nāmā m, (mài) kàzàɍ-kazaɍ idph; be ~ about dùɓufà gà v3.

energy n a. (vitality) kùzārī m: Bon Vita gives you ~! Bòn Bītā nā sâ kùzārī! I don't have the ~ to continue further bâ ni dà kùzārin cî gàba. b. (power) ɓarfī m: electrical ~ ɓarfin (wutaɍ) làntaɍkì; nuclear ~ ɓarfin nūkìliyà. c. (fuel) makāmashī m: solar, nuclear ~ makāmashin zāfin rānā, nūkìliyà.

enforce v zaɍtaɍ (dà) v5, tabbataɍ (dà) v5: the law is not strictly ~d bà à tsanàntâwā wajen zaɍtaɍ dà dòkàɍ.

engage v (so. for work) jìngatā v2.

engaged, be v (to be married) yi baiwā f, yi baikō m: Ladi is ~ an yi wà Lādì baiwā; Ladi is ~ to Sule an yi baiwaɍ Lādì dà Sulè; how long have they been ~? tun yàushè akà yi musù baiwā?

engagement n a. (for marriage) baiwā f, baikō m. b. (appointment) àlkawàɍī m ⟨ai⟩.

engine n a. (motor) injī m ⟨una⟩, [F] mōtâɍ m: don't leave your ~ running kà kashè injìn. b. (apparatus, piece of equipment) nā'ūɍā f ⟨oCi⟩. c. (locomotive) tukunyaɍ jirgī f.

engineer n injìniyà n ⟨oCi⟩, [F] ìnjìnâɍ n: civil ~ injìniyàn gìne-gìne; electrical ~ injìniyàn làntaɍkì.

engineering n ilìmin aikìn injìniyà m.

England n Ingìlà f.

English 1. n Tūɍancī m, [F] Ingìlīshì m: he speaks ~ very well yā iyà Tūɍancī sòsai; Pidgin E. Bùɍōɓā m.
2. adj na Tūɍāwā, na Ingìlà: that is an old ~ custom tsōhuwaɍ àl'ādàɍ Tūɍāwā cè.

Englishman n bà'ingìlīshì m.

engrave v yi zānè dà wutā.

engraving n zānen wutā m.

enjoy v ji dāɗī m, hōlè dà v4, mōrè dà v4, yi nìshāɗī m: we ~ed the celebration mun yi nìshāɗìn bìkìn; I ~ed the game nā hōlè dà wàsân = nā ji dāɗin wàsân; ~ oneself mōrè v4, hōlè v4, shèɓà ayā, (esp. in worldly sense) ci dūniyà.

enjoyable adj (mài) dāɗī m, (mài) aɍmashī m: the game was ~ wàsân yā ji aɍmashī.

enjoyment n jìn dāɗī m, nìshāɗī m; (in social gathering) ànnàshùwā f.

enlarge v ɓārà girmā, fāɗàɗā v1.

enlighten v wāyaɍ dà kân w., wāyè wà kâi, haskàkā v1: ~ the people wāyaɍ dà kân jàma'à; I ~ed him about the ways of the world nā wāyaɍ masà dà kâi gàme dà sha'ànin dūniyà; education ~s our lives ilìmī nā haskàkà ràyuwaɍmù.

enlist v shìga sōjà.

enliven v rāyaɍ (dà) v5: she ~ed the conversation tā rāyaɍ dà hīɍàɍ.

enmity n àdāwā f, gàbā f, ɓìyayyà f.

enormous adj a. (in size) ɓātò m ⟨Ca⟩: an ~ man, box ɓātòn mùtûm, àkwàtì; (often expressed by ideophonic adjs which go with specific nouns): an ~ building fankamēmèn ginī; an ~ hole wafcēcèn rāmì. b. (of amount): an ~ quantity (mài) ɗimbin yawā, (mài) tārìn yawā: an ~ sum of money kuɗī màsu ɗimbin yawā.

enough *adj* a. (*sufficient*) ìsasshē *adj*, cìkakkē *adj*: do you have ~ money? kinā dà kuɗī ìsàssū? be ~ ìsā *v2*: this isn't ~ money kuɗin nàn bà sù ìsā ba; food ~ for 50 people àbincîn dà zâi ìshi mùtûm hàmsin; more than ~ fìye dà kīmà; have ~ (*of food*) ƙoshi *v3*\*: thanks, I've had ~ àlhamdù lillāhì nā ƙoshi = mādàllā nā àmfānà; things have gone far ~, it's time to act (*fig.*) tùrā tā kai bangō. b. (*satisfactory*): be good ~ for gamsař (dà) *v5*: his work is good ~ for me aikìnsà yā gamsař dà nī; it isn't good ~ bài gamsař ba = bài ìsā ba = bài yi ba.

enquire *v, see* inquire.

enraged, be(come) *v* kùfulà *v3*: he is easily ~ yanà dà saurin kùfulà.

enrich *v* a. (*strengthen*) ƙarfàfā *v1*: they ~ the flour with vitamins anā ƙarfàfā fulāwà dà bitàmîn. b. (*oneself, become rich*) afzùtà kâi: ~ oneself at public expense afzùtà kâi dà kuɗin jàma'à.

en route *adv* à kân hanyà, cikin tàfiyà.

enslave *v* bautař (dà) *v5*:

ensure *v* tabbatař (dà) *v5*: I can't ~ that he will come on time bà zân iyà tabbatař dà zuwansà cikin lōkàcī ba; in order to ~ peace and prosperity don à tabbatař dà lùmānà dà zaman lāfiyà.

entangled, be(come) *v* hařɗè *v4*, cukwì- kwìyē *v4*, sarƙàfē *v4*.

enter 1. *vi* (*go in*) shìga *v3*; (*come in*) shigō *v6*.
2. *vt* shigař (dà) *v5*: he ~ed my name in the contest yā shigař dà sūnānā à gàsâř.

enthusiasm *n* a. (*interest*) shà'awà *f*: he has great ~ for his work yanà shà'awàř aikìn dà yakè yî sòsai. b. (*eagerness*) ɗòkī *m*, zàgwàdī *m*: Audu is full of ~ Audù yā fayè zàgwàdī = Audù, àkwai zàgwàdī. c. (*energy*) kùzārī *m*.

enthusiastic *adj* (mài) shà'awà *f*, (mài) kùzārī *m*.

entire *adj & adv* a. (*whole, of sth.*) duk / dukà *adv*: he ate the ~ loaf yā cînyè buřōdì dukà. b. (*in its entirety, esp. of activity*) gàbā ɗaya: he wasted my ~ day yesterday yā ɓātà minì lōkàcī gàbā ɗaya jiyà; he spent the ~ day in bed yanà kwànce gàbā ɗayan rānàř; I read the ~ book nā kařàncè littāfìn gàbā ɗayansà.

entirely *adv, see* completely.

entourage *n* tàwagà *f*: the emir and his ~ sarkī dà tàwagàřsà.

entrails *n* kāyan cikì *m*.

entrance *n* mashigà *f*, (*door*) ƙōfà *f* ⟨oCi⟩: where is the ~? ìnā ƙōfà? = ìnā mashigà?

entrance fee *n* kuɗin shìgā *p*.

entrenched *adj*: laziness has become ~ ragwancì yā zaunà dà gìndinsà.

entrust *v* bā dà àmānà *f*: I ~ my son to you nā bā kà àmānàř dānā.

entry *n* a. (*entrance*) mashigà *f*; no ~! bâ shìga! b. (*in bookkeeping*) shigàřwā *f*.

enumerate *v* lāsàftā / lissàfā *v1*: they ~d the crimes he had committed an lāsàftā masà laifuffukàn dà ya aikàtā.

enumeration *n* lissāfì *m*, ƙìdāyà *f*.

envelope *n* ambùlàn *m* ⟨ambulōlī⟩, [F] àmbùlàf *f*: a self-addressed ~ ambùlàn mài àdìřēshìnsà à kâi.

envious *adj* (mài) baƙin cikì *m*, (mài) hassadà *f*, (mài) ƙyàshī *m*; (& *hostile*) (mài) nukuřà *f*; be ~ of so. yi wà baƙin cikì, yi wà hassadà: he is ~ of my progress, my new car yanà baƙin cikìn cî-gàbānā, sàbuwař mōtàtā; an ~ person won't get anything out of life mài hassadà bà zâi ci řībàř zaman dūniyà ba.

environment *n* màhâllī / mùhâllī *m*: provide the right ~ for sāmař wà màhâllìn dà ya dācè; make efforts to clean up the ~ yi ƙòƙarin tsabtàcè màhâllī.

environs *n* kēwayè *m*: Kano and its ~ Kanò dà kēwayèntà.

envision *v* ƙiyàstā à râi *v1*.

envoy *n* ɗan àikē *m*, wàkīlī *m* ⟨ai⟩.

envy *v* yi hassadàř w., yi kīshìn w., yi wà baƙin cikì, yi ƙyàshī *m*; (*esp. hostile*) yi nukuřà *f*: I ~ his success inà nukuřàř nasařàř dà ya ci.

epidemic *n* ànnōbà *f*, ɓarkēwař cīwò *f*: a cholera ~ has broken out ànnōbař kwalařà tā ɓarkè.

epilepsy *n* fařfāɗiyā *f*.

epileptic *n* mài fařfāɗiyā *n*.

episiotomy *n* yankan gishīrī *m*.

episode *n* karò *m*.

epithet *n, see* praise-epithet.

epoch *n* zāmànī / zàmānì *m*, mařřà *f*.

equal 1. *adj & adv* daidai *adv*: this is not ~ to that wannàn bà daidai dà wàncan ba; divide it into 3 ~ parts ràbà wannàn ukù daidai; mix ~ amounts of sugar and flour kì gauràyà yawàn sukàrī daidai dà na fulāwà; be ~ yi daidai, yi ɗaya: all men are ~ under the law mutànē ɗaya sukè à fuskàř shàři'à; exactly ~ daidai wà daidà.

2. *n*: it has no ∼ bābù kàmařsà = bâ mài kàmařsà.

3. *v* (*in math*): 6 times 2 ∼s 12 shidà sàu biyu shā biyu kè nan.

**equality** *n* dàidaitō *m*, daidaicī *m*: we believe in the ∼ of men munà īmānìn dàidaiton àl'ummā.

**equalize** *v* daidàitā *v1*.

**equator** *n* ìkwaità *f*.

**equip** *v*: each room is ∼ped with an air conditioner an sanyà wà kōwànè dākì iyàkwàndishàn.

**equipment** *n* (*implements*) kāyan aikī *m*; (*piece of* ∼) nā'ūřā *f* ⟨oCi⟩.

**equivalent** *n* & *adj* makwàtàncī *m*: not every English word has its ∼ in Hausa bà kōwàcè kalmàř Tūřancī kè dà makwatancìyařsà à Hausa ba; ∼ to daidai dà: this word is ∼ to that kalmàř nân daidai dà wàccan.

**era** *n* zāmànī / zàmānī *m*, mařřā *f*: during the Roman ∼ à mařřař Rûm.

**eradicate** *v* (*disease*) kau dà / kawař (dà) *v5*: smallpox has been ∼d throughout the world an kawař dà cùtař agànā kō'ìnā cikin dūniyà.

**erase** *v* gōgè *v4*, shāfè *v4*.

**eraser** *n* (*pencil*) řōbà *f*, [F] gwâm *f*; (*blackboard*) magōgī *m*, mashāfī *m*.

**erect** 1. *v* kafà *v1*: ∼ a tent, monument kafà laimā, àbin tunāwā.

2. *adv* sak *idph*: stand ∼ tsayà sak.

**erection** *n* (*sexual*) tādī *m*, tāshī *m*.

**erode** *v* (*of soil*) zōzàyē / zaizàyē *v4*: the rain has ∼d the (mud) wall ruwā yā zaizàyè gàřū; be ∼d (*of mud structure*) zāgè *v4*, rājè *v4*.

**erosion** *n* (*of soil*) zàizayā *f*.

**err** *v* yi kuskurè *m*.

**errand** *n* hidimā *f* ⟨oCi⟩: I have some ∼s to run inà dà wasu hidimōmī.

**error** *n* kuskurè / kurè *m* ⟨kùràkùrai⟩; speech ∼ tsāmin bàkī *m*.

**erupt** *v* ɓarkè *v4*: the volcano ∼ed aman wutā yā ɓarkè à dūtsè; violence has ∼ed in the streets tāshìn hankàlī yā ɓarkè cikin gàrī.

**escalate** *v* tsànantā *v3*: prices have ∼d hàuhawàř fàřāshī tā tsànantā.

**escape** 1. *v* a. (*break loose & flee*) tsērè *v4*, gudù *v3b*: the robbers ∼d without a trace 'yan fashī sun tsērè bâ kō ɓuřɓushinsù. b. (*safely from danger*) tsīra *v3a*, kùskurà *v3*: we ∼d from the fire mun tsīra dàgà gòbařař; (*fig.*) they ∼d by the skin of their teeth dà gùmin gòshī sukà tsīra. c. (*by slipping away*)

ku6ùcē *v4*: he ∼d during the confusion yā ku6ùcē a sanàdin hàrgitsī; ∼ from (*usu. so.'s grip*) ku6ùcē wà *v4*: the soldiers ∼ from the enemy sōjōjī sun ku6ùcē wà àbòkan gàbā; help so. ∼ ku6utař (dà) *v5*.

2. *n* a. tsīrā *f*, gudù *m*: ∼ was impossible tsīrā tā fàskarà; have a narrow ∼ (*fig.*) ƙētàrè rījìyā dà bāya, (*esp. from death*) aunà ařzìkī. b. (*way to avoid doing sth.*) makawā *f*: there is no ∼, it must be done bâ makawā sai an yī shì.

**escort** 1. *v* rakà *v1*, yi wà rakiyā *f*.

2. *n* ɗan rakiyā *m*.

**esophagus** *n* maƙōshī *m*, màƙōgwàrō *m*.

**especially** *adv* a. mùsammàn *adv*: he came ∼ to greet you yā zō mùsammàn don yà gaishē kà; a ram is slaughtered ∼ for the feast anà yankà řàgō nè mùsammàn don bìkîn. b. (*contrastive*) tun bâ...bâ: I want to visit many towns, ∼ Kano inà sôn ìn zìyàrci garūruwà dà yawà tun bâ mā Kanò bâ; the harvest has been good, ∼ of sorghum girbìn hatsī yā yi àlbařkà tun bâ dāwā bâ; you should always wear shoes ∼ if you go where it is dirty kà rikà sâ tàkàlmī tun bà in zā kà shìga wurī mài ƙàzântā bâ. c. (*for no other purpose*) tàkànas (ta Kanò) *adv*: I came most ∼ to speak with you nā zō tàkànas ta Kanò don ìn yi makà màganā.

**espionage** *n* aikìn lèƙen àsīřin ƙasā *m*.

**essay** *n* (*academic*) màƙālā *f*.

**essence** *n* (*basic nature of sth.*) tàkàmaimai *n*, ainihī *m*: I don't know what the ∼ of the matter is bàn san tàkàmaiman màganā ba.

**essential** *adj* a. (*real*) na ainihī *m*, na hàƙīƙanī *m*: the ∼ truth, fact ainihin gàskiyā, màganā. b. (*important*) mùhimmī *adj* ⟨ai⟩, (mài) muhimmancī *m*: it is ∼ that you be present at the meeting mùhimmìn àbù nē kà hàlàřci tàrôn; the ∼ things in life are food, clothing, and shelter dà àbinci dà tufā dà wurin zamā sū nè mùhìmman abūbuwā à ràyuwā.

**establish** *v* (*a school, law, society*) kafà *v1*; ∼ diplomatic ties ƙullà huldàř jakādancì.

**establishment** *n*: a business ∼ kamfànī *m* ⟨oCi⟩.

**estate** *n* a. (*land, property*) kadařā *f*. b. (*inheritance*) gādò *m*.

**esteem** 1. *n* dařajà *f*, girmàmāwā *f*.

2. *v* (*show so. respect*) girmàmā *v1*, ga girman w., ƙaddàřā *v1*; (*value*) kīmàntā *v1*, dařajàntā *v1*: he is highly ∼d as a poet an kīmàntā wàƙōƙinsà = an ɗauki

wāƙōƙinsà dà daṙajà.

**estimate 1.** *v* (*specify a number, quantity*) ƙiyàstā *v1*: it is ~d that a million dollars was spent on the project an ƙiyàstà cêwā an kashè dalà milyàn wajen aikìn. **b.** (*evaluate worth*) kīmàntā / ƙīmàntā *v1*, ƙaddàṙā *v1*: its value is ~d at ₦200 an kīmàntà daṙajàṙsà naiṙā̀ dàrī biyu; he ~d the cost of the repair for me yā kīmàntà minì kuɗin gyārā.
**2.** *n* ƙiyàsì *m*, istìmàn *m*: an ~ for car repairs istìmàn gyāran mōtà̀.

**estranged** *adj*: become ~ yi baṙam-bàṙàm *idph*: they've become ~ sun yi baṙam-bàṙàm.

**et al.** *abbr* dà sauransù.

**etc.** *abbr* dà sauransù, dà makàmàntansù.

**eternal** *adj* (*of God only*) na dàwwamà̀ *f*, madàwwàmī *adj*, dàwwàmammē *adv*: only God is ~ Allàh nē kaɗai dàwwàmammē; God ~ Allàh Madàwwàmin Sarkī.

**eternity** *n* dàwwamà̀ *f*; for ~ haṙ àbàdân àbādìn.

**ethical** *adj* (mài) ɗā'à̀ *f*, (mài) aƙīdà̀ *f*, na hàlàyē nagàri *m*.

**ethics** *n* ɗā'à̀ *f*, aƙīlà̀ *f*.

**ethnic** *adj* na kàbīlà̀ *f*.

**ethnography** *n* ilìmin àl'àdun kàbīlū *m*.

**etiquette** *n*: rules of ~ sanìn yā kàmàtà *m*.

**etymology** *n* ilìmin nazàṙin asalin kalmōmī *m*.

**eucalyptus** *n* tùrārē *m*; ~ oil zaitì *m*.

**eulogy** *n* yàbō *m*.

**eunuch** *n* bà̀bā *m* ⟨anni⟩.

**euphemism** (*in speaking*) sāye *m*; use a ~ sāyà̀ *v1*: he is speaking euphemistically yanà̀ sāyàwā.

**Europe** *n* Tūṙai *m*.

**European** *n* bàtūṙè̀ *m*; bànasāṙè̀ *m*, nàsāṙa *m* ⟨u⟩.

**evacuate** *v* kwāshè̀ *v4*: they ~d the children first sun kwāshè̀ yārā dà farkō.

**evade** *v* **a.** (*escape*) kuɓùcè wà *v4*: he ~d the police yā kuɓùcè wà 'yan sàndā. **b.** (*avoid doing*) gujè̀ wà *v4*, ƙi *v0*: ~ taxes ƙi biyàn hàṙàjì; ~ a question zūṙè̀ wà tàmbayà̀.

**evaluate** *v* kīmàntā / ƙīmàntā *v1*, ƙaddàṙā *v1*: how would you ~ its worth? yà̀yà̀ zā à kīmàntà daṙajàṙsà? = yà̀yà̀ zā à ƙaddàṙà kuɗinsà?

**evaporate** *v* būshè *v4*; (*of large wet area*) tsanè̀ *v4*, turārā *v1*.

**evasive** *adj*: be ~ **a.** (*be devious*) yi kwànekwàne *m*, yi zūƙe-zūƙe *m*, yi kèwàye-kèwàye *m*, yi gòce-gòce *m*, yi wùnī-wunī

*idph*, yi ƙùmbìyā̀-ƙumbiyā *idph*. **b.** (*hide one's real feelings*) yi kinibībì *m*.

**eve** *n* darē *m*: Saturday ~ daren Lahàdì; Christmas ~ daren Kiṙsìmatì; (*of an Islamic holiday*) jājibè̀ṙè̀ *m*: Sallah ~ jājibè̀ṙèn Sallà̀ = daren Sallà̀.

**even**[1] *adv* **a.** kō: he didn't ~ look at us bài kō dùɓē mù ba; ~ a child knows that kō jàrīrì yā san hakà; I don't ~ have a penny bâ ni dà kō kwabò̀ = kō kwabò̀ ɗaya bābù gàrē nì; not ~ a penny! (*fig., emphat.*) kō dà̀ ƙàrfamfànā̀! **b.** (*including*) haṙ *prep*: I gave him some clothes and ~ some money nā bā shì tufāfì haṙ kuɗī; ~ the house burned down haṙ gidàn yā ƙōnè. **c.** (*in fact, moreover*) haṙ mā *prep*: the house ~ burned down gidàn haṙ mā yā ƙōnè; this work is ~ more difficult than I thought aikìn nân haṙ mā yā fi yâddà nakè zàtō wùyā; (*emphat., contrastive*) hàttā...mā: they stole all his goods, ~ his shoes were taken an sàcè masà kāyā dukà hàttā tàkàlminsà mā. **d.** (*other uses*): ~ if (*fut. condition*) kō dà̀: ~ if it were to rain tomorrow, we would still leave kō dà̀ â yi ruwā gòbe zā mù tāshì; ~ so hakà nan; ~ though (*past event*) kō dà̀, duk dà̀: ~ though it rained yesterday, they left duk dà̀ an yi ruwā jiyà sun tāshì.

**even**[2] *adj* **a.** (*level, smooth*) bâi ɗaya *adv*: the floor is ~ dà̀ɓē yā yi bâi ɗaya; an ~ temper mài saukin kâi, mài sanyin zūcìyā. **b.** (*equal, matching*) daidai *adv*: make them ~ with each other kà sâ su daidai dà jūnā; the score was ~ bâ wàndà yi ci wani; get ~ rāmā *v1*, faṙkè *v4*: it you do that to me, I'll get ~ with you in zā kà yi minì hakà fa, zân rāmà̀. **c.** (*in math*): an ~ number cìkā *f*: 4 is an ~ number huɗu cìkā cè.

**evening** *n* (*ca. 5-7 pm*) màràicē *m*; (*dusk till ca. 10 pm*) yàmmā *f*; good ~! baṙkà̀ dà yàmmā! in the ~ dà yàmma *adv*.

**evenly** *adv* bâi ɗaya *adv*: spread it out ~ kà baṙbàzā su bâi ɗaya; arrange the chairs ~ in rows kù jērà kùjèrū bâi ɗaya; the teams are ~ matched ƙarfin ƙungiyōyìn ɗaya nè̀.

**event** *n*: the ~s of the past few days abūbuwàn dà sukà fàru kwānan nàn; in any ~ kō ta yà̀yà̀; in the ~ that ìdan/in *conj*: in the ~ of their death ìdan ajàlinsù yā cìka; a social ~ shagàlī *m* ⟨u-a[2]⟩.

**eventually** *adv* **a.** (*finally*) dàgà bāya, dàgà ƙarshē. **b.** (*sooner or later*) yâu dà gòbe, kō bàdaɗè kō bàjimā̀.

**ever** *adv*: ~ do sth. taɓā̀ *v1*: have you ~ been to Egypt? kā taɓà zuwā̀ Masār̀? hardly ~ do sth. cikà *v1* (+ *neg.*): we hardly ~ watch television bā mà cikà kallon talàbijìn; ~ since tun (dà) *conj*: ~ since I was a child tun inā̀ yār̀ō = tun inā̀ k̃aramī; more than ~ fìye dà kōyàushè; better, worse than ~ mài kyâu, mài tsananī fìye dà na dā̀; (*in admonitions*) kùskurà *v3* (+ *neg. subjunct.*): don't ~ go there! kadà kà kùskurà kà jē can; don't ~ use that word kadà kà kùskurà kà fàɗi kalmàr̀ nân.

**everlasting** *adj* na dàwwamā̀ *f;* be ~ dàwwamà *v3;* God ~ Allàh Madàwwàmī.

**every** *det* a. (*each*) kōwànè *m*, kōwàcè *f*, kōwàɗànnè *p; duk*: ~ month kōwànè watā̀; ~ farmer duk manòmī. b. (*with expr. of time*) kullum *adv*: ~ morning kullum sāfe; I see him ~ day inā̀ ganinsà kullum.

**everybody** *pro* kōwā, *see* everyone.

**everyday** *adj* na yâu dà kullum *adv*: the ~ noise of the city hàyà-hàyàr̀ bir̀nī ta yâu dà kullum.

**everyone** *pro* a. kōwā *m*: ~ knows that kōwā yā san hakà; give ~ his share kà bā kōwā rābonsà; (*emphat.*) kōwā dà kōwā: I saw ~ at the meeting nā ga kōwā dà kōwā à tàr̀ôn. b. (*in subord. cl.*) duk wândà *m*, duk wâddà *f*, duk waɗàndà *p*: ~ who saw the game enjoyed it duk wândà ya ga wàsân yā ji dāɗinsà.

**everything** *pro* a. kōmē / kōmai *m*: he knows ~ about that yā san kōmē gàme dà wànnan; is ~ all right? kōmē yā yi daidai? (*emphat.*) kōmē dà kōmē: I bought ~ there nā sàyi kōmē dà kōmē cân; we were the only one who saw ~ that happened mū kaɗai nè mukà ga kōmē dà kōmē. b. (*whatever*) duk àbîn dà: I did ~ I was told to do nā yi duk àbîn dà akà gayà minì ìn yi; tell me~ you know fàɗā minì duk àbîn dà ka sanì.

**everywhere** *adv* a. kō'ìnā *adv*: you can see them ~ at the market anā̀ ganinsù kō'ìnā à kàsuwā. b. (*in subord. cl.*) duk indà, kō'ìnā: ~ you go, you will meet friendly people duk indà kukè tàfiyà, zā kù hàɗu dà mutànè màsu fàr̀a'à.

**evict** *v* kòr̃ā *v2*, kōr̀è *v4*: they were ~ed from their house an kōr̀è su gàbā ɗaya dàgà gidansù.

**evidence** *n* a. (*Law*) shaidà *f* ⟨u⟩; give ~ at a trial bāyar̀ dà shaidà à

shàr̀i'ā̀; acquit so. for lack of ~ sàki w. sabṑdà rashìn shaidà; false ~ shaidàr̀ zur̀; supporting ~ shaidàr̀ k̃arfàfâwā = k̃wàk̃k̃wārar̀ shaidà. b. (*signs*) àlāmū *p*: all the ~ points to the same conclusion duk àlāmū sun nūnà hukuncī ɗaya.

**evident** *adj* be ~ tàbbatà *v3*: it is ~ that he has lost all sense of shame rashìn kunyā̀ tā tàbbatà gàrē shì.

**evidently** *adv* a. (*clearly*) bā shakkà̀ *f*. b. (*apparently*) gā àlāmā̀ *f*: he ~ left gā àlāmā̀ yā tāshì.

**evil** 1. *adj* mūgū̀ *adj* ⟨miyàgū⟩, mamùgùncī *m*, mak̃ètàcī *m;* an ~ character mài bak̃in râi *n*, mài bak̃in cikī *n*: he is ~ mamùgùncī nè = bak̃in cikī gàrē shì; ~ intention bak̃ar̀ àniyā̀; ~-tempered mài bak̃ar̀ zūcìyā̀; ~ spirit ìbìlîs *m*. 2. *n* a. mùgùntā *f*, k̃ètā *f*, shar̀r̀ī *m*.

**ewe** *n* tunkìyā *f* ⟨tumàkī⟩.

**ewer** *n* tùlū *m* ⟨una⟩.

**exact** *adj & adv* a. (*precise*) daidai *adv*: he gave me the ~ change canjìn dà ya bā nì daidai nè. b. (*real, actual*) ainihin, tàkàmaiman, hàk̃īk̃ànin: he gave me the ~ thing that I needed yā bā nì ainihin àbîn dà nakè bùkātà; the ~ truth ainihin gàskiyā̀; its ~ weight is 5 pounds ainihin nauyinsà lābā̀ bìyar̀ = nauyinsà tàkàmaimai lābā̀ bìyar̀; he doesn't know his ~ age bài san hàk̃īk̃ànin yawàn shèkàrunsà na haihùwā ba.

**exactly** 1. *adv* a. daidai *adv*, (*emphat.*) daidai wà daidà *adv*: he came at ~ 3 p.m. yā zō k̃arfè ukù daidai (wà daidà); that is ~ what I said to him! daidai àbîn dà na gayà masà kè nan! that's ~ right! hakà nē sòsai! b. (*emphat., of countable things*) cur̀ *idph*, cif *idph*: she is ~ 20 years old shèkàruntà àshìr̀in cur̀; it is 2:47 ~ k̃arfè ukù saurā mintī shā ukù cif.

**exaggerate** *v* zugùgùtā / zugwīgwìtā *v1*, k̃ārā wà gishirī, kambàmā *v1*: traders ~ the quality of their goods 'yan kàsuwā nā̀ zugwīgwìtā kyân kāyansù; (*in very loud way*) kurūrùtā *v1*.

**examination** *n* jar̀r̀àbâwā *f;* pass an ~ ci jar̀r̀àbâwā; fail an ~ fāɗì à jar̀r̀àbâwā.

**examine** *v* a. (*give test*) bā dà jar̀r̀àbâwā. b. (*look at*) dūbà / [F] dībā *v1* ⟨dūbā⟩: ~ a patient dūbà maràs lāfiyà; the customs officers will ~ all your goods carefully 'yan kwastàn zā sù dūbà kāyankà à tsànàke.

**example** *n* a. (*illustration*) mìsālī *m* ⟨ai⟩, kwatancī *m*: this is an ~ of what I mean wànnan mìsālìn àbîn dà nakè nufî; for

~ mìsālìn = alal mìsālî. b. (*exemplary character*) hālī *m* ⟨aye⟩: set a good ~ for children nūnà wà yârā hālī mài kyâu; you should follow his ~ kà bi hālinsà.

**excavate** *v* haƙà *v1* ⟨hàƙā⟩ *f*: they are excavating Dala to look for historical artifacts sunà hàƙaƙ Dàla don sāmō kāyan tāřīhì.

**exceed** *v* zaɽcè *v4*, wucè *v4*, fi *v0*: don't ~ the speed limit kadà kà wucè yawàn gudùn dà akà ƙayyàdē; the cost of the repairs won't ~ ₦50 kuɗin gyārân bà zā sù fi naiřà hàmsin ba; ~ one's expectations wucè mìsālī = zaɽcè kīmà; (*slightly*) ɗarà *v1*: my expenses slightly ~ my income bùkātàtā tā ɗarà sāmùnā.

**exceedingly** *adv, see* extremely.

**excel** *v* fîfītā *v3*.

**Excellency** *hon*: His ~ the Governor of Kano State Mài Girmā Gwamnàn Jihàƙ Kanò; His ~ (*esp. an envoy*) Mùƙaddàshinsà.

**excellent** *adj* na ƙwařai, (mài) aƙmashī *m*: ~ work, person aikì na ƙwařai, mùtumìn ƙwařai; the play was ~ wàsân yā yi aƙmashī.

**except** 1. *prep & conj* ban dà *prep*, illā *prep*: every day ~ Sunday kōwàcè rānā ban dà Lahàdì; everyone came ~ Musa kōwā yā zō illā Mūsà; (*after neg.*) sai *prep*: no one can do it ~ him bâ mài yînsà sai shî; I don't have anything ~ this bâ ni dà kōmē sai wannàn.
2. *v* kēɓè *v4*, wāřè *v4*: no one has been ~ed bà à kēɓè kōwā ba.

**exception** *n*: with the ~ of ban dà *prep*, illā *prep*: everyone may enter with the ~ of children kōwā zâi iyà shìgā ban dà yârā; every rule has ~s kōwàcè ƙā'idà takàn baudè; make an ~ kēɓè *v4*, wāřè *v4*.

**exceptionally** *adv* sòsai *adv*, ainùn *adv*, ƙwarai *adv*: ~ painful mài zāfī ainùn; (*emphat.*) nà dà kāfìřin X, nà dà shègèn X: she is ~ beautiful tanà dà kāfìřin kyâu; ~ difficult shēgìyaƙ wàhalà = mài wàhalà sòsai.

**excess** *n* a. (*surplus*) rārà *f*; in ~ of fìye dà: your suitcase may not weigh in ~ of 44 pounds kadà nauyin jàkaƙkà yà kai fìye dà wayà àƙbà'in dà huɗu.

**excessive** *adj*: be ~ wucè kīmà, wucè lambà: the amount was ~ yawànsà yā wucè kīmà.

**excessively** *adv* (mài) tsananī *m*: it is ~ difficult yanà dà wùyā mài tsananī.

**exchange** 1. *v* mùsāyà *v2*: ~ a donkey for a horse mùsàyi jâkī dà dōkì; in ~ for à bàkin, à kân: she gave me some soap in ~ for some canned milk tā bā nì sàbulū à bàkin gwangwanin madařā.
2. *n* mùsāyā *f*: foreign ~ kuɗaɗen mùsāyā; an even ~ mùsāyaƙ tagwàyē; an ~ of views mùsāyaƙ řa'àyī.

**excite** *v* a. (*please*) ƙāyatař / ƙāwatař (dà) *v5*, bâ w. shà'awà: the game ~d the crowd wāsân yā ƙāyatař dà kōwā = wāsân yā bâ kōwā shà'awà. b. be ~d (*be nervous*) tsìma *v3*, yi zùmūdī *m*: he is always ~d before a competition kullum yakàn tsìma kàfin à yi gàsā; why are you so ~d? zùmūdin mè kakè yî?

**excitement** *n* (*from anxiety or eagerness*) zùmūdī *m*: what's all the ~ about? mè akè yi wà zùmūdī? nervous ~ tsìma *f*.

**exciting** *adj* (mài) ban shà'awà.

**exclamation** *n* (*Gram.*) kalmàƙ mõtsin râi *f*; ~ mark àlāmàƙ mõtsin râi *f*.

**exclude** *v* a. (*prohibit*) wāřè *v4*: women were ~d from the meeting an wāřè mātā dàgà tàrôn. b. (*leave out*) fid dà / fitaƙ (dà) *v5*, kēɓè *v4*: they ~d me from the matter sun fid dà nī dàgà màganàƙ; they didn't ~ anyone bà sù kēɓè kōwā ba.

**exclusion** *n* wāriyà *f*.

**exclusive** *adj* a. (*restricted*) kēɓaɓɓē *adj*; ~ oil rights kēɓaɓɓen hakkìn hàƙaƙ mâi. b. (*special*) na mùsammàn: this is an ~ club wannàn kùlâb ta mùsammàn cē.

**excrement** *n* kāshī *m*, (*euphem.*) nàjasà *f*, bāyan gidā *m*; (*human, usu. used in talking to children*) tūtù *m*.

**excrete** *v* yi kāshī *m*, kāsàyē *v4*.

**excuse** 1. *n* a. (*justification*) uzùřī *m*, hujjà *f* ⟨oCi⟩: what is your ~ for doing that? mènē nè uzùřinkà na yîn hakà? look for an ~ nèmi hujjà; your ~ is weak uzùřinkà bâ shi dà makāmā. b. (*pretext*) mafitā *f*, uzùřī *m*, dàlīlī *m* ⟨ai⟩: he is looking for an ~ not to attend the meeting yanà nēman mafitā don gudùn hàlaƙtaƙ tàrôn; laziness is no ~ lālàcì bâ dàlīlī ba nè; give a lame ~ yi kùskùndà *f*.
2. *v* a. (*pardon*) gāfàƙtā wà *v1*, yi wà ahuwà *f*: please ~ me for being late don Allàh kà yi minì ahuwà sabõdà nā màkarà. b. (*for serious offense*) yàfā *v2*, yāfè wà *v1*: I will not ~ his rudeness to me bà zân yàfè masà rashìn kunyàƙ dà ya yi minì ba. c. (*in greetings*): ~ me! (*on entering place, said by women*) gāfàřā dai! = àhuwonkù dai! (*said by men*) sàlāmù àlaikùn! please ~ us! (*on taking leave*) kù yi manà aikìn gāfàřà.

execute *v* a. (*carry out*) zaŕtaŕ (dà) *v5*, ai-wataŕ (dà) *v5*. b. (*kill*) yi wà hukuncìn kisà; (*by firing squad*) haŕbè *v4*, bindìgē *v4*; (*by hanging*) rātàyē *v4*; (*by gas*) bâ w. gubà.

execution *n* a. (*of plan*) zaŕtâŕwā *f*, aiwatâŕwā *f*. b. (*capital punishment*) hukuncìn kisà *m*: the ~ took place last week an yi hukuncìn kisà mākòn dà ya wucè.

executioner *n* hauni *m*.

executive *adj* (mài) zaŕtâŕwā *f*: ~ power īkòn zaŕtâŕwā = cìkakken īkò; chief ~ officer shûgàbā *n* ⟨anni⟩.

exegesis *n* tàfsīŕì *m*.

exemplify kwatàntā *v1*.

exempt *adj*: be ~ dâukē wà *v4*, kēɓè *v4*: they are ~ from taxation an dâukē musù biyàn hàŕàjì = an kēɓè su dàgà biyàn hàŕàjì.

exercise 1. *n* a. (*of body*) mōtsà jìkī *m*: ~ contributes to our health mōtsà jìkī kàn ƙarà manà lāfiyà. b. (*work*) aikì *m* ⟨ayyukà⟩: ~ book littāfìn aikì = littāfìn ŕubùtū. c. (*Mil.*): military ~s rawaŕ dājì *f*.
2. *v* a. (*one's body*) mōtsà jìkī, warwàrè jìkī. b. (*one's rights, power*) bi hakkì *m*.

exert *v* mai dà himmà, mai dà ƙoƙarī; ~ one's utmost yi iyākaŕ ƙoƙarī, ciccìjē *v4*.

exhaust *n* (*of car*) sàlansà *f*, [F] shàfàmā *f*.

exhausted, be *v* a. (*tired*) gàlàbaità *v3*, gàji tiƙis, gàji tilis; (*to the point of collapse*) sārè *v4*. b. (*used up*) ƙārè *v4*; their natural resources are ~ àlbaŕkàtun ƙasaŕsù sun ƙārè.

exhibit, exhibition 1. *n* wàsā *m*, nūnì *m*: an ~ of Hausa arts and crafts nūnìn kāyan fàsāhà dà sanà'ō'in Hàusàwā.
2. *v* gwadà *v1*, nūnà *v1*.

exhort *v* gàŕgaɗà *v2*.

exhortation *n* gàŕgàɗī *m*.

exile 1. *n* a. gudùn hijìŕā *m*: go into ~ yi gudùn hijìŕā; he's living in ~ yanà zaman gudùn hijìŕā; a government-in-~ gwamnatìn gudùn hijìŕā. b. (*psn.*) ɗan gudùn hijìŕā *m*.
2. *v* kōŕā *v2*, kōŕè *v4*: he has been ~d from his homeland an kōŕè shì dàgà ƙasaŕsù.

exist *v* a. (*be in effect*) ci *v0*, yi aikì *m*: the ~ing government gwamnatì mài cî yànzu; that law no longer ~s bā à aikì dà dòkāŕ yànzu. b. (*be in existence*) kasàncē *v4*: the thing once ~ed but it is no longer in existence dâ àbîn

yā kasàncē àmmā yànzu bābù irìnsà; (*in affirm.*) àkwai, dà (+ *n*); (*in neg.*) bābù, bâ (+ *n*): does such a thing really ~? àshē, àkwai àbù kàmaŕ hakà? = àshē dà wannàn? I never knew such a thing ~ed bàn taɓà sanìn dà wannàn ba; no such thing ~s bābù irìn wannàn.

existence *n* a. (*life*) ràyuwā *f*, zamā *m*: a miserable ~ zaman wàhalà = zaman talaucì; in ~ à ràye: there are no more of them in ~ bābù sauransù à ràye. b. (*beingness*) kasàncêwā *f*; come into ~ (*Relig.*) kasàncē *v4*: when God commanded it to come into ~, so was it dà Allàh ya cè yà kasàncē, sai àbìn yā kasàncē.

exit 1. *v* fìta *v3*: you should ~ by the back door sai kà fìta ta ƙōfāŕ bāya.
2. *n* mafìtā *f*.

exonerate *v* yāfè wà *v4*.

expand *v* a. (*develop*) bùnƙàsà *v3*: the city has ~ed tremendously biŕnîn yā bùnƙàsà sòsai. b. (*swell up*) kùmburà *v3*. c. (*increase*) fāɗàɗà *v1*: heat ~s, cold contracts zāfī nằ fāɗàɗâwā sanyī nằ ƙanƙàncêwā.

expatriate *n* bàƙō *m* ⟨i⟩, bàŕe *n*.

expect *v* a. (*wait for*) zubà idò, ƙurà wà idò, sàurārà *v2* ⟨sàuràrē, sàuràrō⟩, sâ rai: I am ~ing him to come at 3 pm inà zubà idòn zuwànsà dà ƙarfè ukù; when do you ~ him to come? yàushè kakè sâ rân zuwànsà? b. (*anticipate*) yi tsàmmānì *m*, zàta *v2* ⟨zàtō⟩: it is ~ed that this year's rainy season will be good bana anà tsàmmānìn dằminà mài àlbaŕkà; I am ~ing a letter from home inà tsàmmānìn wàsīƙà dàgà gidā; I never ~ed such kindness bàn yi tsàmmānìn àlhēŕì irìn wannàn ba; it is just as I ~ed daidai yàddà nakè zàtō kè nan; I've stopped ~ing any good from him nā fid dà ƙaunaŕ zâi yi wani àbin kiŕkì. c. (*a baby*) nà dà jūnā biyu: she is ~ing tanà dà jūnā biyu.

expectation *n* tsàmmānì *m*, zàtō *m*, sâ rāi *m*: according to one's ~s yàddà akè tsàmmānì = yàddà akè sâ rāi; beyond one's ~s fìye dà akè zàtō.

expedient *adj* na gaggāwā *f*: an ~ plan tsārìn gaggāwā.

expedite *v* gaggàutā *v1*, hanzaŕtaŕ (dà) *v5*.

expel *v* kōŕè *v4*: 3 students were ~led from school an kōŕè ɗàlìbai ukù dàgà makaŕantā.

expenditure *n* kàsàssun kuɗī *p*.

expense *n* kuɗī *m/p*: my ~s exceeded my income kuɗîn dà nakè kashèwā sun fi àbìn dà nakè sāmù; at public ~ dà kuɗin jàma'ầ.

**expensive** *adj* (*of thing*) (mài) tsầdā *f*: this gown is ~ rìgař nàn nầ dà tsầdā; (*of price, cost*) dà yawầ: it is too ~ kuɗinsà sun yi yawầ.

**experience** 1. *n* a. (*expertise*) gồguwā *f*, ƙwarềwā *f*: gain ~ in fixing cars sầmi gồguwař gyàrà mōtầ; have a lot of ~, be ~d gồgu *v7*, ƙwarề *v4*: he has had a lot of ~ with cars yā ƙwarề dà mōtầ sōsai; he doesn't have enough ~ bâ shi dà cikakkiyař ƙwarềwā; an ~d person tsōhon hannū *m*, tsōhuwař zumầ *f*: he's an ~d driver shī tsōhon hannū nề wajen tūƙì. b. (*of the world*): worldly ~ dàbầřun zaman dūniyầ; c. (*knowledge*) sanì *m*: the young can benefit from the ~ of their elders sằmầrī sunà iyà ƙàruwà dàgà sanìn magàbầtansù.
2. *v* shā *v0*, ɗanɗànā *v1*: he ~d disappointment yā shā ɓācìn râi; they ~d poverty sun ɗanɗànà talaucì.

**experiment** *n* gwajì *m* ⟨e²⟩: scientific ~s gwàje-gwàjen kìmiyyầ.

**expert** *n* & *adj* gwànī *m*, gwànầ *f* ⟨aye⟩, ƙwàrarrề *adj*: he's an ~ driver shī gwànin matūƙì nề; be an ~ in sth. nàƙaltầ *v2*: she is an ~ at (cooking) bean cakes tā nàƙàlci kōsai.

**expertise** *n* gwànintầ *f*, ƙwarềwā *f*.

**expire** *v* ƙarề *v4*, mutù *v3b*: my license has ~d lāsìn dīnā yā ƙarề.

**explain** *v* bayyànā *v1*, yi bàyānì *m*, gānar̃ (dà) *v5*: he ~ed to me why he was absent yā bayyànā minì dàlīlìn rashìn zuwànsà; please ~ this to me don Allàh kà yi minì bàyānìn wannàn = don Allàh kà gānar̃ minì wannàn.

**explanation** *n* bàyānì *m* ⟨ai⟩, dàlīlì *m* ⟨ai⟩.

**explicit** *adj* (*detailed*) fillā-fillā *idph*, dallā-dallā *idph*: I gave him ~ directions to the hospital nā yi masà kwàtàncen asìbitì fillā-fillā.

**explicitly** *adv* (*unambiguously*) ɓarō-ɓàrō *idph*, ƙarara *idph*: I told him ~ not to do it nā gayầ masà ɓarō-ɓàrō kadà yà yi.

**explode** 1. *vt* (*detonate*) fasà *v1*, sàkā *v2*.
2. *vi* (*of weapons*) fashề *v4*; (*of a tire, heater*) yi bindigầ *f*.

**exploit** *v* cī dà gùmin w.: the plantation owners ~ed the slaves mầsu gandū sun cī dà gùmin bāyī; (*to the extreme*) tātsề *v4*: you allowed yourself to be ~ed for nothing kā zaunà anầ tātsề ka à banzā.

**explore** *v* bincìkā *v1*; (*for discovery*) gānō *v6*.

**explosion** *n* fàshe-fàshe *p*: a loud ~ fàshe-fàshe mài ƙārā; bomb ~ fashèwar̃ bâm = tāshìn bâm.

**explosive(s)** *n* nằkiyầ *f*.

**export** *v* aikầ ƙasầshen wàje: the country ~s cotton and groundnuts ƙasâr̃ tanầ aikà audùgā dà gyàɗā ƙasầshen wàje; ~ed goods kāyan dà akề aikằwā ƙasầshen wàje.

**expose** 1. *v* a. (*a psn., secret*) tōnầ *v1*: he ~d my secret yā tōnầ minì àsīr̃ī; (*with intent to shame*) fàllasầ *v2*. b. (*open up, strip clean*) tsiràità *v1*: the room, matter has been completely ~d an tsiràità ɗākìn, màganầr̃.
2. *n* àbin fàllasầ *m*.

**express¹** *adj* & *adv* a. (*fast*) na ujilầ *f*, na gaggāwā *f*: an ~ train jirgin ujilầ. b. (*of mail*) ta kâr̃-tà-kwāna: he sent it by ~ mail yā aikà dà kâr̃-tà-kwāna.

**express²** *v* (*say*) nūnầ *v1*: ~ a desire nūnầ sô; ~ an opinion bā dà r̃a'àyī.

**express³** *v* (*extract*) mātsầ *v1*.

**expression** *n* (*in language*): an idiomatic ~ salon màganầ *m*; the Hausas have an ~ that... Hàusầwā sunà cêwā....

**expressly** *adv* mùsammàn *adv*, tàkànas (ta Kanồ) *adv*: he went there ~ to buy kolanuts yā jē can tàkànas ta Kanồ don yà sayō gōr̃ồ.

**extend** *v* a. (*lengthen*) ƙārầ *v1*: they ~ed his visa an ƙārầ masà bīzầr̃sà; (*prolong*) tsawàità *v1*. b. (*offer*) mīƙầ *v1*: he ~ed his hand yā mīƙầ hannunsà; ~ thanks to so. mīƙầ wà gồdiyā = isar̃ wà dà gồdiyā; ~ so. a welcome yi wà mar̃àba *f*; ~ so. condolences yi wà tà'àziyyầ *f*; ~ so. credit lầmuntầ *v2*: they ~ed me ₦100 credit sun lầmùncē nì nair̃ầ dàrī.

**extension** *n* ƙārì *m*: grant an ~ of time bā dà ƙārìn wa'àdī.

**extensive** *adj* (mài) yawầ *m*; (*of sth. neg.*) (mài) tsananī *m*: ~ damage ɓar̃nā mài tsananī.

**extent** *n* iyầkacī *m*: the ~ of the damage is not known bā à sàne dà iyầkacin ɓar̃nâr̃ ba.

**exterior** *adj* na wàje, dàgà wàje.

**exterminate** *v* kar̃kàshē *v4*, ƙarề *v4*.

**external** *adj* na wàje, (*outside one's country*) na ƙasầshen wàje, na ƙētar̃è.

**extinct** *adj*: become ~ ƙarề gàbā ɗaya.

**extinguish** *v* kashè *v4*.

**extortion** *v* shar̃r̃ì *m*.

**extra** *adj* (*additional*): ~ charges ƙarìn kuɗī.

**extract** *v* a. (*a tooth*) cirè *v4.* b. (*a little from a mass*) tsāmè *v4*: ~ the main points from his speech tsāmè gundārin àbîn dà ya fàdā. c. (*oils, liquids*) mātsā *v1*: oil is ~ed from the groundnuts anā mātsà gyàdā don à sāmi mâi.

**extradite** *v* mai dà mài lâifī ƙasaŕsù.

**extraordinarily** *adv, see* exceptionally.

**extraordinary** *adj* (*psn. of ~ ability*) hàtsàbībì *m* ⟨ai⟩: he is an ~ man shī hàtsàbībì nē; be ~ wucè kīmā, wucè mìsālì, wucè hankàlì: his knowledge is ~ ilìminsà yā wucè mìsālì; how ~! īkòn Allàh!

**extravagance** *n* almubazzaŕancì *m*, bùshāshā *f.*

**extravagant** *adj* (*psn.*) àlmùbazzàŕī *m* ⟨ai⟩.

**extreme** *adj* matsànàncī *adj*, (mài) tsananī *m*: ~ hunger matsanancìyaŕ yunwā = yunwā mài tsananī; ~ cold sanyī mài tsananī; under ~ conditions à tsànànce.

**extremely** *adv* a. sòsai *adv*, ainùn *adv*, haiƙàn *adv*, ƙwaŕai *adv*, matuƙā (gāyà) *adv*: she is ~ happy tā yi farin cikì matuƙā; it was ~ good of you to come kin kyâutā ƙwaŕai dà kikà zō. b. (*emphat. modifier*) na tsìyā (*modifies preceding word*); (mài) gwànin, màsīfàŕ, ƙàzāmin (*modifies following word*): he is ~ strong, rich yanā dà ƙarfin tsìyā, kuɗin tsìyā; ~ useful mài gwànin àmfànī; the story is ~ interesting làbāŕin nā dà gwànin ban shà'awā; it is ~ hot today yâu anā màsīfàŕ zāfī = yâu anā ƙàzāmin zāfī. c. (*esp. of sth. neg.*) (mài) tsananī *m*, matsànàncī *adj*: it is ~ cold today yâu anā tsananin sanyī = yâu àkwai matsànàncin sanyī; be careful, it is ~ dangerous yi hankàlī yanā dà haɗàŕī mài tsananī.

**extremist** *n & adj* (*Pol.*) (mài) tsàttsauran ŕa'àyī *m.*

**exude** *v* (*liquid, moisture*) yi nàsō *m.*

**ex-wife** *n* mātā ta dâ *f*, tsōhuwaŕ mātā *f*: he married my ~ yā aurè minì màtātā.

**eye** *n* a. idò *m* ⟨idànū⟩: some dust has got into my ~ ƙùrā tā shigam minì idò; it's true, I saw it with my own ~s bà wai ba, dà idònā na ganī; the whites of the ~ farin idò *m*; keep an ~ on so. sâ wà idò; look as far as the ~ can see dūbà haŕ iyākacin ganī = dūbà haŕ bìlā haddìn; in the public ~ à idòn jàma'à; (*fig.*) see ~ to ~ jìtu *v7*: we don't see ~ to ~ on the matter bà mù jìtu ba à kân màganàŕ; give so. the evil ~ (*esp. to frighten chil-* dren) yi wà hàràrà garkè; blood-shot ~s jan idò. b. (*adverbial uses*): in, on the ~ à ido/idò *adv*: don't put it in your ~ kadà kì sâ à ido. c. (*other uses*): ~ of a needle kafaŕ àllūŕà, hancìn àllūŕà; ~ of a potato dùmɓàrun dànkalì *m.*

**eyeball** *n* ƙwàyaŕ idò *f.*

**eyebrow(s)** *n* girā *f*: raise one's ~s (*to show surprise*) ɗagà girā; (*to show insult*) haɗà girā.

**eyebrow pencil** *n* jà-gira *f.*

**eyeglasses** *n* tàbàrau *m*, madūbī / madūbin idò *m*, [F] lùlētì *m*; put on, take off ~ sâ, cirè tàbàrau; prescription ~ tàbàran likità.

**eyelash** *n* gāshìn idò *m.*

**eyelid** *n* fātàŕ idò *f.*

**eye socket** *n* gurbìn idò *m.*

# F

fable n hìkāyà f ⟨oCi⟩.
fabric n yādì m: what kind of ~ is that? wànè irìn yādì nē wànnan?
fabricate v: ~ a lie ƙàgà ƙaryā.
face 1. n a. fuskà f ⟨oCi⟩: hide one's face rufè fuskà; his ~ relaxed yā sàki fuskà; make a ~ (by distorting mouth) yi gàtsìnē m, (by sticking tongue out) yi gwalō m; lie ~ down kwàntā ƙub dà cikì; lie ~ up kwàntā à rìgìngìne; meet ~ to ~ (unexpectedly) yi kìcìɓìs m, yi ařbā f. b. (reputation): lose ~ ji kunyà f, make so. lose ~ zub dà mutuncìn w., ci zařàfin w.; save ~ kārè mutuncì, riƙè mutuncì, kārè girmā.
2. v fùskantà v2, yi kallō m: the post office ~s the station gidan wayà nà kallon tashàř; serious problems are facing us munà fùskantàř mùmmūnan matsalōlī; I'm too ashamed to ~ him inà jìn kunyà hař bā nà sô ìn haɗà idò dà shī.
face cloth n hankicì m.
facilitate v tàimakà v2 ⟨tàimakō⟩: in order to ~ the inquiry don tàimakon bìncìkên.
facing prep daurà dà, kallon, fùskantàř: the house ~ ours gidân dà kè daurà dà nāmù = gidân dà kè kallon nāmù.
fact n a. (truth, reality) gàskiyā / gaskiyā f, dāhìř m: it is a ~, no doubt about it gàskiyā cè bābù shakkà; it's a ~ that men have landed on the moon dāhìř nē mutānē sun sàuka à watà; is that a ~ or an opinion? wannàn gàskiyā cè kō řa'àyī nè? in actual ~ bisà ƙàshin gàskiyā = bisà kân gàskiyā; the ~ of matter is... hàƙīƙànin màganà shī nè... = ainihin màganà shī nè.... b. (data) gàskiyā f, bàyānì m ⟨ai⟩: present the ~s gabātař dà bàyānì. c. (certainty) tabbàcì m: I don't know that for a ~ bàn san tabbàcinsà ba.
faction n (group) ɓangarè m.
factory n (esp. processing) masanà'antā f: a tea-processing ~ masanà'antař sarràfà shāyì; (esp. assembly) ma'aikatā f: a car ~ ma'aikatař hařhàɗà mōtōcì.
factual adj (mài) gàskiyā f.

faculty n (academic ~) sāshèn jāmi'à m.
fad n yàyī m: a ~ among women is to wear 3 earrings wani yàyin mātā sâ 'yan kunne ukù.
fade v ƙōƙè v4, kōɗè v4, kōɗař (dà) v5: the book cover has ~d bangon littāfì yā ƙōƙè; does this color ~? launìn nân yanà kōɗèwā? the sun has ~d the curtain rānā tā kōɗař dà lābulē.
faeces n, see feces.
fail 1. v a. (a test, contest) fāɗì v3b: he ~ed the examination yā fāɗì à jařřàbâwā. b. (be unable to do) kāsà v1, gazà v1: I tried and tried but ~ed nā yi nā yi àmmā nā kāsà; I ~ to understand your point of view nā kāsà gānè řa'àyinkà. c. (refuse, not do) ƙi v0, rasà v1: the car ~ed to start mōtà tā ƙi tāshì; he never ~s to write us once a month bài taɓà rasà řubūtà manà kōwànè watà ba. d. (fall short, not have) kāsà v1, rasà v1: his salary ~ed to meet his needs àlbâshinsà yā kāsà biyā masà bùkātà; his strength ~ed him yā rasà ƙarfinsà. e. (use v in neg.): the crops ~ed because of the drought àmfànin gōnā bài kai ba saɓōɗà farì; all their efforts ~d duk ƙōƙarinsù bài ci nasařà ba.
2. n: without ~ bâ makawā: I'll come tomorrow without ~ zân zō gòbe bâ makawā.
failing n (weakness) aibù / aibì m ⟨oCi⟩, illà f ⟨oCi⟩: he has one great ~, laziness aibùnsà ɗaya, lālācì.
failure n kāsàwā f, gazàwā f, karèwā f: bank ~ gazàwař bankì = karèwař bankì; crop ~ gazàwař àmfànin gōnā.
faint 1. v sūma v3a, sōmè v4: he ~ed yā sōmè = hankàlinsà yā fìta; make so. ~ sōmař/sūmař (dà) v5.
2. adv: feel ~ (weak) ji laƙwas idph.
fair adj a. (just) (mài) ādalcì m: be ~ to so. yi wà ādalcì m, kyàutā wà v1: I do not think I have had ~ treatment bàn yi zàton an yi mini ādalcì ba; a ~ share ràbon gàskiyā. b. (satisfactory) dà dāma-dāma adv: your work is ~, you must work harder aikìnkà dà dāma-dāma yakè, dōlè kà ƙārà ƙōƙarinkà. c. (light in color): a ~-skinned African jàtau n, farī m ⟨aCe⟩.
fairly adv a. (somewhat, use dimin. ɗan m, 'yař f ⟨'yan⟩): the building is ~ tall ginìn nà dà ɗan tsawō; he is ~ rich yanà dà 'yan kuɗī; he speaks English ~ well Tūřancinsà bâ lâifì. b. (justly): treat so. ~ yi wà ādalcì m.

**fairness** *n* ādalcī *m*.

**fairy** *n* àljanā *f* ⟨u⟩.

**fairy tale** *n* làbārìn àljanā *m*.

**faith** *n* a. (*belief*) īmānī *m*: have ~ in God yi īmānī dà Allàh; I have ~ that his coming will help us nā yi īmānìn zuwànsà zâi tàimàkē mù. b. (*trust*) amìncêwā *f*; have ~ in amìncē dà *v4*. c. (*intent*) àniyā *f*: act in good ~ yi dà kyàkkyāwar̃ àniyā.

**faithful** *adj*: a ~ friend àbōkī na k̃war̃ai = àmìntaccen àbōkī; ~ly yours (*in a letter*) (hāzā) wassàlàm, nī nè.

**fake** 1. *n & adj* a. (*counterfeit*) jàbu *m*: this diamond is a ~ daimùn ɗin nàn jàbu nè. b. (*fraudulent*) na k̃aryā *f*: he's not a real doctor but a ~ bà likitàn gàskiyā bā nè, na k̃aryā nè; a ~ passport fàsfô ɗin k̃aryā = jàbun fàsfô. c. (*menacing*) na dōd̃òridò *m*: a ~ gun bindigàr̃ dōd̃òridò.

**falcon** *n* shāhò *m* ⟨una⟩.

**fall**[1] 1. *v* a. fāɗì *v3b*: he fell with a thud yā fāɗì r̃ìm; (*of rain*) sàuka *v3*, saukō *v6*: before the first rains ~ k̃āfìn ruwan fārì yà saukō; (*of prices*) sàuka *v3*, yi k̃asà; night fell darē yā yi. b. (*var. v + prep uses*): ~ down fāɗì *v3b*, tumà dà k̃asà *v1*; ~ down from saukō *v6*: he fell down from upstairs yā fāɗō dàgà bēnè; ~ to, into, onto fāɗà *v1*: the goods fell to the ground kāyā sun fāɗà k̃asà; she fell into the water tā fāɗà ruwa; ~ in(to) disgrace ɓātà k̃âi: he fell in disgrace with the emir yā ɓātà kânsà wajen sarkī; ~ into difficulty shìga cikin wàhalà; ~ off fāɗō dàgà *v6*: the book fell off the shelf littāfìn yā fāɗō dàgà kantà; ~ on (*of time*) kāmà *v1*: Sallah ~s on Monday hūtun Sallà yā kāmà ran Lìttìnîn; ~ out (*of hair, leaves*) zùba *v3*; ~ out of sth. fāɗō dàgà cikin: they all fell out of the canoe duk sun fāɗō dàgà cikin kwàlekwàle; ~ upon so. (*attack*) fāɗà/far̃ wà *v1*. c. (*var. v + adv uses*): ~ apart (*come apart*) ɓaɓɓàllè *v4*; ~ apart (*disintegrate*) r̃agar̃gàjē *v4*, war̃gàjē *v4*; ~ asleep yi barcī *m*; ~ behind in sth. barī à bāya: I've fallen behind in my payments an bar̃ nì à bāya wajen biyàn bāshì; ~ headlong into, off wantsàlà *v1*; ~ short kāsà *v1*, gazà *v1*: the rain ~s short every year ruwàn yakàn kāsà kōwàcè shèkar̃à. 2. *n* fāɗùwā *f*, sàukā *f*: the rise and ~ of prices hawà dà sàukar̃ far̃āshì.

**fall**[2] *n*, see season.

**fallow** *adj* sàurā *f*: that is a ~ field wànnan sàurā cè.

**false** *adj*: the news appears to be ~ làbārìn dai gà àlāmà k̃aryā nè; ~ teeth hak̃ōran r̃ōbà; ~ witness shaidàr̃ zur̃.

**falsify** *v* k̃ar̃yàtā *v1*.

**fame** *n* sūnā *m*, màshàhūr̃àntakà *f*; ~ and fortune sā'à dà ràbo.

**familiar** *adj*: be ~ with sanì *v\**: I'm not ~ with that road bàn san hanyàr̃ ba; he looks ~, perhaps we've met before inà jîn nā san shì, k̃īlà mun taɓà hàɗuwā; be quite ~ with sābà dà *v1*, mayyàzè dà *v4*: I'm still not completely ~ with the town har̃ yànzu bàn mayyàzē dà gàrìn ba; I'm very ~ with this kind of work nā sābà dà irìn wannàn aikì.

**familiarity** *n* sàbō *m*: it was because of ~ that he took you for granted sàbō nè ya sà ya rainà ka; (*fig.*) ~ breeds contempt sàbon idò shī kè sà rainì.

**family** *n* (*one's parents*) iyàyē *p*; (*one's wife & children*) ìyàlì *m*; (*one's relatives*) ɗan'uwā *m* ⟨'yan'uwà⟩, dangì *m* ⟨oCi⟩: he has no ~ bà shi dà dangì; ~ ties zumuncì *m*, zùmùntà *f*.

**famine** *n* yunwà *f*, matsanancìyar̃ yunwà *f*: ~ brings about disease yunwà tanà haddàsà cūtuttukà.

**famous** *adj* (*of things*) sànannē *adj*: the groundnut pyramids used to be a ~ landmark of Kano dâ dālàr̃ gyàɗā sànanniyar̃ àlāmàr̃ Kanò cē; Sokoto is ~ for its leatherwork Sakkwato sànannen gàrī nè wajen dūkancì; (*of people*) màshàhūrì *m* ⟨ai⟩, shàhàr̃r̃ē *adj*: he is a ~ Hausa writer shī màshàhūrìn mar̃ùbūcin Hausa nè; become ~ shàhàr̃à *v3*, yi sūnā *m*.

**fan** 1. *n* (*of raffia*) mafīcī / mafīfīcī *m* ⟨ai⟩, (*of ostrich feathers*) fìginì *m*; (*electric, table model*) fankà *f*, (*ceiling*) fankàr̃ samà *f*, [F] bàntìlàtàr̃ *m*. 2. *v* a. (*cool so., sth.*) yi fītà *f*, fīfītā *v1* ⟨fīfītā⟩ *f*. b. (*a fire into flames*) hūrà *v1*, (*a fire with bellows*) rūrà *v1*.

**fanatic** *n* (*Pol.*) mài tsàttsauran r̃a'àyī *n*.

**fan belt** *n* fambêl *m*, [F] kùr̃wā *m*.

**fantastic** *excl* bà dāmà! *excl*, (*esp. of beauty*) tùbar̃kallà *excl*: what a ~ girl she is! k̃âi, yàrinyàr̃ nan tùbar̃kallà!

**fantasy** *n* (*story*) tàtsūnìyā *f* ⟨oCi⟩.

**far** *adj & adv* a. (mài) nīsā *m*, nēsà *adv*: it is ~ from here yanà dà nīsā dàgà nân = yanà nēsà dà nân; I saw it from ~ away nā gan shì dàgà can nēsà = nā hàngē shì dàgà nēsà; how ~ is it from Kano to Jos? dàgà Kanò zuwà Jàs mîl nawà nè? it is too ~ to walk nīsansà yā fi k̃arfin à

tàfi à ƙasà; their friendship will not go
~ àbòtaƒsù ba zā tà jē nēsà ba. b. as
~ as haƒ *prep*, iyā / iyākaƒ / iyākacin
*prep*: we went as ~ as the post office mun
tàfi haƒ gidan wayà; as ~ as I know à
iyākacin sanīnā dai.

farce *n* mūgùn wàsā *m*.

fare *n* (*transportation*) kudī *m/p*: air ~
kudin jirgin samà.

Far East *n* ƙasàshen Gabàs Mài Nīsā *p*.

farewell *n* ban kwānā *m*: we said ~ to them
and left mun yi musù ban kwānā mun tàfi.

farm 1. *n* gōnā *f* ⟨aki⟩: he removed the
weeds from his ~ yā nōmè gōnaƒsà;
(*large, collectively owned*) gandū *m* ⟨aye⟩;
(*small plot for boys*) gàyaunā *f* ⟨i⟩; (*fallow, disused*) sàurā *f* ⟨uka⟩.
2. *v* yi nōmā *m*; (*to remove weeds*) nōmè
*v4*.

farmer *n* manòmī *m*.

farm hand *n* ɗan bārēmā *m*.

farming *n* nōmā *m*, (*done by temporary help*)
bārēmā *f*.

far-sighted *adj* (*lit. or fig.*) (mài) hàngen
nēsà *m*.

fart *v* yi tūsā *f*, (*euphem.*) hūtà *v1*.

farther *adv*: how much ~ is it to get to
the village? saurā mīl nawà nē mù kai
ƙauyèn? just a little ~ saurā 'yaƒ tazarā
kàɗan.

fascinate *v* bā dà shà'awà *f*, ƙāyataƒ /
ƙāwataƒ (dà) *v5*: clocks ~ me àgōgo yanà
bā nì shà'awà = àgōgo yanà ƙāyataƒ dà
nī = inà shà'awàƒ àgōgo.

fascinating *adj* (*interesting*) (mài) ban
shà'awà *m*, mài ƙāyataƒwā: he was a
~ politician ɗan sìyāsà nē mài ban
shà'awà.

fascination *n* shà'awà *f*.

fascism *n* baƙin mulkī *m*, mulkìn fiƒ'aunà
*m*.

fashion *n* yàyī *m*, salō *m*: it's the latest ~ sābon yàyī nè = sābon salō nè;
this is no longer ~able an dainà yàyin
wannàn; old ~ed (*thing*) tsōhon yàyī,
(*psn.*) mùtumìn dâ.

fashionable *adj* (*psn.*) ɗan kwalliyā *m*,
(*esp. West. style*) ɗan gāyè *m*; (*of clothes*)
sābon yàyī *m*: she wears ~ clothes tanà
sà sābon yàyī = 'yaƒ kwalliyā cè; cotton brocade is very ~ nowadays yànzu anà
yàyin shaddà.

fast¹ *adj & adv* a. (*of action*) (mài) saurī
*m*: don't speak so ~ kadà kà yi màganà
dà saurī hakà; she talks too ~ tā cikà
màganà dà saurī; he works ~er than they
do yā fi sù saurin aikì. b. (*of motion*)

(mài) gudù *m*: do not drive so ~ kadà kà
yi gudù dà mōtà hakà; how ~ are we going? nawà nē yawàn gudùnmù? my watch
is 5 minutes ~ àgōgōnā nà gudùn mintī
blyaƒ. c. (*of passage of time*) dà wuri
*adv*: children grow up ~ yârā nà girmā
dà wuri = yârā nà dà saurin girmā. d.
(*firmly fixed*): this color is not ~ launìn
nân nà zùbà; they are ~ friends sun
shàƙu; be ~ asleep shàrè barcī.

fast² 1. *n* azùmī *m*, ƙishirwā *f*: one of
the five pillars of Islam is the ~ ɗaya
dàgà cikin shìkàshìkan Musuluncī shī
nē azùmī; a day of ~ rānaƒ azùmī; break
a ~ (*for health reasons*) shā azùmī, (*in vi-
olation*) karyà azùmī, ɓātà azùmī.
2. *v* yi azùmī *m*: they ~ for the whole
month anà azùmī gàbā ɗayan watàn.

fasten *v* a. (*join*): ~ a button, snap ɓallà
maɓallī; ~ a buckle, belt jā bōkùl, bêl.
b. (*secure with rope*) ɗaurà *v1*; ~ sth.
securely ɗaurà w.a. kankan; ~ a noose
around so. zargà wà igiyà.

fastener *n* maɓallī *m*; snap ~ maɓallī màcè
dà gōyō; hook ~ maɓallī mài ƙugìyā.

fastidious *adj* (mài) tsantsanī *m*.

fat 1. *adj* a. (*of psn.*) (mài) ƙibà *f*: get
~ yi ƙibà = yi jìkī; get ~ter ƙārà
ƙibà; big and ~ ɓulēlè *adj*, ɓulɓul *idph*,
sùkùtùm *idph*: she's big and ~ ɓulēlìyā
cè = ɓulɓul dà ita = sùkùtùm dà ita.
b. (*of meat*) (mài) mâi *m*: this meat is ~
and juicy wannàn nāmà yā yi mâi.
2. *n* (*of meat, animal*) mâi *m*, kitsè *m*.

fatal *adj*: the disease turned out to be ~
cīwòn yā zama ajàlī.

fatality *n*: were there any fatalities? an rasà
rāyukà?

fate *n* ƙaddaƒà *f*: accept ~ kàrɓi ƙaddaƒà;
as ~ would have it, Audu happened to pass
by just then bisà ƙaddaƒà sai gà Audù ya
wucè; that's my ~! Allàh ya dōrà minì!
when ~ comes knocking, there's no escape
in ƙaddaƒà tā zō, bā makawà = (*fig.*)
kōmē gudùn bàrēwā tā baƒ dājì.

father *n* (*term of ref.*) ùbā *m* ⟨anni⟩; (*most
polite terms of ref.*) mahàifī *m*, bàba *m*,
tsōhō *m*; (*term of addr.*) bàba; like ~ like
son (*fig.*) bàrēwā tā yi gudù ɗantà yà yi
ràrràfē?

father-in-law *n* sùrukī *m* ⟨ai⟩.

fatigue¹ *n* gàjiyà *f*.

fatigue² *n*: ~ duties (*in army, school*)
gwālè-gwālè *m*.

faucet *n* famfò *m* ⟨una⟩: turn on, turn off
a ~ būɗè, rufè famfò; the ~ is dripping
famfò nà ɗìgā.

fault *n* a. (*one's responsibility*) lâifī *m*
⟨uka²⟩: it's not his ~ bằ lâifinsằ ba nề
= bằ shi dằ laîfī; it's all your ~! ai
lâifinkằ nē! b. (*character flaw*) aibū /
aibī *m* ⟨oCi⟩, illằ *f* ⟨oCi⟩: you have one
~, you are too quick-tempered aibùnkằ
ɗaya, kằ fayề zāfin zūcìyằ; find ~ with
so. kūshề wằ *v4*: he found ~ with the way
I dressed yằ kūshề minì adōnā.
faultless *adj* marằs lâifī *m*, marằs aibī *m*.
faulty *adj* (mài) lâifī *m*, (mài) illằ *f*.
favor 1. *n* a. (*service*) tàimakō *m*, àlhēr̃ì
*m*: would you do me a small ~? kō zā kà
yi minì ɗan àlhēr̃ì? return a ~ rāmằ wà
àlhēr̃ì; remind so. of past ~s (*to embarrass him*) yi wà gōrì *m*. b. (*need*) bùkātằ
*f*: I need a ~ done inằ dà bùkātằ. c.
(*preference*): be in ~ of gòyi bāyan: we
are in ~ of the proposed bill munằ gòyon
bāyan shirìn dōkàr̃ì. d. (*so.'s approval*)
farin jinī *m*, fādằ *f*: he's out of ~ with
the teacher bằ shi dà farin jinī wajen
mālằm; he's more in ~ than I yằ fī nì
fādà; he is no longer in the emir's ~ bằ
shi dà fādà wajen sarkī.
2. *v* a. (*give preferential treatment*) nūnằ
wà fīfīkồ: the teacher ~s Sule mālằmīn
yanằ nūnằ wà Sulè fīfīkồ. b. (*bestow
good upon, usu. said of God*) ɗaukàkā
*v1*: God has ~ed him (in life) Allàh yā
ɗaukàkā shi.
favorable *adj*: the conditions are ~ lōkàcìn
yā dācề.
favorably *adv*: speak ~ about so. yi wà
shaidàr̃ kir̃kì; regard so.'s request ~
amìncē dà r̃ồkon w.
favorite 1. *adj*: my ~ story is *Gan-
doki* làbār̃ìn duk dà na fi sồ shi nề
Ganɗoki.
2. *n* (*psn.*) ɗan gàban gồshi *m*, ɗan gātā
*m*: the eldest boy is his ~ bàbban ɗan shì
nề ɗan gātansằ; ~ wife mōwằ *f*: Ladi is his
~ Lādì mōwàr̃sà cē = Lādì 'yar̃ gàban
gồshinsà cē.
favoritism *n* fīfīkồ *m*, gātancì *m*.
fear 1. *n* tsồrō *m*, fàr̃gàbā *f*: she fainted
from ~ tā sūma sabồdà tsồrō; for ~ of
don tsồron kadà, don gudùn kadà: he
didn't tell me for ~ of annoying me bài
faɗà minì ba don gudùn kadà r̃âinā yà
ɓācì; be paralyzed with ~ yi mutuwàr̃
tsàye.
2. *v* tsồratằ *v2*, yi/ji tsồron w.a.:
everyone ~s the secret police kōwā nằ
tsồron 'yan sàndan ciki; God-~ing mài
tsồron Allàh.
fearful *adj* (mài) ban tsồrō *m*: a ~ storm

ruwā dà iskằ mài ban tsồrō.
feast *n* (*banquet*) wàlīmằ *f* ⟨oCi⟩; (*festival,
celebration*) bìkī *m* ⟨uwa²⟩.
feather *n* gāshì *m* ⟨gāsū⟩: peacock ~
gāshìn dāwīsù; as light as a ~ sakwat
*idph*.
feature *n* àlāmằ *f* ⟨oCi⟩, siffằ *f* ⟨oCi⟩; distinctive ~ (*Gram.*) siffàr̃ bayyànâwā.
February *n* Fabur̃air̃ù *m*.
feces *n* kāshī *m*, (*euphem.*) bāyan gidā *m*,
nàjasà *f*.
federal *adj* na tàrayyằ *f*: a ~ government
gwamnatìn tàrayyằ.
federation *n* tàrayyằ *f*.
fed up, be *v* (*with so., sth.*) ƙōsằ *v1*,
gùndurà *v3*: I'm absolutely ~ up with him
nā ƙōsằ dà shī = yā cikà minì cikì =
yā shā minì kâi; the peasants were ~
with the government manồmā sun ƙōsằ dà
gwamnatìnsù.
fee *n* (*any payment*) kuɗī *m/p*: school ~s
kuɗin makarantā; (*payment for work*)
lādā *m*, see wages; court ~s (*for messenger*) ìjār̃à *f*; court ~s (*from property
cases*) ushir̃à *f*.
feeble *adj* (*sickly*) kùmāmā *n* ⟨ai⟩; (*weak-
ened*) (mài) raunī *m*: he was ~ after his
operation bāyan tìyātàr̃ dà akà yi masà
jìkinsà yā yi raunī; be(come) ~ yi
raunī *m*, ràunanà *v3*, kùmantà *v3*.
feed 1. *v* (*oneself, one's family*) cī dà /
ciyar̃ (dà) *v5*; (*animals*) kīwàtā *v1*; be
well fed kīwàtu *v7*.
2. *n* (*for animals*) àbinci *m*.
feel *v* a. (*perceive*) ji *v0*: ~ cold, hungry, sleepy ji sanyī, yunwằ, barcī; how
do you ~? yàyằ ka ji dà jìkī? she
doesn't ~ well today yâu bā tằ jîn
dādìn jìkintà. b. (*touch*) taɓà *v1*: the
hedgehog's coat ~s unpleasant to the
touch gāshìn būshiyā bā shi dà dādìn
taɓằwā; its surface ~s smooth, rough,
slippery jìkinsà yā yi sumul, kaushī,
santsī; ~ one's way (*grope*) lālùbā *v1*,
yi làlùbē *m*: he was ~ing his way along
the wall yanà làlùben bangō. c. (*have an
opinion, emotion*) ganī *v\**, ji *v0*: how do
you ~ about the results? mề kakề ganī
gàme dà sàkàmakôn? = yàyằ kakề jî dà
sàkàmakôn? I really ~ that you are wrong
inà jî à jìkīnā cêwā bâ ka dà gàskiyā;
~ like doing (*be in the mood*) ji yî: they
don't ~ like working today bā sằ jîn yîn
aikì yâu; I really ~ like singing jî nakề
kàmar̃ ìn yi wāƙằ; ~ badly about sth.
ɗauki w.a. mài zāfī; ~ sad about sth.
ji zāfin w.a.

**feeling** *n* a. (*sensation*): my hands have no ~ because of the cold hannầyēnā sun mutù sabồdầ sanyī. b. (*emotion, intuition*): I have a ~ that... jìkīnā yā bā nì cêwā...; I have mixed ~s about that inầ dà zūcīyā biyu gầme dà wầnnan; hide one's real ~s yi kinibībì *m;* be considerate of so.'s ~s yi wầ kầrā *f;* hurt so.'s ~s 6ātầ wâ rāi.

**fellow** *n* tālìkī *m* ⟨ai⟩: he is a nice ~ ɗan tālìkin nan yanầ dà kifkì.

**fellowship** *n* zùmùntā *f,* ƙầwầncē *m.*

**felony** *n* bầbban lâifī *m.*

**female** *n & adj* mầcè *f* ⟨mātā⟩, tamàta *adj*: a ~ child 'yā mầcè, ~ children 'yā'yā mātā; a ~ elephant gīwā tamàta.

**feminine** *adj* tamàta *f.*

**femininity** *n* mātūcì / mātuncì *m.*

**femur** *n* kàsangalì *m.*

**fence**[1] 1. *n* (*around farm*) shingē *m* ⟨aye⟩; (*around compound, of cornstalk or matting*) dangầ *f* ⟨oCi⟩, dầfnī *m* ⟨uka⟩.
2. *v* shingề *v4*, kangề *v4*, dangàcē *v4*: they ~d off their compound with mats sun shingề gidansù dà zānā.

**fence**[2] *n* (*one who sells stolen goods*) 6àrāwòn zàune *m.*

**fender** *n* (*of car, bicycle*) mutầgādì *m,* [F] gầfdầbû *m.*

**fend off** *v* tarè *v4*: we ~ed off the enemy mun tarè àbòkan gầba.

**fennec** *n* yânyāwầ *f* ⟨i⟩.

**ferment** *v* ru6ầ *v1*, ru6ař (dà) *v5*: they ~ grain to make beer sukàn ru6ầ hatsī sù yi giyầ dà shī; be(come) ~ed rù6a *v3*.

**ferry** 1. *v* yi fitồ *m*: we were ferried across the river an yi manầ fitồ mukà hayầ kồgī.
2. *n* jirgin fitồ *m.*

**fertile** *adj* (mài) àlbařkầ *f*, (mài) ni'imầ *f.*

**fertility** *n* àlbařkầ *f.*

**fertilize** *v* zuzzùbà tākì *m.*

**fertilizer** *n* (*manure*) tākì *m,* tầrōsō *m;* (*chemical*) tākìn zāmànī *m;* (*superphosphate*) tākìn sūfầ *m.*

**festival** *n* bìkī *m* ⟨uwa[2]⟩: ~ of culture bìkin àl'àdun gařgājiyầ; (*Muslim*) (rānař) sallầ *f*, Ìdì *m, see* Id.

**fetch** *v* nēmō *v6*: go ~ the police for us jè ka kà nēmō manầ 'yan sàndā; water ~ dēbō ruwā.

**fetish** *n* àbin tsāfì *m.*

**fetus** *n* ɗan tầyī *m.*

**fever** *n* zàzzà6ī *m*: she has a ~ tanầ zàzzà6ī; hay ~ màshasshařā / màsassařā *f.*

**few** *quant* a. (*not many*) kàɗan *adv*: he has ~ friends àbòkansà kàɗan nề; ~ people

know him mutầnē kàɗan sun san shì; after a ~ days bāyan 'yan kwầnàkī kàɗan; a ~ days ago kwānakin bāya; ~ of them are any good dàgà cikinsù kàɗan nề kề dà kyâu; there were ~er than 50 people mutầnên bà sù kai hàmsin ba. b. (*some*) waɗansu / wasu *det*: a ~ people have come to see you waɗansu mutầnē sun zō ganinkà; quite a ~ dà dāmā, bâ lâifī: he has quite a ~ friends àbòkansà dà dāmā = yanầ dà àbòkai bâ lâifī; just a ~ (*dimin.*) wasu 'yan: just a ~ belongings wasu 'yan kāyā.

**fez** *n* hûlař dầfā *f.*

**fiancé** saurầyī *m.*

**fiancée** *n* bùdurwā *f.*

**fiction** *n* ƙầgaggen lầbāřī *m;* non-~ lầbāřī *m.*

**fiddle** *n* (*approx. Hausa equivalents*): (*single-stringed*) gồgē *m*, (*smaller*) kūkūmầ *f;* play the ~ yi gồgē, yi kūkūmầ.

**fidgeting** *n* (*restlessness*) mùtsùniyā *f,* mùtsù-mutsū *idph*: what are you ~ about! mùtsù-mutsun mề kikề! (*esp. by children*) gîggīwầ *f.*

**field** *n* a. (*farm*) gōnā *f* ⟨aki⟩; (*fallow*) sàurā *f* ⟨uka⟩. b. (*esp. Sport*) fīlī *m* ⟨aye⟩: playing ~ fīlin wầsā. c. (*any open area*) fagē *m* ⟨aCe⟩: battle~ fagen yầƙì = fīlin dāgā. d. (*subject of study*) fannì *m* ⟨oCi⟩.

**field hand** *n* ɗan bārēmầ *m.*

**fifteen** *quant* (gōmầ) shâ bìyař *f.*

**fifth** *quant* na bìyař; one-~ humùsī *m.*

**fifty** *quant* hàmsin *f.*

**fig** *n* (*Ficus thonningii*) cēdiyā *f* ⟨oCi⟩, (*F. gnaphalocarpa*) 6aurē *m* ⟨aye⟩.

**fight** 1. *v* a. (*quarrel or physical*) yi faɗầ *m.* b. (*a war*) yi yầƙì *m*, yầƙầ *v2*: the army is ~ing the rebel forces sōjà tanầ ta yầƙì dà 'yan tāwāyề.
2. *n* (*quarrel*) faɗầ *m*, gařdamầ / gaddamầ *f* ⟨gařdàndamī⟩.

**figure**[1] *n* a. (*any form*) siffầ / sifầ *f* ⟨oCi⟩. b. (*human form*) ƙīrầ *f*: she has a good ~ kyân ƙīrầ gàrē tà; she has a full ~ tā cìka. c. (*a drawing in book*) zānē *m* ⟨e[2]⟩. d. (*in math*) adàdī *m* ⟨ai⟩: this ~ is incorrect adàdin nàn bài yi ba; I am bad at ~s bàn iyầ lìssāfì ba. e. ~ of speech fàsāhầř màganầ *f.*

**figure**[2] *v* (*reckon, estimate*) ƙiyàstā *v1*: I ~d that this would be enough nā ƙiyàstā wannàn zâi ìsa; ~ out sth. gānề *v4.*

**file**[1] 1. *n* (*of metal*) zařtồ *m* ⟨una⟩, magāgarī *m.*
2. *v* a. (*abrade*) gōgề *v4*: I ~d it down

with a ~ nā gōgè shi dà zařtò; ~ one's
nails gōgè farcè. b. (*sharpen*) wāsā *v1*.
file² *n* (*dossier*) fāyìl *m* ⟨oCi⟩, [F] dōsè
*m*: your ~ has been lost an ɓatař makà
dà fāyìl = fāyìl ɗinkà yā ɓacè.
fill 1. *vt* a. (*sth.*) cikà *v1*: ~ a water pot
cikà ràndā; ~ in a form, a tooth cikè
fōm, rāmìn haƙōrī; ~ sth. to the brim
bātsè *v4*, cikà māƙil: she ~ed the glass
to the brim tā bātsè tambùlàn; ~ sth.
up yi cikò *m*. b. (*a place to capacity*)
māƙarā *v1*: horsemen ~ed the entire field
māsu dawākī sun māƙarà fīlìn = fīlìn
yā yi cìkōwā dà māsu dawākī.
2. *vi* cika *v3*, see full.
3. *n*: eat one's ~ ƙoshi *v3\**; have one's
~ of sth. gùndurā *v2*: I've had my ~ of
this kind of food irìn àbincin nàn yā
gùndùrē nì.
fillet *n* (*of beef*) tàƙandā *f*.
filling *n* (*in tooth*) cikò *m*.
filly *n* dùƙusā *f* ⟨ai⟩.
film¹ *n* (*scum, thin coating or covering*) yānā
*f*.
film² *n* (*for camera*) fîm *m*, [F] filìm *m*;
(*movie*) fîm *m*, sìlìmā *f*, [F] filìm *m*:
cowboy ~ fîm ɗin kābòyī; spy ~ fîm
ɗin sì'aidî; reel of ~ faifan fîm; ~
show (*outdoors*) mājìgī *m*; show a ~ bugà
sìlìmā.
filter 1. *n* a. (*for oil, cigarettes*) filtà *f*,
[F] filtìř *m*: a ~ cigarette sìgārì mài
filtà. b. (*for water*) matācī *m*.
2. *v* tācè *v4*.
filth *n* ƙazântā *f*, daudà *f*, dàtti *m*, [F]
saltè *m*: there is too much ~ here daudàř
nàn tā yi yawà.
filthy *adj* a. (*of psn.*) ƙazāmī *adj* ⟨ai⟩,
duƙun-duƙun *idph*: his clothes are ~
kāyansà duƙun-duƙun sukè; (*fig.*) be ~
rich nā dà ƙazāmin kuɗī. b. (*of place*)
(mài) daudā *f*, kaca-kaca *idph*: the room
was ~ dākìn yā yi kaca-kaca.
final *adj* na ƙarshē *m*: the ~ chapter bābì
na ƙarshē.
finally *adv* dàgà ƙarshē: they ~ agreed
dàgà ƙarshē sun yàřda; the plan was ~
approved an tabbatař dà shirìn dàgà
ƙarshē; what ~ became of him? yàyà akà
ƙarè dà shī?
finance *n* sha'ànin kuɗī *m*.
financial *adj*: he's in ~ difficulties yanā
cikin matsī; ~ troubles matsalōlin
kuɗī.
finch *n* bâiwař Allāh *f*, tsādā *f*.
find 1. *v* a. (*get*) sāmù *v2\**: I didn't ~ any
at the market bàn sāmē shì à kàsuwā

ba; he couldn't ~ the time to visit us
yā kāsà sāmùn dāmař kai manà zìyāřā;
~ out (*information*) tàmbayā *v2*: ~ out
when the bus leaves kà jē kà tàmbàyi
lōkàcin tāshìn bâs. b. (*by searching,
discovering*) gānō *v6*: ~ a cure for a disease gānō māgànin cîwò; they could not
~ their way bà sù gānō hanyàřsù ba; I
found my (lost) knife nā gānō wuƙātā; go
~ out what he is up to jè ka kà gānō
àbîn dà yakè shirî. c. (*come upon accidentally, by chance*) tsìntā *v2*: I found
₦5 in the street nā tsìnci naiřā bìyař
à hanyà. d. (*come across sth.*) tař dà /
tarař (dà) *v5*: they found (out) that he
wasn't home an tarař bā yà gidā; on
our return, we found out that someone had
died dà dāwôwařmù, sai mukà tarař an
yi ràsuwā. e. ~ so. guilty sāmi w. dà
laîfī.
2. *n*: a lucky ~ tsìntuwā *f*.
fine¹ 1. *adj* a. (*good, lovely*) (mài) kyâu *m*:
that's ~! dà kyâu! he loves ~ clothes yanā
sôn tufāfî māsu kyâu. b. (*soft in texture*) (mài) taushī *m*: this cloth is much
~r than that wannàn yādìn yā fi wancàn
taushī.
2. *adv* a. (*well*) lāfiyā: how are you? ~
thank you kanā lāfiyà? lāfiyà lau; at
first, everything was ~ dà farkō, kōmē
lāfiyà. b. (*in small pieces*) ƙananā *p*:
she chopped up the okra ~ tā yayyànkà
kuɓèwā ƙananā.
fine² 1. *n* tārā *f*: a stiff ~ tārā mài
tsananī.
2. *v* ci w. tārā: the judge ~d him ₦50
àlƙālī yā cī shi tārā naiřā hàmsin.
finger *n* yātsā *m* ⟨yātsū⟩; index ~ ɗan
alì = ɗan nūnì; little ~ ɗan ƙurì/ƙurè;
point a ~ nūnà yātsā; snap one's ~s kaɗà
hannū; ~ disease (*whitlow*) kàkkařai *m*.
fingernail *n* farcè *m* ⟨a-a⟩, akaifā *f* ⟨u⟩,
ƙùmbā *f* ⟨una⟩.
fingerprint *n* zānen yātsā *m*: ~s were
found everywhere an gānō zānen yātsū
kō'ìnā.
finicky *adj*: be ~ yi tārā *f*: he's not ~
about food bā yà tārař àbinci.
finish 1. *v* a. gamā *v1*: ~ school gamà
makařantā; ~ on time gamà cikin
lōkàcī; ~ one's studies saukè kàřātū.
b. (~ *completely*) ƙarè *v4*, ƙaràsā *v1*:
when you have ~ed it, I want to see it
in kā ƙarè shi inā sôn ìn ganī; I ~ed
reading it last night nā ƙaràsà kařàntā
shi jiyà dà dare; the work isn't completely ~ed, here's some more aikìn bài

ƙārè ba, gằ saurā; it's completely ~ed
yā ƙārè kakaf. c. (*accomplish a duty*)
iyař/idař (dà) *v5*: they have ~ed their
prayers sun idař dà sallằ.
**2.** *n*: from start to ~ dàgà farkō hař
ƙàrshē; a fight to the ~ fadằ na hař
àbàdā.

**fire[1] 1.** *n* a. wutā *f*: a ~ broke out wutā
tā tāshì; the ~ is burning brightly wutā
tanằ cî sòsai; the ~ has gone out wutā
tā mutù; the house is on ~ gidā yanằ
cîn wutā = gidā yā kằmu dà wutā; put
more wood on the ~ ƙarà wà wutā itàcē;
put out a ~ kashè wutā; light, start a ~
kunnà wutā; fan a ~ hūrà wutā; set ~ to
sth. cinnà wà wutā, sâ wà wutā, dòsànà
wutā à: he set the house on ~ yā cinnà
wà ɗākì wutā = yā dòsànà wutā à ɗākì ;
(*fig.*) where there's smoke there's ~ ruwā
bā yằ tsāmī banzā; ~ mound (*for roast-
ing meat*) tukùbā *f*. b. (*adverbial uses*):
in the ~ (à) (cikin) wuta *adv*: don't put
it in the ~ kadà kà sâ shi cikin wuta;
he entered, came out of the ~ yā shìga,
fìta wuta. c. (*conflagration*) gòbařā *f*:
a ~ broke out last night wata gòbařā tā
tāshì jiyà dà dare. d. (*from a weapon*)
wutā *f*: open ~ on so. būɗè wà wutā.
**2.** *v* a. (*a weapon*) bugằ *v1*, hařbằ *v1*. b.
(*an engine, rocket*) tā dà *v5*. c. (*pottery*)
tòyằ *v1*; this pot is not well ~d wannàn
tukunyā bà tā tòyu sòsai ba.

**fire[2]** *v* (*dismiss*) kòrā *v2*: he was ~d from his
job for stealing an kòrē shì dàgà aikìn
sabòdà sātā.

**fire department** *n* ma'aikatař kashè
gòbařā *f*.

**fire engine** *n* mōtàř kwāna-kwāna *f*, [F] pīpằ
*f*.

**firefly** *n* màƙèsu *f*, màƙèsuwā *f*, ƙyàllu-
ƙyàllu *f*, wutař 'Yōlà *f*.

**fireman** *n* ɗan kwāna-kwāna *m*, [F] sōjàn
kashè wutā *m*.

**firewood** *n* itàcē / icè *m*, (*esp. twigs*)
ƙirằrè *p*: a load of ~ ƙunshìn itàcē;
chopped up ~ fàskàrè *m*.

**fireworks** *n* wằsan wutā *m*.

**firm[1]** *adj* a. (*hard*) (mài) taurī *m*: the
earth is ~ here but soft there ƙasâř
nân taurī cân taushī. b. (*determined*)
tāshì tsàye à kân: she was ~ about not
letting the children eat candy tā tāshì
tsàye à kân kadà yârā sù shā àlēwā.

**firm[2]** *n* (*business*) kamfànin cìnikī *m*.

**firmly** *adv* (*often expressed by ideophones
which go with specific verbs*): the door has
been closed ~ ƙōfằ tā dànnu dandan; the

rope is ~ tied igiyằ tā ɗauru tsantsan.

**first 1.** *quant* farkō *m*, na farkō, na
fārì: the ~ day of the month rānā
ta farkon watằ; the ~ time we met
farkon sằduwařmù = sằduwařmù ta fārì;
~ name (*Islamic*) sūnan yankā = sūnan
řằgō = sūnan gàskiyā, (*non-Islamic*)
sūnan rānā; I bought the ~ one that I
saw nā sàyi àbîn dà na fārà ganī; the
~ time that I saw him ganīnā na farkō dà
shī; it is the ~ big building you'll come
to shī nề bàbban ginìn dà zā kà fārà
ìsā; from ~ to last (tun) dàgà farkō hař
(zuwà) ƙàrshē.
**2.** *adv* a. (*beginning*): at ~ dà farkō = dà
fārì; in the ~ place... dà farkō dai...;
when we ~ arrived dà farkon isôwařmù.
b. (*before doing sth. else*) tùkùna / tùkùn
*adv*: let's eat ~ bàri mù ci àbinci
tùkùna; do sth. ~ fārà *v1* (+ *action n*):
~ read then write kà fārà kàřàtū kānà kà
yi řùbūtū. c. be the ~ to do sth. tsìrā
*v2*: who was the ~ to introduce Hausa
written in Roman script? wằ ya tsìri
řùbūtun Hausa dà bōkò?

**first aid** *n* tàimakon farkō *m*, tàimakō wajen haɗàřī.

**first-born** *n* ɗan fārì *m*.

**first-class** *adj* a. (*in quality*) làmbàwân *m*:
the best ~ hotel in the city hòtâl mafì
duk làmbàwân à gàrîn. b. (*of tickets*)
faskìlà *m*.

**firstly** *adv* dà farkō, dà fārì.

**first-rate** *adj* (mài) nàgàřtā *f*.

**fiscal year** *n* shèkaràř kasàfin kuɗī *f*.

**fish 1.** *n* kīfī *m* ⟨aye⟩.
**2.** *v* (*with nets*) sùntā *v2*, yi sû *m*, (*with
line & hook*) yi fatsa *f*.

**fishbone** *n* ƙayằ *f* ⟨oCi⟩.

**fisherman** *n* masùncī *m*, mài sû *n*.

**fish-hook** *n* (*with line*) fatsa *f*: cast a ~
into the river jēfà fatsa à kòg̣ī.

**fishing** *n* sû *m*, kāmùn kīfī *m*.

**fish-net** *n* (*small*) hōmā *f* ⟨aye⟩; (*large*) tārū
*m* ⟨aye⟩.

**fist** *n* dunƙulèn hannū *m*; clench a ~ dunƙùlā
*v1*; crush sth. in ~ dunƙùlē *v4*; raise a ~
in salute yi jìnjinằ *f*.

**fit[1] 1.** *v* a. (*be right size*) yi wà daidai: the
blouse ~s her perfectly rìgā tā yi matà
daidai cif; these things will not ~ into
the box kāyan nàn bà zā sù shìga cikin
àkwàtì ba. b. (*suit*) dācè dà *v4*: his qual-
ifications ~ the job ƙwarèwařsà tā dācè
dà aikìn.
**2.** *adj* a. (*suitable*): be ~ dācè *v4*: this
water is not ~ to drink ruwan nàn bài

dācè dà à shā shì ba; be ~ for so. (befitting) kàmātà v2: this place is not ~ for
women (to be in) wurin nàn bài kàmàci
mātà ba; be ~ting kyàutu v7, càncantà v3
(+ 3rd pers. subj pro): it would be ~ing to
praise him for his work zâi kyàutu à yabà
masà dà aikinsà = zâi càncantà ìdan an
yabà masà dà aikinsà. b. (healthy): he
doesn't feel ~ today yâu bā yà jîn dādī;
he is really feeling ~ (fig.) yanà būsàr
iskà.
fit[2] n (epileptic) farfàɗiyā f: he had an
epileptic ~ farfàɗiyā tā bùgē shì.
five quant biyar f.
fix 1. v a. (repair) gyārà v1 ⟨gyārā⟩, gyártà
v1: I have to get my car ~ed yā kàmātà ìn
kai mōtà gyārà; can you ~ my flat tire?
kà iyà yi wà tāyà fācì? b. (prepare)
shiryà v1: ~ dinner shiryà àbinci. c.
(restrict) ƙayyàdē v4: prices are ~ed by
the market kàsuwā kè ƙayyàdè kuɗin
abūbuwà; there is no ~ed rule about that
bàbù wata ƙayyàdaddiyar dòkà gàme dà
wannàn; ~ a date sà rānā.
2. n: (fig.) be in a ~ shìga ukù.
fizzle out v shirīrìcē v4: the plan ~d out
shirìn yā shirīrìcē.
flabby adj: be ~ yi laƙwas idph.
flag n tūtà f ⟨oCi⟩: ~s flew everywhere
tūtōcī nà tāshì kō'ìnā.
flagpole n sàndar tūtà f.
flake 1. n (crumb, bit) ɓarɓashī m, bùrbùdī
m.
2. v ɓamɓàrē v4: the paint has started to
~ off fentì nà ɓamɓàrêwā.
flame n harshèn wutā m; it burst into ~s yā
kāmà dà wutā.
flap v (of sth. in wind) kaɗà v1: the flag
is ~ping in the wind tūtà nà kaɗàwā à
iskà; the bird flew up ~ping its wings
tsuntsū yā kaɗà fìkàfìkai yā tāshì
fìr.
flare up v (of fire, temper, dispute) kùfulà
v3.
flash n (of light) haskē m.
flashlight n tōcìlàn f, [F] cōcìllà f.
flask n (of gourd, for water) būtàr gòran
ruwā f; (thermos) fìlâs m, tàrmûs m.
flat[1] n (apartment) gidā m ⟨aCe⟩, (in a
building with upper storey) bēnē m ⟨aye⟩.
flat[2] n (tire) fancà f, fācì m, [F] kìrèbê m;
have a ~ yi fancà = yi fācì.
flat[3] adj (mài) bâi ɗaya, (mài) lēbùr m; be
~ yi lēbùr.
flatter v a. yi wà dādin bàkī m, yi
wà rōmon bakà; (esp. to win favor) yi
fādancī m. b. (praise excessively) zugà

v1: she ~s him shamelessly tanà zugà shi
bà kunyà bà tsòron Allàh.
flattery n dādin bàkī m, rōmon bakà m; (to
win favor) fādancī m.
flatulence n tūsà f.
flavor n ɗanɗanō m: it has a salty ~ yanà
dà ɗanɗanon gishirī; this soup doesn't
have any ~ wannàn miyà salaf takè.
flaw n (esp. of character) aibù / aibì m
⟨oCi⟩, layànī m, illà f ⟨oCi⟩.
flay v fēɗè v4.
flea(s) n ƙùmā m, tùnkùyau m.
flee v gudù v3b, shēƙà dà gudù v1: the thief
fled on foot ɓàrāwòn yā gudù dà ƙafà;
~ to gudō v6: he fled to Nigeria to take
refuge yā gudō Nìjēriyà don yà faƙè.
flesh n tsōkà f.
flex v lanƙwàsà v1, tanƙwàrā v1.
flexible adj a. (of material) (mài) lànƙwàsuwā f, (mài) tànƙwàruwā f: this metal is
not ~ ƙarfèn nân bā yà tànƙwàruwā. b.
(of personality) (mài) sauƙin kâi m: he'll
agree because he is ~ zâi yàrda sabòdà
yanà dà sauƙin kâi.
flick v kaɓè v4: ~ dust off a robe kaɓè ƙùra
dàgà rìgā; (with one's fingers) ɗallà v1:
he ~ed some gravel at me ya ɗallà minì
tsakuwà.
flight n a. (of bird) tāshì m; (of airplane)
tàfiyà ta jirgin samà f. b. (escape to
avoid persecution) hìjìrà f.
flimsy adj: your excuse is ~ uzùrinkà bâ
shi dà makāmā.
fling v wātsar (dà) v5, wurgar (dà) v5: they
flung their clothes on the floor sun wātsar
dà kāyansù à ƙas.
flint n ƙanƙarā f: ~ of lighter ƙanƙarar
ƙyàstū.
flip v: let's ~ a coin zō ìn yi makà kân
sarkī kō dàmarà.
flip-flops n (rubber sandals) silīfà m.
flirt v yi kwàrkwasà f.
float v (of psn.) yi iyò m; (of sth.) tāsō kân
ruwā.
flock 1. n: ~ of birds tārìn tsuntsàyē m,
~ of sheep garkèn tumākī; leader of the
~ ùban garkè.
2. v: everyone ~ed to the prayer grounds
kōwā yā yi jērìn gwānò zuwà fīlìn ìdì.
flog v fyāɗà wà būlālà, fyàɗè w. dà
būlālà.
flood v & n yi ambàliyà f, yi amāguwà f:
the rains ~ed the farms ruwan samà yā yi
wà gònàkī ambàliyà; ~waters ambàliyàr
ruwā; the river is at ~ level kògī yā cikō
= kògī yā kai yā kāwō = kògī yā bàtsè.

**floor** *n* a. (*of room*) dàɓē *m*: sweep the ~ shàrè dàɓē. b. (*storey*) hawā *m*: the building has three ~s ginìn yanà dà hawā huɗu; the ground ~ jàkin bēnē.

**flour** *n* (*finely ground*) gàrī *m*, (*coarsely ground*) tsàkī *m;* whole wheat ~ (*locally grown*) gàrin alkamà; white ~ (*refined, imported*) fulāwà *f;* cassava ~ kwàkī *m*, gàrin rōgò *m*.

**flow** *v* a. gùdānà *v3*: there is water ~ing through the pipe àkwai ruwā yanà gùdānà ta famfò; stop ~ing ɗaukè *v4*, (*recede*) jànyē *v4*. b. (*v + adv/prep uses*): ~ down (*heavily*) kwàràrà *v3;* ~ into màlàlà *v3*: the water ~ed into the hut ruwā yā màlālà cikin ɗàkì; ~ out into malàlē *v4*: this stream ~s out into the River Niger ƙòramàr̃ nan tanà malàlēwà zuwà Kògin Kwàrà; ~ over, beyond tumbàtsē *v4*: the river has ~ed beyond its banks kògîn yā tumbàtsē har̃ bāyan gàɓà; ~ past, ~ toward bi *v0*: the river ~s past the factory kògîn yā bi ta ma'aikatàr̃; ~ through (*flood*) kwàràrà wà *v1*: the floodwaters ~ed through the town ambàliyàr̃ ruwā tā kwàràrō wà gàrîn.

**flower** 1. *n* fùrē *m* ⟨anni⟩, fulāwà *f;* ~ bud (*on tree*) hùɗà *f*.
2. *v* (*of plant, tree*) fid dà fùrē.

**fluctuate** *v* canzà *v1*: his mood ~s between hope and despair hàlìnsà yanà canzàwā tsàkānin bùrì dà yankè ƙaunā.

**fluctuation** *v* (*of prices*) hawā dà sàukā *f*: there is ~ in the price of commodities àkwai hawā dà sàukar̃ fàr̃àshìn kāyan màsàr̃ūfì.

**fluent** *adj*: he is ~ in several languages yanà jîn harsunà dà dāmā = yā iyà harsunà dà yawà; (*fig., re. Hausa only*) he speaks Hausa ~ly yā iyà Hausa kàmar̃ jàkin Kanò.

**fluid** *n* ruwā *m*.

**fluke** *n* màtsàttsàku *f*.

**flustered, be(come)** *v* gìgìcē *v4*, kidìmē *v4*: their questions ~ed her tambayōyinsù sun sà tā gìgìcē; (*esp. out of fear*) ɗimàucē *v4*.

**flute** *n* (*of cornstalk*) sìrīƙì *m* ⟨ai⟩, (*end-blown, of cornstalk or metal*) sàrēwà *f*, (*transversely blown*) tìlìɓòr̃o *m*.

**flutter** *n* yi filfilwà *f*: paper is ~ing through the air takàr̃dā nà filfilwà à samà; the flag is ~ing in the wind tūtà tanà tāshì fil-fil-fil.

**flux** *n* (*for solder*) sìnàdàr̃ī *m*.

**fly**[1] *n* ƙudà *m* ⟨aCe⟩: the flies are really bothering us ƙudàjē sunà dāmùnmù sòsai;

(*large biting* ~) bōbuwā *f;* tsetse ~ ƙudan tsandō *m*.

**fly**[2] *v* tāshì *v3b*: the birds suddenly flew up tsuntsàyē sun tāshì fìr̃; (*by plane*) yi tàfiyà ta jirgin samà; (*fig.*) time flies lōkàcī yanà gudù; the door flew wide open ƙōfàr̃ tā wàgè; ~ into a rage hàrzuƙà *v3*.

**fly swatter** *n* (*tradit. horsehair*) izgā *f*.

**foal** *n* dùƙushī *m* ⟨ai⟩.

**foam** 1. *n* (*from soap*) kumfā *m;* ~ rubber r̃ōbà *f*, [F] ìpanjì *f*: a ~ rubber mattress kàtīfàr̃ r̃ōbà.
2. *v* yi kumfā *m*: he's ~ing at the mouth bàkinsà nà kumfā.

**focus** *v* ƙurà idò, zurà idò: we ~sed our hopes on him mun ƙurà idò à kânsà; everyone's attention was ~sed on him an ƙurà masà idò.

**fodder** *n* ìngirìcī *m*.

**foetus** *n, see* fetus.

**fog** *n* hazō *m*: it is ~gy today yâu dà hazo-hazo.

**fold** 1. *v* a. ninkè *v4*, karyà *v1*: he ~ed his clothes and put them away yā ninkè kāyansà yā ajìyē; ~ one's arms across chest maƙàlè hannū, (*in prayer*) kāmà ƙìrjī; ~ down, ~ over lanƙwàsà *v1*, kalmàsà *v1*: ~ down the corner of the paper lanƙwàsà takàr̃dā dàgà kusurwà; ~ing chair kujèrā mài ninkèwā. b. (*into equal parts*) ninkà *v1*: he ~ed the paper in 4 yā ninkà takàr̃dā huɗu.
2. *n* (*crease*) kàlmasà *f*, karì *m*.

**folder** *n* (*file*) fāyìl *m* ⟨oCi⟩, [F] shàmîs *m*.

**foliage** *n* ganyàyē *p*.

**folk** 1. *n* a. jàma'à *f/p*, mutànē *p;* (*of a nation*) àl'ummà *f*. b. (*kinsmen*) 'yan'uwā *p*, dangì *m*.
2. *adj* na gàr̃gàjiyā *f*: ~ medicine màgànin gàr̃gàjiyā.

**folklore** *n* ilìmin hikimōmin àl'ummà *m*.

**folk song** *n* wāƙar̃ gàr̃gàjiyā *f*.

**folktale** *n* tàtsūnìyā *f* ⟨oCi⟩; come and tell us a ~ zō kì yi manà tàtsūnìyā; this ~ is about the trickster Gizo wannàn tàtsūnìyar̃ Gizò cē.

**follow** *v* a. bi *v0*: ~ this road straight on kà bi wannàn hanyà sak; he refused to ~ my instructions yā ƙi bîn ùmàr̃nīnà; ~ed by biye dà: the people were ~ed by their animals mutànē nà biye dà dabbōbinsù; the subject is ~ed by the verb fi'ìlī yanà biye dà mìƙau = fi'ìlī yanà gàbātar̃ mìƙau; one ~ing the other kâi dà kâi, bì dà bì, biye dà jūnā; the ~ing day kàshēgàrī / wàshēgàrī *f;* ~ closely màtsā *v2*: don't ~ that car so closely kadà kà màtsi waccàn mōtàr̃; ~ through on a promise cikà àlkawàr̃ī. b. (*understand*) gànè *v4*: he could not ~ my explanation yā kāsà gànè bàyānīnā.

**foment** *v* izà wutà: they did their best to ~ rebellion sun yi iyā yīnsù sù izà wutar̃ tāwāyèn.

**fond** *adj*: be ~ of sō *v0*, yi k̃aunā *f*: he is ~ of reading yanà sôn kàr̃ātū = sôn kàr̃ātū gàrē shì; (*of one ano.*) shàk̃u *v7*, sàr̃k̃u *v7*: he and Audu are ~ of each other dà shī dà Audù sun shàk̃u = jininsù yā hàɗu.

**fondle** *v* yi tsàràncē *m*.

**fonio** *n* accà *f*.

**fontanelle** *n* maɗigà *f*.

**food** *n* àbinci *m*: ~, clothing and shelter dà àbinci dà tufà dà wurin zamā; without ~ or water bâ cî bâ shâ; (*staple ~*) cīmā *f*, [F] cīmakà *f*: what kind of ~ do the Hausa have? mènē nè cīmar̃ Hàusàwā? unsold ~stuffs kwantai *m*; (*fig.*) ~ for thought àbin tùnānī.

**fool** 1. *n* wāwā *n* ⟨aye⟩, sākar̃ai *n*, ⟨sākàr̃kàr̃ī⟩, saunā *n* ⟨oCi⟩, dōlō *m* ⟨aye⟩, shāshàshā *n*: an absolute ~ wāwā nè sòsai = wāwā nè na k̃in k̃āràwā = wāwā nè na innānàhà; what a ~ that person is! wànnan àkwai shāshàshā! behave like a ~ mūzàncè *v4*, yi sākar̃cī; make a ~ of so. mūzàntā *v1*; take so. for a ~ mai dà w. wāwā, rainà wà wàyō, rainà wà hankàlī: no one likes to be taken for a ~ bā mài sôn yà mai dà kânsà wāwā.

2. *v* (*trick, outwit*) r̃ūɗà *v2*, zàmbatà *v2*: his appearance ~ed me shìgar̃sà tā r̃ūɗē nì; ~ around yi wàsā *m*: stop ~ing around kà dainà wàsā; you can't ~ someone clever (*fig.*) bā à yi wà birì bur̃tū.

**foolhardy** *adj*: do sth. ~ yi kàsadà *f*.

**foolish** *adj* a. (*psn.*) saunā *n*; be, do sth. ~ yi wàutā *f*, zama wāwā: I was ~ to trust him nā yi wàutā dà na yàr̃da dà shī; I am not so ~ as that wàutātā bà tà kai hakà ba; make so. look ~ mūzàntā *v1*. b. (*in speech*): what a ~ thing to say! shìrmē nè!

**foolishness** *n* wàutā *f*, wàwancì *m*, sūsancì *m*, saunancì *m*, sākar̃cì *m*; (*esp. in speech*) shìrmē *m*.

**foot** *n* a. k̃afà *f* ⟨k̃afàfū, uwa²⟩, sau / sāwū *m* ⟨sāwàyē⟩: she hurt her ~ tā ji cīwò à santà; (*fig.*) get cold feet shā jinin jìkī. b. (*adverbial uses*): in, on the ~ (à) k̃afà *adv*: go on ~ tàfi à k̃asà = tàfi dà k̃afà; he always goes to the office

on ~ kullum yanà zuwà ōfìs à k̃asà. c. (*base of sth.*) gìndī *m*: at the ~ of a tree à gìndin bishiyà. d. (*unit of measurement & in poetic meter*) k̃afà *f* ⟨k̃afàfu, uwa²⟩: this table is 5 feet long tsawon tēbùr̃in nàn k̃afà bìyar̃ nè.

**foot and mouth disease** *n* bōr̃ù / baur̃ù *m*.

**football** *n, see* soccer.

**footpath** *n* turbà *f*.

**footprint** *n* sāwun k̃afà *m*.

**footstep** *n* (*of partic. psn.*) tākù *m*: I recognized his ~ nā gànè tākùnsà; I hear some ~s outside nā ji anà mòtsī à wàje.

**for** *prep* a. (*to indicate ind obj*) wà/mà (+ n), ma- (+ *pro, see* Appendix A), gà *prep*: I bought some soap ~ Ladi nā sayō wà Lādì sàbulù; please greet your wife ~ me kà gayar̃ minì dà uwar̃gidā; milk is good ~ children madàr̃ā nà dà àmfànī gà yârā. b. (~ *the purpose of*) (*use genitive constr.*): a knife ~ cutting meat wuk̃ar̃ yankà nāmà; a box ~ clothing àkwàtìn kāyā; where is the key ~ this door? ìnā makullin k̃ōfàr̃ nân? c. (*on account of*) sabòdà *prep*, dòmin / don *prep*, wajen *prep*: they imprisoned him ~ stealing sun ɗaurè shi sabòdà sātà; he was rewarded ~ bravery an yi masà kyàutā don jàr̃ùntakà; this hoe is good ~ digging it up far̃tanyàr̃ nân tanà dà àmfànī wajen tōnàwā. d. ~ the sake of dòmin / don *conj*, sabòdà *conj*: they bought it ~ my sake (to please me) sun sàyē shì dòmīnā; ~ what? don mè? = sabòdà mè? e. (*for use as particles with verbs, see relevant verb entries*): wait ~ Ladi jirà Lādì; pay ~ the robe biyā kuɗin r̃ìgā; send ~ a doctor aikà wà likità yà zō; go ~ a walk fìta yāwò. f. (~ *a period of time, usu. not translated*): the meeting lasted ~ 2 hours tàrôn yā kai awà biyu; I haven't seen her ~ 3 days kwānā ukù bàn gan tà ba; they stayed ~ 3 months sun zaunà watà ukù. g. (*other uses*): ~ Garba, it is a lot of money gà Gar̃bà kuɗī nè màsu yawà; it is good ~ nothing bâ shi dà àmfànī; is this letter ~ you? wànnàn wàsīk̃àr̃kà cē? it costs ₦2 ~ the first 10 words kuɗinsà naír̃à biyu à kân kalmōmī gōmà na fark̃ō.

**forbearance** *n* dauriyà *f*, jūrèwā *f*.

**forbid** *v* a. hanà *v1*: the children's mother forbade them to go out mahaifìyar̃ yârā tā hanà su fìtā wàje; smoking is ~den here an hanà shân tābà à nân. b. (*in Islam*) har̃àmtā *v1*; God ~ (that it should happen)! Allàh yà kiyàyē!

force[1] 1. *n* (*strength*) ƙarfī *m*: do not use ~ kadà kà nūnà ƙarfī; brute ~ ƙarfin tsìyā; join ~s hadà ƙarfī = hadà gwīwà.
2. *v* a. (*use force*): ~ apart, open tàɓè *v4*: I ~ed open the lid of the box nā tàɓè murfin àkwàtì. b. (*require, constrain*) tīlàstā wà *v1*: they ~d him to give up his job sun tīlàstā masà dà yà baƙ aikìnsà; engine trouble ~d the plane to land ɓācìn injìn yā tīlàstā wà jirgîn yà saukō.

force[2] *n* (*group*) rùndunā *f* ⟨oCi⟩: the armed ~s rùndunaƙ sōjà/sōjōjī; the air ~ sōjōjin mayàƙan samà; peace-keeping ~ rùndunaƙ tabbataƙ dà zaman lāfiyà; the police ~ 'yan sàndā; the special ~s sōjōjin ƙùndùmbālā; the labor ~ 'yan ƙwādagō.

forced *adj* na tīlàs, na dōlè: a ~d landing sàukaƙ tīlàs; ~ labor aikìn dōlè.

forceps *n* hàntsakī *m* ⟨ai⟩, màtsēfatà *f* ⟨ai⟩.

ford 1. *v* (*a river*) hayè *v4*, ƙētàrē *v4*.
2. *n* mahayī *m*, maƙētarī *m*.

forearm *n* hannū *m* ⟨aye, uwa⟩.

forecast 1. *v* kìntātà *v2*.
2. *n* kìntàcē *m*.

forefathers *n* kàkā dà kàkànnī *p*.

forehead *n* gòshī *m*.

foreign *adj* a. (*external to one's country*) na (ƙasàshen) wàje *adv*, na ƙētarè *m*: ~ affairs haƙkōkin ƙasàshen wàje; a ~ country ƙasaƙ wàje = ƙasaƙ ƙētarè; ~ exchange kudàɗen mùsāyā; a ~ language (*outside Nigeria, Niger*) harshèn ƙasaƙ wàje, (*within Nigeria, Niger*) bàƙon harshè. b. (*from another culture*) bàƙō *adj* ⟨i⟩: a ~ car, custom bàƙuwaƙ mōtà, àl'ādà.

foreigner *n* bàƙō *m* ⟨i⟩.

foreman *n* hēlùmà *m*, hōmàn *m*, [F] kwàntìƙmētìƙ *m*.

foremost *adj*: he is the ~ writer in the Hausa language shī nè maƙùbùcī mafī shàhaƙà à harshèn Hausa.

foresee *v* tsìnkàyà *v2*, hàngā *v2*, hangō *v6*, yi hàngē *m*: I foresaw the difficulties I would get into nā tsìnkàyi wàhalàƙ dà zân shìga; they ~ trouble ahead for him anà yi masà hàngen wàhalà; I ~ a trip to Europe nā hangō tàfiyà zuwà Tūƙai.

foresight *n* a. (*insight*) tsìnkàyā *f*, tsìnkàyē *m*, hàngen nēsà *m*: he has ~ yanà dà tsìnkàyē. b. (*advanced planning*) tānàdī *m*.

foreskin *n* lōɓā *f*.

forest *n* dājì / jējì *m* ⟨dāzuzzukà⟩; ~ reserve gandun dājì; (*esp. tropical*) kurmì *m* ⟨a-u⟩.

forever *adv* a. (*permanently*) haƙ àbàdà *m*, dindìndin *adv*: they became friends ~ sun ɗaurà àɓōtā haƙ àbàdà. b. (*continually*) kullum *adv*: he is ~ pestering me kullum yanà ta fìtinàtā.

foreword *n* gabātàƙwā *f*, ƙaddamàƙwā *f*.

forge 1. *v* a. (*metal, a document*) ƙērà *v1* ⟨ƙīrà⟩ *f*: he ~s iron yanà ƙīrà dà baƙin ƙarfè. b. (*document*): ~ a check bugà câk na jàbu.
2. *n* maƙērā *f*.

forged *adj* (*faked*) na ƙīrà, na jàbu: this is passport is ~ wannàn fàsfō na ƙīrà nē; a ~ check câk na jàbu.

forger *n* ɗan kantàfìs *m*.

forget *v* mântā *v1*, yi mantuwā *f*, mâncē *v4*, ƙàfkanà *v3*: have you forgotten about our appointment? kin yi mantuwā dà àlkawàƙinmù? don't ~ to give him my message kadà kà mâncē dà bā shì sàƙōnā; ~ completely mâncē shaf; ~ momentarily shà'afà *v3*: I have forgotten his name for the moment af, nā shà'afà dà sūnansà = sūnansà yā kwântā minì.

forgetful *adj* (mài) mantuwā *f*, màntau *n*: he is very ~ yā fayè mantuwā = shī màntau nè.

forgive *v* yàfè wà *v4*, haƙùrà wà *v1*: I will never ~ him for his rudeness to me bà zân taɓà yàfè masà rashìn kunyàƙ dà ya yi minì; he does not ~ people easily bà shi dà saurin yàfè wà mutànē; (*in formal context*) gàfaƙtà *v2*, gàfàƙtā wà *v1*: please ~ me for being late à gàfàƙcē nì sabòdà rashìn zuwànā cikin lōkàcī.

forgiveness *n* gàfaƙà *f*: beg for ~ rōƙi gàfaƙà, tūba *v3a*; he begged our ~ yā rōƙi gàfaƙà à gàrē mù.

fork *n* a. cōkàlī mài yātsū *m*, fôk *m*, [F] kùƙshêt / hùƙshētì *f*; a ~ed stick gwàfā *f* ⟨anni⟩. b. (*in road*) mararrabaƙ hanyà *f*.

form[1] 1. *n* a. (*shape*) siffà / sifà *f* ⟨oCi⟩: make into the ~ of sth. yi à siffàƙ w.a. b. (*structure, Gram.*) sīgà *f* ⟨oCi⟩: Hausa verbs have many different ~s àikàtan Hausa nà dà sīgōgī dà dāmā. c. (*type*) nau'ì *m* ⟨oCi⟩: ice is a ~ of water ƙanƙarā wani nau'in ruwā cè. d. (*orderliness*) tsārì *m*: ~ and function tsārì dà aikì.
2. *v* (*an organization*) kafà *v1*: a commission of inquiry was ~ed to look into the matter an kafà kwàmìtîn bìncìkē don

duddǔbà màganàř.

form[2] n (any document) fôm m, [F] fîsh f:
fill out a ~ cikà fôm.

form[3] n (in school) ajî m ⟨uwa[2]⟩: she's in
second ~ tanà ajî biyu.

former adj a. (from before) na dâ: the ~
ambassador jàkādà na dâ; his ~ wife
màtařsà ta dâ. b. (first mentioned) na
dayân: there go Audu and Sule, the ~ is
a teacher, the latter a doctor gà Audù dà
Sulè, na dayân mālàmī nè na ƙàrshên
kuma likità nē.

formerly adv à (zāmànin) dâ adv: ~ this
town was an important trade center à
zāmànin dâ gàrin nàn bàbbař cībìyař
cìnikī nè; ~ he would come in the morn-
ings dâ yakàn zō dà sāfe.

formidable adj gàgàrùmī adj ⟨ai⟩.

fornication n zìnā f, làlātà f.

fornicator n mazìnàcī m.

forth adv: go back and ~ yi kai-dà-kàwō
m, yi kai-kàwō m, yi zìřgà-zir̃gā f:
people are going back and ~ mutànē nà
kai-dà-kàwō; carry sth. back and ~ kai
dà kāwō: they are carrying things back
and ~ mutànē sunà kâiwā sunà kāwôwā;
and so ~ dà dai sauransù.

forthcoming adj (mài) zuwà: the ~ celebration bìkī mài zuwà.

fortnight n mākò biyu m.

fortunate adj a. (wealthy) (mài) dūkìyā f,
(mài) ařzìkī m. b. (lucky) (mài) sā'à f,
(mài) ràbō m: he is ~ yā yi sā'à = yanà
dà sā'à.

fortune n a. (wealth) dūkìyā f, ařzìkī m:
inherit so.'s ~ gàji dūkìyař w. b. (good
luck) sā'à f: may God bring you good ~!
Allàh yà bā dà sā'à! I once had the good
~ to meet him nā yi sā'à dà na taɓà
hàduwà dà shī. c. (one's future): to tell
so.'s ~ yi wà dūbà m, bugà wà ƙasā.

fortune-teller n mài dūbà n.

forty quant àřbà'in f.

forward 1. adv gàba adv: go ~ ci gàba =
yi gàba; rush ~ shèƙà gàba; look ~ to
yi allà-allà m, zubà idò, sâ râi: I
am looking ~ to his arrival inà zubà idòn
zuwànsà; I'm looking ~ to vacation coming inà allà-allà hūtū yà zō; we are
looking ~ to our trip to Nigeria munà sâ
rân tàfiyàřmù zuwà Nìjēřiyà; from this
day ~ dàga yànzu; two steps ~ one step
backward (fig.) kwàn gàba, kwàn bāya.
2. v tūrà v1: they will ~ the mail to
your new address zāsù tūrà makà tàkàřdū
zuwà sābon àdìřēshì.

foster v (a child) dàuki řènon w.

foster-father n ùban rāna m.

foster-mother n uwař rāna f.

foster-parents n iyàyen-rāna p, iyàyen
riƙò p.

foul 1. adj: ~ odor (from decayed organic
matter) dòyī m, (e.g. of chemicals) wārī
m; speak ~ language yi mūgùn bàkī m, yi
danyen bàkī m; ~ play làifī m.
2. n (Sport) fāwùl m, fànāřētì m.

found v (establish) kafà v1: the university was ~ed in 1970 an kafà jāmi'à
cikin shèkarà ta alìf dà dařī tařà dà
sàbà'in.

foundation n a. (base of building) hàřsāshì
m: lay a ~ sà hàřsāshì. b. (source)
tūshè m: the rumors were without ~
jìta-jìta bâ ta dà tūshè. c. (charitable
organization) gìdaunìyā f ⟨u⟩.

fountain pen n àlƙalàmī m ⟨ai⟩, [F]
ìstìlô m.

four quant huɗu f; ~ each huřhuɗu.

fourteen quant (gōmà) shà huɗu f.

fourth quant na huɗu; one-~ řubù'ī m.

fowl n (no gen'l term); (chicken) kàzā f ⟨i⟩;
bush ~ makwarwā f ⟨makwàrē⟩; guinea-~
zàɓō m, zàbuwā f ⟨i⟩.

fowl lice n ƙuddumùs m.

fowl pox n agànař kàjī f.

fox n (fennec) yânyāwà f ⟨i⟩.

fracture 1. n kàrayà f; set a ~ dōrà
kàrayà.
2. v karyè v4: he ~d his leg ƙafàřsà tā
karyè = àkwai kàrayà à ƙafàřsà.

fragile adj: ~ goods kāyan ařas m.

fragment n (of sth. breakable) gutsurè m
⟨gutsàttsarī⟩: a ~ of glass gutsurèn
gìlāshì; (~ of broken pot) tsìngārò m
⟨u⟩, see potsherd.

fragrance n ƙanshī m: the ~ of perfume
ƙanshin tùràrē.

frame 1. n (of car) fìřâm m, [F] shàsî m;
(of bicycle) gàngař jìkī m, [F] kādìř m;
(for thatched roof) tsaikò m; (for picture,
photograph) kātākò m.
2. v (accuse falsely) dafà wà làifī, yi
wà ƙāge m, maƙalà wà v1.

framework n sīgà f ⟨oCi⟩.

franc n (CFA ~, the basic unit of currency
in Niger, see Appendix F): 5 ~s [F] dalà
f ⟨oCi⟩; 100 ~s dalà àshìřin; 1000 ~s
[F] jìkā f ⟨una⟩.

France n Fàřansà / Fàřanshì f.

francolin n makwarwā f ⟨makwàrē⟩, fàkarā
f ⟨u⟩.

francophone adj: ~ country ƙasā řènon
Fàřansà.

**frankly** adv (openly, without hiding) à fīlī adv, (boldly, bluntly) ɓarō-ɓàrò idph: I told him ~ that I considered him a liar nā fitō masà ɓarō-ɓàrò cêwā nā dàukē shì kàmaɽ maƙàryàcī.

**fraternal** adj na 'yan'uwā.

**fraud** n zàmba f, hā'incì m; (by adulterating goods) àlgushù / àlgûs m; (by breach of trust) màgudī m. b. (psn.) mazàmbàcī m, mài màgudī n.

**fraudulent** adj (mài) zàmba f; ~ly bisà zàmba.

**fray** v zaizàyē v4.

**free** 1. adj 'yàntaccē adj: ~d slaves 'yàntàttun bāyī; a ~ man dā m; am I ~ to go or not? kā yàɽda ìn tàfi kō kùwa? 2. adv a. (for nothing, gratis) à fàyû, à banzā, à kyàutā: the food is ~ anā bā dà àbincîn kyàutā; he got it ~ yā sàmē shì à fàyû. b. (loose, released) à sàke adv; he was given a ~ hand an sakam masà sha'ànîn. 3. v (give freedom) 'yàntā v1; sàkā v2: they have ~d all the prisoners sun sàki fuɽsunōnī dukà.

**freedom** n 'yancì m: what is the use of ~ without the opportunity to work? ìnā àmfànin 'yancì in bā à sāmùn aikì? ~ fighter ɗan ƙwàtaɽ 'yancì; ~ of religion 'yancìn àddīnì; ~ of speech 'yancìn fàɗaɽ ɽa'àyī.

**freely** adv (openly) ƙurū-ƙùrù idph: he admitted ~ that he had been drinking yā fàɗā ƙurū-ƙùrù cêwā yā shā giyà.

**freeze** v daskàrā v1: the cold ~s the water and turns it into ice sanyī nà daskàrà ruwā yà zama ƙànƙarā; (fig.) I'm frozen stiff from the cold nā kangàrē sabòdà sanyī.

**freight** n jigilaɽ kāyā f, sufùɽin kāyā m: ~ charges kuɗin sufùɽin kāyā; ~ train jirgin kāyā.

**French** 1. n a. (the language) Faɽansancī m, [F] Tùɽancī m. b. (a psn.) bàfaɽanshè m. 2. adj na Fàɽansà / na Fàɽanshì: a ~ custom àlādàɽ Fàɽansà.

**frequency** n (of radio) mītà f.

**frequent** v làzimtà v2.

**frequently** adv sàu dà yawà; do sth. ~ yi yawàn (+ action n or v phr.): I go to their house ~ inà yawàn zuwà gidansù = inà zuwà gidansù sàu dà yawà; it happens ~ yanà yawàn àukuwà; they raid that village ~ sunà yawàn kai wà ƙauyèn harì; not ~ bà sàfài ba.

**fresh** adj (raw) ɗanyē adj ⟨u⟩: (new) sābō

adj ⟨sàbàbbī⟩: ~ eggs, paint sābon ƙwai, fentì; ~-cut meat nāmà sābon yankà; ~ air iskà mài dāɗī.

**Friday** n Jumma'à f: everyone goes to the mosque on Friday kōwā nà tàfiyà masallàcī ran Jumma'à.

**fridge** n fiɽjì / fìɽîj m, [F] pìɽîgô m.

**friend** n àbōkī m, àbōkìyā f ⟨ai⟩ ⟨àbōkànai⟩, ɗan'uwā m; (close ~) àmīnì m ⟨ai⟩; (a woman's ~) ƙawā f ⟨aCe⟩, àbūyà f; they are ~s sū 'yan'uwan jūnā nè; he is a good ~ of mine shī àbōkīnā nè na ƙwaɽai; be very close ~s shàƙu v7; become ~s ƙullà àbōtà, ɗaurà àbōtà; make ~s sàmi àbōkī, yi àbōkī: he makes ~s easily yā yi àbōkai bâ wùyā; we've been ~s since school àbòtaɽmù tun munà makaɽantà; they are no longer ~s sun ɓātà tsàkāninsù.

**friendly** adj (mài) fàɽa'à f, (mài) sôn mutànē: he is a ~ person yanà dà fàɽa'à; have ~ relations with yi ƙawàncē dà: those countries do not have ~ ties ƙasàshên bā sà ƙawàncē dà jūnā.

**friendship** n àbōtà / àbūtà f, àbōkàntakà f, sô m, amincì m; (esp. between women) ƙawàncē m; (esp. close) zùmùntà f; break a ~ ɓātà àbōtà; cement a ~ ƙàrà danƙòn àbōtà; form a ~ ƙullà àbōtà = ɗaurà àbōtà.

**fright** n tsòrō m, fàɽgàbā f: I almost died of ~ tsòrō yā kusa kashè ni.

**frighten** v bâ w. tsòrō m, tsōràtā v1: the thunder ~ed the children tsāwā tā bâ yârā tsòrō; ~ so. away tsōrataɽ (dà) v5; be ~ed ji tsòrō, tsòratà v3.

**frisk** v lālùbē v4: the police ~ed him all over 'yan sàndā sun lālùbē shi kakaf.

**frivolous** adj be ~ (esp. with time, money) salwàntā v1: his ~ness with money has made him poor salwàntà kuɗîn dà ya yi yā talàutā shi.

**fro** adv go to and ~ yi kai-dà-kàwō m, yi zìɽgà-zìɽgà f, see forth.

**frog** n kwàɗō m ⟨i⟩; (large, smooth skin) bùdiddìgī m ⟨ai⟩, (large, rough skin) ƙōzō m.

**from** prep a. (directional) dàgà prep: they arrived ~ Sokoto sun isō dàgà Sakkwato; we took shelter ~ the rain mun fakè dàgà ruwā; (~ inside) dàgà cikin: he came out ~ the room yā fitō dàgà cikin dākì; (~ so.) dàgà gàrē (+ pro): I haven't heard anything ~ him bàn ji kōmē dàgà gàrē shì ba. b. (by way of, via) ta prep: I saw them ~ the window nā gan sù ta tāgà. c. (temporal) tun dàgà: I read the book ~ beginning to end nā kařàncē littāfìn tun dàgà farkō hař ƙarshē; he works ~ morning to night yanà aikì tun dàgà sāfe hař dare; 2 weeks ~ now nân dà sātī biyu; ~ now on nân gàba, dàgà yànzu. d. (for use as particle with verbs, see relevant verb entries; v4 verbs with ind. obj often indicate 'away from'): he stole ₦10 ~ me yā sācè minì naiřā gōmà; they grabbed the purse ~ her sun ƙwācè matà jàkā. e. (in subtraction) à ɗēbè: 7 ~ 10 leaves 3 gōmà à ɗēbè bakwài ukù kè nan. f. (to designate inhabitant of an area) ɗan m, 'yař f, 'yan p; mài n, màsu p: a girl ~ Daura 'yař Dàurā; the people ~ the village màsu ƙauyè.

**frond** n (of dum palm) kabà f ⟨oCi⟩, (of deleb palm) karī m.

**front** n a. (of body or sth.) gàbā m: the ~ of the house gàban gidā; ~ and back (e.g. of piece of paper) cikì dà bâi. b. (adverbial uses): in, on the ~ (à) gàba adv: they sat in ~ sun zaunà à gàba; the ~ page shāfì na gàba = shāfìn farkō; the ~ door ƙōfà ta gàba; in ~ of (à) gàban prep: they're in ~ of the door sunà gàban ƙōfà; he bowed down in ~ of the emir yā sunkùyā à gàban sarkī; he was shot in ~ an hàřbè shì dàga gàba.

**frontier** n (border) iyàkā f ⟨oCi⟩.

**froth** n kumfā m.

**frown** v (in thought) gamà girā f; (esp. from anger, sadness) ɓātà fuskà, daurè fuskà, muřtùkè fuskà: he ~ed at me yā ɗaurè minì fuskà; ~ upon (disapprove of) ƙi jinin: they ~ upon women wearing shorts an ƙi jinin mātā sù sâ gàjēren wàndō.

**frozen** adj (of liquids) dàskàrarrē adj; (stiffened) sàndàrarrē adj, kàngàrarrē adj.

**fruit** n 'yā'yan itàcē p; (fig.) your work will bear ~ aikìnkà zâi haifà.

**frustrated, be** v ji tàkàicī m.

**frustration** n tàkàicī m: the frustrating thing is... àbin tàkaîcī shī nè...; source of ~ alàƙaƙài m, jìdālī m: the matter has become a great source of ~ to us àbin yā zamè manà alàƙaƙài.

**fry** v (any food in oil except fried cakes) sōyà v1 ⟨sūyà⟩ f: French-fried potatoes sòyayyen dànkalì; (esp. any Hausa cake made from batter) tōyà v1 ⟨tūyà⟩ f.

**frying pan** n kwānòn tūyà m; (tradit., of clay with indentations) kaskon tūyà m, tàndèřū m, tandà f.

**fuel** n makāmashī m: wood is the main ~ in Africa itàcē shī nè mùhimmìn

makāmashī à ƙasàshen Afiřkà; (esp. gasoline, petroleum) mâi m: ~ pump famfòn mâi; ~ tank tankìn mâi.

**fugitive** n ɗan gudùn hijiřā m, magùjī m.

**Fulani** 1. n a. (member of ethnic group) bàfilātànī / bàfilācè m ⟨filànī⟩: pastoral, nomadic ~ Filànin dājì; town ~ Filànin gidā. b. (language) Filātancī / Fillancī m: they are ~ing ~ sunà màganà dà Filātancī. 2. adj na Filànī p.

**fulfill** v a. (a promise, obligation) cikà v1, cika v3: he did not ~ his promise to repay me bài cikà àlkawàřinsà na biyànā bāshī ba. b. (a goal, wish) biyā v0: God has ~ed our wishes Allàh yā biyā manà bùkātà = bùkātàřmù tā biyā.

**fulfillment** n a. (of wish) biyàn bùkātà m. b. (satisfaction) gàmsuwā f, ƙōshī m.

**full, be** 1. v a. cika v3: be chock ~, ~ to the brim cikà fal = cìka tìnjim = cìka màƙil = bàtsè v4; be ~ (congested) yi cìkōwà f: the room was absolutely ~ of people ɗākì yā yi cìkōwà dà mutànē; be ~ of à cìke dà: the calabash was ~ of milk ƙwaryā à cìke takè dà nōnò = ƙwaryā tā bàtsè dà nōnò; become ~ cikō v6: shut off the water, the bucket is ~ kà rufè famfò, bōkitì yā cikō. b. (after eating) ƙōshi v3*, gyàtsè v4: thanks, I am ~ àlhamdù lillāhì nā ƙōshi. 2. adj a. cìkakkē adj: a ~ report cìkakken làbāřī; write your name in ~ here kà řubùtà cìkakken sūnankà à nân; ~ speed ahead! kà ƙārà mâi! = kà ƙārà wutà! b. (completely developed) ƙàsàitaccē adj, gàwùřtaccē adj: a ~-scale war ƙàsàitaccen yāƙì.

**full stop** n (in orthography) āyà f ⟨oCi⟩.

**fumes** n a. (visible) hayāƙī m: poisonous ~ hayāƙī mài gubà. b. (invisible) wārī m: gasoline, petrol ~ wārin fētùř.

**fun** n a. (enjoyment) nìshāɗì m: horseback riding is great ~ hawan dōkì àbin nìshāɗì nē; have ~ yi nìshāɗì, shàƙàtā v1. b. (jest): in ~ dà wàsā, dà gàngan: I said it in ~ dà gàngan nakè; make ~ of so. yi wà ba'à f, yi wà jàfa'ì m; mūzàntā v1; poke ~ at so. zòlayà v2.

**function** n a. (job) aikì m: its ~ is to prevent people from entering aikìnsà shī nè hanà mutànē shìgā. b. (social event) bìkī m ⟨uwa²⟩, shagàlī m ⟨u-a²⟩.

**functionary** n (usu. used in pl) mânyan ƙūsōshī p: important government functionaries mânyan ƙūsōshin gwamnatì.

**fund** n asūsù m: relief ~ asūsùn àgàjī;

a ~ for the destitute asūsùn tàimakon
gàjìyàyyū; public ~s kuɗin bàitùlmālì,
kuɗin jàma'ā.
fundamental *adj* mùhimmì *m* ⟨ai⟩, (mài)
muhimmancì *m*: a ~ difference mùhimmìn
bambancì.
fundamentalist *n* mài r̃a'àyin rìk̃au *m*.
funeral *n* jànā'izā̀ *f*.
funnel *n* mazurārī *m*, maɗūrī *m*, būtūtū *m*.
funny *adj* (*comical*) (mài) ban dà̀riyā *m*:
I heard a ~ story about him nā ji wani
làbārìnsà mài ban dà̀riyā.
fur *n* gāshì *m* ⟨gāsū⟩.
furious *adj*: get ~ hàr̃zuk̃à *v3*, hàsalà
*v3*: she gets ~ whenever his name is
mentioned tanà̀ hàsalà̀ duk lōkàcîn dà
akè̀ àmbatà̀r̃ sūnansà; a ~ look kallon
hadarìn kàjī = kallon banzā.
furlough *n* lifì *m*, [F] far̃masō *m*.
furnish *v*: ~ a room sā kāyā à ɗākì; the
room was ~ed with only a table and a chair
àkwai tēbù̀r̃ dà kujè̀rā kawài à cikin
ɗākì.
furniture *n* kāyan ɗākì *m*.
furrow *n* kunyā *f* ⟨oCi⟩; make a ~ hūɗà̀ *v1*,
yi hùɗā *f*.
further *adv & adj*: go ~ yi gàba, ci gàba:
it's dangerous to go any ~ àkwai haɗà̀r̃ī
à ci gàba; without ~ notice bâ wata
sanàr̃wā; I have no ~ use for this bâ ni
dà sauran àmfànī dà wannàn; let's not
discuss the matter ~ mù dainà màganàr̃.
furthermore *adv* daɗìn daɗàwā, bugù dà
k̃ārì *conj*.
fuse *n* fîs *m*: spare ~ fîs sàfiyā̀; the ~
has blown fîs ɗîn yā mutù.
fuss *n* **a.** (*sth. trivial*) k̃ōràfī *m*, (*exaggeration of discomfort*) kwàkwāzò *m*: stop
all that ~ing! kì bar̃ wannàn k̃ōràfī.
**b.** (*commotion*) rìgimā̀ *f*, hàyàniyā *f*,
hàtsàniyā *f*: what is all the ~ about? mènē
nè̀ dàlīlìn wannàn rìgimā̀?
futile *adj* à banzā *adv*.
future **1.** *adv & adj* gàba *adv*: our ~ plans
shirìnmù na gàba; in (the) ~ nân gàba,
dàgà gàba: be careful in the ~ nân gàba
kà yi hankàlī; only God knows what will
happen in the ~ sai Allàh kaɗai yā san
àbîn dà zâi zō nân gàba.
**2.** *n* gòbe *f*, gàba *adv*: let's work hard for
the ~ mù yi aikì tuk̃ùru don gòbe; our
children are our ~ yàrā mânyan gòbe; no
one knows what the ~ holds (*fig.*) gòbe ta
Allàh cē.

# G

gaffe n (verbal blunder) kàtōɓarā f, kaɓɓà f.

gain 1. n (profit) r̃ībā f ⟨oCi⟩: a ~ of 10 percent r̃ībā ta kashī gōmà cikin d̃arī; one man's loss is another man's ~ (fig.) fàd̃ùwar̃ wani tāshìn wani.
2. v sāmù v2*: ~ so.'s confidence sàmi yàr̃dar̃ w.; ~ popularity, experience sàmi shàhar̃à, k̃war̃ềwā; ~ weight yi k̃ībà f; ~ from sth. àmfānà dà v3: what have you ~ed from it? mề ka àmfānà dà shī?

gall bladder n mad̃acìyā f, màtsarmamā f.

gallon n galàn m.

gallop v yi sukùwā f; at a ~ à sùkwằne; they ~ed up the hill sun hau tsaunìn à sùkwằne.

gamble v a. yi cāca f: ~ at horses, cards yi cācar̃ dawākī, kar̃tà; he ~d his salary away yā kad̃è àlbâshinsà. b. (take a risk) yi cāca f, yi kàsadà f.

gambler n d̃an cāca m.

gambling n cāca f: he won at ~ yā ci cāca; he lost at ~ cāca tā cī shì; (var. types): (esp. with cards) mōd̃ì m; (lottery, raffle) r̃ēhùl m, tàmbōlà f, [F] tàmbōlà f; (football pool) cācar̃ pûl f.

game¹ n (sports, playing) wàsā m ⟨anni⟩: play a ~ yi wàsā; it is a ~ of chance, not of skill wàsā nè na sā'à bà na gwànintà ba; the ~ is over (fig.) darà tā ci.

game² n (wild animals) nāmun dājì p; hunt big ~ fàràuci mânyan nāmun dājì.

gang n (of youths, thugs) 'yan dabà p, 'yan iskà p.

gap n a. gīɓì m ⟨giyàɓū⟩: he has a ~ because he lost a tooth yanà dà gīɓì sabòdà hak̃ōrinsà yā fàd̃ì; (natural ~ between the two front teeth) wushiryā f. b. (distance between oneself & so. ahead) rātà f, tazarā f: the ~ between the rich and the poor rātar̃ dà kề tsàkānin màsu kud̃ī dà talakāwā; bridge a ~ between daidàità rātà tsàkānin.

gape v yi ɓalàu idph, yi gàlàu idph: his mouth was gaping wide open yā sàki bàkinsà ɓalàu = yā yi gàlàu dà bàkī; there was a gaping hole in the wall àkwai wani wafcēcèn rāmì à bangō.

garage n gàr̃ējì m, [F] gàr̃âj m.

garbage n shằrā f: take out the ~ kwāshè shằrā = zub dà shằrā; ~ can garwar̃ shằrā; ~ heap jūjì m.

garden n (ornamental) gādìnà f, (esp. for fruit, vegetables) làmbū m ⟨una⟩, [F] garkā f ⟨a-e⟩.

garden egg n, see eggplant.

gardener n gādìnà n, mài aikìn làmbū n, [F] mài garkā n.

gardening n aikìn làmbū m.

gargle v kurkùrā v1: he ~d with some medicine yā kurkùrà māgànī à bakà.

garlic n tàfar̃nuwā f.

garment n tufā f ⟨tufàfī⟩.

gas n a. (gasoline, petrol) mâi m, fētùr̃ m, [F] ìsansì m; (premium gasoline) sūfà m, [F] sùpâr̃ m: this car uses a lot of ~ mōtàr̃ nân tanà shân mâi dà yawà; fill up on ~ shā mâi; step on the ~ (speed up) tākà mōtà. b. (natural ~, bottled ~) gâs m. c. (chemical) hayāk̃ī m: poisonous ~ hayāk̃ī mài gubā; tear ~ bàr̃k̀onon tsōhuwā m, tiyàgâs m. (stomach~) k̃wàr̃nàfì

gasoline see gas.

gasp v (pant, of animals) yi hàkī m; (for air, e.g. after crying) yi shàsshềk̃ā f, (fig.) had̃ìyè zūcìyā.

gas station n gidan mâi m.

gate, gateway n k̃ōfà f ⟨oCi⟩: Kano city has 17 gates àkwai k̃ōfōfī shâ bakwài à bir̃nin Kanò.

gather 1. vt a. (collect) tārà v1: ~ wood, people tārà itàcē, mutằnē; ~ up tattārà v1: let's ~ up all the papers and put them in one stack mù tattārà tàkàr̃dū dukà mù yi tārì d̃aya dà sū. b. (harvest), see harvest, pick; ~ rubber tārà dank̃ō.
2. vi tằru v7: people ~ed to hear him speak jàma'à sun tằru sù ji màganàr̃sà; (of clouds) had̃u v7.

gathering n tàr̃ō m, hàd̃uwā f: a ~ of people from every village hàd̃uwar̃ jàma'à dàgà k̃ōwànè k̃auyè.

gauge 1. n ma'aunì m, gējì m, [F] kwàntâr̃ m: tire, air ~ gējìn tāyà, iskà; gas ~ gējìn nūnà mâi.
2. v a. (measure) aunà v1 ⟨awò⟩. b. (estimate) kīmàntà v1, k̃iyàstà v1: it's hard to ~ how hard the wind is blowing dà wùyā à kīmàntà k̃arfin iskà.

gauze n (compress for wounds) lintì m, [F] kwàmfàr̃âs f.

gay adj a. (happy) (mài) far̃a'à f. b. (homosexual male) d̃an daudù m, d̃an

lùwādî/lūɗù *m;* (*homosexual female*)
'yař mādigò *f.*

gaze at *v* (*expectantly*) zubã wà idò.

gazelle *n* bàrēwā *f* ⟨i⟩.

gear *n* (*e.g. of car*) giyã *f:* what ~ is it in?
à giyã ta nawà takè? third ~ giyã ta
ukù; put the car in first ~! kà sâ mōtã à
ɗaya! shift ~s sākè giyã = sâ giyã; *see*
neutral, reverse.

gearbox *n* giyã bôs *m,* [F] kàřtāř *m.*

gearshift *n see* gear.

gecko *n* tsakā *f,* (*bigger*) sàri-kutuf *m.*

gelignite *n* nãkiyã *f.*

gem *n* (*precious stone*) lu'ùlu'ù *m.*

gemination *n* (*Gram.*) shaddã *f,* tagwai *m:*
geminate consonants tagwan hařuffã.

gendarme *n* [F] jandařmà *m.*

gender *n* jinsì *m:* most Hausa words ending in the letter 'a' have feminine ~
yawancin kalmōmin Hausa mãsu 'a' à
ƙarshē jinsìnsù na màcè nē.

genealogy *n* salsalã *f:* he can trace his
~ to Usman dan Fodio salsalàřsà tā
dangànā gà Shēhù.

general[1] *n* (*Mil.*) janàř *m,* [F] jànàřâl *m.*

general[2] *adj* na kōwã: it is ~ knowledge
sanìn kōwã nè = kōwã yā sanì; give me
a ~ idea of what the book is about kà
faɗà mini à tàƙaice àbîn dà littāfìn
ya ƙùnsã; a ~ meeting bàbban tàrō; in
~, ~ly gālìbī, gālìbàn, yawancì: as a
~ rule they arrive at 8 a.m. gālìbī sukàn
zō nân à ƙarfè takwàs na sāfe.

generate *v:* ~ electricity bā dà wutař
làntařkì.

generation *n* sa'ã *f* ⟨oCi⟩; she is of my ~
ita sa'àtā cè; the preceding ~ mutànen
dã; the present ~ mutànen yànzu; that
custom has been practiced for ~s àl'ādã
cē ta kàkā dà kàkànnī.

generator *n* jànàřētô *m,* [F] dìnàmô *m.*

generosity *n* kařimcì *m,* hālin kyàutā *m;*
(*given by God*) baiwā *f.*

generous *adj* (mài) kařimcì *m,* kàřīmì *m*
⟨ai⟩, (mài) kyàutā *f:* be ~ to so. nūnà
wà kařimcì: although he is poor he is ~
kō dà yakè matàlàucī nề àmmā yanà dà
kařimcì.

genes *n* ƙwāyōyin hālī *p.*

genet *n* inyāwařã *f.*

genetics *n* ilìmin ƙwāyōyin hālī *m.*

genitals *n* (*gen'l term*) àl'auřã *f;* (*euphem.*
*of either sex*) gàbā *m,* gìndī *m.*

genius *n* ɗan baiwā *m:* Einstein was a ~
Einstein ɗan baiwā nề.

genocide *n* kisàn ƙàrè-dangì *m:* war of ~
yāƙìn ƙàrè-dangì.

gentle *adj:* a ~ person mùtûm mài hankàlī;
a ~ breeze iskã mài dādī; be ~ with so.
yi hankàlī dà w., lallàɓā *v1.*

gentleman *n* dattījò *m* ⟨dàttāwā, ai⟩: he
has the qualities of a ~ yanà dà dattākò;
Ladies and Gentlemen Jàma'ã, Mazā dà
Mātā.

gently *adv:* knock ~ on a door ƙwanƙwàsà
ƙōfã à hankàlī; smile ~ yi ɗan
mùřmùshī; treat so. ~ lallàɓā *v1.*

genuine *adj* a. (*real, original*) na gàske,
na ainihī *m:* this is ~ Holland wax
cloth wannàn àtàmfā 'yař Hōlàn cē ta
ainihī. b. (*pure, unmixed*) gangàriyã *f:*
it is made of ~ gold zīnāřì nē na gàske =
na zīnāřì nē gangàriyã; ~ democracy
gangàriyàř dìmòkùřàɗiyyã.

geography *n* làbāřìn ƙasā *m.*

geology *n* ilìmin sanìn mà'àdìnai *m.*

germ *n* ƙwàyař cùtā *f* ⟨oCi⟩.

germinate *v* tsirō *v6.*

germination *n* tsìre-tsìre *m.*

gesture *n* (*movement*) mòtsī *m;* make an
insulting ~ (*esp. to children*) yi daƙuwã *f,*
yi àmbōlã *f.*

get *v* a. (*obtain*) sāmù *v2\*:* we got them at
the market mun sãmē sù à kàsuwā; she
got me some cold water tā sāmō mini
ruwan sanyī. b. (*cause, ~ sth. done*) sâ
*v1\*:* ~ this chair fixed for me kà sâ à
gyārà mini kujèrař nàn; we got him to
help us mun sâ shi yā tayã mu; fail to
~ sth. done kāsà *v1:* I can't ~ the door
open nā kāsà bûɗe ƙōfàř. c. (*var. v +
adj uses*): ~ angry yi fushì *m;* ~ better
sàmi sauƙì; ~ fat yi ƙibà *f;* ~ hot, cold
fārà zāfī, sanyī; ~ hurt ji cīwò; ~
lost 6acè *v4;* (*fig.*) ~ lost! ɓàcē manà dà
ganī! ~ ready shiryà *v1;* ~ rich wàdātà
*v3,* àřzutà *v3;* ~ tired gàji *v3\*.* d. (*var.
v + adv/prep uses*): ~ along yi shirì *m,*
jìtu *v7:* he doesn't ~ along with his in-
laws bā yà shirì dà sùrùkansà; we really
~ along with each other mun jìtu sòsai
= jininmù yā hàɗu sòsai; ~ back (*return*) dāwō *v6;* ~ back at so. (*get revenge*)
rāmà wà *v1;* ~ into trouble shìga cikin
wàhalà; ~ away from kau dàgà; ~ on,
onto (*mount*) hau *v\*;* ~ on with (*continue*)
ci gàba; ~ off (*dismount*) sàuka dàgà; ~
out of fìta dàgà: he couldn't ~ out of the
hole yā kāsà fìtôwā dàgà rāmìn; ~ out
of the way kaucè dàgà; ~ to (*a place*) ìsa
*v3,* kai *v\*:* we'll ~ to Jos before dark zā
mù kai Jàs kàfìn darè yà yi; we got
home safely mun ìsa gidā lāfiyã; how
do you ~ to Maradi? ìnā nề hanyàř zuwà

Marādi? ~ up tāshì v3b: what time do
you ~ up? ƙarfè nawà kakè tāshì dàgà
barcī? ~ up suddenly tāshì faɼat.

ghost n fàtalwā f ⟨oCi⟩.

giant n & adj ƙātō adj ⟨Ca⟩.

gibberish n (unintelligible speech) bàdà-
bàdà idph: he is talking ~ yanà màganà
bàdà-bàdà.

giddiness n jùwā f, hàjījiyà f.

gift n a. kyàutā f ⟨uka²⟩, (souvenir)
tsàrabà f ⟨oCi⟩: she gave me a ~ of perfume tā bā nì kyàutaɼ tùrằrē; at Sallah, the rich give ~s to the poor ran Sallà
màsu hālī sunà yi wà talakāwā kyàutā.
b. (God-given talent) baiwā f: God has
given him the ~ of poetry Allàh yā yi
masà baiwaɼ wallàfà wāƙōƙī.

gigantic adj (often expressed by ideophonic
adjs which go with specific nouns, see
enormous, huge, massive).

giggle v ƙyalƙyàlā v1, ƙyalƙyàlē dà
dằriyā.

gills n hàrzā f.

gin¹ v (cotton) guɼzà v1.

gin² n (locally brewed) kōkinō f.

ginger n (from a root) cìtta mài yātsū
f; (from Melegueta pepper) cìttaɼ àhò f,
cìtta mài 'yā'yā f.

gingivitis n cìzaɼ / cìzal m.

ginnery n (cotton) ma'aikataɼ guɼzà
audùgā f.

giraffe n ràƙumin dawà m.

girl n yārinyà f ⟨'yammātā⟩; baby-~ 'yā
màcè; boys and ~s yârā mazā dà mātā:
he has 5 children, 2 boys and 3 ~s yanà dà
'yā'yā bìyaɼ, mazā biyu dà mātā ukù;
school for ~s makaɼantā ta 'yammātā;
(unmarried) bùdurwā f ⟨oCi⟩.

girlfriend n (of boy) bùdurwā f ⟨oCi⟩; (of
girl) ƙawā f ⟨aCe⟩, àbōkìyā f, (close)
àmīnìyā f; see friend.

gist n gundārī m: the ~ of the story is...
gundārin làbāɼìn shī nè... = làbāɼìn à
tàkàice shī nè....

give v a. (sth. to so.) bâ w. v*, bai wà
vdat, sam mà vdat: they gave the beggars
some food sun bâ àlmằjìɼai àbinci =
sun bai wà àlmằjìɼai àbinci; who gave
it to them? wằ ya bā sù? whom did you
~ it to? wằ kikà bâ? he gave me some
kolanut yā sam mnì gōɼò. b. (sth.) bā dà
/ bāyaɼ (dà) v5: they gave ₦10 sun bā dà
naiɼā gōmà; how much did they ~? nawà
sukà bāyaɼ? c. ~ birth haifù v3b; ~ birth
to hàifā v2: she gave birth to a daughter
tā hàifi 'yā màcè. d. (var. v + adv/prep
uses): ~ so.'s secret away tōnà wà àsīɼī;

~ sth. back mai dà / mayaɼ (dà) v5; ~
in to so. (in a discussion) sakaɼ wà vdat:
I gave in to her wishes nā sakam matà
àbîn dà takè sô; ~ up (be resigned after
making an effort) hàƙurà v3, dànganà v3,
sàdūdà v3; ~ up (in guessing, riddling) bā
dà gàrī: I ~ up! nā bā kà gàrī! = nā
kāsà! ~ up sth. (leave) barī v*: he gave
up his job yā baɼ aikìnsà; ~ up hope
fid dà râi, yankè ƙaunà, sàrē v4; ~ up
doing sth. (quit doing) dainà v1: he has
~n up smoking yā dainà shân tābà.

gizzard n ƙùndū m.

glad adj (mài) farin cikì m, (mài) muɼnà
f: be very ~ yi matuƙaɼ farin cikì = yi
muɼnà ƙwarai; I am ~ you were able to
come nā yi muɼnà dà kukà sằmi dāmaɼ
zuwằ.

gladly 1. adv cikin farin cikì, cikin
muɼnà.
2. excl: would you do me a favor? ~! kō
zā kà yi minì wani ɗan tàimakō? ƙwarai
kùwa!

glance v: ~ at ɗan dūbằ v1, ɗan kàllā
v2: I ~d at the newspaper nā ɗan dūbà
jàɼīdằ; he ~d sideways at her yā kàllē
tà à sằce.

gland n (swollen ~ in groin, armpit)
kằlūluwằ f.

glare v hàrārā v2, yi hàrārā f: he ~d at us
in a menacing way yā yi manà wata irìn
hàrārā mài ban tsòrō.

glass n a. (for drinking) tambūlàn m
⟨tambulōlī, tambulằ⟩, gìlāshì m ⟨oCi⟩,
[F] fìnjālì m ⟨ai⟩; (of plastic) kwâf na
ɼōbằ m. b. (material) gìlāshì / gìlās m,
[F] na kwalabā: ~ breaks easily gìlāshì
nà dà saurin fashèwā.

glasses n tàbằrau m, madūbin idò m, [F]
lùlētì m: he must wear ~ tīlàs yà
sâ tàbằrau; reading ~ tàbằran kàɼàtū;
prescription ~ tàbằran likità.

gleam v yi wàlƙiyā f: the metal bowls are
so clean they are ~ing tāsōshì sun wànku
tas haɼ sunà wàlƙiyā.

glean v tsìntā v2: did you ~ any information from his speech? kō kā tsìnci ɗan
wani àbù dàgà cikin jàwābìnsà?

glimpse n: get a ~ of tsìnkāyā v2, hàngā
v2: we got a ~ of the emir on horseback
mun tsìnkằyi sarkī kân dōkì.

glitter v yi ƙyàlƙyàlī m.

globe n a. (the world) dūniyà f: global
economy tattalin aɼzìkin dūniyằ. b.
(bulb, esp. for car, flashlight) gùlâb m, [F]
gwàlâf m; see lightbulb.

gloomy adj (of weather) dùkùkù idph: the

weather is ~ today yâu gàri yā yi
dùkùkù; (of psn.) dùkū / dùkum idph:
what's made you so ~? mè ya sằmē kà na
gan kà dùkū hakà?

glorify v girmàmā v1, ɗaukàkā v1.

glorious adj: God the most ~ Allàh
Maɗàukàkin Sarkī.

glory n (honor) sūnā m, yàbô m.

glossary n tsārìn kalmōmī m.

glossy adj (mài) wàlƙiyā f, (mài) shèƙī m:
a ~ photograph hōtō mài shèƙī.

glottal stop n (Gram.) baƙin ɓòye m.

glove n sàfaƙ hannu f.

glow v yi haskē m: this watch ~s in the
dark wannàn àgōgôn nà haskē à cikin
duhù.

glue 1. n līƙì m, (of gruel) kōko m, (white)
gùlû m, [F] kwâl m, (clear) gâm m: the ~
has come off līƙin yā tāshì; put ~ on
sth. mannà dà kōko.
2. v: ~ sth. together līƙà v1, līƙè v4:
he ~d the envelope shut yā līƙè bàkin
ambùlàn.

glum adj, see gloomy.

glut n rārā f: there was an oil ~ worldwide
an yi rāraƙ mâi kō'ìnā à dūniyà.

glutton n hàndàmau m.

gluttony n zàrī m, hàdamà f.

gnaw at v gwàgwiyà v2, gurgùrē v4.

go v a. tàfi v3* ⟨tàfiyà⟩ f, jē v0: we're
~ing to the market munà tàfiyà kàsuwā;
~ on foot, by car, by air tàfi à ƙasà, à
mōtà, à jirgin samà. b. (in commands):
~! (m/f) jè ka/ki! ~ and see! jè ki kì
ganī = kì jē kì ganī. c. (leave) tāshì
v3b: he's already gone yā rigā yā tāshì.
d. (be off to a place) zâ (+ pro): where
are you ~ing? ìnā zâ ka? = ìnā zuwà?
she's not ~ing home bà zâ ta gidā ba.
e. (var. v + adv/prep uses): ~ ahead (continue) ci gàba; ~ around kēwàyā v1; ~
away tàfi v3*: ~ away! get ~ing! tàfi
àbinkà! = yi tàfiyàƙkà! ~ back kōmà
v1; ~ back and forth, come and ~ yi kai-
dà-kàwō, yi zìƙgà-zìƙgà f: people have
been coming and ~ing all day jàma'à sun
yinì sunà kai-dà-kàwō; ~ by way of, via
bi ta v0: we went by a short-cut mun bi
ta yànkē; ~ down (from above) sàuka v3;
~ down (descend) gangàrā v1: he went
down into the stream yā gangàrā ràfī;
~ in, into shìga v3; ~ on (happen) gùdànà
v3: what's going on? mè yakè gùdānà? =
mè akè yî? ~ on (continue) ci gàba; ~
over sth. again sākè v4: let's ~ over the
lessons again mù sākè bìn daƙussànmù =
mù yi bìtaƙ daƙussànmù; ~ out fìta v3;

~ out (of lights, fire) mutù v3b: all of a
sudden the lights went out faƙat ɗaya
fìtìlun nàn sukà mutù; ~ through (cross
through) kētà v1: the road goes through
town hanyàƙ tā kētà gàrī; ~ through
(pass through) rātsà v1: liquid won't ~
through plastic ruwā bà yà rātsà ƙōbà;
~ to (a place) nùfā v2: this road ~es
to Zaria wannàn hanyà tā nùfi Zāriyà;
~ to, toward (as a group) ɗungumà v3:
the pilgrims went to Mecca àlhàzai sun
ɗungumà zuwà Makà; ~ toward (a destination) tìnkārà v2; ~ with (suit) dācè dà
v4: the blouse doesn't ~ with the wrapper
rìgâƙ bà tà dācè dà zanèn ba; let sth.,
so. ~ sakì v2*: he let the boy ~ yā sàki
yārò.

goad v izà v1, tūrà v1, zugà v1: I ~ed him
into insulting the merchant nā izà shi
haƙ yā zàgi mài sayâƙwā.

goal n a. (hope) bùrì m, bùkātà f ⟨u⟩:
maƙàsūdì m, mùƙādì m: he achieved his ~s
yā cim mà bùrìnsà = bùrìnsà yā cìka =
bùkātàƙsà tā biyā. b. (philosophical ~
in life) àlƙiblà f, manufā f: he has no ~s
in life bà shi dà àlƙiblà = bà shi dà
manufā cikin ràyuwaƙsà. c. (Sport, esp.
soccer, hockey) gwâl m, [F] bî m; score a
~ ci gwâl = ci gōlà = sâ bî.

goalkeeper n gōlà m, [F] gòlê m.

goalpost n gidā m, sàndaƙ gōlà f.

goat n (gener. & she-~) àkuyà f ⟨awākī⟩;
(he-~) bùnsurū m ⟨ai⟩; (long-haired)
buzurwā f ⟨oCi⟩; kid ~ 'yaƙ àkuyà.

goatee n gēmù m ⟨una⟩.

gobble v: ~ up food ci àbinci hàyàm-
hàyàm.

goblin n dòdō m ⟨anni⟩.

God n Allàh m, Ùbangijì m: ~ Almighty
Allàh Maɗàukàkin Sarkī; it is up to
~ yanà gà Īkòn Allàh; may ~ bless
you! Allàh yà yi makà àlbaƙkà! I swear
to ~! nā rantsè dà Allàh! thanks
be to ~! àlhamdù lillāhì! ~ willing!
inshā'àllāhù! by ~! wàllāhì (tàllāhì)!

goggles n tàbàrau m.

goiter n màƙoƙò m.

gold n zīnàƙì m, zīnàƙìyā f, gwâl m: make
a ring of ~ ƙerà zōbè dà zīnàƙì; this
ring is made of ~ wannàn zōbèn gwâl nē;
~-colored ruwan gwâl; ~-plating kumfan
zīnàƙì.

golden adj na zīnàƙì; (fig.) a ~ opportunity bàbbaƙ dāmā.

goldsmith n maƙèrin farfarū m,
guƙsùmētì m, [F] maƙèrin zīnàƙì m.

gong *n* gwàrjen shêlà *m*, (*V-shaped, of metal*) kùgē *m*.

gonorrhoea *n* cīwòn sanyī *m*.

good 1. *adj* a. (*of quality, beauty*) (mài) kyâu *m*, kyàkkyāwā *adj*: ∼ advice kyàkkyāwař shāwařà; separate the ∼ from the bad bambàntà mài kyâu dàgà mùmmūnā; make sth. look ∼ ƙāyatař / ƙāwatař (dà) *v5*. b. (*moral, of behavior*) na kiřkì *m*, sālìhī *m* ⟨ai⟩, nagàri *m*, tagàri *f* ⟨nagàrgàrū⟩ he is a ∼ person nagàri nè = mùtumìn kiřkì nē = sālìhī nè; a ∼ deed aikìn kiřkì = àbin kiřkì; come to no ∼ ɓalɓàlcē *v4*, lālācē *v4*; do so. a ∼ turn yi wà àlhēřì *m*, yi wà àbin kiřkì. c. (*skillful*): be ∼ at doing sth. nàƙaltà *v2*, iyà *v1*: she's a ∼ cook tā nàƙàlci girkì = tā iyà girkì; he is ∼ at mathematics yā iyà lìssāfì. d. (*pleasant*) (mài) dādī *m;* today we're having very ∼ weather yâu gàrîn dà dādī; be in ∼ health ji dādin jìkī; be in a ∼ mood nā cikin ànnàshuwā, nā cikin wàlwàlà; have a ∼ time (*fig.*) kēcè rainì, shēƙà ayà; I've got ∼ news for you! àlbishìřinkà! (*to which the reply is* gōřò!). e. (*useful*) (mài) àmfānī *m*: milk is ∼ for children madařā nà dà àmfānī gà yârā; do so. ∼ àmfānà *v2*: the medicine did me ∼ māgànîn yā àmfānē nì; it won't do you any ∼ bà zāi yi makà àmfānī ba. f. (*close, intimate*) na ƙwařai: he is a ∼ friend àbōkī nè na ƙwařai; be on ∼ terms with yi shirì dà. g. (*in greetings*): ∼ morning! bařkà dà sāfiyà! = bařkà dà àsùbâ! = bařkà dà hàntsī! = bařkà dà kwānā! ∼ afternoon! bařkà dà rānā! = bařkà dà yâmmā! ∼ evening! bařkà dà yâmmā! = ìnā wunì! ∼ night! mù kwan lāfiyà! = sai dà sāfe! = sai gòbe! = àsùbā tagàri! = àsùbā àlhēřì!
2. *n* àlhēřì *m*, àbin kiřkì *m*, aikìn kiřkì *m*: do ∼ or evil yi àlhēřì kō shařřì; come to no ∼ (*of psn.*) ɓalɓàlcē *v4*, lālācē *v4*: his son came to no ∼ ɗansà yā ɓalɓàlcē.

goodbye 1. *n*: say ∼ yi ban kwānā *m*, yi sallamà *f*: let's go say ∼ to them mù jē mù yi musù ban kwānā; wave ∼ yi wà adàɓô *m*.
2. *excl* (*when expecting to meet again soon*) sai an jimà! = sai an kwan biyu! (*when unsure about next meeting*) sai wata rānā! (*when separation will be long*) sai wani lōkàcī! = sai yâddà ta yìwu!

good-for-nothing *n* wòfī *n*, lūsàřī *m* ⟨ai⟩, sākařai *n* ⟨sākàřkařī⟩, ƙatòn banzā *m*.

good-looking *adj* (*of people*) kyàkkyāwā *adj;* (*of things*) (mài) kyân ganī *m*: it is a ∼ car mōtà tanà dà kyân ganī.

good-natured *adj* (mài) fàřa'à *f*, (mài) sauƙin kâi *m*, (mài) lāfiyà *f*.

good-tempered *adj* (mài) sanyin zūcìyā *m*, (mài) lāfiyà *f*.

goodness *n* kyâu *m;* (*esp. moral*) nàgàřtā *f;* for ∼' sake! don Allàh!

goods *n* kāyā *m* ⟨aki²⟩: he sells leather ∼ yanà sai dà kayàyyakin fātà; smuggled ∼s kāyan sùmōgà; (*merchandise*) hàjà *f*: during hard times, you see piles of ∼ in the stores lōkàcin matsì, akàn ga tulìn hàjà à kantunà.

good will *n* fātan àlhēřì *m*, farař zūcìyā *f*.

goose *n* dinyā *f* ⟨oCi⟩.

gore *v* tùnkuyà *v2*: a bull ∼d him bìjimī yā tùnkùyē shì.

gorge *n* (*ravine*) kwàzazzabò *m* ⟨ai⟩.

gorgeous *adj* kyàkkyāwā *adj;* what a ∼ girl! yārinyàř nân tùbařkallà!

Gospel(s) *n* (*New Testament*) Lìnjīlā *f*: there's a new translation of the ∼ into Hausa an yi sàbuwař fassařař Lìnjīlā zuwà Hausa; preach the ∼ yi wa'azin Lìnjīlā.

gossip 1. *n* (*rumor*) jìta-jìta *f;* here's the very latest ∼ gà jìta-jìta dà ɗumidùmintà; (*malicious*) tsēgùmī *m*, gulma *f* ⟨gùlmànce-gùlmànce⟩: let me give you some juicy ∼ bàri ìn tsēgùntà mikì; his reputation was ruined by malicious ∼ an ɓātà masà sūnā dà gùlmànce-gùlmànce.
2. *v*: ∼ about so. yī dà w., ci nāmàn w., yi tsēgùmin w.: I caught them ∼ing about me nā tař dà sū sunà yî dà nī = ...sunà cîn nāmānà; ∼ to so. about so. yi wà tsēgùmin w.: she was ∼ing to me about Ladi tā yi minì tsēgùmin Làdì; ∼ to so. about sth. tsēgùntà wà dà w.a.

got to *v* dōlè (+ *subjunct.*), tīlàs (+ *subjunct.*): it has ∼ to be done dōlè nē à yī shì = dōlè nē sai an yī shì; you have ∼ to finish this at once yā zama tīlàs kà ƙàràsà wannàn nan dà nan.

gourd *n* a. (*gen'l term*) dumā *m* ⟨aCe⟩. b. (*var. whole types*): (*small, bottle-shaped, for water*) būtà *f* ⟨oCi⟩; (*large, used as a float*) gòrā *m* ⟨una⟩; (*small, used as container for milk, honey, or as inkpot*) kùřtū *m* ⟨una⟩; (*type of warty* ∼) ƙùrzunū *m;* (*elongated, used as musical instrument*) shàntū *m* ⟨una⟩; (*long, for dyeing hands with henna*) zùngùřū *m*. c. (*var. split types used as containers*): (*medium, round, for food*) ƙwaryā *f* ⟨ƙôrai⟩; (*large, round, for feeding animals or for bathing*) masakī *m* ⟨ai⟩; (*small, for measuring out liquids*) ƙôƙo *m* ⟨una⟩; (*used as ladle, spoon*) lūdàyī *m* ⟨luwâdū⟩.

**govern** *v* yi mulkī *m*, riƙè ragàmař mulkī: who ~s the country? wà kè mulkìn ƙasâř?

**government** *n* a. mulkìn ƙasā *m*: most people don't have a say in the ~ of their country yawancin mutànē bâ su dà ta cêwā cikin mulkìn ƙasařsù; (*of a partic. country*) gwamnatì *f*, [F] gùhùřnùmâ *f*: form a ~ kafà gwamnatì; the federal ~ gwamnatìn tàrayyà; ~ house gidan gwamnatì.

**governor** *n* gwamnà *m* ⟨oCi⟩, [F] gwamnàn jahà *m*.

**governor-general** *n* gwàmnà-janàř *m*.

**gown** *n* (*men's or women's*) rìgā *f* ⟨una⟩, *see* **robe**.

**grab** *v* a. fìgè *v4*, warcè *v4*: she jumped up, ~bed her things and fled tā yi wuf ta fīgō kāyantà ta tsērè; (*rush to* ~) ràrumà *v2*: she quickly ~bed the child so he wouldn't fall tā ràrùmi jàrīrī kadà yà fàɗì; the bandits ~bed my horse 'yan fashì sun ràrumi dōkìnā. b. (*var. uses*): ~ sth. from so. ƙwàcè wà *v4* fizgè dàgà *v4*: be careful someone doesn't ~ your purse yi hankàlī kadà wani yà ƙwàcè mikì jàkā; ~ hold of dànƙā *v2*: he ~bed hold of a branch to keep from falling yā dànƙi rēshè don gudùn fàɗuwā; he ~bed a handful of peanuts and began tossing them into his mouth yā dànƙi gyàɗā yanà ta afàwā.

**grace** *n* a. (*esp. of God*) àlhērì *m*, yàřdā *f*: by the ~ of God dà yàřdař Ùbangijì = da yàřdař Allàh. b. (*majesty, graciousness*) àlfařmā *f*: she walks with ~ tanà tàfiyàř àlfařmā. c. (*favor*): be in the good ~s of nà dà farin jinī wajen, nà da fàɗà wajen: he is in the teacher's good ~s yanà dà farin jinī wajen màlàmîn. d. (*benefit*): through the good ~s of àlbařkàcin w.: we got it through the good ~s of his father mun sàmi àlbařkàcin tsōhonsà.

**gracious** 1. *adj* (mài) àlfařmā *f*. 2. *excl* good ~! sùbàhānàllāhì!

**grade**[1] *n* a. (*rank*) dařajà *f*: major is one ~ higher than sergeant-major manjà yā darà sàmanjà dà dařajà ɗaya; (*quality*): top-~ gangàriyà *f*: this is top-~ cotton audùgař nàn gangàriyà cē. b. (*class level in school*) ajì *m* ⟨uwa²⟩. c. (*school exam results*) mākì *m*: his ~ was 70 am bā shì mākì sàbà'in.

**grade**[2] 1. *v* (*a road*) yi wà hanyà lēbùř. 2. *n* (*incline*) gangarè *m*.

**grader** *n* (*for roads*) kàtàfīlà *f*, [F] kàtàřfīlà *f*.

**grade school,** *see* **school.**

**gradually** *adv* a. sànnu-sànnu *adv*, sànnu à hankàlī: he recovered ~ yā sàmi saukī sànnu-sànnu. b. (*over long period of time, in past*) à kwāna à tāshì *adv*: the town ~ became a city à kwāna à tāshì, gàrîn ya zama biřnī. c. (*in the fut.*) yâu dà gòbe (+ *indef. fut.*): you will ~ understand what I mean yâu dà gòbe kà gànè àbîn dà nakè nufî.

**graduate** 1. *n* (*at university level*) mài dìgìřî *n*, [F] mài dìfìlâm *n*; (*of partic. institution*) dā *m*, 'yā *f*, 'yan *p*: a ~ of Bayero University ɗan jāmi'àř Bàyarò. 2. *v* (*post-secondary level*) sàmi dìgìřî; (*lower level*) saukè kàřàtū, gamà kàřàtū.

**graduation** *n* sàukař kàřàtū *f*.

**graft**[1] *n* (*corruption*) hàndamà *f*.

**graft**[2] *v* (*plants*) gwàmà *v1*, yi wà w.a. aurē *m*.

**grafting** *n* gwàmiyā *f*, aurē *m*.

**grain** *n* a. (*only sorghum & millet*) hatsī *m*: the ~ is ripe enough to harvest hatsîn yā ìsa girbì; thresh ~ from the chaff by pounding sussùkè hatsī ta hanyàř càsà; (*after threshing*) tsàbā *f*. b. (*var. types*): (*sorghum*) dāwà *f*, (*bullrush-millet*) gērō *m*, (*late millet*) màiwā *f*, (*wheat*) alkamà *f*, (*fonio*) àccà *f*. c. (*single ~ of cereal*) ƙwāyā *f* ⟨oCi⟩: a ~ of rice ƙwàyař shìnkāfā; ~s of sand yàshī kàɗan; (*fig.*) there is a ~ of truth in what you say àkwai ƙanshin gàskiyā à cikin màganàřkà; there's not one ~ of truth in it kō 6àř6ashin gàskiyā bābù.

**grammar** *n* nahawù *m*: there is no language without a ~ bābù harshèn dà bâ shi dà nahawù.

**grammatical** *adj* kàř6a66ē *adj*.

**gramophone** *n*, *see* **phonograph.**

**granary** *n* rùmbū *m* ⟨una⟩.

**grandchild** *n* jìkā *n* ⟨oCi⟩: he has 5 ~ren, 3 boys and 2 girls jìkōkinsà bìyař, ukù mazā biyu mātā; great-~ tàttà6à-kunne *n*.

**granddaughter** *n* jìkā / jìkanyà *f* ⟨oCi⟩.

**grandfather** *n* kàkā *m* ⟨anni⟩.

**grandmother** *n* kàkā *f* ⟨anni⟩: my ~ on my father's side kàkātā ta wajen ùbā.

**grandparent** *n* kàkā *n* ⟨anni⟩.

**grandson** *n* jìkā *m* ⟨oCi⟩.

**granite** *n* dūtsè *m*.

**grant**[1] *n* (*of money*) tàimakon kuɗī *m*.

grant[2] v: ~ so. a divorce (by judge) rabà wà
aurē, sawwàk̃ē wà aurē; ~ so. a request
biyā bùkātàr̃ w.; ~ so. an interview bâ
w. izìnin gānàwā; take so. for ~ed rainà
/ r̃ēnà v1.

grape n inàbī m.

grapefruit n gar̃ēhùl m, [F] fànfàlèmûs m.

grapevine n: (fig.) hear sth. through the ~
ji à wayàr̃ iskà = ji à tashàr̃ dājì.

grasp v lālùbā v1, yi làlùbē m: he was
~ing for any means to cheat us yanà
làlùben duk wata hanyàr̃ dà zâi cùcē
mù; (fig.) ~ at straws yi k̃àme-k̃àme.

grass n cìyāwà f ⟨i⟩: cut the ~ sàrè
cìyàyī; (dried) hak̃ì m; (dried, for
thatching) shūcì m; prepare ~ for thatching yantà v1.

grasshopper n fàr̃ā f ⟨i⟩.

grate v gōgè v4.

grateful adj (mài) gōdiyā f: I am very ~
to you for your help inà makà matuk̃ar̃
gōdiyātà sabòdà tàimakòn; be ~ for
yabà dà v1: we are ~ for what he has done
for us mun yabà dà àbin dà ya yi manà.

gratify v gamsar̃ (dà) v5.

gratis adv à fàyû, à banzā, à kyàutā.

gratitude n gōdiyar̃ zūci f; (to God)
hamdalà f.

gratuity n, see tip[2].

grave[1] n kabàr̃ī m ⟨u-a[2]⟩, makwancī m:
bury so. in a ~ rufè w. cikin kabàr̃ī;
(of important psn.) kùshēwā f ⟨i⟩.

grave[2] adj: a ~ error bàbban kuskurè; a ~
situation hālì mài ban tsòrō; his situation has become ~ hālìnsà yā tsànantà.

gravel n tsakuwā f, bur̃jì m.

graveyard n makabar̃tā f, hur̃ùmī m.

gravity n a. (seriousness): the ~ of his
illness tsananin cīwònsà. b. force of ~
k̃arfin màgànādīsùn k̃asā m.

gravy n miyà f, see stew.

gray, grey adj tòka-tòka adj; go ~ (of hair
due to old age) yi furfurā f: his hair is
completely ~ furfurā cè fat à kânsà.

graze[1] v (eat grass) yi kīwò m.

graze[2] v (scrape skin) kūjè / k̃ūjè v4, daujè
v4.

grease 1. n a. (esp. in food) maik̃ò m, mâi
m. b. (for engine) gìr̃îs m.
2. v: ~ an engine sâ wà mōtà gìr̃îs.

greasy adj a. (of food) (mài) maik̃ò m, (mài)
mâi m: the doctor told her not to eat
~ food likità yā hanà ta cîn maik̃ò;
the soup is very ~ miyà tā cikà mâi;
his hands are ~ hannunsà nà dà mâi. b.
(from engine oil) (mài) gìr̃îs m.

great 1. adj a. (serious) bàbba adj ⟨mànyā⟩:
they were discussing a matter of ~ importance sunà wata bàbbar̃ màganà. b. (remarkable, important) gàgārùmī adj ⟨ai⟩,
k̃àsàitaccē adj, mùhimmì adj ⟨ai⟩: they
won a ~ victory sun ci gàgārùmar̃ nasa-
r̃à; he was a ~ soldier shì k̃àsàitaccen
sōjà nē; it is one of the world's ~est
books yanà dàgà cikin mùhimman lìt-
tàttàfan dūniyà. c. (noble, esp. of relig. figures) (mài) dar̃ajà f: Muhammadu
Rumfa was a ~ emir Mùhammadù Rùmfa
sarkī nề mài dar̃ajà sòsai. d. for the
~er part yawancī m, mafì yawà.
2. excl tùbar̃kallà! excl.

greatly adv k̃war̃ai adv: I admire him ~ inà
shà'awàrsà k̃war̃ai.

grebe n k̃àzar̃ ruwa f.

greed n kwàd̃ayī m, hàndamà f, k̃awà-zūci
m; (esp. for food) zàr̃ī m, hàdamà f.

greedy adj (mài) zàr̃ī m, hàndàmau n, (mài)
hàdamà f; be ~ about hàndamà v2.

green adj a. k̃ōr̃è adj ⟨kwàr̃r̃à⟩; dark, deep
~ k̃ōr̃è shar̃ = k̃ōr̃è fatau; light ~
tsanwā f: bright, vivid ~ tsanwā shar̃.
b. (of unripe fruit) d̃anyē adj ⟨u⟩.

greet v gai dà / gayar̃ (dà) v5, yi wà
gaisuwā f: please ~ your wife for me
kà gayar̃ minì dà uwar̃gidā = kà cê wà
uwar̃gidā inà gaishē tà; they ~ed him
on his arrival sun yi masà sànnu dà zuwà;
(one ano.) gaisà v1, yi sallamà f: after
~ing each other, they went inside dà sukà
gaisà = dà sukà yi sallamà, sai sukà
shìga ciki.

greetings n gaisuwā f ⟨oCi⟩: ~ to you! inà
gaisuwā! give, send ~ to so. gai dà /
gayar̃ (dà) v5: give my ~ to everyone inà
gai dà duk idòn sanì = gàyar̃ minì dà
duk idòn sanì; extend one's ~ to isar̃
dà v5: please extend my ~s to your family
kà isar̃ minì dà gaisuwā gà ìyālìnkà.

grenade n gùr̃nât m, nàkiyà f.

grey adj, see gray.

grief n bak̃in cikì m, tàusàyī m: express
one's ~ over nūnà tàusàyī gàme dà.

grievance n (complaint) k̃àrā f, kūkā m.

grieve v yi bak̃in cikì m.

grill v (roast meat) gasà v1: meat ~ed over
a fire mound is called tsire nāmàn dà akè
gasàwā kân tukùbā anà kirànsà tsìr̃ē.

grim adj: look ~ d̃aurè fuskà = mur̃tùkè
fuskà.

grimace v a. (in pain) yàtsìnē v4, yi
yàtsìnà f. b. (sneer by distorting mouth)
gàtsìnà v1, yi gàtsìnē m; (by sticking
tongue out) yi gwālō m.

grin v (*esp. from happiness*): he's ∼ning (*fig.*) bằkinsà hař kunne.

grind v a. (*coarsely*) ɓařzā v1, (*into fine flour*) niƙằ v1 ⟨niƙằ⟩: it was finely ground an niƙằ shi lilis. b. (*sth. fresh or with liquid, esp. tomatoes, chillies*) markằdā v1. c. (*sharpen a tool*) wāsā v1.

grinder n (*mechanical*) injìn niƙằ m, [F] màshîn kin niƙằ m.

grindstone n a. (*for grinding cereals*) dūtsèn niƙằ m: a ∼ consists of a large stone and a smaller one dūtsèn niƙằ yā ƙùnshi uwā dà ɗā. b. (*whetstone*) dūtsèn wāshī m.

grip 1. v riƙè kankan v4: he ∼ped the bottle and wouldn't let go yā riƙè kwalabař kankan bà yằ sô yà sàkē tà. 2. n riƙō m; (*fig.*) she's got a ∼ on her husband tā sằmi kân mijìntà.

gristle n gurunguntsī m.

grit v: ∼ one's teeth cījè haƙòrā.

groaning n gunằgunī m, (*esp. from pain*) nīshī m: the patient was ∼ with pain majìyyàcī nằ nīshī sabòdà zāfin cīwò.

groceries n kāyan cèfànē m: go to buy ∼ tàfi cèfànē.

groom n a. angò m ⟨aye⟩. b. (*for horses*) ɗan bàřga m.

grope v lālùbā v1, yi lằlùbē m, fằfakằ v2, ⟨fằfàkē⟩: she's groping along the wall tanằ lằlùben bangò; he groped in the drawer for a pencil yā fằfàki fensìř cikin àljīhun tēbùř.

gross adj: it weighs 10 kilos ∼ including the container nauyinsà kilò gōmà duk dà tiyằ; ∼ earnings àlbâshī kằfin ɗebe-ɗebe; (*Econ.*) ∼ national product jimlàř dūkìyař ƙasā.

ground n a. ƙasā f ⟨aCe⟩: the ∼ is hard ƙasā tā yi taurī; barren ∼ faƙò m: the ∼ becomes barren in the dry season ƙasā takàn zama faƙò dà rānī; high ∼ tudù m; low ∼ kwarì m; sloping ∼ gàngarā f: rising and falling ∼ tudù dà gàngarā. b. (*adverbial uses*): on, to the ∼ (à) ƙas(à) adv: put it down on the ∼ kà sàukē shi à ƙasà; he fell on the ∼ yā fāɗā ƙas.

groundnut(s) n gyàɗā f, (*Bambara* ∼) gujiyā f, 'yař ƙùrigà f: grow ∼ nōmà gyàɗā; ∼ balls (*with oil extracted & fried*) ƙulìƙulì m; ∼ paste, butter tùnkūzā f; ∼ stew miyàř gyàɗā.

grounds[1] n (*basis*) dàlīlì m ⟨ai⟩.

grounds[2] n (*area of a partic. place*) hàřābà f: the ∼ of the palace hàřābàř fādà; prayer ∼ fīlin ìdì m.

group 1. n a. (*small* ∼) gungù m: a ∼ of people gungùn mutằnē. b. (*partic. association of people*) ƙungìyā f ⟨oCi⟩: a farmers' ∼ ƙungìyař manōmā. c. (*of like things, beings*) guřguzū m: a ∼ of fish, birds guřguzun kīfằyē, tsuntsằyē. d. (*of people going someplace together*) tàwagằ f: a ∼ of pilgrims tàwagàř àlhàzai; a whole ∼ of people came to watch mutằnē tàwagằ gùdā sun zō kallō. e. (*pile*) tārì m. 2. v tārā v1: she ∼ed them together into different piles tā tārā su tārì-tārì.

grove n kurmì m ⟨a-u⟩.

grow 1. vi a. (*increase*) ƙằru v7: the noise grew louder ƙārâř tā ƙằru; he is ∼ing richer and richer ařzìkinsà nằ ta ƙằruwā; ∼ long yi tsawō m: they let their hair ∼ long sunằ barìn gāshìnsù yà yi tsawō; ∼ increasingly older daɗà tsūfā. b. (*get bigger, older*) girma v3a: children ∼ fast yārā sunằ girmā dà wuri. c. (*reach adulthood*): ∼ up ìsa mùtûm, zama bàbba: his daughter is ∼n up 'yařsà tā ìsa mùtûm; his sons are all ∼n up 'yā'yansà duk sun ìsa mùtûm = 'yā'ansà duk sun zama sàmằrī. d. (*reach puberty, tradit. legal status*): ∼ up bàlagà v3. e. (*spend one's childhood*): ∼ up tāshì v3b: I grew up at my uncle's à gidan ƙanèn bàbānā na tāshì. f. (*of plants*) fitō v6, tāshì v3b: plants ∼ quickly after the rains bāyan an yi ruwā, shùke-shùke nằ fitōwà dà wuri. 2. vt (*foodstuffs*) nōmā v1 ⟨nōmà⟩: which cereals do they ∼ in Nigeria? wànè irìn hatsī akè nōmằwā à Nìjēřiyằ?

growl v yi gùřnằnī m: lions, hyenas, and dogs all ∼ dà zākì dà kūrā dà kàrē duk sunằ gùřnằnī; (*in stomach from hunger*) yi mùřdā f, yi tùƙā f: my stomach is ∼ing from hunger cikìnā nằ mùřdā sabòdà kùmallō.

grown-up n & adj a. (*in Hausa society, one who has reached puberty*) bàlàgaggē adj; become ∼ bàlagà v3; act ∼ (*of a child*) yi wằyō m, nằ dà nìtsuwā f. b. (*adult*): be ∼ ìsa mùtûm.

growth n a. (*maturity*) girmā m: the tree hasn't yet reached its full ∼ bishiyằ bà tà kai girmā ba. b. (*expansion*) hàɓakà f: there's been a rapid ∼ of trade an sằmi hàɓakàř cìnikī mài yawằ.

grub n tsūtsā f ⟨oCi⟩.

grudge n: bear, hold a ∼ against so. ƙùllatā v2, riƙè w. à zūci, ji haushin w.: he holds a ∼ against me yā riƙè ni à zūci = yanằ ƙùllatằtā; I still bear a ~ against him haɍ yànzu inà ƙùllàce dà shī = haɍ yànzu inà rìƙe dà shī à zūci.

gruel n (from millet, guinea corn) kùnū m, (with millet balls in sour milk) furā f, (from fermented millet) kōko m.

grumble v yi mītã f, yi gùngùnī / gunãgunī m, (esp. about sth. trivial) yi ƙōràfī m.

grunt v yi gùɍnãnī m.

guarantee 1. n gàɍàntî m: the ~ has expired gàɍàntîn yā ƙàrè; this battery has a 6-month ~ wannàn bātìr dîn nã dà gàɍàntîn watã shidà.
2. v (assure) bā dà tabbàcī: I ~ that you will be satisfied with this nā bā kà tabbàcin cêwā zā kà gàmsu dà wannàn.

guarantor n: be ~ for so. tsayã wà v1.

guard 1. n a. (night watchman) mài gādì m, [F] gàɍdìnyê m. b. (in emir's palace) dõgarì m ⟨ai⟩. c. national ~ 'yan tsàron ƙasà p, [F] gàɍ-dà-sarki m.
2. v a. (keep watch) yi gādì m, jirā v0: the building is ~ed day and night àkwai mãsu gādìn ginìn darē dà rānā. b. (defend, protect) tsarè v4; (shield off) kārè v4, yi gàrkuwā f: two soldiers ~ the entrance sõjõjī biyu sunã kārè ƙõfàɍ; be on one's ~ against so. kìyāyã v2: be on your ~ against strangers kà kìyāyi bàƙī; ~ against sth. kiyāyè v4: ~ against danger kiyàyè hadàɍī; catch so. off ~ (fig.) fàki idòn w., fàki numfāshin w.

guardian n (legal) mài riƙòn w.

guava n gwaibã / gōbã f ⟨oCi⟩.

guerilla n ɗan sàri-kà-nõƙè m, ɗan sùnƙūrù m; ~ warfare yāƙìn sàri-kà-nõƙè = yāƙìn sùnƙūrù.

guess 1. v a. (make a ~) cìtā / cìntā v2, yi kà-cīci-kà-cīci m, cànkā v2: ~ what I have in my pocket kà cìnci àbîn dà nakè dà shī à àljīhū; you ~ed right, wrong (in answer to puzzle, word game) kā sāmō, bà kà sāmō ba. b. (estimate roughly) kìntātã v2: I ~ he'll be arriving tomorrow nā kìntàci zuwànsà gòbe.
2. n cìntā f, cànkē m, zàtō m: you made a good ~ cìntaɍkà tā yi daidai; a wild ~ kãme-kãme m.

guest n bàƙō m ⟨i⟩: how many ~s have been invited? bàƙī nawà akà gàyyatã? be a ~ of so. bàƙuntã v2: he was our ~ for a week yā bàƙùncē mù haɍ kwānā bakwài.

guide 1. n jà-gōrà n.
2. v nūsaɍ (dà) v5, yi wà jà-gōrà, sã w. hanyà: he ~d us to the road yā nūshē mù hanyã.

guile n wãyō m, (esp. of women vis-a-vis men) kissã f.

guilt n lâifī m ⟨uka²⟩: admit one's ~ amsà lâifī; burden of ~ àlhakī m.

guilty adj (mài) lâifī m: he is the ~ one, not me shī yakè dà lâifī, bã nī ba; she is not ~ in the least bã ta dà lâifī kō ƙwaɍzanè; find so. ~ sãmi w. dà lâifī; plead ~ amsà lâifī; have a ~ look yi wuƙī-wùƙī idph: he's looking ~ as if he were the thief yanã wuƙī-wùƙī sai kà cê ɓàrāwòn.

guinea-corn n dāwã f, (red. var.) ƙaurã f: ~ is one of the staples of the Hausa people dāwã tanã daya dàgà cikin kāyan màsàɍūfīn Hàusàwã.

guinea-fowl n zàbō m, zàbuwā f ⟨i⟩.

guinea-pig n ɓēɍan Masàɍ m.

guinea-worm n kùɍkunū m.

gullet n màƙōgwàrō m.

gully n mazurārī m.

gulp 1. n (of water) maƙwàrwā f.
2. v: ~ down (liquids) kwànkwadã v2: it was only after ~ing down some water that we quenched our thirst sai dà mukà kwànkwàdi ruwā mukà kashè ƙishirwā; (food) zàƙā v2: he ~ed his food down yā zàƙi àbinci.

gum n a. (rubbery substance) danƙō m; (chewing ~) cìngâm m. b. (glue) gùlû m, [F] kwâl m. c. (eraser) ɍōbã m, gwâm m, [F] gâm f.

gum Arabic n ƙārō m.

gums n dāsàshī m: my ~ are aching dāsàshīnā nã minì cīwò.

gun n bindigã f ⟨oCi⟩; artillery ~ ìgwā f ⟨oCi⟩; Dane ~ àdakã f ⟨u⟩, bindigàɍ tōkā f; machine ~ bindigã mài ruwā, bindigã mài jìgìdā, mãshingàn f; fire a ~ bugà bindigã = haɍbà bindigã; load a ~ dūrà hàɍsāshī = yi wà bindigã ɗurì: is the ~ loaded? bindigàɍ a ɗùre takè? = dà hàɍsāshī à bindigàɍ? (fig.) he's sticking to his ~s yanã nân à kân bàkansà.

gunfire n ruwan hàɍsāshī m, hàɍbe-hàɍbe m.

gunpowder n àlbàɍūshì m.

gush v ɓulɓulō v6: oil ~ed forth from the well mâi yā ɓulɓulō dàgà rījìyā.

gusset n (of robe, trousers) shìge m.

gust n: there was a sudden ~ of wind sai iskà tā tāsō nan dà nan.

guts n hanjī m; (fig.) he's got ~ ƙarfin zūcìyā gàrē shì; (fig.) he hates my ~ yā ƙi jinīnā.

gutta percha n (tree) gamjì m.

gutter *n* (*in street*) magudānar̃ ruwā *f*,
  làmbàtū *m*, kwatã̀ *f*, [F] gōtã̀ *f*: he fell into
  the ~ yā fāɗã̀ kwatã̀; (*on roof*) ìndar̃ar̃ō
  *m*.
gymnasium *n* dākìn mōtsà jìkī *m*.
gymnastics *n* wằsànnin mōtsà jìkī *p*.
gynecologist *n* likitàn mātā *n*.

# H

**habit** *n* ɗàbī'ầ *f* ⟨u⟩, (*character*) hālī / halī *m* ⟨aye⟩: good ~s halī nagàri; bad ~s mùmmūnaɽ ɗàbī'ầ; he has bad ~s ɗàbī'aɽsà bâ ta dà kyâu = yanầ dà mūgùn hālī; it's their ~ to get up early ɗàbī'aɽsù cē tāshì dà wuri; smoking is a bad ~ shân tābầ mùmmūnaɽ ɗàbī'ầ cē; acquire, get into the ~ of sābầ dà *v1*: you'd better get into the ~ of turning out the lights gwằmmà kà sābầ dà kashè wutâ; become a ~ with so. zamề wà jìkī: lying has become a ~ with him ƙaryā tā zamề masà jìkī.

**habitual** *adj*: he's a ~ liar yā sābầ dà ƙaryā = hālinsà ƙaryā.

**hack at** *v* (*a tree, log*) sassàrā *v1*.

**haft 1.** *n* ƙōtầ *f* ⟨oCi⟩.
**2.** *v* kwaɓầ *v1*: he ~ed the axe yā kwaɓà gàtarī à ƙōtầ.

**hail**[1] *n & v* ƙànƙarā *f*: it rained and even ~ed an yi ruwā haɽ dà ƙànƙarā; ~storm iskầ mài ƙànƙarā.

**hail**[2] *v* (*a taxi*) tsai dà / tsayaɽ (dà) *v5*; (*a psn.*) gai dà / gayaɽ (dà) *v5*.

**hair** *n* (*of psn., animal*) gāshì *m* ⟨gāsū⟩, (*head ~ of men*) sùmā *f*; ~ on chest gāshìn ƙìrjī; pubic ~ gāshìn gàba; gray ~ furfurā *f*: my ~ is very gray duk kâinā furfurā cē; curly ~ nànnàɗaɗɗen gāshì; short tightly curled ~ gāshì mài taurī; long ~ gāshì mài yawầ = gāshì mài tsawō; wear one's ~ long tārà gāshì; straight ~ mīƙaƙƙen gāshì; do, fix one's ~ (*of women*) yi kitsồ *m*, kitsề *v4*: she had her ~ done tā yi kitsồ = an yi matà kitsồ.

**haircut** *n* (*for men*) askì *m*: I want to have a ~ inầ sôn yîn askì = inầ sô à ragề minì sùmā.

**hairdo** *n* (*for women*) kitsồ *m*: she has a special ~ tā yi wani irìn kitsồ.

**hairy** *adj* (*esp. of body*) gàɽgāsā *adj*.

**Hajj** *n* Hajì *m*: they went on the ~ sun tàfi Hajì.

**half** *n* **a.** rabì *m*: it weighs 2 and a ~ pounds nauyinsà wayầ biyu dà rabì nē; ~ an hour rabìn awầ; ~ price rabìn kuɗī; the

board was ~ an inch thick kaurin kātākồn rabìn incì nē; we've gone ~-way mun ci rabìn tàfiyầ. **b.** (*of sth. that can be split*) ɓārì *m*: ~ a kolanut ɓārìn gōɽồ.

**half-brother, half-sister** *n*: he, she is my ~ (*same father, different mother*) ùbanmù ɗaya; (*same mother, different father*) uwaɽmù ɗaya.

**half-heartedly** *adv* dà zūcìyā biyu.

**half-way** *adv* rabì *m*: Garko is almost ~ between Wudil and Rano Gaɽkồ tanầ rabìn Wùdil dà Rano; reach the ~ point kai rabì, ci rabì: he is ~ through his work yā kai rabìn aikìnsà; we're ~ through on our trip mun ci rabìn tàfiyầ.

**halt 1.** *v* tsayầ *v1*, dākàtā *v1*; tsai dà / tsayaɽ (dà) *v5*, dākataɽ (dà) *v5*.
**2.** *n*: all traffic came to a ~ mōtōcī duk sun tsayầ cak.

**halter** *n* (*for horse*) ragàmā *f*.

**halve** *v* rabà biyu *v1*.

**ham** *n* nāmàn àladề *m*.

**hamlet** *n* ƙàramin ƙauyề *m*.

**hammer 1.** *n* gùdumā *f* ⟨oCi⟩, hamầ *f*, [F] màɽtô *m*; sledge-~ hamầ *f*, [F] mâs *m*; (*var. types used by blacksmiths*): muntàɽagầ *f*, masàɓā *f* ⟨ai⟩, maskồ *m* ⟨a-e⟩.
**2.** *v* bugầ *v1*: ~ in a nail bugà ƙūsā.

**hamper** *v* tsai dà / tsayaɽ (dà) *v5*: the rains have ~ed the road work ruwā yā tsai dà aikìn hanyầɽ.

**hand 1.** *n* **a.** hannū *m* ⟨uwa, aye⟩: my ~s are cold hannūnā nằ dà sanyī; where can I wash my ~s? ìnā zân iyà wankè hannū? = àkwai būtàɽ ruwā kusa? my ~ hurts nā ji cīwồ à hannu; ~ in ~ hannū dà hannū = rìƙe dà hannun jūnā; I had no ~ in the matter bā nằ cikin sha'ànī = bā nằ cikin màganàɽ = hannūnā suluf cikin màganàɽ; we are all in God's ~s mū dukà munầ hannun Allàh; (*fig.*) an old ~ tsōhon hannū *m*: he's an old ~ at fixing tires shī tsōhon hannū wajen yi wầ tāyầ fācì. **b.** (*adverbial uses*): in, on the ~ à hannu *adv*: she cut herself on the ~ tā yankè à hannu; cash in ~ kuɗī hannu; the matter at ~ àbîn dà akề ciki yànzu = àbîn dà kề àkwai; ~-made work aikìn hannu; this bag is made by ~, not by machine jàkaɽ nàn dà hannu akà yī tà bầ dà injì ba; empty-~ed hannū banzā; on the one ~..., on the other ~... ta wani ɓangarèn..., àmmā ta wani ɓangarèn kuma. **c.** (*direction*): on the right-~, left-~ dà hannun dāma, hagu; he is right-~ed, left-~ed shī bàdāmayề, bàhagồ nē; it is improper to give or ac-

cept anything with your left ~ bâ kyâu mîƙà kō kàrɓaȓ àbù dà hannun hagu. d. (*of watch, clock*) hannū *m*: minute, hour ~ dōgon, ƙàramin hannū. e. (*var. v + n uses*): clap ~s yi tâfī *m*, tāfà *v1*; slap so.'s ~ in greeting tāfà *v1*; get out of ~ gâgarà *v3*; hold so.'s ~ kāmà hannū: they are walking along holding ~s sunà tàfiyà kàme dà hannū; lend, give a ~ tayà *v1*, bā dà hannū: please lend me a ~ with this box don Allàh kà tayà ni ɗaukàȓ wannàn àkwātìn; shake ~s gamà hannū, haɗà hannū, (*tradit. Hausa style*) yi mùsāfahà *f*.
2. *v* danƙà wà *v1*: I ~ed him the keys to the room nā danƙà masà màbùɗan dākì; (*surreptitiously*) sunnà *v1*: he ~ed the money to me secretly yā sunnō minì kuɗîn; ~ sth. over to so. mîƙà wà *v1*; ~ out (*distribute*) rabà *v1*; the custom has been ~ed down for generations àl'ādà tun ta kàkā dà kàkànnī.

**handbag** *n* jàkaȓ hannu *f* ⟨una²⟩, jàkaȓ mātà *f*, [F] sàkwât *f*.

**handball** *n* ƙwallon hannu *m*.

**hand-brake** *n* biȓkìn hannu *m*: pull the ~ jā biȓkìn hannu; release the ~ sakaȓ dà biȓkì.

**handcuffs** *n* ankwà *f*, [F] ankwâȓ *m*.

**handful** *n* danƙì *m*, dintsì *m*; give so. a ~ of dintsà wà *v1*: he gave me a ~ of groundnuts yā dintsà minì gyàɗā = yā bā nì dintsìn gyàɗā; (*fig.*) only a ~ of people attended the meeting mutànē 'yan kàɗan sukà hàllàȓci tàrôn.

**handicraft** *n* aikìn hannu *m*.

**handicap** *n* (*in contest*) rātā *f*.

**handicapped** *n & adj* (*mentally*) tàɓaɓɓē *adj*; (*physically*) nàƙàsasshē *adj*.

**handkerchief** *n* mayānī *m*, hankicì *m*, [F] mùshùwâȓ *m*: she tied the money up in a ~ tā ƙullè kuɗîn cikin hankicì.

**handle** 1. *n* a. mariƙì *m*: she broke the ~ of the cup tā karyà mariƙin kwâf; (*twin ~s on any vessel, container*) kûnnē *m* ⟨uwa⟩: a pot with 2 ~s tukunyā mài kunnuwà. b. (*shaft of hoe, axe*) ƙōtà *f* ⟨oCi⟩.
2. *v* a. (*touch*) taɓà *v1*, tàɓu *v7*: this pot is too hot to ~ tukunyaȓ nàn bā tà tàɓuwā sabòdà zāfī. b. (*cope with*) iyà *v1*: he'll be able to ~ the job with no trouble zâi iyà aikìn bà tàre dà wata màtsalà ba. c. (*not cope with*) gàgarà *v2*: she can't ~ her children any more yànzu yârân sun gàgàre tà = yârân sun fi ƙarfintà yànzu.

**handlebar(s)** *n* (*of bicycle*) hannun kèkè *m*, kân kèkè *m*.

**handrail** *n* hannū *m*.

**handshake** *n* (*Hausa-style*) mùsāfahà *f*, ban hannū *m*.

**handsome** *adj* a. (*of looks*) (mài) kyâu *m*, kyàkkyāwā *adj*: they have 3 ~ boys yâransù ukù kyāwàwā. b. (*of quantity*) (mài) yawà *m*: a ~ sum of money jimlàȓ kuɗī mài yawà.

**handwriting** *n* ȓùɓùtū *m*: his ~ is difficult to read ȓùɓùtunsà nà dà wùyaȓ kaȓàntâwā = ȓùɓùtunsà bā yà kàȓàntuwā; good ~ mài fàsāhàȓ ȓùɓùtū; small ~ ȓùɓùtū ƙanànā.

**hang** 1. *vt* a. (*sth. onto a place*) rātàyā *v1*: ~ the gown on a door yā rātàyà rìgâȓ à jìkin ƙōfà; ~ out the wash shânyà wankì: the wash was hung on the clothesline an shânyà wankì à igiyàȓ shânyā = wankìn yanà ràtàye à igiyàȓ shânyā; ~ up the telephone ajìyè tàȓhô. b. (*a psn.*) rātàyè *v4*; ~ one's head sunkuyaȓ dà kâi.
2. *vi* (*dangle*) yi rētò *m*: a chain was ~ing from the dog's neck sarƙà nà rētò à wuyàȓ kàrē; ~ around (*a place*) yi shâwāgì *m*: he's been ~ing around the office all day yanà shâwāgìn ōfìs gàbā ɗayan rānâȓ; ~ back (*conceal oneself, be aloof*) rāɓè *v4*, yi ràɓe-ràɓe, tōgè *v4*, yi tōgiyà *f*: why are you ~ing back like that at the door? don mè kikè tōgiyà hakà à bàkin ƙōfà?

**hanger** *n* (*for clothes*) marātayī *m*, hangà *f*.

**hangnail** *n* ɗan ùbā *m*.

**haphazardly** *adv*: do sth. ~ yi gàràjē dà *m*: he does his work ~ yanà gàràjē dà aikìnsà.

**happen** *v* a. (*occur*) aùku *v7*, fàru *v7*, wàkānà *v3*: when did the accident ~? yàushè haɗàrìn ya àuku? what ~ed? mè ya fàru? don't let it ~ again kadà kà baȓ àbîn yà sākè fàruwā; it often ~s that letters are lost in the mail yanà yawàn àukuwā wàsìƙū sù ɓatà à gidan wayà; ~ by chance yi gàm-dà-Kàtaȓ, *see* chance, coincidence. b. (~ *to so.*) sāmù *v2\**: what ~ed to you? mè ya sàmē kà? c. (*be possible*) yìwu *v7*: it might ~ zâi yìwu; it may ~ that he will come mài yìwuwā nè yà zō. d. (*come to be*) kasàncē *v4*, zàmanà *v3*, zamantō *v6* (*all used with indef. subj pro* yā *in past*): I ~ed to be sick at the time yā kasàncē inà rashìn lāfiyà à lōkàcîn; we ~ed to be there when he got back yā zamantō munà cân lōkàcîn dà ya kōmō.

**happily** *adv*: they lived ~ ever after sun

zaunā tāre hař àbàdā.

**happiness** n farin cikī m, muřnā f: our children bring us ~ yāranmù sunā sâ mu farin cikī.

**happy** adj (mài) farin cikī m, (mài) muřnā f; be ~ yi farin cikī, yi muřnā; I'm ~ to see you inā farin cikī dà ganinkì = inā muřnâř ganinkì; he's extremely ~ yanā matuƙař muřnā = (fig.) bàkinsà hař kunne; make so. ~ faràntā wà râi, dādàdā wà v1, sâ w. farin cikī; ~ birth-day! many ~ returns! Allàh yà maimàitā!

**harass** v shā wà kâi, matsā wà (lambā) v1, tsanàntā wà v1, ƙwàřzabā v2.

**harbor** n (natural) bākin ruwā m; (port) tashàř jirgin ruwa f.

**hard** 1. adj a. (not soft) (mài) taurī m, tàttaurā adj: the ground is very ~ ƙasā tā yi taurī. b. (difficult) (mài) wùyā f, (mài) wàhalā f: ~ questions tambayōyī māsu wùyā; it is ~ to please everyone dà wùyā à dādàdā wà kōwā; have a ~ time, be ~ up (financially) nā cikin matsī, nā cikin màtsuwā: the farmers are having a ~ time these days manōmā sunā cikin matsī yànzu; give so. a ~ time (fig.) bā w. kāshī; it's a ~ life (fig.) dūniyā gidan wàhalā.
2. adv a. (esp. ref. to work) tuƙùru adv: progress comes only with ~ work cī-gàba sai dà aikī tuƙùru; he works the ~est of all yā fi kōwā aikìn tuƙùru. b. (very much) ƙwařai adv, sōsai adv: he studies ~ yanā kàřàtū ƙwařai; they are play-ing ~ sunā wāsā sōsai. c. (a lot of); (use specialized verbs which indicate 'do-ing a lot of sth.'): it rained ~ an shēƙà = māƙà = labtà ruwā; he beat the donkey ~ with a stick yā dìřki jàkī dà sàndā = yā dìřƙà wà jàkī sàndā; she slapped him ~ tā kwàɗē shi dà marī = tā kwàɗà masà marī.

**hard-boiled** adj: a ~ egg dàfaffen ƙwai.

**harden** v (stiffen) ƙandàrē v4.

**hard hat** n hūlař kwanō f.

**hard-hearted** adj maràs tàusàyī m, maràs īmānī m.

**hardly** adv a. (almost not) dà ƙyař/kyař (+ rel. complet.), dà wùyā (+ subjunct.): we could ~ understand what he said dà ƙyař mukà gānè àbîn dà ya fàɗā = dà wùyā mù gānè àbîn dà ya fàɗā. b. (almost none, almost never) kusan bābù: there was ~ any food left kusan bābù sauran àbinci; ~ ever bā sàfài ba: I ~ ever see him bā sàfài nakàn gan shì ba = bàn cikà ganinsà ba. c. (barely): ~ do X when Y X

kè dà wùyā sai Y: we had ~ gone outside when it began to rain fìtařmù wàje kè dà wùyā sai akà fārà ruwā.

**hardship** n wàhalā f ⟨oCi⟩, wùyā f: en-dure ~ during the drought daurè wàhalā lōkàcin farī.

**hare** n zōmō m ⟨aye⟩.

**hare-lip** n lēɓèn ràƙumī m.

**harm** 1. n a. (fault) lâifī m ⟨uka²⟩, illà f ⟨oCi⟩: there's no ~ in trying bā lâifī à gwadà à ganī; there's no ~ in it bā illà à cikinsà. b. (Law, a wrongful act) lahànī m: with intent to cause ~ dà niyyàř à yi sanàdin lahànī.
2. v yi wà illà f, yi wà lâifī m; lahàntā v1, jāwō lahànī gà.

**harmattan** n (wind) hùntūřù m, [F] bùjī m: the ~ blows from the north hùntūřù nā tāsôwā dàgà arêwa.

**harmful** adj (mài) lahànī m: is this plant ~ to people? shūkàř nân tanā dà lahànī gà mutànē? smoking is ~ to your health shân tābà yanā jāwō lahànī gà lāfiyàř jìkī.

**harmless** adj maràs lahànī m.

**harmony** n dàidàituwā f.

**harness** n kāyan dōkī m.

**harpoon** n hargī m, (large, barbed) sàngō m.

**harsh** adj matsànàncī adj.

**hartebeest** n (West African) kankī m; (Senegal) darī m, daranyā f.

**harvest** 1. n (season) kàkā f; the ~ will be good this year wannàn shēkarā zā tà yi àlbařkà; (of grain) girbī m; (of beans, groundnuts) rōrō m.
2. v (use specific verbs for specific crops): (standing crops) gìrbā v2 ⟨girbī⟩: the men went out to ~ the corn mutànē sun tàfi girbìn hatsī; (low-lying crops, beans) rōrā v2 ⟨rōrō⟩; (cotton, tobacco) cìrā v2; (groundnuts) fàřtā v2 ⟨fařtā⟩ f, rōrā v2 ⟨rōrō⟩; (rice, wheat) yankā v1; (tubers, root crops) tōnā v2 ⟨tōnō⟩.

**harvest season** n kàkā f.

**hashish** n, see marijuana.

**hasp** n àlhařgà f; ~ and staple hancì dà sarƙà.

**hassle** n kàcàniyā f, màtsalā f: it's a ~ to get a license sāmùn lāsìn àkwai màtsalā.

**hassock** n, see pouf.

**haste** n saurī m, hanzarī m; (urgency) gaggāwā f; in ~ dà saurī = dà gaggāwā; make ~ yi saurī m, yi hanzarī m, gaggàutā f; ~ makes waste saurī yā hàifi nàwa.

hasten v yi saurī m, gaggàutā v1; (to a place) gařzàyā v1: she ~ed to the market tā gařzàyā zuwā kàsuwā.

hasty adj (esp. with neg. result) (mài) gaggāwā f: make a ~ decision yankè shāwařā cikin gaggāwā; (& poorly done) (mài) gàràjē m: don't be ~ with your work kadà kà yi gàràjē dà aikìnkà.

hat n hūlā f ⟨una⟩, (straw) màlàfā f ⟨u⟩, (European style) shàhò f, [F] shàppò f; (for Hausa styles, see cap).

hatch v ƙyanƙyàshē v4: the hen ~ed the eggs kàzā tā ƙyanƙyàshè ƙwai; the egg ~ed ƙwai yā ƙyanƙyàshē; ~ a plot yi ƙullī m.

hatchet n bàrandamī m ⟨ai⟩, ɗan gàtarī m.

hate v tsanā v2, ƙi v0, ƙi jinin w.a.: he has ~d me since childhood tun munà yārā ya tsànē nì; I ~ the cold, noise bā nà sôn sanyī, hàyàniyā; I ~ violence nā ƙi jinin tāshìn hankàlī.

hatred n àdāwā f, gàbā f, ƙìyayyà f.

haughty adj (mài) jī-jī dà kâi m, (mài) girman kâi m.

Hausa n a. (language) Hausa f: he speaks ~ (said of a Hausa psn.) bàhaushè nē, (said of non-Hausa psn.) yanà jîn Hausa. b. (member of ethnic group) bàhaushè m, bàhaushìyā f ⟨Hàusàwā⟩; he is not a ~ shī kàbīlā nē = shī yàřē nè.

have[1] v a. (as a modal v to form tenses, use complet. asp. pro, see Appendix A): ~ you finished? kun gamà? yes, we ~ done it ī, mun yī shì; he hasn't finished yet bài gamà ba tùkùna. b. (over a period of time): ~ been doing (use time expr. in past cl. plus contin. cl.): she has been working for me for 3 weeks tā yi mākò ukù tanà minì aikī; they ~ been working all day sun yinì sunà aikī; I ~ been living here for 10 years nā shèkarà gōmà inà zàune à nân. c. (cause to be done) (use subjunct.): I need to ~ this repaired inà bùkātā à gyārà minì wannàn; Musa doesn't want to ~ his tooth pulled Mūsā yà sô à cirè masà haƙōrī. d. (must do): ~ to do sth. dōlè (+ subjunct.), wājìbī nè (+ subjunct.), wàjabà v3: you ~ to change trains at Kaduna dōlè kà sàkè jirgī à Kàdūna; you do not ~ to do that bài wàjabà kà yi hakà ba.

have[2] v a. (own) (use contin. asp. pro. + dà): he has a bicycle yanà dà kèkè; do you ~ any money? kanà dà kuɗī? he has no children bâ shi dà 'yā'yā; how many do you ~? gùdā nawà kakè dà sū? (fig.)

the ~s and ~ nots màsu shī dà maràsā shī. b. (possess) màllakà v2: women like having lots of jewelry mātā sunà sôn sù màllàki sarƙōƙin adō. c. (an illness) (use contin. asp. pro + n): she has a cold, a headache tanà mura, tanà cīwòn kâi. d. (non-possessive meaning, often formed with yi + n, see that noun entry): ~ a quarrel, a rest, a bath, patience yi faɗā, hūtū, wankā, haƙurī.

havoc n biji-biji idph: the tornado wreaked ~ at the market gùguwà tā yi biji-biji à kàsuwā.

hawk[1] n shàhò m ⟨una⟩, (black crested ~-eagle) karàmbatà f.

hawk[2] v yi tàllà m: he is ~ing his wares yanà tàllàn kōlìnsà.

hay n ìngirìcì m, bùsasshiyař cìyāwā f.

hay fever n màsassarā / màshassharā f, haɓɓōjè m.

haze n hazō m: it's very hazy today yâu àkwai hazō dà yawà.

he pro, see Appendix A.

head 1. n a. (of body) kâi m ⟨kàwunā⟩; nod one's ~ kaɗà kâi = gyaɗà kâi; put one's ~ down, lower one's ~ kifè kâi, sunkuyař dà kâi: they lowered their ~s and wept sun kifè kâi sunà ta kūkā; rest ~ on hand (in thought) yi tàgumī m; turn one's ~ around waigà v1, waiwàyà v1; ~s or tails kân sarkī kō dàmarà; (fig.) let's put our ~s together mù haɗà kâi; (fig.) he has a good ~ for numbers yā iyà lìssāfì. b. (adverbial uses): on the ~ à kā/ka adv: he carried the load on his ~ yā dàuki kāyā à ka. c. (senses) hankàlī m ⟨u-a⟩: he lost his ~ yā fìta dàgà hankàlinsà; he kept his ~ hankàlinsà nà kwàncè. d. (admin. ~) shùgàbā n ⟨anni⟩: he is still ~ of the committee hař yànzu shī shùgàban kwàmìtîn nē; ~ of state shùgàban ƙasā; ~ of the house màigidā m; village ~ mài gàrī m, dagacī m ⟨ai⟩. e. (of grain, corn, millet) zangařnìyā f. 2. v a. (lead) shùgàbantā v2: he ~ed the company for 10 years yā shèkarà gōmà yanà shùgàbantař kamfànîn. b. (go in a direction): ~ for a place dōsa v2, nùfā v2: the fishermen ~ed for the river masùntā sun dòshi kògîn; let's ~ for home mù kàmà hanyà zuwà gidā; ~ so. off shāwō kâi: I ran after the goat and managed to ~ it off nā bi àkuyà dà gudù nā shāwō kàntà. 3. adj a. (main, top) bàbba adj ⟨mânyā⟩: ~ clerk bàbban àkàwu; ~ office bàbban kamfànī: their ~ office is in Kano bàbban kamfàninsù à Kanò yakè.

**headache** n cīwòn kâi m: I have a ~ inà cīwòn kâi = inà fāmā dà cīwòn kâi = cīwòn kâi yanà dāmŭnā.

**heading** n (title) kân bàyānì m, matāshìyā f.

**headlight** n fìtilầř mōtầ f, [F] idòn mōtầ m, [F] fâř m.

**headline** n kân làbāřì m ⟨kānun làbầřai⟩.

**headman** n hēlùmà m ⟨oCi⟩, hōmàn m, [F] kwàntìř-mētìř m.

**headmaster, headmistress** n, see principal.

**head-on** adj gàbā dà gàbā: they had a ~ collision sun yi karò gàbā dà gàbā.

**head-pad** n gammō m ⟨aye⟩.

**head-pan** n (for carrying loads) kwānòn sarkī m.

**headquarters** n (government, police) hêdkwatầ / shâlkwatầ f; (police) [F] kwàmsầřiyầ f.

**head-start** n rātā f.

**headstrong** adj (mài) taurin kâi m.

**head-tie** n, see kerchief.

**heal** v warkè v4, warkař (dà) v5: the wound ~ed within a week ràunîn yā warkè cikin mākò daya; this medicine will help ~ the wound wannàn māgànī zâi sâ ràunī yà warkè; if it is covered, it will ~ faster in an rufè shi, yâ fi warkèwā dà wuri; the doctor has ~ed many people bōkā yā warkař dà mutầnē dà dāmā.

**healer** n (tradit. doctor) bōkā n ⟨aye⟩.

**health** n lāfiyầ f: good ~ kòshin lāfiyầ; in poor ~ cikin rashìn lāfiyầ; he is not in good ~ bà shi dà kòshin lāfiyầ; exercise will make you ~ier mōtsà jìkī zâi kārầ makà kòshin lāfiyầ; ~ is wealth (fig.) lāfiyầ uwař jìkī.

**health inspector** n dùbà-gàri n.

**heap** 1. n tārì m, tulì m, tsibì m: there was a ~ of corn on the floor àkwai tārìn hatsī à dàbên; (of tied bundles of grain in field) būshiyā f, bāgā f; garbage, rubbish ~ jūjì m.
2. v (make a ~) tārà v1; ~ sth. on tulà wà v1, labtà wà v1: she ~ed the food on his plate tā tulà masà àbinci; ~ abuse on so. dankàrā wà zāgì.

**hear** v a. ji v0: I ~d all about it nā ji duk àbîn dà akè ciki; ~ news of so. ji làbāřìn w. = sàmi làbārìn w. b. (listen to) sàurārà v2 ⟨sàurārō, sàurầrē⟩: everyone came to ~ him speak kōwā yā zō sàurāronsà. c. (indirectly, from speculation or rumor) ji kishin-kishin, ji à

wai: we ~d it said that he'll be inaugurated next month mun ji kishin-kishin zā à nadà shi watầ mài zuwầ; I ~d that... nā ji à wai... = an cê wai....

**hearing** n a. jî m; he is hard of ~ shī kurma-kurma nè; lose one's ~ kurùmcē v4, zama kurmā. b. (in court) sàurāron kārā m: the ~ is set for June 1 an sâ rānař sàurāron kārầř daya gà watàn Yūnì.

**hearsay** n kishin-kishin m, kīlà-wàkālà f.

**heart** n a. zūcìyā f ⟨oCi⟩: her ~ was pounding from fear zūcìyařtà nà dầřdầř; learn by ~ haddàcē v4; set one's ~ on kwallàfà râi à kân; she is kind-~ed, good at ~ tanầ dà kiřkì = tanầ dà sôn mutầnē; he was broken-~ed yā yi kàrāyař zūcìyā; half-~edly dà zūcìyā biyu; whole-~edly dà zūcìyā daya; ~ palpitations (from illness) bàlli-bàlli m. b. (adverbial uses): in the ~ à zūci adv: they shot him in the ~ sun hàřbē shì à zūci. c. (fig. uses): the ~ of the matter is... ainihin gàskiyā ita cè...; ~ of the city marāyař gàrī; have a ~-to-~ talk yi zùbē-ban-kwaryātā m.

**heart attack** n cīwòn zūcìyā m.

**heartbeat** n bugùn zūcìyā m: ~ rate saurin bugùn zūcìyā.

**heartburn** n kwầřnàfī m; have ~ ji kwầřnàfī.

**heart-felt** adj: extend one's ~ thanks mīkầ matukầř gòdiyā.

**hearth** n murfù m ⟨a-u⟩.

**heartless** adj maràs tàusàyī m, maràs īmānì m.

**hearts** n (in cards) kubbì m, yātì m.

**heat** 1. n a. (of sun, fire) zāfī m: the ~ of the fire makes me feel sleepy zāfin wutā yā sâ ni jîn barcī; (extreme ~) kūnầ f: the ~ of the sun kūnầř rānā = zāfin rānā. b. (hot weather) zufầ/zuffầ m: I suffer from the ~ inà fāmā dà zufầ.
2. v dumầmā v1, zāfàfā v1.

**heater** n (electric) hītầ f.

**heathen** n ařnè m ⟨ařnā⟩.

**heating coil** n (for boiling water) hītầ f, [F] řēshô m.

**heaven** 1. n a. (sky) samà m ⟨Cai⟩: God created ~ and earth Allàh nē mahàlìccin sàmmai dà kàssai; (fig.) I'll move ~ and earth to do it samà dà kasa sù hàdu, sai nā yī shì. b. (Paradise) Àljannà f, (the Next World) Lāhiřầ f: his soul has gone to ~ rânsà yanà Àljannà.
2. excl: good ~s! sùbàhānàllāhì!

**heavy** *adj* a. (*in weight*) (mài) nauyī *m*: the box is ~ àkwàtìn nã dà nauyī; how ~ is it? mḕnē nḕ nauyinsà? it is too ~ for me to carry nauyinsà yā fi ƙarfīnā. b. (*in quantity*): a ~ debt ɗimbin bāshì; a ~ smoker mashàyin tābà; a ~ sleeper mài dōgon barcī; there was a ~ rain an shḗƙa ruwā.

**heavily** *adv*: rain ~ shḗƙa = mākà = gabcè ruwā; be ~ in debt ci bāshì har̃ iyā wuyà.

**Hebrew** *n* Yahūdancī *m*.

**hectare** *n* sābuwar̃ ēkà *f*, [F] ēkà *f*.

**heddle** *n* (*in weaving*) andīr̃ā *f* ⟨ai⟩, allēr̃ā *f*.

**hedge** *n* shingē *m* ⟨aye⟩.

**hedgehog** *n* būshiyā *f* ⟨oCi⟩.

**hedonism** *n* aƙīdar̃ jîn dāɗī *f*.

**heed** *v* bi *v0*: ~ advice bi shāwar̃ā.

**heel** *n* (*back of foot*) diddigḕ / digàdigī *m* ⟨a..ai⟩; (*sole of foot at the* ~) dundūnìyā *f* ⟨oCi⟩; (*of shoe*) dundūnìyar̃ tàƙàlmī *f*; high ~ shoes cōge *m*, tàƙàlmī mài dōguwar̃ dundūnìyā; (*fig.*) take to one's ~s shḗƙà dà gudù = yankè à gùje = ar̃cè dà gudù.

**heifer** *n* kàr̃sanā *f* ⟨u⟩.

**height** *n* a. tsawō *m*, (*esp. of people*) tsayì *m*: the ~ of the building is 60 meters tsawon ginìn mītà sìttin nḕ; a man of average ~ mùtûm mài matsàkàicin tsayì. b. (*acme, peak*) gàniyā *f*: at the ~ of his political power à cikin gàniyàr̃ mulkìnsà; the ~ of folly iyākar̃ wàutā.

**heighten** *v* (*increase*) ƙārā *v1*: what he said ~ed my fears màganàr̃sà tā ƙārā bā nì tsōrō.

**heir** *n* magàjī *m*: they divided the estate among the ~s sun rabà wà magàdan gādò; ~-apparent mài jiràn gādò.

**Hejira** *n* Hijir̃ā *f*.

**helicopter** *n* jirgin samà mài sàukar̃ ùngùlu *m*, helìkaftà *f*, [F] èlìkàptàr̃ *m*.

**hell** *n* (*the underworld*) Wuta *f*, Jahànnamà *f*; to ~ with you! to ~ with it! tir̃ dà kai! tir̃ dà wannàn!

**hello** *excl* (*on entering a place*) sàlāmù àlaikùn (*to which reply is*: yâwwā, àmin wà àlaikùn sàlām); (*used esp. by women*) gāfar̃ā dai! = àhuwonkù dai! say ~ to gai dà / gayar̃ (dà) *v5*: say ~ to Sule for me gàyar̃ minì dà Sulè.

**helmet** *n* hùlar̃ kwānō *f*.

**help** 1. *v* a. tàimakà *v2* ⟨tàimakō⟩: he ~ed me get a job yā tàimàkē nì nā sàmi aikì; (*lend a hand*) tayà *v1*, bā dà hannū: ~ me lift this box tàyā ni ɗagà àkwàtìn

nân; life means that everyone should ~ each other (*fig.*) zaman dūniyà cùɗan nì ìn cùɗē kà nē. b. (*in an emergency*) yi gudùmmawā *f*; ~! thief! kù tarè! ɓar̃āwò! c. (*support*): ~ so. out tàllafà *v2*, yi tallàfin *w*.: I ~ed put my younger brother through college nā yi tallàfin ƙanḕnā lōkàcin kàr̃àtunsà à jāmi'à. d. (*avoid, in neg. sent.*) can't ~ doing sth. kāsà *v1*: we couldn't ~ laughing mun kāsà haɗìyè ɗàriyā; I cannot ~ feeling that he is dishonest nā kāsà dainà jîn cêwā shī macùcī nḕ; I can't ~ worrying about her tīlàs nē ìn ɗàmu dà ita; it's all right, you couldn't ~ it shī kḕ nan tun dà àbîn yā fi ƙarfinkà; it can't be ~ed bâbù yâddà zā à yi; I won't go if I can ~ it bà zân tàfi ba sai tīlàs.

2. *n* a. tàimakō *m*: thank you for all your ~ nā gōdḕ mukù duk tàimakôn dà kukà yi; give ~ bā dà tàimakō; self-~ project aikìn tàimakon kâi dà kâi. b. (*aid in an emergency*) gudùmmawā *f*, (*esp. relief*) àgàjī *m*: get some ~! à yiwō àgàjī! = à yiwō gudùmmawā!

**helper** *n* matàimàkī *m*, matàyī *m*.

**helpful** *adj* (mài) tàimakō *m*, (mài) àmafànī *m*: this pamphlet is ~ ƙàsīdar̃ nân tanà dà tàimakō; you've been very ~ kā bā dà tàimakō ƙwar̃ai.

**helter-skelter** *adv* fata-fata *idph*: they were scattered ~ sun wàtsu fata-fata.

**hem** 1. *v* a. (*sew edge*) kalmàsà *v1*, (*by facing with piece of cloth*) lāfè *v4*. b. (*surround*) ritsà *v1*: they've ~med in the enemy an ritsà àbōkan gàba.

2. *n* kàlmasà *f*, cîn bàkī *m*, lāfì *m*.

**hemisphere** *n*: the southern ~ ɓangarèn kudancin dūniyà.

**hemorrhage** *n & v* zub dà jinī.

**hemorrhoids** *n* bāsùr̃ *m*, fìtar̃ bāyā *f*, ɗan kanōma *m*; (*euphem.*) zāfī *m*, (*in women*) angùryā *f*: I'm suffering from ~ inà fāmà dà zāfī.

**hemp** *n* a. ramà *f*: sacks are made of ~ anà bùhū dà ramà. b. (*cannabis*), see **marijuana**.

**hen** *n* kàzā *f* ⟨i⟩: keep ~s yi kīwòn kàjī; a laying ~ daƙwalwā *f* ⟨daƙwālē⟩.

**hence** 1. *conj* don hakà, sabõdà hakà; ~ they reimbursed us don hakà sun mayar̃ manà dà kuɗī.

2. *adv* a. (*of time*) nân dà (+ *expr. of time*): 10 weeks ~ nân dà mākò gōma. b. (*within a week*): 2 days ~ jībi *f*, 3 days ~ gàtà *f*, 4 days ~ città *f*.

**henceforth** *adv* nân gàba, dàgà yâu, dàgà

yànzu.

**henna** *n* lallè *m;* she is staining her hands with ~ tanà ƙunshì à hannu.

**hen-pecked** *adj:* he is a ~ husband shī mijìn ta-cè nē.

**hepatitis** *n* cīwòn shāwarà *m,* cīwòn hantà *m.*

**her, hers** *pro, see* Appendix A.

**herb(s)** *n* a. (*medicinal*) māgànin gar̃gājiyā *m;* (*from leaves*) ganyē *m* ⟨aye⟩, tsìre-tsìre *m;* (*from roots*) sauyà *f* ⟨oCi⟩. b. (*culinary*) kāyan miyà *m.*

**herbalist** *n* bōkā *m,* bōkanyà *f* ⟨aye⟩, magōrī *m.*

**herd** 1. *n* garkè *m* ⟨u-a⟩: a ~ of buffalo garkèn ɓakànē; leader of the ~ ùban garkè.
2. *v* yi kīwò *m;* ~ together tārà *v1:* he ~ed the cattle together yā tārà shānū wurī gùda.

**herder, herdsman** *n* makìyàyī *m.*

**here** *adv* a. (*nearby*) nân *adv:* I live ~ inà zàune à nân; he doesn't live far from ~ gidansà bâ nīsā dàgà nân; right ~ nân-nân; ~ and there (*not close together*) jẽfī-jēfī / jīfà-jīfà *adv:* in the countryside, hamlets are scattered ~ and there à jẽjī anà sāmùn 'yan ƙanānàn ƙauyukà jẽfī-jēfī. b. (*in pointing at sth., so.*) ~ X is, are gà X: ~'s the pencil you were looking for gà fensìr̃ ɗîn dà kakè nēmā. c. (*in handing sth. to so.*): ~ you are! ungo/ùngo! *excl:* ~ take it! ungō shì!

**hereafter¹** *adv* dàgà yànzu, nân gàba.

**hereafter²** *n:* the ~ lāhirà *f.*

**hereditary** *adj* na gādò *m:* a ~ disease cùtar̃ dà akè gādò.

**heredity** *n* gādòn hālī *m.*

**heresy** *n* zindīƙancì *m,* bìdi'à *f.*

**heretic** *n* zìndīƙì *m* ⟨ai⟩.

**hermit** *n* mài ƙîn dūniyà *n,* mài gudùn dūniyà *n;* (*Relig., ascetic*) sūfī *m* ⟨aye⟩.

**hernia** *n* (*scrotal*) gwaiwā *f,* ɗaɗàlī *m;* (*umbilical*) cībì *m.*

**hero** *n* a. jār̃ùmī *m* ⟨ai⟩. b. (*character in a narrative*) gōgà *m:* 'our ~' gōgan nākà.

**heroin** *n* hōdàr̃ ìbilîs, hōdàr̃ àljànū *f.*

**heron** *n* (*grey*) zalɓè *m.*

**herpes** *n* (*zoster*) būlālìyā *f.*

**herself** *pro, see* self, Appendix A.

**hesitate** *v:* don't ~ to ask for whatever you need kadà kà ƙi tàmbayàr̃ duk àbîn dà akè sô; I ~ to do such a thing inà jîn nauyin yîn hakà; he ~d at the door yā jā dà bāya à bàkin ƙōfà.

**hesitant** *adj:* she is ~ about speaking Hausa tanà jîn kunyà tà yi màganà dà Hausa.

**hesitation** *n:* he did it without a moment's ~ yā yī shì bâ wata-wata.

**hessian** *n* (*cloth*) àlgàr̃ār̃à *f.*

**hey** *excl* (*used esp. to children*) ~ you (*m/f/p*)! kai/kē/kū!

**hiccough, hiccup** *n* shaƙuwà *f:* have the ~s yi shaƙuwà; I can't stop ~ing bà zân iyà dainà shaƙuwà ba.

**hide¹** *n* (*rawhide*) ƙirgī *m* ⟨a-a⟩; (*prepared ~ of goat, sheep, used as prayer mat*) būzū *m* ⟨aye⟩; (*tanned*) fātà *f* ⟨fātū⟩: he deals in ~s and skins yanà cìnikin ƙirgī dà fātà; tan a ~ jēmà *v1* ⟨jīmà⟩ *f.*

**hide²** 1. *vt* a. (*conceal*) ɓōyè *v4:* we hid the medicine from the children so they wouldn't find it mun ɓōyè wà yârā māgànī kadà sù sàmē shì; I hid my grief nā ɓōyè baƙin cikīnà; a hiding place maɓōyà / maɓūyà *f;* ~-and-seek wàsan ɓōyō/ɓūyā *m.* b. (*conceal sth. held in the hand*) sunnè *v4:* they hid their swords under their robes sun sunnè takubbànsù à rīgunà. c. (*by covering*) rufè *v4:* the clouds hid the sun gìzàgìzai sun rufè rānā; she hid her face in her hands tā rufè fuskàr̃tà dà hannu. d. (*withhold*) tōgè *v4:* ~ the truth tōgè gàskiyā; ~ one's true feelings tōgè *v4,* yi tōgiyà *f,* yi kinibībī *m.*
2. *vi* a. ɓūya *v3a,* ɓōyè *v4:* he hid yā ɓūya = yā ɓōyè kânsà; ~ from so. ɓōyè wà: he hid from the police yā ɓōyè wà 'yan sàndā; he went into hiding yā shìga wani lungù.

**high** *adj* a. (*tall*) dōgō *adj* ⟨aye⟩, (mài) tsawō *m,* (mài) tsayī *m:* the building is 100 feet ~ tsawon ginìn yā kai ƙafà dàrī; how ~ is that mountain? mēnè nè tsawon dūtsèn can? a region with ~ mountains jihà mài dōgàyen tsaunukà; ~ in the sky can samà. b. (*var. adj + n uses*): the ~ jump gàsar̃ tsallè; ~ official bàbban ma'àikàcī; ~ price kuɗī màsu yawà; ~-ranking mài mar̃tabà *f;* at ~ speed dà gudùn gàske; a ~ wind iskà mài ƙarfī. c. (*intoxicated*): be ~ (*on liquor or drugs*) bùgu *v7.*

**highly** *adv* sòsai *adv:* he is ~ recommended an yàbē shì sòsai; he is ~ skilled gwànī nè sòsai.

**highness** *n:* His H. the Emir of... Mài Mar̃tabà Sarkin....

**high school** *n* makar̃antar̃ sakandàr̃è *f, see* school.

**highway** *n* bàbbar̃ hanyà *f,* hanyà fàffāɗā *f.*

**highway code** *n* dōkar̃ hanyà *f.*

**hijack** *v* yi fashìn jirgin samà.

**hijacker** *n* ɗan fashìn jirgin samà.

**hill** *n* tudù *m* ⟨Cai⟩, tsaunī *m* ⟨uka⟩.

**hilt** *n* (*of sword*) marik̃in tak̃ōbī *m.*

**hilly** *adj* hawā dà gàngarà: the road to Jos is very ~ à hanyàr̃ Jàs àkwai hawā dà gàngarà.

**him** *pro*, *see* Appendix A.

**himself** *pro*, *see* self, Appendix A.

**hinder** *v* hanà *v1*, tauyè *v4*: lack of funds has ~ed completion of the work rashìn kuɗī yā hanà kammàlâwar̃ aikìn; the delay ~ed our progress jìnkirìn yā tauyè cî-gàbanmù.

**hindquarters** *n* kutùr̃ī *m.*

**hint 1.** *v* nūnà *v1*: what are you ~ing at? mè kakè sô kà nūnà? (*through indirect means*) yi k̃ishin-k̃ishin *m*: it's been ~ed that he will come anà k̃ishin-k̃ishin zâi zō.
**2.** *n* a. (*sign*) àlāmà *f* ⟨u⟩: he left town without giving a ~ yā bar̃ gàrîn bà tàre dà ya nūnà àlāmà ba. b. (*reminder*) matāshìyā *f*: I gave him a ~ nā yi masà matāshìyā.

**hip(s)** *n* ɗuwàwū *m* ⟨ɗuwàiwai⟩, (*euphem.*) gìndī *m*: she has wide ~s tanà dà fāɗin ɗuwàwū; wriggle, sway one's ~s kaɗà gìndī = karyà gìndī.

**hip-joint** *n* kwàtangwalô *m.*

**hippopotamus** *n* dòrinā *f*: ~es like wallowing in the mud dòrinā nà sôn tùr̃buɗà cikin càɓi; pygmy ~ wàɗar̃ dòrinā *f.*

**hire** *v* a. (*lodging, equipment*) yi hayà *f*: we ~d a car to go to Sokoto mun yi hayar̃ mōtà zuwà Sakkwato. b. (*a psn.*) daukà *v2\**, jìngatà *v2*: we ~d a cook and a steward mun ɗauki kūkù dà bòyi.

**his** *pro*, *see* Appendix A.

**historian** *n* masànin tār̃īhì *m.*

**historic, historical** *adj* na tār̃īhì: it was an ~ occasion mùhimmìyar̃ rānar̃ tār̃īhì cē.

**history** *n* tār̃īhì *m*: he studied ~ at the university yā kar̃àntà tār̃īhì à jāmi'à.

**hit** *v* a. (*sth. or so.*) bùgā *v2* ⟨bugù⟩: the car ~ the bridge, a donkey mōtàr̃ tā bùgi gadàr̃, jākī. b. (*so.*) dòkā *v2* ⟨dūkà⟩, dàkā *v2*; (*esp. a child, lightly for punishment*) lallàsā *v1*; (*with fist*) nàusā *v2* ⟨naushì⟩; ~ so. hard k̃umè *v4*: the coconut fell down and ~ him hard on the head kwākwà tā fāɗō tā k̃umè shi à ka = kwākwà tā fāɗō tā k̃umè masà kâi.

**hitch¹** *n* tangar̃ɗà *f*: the work is proceeding without a ~ aikìn nà tàfiyà bâ tangar̃ɗà.

**hitch²** *v* haɗà *v1*: the plow has been ~ed to the bull an haɗà wà bìjimī gàr̃mā; (*by hooking around sth.*) sark̃àfā *v1*.

**hither** *adv*: ~ and thither nân dà cân; go ~ and thither yi kai-dà-kāwō *m*, yi zìr̃gà-zìr̃gā *f.*

**hitherto** *adv* (à) dā *adv*: ~ there wasn't any electricity in the village dā bābù làntar̃kì à k̃auyèn.

**hive** *n*, *see* beehive.

**hives** *n* k̃uràjē *p.*

**hoard** *v* 6ōyè *v4*: it is forbidden by law to ~ essential commodities dòkā tā hanà à 6ōyè kāyan màsàr̃ūfì.

**hoarse** *adj*: be(come) ~ dushè *v4*, shāk̃è *v4*: her voice was ~ from crying so much muryàr̃tà tā dushè sabòdà yawàn kūkā.

**hoax** *n* girì *m*: play a ~ on so. yi wà girì.

**hobble** *v* (*tie front legs together*) dabaibàyē *v1*, yi wà dàbaibàyī *m*: ~ the horse so it won't run away kà dabaibàyè dōkìn don kadà yà gudù; (*tie front legs to back*) tar̃nak̃ē *v4*, yi wà tàr̃nak̃ī *m.*

**hockey** *n* k̃wallon gōrà *m.*

**hoe 1.** *n* (*small, with triangular blade*) far̃tanyà / fatanyà *f* ⟨far̃ètanī, u⟩, hauyā *f* ⟨oCi⟩: their ~s are well-made fàr̃tànyunsù màsu amincì nē; in many areas ~s have given way to plows à wur̃àrē dà yawà gàr̃mar̃ shānū tā kashè wà far̃tanyà k̃àsuwā; (*large with short handle, for plowing*) gàr̃mā *f* ⟨gar̃èmanī⟩; (*for harvesting*) masassabī *m*, magirbī *m*; (*long handled, for sowing*) sùngumī *m* ⟨u-a⟩: take this ~ and make holes for planting ɗauki sùngumin nàn kà yi ta sārì.
**2.** *v* (*remove weeds*) yi nōmā *m*, nōmè *v4*; he has ~d the whole farm yā nōmè gōnā dukà.

**hog** *n* a. àladè *m*; *see* warthog. b. (*greedy psn.*) hàndàmau *n.*

**hold 1.** *v* a. rik̃è *v4*, kāmà *v1*: ~ it tightly rik̃ē shi dà k̃arfī = rìk̃ē shi kankan; ~ this for me for a moment kà ɗan rik̃è minì wannàn; be ~ing sth. nà rìk̃e dà: he is ~ing a spear, book yanà rìk̃e dà māshī, littàfī. b. (*var. v + adv/prep uses*): ~ back (*keep secret*) tōgè *v4*: they held back the truth sun tōgè gàskiyā; ~ back (*hinder*) tauyè *v4*; ~ sth. down dannè *v4*; ~ sth. up (*lift*) ɗagà *v1*. c. (*var. v + n uses*): ~ so.'s attention jāwō hankàlin w.: his speech failed to ~ their attention jàwābìnsà yā kāsà jāwō hankàlinsù; ~ one's breath (*from fear*) ɗaukè numfāshī; ~ one's nose (*from bad smell*) rik̃è hancì; ~ an enquiry yi bìncìkè *m*; ~ (a grudge)

against so. riƙè à zūci: he'll ~ it against
me as long as he lives zâi riƙè ni à zūci
haƙ àbàdā; ~ hands kāmā hannū; ~ out
one's hand to so. mīƙà wà hannū; ~ a
meeting gamà tàrō; ~ office (Pol.) riƙè
mùƙāmì. d. (of volume, quantity) ci v0,
ɗaukà v2*: how much does this box ~?
nawà nē àkwàtìn nân kè cî? the drum ~s
40 gallons of water dùƙô dîn kàn ci galàn
àƙbà'in na ruwā; the box will not ~ all
these things àkwàtìn bà zâi ɗauki duk
kāyan nàn ba. e. (stay) kāmà v1: this glue
doesn't ~ wannàn gâm dîn bā yà kāmàwā.
**2.** n: get a ~ of so. nèmā v2; have a ~
over so. mallàkē v4: his older brother has
a strong ~ over him wânsà yā mallàkē
shi.
**holder** n a. (handle) mariƙī m. b. (one who
possesses) mài àkwai n.
**hole** n rāmì m ⟨uka⟩: dig a 6 foot ~ haƙà
rāmì mài zurfin ƙafà shidà; a gaping
~ wafcēcèn rāmī; (with narrow opening)
kafā f ⟨oCi⟩; (small ~ made by piercing)
hūjì m, hūdà f: have a ~ in it hūjè v4; be
full of ~s huhhūjè v4; make a small ~ in
sth. hūdà v1; make a big ~ (e.g. in wall)
ɓusà v1; make ~s for planting yi sārì m.
**holiday** n (official) rānaƙ hūtū f, [F] ƙaffô
m: tomorrow is a ~ gòbe rānaƙ hūtū cè;
(secular school vacation) hūtū / dōgon
hūtū m, [F] bàkâns f: where will you
go for your ~? ìnā zā kù jē hūtū?
Muslim ~ Sallà f, Īdì m; Christmas ~
Sallàƙ Kiƙsìmatì = hūtun Kiƙsìmatì =
[F] Nòwâl m; (Koranic school ~) tàshē m.
**holiness** n tsarkī m.
**hollow 1.** n (of tree) kògon bishiyà m.
**2.** adj hōlòƙō m: the trunk of the baobab
tree is often ~ yawancī gàngaƙ kūkà
hōlòƙō cè.
**3.** v: ~ out rāràkē v4: he ~ed out the
cornstalk yā rāràkè karā.
**holy** adj (mài) tsarkī m, tsàrkàkakkē adj:
Mecca is a ~ city Makà tsàrkàkakken gàrì
nè; the ~ Koran Àlƙùƙ'ānì Mài Girmà
m, Àlƙùƙ'ānì Mài Tsarkī m; the ~ Bible
Littāfì Mài Tsarkī m; a ~ war jìhādì
m.
**homage** n fādancī m, girmàmâwā f.
**home** n a. gidā m ⟨aCe⟩: he is on his way ~
yanà kân hanyàƙsà ta zuwà gidā; there's
no one at ~ gidàn bâ kōwā; please make
yourself at ~ maƙàba, kà sàki jìkinkà.
b. (institution) gidā m ⟨aCe⟩: ~ for the
infirm gidan gàjìyàyyū; ~ for the insane
gidan mahàukàtā; ~ for the mentally dis-
turbed gidan màsu tàɓaɓɓen hankàlī.

**homeland** n ƙasā f.
**homesickness** n kēwaƙ gidā f.
**homework** n (school) aikìn gidā m.
**homicide** n kisàn kâi m.
**homosexual** n (male) ɗan daudù m,
ɗan lùwādì/lūɗù m; (male who affects
women's manners, speech) ɗan hàmsin m;
(female) 'yaƙ mādigō f.
**hone** v wāsà v1 ⟨washī⟩.
**honest** adj a. (psn.) mài gàskiyā n, mài
kiƙkì n, sālìhī m ⟨ai⟩, nagàri m,
tagàri f ⟨nagàrgàrū⟩: an ~ man mùtumìn
kiƙkì = nagàri = mùtûm mài gàskiyā;
you can trust her, she is ~ zā kì iyà
amìncêwā dà ita, tanà dà gàskiyā; that
is the ~ truth wannàn dà gàsken gàskiyā
nè; he looks ~ yanà dà àlāmaƙ gàskiyā;
he gave me an ~ answer yā bā nì amsà
ta gàskiyā. b. (legitimate) na hàlâl m.
**honestly 1.** adv dà gàske adv, à kân
gàskiyā; do you ~ believe that? kā yàrda
haƙ zūcìyaƙkà? he came by it ~ yā sàmē
shi ta hanyaƙ hàlâl.
**2.** excl tsàkānī dà Allàh!, wàllāhì
tàllāhì! that's all I know, ~! shî nè duk
àbîn dà na sanì, tsàkānī dà Allàh!
**honesty** n gàskiyā / gaskiyā f: I do not
doubt his ~ bā nà shakkàƙ cêwā shî mài
gàskiyā nè; I doubt his ~ bàn amìncē dà
shî ba; ~ is the best policy (fig.) gàskiyā
tā fi kwabô = gàskiyā tanà dà rānaƙtà.
**honey** n zumà f, ruwan zumà m.
**honeycomb** n sāƙaƙ zumà f.
**honk** v: ~ a horn matsà hâm m, [F] yi ōdà
f.
**honor 1.** n a. (respect for others) daƙajà
f, girmàmâwā f, maƙtabà f: a reception
was given in ~ of the President an yi
wà shùgaban ƙasā lìyāfàƙ girmàmâwā;
with ~ cikin girmà dà aƙzìkì; Your H.!
Yallàɓai! (for royalty) Mài Maƙtabà! b.
(human dignity, self-respect) mutuncì m,
iƙìlī m: lose one's ~ zub dà mutuncì.
**2.** v a. (pay respect to) girmàmā v1, bâ w.
girmà, daƙajàntā v1: you should ~ your
parents at all times wājìbī nè kà girmàmà
mahàifankà kōyàushè. b. (fulfill): ~ a
promise, pledge cikà àlkawàƙī.
**honorable** adj: achieve an ~ treaty cim mà
yaƙjējēnìyā cikin girmà dà aƙzìkì.
**honorary** adj na girmàmâwā f: an ~ degree
dìgìƙìn girmàmâwā.
**hood** n a. (of garment) ƙōƙuwà f. b. (of car)
bōnèt m, [F] kàpô m.
**hoodlum** n ɗan iskà m, ɗan dabà m,
àshàƙāƙì m ⟨ai⟩.
**hoodwink** v yi wà girì m.

hoof *n* kòfatò *m* ⟨ai⟩.

hook 1. *n* a. k̃ùgìyā *f* ⟨oCi⟩: hang sth. on a ~ rātàyā à k̃ùgìyā; ~ fastener (*for clothes*) maɓallī mài k̃ùgìyā. b. (*for securing door*) mak̃atā *f*.
2. *v*: become ~ed sark̃àfē *v4*: my gown got ~ed on a nail rìgātā tā sark̃àfē à k̃ūsā.

hooked *adj* a. (*having a hook*) (mài) k̃ùgìyā *f*, (*having a crook*) (mài) lànk̃wasā *f*: a ~ letter (*in Hausa alphabet*) bak̃ī mài lànk̃wasā.

hookworm *n* farar̃ tsūtsā *f*, tsūtsàr̃ cikì *f*.

hoop *n* (*rolled along as toy*) gar̃e *m*.

hoopoe *n* (*Senegal*) àlhudàhudà *f*.

hoot *v* yi kūkā *m*.

hop *v* tsallàkē *v4*, yi tsallē *m*: a hare ~ped across the field wani zōmō yā tsallàkē ta fīlī; she ~ped like a frog tā yi tsallen kwàdō.

hope 1. *n* a. fātā *m*, râi *m*; (*expectation*) sâ râi *m*: there is no ~ left that he is still alive yànzu bābù sauran sâ râi cêwā yanā dà rai; lose, give up ~ fid dà tsàmmànī, yankè k̃aunā, dànganà *v3*: we lost ~ that he would be found mun yankè k̃aunā à kân sāmùnsà; have false ~s yi tsàmmānìn banzā; lose ~ (*become doubtful*) kàrayà *v3*: I'm losing ~ of getting the job nā kàrayà gà sāmùn mùk̃āmìn.
b. (*strong desire, aim*) būrī / gūrì *m*: my ~ is to go to college būrīnā ìn shìga jāmi'à. c. (*support*) dōgarà *f*: he's our only ~ shī nè dògarar̃mù.
2. *v* yi fātā *m*, sâ râi: we ~ you and your family are well munà fātā kai dà ìyālìnkà duk kunā lāfiyā; we are hoping to see you munà fātan ganìnkà = munà sâ râi mù gan kà; I'm hoping to get a letter from home inà sâ rân sāmùn wàsīk̃à dàgà gidā; he ~s to go abroad yanā fātan zuwà k̃asāshen wàje; ~ for the best yi fātan àlhēr̃ì.

hopeful *adj*: be ~ yi fātā *m*, sâ râi.

hopeless *adj*: it's a ~ situation bâ àbîn dà zā à iyā yî = bābù sauran sâ rai; become ~ (*useless*) zama banzā.

horde *n*: ~s of people dìmbin mutànē = cìncìrindòn mutànē.

horizontal *adj* à kwànce *adv*: a ~ line lāyìn kwànce.

horn *n* a. (*of animal*) k̃āhō *m* ⟨k̃āhònī⟩. b. (*of car*) hàm *m*, [F] ōdà *f*: honk the ~ matsà hàm = būsà hàm. c. (*long metal ~ blown for chiefs*) kàk̃àkī *m*.

hornbill *n* (*var. types*) bur̃tū *m* ⟨aye⟩, cilàkōwà *f*.

hornet *n* rinā *f*, (*black type*) zìr̃nàk̃ō *m*.

horrible *adj* a. (*bad, severe*) *see* terrible. b. (*cruel*) mak̃ètàcī *adj*.

horrify *v* rāzànā *v1*, gìgìtā *v1*, firgìtā *v1*; a ~ying story làbār̃ì mài firgìtâwā; be horrified ràzanà *v3*, gìgītà *v3*, fìrgìtà *v3*: she was horrified to see it dà ganinsà tā gìgītà.

horror *n* tsōr̃ō *m*, r̃àzanā *f*.

horse *n* a. dōkì *m* ⟨dawākī, dàwākai⟩; (*colt*) dùk̃ushī *m* ⟨ai⟩; (*mare*) gōdìyā *f* ⟨oCi⟩; (*stallion*) ìngar̃mā *m* ⟨u⟩; ~ trappings kāyan dōkì; break in a ~ hòri dōkì. b. (*var. types*): (bay) bikilì *m*; (black) akawàl *m*; (light dun) gunyā *m*; (light grey) kìlî *m*; (piebald) dànda *m*; (dark grey roan) bìdi *m*; (strawberry roan) jūr̃û *m*.

horseback *adv* (à) kân dōkì; ~ riding kìlīsā *f*, hawan dōkì *m*.

horseman *n* mahàyin dōkì *m*, mài dōkì *m*.

horse-racing *n* sukùwā *f*.

horseradish tree *n* zōgalāgandì / zōgale *m*.

horseshoe *n* tàkàlmin dōkì *m*.

horticulture *n* ilìmin shùke-shùke *m*.

hose *n* (*rubber*) mēsà *f* ⟨oCi⟩, tìyō *m*, [F] tìyô *m*.

hospitable *adj* (mài) kar̃imcì *m*: they were very ~ to us sun nūnā manà kar̃imcì; be ~ to so. kàrɓi w. dà hannū bībiyu.

hospital *n* asìbitì *m* ⟨oCi⟩, [F] ōpìtâl *m*; ~ aide [F] lakwàtar̃ò *m*.

hospitality lìyāfà *f*.

host *n* (*one who provides lodging*) mài masaukī *m*; be a ~ to so. sàukā *v2*: Audu was my ~ Audù yā sàukē nì.

hostage *n*: take so. as ~ rìk̃è w. kāmuwā, yi gàrkuwā dà w.: he was held as a ~ for ransom an rìk̃è shi kāmuwar̃ kudī.

hostel *n* (*student quarters*) mazaunin dàlìbai *m*.

hostile *adj* a. (*not friendly*) (mài) fadà *f*: the area is surrounded by ~ tribes yankìn à zāgàye yakè dà mutànē màsu fadà; become ~ to so. yi wà zaman gàbā; exchange ~ words yi sā-ìn-sā *m*; a ~ look (*fig.*) kallon hadarìn kājì. b. (*opposed to*) (mài) àdāwà *f*: they are ~ to the government sunā àdāwà dà gwamnatì.

hostility *n* a. (*enmity*) gàbā *f*, àdāwà *f*: they live in mutual ~ sunā zaman gàbā dà jūnā. b. (*social, political disruption*) rìkicī *m*, jàyayyà *f*: hostilities broke out at the border an tā dà rìkicī à kân iyàk̃âr̃.

**hot** *adj* a. (*of temperature*) (màì) zāfī *m*, (màì) gùmī *m*, *see* heat: it's ~ today yâu anā zāfī = anā zufā = àkwai gùmī; ~ water ruwā màì zāfī = ruwan zāfī; his body is ~, he may have a temperature jìkinsà nā dà zāfī, k̃īlà yanā zàzzàɓī; burning ~ (màì) k̃ūnā *f*: this water is burning ~ ruwan nàn nā dà k̃ūnā; it is blazing ~ today yâu rānā tanā dà k̃ūnā = yâu anā kwādā rānā; red-~ zāfī jā-zir̃, màì tsananin zāfī: the metal is red-~ k̃arfèn yā yi zāfī jā-zir̃; (*fig.*) news ~ off the press làbār̃ì màì dùmi-dùminsà. b. (*of spices*) (màì) yājī *m*: they prefer ~ spicy food sun fi sôn àbinci màì yājī.

**hotel** *n* masaukī *m* ⟨ai⟩, hôtâl *m*.

**hotplate** *n* (*small burner*) r̃àshô *m*, [F] r̃êshô *m*.

**hot season** *n* bazarā *f*, *see* season.

**hot-tempered** *adj* (màì) zāfin zūcìyā *m*: she is really ~ tā fayè zāfin zūcìyā.

**hour** *n* sā'à *f* ⟨oCi⟩, awā *f* ⟨oCi⟩: there are 24 ~s in a day àkwai sā'à àshìr̃in dà huɗu cikin kwānā ɗaya; the bus leaves every ~ bâs tanā tāshì bāyan duk awā ɗaya; Kaduna is 2 ~s away from here nân dà Kàdūna awā biyu; within half an ~ nân dà rabìn awà; I waited for ~s and ~s nā daɗè inā ta jirà; working ~s lōkàcin aikì.

**house** *n* (*compound & buildings inside*) gidā *m* ⟨aCe⟩; (*flat roofed*) sōrō *m* ⟨aye⟩: go from ~ to ~ bi gidā-gidā; head of the ~ màigidā *m*.

**house arrest** *n* ɗaurìn tālàlā *m*.

**houseboy** *n* yāròn gidā *m*, bòyi *m* ⟨x²⟩, [F] bōyì *m*.

**household** *n* gidā *m*: members of the ~ mutànen gidā.

**housewife** *n* uwar̃gidā *f*.

**housework** *n* aikìn gidā *m*, hidimā *f* ⟨oCi⟩.

**housing** *n* (*in gen'l*) màhàllī / mùhàllī *m*: we must provide better ~ for our people tīlàs nē mù sāmar̃ wà jàma'à màhàllī àmìntaccè; (*partic. place to stay*) masaukī *m*, wurin kwānā *m*.

**hover** *v* yi shāwāgì *m*: ~ around the office yi shāwāgìn ôfìs; (*in order to prey*) yi jēwā *f*.

**how 1.** *interrog adv* a. (*in what way*) yàyà, k̃àk̃à: ~ does he know? yàyà ya sanì? ~ do you spell it? yàyà akè r̃ubùtā ta? ~ do you like this? yàyà ka ga wannàn? = mè ka

ganī gàme dà wannàn? b. (*by what means*) ta yàyà: ~ is it done? ta yàyà akàn yī shì? ~ can that be! inā/anā! *excl;* and ~! kàmar̃ mè! c. (*for quantity*): ~ many, much? nawà: ~ many days did you stay there? kwānā nawà ka yi à cân? ~ many are there? gùdā nawà kè àkwai? ~ much does this bottle hold? nawà kwalabar̃ nàn kè ɗaukà? I don't know ~ many people came bàn san kō mutànē nawà sukà zō ba; ~ much is it all together? nawà nē dukà? ~ often does he come? sàu nawà yakàn zō? no matter ~ much kō nawà: I'll buy it no matter ~ much it costs zân sàyā kō nawà kuɗinsà. d. (*in greetings*): ~ are you? ~ do you do? kanā lāfiyà? (*used in morning*) inā kwānā? = kā kwan lāfiyà? (*used in evening*) inā yinì/wunì?

**2.** *rel pro* yâddà/yândà/yaddà: he doesn't know ~ he can fix it bài san yâddà zâi iyà gyārā shi ba; this is ~ it happened gà yâddà àbîn ya fàru.

**3.** *adv* hakà *adv*: this is ~ it is done hakà akè yînsà; that is ~ it is hakà nè = hakà dai nè; no matter ~ kō ta yàyà / kō ta k̃àk̃à, ta kō yàyà / ta kō k̃àk̃à: you must finish it today, no matter ~ dōlè kù k̃āràsā shi yâu kō ta yàyà.

**however 1.** *adv* kō yàyà, duk yâddà: ~ hard he tries he will not finish kō yàyà ya yi k̃ōk̃arī bà zâi gamà ba; ~ you look at it, what she did was wrong duk yâddà kikà ɗaukē shì àbîn dà ta yi bà daidai ba nè; ~ many kō nawà: ~ many you see, you must count all of them kō nawà ka ganī, kà k̃irgà dukànsù.

**2.** *conj* (*nevertheless*) (àmmā) duk dà hakà: it is getting late, ~ we should make an effort to visit him before dark darē yā kusa àmmā duk dà hakà mù yi k̃ōk̃arī mù zìyàr̃cē shì kàfìn darē yà yi.

**howl** *v* yi kūkā *m* ⟨k̃ōke-k̃òke⟩; (*esp. of pain*) yi k̃ārā *f*; (*of wind*) yi k̃ūgì *m;* (*of a dust storm*) yi hōlōk̃ō *m*.

**hub** *n* a. (*of wheel*) hôb *m*. b. (*center*) cībìyā *f* ⟨oCi⟩: Kano is the ~ of Hausaland Kanō ita cè cībìyar̃ k̃asar̃ Hausa.

**hubbub** *n* hàyàniyā *f*, hàyà-hàyà *f*, hàdà-hadā *f*: what is all the ~ about? mè akè yi wà hàyàniyā? = hàyàniyar̃ mè akè yî? there's always a lot of ~ on market day ran k̃àsuwā àkwai hàdà-hadā dà yawà.

**hubcap** *n* murfin wīlì *m*, [F] ànjàlìbàr̃ *m*.

**huddle** *v* tākùrā *v1*, tàkurà *v3*: the cold made them ~ up together sanyī yā tākùrā su; they were sitting ~d together sunā zàune à tàkùre.

hug v a. (embrace) rùngumã v2, rungùmē v4: the mother ~ged her children uwâř tā rungùmè 'yā'yantà. b. (stay close to) bi v0: the road ~s the side of the mountain hanyà tā bi gēfèn tsaunĩ.

huge adj a. ƙātõ adj ⟨Ca⟩: a ~ man ƙātòn mùtûm = bìjimĩ; (often expr. by ideophonic adjs which go with specific nouns): a ~ sword shařtaɓēɓèn takõbĩ; a ~ horse firɗēɗèn dōkĩ; a ~ kolanut gōřò guřsumēmè; a ~ lake mākēkèn tafkĩ; a ~ tree gabjējìyař bishiyà; a ~ person jibgēgèn mùtûm = mùtûm ribɗēɗè. b. (formidable) gàgārùmī adj ⟨ai⟩: a ~ task, crowd gàgārùmin aikĩ, tàrō. c. (of quantity) mài ɗimbin yawã, mài tārìn yawã: a ~ amount of rice shìnkāfā mài ɗimbin yawã.

hum 1. v (a song) yi wāƙã f.
2. n: ~ of an engine amon injĩ; ~ of bees, wasps zĩzař zumã, zànzarō; ~ of mosquitos kūkan saurō.

human adj na ɗan Adàm: the ~ race jinsìn ɗan Adàm = 'yan Adàm; ~ nature hālin ɗan Adàm, mùtùntakã f; the accident was due to ~ error haɗařīn yā fàru sabõdà lâifin mùtûm.

human being n ɗan Adàm n, bìl Adamà n, mùtûm m ⟨mutànē⟩.

humane adj (mài) mutuncĩ m, (mài) īmānĩ m, (mài) kàmālã f; (compassionate) (mài) tàusàyĩ m, (mài) jîn ƙai m; be ~ to one's fellow beings tausàyā wà àl'ummã.

humanitarianism n tàusàyin ɗan Adàm m.

humanity n a. (mankind) 'yan Adàm m, bìl Adamà m. b. (being humane) kàmālã f, mutuncĩ m: he's a writer of great ~ mařùbùcī nè mài mutuncĩ ƙwařai.

humble adj (psn.) mài tàwāli'ũ m; be ~ nūnà tàwāli'ũ, ƙasƙantař dà ƙâi.

humid n (mài) laimã f: the weather in the south is very ~ yanàyin kudancin ƙasā nà dà laimã dà yawã.

humiliate v ci mutuncìn w., wulāƙàntā v1, wulāƙantař (dà) v5, ƙasƙàntā v1, zubař dà mutuncìn w.: they ~d me sun ci mutuncĩnā = sun wulāƙàntā ni = sun wulāƙantař dà nĩ; his behavior ~d his family dàbī'ařsà tā zubař dà mutuncìn dangìnsà; (esp. face-to-face) ci fuskàř w., cī wà fuskà.

humiliation n cîn mutuncĩ m, cîn fuskà m, wulāƙancĩ m, ƙankancĩ m.

humility n tàwāli'ũ m; show one's ~ nūnà tàwāli'ũ, ƙasƙantař dà ƙâi.

humor n ban dàriyā m, bařkwancĩ m: he has no sense of ~ bài iyà ban dàriyā ba.

humorous adj (mài) ban dàriyā: a ~ story làbārĩn ban dàriyā; (psn.) (mài) bařkwancĩ m, (mài) sôn wàsā m.

hump n (of animal) tōzō m ⟨aye⟩: the dromedary has one ~ rāƙumī nà dà tōzō ɗaya; (of psn.) dōrō m ⟨aye⟩.

hunch[1] v yi dōrō m.

hunch[2] n: have a ~ that kyautàtā zàtō cêwā: I have a ~ that he will change his mind and come nā kyautàtā zàtō cêwā zâi sākè shāwařã zâi kuma zō.

hunchback n (from spinal deformity) mài ƙùsumbī m.

hundred quant ɗarī f ⟨uka²⟩: two ~ ɗarī biyu = mētan; ~s of people ɗarurrukàn mutànē; in the year 1804 à cikin shēkarã ta alìf dà ɗarī takwàs dà huɗu.

hunger n yunwã f: I'm dying of ~ inà jîn yunwã kàmař tā kashè ni; ~ strike yājìn ƙîn cîn àbinci; ~ for power màitař īkõ.

hungry adj: be ~ ji yunwã f: I'm ~ inà jîn yunwã; we went ~ mun zaunà dà yunwã.

hunt, hunting 1. n fàrautã f.
2. v fàrautã v2, yi fàrautã f; ~ big game fàraùci mânyan nāmun dājĩ; ~ for sth. duddùɓā v1, nànnēmã v2.

hunter n mafàràucī m.

hunting grounds n mafarautã f.

hurdles n (Sport) gudùn tsallàkè shingē m.

hurray excl yâwwā! excl.

hurricane lamp n fìtilàř ƙwai f.

hurry 1. n saurī m, hanzarī m: I'm sorry I can't stay, I'm in a ~ ayyà, bà zân iyà zamā ba, inà saurī; I need it in a ~ dà hanzarī nakè bùkātàřsà; (esp. urgent) gaggāwā f: don't be in such a ~ so as to ruin your work kadà kà yi gaggāwā kà ɓātà aikìnkà.
2. v a. yi saurī m, yi hanzarī m, gaggàutā v1: let's ~ so we won't be late mù yi saurī kadà mù màkarà; ~ up! yi saurī mànà! b. (to a place) gařzàyā v1: ~ to the market before they close kì gařzàyā (zuwà) kàsuwā kàfìn à rufè. c. (usu. used as a command) yi maza adv: ~ up and go to the market yi maza kì tàfi kàsuwā.

hurt 1. vt a. (oneself) ji cīwò m: I ~ my hand nā ji cīwò à hannu; (so.) jī wà cīwò m, yi wà ràunī m: he ~ my finger yā jī minì cīwò à yàtsà; ~ so.'s feelings ɓātà wà râi, jī wà cīwò; ~ so. violently (cause bodily injury) yi wà àikà-aikà f. b. (do harm) yi wà lâifī m, yi wà lahànī m.

**2.** *vi (be painful)* yi zāfī *m,* yi r̃àdàdī *m:* the burn on my leg ~s k̃ūnan dà k̃è k̃afàtā nà̃ zāfī.

**husband** *n* mijì *m* ⟨mazā, mazàjē⟩; *(term of addr. ref. to one's own* ~) màigidā *m.*

**hush** *n (of a crowd)* tsit *idph:* a ~ came over the crowd tàron mutànē yā yi tsit.

**husk** *n (of maize)* ɓawō *m.*

**hut** *n* dākì *m* ⟨una⟩; entrance ~ *(to a Hausa compound)* zaurè *m* ⟨uka⟩; *(of grass, cornstalk)* bukkà *f* ⟨oCi⟩; *(round, with thatch)* kagò *m.*

**hyena** *n (spotted)* kūrā *f* ⟨aye⟩, *(male)* kūrè *m;* *(striped)* sìyākī *m* ⟨ai⟩; ~ cub kwīkwiyò *m.*

**hygiene** *n* kīwòn lāfiyà *m,* aikìn tsabtà *m.*

**hymn** *n* wāk̃àr̃ yàbō *f,* wàk̃ē *m* ⟨oCi⟩.

**hypertension** *n* hàuhawàr̃ jinī *f.*

**hyphen** *n* karan-dōrì *m,* gadà *f.*

**hypochondriac** *n* mài lambō *n.*

**hypocrisy** *n* munāfuncì *m,* fuskà biyu *m.*

**hypocrite** *n* munāfùkī *m* ⟨ai⟩, mài fuskà biyu *n.*

**hypothesize** *v* yi hàsàshē *m.*

**hyrax** *n* rēmā *f* ⟨aye⟩, agwadā *m* ⟨oCi⟩.

**hysterical** *adj (uncontrollable):* become ~ rūdè *v4,* haukàcē *v4.*

# I

I *pro, see* Appendix A.

ibis *n* (*white*) dûddufā̃ *f*, jinjimī *m*, (*Hadada or wood* ~) tsagagī *m*.

ice *n* (*naturally formed*) k̃ank̃arā *f*, (*from refrigerator*) āyàs *f*, [F] gàlâs *f*: this feels as cold as ~ sanyin wannàn kàmar̃ k̃ank̃arā.

icon *n* gumkī *m* ⟨a-a⟩.

Id *n* (*Muslim holiday*) (r̃anar̃) sallā̀ *f*, īdī *m*: Id-al-Kabir (*greater*) Bàbbar̃ Sallā̀ = Sallā̀ Layya; Id-al-Fitr (*lesser*) K̃àramar̃ Sallā̀ = Sallār̃ Azùmī; there are 2 major festivals, the greater ~ and the lesser ~ àkwai bìkin sallā̀ biyu, bàbba dà k̃àramī.

idea *n* a. (*plan*) shirī *m*, shāwar̃ā̀ *f*: that's a good ~ shāwar̃ā̀ cē mài kyâu; we rejected the ~ of doing it that way mun wātsar̃ dà shirìn yînsà hakà. b. (*esp. a clever one*) dàbār̃ā̀ *f* ⟨u⟩: you had a good ~ dàbar̃ā̀r̃kà tā yi kyâu; an ~ just came to me wata dàbār̃ā̀ tā fādō minì à rai. c. (*opinion, conviction*) r̃a'àyī *m*: he has his own ~s about this yanà dà nāsà r̃a'àyîn gàme dà wannàn. d. (*knowledge of sth.*) masanìyā *f*: have you any ~ where they could be? kō kanà dà masanìyar̃ indà sukè? I haven't the slightest ~ bàn sanī ba kō kàɗan.

ideal 1. *n* àk̃īdā *f*: the ~s of Islam, democracy àk̃īdar̃ Musuluncì, dìmòkùr̃àɗiyyà.
2. *adj*: be ~ dācè *v4*: the location is ~ wurī nḕ wândà ya dācè; it is an ~ job for him aikìn yā dācè dà shī sòsai.

idealistic *adj*: he is ~ yanà dà àk̃īdà kyàkkyāwā.

identical *adj*: this hat is ~ to that one hùlar̃ nàn irìnsù ɗaya dà waccàn.

identification *n* (*card*) kātìn shaidā̀ *m*, [F] kar̃tìɗàndîtê *f*: can you show me some ~? kanà dà kātìn shaidā̀? = kanà dà wata shaidā̀? my passport is my form of ~ kātìn shaidātā fàsfô.

identify *v* a. (*recognize*) gānè *v4*, shâidā *v1*: the witness failed to ~ the accused shaidār̃ yā kāsà gānè wândà akè tùhumā̀; she identified the purse as being Kande's tā shâidà jàkâr̃ ta Kànde cḕ. b. (*ascertain, confirm*) tabbatar̃ (dà)

*v5*: no one has identified the body yet bâ wândà ya tabbatar̃ dà gāwar̃ ba tùkùna.

ideology *n* manufā *f*, r̃a'àyī *m*: Communist ~ manufar̃ 'yan gur̃guzū.

ideophone *n* (*Gram.*) àmsà-kàma *m*, jēmāgè *m*.

idiocy *n* a. (*foolishness*) sākar̃cī *m*, wāwancī *m*. b. (*retardedness*) gaulancī *m*.

idiom *n* (*Gram.*) màganàr̃ fàsāhā̀ *f*: Hausa ~s are difficult to learn màgàngànun fàsāhàr̃ Hausa sunà dà wùyā kòyō.

idiot *n* a. (*fool*) sākar̃ai *n* ⟨sākàr̃kar̃ī⟩, wāwā *n* ⟨aye⟩, shāshāshā *n*, sūsùsū *n*. b. (*retarded psn.*) gaulā *n* ⟨aye⟩.

idle *adj* a. (*useless*) na banzā *f*: ~ talk màganàr̃ banzā; be ~ yi zaman banzā: the machines are lying ~ nā'ūr̃ōr̃în sunà zaman banzā. b. (*aimless, shiftless*): an ~ person ragō *m* ⟨aye⟩, sākar̃ai *n* ⟨sākàr̃kar̃ī⟩. c. (*unemployed*) mài zaman kashè-wàndō *m*.

idleness *n* ragwancī *m*, zaman banzā *m*, sākar̃cī *m*.

idly *adv* (*without aim, purpose*): he is sitting ~ yanà zàune ɓàkàtàn; he is staring ~ yanà kallō gàlau.

idol *n* gumkī *m* ⟨a-a⟩: in Islam, it is heresy to worship ~s bâutā wà gumàkā zindīk̃ancī nḕ à Musuluncì.

i.e. *abbr* wàtàu: he's a European, ~ a person from Europe bàtūr̃ḕ nḕ wàtàu mùtumìn Tūr̃ai.

if *conj* a. (*for real present condition*) in/ìdan/kàdan *conj*: ~ it rains, we won't go in anā̀ ruwā, bà zā mù tàfi ba; you will break it ~ you are not careful zā kì fasà shi ìdan bà kì yi hankàlī ba; ~ it costs too much, do not buy it ìdan yanā̀ dà tsàdā dà yawà kadà kà sàyā; ~ it is not so in bā̀ hakà ba. b. even ~ (*for fut. event*) kō dà: even ~ it rains, we must go kō dà anā̀ ruwā dōlè mù tàfi. c. (*for hypothetical past condition*) (in) dā X dā Y: ~ you had seen it, you would have cried in dā kin gan shì dā kin yi hawàyḕ; ~ you had told us, we would have helped you dā kun faɗà manà dā mun tàimàkē kù; ~ I had been you, I would not have gone dā nī nḕ kai, dā bàn tàfi ba; ~ only dā mā (+ *complet.*): ~ only I'd been able to go! dā mā nā tàfi! ~ only I hadn't done it! ai dā mā bàn yi hakà ba! = ìnā mā bàn yi hakà ba! d. even ~ (it were)... kō dā (+ *complet.*): even ~ it were to rain, we would go ko dā an yi ruwā sai mun tàfi; I wouldn't know him even ~ I saw him kō dā nā gan shì bà zân gānè shi

ba. e. as ~ sai kà cê, kàmař: he talks
as ~ he knows yanà màganà sai kà cê yā
sanÌ; it looks as ~ it is going to storm sai
kà cê zā à yi ruwā dà iskà; he treated
me as ~ he didn't know me yā dàukē nÌ
kàmař bài san nÌ ba. f. (whether) kō (+
complet. or fut.): he asked me ~ I knew
her yā tàmbàyē nÌ kō nā san tà; I would
like to know ~ he is going or not inà sô
Ìn san kō zâi jē kō bà zâi jē ba.

**Igbo** n a. (member of ethnic group)
ìnyāmuři m, ìnyāmuřā f ⟨ai⟩. b. (language) InyāmuřancÌ m.

**ignite** v kunnà v1, hasà v1.

**ignition** n (of car) makunnin mōtà m.

**ignoramus** n jāhìlÌ m ⟨ai⟩: he is a total
~ jāhìlÌ nè na innānàhā.

**ignorance** n a. (lack of knowledge, aware-
ness) rashìn sanÌ m, duhù m: it was simple ~ that made him do it rashìn sanÌ
nē ya sà shi aikàtà hakà; ~ of the
law is no excuse bâ ruwan shàři'à dà
rashìn sanÌ; nothing is worse than ~
(fig.) rashìn sanÌ yā fi darē duhù. b.
(lack of education) duhùn kâi m, jāhilcÌ
m: to praise oneself is sheer ~ yàbon kâi
jāhilcÌ.

**ignorant** adj (mài) duhùn kâi m, (pejor.)
jāhìlÌ m ⟨ai⟩; be ~ of jàhiltà v2: they
are ~ of our plans sun jàhìlci shirìnmù
= sunà cikin duhù gàme dà shirìnmù.

**ignore** v (pay no attention) ƙyālè v4, ràbu
dà v7: ~ him, he's just being rude ràbu
dà shÌ, rashìn kunyà kawài yakè yî;
(totally) yi banzā dà, yi bÌřis dà: they
completely ~d his cries for help sun yi
bÌřis dà Ìhùnsà na nēman gudùmmawā.

**ilk** n: and their ~ dà màkàmàntansù.

**ill** adj maràs lāfiyà f, (mài) cīwò m: I
am ~ inà cīwò = bâ ni dà lāfiyà
= inà rashìn lāfiyà; become ~ kàmu
dà rashìn lāfiyà; the food made us ~
àbincìn yā sà mu rashìn lāfiyà.

**ill-at-ease** adv dàri-dàri adv: I'm ~ with
him inà dàri-dàri dà shī.

**ill-bred** adj (psn.) sàkakkè adj.

**illegal** adj hàřàmtaccē adj, hàřām / hàřāmùn
m; make sth. ~ hanà v1: it is ~ to smoke
here an hanà shân tābà à nân; (esp. in
Islam) hařàmtà v1, hàřamtà v3: it is ~ to
accept bribes kàrɓař hancì yā hàřamtà.

**illegible** adj: the writing was faded and ~
řùbùtun yā ƙōƙè kuma bâ yà kàřàntuwā.

**illegitimate** adj (psn.) shēgè m ⟨u⟩: an ~
child cannot inherit anything shēgè bâ yà
gādòn kōmē.

**illiteracy** n rashìn iyà řùbùtū dà kàřàtū.

**illiterate** adj a. (unable to read or write,
lacking education) (mài) baƙin kâi n: he
is ~ bâ shi dà kàřàtū; they may be ~
but they know many things kō dà yakè sū
baƙin kâi nē àmmā sun san abūbuwà dà
yawà. b. (ignorant) (mài) duhùn kâi m,
(pejor.) jāhìlÌ m.

**illness** n a. (disease) cīwò m, cùtā f
⟨cÌwàce-cÌwàce⟩, màlātÌ m: he's come
down with some ~ wani cīwò yā kāmà
shi; a serious ~ mūgùn cīwò; suffer from
~ yi fāmā dà cīwò; cause ~ haddàsà
cùtā; recover from ~ warkè v4. b. (lack
of good health) rashìn lāfiyà m: he was
absent due to ~ bài zō ba sabòdà rashìn
lāfiyà.

**ill-tempered** adj tsagèrā n ⟨u⟩, (mài)
baƙin râi m.

**illuminate** v haskàkā v1: the room was
~d with candles an haskàkà dàkìn dà
kyandìř.

**illusion** n shūcìn gizo m: his ~s were shat-
tered shūcìn gizòn dà ya yi yā wařgàjē.

**illustrate** v a. (exemplify) misàltā v1: he
~d his point by telling a fable yā misàltà
manufařsà dà wata tàtsūnìyā. b. (draw)
zānà v1: the book is ~d with drawings and
photographs littāfÌ yanà dà zàne-zàne
dà hōtunà.

**illustration** n a. (example) mìsālÌ m ⟨ai⟩,
kwatancÌ m: let me give you an ~ of what
I mean bàri Ìn bā dà kwatancìn àbìn dà
nakè nufÌ. b. (drawing) zànē m ⟨e²⟩.

**illustrious** adj màshàhūřÌ adj ⟨ai⟩: he is
one of the country's most ~ writers yanà
daya dàgà cikin màshàhùřan mařubùtan
ƙasàř.

**image** n a. (model) sūřà f ⟨oCi⟩: he drew
an ~ of a horse yā zānà sūřař dōkÌ. b.
(likeness) kàmā m/f ⟨anni⟩: he is the ~ of
his father yā yi kàmā dà mahàifinsà.

**imaginary** adj: all the characters in this
book are purely ~ duk wadàndà sukà fito
cikin littāfìn nân bâ na gaskiyā ba
nè.

**imagine** 1. v: ~ that you are going to take
a trip to England kà kwatàntà à zūci zā
kà tàfi Ingìlà; I can ~ how badly he
feels nā san yàddà yakè jî; you're just
imagining things mafařkÌ kakè.
2. excl ~ that! tabdì! excl.

**imam** n (Relig.) lìmām / lìmāmÌ m ⟨ai⟩.

**imbecile** n, see idiot.

**imitate** v kwàikwayà v2 ⟨kwaikwayō⟩: a comedian really knows how to ~ other people dan kāmà yā iyà kwaikwayon mutànē
sòsai; he knows how to ~ bird calls yā

iyà kūkan tsuntsåyē.

**imitation** *n* a. kwaikwayō *m.* b. (*fake*) jàbu *m*: this is ~ leather wannàn jàbun fātā nē.

**immediate** *adj* dà gaggāwā, cikin hanzarī: I need an ~ reply inà bùkātảƙ amsā dà gaggāwā; in the ~ future nân dà ƙyas.

**immediately** *adv* a. (*ref. to present time*) yànzu-yànzu *adv*: come ~ kà zō yànzuyànzu. b. (*at that moment*) nan dà nan *adv*: then the car started ~ nan dà nan mōtā ta tāshì.

**immemorial** *adj*: from time ~ tun kàkan kằkànnī = tun fil àzal = tun shěkarā àƙu-àƙu.

**immense** *adj* a. (*of quantity*) (mài) ɗimbin yawā: an ~ quantity of food àbinci mài ɗimbin yawā; he is ~ly wealthy yanā dà ɗimbin dūkìyā. b. (*of size*) (*often expressed by ideophonic adjs which go with specific nouns, see* huge): an ~ lake, forest mākēkèn tafkì, kurmì; an ~ house gabjējèn gidā.

**immigrant** *n* bàƙō *m* ⟨i⟩; illegal ~ bàƙon hàurē.

**immigrate** *v*: many people want to ~ to this country mutànē dà dāmā sunā sô sù zaunā à ƙasař nàn.

**immigration** *n*: department of ~ ma'aikatař kwastàn.

**immodest** *adj* (mài) sôn à sanī *m*, (*shameless*) maràs kunyà *f*: she is ~ sôn à sanī gàrē tà = bā ta dà ta ido.

**immoral** *adj* (*Relig., of psn.*) fāsìƙī *m* ⟨u⟩; (*socially*) malàlàcī *m*, maràs dā'à *f*: an ~ book littāfì maràs dā'à; an ~ act aikìn māshā'à; be(come) ~ làlàcē *v4*: he is ~ yā làlàcē.

**immorality** *n* (*Relig.*) hařamcì *m*, fāsìƙancì *m*; (*social*) māshā'à *m*, làlātā *f*, rashìn dā'à *m.*

**immunization** *n* lambà *f* ⟨oCi⟩, [F] shàsshāwā *f*: ~s protect us from diseases lambà tanà tsarè mu dàgà cūtuttukā.

**impact** *n*: have an ~ on shāfà *v2*: the new ruling has no ~ on us sābuwař dòkā bà tà shāfē mù ba.

**impale** *v* tsīrè *v4.*

**impartial** *adj* maràs sôn kâi *m*: a judge must be ~ tīlàs àlƙālī yà nūnà rashìn sôn kâi.

**impartiality** *n* rashìn sôn kâi *m.*

**impassable** *adj*: the road is ~ hanyař bā tā bìyuwā; the river is ~ kògìn bā yà ƙètàruwā.

**impasse** *n*: be at an ~ shìga hālin ƙàƙànikà-yi.

**impatience** *n* rashìn hàƙurī *m*, gajen hàƙurī *m*, cî-dà-zūci *m.*

**impatient** *adj* a. (*easily irritated*) maràs hàƙurī *m*, (mài) gajen hàƙurī *m*: he is an ~ person bā shi dà hàƙurī = yanā dà gajen hàƙurī; I was ~ with him nā kāsà yîn hàƙurī dà shī. b. (*of waiting*) ƙàgarà *v3*: she was ~ to get a letter from home tā ƙàgarà tà sàmi wàsīƙà dàgà gidā.

**impeach** *v* tūɓè *v4*, tsīgè *v4*: the president was ~ed from office an tūɓè shùgàbān dàgà mùƙāmìnsà.

**imperative** *adj* wājìbī *m*, tīlàs *m*: it is ~ that he be seen by a doctor wājìbī nè likità yà dūbà shi.

**imperialism** *n* mulkìn màllakà *m.*

**impersonate** *v* yi sōjàn gōnā *m*: he ~d a policeman yā yi sōjàn gōnā ya cè shī ɗan sàndā nè.

**impersonator** *n* sōjàn gōnā *m.*

**impertinent** *adj* (mài) tsīwā *f*: be ~ to so. yi wà tsīwà.

**impetuous** *adj* (mài) gajen hàƙurī *m.*

**implement**[1] *v* aiwatař (dà) *v5*, zařtař (dà) *v5*: after much delay, the plan was finally ~ed bāyan jìnkirì mài yawà, an aiwatař dà shirìn.

**implement**[2] *n* (*tool*) kāyan aikì *m.*

**implicate** *v* (*fig.*) shāfà wà kāshin kàjī: he ~d 3 other people yā shāfà wà wasu mutànē ukù kāshin kàjī; (*an innocent psn.*) ɗafà wà lâifī *v1.*

**imply** *v* nūnà à fàkàice: what he said implied that he wanted to come zàncensà yā nūnà à fàkàice yanā sôn zuwà.

**impolite** *adj* maràs ladàbī *m.*

**impoliteness** *n* rashìn ladàbī *m*, maràs dā'à *f.*

**import** *v* shigō dà kāyā: they ~ goods from abroad sunā shigōwā dà kāyan wàje; they are not allowed to ~ food an hanà shigōwā dà àbinci; ~-export business jigilař kāyā dà ƙasàshen wàje; ~ed goods kāyan wàje.

**importance** *n* a. (*value*) muhimmancì *m*, àmfànī *m*: that is of no ~ to me wànnan bā shi dà wani muhimmancì à wurīnā. b. (*eminence*) girmā *m*: a person of great ~ mài girmā; self-~ girman kâi *m.*

**important** *adj* a. (*significant, valued*) mùhimmì *adj* ⟨ai⟩, (mài) muhimmancì *m*, bàbba *adj* ⟨mânyā⟩: it is an ~ matter mùhimmìyař màganà cē = màganà cē bàbba; the most ~ thing àbìn dà ya fi muhimmancì = àbù mafì muhimmancì; it is one of the most ~ crops yanā

immortal see everlasting

ɗaya dàgà cikin mùhìmman shŭke-shŭke.
b. (in rank) bàbba adj (mànyā): he is
an ~ government official shī bàbban
ma'àikàcin gwamnatì nē; the ~ people mânya-mânya p, gâggā p: all the ~
people attended mânya-mânya duk sukà
hàllàřà. c. (eminent) (mài) girmā m: he
thinks he is more ~ than me yanā nūnā
kàmař yā fī nì girmā. d. (impressive,
of things) gàgārùmī adj (ai): an ~ book,
discovery gàgārùmin littāfì, gàgàrùmař
gānŏwā; become ~ (developed) gàwuřtà
v3, kàsaità v3.

impose v a. (a tax) ɗōrā wà v1: during that
period, the government ~d a special tax on
everyone à lōkàcìn, gwamnatì tā ɗōrā
wà kōwā dà kōwā hàřàjì na mùsammàn; ~
economic sanctions sâ tàkunkùmin tattalin ařzìkī. b. (a law, curfew) kafà
v1: ~ a curfew because of the disturbances
kafà wata dòkař hanà fìtā sabŏdà
tāshìn hankàlī. c. (force) tīlàstā wà
v1, wahalař (dà) v5: he ~d the burden on
us yā tīlàstā manà ɗàwàiniyā. d. (an
opinion) cūsā v1: he is always imposing
his opinions on others kullum yanā cūsā
wà wasu řa'àyinsà.

imposing adj (impressive): ~ buildings
fankamā-fànkàmàn gìne-gìne; an ~ granary ribɗēɗèn rùmbū.

impossible adj: be ~ (cannot be done) yìwu
v7 (+ neg.): it will be ~ for us to finish by tomorrow bà zāi yìwu ba mù gamà
gòbe = maràs yìwuwā nè mù gamà gòbe;
it is ~ I give up àbin nàn bā yā yìwuwā
nā hàkurà; be ~ (be beyond so., out of
reach) fàskarà v3, bùwāyà v3: it was ~
to catch him kāmùnsà yā fàskarà; the
thief was ~ to catch ɓàrāwòn yā fàskarà
kàmuwā; be ~ for so. to gàgarà v2, bùwāyà
v2, fàskarà v2: it was ~ for the police to catch the thief ɓàrāwòn yā gàgàri
'yan sàndà kāmù; this work is ~ for me
to do aikìn nàn yā bùwàyē nì = aikìn
nàn yā fi kařfīnā; ~ work, an ~ child
gàgàrarren aikì, yārŏ.

impostor n sōjàn gōnā m.

impotent adj là'īfì m (ai); he is ~ (euphem.) bà namijì ba nè = bā yā ɗakà.

impoverish v talàutā v1; be ~ed talàucē
v4, tsiyàcē v4.

impractical adj: your plan is ~ shirìnkà
bà zāi yìwu ba.

impress v a. (make so. admire) buřgè v4:
his clothes really ~ed us kāyansà sun
buřgè mu sòsai. b. (please, interest)
kāyatař / kāwatař (dà) v5: his talk ~ed

the voters jàwābìnsà yā kāwatař dà màsu
jēfà kùři'à.

impression n a. (feeling of admiration)
bùřgā f: he's always trying to make an
~ yā cikà bùřga = yanā kòkarin buřgè
mutànē; make a good ~ kāyatař/kāwatař
(dà) v5. b. (mark) shaidà f (u), àlāmà f
(oCi): the wheels left deep ~s in the mud
tāyōyìn sun bař bàbbař àlāmà cikin
tàɓō.

impressive adj a. (causing admiration)
(mài) buřgèwā f, (mài) ban màmākì m:
his intelligence is ~ hàzākàřsà tanà bā
dà màmākì = hàzākàřsà abař màmākì
cē; his speech was very ~ jàwābìnsà
yā buřgè sòsai. b. (outstanding, significant) gàgārùmī adj (ai): ~ work
gàgārùmin aikì; an ~ person bìjimī adj
(ai): she is ~ bìjimā cē.

imprison v ɗaurè v4: he was ~ed for 5 years
an ɗaurè shi shèkarà bìyař.

imprisonment n ɗaurī m: he was sentenced to 3 years' ~ an hukùntā shi dà
ɗaurìn shèkarà ukù à gidan yārì; life
~ ɗaurìn rāi dà râi.

improper adj maràs kyâu m: it is ~ to
give or accept anything with your left hand
bà kyâu mīkà kō kàrɓař àbù dà hannun
hagu.

improve 1. vt a. (make better, of concrete
things) gyārā v1, ingàntā v1: they have
~d their house by putting a fence around
it sun gyārà gidansù dà sukà kēwàyē
shi; the government promised to ~ the
roads gwamnatì tā yi àlkawàřī zā à
ingàntà hanyōyì. b. (make better, of abstract things) kyautàtā v1: ~ one's behavior, the welfare of the people kyautàtā
hālī, ràyuwař àl'ummà.
2. vi a. (get, become better) ìngantà v3,
kyàutatà v3, kāru v7: the economy ~d
in 5 years tattalin ařzìkin kasà yā
ìngàntà cikin shèkarà bìyař; the students are improving all the time ɗàlìbai
sunà ta kàruwā kōyàushè; your Hausa
is steadily improving Hausařkà tanà kārà
ìngàntà. b. (recover from illness) ji
saukī m, sàmi saukī.

improvement n gyāruwā f, ìngantà f,
kāruwā f.

impudence n shègàntakà f, shakiyyancì
m.

impudent adj shàkiyyì m (ai).

impulsive adj (psn.) jigìlī m (ai).

impure adj maràs tsabtà f: this water is ~
ruwân nan bâ shi dà tsabtà; (of metals)
(mài) gamì m: this is an ~ metal kařfèn

nân yanā̀ dà gamī̀.

in 1. *prep* a. (*within, contained* ~) (à) cikin *prep*: ~ the box, car, water cikin àkwàtì, mōtā̀, ruwa; what is ~ it? mè kè̀ cikinsà? he did it ~ a hurry yā yī shi cikin hanzarī. b. (*at a place*) à *prep*: ~ school, the hospital à makar̃antā̀, asìbitì; he lives ~ Kano yanā̀ zàune à Kanò; I read it ~ the newspaper nā kar̃àntā shi à jar̃īdā̀; ~ place of à madàdin; ~ public à idòn jàma'ā̀. c. (*with expr. of time*): ~ the rainy season lōkàcin dāminā̀; ~ May cikin watàn Māyù; ~ 1989 à cikin shè̀kar̃à ta alìf dà dàrī tar̃à dà tàmā̀nin dà tar̃à. d. (*with time adv*) dà *prep*: ~ the morning, the afternoon dà sāfe, rāna; ~ an hour's time (*within*) nân dà awā̀ gùdā; ~ an hour's time (*after*) bāyan awā̀ gùdā. e. (*using*) dà *prep*, à *prep*: he is speaking ~ English yanā̀ màganā̀ dà Tūr̃ancī = yanā̀ màganà à Tūr̃ance; write sth. ~ pencil r̃ubū̀tā w.a. dà fensìr̃. f. (*with respect to*) wajen *prep*, gurin/gûn *prep*: he is an expert ~ carpentry gwànī nè̀ gûn aikìn sàssaƙā̀.
2. *adv* (*inside*) à ciki/cikī *adv*: here it is, put it ~ gā̀ shi nân kà sā shi ciki.

in- (*neg. prefix for n & adj, see* un-) a. (*for nouns, usu. use* rashìn + *n*): inequality rashìn dàidaitō. b. (*for attrib. adj, usu. use* maràs (+ *n*)): an insignificant matter màganā̀ maràs muhimmancī; an impatient person mùtûm maràs hàƙurī. c. (*for pred. adj, usu. use neg. sent. or neg. v*): he was incorrect bài yi daidai ba; it was inadequate bài ìsa ba; he was incapable of doing it yā kāsà yînsà = bài iyà yînsà ba.

inaccurate *adj*: his statement was ~ màganar̃̀sà bā̀ daidai ba cè; the estimate was ~ lìssāfìn bài yi daidai ba.

inadequate *adj*: ~ housing is a serious problem rashìn ìsasshen màhâllī gāgàrùmar̃ màtsalā̀ cē.

inadvertently *adv* bā̀ dà gàngan ba, bā̀ dà sanī̀ ba: I wronged him ~ nā sā̀ɓā̀ masà bā̀ dà sanīnā̀ ba.

inanimate *adj* maràs râi *m*.

inappropriate *adj*: be ~ to càncantà *v3*, kyàutu *v7* (+ *impers. 3rd pers. subj pro*): it would be ~ for us to persuade him bài kyàutu mù làllā̀shē shì ba; be ~ dācè *v4* (+ *neg.*): it was an ~ time lōkàcîn bài dācè ba; speak ~ly (*out of context*) cā̀ɓà màganā̀, yi ɗanyar̃ màganā̀.

inasmuch as *conj see* since.

inaugurate *v* naɗā̀ *v1*.

inauguration *n* naɗī *m*: ~ of the chief, district head naɗìn sarkī, hākìmī.

incantation *n* sùrƙullē *m*.

incense *n* tùr̃àren wutā *m*.

incentive *n*: he has no ~ to work bā yā̀ jîn ƙarfin yîn aikì.

incessantly *adv* bâ tsayā̀wā, bâ jî bâ ganì.

incest *n*: commit ~ yi jìmā'ī̀ dà ɗan'uwā kō 'yar̃'uwā.

inch *n* incì *m*: it is 12 ~es high tsawonsà incì shâ biyu.

incident *n* a. (*event*): the ~ happened long ago wannàn àbù yā àuku tun tùni. b. (*minor disturbance*) ɗan tāshìn hankàlī *m*, 'yar̃ fìtinā̀ *f*.

incidentally *adv* af *excl*: ~, before I forget... af, kàfìn ìn mântā...; ~, did you know that...? af, kō kā san...?

incinerator *n* bōlā̀ *f*.

incite *v* zugā̀ *v1*, hanzùgā *v1*, ingìzā *v1*: ~ a crowd to riot hanzùgà jàma'ā̀ tà yi tar̃zōmā̀.

incline *n* ɗan tudū *m*.

include *v* a. (*comprise*) haɗā̀ (har̃) dà *v1*: the organization ~s writers and teachers ƙungìyar̃ tā haɗā̀ dà mawàllàfā lìttàttàfai dà kuma màlàmai; your duties also ~ watering the garden ayyukànkà sun haɗā̀ har̃ dà ban ruwan làmbū. b. (*contain*) ƙunsā *v2*: the dictionary even ~s technical terms ƙāmùs dîn yā ƙunshi har̃ kè̀ɓàɓɓun kalmōmī. c. (*be part of*) sâ w. ciki: are we also ~d in the invitation? mū mā an sâ mu cikin waɗàndà akà gàyyatā̀?

including *prep* har̃ *prep*, duk dà *prep*: the stores are open ~ Sundays anā̀ būɗè kantunā̀ har̃ ran Lahàdì; the cost is ₦90 ~ tax kuɗinsà nair̃ā̀ càsà'in duk dà har̃ājì.

inclusive *adv* har̃ zuwā̀: from Tuesday to Friday ~ dàgà ran Tàlātā̀ har̃ zuwā̀ ran Jumma'ā̀.

incoherent *adj* a. (*lacking coherence*) bâ kâi bâ gìndī: what he said was ~ màganar̃̀sà bâ kâi bâ gìndī; speak ~ly (*unintelligibly*) yi gwàlàn-gwalan *idph*. b. be ~ (*mumble*) yi gùngùnī *m*; (*speak too fast*) yi bada-bada *idph*, yi bàdàm-badam *idph*.

income *n* (*wages, earnings*) àlbâshī *m*, kuɗī *m/p*: gross ~ àlbâshī gàbā ɗaya.

income tax *n* har̃ājì *m*.

incomparable *adj*: it is ~ yā wucè mìsālì = yā wucè kīmā̀ = bâ yā̀ mìsàltuwā.

incomplete *adj*: your report is ~ r̃àhōtònkà
bài cìka ba = r̃àhōtònkà bǎ cìkakkē ba
nề.

incomprehensible *adj*: his lecture was
quite ~ to us bà mù gānè laccàr̃sà ba
sam.

inconsiderate *adj*: he is an ~ person bâ shi
dà sanìn yā kàmātà = bā yǎ dà lìssāfì
= bâ shi dà kǎrā; he is very ~ of his wife
bài dǎmu dà màtar̃sà sôsai ba.

inconsistent *adj*: be ~ sā6ǎ dà *v1*, yi
sā6ānī dà: your story is ~ with his
làbār̃ìnkà yā sā6ǎ dà nāsà.

inconvenient *adj*: be ~ ƙuntàtā wà *v1*: it
is ~ for us to live far from work zamā nēsà
dàgà wurin aikì kàn ƙuntàtā manà.

incorrect *adj* bà daidai ba: his answers
are always ~ kōyaùshè amsōshinsà bà
daidai ba.

incorrigible *adj* kàngàrarrē *adj*, gàgàrarrē
*adj*.

increase 1. *n* ƙārì *m*: an ~ in wages, tax
ƙārìn àlbâshī, har̃ajì.
2. *vt* a. (*make more*) ƙārà *v1*: ~ taxes
ƙārà har̃ajì; fertilizer helps ~ crop production tākì nà dà àmfānī wajen ƙārà
yawàn àmfānin gōnā. b. (*make greater
in number, frequency*) yawàitā *v1*, dad̃à
*v1*: we want them to ~ the number
of programs about Hausa culture munà
sô à yawàitā shìrye-shìryen àl'àdun
Hàusàwā.
3. *vi* yàwaitā *v3*, ƙaru *v7*, dad̃u *v7*: crime
has ~d laifuffukà sun yàwaitā; my expenses have ~d this year kashè kud̃īnā
yā ƙàru bana; the herd of cattle has ~d
garkèn shānū yā dàd̃u.

increment *n* ƙārì *m*.

incubate *v* (*an egg*) yi kwâncī *m*.

incumbent *adj*: be ~ on wàjabà gà *v3*.

incur *v*: ~ a debt ci bāshì; ~ hardship ji
jìkī.

incurable *adj*: this disease is ~ wannàn cǔtā
bâ ta dà māgànī.

indebted *adj*: he is heavily ~ to the bank
bankìn yanà bînsà bāshì mài yawà.

indecent *adj*: ~ exposure wāwan zamā *m*,
bàd̃ō *m*, gàhō *m*; she was sitting ~ly tā
yi wāwan zamā = tā zaunà bàd̃ō; ~ talk
bātsa *f*, d̃anyen bàkī *m*.

indecisive *adj*: be ~ yi wàswāsì *m*, yi
ruwan idò *m*: don't be so ~, make up
your mind kà bar̃ wàswāsì, kà tsai
dà shāwar̃à; he's always so ~ yā fayè
wàswāsì = kullum yanà cikin wàswasì
= kullum yanà ruwan idò.

indeed 1. *adv* a. (*truly*) ƙwar̃ai *adv*, lallē
*adv*: it was ~ kind of you to come kun
kyâutā ƙwar̃ai dà kukà zō = lallē kun
kyâutā dà kukà zō.
2. *excl* habà! *excl*; (*in doubting sth.*): ~? is
that so? àshē? hakà nē? (*esp. confirming
sth.*) ƙwar̃ai dà gàske! = sôsai! = hakà
fa!

independence *n* a. (*Pol.*) mulkìn kâi *m*,
'yancìn kâi *m*: Nigeria achieved ~ in
1960 Nìjēr̃iyà tā sàmi 'yancìn kâi à
cikin shèkarà ta alìf dà d̃àrī tar̃à
dà sittin; celebrate I. Day yi shagàlin
bìkin mulkìn kâi. b. (*autonomy*) zaman
kâi *m*. c. (*financial*) cîn gashìn kâi *m*.

independent *adj* a. (*self-governing*) (mài)
mulkìn kâi; become ~ sàmi mulkìn kâi.
b. (*not dependent*) (mài) zaman kâi *m*:
he is an ~ person mùtumìn kânsà nē. c.
(*financially*) (mài) cîn gashìn kâi *m*:
everyone likes being ~ kōwā nà sôn cîn
gashìn kânsà.

index *n* a. (*of book*) fìhìr̃isà *f*. b. ~ finger
d̃an alì *m*.

indicate *v* nūnà *v1*: he ~d his disapproval yā
nūnà rashìn yàr̃dar̃sà; on the map, the
towns are ~d by dots an nūnà garūruwàn
dà dìge-dìge à tàswīr̃à.

indication *n* a. (*sign*) àlāmà *f* ⟨u⟩: by all
~s, he'll win the election gà dukàn àlāmū
zâi cînyè zā6ên. b. (*warning, omen*)
ishār̃à *f* ⟨oCi⟩: there were many ~s of
the danger àkwai ishār̃ōr̃ī dà yawà gàme
dà had̃àr̃ìn.

indicator *n* (*in car*), *see* turn signal.

indict *v* tùhumà *v2*: ~ so. for graft tùhùmi
w. dà hàndamà.

indifference *n* hālin kurùm *m*.

indigenous *adj* a. (*ref. to Hausa with no Fulani ancestry*) kàd̃ò *m*, kàd̃ùwā *f* ⟨hā6è⟩. b.
(*to a country*) na asalī *m*, na ƙasā *m*.

indigestion *n* 6àcìn cikì *m*: the food gave
me ~ àbincîn yā 6ātà minì cikì; he has
~ cikìnsà yā rūd̃è.

indignant *adj*: be ~ ji tàkâicī *m*: I was ~
at the humiliation they had to suffer nā ji
tàkâicin cîn mutuncìn dà akà yi musù.

indigo *n* (*plant or its dye*) bābà *m*; (*prepared
~*) shūnī *m*; deep ~ color shùnayyà *f*; (~
*residue*) dagwalò *m*.

indirect *adj* kàikàitaccē *adj*: an ~ question kàikàitacciyar̃ tàmbayà; be ~ (*in
speech, manner*) yi tàfiyàr̃ kūr̃ā, yi
6òye-6òye *m*: stop being so ~ and come
out with it kà dainà tàfiyàr̃ kūr̃ā kà
fitō fīlī; go by an ~ route yi kèwàyē
*m*: we came to Kano by an ~ route mun

yi kĕwàyē mun tahō Kanō.

**indirectly** adv (in concealed way) à fàkàice adv, à sằce adv: he asked me ~ yā tằmbàyē nì à fàkàice; he glanced at me ~ yā kàllē nì à sằce; refer, talk ~ about sth. yi habaicī m.

**indiscipline** n rashìn ɗā'ằ m: campaign against ~ yằƙī dà rashìn ɗā'ằ.

**indiscreet** adj (of a psn.) maràs àsīƙī m: he is very ~ bā yằ dà àsīƙī; an ~ remark ɗanyaƙ màganằ f.

**indoctrinate** v cūsằ wằ v1: they have ~d us with foreign ideas sun cūsằ manằ bằƙin àl'ằdū.

**indolence** n sôn jìkī m.

**indoors** adv (à) ciki/cikī adv: where are they? they are ~ inằ sukè? sunằ ciki; it is best to stay ~ during the heat of the day dà tsakaƙ rānā gwammằ à zaunằ ciki.

**indulge** v (spoil so.) shagwaɓaƙ (dà) v5.

**industrialized** adj: an ~ nation ƙasā mài aƙzìkin màsànằ'àntū.

**industry** n màsànằ'àntū p: the car, steel ~ màsànằ'àntun mōtōcī, ƙaràfā; the tourist ~ haƙkaƙ yàwòn shằƙàtâwā.

**inequality** n rashìn dàidaitō m, rashìn daidaicī m.

**inevitable** adj: it is ~ that... bâ makawā sai (+ complet.): the thing was ~ àbù nē bâ makawā sai an yī shì; death is ~ bâ makāwā sai mun mutù.

**inexperience** n ɗanyàntakằ f.

**inexperienced** adj ɗanyē adj ⟨u⟩: an ~ driver ɗanyen diƙēbằ.

**infamous** adj rìƙaƙƙē adj.

**infant** n jằrīrī m ⟨ai⟩, jinjìrī m ⟨jìrằjìrai⟩; (esp. one carried on one's back) gōyō m.

**infantry** n dằkằrai / dằkằrū p.

**infect** v hàƙbā v2: he ~ed her with syphilis yā hàƙbē tà dà tùnjērē; become ~ed kằmu dà cīwồ.

**infectious** adj (mài) kằmuwā f: an ~ disease cīwồ mài kằmuwā.

**infer** v ɗaukằ cêwā: I ~ that you are not going to do it nā ɗaukằ cêwā bà zā kà yī shì ba.

**inferior** adj a. (in rank, hierarchy) ƙasà dà: he's my ~ yanằ ƙasà dà nī = shī mabìyīnā nè. b. (in quality) maràs amincì m: an ~ bicycle kẽkè maràs amincì.

**infertile** adj (woman) jūyằ f ⟨oci⟩: she's ~ jūyằ cē = bā tà haihùwā.

**infest** v hàƙbā v2, hàƙbu v7: the beans are ~ed with insects wākè yā hàƙbu dà ƙwằrī.

**infidel** n (esp. non-believer in Islam) kāfìƙī m ⟨ai⟩: act like an ~ yi kāfiƙcì m.

**infinite** adj bìlā haddìn adv: there seem to be an ~ number of insects in the world gằ àlāmằ àkwai ƙwằrī bìlā haddìn à dūniyằ; the power of God is ~ ìkòn Allàh bā yằ ƙarēwā.

**infirm** adj kùmāmā adj ⟨u⟩: care for the aged and the ~ kùla dà tsồfàffī dà kùmằmū.

**infirmity** n kumāmancì m.

**inflame** v zugằ v1, tunzùrā v1: his eloquence ~d the crowd zàlāƙàƙsà tā tunzùrà tằrôn.

**inflammation** n kùmburī m: the ~ has subsided kùmburī yā sacè.

**inflammatory** adj: an ~ speech jàwābì mài zugà mutằnē.

**inflammed** adj (from infection): be ~ yi fushī m, (& swollen) kùmburà v3: her finger is ~ yātsằƙtà tā yi fushī.

**inflate** v a. (a balloon) hūrà v1, būsà v1; (a tire, ball) sâ wà iskằ, cikà dà iskằ. b. (Econ.): ~ prices ɗagà fàƙāshì.

**inflation** n (Econ.) hàuhawàƙ fàƙāshìn kāyā f.

**inflection** n (Gram.) kùmbùrau m.

**inflexible** adj (sth. or so.) maràs lànƙwàsuwā f: this stick is ~ sàndaƙ nàn bā tằ lànƙwàsuwā.

**influence** 1. n tāsīƙì m: Western ~s tāsīƙìn ƙasằshen Tūƙai; wield ~ over so. yi wà tāsīƙì; he has ~ with the committee yanằ dà hanyằ wajen kwàmìtî. 2. v yi wà tāsīƙì m; be ~d by sāmō tāsīƙì dàgà: my way of thinking has been ~d by him tùnằnīnā yā sāmō tāsīƙì dàgà gàrē shì.

**influenza** n muƙà f.

**inform** v sanaƙ (dà) v5, shâidā wà v1: he ~ed me of the committee's decision yā sanaƙ dà nī gàme dà shāwaƙàƙ kwàmìtîn; let everyone be ~ed that... anằ sanaƙ dà kōwā dà kōwā cêwā...; be ~ed of sàne dà: he has been ~ed of our arrival yanằ sàne dà isôwaƙmù.

**information** n a. (news) lằbārī m ⟨ai, u⟩: I don't have any ~ about her bâ ni dà lằbārìntà; disseminate ~ yàdà lằbằƙai; get, look for ~ nẽmi lằbāƙī; inquire somewhere for ~ tùntuɓà v2: I asked at the police station for ~ nā tùntùɓi ôfîshin 'yan sàndā; ministry of ~ ma'aikataƙ yàdà lằbằƙai. b. (knowledge of sth.) masaniyā f: they had no ~ at all about that bâ su dà wata masaniyā kân wànnan. c. (explanation) bàyānì m ⟨ai⟩; we need some ~ on how to use this munǎ bùkātàr̃ bàyānìn yǎddà akè àmfǎnī dà wannàn.

**informer** *n* ɗan r̃ahōtò *m*.

**infrequently** *adv* bǎ sàfài ba.

**infringe** *v*: ~ on so.'s rights kētà hakkìn w.

**infuriate** *v* tunzùrā *v1*; be(come) ~d hàr̃zuƙà *v3*, hàsalà *v3*.

**infusion** *n* (*of herbs for medicinal use*) tsimī *m*, jiƙò *m*.

**ingenious** *adj*: (mài) fàsāhǎ *f*: that's really ~ lallē an nūnā fàsāhǎ.

**ingrate** *n* bùtùlu *n* ⟨ai⟩.

**ingratitude** *n* butulcī *m*, rashìn gòdiyā *m*, bǎkin kǎzā *m*.

**ingredients** *n* (*of food*) kāyan miyǎ *m*.

**inhabit** *v*: the house is ~ed dà mutǎnē à gidân; the house is not ~ed gidân bâ kōwā; it is an ~ed area dà mutǎnē zàune à wurîn.

**inhabitant** *n* mazàunī *m*.

**inhale** *v* (*through nose*) shǎƙā *v2*: it is dangerous to ~ gasoline fumes shǎƙar̃ wārin fētùr̃ yanǎ dà haɗàr̃ī; ~ snuff shèƙi anwùr̃u; (*deeply through mouth*) zùƙā *v2*: he ~d the cigarette yā zùƙi tābǎ.

**inherently** *adv*: he is ~ that way an hàlìccē shì hakà = ɗabī'àr̃sà cē.

**inherit** *v* gǎdā *v2*, ci gādò *m*: he ~ed his father's wealth yā gǎji dūƙìyar̃ mahàifinsà; we ~ed his house mun ci gādòn gidansà; it is said that character is ~ed an cê wai anǎ gǎdar̃ hālī.

**inheritance** *n* gādò *m*.

**inhumanity** *n* rashìn tàusàyī *m*, rashìn īmānì *m*.

**initial**[1] *v* (*sign*) sâ hannū.

**initial**[2] *adj* (*first*) na farkō: the ~ decision shāwar̃ǎ ta farkō.

**initiate** *v* fārā *v1*.

**inject** *v* yi wà àllūr̃ǎ *f*, ɗūrà wà àllūr̃ǎ.

**injection** *n* àllūr̃ǎ *f* ⟨ai⟩: she went to the clinic to get an ~ tā jē asìbitì don à yi matà àllūr̃ǎ.

**injure** *v* jī wà cīwò *m*, jī wà ràunī *m*: the accident ~d 3 people haɗàr̃ī yā jī wà mùtûm ukù ràunī; ~ oneself jī wà kâi: the child ~d his shoulder yārò yā jī wà kânsà ràunī à kàfaɗà; (*on the head*) rōtsǎ wà *v1*, yi wà rōtsì *m*; be ~d ji ràunī *m*, yi ràunī *m*, ji cīwò *m*: those who were ~d have recovered waɗàndà sukà ji ràunī sun warkè; ~ so.'s reputation 6ātà wà sūnā.

**injury** *n* ràunī *m* ⟨uka⟩, cīwò *m* ⟨cīwàce-cīwàce⟩; (*on head*) rōtsì *m*: he has a head ~ an yi masà rōtsì.

**injustice** *n* rashìn ādalcì *m*: you do him an ~ in saying that bà kà yi masà ādalcì ba dà ka fàɗi hakà.

**ink** *n* (*esp. used in Koranic schools*) tàwadǎ *f*, (*manufactured*) inkì *m*.

**inkwell, inkpot** *n* (*made from a gourd*) kùr̃tun tàwadǎ *m*.

**in-law** *n* (*any parent or sibling of spouse*) sùrukī *m*, sùrukā *f* ⟨ai⟩; *see* brother-in-law, sister-in-law.

**inner** *adj* na ciki *adv*: the ~ room ɗākìn ciki; the ~most room ɗākì na can ciki = ɗākìn ƙuryà; the ~ city cikin gàrī.

**inner tube** *n* tîf *m*, [F] shambûr̃ *m*.

**innocence** *n* rashìn lâifī *m*; prove one's ~ wankè kâi.

**innocent** *adj* a. (*not guilty*) maràs lâifī *m*: he insisted that he was completely ~ yā dāgè kân bâ shi dà lâifī fes; prove oneself ~ wankè kâi. b. (*not involved*): the soldiers killed some ~ people sōjōjì sun kashè mutǎnē bāyin Allàh.

**innovation** *n* sābon àbù *m*; (*in Relig.*) bìdi'ǎ *f* ⟨oCi⟩.

**innuendo** *n* habaicī *m*, shǎgu6ē *m*, gūgàr̃ zānā *f*: did you hear what he said? that was an ~ about me kā ji àbîn dà ya fàɗā? yanǎ minì habaicī.

**innumerable** *adj*: the stars (in the sky) are ~ tàur̃àrī bà zā sù ƙìrgu ba.

**inoculate** *v* a. (*people*) yi wà lambǎ *f*, yi wà àllūr̃ǎ *f*, [F] yi wà shàsshāwā *f*: all the children must be ~d dōlè nē à yi wà yârā dukà lambǎ. b. (*animals*) yi wà hūjì *m*.

**inoculation** *n* lambǎ *f*, àllūr̃ǎ *f*, [F] shàsshāwā *f*, hūjì *m*.

**inquest** *n* bìncìken sanàdin mutuwǎ *m*.

**inquire** *v*: ~ about so. yi tàmbayàr̃ w.: he is inquiring about you yanǎ tàmbayàr̃kì; ~ about sth. lost or needed yi cigiyàr̃ w.a.: I'm inquiring about for a cook inà cigiyàr̃ kūkù; ~ at (*for information*) tùntu6ā *v2*: I ~d at the embassy for visa information nā tùntù6i òfîshin jakàdancì don bàyànìn bīzǎ; ~ into bincìkā *v1*, yi bincìkē *m*: the police are inquiring into the matter 'yan sàndā sunà bincìken màganàr̃.

**inquiry** *n* bincìkē *m*: an ~ into the disaster has been been ordered an sâ à yi bincìken bàlā'ìn.

**inquisitive** *adj* (mài) ganin ƙwaf *m*; being very ~ (mài) ƙwàƙwā *f*; an ~ look kallon ƙùrullǎ.

**insane** *adj* mahàukàcī *adj*, tà6a66ē *adj*: he's completely ~ shī mahàukàcī tubùr̃àn; become ~ yi hàukā *m*, haukàcē *v4*, tà6u *v7*: he has become ~ hankàlinsà yā tà6u = yā haukàcē.

insane asylum *n* gidan mahàukàtā *m*, gidan màsu tà6a66en hankàlī.

insanity *n* hàukā *m*, tà6uwař hankàlī *f*.

insect *n* ƙwàrō *m* ⟨i⟩.

insecticide *n* māganin ƙwàrī *m*, (*in powdered form*) hōdàř ƙwàrī *f*, [F] hūdîř *m*.

insert *v* a. (*between 2 things*) tsarmà *v1*: ~ a vowel between the consonants tsarmà wasàlī tsàkānin baƙàƙên. b. (*a thread, rope, wire through small opening*) zurà *v1*: here is how to ~ the drawstring (into the trousers) gà yàddà zā à zurà mazāgī. c. (*a tool into its handle*) kwa6à *v1*.

inside 1. *adv* ⟨à⟩ ciki/cikì *adv*: he looked, went ~ yā dūbà, shìga ciki; ~ and out cikì dà bâi; ~-out bài-bâi *adv*: wear a shirt ~-out sâ taguwā bài-bâi. 2. *prep* à cikin *prep*: it is ~ the box, the town yanà cikin àkwàtìn, gàrîn.

insight *n* bàsīřà *f*: this is an ~ful plan wannàn shirì nē mài bàsīřà; very ~ful mài kaifin bàsīřà.

insignia *n* lambà *f* ⟨oCi⟩; (*on sleeve of uniform*) igiyà *f* ⟨oCi⟩: the ~ of a sergeant igiyàř sājà.

insignificant *adj* (*unimportant*) maràs muhimmancì; (*of negligible importance, esp. a psn.*) ƙaramin àlhakì *m*: he is ~ in the organization shī ƙaramin àlhakì nē à ƙungìyā.

insincerity *n* (*flattery*) rōmon bakà *m*, dādin bàkī *m*; (*esp. to win favor*) fādancì *m*.

insinuation *n* habaicì *m*, gūgàř zānā *f*: he's making ~s against my father yanà yi wà mahàifīnā habaicì.

insipid *adj* (*tasteless*) salaf *idph*: the tea is ~ shāyìn nân salaf dà shī; (*having no salt or meat*) (mài) lāmī *m*.

insist *v* dàgè *v4*, kafè *v4*, nācè *v4*, yi tsàye *m*: I ~ on seeing the manager nā dàgè sai nā ga manajà.

insistent *adj* (mài) nācì *m*.

insistently *adv* bâ jî bâ ganì.

insolence *n* rashìn kunyà *m*, tsaurin idò *m*, (*esp. by women*) tsīwà *f*, (*esp. by men*) tsagērancì *m*: I was met with nothing but ~ bàn taràř dà kōmē ba sai rashìn kunyà; treat so. with ~ rainà / rēnà *v1* ⟨rainì / rēnì⟩.

insolent *adj* matsìwàcì *adj*, (mài) tsaurin idò *m*, tsagèrā *n* ⟨u⟩; (*assertive*) (mài) iyà yî *n*; she is really ~ tā cikà tsīwà = tsīwà gàrē tà.

insomnia *n* rashìn barcī *m*: suffer from ~ yi fāmā dà rashìn barcī.

inspect *v* dūbà *v1*: the president ~ed the troops shùgaban ƙasā yā dūbà sōjōjī.

inspector *n* a. (*of police*) sùfētò *m*; ~-general bàbban sùfētòn 'yan sàndā. b. (*of schools*) mài dūbà màkàřàntū *n*. c. sanitation, health ~ dūbà-gàri *n*, [F] ɗan lařwai *n*.

inspiration *n* ìlhāmà *f*, būdì *m*.

inspire *v* tsimà *v1*: his poetry ~d us wāƙōƙinsà sun tsimà mu.

install *v* a. (*connect equipment*) sâ *v1\**: ~ a phone sâ wayàř tàřhò; (~ *upright equipment*) girkà *v1*: ~ a refrigerator girkà fiřjì. b. (*an official*) nadà *v1*: the emir will be ~ed next month zā à nadà sarkī watà mài zuwà.

installation *n* (*of official*) nadì *m*.

instance *n* a. (*example*) mìsālì *m* ⟨ai⟩: I'll give you an ~ zân yi makà mìsālì; for ~ alàl mìsālì = mìsālìn; in the first ~ dà farkō dai.

instant 1. *adj* nan tàke: it was an ~ dismissal kòrā cè nan tàke. 2. *n*: come this very ~ zō nan dà nan = zō yànzu-yànzun nàn = zō dàzu-dàzun nàn.

instantly *adv* nan tàke: he died ~ yā ràsu nan tàke.

instead of *prep* ⟨à⟩ màimakon *prep*, à madàdin *prep*: take this ~ of that ɗauki wannàn màimakon wancàn; Musa came ~ of Audu Mūsā yā zō à madàdin Audù; ~ of doing as I told him, he did just the opposite màimakon yà yi àbîn dà na sâ shi, akàsinsà nē ya yi.

instinct *n* ìlhāmì *m*.

institute *n* tsàngayà *f* ⟨oCi⟩.

instruct *v* a. (*command*) ùmařtà *v2*: I have been ~ed to wait an ùmàřcē nì ìn dàkàtā. b. (*show*) gwadà wà *v1*, nūnà wà *v1*: we will ~ you how to use it zā mù gwadà mukù yàddà zā à yi àmfànī dà shī. c. (*teach*) kōyà wà *v1*.

instruction *n* a. (*order*) ùmàřnī / ùmùřnī *m*: he gave us explicit ~s yā bā mù ùmàřnī 6arō-6àrò; here are the doctor's ~s gà ùmàřnin likità. b. (*teaching*) kōyàřwā *f*, kàřātū *m*: the ~ of mathematics kōyàřwař ilìmin lìssāfì. c. (*of morals*) tàřbiyyà *f*.

instructor *n* màlàmì *m* ⟨ai⟩, mài kōyàřwā *n*.

instrument *n* (*apparatus*) nā'ūřā *f* ⟨oCi⟩; (*for work*) kāyan aikì *m/p*; musical

~s kāyan kiɗā̀ = kāyan kìɗe-kìɗe dà
bùshe-bùshe.

**insubordinate** *adj*: be ~ ƙi bî, kàngarà
*v3*.

**insubordination** *n* rashìn bìyayyā̀ *m*,
kàngarà *f*.

**insult** 1. *n* zāgì *m* ⟨e²⟩, cîn mutuncî *m*.
2. *v* a. zā̀gā *v2*, (*a lot*) dūrā̀ wà zāgì *m*.
b. (*humiliate*) yi wà rashìn kunyā̀, ci
mutuncìn w.; an ~ing remark màganā̀ mài
rashìn kunyā̀; ~ so.'s intelligence rainà
/ rēnā̀ *v1*.

**insurance** *n* ìnshōřā̀ *f*, [F] àssìřâns *f*:
national health ~ ìnshōřàř lāfiyā̀ ta
ƙasā̀; buy ~ yi ìnshōřā̀, [F] cìri
àssìřâns; ~ agent wàkīlìn kamfànin
ìnshōřā̀.

**insure** *v* (*sth.*) yi wà w.a. ìnshōřā̀ *f*.

**integrate** *v* haɗè *v4*, gamè *v4*: ~ blacks and
whites haɗè baƙář fātā̀ dà jař fātā̀.

**integration** *n* (*social, polical*): national ~
gamèwař ƙasā̀ *f*, haɗèwař jàma'ā̀ *f*; racial
~ haɗèwař al'ummōmī.

**integrity** *n* mutuncî *m*: protect one's ~
kārè mutuncî.

**intellectual** *n* mài ilìmī *n*: he was one
of the ~s of the period yanā̀ ɗaya dàgà
cikin màsu ilìmī à lōkàcîn.

**intelligence** *n* a. (*mental skill*) hàzāƙā̀ *f*,
azancī *m*; (*common sense*) hankàlī *m*,
tùnànī *m*, wā̀yō *m*, kân gadō *m*; (*insight-
fulness*) bàsīřā̀ *f*. b. (*Mil.*) aikìn lèƙen
àsīřī *m*: ~ agency sāshèn lèƙen àsīřī.

**intelligent** *adj* hāzìƙī *adj* ⟨ai⟩, (mài)
azancī *m*, (mài) ƙwalwā / ƙwaƙwalwā *f*,
(mài) kâi *m*, (mài) kân gadō *m*: he is ~
ɗan ƙwalwā nè = yanā̀ dà kâi.

**intelligibility** *n* fàhimtā̀ *f*: mutual ~
fàhimtàř jūnā.

**intelligible** *adj*: this paragraph is not ~
sakìn lāyìn nân bâ shi dà sauƙìn
gānèwā.

**intend** *v* nùfā̀ *v2* ⟨nufî⟩, yi niyyā̀ *f*: I ~ to
go inā̀ dà niyyàř tàfiyā̀; he ~ed to give
you this yā yi niyyàř bā kà wannàn; he
~ed to harm us yā nùfē mù dà mūgùn àbù
= yā yi niyyàř yi manà lahànī.

**intense** *adj*: the heat of the fire was ~ wutā̀
tā yi mūgùn zāfî; (*serious*) the game became more ~ wàsân yā yi tsāmārī.

**intent** *n* niyyā̀ *f* ⟨oCi⟩, nufî *m*: with ~ to
cause injury dà niyyàř yîn lahànī.

**intention** *n* a. niyyā̀ / àniyā̀ *f*, nufî *m*: he
came with the ~ of helping me yā zō dà
nufìn tàimakōnā̀; it was our ~ to come
and see you nufìnmù mù zō mù gaishē
kà; with good ~s dà kyàkkyāwař àniyā̀.

b. (*esp. evil*) àlƙàbā'ì *m*: he has evil ~s
yanā̀ dà mūgùn àlƙàbā'ì. c. (*aim, objective*) manufā *f*.

**intentionally** *adv* dà gàngan.

**inter** *v* sutùřtā *v1*.

**interact** *v* yi huldā̀ *f*, yi mà'ammalā̀ *f*: I
don't ~ with him bā nà huldā̀ dà shī.

**intercept** *v* taryè *v4*, ci tārè *m*: the message was ~ed before it could reach the general an taryè sāƙòn kàfìn yà kai wurin
janář.

**interest**[1] 1. *n* a. (*affair*) hařkā̀ *f* ⟨oCi⟩: economic ~s hařkōkin tattalin ařzìkī. b.
(*sth. one likes*) shà'awā̀ *f*: I have an ~
in music inā̀ shà'awàř wāƙā̀; a selfish ~
sôn zūcìyā *m*, sôn râi *m*: he has a selfish
~ in the matter yanā̀ dà sôn râi cikin
màganàř; in the public ~ don àmfànin
jàma'à̀; lose ~ in gùndurà *v2*: I lost ~
in the game wàsân yā gùndùrē nì = nā
dainà shà'awàř wàsân.
2. *v* bā dà shà'awā, ƙāyatař/ƙāwatař
(dà) *v5*: the matter ~ed me àl'amārìn yā
bā nì shà'awā̀; this poem ~s me more
wannàn wāƙā̀ tā fi ƙāyatař dà nī; be
~ed in yi shà'awàř w.a.: I'm ~ed in
weaving inā̀ shà'awàř sāƙā̀; I was not at
all ~ in it kō kàɗan bàn yi shà'awářsà
ba.

**interest**[2] *n* (*of loan*) (kuɗin) ruwā *m*: 10 per
cent ~ kuɗin ruwā na kashì gōmà dàgà
cikin ɗàrī; an ~-free loan bāshì maràs
ruwā.

**interesting** *adj* (mài) ban shà'awā *m*, mài
ƙāyatářwā / ƙāwatářwā: have a very ~
talk yi tàdī̀ mài ban shà'awā; the topic
is especially ~ to us zàncēn yanā̀ dà ban
shà'awā matuƙā gàrē mù; make sth. ~
ƙāyatař/ƙāwatař (dà) *v5*: he made his
lecture ~ yā ƙāyatař dà laccàřsà; his
lecture was very ~ jàwābìnsà yā ƙāyatař
sòsai.

**interfere** *v* tsōmà bàkī, kūtsà kâi, shìga
ciki, yi kàřàmbànī *m*, yi shisshigī *m*:
don't ~ in what does not concern you kadà
kà tsōmà bàkinkà indà bâ ruwankà.

**interference** *n* (*meddling*) kàřàmbànī *m*,
shisshigī *m*.

**interim** *adj* na wucìn gādì: an ~ government gwamnatìn wucìn gādì.

**interjection** *n* kalmàř mòtsin râi *f*.

**intermarriage** *n* àuràtayyā̀ *f*.

**intermediate** *adj* matsàkàicī *adj*, (*in size*)
màdàidàicī *adj*: an ~ Hausa course kwâs
ɗin Hausa matsàkàicī.

**intermission** *n* (*pause*) ɗan hūtū *m*.

internal *adj* na ciki: an ~ affair àl'amàřin cikin gidā.

international *adj* na dūniyà *f*: international ~ cìnìkayyàř ƙasàshen dūniyà; an ~ trade conference tàron 'yan kàsuwā na dūniyà; ~ trade is beneficial sàyē dà sayářwař ƙasàshen dūniyà nà dà àmfànī; ~ relations huldōdin ƙasàshen dūniyà.

interpret *v* a. (*clarify*) bayyànā *v1*. b. (*translate*) fassàřā *v1*, yi tāfintà *f*.

interpretation *n* a. (*meaning*) mà'ànā *f*. b. (*translation*) fassařā *f*.

interpreter *n* tāfintà *n* ⟨oCi⟩, [F] àntàmfîřētî *n*: who will be my ~? wà zâi yi minì aikìn tāfintà?

interrogate *v* tùhumtà *v2*: the police ~d him closely 'yan sàndā sun tùhùmcē shì sòsai.

interrogation *n* tùhumà *f*.

interrupt *v* a. (*so.'s speech*) katsè wà màganà, tūrà màganà (ciki): I was speaking when Audu ~ed me inà màganà sai Audu yā katsè minì màganà = ...sai Audù yā tūrà màganàtā ciki. b. (*so.'s action*) katsè wà hanzarī.

interruption *n* a. (*esp. in speaking*) katsèwā *f*. b. (*pause*) fāshì *m*: without ~ bà tàre dà fāshì ba = bâ fāshì.

intersection *n* mahaɗà *f*.

intersperse *v* tsarmà *v1*: ~ black with white tsarmà baƙī dà farī; hair ~d with gray gāshì mài tsarmìn furfurā.

interval *n*: at 10 minute ~s kōwànè mintì gōmà-gōmà.

intervene *v* sâ bàkī: I don't want to ~ in their quarrel bā nà sô ìn sâ bàkī cikin gařdamařsù.

interview 1. *v* gānà dà *v1*: he has been ~ed on radio 'yan jàřīdù sun gānà dà shī ta řēdiyò.
2. *n* (*by media*) gānàwā *f*, hīřa *f*; (*for job placement*) intàbìyû *f*.

intestine(s) *n* hanjī *m*: large ~ uwař hanjī *m*, màkyarwayà *f*; small ~ ƙàramin hanjī.

intimate *adj* (*close*): an ~ friend àmīnì *m*, àmīnìyā *f* ⟨ai⟩; they are ~ friends sun shàƙu dà jūnā sòsai.

intimidation *n* kùřařī *m*, kūrī *m*, bùřgā *f*.

intimidate *v* tsōràtà *v1*, yi wà kūrī *m*, ci w. dà bùřgā: he was trying to ~ me yā cī nì dà bùřgā; (*esp. to children to make them quiet*) yi wà dòdòřidò *m*.

into *prep* a. (à) cikin *prep*: peek ~ a room lēƙà cikin dākì. b. (*for use as a particle with verbs, see partic. verb entries*): divide ~ rabà *v1*; turn ~ mai dà *v5*; fall, jump ~ fāɗà *v1*; go ~ shìga *v3*; run ~ (*collide with*) yi karō dà.

intolerance *n* rashìn girmàmàwā *m*.

intonation *n* ràusayàř sautì *f*.

intoxicate *v* sâ w. yà bùgu; be ~d bùgu *v7*, shàwu *v7*.

intoxication *n* bùguwā *f*, māyē *m*: alcohol causes ~ giyà nà sâ māyē.

intransigent *adj* (*psn.*) tsagèrā *n* ⟨u⟩: the strikers were ~ màsu yājìn aikì tsàgèrū nè.

intransitive *adj*: an ~ verb àikàtau ƙ̀ī-kàrɓau *m*.

intrigue[1] *n* a. (*bad, evil*) mākiřcì *m*, jàmhūřù *m*: political, palace ~ mākiřcìn sìyāsà, fādà. b. (*mild plot, esp. done by women to men*) kissà *f*: they are planning some ~ against their husband sunà wà mijìnsù kissà.

intrigue[2] *v* (*fascinate*) ƙāyatař / ƙāwatař (dà) *v5*: folktales ~ most children tātsūniyōyī nà ƙāyatař dà mafì yawàn yârā.

introduce *v* a. (*people*) haɗà w. dà w., sàdà w. dà w.: he ~d me to Bello yā haɗà ni dà Bellò; I would like to ~ my wife tô, gà mài dākìnā, Mālàmā X; (*formally*) gabātař (dà) *v5*. b. (*put forth, e.g. a topic*) gabātař (dà) *v5*. c. (*initiate sth.*) tsìrā *v2*, fārà àmfànī dà: he ~d a new system of writing Hausa yā tsìri sābon tsārìn řubùtà Hausa.

introduction *n* gabātářwā *f*.

intrusiveness *n* kàřàmbànī *m*, katsalandàn *m*, shisshigī *m*.

intuition *n* ìlhāmì *m*; my ~ tells me that... jìkīnā yā bā nì....

invade *n* màmayà *v2*, kai wà harì.

invalid[1] *n* (*handicapped*) nàƙàsasshē *m*.

invalid[2] *adj* maràs ƙarfī *m*: that's an ~ excuse hujjà bâ ta dà ƙarfī.

invaluable *adj*: his help has been ~ tàimakonsà yā wucè mìsālì.

invent *v* ƙāgà *v1*: ~ a story ƙāgà làbārì; ~ a lie zūƙà ƙaryā, haifà ƙaryā; (*esp. things*) ƙirƙìrā *v1*: the telephone was ~ed in America an ƙirƙìrà tàřhô à Amìřkà.

invention *n* ƙirƙìrā *f*, sābuwař dàbāřà *f*.

inventor *n* mài ƙirƙìrōwā *n*.

inventory *n*: take ~ lāsàftà kāyā, ƙidàyà kāyā.

invert *v* kifà *v1*: she ~ed the calabash and sat on top of it tā kifà ƙwaryā tā zaunà à kâi.

invest *v* zubà jàřì, sakà jàřì: I ~ed some money in his business nā zubà jàřì cikin haɽkàɽ cìnikinsà.

investigate v a. yi bìncìkē m, bincìkē v4.
b. (trace origin of sth.) bi diddigī m, bi
sanàdī m: ~ the source of the rumors bi
sanàdin jìta-jìta.

investigation n bìncìkē m, bìn diddigī m,
bahàsī m: you should make a thorough ~
kà yi zùzzurfan bìncìkē = kà bincikō
kàmā dà kàmā; conduct an ~ gudānaɽ dà
bìncìkē.

invisible adj: it is ~ bā yà gànuwā; become
~ (esp. through magic) yi lāyàɽ zānā.

invitation n gàyyā f ⟨gàyyàce-gàyyàce⟩,
takàɽdaɽ gàyyatà f: send out ~s aikà dà
tàkàɽdun gàyyatà.

invite v gàyyatà v2, kirā v0: ~ so. to
a party gàyyaci w. lìyāfà = kirā w.
lìyāfà.

invocation n (Relig.) àddu'à f ⟨oCi⟩.

involve v shàfā v2: we are all ~d in this
màganàɽ tā shàfē mù dukà.

iodine n àidîn m, [F] tantalajī m.

irascible adj (mài) saurin fushī m,
fùsàtaccē adj.

iris n (of eye) ƙwàyaɽ idò f.

iron[1] n (metal) baƙin ƙarfè m; ~ ore tamā
f; corrugated ~ (building material) kwānò
m.

iron[2] 1. n (for ironing) dūtsèn gūgā m, āyàn
m, [F] fêɽ m.
2. v gōgè v4, yi gūgā m, [F] yi pāshē m:
~ these pants for me gògē minì wàndon
nàn.

ironic(al) adj: say sth. ~ to so. yi wà gàtsē
m, yi wà baƙaɽ màganà f; isn't it ~ that
man invents things to destroy himself àbin
màmākì nē mùtûm yà ƙirƙìri àbîn dà zâi
halàkā shi.

irony m gàtsē m, baƙaɽ màganà f; (mockery) ba'à f.

irrational adj: he has become ~
hankàlinsà yā gushè.

irrelevant adj: what he says is ~ to
our discussion màganàɽsà bà tà dācè dà
zàncenmù ba.

irresponsible adj: he is ~ bài san cīwòn
kânsà ba.

irrigate v yi ban ruwā m.

irritate v a. (annoy) bā w. haushī m, ji
haushī m: he ~s me yā bā nì haushī =
nā ji haushinsà; we were ~d by what
he said mun ji haushin màganàɽsà. b.
(physically bother): this sweater ~s me
inà jîn ƙàiƙàyin rìgaɽ sanyin nân; the
smoke ~s my eyes hayāƙī yā sâ idònā
ruwā.

irritation n (annoyance) haushī m,
tàkàicī m.

Islam n Musuluncì m; according to ~ à
Mùsùlùnce: that is a sin according to ~
zunùbī nè à Musuluncì = à Mùsùlùnce;
they believe in ~ sū Mùsùlmī nè.

Islamic adj na Musuluncì m.

island n tsìbirì m ⟨ai⟩.

isolate v wārè v4, kēɓè v4; (oneself) kaɗàità
kâi v1.

isolation n kaɗaicì m; they live in ~ sunà
zàune à kàɗàice.

issue 1. v a. (an order) kafà v1; ~ a direc-
tive bā dà ùmàɽnī. b. (currency) fitō dà
v6: new currency has been ~d an fitō dà
sàbàbbin kuɗī.
2. n (matter) màganà f ⟨u²⟩, sha'ànī m
⟨oCi⟩: poverty is a complex ~ talaucì
rìkìtacciyaɽ màganà cē; the thing at ~
àbîn dà akè màganà à kâi.

it pro, see Appendix A.

italics n ɽùbùtun tàfiyàɽ tsūtsà m.

itch n ƙàiƙàyī m: feel an ~ ji ƙàiƙàyī;
make so. ~ yi wà ƙàiƙàyī; scratch an ~
sōsà v1 ⟨sūsà⟩ f; this cloth is ~y yādìn
nân nà dà ƙàiƙàyī.

itself pro, kânsà m, kàntà f see Appendix
A: the machine works by ~ injì dà
kânsà yakè aikì.

ivory n haurèn/haƙòrin gīwā m.

# J

jab v zùngurà v2: he kept ~bing me with his elbow yā yi ta zùngurātā dà gwīwàr̃ hannu.

jabber v yi sùr̃ūtù m: ~ about nothing yi sùr̃ūtùn banzā.

jack[1] 1. n (of car) jâk m, [F] kìr̃îk m.
2. v ɗagà dà jâk v1: ~ up the car to remove the tire ɗagà mōtā̀ dà jâk ɗòmin cirè tāyā̀.

jack[2] n (in cards) ɗan biyu m.

jackal n dilā m ⟨oCi⟩.

jacket n kwât f, jā̂kêt / jākèt m, [F] bês f.

jack-of-all-trades n gā̀tarin gwār̃i m, ɗan ƙwālè-ƙwālè m.

jail 1. n kūr̃kukù m, gidan yārī m, gidan mazā m, [F] kasò m; he was sentenced to 90 days in ~ an yankè masà hukuncìn ɗaurìn kwānā càsà'in.
2. v ɗaurè v4: he was ~ed for 90 days an ɗaurè shi kwānā càsà'in.

jailer n gàndur̃ōbà m ⟨oCi⟩, [F] mài gādìn 'yan kasò m; (chief warden) yārī m.

jam[1] n (sweet) jâm m, [F] kwànfìtîr̃ f.

jam[2] 1. v a. (push, crowd sth. together) cunkùsā v1, cūsā v1: she ~med her clothes into a small case tā cunkùsà kāyantà cikin 'yar̃ jàkā: the streets were ~med with cars hanyōyi sun cunkùshē dà mōtōcī. b. (get stuck, of sth. movable or with teeth) cījè v4: the lock, gear has ~med kūbā̀, giyà tā cījè.
2. n (of traffic) cùnkōson mōtōcī m, gô-sùlô m.

January n Jànair̃ù m.

jar[1] n kwalabā f ⟨a-e⟩.

jar[2] v gìr̃gìzā v1: don't ~ the table when you sit down in kā zaunà, kadà kà gìr̃gìzà tēbù̂r̃.

jargon n sā̀rā f, zàuràncē m: prisoners have their own ~ fur̃sunōnī sunà dà tāsù sā̀rā̂r̃.

jaundice n shāwar̃ā̀ f, ta jikà f.

javelin n (Sport) jîfàn māshī m.

jaw n mummuƙè̀ / muƙàmuƙī m ⟨a..ai⟩.

jealous adj a. (possessive) (mài) kīshì m: he is ~ of his wife yanà kīshìn

amaryar̃sà. b. (envious) (mài) ƙyàshī m, (mài) hassadā̀ f, (& hostile) (mài) nukur̃ā̀ f: I am ~ of his new car inā̀ ƙyàshin sābuwar̃ mōtàr̃sà.

jealousy n kīshì m; (envy) ƙyàshī m, hassadā̀ f, nukur̃ā̀ f.

jeans n jìn m.

jeep n jîf f.

jeer v yi ēhò m.

jerk v (move abruptly) kar̃kàdā v1.

jerry can n jar̃kà f, [F] jàr̃kâl m.

jersey n (worn by sports teams) jēsì f ⟨una⟩.

jester n wāwan sarkī m.

jet n (plane) jirgin samā m ⟨aCe⟩; ~ fighter jirgin yāƙī.

jet-black adj baƙī ƙirin, baƙī wuluk.

Jew n yàhūdù m, bàyahūdè̀ m.

jewel n dūtsè̀ m ⟨duwàtsū⟩.

jewelry n kāyan adō m, dūtsèn wuyà m.

Jew's harp n (metal) bàmbarō m, (of cornstalk) zàgàdū m.

jiffy n: in a ~ kā̀fìn ƙyaftāwā dà bìsmillà.

jigger n (insect) jìgā f.

jingle v kar̃kàɗā v1: he ~d the keys in his pocket yā kar̃kàɗà màkùllansà à àljīhù.

jinn n àljanī m ⟨u⟩.

job n a. (work in gen'l) aikī m ⟨ayyukà̀⟩: a good ~ aikī mài kyâu; apply for a ~ r̃ubū̀tà takàr̃dar̃ nēman aikī; fill a ~ cikà gurbī; find, get a ~ sāmi aikī; look for a ~ nèmi aikī. b. (partic. position) matsayī m, muƙāmī m: I have a ~ as an accountant matsayīnā àkantà; a ~ opening gurbìn aikī m.

jockey n mahàyin dōkìn sukùwā m.

join v a. (bring, come together) haɗà v1, hàɗu v7: he ~ed the sleeve to the gown yā haɗà hannun r̃īgā dà uwar̃ r̃īgā; ~ forces, ~ in a venture haɗà gwīwā̀; where do the two streams ~? inā̀ kōgunàn biyu sukà hàɗu? b. (with adhesive substance) mannà v1: use some glue to ~ the fragments together kà sā līƙī kà mannà gutsàttsarī. c. (become member of) shìga v3: ~ the army, a club, a political party shìga sōjà, ƙungìyā, jàm'iyyà̀; ~ in a conversation shìga zàncē.

joint 1. n a. (in body) gaɓā̀ f ⟨oCi⟩: all my ~s ache duk gaɓōɓī nā minì cīwò. b. (place where two things meet) magamī m: the ~s need to be oiled magamîn nā̀ bùkātar̃ mâi.
2. adj: take ~ action haɗà kâi bisà sha'ànîn.

jointly 142 just

jointly *adv* tằre *adv.*

joke 1. *n* wằsā *m*, àbin (bā dà) dằriyā *m*:
that was a good ~! kâi wannàn àbù yā
bā dà dằriyā! I fail to see the ~ bàn ga
àbin dằriyā à ciki ba; he cannot take
a ~ bā yằ sôn wằsā; play a ~ on so. yi
wằ wằsā = yi wằ wằyō; tell a dirty ~ yi
shaƙiyyancì *m*; make a ~ about so. yi
ba'àƙ w.
2. *v* yi baƙwancì *m*, yi wằsā *m*: all joking aside ban dà wằsā; I'm only joking!
wằsā nakè! = dà gàngan nakè! ~ about
so. yi ba'àƙ w.: they are joking about
Audu sunằ ba'àƙ Audù.

joker *n* a. (*in cards*) jōkằ *m*, [F] jòkêƙ *m*.
b. (*psn.*) mằi baƙwancì *n*, bàkwanīkề *m*.

joking *n* baƙwancì *m*, (*done by emir's
jester*) kwanīkancì *m*.

Jollof rice *n* dằfà-dukằ *m*.

jolly *adj* (mài) fằƙa'ằ *f*.

jolt *v* kaƙkàɗā *v1*: the car ~ed a lot because
of the bumpy road mōtằ nằ kaƙkàɗâwā
sabòdà gaƙgadà.

journal *n* mùjallằ *f* ⟨oCi⟩: it is a monthly
~ mùjallaƙ watằ-watằ cē.

journalism *n* aikìn jàƙīdằ *m*.

journalist *n* ɗan jàƙīdằ *m*.

journey *n* tằfiyằ *f* ⟨e²⟩: the ~ was long
and dangerous tằfiyàƙ nằ dà tsawō, gằ
kuma haɗàƙī; (*overnight* ~) zangò *m*: a
3-day ~ tằfiyằ ta zangò ukù = tằfiyằ
ta kwānā ukù; break a ~ yā dà zangò;
I wished him a safe ~ nā yi masà fātan
Allàh yà kiyằyē.

joy *n* muƙnằ *f*, jîn dāɗī *m*, farin cikì *m*:
jump for ~ dakà tsallē don muƙnằ; be
full of ~ yi muƙnằ = ji dāɗī.

joyous *adj* na muƙnằ *f*: this is a ~ occasion
wannàn lōkàcī nề na muƙnằ; the end of
the war was a ~ occasion for everyone gamà
yàƙìn yā sâ kōwà muƙnằ.

judge 1. *n* a. (*Law*) mài shàƙi'ằ *m*,
mahùkùncì *m*; (*of tradit. court*) àlƙālī *m*
⟨ai⟩, (*of modern court*) jōjì *n*, [F] jūjù
*n*; chief ~ cîf-jōjì *m*; *see* magistrate.
b. (*one who can* ~ *sth.*) mahùkùncì *m*.
2. *v* (*Law*) yankè hukuncì; as far as I
could ~ àbin dà na ganì dai.

judgment *n* hukuncì *m*: pass, exercise
~ yankè hukuncì; he exercised poor ~
in the matter bài yankè hukuncìn dà
ya kàmātà ba; (*Relig.*) day of ~ rānaƙ
hìsābì = rānaƙ kìyāmà.

judicial *adj* na shàƙi'ằ *f*.

judo *n* jīɗò *m*, [F] jìɗô *m*.

jug *n* (*clay or gourd*) būtằ *f* ⟨oCi⟩.

juice *n* ruwā *m*: orange ~ ruwan lèmon
zāƙī.

juicy *adj* (mài) ruwa-ruwa *adv*.

juju *n* tsāfì *m*, māgànī *m*, jùjū *m*: he did
some ~ on her yā yi matà jùjū = yā yi
matà māgànī.

jujube *n* (*tree*) *n* magaryā *f*.

July *n* Yūlì *m*.

jumble *n* bàƙkàtài *adv*: his room was a ~
of clothes and papers ɗākìnsà à bàƙkàtài
yakè dà kāyā dà tàkàƙdū.

jump 1. *n* tsallē *m*; (*Sport*) high ~
tsallen samà; long ~ tsallen ƙasà.
2. *v* a. yi tsallē *m*, tùma *v3*: ~ for
joy dakà tsallē don muƙnằ; ~ down
dirō *v6*: the cat ~ed down from the wall
kyânwā tā dirō dàgà kân katangā; ~
over tsallàkē *v4*: the thief ~ed over the
wall and escaped ɓàrāwòn yā tsallàkè
katangā yā tsērề; how far can you ~?
dà ƙafà nawà zā kà iyà tsallàkêwā? ~
up suddenly yi wuf *idph*: he suddenly ~ed
up yā yi wuf yā tāshì. b. (*of train*) gōcè
*v4*: the train ~ed the tracks jirgin ƙasà
yā gōcè dàgà kân dōgō.

junction *n* (*intersection*) mahaɗā *f*.

June *n* Yūnì *m*.

jungle *n* kurmì *m* ⟨a-u⟩.

junior *adj* a. (*of sibling*) ƙanè *m*, ƙanwà *f*
⟨ƙannē⟩: he is my ~ brother ƙanēnā nề.
b. (*in rank, ability, etc.*) ƙasà dà *prep*:
he's ~ to us yanà ƙasà dà mū.

junk *n* tàrkàcē *m*, tàrkàcen banzā *m*; (*odds
& ends*) kàrìkìtai *p*, kòmàtsai *p*: some
people like to collect ~ wasu sunà sôn
tārà tàrkàcē.

junta *m* mulkìn sōjà *m*.

jurisdiction *n* īkò *m*: Maradi has ~ over
Tasawa Maràdi tanà īkòn Tāsāwā.

jurisprudence *n* (*Islamic*) fiƙihù *m*.

just¹ *adv* a. (*exactly*) daidai *adv*: ~ at
that moment daidai lōkàcīn; ~ as (*at
that moment*) daidai lōkàcin: ~ as I
was about to speak, it happened daidai
lōkàcīn dà zân yi màganà, àbîn yā
fàru; the thief was climbing over the
wall ~ as we returned ɓàrāwòn nà haurà
katangā daidai lōkàcin dāwôwaƙmù; ~
on time daidai cikin lōkàcī; ~ so
daidai hakà; ~ now dằzun nàn, yànzun
nàn: she was here ~ a second ago tanà
nân dàzu-dàzun nàn; be ~ right yi
daidai wà daidà; that's ~ what I told
him! àbîn dà na gayà masà kề nan! that's
~ what I was hoping to find! àbîn dà
dà mā nakề nēmā ìn sāmù kề nan! b.
(*merely*) kawài *adv*: he's ~ a poor man

shī talàkà nē kawài. c. (*barely*) dà ƙyaƙ
(+ *rel. complet.*): we only ~ caught the
train dà ƙyaƙ mukà sàmi jirgîn; they ~
managed to finish on time dà ƙyaƙ sukà
gamà cikin lōkàcī. d. (*other uses*): ~
as X so Y (*in comparing*) kàmaƙ yàddà X
mā Y: ~ as they have done it so should
we kàmaƙ yàddà sū sukà yi, mū mā sai
mun yi; ~ as if sai kà cê: it's ~ as if he
hadn't heard anything sai kà cê bài ji
kōmē ba; be ~ about to do X when Y (*fut.
event*) X kè̃ nan sai Y: we were ~ about
to leave when we heard someone calling
us zā mù tāshì kè̃ nan sai mukà ji anà̃
kirànmù = munà̃ gab dà tāshì sai mukà
ji anà̃ kirànmù; ~ prior to (à) gòshin:
it was ~ prior to her wedding that she died
anà̃ gòshin bīkin aurentà ta mutù.

just[2] *adj* a. (*having fairness*) (mài) ādalcī
*m;* a ~ person ādàlī *m:* he is a ~ man and
will listen to all of you shī ādàlī nè̃, zâi
sàuràrē kù dukà. b. (*suitable, appropriate*): it was a ~ decision shāwaƙà cē dà
ta dācè̃.

justice *n* a. (*the law*) shàƙi'à̃ *f;* bring so.
to ~ hukùntā *v1.* b. (*judge*), *see* judge,
magistrate. c. (*fairness*) ādalcī *m;* in
the name of ~, listen to my cause don
Allàh, kà sàuràri jàwābīnā; there's
no ~ in this world (*fig.*) dūniyà̃ tā ƙi
gàskiyā.

justification *n* dàlīlì *m* ⟨ai⟩, hujjà̃ *f*
⟨oCi⟩: is there any ~ for committing terrorism? àkwai hujjàƙ yîn ta'àdda?

justify *v:* you were justified in saying that
kanà̃ dà hujjàƙ fàɗaƙ hakà; is it true
that the end justifies the means? (*fig.*)
gaskiyā nè̃ kwalliyā tā biyā kuɗin
sàbulũ?

justly *adv* a. (*fairly*) (mài) ādalcī *m:* rule
~ yi mulkì cikin ādalcī. b. (*suitably*):
he was ~ punished an yi masà hukuncìn
dà ya dācè̃.

jute *n* tùƙgunnìyā *f*, lālò *m*.

juvenile *adj:* don't act in such a ~ manner kadà kà yi yà̃rìntā; he's still a
~ and should not be tried in court haƙ
yànzu yārò̃ nē bài ìsa à kai shì gàban
shàƙi'à̃ ba; ~ delinquent fàndàrarrē
*adj,* kàngàrarrē *adj.*

# K

**Kanuri** *n* a. (*member of ethnic group*) bàbar̃barè *m* ⟨barèbarī⟩. b. (*language*) bar̃bar̃cī *m*.

**kapok** *n* rīmī *f*, audùgar̃ rīmī *f*: ~ is used in making pillows anā matāshin kâi dà rīmī.

**karate** *n* kàr̃êt *m*, [F] kàr̃àtê *m*.

**kebab** *n* tsìr̃e *m*: ~s are grilled over a fire mound anā gasà tsìr̃e bisà kân tukùbā; ~ skewer tsinken tsìr̃e.

**keen** *adj*: a ~ mind mài kaifin tùnànī; a ~ desire matuɓar̃ sô; a ~ pupil yàr̃ò mài himmà; be ~ to do sth. ɓallàfà rài: she is ~ to travel abroad tā ɓallàfà rântà tà yi tàfiyà ɓasàshen wàje.

**keep** *v* a. (*retain, hold, set aside*): ~ a promise cikà àlkawàr̃ī; can you ~ a secret? anā sir̃r̃ì dà kai? ~ this for me until next week kì ajìyē minì wannàn sai màkò mài zuwà; may I ~ this newspaper? ìn ɗauki wannàn jàr̃īdà? ~ the rest of the change kà riɓè sauran canjì; ~ sth. safely ādànà *v1*: the head of the house ~s the money safe in his room màigidà yanà ādànà kuɗîn à tùrākà; ~ in mind yi là'akàr̃ī *m*, ànkarà *v3*: we should ~ this in mind before making our decision mù ànkarà dà wannàn kàfìn mù yankè shāwar̃à. b. (*remain*): ~ calm yi hàɓurī; how many days will this meat ~ before it goes bad? kwānā nawà nāmàn nân zài kai bài ɓàcì ba? let's ~ together so we don't get lost mù tàfi tàre don kadà mù ɓatà. c. (*support so., maintain sth.*): ~ a family riɓè ìyālì = cī dà ìyālì; ~ accounts yi lìssāfìn kuɗī; ~ animals yi kīwò; the watch ~s good time àgōgo yanà tàfiyà daidai. d. (*keep so. or sth. in some state*) barì *v\**, sâ *v1\**: this must be kept cool à bar̃ wannàn yà yi sanyī = kà sâ wannàn yà yi sanyī; I kept them waiting nā bar̃ sù sunà jirà = nā sâ su jirà; ~ quiet yi shirū *m*: can't you ~ the children quiet? bà zā kì iyà sâ yàrā sù yi shirū ba? e. (*continue same action*) dingà / ringà *v1*, riɓà *v1*, yi ta: he kept (on) reading, crying yā dingà kàr̃àtū, kūkā = yā yi ta

kàr̃àtū, kūkā; don't ~ doing that kâr̃ kà riɓà yîn hakà; we'll ~ on trying until we succeed zā mù yi ta ɓòɓarī har̃ mù ci nasar̃à; unfortunately, I ~ forgetting to do it wàllāhì inā ta màntâwā ìn yī shì. f. (*var. v + adv/prep uses*): ~ apart from ɓauràcē/ɓauyàcē wà *v4*: they kept apart from one another sun ɓauràcē wà jūnā; ~ at, to dàgè kân: we must ~ to our work schedule tīlàs sai mun dàgè kân tsàr̃in aikìnmù; ~ away from yi nēsà dà: children should ~ away from fire yā kàmàtà yàrā sù yi nēsà dà wutà; ~ so. away from nīsàntà *v1*: they kept her away from him sun nīsàntà ta dà shī; ~ back jā dà bāya: the crowd kept back to let the chief pass jàma'à sun jā dà bāya don sarkī yà wucè; the police kept the crowd back 'yan sàndā sun sâ jàma'à sun jā dà bāya; ~ so. from sth. hanā *v1*: the work kept me from attending the meeting aikìn yā hanā ni hàlar̃tar̃ tàr̃ôn; they kept us from entering the building sun hanā mu shìgā ginìn; ~ off the grass! kadà kà tākà cìyāwà! = kâr̃ kà bi ta cìyāwà! ~ out (*shield*) kār̃è *v4*: this curtain should ~ out the light lābulen nàn zâi kār̃è haskē; the sign read, '~ out!' sanàr̃war̃ tā cê, 'bà shìgā!' ~ straight on (*in a certain direction*) bi sak: ~ straight on this road bi hanyàr̃ nân sak; (*fig.*) ~ up with the Joneses dakà ta w.: stop trying to ~ up with me! kadà kà dakà tàwa!

**kerchief** *n* (*woman's head-tie*) kallàbī *m* ⟨u-a⟩, ɗan kwālī *m*, àdīkò *m* ⟨u⟩, (*wound around head*) gwaggwar̃o *m*: put on a ~ ɗaurà kallàbī; women wear many different kinds of ~s mātā kàn ɗaurè kallubà irì-irì.

**kernel** *n* (*single grain*) ɓwàyā *f* ⟨oCi⟩.

**kerosene** *n* (*paraffin*) kànànzîr̃ *m*, [F] kàlànzîr̃ *m*, [F] fìtàr̃ô *m*; ~ can garwar̃ kànànzîr̃.

**kestrel** *n* (*lesser*) cì-fàra *m*, (*mountain*) kar̃àmbatà *f*.

**kettle** *n* būtà *f* ⟨oCi⟩, sàhānì *m* ⟨ai⟩, (*electric*) būtàr̃ làntar̃kì *f*: put a ~ on the fire ɗōrà būtà kân wutà.

**key** *n* makullī *m*, mabūɗī *m*, [F] làkilê *m*; (*for door lock*) ɗan kūbà *m*: leave the ~ in the lock kà bar̃ mabūɗī cikin kwàɗôn; lose one's ~ yar̃ dà mabūɗī.

**keyhole** *n* kafar̃ makullī *f*.

**khaki** *n* kàkī *m*, [F] kàkî *m*: army uniforms are made from ~ anā kāyan sōjà dà kàkī.

**kick 1.** *v* **a.** (*a ball*) hàr̃bà *v1*, dōkà *v1*, bugà *v1*: ~ a ball into the net dōkà ƙwallō à ràgā; ~ a ball into the air bugà bâl d̃in samà; (*one's foot forward*) shūrà *v1*: he ~ed his foot forward yā shūrà ƙafà; (*by psn. to so. or animal*) hàurà *v2*, shūrà *v2*: she ~ed the dog tā shùri kàrē; (*by animal to so.*) hàr̃bà *v2*: the donkey ~ed me in the stomach jàkī yā hàr̃bē nì à cikì; ~ so. out kòrà *v2*: he was ~ed out of the club an kòrē shi dàgà ƙunglyā; ~ up dust tā dà ƙùrā.
**2.** *n* hàr̃bì *m* ⟨e²⟩, shūrì *m* ⟨e²⟩: he gave me a mean ~ in the stomach yā yi mini mūgùn hàr̃bì à cikì.
**kid** *n* **a.** (*goat*) d̃an àkuyà *m*, 'yar̃ àkuyà *f*. **b.** (*child*) yārò *m*, yārinyà *f* ⟨yārā⟩.
**kidding** *n*: I'm only ~ dà gàngan nakè = dà wàsā nakè; no ~! bâ dāmā!
**kidnap** *v* sācè *v4*.
**kidney** *n* ƙōdà *f* ⟨oCi⟩.
**kill** *v* **a.** (*psn., animal*) kashè *v4*: he was ~ed in the war an kashè shi lōkàcin yāƙì; he ~ed himself yā kashè kânsà. **b.** (*slaughter*) yankà *v1*. **c.** (*fig. uses*): this heat is ~ing me zāfin nàn kàmar̃ yà kashè ni; ~ a rumor kwantar̃ dà jìta-jìta = kawar̃ dà jìta-jìta; ~ time yi zaman jiràn lōkàcī; be dressed to ~ ƙurè àdakà, cāɓà adō.
**killer** *n* mài kisàn kâi *n*: he's not the ~ bà shī ya yi kisàn kân ba; a ~ disease cùta mài kisà = cùtar̃ ajàlī.
**kiln** *n* (*tradit.*) tàndèr̃ū *m*.
**kilogram** *n* kilò / kìlò *m*.
**kilometer** *n* kilòmītà *f*, kilò *m*, [F] kìlòmētìr *m*.
**kin** *n* dangì *m*: notify next of ~ sanar̃ dà dangìn w.
**kind¹** *n* **a.** irì *m* ⟨e²⟩: which ~ do you want? wànè irì kakè sô? do you have any other ~? kanà dà wani irì dàbam? we don't have that ~ here bâ mu dà irìnsà nân; I want one of the same ~ inà sôn d̃aya irìnsà; what ~ of car do you have? wàcè irìn mōtà kakè dà ita? those ~s of people are shameless ìre-ìren mutànē bâ su dà kunyà; what ~ of a man is that? (*expr. of wonder or disapproval*) wànè irìn mùtûm nē shī? what ~ of person do you take me for anyway! mè ka d̃aukē nì? he's not the ~ of person to refuse shī bà irìn mutànên dà zā sù ƙi ba nè; squash is a ~ of vegetable kàbēwà tanà dàgà cikin kāyan làmbū; all ~s of, any ~ at all kōwànè irì; you'll find all ~s of printed cloth there zā kì sàmi

kōwàd̃annè irìn atamfōfì cân; they are two of a ~ (*fig.*) duk tàfiyàr̃sù d̃aya = duk jirgī d̃aya ya kāwō sù. **b.** various, different ~s irì-irì, dàbam dàbam; (*esp. of things having color*) kalà-kalà: all ~s of goods kāyā irì-irì; she bought many ~s of cloth tā sàyi yàdì kalà-kalà; you'll see many different ~s of pots zā kà ga tukwànē dàbam dàbam.
**kind²** *adj* (mài) kir̃kì *m*: he is a ~ person mùtûm nē mài kir̃kì; he is one of the ~est men yanà dàgà cikin mutànē maflyā kir̃kì; be ~ (to so.) yi (wà) kir̃kì *m*, kyàutā (wà) *v1*, yi (wà) àlhēr̃ì *m*: it was very ~ of you to come lallē kin kyàutā dà kikà zō; he was ~ to us yā yi manà àlhēr̃ì = yā kyàutā manà; he did not act ~ly toward us bài yi manà aikìn kir̃kì ba; a ~ act àbin kir̃kì = aikìn kir̃kì = àlhēr̃ì; be ~ to animals tausàyā wà dabbōbī.
**kindergarten** *n* (*school*) makar̃antà ta ƙanānàn yârā *f*, nāsàr̃è *f*, [F] màtàr̃nâl *f*.
**kindhearted** *adj* (mài) hālin kir̃kì *m*.
**kindle** *v*: ~ a fire kunnà wutā = had̃à wutā.
**kindling** *n* makāmashī *m*, (*of twigs*) ƙiràr̃ē *p*, (*of dried leaves, grass, odds and ends*) būyāgī *m*.
**kindness** *n* kir̃kì *m*, àlhēr̃ì *m*: do so. a ~ yi wà àlhēr̃ì = yi wà àbin kir̃kì; may God repay you for your ~ Allàh yà sākà makà dà àlhēr̃ì.
**king** *n* **a.** sarkī *m* ⟨sarākunà⟩: long live the ~! rân sarkī yà dad̃è! God save the ~! Allàh yà kiyàyè sarkī! **b.** (*in cards*) rayyà *f*.
**kingdom** *n* daulà *f* ⟨oCi⟩; the ~ of God Àljannà *f*.
**kingfisher** *n* cī-na-wùya *f*, mar̃ōƙin ruwa *m*.
**kinship** *n* dàngàntakà *f*, 'yàn'ùwàntakà *f*; ~ ties zumuncì *m*, zùmùntà *f*: he has no close ties of ~ bâ shi dà zumuncì.
**kinsman** *n* d̃an'uwā *m*: they are kinsmen sū 'yan'uwan jūnā nè.
**kiosk** kiyâs *m*.
**kiss 1.** *v* sùmbatà *v2*.
**2.** *n* sumbà *f*.
**kitchen** *n* (*tradit.*) madafà *f*, dākìn girkì *m*, gwàdalà *f*; (*modern*) kicìn *m*, [F] kìzîn *f*.
**kite¹** *n* (*bird*) shirwà *f*, 'yar̃ bazarà *f*.
**kite²** *n* (*toy*) filfilwà *m*, filfilò *m*.
**kitten** *n* 'yar̃ kyânwā *f*, ùlle *f*.
**knead** *v* (*mix with fingers*) cūd̃à *v1*: ~ the dough for 10 minutes kì cūd̃à ƙwàbabben fulàwā mintì gōmà; (*into balls with fingers*) cūr̃à *v1*, mulmùlà *v1*, dunƙùlà *v1*,

lailàyā *v1*: the *fura* has been ~ed into balls an dunƙùlà furā cūrì-cūrì.

knee *n* gwīwà *f* ⟨oCi⟩; I've hurt my ~ nā ji cīwò à gwīwà; at, on the ~ à gwīwà *adv*; the water came up to the ~s ruwân yā kai iyā gwīwà.

knee-cap ƙōƙon gwīwà *m*.

kneel *v* durƙùsā *v1*, yi dùrƙusō *m*: they knelt before the chief sun durƙùsā gàban sarkī; (*on all fours or with elbows on knees*) gùřfānà *v3*.

knee-pad *n* (*Sport*) sàfař gwīwà *f*.

knife 1. *n* wuƙā *f* ⟨aCe⟩: a sharp ~ wuƙā mài kaifī; a serrated ~ wuƙā mài haƙòrā; a shaving ~ askā *f*; (*small, for household use*) wuƙař maƙērā *f*; (*large, used to cut sugar cane*) bàřhō *m*.
2. *v* sōƙā wà wuƙā, lumā wà wuƙā.

knit *v* sāƙā *v1*, ⟨sāƙà⟩ *f*: ~ so. a sweater sāƙā wà sùwaità; (*fig.*) ~ one's brow gamà girā.

knitting needle *n* tsinken sāƙā *m*.

knob *n* mariƙī *m*, (*which turns*) mamuřdī *m*.

knock *v* a. (*on a door*) ƙwanƙwàsā *v1*, ƙyanƙyànā *v1*, bugā *v1*: you should ~ before you enter the room kà ƙwanƙwàsà ƙōfà kāfin kà shìga; did you hear someone ~ing on the door? kā ji ƙwànƙwasàř ƙōfà? without ~ing bā sallamà: he burst into the room without ~ing yā kūtsà kâi ya shigō ɗākì bā sallamà. b. (*var. v + adv/prep uses*): ~ so. down (*by psn.*) bankàɗē *v4*; ~ so. down (*by thing*) bankè *v4*, bugè *v4*, kaɗè *v4*: the car ~ed him down mōtà tā bankè shi = an bankè shi dà mōtà; ~ against bankō *v6*; to ~ sth. down (*destroy*) rūshè *v4*: the city wall was ~ed down to widen the road an rūshè gānuwā don fāɗàɗà hanyà; ~ so. out dōkè *v4*: the boxer ~ed out his opponent ɗan dambên yā dōkè àbōkin karàwařsà; ~ sth. over (*& spill*) 6ař dà / 6arař (dà) *v5*: she ~ the beans over and spilled them tā 6ař dà wākē; ~ a hole in sth. hūɗà *v1*; (*fig.*) ~ on wood kadà kà fid dà tsàmmànì.

knock-kneed *adj* gwāmē *m* ⟨aye⟩; become ~ zama gwāmè, gwāmùncè *v4*.

knot *n* a. ƙullī *m*; tie, make a ~ yi ƙullì, ƙullà *v1*, ƙudùrā *v1*: he tied a ~ in the string yā yi ƙullì à zàrēn = yā ƙullà zàrēn; untie a ~ kwancè / kuncè *v4*, suncè *v4*: the ~ has become untied ƙullì yā suncè; a slip-~ (*noose*) zàrgē *m*; the Northern ~ (*heraldic design of Hausaland*) dàgī *m*. b. (*in wood, tree*) idòn itàcē *m*.

know *v* a. sanì *v*\*: I do not ~ him, but I

~ of him bàn san shì ba àmmā inā jîn làbāřìnsà; I ~ Ladi very well, superficially nā san Lādì farin sanì, sanìn shānū; I don't really ~ what he's like bàn san shì tàkàmaimai ba; I don't ~ him well enough to ask bàn san shì ba sòsai bàllē ìn tàmbàyē shì; ~ about sth. ji làbāřìn w.a., san dà: Audu ~s something about it Audù nā dà làbāřìnsà = Audù yā san dà shī; do you ~ whether he returned? shin yā dāwō? let so. ~ sanař (dà) *v5*, shaidà wà *v1*; as far as I ~... à iyā sanīnā dai...; ~ sth. clearly, for certain tantàncē *v4*: ~ clearly the difference between good and evil tantàncē tsàkānin nagàri dà mūgù. (*fig.*) he ~s me like the back of his hand yā san nì kàmař yunwàř cikìnsà. b. (*e.g. a language*) ji *v0*, iyā *v1*: he doesn't ~ English bā yā jîn Tūřancī = bài iyà Tūřancī ba; ~ how iyā *v1*: he doesn't ~ how to read and write bài iyà kàřàtū dà řùbùtū ba; ~ by heart haddàcē *v4*.

knowledge *n* a. (*knowing sth.*) sanì *m*: to the best of my ~ à iyākař sanīnā dai; without so'.s ~ bā dà sanìn w. ba; it's common ~ sanìn kōwā nè. b. (*learning*) ilìmī *m*, sanì *m*: he was respected for his great ~ an girmàmā shi sabòdà zurfin ilìminsà; a very ~able person mùtûm mài dìmbin sanì. c. (*information*) masanìyā *f*: he had some ~ of the events which took place yanā dà masanìyař abùbuwàn dà sukà fàru.

known *adj* sànannē *adj*: it is a well-~ fact sànannen àbù nē.

knuckle *n* ga6ā *f* ⟨oCi⟩; rap so. with one's ~s řànƙwasà *v2*; crack one's ~s 6allà yàtsū.

kob *n* māràyā *f* ⟨oCi⟩.

kobo *n* (*unit of currency in Nigeria, abbreviated as k, see* Appendix F) kwabō *m* ⟨Cai, Cuna⟩: 30k kwabō tàlàtin; ₦3.50 naiřā ukù dà kwabō hàmsin.

koko-yam *n, see* coco-yam.

kolanut *n* gōřò *m*; (*wrapped in leaves & burlap*) hūhùn gōřò; huge round ~s gōřò řugū-řùgū; most ~s have 2 sections yawancin gōřò ƙwàř biyu nè.

Koran *n* Àlƙùř'ānī Mài Girmā *m*, Àlƙùř'ānī Mài Tsarkī *m*; read the ~ aloud in a group yi tàkàřā *f*.

Koranic school *n* makařantař àllō *f*, Mùhammadiyyà *f*.

kwashiorkor *n* tsīla *f*: he has ~ tsīla tā kāmā shi.

# L

**label** *n* lambà *f* ⟨oCi⟩, àlāmà *f* ⟨oCi⟩.

**labor** *n* a. (*work*) aikì *m*: a huge amount of ~ is involved in building a dam àkwai gàgàrùmin aikì wajen ginà madatsar̃ ruwā; b. (*manpower*) ƙwādagō *m;* the ~ force 'yan ƙwādagō, ma'àikàtā *p:* ~ union ƙungìyar̃ 'yan ƙwādagō; we are short of ~ today munà dà ƙarancin ma'àikàtā yâu; unskilled, manual ~ lēbùr̃ancì *m;* farm ~ (*temporary*) bārēmà *m.* c. (*pains of childbirth*) nāƙudà *f:* she is in ~ tanà nāƙudà = tanà kân gwīwà.

**laboratory** *n* ɗākìn bìncìkē *m*, ɗākìn gwajì *m.*

**laborer** *n* (*daily paid, doing manual work*) lēbùr̃à *m* ⟨oCi⟩, ɗan ƙwādagō *m*, [F] mànēbîr̃ *m;* (*for loading vehicles*) ɗan lōdì *m;* casual ~ ɗan ìnā-dà-aikì.

**lace** *n* lēshì *m*: a ~ gown r̃ìgar̃ lēshì.

**laces** *n:* shoe ~ maɗaurin tàkàlmī *m.*

**lack** 1. *n* rashì *m*: a ~ of rain rashìn ruwā = ƙarancin ruwā; they've gotten lazy through ~ of work rashìn aikì yā sâ sun zama malàlàtā.
2. *v* rasà *v1*: I didn't ~ anything there bàn rasà kōmē à cân ba.

**ladder** *n* tsānì *m* ⟨uka⟩, kwàrangà *f:* lean a ~ against the wall jingìnà tsānì à (jìkin) bangō.

**ladle** *n* (*made from small gourd*) lūdàyī *m* ⟨luwàɗū⟩; (*from large gourd with straight handle*) gàgò *m* ⟨Ca⟩; (*large, of wood*) ƙòshiyà *f* ⟨oCi⟩.

**lady** *n* màcè *f* ⟨mātā⟩ (*in the genitive, use* màtar̃): a ~ came looking for you wata màcè tā zō nēmankì; is that ~ your teacher? màtar̃ càn màlàmar̃kù cē? ~ of the house uwar̃gidā *f;* Ladies and Gentlemen jàma'à mazā dà mātā.

**lair** *n* kùr̃fī *m.*

**lake** *n* tafkì *m* ⟨una⟩.

**lamb** *n* ɗan r̃àgō *m*, 'yar̃ tunkìyā *f*, ⟨'yā'yan tumākī⟩; leg of ~ cinyar̃ r̃àgō *f.*

**lame** *adj* (*psn.*) gurgù *m* ⟨a-u⟩: he limps because he is ~ yanà ɗingishī sabòdà shī gurgù nē; (*fig.*) that's a ~ excuse uzùr̃in nàn bâ shi dà makāmà.

**lamp** *n* fìtilà *f* ⟨u⟩; bush-~, hurricane ~ fìtilar̃ ƙwai; kerosene ~ (*made from tin can*) à-ci-bàlbàl *f;* oil ~ (*using shallow clay dish*) fìtilar̃ kaskō; pressure ~ fìtilar̃ ruwā, [F] lampèdā *f.*

**lampshade** *n* murfin fìtilà *m.*

**lance** 1. *v* (*a wound*) yankà *v1.*
2. *n* māshì *m* ⟨māsū⟩.

**lance-corporal** *n* lâskōfùr̃ *m.*

**land** 1. *n* a. ƙasā *f:* the ~ is very mountainous ƙasar̃ tā cikà duwàtsū; the ship reached ~ jirgin ruwa yā ìsa bàkin ruwā. b. (*property*) gōnā *f* ⟨aki⟩, fīlī *m* ⟨aye⟩: he owns a lot of ~ yanà dà fīlàyē dà yawà. c. (*uncleared, uninhabited*) sùnƙūrù *m.*
2. *v* (*of plane*) sàuka *v3;* a forced ~ing sàukar̃ tīlàs; (*of boat*) ìsa gābà, ìsa bàkin ruwā.

**lane** *n* lāyì *m* ⟨uka⟩.

**landlady** *n* uwar̃ ɗākì *f.*

**landlord** *n* màigidan hayà *m*, ùban ɗākì *m.*

**language** *n* a. harshè *m* ⟨una⟩: they speak the same ~ harshènsù ɗaya; be able to speak a ~ iyà harshè; the same ~ is spoken throughout the country harshè gùdā nè akè màganà dà shī à duk ƙasar̃; he is good at learning ~s yanà dà saurin kòyon harsunà; understand a ~ ji harshè = gānè harshè; ~ policy tsārìn àmfànī dà harshè; a local, vernacular ~ (*esp. of an ethnic minority*) yàr̃ē *m* ⟨uka⟩, lahajà *f* ⟨oCi⟩; vulgar ~ (*sexually explicit*) bātsa *f*, ɗanyen bàkī *m*, mūgùn bàkī *m.*

**languid** *adj* (*mài*) kàsàlà *f.*

**lap**[1] *n* (*of body*) cinyà *f:* sit on so.'s ~ zaunà à kân cinyar̃ w.; bounce a baby on one's ~ jijjìgà ɗā à cinyà.

**lap**[2] *n* (*Sport*) kèwàyen fīlì *m*: each ~ is 400 meters kōwànè kèwàyen fīlì mītà dàrī huɗu nè.

**lap**[3] *v* (*drink*): ~ up lāshè *v4.*

**lapse** *v* ƙār̃è *v4*: the warranty has ~d gàr̃antîn yā ƙār̃è.

**lard** *n* kitsèn àladè *m.*

**large** *adj* a. (*big*) bàbba *adj* ⟨mànyā⟩, (*mài*) girmā *m*: they have a ~ house sunà dà bàbban gidā; the house is ~r than all the others gidân yā fi duk saurân girmā; make the trousers ~r ƙār̃à girman wàndō; it is about as ~ as this one girmansà kusan wannàn nè; be slightly ~r than darà *v1:* it is a little ~r than this yā ɗan darà wannàn. b. (*in number, quantity*) dà dāmā: he has quite a ~ family yanà dà ìyālì dà ɗan dāmā.

**lark** *n* tsīgī *m.*

laryngitis n shāƙēwaƙ muryà f.

larynx n màƙwallatò m.

last[1] adj (final) na ƙàrshē m: his ~ speech jàwābìnsà na ƙàrshē; this is the ~ day of the month yâu nē rānaƙ ƙàrshen watā; the ~ news I heard was... làbārìn ƙàrshē dà na ji shī nè...; ~ night jiyà dà dare = daren jiyà; ~ month watàn jiyà; ~ year bāƙa f; ~ week màkòn jiyà = màkòn dà ya wucè; ~ Sunday Lahàdìn dà ta wucè; when did you see him ~? tun yàushè ràbonkà dà ganinsà? at ~ (lastly) dàgà ƙàrshē.

last[2] v a. (endure) dōrè v4: their friendship will not ~ àbòtaƙsù bà zā tà dōrè ba; ~ a long time dadè v4: their marriage didn't ~ long aurensù bài dadè ba = aurensù bài yi ƙarkō ba; ~ forever dàwwamā v3. b. (esp. of goods) yi ƙarkō m, yi ƙwārī m: this cloth, watch will ~ a while yādìn nân, àgōgon nàn zâi yi ƙarkō; will the cloth ~? yādìn yanà dà ƙwārī? c. (a specific amount of time) kai v*: the war ~ed 3 years yāƙìn yā kai shèkarà ukù; how long will the food ~ us? àbincîn zâi kai mù haƙ yàushè? nothing ~s forever kōmē na dūniyà mài ƙarèwā nè.

lastly adv dàgà ƙàrshē.

latch n sàkatà f ⟨u⟩: make sure the door is fastened with the ~ kà tabbataƙ cêwā kā rufè ƙōfaƙ dà sàkatà.

late adj a. be ~ màkarà v3, yi lattì m: the plane was 3 hours ~ jirgîn yā màkarà dà awā ukù; you are ~ kā màkarà = kā yi lattì = kā zō à màkàre; today you came ~r than yesterday yâu kā màkarà fìye dà jiyà; it is too ~ to start now lōkàcin fāràwā yā wucè; it is too ~ to do anything about it bâ yâddà zā à iyà yî; I'm ~ (in doing sth. early in the day) darē yā yi minì; we were ~ to school mun yi daren zuwà makaƙantā; I was ~ getting to the farm nā yi rānaƙ zuwà gōnā; it is getting ~ (getting dark) darē yā yi; don't stay out, up too ~ kadà kà cikà darē; by Friday at the ~st nân dà Jumma'à; better ~ than never (fig.) gàra màkarà dà ƙìn zuwà. b. (recently deceased) marìgàyī m: the ~ writer Sa'adu Zungur marìgàyī maƙùbùcī Sà'àdù Zungùƙ; it was a picture of the ~ chief hòton sarkī marìgàyī nè.

lately adv kwānan nàn: I have not seen much of him ~ kwānan nàn bàn cikà ganinsà ba.

later adv a. (afterward) dàgà bāya: he said he would finish ~ yā cê zâi gamà dàgà bāya; they arrived two days ~ sun isō

kwānā biyu dàgà bāya. b. (after X time has passed) bāyan X: a fews days ~ bāyan an kwan biyu; 10 years ~, he became wealthy bāyan shèkarà gōmà yā zama mài kudī. c. (in a while): he came back a little ~ jìm kàɗan ya dāwō; see you ~ sai an jimà; sooner or ~ kō bàdaɗè kō bàjimà; a tiny bit ~ ƙiris idph: just a little bit ~ and we would have missed him saurā ƙiris dà mun kuskùrè ganinsà.

laterite n marmarā f.

latest adj (newest, most modern) na dàgà yàu-yau: the ~ style, invention salon, ƙìrƙiràƙ dàgà yàu-yau; (e.g. news) (mài) ɗùmi-ɗùmi: the ~ information, gossip làbārì, jìta-jìta mài ɗùmi-ɗùminsà.

lather n kumfā m.

latrine n (pit) salgā f, shàddā f; (in building) bāyan gidā m, see toilet.

latter n (last mentioned): the ~ na ƙàrshēn: there are Audu and Sule, the former is a teacher, the ~ a doctor gà Audù dà Sulè, na ɗayàn mālàmī nè, na ƙàrshēn kō likità nè.

laugh 1. n dàriyā f: he said it with a ~ yā fàɗē shì cikin dàriyā.
2. v yi dàriyā f, dārā v1; ~ about sth. yi dàriyaƙ w.a.: I ~ed a lot about it nā yi dàriyaƙ àbîn sòsai; what are you ~ing about? dàriyaƙ mè kakè yî? it is nothing to ~ about bâ àbin dàriyà ba nè; ~ at so., sth. yi wà dàriyà; who are you ~ing at? wà kakè yi wà dàriyà? make so. ~ bâ w. dàriyā: it made me ~ a lot àbin nàn yā bâ nì dàriyā ainùn; burst out ~ing fashè = ɓarkè = būshè dà dàriyā.

laughter n dàriyā f, (of women expressing joy) shēwā f; roar with ~ (of many) rūɗè dà dàriyā: the audience roared with ~ 'yan kallō sun rūɗè dà dàriyā.

launch v a. (present) gabātaƙ (dà) v5, ƙaddamaƙ (dà) v5: there'll be a party to ~ the new books zā à yi bìkin gabātaƙ dà sàbàbbin lìttàttàfai. b. (Mil.) haƙbà v1: ~ a rocket, satellite haƙbà ƙōkà, kumbò.

launching pad n turkèn haƙbà ƙōkà m.

laundry n (kāyan) wankì m; ~ area mawankā f.

lava n aman wutaƙ dūtsè m.

lavatory n, see toilet.

law n a. shàƙi'à f; (academic subject) ilimin shàƙi'à m; (Islamic ~ as academic subject) ilimin fùƙu'à m; ~ful act (in Islam) hàlāl m; un~ful act (in Islam) hàƙām m. b. (rule, edict) dōkā f ⟨oCi⟩:

that ~ is still in effect dŏkâr̃ tanâ nân har̃ yànzu; according to the ~... dŏkā tā cê...; break a ~ karyà dŏkā; implement a ~ zar̃tar̃ dà dŏkā; obey the ~ bi dŏkā; pass a ~ kafà dŏkā; maintain, respect ~ and order kiyâyè dŏkā.

**lawsuit** n k̃ārā f: file a ~ kai k̃ārā; dismiss a ~ wātsar̃ dà k̃ārā.

**lawyer** n lauyà n ⟨oCi⟩, [F] àbŏkâ m ⟨oCi⟩; defense ~ lauyà mài kārè wândà akè tùhumā; prosecuting ~ lauyàn gwamnatì.

**laxative** n māganin wankè cikì m.

**laxity** n (moral) rashìn d̃a'à m.

**lay** v a. (put) (var v + adv/prep uses): ~ sth. across (diagonally) gittà̃ v1: he ~ the stick across the road yā gittà sàndā kân hanyà̃; ~ down arms ajìyè màkà̃mai; ~ down a rule kafà k̃a'idà̃; ~ so. off (from work) sàllamā v2; ~ sth. on top of sth., so. d̃ōr̃à v1: she laid the child on the bed tā d̃ōr̃à yār̃ŏ kân gad̃ō; they laid the blame on me sun d̃ōr̃à minì lâifī; ~ sth. flat on a place shimfìd̃à v1: first, ~ a mat on the floor dà farkō kà shimfìd̃à tàbarmā à d̃aɓē; ~ so. to rest (in grave) kwantar̃ dà w. à kabàr̃ī. b. ~ an egg nasà k̃wai = sakà k̃wai.

**layer** n: a ~ of oil kwànciyar̃ mâi; wear several ~s of clothing yi hàd̃e m.

**laziness** n k̃yûyā / k̃îwā f, lālācì m, ragwancì m.

**lazy** adj malà̃lacì adj, (esp. about one's duties) (mài) k̃yûyā / k̃îwā f: he is both ~ and dirty malà̃lacì nè̃ kuma gà shì k̃azāmì; he was the laziest boy of all yā fi kōwā lālācì; be ~ yi lālācì m, yi k̃yûyā f; I feel ~ about working today yâu inà jìn k̃yûyar̃ yîn aikì.

**lead**[1] n (metal) dar̃mā / dalmā f.

**lead**[2] n (head start) rātā f: he's in the ~ yā bā sù rātā.

**lead**[3] 1. vt a. (guide) yi wà jà-gōrà, yi wà jà-gàba: this man will ~ you into town mùtumìn nân zâi yi mukù jà-gōrà zuwà gàrī; (a caravan, convoy) yi jà-gàba: he led the caravan yā yi wà ayàrī jà-gàba; (an animal) jā v0; ~ so. astray ɓad dà / ɓatar̃ (dà) v5. b. (direct a group, organization) shũgàbantà v2. c. (give rise to) haifar̃ (dà) v5: the discussion led only to confusion tattàunâwâr̃ tā haifar̃ dà hàrgitsì kawài.

2. vi (go in direction of) nùfā v2, d̃ōsà v2, bi v0: where does this road ~ to? ìnā hanyàr̃ ta nùfā? = ìnā hanyàr̃ ta bi?

**leader** n shũgàbā n ⟨anni⟩, (esp. caravan ~) màdugū m ⟨ai⟩; he was a great ~

shàhàr̃ar̃r̃en shũgàbā nè̃; the ~ of the rebels màdugun 'yan tāwāyè.

**leadership** n shũgabancì m, jāgōrancì m; ~ qualities kwàrjinin shũgabancì.

**leading** adj (famous) shàhàr̃ar̃r̃ē adj: he is a ~ statesman yanà̃ dàgà cikin shàhàr̃ar̃r̃un 'yan sìyāsà.

**leaf** n a. (of tree) ganyē m ⟨aye⟩; shed leaves kad̃è ganyē. b. (of book) war̃k̃à f ⟨oCi⟩, takàr̃dā f ⟨u⟩: some leaves have been torn out of the exercise book an yāgè wad̃ansu war̃k̃ōk̃ī dàgà littāfìn r̃ùbūtū; (fig.) turn over a new ~ sākè hālī.

**leak** 1. v a. yi yŏyō m, zùba v3: the bucket has a hole and ~s bōkitì yā hūjè yanà̃ zùbā; (drip) d̃iga v3. b. (~ & flow out) malā̃lē v4: water is ~ing out of the tank ruwā nà̃ malā̃lêwā dàgà cikin tankì. c. (a secret to so.) kwarmàtā wà v1, yi wà kwàrmatŏ m: it has been ~ed to the press an kwarmàtā wà 'yan jàr̃îdū.

2. n a. yŏyō m. b. (secret revealed) kwàrmatŏ m.

**lean**[1] v jìnginà v3: he ~ed on the table, against the tree yā jìnginà dà tēbùr̃, dà bishiyà̃; stop ~ing on me kà bar̃ jìnginà dà nī; ~ sth. against sth. jìnginà v1, dangànā v1: I ~ed the ladder against the wall nā jìnginà tsānì à jìkin bangō; ~ on sth. (for support) d̃ōgàrā v1: the old man ~ed on his stick tsōhōn yā d̃ōgàrà sàndar̃sà; ~ towards kar̃kàtā v1: he ~ed forward to hear what I had to say yā kar̃katŏ don yà ji àbîn dà zân fàd̃ā; (fig.) I'm ~ing more towards his way of thinking nā fi kàr̃katà gà r̃a'àyinsà; ~ out of kunnà kâi: don't ~ out the window kadà kà kunnà kâi ta tāgà.

**lean**[2] adj a. (thin psn.) sīr̃īr̃ì adj ⟨sīr̃àr̃à⟩. b. ~ meat nāmà maràs kitsè.

**leap** 1. n tsallē m ⟨e²⟩.

2. v yi tsallē m, dakà tsallē; ~ down d̃ìra v3: he ~ed down from his horse yā d̃ìra dàgà dōkìn; ~ over tsallàkē v4: ~ over a fence tsallàkè katangà; ~ to one's feet zàbur̃ā v3.

**learn** v a. (a subject) kŏyā v2 ⟨kŏyō⟩: they ~ arithmetic in second grade anà̃ kòyon lìssāfì à ajì na biyu; he ~s quickly yanà̃ kŏyō dà saurī; he ~ed geography very easily yā kŏyi làbār̃ìn k̃asā cikin sauk̃ī; math is not easy to ~ lìssāfì bā yà dà saukin kŏyō; ~ by heart haddàcē v4. b. (increase one's knowledge of sth.) k̃āru v7: I've ~ed something more today yâu nā k̃āru. c. (a skill) iyà v1: he wants to ~ carpentry yanà sô yà iyà aikìn kāfintà. d. (*get news, information*) ji (làbārì) wai: I ~ed that there will be a celebration next week nā ji wai zā à yi bìkī mākò mài zuwà.

**learned** *adj* (*psn.*) masànī *m*, (mài) ilìmī *n*: he is a ~ man shì masànī nē.

**learner** *n* mài kòyō *n*, ɗan kòyō *m*, ɗan dāgājī *m*: watch out for his driving, he is only a ~ yi hankàlī dà tūkìnsà, ɗan kòyō nè.

**learning** *n* a. (*knowledge*) ilìmī *m*, sanì *m*: he is a man of great ~ mùtumìn nē mài ɗimbin sanì; (*fig.*) a little ~ is a dangerous thing kāramin sanì kukùmī nè. b. (*act of* ~) kòyō *m*: ~ a language is not easy kòyon wani harshè nà dà wùyā. c. (*education*) kārātū *m*.

**leash** *v* (*an animal*) ɗaurè *v4*; ~ law dòkar ɗaurē.

**least** 1. *quant & det* a. (*use compar. constr. such as* fi duk(à) rashì, mafì kankantà, mafì kàɗan): he has the ~ money of all of us dàgà cikinmù kuɗinsà yā fi kankantà = kuɗinsà mafì kàɗan nè; the ~ amount mafì kankantà = mafì kàɗan; this is the ~ useful of all wannàn yā fi dukà rashìn àmfànī = wannàn nē mafì duk rashìn àmfànī.
2. *adv*: at ~ akallà *adv*, à takàice *adv*: he should give you at ~ ₦5 yā kàmātà akallà yà bā kà naifà bìyar; not in the ~ kō kàɗan, kō kusa: he was not in the ~ angry bài yi fushī ba kō kusa; that is the ~ of my worries bàn dàmu dà wannàn kō kàɗan ba.

**leather** *n* fātà *f* ⟨fātū⟩; (*dried, untanned*) kirgì *m* ⟨a-a⟩; ~ worker bàdūkù *m*.

**leatherwork** *n* dūkancì *m*, aikìn fātà *m*.

**leave** 1. *v* a. (*let*) barì *v\**: ~ it like that kà bar shì hakà; he left the door open yā bar kōfà à bùɗe; he didn't ~ me enough room bài bar minì ìsasshen wurī ba; I will ~ you to deal with him zân bar kà dà shī = zân kyàlè ka dà shī; I'll ~ it for you zân bar makà shī; ~ sth., so. alone barì *v\**: just ~ those things alone, they're not yours kà bar abūbuwàn nan kawài bà nākà ba nè; just ~ him alone (*pay no attention to him*) kà ràbu dà shī kawài; just ~ him alone and stop bothering him (*fig.*) kà shāfà masà lāfiyà. b. (*stop going*) barì *v\**: ~ school, a job bar makarantà, aikì. c. (~ *behind*) barì *v\**, barō *v6*: I left my family behind at home nā barō ìyālìnā gidā; he died leaving 2 wives and 6 children yā ràsu yā bar

mātā biyu dà 'yā'yā shidà; I have left word for him to follow us nā bar masà sàllāhù yà biyō mù. d. (*depart*) tāshì *v3b*, tàfi *v3\**: when does the train ~? yàushè jirgī kè tāshì? he's already left from work yā rigā yā tāshì dàgà aikì; I caught him just as he was about to ~ nā sàmē shì daidai lōkàcîn dà yakè hafamàr tàfiyà. e. (*separate, divorce*) ràbu *v7*: his wife has left him màtarsà tā ràbu dà shī. f. (*remain*) ragè *v4, see* left[2]: they didn't ~ me any bà sù ragè minì kōmē ba.
2. *n* a. (*permission*) izìnī *m*. b. (*vacation*) hūtū *m*, lifì *m*, [F] kwànjê *m*: a few days' ~ hūtū na 'yan kwànàkī; go on, take ~ tàfi, ɗau hūtū; ~ of absence (*esp. Mil.*) lifì *m*, [F] fafmasō *m*: get, take ~ ɗauki lifì; maternity ~ hūtun haihùwā = hūtun jēgò. c. (*farewell*) ban kwānā *m*; take ~ of so. yi wà ban kwānā *m*, yi sallamà dà *f*: he came to take ~ of us yā zō yà yi manà ban kwānā.

**lecture** *n* (*academic*) laccà *f* ⟨oCi⟩, [F] kûr *m*; (*public speech*) jàwābì *m* ⟨ai⟩: deliver a ~ gabātar dà jàwābì = kaddamar dà jàwābì.

**lecturer** *n* (*university*) mālāmin jāmi'à *m*: he's a ~ in history shì mālāmin jāmi'à nē à fannìn tārīhì; (*any speaker*) mài bā dà laccà *n*.

**ledger** *n* (*accounting book*) lajà *f*.

**leech** *n* màtsàttsàku *f*.

**left**[1] *adj & adv* hagu *m*, hauni *m*: it is on the ~ yanà (dàgà) hagu = yanà hannun hagu; follow, turn to the ~ bi, jūyà hagu; the road on the ~ hanyàr dà ta bi hagu; his ~ arm hannunsà na hagu; to the ~ of hagu dà: his house is to the ~ of mine gidansà nà hagu dà nàwā; on the ~ side of à haguncin: the house is on the ~ side of the road gidân yanà haguncin hanyà.

**left**[2], be *v* (*remain*) ragè *v4*, ràgu *v7*, saura *v3a*: I ate up what was ~ nā cînyē àbîn dà ya saura; there is just a little ~ kàɗan ya ragè; there are only ₦3 ~ àbîn dà ya saura naifà ukù kawài; how many are ~? saurà nawà? there isn't any ~ bàbù saurà = bābù ràgōwà = bâ àbîn dà ya ràgu = bà à ragè kōmē ba.

**left-handed** *adj* (*psn.*) bàhagò *m* ⟨ai⟩: he is ~ shì bàhagò ne.

**leftist** *n, see* left-wing.

**leftovers** *p* (*warmed up for breakfast*) dùmāmē *m*, [F] zàzàfē *m*.

**left-wing** *adj* (mài) nēman sauyì *m*, (mài) ra'àyin sauyì *m*.

**leg** *n* ƙafà *f* ⟨ƙafàfū, uwa²⟩: break a ~ karyè ƙafà; a broken ~ kàryayyiyař ƙafà; hurt one's ~ yi ràunī à ƙafà = ji cīwò à ƙafà; fix the ~ of this table kà gyārà ƙafař tēbùřin nàn; stretch one's ~s mī̀ƙè ƙafà.

**legal** *adj* (*any lawful act in Islam*) hàlâl *m*: it is ~ to have 4 wives under Islamic law auren mātā huɗu gà Mùsùlmī hàlâl nē; declare, make sth. ~ halàttā *v1*; (*pertaining to law*) na shàři'à *f*: ~ affairs hařkōkin shàři'à.

**legend** *n* (*tale*) àlmàřà *f* ⟨u⟩.

**legible** *adj* (mài) kàřàntuwā *f*.

**legislature** *n* màjàlisàř dōkōkī *f*.

**legitimate** *adj*: a ~ child ɗan hàlâs/hàlâk *m*; be ~ (*in Islam*) hàlattā *v3*.

**leisure** *n* (*opportunity*) dāmā *f*, sùkūnī̀ *m*: at your ~ in kā ga dāmā = lōkàcîn dà kakè dà dāmā; ~ time lōkàcin shàƙàtâwā *m*.

**lemon** *n* lèmon/lèmun tsāmī *m*.

**lemonade** *n* ruwan lèmon tsāmī *m*.

**lend** *v* a. (*esp. money*) rântā *v1*, bā dà ràncē *m*, *see* borrow: could you ~ me ₦20? kō zā kà iyà rântā minì naiřà àshìřin? = kō zā kà bā nì ràncen naiřà àshìřin? b. (*anything except money, food*) arà wà *v1*, bā dà arò *m*: he lent me a flashlight yā arà minì tōcìlàn = yā bā nì aron tōcìlàn. c. (*of vehicle for temporary use*) bā dà dānī̀: he lent me his bicycle yā bā nì dānìn kèkènsà. d. ~ a hand tayà *v1*, bā dà hannū: please ~ us a hand to push this car don Allàh kù bā mù hannū mù tūrà mōtàř nân = don Allàh kù tayà mu wajen tūrà mōtàř nân.

**lender** *n* (*money*) mài bā dà bāshì *m*.

**length** *n* a. tsawō *m*, tsayī̀ *m*: what is the ~ of the table? mènē nè tsawon tēbùř dîn? a plank 3 meters in ~ kātākō mài tsawon mītā ukù; the ~ of time I spent there was 3 weeks tsawon zamānā cân màkò ukù nē; speak at ~ yi màganā mài tsawō = yi dōgon bàyānì. b. (*of pre-cut printed yardage*) turmì *m*. c. (*Gram.*) tsawō *m*, tsayī̀ *m*: vowel ~ tsawon wasàlī = jan wasàlī.

**lengthen** *v* a. (*a garment, thing*) ƙārà tsawō. b. (*prolong*) tsawàitā *v1*.

**lengthwise** *adv* à tsàye *adv*.

**leniency** *n* sassaucì *m*, rangwamè *m*.

**lenient** *adj*: be ~ rangwàntā wà *v1*, sassàutā wà *v1*, yi wà rangwamè *m*, yi wà saukī̀ *m*, yi wà sassaucì *m*: the judge was ~ and gave him only 30 days àlƙālī yā yi masà rangwamè dà ya bā shì kwānà tàlàtin kawài; he gave him a ~ sentence yā yi masà hukuncì mài saukī̀; she is too ~ with her children tā cikà yi wà 'yā'yàntà sassaucì.

**lens** *n* (*of eyeglasses*) ruwan tàbàrau *m*.

**leopard** *n* dàmīsà *f* ⟨oCi, u⟩.

**leper** *n* kuturū *m*, kuturwā *f* ⟨a-e⟩.

**leprosy** *n* kuturtà *f*.

**lesbian** *n* 'yař mādigò *f*.

**less** 1. *quant & det*: (*in gen'l, use the compar. verb* kai *v* * *in the neg. or neg. verbs such as* ragè *v4 or* kàsà *v1*): he has ~ patience than I bài kai nì hàƙurī ba; he earns ~ money than you àlbâshinsà bài kai nākà ba; they came back in ~ than an hour bà sù kai kō awà ɗaya ba sukà dāwō; there is ~ than you think yā kāsà yàddà kakè zàtō; 7 is ~ than 10 bakwài bà tà kai gōmà ba = bakwài yanà ƙasà da gōmà.

2. *adv* a. do ~ ragè *v4*: you should think more and talk ~ kù ragè màganà kù ƙārà tùnànī; how is it that you gave me 2 ~ (than what I expected)? yàyà ka ragè minì biyu? he sold it to me for ~ yā ragè minì = yā yi minì rangwamè; it gets increasingly ~ kullum ràguwā yakè yî; this bus is ~ crowded than that one wannàn bâs bà tà yi cìkōwā kàmař waccàn ba. b. more or ~ kusan *prep*: there were 50 more or ~ sun kai kusan hàmsin; that is more or ~ correct wannàn kusan daidai nè; c. ~ than (*below*) ƙasà dà *prep*: ~ than 3 years ƙasà dà shèkarà ukù. d. much ~ (*for neg. contrast*) bàllē / bàllàntànā: he can't read, much ~ write bài iyà kàřàtū ba bàllē mā řubùtū.

3. *prep*: 6 ~ 2 is 4 shidà à ɗebè biyu huɗu kè nan.

**lessen** *v* a. (*subside*) tsagàitā *v1*. b. (*relieve*) saukàƙā *v1*: this medicine will ~ the pain màgànin nàn zâi saukàƙā makà zāfī.

**lesson** *n* dařàsī̀ *m* ⟨u-a⟩: a math ~ dařàsin lìssāfī̀; driving ~s dařussàn kòyon tūƙī̀.

**lest** *adv* (don) kadà: take an umbrella ~ you get soaked kà tàfi dà laimā don kadà ruwā yà bā kà kāshì.

**let¹** *v* a. (*allow*) barì *v* *: ~ him enter bàř shi yà shigō = sai yà shigō; ~ me help you bàri ìn tàimàkē kì; he will not ~ you do that bà zâi bař kà kà yi hakà ba; don't ~ the food get cold kâř kà bař àbinci yà hūcè. b. (*var. v + v uses*): ~ so. go (*release*) sàkā *v2*: ~ me go! sàkē ni! he ~ them go without punishment yā sàkē sù bằ tằre dà wani hồrō ba; ~ so. go (dismiss) sàllamằ v2; ~ so. know sanaȓ (dà) v5: I will ~ you know what happens zân sanaȓ dà kai àbîn dà ya fằru. c. (var. v + adv/prep uses): ~ so. alone (ignore) ƙyàlē v4; ~ so. down (disappoint) bā dà / bāyaȓ (dà) v5; ~ so. off (forgive) yāfē wà v4, baȓ wà: I'll ~ you off this time nā yāfē makà wannàn karòn = nā baȓ makà wannàn karòn; ~ go of sth. (release) sakì v2*; ~ up (lessen) tsagàitā v1: after a while, the rain ~ up jimằwā kàɗan ruwān yā tsagàitā. d. ~ alone bàllē / bàllàntànā: there's no water, ~ alone food bābù ruwā bàllàntànā àbinci; I can't swim, ~ alone you bàn iyà iyồ ba bàllē kai.

**let²** v, see rent.

**lethargic** adj (temporarily) (mài) kàsālằ f, laƙwas idph: feel ~ ji kàsālằ, yi laƙwas: I'm feeling ~ today yâu inà jîn kàsālằ; (naturally sluggish) nằ dà sanyin jìkī m: he is ~ by nature sanyin jìkī gàrē shì.

**letter** n a. (of alphabet) haȓàfī m ⟨u-a⟩, baƙī m ⟨aCe⟩: capital ~ bàbban baƙī; the English alphabet has 26 ~s baƙàƙen Ingìlīshì àshīȓin dà shidà nē. b. (correspondence) wàsīƙà f ⟨u⟩, takàȓdā f ⟨u⟩, [F] lètìȓ f ⟨oCi⟩: I received a ~ from him nā sằmi wàsīƙà dàgà gàrē shì; are there any ~s for me? inà dà wàsīƙū? mail a ~ sakà wàsīƙà à gidan wayằ; an express ~ wàsīƙà kàȓ-tà-kwàna = wàsīƙà mài gaggāwā; registered ~ wàsīƙà ta ȓajistà = wàsīƙaȓ hannū-dà-hannū.

**lettuce** n latàs m, sàlâk m, [F] sàlātì m; water ~ (found in ponds) kainuwā f.

**leukoma** n hakiyằ f, tsāwuryằ f.

**level¹** 1. v & adj (even) yi lēbùȓ m, [F] yi nìbô m: the floor is ~ with the street dàɓên yā yi lēbùȓ dà hanyằ; ~ a place to make it even yi wà wurī lēbùȓ don yà zama bâi ɗaya.
2. n a. (height) tsawō m: the water reached the ~ of my knees ruwân yā kai haȓ tsawon gwīwằtā = ruwân yā kai yà gwīwằtā. b. (surveyor's) madūbin lēbùȓ m, [F] nìbô m; (carpenter's) sàndaȓ lēbùȓ f.

**level²** v (destroy) rūsaȓ (dà) v5, rūshē v4: the storm ~led the house iskằ tā rūsaȓ dà gidân.

**lever** n lībằ f.

**lewd** adj na bātsa f: a ~ photograph hồton bātsa; ~ talk ɗanyen bằkī m, mūgùn bằkī m.

**lexicography** n ilìmin tsārà ƙāmùs m.

**lexicon** n tsārìn ƙāmùs m.

**liabilities** n bāsūsukằ p.

**liar** n maƙàryàcī m; you're a ~! ƙaryā kakè!

**libel** n shaȓȓì m.

**liberal** n & adj (Pol.) (mài) sassaucin ȓa'àyī m.

**liberate** v 'yântā v1: the army ~d the town sōjōjī sun 'yantō gàrîn.

**liberty** n 'yancì m: the right to ~ hakkìn 'yancì; I am not at ~ to speak bâ ni dà 'yancìn màganằ.

**librarian** n ma'àikàcin lābùȓàȓē m.

**library** n lābùȓàȓē m ⟨oCi⟩, [F] malittāfà f, [F] bìbìlòtêk f; (reading room) dākìn kàȓàtū m.

**lice** n kwâȓkwatằ / ƙwâȓƙwatằ f: his hair was infested with ~ gāshìnsà cìke yakè dà kwâȓkwatằ; crab ~ dànkà-ɗafi m; sand ~ kûȓkudù m.

**license** n (auto) lāsìn / lāsīsì m, [F] fàȓmî m: driver's ~ lāsìn tūƙì; (for business, trade) takàȓdaȓ izìnī f, [F] lìsâns f: medical ~ takàȓdaȓ izìnin aikìn likità; ~ bureau ōfìshin lāsīsì; apply for a ~ nềmi lāsīsì; obtain a ~ yi lāsìn; revoke a ~ ƙwàcè lāsīsì.

**license plate** n lambàȓ mōtằ f, [F] limaȓon mōtằ m.

**lick** v a. làsā v2, tàndā v2: the dog ~ed his wounds kàrē yā làshi gyàmbonsà; (one's fingers after eating) sudề v4; (moisten with tongue) jiƙà dà miyau: he ~ed the envelope to seal it yā jiƙà ambùlàn dà miyau don yà līƙề shi. b. (fig., defeat) ci v0, lāshē v4: they ~ed us 4 to 1 sun lāshề mu huɗu dà ɗaya; they gave us a real ~ing sun cī mù mūgùn cî.

**lid** n murfī m ⟨ai⟩: put the ~ on a pot sânyà murfī à kân tukunyā = rufề tukunyā dà murfī; take the ~ off ɗaukè murfī = būɗề tukunyā.

**lie¹** v kwântā v1, yi kwànciyā f: I lay (down) on the bed to rest nā kwântā à gadō don ìn hūtà; be lying down à kwànce adv: he is still lying in bed haȓ yànzu dai à kwànce yakè à gadō; ~ face down yi ȓûb-dà-cikì m; ~ on one's back yi rìgìngìne m; ~ on one's elbow kìshìngìɗà v3, yi kìshìngìɗe m; ~ in wait yi kwantō m, yi fàkō m: the cat is lying in wait for the mouse kyânwā tanà fàkon 6ēȓā; lying across à gìcce adv: a log was lying across the road wani gungumề yanằ gìcce à hanyằ; lying around (scattered) à wầtse adv: there were clothes

lying all around the room tufāfī sunā
wāřwàtse à cikin dākī.

**lie²** 1. *v* yi ƙaryā *f*, (*emphat.*) zūƙà ƙaryā,
shārà ƙaryā: he ~d to the court yā yi
ƙaryā gàban àlƙālī; you're lying! zūƙà
ƙaryā kakè!
2. *n* ƙaryā *f* ⟨ƙaràirai⟩: don't tell ~s
kadà kà yi ƙaryā; tell a ~ about, to
so. yi wà ƙaryā; his ~s were found out
ƙaryařsà bà tà ci ba; he fed us with ~s
yā shārā manà ƙaràirai; what a whop-
ping ~! ji ƙaryař wòfī!

**lieutenant** *n* làftanàn *m*, [F] lìtìnân *m*.

**life** *n* a. râi *m* ⟨rāyukà⟩: he is ~less bâ shi
dà râi; lose one's ~ rasà râi: many lives
were lost an rasà rāyukà dà yawà; he
lost his ~ saving someone yā rasà rânsà
gàrin cêton wani; it is a question of
~ and death àbù nē na à yi râi kō à
mutù; he was sentenced to ~ imprisonment an ɗaurè shi râi dà râi; friends
for ~ àbòtař râi dà râi; president for
~ shùgàban dindìndin; he is crippled for
~ yā nàƙasà hař àbàdà; come back to ~
(*from fainting*) fařfaɗō *v6*; run for one's
~ yi gudù don tsērař dà râi; save so.'s
~ cêtā *v2* ⟨cêtō⟩; spare one's ~ yi wà
râi; may God prolong your ~! (*said esp.
to important people*) Allàh yà jā zāmānī!
where there is ~, there is hope (*fig.*) in
dà râi dà râbō. b. (*pre-ordained span
of* ~) ajàlī *m*: his ~ came to an end yā
kai ajàlī = ajàlinsà yā ƙarè. c. (*one's
way of* ~) ràyuwā *f*: people today have an
easier ~ than in the past mutànen yànzu
sun fi na dâ jîn dāɗin ràyuwā; he leads
a busy ~ ràyuwařsà tā cikà hidimā dà
yawà; he led a good ~ yā shā daulà à
ràyuwařsà; the Hausa way of ~ hālin
ràyuwař Hàusàwā; never in my ~ have I
heard of such a thing tun dà nakè, bàn
taɓà jîn irìn wannàn ba. d. (*existence*)
zamā *m*: ~ is very pleasant here zaman nàn
nā dà dāɗī; a ~ of trouble zaman màsīfà;
how's ~? yàyà zaman gàrī? ~ has its ups
and downs (*fig.*) zaman dūniyà hawā dà
gàngarà = wata rānā à shā zumà wata
rānā maɗàcī; ~ is full of troubles dūniyà
gidan wàhalà; that's ~! sha'anin dūniyà
kè nan! = hālìn dūniyà kè nan! e. (*any
living creature*) màhàlūkì *m* ⟨ai⟩, àbù mài
râi *m*: there is no ~ on the moon bābù
wani màhàlūkì à kân watà.

**lifeless** *adj* maràs râi *m*.

**lifespan** *n* ajàlin mùtûm *m*.

**lifestyle** *n* hālin ràyuwā *m*.

**lifetime** *n* ràyuwā *f*: it won't happen within

our ~ bà zāi fàru cikin ràyuwařmù ba.

**lift¹** *v* (*raise*) ɗagà *v1*: he ~ed his head to
speak yā ɗagà kâi don yà yi màganà; the
state of emergency has been ~ed an ɗagà
dòkař-tā-ɓācìn; (*sth. heavy*) cìccìɓà *v2*,
sùngumà *v2*: would you help me ~ this
heavy box? kō zā kù tayà ni mù cìccìɓi
wannàn àkwàtì? it is too heavy to ~ bâ yà
cìccìɓuwà; ~ up sth. yi samà dà: they
~ed up the box sun yi samà dà àkwàtì;
~ up edge of sth. bankàɗà *v1*: she ~ed
the edge of the carpet to sweep under it
tā bankàɗà dàřdūmā don tà yi shārā.

**lift²** *n* (*elevator*) lîf *m*; (*ride in car*) dānì
*m*, lîf *m*: he gave me a ~ to town yā bā
nì dānì zuwà gàrī.

**ligament** *n* jījìyā *f* ⟨oCi⟩.

**light¹** 1. *n* a. (*brightness*) haskē *m*: by the
~ of a candle dà hasken kyandìř. b. (*of
a fire or from electricity*) wutā *f*: turn on
a ~ kunnà wutā = kunnà fìtilà; turn
off a ~ kashè wutā; give me a ~ for my
cigarette sam minì wutā ìn kunnà tābà.
c. (*electric*) fìtilà *f* ⟨u⟩: the ~ has gone
out, let's get a new bulb fìtilà tā mutù,
mù nèmi sābon ƙwan làntařkì; street ~
fìtilař tītì = fìtilař gàrī. d. (*of
day*): let's work while there is still ~ mù
yi aikì tun gàrī yanà ganì.
2. *v* a. (*any fire*) kunnà *v1*: he lit a fire,
cigarette yā kunnà wutā, tābà; (*a fire, by
blowing or fanning*) hūrà *v1*; ~ a match
ƙyastà àshānā; ~ a pipe dānà wutā à
tukunyař tābà. b. (*a place*) haskàkà *v1*:
he lit the room with a candle yā haskàkà
dākì dà kyandìř; we found the room all
lit up mun sàmi dākì à hàskàke.
3. *adj* a. (*of colors*) (mài) haskē *m*, bàu
*idph*: ~ blue shūdì mài haskē = shūdì
bàu. b. (*of skin color*) (mài) wankan
tařwadà *m*, (*very* ~) farī *m*, jàtau *n*.

**light²** *adj* a. (*not heavy*) maràs nauyī *m*:
the load is ~ kāyân bâ nauyī; (*very* ~)
sakwat *idph*, sayau *idph*, sakayau *idph*:
this is as ~ as a feather wannàn sakwat dà
shī; how can this box be so ~? yàyà na
ji àkwàtìn nân sakayau? b. (*easy*) (mài)
saukī *m*: ~ work, punishment aikì, hòrō
mài saukī.

**lightbulb** *n* ƙwan làntařkì *m*, [F] àmpûl *f*;
(*fluorescent*) kyandìř *m*; (*for car, flashlight*) gùlâb *m*, [F] gwàlâf *m*.

**lighten** *v* a. (*weight*) ragè nauyī: we must
~ the donkey's load yā kàmatà mù ragè
nauyin kāyan jàkī. b. (*make easier*)
saukàƙà *v1*, yi sassaucì *m*: he has ~ed
our work yā saukàƙà manà aikìn = yā yi

manà sassaucì gà aikìn.

**lighter** n (*for cigarettes*) lētà f, k̃yàstū m, [F] bìr̃ìk̃ê m.

**light-hearted** adj (mài) fàr̃a'à f, (mài) sakìn fuskà m.

**lightly** adv (*gently*) à hankàlī: he knocked ~ on the door yā k̃wank̃wàsà k̃ōfà à hankàlī; take sth. ~ (*not seriously*) yi gàràjē m: he takes his studies ~ yanà gàràjē dà kàr̃àtunsà.

**lightning** n (*sheet*) wàlk̃iyā f, (*bolt*) àr̃ādù f, (*euphem.*) àbar̃ samà f, ta samà f: a bolt of ~ gàtarin àr̃ādù; if you hear the sound of thunder, it means ~ has struck in kā ji tsāwā, tô, àr̃ādù tā fàdì.

**like**[1] 1. *v a.* (*be fond of*) sō *v0* (*used mostly in contin.*): I ~ him inà sônsà; I don't ~ it bā nà sônsà; most people ~ music yawancin mutànē nà sôn kàde-kàde; ~ very much kwàntā wà à râi: I really ~ her child yāròntà yā kwàntā minì à râi; well, I really don't ~ it very much kâi, bàn cikà sônsà ba; ~ it or not, you have do it kō kā sō kō kā k̃i sai kā yī shì; do just as you ~ yi kàmar̃ dai yàddà kakè sō = yi kàmar̃ yàddà ka ga dāmā; if you would ~ to, you may go with us in kā ga dāmā, munà iyà tàfiyà tàre. b. (*think of, have an opinion of*) ganī *v\**, ji *v0*: how do you ~ Kano? yàyà ka ga Kanò? = yàyà kakè jî dà Kanò? how do they ~ that? yàyà sukà ga wannàn? = mè sukà ganī gàme dà wannàn? = mè sukè jî dà wannàn?

2. *n a.* (*desire*): he has his ~s and dislikes yanà dà abūbuwàn dà yakè sô dà wadàndà bā yà sô. b. (*kind, ilk*): and their ~ (*ilk*) dà makàmàntansù: I don't care for lazy people and their ~ bā nà sôn malàlàtā dà makàmàntansù; this place is for the ~s of you, not us wannàn wurī sai yà kū yà kū, bà mū ba.

**like**[2] *prep a.* (*similar to*) kàmar̃ *prep*: it smells ~ an onion wàrinsà kàmar̃ àlbasà; it looks to me ~ rain nā ga kàmar̃ zā à yi ruwā; do it ~ this kà yī shì kàmar̃ hakà; what is it ~? yàyà yakè? b. (*esp. physical resemblance*) kàmā dà *prep*: a roar ~ a lion's rūr̃ì kàmā dà na zākì; he is not ~ his brother bài yi kàmā dà dan'uwansà ba; one who is ~ me mài kàmā dà nī. c. (*of equivalent status*) yà *prep*: you're ~ me and I'm ~ you kai yà nī, nī yà kai; how is it that someone ~ you has been given such (lowly) work? mùtûm yà kai à bā shì wannàn aikìn? someone ~ X kàmar̃ X, tàmkar̃ X: someone ~ you

wouldn't do such a thing tàmkar̃kà bà yà yi hakà ba; ~ father ~ son (*fig.*) bàrēwā tà yi gudù dantà yà yi ràrràfē? d. (*of that kind*) irìn na: trousers ~ those of old wàndō irìn na dâ; he walks just ~ his father yanà tàfiyà irìn ta bàbansà. e. (*in outward appearance*) shigen na: the skink looks ~ a snake jìkin kul6à shigen na macìjī nè; hers is ~ mine tātà shigen tàwa; be dressed ~ yi shìgar̃: he is dressed ~ a European yā yi shìgar̃ Tūr̃āwā. f. (*simile*) sai kà cê: he swims ~ a fish yā iyà iyò sai kà cê kīfī nè. g. feel ~ doing ji *v0* : he feels ~ seeing a movie yanà jîn kallon sìlimà; I don't feel ~ studying today bā nà jîn yîn kàr̃àtū yâu.

**likely** adj & adv (*possible*) (mài) yìwuwā: it is ~ that we will spend 2 years there mài yìwuwā nè mù yi shēkarà biyu à cân; it is ~ to gà àlāmà: it's ~ to rain gà àlāmà zā à yi ruwā; it is not ~ to happen bâ àlāmàr̃ yìwuwar̃sà; it is not at all ~ dà kyar̃ zâi yìwu.

**likelihood** n àlāmà f ⟨u⟩: is there any ~ of his coming? kō àkwai àlāmàr̃ zuwànsà?

**liken** v misàltà *v1*: he ~ed his stay to being in prison yā misàltà zamân dà na kûr̃kukù.

**likeness** n shigē m, shìgā f.

**likewise** adv kàzālikà adv, mā hakà(nan): she went and I did ~ tā jē nī mā kàzālikà = tā jē nī mā hakànan.

**lily** n (*water-*~) badò m.

**lilytrotter** n (*bird*) tàkà-badò m.

**limb** n (*of tree*) rēshè m ⟨Ca⟩.

**limbo** n: the matter is in ~ (*fig.*) màganà tanà k̃asà tanà dabò.

**lime**[1] n (*fruit*) lèmon tsāmī m.

**lime**[2] n (*mineral*) farar̃ k̃asā f.

**limit** 1. *n a.* (*specific boundary*) iyàkā / iyākā f ⟨oCi⟩: Kano city ~s iyàkar̃ bìr̃nin Kanò; a credit ~ iyàkar̃ bāshì; his love knows no ~ k̃àunar̃sà bâ ta dà iyàkā; to the ~ iyà / iyàkar̃ / iyàkacin *prep*: he worked to the ~ of his abilities yā yi aikì iyàkacin k̃ōk̃arinsà = iyàkar̃ k̃ōk̃arinsà; indebt oneself to the ~ ci bāshì iyà/iyàkar̃ wuyà; that's the ~! iyàkar̃sà kè nan! = iyàkacinsà kè nan! set a time ~ k̃ayyàdè lōkàcī, iyàkàncè lōkàcī: they have given us a time ~ sun iyàkàncè lōkàcinmù = sun k̃ayyàdē manà lōkàcì. b. (*endpoint to be reached*) mak̃urā f: he reached the ~ of his endurance yā kai mak̃urar̃ jìmirinsà = yā kai iyàkar̃ jìmirinsà. c. (*esp. le-*

*gal*) haddì *m*, ƙā'idà *f* ⟨oCi⟩: exceed the ~ kētà haddì = wucè ƙā'idà; age ~ yawàn shèkàrun dà akà yankè; speed ~ ƙàyyàdadden yawàn gudũ; go beyond the ~s of propriety (*fig.*) wucè gōnā dà irì = shìgè makàdì dà rawā.

2. *v* iyākàncē *v4*, ƙayyàdē *v4*; be too ~ed (*of time*) ƙurè *v4*: the time is too ~ed to finish up lōkàcī yā ƙurè, bà zā mù iyà gamāwā ba.

limitless *adj* a. (*without limit*) maràs iyàkā *f*, maràs maƙurā *f*. b. (*infinite*) bìlā haddìn.

limp[1] *v* yi dìngishì *m*: he is ~ing due to the accident yanà dìngishì sabòdà hadàřìn.

limp[2] *adj* (*sluggish*) laƙwas *idph*: I feel ~ jìkīnā yā yi laƙwas; (*drooping*) (mài) yaushī *m*, làngàɓaɓɓè *adj*; be(come) ~ langàɓè *v4*.

line 1. *n* a. lāyì *m* ⟨uka⟩: draw a straight ~ from here to there kà jā lāyì mìƙaƙƙè dàgà nân zuwà cân; sign on the ~ sâ hannu à lāyì; read from ~ 8 kà kařàntā dàgà lāyì na takwàs; arrange things in a ~ jērà abūbuwà à lāyì gùdā; form a ~, stand in ~ yi lāyì *m*, yi jērìn gwànō *m*: you stand in ~ when you vote anà lāyì lōkàcin jēfà ƙùři'à; (*fig.*) make them toe the ~ kà sâ su à lāyì. b. (*of individuals in a row*) jērì *m*, *see* row. c. (*telephone, electrical*) wayà / wayàř tàřhō *f*: the ~ is busy tàřhō nà aikì; someone is on the ~ anà wayà. d. (*clothesline*) wayà *f*, igiyàř shânyà *f*: the clothes were hanging on the ~ tufāfìn sunà ràtàye kân wayà. e. (*for fishing*) fatsa *f*. f. (*in poetry*) ƙwàyā / ƙwař *f*. g. (*lineage*) jinī *m*, asalī *m*: he comes from a ~ of blacksmiths shì jinin maƙèrā nè = asalinsà maƙèrī nè.

2. *v* a. (*make a ~*): ~ sth. up jērà *v1*, yi lāyì *m*: he ~d them up in rows yā jērà su lāyì-lāyì = yā jajjērà su; a road ~d with trees hanyà mài jērìn itàtuwà. b. (*a garment*) sâ shāfì *m*.

lineage *n* jinī *m*, asalī *m*.

lingua franca *n*: Hausa is the major ~ of West Africa Hausa ita cè harshèn dà akà fi àmfànī dà shī à Afiřkà ta Yàmma.

linguist *n* masànin harsunà *m*.

linguistics *n* ilìmin harsunà *m*.

liniment *n* māganin shāfàwā *m*, lilimàn / lilimantì *m*, [F] mân màsâj *m*.

lining *n* (*of garment*) shāfì *m*.

link *v* haɗà *v1* ⟨haɗì⟩: the new road will ~ all the villages sàbuwař hanyà zā tà haɗà

duk ƙauyukà.

linoleum *n* lēdàř dàɓen ɗākì *f*.

lint *n* (*inside a pocket*) ƙařfamfànā *f*.

lintel *n* lintà *f*.

lion *n* zākì *m* ⟨oCi⟩; ~ cub kwìkwiyò *m*; ~ess zākanyà *f*; (*fig.*) the ~'s share kashì mafì tsōkà.

lip *n* lēɓè *m* ⟨Ca, una⟩: my ~s are cracked from the wind làɓɓānā sun būshè sabòdà iskà; point with one's ~s yi zùndē *m*, nūnà dà bàkī.

lip-service *n* ladàbin kūrā *m*.

lipstick *n* jàn-bàki *m*.

liquid *n* ruwā *m*.

liquidate *v* (*Econ.*) yi kàrayàř ařzìkī.

liquor *n* (*any strong alcoholic drink*) bàřàsā *f*.

lisp *v* yi tsāmin bàkī *m*.

list 1. *n* (*of names, numbers*) tsārì *m*, jērì *m*.

2. *v* lāsàftā / lissàfā *v1*: he ~ed our names one after the other yā lissàfà sūnàyenmù ɗai-ɗai dà ɗai-ɗai.

listen *v* sàurārà *v2* ⟨sàurārō, sàurārè⟩: I ~ed to what he was saying nā sàuràri àbin dà yakè fàɗā sòsai; we are ~ing to him munà sàurāronsà = munà sàurārensà; he ~s regularly to this program yakàn sàuràri wannàn shirì à kâi à kâi; ~ attentively kasà kûnnē, yi kàsàkē *m*.

listener *n* mài sàurārō *m*, mài sàurārè *m*: radio ~s in Niger màsu sàurāron řēdiyò à Nìjàř.

liter *n* lītà *f*, [F] lītìř *m*.

literacy *n* kàřātū dà řubūtū: the government's goal is to achieve universal ~ būřin gwamnatì shī nè kōyà wà jàma'à kàřātū dà řubūtū; ~ campaign yàƙì dà jāhilcì *m*, ilìmin mânyā *m*, [F] kuřdàdī *m*.

literal *adj*: ~ meaning of a word mà'ànař kalmà ta fīlì = mà'ànař kalmà ta zāhìřì; a ~ translation fassařàř kâi tsàye.

literally *adv*: translate ~ (*word by word*) jūyà kalmà dà kalmà.

literary *adj* na adàbī *m*.

literature *n* adàbī *m*: comparative ~ nazàřin kwatàntà adàbī; oral ~ adàbin bàkà; written ~ řubūtaccen adàbī.

litre *n* lītà *f*, [F] lītìř *m*.

littered *adj* řàkàcàm / řàkwàcàm *idph*: his room is ~ dākìnsà yanà nan řàkàcàm.

little 1. *adj* a. (*in size*) ƙaramì *adj* ⟨ƙanànà⟩; ƙànƙanè *m*, ƙànƙanùwā *f* ⟨ƙanànà⟩: a ~ rabbit ƙaramin zōmō; I want a big one, not a ~ one inà sôn bàbba bà ƙaramì ba

**nē. b.** (*young in age*) yārṑ *m*, yārinyȃ *f* ⟨yārā⟩: when I was ∼ lōkàcîn dà nakè yārṑ = tun inȃ ƙàramî; I haven't seen him since we were ∼ ràbonmù tun munȃ yārā. **c.** (*as dimin.*) ɗan *m*, 'yaȓ *f* ⟨'yan⟩: a very ∼ girl wata 'yaȓ ƙàramaȓ yārinyȃ. **2. adv a.** kàɗan *adv*: there is just a ∼ water left ruwàn dà ya ragè kàɗan nè; let me have a ∼ of that sam minì wannàn kàɗan; I know very ∼ about her àbîn dà na sanì gàme dà ita kàɗan nè; a ∼ bit ɗan kàɗan = kàɗan kàɗan; I have a ∼ bit of money inȃ dà kuɗī 'yan kàɗan. **b.** (*as dimin. preceding a v*) ɗan: she knows a ∼ Hausa tā ɗan iyà Hausa = tā iyà Hausa kàɗan; please wait a ∼ don Allàh kà ɗan dākàtā = don Allàh kà dākàtā kàɗan; ∼ by ∼ (*incrementally*) dà kàɗan kàɗan: children grow up ∼ by ∼ dà kàɗan kàɗan yârā kè girmā; ∼ by ∼ (*gradually over time*) à kwāna à tāshì, kwànci-tàshi: ∼ by ∼ the company became successful à kwāna à tāshì kamfànī yā ci nasarȃ.

**live 1. v a.** (*reside*) zaunȃ *v1* yi zamā *m*: he ∼s in Yakasai quarter yanà zàune nè à ùnguwaȓ Yàkàsai; where do you ∼? à ìnā kakè dà zamā? have you ∼d here long? kā daɗè dà zama à nân? fish ∼ in water kīfàyē sunà zamā à ruwa nè; ∼ peacefully yi zaman lùmānȃ; they ∼ in peace and happiness sun zaunà cikin lùmānȃ dà jîn dāɗī. **b.** (*during a certain epoch*) yi zāmànī *m*: he ∼d 100 years ago yā yi zāmàninsà shèkarà ɗarī dà sukà wucè. **c.** (*have life*) nà dà râi, see **alive**: is he still living? yanà nân dà râi? **d.** (*survive*) ràyu *v7*: the doctors don't think he will ∼ likitōcī bā sà tsàmmānìn zâi ràyu; one cannot ∼ without air ràyuwà bā tà yìwuwā sai dà iskà; he ∼d to the age of 90 yā ràyu haȓ shèkarà càsà'in; ∼ with sth. (*be resigned to*) hàƙurà dà *v3*, dànganà dà *v3*: it's a loss that we have to ∼ with rashì nē dà yā zama tīlàs mù hàƙurà dà shī. **2. adj** (mài) râi *m*.

**livelihood** *n* gātā *m*: teaching is his ∼ aikìn màlàntā shî nè gātansà.

**liver** *n* hantȃ *f* ⟨oCi, una⟩.

**livestock** *n* dabbōbin kīwò *p*; ∼ market kàsuwaȓ dabbōbī.

**living** *n*: make a ∼ nèmi àbinci; how does he make his ∼? mḕnē nè hanyàȓ nēman àbincinsà? what does he do for a ∼? mḕ yakè yî à ràyuwaȓsà? he earns an honest ∼ yanà cîn gùminsà.

**lizard** *n* ƙàdangarè *m* ⟨u⟩; (*blue with orange back*) jan kwatakwàrē *m*, jan gwādā *m*; see **chameleon, gecko, monitor lizard, skink.**

**load** *n* (*goods*) kāyā *m* ⟨aki²⟩; a ∼ of (*n depends on type of goods*): a ∼ of corn damìn hatsī; a ∼ of firewood ƙunshìn itàcē. **2. v a.** (*a psn. or animal into*) hau dà *v5*: they ∼ed the cattle into the wagon sun hau dà shānū à cikin tàȓagū. **b.** (*a pack animal, vehicle*) azȃ wà *v1*; (*a vehicle*) yi wà lōdì *m*; (*excessively*) labtȃ wà *v1*: (*fig.*) they ∼ed me with gifts sun labtȃ minì kyàutā. **c.** (*a gun*) dūrȃ *v1*.

**loaf¹** *n* (*of bread*) buȓōdì *m*, (*sliced*) buȓōdì mài yankā-yankā: buy me two loaves of bread kà sayō minì buȓōdì biyu; (*fig.*) half a ∼ is better than none à rashìn tuwō akàn ci wākē à kwāna.

**loaf²** *v* yi sākaȓcī *m*, yi ragwancī *m*.

**loafer** *n* ragō *m* ⟨aye⟩, sākaȓai *n* ⟨sākàȓkaȓī⟩.

**loan 1. n a.** (*sth. for temporary use to be returned*) arō *m*: this flashlight is not mine, it's a ∼ wannàn tōcìlàn bā tàwa ba cè, ta arō cè. **b.** (*esp. money*) ràncē *m*; (*esp. long-term* ∼ *of money*) bāshì *m* ⟨uka²⟩: take out a ∼ ci bāshì, karɓō bāshì; pay back a ∼ biyā bāshì. **2. v,** see **lend.**

**loanword** *n* kalmàȓ arō *m*.

**loathe** *v* yi ƙyāmā *f*, tsànā *v2*: they ∼ each other sunà ƙyāmaȓ jūnā.

**lobbying** *n* fādancī *m*, kāmùn ƙafȃ *m*.

**lobe** *n*, see **earlobe.**

**local** *adj*: a ∼ custom àl'ādàȓ gaȓgājiyā *f*; ∼ government ƙaramaȓ hùkūmȃ *f*; ∼ administrator kàntōmà *f* ⟨oCi⟩; it is ∼ly made an yī shì à wurîn.

**locate** *v*: I can't ∼ the town on the map nā kāsà ganin gàrîn à tàswīȓȃ; his office is ∼d in that building ōfìshinsà nà cikin wancàn ginìn.

**location** *n* wurì *m* ⟨aCe⟩: this is a suitable ∼ for a school wurin nàn zâi dācè dà makaȓantā.

**lock 1. n** makullī *m*; (*with spring, for door*) kūbȃ *f* ⟨oCi⟩: the ∼ is broken kūbȃ tā karyè; (*padlock*) kwàɗō *m* ⟨i⟩. **2. v** kullè *v4*: shut the door and ∼ it kà jāwō ƙōfȃ kà kuma kullè ta; I found the house ∼ed nā tarar dà gidā à kùlle.

**lockjaw** *n* sarƙḕwaȓ haƙōrā *f*.

**locksmith** *n* mài makullī *m*.

**locomotive** *n* tukunyaȓ jirgī *f*.

**locust** *n* fārȃ *f* ⟨i⟩: ∼s have attacked the crops fārī sun faȓ wà shùke-shùke;

(*newly hatched*) fàrař ɗangō *f;* (*large, non-gregarious type*) bābè *m* ⟨Ca⟩.

**locust-bean** *n* (*tree*) ɗòrawā *f* ⟨i⟩; ~ cakes dàddawā *f.*

**lodge** *v* a. (*provide lodgings*) saukař (dà) *v5;* (*get lodgings*) sàuka *v3,* (*esp. overnight*) yā dà zangò. b. (*get stuck*) maƙàlē *v4:* the bone ~d in his throat ƙashī yā maƙàlē masà à màƙōgwàro. c. (*a complaint*) kai ƙārā: she ~d a complaint against him tā kai ƙārařsà.

**lodgings** *n* masaukī *m.*

**log** *n* gungumè *m* ⟨a..ai⟩.

**logic** *n* a. (*sense*) hankàlī *m*, azancī *m.* b. (*academic subject*) ilìmin mandìƙī *m.*

**loincloth** *n* bàntē *m* ⟨una⟩, (*of leather*) wàřkī *m* ⟨una⟩.

**loins** *n* tsatsò *m.*

**loiter** *v* yi shàwāgì *m*, yi yāwòn banzā *m*, (*esp. when sent on errand*) shantàkē *v4*, yi nàwā *m.*

**lonely** *adj* (mài) kaɗaicì *m:* feel ~ ji kaɗaicì.

**loneliness** *adj* kaɗaicì *m:* suffer from ~ yi fāmā dà kaɗaicì.

**loner** *n* makàɗàicī *m.*

**long** 1. *adj* a. (*of space or time*) (mài) tsawō *m,* (mài) tsayī *m:* how ~ it is? mēnē nè tsawonsà? the room is 10 feet ~ tsawon ɗākì ƙafà gōmà nē; a ~ visit zìyàřà mai tsawō; after a ~ time bāyan wani lōkàcī mài tsawō; all day ~ rānā gàbā ɗayansà. b. (*of shape or time*) dōgō *adj* ⟨aye⟩: a ~ stick, journey dōguwař sàndā, tàfiyà; ~ hair gāshì mài yawà = gāshì mài tsawō; donkeys have ~ ears jàkī nà dà kunnuwà dōgwàyē; a ~ vowel dōgon wasàlī = wasàlī mài jā. c. (*lasting over time*): be a ~ time daɗè *v4:* I have been here for a ~ time nā daɗè inà nân = inà nân dà daɗèwā; have you had the backache for a ~ time? kā daɗè kanà fāmā dà cīwòn bāyân? I haven't seen him for a ~ time nā daɗè bàn gan shi ba = ràbonmù dà ganinsà yā daɗè. d. (*of distance*) (mài) nīsā *m:* a ~ journey tàfiyà mài nīsā.

2. *adv* a. (*of time*) dà daɗèwā: not ~ ago ban dà daɗèwā: he went out not ~ ago yā fìta ban dà daɗèwā; before ~ (*in a short while*) bà dà daɗèwā ba: I'll finish it before ~ zân gamà bà dà daɗèwā ba; ~ after his death bāyan mutuwàřsà dà daɗèwā; ~ ago, a ~ time ago (*some time ago*) tun dà daɗèwā, tun tùni, tun tuntùni: he left this country a ~ time ago yā bař ƙasař nàn tun tùni; ~ ~ ago (*in olden times*)

dā dā, can dā, tun dā can. b. be ~, last ~ daɗè *v4:* I won't be ~ bà zân daɗè ba; you may go out but not for ~ kā iyà fìtā àmmā kadà kà daɗè; it is ~ past midnight shā biyun darē tā daɗè dà wucèwā; ~ live the Emir! rân Sarkī yà daɗè! c. how ~? (*ref. to fut. event*) hař yàushè: how ~ will it continue to rain? hař yàushè zā à kai anà ruwā? how ~? (*ref. to past event*) tun yàushè: how ~ have you known it? tun yàushè ka sanī? d. as ~ as hař *prep:* as ~ as I live hař iyākař râinā = hař rānař mutuwàtā; stay as ~ as you like zàunā hař lōkàcîn dà ka ga dāmā. e. so ~ as muddìn *conj:* so ~ as I'm alive muddìn dai inà dà râi; so ~ as you come, I won't be annoyed muddìn kā zō, bà zân 6àtà râi ba.

**long for** *v* yi kēwā *f:* he is ~ing for his family, home yanà kēwař ìyālìnsà, gidā; they ~ for him to return sunà kēwař dāwôwařsà; (*esp. by husband who no longer has wife*) yi bègè *m:* he divorced his wife but now he is ~ing for her sun ràbu dà màtařsà àmmā yànzu yanà bègentà.

**longing** *n* kēwā *f*, bègē *m.*

**loofah** *n* sòsò *m.*

**look** 1. *v* a. dūbà / dībā *v1* ⟨dūbā⟩: if you had ~ed you would have found it dà kin dūbà dà kin sàmē shì; ~ before you leap (*fig.*) à dingà sārā anà dūban bàkin gàtarī. b. ~ at so., sth. dùbà / dībā *v2* ⟨dūbā⟩: he ~ed at himself in the mirror yā dùbi kânsà à madūbī; ~ at (*watch*) kàllā *v2* ⟨kallō⟩, kàllatà *v2:* they are ~ing at us sunà kallonmù; ~ at (*pay attention to*) lùřa dà *v1:* you should ~ at the traffic before crossing the street kà lùřa dà mōtōcī kàfin kà ƙētàrè hanyà. c. ~ for (*seek*) nèmā *v2* ⟨nēmā⟩, bìdā *v2:* they went to ~ for him sun jē nēmansà; come help me ~ for my book zō kà tayà ni bìdař littāfīnà; ~ desperately for sth. nèmi w.a. ruwā à jàllō = nèmi w.a. idò rùfe; ~ for sth. lost, needed yi cigiyàř w.a.: everyone is looking for the lost boy kōwā nà cigiyàř yāròn dà ya 6acè. d. (*appear, have appearance of*): ~ like so. yi kàmā dà *f:* he ~s just like his father yanà kàmā dà ùbansà = kàmařsà ɗaya dà ta ùbansà = siffàřsà kàmař ùbansà; ~ like, as if gà àlāmà (kàmař), nūnà àlāmà: he ~s like an honest man gà àlāmà mùtumìn kiřkì nē; the fruit ~s ripe gà àlāmà ɗan itàcē yā nùna; she ~s as if she is not feeling well tā nūnà àlāmà kàmař bā tā jîn dādī; ~ nice (of things only) nà dà kyân ganī: the picture ~s nice zànên yanā dà kyân ganī; it is not as good as it ~s kyânsà bài kai yàddà akè ganī ba; ~ nice (of people) nà dà kyâu: she is nice-~ing tanà dà kyâu. e. (var. v + adv/prep uses): ~ after sth., so. kulà dà v1, lùřa dà v3, (with great care) ādànà v1: some nurses were ~ing after the patients màsu jiyyà sunà kulàwā dà maràsà làfiyà; she ~s after her things properly tanà ādànà kāyantà = tanà dà ādànī; ~ after so. (family) rìřā v2 ⟨riřò⟩: he is ~ing after his nephew yanà riřòn ɗan řanènsà; he is ~ing after his household yanà rìře dà gidansà; ~ around, behind waiwàyà v1; ~ down on so. rainà / rēnà v1, řasřàntā v1; ~ forward to sà idò gà, zubà idò gà, sà rài: I'm ~ing forward to your coming inà sà rân zuwànkà idò gà zuwànkà = inà sà rân zuwànkà = inà ɗòkin zuwànkà; ~ into (a matter) bincìkà v1; ~ so. over (examine) dūbà v1: the doctor is ~ing over the patients likitàn nà dūbà majìyyàtā; ~ out (be careful) mai dà hankàlī, yi hankàlī; ~ to so. for zubà wà idò: he ~s to his older brother for guidance yanà zubà wà wànsà idò don shāwarà; ~ out quickly (peek) lēřà v1: ~ out the window to see if they're on their way here kà lēřà ta tāgà kà ga kō sunà tahòwā; ~ up sth. (in a book) nēmà v2 ⟨nēmā⟩: he ~ed up the word in the dictionary yā nēmi kalmàř cikin řāmùs; ~ up to so. (respect) girmàmà v1, ga girman w.

2. n a. kallò m, dūbà m: a dirty ~ kallon wulàřancì, kallon banzà, dūban wùlàkài. b. (appearance of sth.) ganì m, siffà / sifà f ⟨oCi⟩: I don't like its ~s bā nà sôn siffàřsà; it has a nice ~ yanà dà kyân ganī; it has the ~ of a Mercedes siffařtà kàmař ta Mařsandī; good ~s (beauty) kyâu m: Audu has good ~s Audù nà dà kyâu.

looking-glass n madūbī m.

loom n masāřā f.

loop n (for fastening) maɗaukī m.

loophole n kafā f ⟨oCi⟩, mafitā f.

loose adj & adv a. (slack) sako-sako idph, à sàssàuce adv, à sàke adv: the rope is ~, tie it securely igiyà à sàssàuce takè, kà ɗaurà ta kankan; the belt is ~ bêl bài ɗauru sòsai ba; (fig.) a ~ woman làlàtacciyā adj. b. (free): become ~ sakì v2*: the screw is ~ řūsà tā sakì = řūsà à sàke takè; shake sth.

~ gìřgìdā v1. c. (of sth. woven, braided) maràs tsaurī m. d. (~ but connected) yi rawā f: my tooth is ~ hařōrīnā yanà rawā = yanà mòtsī. e. (untied): let sth. ~ kwancè v4, suncè v4: the goat was let ~ for grazing an kwancè àkuyà don tà yi kīwò.

loosely adv sako-sako idph, (very ~) sàkwàf idph: it is ~ tied an ɗaurè shi sako-sako.

loosen v sassàutā v1: he ~ed the rope yā sassàutà igiyā; (by shaking or using force) gìřgìdā v4.

loot 1. n (booty) gànīmà f.
2. v wāshè / wāsàshē v4, yi wàsōsò m: they ~ed the palace sun wāshè kāyā dàgà fādà; the demonstrators began ~ing the shops màsu zàngà-zangà sun fārà wàsōsòn kantunà.

lop off v sārè v4, fillè v1.

lopsided adj: be(come) ~ kařkàcē v4.

lord n: the L. God Allàh Maɗaukàkin Sarkī; good ~! Allàh sarkī!

lorry n bàbbař mōtà f, see truck.

lorry park n tashàř mōtà f.

lose v a. (accidentally) yā dà / yař (dà) v5, ɓacè wà v4: have you lost something? kā yā dà wani àbù nē? she lost her keys tā yā dà makullìntà = makullī yā ɓacè matà; (cause to ~) ɓad dà / ɓatař (dà) v5: they lost my luggage an ɓatař mini dà kāyā. b. (no longer have sth.) rasà v1: he lost his 2 sons yā rasà 'yā'yansà biyu. c. (through misfortune) yi hàsāřà f: he lost all his money yā yi hàsārař duk kuɗinsà. d. (Sport) ci v0: the Kano team lost an ci 'yan řungìyař Kanò; (in games) kasà v1: I lost the game an kasà ni à wàsân. e. (var. v + n uses): ~ one's balance yi tàngaɗī m, tangàɗā v1; ~ hold of suɓùcè wà v4, kuɓùcè wà v4: he lost hold of the wheel sìtìyàřī yā kuɓùcè masà; ~ hope fid dà rài, yankè řaunā, sārè v4: I've lost hope of getting a job; nā fid dà rài gà sāmùn aikì; he lost hope when he saw his crops destroyed by the storm yā yankè řaunā dà ya ga iskà tā halàkà masà shùke-shùkên; ~ one's life rasà rài; ~ one's bearings yi ɗīmuwà f, ɓacè wà v4, yi ɓatàn kâi; I lost my way hanyà tā ɓacè minì; ~ one's sight makàncē v4; ~ time (waste time) ɓātà lōkàcī: we lost a lot of time waiting for him mun ɓātà lōkàcī dà yawà munà jirànsà; ~ time (of clock, watch) yi lattì m: this watch ~s 2 minutes a day àgōgon nàn nà lattìn mintì biyu

kullum; ~ weight (*slim down*) ragè ƙibà,
saɓè *v4;* ~ weight (*due to illness, worry*)
rāmè *v4*, ƙanjàmē *v4*, yanƙwànē *v4*.

**loss** *n* a. (*lack*) rashì *m*: this was a great
~ to me wannàn bàbban rashì nē gàrē
nì; be at a ~ for words rasà ta cêwā.
b. (*of property, life*) hàsārà *f*: there was
a great ~ of life an yi hàsāràr̃ rāyukà
= an rasà rāyukà dà yawà. c. (*esp. in
money transactions*) fāɗùwā *f*: his ~es
have been very great fāɗùwar̃sà tanà dà
yawà; sell at a ~ karyar̃ (dà) *v5*: he had
to sell his house at a ~ tīlàs tā sà yā
karyar̃ dà gidansà; suffer a double ~ yi
ɓatàn ɓàkàtantàn; one man's ~ is another man's gain fāɗùwar̃ wani tāshìn
wani.

**lost, be(come)** *v* a. ɓatà *v3b*, ɓacè *v4*, *see*
lose: her keys are ~ makullintà yā ɓacè
= makullī yā ɓacè matà; some children
got ~ in the crowd wasu yârā sun ɓatà
cikin tàron mutànē; get ~! ɓacè manà
dà ganì! inquire about sth. ~ yi cigiyà
*f*: I inquired about my ~ watch nā yi
cigiyàr̃ àgōgōnā; ~ and found department sāshèn cigiyà dà sanar̃wā.

**lot**[1] *n* a. a ~ of, ~s of (mài) yawà *m*, dà
yawà, dà dāmā, bâ lâifī: we still have
a ~ of work to do har̃ yànzu munà dà
aikì dà yawà; that store has a ~ of
goods kàntin nàn nà dà kāyā bâ lâifī;
quite a ~ dà ɗan dāmā; ~s and ~s of
(mài) tārìn yawà, (mài) ɗimbin yawà,
ninkìn bàninkìn: he has ~s and ~s of
money yanà dà kuɗī màsu ɗimbin yawà;
there are ~s and ~s of goods at the
market àkwai kāyā ninkìn bàninkìn à
kàsuwà. b. (*with verbs*): do a ~ of yi
yawàn: he watches a ~ of television yanà
yawàn kallon talàbijìn; they come to
our house a ~ sunà yawàn zuwà gidanmù;
do a ~ of (*by nature, characteristically*)
fayè *v4*, cikà *v1*: he smokes a ~ yā fayè
shân tābà; she talks a ~ tā cikà sùr̃ūtù.

**lot**[2] *n* (*one's fate*) ràbo *m*.

**lot**[3] *n* (*open space*) fīlì *m* 〈aye〉; parking
~ fīlin ajìyè mōtōcī.

**lottery** *n* tàmbōlà *f*, [F] tàmbòlà *f*, lōtàr̃è
*f*.

**loud** *adj* (mài) ƙarfī *m*: a ~ voice, noise
muryà, ƙārā mài ƙarfī; read out ~
kar̃àntā dà ƙarfī, kar̃àntā à fīlī;
grow, become ~er kaurè *v4;* the argument,
drumming got ~er faɗà, kiɗì yā kaurè;
speak ~er ɗagà muryà.

**loudspeaker** *n* lāsìfīkà *f* 〈oCi〉, [F]
ōpàr̃làr̃ *m*.

**louse** *n see* lice.

**love** 1. *v* a. sō *v0*, ƙàunatà *v2*: he really
~s her yanà sôntà ƙwar̃ai. b. (*enjoy*) ji
dàɗī *m*: she ~s knitting tanà jîn dàɗin
sāƙà.
2. *n* sô *m*, ƙàunā *f*, (*mutual*) sòyayyà *f*:
he is in ~ with her yanà sôntà; there's
no ~ lost between them bā sà sôn jūnā;
she is his ~ ita àbar̃ ƙàunar̃sà cē; a
~ story làbār̃in sòyayyà; make ~ (*euphem.*) tārà dà, yi jìmā'ì *m*, (*vulg.*) ci
*v0;* ~ of country kīshìn ƙasā *m*; (*fig.*) ~ is
blind mài sô màkàhò nē; (*fig.*) ~ conquers
all sòyayyà ruwan zumà.

**lovebird** *n* kàlō *m*.

**lovely** *adj* kyàkkyāwā *adj*.

**lover** *n* masòyī *m*, (*pejor.*) fàr̃kā *n*
〈far̃èkanī〉, kwar̃tō *m* 〈aye〉.

**low** *adj* a.(*of height*) maràs tsayì *m*: the
table is ~ tēbùr̃ dîn bâ shi dà tsayì. b.
(*in worth*) maràs dar̃ajà *f*, maràs mar̃tabà
*f*: I have a ~ opinion of him bâ shi dà
dar̃ajà à idònā; he's a ~ type, pay no
attention to him ƙàramin mùtûm nē, ràbu
dà shī; ~ prices far̃àshìn mài r̃àhūsà.
c. (*near the ground*) ƙasà-ƙasà *adv*: the
branches are ~ r̃àssā sunà ƙasà-ƙasà.
d. (*softly*): they are talking in a ~ voice
sunà màganà dà taushī = sunà màganà
ƙasà-ƙasà.

**lower** 1. *v* a. (*to ground*) yi ƙasà-ƙasà dà:
~ it down carefully yi ƙasà-ƙasà dà shī
à hankàlī. b. (*bring down from above*)
saukar̃ (dà) *v5;* ~ a bucket into a well
zurà gùgā à rījìyā. c. (*value, quantity
of sth.*) ragè *v4*: ~ the price ragè kuɗī =
yi rangwamèn kuɗī; he ~ed the price for
me yā yi mini rangwamè; ~ the value of
the currency ragè dar̃ajàr̃ kuɗī; ~ oneself in others' esteem ƙasƙàntā dà kâi. d.
~ one's head sunkuyar̃ dà kâi; ~ one's
voice tausàsà muryà.
2. *adj* na ƙasà: the ~ shelf kantà ta
ƙasà.

**lowlands** *n* kwarì *m*.

**loyal** *adj* (mài) bìyayyà *f*: a traitor is not ~
to his country macì àmānà bā yà bìyayyà
gà ƙasar̃sù; he is ~ to the emir yanà bîn
sarkī; he is a ~ friend àbōkī nagàri nè
= àmīnì nè.

**loyalty** *n* bìyayyà *f*.

**lubricate** *v* (*a vehicle*) sâ wà mōtà gir̃īs.

**luck** *n* sā'à *f*: good ~! Allàh yà bā dà
sā'à! may God bring good ~! (*esp. on
hearing of a birth*) Allàh yà amfànā! bad
~ rashìn sā'à; I am out of ~ today yâu
bā ni dà sā'à; we wish you the best of

~ munã makà fātan kyàkkyāwan àlhēr̃ĩ;
let's try our ~ mù jar̃r̃àbà hannunmù; it's
a matter of ~ sai mài r̃àbō; a stroke of
~, sheer ~ gàm dà Kàtar̃, kàtar̃ī m: it
was sheer ~ that I saw him at the market ganinsà à kãsuwā dà na yi gàm dà
Kàtar̃ nẽ = nā yi kàtar̃in ganinsà à
kãsuwā; (one's persistent ~) r̃àshī m:
it's just his ~ to be rich, poor yanã dà
r̃àshin ar̃zìkī, tsìyā; that's just your
~! r̃àshinkà nē!

**lucky** adj a. (for good events): be ~ tãki
sā'ã f, yi sā'ã f: he was ~ and found
some money on the road yā tãki sā'ã yā
tsìnci kuɗī à hanyã; we were ~ he was
still around when we arrived an yi sā'ã
yanã nan lōkàcîn dà mukà isō; he had a
~ day yā sãmi rānā. b. (in avoiding neg.
events): be ~ yi ar̃zìkī m: he was ~ that
he didn't get hurt yā yi ar̃zìkī dà bài
ji cīwõ ba. c. (by coincidence): be ~ yi
gàm-dà-Kàtar̃ m, yi kàtar̃ī m, yi dãcē
m: if you are ~ enough to see him, greet
him for me ìdan kā yi kàtar̃in ganinsà,
kà gayar̃ minì dà shī; it was really ~ a
policeman appeared at that very moment
an yi gàm-dà-Kàtar̃ wani ɗan sàndā yā
ɓullō daidai lōkàcîn.

**ludo** n lìdô m, [F] lìdô m.

**luggage** n kāyā m ⟨aki²⟩, r̃unshĩ m: do you
have much ~? kanã dà kāyā dà yawã? 3
pieces of ~ r̃unshĩ gùdā ukù.

**lukewarm** adj (mài) ɗan ɗùmī m, (mài)
ɗùmi-ɗùmi.

**lumbar region** n kwànkwasõ m.

**lumber** n icèn kātākō m, (from deleb palm)
azãr̃a f ⟨u⟩.

**lump** n a. gùdā f ⟨gùdãjī⟩; (made by knead-
ing) cūr̃ĩ m: a ~ of rice cūrìn shìnkāfā;
~ of butter dunr̃ulèn mâi; ~ of sugar
r̃wãyar̃ sukàr̃ī. b. (swelling on body)
r̃ùllūtù m: I bumped into the wall and
got a ~ on my head nā r̃umẽ dà bangō
har̃ kâinā yā yi kùmburī. c. pay in a ~
sum biyā gàbā ɗaya.

**lunacy** n hàukā m, tàɓuwā f.

**lunar** adj na watã m: ~ eclipse hùsūfìn
watã m, zàzzàɓin watã m.

**lunatic** n mahàukàcī m, tàɓaɓɓē m,
mõtsattsē m.

**lunch** n àbincin rāna m.

**lung** n hũhū m: ~ disease cùtar̃ hũhū.

**lunge at** v kai wà bãr̃ā: the lion ~d at the
hunter zākìn yā kai wà mahàr̃bîn bãr̃ā.

**lungfish** n gâiwā f.

**lurch** v tangàɗā v1.

**lurk** v laɓẽ v4.

**lust** n kwàɗàyī m, (esp. sexual) jàr̃abã f.

**lute** n (no gen'l term; for plucked instruments, see banjo; for bowed instruments,
see fiddle).

**luxury** n ālātù m: the room is luxuriously
furnished ɗākìn nã dà kāyan ālātù; he
leads a life of ~ yanã r̃ãyuwar̃ jîn dāɗī.

# M

**macaroni** *n* màkàr̃ōnî *f*, tàliyà *f*, [F] màkà *f*.

**machete** *n* àddā *f* ⟨una⟩.

**machine** *n* a. (*with engine*) injî *m* ⟨una⟩; grinding ~ injìn nik̃à; sewing ~ kèkèn dìnkî *m*. b. (*for office*) nā'ūr̃ā *f* ⟨oCi⟩: adding ~ nā'ūr̃ar̃ lìssāfî; photocopy ~ nā'ūr̃ar̃ d̃aukàr̃ hòto.

**machine gun** *n* bindigà mài ruwā *f* ⟨oCi⟩, màshingàn *f*, [F] màtir̃yāshî *f*; automatic ~ bindigà mài jìgìdā; ~ fire ruwan hàr̃sāshî.

**machinery** *n* injunà *p*: heavy ~ mânya-mânyan injunà.

**mad** *adj* a. (*angry*) (mài) fushī *m*: I was ~ at him nā yi fushī dà shī. b. (*mentally unbalanced*) mahàukàcī *adj*: become, go ~ yi hàukā *m*, haukàcē *v4*, zama mahàukàcī; go stark-raving ~ haukàcē tubur̃àn. c. (*enthusiastic*): be ~ about nà mūgùn sô, nà (dà) màsīfàr̃ sô: he's ~ about soccer yanà màsīfàr̃ sôn k̃wallon k̃afà.

**madam** 1. *hon* rânkì-yà-dad̃è, màdân; (*term of addr. for mistress of the house*) uwar̃gidā *f*. 2. *n* (*of brothel*) magājìyā *f*.

**madly** *adv*: he's ~ in love with her yanà mūgùn sôntà = yanà hàukan sôntà.

**madman** *n* mahàukàcī *m*: he was acting like a ~ yanà àbù kàmar̃ mahàukàcī.

**madness** *n* hàukā *m*: utter ~ hàukā tubur̃àn = hàukā jā.

**magazine** *n* mùjallà *f* ⟨oCi⟩.

**magenta** *n* gàr̃ūr̃à *f*.

**maggot** *n* tsūtsà *f* ⟨oCi⟩.

**magic** *n* (*animistic practices*) tsāfī *m*, (*combining Islam & animism*) tsubbù *m*, (*esp. trickery*) dabò *m*; a ~ spell sihìr̃ī *m*.

**magician** *n* mài dabò *n*, d̃an tsubbù *m*, d̃an rùf̃à-ido *m*; (*psn. of extraordinary ability*) hàtsàbībî *m* ⟨ai⟩.

**magistrate** *n* majistàr̃è *n*, [F] màjìstàr̃â *n*, see **judge**; ~'s court kōtùn majistàr̃è *f*, [F] jàstîs *f*.

**magnet** *n* māyèn k̃arfè *m*, màgànād̃īsù *m*.

**magnify** *v* k̃ārà girman w.a.

**Mahdi** *n* Màhàdī *m*.

**mahogany** *n* (*tree*) mad̃ācī *m*.

**maiden** *n* bùdurwā *f* ⟨oCi⟩.

**mail** 1. *n* wàsīk̃ū *p*, [F] kùr̃ê *m*: has the ~ gone? an d̃au wàsīk̃ū? deliver the ~ kai wàsīk̃ū; express ~ wàsīk̃à k̃âr̃-tà-kwāna = wàsīk̃à mài gaggāwā; registered ~ ta r̃ajistà *f*. 2. *v* aikà dà *v1*, jēf̃à *v1*, sakà *v1*: when did she ~ it? yàushè ta aikà dà ita? he ~ed the letters at the post-office yā sakà wàsīk̃ū à gidan wayà.

**mailbox** *n* àkwàtìn wàsīk̃ū *m* ⟨una⟩.

**mailman** *n* māsinjàn gidan wayà *m*.

**maim** *v* lahàntā *v1*, (*deform*) nak̃asā *v1*.

**main** *adj* bàbba *adj* ⟨mânyā⟩: the ~ reason for my coming bàbban dàlīlìn zuwānā; the ~ road bàbbar̃ hanyà.

**mainly** *adv* gālìbàn *adv*, yawancī *m*: it's ~ rice they eat gālìbàn shìnkāfā sukè cî; the book is ~ about history yawancin littāfìn yā k̃unshi tār̃īhì.

**maintain** *v* a. (*a family*) rik̃è *v4*: he's struggling to ~ his family yanà wàhalà wajen rik̃è ìyālìnsà. b. (*a building, road*) ādànā *v1* ⟨ādànī⟩, gyārā *v1* ⟨gyārā⟩, kulà dà *v1*: they don't ~ the buildings properly bā sà ādànà gìne-gìnên sòsai; ~ law and order kiyàyè d̃òkā.

**maintenance** *n* ādànī *m*, aikìn kùlā *m*: spend money for the ~ of the buildings kashè kud̃in wajen ādànin gìne-gìne.

**maize** *n* masàr̃ā *f*.

**majesty** *n* àlfar̃mā *f*: his ~ the emir mài àlfar̃mā sarkī; a majestic poem wāk̃à mài àlfar̃mā.

**major**[1] *n* (*Mil.*) manjà / manjò *m* ⟨oCi⟩, [F] màjâr̃ *m*.

**major**[2] *adj* (*important*) gàgārùmī *adj* ⟨ai⟩, mùhimmī *adj* ⟨ai⟩: win a ~ victory ci wata gàgārùmar̃ nasar̃à.

**majority** *n* a. mafî yawà, yawancī *m*, gālìbī *m*: the ~ was in favor of the decision mafî yawansù = yawancinsù sun yàr̃da dà shāwar̃àr̃. b. (*Pol.*) màsu rinjāyè *p*: ~ rule mulkìn màsu rinjāyè.

**make**[1] *v* a. (*construct*) yi *v0*: what are they made of? dà mè akè yînsù? paper is ~ from trees anà yîn takàr̃dā dà itàcē; ~ into sth. (*convert, produce*) mai (dà) *v5*: carve wood to ~ chairs sàssak̃ì itàcē à mai dà shī kujèrā; ~ a box into a seat mai dà àkwàtì àbin zamā. b. (*manufacture or ~ by hand*) k̃ēr̃ā *v1* ⟨k̃īr̃à⟩ *f*: I want him to ~ me a round table inà sô yà k̃ēr̃à minì wani zàgàyayyen tēbùr̃. c. (*cause*) sâ *v1**: the teacher made them sweep the classroom mālàmī yā sâ sun shārè ɗākìn ajī; the food made him ill àbincîn yā sâ shi rashìn lāfiyằ; the medicine will ~ you feel better māgànîn zâi sâ ka jîn sauƙī; ~ so. look like a fool sâ w. kunyằ, mūzàntā *v1;* it ~s no difference (to me) duk ɗaya nè (gàrē nì). d. *(appoint)* naɗā *v1:* he was made chief, chairman an naɗā shi sarkī, shùgàbā. e. *(var. v + n uses):* ~ a confession amsà lâifī, yi ìƙìřāřī *m;* ~ an effort yi ƙōƙarī *m;* ~ friends yi àbòtā *f,* yi àbōkī *m;* ~ fun of so. *(tease)* zòlayằ *v2;* ~ a law kafà dòkā; ~ love *(euphem.)* tārằ dà, yi jìmā'ì *m,* *(vulg.)* ci *v0;* ~ money sằmi kuɗī: ~ peace between yi sulhū tsàkānī; ~ a speech yi jàwābì; ~ war yi yāƙì. f. ~ up *(reconcile)* daidàitā *v1,* shiryà *v1:* they made up after their quarrel sun shiryā bāyan faɗàn dà sukà yi. g. ~ up *(compensate)* rāmà *v1:* ~ up for missed prayers, lost time rāmà sallā, lōkàcîn dà akà ɓatà. h. ~ up *(apply cosmetics)* yi kwalliyā *f.* i. ~ up sth. *(invent)* ƙāgà làɓāřì, shiryà làɓāřì: that's a made-up story wannàn làɓāřì shirì nè. j. ~ up one's mind tsai dà shāwařằ: he made up his mind to stay yā yankè shāwařằ zâi zaunằ. make² *n (brand, type)* irì *m* (e²), samfùř *m* (oCi); *(esp. large factory-made goods)* ƙīrằ *f:* what ~ is your car? mōtàřkà wàcè ƙīrā cē? = mōtàřkà wàcè irì cē?

make-up *n (cosmetics):* pancake ~ *(powdered)* fankèkè *m,* [F] fànkēkē *m;* *(liquid)* hōdàř ruwā *f;* apply ~ yi kwalliyā *f.*

malaria *n* zàzzàɓin cīzòn saurō *m,* [F] zàzzàɓin dằminā *m:* he's got ~ yā kằmu dà zàzzàɓin cīzòn saurō.

male *adj* namijì *adj* (mazā): a ~ child ɗā namijì; ~s are generally taller than females yawancī mazā sun fi mātā tsawō.

malice *n* ƙètā *f,* mūgùn halì *m,* mùgùntā *f.*

malicious *adj* maƙètàcī *adj,* mamùgùncī *adj;* ~ gossip tsēgùmī *m,* gulma *f.*

malignant *adj* (mài) yằɗuwā *f.*

mallet *n (for beating dyed cloth)* ɗan bugù *m.*

malnutrition *n* rashìn ìsasshen àbinci; severe ~ *(kwashiorkor)* tsīla *f:* he has severe ~ tsīla tā kāmā shi.

malpractice *n* māgudī *m,* àlgûs *m.*

mammal *n* shằ-nōnò *m,* bằ-dà-nōnò *m.*

mammary gland *n* nōnò *m.*

mammy wagon *n* mōtằ mài bōdìn kàtākō *f,* gingimāri *f; see* truck.

man *n* a. mùtûm *m* (mutằnē): this is not

the ~ wannàn bà shī nè mùtumìn ba. b. *(male)* namijì *m* (mazā): was it a ~ or a woman? namijì nē kō màcè? c. *(human being)* ɗan Adàm *m:* all men are mortal duk ɗan Adàm mamàcī nè; the '~-in-the-street' talàkà *n* (awa). d. *(from a partic. place)* *(use ethnonymic* ba- (awa) *prefix + place name, or use* ɗan ('yan) *or* mùtumìn (mutầnen) *+ place name):* those men are all from Katsina mutànên nan duk Katsināwā nè; I am a Kano ~ whereas he is a Yola ~ nī bàkanè nē shī kùwa mùtumìn 'Yōlà.

manage *v* a. *(control)* sařřàfā *v1:* he can't ~ that horse bài iyà sařřàfà dōkìn ba. b. *(run, administer)* tafiyař (dà) *v5,* gudānař (dà) *v5:* he knows how to ~ his business yā iyà tafiyař dà hařkōkin cìnikinsà; he ~s the store sha'ànin kàntîn yanà hannunsà. c. *(make do)* lallàɓā *v1:* my car is not working well but I'll ~ even so mōtātā bā tà aikì sòsai àmmā zān lallàɓā hakà nan mā; ~ to do sth. sāmù *v2*: I didn't ~ to see him bàn sằmi ganinsà ba; just ~ to do sth. dà ƙyař/kyař *(+ rel. complet.):* we just ~d to escape dà ƙyař mukà kuɓùcē.

manager *n* manajà *n* (oCi), [F] dàřaktàř *n.*

managing director *n* manajàn dàřaktằ *m.*

mandatory *adj* na dōlè, na tīlàs: a ~ fine tàrař dōlè.

mane *n* gềzā *f.*

maneuvers *n (Mil.)* rawař dàjì *f.*

mango *n* mangwàřò *m.*

maniac *n* mahàukàcī tuburàn *m.*

manicure *v* yankà farcè.

manioc *n, see* cassava.

manipulate *v* a. *(handle, esp. a machine)* sařřàfā *v1.* b. *(influence, control)* màllakà *v2.*

mankind *n* ɗan Adàm *m,* bìl Adamà *m.*

manliness *n* màzằkutà *f.*

man-made *adj* na ƙīřàř ɗan Adàm.

mannequin *n* mùtum-mùtumī *m.*

manner *n* a. *(way)* hanyà *f* (oCi): in a different ~ ta wata hanyằ dàbam; in this ~ ta hakà. b. *(character, a psn.'s way)* hālī / halī *m* (aye), hàlayyằ *f:* I don't like his ~ bā nằ sôn irìn halinsà; ~ of speech lafàzī *m:* his ~ of speech is crude lafàzinsà bâ dādī.

manners *n* ladàbī *m,* ɗā'à *f:* lack of ~ rashìn ladàbī; he has no table ~ bâ shi dà ɗā'à wajen cîn àbinci; mind your ~! kà kùla!

mannerism *n* dàbī'ằ *f* (u), hālì *m* (aye): he has some very strange ~s yanà dà waɗansu irìn ɗàbî'ū ɗàbam.

manpower n (work force) ma'àikàtā p, 'yan ƙwādagō p.

mantis n ƙōƙì-ƙōƙì m, (term used esp. by children) dōkìn Allàh m.

manual[1] adj na hannu, dà hannu: ~ work aikìn hannù; ~ labor lēbuřancì m.

manual[2] n (instruction book) littāfìn bàyānì m.

manufacture v ƙērā v1 ⟨ƙīrā⟩ f: this company ~s refrigerators wannàn ma'aikatāř tanà ƙīrāř fiřjì.

manufacturer n kamfànin ƙīrā m: I sent it back to the ~ nā mai dà shī kamfànin ƙīrā.

manure n tàrōsō m, tākì m, see fertilizer; spread, put on ~ zubà, bazà tākì.

many adj a. (mài) yawà m, dà yawà, dà dāmā: ~ of the bottles were broken kwalàbē dà dāmā sun fařfàshē; I do not need so ~ of them bā nā bùkātàřsù dà yawà hakà; ~ times sàu dà yawà; a great ~ māsu yawàn gàske; very ~ mài ɗimbin yawà, mài tārìn yawà. b. how ~? (gùdā) nawà? how ~ does she want? gùdā nawà takè sô? how ~ children do you have? yârā nawà gàrē kà? how ~ times have you been there? sàu nawà kikà tàfi can? as ~ as, however ~ kō nawà: take as ~ as you need ɗauki kō nawà kakè bùkātà.

map n tàswīřà f ⟨oCi⟩: the village is not shown on the ~ bà à nūnà ƙauyèn à tàswīřà ba.

marabou stork n bòrin tinkè m.

marabout n bōkā m ⟨aye⟩.

marathon n gudùn dōgon zangò m.

march v a. (Mil.) yi mācì m, [F] yi dēpilē/dipilē m: ~ left-right-left-right yi mācì řàf řàf řàf. b. (demonstration) zàngà-zangà f.

March n Māřìs m.

mare n gōdìyā f ⟨oCi⟩.

marijuana n ganyē m, wî-wî m, tābàř-Àljànnū f, [F] màndūlà f: he smokes ~ yanà shàn wî-wî = mashàyin ganyē nè.

mark 1. n a. (sign) àlāmà f ⟨oCi⟩: exclamation, question, quotation ~ àlāmàř mòtsin râi, tàmbayà, zàncen wani. b. (stamp on goods, animals) shaidà f ⟨u⟩, lambà f ⟨oCi⟩. c. (school exam result) mākì m. d. (stain) tabò m ⟨Cuna⟩: what are these ~s on the wall? tabbunàn mènē nè à bangon nàn?
2. v a. sâ àlāmà f, yi lambà f. b. (homework, exam) gyārà v1, dūbà v1. c. ~ out (outline an area) shātà v1, yi shācì m.

market 1. n kàsuwā f ⟨oCi⟩, (small wayside ~) maciyā f: when is the ~ held? yàushè kàsuwâř takè cî? the ~ is in full swing kàsuwā tanà cî sòsai; establish a ~ kafà kàsuwā; there's always a ~ for skin cream mân shāfàwā yanà dà kàsuwā kōyàushè; black ~ (esp. for currency) kàsuwař shunkù f.
2. v (a product) yi kiràn kàsuwā.

marketing n kāsuwancì m: ~ board hùkūmàř kāsuwancì; go ~ ci kàsuwā, (esp. for groceries) yi cèfànē m.

maroon n ruwan màkubà m.

marriage n aurē m; ~ ceremony ɗaurìn aurē; ~ celebration bìkin aurē.

married adj: he is ~ yanà dà aurē; a ~ woman màtař aurē; get ~ yi aurē m; get ~ to àurā v2, yi aurē dà (with pl subj): he's getting ~ to her zā sù yi aurē dà ita; they have been ~ 30 years shèkàrunsù tàlātin dà aurē.

marrow[1] (of bone) 6ařgō m.

marrow[2] n (squash) kàbūshì / kàbûs m.

marry v a. (get married) yi aurē m: he did not ~ till he was 30 bài yi aurē ba sai dà ya kai shèkarà tàlàtin. b. (so.) aùrā v2, yi aurē dà (with pl subj): he married a girl from Daura yā aùri wata yāřinyà 'yař Dàurā; he married Ladi yā aùri Lādì = sun yi aurē dà Lādì; ~ off so. yi wà aurē, aurař (dà) v5: he married off his daughter to a rich trader yā aurař dà 'yařsà gà wani àttājìřī. c. (perform marriage ceremony) ɗaurà wà aurē: in Hausaland, it is the imam who marries people à ƙasař Hausa, lìmân kè ɗaurà wà mutànē aurē.

marsh n fàdamà f ⟨oCi⟩.

martial adj na sōjà: ~ law dòkař sōjà.

martyr n shàhīdì m ⟨ai⟩.

martyrdom n shàhādà f.

marvelous adj àbin buřgèwā m, àbin àl'ajàbī m.

masculine adj namijì m.

masculinity n màzàkutà f.

mash v markàdā v1.

mask n: a ~ed person dòdō m ⟨anni⟩.

mason n magìnī m, [F] màsôn m.

mass[1] n ɗimbì m: a ~ of people, birds ɗimbin mutànē, tsuntsàyē; the ~es talakāwā p, yākūbāyī p.

mass[2] n (sermon) wa'àzī m.

massacre n kisàn gillà m.

massage 1. n tàusā f, mùřzā f: she gave him a ~ tā yi masà tàusā.
2. v tàusā v2, muřzà wà v1: she ~d his back tā muřzà masà bāyā.

massive *adj* (*often expr. by ideophonic adjs which go with specific nouns*): a ~ wall mākēkìyař gānuwà; ~ rocks gabzā-gàbzàn duwàtsū.

mass media *m* kafōfin wātsà làbàřai *p*.

master[1] *n* a. (*of house*) màigidā *m*: he is his own ~ màigidan kânsà nē. b. (*expert*) gwànī *m* ⟨aye⟩; a Master's degree dìgìřī na biyu *m*, [F] mètìřîs *f*.

master[2] *v* (*acquire skill*) ƙwarè *v4*, nàƙaltà *v2*: he has not ~ed English grammar yet bài ƙwarè à nahawùn Tūřancī ba tùkùna.

mastitis *n* cīwòn màma *m*.

mat *n* a. (*gen'l term for floor* ~) tàbarmā *f* ⟨i⟩; spread out a ~ shimfìɗà tàbarmā; roll up a ~ naɗè tàbarmā; weave a ~ sāƙà tàbarmā. b. (*var. types*): (*rectangular, room-sized*) būjù-kurà *f*; (*of straw, round*) wundī *m* ⟨aye⟩; (*of straw, oval, multi-colored*) fīginī *m*; (*of plaited grass, used for fencing, roofing*) zānā *f* ⟨zànàikù⟩; (*of plaited grass to cover kolanuts*) àshàsha *f*; (*of coarse grass, used to screen doorway*) tufānìyā *f*; (*of reeds to cover window, door*) asabàřī *m*; (*old, worn, of grass*) kēsò *m* ⟨una⟩; (*round, coiled, varying in size*) faifai *m* ⟨a..ai⟩: make a coiled ~ ɗinkà faifai.

match[1] *n* àshānā *f*, [F] àlìmētì *m*; strike a ~ ƙyastà àshānā; light a cigarette with a ~ kunnà tābà dà àshānā; a box of ~es fànkon àshānā.

match[2] *n* (*Sport*) karàwā *f*: have a ~ with sàmi karàwā dà = karà dà; our team was eliminated in the 3rd ~ an fid dà tîm ɗinmù à karàwā ta ukù.

match[3] *v* a. (*fit, go with*) dācè dà *v4*: the cap doesn't ~ the robe hùlâř bà tà dācè dà rìgâř ba; his energy ~es his work ƙwàzonsà yā dācè dà aikìnsà; (*esp. of clothes*) yi àsun dà àsun: her clothes ~ed completely tā yi àsun dà àsun. b. (*be equal, alike*) yi daidai.

matchbox *n* gidan àshānā *m*, fànkō *m*.

matchet *n* àddā *f* ⟨una⟩.

mate[1] *n* a. (*one's counterpart*) àbōkī *m* ⟨ai⟩: office ~ àbōkìn aikì; room~ àbōkin hayà; a driver's ~ kàren mōtà *m*. b. (*one of a pair*) wàrī *m*: where is the ~ to this sock? ìnā wàrìn sàfař nàn?

mate[2] *v* (*of animals*) yi barbarā *f*.

material *n* a. (*yardage*) yādì *m*, [F] tìsì *m*; pre-cut length of printed ~ turmī *m* ⟨a-e⟩; shirting ~ zàwwātì *m*; one yard of ~ sàndā *f*; any piece of ~ ƙyallē *m*. b. (*for

construction*) kāyā *m* ⟨aki[2]⟩: building ~s kāyan ginì.

materialism *n* sôn àbin dūniyà *m*.

materialistic *adj*: he is very ~ yā cikà sôn àbin dūniyà.

maternal *adj*: ~ uncle kàwu *m* ⟨kàwùnai⟩, řàfànī *m* ⟨ai⟩; ~ aunt innà *f*, gòggo *f*; ~ love sôn yârā *m*.

mathematics *n* ilìmin lìssāfì *m*.

mating *n* (*of animals*) barbarā *f*.

matter 1. *n* a. (*affair*) sha'ànī *m* ⟨oCi⟩, hařkà *f* ⟨oCi⟩, àl'amàřī / lamàřī *m* ⟨u-a⟩, màganà *f* ⟨u[2]⟩: look into the ~ bincìkà àl'amàřīn; take a ~ seriously kulà dà àl'amàřī; make ~s worse cā6à sha'ànī = rikìtà sha'ànī; business ~s hařkōkin cìnikī; worldly ~s al'amuřàn dūniyà; the fact of the ~ is... hàƙīƙànin màganà shī nè... = ainihin màganà shī nè...; the subject ~ is... àbîn dà àbù ya ƙùnsā shī nè...; it is a ~ of opinion àbîn dà ya shàfi řa'àyī kè nan. b. (*difficulty*) màtsalà *f* ⟨oCi⟩: is anything the ~? àkwai wata màtsalà? = àkwai àbîn dà ya fàru? it's a ~ of money that is bothering me màtsalàř kuɗī cè kè dàmūnā; what's the ~ with this car? mè ya sàmi mōtàř nân? c. (*in forming indefinites*): no ~ what kōmē, duk àbîn dà, *see* whatever: no ~ what, I won't give it to you kōmē àbinkà, bà zân bà kà shī ba; no ~ what I do, I can't fix it kōmē àbîn dà nakè yî, bā yà gyàruwā; no ~ when kōyàushè, duk lōkàcîn dà, *see* whenever: no ~ when you return, I'll be here kōyàushè kukà dāwō, inà nân; no ~ where kō'ìnā, duk indà, *see* wherever: no ~ where I go, I see them kō'ìnā nakè tàfiyà, inà ganinsù; no ~ who duk wândà, *see* whoever: no ~ who I asked, no one knew where the place was duk wândà na tàmbayà bà wândà ya san wurîn; no ~ how duk yàddà, *see* however: no ~ how difficult it is, I will do it kōmē wùyā tasà sai nā yi. d. (*the material world*) hàlittà *f*.
2. *v* (*be important*): what they do ~s to me inà jîn àbin dà sukè yî; it doesn't ~ (*not important*) bà kōmē = bà dàmuwā; it doesn't ~ to me (it's all the same) duk ɗaya gàrē nì.

mattress *n* kàtīfà *f* ⟨u⟩, [F] màtàlà *f*: air ~ kàtīfàř iskà; foam-rubber ~ kàtīfàř řōbà; ~es are stuffed with kapok anà cunkùsà kàtīfà dà rīmì.

mature 1. *v* (*reach puberty*) bàlagà *v3*: girls ~ faster than boys 'yammātā sun fi mazā saurin bàlagà.

**2.** *adj* a. (*reached puberty*) bàlàgaggē *adj*; (*fully developed*) rìƙaƙƙē *adj*: a ~ writer rìƙaƙƙen maṙùbùcī. b. (*self-sufficient*) (mài) zaman kâi: he is a ~ person mùtumìn kânsà nē. c. (*wise*) (mài) hālin dattījò *m*, (mài) dattākò *m*.

**maximum** *n* iyākā / iyākā *f*, bàkī *m*, maƙurā *f*: the ~ amount you will get iyākaṙ àbîn dà zā kà sāmù; the ~ speed of this car is 100 mph maƙuraṙ gudùn mōtaṙ nân mîl dàrī.

**may** *v aux* a. (*be possibly*) mài yìwuwā (+ *subjunct.*), yìwu *v7, see* might[2]: they ~ be late mài yìwuwā nè sù màkarà; he ~ come mài yìwuwā nè yà zō = yā yìwu zâi zō; I'll take it, I ~ need it zân ɗaukē shì, yâ yìwu ìn bùkàcē shì. b. (*in polite question, use subjunct.*): ~ I sit here? don Allàh ìn zaunà nân? c. (*for invoking good wishes, use* Allàh + *subjunct.*): ~ you prosper! Allàh yà bā dà aṙzìkī; ~ your life be long! Allàh yà jā zàmānī (*said esp. to important people*).

**May** *n* Māyù *m*.

**maybe** *adv* wàtàkīlà / kīlà *adv*, mài yìwuwā: ~ we'll see him wàtàkīlà zā mù gan shì = mài yìwuwā nè mù gan shì.

**mayonnaise** *n* mân sàlàk *m*, [F] ruwan sàlātì *m*.

**mayor** *n* magājin gàrī *m*, [F] mêṙ *m*.

**me** *pro, see* Appendix A.

**meal** *n* a. (*from grain*) gàrī *m*; corn~ gàrin masàṙā. b. (*time for eating*) kàlàcī *m*; have a ~ yi kàlàcī; we eat 3 ~s a day munā cîn àbinci sàu ukù à rānā.

**mean**[1] *v* a. (*denote, signify*) nùfā *v2* ⟨nufì⟩, nūnà àlāmā: what does this word ~ in Hausa? kalmāṙ nân mè takè nufì dà Hausa? it ~s 'good' in Hausa tanā nufìn 'kyâu' dà Hausa; what do you ~ by that? mè kìkè nufì dà hakà? he usually ~s what he says yawancī àbîn dà ya faɗì shī yakè nufì; that ~s she is angry wannàn yanā nūnà àlāmàṙ fushintà = àlāmàṙ fushintà kè nan. b. (*intend*) yi niyyà *f*, nùfā *v2* ⟨nufì⟩: he ~t for you to have this yā yi niyyàṙ bā kà wannàn; he ~t you no harm bài nùfē kà dà cùtā ba; I didn't ~ to do it bà dà gàngan na yi hakà ba; (*intend, when speaking*): I don't know what you ~ ban gānè hausaṙkà ba = bàn ji àbîn dà kakè nufì ba.

**mean**[2] *adj* a. (*small-minded psn.*) ƙàramin mùtûm *m*. b. (*unkind, hurtful*) (mài) baƙin cikì *m*, mūgù *advj*: he's a ~ person baƙin cikì gàrē shì; a ~ kick mūgùn

haṙbì; he is ~ to animals bā yà tàusàyin dabbōbī; a ~ look kallon banzā = kallon wulāƙancì. c. (*miserly, stingy*) bàhīlì *m* ⟨ai⟩ maṙōwàcī *adj*, (mài) rōwà *f*.

**mean**[3] *adj* (*average*) matsàkàicī *adj*: the ~ income of teachers is... matsàkàicin àlbâshin màlàmai shī nè....

**meaning** *n* a. (*semantic*) mà'ànā *f* ⟨oCi⟩: a dictionary gives the ~ of words ƙāmùs yanà bā dà ma'anōnin kalmōmī; the word has a double ~ kalmàṙ tanà dà mà'ànā biyu. b. (*intention*) niyyà *f*, nufì *m*: what is the ~ behind all his insults? mè yakè nufì dà zàge-zàgensà? c. (*underlying significance, purpose*) manufā *f*: the ~ of life manufaṙ ràyuwā.

**meaningful** *adj* (mài) mà'ànā *f*: what he said was very ~ jàwābìnsà yā yi mà'ànā sòsai.

**meaningless** *adj* a. (*having no sense*) maràs mà'ànā *f*, maràs azancī *m*: what you are saying is ~ màganàṙkà bā ta dà azancī. b. (*worthless*) na wōfì *m*: what he said was ~ zàncensà wōfì nè.

**means** *n* a. (*way*) hanyà *f* ⟨oCi⟩: is there another ~ of doing it? àkwai wata hanyàṙ dàbam dà zā à yī shì? by ~ of ta hanyàṙ: by oppressive ~ ta hanyàṙ zāluncì; by whatever ~ possible ta kōwàcè hanyà = ta hanyà kō yàyà; the end justifies the ~ (*fig.*) kwalliyā tā biyā kuɗin sàbulù. b. (*resources, wealth*) zaṙàfī *m*, dāmā *f*, hālī *m* ⟨aye⟩: I don't have the ~ to take the trip bâ ni dà zaṙàfin yîn tàfiyàṙ; a man of ~ mài zaṙàfī = mài hālī = mài hannū dà shūnī.

**meantime** *adv*: in the ~ kàfìn nan: I'm off to the market, in the ~, you should sweep the rooms zâ ni kàsuwā, kàfìn nan kì shārè dākunà.

**measles** *n* ƙyândā *f*, (*German* ~) baƙon dàurō *m*.

**measure** **1.** *n* a. ma'aunī *m*, magwajì *m*, mīzānì *m*: a foot is a ~ of length lūṙà ma'aunī nè na tsawō. b. (*bowls of specific sizes used at market*): mūdù *m*, kwānò *m*, tiyà *f*: I want 6 ~s of flour inà sôn gàrin fulāwà mūdù shidà.

**2.** *v* aunà *v1* ⟨awò⟩, gwadà *v1*: we ~d the distance between the house and the tree mun aunà nīsan tsàkānin gidā dà bishiyà; rulers are used for measuring length anā àmfànī dà lūṙà wajen aunà tsāwō; have you ~d the window? kā gwadà tāgàṙ? (*for clothing*) aunà *v1*, [F] ɗauki mĕzîř m.

**measurement** n awŏ m ⟨àune-àune⟩: what are the precise ∼s of the room? nawà nē àune-àunen ɗākìn daidai? take so.'s ∼s aunà v1: let me take your ∼s bàri ìn aunà ka.

**measuring tape** n têf m, [F] mētlř m.

**meat** n nāmà m ⟨nāmū⟩; (good quality ∼ with some fat) wàjiyà f; boneless ∼ tsōkà f; ground ∼ nìƙaƙƙen nāmà; a piece of ∼ tsōkàř nāmà.

**meat-grinder** n injìn niƙà nāmà m.

**mechanic** n màkānikè / bàkānikè m ⟨ai⟩, [F] màkànìsê m: he is a ∼ sànā'àřsà makānikancì nē.

**mechanical** adj na injì m.

**medal** n lambà f ⟨oCi⟩: gold, silver, bronze ∼ lambàř gwâl, azùřfā, tagùllā; ∼ of honor lambàř girmā.

**meddle** v yi kàřàmbànī m, yi shisshigī m, yi katsalandàn m: stop meddling in my affairs! kà dainà yi minì kàřàmbànī! = kà dainà shìga sha'anīnā!

**meddlesome** adj (psn.) kařambānà n, (mài) kankambà f.

**media** n (the press) 'yan jàřìdū p.

**mediate** v yi sulhù tsàkānī, shìga tsàkānī: ∼ between workers and employers yi sulhù tsàkānin ma'àikàtā dà mà'àikàtū.

**medical aide** n (in hospital) ma'àikàcin asìbitì n, [F] làkwàtařò n.

**medicinal** adj na māganī m: ∼ roots saiwōyin māganī.

**medicine** n a. māganī m ⟨u-a²⟩: cold ∼ māganin mufà; ∼ for hemorrhoids māganin bāsùř; take ∼ shā māganī; the ∼ didn't work māganîn bài yi àmfānī ba; the ∼ works fast māganîn nà dà ƙarfī; the ∼ did me no good bài māgàntà minì kōmē ba; he got a dose of his own ∼ (fig.) ƙàiƙàyī yā kōmō kân mashēƙìyà. b. (academic subject) ilìmin aikìn likità m: practice ∼ yi aikìn likità; he is studying ∼ yanà kôyon aikìn likità.

**medicine man** n (native doctor) bōkā m ⟨aye⟩, magòrī m.

**meditate** n yi tsōkàcī m, yi tùnànī m.

**medium** adj (not large, not small) madàidàicī m: I need a ∼ size blouse inà nēman madaidaicìyař rìgā; (average) matsàkàicī m: a person of ∼ height, build mùtûm mài matsàkàicin tsawō, jìkī.

**meek** adj (mài) tàwāli'ù m.

**meet** 1. v a. gàmu dà v7, hàɗu dà v7, sàdu dà v7: I am very pleased to ∼ you nā yi muřnàř gàmuwā dà kai; I have never

met him bàn taɓà hàɗuwā dà shī ba; I would like you to ∼ my friend inà sôn ìn haɗà ka dà àbōkīnā; this is the first time that I've met him wannàn farkon sàduwařmù dà shī; agree to ∼ at a place yi magamà f; ∼ face to face with yi ařbà dà, yi idò huɗu dà; ∼ unexpectedly yi kìciɓìs dà: the boy was dawdling along when he unexpectedly met his father yārò nà shantàkèwā sai ya yi kìciɓìs dà bàbansà. b. (go to ∼ so.) taryè v4, tàřbā v2: I went to the station to ∼ my brother nā tàfi tashàř ìn taryō ɗan'uwānā. c. (of a committee) yi zaman tàrō. d. (encounter) sāmù v2*: ∼ with kindness sàmi àlhēřì; ∼ with success ci nasařà. 2. n (Sport) karàwā f.

**meeting** n a. tàrō m: hold a ∼ yi zaman tàrō; a ∼ of council members tàron 'yan màjàlisà; summit ∼ tàron ƙòli; (esp. of a committee) mitìn m, [F] řànyô f. b. (appointment) àlkawàřī m: I have a ∼ with him munà dà àlkawàřī. c. (becoming acquainted) sàbō m: ever since their first ∼, he has been wanting to marry her tun sàbonsù yanà nēmà yà àurē tà.

**megaphone** n būtūtun ƙārà màganà m, lāsìfīkà f ⟨oCi⟩.

**melancholy** n baƙin cikì m, tàsàlīmà f.

**melody** n karìn wāƙà m.

**melon** n (watermelon) kankanā f; (round, yellow, sweet) màlō m; (round, used in stews) gunà f; ∼ seeds (esp. used in stews) àgūsi m.

**melt** v narkè v4; (sth.) narkař (dà) v5.

**member** n (any kind) ɗan m, 'yař f, 'yan p: ∼ of a household ɗan gidā; ∼ of a club ɗan ƙungìyā; ∼ of the NPN party ɗan jàm'iyyàř NPN; ∼ of opposition party àbōkin hàmayyà; (esp. of club, society) membà n ⟨oCi⟩: become a ∼ of shìga ciki, zama membà.

**membrane** n tantānī m.

**memento** n tsàřabà f ⟨oCi⟩.

**memorial** n (ceremony) bìkin tunàwā m; (object) àbin tunàwā m.

**memorization** n haddà f.

**memorize** v haddàcè v4: he can ∼ quickly yanà dà saurin haddà.

**memory** n: he has a good ∼ bā yà dà mantuwà; he has a short ∼ yanà dà mantuwà; let me refresh your ∼ bàri ìn tunà makà = bàri in yi makà matāshìyā; in ∼ of don tunàwā dà.

**menacing** adj: a ∼ glare hàrārā mài ban tsòrō.

**mend** *v* a. gyārā̀ *v1* ⟨gyārā⟩, gyârtā *v1;*
(*fig.*) ~ one's ways gyārā hālī. b. (*by
sewing*) ɗinkḕ *v4;* ~ a hole (*in clothing*) daddàgē *v4*: she ~ed the hole in the
trousers, socks ta daddàgè hūɗar̃ wàndō,
sāfā; (*by patching*) yi wà mahō̃ *m.*

**meningitis** *n* sànk̃àrau *m.*

**menopause** *n*: reach ~ dainà hailā̀, (*euphem.*) dainà wankī̀.

**menstruate** *n* yi hailā̀ *f,* (*euphem.*) yi
àl'àdā̀ *f,* yi wankī̀ *m;* miss menstruation
yi ɓatàn watā̀; she has finished menstru-
ating (*for the month*) hailā̀ tā ɗaukḕ.

**mental** *adj*: ~ illness tàɓuwā *f,* hàukā *f;* ~
hospital asìbitìn mahàukàtā = asìbitìn
tàɓàɓɓū; ~ health hankàlī *m;* ~ly ill
tàɓàɓɓē *adj;* ~ly retarded person gaulā
*n* ⟨aye⟩.

**mentholatum** *n* màntàlētā̀ *m,* [F]
màntàlētī̀ *m.*

**mention** *v* àmbatā̀ *v2* ⟨ambatō⟩, fur̃tā̀ *v1,*
fàɗā / faɗī̀ *v2\*;* she ~ed your name
tā àmbàci sūnankì; they don't like to
~ their age bā sà sōn faɗìn yawàn
shḕkàrunsù; they didn't ~ a word kō
kalmā̀ ɗaya bà sù fur̃tā̀ ba; don't even
~ to him that... kadà mā kà àmbàta masà
cêwā...; he ~ed that... yā àmbàta cêwā
= yā fur̃tā̀ cêwā...; ~ sth. to so. faɗā̀
wà *v1,* gayā̀ wà *v1:* I'll ~ it to him zân
gayā̀ masà; don't make a mistake and ~
it to him kadà kà kùskurà kà faɗā̀ masà
wannàn; don't ~ it! (*reply to thanks*) tô
màdàllā! = habā̀!

**mercenary** *n* sōjàn hayà *m.*

**merchandise** *n* hājā̀ *f* ⟨oCi⟩, kāyan
sayâr̃wā *m.*

**merchant** *n* ɗan k̃àsuwā *m.*

**merciful** *adj* (mài) tàusàyī *m,* (mài) īmānì
*m;* (*of God*) (mài) jîn k̃ai *m.*

**merciless** *adj* maràs tàusàyī *m,* maràs
īmānì *m.*

**mercury** *n* zaibā̀ *f.*

**mercy** *n* a. tàusàyī *m,* īmānì *m;* I'm totally at your ~ sai yàddà kà yi dà nī.
b. (*used on occasion of death*) jîn k̃ai *m,*
r̃ahamā̀ *f:* may God have ~ on her soul
Allàh yà ji k̃antà = Allàh yà r̃ahamshē
tà.

**merely** *adv* kawài *adv:* he's ~ a boy ɗan
yārṑ nē kawài.

**merge** *v* haɗḕ *v4,* gamḕ *v4.*

**merger** *n* haɗēwā *f,* gamēwā *f.*

**merit** *n* àmfànī *m.*

**merriment** *n* ànnàshùwā *f.*

**merry** *adj* (mài) fàr̃a'ā̀ *f;* ~ Christmas!
bar̃kā̀ dà Kir̃sìmatì!

**mess** 1. *n* a. (*disorder*): in a ~ à bàr̃kàtài
*adv,* kaca-kaca *idph*: this room is in a ~
dākìn nân à bàr̃kàtài yakè = dākìn nân
yā yi kaca-kaca; (*messy child*) kùcākī
*m,* kùcākā *f* ⟨ai⟩: you're a ~! kē kùcākā!
b. (*muddle, confusing situation*) rìkicī
*m*: get into a ~ shìga cikin rìkicī;
make a ~ of sth. dāgùlā *v1,* ɓātā̀ *v1:*
he made a ~ of the matter yā dāgùlā
àl'amàr̃in; make a ~ of a place ɓātā̀
wurī.
2. *v* a. (*spoil*): ~ up dāgùlā *v1*: the
children have ~ed up our writing yârā
sun dāgùlā manà r̃ubùtū; (*esp. with food*)
dagwalgwàlā / jagwalgwàlā *v1*: don't
~ up your blouse kadà kì dagwalgwàlā
rìgar̃kì. b. (*muddle, confuse*): ~ up
dāmā̀ *v1,* rikìtā *v1:* he has ~ed up our
plans yā dāmà manà shirìnmù.

**message** *n* sā̀k̃ō *m* ⟨anni⟩; send a ~ to so.
aikà wà dà sā̀k̃ō; deliver a ~ to so. isar̃
dà sā̀k̃ō à wurin w.; (*verbal*) sàllahù̃ *m:*
did he leave a ~ for me? kō yā bar̃ mini
sàllahù̃?

**messenger** *n* (*in office*) māsinjà *m* ⟨oCi⟩,
[F] fàlàntô *m;* (*in emir's court*) jàkādā̀
*m* ⟨u⟩; (*of God*) mànzo *m* ⟨anni⟩.

**Messiah** *n* (*Jesus*) Àlmàsīhù *m;* (*Mahdi*)
Màhàdī *m.*

**messy** *adj* kaca-kaca *idph,* (*filthy*) dukun-
dukun *idph,* (*sticky, greasy*) dank̃wan-
dànk̃wàn *idph;* (*of mouth covered with food*)
dumū-dùmū̃ *idph.*

**metal** *n* k̃arfè *m* ⟨a-a⟩.

**metallic** *adj*: ~ thread, paint zàrē, fentì
mai shēk̃ī.

**metaphor** *n* kàmàncē *m;* a ~ical meaning
ɓò̃yayyiyar̃ mà'ànā.

**meteor** *n* māshī *m.*

**meteorology** *n* ilìmin yanàyī *m.*

**meter** *n* a. (*unit of length*) mītā̀ *f,* [F] mētìr̃
*m,* (*wavelength band*) mītā̀ *f.* b. (*gauge*)
mītā̀ *f,* [F] kwàntar̃ *m*: gas ~ mītàr̃ gâs.
c. (*Lit.*) karī̀ *m* ⟨uwa²⟩.

**method** *n* a. (*way, technique*) hanyà *f*
⟨oCi⟩, dàbār̃ā *f* ⟨u⟩: the latest ~ hanyà
mafì sàbùntakā̀; teaching ~s hanyōyin
kō̃yâr̃wā; use a ~ bi hanyà. b. (*orderliness*) fasàlī *m,* tsàrī *m.*

**methodical** *adj* (mài) fasàlī *m,* (mài)
tsārī *m*: he's not ~ in his work aikìnsà
bā fasàlī.

**metre** *n, see* **meter.**

**microphone** *n* màkàr̃ùfô *m,* [F] mìkùr̃ô *m.*

**microscope** *n* madūbin likità *m,* madūbin
kìmiyyā̀ *m,* [F] madūbin k̃wāyōyin cùtā
*m.*

midday *n* tsakař rānā *f;* at ~ dà tsakař rānā = dà rānā tsakà.

middle *n* a. tsakiyà *f,* (*in the genitive, may use* tsakař): ~ finger ɗan yātsàn tsakiyà; he is ~-aged yanà tsakař ƙarfinsà = yanà tsakiyàř ƙarfinsà; in the ~ of the room à tsakiyàř dākì = à tsakař dākì; in the ~ of the confusion à cikin tsakiyàř rìkicī; in the ~ à tsakà *adv:* I put it in the ~ nā sâ shi à tsakà; in the ~ of the day dà rānā tsakà = dà tsakař rānā. b. (*in the midst of doing sth.*): she was in the ~ of cooking when he entered tanà tsakař girkì ya shigō; he was in the ~ of his speech when he stopped yanà tsakař màganà sai ya tsayà.

Middle East *n* ƙasàshen Gabàs ta Tsakiyà *p.*

middleman *n* ɗan bařàndà *m.*

middle school *m, see* school.

midget *n, see* dwarf.

midnight *n* tsakař darē *f,* shâ biyun darē *m;* at ~ dà tsakař darē = dà dàddare.

midst *n* tsakiyà *f, see* middle.

midway *adv:* his farm is ~ between the 2 towns gōnařsà yanà tsàkānin garūruwàn biyu.

midwife *n* ùngōzòmà *f.*

might[1] *n* ƙarfī *m;* with all one's ~ bâ jî bâ ganī, gàdàn-gàdàn *idph:* he set to work with all his ~ yā kāmà aikì bâ jî bâ ganī.

might[2] *v aux* yìwu *v7* (+ *complet. or fut.*), *see* may: we ~ see him there yā yìwu zā mù gan shì can; he told me he ~ not come yā gayà minì mài yìwuwā nè bà zâi zō ba.

migrant *n* bàƙō (dàgà wata ƙasà) *m.*

migrate *v* ƙaura *v3a,* yi ƙaurā *f;* ~ to yi ƙaurā zuwà.

migration *n* ƙaurā *f;* forced ~ gudùn hijiřā *m.*

mild a. (*of food*) maràs yājì *m.* b. (*not harsh*) maràs tsananī *m.*

mildew *n* rìmā *f;* be(come) ~ed yi rìmā: the wall is ~ed bangō nà rìmā.

mile *n* mîl *m* ⟨oCi⟩; a 100 ~s from here mîl ɗàrī dàgà nân; don't go over 45 ~s per hour kadà gudùnkà yà wucè àřbà'in dà bìyař; this car gets 30 ~s to the gallon mōtàř nân tanà cîn mîl tàlàtin dà galàn gùdā.

mileage *n* nīsan milōlī *m,* mālējì *m;* ~ chart jadawàlin mālējì.

milestone *n* turkèn mîl *m.*

militant *n* tsagèrā *n* ⟨u⟩.

military 1. *n:* the ~ sōjà *m/p,* [F] sōjì *m/p:* Nigeria has a strong ~ force Nìjēřiyà nà dà sōjà mài ƙarfī. 2. *adj* na sōjà *m:* ~ court kōtùn sōjà; ~ government gwamnatìn mulkìn sōjà; ~ maneuvers rawař dājì *f.*

military police *n* kùrfau *m/p.*

milk 1. *n* (*breast ~, sour ~*) nōnò *m;* (*cow's ~*) madařā *f:* evaporated, condensed ~ madařař gwangwanī; powdered ~ gàrin madařā; (*curdled, usu. with fat*) sàrē *m;* (*yogurt-like sour ~*) kìndìřmō *m;* (*fig.*) cry over spilt ~ yi ìhù bāyan harì = yi fařgař Jàjì. 2. *v* tàtsā *v2:* she's ~ing (the cow, goat) tanà tàtsař nōnò; (*fig.*) ~ so. dry tàtsē *v4.*

milk teeth *n:* shed ~ yi fàmfarà *f.*

mill *n* ma'aikatā *f:* flour, groundnut ~ ma'aikatař fulāwà, mân gyàdà; cotton ~ ma'aikatař gyàrà audùgā.

millet *n* (*planted early*) gērō *m,* (*planted late*) màiwā *f,* dàurō *m;* roasted ~ (*from newly ripened heads*) tumù *m.*

million *quant* miliyàn *f,* [F] mìlìyân *f.*

millionaire *n* mìlōniyà *n.*

millipede *n* ƙàdandòniyà *f.*

millstone *n* bàbban dūtsèn niƙà *m.*

mime *n* bèbàncè *m;* (*psn.*) mabèbàncī *m.*

mimic *v* kwaikwàyà *v1.*

mimicry *n* kwaikwayō *m.*

mimosa *n* gàbàruwā / bàgàruwā *f* ⟨gàbàrī / bàgàrī⟩.

minaret *n* hàsūmiyà *f.*

mince *v* yayyànkà *v1:* she ~d the garlic into tiny pieces tā yayyànkà tàfařnuwā mitsī-mitsī.

mind[1] *n* a. (*intellect*) tùnànī *m,* ƙwalwā *f,* bàsīřà *f:* he has a sharp ~ yanà dà kaifin tùnànī = ɗan ƙwalwā nè. b. (*state of ~*) hankàlī *m:* my ~ is in turmoil, at rest hankàlīnā yā tāshì, yā kwàntā; lose, go out of one's ~ tà6u *v7,* mòtsu *v7,* fìta dàgà hankàlī; his ~ is going yā fàrà mòtsuwā. c. (*thoughts, feelings*) râi *m,* zūcìyā *f:* an idea came to my ~ wata dàbàřà tā fàdō minì à râi; broad-~ed mài sauƙin kâi; open-~ed mài jîn shāwařà, mài kàr6ař shāwařà; strong-~ed mài taurin râi; bear, keep in ~ riƙè à zūci; set one's ~ on sâ râi à kân; change one's ~ sàkè shāwařà; make up one's ~ yankè shāwařà = tsai dà shāwařà: make up your ~ once and for all! kà tsai dà màganà gùdā!

mind[2] *v* a. (*pay attention*) lùřa dà *v3:* kulà dà *v1,* ànkarà dà *v3:* ~ what you

are doing kà kulà dà àbîn dà kakè yî.
b. (object to) dầmu dà v7: I don't ~ the
heat bàn dầmu dà zāfîn ba. c. (one's
business): he ~s his own business yanà
sha'ànin gàbansà = yanà kasàfinsà =
yā shàgalà dà àbin kânsà; ~ your
own business! shìga sha'àninkà! = yi
kasàfin gàbankà! never ~! (don't worry)
kadà kà dầmu! = bâ kōmē! d. (polite request): do you ~ if I...? don Allàh kō zân
iyà...? would you ~ lending me a hand
to lift this? don Allàh kō zā kà tayà ni
daukầr wannàn?
mine¹ 1. v (coal, minerals) hakō v6 ⟨hàkā⟩
f: in that country, they ~ gold à kasàr
can anà hàkar gwâl.
2. n mahakā f, wurin hakā m: a tin ~
mahakar kùzà = wurin hakàn kùzà.
mine² pro, see Appendix A.
minerals p a. (geological) mà'àdinai p. b.
(soft drinks) lèmō / lèmū m.
miner n mài hakàn mà'àdinai n.
mineral water n sōdā f, [F] bùlbît m.
mingle v shìga mutầnē, yi cùdanyà dà
mutầnē.
minibus n hayìs f, [F] hìyâs f.
minimum n: the ~ amount you will get
àbin dà zā kà sāmù à kallà; the ~ age
for going to school is 6 bā à sâ yârā
makarantā kasà dà shèkarà shidà.
mining n hakàn mà'àdinai m; gold, coal ~
hakàn zīnàrī, kwâl.
minister n a. (Pol.) ministà m ⟨oCi⟩,
[F] mìnistîr m; M. of State for External Affairs Kàramin Ministàn Harkōkin
Wàje; M. of State for Planning and Budget Kàramin Ministàn Shìrye-Shìryen
Gwamnatì dà Kasàfin Kudī. b. (Relig.,
priest) fādà m, [F] àlmàsīhù m.
ministry n (government office) ma'aikatā f,
see Appendix E.
minor 1. adj kàramī adj ⟨kanānà⟩, kànkanè
m, kànkanùwā f ⟨kanānà⟩: a ~ accident
kàramin hadàrī.
2. n (child) yārò m, yārinyà f ⟨yârā⟩.
minority (Pol.) marasà rinjāyè p: ~ leader
shùgàban marasà rinjāyè; ethnic minori-
ties kàbìlū marasà yawà.
minstrel n marōkī m, dan ma'abbà m.
mint n (flavor, candy) mintì m; (plant)
nà'anà'a / nànà f, [F] ànànâ f.
minus prep: 20 ~ 4 is 16 àshìrin à dèbè
hudu shà shidà kè nan; ~ sign àlāmàr
dēбēwā f.
minute¹ n a. (unit of time) mintì m ⟨oCi⟩:
it is now 10 ~s past 8 yànzu karfè takwàs
dà mintì gōmà; my watch is 5 ~s fast

àgōgōnā yanà gudùn mintì bìyar. b. (a
moment): wait a ~! dàkàtā kàdan! in a
~ in an jimà, nân dà kyas, dầzu adv; in
just a ~ yànzu-yànzu = dầzu-dầzu; I'll
be finished in a ~ nā gamà nân dà kyas;
he left just a ~ ago yā tàshì dầzun nàn.
minute² adj dan mitsilī adj: there was a ~
amount of salt in it dà gishirī dan mitsilī à ciki.
miracle n àbin mầmākì m, àbin àl'ajàbī
m; (performed by prophet) mù'ùjizā f
⟨oCi⟩; (performed by saint) kàrāmā f;
perform a ~ yi àbin mầmākì, nūnà
mù'ùjizā, nūnà kàrāmā.
mirage n kàwalnēnìyā f.
mired, be v (in mud) kafè à cầбī.
mirror n madūbī m: he looked at himself in
the ~ yā dùbi kânsà à madūbī.
misbehave v yi rashìn ladàbī m.
miscarriage n бàrī m; she had a ~ tā yi
бàrī = tā zub dà cikì = cikìntà yā
zubè.
miscellany adj tàrkàcē m, kàrìkìtai p,
kōmàtsai p: miscellaneous items kāyan
tàrkàcē.
mischief m n fìtinà f.
mischievousness m (playful, by children)
kìrìnìyā f.
misdemeanor n kàramin lâifī m.
miser n marōwàcī m, mài rōwā n, mài
tsumulmulā n, bàhīlì m ⟨ai⟩; he is a ~
mài tsumulmulā nè = makō gàrè shì.
miserable adj: he is ~ rânsà à бàce yakè;
he feels ~ bā yà jîn dādī.
misfortune n rashìn sà'à m; (physical, financial) tsàutsàyī m: suffer a ~ shā
tsàutsàyī.
mishear v yi jîn kûnnē.
mislead v a. (lead astray) бad dà / бatar
(dà) v5, sâ w. бatàn hanyà, sâ w. dājì.
b. (deceive) rūdā v1: he ~d us by saying
he had bought it yā rùdē mù dà ya cè yā
sàyā.
mispronunciation n tsàmin bàkī m.
miss 1. v a. (fail to do) kuskùrē v4: he shot
at the gazelle but ~ed it yā harbi bàrēwā
àmmā yā kuskùrē = ...àmmā bài sàmē tà
ba; he ~ed his chance dāmā tā kuбùcē
masà. b. (not meet) sāбà v1, yi sàбānī
m: we ~ed each other on the road mun
sāбà à hanyà = mun yi sàбānī à hanyà =
mun shā bambam à hanyà. c. just ~ (escape sth. unfortunate) aunà arzìkī: I just
~ed breaking my arm nā aunà arzìkī dà
bàn karyè hannūnā ba; just ~ (narrowly
avoid) saurà kàdan dà: the bus just ~ed
colliding with the car saurà kàdan dà bâs

dîn tā yi karð dà mōtàř; we almost ~ed
the train saurā kàdan dà jirgī yā bař
mù. d. (long for) yi kēwař w.: she ~es
her family tanā kēwař iyàyentà; I shall
~ you zân yi kēwařkì = zā kì bā nì kēwā
= zā kì bař nì cikin kēwā; (esp. by husband whose wife has left him) yi bēgē m.
2. n kuskurè/kurè m ⟨kùràkùrai⟩.

Miss hon (term of ref. or addr.) Mālàmā (+
first name) f: M. Ladi Mālàmā Lādì.

missile n hàřsāshì mài lìnzāmì m.

missing adj: be ~ (misplaced) ɓacè v4:
when did you realize it was ~? yàushè
ka fařga cêwā yā ɓacè? (short, not ac-
counted for) there is one ~ daya tā ragè.

mission n a. (Relig.) mishàn m. b. (delegation) ƙunglìyā f ⟨oCi⟩.

missionary n mishàn m, [F] mashàn m, [F]
àlmàsīhù m.

mist n hazō m: the hills are hidden by the ~
tsaunukàn nā rùfe dà hazō; it was ~y
at the airport hazō yā rufè fīlin jirgin
samà.

mistake 1. n kuskurè/kurè m ⟨kùràkùrai⟩,
mìstîn m: I made a serious ~ nā yi
bàbban kuskurè; you made a foolish ~
kuskurènkà wâutā nè; make a ~ (through
oversight) řàfkanà v3; (in cautioning so.)
kùskurà v3 (+ neg. subjunct.): don't ever
make the ~ of mentioning his name kadà
kì kùskurà kì fàdi sūnansà; by ~ bisà
kuskurè, bā dà sanì ba, bā dà niyyà
ba: someone has taken my bag by ~ wani
yā dàuki jàkātā bā dà saninsà ba.
2. v (misunderstand): she mistook my intentions bà tà fàhìmci àbîn da nakè
nufî ba.

mistaken adj bā daidai ba; you are ~ bà
kà yi daidai ba.

Mister hon, see Mr.

mistletoe n kaucì m.

mistreat v gānā wà wùyā, dàuki àlhakin
w., wulàƙantař (dà) v5, zàluntà v2:
you should try to forgive those who have
~ed you sai kà yi hàƙurī kà yàfè wà
wadàndà sukà zàlùncè kà.

mistress n a. (of a school) mālàmař
makařantā f; (of household) uwařgidā f.
b. (lover) fàřkā f ⟨fařèkanī⟩, kwařtuwā
f ⟨kwařtàyē⟩.

mistrust v ƙi amìncêwā dà, ƙi yàřdā dà.

misunderstand v a. (not understand): he
misunderstood what I said bài gànè àbîn
dà na fàdā ba = yā yi minì mùmmūnař
fàhìmtà. b. (misinterpret): he misunderstood the matter yā kuskùrè àbîn = yā
dàuki àbîn à hàgùnce.

misunderstanding n rashìn fàhìmtà m.

misuse v (take advantage of) yi àmfànī dà:
he ~d his position to get rich yā yi àmfànī
dà mùƙāmìnsà don yà ařzùtà kâi.

mix n a. (gen'l term) hadà v1; (dry or
liquid) garwàyā / gauràyā v1: ~ sand
and cement garwàyà yàshī dà sùmuntì;
oil and water do not ~ (lit.) mâi bā yà
gàuràyuwā dà ruwā, (fig.) wutā dà shiɓà
bā sà hàduwā; (sth. dry by adding liquid to make paste) kwaɓà v1: he ~ed
the earth with water yā kwaɓà ƙasā; ~
with people (mingle) yi cùdanyà f, shiga
mutànē. b. (~ var. foods): (different foods
together) cākùdā v1: ~ rice with beans
cākùdà shìnkāfā dà wākē; (dry & wet
foods to make gruel) dāmà v1: ~ flour (and
water) dāmà fulāwā; ~ balls of fura dough
(and milk) dāmà furà. c. get ~ed up (confused) rikìcē v4: he got ~ed up about
the departure date yā rikìcē dà rānař
tàfiyà; get ~ed up (involved in) shiga
cikin sha'ànī; I don't want to get ~ed
up with him bā nà sôn à hadà ni dà shī.

mixture n hadì m, gamì m, garwayè m: a
~ of flour and sugar garwayèn fulāwā dà
sukàřī; yaji is a ~ of different spices yājì
garwayèn kāyan ƙanshī irì-irì.

moaning n nīshì m, (by animal) gùřnànī
m.

mob 1. n (mass): a ~ of people mutànē
tìnjim = dimbin mutànē = cìncìrindòn
mutànē; (demonstrators) 'yan zàngà-
zàngà p, màsu zàngà-zàngà p.
2. v: the streets were ~bed with people
hanyōyī sun cunkùshē dà mutànē.

mobile adj na tàfi-dà-gidankà: ~ bank,
hospital bankìn, asìbitìn tàfi-dà-gidankà; ~ home gidan kātākō, gidan tì-
řēlà.

mock v (deride) yi wà ba'à f, mūzàntà
v1; (by using disrespectful language) yi wà
jàfā'ì m; (esp. imitate so.'s manner or
speech) kwatà v1, yi kwatā f.

mockery n (derision) ba'à f, kwatā f.

model n a. (partic. design) samfùř m, [F]
mōdàl m: make me a blouse of this ~ kà
dinkà minì rìgā irìn wannàn samfùř;
it is a ~ of a train samfùřin jirgin ƙasà
nē. b. (style) yàyī m: this is the latest ~
radio wannàn řēdiyò sābon yàyī nè.

moderate 1. adj (average) matsàkàicī adj:
the price is ~ kudìn matsàkàicī nè;
(medium amount) madàidàicī adj: a ~
quantity of rice madaidaicìyař shìnkāfā;
he ate a ~ amount of food yā ci àbinci
daidai kīmà.

2. *n & adj* (*Pol.*) (mài) tsàkàitaccen ŕa'àyī *m.*

**moderation** *n*: in ~ kīmà *adv.*

**modern** *adj* na zāmànī/zằmằnī *m*, na yâu: ~ Hausa Hausa ta zāmànī = Hausaŕ yâu dà kullum; a ~ man mùtumìn zāmànī = ɗan yâu; in ~ times à zāmànin nàn; he built a ~ house yā ginà gidā ginìn zāmànī.

**modest** *adj* a. (*not boastful*) (mài) kunyà *f*: she's a ~ person tanà dà kunyà. b. (*shy*) (mài) jîn kunyà *m*, (mài) jîn nauyī *m*: we felt ~ in front of him munà jîn kunyàŕsà. c. (*moderate*) dà dāma-dāma: he earns a ~ salary àlbâshinsà dà dāma-dāma = yanà sāmùn àlbâshī madàidàicī.

**modesty** *n* (*sensitivity, shyness toward others*) kàrā *f*, jîn kunyà *m*, filākò *m*: she wasn't able to tell him out of ~ tā kāsà gayà masà sabòdà kàrā; lack of ~ sòn à sanì *m*: they have no ~ sòn à sanì gàre sù.

**modification** *n* gyàre-gyàre *p*: the building has had a few ~s an yi wà ginì waɗansu gyàre-gyàre.

**modifier** *n* (*Gram.*) sìffàntau *m.*

**modify** *v* a. (*change*) gyaggyàrā *v1.* b. (*Gram.*) siffàntā *v1*, bayyànā *v1*: the function of adjectives is to ~ nouns aikìn siffōfī bayyànà sūnàyē.

**moist** *adj* (mài) danshī *m*, (mài) laimà *f*; become ~ jìƙa *v3.*

**moisten** *v* jiƙà *v1*, laimàtā *v1*; (*esp. ground*) dansàsā *v1*: they ~ed the field in preparation for the game sun dansàsà fīlī don wàsân.

**moisture** *n* laimà *f*, (*dew of early morning*) rāɓā *f*, (*seeping through a surface*) nàsō *m.*

**molar** *n* mataunī *m.*

**mold**[1] *n* (*on foods*) fùmfùmnā / hùnhùnā *f*; become ~y (*& discolored*) dùnànà *v3.*

**mold**[2] *n* (*for casting metal*) zubī *m.*

**mole**[1] *n* (*on skin*) tàwadàŕ Allàh *f*, mawankī *m.*

**mole**[2] *n*, *see* shrew.

**moment** *n* a. (*in time*): at the ~ yànzu *adv*: he's very busy at the ~ aikì yā yi masà yawà yànzu; at this very ~ yànzu-yànzun nàn; a ~ ago dàzu *adv*: just a ~ ago dàzu-dàzun nàn; in a ~ in an jimà = nân dà ƙyas; he will come at any ~ zâi zō in an jimà = zâi zō nân dà ƙyas; wait a ~! dàkàtā kàɗan! b. (*partic. time*) lōkàcī *m*: at that ~ à lōkàcîn: at that very ~ à daidai lōkàcîn nan; I came the ~ I heard the news nan dà nan dà

jîn làbāŕìn na zō; at the present ~ à lōkàcin yànzu; now is the right ~ to ask him yànzu daidai lōkàcin tàmbayàŕsà; at the same ~ à lōkàcī daya = à lōkàcī gùdā; at the propitious ~ à kân karī; at precisely the wrong ~ à karìn banzā.

**monarchy** *n* mùlūkiyà *f.*

**Monday** *n* Lìtinîn *f.*

**money** *n* kuɗī *m/p*; I've lost my ~ kuɗī sun ɓacè minì; he has lost all his ~ yā yi bàbbaŕ hàsāŕà it is worth a lot of ~ yanà dà daŕajà sòsai; make, spend, save ~ sàmi, kashè, ajìyè kuɗī; waste, squander ~ ɓad dà / ɓataŕ (dà) *v5*; he has no ~ whatsoever bâ shi dà kuɗī kō ànīnī; (*fig.*) ~ talks kuɗī màgànin tàkàicī.

**money-lender** *n* mài bā dà bāshì *n*: he is in business as a ~ cìnikinsà bā dà bāshì.

**money order** *n* fàs-ōdà *f*, [F] màndâ *f.*

**mongoose** *n* tùnkū *m* ⟨una⟩.

**monitor lizard** *n* (*land*) damō *m*; (*water*) guzà *m*, tsàrī *m.*

**monk** *n* sūfī *m* ⟨aye⟩.

**monkey** *n* birì *m* ⟨birai⟩; (*small, blue*) tsūlà *f*, (*red*) àtalà *m.*

**monopolize** *v* kankànē / kyankēnē *v4*: ~ a conversation kankànè hīŕa; (*Econ.*) yi bàbàkēŕē *m.*

**monopoly** *n* (*Econ.*) bàbàkēŕē *m*: he has a ~ on the kolanut trade yā yi bàbàkēren kàsuwaŕ gōŕò.

**monotheism** *n* tàuhīdì *m.*

**monotonous** *adj* (mài) cîn râi *m*, (mài) gùndurà *f*: a ~ book littāfì mài cîn râi.

**monotony** *n* cîn râi *m*, gùndurà *f.*

**monster** *n* (*any fearful thing*) dòdō *m*, dòdannìyā *f* ⟨anni⟩.

**month** *n* watà *m* ⟨anni⟩: he is paid ₦600 a ~ anà biyànsà àlbâshin naiŕà ɗarì shidà à watà; he lived there for 8 ~s yā yi zaman watà takwàs à can; what day of the ~ is it? yâu nawà gà watà? last ~ watàn jiyà; next ~ watàn gòbe = watà mài zuwà; ~ after next watàn jībi.

**monthly** *adv* watà-watà *adv*: the magazine appears ~ mùjallaŕ nà fitôwā watà-watà.

**monument** *n* àbin tunàwā *m.*

**mood** *n*: a good ~ ànnàshùwā *f*, wàlwàlā *f*: today I'm in a good ~ yâu inà ànnàshùwā; a bad ~ baƙin cikì *m*; be in the ~ for ji *v0*: I'm in the ~ for a walk, to read a book inà jîn shân iskà, kaŕàntà littāfì.

moon *n* watã *m* ⟨anni⟩: there's a new ∼ watã yā tsayã; there's a full ∼ tonight yâu daren shâ huɗun watã.

moonlight *n* farin watã *m*.

moor *v* (*a boat*) daurè *v4*.

mop 1. *n* magōgin dàɓē *m*, àbin tsanè ruwā *m*.

2. *v*: ∼ a floor gōgè dàɓē dà àbin tsanè ruwā.

moral[1] *adj* (*psn.*) (mài) aƙīdã *f*, (mài) dā'ã *f*.

moral[2] *n* (*of a tale*) daɽàsī *m* ⟨u-a⟩.

morale *n* ƙarfin gwīwã *m*: our ∼ is good munã dà ƙarfin gwīwã.

morality, morals *n* àƙīdã *f*, dā'ã *f*: he has no morals bâ shi dà dā'ã.

more 1. *quant & det* a. (*additional*): (*in gen'l, use the compar. verb* fi *v0 and its derivatives, or verbs of repetition such as* daɗã *v1,* ƙārā *v1, or* sākè *v1.*): he has ∼ experience than the others yā fi saurân ƙwarèwā; I have ∼ clothes than he nā fi shî kāyan jìkī; give him some ∼ water à daɗã masà ruwā; do you want ∼ tea? ìn daɗō makà shāyì? I need ∼ time inã bùkātàɽ à ƙārã minì lōkàcī. b. (*remaining*): there are no ∼ stamps bābù sauran kân sarkī.

2. *adv*: you must work ∼ lallē kì ƙārà aikī; be ∼ careful kà ƙārà kùlā; nothing is ∼ important than health bābù àbîn dà ya fi lāfiyã muhimmancī; which box holds ∼? wànè àkwàtà ya fi cî? tell it to me once ∼ kà sākè gayã minì; ∼ than (*in excess of*) fìye dà, samà dà: he gave me ∼ than that yā bā nì fìye dà hakà; there are ∼ than 50 inside àkwai samà dà hàmsin ciki; he can't be ∼ than 10 years old bà zâi fi shèkarã gōmà dà haihùwā ba; ∼ than anything else fìye dà dukà; ∼ than ever fìye dà kullum = fìye dà kōyàushè; ∼ or less kusan *prep*, wajen *prep*: there are 20 ∼ or less àkwai dai kusan àshìɽin; that is ∼ or less correct wannàn kusan daidai nè; or ∼ kō mā fi: there are 20 people or ∼ on the way àkwai mutànê àshìɽin kō mā fi à tàfe.

3. *pro* a. (*additional ones*) ƙārì *m*: she gave me 3 ∼ tā bā nì ƙārì na gùɗà ukù; she gave them some ∼ tā ƙārā musù; I have nothing ∼ to say bâ ni dà ƙārìn màganã = bâ ni dà àbîn dà zân ƙārà cêwā = bâ ni dà sauran màganã. b. (*remaining ones*) saurā *m*, ràgōwã *f*: there are only 3 ∼ left àkwai saurā gùɗà ukù kawài = ukù kawài ya ragè; do you have any ∼? kanà dà ràgōwã?

moreover *conj* daɗin dadãwā, bugũ dà ƙārì *conj*: I saw her do it, ∼ she told me about it nā gan tà tanã yî, daɗin dadãwā, tā gayã minì.

morning *n* sāfiyā *f*: good ∼! barkà dà sāfiyā! = barkà dà àsùbâ! early ∼ (*from 8-10 am*) hàntsī *m*; in the wee hours of the ∼ dà tsakaɽ darē; the ∼ after wàshègàrī / kàshègàrī *f*; in the ∼ dà sāfe *adv*: early in the ∼ dà sassāfe; this ∼ yâu dà sāfe; he works from ∼ till night yakàn yi aikì tun dàgà sāfe haɽ dare; the ∼ meal kàlàcin sāfe.

morning sickness *n* laulàyin cikì *m*.

morphology (*Gram.*) tàsàɽīfì *m*.

mortal *adj* mamàcī *m*: all men are ∼ ɗan Adàm duk mamàcī nè.

mortality *n*: ∼ rate yawàn màce-màce.

mortar[1] *n* turmī *m*: ∼ and pestle turmī dà taɓaryā; pound grain in the ∼ dakà hatsī cikin turmī.

mortar[2] (*for construction*) kwaɓī *m*.

mortgage *n* jìnginàɽ gidā *f*.

Moslem *n, see* Muslim.

mosque *n* masallācī *m* ⟨ai⟩: Friday, central ∼ masallācin Jumma'à.

mosquito *n* saurō *m*: ∼ bite cīzòn saurō; we were bitten by ∼es all night long mun shā cīzòn saurō dà dare gàbā ɗayansà; ∼ coil māgànin saurō = [F] igiyàɽ lēgàs; ∼ net gidan saurō.

most 1. *quant & det* a. (*in pred. position, use compar. constr. such as* fi duk yawà, mafì yawà): she has the ∼ jewelry of all tā fi duk yawàn kāyan adō = tanã dà kāyan adō mafì yawã; they scored the ∼ goals sun fi dukà yawàn cîn gwàl. b. (*in subj. position, use* yawancī *m/adv*): ∼ students have to study a lot dōlè yawancin dàlìbai su' yi kàɽàtū dà yawà.

2. *adv*: the ∼ comfortable chair kujèrã mafì dāɗin zamā; ∼ of the time, for the ∼ part gālibàn *adv*, yawancī *m/adv*: ∼ of the time he gets up early yawancī yanã tashì dà wuri; for the ∼ part they are honest gālibàn sunã dà gàskiyã; that is what troubles us ∼ shī nè àbîn dà ya fi dāmùnmù; his plan was the ∼ suitable dàbāɽàɽsà tā fi dācêwā; ∼ of all (*above all*) fìye dà dukà: ∼ of all they want to return home fìye dà dukà sunã sôn sù kōmà gidā.

3. *pro* a. (*majority*) mafì yawà, yawancī *m*, kusan dukà: ∼ (of the people) agree mafì yawà sun yàrda; I understood ∼ of what he said nā gānè kusan duk

màganàr̃sà. b. (*maximum*) iyākā / iyākā
f, bàkī m: this is the ~ I can give you
iyākar̃ àbîn dà na iyā bā kà kè nan;
he did the ~ that he could yā yi bàkin
k̃òk̃arinsà.

**mostly** *adv* gālibàn *adv*, yawancī m: ~ I
prefer city life gālibàn à bir̃nī na fi
sôn zamā; the people here are ~ Hausa
mutànên dà kè nân gālibàn Hàusàwā nè.

**moth** *n* fàdà-wuta m.

**mother** *n* (*term of ref.*) uwā f ⟨iyàyē⟩; (*most
polite terms of ref.*) mahaifìyā f, bābà
f, màma f, tsōhuwā f, gyàtumā f: how is
your ~? yàyà mahaifìyar̃kì? my ~ is well
gyàtumātā tanà lāfiyà; (*term of addr.
to one's own*) innà, iyà, bàbà.

**mother-in-law** *n* sùrukā / sàràkuwā f
⟨ai⟩; (*term of addr.*) iyà.

**mother tongue** *n* (*one's own*) harshèn
gidā, harshèn uwā m; (*esp. of an ethnic
minority*) yàr̃ē m ⟨uka⟩: his ~ is Jukun
yàr̃ensà jukunancī nè.

**motion** *n* a. (*movement*) mòtsī m, gushì
m; ~ sickness tāshìn zūcìyā m. b. (*in a
meeting*) bàtū m, mōshàn m: make, withdraw a ~ kāwō, jànyē bàtū; second a ~
gòyi bāyan bàtū.

**motive** *n* dàlīlì m ⟨ai⟩: a strong ~
k̃wàk̃k̃wāran dàlīlì; have an ulterior ~
cī dà cètō: does he have an ulterior ~?
yanà cî dà cètō?

**motor** *n* (*engine*) injì m ⟨una⟩.

**motorcycle** *n* bàbûr̃ m ⟨u-a⟩, màshîn m.

**motor scooter** *n* bàbûr̃ m, basfà m, [F]
bàspà m, [F] mòtô m, [F] mòbìlât m.

**motto** *n* tākè m: their ~ is 'unity' tākensù
'hadìn kâi'.

**moult** *v* zub dà gāshì.

**mound** *n* dan tudù m; a fire ~ (*for grilling
meat*) tukùbā f.

**mount** *v* (*animal*) hau *v*\* ⟨hawā⟩.

**mountain** *n* dūtsè m ⟨duwàtsū⟩, bàbban
tsaunì m ⟨uka⟩: which is the highest ~
in Africa? wànè dūtsè nē mafì tsawō
à Afir̃kà? the province is very ~ous
duwàtsū sun yi yawà à lar̃dìn.

**mourn** *v* (*gen'l 3-day period*) yi makōkī m;
(*by widow, for 3 months*) yi tàkabà f.

**mourning** *n* (*gen'l 3-day period*) zaman
makōkī m; (*of widow, for 3 months*)
tàkabà f: she is in ~ tanà tàkabà; finish ~ shàrè makōkī.

**mouse** *n* ɓērā m ⟨aye⟩, kūsù m ⟨kūsā⟩;
(*fig.*) be as quiet as a ~ yi tsit kàmar̃
an yi mutuwà = yi tsit kàmar̃ ruwā yā
cī sù.

**mouse-trap** *n* almìnjîr̃ m.

**moustache** *n* gàshìn bàki m.

**mouth** *n* a. bàkī m ⟨una⟩: we stood
there with our ~s wide open munà nan
bàkī sàke; ~ of a pot, calabash bàkin
tukunyā, k̃waryā; what town is at the ~
of the Niger? wànè gàrī kè bàkin Kōgin
Kwār̃à? make one's ~ water sâ miyau yà
gudà. b. (*adverbial uses*): in, on the ~
(à) bakà, à bàki *adv*: he was hurt on the
~ yā ji ràunī à bakà; don't put it in
your ~! kadà kì sâ à bàki! by word of
~ dà bakà.

**mouthful** *n* lōmà f ⟨oCi⟩: he's eating big
~s of rice yanà cîn shìnkāfā dà bàbbar̃
lōmà.

**move** 1. *vi* a. (*make a movement*) mōtsà
*v1*, yi mòtsī m: don't ~, there's a
snake kadà kà mōtsà, àkwai macìjī. b.
(*change position*) gusà *v1*, gushè *v4*; ~
aside kaucè *v4*; ~ close matsà *v1*: let's
~ closer together mù matsà dà jūnā. c.
(*go, function*) tàfi *v3*\* ⟨tàfiyà⟩ f: the
minute hand isn't moving dōgon hannun
àgōgo bā yà tàfiyà. d. (*change residence*) sākè gidā: they've ~d to another
neighborhood sun sākè gidā zuwà wata
ùngùwā dàbam; (*of bride to husband's residence*) tārè gidā *v4*. e. (*migrate, emigrate*) k̃aura *v3a*, yi k̃aurā f.
2. *vt* a. (*remove*) kau dà / kawar̃ (dà) *v5*,
gusar̃ (dà) *v5*: someone has ~d my tools
wani yā kau dà kāyan aikìnā; the police
made me ~ my car 'yan sàndā sun sâ nā
gusar̃ dà mōtātà. b. (~ *nearer to*) matsà
dà *v1*: he ~d the chair closer to the door
yā matsà dà kujèrā kusa dà k̃ōfà. c.
(*many things in several trips*) jìdā *v2*: the
men have ~d all the bundles of guinea corn
mutànē sun jìdi dâmman hatsī dukà. d.
(*invoke sympathy*) sōsà wà zūcìyā, bâ w.
tàusàyī: the story ~d us làbārìn yā bâ
mù tàusàyī.

**movement** *n* a. (*motion*) mōtsī m, gushì
m; freedom of ~ wàlàwā f. b. (*ideology*)
r̃a'àyī m: the women's ~ r̃a'àyin cî-
gàban mātā.

**movie(s)** *n* sìlimà m, fîm m, *see* cinema;
~ theater (gidan) sìlimà / sìlìmân m.

**moving** *adj*: it was a ~ story làbàr̃ì nē mài
ban tàusàyī.

**mow** *v*: ~ the lawn yankè cìyāwà.

**Mr.** *hon* (*term of ref. or addr.*) Mālàm, [F]
Mùshe: Mr. Sale Mālàm Sālè = Mùshe
Sālè.

**Mrs.** *hon* (*term of ref. or addr.*) Mālàmā
(+ *given name*): Mrs. Ladi Mālàmā Lādì;
(*term of addr. to so.'s wife*) Uwar̃gidan

Mālàm X.
much 1. *quant* a. (mài) yawã *m*: we haven't
~ time bâ mu dà lōkàcī mài yawã; there
is too ~ sugar (in it) sukàřī yā yi yawã;
this work is too ~ for me aikìn nân yā yi
minì yawã.
2. *adv* a. (*in compar. constr., use verb* fi
*v0*): he is ~ better at English than I am
yā fī nì iyà Tūřancī sòsai. b. (*a lot*)
dà yawã: we need ~ more munã bùkātà dà
yawã; do you see ~ of him? kakàn gan shì
dà yawã? do too ~ of sth. cikã *v1*, fayè
*v4*: he smokes too ~ yā fayè shân tābã;
I do not take ~ interest in birds bàn cikà
shà'awàř tsuntsàyē ba; take as ~ as you
want ɗauki bàkin àbîn dà kakè sô. c.
(*in neg. contrastive sent.*) ~ less bàllē /
bàllàntànā: I didn't see him ~ less speak
to him bàn gan shì ba bàllàntànā ìn yi
masà màganà. d. how ~? nawà *adv*: how
~ does a bag cost? nawà akè sai dà bùhū
gùdā? e. however ~ kō nawà: however ~
it costs I'll buy it kō nawà nē kuɗinsà zân
sàyā.
mucus *n* (*from nose*) mãjinā *f*, (*dried*)
tàsōnō *m*, (*phlegm*) kãkī *m;* (*discharge
from eye*) kwantsã *f*.
mud *n* a. (*natural state*) tàɓō *m*: become
stuck in the ~ kafè cikin tàɓō; (*slushy*)
cãɓī *m*, càɓàlɓàlō *m*. b. (*clay from pond
for building*) lākà *f*: the houses are built
of ~ anã ginà gidàjē dà lākà; (*soil esp.
mixed for building*) kasà *f*: a ~ house
gidan kasà; mix ~ (*for building*) kwãɓà
kasà.
muddle *n*: he made a ~ of the whole thing
yā rikìtà sha'ànī duk.
muddy 1. *adj* (mài) cãɓī *m;* be(come) ~ yi
cãɓī *m*, cāɓè *v4*, yi càɓàlɓàlō *m*.
2. *v* (*by stirring up sediment*) guřɓàtà *v1*,
dāmà *v1*: the cattle have muddied the water shānū sun guřɓàtà ruwā.
mudfish *n* gâiwā *f*, (*resembling a catfish*)
tařwadà *f* ⟨tařèwadī⟩.
mudguard *n* mutàgàdì *m*, [F] gàřdàbû *m*.
muezzin *n* làdân / làdānī *m* ⟨ai⟩.
muffler *n* (*of car*) sàlansà *f*, [F] shàmfàmà
*f*.
mug *n* mōdà *f* ⟨aye⟩.
mulatto *n* barbarař yânyāwà *n*.
mule *n* àlfadàřī *m* ⟨ai⟩.
mulish *adj*: be ~ dãgè *v4*, yi kafiyà *f*.
multilingualism *n* iyà harsunà.
multiple *n* ninkì *m*, riɓì *m*: a ~ of 3 ninkì
ukù.
multiplication *n* sàu *m*: she has trouble
with ~ sàu yanà bā tà wàhalà; ~ sign

àlāmàř sàu; ~ table jadawàlin lìssāfì
*m*.
multiply *v* riɓà / riɓànyā *v1*, ninkà *v1*: his
wealth multiplied threefold dūkìyařsà tā
ninkà ukù; our difficulties have multiplied
because of the bad weather matsalōlinmù
sun ninkà sabòdà mūgùn yanàyī; know
how to ~ iyà sàu; how much is 2 multiplied by 3? biyu sàu ukù nawà kè nan?
multitude *n*: a ~ of people mutànē tìnjim
= ɗimbin mutànē = cìncìrindòn mutànē
= cùnkōson mutànē.
mumble *v* (*grumble or speak low*) yi
gùngùnī/gunàgunī *m;* (*speak fast, unintelligibly*) yi bàdà-bàdà *idph*, yi bàdàm-
badam *idph*.
mumps *n* hàngum *m*.
municipal *adj* na biřnī *m*.
murder *v* kashè *v4*, yi kisàn kâi *m;* a terrible ~ kisàn gillà.
murderer *n* mài kisàn kâi *n*.
muscle *n* tsōkà *f;* biceps ~ kwànjī *m;* I've
pulled a ~ in my leg kafàtà tā ɗaurè.
muscular *adj* muřɗēɗè *adj*: he is huge and ~
muřɗēɗèn kàtò nē; they are very ~ kàttā
nè muřɗā-mùřɗà.
museum *n* ma'àdanař kāyàyyakin tāřīhì
*m*, gidan tāřīhì *m*.
mush *n* (*stiff porridge made from various
grains, the staple food of the Hausa*) tuwō
*m*.
mushroom *n* nāmàn kàzā *m*.
mushy *adj* (*of cooked food*) làngàɓaɓɓè *adj;*
be(come) ~ langàɓè *v4*, jikɓè *v4*.
music *n* (*esp. instrumental*) kiɗà *m*, (*song,
singing*) wākà *f*.
musical *adj* na kiɗà.
musician *n* makàɗī *m*, mabùshī *m:* Hausa
~s makàɗan Hàusàwā; band of ~s màsu
bùshe-bùshe dà kàɗe-kàɗe.
musk *n* tùràren jūdà *f*.
musk shrew *n* jāɓà *f*.
Muslim *n & adj* Mùsùlmī *m:* they are ~ sū
Mùsùlmī nè; it is a ~ custom dàbī'à cē
ta Mùsùlmī; become a ~ mùsùluntà *v3*.
muslin *n* àkōko *m*, namūzù *m*, maltì *m*.
mussel shell *n* kùmbà *m*.
must *v* a. (*be necessary*) dōlè *adv*, tīlàs
*adv*, wājìbī *m*, wàjabà *v3*: you ~ go dōlè
kà tàfi = wājìbī nè kà tàfi; you ~
type the report again dōlè kà sākè bugà
řàhōtòn nân; it is something that everyone ~ do àbù nē dà ya wàjabà kōwà yà
yi. b. (*for polite request or suggestion*)
sai (+ *complet.*): ~ you really go? stay a
little longer dōlè nē sai kà tàfi? kà ɗan
jimà. c. (~ *not*) kadà/kâř (+ *subjunct.*):

you ~ not do it kadà kà yi. d. (*probably*)
lallē *adv*: there ~ be some mistake lallē
dà kuskurè; he ~ be crazy lallē hàukā
yakè yî; he ~ have lost his way lallē yā
rasà hanyà = lallē yā 6atà.
mute *adj*: deaf-~ bēbē *m* ⟨aye⟩.
mutilate *v* naƙàsā *v1*, yi wà mūgùn ràunī.
mutiny *n* tāwāyèn sōjà *m*.
mutter *v* yi gunàgunī *m*.
mutton *n* nāmàn ràgō *m*.
mutual *adj* (*use suffixes* -ayyà *&* -ēnìyā
*on the verb*): ~ hatred ƙìyayyà *f*; ~ love
sòyayyà *f*; ~ agreement yàrjējēnìyā *f*.
muzzle *v* (*an animal*) sâ wà tàkunkùmī
*m*; (*fig.*) ~ the press yi wà 'yan jàrîdū
tàkunkùmī.
my *pro, see* Appendix A.
myself *pro, see* self, Appendix A.
mystery *n* a. àbin màmākì *m*; it's a ~
to me àbin màmākì nē gàrē nì = nā
kāsà gānèwā; this affair is a ~ àl'amàrin
nàn ƙwaryā rùfe nè = àl'amàrin nàn
nà dà ɗaurèwar kâi. b. (*detective story*)
làbārìn ɗan sàndan ciki *m*.
mystic *n* (*Relig.*) sūfī *m* ⟨aye⟩.
mystify *v* ɗaurè wà kâi, shigè wà à duhù:
the whole affair mystified them sha'ànī
duk yā shigè musù à duhù.
myth *n* hìkāyàr mafārī *f*.

# N

nag *v* fìtinằ *v2*, dằmi w. dà fìtinằ, matsằ wằ *v1*.

nail *n* a. (*fingernail*) farcè *m* ⟨a-a⟩; bite one's ~s ci yātsū; cut one's ~s yankè farcè = ragè farcè. b. (*carpentry*) ƙūsā *f* ⟨oCi⟩: I need more ~s inằ bùkātằ ƙārìn ƙūsōshī; drive a ~ into a box bugằ wằ àkwằtì ƙūsà; (*fig.*) you've hit the ~ on the head kā yi sūsā indà yakè ƙaiƙayī. 2. *v* (*into sth.*) bugà ƙūsằ; (*fasten onto, e.g. wall*) kafằ *v1*.

nail polish *n* jàn-farcè *m*.

naira *n* (*basic unit of currency in Nigeria, abbreviated as* ₦, *see* Appendix F) naiřằ *f* ⟨oCi⟩: ₦5.50 naiřằ bìyař dà kwabò hàmsin.

naive *adj* (*psn.*) bàƙauyè *adj*, bàgidàjè *adj*: he's totally ~ about women bàgidàjè fitik gàme dà mātā; (*unworldly, never travelled*) (*fig.*) kīfin rījìyā *m*.

naiveté *n* ƙauyancī *m*, gidādancī *m*, kidāhumancī *m*.

naked *adj* (*psn.*) (mài) tsìrārằ *f*; (*half-~, insufficiently dressed*) huntū *m* ⟨aye⟩: I found him ~ to the waist nā sằmē shì huntū = nā sằmē shì à hùnce; stark ~ zìgìdiř *idph*, zìndiř *idph*: I saw him stark ~ nā gan shì zìgìdiř; be ~, strip oneself ~ tsìraitā *v3*, yi tsiraicì *m*; (*fig.*) it's the ~ truth! hàkīkànin gaskiyā nè!

name 1. *n* a. sūnā *m* ⟨aye⟩: what is the ~ of this village? yàyằ sūnan wannàn ƙauyè? I cannot remember his ~ nā kāsà tunà sūnansà = sūnansà yā 6acè minì; I know him only by ~ inằ jîn sūnansà kawài; I don't know anyone of that ~ bàn san wani mài sūnā hakà ba; he has the same ~ as I shī mài sūnānā nè = shī tàkwàřānā nè; personal, given ~ (*Islamic*) sūnan yankā = sūnan rằgō = sūnan gàskiyā, (*non-Islamic*) sūnan rānā; last ~, official ~ sūnan mahàifī; ~ avoidance (*Hausa custom*) àlkunyà *f*: she avoided mentioning his ~ (*out of deference to him*) tā yi masà àlkunyà. b. (*reputation*) sūnā *m*, shaidà *f*; have, make a good ~ yi sūnā; have a bad ~ yi mūgùn sūnā = yi ƙaurin sūnā;

that company has a bad ~ kamfànîn nan bā yằ dà shaidằ mài kyâu; if you do that, you'll give yourself a bad ~ in zā kì yi hakà zā kì 6ātà kânkì; call so. ~s zằgā *v2* ⟨zāgì⟩, zàzzāgằ *v2*: he called me all kinds of ~s bâ zāgìn dà bài yi minì ba. 2. *v* a. (*a newborn*) raɗằ wà sūnā: the child has been ~d Musa an raɗằ wà ɗā sūnā Mūsā; a man ~d Musa wani mùtûm mài sūnan Mūsā; he was ~d after his uncle an sâ masà sūnan kàwunsà. b. (*appoint*) naɗằ *v1* ⟨naɗì⟩: he has been ~d police inspector an naɗằ shi sùfētò.

namely *adv* wằtàu / wằtò: only one person didn't come, ~ Adamu mùtûm ɗaya nè kawài bài zō ba, wằtàu Àdàmu.

namesake *n* tàkwàřā *n* ⟨oCi⟩: he is my ~ shī tàkwàřānā nè; she is my ~ ita tàkwàřātà cè.

naming day ceremony *n* sūnā *m*: tomorrow there is a ~ at so-and-so's house gòbe zā à yi sūnā à gidan wānè.

nap *n* (*early afternoon*) barcin rāna *m*, ƙailūlā *f*; take a little ~ (*anytime*) rintsà *v1*: I'm going to take a little ~ zân ɗan rintsà.

nape *n* ƙēyằ *f*.

narrate *v* bā dà lằbāřì, warwàrè lằbāřì, ruwàitā *v1*.

narration *n* wàrwarằ *f*.

narrative *n* lằbāřì *f*.

narrator *n* mài bā dà lằbāřì *n*.

narrow 1. *adj* a. (*not wide*) maràs fāɗī *m*: the river is very ~ here kồgin bâ shi dà fāɗī à nân. b. (*constricted*) (mài) ƙuncī *m*, màtsattsē *adj*, (mài) matsī *m*: the room is ~ dākìn yā yi ƙuncī; the gown is too ~ rīgā tā yi matsī; a ~ path màtsattsiyař hanyằ; he is ~-minded bā yằ kàr6ař shāwařằ. c. have a ~ escape (*fig.*) aunà ařzìkī: they had a ~ escape from death sun aunà ařzìkī dằ sun mutù. 2. *v*: ~ one's eyes kannè idò.

nasty *adj*: he's a ~ person baƙin cikì gàrē shì; a ~ remark màganằ mài rashìn kunyằ; a ~ wound mūgùn ràunī.

nation *n* àl'ummằ *f* ⟨oCi⟩, ƙasā *f* ⟨aCe⟩: there are over 50 different African ~s àkwai al'ummōmī fìye dà hàmsin à Afiřkà.

national *adj* na ƙasā *f*: in ~ dress sànye dà kāyan ƙasā = sànye dà kāyan gařgājiyā; ~ anthem tākè *m*; ~ defense tsàron ƙasā; ~ guard 'yan tsàron ƙasā *p*, [F] gàř-dà-sarki *m*; ~ government gwamnatìn ƙasā bằkī ɗaya; ~

languages harsunàn ƙasā; ~ security tsàron lāfiyaȓ àl'ummā; N. Youth Service Corps ƙungiyaȓ 'Yan Bāutā wà ƙasā.

**nationalism** *n* kīshìn ƙasā *m*.

**nationalist** *n* ɗan kīshìn ƙasā *m*.

**nationalize** *v* mai dà w.a. hannun 'yan ƙasā.

**nationality** *n* ƙasā *f*: what is your ~? ìnā nē ƙasaȓkù? = dàgà wàcè ƙasā kakè?

**native** *n* & *adj* (*ethnonymic prefix*) bà-⟨awa⟩ (+ *place name*); ɗan *m*, 'yaȓ *f* ⟨'yan⟩ (+ *place name*); mùtûm *m*, mùtūnìyā *f* ⟨mutằnē⟩ (+ *place name*): I am a ~ of Kano but they are a ~s of Yola nī bàkanè nē àmmā sū mutằnen 'Yōlà nē; she is a ~ of that village ita mùtūnìyaȓ ƙauyèn nan; (*of a particular country*) ɗan ƙasā *m*: she is a ~ of Mali ita 'yaȓ ƙasaȓ Mālì cē; this is my ~ land wannàn ita cè ƙasaȓmù; a ~ speaker mài harshèn gidā; he speaks Hausa like a ~ (*fig.*) yā iyà Hausa kàmaȓ jàkin Kanò.

**natural** *adj*: ~ history làbāȓìn hàlittā; ~ resources aȓzìkin ƙasā; he died a ~ death mutuwā̀ cē dai ta Allàh; it is ~ to be afraid of death hakà Allàh ya yi sai mun ji tsòron mutuwā̀; you don't look ~ in that picture cikin wannàn hòtō, kàmaȓ bā̀ kai ba.

**naturally** *adv* a. (*of course, obviously*) dâ mā, àlhālī kùwa: ~ I knew (it would happen) dâ mā nā sanì; ~, I've known him since he was a boy dâ mā, nā san shì tun yanà̀ yārò; ~ he didn't tell me àlhālī kùwa bài gayà minì ba. b. (*by nature or habit*): he is ~ that way hakà hālinsà yakè.

**nature** *n* a. (*behavior*) hālī / halī *m* ⟨aye⟩: that's his ~ halinsà kè nan; be(come) second ~ zama jìkī: turning out the lights has become second ~ to me kashè wutā yā zamè minì jìkī; human ~ mùtùntakā̀ *f*. b. (*the natural world*): that's its ~ haka akà halìttā shi. c. (*essence of sth.*) tàkàmaimai *m*, ainihī *m*: I don't know the precise ~ of his business bàn san tàkàmaiman haȓkàȓsà ba.

**naught** *n*: come to ~ sūlàncē *v4*, wātsè *v4*: his hopes came to ~ fātansà yā sūlàncē; their plans came to ~ shìrye-shìryensù duk sun wātsè.

**naughty** *adj* shàƙiyyī *n* ⟨ai⟩, (mài) fìtinà *f*, (mài) hālin banzā *m*, (mài) ƙìn jî: I've never seen such ~ boys bàn taɓà ganin yârā màsu ƙìn jî kàmaȓsù ba; you were very ~ and will be punished kin cikà hālin banzā zā à hòȓē kì.

**nausea** *n* tāshìn zūcìyā *m*; (*from not having eaten*) kùmallō *m*.

**nauseous** *adj*: feel ~ ji tāshìn zūcìyā, ji amai *m*; make so. ~ tā dà zūcìyaȓ w.: flying makes me ~ tàfiyà ta jirgin samà kàn sâ ni tāshìn zūcìyā = tàfiyà̀ ta jirgī kàn tā dà zūcìyātā; (*from not having eaten*) ji kùmallō *m*.

**navel** *n* cībìyā *f* ⟨oCi⟩; (*enlarged*) cībì *m*.

**navy** *n* (*Mil.*) rùndunaȓ mayằƙan jirằgen ruwa *f*.

**near** *adv* & *prep* kusa dà *prep*, dab dà *prep*: it is ~ the post office yanà kusa dà gidan wayā̀; it is quite ~ here dab dà nân yakè = bā̀ nīsā dàgà nân; from here, which is the ~est town? dàgà nân wànè gàrī ya fi kusa? from ~ and far na kusa dà na nēsà; very ~ kuȓkusa *adv*; go ~ (*approach*) rā̀6ā *v2*: he shouldn't go ~ the patient kadà yà rā̀6ì mài cīwòn; come ~ (*of space*) zō kusa, matsō *v6*; draw ~ (*of time*) matsō *v6*, ƙarātō *v6*, kusa *v*\*: harvest season is drawing ~ ƙāƙā tā ƙarātō.

**nearby** *adv* nân kusa.

**Near East** *n* ƙasằshen Gabàs ta Tsakiyā̀ *p*.

**nearly** *adv* a. (*almost*) kusan *prep*: it is ~ 10 o'clock now yànzu kusan ƙarfè gōmà; ~ every day kusan kōwàcè rānà; it's ~ 5 miles from here yā yi kusan mîl bìyaȓ dàgà nân; in ~ every village kusan à kōwànè ƙauyè; not ~ (*not adequate*) kō kusa: there are not ~ enough bā̀ sù ìsa ba kō kusa. b. (*on the point of*): be ~ gab dà *prep*, bằkin *prep*, kusan *prep*, kusa *v*\*: they were ~ dead from the cold sunà̀ bằkin mutuwā̀ sabòdà sanyī = sunā̀ gab dà mutuwā̀ sabòdà sanyī; he's ~ finished yā kusa gamằwā = yanà̀ gab dà gamằwā; be ~ ready to yi shirin: she is ~ ready to go tanà̀ shirìn tàfiyà̀ = tanà̀ kusan tàfiyà̀ = tā kusa tàfiyà̀. c. (*imminently*) saurā kàɗan dà (+ *complet.*), saurā kàɗan (+ *subjunct.*): he ~ died saurā kàɗan dà yā mutù = saurā kàɗan yà mutù; the water is ~ gone saurā kàɗan ruwā yà ƙārè.

**near-sighted** *adj*: he is ~ bā̀ yà ganin nēsà = yanà̀ ganī garma-garma.

**neat** *adj* kintsattsē *adj*, tsàbtàtaccē *adj*, tsaf *idph*: his work is very ~ aikìnsà kintsattsē nē = aikìnsà tsaf dà shī; be ~ly done yi tsaf, very ~ly tsaf-tsaf; ~ness tsabtā̀ *f*.

**necessary** *adj* dōlè *adv*, tīlàs *adv*: it has become ~ yā zama tīlàs; be ~ that wājìbī nè dōlè nè: if you want to travel

abroad, it is ~ to get a visa first ìdan kanã
sô kà tàfi ƙasàshen wàje, wājìbī nè kà
sàmi bīzã tùkùna. is it ~? na dōlè nē?

necessarily adv lallē adv: that is not ~ so
bã lallē ba nè sai yā zama hakà.

necessity n a. (sth. essential, required)
wājìbī m: water is a ~ of life ruwã wājìbī
nè à rãyuwā. b. (sth. unavoidable) tīlàs
f, dōlè f: ~ made me do it tīlàs cē ta
sã na yi hakà; (fig.) ~ is the mother of
invention dōlè ƙanwàř 'nā-ƙi'. c. (esp.
sth. unforeseen) làřūřã f ⟨oCi⟩: in case of
~ call me at once in dai làřūřã tā sãmē
kà kà yi gaggāwā kà kira nì.

neck n a. wuyã m ⟨oCi⟩: I have a stiff ~
wuyãnā yā ƙagè. b. (adverbial uses): on
the ~ (à) wuyà adv; (fig.) be in debt up
to one's ~ ci bāshì hař yà wuyà = ci
bāshì iyā wuyà. c. (of musical instrument) sàndā f.

necklace n a. àbin wuyà m: put on a ~
ɗaurà àbin wuyà. b. (var. types): (with a
chain) sarƙàř wuyà f; (with beads, stones)
dūtsèn wuyà m; coral ~ mùřjānì m; cornelian ~ tsàkiyã f.

necktie n tāyè m.

need 1. v a. bùkātã v2: I ~ some thread
inã bùkātàř zàrē; put it aside until you
~ it kà ajìyē shi sai kā bùkàcē shì
= kà ajìyē shi sai lōkàcîn dà kakè
bùkātàřsà; what I ~ most of all is... àbîn
dà na fi bùkātã shī nè.... b. (ought to)
kàmātã v3 (with indef. subj pro yā): this
~s to be done yā kàmātã à yi wannàn; we
~ not tell him bài kàmātã mù faɗà masà
ba = bã sai mun faɗà masà ba.
2. n a. (want, desire) bùkātã f, mùřādì m:
my ~s have been met bùkātãtã tā biyā.
b. (necessity, requirement) làřūřã f: he
looked after the ~s of his master yā tsarè
làřūřàř maìgidansà. c. (concern): there
is no ~ to be angry bābù wani àbin fushī
à ciki.

needle n àllūřã f ⟨ai⟩; thread a ~
zurà àllūřã; eye of a ~ kafař àllūřã;
(large, for stiff materials) bàsillã f ⟨u⟩;
(for thatching) bìdā m; (for hairdress-
ing) kibiyàř kitsò f; knitting, crochet
~ tsinken sāƙã m, kwàřashī m, [F]
kwàřashê m; (fig.) pins and ~s minjiryã
f: I have pins and ~s in my foot ƙafã tanà
minì minjiryā.

needless adv (not necessary): ~ to say bã
sai an fàdā ba: ~ to say they refused
bã sai an fàdā ba sun ƙi yàřdā; it's ~
to tell you that he was late bã sai an cê
makà yā màkarà ba.

needlework n ɗinkìn hannu m.

needy n: the poor and ~ gàjìyàyyū p.

neem n (tree) dàřbējiyà f, dōgon yārò m,
mainã f, nîm f.

negation n (Gram.) kōrēwā f.

negative[1] adj (Gram.) kòrau m: a ~ sentence jimlã kòrau.

negative[2] n (of film) dòdon hòtō m, [F]
kìlìshê m.

neglect v a. (ignore so.) ƙyālè v4: he ~ed
his friends yā ƙyālè àbòkansà; (ignore
sth.) yi banzā dà f, yi wàsā dà m: he
~ed his duties yā yi banzā dà aikìnsà.
b. (be careless) yi sakacī m, yi wàsā m:
do not ~ your health kâř kà yi wàsā dà
lāfiyàř jìkī; his education was ~ed bà
à kula dà nēman ilìminsà ba.

negligence n sakacī m, rashìn kùlā m,
nàwā f.

negotiate v tattaunã v1, yi shāwàřwařī p;
(over wages) yi jìngā f.

negotiations n tattàunâwā f, shāwàřwařī
p: peace ~ shāwàřwařin lùmānã.

Negro n baƙar fātā n/p.

neigh v yi hànīniyã f.

neighbor n maƙwàbcī m: he used to be our
~ shī maƙwàbcinmù nē à dā.

neighborhood n ùnguwã f ⟨oCi⟩, [F] kàřcê
m: the court and the prison are in the
same ~ gidan shàři'ã dà kûřkukù à
ùnguwā ɗaya sukè.

neighborly adj: be ~ yi zumuncî m, yi
maƙwàbtakã f.

neither 1. conj a. (for action, use conjoined
neg. sent.): he ~ saw nor heard anything
bài ga kōmē ba, bài kuma ji kōmē ba;
I have ~ seen him nor written to him
bàn gan shì ba kuma bàn řubūtã masà
ba; the noise has ~ decreased nor stopped
ƙāřař bà tà ràgu ba kuma bà tà tsayà
ba. b. (with nouns, usu. use conjoined bã
phrases): I have ~ food nor money bã ni
dà àbinci, bã kuma kuɗî; ~ praise nor
blame bã yàbō bã fàllasã; ~ she nor I
went tsàkānin nī dà ita bã wàddà ta
tàfi.
2. pro: ~ one bã kōwànnē m, bã kōwàccē
f, kō ɗaya: ~ one nor the other bã
kōwànnensù; which book do you want? ~
one (of them) wànè littāfì kakè sô? bã
kō ɗaya (dàgà cikinsù); ~ of them came
kō ɗaya dàgà cikinsù bài zō ba. and
~ did X, and ~ was X X hakà mā: I did
not see it, and ~ did she bàn gan shì ba
ita mā hakà; the first was not useful and
~ was the second na farkō bã shi dà
àmfànī hakà mā na biyùn.

nephew n (use ɗan 'son of' + term for the specific sibling): (son of older brother) ɗan wā, (son of younger brother) ɗan ƙanè, (son of older sister) ɗan yā, (son of younger sister) ɗan ƙanwā.

nepotism n hālin hannū-yā-san-na-gidā m.

nerve n jījìyā f ⟨oCi⟩; (fig.) get on so.'s ∼s shā wà ƙai, ɗami w. dà fìtinà: (fig.) he lost his ∼ gàbansà yā fāɗì.

nervous adj a. (anxious, worried): be, feel ∼ yi jừyàyī m, ɗāmā v2: we were starting to get ∼ seeing that they might beat us mun fārà ɗàmuwā ganìn cêwā zā sù rìnjàyē mù; she was feeling ∼ about the examination tanà jừyàyin jařřàbâwā; I was ∼ gàbānā yā fāɗì. b. (excited): be ∼ tsìma v3, yi zùmūɗī m: they are always ∼ before a game kullum sukàn tsìma kàfìn sù yi wàsân.

nervousness n jừyàyī m, fāɗùwař gàbā f, ɗàmuwā f.

nest n (of bird) shèƙā f ⟨una⟩: build a ∼ yi shèƙā; (of wasp) gidan zànzarō m; (esp. of hen) gurbì m ⟨a-a⟩.

net n rāgā f ⟨oCi⟩; tennis ∼ rāgař tanìs; (large, for fishing) tārū m; (small, for fishing) kōmā f; mosquito ∼ gidan saurō m.

netball n ƙwallon rāgā m.

netting n rāgā f.

network n sādařwā f: communications ∼ hanyōyin sādařwā.

neutral 1. adj (Pol.) na 'yan bâ-ruwanmù; a ∼ country ƙasař 'yan bâ-ruwanmù.
2. n (of gears) fìřī f: put the car in ∼ kà sà giyà à fìřī; the car is in ∼ giyà tanà fìřī.

neutrality n (Pol.) tsakà-tsakancì m.

never adv, see ever. a. (not ever do) taɓà v1 (in neg. sent.): I've ∼ met him before bàn taɓà hàɗuwā dà shī ba; he's ∼ been abroad bài taɓà tàfiyà ƙasàshen wàje ba; ∼ do again sākè v4 (in neg. sent.): we ∼ saw him again bà mù sākè ganinsà ba; ∼ do that again! kadà kù sākè yîn wannàn ba! ∼ mind! (don't worry) bâ kōmē! = kâř kà ɗàmu! b. (in times past) dā mā (in neg. sent.): it was ∼ like that dā mā bà hakà ba nè. c. (forever) hař àbàdā (in neg. sent.): we shall ∼ forget your kindness hař àbàdā bà zā mù màncē dà àlhēřìnkù ba; I ∼ want to see him again hař àbàdā bā nà sôn ìn sākè ganinsà. d. (emphat.) fàufau idph, sam idph: I'll ∼ tell it to him! fàufau bà zân gayà masà ba! = sam bà zân gayà masà ba!

nevertheless conj (àmmā) duk dà hakà:

they did their best, ∼ they failed sun yi iyā ƙôƙarinsù àmmā duk dà hakà bà sù ci ba.

new adj a. (recent) sābō adj ⟨sàbàbbī, sàbbī⟩: a ∼ bicycle, friend, president sābon kèkè, àbōkī, shừgàbā; I wished him a happy ∼ year nā yi masà bařkà dà sābuwař shèkarà; brand-∼ sābō ful idph, sābō ƙau idph. b. (ano. one, a different one) wani m, wata f, wasu/waɗansu p: I have a ∼ bicycle inà dà wani kèkè dàbam. c. (in greetings): what's ∼? ìnā làbāřì? (to which reply is sai àlhēřì).

newborn adj (baby) jàrīrī m ⟨ai⟩, jinjìrī m ⟨jìràjìrai⟩.

newcomer n bàƙō m ⟨i⟩, sābon zuwà m ⟨sàbàbbin zuwà⟩: he is a ∼ in town shī bàƙō nè à gàrîn = shī sābon zuwà nē à gàrîn.

news n làbāřì m ⟨ai, u⟩: the ∼ is at 1 o'clock anà bā dà làbāřì dà ƙarfè ɗaya; I have had no ∼ from him for a long time nā daɗè bàn ji làbāřìnsà ba; bad ∼ làbāřìn bâ dāɗī; I've good ∼ for you! àlbishìřìnkà! (to which reply is gōřò!)

newscaster n mài kařàntà làbàřai n, mài bā dà làbàřai n.

newspaper n jàřīdà f ⟨u⟩.

next 1. adj a. (in time) mài zuwà, na gàba: ∼ week mākò mài zuwà; ∼ Saturday Sātī mài zuwà = Sātī ta gàba; ∼ month watà mài zuwà = watàn gòbe; Saturday after ∼ Sātī ta samà; by the same time ∼ month watà mài zuwà wař hakà; ∼ day kàshègàrī / wàshègàrī f: he came the ∼ day yā zō kàshègàrī; ∼ year bàɗi adv; until the ∼ time! sai wani lōkàcī! the ∼ world lāhiřà f, makōmā f, gidan gàskiyā m. b. (in space) na gàba: we get off at the ∼ station zā mù sàuka à tashà ta gàba; ∼ to kusa dà prep: it's ∼ to the market yanà kusa dà kàsuwā; right ∼ to, just ∼ to dab dà, kuřkusa dà: he was standing right ∼ to me yanà tsàye dab dà nī; the shop is just ∼ to the post office kàntîn kuřkusa yakè dà gidan wayà; he lives ∼ door maƙwàbcinmù nè; we live ∼ door to them gà gidanmù gà nāsù; (fig.) it cost us ∼ to nothing kàmař kyàutā mukà sàmē shì.
2. adv (after, in time or space) dàgà bāya, dàgà nan, bāyan hakà: ∼, add some water dàgà bāya kì daɗà ruwā = kì daɗà ruwā dàgà nan; what should we do ∼? mè zā mù yi bāyan hakà? = mè kuma zā mù yi?

nib n (of pen) kân àlƙalàmī m, bàkin

àlƙalàmī *m*.

**nibble** *v* gàigayà *v2*: the mouse ~d at the potato ɓēr̃ā yā gàigàyi dànkalī.

**nice** *adj* a. (*of people*) (mài) kyâu *m*, (mài) kir̃kī *m*: he's a very ~ person mùtumīn kir̃kī nē; be ~ to so. kyâutā wà *v1*: he wasn't very ~ to me bai kyâutā minì ba kō kàɗan. b. (*to see*) (mài) kyâu *m*; make sth. ~-looking ƙāyatar̃/ƙāwatar̃ (dà) *v5*. c. (*to the senses*) (mài) dāɗī *m*: he has a ~ house gidansà yanã dà dāɗī = yanã dà kyâu; it is the ~st one I have ever seen shī nē mafī dāɗī duk dàgà cikin waɗàndà na taɓà ganī.

**niche** *n* (*in wall*) àlkūkī *m* ⟨ai⟩.

**nick** *n* gīɓī *m*: the calabash has a ~ in it ƙwaryā tā yi gīɓī; (*fig.*) in the ~ of time à kân karī.

**nickname** *n* laƙàbī *m*: her name is Mary but her ~ is Kande sūnantà Mar̃yamù àmmā laƙàbintà Kànde; Mai Kano is the ~ for anyone named Abdullahi Mài Kanò laƙàbin mài sūnan Abdullāhī nē.

**niece** *n* (*use* 'yar̃ '*daughter of*' + *term for the specific sibling*): (*daughter of older brother*) 'yar̃ wâ, (*daughter of younger brother*) 'yar̃ ƙanè, (*daughter of older sister*) 'yar̃ yâ, (*daughter of younger sister*) 'yar̃ ƙanwà.

**Niger** *n* Nìjēr̃ *f*.

**Nigeria** *n* Nìjēr̃iyà / Nàjēr̃iyà *f*.

**night** *n* a. darē *m* (aCe): it is ~ darē yā yi; I want it done before ~ falls inà sôn à gamã kāfìn darē yà yi; day and ~ darē dà rānā; last ~ jiyà dà dare; the ~ before last shēkaranjiyà dà dare; Saturday ~ (*i.e. eve of Sunday*) daren Lahàdì; spend the ~ kwāna *v3a*; good ~! mù kwan lāfiyà! = sai dà sāfe! = sai gòbe! = àsùbâ tagàri! = àsùbâ àlhēr̃ī! b. (*adverbial uses*): at ~ dà dare *adv*; very late at ~ dà dàddare *adv*; day and ~ (*without interruption*) bâ darē bâ rānā: the machine works day and ~ injìn nã aikì bâ darē bâ rānā; in the dead of ~ dà tsakar̃ darē = dà dàddare.

**night blindness** *n* dìndimī *m*.

**nightclub** *n* hòtâl *m*.

**nightjar** *n* (*bird*) yautai *m*.

**nightmare** *n* mafar̃kin àbin tsòrō.

**night watchman** *n* mài gādī *m*, [F] gàr̃dìnyê *m*.

**nincompoop** *n* shāshàshā *n*.

**nine** *quant* tar̃à *f*.

**nineteen** *quant* (gōmà) shâ tar̃à, àshìr̃in bâ ɗaya.

**ninety** *quant* càsà'in / tìs'in *f*.

**ninth** *quant* na tar̃à.

**nipple** *n* kân nōnò *m*.

**no** 1. *excl* a. (*in answer to affirm. question*) ā'ã *excl*: when I asked him, he said '~' dà na tàmbàyē shì sai ya cè 'ā'ã'. b. (*in answer to neg. question*) ī *excl*: hasn't he come yet? ~ (he hasn't) bài zō ba tùkùna? ī (bài zō ba). 2. *quant* a. (*not any*) bābù, bâ (+ *n*): there's ~ money bābù kuɗī = bâ kuɗī; is there any left? ~ (there isn't) àkwai saurā? bābù. b. (*used as gen'l admonition, prohibition*) ban dà: ~ smoking here! ban dà shân tābã nân! = bā ã shân tābã nân! = kadà à shā tābã nân! ~ swearing in the classroom ban dà ràntse-ràntse dà Allàh cikin ajì. c. (*other uses*): ~ sooner had I arrived than they called me bàn daɗè dà isôwā ba sukà kirā nì; in ~ time at all (*fig.*) kāfìn ƙiftàwar̃ idò; ~ matter who, what, when, where, how, *see* matter 1c.

**nobility** *n* (*ruling class*) sàrākai *p*.

**noble** 1. *n* a. (*belong to the emir's court*) bàfādè / bàfādã *m*, sàrākī *m* ⟨ai⟩. 2. *adj* a. (*of high rank*) (mài) mar̃tabã *f*, (mài) mùƙāmì *m*. b. (*kind*) na kir̃kī *m*.

**nobody** *pro*, *see* no one, anyone.

**nod** *v* a. (*up & down, to agree or keep rhythm*) gyaɗã *v1*; (*from side to side, to disagree*) kaɗà kâi. b. (*from sleepiness*) yi gyàngyaɗī *m*, gyangyàɗā *v1*.

**noise** *n* a. (*gentle, pleasant sound*) amō *m*; (*loud sound*) ƙārā *f*: what was that ~? wàcè irìn ƙārā cè wànnan? (*loud banging*) kwàràmniyā *f*. b. (*of people talking*) sùrūtù *m*; (*din of crowd, people*) hàyàniyā *f*, hàyà-hàyà *f*. c. (*of contempt, made with lips*) tsàkī *m*.

**noisy** *adj* (mài) ƙārā *f*, (mài) kwàràmniyā *f*.

**nomad** *n* (*pastoralist*) makìyàyī *m*.

**nominate** *v* tsai dà / tsayar̃ (dà) *v5*: he was ~d for president an tsayar̃ dà shī shùgàbā.

**non-aligned** *adj* (*Pol.*): ~ nations ƙasàshen 'yan bâ-ruwanmù.

**non-believer** *n* (*esp. in Islam*) kāfìr̃ī *m* ⟨ai⟩.

**none** *pro* bâ wândà: ~ of us can ride a horse bâ wândà ya iyà dōkì à cikinmù; I saw ~ of them bàn ga kōwànnensù ba; there are ~ at all bâ kō ɗaya; there are ~ left bâ saurā = bâ ràgōwà; I have ~ bâ ni dà kōmē; ~ whatsoever kō ƙyas *idph*: we've had no news, ~ whatsoever kō ƙyas bâ mu dà làbār̃ī.

**nonsense** *n* a. (*having no sense, meaning*)

rashìn hankàlī m. b. (incoherent talk) bâ
kâi bâi gìndī: what he's saying is just ~
màganàr̃sà bâ kâi bâi gìndī. c. (foolish
talk) shìrme m, màganàr̃ banzā f, sùr̃ūtùn
banzā m, shìftamā f: you're talking ~
shìrme kakè yî = shìrmenkà kakè; I've
never in my life heard of such ~ tun dà
nakè bàn tabà jîn shìrme irìn wannàn
ba.

non-stop adv a. (without stopping) bâ
tsayàwā, bâ jî bâ ganī: a ~ flight
tàfiyar̃ jirgī bâ tsayàwā. b. (without
interruption) bâ tsinkèwā, bâ katsèwā:
he spoke ~ for one hour yā yi màganā awā
ɗaya bâ katsèwā.

noodles n tàliyà f.

nook n sāƙò m, lungù m, lōkò m: go and
look for it in every ~ and cranny kà jē
nēmansà sāƙò-sāƙò; (esp. most inaccessible corner of room) ƙuryà f.

noon n tsakar̃ rānā f: he came before ~ yā
zō kāfìn tsakar̃ rānā; at ~ dà tsakar̃
rānā.

no one pro, see anyone. a. (as obj. of sent.)
kōwā (in neg. sent.): I met ~ on the way
bàn hàɗu dà kōwā à hanyà ba = bâ wândà
na hàɗu dà shī à hanyà. b. (as subj.
of sent.) bâ wândà, bâ wâddà: ~ knows
the real story bâ wândà ya san ainihin
làbār̃ī; ~ (f.) wants to deal with her bâ
wâddà kè sôn mà'āmalà dà ita. c. (in
'there is/are' clauses) bâ kōwā: there is
~ in the room bâ kōwā cikin dākìn = bâ
wândà kè cikin dākìn.

noose n zàrgē m; fasten a ~ to zargà wà
v1: he fastened the ~ around the goat yā
zargà wà àkuyà zàrgē.

nor conj, see neither.

normal adj: ~ working hours lōkàcin aikī
na kullum; he's a ~ child yārò nē kàmar̃
kōwànè; it is below ~ bài isa ba; this
is our ~ work wannàn aikìnmù nē na yâu
dà kullum; this is how it is ~ly done hakà
akà sābà yînsà.

north n & adv arèwa f: the wind is blowing
from the ~ iskà nà bugôwā dàgà arèwa;
we are travelling ~ munà tàfiyà gàba
arèwa; they entered the town from the ~
sun shigō gàrîn ta arèwa = sun shigo
gàrin ta arèwacinsà; N. Africa Afir̃kà
ta Arèwa; it is ~ of town yanà arèwacin
gàrī = yanà arèwa dà gàrī.

northeast adv arèwa masò gabàs: the village lies ~ of town ƙauyèn yanà arèwa
masò gabàs dà gàrîn.

northern adj na arèwa, arēwacin prep: in
the ~ part of the state à arēwacin jihà;

the ~ states jihōhin arèwa; the ~ states
of Nigeria jihōhin arēwacin Nìjēr̃iyà;
~ Niger Nìjar̃ ta arèwa.

northerner n bà'arè m.

northwest adv arèwa masò yâmma.

nose n hancì m (una); pick one's ~ ƙwàƙùli
hancì; blow one's ~ fyàcè màjinà; wipe
one's ~ gōgè hancì, (with back of hand)
yi dàjìnē m; bridge of the ~ karan hancì
m; in, on the ~ à hanci adv: he was
hurt on the ~ yā ji ràunī à hanci;
(fig.) don't poke your ~ into someone else's
business kadà kà tsōmà bàkī indà bâ
ruwankà. (fig.) she cut off her nose to spite
her face tā cùci kântà.

nosebleed n habò m: I have a ~ inà habò.

nostalgia n bègē m: be nostalgic about
childhood yi bègen ƙùrùciyà.

nostril n kafar̃ hancì f.

nosy adj: be ~ yi kàr̃àmbànī m, yi
shisshigī m, yi katsalandàn m, tsōmà
bàkī.

not adv a. (in a noun phr. or non-vbl. sent.)
bâ...ba: ~ now, here, them bâ yànzu ba,
bâ nân ba, bâ sū ba; today is ~ Tuesday yâu bâ Tàlātā ba cè; it's a cat ~ a
dog kyânwā cè bâ kàrē ba; that's ~ what
I want bâ àbîn dà nakè sô ba. b. (in
sent. in past & fut.) bâ...ba: they didn't
know bâ sù sanì ba; the children will not
come yârā bâ zā sù zō ba. c. (in sent.
in habit.) bâ (+ adv) ...ba: I don't usually
eat lunch bâ kàsàfài nakàn ci àbincin
rāna ba; they don't come often bâ sàfài
sukàn zō ba. d. (in contin., locative or
stative sent.) bā: we do ~ like him bā
mà sônsà; he isn't seated bā yà zàune;
many people don't work mutànē dà yawà
bā sà aikì; Ladi isn't here Lādì bā tà
nân. e. (in 'have' sent.) bā: Musa doesn't
have a bicycle Mūsā bâ shi dà kèkè. f. (in
'there is/are' sent.) bâ (+ n), bābù: there
isn't any oil in the bottle bâ mâi cikin
kwalabà; is there a doctor here? no, there
isn't àkwai likità nân? ā'à bābù. g.
(in neg. command, subjunct.) kadà/kâr̃:
don't quarrel with him kadà kà yi fadà
dà shī; I told him ~ to go nā cê masà
kadà yà tàfi. h. (in tag questions) kō
kùwa, kō bābù, kō bà hakà ba: today is
Sunday, is it ~? yâu Lahàdì cē kō kùwa?
are there some or ~? kō àkwai waɗansu
kō bābù? is he going or ~? zâi jē kō bà
zâi jē ba? you told them didn't you? kin
gayà musù kō bà hakà ba? i. ~ yet tùkùna
/ tùkùn: we haven't done it yet bà mù yī
shì ba tùkùna; ~ at all sam-sam idph: I

didn't see him at all sam-sam bàn gan shì
ba.
**note** 1. *n* a. (*of paper*) 'yař wàsīƙā *f* ⟨u⟩;
currency ~ takařdař kudī. b. (*notice*)
kùlā *f*, lùřa *f*: take ~ of kulā dà *v1*, lùřa
dà *v3*.
2. *v* a. (*notice*) kulā dà *v1*, lùřa dà *v3*; ~
carefully kiyàyē *v4*: I carefully ~d what
he said nā kiyàyè àbîn dà ya cê. b.
(*write down*) řubùtā *v1*: ~ it down so you
don't forget kà řubùtā don kadà à màntā.
**notebook** *n* littāfìn řubùtū *m*, [F] kàyè
*m*.
**noteworthy** *adj*: sth. ~ àbin lùřa.
**nothing** *pro*, *see* anything. a. (*as obj of
vbl. sent.*) kōmē: he did ~ bài yi kōmē
ba; she has ~ bâ ta dà kōmē; I want ~
to do with him bā nà sôn wata mà'āmalà
dà shī; it adds up to ~ bài dadà kōmē
ba; it has ~ to do with me bài shāfē nì
ba = bâ ruwānā. b. (*with verbs of saying in neg.*): he said ~ at all bài cê kō
ƙàlā ba = bài cê kō uffàn ba; there is
~ more to be said bābù sauran ta cêwā;
I have ~ to say bâ ni dà ta cêwā. c. (*as
subj of vbl. sent.*) bâ àbîn dà: ~ can be
done about it bâ àbîn dà zā à iyà yî;
there is ~ wrong with it bâ àbîn dà ya
sāmē shì. d. (*in 'there is/are' clauses*)
bâ kōmē: there was ~ in the box bâ kōmē
cikin àkwàtì; there's ~ that he hasn't
done bâ àbîn dà bài yi ba. e. (*in equational sent.*): it is ~ bà wani àbù ba nè
= bâ kōmē; that is ~ new to me wannàn
bâ sābon àbù ba nè gàrē nì. f. (*other
uses*): come to ~ (*e.g. of plan, matter*)
sūlàncē *v4*: all our work came to ~ duk
shirìnmù yā sūlàncē; for ~ à banzā: he
insulted me for ~ yā zāgē nì à banzā;
buy for almost ~ sàyā à gàrāɓàsà: it cost
me next to ~ à gàrāɓàsà na sayō = à
àràhā banzā na sayō; to say ~ of... bàllē
/ bàllàntànā, à bař zàncen: there's no
water, to say ~ of food bâ ruwā bàllē
àbinci = bâ ruwā à bař zàncen àbinci.
**notice** 1. *n* a. (*announcement*) sanâřwā *f*,
faɗakāřwā *f*: the ~s have been posted
all around town an kafà sanâřwā kō'ìnā
cikin gàrī; ~ is hereby given that... anā
sanař dà cêwā...; without ~ bâ tàre dà
sanâřwā ba = bâ làbārì; on short ~
dà sanâřwā cikin ƙùrarren lōkàcì. b.
(*esp. of dismissal*) nōtìs *m*: he was given
2 weeks' ~ an bā shì nōtìs ɗin mākò
biyu; c. (*attention*): take ~ of kulā dà
*v1*, ànkařà dà *v1*: don't take any ~ of him
kadà kà kulā dà shī = kà ƙyàlē shi =

yi banzā dà shī.
2. *v* lùřa dà *v3*, kulā dà *v1*: did you ~
what he said? kā kulā dà àbîn dà ya
fàdā? I ~d that she was angry nā lùřa
cêwā tanà fushī; (*usu. ref. to sth. past*)
ànkařà dà *v3*: I didn't ~ that it was already 2 o'clock bàn ànkařà dà cêwā ƙarfè
biyu tā yi ba.
**notification** *n* sanâřwā *f*, he was dismissed
without any ~ an sàllàmē shì bâ dà wata
sanâřwā ba; ~ is hereby given that... anā
sanař dà kōwā dà kōwā cêwā....
**notify** *v* a. (*inform*) sanař (dà) *v5*, shâidā
wà *v1*: we were not notified that he was
coming bà à sanař dà mū cêwā zâi zō
ba. b. (*alert*) faɗakař dà *v5*.
**notorious** *adj* rìƙaƙƙē *adj*, gàwùřtaccē *adj*:
a ~ robber rìƙaƙƙen ɓàrāwò.
**nought** *quant* sifìřī *m*.
**noun** *n* sūnā *m* ⟨aye⟩: common ~ sūnan
gàmà-gàri; proper ~ (*personal*) sūnan
yankā; proper ~ (*place*) sūnan wurī.
**nourish** *v* a. (*feed*) cī dà / ciyař (dà) *v5*.
b. (*provide nourishment*) ginā jìkī: this
food is very ~ing àbincin nàn nà ginā
jìkī sòsai.
**novel**[1] *adj* (*new*) sābō *adj* ⟨sàbàbbī,
sàbbī⟩.
**novel**[2] *n* ƙàgaggen làbārì *m*.
**novelty** *n* sābon àbù *m*.
**November** *n* Nùwambà *m*.
**novice** *n* dan kòyō *m*, sābon kòyō *m*; (*pejor.*)
ɗan dāgàjī *m*.
**now** *adv* yànzu *adv*: just now yànzun nàn,
dàzun nàn: he left just ~ yànzun nàn ya
tāshì; from ~ on nân gàba, dàgà yànzu;
up till ~ (*still*) haƙ yànzu: he hasn't paid
me up till ~ bài biyā nì ba haƙ yànzu;
~ and again, ~ and then lōkàcī-lōkàcī;
~ that tun dà (+ *complet. or rel. complet.*): ~ that we know where she is tun
dà mun san indà takè.
**nowadays** *adv* yànzu *adv*, à zāmànin yâu,
à mařřař yâu: ~ this is quite common
wannàn ai yànzu yā zama gàmà-gàri; ~
we don't do that any more à zāmànin yâu
an dainà yîn hakà; even ~ haƙ wà yâu:
scarification is done in the villages even ~
haƙ wà yâu, anā shàsshāwà à ƙauyè.
**nowhere** *adv* kō'ìnā, *see* anywhere; (*in
neg. sent.*) indà (+ *neg.*): this will get you
~ bâ indà wannàn zâi kai kà; he was ~
to be seen bâ indà akà gan shì ba; there
is ~ that he hasn't been bâ indà bài jē
ba; the old man has ~ to live tsōhō bâ
shi dà wurin zama.
**nozzle** *n* būtūtun ƙarfè *m*.

nuclear *adj* na nūkìlìyằ *f*: ∼ energy makāmashin nūkìlìyằ; ∼ deterrent
rìgằkafìn màkằman nūkìlìyằ; ∼ fallout
bùr̃bùɗin atằm; ∼ proliferation yằɗuwar̃
màkằman nūkìlìyằ; ∼ weapons màkằman
ƙằr̃è-dangì.

nude *adj* (mài) tsìrārằ *f*.

nudge *v* ɗan zùngurằ *v2*: he ∼d me to remind me yā ɗan zùngùrē nì don yà yi
mìnì matāshìyā.

nudity *n* tsìrārằ *f*.

Nufe *n* a. (*member of ethnic group*) bànufè
*m*. b. (*language*) Nufancī *m*.

nuisance *n* fìtinằ *f*, àbin fìtinằ *m*, àbin
dằmuwā *m*: that child is a ∼ yāròn nan yā
cikà fìtinằ.

numb *adj* (*stiff*): be ∼ ƙagè *v4*, sagè *v4*,
sandàrē *v4*, yi dùndùrùs *idph*.

number 1. *n* a. (*any written numeral*)
àlƙalàmī *m* ⟨u-a⟩, [F] limar̃ō *m*; odd
∼ màrā *f*; even ∼ cìkā *f*; be ∼ one ci
làmbàwàn, [F] yi limar̃ō ân. b. (*for identification*) lambằ *f* ⟨oCi⟩: what is your
license plate ∼? mècē cè lambàr̃ mōtàr̃kà?
telephone, house ∼ lambàr̃ wayằ, gidā;
take bus ∼ 6 shìga bâs mài lambằ shidà.
c. (*sum, total*) jimlằ / jumlằ *f* ⟨oCi⟩,
adàdī *m* ⟨ai⟩: count up the ∼ of people here kà ƙidàyà jimlàr̃ mutằnên dà kè
nân; there were 7 in ∼ adàdinsù bakwài
nē; he has a good head for ∼s yanằ dà ƙâi
ƙwar̃ai wajen lìssāfì = yā iyà lìssāfì
ƙwar̃ai. d. (*quantity*) yawằ *m*: their ∼s
were small yawànsù kàɗan nề; a large ∼
of dà yawằ, dà dāmā: a large ∼ of people went to look mutằnē dà dāmā sukà jē
kallō; I haven't seen him for a ∼ of years
an yi shèkàrū dà yawằ bàn gan shì ba;
a small ∼ of kīmằ *f*: a small ∼ of people came mutằnē kīmằ sun zō. e. (*Gram.*)
jam'ì *m*: an adjective agrees in ∼ with its
noun jam'ìn siffằ dà na sūnā dōlè yà
kasàncē ɗaya.
2. *v*: they ∼ed up to a 1000 sun kai dubū;
(*fig.*) his days are ∼ed kwānansà yā kusa
ƙār̃èwā = ajàlinsà yā kusa.

number plate *n*, *see* license plate.

numeral *n* àlƙalàmī *m* ⟨u-a⟩, [F] limar̃ō
*m*: 3 and 10 are both ∼s ukù dà gōmà
alƙalumằ nē.

numerical *adj*: in ∼ order cikin tsārìn
lambōbī.

numerology *n* hìsābì *m*.

numerous *adj* màsu yawằ; very ∼ màsu
yawàn gàske.

nurse 1. *n* mài (aikìn) jiyyằ *n*, nâs *n*, [F]
likità *n*, [F] làkwàtar̃ò *n*, [F] màdân kin

likità *f*.
2. *v* a. (*look after sick psn.*) yi jiyyàr̃ *w*.
b. (*suckle a child*) shā dà / shāyar̃ (dà)
*v5*: she is nursing her child tanằ shāyar̃
dà ɗantà nōnồ.

nursery *n* (*school*) makar̃antā ta ƙanānàn
yārā *f*, nāsàr̃è *f*, [F] màtàr̃nâl *f*.

nursing *n* a. (*by mother*) jēgồ *m*: she is
still ∼ her child har̃ yànzu tanằ jēgồ; a
∼ mother màcè mài jēgồ; (*by child*) shân
nōnồ: this child is still ∼ har̃ yànzu yāròn
nân nằ shân nōnồ. b. (*field of study*)
aikìn nâs *m*.

nut *n* a. (*hard-shelled fruit, no gen'l term,
see specific nouns*). b. (*used with bolt*)
nōtì *m*, [F] bùlô *m*.

nutshell *n* kwàfsā / kwàsfā *f*; (*esp. of
peanuts*) ɓāwō *m*; (*fig.*) in a ∼ à tàƙàice,
à dùnƙùle.

nylon *n* (*fabric*) nailàn / lēnàn *m*; (*thick
thread*) lìlō *m*, [F] lìlô *m*.

# O

**oasis** *n* zangŏ *m* ⟨una⟩.

**oath** *n* rantsuwā *f*: take an ∼ yi rantsuwā; ∼ of allegiance rantsuwař mīƙà wuyằ; break, violate an ∼ karyà àlkawàřī.

**obedience** *n* bìyayyằ *f*.

**obedient** *adj* (mài) bìyayyằ *f*.

**obey** *v* bi *v0*, kiyằyē *v4*: ∼ the law bi dŏkā; he ∼ed his parents yā bi ùmàřnin iyằyensà.

**object**[1] *n* a. (*thing*) àbù *m*, àbā *f* ⟨uwa[2]⟩ (*in the genitive, use* àbin): there was a strange ∼ lying on the road àkwai wani irìn àbù à kân hanyằ. b. (*purpose*) màƙàsūdì *m*: the ∼ of his visit màƙàsūdìn zìyāřàřsà. c. (*Gram.*) kàrɓau *m*.

**object**[2] *v* a. (*oppose*) yàřda (+ *neg.*) *v3*, amìncē (+ *neg.*) *v4*: I ∼ to the proposal bàn yàřda dà shirìn ba. b. (*dislike*) ƙi *v0*: I don't ∼ to the cold bàn ƙi sanyī ba.

**objection** *n*: there were no ∼s to the plan an amìncē dà shirìn = bà à ƙi shirìn ba; I have no ∼ to what he said nā yàřda dà àbîn dà ya fàdā.

**objective** *n* a. (*primary goal*) màƙàsūdì *m*: his ∼ is to confuse you màƙàsūdìnsà shī nè yà rūdà ka. b. (*strong wish*) būrì / gūrì *m*: my ∼ is to finish this month būrìnā ìn gamà watàn nân.

**obligation** *n* a. (*duty*) dōlè *f*, wàjìbī *m*: I had an ∼ to do it dōlè cē ta sà na yi hakà; it is an ∼ for everyone wàjìbī nè gà kōwā. b. (*esp. toward family*) nauyī *m*; fulfill one's ∼ saukè nauyī. c. (*moral* ∼ *to others*) àlhakī *m*: it is his ∼ to look after these people àlhakinsà nē yà kulà dà wadànnân mutằnē; he failed in his ∼s toward me yā dàuki àlhakīnā. d. (*Relig.*) fàřillằ *f* ⟨ai⟩: it is an ∼ for all Muslims to perform the daily prayers sallà fàřillằ cē à kân kōwànè Mùsùlmī.

**obligatory** *adj* na tīlàs, na dōlè; attendance at the lectures is ∼ zuwằ laccōcîn yā zama tīlàs = wàjìbī nè kōwā yà zō laccōcîn.

**oblige** *v* (*require*) tīlàstā wà *v1*, kāmà tīlàs, wàjabà *v3* (+ *3rd pers. impers.*

*pro*): I was ∼d to attend the meeting an tīlàstā minì hàlařtằř tằrôn = tīlàs tā sà ni hàlařtằř tằrôn; we were ∼d to return home yā kāmà tīlàs mù kōmằ gidā = tīlàs ta sà mukà kōmằ gidā = yā wàjabà mù kōmằ gidā.

**oboe** (*tradit. Hausa type*) àlgaitằ *f* ⟨u⟩.

**obscene** *adj* (*sexually explicit*) na bātsa *f*: an ∼ book littāfìn bātsa; an ∼ movie fîm dîn bātsa; ∼ language mūgùn bằkī *m*, danyen bằkī *m*: he said sth. ∼ to me yā yi minì mūgùn bằkī = yā yi minì bātsa; use an ∼ gesture yi shaƙiyyancì *m*.

**obscure** 1. *adj* (*hidden*) ɓŏyayyē *adj*: the word has an ∼ meaning kalmằř nằ dà ɓŏyayyiyař mà'ànā. 2. *v* (*be in the way*) kārè *v4*: he ∼d my view yā kārè minì.

**obsequiousness** *n* fādancī *m*, ƙanƙan dà kâi *m*.

**observant** *adj* a. (*quick to observe*) (mài) lùřā *f*, (mài) kùlā *f*. b. (*Relig.*) (mài) yîn fàřillā *m*.

**observation** *n* lùřā *f*, kùlā *f*.

**observe** *v* a. (*look at*) lùřa dà *v3*, dūbằ *v1*: the doctors were observing his condition likitōcī sunà lùřā dà hālìn dà yakè ciki. b. (*obey*) bi *v0*, kiyằyē *v4*: ∼ the law kiyằyè dōkā.

**observance** *n* (*Relig.*) fàřillằ *f* ⟨ai⟩.

**observer** *n* dan kallō *m*, mài kallō *n*.

**obsession** *n* jàřabằ *f*.

**obstacle** *n* cīkàs *m*: his youthfulness was an ∼ to his getting the job ƙùřuciyařsà tā yi masà cīkàs wajen sāmùn aikìn.

**obstinate** *adj* (mài) taurin kâi *m*, (mài) tsàyayyằ *f*, (mài) kafiyā *f*; be ∼ yi taurin kâi, yi kafiyā, dàgè *v4*: he was ∼ about staying yā dàgè à kân sai yā zaunằ.

**obstruct** *v* (*block*) tsarè *v4*: a truck was ∼ing the road wata bàbbař mōtà nà tsarè hanyằ.

**obstruction** *n* a. (*blockage e.g. in pipe*) tōshèwā *f*. b. (*difficulty*) tangařdằ *f*.

**obtain** *v* sāmù *v2\**: ∼ permission sàmi izìnī.

**obtainable** *adj* (mài) sàmuwā *f*: it's not ∼ anywhere bā yà sằmuwā kō'ìnā.

**obvious** *adj* à fīlì, fìtaccē *adj*: an ∼ reason fìtaccen dàlīlì; it's meaning is ∼ mà'ànařsà à fīlì takè; he is the ∼ choice for the job shī nè mafì dācèwā dà aikìn.

**obviously** *adv* tabbàs *adv*, à hàƙīƙà: I was ∼ disappointed tabbàs râinā yā ɓacì; he said that he had done it but ∼, he

hadn't yā cē yā yī shì àmmā à hàƙīƙā
bài yi ba.

**occasion** n a. (event) karð m: on that ∼,
everyone will receive a certificate à wànnan
karð, kōwā zâi sāmi sàtifikàt; on this
important ∼ à wannàn bàbbaƙ rānā. b.
(time) lōkàcī m ⟨ai⟩: it was a happy ∼
lōkàcîn farin cikì nē; on certain ∼s
wani lōkàcì, wani bî.

**occasionally** adv lōkàcī-lōkàcī adv, sā'ì-
sā'ì adv, lōtò-lōtò adv: we see them ∼
munà ganinsù lōkàcī-lōkàcī.

**occupant** n a. (of rented quarters) ɗan hayà
m. b. (passenger) the ∼s of the car were
not hurt wadàndà kè cikin mōtà bà sù
ji ràunī ba.

**occupation** n a. (job, profession) aikì m,
sànā'à f ⟨oCi⟩: he is a smith by ∼
sànā'aƙsà ƙīrà cē. b. (Mil.) màmayà f.

**occupy** v a. (Mil.) màmayē v4: the army occupied the town for 2 months sōjōjìn sun
màmàyè gàrîn haƙ watà biyu. b. (preoccupy): be occupied in one's affairs yi
kasàfī m, shàgalà dà v3: they are occupied in their own affairs sunà kasàfinsù
= sunà shàgalà dà àbin kânsù.

**occur** v aùku v7, wàkānā v3: when did that
∼? yàushè àbin nàn ya àuku? make sure
that it won't ∼ again kà tabbataƙ dà àbîn
bài sākè àukuwā ba; ∼ to so. fàɗō wà à
râi: an idea ∼red to me wata dàbāƙà tā
fàɗō minì à râi.

**occurrence** n: it's a common ∼ àbù nē dà
akà sābà.

**ocean** n tèku f.

**o'clock** adv ƙarfè m: he came at 6 ∼ yā zō
dà ƙarfè shidà; it's 2 ∼ ƙarfè biyu tā
yi.

**October** n Òktōbà m.

**odd** adj a. (peculiar, of psn.): bàhagòn
mùtûm, hūtsū m ⟨aye⟩: he's an ∼ kind of
person shi bàhagòn mùtûm nē = shī wani
irìn mùtûm nē. b. (not regular): be at ∼s
with sā6à dà v1; ∼ man out (not member
of group) bàƙē m: he's the ∼ man out here
shī bàƙē nè à cikinmù. c. (in math): an
∼ number màrā f: 7 is an ∼ number bakwài
màrā cè.

**odds and ends** n kàrìkìtai p, kòmàtsai p:
tàrkàcē m, kwàƙànkwàtsai p: please clear
out all these ∼ of yours don Allàh kà kau
dà duk tàrkàcen nàn nākà.

**odor** n (fragrant) ƙanshī m; (smelly, foul,
e.g. animal feces) wārī m; (of sth. rotten or
of human faeces) dòyī m; (acrid, of smoke
) ƙaurī m; (of urine, ammonia) zaurī m;
(of body, sweat) ƙārī m.

**of** prep a. (genitive constr., use linkers na m,
ta f, na p, or corresponding short variants
n/ƙ/n): a bundle ∼ millet damìn gērō;
a cake ∼ soap ƙwàyaƙ sàbulū; the people ∼ the village mutànen ƙauyè; my letter ∼ last week wàsīƙàtā ta mākòn jiyà;
a dress ∼ silk rìgaƙ sìlikì; the side
∼ the road bàkin hanyà; the aim ∼ the
government būrìn gwamnatì; all ∼ them
dukànsù. b. (possessive constr., use poss.
pro, see Appendix A): a friend ∼ theirs
wani àbōkinsù; that friend ∼ theirs (emphat.) nāsù àbōkîn; this country of ours
tāmù ƙasâƙ. c. (after adj, oft. expr. by
genitive or dà): I am doubtful ∼ it inà
shakkàƙsà; don't be afraid ∼ the dog
kadà kà ji tsòron kàrên; we were aware
∼ her arrival munà sàne dà isôwaƙtà; we
are tired ∼ them mun gàji dà sū; east ∼
town gabàs dà gàrī = gabashin gàrī. d.
(other uses): west, north ∼ yâmma, arèwa
dà; in spite ∼ duk dà; the third day ∼
the month ran ukù gà watà; a quarter ∼
five ƙarfè bìyaƙ saurā kwatà; 3 ∼ them
were no good ukù dàga cikinsù bâ kyâu.

**off** adv a. (for use as particle with verbs, see
relevant verb entries; v4 verbs oft. include
the meaning of 'off'): chop ∼ a branch
sārè rēshè; turn ∼ the electricity kashè
wutā; shake ∼ the dust kakkà6è ƙùrā;
scrape the food ∼ the pot kankàrè àbinci
dàga tukunyā. b. (var. uses): where are
you ∼ to? inà zâ ki? = inà zuwà? (∼
of) dàgà prep: he jumped down ∼ the wall
yā dirō dàgà kân katangā; he fell ∼ the
horse yā fàɗō dàgà kân dōkì.

**offence** n (Law) làifī m ⟨uka²⟩: commit
an ∼ yi làifī; charge so. with an ∼ kāmà
w. dà làifī.

**offend** v 6àtà wà râi, jī wà cīwð, ci mutuncìn w.: he has deeply ∼ed me yā 6àtà
minì râi matuƙà; feel ∼ed ji zāfī.

**offensive** adj (mài) cîn mutuncì, (mài)
rashìn kunyà: an ∼ remark màganà mài
rashìn kunyà.

**offer** 1. v a. (in bargaining) tayà v1, yi
tayì m: he ∼ed me ₦150 for my radio yā
tayà ƙēdiyōnā naiƙā dàrī dà hàmsin.
b. (to do sth.) cê v*: he ∼ed to go yā
cê zâi tàfi; he ∼ed to give me a ride
to Kaduna yā cê zâi dàukē nì zuwà
Kàdūna; he was ∼ed the job but he didn't
accept an bā shì aikìn àmmā bài kàr6ā
ba.
2. n (in bargaining) tayì m: he refused
my ∼ yā ƙi tayìnā; make an ∼ for sth.
tayà v1: I made an ∼ of ₦70 for the blan-

ket na tayà lūr̃ū nair̃ā sàbà'in.

offering n (*Relig.*) hadāyā *f.*

office n a. (*place of work*) ōfìs *m* ⟨oCi⟩, [F] bùr̃ô *m*: the files are in his ~ fāyilōlîn sunā ōfîshinsà; ~ hours lōkàcin aikĩ; ~ mate àbōkin aikĩ; ~ supplies kāyan aikîn ōfìs. b. (*Pol.*) mùr̃āmĩ *m*: hold ~ rìr̃e mùr̃āmĩ; he holds an ~ in the ministry yanā rìr̃e dà mùr̃āmĩ à ma'aikatâr̃; the party now in ~ jàm'iyyàr̃ dà kè rìr̃e dà mulkĩ; they are running for ~ sunā cikin tākar̃ar̃ mùr̃āmìn.

officer n a. (*admin. official*) ma'àikàcī *m*, jāmì'ī *m* ⟨ai⟩: education, commercial ~ jāmì'in ilìmī, cìnikī; I want to see the ~ in charge inā sôn ganin bàbban jāmì'în; agricultural ~ bàtūr̃èn gōnā *m*. b. (*in special forces*) army ~ hafsà *m* ⟨oCi⟩; customs ~ ɗan kwastàn *m*, jāmì'in kwastàn *m*, [F] sōjàn dùwân *m*; police ~ (*gen'l policeman*) ɗan sàndā *m*, (*at divisional level*) dīfì'ò *m*; traffic ~ tar̃āfìs *n*, mài bā dà hannū *n*.

official 1. n (*admin.*) jāmì'ī *m* ⟨ai⟩, ma'àikàcī *m*.
2. adj na aikĩ: ~ visit zìyār̃àr̃ aikĩ; ~ language (*for admin.*) harshèn gudānar̃ dà ayyukà: English has been made the ~ language an mai dà Ingìlīshĩ harshèn gudānar̃ dà ayyukà.

offspring n 'yā'yā *p*; (*descendants*) zūr̃iyā *f.*

often adv sàu dà yawà: they came ~ sun zō sàu dà yawà; not ~ bã sàfài ba, bã kàsàfài ba: I don't see him very ~ bã kàsàfài nakàn gan shì ba; do sth. ~ shā *v0*, yi yawàn: he ~ came to our house yā shā zuwà gidanmù; he ~ listens to that program yakàn yi yawàn sàurār̃en shirìn nan.

ogre n (*any fearful thing*) dōdō *m*, dōdannìyā *f* ⟨anni⟩.

oh excl àshē!: ~ he's here, is he? àshe yana'a nân?

oil 1. n a. mâi *m*: palm ~ mân jā; peanut ~ mân gyàdā; put some ~ on the joint kà sâ mâi a magamī; (*fig.*) ~ and water do not mix bā ā gamà wutā dà shìɓā. b. (*petroleum*) mân fētùr̃ *m*; drill for ~ har̃ō *v6* ⟨har̃ā⟩ *f*; they are drilling for ~ sunā har̃ō mâi = sunā hàr̃ar̃ mâi; ~ rights hakkìn hàr̃ar̃ mâi; an ~ spill zubèwar̃ mân fētùr̃. c. (*engine grease*) bar̃in mâi *m*, [F] mân mōtà *m*: ~ change jùyen bar̃in mâi *m*, [F] bìdanjì *m*.
2. v: the joint needs to be ~ed magamîn nā bùkātàr̃ mâi.

oil-can n (*for motor oil*) gwangwanin bar̃in mâi *m*, [F] bìdô *m*; (*for sewing machine*) tùr̃umbā *f.*

oilfield n wurin hàr̃ar̃ mâi *m*.

oil refinery n matātar̃ mâi / matātar̃ mân fētùr̃ *f.*

oil rig n injìn hàr̃ar̃ mâi *m.*

oil well rījìyar̃ hàr̃ar̃ mâi *f*, mahar̃ar̃ mâi *f.*

oily adj (mài) mâi *m*; (*from animal fat*) (mài) mair̃ō *m.*

ointment n māgànin shāfàwā *m*, lilimàn / lilimantĩ *m*, [F] mân màsâj *m.*

OK, okay 1. excl a. (*confirming*) tô: let's go, ~? mù tàfi, tô? b. (*expressing finality*) shī kè nan!
2. adv (*satisfactorily*) bâ lâifī: the work is going ~ aikìn nā tàfiyà bâ lâifī.

okra n kuɓèwā *f.*

old adj a. (*in age*) tsōhō *adj* ⟨tsòfàffī⟩; ~ man (*term of addr. or ref.*) bàba *m*, dattìjò *m*; ~ woman (*term of addr. or ref.*) iyā *f*, tsōhuwā *f*, dattìjùwā *f*; ~ people tsòfàffī *p*, dàttìjai *p*, mânyā *p*; young and ~ yârā dà mânyā; how ~ is he? shèkàrunsà nawà dà haihùwā? he is 10 years ~ shèkàrunsà gōmà; she was 3 years ~ when her mother died shèkar̃àrtà ukù mahaifìyar̃tà ta mutù; you must be 18 years ~ before you can drive sai mùtûm yā kai shèkarà shā takwàs kàfin yà yi tūr̃ĩ; be ~ tsūfa *v3a*; be very ~ tsūfa tukuf; become ~ mànyantà *v3*; ~ age tsūfā *f*, hālin mànyàntakà *m*; be ~er than gìrmā *v2*, girmè wà *v4*: he is 3 years ~er than her yā gìrmè tà dà shèkarà ukù = yā girmè matà dà shèkarà ukù. b. (*lasting a long time*) (mài) daɗèwā *f*; this shirt of mine is ~ tagùwar̃ nàn tā daɗè à wurīnā; we are ~ friends mun daɗè munà àbōtà; this rampart is over 200 years ~ gānuwar̃ nàn tā daɗè fìye dà shèkarà ɗàrī biyu. c. (*former*) na dā: here is my ~ bicycle and there is my new one nân nē kèkènā na dā càn kuma gà sābôn; in the ~(en) days à zāmànin dā.

old-fashioned adj na dā: an ~ person, way mùtumìn, hanyàr̃ dā.

olive n (*tree or fruit*) zàitûn *m*; ~ oil mân zàitûn.

omelette n wàinar̃ kwai *f.*

omen n ìshār̃à *f* ⟨oCi⟩, àlāmà *f* ⟨u⟩: bad ~ mūgùwar̃ ìshār̃à.

omit v a. (*skip*) r̃ètàr̃ē *v4*, tsallàkē *v4*: his name was inadvertently ~ted an r̃ètàr̃è sūnansà bã dà gàngan ba = an yi kuskurèn tsallàkè sūnansà. b. (*fail to do*) rasã *vI*.

**on 1.** *prep* **a.** à *prep*: ~ the wall, the way, page 3 à jìkin bangō, kân hanyã, shāfì na ukù; see sth. ~ television ga w.a. à talàbijìn. **b.** (*upon*) (à) kân *prep*: it is ~ the table yanà kân tēbùr̃; she laid the child on the bed tā d̃ōrà yārò kân gadō. **c.** (*oft. included in the meaning of a verb & not translated*): get ~ a bus shìga bâs; knock ~ a door ƙwanƙwàsà ƙōfã; put ~ a turban nad̃à rawànī; pounce ~ a mouse faucè 6ēr̃ã; depend ~ it d̃ògarà dà shī. **d.** (*oft. expressed as ind. obj*): put responsibility ~ Audu d̃ōrà wà Audù nauyī; pay a visit ~ the emir kai wà sarkī zìyār̃à; spit ~ him tōfã masà yau. **e.** (*by means, way of*) à *prep*: they came ~ foot, a bicycle sun zō à ƙafà, à kèkè. **2.** *prep* (*to intro. subord. phr. or cl.*) dà *prep*: ~ his arrival he went straight to the palace dà isôwar̃sà yā tàfi fādà kâi tsàye; ~ opening the door, she saw what was going on dà ta būd̃è ƙōfã sai ta ga àbîn dà akè tàfe; ~ seeing the hyena, she began to tremble dà ganìn kūrā, jìkintà yā yi ta 6ar̃ī.

**once** *adv* **a.** sàu d̃aya: he hit me only ~ yā dàkē nì sàu d̃aya tak; ~ a day sàu d̃aya à rānā. **b.** at ~ (*immediately*) nan dà nan, yànzun nàn, yànzu-yànzu *adv*: you should go at ~ lallē nè kà tàfi yànzu-yànzu; all at ~ (*simultaneously*) gàbā d̃aya: they left all at ~ sun tāshì gàbā d̃aya; ~ upon a time, there was... wata rānā an yi wani... = wata rānā an ta6à yi....

**one¹ 1.** *quant* **a.** (*in counting*) d̃aya *f*: ~, two, three... d̃aya, biyu, ukù...; ~ only d̃aya tak = d̃aya kad̃ai: ~ is less than two d̃aya bà tà kai biyu ba; it costs ₦1.50 kud̃insà nair̃ã d̃aya dà kwabō hàmsin; they beat us by ~ point sun cī mù dà d̃igō d̃aya; in ~ place à wurī d̃aya; there is only ~ correct answer amsã d̃aya cè kad̃ai. **b.** (*among*): ~ of (d̃aya) dàga cikin: she is ~ of my best friends tanà d̃aya dàga cikin ƙawàyēnā na ƙwar̃ai; lead is ~ of the heaviest metals dar̃mã tanà dàga cikin ƙarãfan dà sukà fi nauyī. **2.** *pro* **a.** (*a single unit*) gùdā *m*, d̃aya *m/f*: he gave me ~ yā bā nì d̃aya = yā bā nì gùdā = yā bā nì gùdā d̃aya; ~ of them d̃ayansù (*m*), d̃ayar̃sù (*f*). **b.** (*contrasting the first of two*): the ~...the other... wani...wani (kuma)..., d̃aya...d̃ayân (kuma)...: ~ went east and

the other went west wani yā yi gabàs, wani kuma ya yi yâmma. **c.** (*other uses*): ~ after the other (*following*) bî dà bî, kâi dà kâi: they entered the room ~ after the other sun shigō d̃akī bî dà bî; ~ at a time d̃aya-d̃aya / d̃ai-d̃ai: they entered the room ~ at a time sun shigō d̃akī d̃aya-d̃aya; ~ by ~ d̃ai-d̃ai dà d̃ai-d̃ai: unload them ~ by ~ kà saukè su d̃ai-d̃ai dà d̃ai-d̃ai. **3.** *det & pro* **a.** (*a certain, some*) wani *m*, wata *f*: ~ day they'll return wata rānā sã dāwō; I want another ~ in addition to this inà sôn wani ban dà wannàn. **b.** (*a specific* ~): this ~ wannàn, see this, that, other: this ~ is better than that ~ wannàn yā fi wancàn; any ~ (of) kōwànnē *m*, kōwàccē *f*: any ~ of them can do it kōwànnensù nà iyà yînsà.

**one²** *pro* **a.** (*indef. subj pro, see* **Appendix A**): ~ usually writes it this way anà r̃ubùtā shi hakà; ~ must not forget that... kadà à mântā cêwā.... ~ another jūnā *pro*: they love ~ another sunà sôn jūnā. **b.** (*a particular* ~) shī *m*, ita *f*, sū *p*: those are not the ~s I was looking for bà sū nè nakè nēmā ba. **c.** no ~ see **no one, anyone**: no ~ knows bà wàndà ya sanī; there is no ~ who can stop him bà mài hanà shi.

**one-way** *adj*: a ~ street wanwê *f*, [F] hanyã mài kâi d̃aya: this is a ~ street tītìn nân wanwê nē; a ~ ticket tikitìn zuwà.

**oneself** *pro, see* **self, Appendix A.**

**onion** *n* àlbasà *f*; green ~ lawàshī *m*.

**onlooker** *n* d̃an kallō *m*, mài kallō *n*.

**only 1.** *adj & adv* **a.** (*merely*) kawài *adv*, kurùm *adv*: ~ this one sai wannàn kawài; he ~ said that he was looking for you àbîn dà ya cè kurùm shī nè yanà nēmankà; he ~ smiled but didn't utter a word yā yi mùr̃mushī kawài bài cê uffàn ba; not ~ clothes but money bà tufāfī ba kawài, kud̃ī mā; I ~ got 10 gōmà kawài na sāmù. **b.** (*alone*) kad̃ai: we were not the ~ ones there bà mū kad̃ai mukè nan ba; it's ~ you and me (we are the ~ ones) dàga nī sai kai; ~ he can tell you what to do shī kad̃ai zâi iyà gayà mukù. **c.** (*sole, unique*): I am his ~ son nī d̃ansà t̃ilō; he is the ~ one who can do it bà wàndà zâi iyà yînsà sai shī; this is our one and ~ chance wannàn ita cè dāmar̃ dà mukè dà ita kè nan; (*to emphasize the number one*) tak *idph*: I saw 1 and 1 ~ nā ga d̃aya tak. **d.** (*to emphasize immediate time, use reduplicated adv*): I arrived ~

yesterday jiyà-jiyà na isō; I saw him
~ a second ago nā gan shì d̃àzu-d̃àzun
nàn.
2. *conj*: if ~ (*hypothetical past condition*)
(in) dã (+ *complet.*): if ~ you had told us
dã kun gayã manã, *see* if; it was ~ after...
sai dà (+ *rel. complet.*): it was ~ after we
returned that we saw it sai dà mukà dāwō
mukà gan shì.
onomatopoeia *n* àmsà-kàma *f*, àmsà-muryà
*f.*
onwards *adv*: from that time ~ dàgà nan.
open 1. *v* būd̃ē *v4*: ~ a letter, a new hospital, a bank account būd̃ē littāfì, sābon
asìbitì, àjiyàr̃ bankì; when do the
shops ~? yàushè akè būd̃ē kantunã? ~
your mouth wide! (*usu. said to children*)
hã!
2. *adv* à bùd̃e *adv*: I left the door ~ nā
bar̃ k̃ōfã à bùd̃e; the door is wide ~ k̃ōfã
tanã bùd̃e hànhai; he was staring with
his mouth wide ~ yanã kallō bàkinsà
6àlàu; in the ~ (air) à fīlī = à sararī.
opener *n*, *see* can opener.
opening 1. *n* k̃ōfã *f* ⟨oCi⟩, mashigī *m*, kafā
*f* ⟨aCe⟩.
2. *adj*: the ~ chapter bābì na farkō;
~ remarks gabātar̃wā *f*; an ~ ceremony
bìkin būd̃ēwā = bìkin k̃addamar̃wā.
openly *adv* (*frankly, unequivocally*) à fīlī
*adv*, 6arō-6àrō *idph*, farau-fàrau *idph*:
he spoke ~ and said he didn't like it yā
fitō à fīlī ya cê bà yã sō.
operate *v* a. (*a machine*) sar̃r̃àfā *v1*. b.
(*Med.*) yi wà tìyātã *f*, [F] yi wà ôpèr̃ê
*m*; ~ on so. for sth. (*& remove*) yankè
wà *v4*: she was ~d on for appendicitis an
yankè matà tsirò à uwar̃ hanjī; operating room d̃ākìn tìyātã *m*, [F] d̃ākìn
ôpèr̃ê *m*.
operation *n* (*Med.*) aikì *m*, tìyātã *f* [F]
ôpèr̃ê *m*: perform an ~ yi aikìn tìyātã;
she had an eye ~ an yi matà tìyātã à
ido.
operator (*telephone, movie projector*) àfà-
r̃ētã *n*, [F] mài bugà sìlìmā *n*.
opinion *n* r̃a'àyī *m* ⟨oCi⟩: he asked me for
my ~ yā tàmbàyē nì r̃a'àyīnā; express
an ~ bà dà r̃a'àyī; we hold different ~s
mun shā bambam à r̃a'àyī; there's been a
difference of ~ an sàmi sà6ānin r̃a'àyī;
in so's. ~ à r̃a'àyin w., à ganin w.: in
my ~ à ganīnā = yàddà nakè ganī; have
a high ~ of so. k̃addàr̃ā *v1*: I have a high ~
of them inà k̃addàr̃ā su = sunã dà k̃īmā
à idònā.
opponent *n* (*Pol.*) àbōkin hàmayyà *m*;

(*Sport*) àbōkin karãwā *m*.
opportune *adj*: at the ~ moment à kân
karì.
opportunity *n* a. (*chance, means*) dāmā *f*,
hālī *m*, fīlī *m*: will you get the ~ to
learn Hausa? kō zā kì sàmi dāmar̃ k̃òyon
Hausa? he didn't give me an ~ to speak
bài bā nì fīlī ìn yi màganã ba; may
God provide us the ~ Allàh yà yi manà
būdì. b. (*spare time*) sùkūnì *m*.
oppose *v* a. (*not support*) k̃i gōyon
bāyan w.a.: he ~d the decision yā k̃i
gōyon bāyan shāwar̃àr̃ = bài yàrda dà
shāwar̃àr̃ ba. b. (*criticise*) sòkā *v2*: they
~ the idea of changing the constitution
sun sòki r̃a'àyin sauyà tsarìn mulkì.
c. (*Pol.*) yi àdāwã dà *f*: they are ~d to
the government sunã àdāwã dà gwamnatì.
opposite *n* (*polar*) akàsī *m*, kīshìyā *f*
⟨oCi⟩: black is the ~ of white bak̃ī akàsin
farī nè = bak̃ī kīshìyar̃ farī nè; that
is the ~ of what I told you shī nè akàsin
àbin dà na gayà makà; be in ~ direction
of yi kallō *m*, fùskantã *v2*, yi daurà
dà: we sat ~ each other mun zaunã munà
fùskantar̃ jūnā; the bank is ~ the station bankìn nã kallon tashã = bankìn nã
daurà dà tashã; be completely ~ (*fig.*)
yi hannun r̃īgā dà: from there we went
in ~ directions, he went east and I went
west dàgà nan sai mukà yi hannun r̃īgā,
ya yi gabàs na yi yâmma; Audu and I
have completely ~ views (on the issue)
mun yi hannun r̃īgā dà Audù (gàme dà
sha'ànìn).
opposition *n* a. (*lack of agreement*): there
was no ~ to the decision bâ wàndà ya k̃i
gōyon bāyan shāwar̃ã. b. (*Pol.*) hàmayyà
*f*: the ~ àbōkan hàmayyà; the ~ party
jàm'iyyàr̃ dà kè hàmayyà.
oppress *v* zàluntã *v2*, dannè *v4*: he ~ed
his people and treated them cruelly yā
zàlùnci jàma'àr̃sà yā kuma wulāk̃àntã
su.
oppression *n* zàluncì *m*, cîn zālī *m*, danniyā *f*.
oppressive *adj* àzzàlùmī *adj*, na danniyā *f*:
an ~ ruler àzzàlùmin sarkī; an ~ regime
mulkìn danniyā.
optimism *n* kyàkkyāwan fātā *m*, fātā
nagàri *m*.
optimistic *adj*: be ~ kyautàtà zàtō: I'm
~ that I'll finish soon inà kyautàtà zàtō
zân gamã dà wuri.
option *n* zā6ì *m*.
optional *adj* na ganin dāmã *m*: that course
is ~, it is not required kwâs d̃în nan na

ganin dāmā nè bǎ na dōlè ba nè; (esp. ref. to Relig. practices) na nāfilǎ f: ~ fasting, prayer azùmin, sallāf nāfilǎ.

or conj kō conj: black ~ white bakī kō farī; he may ~ may not come mài yìwuwā nè yà zō kō kadà yà zō; either...~ kō...kō: I prefer either Fanta ~ tonic water nā fi sôn kō fantǎ kō tōnìk; either you go ~ you stay kō kà tàfi kō kà zaunǎ.

oral adj na bakà: ~ literature adàbin bakà; an ~ test jaffàbâwaf bakà = jaffàbâwaf ka.

orange 1. n (fruit) lèmon zākī m, [F] lèmon Kanō m, ofanjì m; ~ juice ruwan lèmon zākī.
2. adj (color) ruwan gōfò m; reddish-~ jāwǎ f.

oratory n zàlākǎ f, fàsāhǎ à màganǎ f.

orbit 1. n (of planets) falàkī m ⟨ai⟩.
2. v zāgàyā v1, yi zàgàyē m.

orchard n garkā f ⟨a-e⟩.

order 1. n a. (command) ùmàfnī / ùmùfnī m: give an ~ bā dà ùmàfnī; follow an ~ bi ùmàfnī = kiyàyè ùmàfnī; you must follow the doctor's ~s dōlè kì kiyàyè ùmàfnīn dà likità ya bāyaf. b. (business & admin.) ōdǎ f ⟨oCi⟩: I've placed an ~ for a typewriter nā yi ōdàf tāfìfētā. c. (Law) dōkā f ⟨oCi⟩: preserve law and ~ kiyàyè dōkā. d. (peace) hankàlī m; a disruption of ~ tāshìn hankàlī, hàrgitsī m: after the disruption, ~ was restored bāyan hàrgitsī hankàlī yā kwàntā. e. (arrangement, sequence) tsàrī m: in alphabetical, numerical ~ ta tsàrìn abjàdì, lambōbī; put sth. in ~ tsàrǎ v1; in ~ (one after the other) bî dà bî adv: now here are the news stories in the ~ presented yànzu gà làbàfūn bî dà bî; a sense of ~ lìssāfī m: look what a mess he's made, he has no sense of ~ dùbi yâddà ya sâ kōmē bàfkàtài, bâ shi dà lìssāfī; be in ~ yi daidai: are all your papers in ~? duk tàkàfdunkà daidai sukè? in (their) ~ dakì-dakì adv, bî dà bî adv: put them in ~ kà shiryà su dakì-dakì. f. (working): my telephone is out of ~ wayàtā bā tǎ aikì. g. in ~ to dòmin / don conj: I went there in ~ to see him nā jē cân dòmin ìn gan shì; he said that in ~ to frighten us hakà ya fàdā don yà tsòràtā mu; in ~ not to don kadà, don gudùn (+ subjunct.): in ~ not to quarrel don gudùn fadǎ; in ~ not to waste time don kadà à 6àtā lōkàcī.
2. v a. (command) ùmàftǎ v2, bā dà

ùmàfnī: he ~ed the men to be silent yā bā sōjà ùmàfnī sù yi shirū; he likes to ~ people around yā cikà sôn mulkī. b. (arrange) tsàrǎ v1.

orderly[1] adj (mài) tsàrī m, (mài) lìssāfī m: his work is very ~ aikìnsà nǎ dà tsàrī; in an ~ manner dakì-dakì, à tsàre.

orderly[2] n (Mil.) ōdàlè m, [F] fàlàntô m.

ordinary adj na kullum, na yâu dà kullum; that noise is nothing out of the ~ hàyàniyâf nan àbā cè ta yâu dà kullum; (of things) gàmà-gàri m: this is an ~ watch wannàn àgōgo gàmà-gàri nè; (of people): he's just an ~ person shī talàkà nē = bā wani mùhimmìn mùtûm ba nè.

ore n (iron) tamā f; (tin) kùzà m.

organ n (of body) hàlittǎ f.

organization n a. (arrangement) tsàrī m: his thinking lacks ~ bâ shi dà tsàrī wajen tùnànī; lack of ~ bâ kâi bâ gìndī. b. (preparation) shirī m, tānàdī m: travelling requires a lot of ~ yi tàfiyà yanà bùkātàf tānàdī dà yawà. c. (society) kungìyā f ⟨oCi⟩: a relief ~ kungìyaf ('yan) āgàjī; an international ~ kungìyā ta dūniyà.

organize v (arrange) shiryà v1 ⟨shirì⟩, tsàrǎ v1: he has ~d his room very neatly yā tsàrà dàkìnsà tsaf-tsaf; ~ a conference for next year shiryà bàbban tàrō na bàdi.

organizer n (esp. Pol.) ògànēzǎ m.

orgasm n ìnzālī m.

oribi n batsiyà f ⟨oCi⟩.

Orient n: the ~ Kasàshen Gabàs Mài Nīsā p.

origin n a. (ancestry) asalī m, tūshè m: he is Nigerian by ~ asalinsà ɗan Nìjēfiyà nē = asalìnsà dàgà Nìjēfiyà yakè; they are studying the ~s of the Hausa language sunà nazàrin tūshèn harshèn Hausa; what is the ~ of this word? mènē nè tūshèn wannàn kalmà? b. (beginnings) mafārī m: I don't know the ~ of that rumor bàn san mafārin jìta-jìtāf ba; the ~ of species mafārin nau'ō'in hàlìttū.

original adj a. (earliest) na asalī m: Rano was one of the 7 ~ Hausa states Rano tanà dàgà cikin Hausa bakwài na asalī; b. (genuine, real) na ainihī m: this is the ~, not a copy wannàn takàfdā ta ainihī cè, bā kwafè ba. c. (creative, talented) (mài) hikimà f, (mài) azancī m.

originality n hikimà f, azancī m.

originally adv: we are ~ from Katsina asalinmù Kàtsinà.

ornament *n* àbin adō *m*, kāyan adō *m*.

ornamentation *n* adō *m*, kwalliyā *f*.

ornithology *n* ilĭmin nazàrin tsuntsāyē *m*.

orphan *n* màrāyà *m*, màrainìyā *f* ⟨u⟩.

orthography *v* ƙā'idōjin ƙùbùtū *p*.

orthopedic *adj* na ƙashī *m*.

oryx *n* màrīrì *m* ⟨ai⟩,

ostentatious *adj*: be ∼ yi gàdāřà *f*, yi řìya *f*, nūnà ařzìkī *m*.

ostracize *v* tsàřgā *v2*.

ostrich *n* jìminā *f* ⟨u⟩, (*male*) bàrōdō *m*.

other *det & pro* a. (*that one nearby*) wancàn *m*, waccàn *f*, wadàncân *p*; (*that one in question*) wànnan *m/f* wadànnan *p*: I want the ∼ one inà sôn wancàn; here is one but where is the ∼ (one)? gà ɗaya nân àmmā ìnā wànnan? the ∼ day kwānan bāya. b. (*contrasting the second of two*) ɗaya, ɗayân: they were playing with the ∼ sunà wāsā dà ɗayân; hold the knife with this hand and the chicken with the ∼ kà riƙè wuƙā dà wannàn hannū sàn nan kà riƙè kāzā dà ɗayân; his farm is on the ∼ side of the river gōnařsà tanà ɗaya gēfèn kōgîn; in the ∼ box cikin ɗaya àkwàtìn. c. (*contrasting two actions*): the one did X and the ∼ did Y wani X wani (kuma) Y, ɗaya X ɗayân (kuma) Y: one stayed and the ∼ left ɗaya yā zaunà ɗayân kuma yā tàfi. d. some ∼ (*different*) wani dàbam: some ∼ people came looking for you wasu mutànē dàbam sun zō nēmankà. e. each ∼ jūnā *m*: they respect each ∼ sunà ganin girman jūnā. f. X and the ∼s (*belonging to a group*) su X: I saw Audu and the ∼s at the market nā ga su Audù à kàsuwā. g. (*the remainder*) saurā *m*: where are the ∼s? ìnā saurân?

otherwise *conj* in bà hakà ba.

otter *n* kàren ruwa *m*.

ottoman *n* (*stuffed leather cushion*) tìntìn / tùntùn *m*, kushìn *m*.

ought *v* a. (*indicating surmise, what is expected*) yā kyàutu à cê: they ∼ to be back by now yā kyàutu à cê sun dāwō yànzu. b. (*expressing desirablilty*) yā kàmàtā à cê: everyone ∼ have the right to vote yā kàmàtā à cê kōwā yanà dà haƙƙìn zàɓè. b. (*expressing obligation*) yā kàmàtā (+ *subjunct.*): we ∼ to hurry yā kàmàtā mù yi saurī = ai sai mù yi saurī; they ∼ to be punished yā kàmàtā à hòrè sù.

ounce *n* ōzà *m* ⟨oCi⟩.

our, ours *pro*, see Appendix A.

ourselves *pro*, see self, Appendix A.

out *adv* a. (*outdoors*) wàje *adv*: he has gone ∼ yā fìta wàje; inside ∼ bài-bâi: he wore his shirt inside ∼ yā sâ rìgā bài-bâi. b. (*from among, from inside*): ∼ of dàgà (cikin): 3 ∼ of 10 ukù dàgà cikin gōmà; his wallet fell ∼ of his pocket wàlàt dìnsà tā fāɗì dàgà àljīhunsà; she came ∼ of the room tā fitō dàgà cikin ɗākì. c. (*from sth.*): ∼ of dà: it is made ∼ of wood, ivory an yī shi dà kātākō, haurè. d. (*for use as particle with verbs, see relevant verb entries; v5 verbs oft. include the meaning of 'out'*): take ∼ the trash fid dà shàrā; throw ∼ the water zubař dà ruwa. e. (*lacking*): be ∼ of rasà *v1*, yi rashì *m*: I'm ∼ of gas, money inà rashìn mâi, kuɗī.

outbreak *n* ɓarkèwā *f*: an ∼ of violence ɓarkèwař hàrgitsī.

outcast *n* bàřē *m*: he's an ∼ in his own house an mai dà shī bàřē à gidansù.

outcome *n* sàkàmakō *m*.

outdo *v* tsērè wà *v4*: he outdid me in running yā tsērè mini wajen guɗù.

outdoors *adv* (à) wàje *adv*: let's sit ∼ mù zaunà wàje; (*esp. in the open*) à fīlī, à sararī.

outer *adj* na (dàgà) wàje: an ∼ room ɗākì na dàgà wàje.

outlet *n* mafitā *f*.

outline 1. *n* shācì *m*: we could see the ∼ of the mountain in the distance munà iyà ganin shācìn dūtsèn dàgà nēsà; he drew the ∼ of the farm with his feet ya shàtà iyàkař gōnā dà ƙafàřsà; tell the ∼ of a story bā dà làbārì à taƙàice. 2. *v* shàtà *v1*, yi shācì *m*.

outnumber *v* rìnjāyà *v2*: they ∼ed us 3 to 1 sun rìnjāyē mù ukù dà ɗaya.

out-of-date *adj*: that style is ∼ bā à yàyinsà yànzu; that dictionary is ∼ ƙamùs dîn nan yā tsūfa.

outraged, be(come) *v* hàsalà *v3*.

outright *adj* ƙai tsàye: he refused me ∼ yā ƙī nì ƙai tsàye.

outside 1. *adv* wàje *adv*: he went ∼ yā fìta wàje; ∼ Nigeria wàje dà Nìjēřiyà. 2. *n* (*outer surface*) bāyā *m*: ∼ of a pot bāyan tukunyā.

outsider *n* bàřē *n*: they are ∼s, not one of us sū bàřē nè à cikinmù.

outskirts *n* wàjen gàrī *m*, kēwayèn gàrī *m*, bāyan gàrī *m*.

outsmart *v* yi wà shirì *m*.

outstanding *adj* (*impressive*) gàgārùmī *adj* ⟨ai⟩; ∼ qualities bàjintà *f*; what he did proves how ~ he is àbîn dà ya yi yā nūnà bàjintàr̃sà.

**outstrip** v tsērè wà *v4*: they ~ped us in tying the bundles of corn sun tsērè manà wajen ɗaurìn dammunàn hatsī.

**outwit** v yi wà shirì m, yi wà dàbār̃à f, ƙullà wà dàbār̃à.

**ovaries** n ƙwan màcè m.

**oven** n (*in modern stove*) ōbìn m, [F] hūr̃ù m. (*tradit., made of clay*) tàndèr̃ū m.

**over** 1. adv a. (*in excess of*) samà dà prep, fìye dà: she is ~ 20 years old shèkàruntà samà dà àshìr̃in (fig.) = tā bā àshìr̃in bāyā; he was driving ~ 90 yanà gudù dà mōtà fìye dà càsà'in; ~ the limit fìye dà yàddà akà ƙayyàdē. b. (*during*): ~ a period of time dà kàɗan kàɗan: the water in the well collects ~ a period of time ruwan rìjìyā yanà tàruwā dà kàɗan kàɗan; c. (*again, repeatedly*): do sth. ~ and ~ shā (+ action n): I blinked my lights at him ~ and ~ nā shā yi masà dìm; I've asked him ~ and ~ for the information nā tùntùɓē shi bà sàu ɗaya bà sàu biyu ba. d. (v + adv uses; see also particular verb entries): be ~ ƙārè *v4*, gamà *v1*: is the meeting ~? an gamà tàrôn? = tàrôn yā ƙārè? be left ~ ragè *v4;* do sth. ~ sākè *v4*: this report will have to be typed ~ dōlè sai an sākè bugà wannàn r̃ahōtò. e. (*at a distance*) can: way ~ there can nēsà; ~ in Europe can Tūr̃ai.
2. prep a. (*above*) bisà kân: there was a sign ~ the door àkwai àlāmà bisà kân ƙōfà; the water was ~ their heads ruwā yā kai har̃ iyā kânsù. b. (*across*) (à) kētarèn: a village ~ the border ƙauyèn dà kè ƙētarèn iyàkā.

**overbearing** adj: be ~ zaƙè *v4*, fiffìƙè *v4*.

**overcast** adj: be(come) ~ lumshè *v4*, dushè *v4*: the sky is ~ gàrī yā lumshè.

**overcharge** v ƙwār̃ā *v2*.

**overcoat** n òbàkwât f, [F] kàppōtì f.

**overcome** v a. (*solve*) shāwō kân w.a.: ~ the problem of drugs shāwō kân màtsalàr̃ shân ƙwāyà. b. (*overpower*) rìnjāyà *v2* ⟨rìnjāyè⟩, ī wà *vdat*, kā dà / kāyar̃ (dà) *v5*: ~ one's opponents rìnjāyi àbōkan gàbā; I was ~ with sleep barcī yā rìnjāyē nì; we were ~ by smoke, grief hayāƙī, baƙin cikì yā ī manà = yā kā dà mū.

**overconfident** adj: be ~ nūnà iyà yî.

**overcrowded** adj: be ~ yi cùnkōsō m, yi cìkōwà f: the city is ~ gàrîn yā yi cùnkōsō.

**overdo** v yi fìye dà kīmà, zar̃cè *v4*, wucè gōnā dà irì.

**overeat** v yi mūgùn cî, yi cîn tsìyā.

**overflow** v a. (*flood*) yi ambàliyà f, yi amāguwā f. b. (*be crowded*) tumbàtsē *v4*, yi cìkōwà f: the market is ~ing with people kàsuwā tā tumbàtsē dà mutànē.

**overgrown** adj: the place is ~ (*with weeds*) wurîn yā sarƙè.

**overhaul** n (*of organization or engine*) gar̃ambāwùl m.

**overhear** v ji ƙishin-ƙishin: I overheard it said that... nā ji ƙishin-ƙishin cêwā....

**overjoyed** adj: I was ~ mur̃nà tā kashè ni = dàdī yā kashè ni.

**overlap** v zōɓà *v1*.

**overload** v labtà wà *v1*, tulà wà *v1*: the donkey has been ~ed with firewood an labtà wà jàkī itàcē; I am ~ed with work an tulà mini aikì.

**overlook** v (*pardon*) haƙùrē *v4*, yāfè wà *v4*: they agreed to ~ his petty thefts sun yāfè masà sàce-sàcēn dà ya yi; I'll ~ it this time but don't do it again zân haƙùrē makà wannàn kàm àmmā kâr̃ kà sākè.

**overnight** adv: stay ~ yā dà zangò: on the way from Sokoto to Kaduna, we stayed ~ in Gusau dà zâ mu Kàdūna dàgà Sakkwato, mun yā dà zangò à Gùsau.

**overpower** v a. (*overcome*) kā dà / kāyar̃ (dà) *v5*: they ~ed the enemy sun kā dà àbōkan gàbā; the huge man was difficult to ~ ƙātòn yanà dà wùyar̃ kāyâr̃wā. b. (*dominate*) rìnjāyà *v2* ⟨rìnjāyè⟩.

**override** v màllakà *v2*.

**overripe** adj rùɓaɓɓè adj.

**overrule** v sōkè hukuncì.

**overseas** adv à ƙasàshen ƙētarè: he is working ~ yanà aikì à ƙasàshen ƙētarè.

**overseer** n (*of road crew*) àbàsiyà m, [F] kwàntîr̃-mètîr̃ m.

**oversight** n r̃àfkanà f: it was just an ~ ai r̃àfkanà cē kawai.

**oversleep** v yi mūgùn barcī.

**overtake** v cim mà *vdat*, rìskà *v2*: he overtook me in the race ya cim mini à tsērēn; the times have ~n us zāmànī yā rìskè mù.

**overthrow** v hamɓàrē *v4*, hamɓarar̃ (dà) *v5*, yi jūyìn mulkì m: the government has been ~n an yi jūyìn mulkì = an hamɓarar̃ dà gwamnatì.

**overtime** n àbàtayà m: work ~ yi aikìn àbàtayà = yi aikì bāyan lōkàcī; we've gone half an hour ~ mun zar̃cè lōkàcī dà rabin awà.

**overturn** *v* a. (*capsize*) kifè *v4*, kifař (dà)
*v5*: kaɓàncē *v4*: the car ~ed on us mōtā̃ tā
kifè dà mū; she ~ed the calabash, spilling
the grain tā kifař dà ƙwaryā hař hatsī
yā zubè. b. (*revoke*) kā dà / kāyař (dà)
*v5*: ~ a verdict kā dà hukuncì.

**overweight** *adj*: she is ~ tā cikà ƙibà;
the suitcase is terribly ~ nauyin jàkâř yā
wucè kīmà̃.

**overworked** *adj*: I'm ~ aikì yā yi minì
yawà̃.

**ovulate** *v* yi sàukař ƙwai.

**ovum** *n* ƙwan màcè *m*.

**owe** *v* a. (*money*) bi (bāshì̃) *v0*: he ~s me
₦10 inà bînsà naiřà̃ gōmà; how much
does Audu ~ you? nawà kakè bîn Audù?
be patient, I will pay everything that I
~ you yi hàƙurī zân biyā duk àbîn dà
kakè bînā bāshì̃. b. (*fig.*): I ~ my success to him àlbařkàcinsà nē na sàmi cî-
gàba.

**owing to** *prep* sabòɗà *prep*: the game was
cancelled ~ to bad weather an sōkè wàsân
sabòɗà rashìn kyân yanàyī.

**owl** *n* mūjìyā *f* ⟨oCi⟩: among the Hausa
~s are considered evil wajen Hàusàwā,
mūjìyā mūgùwař àbā cè; (*male*) dūjì̃
*m*; (*horned*) ɗùskwī *m*; (*spotted eagle* ~)
ƙururū *m*.

**own**¹ *v* a. màllakà̃ *v2*: he ~s a lot of property yā màllàki kadařà̃ dà yawà̃; previously, foreigners ~ed most of the fac-
tories à dâ bàƙī kè màllakâř yawancin
mà'àikàtū. b. (*use genitive constr. with
linkers*): who ~s this car? mōtář nân ta
wànē nè? = wà̃ kè dà mōtář nân?

**own**² *pro* a. (*possessed by one, use poss. pro
with linkers* na *m*, ta *f*, na *p*): he carried
my case as well as his ~ yanà̃ ɗàuke dà
jàkātā hàɗe dà tāsà. b. (*emphat. constr.*): they have their ~ method, jargon:
sunà̃ da tāsù hanyàř, sàřâr. c. (*of, by
oneself*) kân (+ *pro*.): she has money of
her ~ tanà̃ dà kuɗin kântà = kuɗintà
sunà̃ kântà; on one's ~ dà ƙashin ƙâi:
no one told her to do it, she did it on her ~
bâ wàndà ya gayà̃ matà tā yi, dà ƙashin
kântà nē ta yi.

**owner** *n* mài *n* ⟨màsu⟩: where's the ~ of this
bicyle? ìnā mài kèkèn nân? = wà̃ kè dà
kèkèn nân?

**ox** *n* tàkarkàrī *m* ⟨ai⟩.

**oxcart** *n* kèkèn shānū *m*, amālanke *m*.

**oxpecker** *n* (*bird*) càřki *m* ⟨una⟩: ~s follow
cattle càřki nà̃ bîn shānū.

**oxygen** *n* iskàř shàƙā̃ *f*.

# P

pace 1. n tākì m: he took 3 ~s to the left
yā yi tākì ukù à hagu; it is more than
10 ~s across fādìnsà yā fi tākì gōmà.
2. v yi tākì m; ~ up and down yi kai-
dà-kàwō m.

pacify v a. (calm so.) làllāsà v2 ⟨lallā-
shī⟩, sanyàyā wà zūcìyā. b. (restore order) kwantar̃ dà hankàlī, sâ wà amincì.

pack 1. n (packet) fākitì m ⟨oCi⟩, [F] fàkê
m: a ~ of cigarettes fākitìn tābà.
2. v a. (a suitcase, box) kimsà v1: he ~ed
his box for the trip yā kimsà àkwàtìnsà
don tàfiyà; ~ up tattàrà v1: everything
is ~ed up an tattàrà kōmē dà kōmē. b.
be ~ed (crowded) cūshè v4, cìka v3: the
place was ~ed with people wurîn yā cūshè
dà mutànē.

package n ƙunshì m, (esp. postal) [F] kwàlî
m ⟨uka²⟩: he was carrying a ~ yanà
ɗauke dà ƙunshì; the postman delivered
a ~ māsinjàn gidan wayà yā kāwō wani
ƙunshì.

packet n, see pack.

pack-ox n tàkarkàrī m ⟨ai⟩.

pact n yàr̃jējenìyā f, àmānà f: make a ~
ƙullà yàr̃jējenìyā = ƙullà àmānà.

pad n (round, used on head for carrying loads) gammō m ⟨aye⟩; ~ of paper
littāfīn r̃ùbùtū.

paddle 1. v (a boat) tūƙà v1.
2. n matūƙī m.

padlock n kwàɗō m ⟨i⟩: keep your bicycle
locked with a ~ kà riƙà kullè kèkènkà
dà kwàɗō.

pagan adj ar̃nè m ⟨ar̃nā⟩; (non-Muslim
Hausa) bàmāgujè m; (any non-believer in
Islam) kāfìr̃ì m ⟨ai⟩.

page n (in book) shāfì m ⟨uka²⟩: turn to
~ 16 kù dùbi shāfì na shā shidà; on
which ~? à shāfì na nawà?

pail n bōkitì m ⟨ai⟩.

pain 1. n cīwò m, zāfī m; (severe, sharp)
r̃àɗàɗī m, zògī m, sūkà f, (abdominal)
tūƙà f: aspirin is good for ~ asfìr̃ìn yanà
māganìn r̃àɗàɗī; do you feel any ~? kinà
jîn zāfī? the ~ has almost gone zāfī
yā kusa dainàwā; I'm feeling a sharp ~

jìkīnā nà minì sūkà; reduce, ease ~
sauƙàƙà zāfī; suffer ~ shā zāfī; (fig.)
take ~s with mai dà hankàlī à kân.
2. v yi wà zāfī m, jī wà cīwò m.

painful adj (mài) cīwò m, (mài) zāfī m: my
leg is very ~ ƙafà nà minì cīwò ainùn.

paint 1. n shāfē m, fentì m, [F] fàntîr̃ m:
wet ~ sābon fentì = ɗanyen fentì.
2. v a. yi wà fentì m: ~ the door green
yi wà ƙōfà fentì kōr̃è. b. (illustrate)
zānà v1, yi zàne-zàne.

painter n a. (of building) mài fentì n, mài
shāfē n, fentà n. b. (artist) mài zànē n.

painting n (art) zànē m ⟨x²⟩.

pair n (a. of socks or shoes) ƙafà f, tākì m:
5 ~s of shoes tàkàlmī ƙafà bìyar̃; one
of a ~ wārì m: where is the other one to
this ~ of shoes? ìnā wārìn tàkàlmin nàn?
b. (not translated in the following): a ~
of scissors àlmakàshī m; a ~ of trousers
wàndō m; in ~s bìbiyu adv: they entered
the room in ~s sun shigō ɗākì bìbiyu.

palace n fādà f, gidan sarkī m.

palate n gàndā f: hard ~ gàndā tsàttsaurā; soft ~ gàndā tàttausā.

pale adj kòɗaɗɖē adj; become ~ kòɗè v4: he
became ~ fuskàr̃sà tā kòɗè.

palm¹ n (trees): coconut-~ kwākwā f; date-
~ dàbīnò m ⟨ai⟩; deleb-~ giginyà f ⟨u⟩;
dum-~ gòrubà f ⟨ai⟩; oil-~ kwākwà f;
raffia-~ tukurwā f ⟨oCi⟩.

palm² n (of hand) tàfin hannu m.

palm oil n mân jā m.

palm wine n bàmmī m.

palpitate v (from fear) yi ɗar̃-ɗar̃ idph,
(from illness) yi 6àlli-6àlli idph, yi
6àl-6àl-6àl idph: she has heart palpitations zūcìyar̃tà tanà 6àl-6àl-6àl.

pampered adj: he is a ~ child ɗan gàtā nè.

pamphlet n ƙàsīdà f ⟨u⟩.

pan n (enamelware) kwānò m ⟨uka⟩; (var.
types): frying ~ kwānòn tūyà m; sauce~
tukunyā f ⟨tukwànē⟩; head-~ (large, for
heavy loads) kwānòn sarkī m; (tradit., of
clay, with indentations for frying cakes)
tàndēr̃ū m, kaskon tūyà m.

pancake n (sweet, from refined white flour)
fànkē m.

pancake make-up n (powdered) fankèkè
m, [F] fànkēkē m; (liquid) hōdàr̃ ruwā f.

pancreas n tùmbur̃kùmā f.

panic 1. n tsòrō m, ràzanà f.
2. v tsòratà v3, fìrgità v3, ràzanà v3,
tùnzurà v3.

pannier n mangalà f ⟨oCi⟩.

pant v (by animal) yi hàkī m; (gasp for air)
yi shàsshèƙà f.

panties *n, see* underpants.

pants *n* wàndō *m* ⟨una⟩, (*short*) gàjēren wàndō *m,* (*West. style*) tùr̃ōzà *m.*

papa *n* (*term of addr.*) bàba *m;* (*term of ref.*), *see* father.

papaya *n* (*tree or fruit*) gwandà *f* ⟨oCi⟩.

paper *n* a. takàr̃dā *f* ⟨u⟩: a sheet of ∼ war̃k̃àr̃ takàr̃dā = fallen takàr̃dā. b. (*newspaper*) jàr̃īdā *f* ⟨u⟩. c. (*academic essay, lecture*) màk̃ālà *f.*

paper clip *n* kìlîf *m,* [F] tàr̃ambân *m.*

parable *n* àlmàr̃à *f* ⟨oCi⟩; (*in the Gospels*) mìsālì *m.*

parachute 1. *n* laimà mài sàukar̃ ùngùlu *f.*

 2. *v* yi sàukar̃ laimà.

parade *n* fàr̃ētì *m,* [F] dēpilē *m;* (*durbar*) dābà *f.*

Paradise *n* Àljannà *f.*

paraffin *n, see* kerosene.

paragraph *n* sakìn lāyì *m.*

parakeet *n* tsiryā *f,* bibbigā *f.*

parallel *adj:* the streets are ∼ tītunà à lāyì ɗaya sukè.

paralysis *n* shān Innà *m,* shānyêwar̃ jìkī *f.*

paralyzed, be *v* shānyē *v4:* his arm is ∼ hannunsà yā shānyē = Innà tā shānyē masà hannū.

paraphrase *v* tak̃àità bàyānì.

parasite *n* a. (*insect*) kaskà *f;* (*plant*) kaucì *m.* b. (*psn.*) cì-mà-zàune *m,* ɗan r̃àrakà *m,* càr̃ki *m,* kaskà *f.*

paratrooper *n* sōjàn laimà *m.*

parcel *n, see* package.

pardon 1. *v* gāfàr̃tā wà *v1,* yāfè wà (làifī) *v4:* the king ∼ed them sarkī yā gāfàr̃tā musù; I begged him to ∼ me nā r̃ôk̃e shì gāfàr̃à = nā r̃ôk̃i gāfàr̃à gàre shì; (*give amnesty*) yi wà ahuwà *f.*

 2. *n* a. (*forgiveness*) gāfàr̃à *f,* yāfèwā *f,* ahuwà *f;* I beg your∼! (*for sth. done wrong*) (*said to one's superior*) à gàfàr̃cē nì! (*said to one's equal*) don Allàh, kà yi hàk̃urī! b. (*polite request for repetition*) ∼ me? I beg your ∼? mè akà cê? = bàn ji ba.

pare *v* fēr̃è *v4.*

parentheses *n* bàkā-biyu *m.*

parents *n* mahàifā *p,* iyàyè *p:* he lost his ∼ when he was very young iyàyensà sun r̃àsu tun yanà k̃àramī.

park 1. *n* a. (*car, lorry* ∼) tashàr̃ mōtà *f.* b. (*for relaxation*) wurin shàk̃àtâwā *m,* mashàk̃atà *f,* [F] jàr̃dân *m;* game ∼ gandun dājì *m.*

 2. *v* (*a vehicle*) ajìyè mōtà, yi fākìn *m,*

[F] yi gàr̃ê *m:* he ∼ed badly bài yi fākìn sòsai ba = [F] yā yi mal-gàr̃ê.

parking *n* (*area*) wajen ajìyè mōtà *m,* (*off side of road*) kìliyà *f;* no ∼ here ban dà ajìyè mōtà à nân.

parliament *n* màjàlisà *f* ⟨u⟩: member of ∼ ɗan màjàlisà *m.*

parlor *n* fālò *m,* [F] bàr̃andà *f:* room with a ∼ cikì dà fālò.

parody *n* ba'à *f,* shàgùɓē *m.*

parrot *n* àku *m.*

part 1. *n* a. (*measure, unit*) kashì *m:* one ∼ rice, two ∼s water shìnkāfā kashì ɗaya, ruwā kashì biyu; divide sth. into 3 ∼s rabà w.a. kashì ukù. b. (*geographical area*) yankì *m* ⟨una⟩, shiyyà *f* ⟨oCi⟩, sāshē / sāshì *m* ⟨Ca⟩: he lives in a different ∼ of the country yanà zàune à wani yankì dàbam. c. (*section*) ɓangarè *m:* in what ∼ of town do you live? à wànè ɓangarèn gàrîn kakè da zamā? (*of town*) ùnguwā *f* ⟨oCi⟩: in what ∼ of town do you live? à wàcè ùnguwā kakè? d. (*unit within a whole*) r̃ukùnī *m:* WHO is a ∼ of the United Nations K̃ungìyar̃ Kiyàyè Lāfiyà wani r̃ukùnin Màjàlisàr̃ Ɗinkìn Dūniyà cē. e. (*piece belong to machine, equipment*): this is a ∼ of the engine wannàn à cikin injìn mōtà yakè; spare ∼ kāyan gyārā *m,* sàfiyà *f.* f. (*Gram.*) ∼ of speech sāshèn màganà *p:* a verb is a ∼ of speech fi'illì yanà dàgà cikin sâssan màganà. g. (*other uses*): I had no ∼ in the matter bâ ni dà hannū à cikinsà = bā nà cikin sha'ànī; a small ∼ of kàɗan dàgà cikin; for the most ∼ yawancī *m,* gālìbī *m,* gālibàn *adv:* that is true for the most ∼ gālìbī wànnan gàskiyā cè; the people here are for the most ∼ Hausa mutànên nân gālibàn Hàusàwā nè; I'll accompany you ∼ of the way zân rakà ka har̃ zuwà wani wurī.

 2. *v* a. (*separate*) rabà *v1,* r̃àbu *v7:* it will be difficult to ∼ them zâi yi wùyā à rabà su; they ∼ed a long time abo sun r̃àbu tun tùni; I don't want to ∼ with it bā nà sôn r̃àbuwā dà shī. b. (*make way for so. to pass*) būɗà *v1:* the crowd ∼ed to let him pass jàma'àr̃ sun būɗà sù bā shì hanyà yà shìge.

partially *adj:* that is only ∼ true wannàn bà gàskiyā ba cē cìkakkiyā.

participate *v* shìga *v3:* ∼ in a discussion shìga màganà.

particle *n* (*remainder of sth.*) ɓar̃ɓashī *m,* bùr̃bùdī *m,* dìddigà *f.*

particular *adj* a. (*special*) na mùsammàn: I

have a ~ reason for going there inã dà
wani dàlīlī na mùsammàn dà zân jē can.
b. (essential) tàkàmaimai adv, na ainihī
m: he has no ~ reason for refusing to
come bã shi dà wani dàlīlī tàkàmaimai
na ƙīn zuwã = bã shi dà wani ainihin
dàlīlīn ƙīn zuwã.

particularly adv (for contrastive effect, see
especially) tun bã (mā) X bâ: I like
fruits, ~ papaya inã sôn 'yā'yan itàcē,
tun bã mā gwandã bâ.

partition 1. n ɓangarẽ m.
2. v: ~ a country rabà ƙasā ɓangarè-
ɓangarẽ.

partner n àbōkin tàrayyã m.

partnership n tàrayyã f, haɗin gwiwã m.

partridge n (francolin) fàkarā f ⟨u⟩, makwarwā f ⟨makwãrē⟩; stone ~ kàzaƙ dūtsè
f.

party n a. (Pol.) jàm'iyyã f ⟨u⟩: establish a political ~ kafà jàm'iyyaƙ sìyāsã;
join a ~ shìga jàm'iyyã; ~ member
ɗan jàm'iyyã; opposition ~ jàm'iyyã
mài àdāwā = jàm'iyyaƙ àbōkan hàmayyã.
b. (social group or organization) ƙungìyā
f ⟨oCi⟩: a ~ of tourists ƙungìyaƙ 'yan
yāwòn shāƙàtāwā. c. (Law, psn. involved
in case) àbōkin shàri'à m. d. (social
gathering) bìkī m ⟨uwa²⟩, lìyāfà f, fātì
f, (esp. with food) wàlīmã f.

pass¹ n a. (permit) izìnī m. b. (of a mountain) wurin ƙētàrè duwàtsū m.

pass² 1. vi a. (~ by) wucè v4, ficè v4, shigè
v4: the stormclouds have ~ed hadarī yā
wucè; he ~ed me without saying a word yā
shigè bài cê minì ƙalà ba. b. (of time)
wucè v4, ficè v4, shigè v4, shūdè v4. c.
(var. v + adv/prep uses): ~ away ràsu v7,
shūdè v4, kwàntà dāma; ~ by (a place)
zarcè v4, shigè ta v4; ~ in front (suddenly, quickly) giftã (ta) v1, gilmã (ta)
v1: the donkey ~ed right in front of the
car jàkī yā giftã ta gàban mōtã; ~ out
(become unconscious) sūma v3a; ~ on the
news bazã làbāƙī; ~ through (a place)
kētã v1: the road ~es through the town
hanyã tā kētã gàrī; ~ through (cross
through) rātsã ta v1: we ~ed through the
market mun rātsã ta kàsuwā.
2. vt (var. v + obj uses): ~ an examination ci jaƙƙabãwā f, yi fāsìn m, [F] yi
pàsè m; ~ the bread, salt mīƙà buƙōdì,
gishirī; ~ the day yinì / wunì v3b; ~
a law kafà dòkā, ƙayyàdē v4; ~ the night
kwāna v3a: ~ sentence yankè hukuncì; ~
wind yi tūsã f, (euphem.) hūtã v1; ~ a
vehicle (overtake) wucè v4, [F] yi dùbulê

m.

passable adj (traversable) (mài) ràtsuwā,
(mài) ƙētàruwā.

passenger n fāsinjà n ⟨oCi⟩, [F] pàsàjê
n.

passer-by n mài wucèwā n, mài gittãwā n.

passion n a. (strong desire, sexual) jàƙabã
f: he has a ~ for football yanã jàƙabàƙ
ƙwallon ƙafã = yanã màsīfàƙ sôn
ƙwallon ƙafã; he is very ~ate yā fayè
jàƙabã. b. (religious ecstasy) shauƙì m.

passport n fàsfô m, [F] pàspâƙ m: confiscate so.'s ~ ƙwācè wà fàsfô.

past 1. n: (in) the ~ (à) dã adv, zāmànin dâ
adv: it was always so in the ~ hakà yakè
à dã kōyaùshè.
2. adj a. (of passage of time): the ~ 3
weeks mākò ukù dà sukà wucè = mākò ukù
dà sukà gàbātã; these ~ few days 'yan
kwānàkin nàn. b. (Gram.): ~ tense, aspect shūdaɗɗen lōkàcī.
3. prep: it is 20 minutes ~ 2 ƙarfè biyu
yā wucè dà mintì àshīƙin; half-~ 2
ƙarfè biyu dà rabì.

pasta n tàliyã f.

paste 1. v mannã v1, līƙã v1: ~ a picture in
a book mannã zānē à littàfī.
2. n a. līƙì m, (white) gùlû m, (of gruel)
kōko m. b. (puree): tomato ~ tùmātìƙin
gwangwanī.

pastor n fàdã m, [F] àlmàsīhù m.

pastoral adj na dājì m: ~ Fulani Filãnin
dājì.

pastoralist n makìyàyī m.

pasturage n (for nomadic pastoralists):
dry-season ~ cīn rānī m; wet-season ~
mashēkarī m.

pasture n makiyāyã f, (well-watered) dau-
sàyī m; put (animal) out to ~ kīwàtã v1.

pat v dàddaɓã v2: I ~ted him gently to wake
him up nā dàddàɓè shì don yà tāshì
dàgà barcī.

patch 1. v a. (a tire) līƙè v4, yi līƙì m: I
~ed the hole nā līƙè hūdã dà facì = nā
līƙà facì à hūdã. b. (clothing) yi facì
m: in a ~ed state, having ~es (of clothes)
mahò m: his trousers have been ~ed àkwai
mahò à wàndonsà.
2. n (on tire, clothes) facì m: his clothes
were full of ~es kāyansà duk facì =
kāyansà duk à fàce sukè.

paternal adj: ~ aunt bābà f, ~ uncle bàba
m.

path n turbã f, 'yaƙ hanyã f; (esp. used
metaph.) tafarkì m: may God show us
the right ~ Allàh yà bã mù tafarkì
madàidàicī.

pathetic *adj* (mài) ban tàusàyī *m*.

patience *n* a. hàƙurī *m*, jìmirī *m*: great ~
hàƙurī matuƙā; have ~ with yi hàƙurī
dà, hàƙurà dà *v3*, jūrè wà *v4*, daurè
wà *v4*: she has a lot of ~ with children
tanà hàƙurā matuƙā gàyà dà yârā; he
doesn't have the ~ to deal with people
bâ shi dà hàƙurin huldà dà mutānē =
bā yà hàƙurī dà mutānē. b. (*endurance*)
daurèwā *f*, jūriyà *f*, jìmirī *m*; lose ~ with
so. gàji dà *v3*\*; have ~ and you'll get far
(*fig.*) sànnu-sànnu kwānā nēsà.

patient[1] *adj* (mài) hàƙurī *m*, (mài) jìmirī
*m*; be ~ with yi hàƙurī dà, hàƙurà dà
*v3*.

patient[2] *n* majìyyàcī / majìnyàcī *m*,
maràs lāfiyà *n*, [F] ɗan màlātì *m*: examine a ~ dūbà majìyyàcī.

patriot *n* ɗan kīshìn ƙasā *m*.

patriotism *n* kīshìn ƙasā *m*.

patrol 1. *n* (*group*) 'yan sintirī *m*, [F]
'yan pàtìrī *m*.
2. *v* yi sintirī *m*.

patron *n* a. (*supporter*) màigidā *m*; he is my
~ inà cîn àlbarƙàcinsà. b. (*customer*)
àbōkin cìnikī *m*.

pattern *n* a. (*abstract design*) samfùr /
samfùrī *m* (oCi); (*esp. of garments*) [F]
mòdâl *m*; a cloth with a bird ~ àtàmfā mài
tsuntsū. b. (*drawing*) zânē *m* (e²).

pauper *n* matàlàucī *m*, (*pejor.*) matsìyàcī
*m*.

pause 1. *n* (*rest*) 'yar shàƙàtâwā *f*, ɗan
hūtū *m*.
2. *v* shàƙàtā *v1*, tsayà kàɗan, dākàtā
kàɗan.

pave *v* yi wà hanyà kwàltâ *f*.

paw *n* dàgī *m* (una).

pawn *v* jingìnà *v1*, jinginar̃ (dà) *v5*, kai
w.a. jìnginà *f*: I ~ed my watch nā kai
àgōgōnā jìnginà.

pawnbroker *n* mài jìnginà *m*, ɗan kàrɓar̃
jìnginà *m*.

pawpaw *n* (*papaya tree or fruit*) gwandà *f*
(oCi).

pay 1. *v* a. (*money*) biyā *v0*: ~ a bill biyā
kuɗī; ~ off a debt biyā bāshì, far̃kè
bāshī: I've paid off the debt I owed nā
far̃kè bāshin dà akè bînā; ~ off a debt
(*commercial*) yi balàs dà w.; ~ money
into the bank zubà kuɗī à bankì; ~ in
advance (*for services*) bā dà àdìbâs; (a
*psn.*) biyā *v0*, bâ w. kuɗī: he paid me
the exact amount yā bā nì kuɗī cif-
cif = yā biyā nì cif-cif; ~ what you
think is right (*in bargaining*) kì biyā àbîn
dà kikà ga yā kàmātà = kì sàyā dà

dar̃ajà. b. (*var. v + n uses*): ~ attention
yi hankàlī, mai dà hankàlī; ~ attention
to (*consider carefully*) lūr̃a dà *v3*, kulà
dà *v1*; ~ attention to (*listen*) sàurārà
*v2* (sàurārō); ~ a visit on so. kai wà
zìyar̃à. c. ~ so. back for a kindness sàkà
wà dà àlhēr̃ì; ~ so. back with evil r̃āmà
wà dà shar̃r̃ì: I did him a good turn but
he paid me back with harm nā yi masà
àlhēr̃ì yā r̃āmà minì dà shar̃r̃ì.
2. *n* biyà *m*: a raise in ~ ƙārìn biyà
= ƙārìn àlbâshī; (*hourly, piecework*)
lādan aikì *m*, kuɗin ƙwādagō *m*; (*weekly*)
kuɗin sātī *m*; (*monthly, semi-monthly*)
àlbâshī *m*; retirement ~ (*from civil service, industry*) gàr̃àtūtì *m*, [F] pìr̃îm *f*.

payday *n* rānar̃ biyà *f*.

payment *n* biyà *m*; cash ~ kuɗī hannu *m*;
partial, advance ~ (*for services*) àdìbâs
*m*: I gave the mechanic ₦50 advance ~ nā
bâ màkānikè àdìbâs na nair̃à hàmsin.

peace *n* a. lùmānà *f*, zaman lāfiyà *m*,
amincì *m*: ~ and stability zaman lāfiyà
dà lùmānà; breach the ~ ɓàtà zaman
lāfiyà; keep the ~ tsarè zaman lāfiyà;
live in ~ yi zaman lùmānà = yi zaman ar̃zìkī; live in ~ and harmony yi
zamā cikin girmā dà ar̃zìkī; is it war
or ~? àmānā kō gàɓā? ~ negociations
shāwàr̃wàr̃in lùmānà; ~ talks shìrìn
sulhù; ~ treaty yàr̃jējēnìyar̃ zaman
lāfiyà; make ~ between (*2 parties*)
sulhùntà *v1*. b. (*state of rest*) kwànciyar̃
hankàlī *f*; I am at ~ hankàlīnā à kwànce
yakè. c. (*in condolences*): may he rest
in ~ Allàh yà ji ƙansà = Allàh yà
r̃ahamshē shì (*to which response is* àmin);
sànnu dà rashì = sànnu dà kēwā (*to
which response is* sànnu).

peaceful *adj* (mài) kwànciyar̃ hankàlī,
(mài) hankàlī kwànce, (*quiet psn.*) mài
shiru-shiru: he always looks ~ kōyàushè
ka gan shì hankàlinsà kwànce; in a ~
manner (cikin) girmā dà ar̃zìkī: tell
him ~ly that he should pay me gàyā masà
girmā dà ar̃zìkī yà biyā nì.

peacock *n* dāwīsù *m*, tsuntsun Makà *m*.

peak *n* a. (*of mountain*) ƙōlōluwā *f*, tulluwā *f*. b. (*acme, apogee*) gāniyà *f*: he's
at the ~ of his political power, popularity yanà cikin gāniyar̃ mulkìnsà,
tāshensà. c. (*of development*): reach a
~ gàwur̃tà *v3*, ƙàsaità *v3*; the traffic was
at its ~ mōtōcī sun cunkùshē sòsai.

peal *n* (*of thunder*) tsāwā *f*.

peanut(s) *n* gyàdā *f*, *see* groundnut(s).

peanut butter *n* tùnkūzà *f*.

**peasant** *n* bàƙauyè *m*, manòmī *m*.

**pebble** *n* tsakuwā *f* ⟨oCi⟩.

**peck** *v* (*by chickens*) càccakā *v2*, tsàttsagā *v2*; (*by birds*) yi ƙōtō *m*.

**peculiar** *adj* wani irìn X: he is a ~ person shī wani irìn mùtûm nē; this is a ~ plant wannàn wata irìn shūkā cē; what a ~ way to behave! kā ji wani irìn hālī!

**pedal** *n* (*of bicycle*) fēdā *f* ⟨oCi⟩.

**peddle** *v* yi tàllà *m*.

**peddler** *n* (*of small wares*) ɗan kirī *m*, ɗan jaur̃a *m*; (*usu. seated at market*) ɗan kōlì *m*.

**peddling** *n* kirī *m*, jaur̃a *f*, kōlì *m*.

**peek at** *v* lēƙā *v1*.

**peel 1.** *n* ɓāwō *m*.
   **2.** *v* ɓārè *v4*: ~ a banana, orange ɓārè ɓāwon àyàbà, lèmō; (*pare with knife*) fērè *v4*: ~ yams, sweet potatoes fērè ɓāwon dōyā, dànkalì; ~ off (*by erosion, moisture*) zāgè *v4*: the plaster is ~ing off the wall yàɓē nā zāgèwā dàgà jìkin bangō; ~ off (*of skin*) sàlùɓē *v4*, sālè *v4*.

**peep at** *v* lēƙā *v1*: he ~ed through the window at the crowd yā lēƙā tàrôn jàma'à ta tāgà.

**peer**[1] *n* (*age group*) tsārā *n* ⟨aki[2]⟩, sa'à *n* ⟨oCi⟩: he is my ~ sa'ànā nè; he has no ~ when it comes to doing math bâ shi dà sa'à wajen lìssāfì = bābù kàmar̃sà wajen lìssāfì.

**peer**[2] *v* duddùɓā *v1*.

**peg** *n* (*stake*) fēgì *m* ⟨una⟩: drive a ~ into the ground kafà fēgì à ƙasà; (*for hanging sth.*) marātayī *m*.

**pelican** *n* kwàsākwàsā *f*.

**pelt** *n* fātā *f* ⟨fātū⟩.

**pelvis** *n* kwàtangwalō *m*.

**pen**[1] *n* àlƙalàmī *m* ⟨u-a⟩, [F] ìstìlô *m*; (*ball-point*) bīr̃ò *m* ⟨una⟩, [F] bîk *m* ⟨oCi⟩.

**pen**[2] *n* (*coop for fowl*) akurkī *m* ⟨ai⟩.

**penalize** *v* hòrā *v2*.

**penalty** *n* **a.** (*punishment*) hòrō *m*. **b.** (*Sport, esp. soccer*) fànār̃ētì *f*, [F] fàr̃nàtî *m*. **c.** (*Law, sentence*) hukuncī *m*: the ~ for murder is death hukuncìn kisàn kâi shī nē kisā.

**pence** *n*, *see* **penny.**

**pencil** *n* fensìr̃ *m* ⟨oCi⟩, [F] kàr̃anyô *m* ⟨oCi⟩: sharpen a ~ fēr̃è fensìr̃.

**pencil sharpener** *n* shāfanā *f*.

**pending** *adj*: the matter is still ~ anā cikin màganàr̃ bà à yankè ba tùkùna.

**penetrate** *v* **a.** (*by squeezing through*) kūtsā *v1*: ~ enemy lines kūtsā cikin àbòkan gàbā; a bit of light ~d the room haskē

yā ɗan shìgō dākìn. **b.** (*pierce*) hūɗā *v1*, sōkè *v4*: the needle ~d the skin àllūr̃ā tā hūɗā fātā. **c.** (*permeate, of liquid*) rātsā *v1*.

**penis** *n* àzzakàr̃ī *m*; (*euphem.*) màzàkutā *f*, kāyan mazā *m*, gìndī *m*, gàbā *m*; (*vulg.*) bùr̃ā *f*, wutsiyā *f*, jèlā *f*, kutumā *f*.

**penknife** *n* askā *f* ⟨a-e⟩.

**penniless** *adj* mìskīnī *m* ⟨ai⟩ fàƙīrì *m* ⟨ai⟩ I'm absolutely ~ nī mìskīnī nē fìtik.

**penny** *n* (*in old or new currency*) kwabō *m* ⟨Cai, Cuna⟩; he hasn't a ~ to his name bâ shi dà kō ɗarī = (*fig.*) bâ shi dà kō kàr̃famfànā.

**pension** *n* fanshò *m*, [F] antar̃ē *m*: go on ~ yi fanshò.

**pensioner** *n* mài kàrɓar̃ fanshò *n*, mài r̃ìtāyà *n*, [F] ɗan antar̃ē *m*.

**pensive** *adj*: be ~ yi zùgum / yi jùgum *idph*; sit ~ly (*with head on hand*) yi tàgumī *m*.

**people** *n* **a.** (*persons*) mutànē *p*, 'yan *p*, *see* **person;** (*collectively*) jàma'à *f/p*: Kano has more ~ than anywhere else Kanò tā fi kō'ìnā yawàn jàma'à; the English-speaking ~ màsu màganà dà Tūr̃ancī; (*the masses*) talakàwā *p*. **b.** (*of a common descent*) mutànē *p*, (*or use suffix* -àwā *with place or ethnic designation*): the Chinese ~ mutànen Sin; the ~ of Ghana mutànen Gànà; the Hausa ~ Hàusàwā.

**pepper** *n* **a.** (*chillies, gener.*) bàr̃kōnō *m*, *see* **chillies;** cayenne ~ (*ground*) gàrin bàr̃kōnō *m*. **b.** (*black, whole*) màsòr̃o *m*; (*Melegueta*) cìttar̃ àhò *f*, cìtta mài 'yā'yā *f*, *see* **ginger.**

**peppermint** (*flavor, candy*) mintì *m*.

**per** *prep* à *prep*: how many times ~ day? sàu nawà à rānā? how much do you pay ~ hour? nawà akè biyà awà gùdā?

**perceive** *v* gānè *v4*: I couldn't ~ any difference between them bàn gānè bambancinsù ba.

**percent** *n* kashì X (dàgà) cikin ɗarī: 15 ~ kashì gōmà shâ bìyar̃ cikin ɗarī; a reduction of 10 ~ ragì na kashì gōmà cikin ɗarī.

**perceptive** *adj* (*psn.*) fāhìmī *m* ⟨ai⟩.

**perch** *n* (*Nile* ~) gīwar̃ ruwa *f*; (*cichlid*) gàr̃gazā *f*.

**percolate** *v* digà *v1*.

**perfect 1.** *adj*: he speaks ~ English yā iyà Tūr̃ancī sòsai; his manners are ~ mùtumìn kir̃kì nē; nobody is ~ (*fig.*) mùtûm tar̃à yakè bài cikà gōmà ba.
   **2.** *v* (*improve*) ingàntā *v1*.

**perfectionist** n: he is too much of a ~ yā cikà sôn iyâwā = fēlēƙē gàrē shì.

**perfectly** adv a. (exactly) daidai wà daidà: he did the work ~ aikinsà daidai wà daidà. b. (completely) sōsai adv: I understand ~ nā gānè sōsai.

**perform** v yi v0: ~ a miracle, operation, play yi àbin àl'ajàbī, aikìn tìyātà, wàsan kwaikwayō.

**performance** n (theatrical) wàsan kwaikwayō m, [F] tìyātìr̃ m.

**perfume** n tùr̃ár̃ē m: put ~ on shàfà tùr̃ár̃ē; a whiff of ~ ƙanshi-ƙanshin tùr̃ár̃ē.

**perhaps** adv mài yìwuwā, wàtàƙīlà / wàtàkīlà / kīlà: ~ we will see them mài yìwuwā nē mù gan sù = kīlà zā mù gan sù.

**period**[1] n a. (time) lōkàcī m ⟨ai⟩, sā'ì m: hold office up to a ~ of 4 years yi mulkī na ƙàyyàdadden lōkàcī na shèkarà huɗu. b. (era, epoch) mar̃r̃à f: during the Roman ~ à mar̃r̃àr̃ Rûm. c. (~ of time fixed in advance) ajàlī m: he stayed for a ~ of 3 months yā zaunà har̃ ajàlin watà ukù. d. (menstruation) àl'ādà f, hailà f; miss a ~ yi ɓatàn watà.

**period**[2] n (in orthography) āyà f ⟨oCi⟩.

**perish** v hàlakà v3: they almost ~ed saurā kàɗan sù hàlakà.

**perjury** n shaidàr̃ zur̃ f.

**permanent** adj na dindìndin adv: a ~ secretary sakatar̃èn dindìndin; a ~ address àdìr̃ēshìn dindìndin.

**permanently** adv har̃ àbàdā adv, dindìndin adv: I don't want to live here ~ bā nà sô ìn zaunà nân har̃ àbàdā.

**permeate** v a. (of pleasant smell) ɗumè v4: perfume ~d the room ɗākì yā ɗumè dà ƙanshin tùr̃ár̃ē; (of unpleasant smell) gumè v4. b. (of moisture, liquid spreading) nāshè v4: dampness ~d the house laimà tā nāshè ɗākì.

**permission** n izìnī m: leave without ~ fìta bà tàr̃e dà izìnī ba; seek ~ nèmi izìnī; give ~ to bâ w. izìnī, yar̃dar̃ wà vdat: did you give him ~ to go? kā yar̃dam masà yà tàfi?

**permit** 1. v yàr̃da v3: he didn't ~ us to take it bài yàr̃da mù ɗaukè shì ba. 2. n takàr̃dar̃ izìnī f, fàmît m, [F] fàr̃mì m; issue a ~ bā dà takàr̃dar̃ izìnī; learner's ~ (for driving) lānà f.

**perpetrate** v: ~ a crime aikàtà lâifī.

**perpetually** adv kō dà yàushè, kullum adv.

**perpendicular** adj à tsàye adv: draw a ~ line zānà lāyì à tsàye.

**perplex** v dābùr̃tā v1, dābùr̃cē v4, rikìtā v1, (esp. sth. unresolvable) àddabā v2: drug abuse is a ~ing problem worldwide shân ƙwàyā àbù nē dà ya àddàbi kōwā à dūniyà.

**persecute** v zàluntā v2, tsanàntā v1.

**persevere** v nācè v4, tāshì tsàye, dāgè v4: we must ~ until we have finished dōlè mù tāshì tsàye sai mun gamà.

**perseverance** n nācì m, jìmirī m, daurèwā f, himmà f.

**persist** v a. (persevere) nācè v4. b. (insist) kafè v4, dāgè v4: he ~ed in following us yā kafè à kân sai yā bī mù; he ~ed in teasing her yā dāgè wajen zòlayàr̃tà.

**persistence** n nācì m, dāgèwā f.

**person** n mùtûm m, mùtūnìyā f ⟨mutànē⟩; a ~ of (having some quality, trait) mài ⟨màsu⟩: a ~ of high rank, good character mài mùƙāmì, mài nàgàr̃tà; a ~ from (of a partic. place, use ethnonymic bà- ⟨awa⟩ prefix + place name, or ɗan ⟨'yan⟩ or mùtûm m, mùtūnìyā f ⟨mutànē⟩ (+ place name): a ~ from Sokoto bàsakkwacè; a ~ from Africa ɗan Afir̃kà = mùtumìn Afir̃kà; in ~ dà kâi: the emir attended in ~ sarkī dà kânsà ya hàllar̃à.

**personality** n: force of ~ kwàr̃jinī m: he has the force of ~ to be a leader yanà dà kwàr̃jinin shūgabancì.

**personnel** n ma'aikatā p.

**perspire** v yi gùmī m, yi jìɓī m, yi zufà/zuffà f.

**persuade** v a. (convince) shāwō kân w., cīwō kân w.: they ~d me to join the group sun shāwō kâinā ìn shìga ƙungìyâr̃. b. (coax) làllāsà / r̃àrrāsà v2 ⟨lallāshī⟩.

**persuasion** n lallāshī m.

**perturb** v dāmā v1, dāmu v7: he was ~ed hankàlinsà yā dāmu.

**pessimism** n mūgùn fātà m.

**pest** n (insect) ƙwar̃ō m ⟨i⟩; (fig.) he's a ~ yā shā minì kâi.

**pester** v hàyyatà v2, matsà wà v1, ƙuntàtà wà v1, fìtinà v2: the children kept on ~ing their mother yârā nà ta hàyyatàr̃ uwar̃sù; he is always ~ing me with foolish questions kōyàushè yakàn matsà minì dà tambayōyin wòfī; ~ so. for food or money dàmi w. dà màyātà.

**pestle** n taɓaryā f ⟨taɓàr̃ē⟩.

**pet** 1. n a. (a favorite) ɗan lèlē m, ɗan gātā m, (esp. wife, child) mōwà f. b. (domestic animal) dabbàr̃ gidā f. 2. v (fondle) yi tsàr̃àncē m.

petition 1. n k̄ārā f; (document) takār̃dā kai k̄ārā f.
2. v yi k̄ārā f.

petting n tsàràncè m.

petrol n (gasoline) mâi m, [F] ìsansì m; (super) sūfà m, [F] sùpâr̃ m.

petroleum n mân fētûr̃ m, [F] pìtār̃ô m; (crude) danyen mâi m.

petty trader n dan kōlì m.

phantom n fàtalwā f ⟨oCi⟩.

pharmacology n ilìmin har̃hàdà māgungunà m.

pharmacist n kyamìs m, [F] mùshen fàr̃màsî m.

pharmacy n kàntin māgànī m, kyamìs m, [F] fàr̃màsî f.

Pharaoh n Fìr̃'aunà m.

philosophy n ilìmin falsafà m.

phlegm n màjinā f, k̀àkī m: spit out ∼ yi k̀àkī.

phone n, see telephone.

phonetics n (Gram.) ilìmin fur̃ùcī m.

phonograph n canjà f, [F] èlêk m; (manually wound) gàr̃màhô m.

phonograph record n faifai m ⟨a..ai⟩, faifan gàr̃màhô m.

phonology n (Gram.) ilìmin tsārìn sautì m.

photocopy v yi hòtō m, yi kwafè m, [F] yi k̀òpî f.

photograph 1. n hòtō m ⟨una⟩.
2. v dauki hòtō, yi hòtō m.

photographer n mài daukàr̃ hòtō n.

photography n daukàr̃ hòtō f.

phrase n jimlà f ⟨oCi⟩; (Gram.) yankì m ⟨una⟩: a verb, noun ∼ yankìn àikàtau, sūnā.

physical adj: ∼ education ilìmin mòtsà jìkī m; ∼ exercise mòtsìn jìkī m; ∼ therapy gashì m.

physician n likità n ⟨oCi⟩, [F] dàktâr̃ m ⟨oCi⟩.

physiotherapy n gashì m.

pick 1. v a. (choose) zàbā v2 ⟨zàbē⟩: ∼ the ones you need zàbi wadàndà kakè sô.
b. (harvest) (use various verbs for specific crops): (cotton) cìrā v2: they are in the fields ∼ing cotton sunā gōnā sunā cìrar̃ audùgā; (guava, citrus fruit) dìbā v2*, tsinkà v1; (banana, mango, date) cirè v4.
c. (var. v + n uses): ∼ a pocket yankè wà àljīhū; ∼ a quarrel jā fadà; ∼ one's nose k̀wàk̀ùlè hancì; ∼ one's teeth sākàcè hak̀òrā. d. (var. v + prep uses): ∼ on so. (tease) zòlayà v2; ∼ out (from a mass) tsāmè v4, tsāmō v6: they ∼ed him out of the water, the crowd an tsāmō shi dàgà

cikin ruwa, tàron mutànē; ∼ up (lift up) dagà v1, daukō v6; ∼ so. up (in a car) daukà v2*: when will you come to ∼ me up? yàushè zā kà zō kà daukō nì?
2. n: take your ∼ zàbi sônkà.

pickaxe n digà f ⟨oCi⟩.

pickpocket n dan sànē m, dan yankan àljīhū m: beware of ∼s yi hankàlī dà 'yan sànē.

pickup n (type of truck) à-k̀òri-kūrā f.

picture n (photograph) hòtō m ⟨una⟩; (drawing) zànē m; (likeness) sūr̃à f: he drew a ∼ of a horse yā zānà sūr̃àr̃ dōkì.

Pidgin English n Bùr̃ōk̀à m: he speaks ∼ Bùr̃ōk̀à yakè yî.

Pidgin French n [F] Far̃ansanshin tsōhon sōjì m.

piece 1. n a. (fragment, sth. broken off) gutsurè m ⟨gutsattsàrī⟩: a ∼ of bread, kolanut, glass gutsurèn bur̃ōdì, gòr̃ò, gìlāshì; a ∼ of calabash sàkainà f; a ∼ of pottery tsìngār̃ō m, kaskon tukunyà m; break sth. into ∼s kakkàryā v1; come to ∼s r̃agàr̃gàjē / r̃ugur̃gùjē v4. b. (of cloth, paper) guntū m ⟨aye⟩, yankì m ⟨una⟩; a small ∼ of cloth k̀yallē m ⟨aye⟩; tear sth. into ∼s yayyàgā v1. c. (unit of counting) gùdā m ⟨gùdàjī⟩: how many ∼s do you what? 6 ∼s gùdā nawà akè sô? gùdā shidà. d. (as diminutive) dan m, 'yar̃ f ⟨'yan⟩: a ∼ of news wani dan làbārì m.
2. v: ∼ sth. together har̃hàdā v1.

piebald adj (horse) dànda m.

pier n kwàtā f.

pierce v a. (bore a very small hole) hūdà v1, yi hūjì m; ∼d ears hūjìn kûnnē; ∼d nose hūdàr̃ hancì f. b. (stab) sòkā v2: they ∼d his hand with a needle an sòkē shi dà àllūr̃à à hannu; give a piercing cry k̀wālà ìhù. c. (with spear or skewer) tsīrè v4.

piety n tsòron Allàh m.

pig n àladè m ⟨ai, u⟩.

piggy bank n asùsù m.

pigeon n tàttabàr̃ā / tàntabàr̃ā f ⟨ai⟩, (speckled) hazbiyà f ⟨oCi⟩; (young) dan shilà m ⟨'yan shilōlī⟩.

pile 1. v tārà v1: they ∼d the grass in one place sun tārà cìyàwā wurī daya; ∼ up jibgà v1, tsibà v1.
2. n tārì m, tsibì m: he fell over a ∼ of stones yā fàdà kân tārìn duwàtsū; in a ∼ tuli adv: there they are in a ∼ gà su cân tulì.

piles n, see hemorrhoids.

pilfering n bùruntū m.

pilgrim n (intending) manìyyàcī m, mahàjjàcī m; (returned from Mecca) àlhajì m, hajìyā *f* ⟨ai⟩.

**pilgrimage** *n* (*to Mecca*) (aikìn) hajì *m*: they went on the ~ sun jē hajì= sun yi aikìn hajì = sun jē Makà; it is obligatory for every able-bodied Muslim to make the ~ yā wàjabà gà dukkàn Mùsùlmī dà yakè dà īkò yà yi hajì.

**pill** *n* ƙwàyā/ƙwàyaȓ māgànī *f* ⟨oCi⟩: take 2 ~s every 4 hours kà shā ƙwàyā biyu kōwàcè awā huɗu.

**pillage** *v* wāshè *v4*.

**pillar** *n* gìnshiƙì *m* ⟨ai⟩; (*esp. ref. to religion*) shisshikè *m* ⟨a..ai⟩: the 5 ~s of Islam shìkàshìkai bìyaȓ na Musuluncì.

**pillow** *n* matāshin kâi *m*, filò *m* ⟨oCi⟩, [F] hulò *m* ⟨oCi⟩: a soft ~ matāshin kâi mài taushī.

**pillowcase** *n* rìgaȓ matāshin kâi *f*, jàkaȓ filò *f*.

**pilot** *n* matùƙin jirgin samà *m*.

**pimp** *n* kàwālì *m* ⟨ai⟩.

**pimple** *n* ƙurjī *m* ⟨a-e⟩, ⟨ƙuràrrajī⟩; (*acne*) bàȓ-ni-dà-mūgù *m*.

**pin** *n* (*safety*) fìl *m*, [F] fangìl *m* ⟨oCi⟩; (*straight*) fìn *m*, [F] àllūȓà *f*.

**pincers** *n* (*of blacksmith*) hàntsakī *m* ⟨ai, u-a⟩; (*of carpenter*) fincìs *m*.

**pinch** *v* mùntsunā *v2*; ~ off a piece of sth. ɓincìnā *v1*.

**pineapple** *n* àbàrbā *f*.

**ping-pong** *n* ƙwallon tēbùȓ *m*; a ~ ball bâl ɗin ƙwallon tēbùȓ.

**pink** *n* ruwan hōɗā *m*.

**pins and needles** *n* minjiryā *f*: I have ~ in my foot ƙafà tanà minì minjiryā.

**pint** *n* sumùnin galàn *m*.

**pious** *adj* (*mài*) tsòron Allàh *m*, (*mài*) àd-dīnì *m*, a ~ leader shēhù *m* ⟨shèhùnnai⟩.

**pip(s)** *n* (*in fruits, vegetables*) 'yā'yā *p*.

**pipe** *n* a. (*metal tube*) būtūtū *m*, [F] tìyò *m* ⟨oCi⟩. b. (*for water*) famfò *m*: ~ed water ruwan famfò. b. (*tobacco*) lòfè *m*, tukunyaȓ tābà *f*: smoke a ~ shā lòfè.

**pistol** *n* ƙàramaȓ bindigà *f* ⟨oCi⟩, lìbaȓɓà *f*, [F] pìstòlê *m*.

**piston** *n* fistìn *m*, [F] pìstân *m*; ~ ring ȓingì *m*, [F] sàgìmā *m*: the ~ rings are worn out ȓingì yā cìnyē = mōtà tā ci ȓingì.

**pit¹** *n* rāmì *m* ⟨uka⟩; (*used as trap*) haƙò *m*; borrow-~ kùduddufī *m* ⟨ai⟩; dye-~ karōfī *m* ⟨ai⟩.

**pit²** *n* (*small stone, seed of fruit*) ɗā *m* ⟨'yā'yā⟩; (*large*) ƙwallō *m* ⟨aye⟩.

**pitch¹** *n* (*in language*) kaifin sautì *m*; a high ~ed voice muryà mài ƙwārī.

**pitch²** *v*: ~ a ball jēfà ƙwallō = wuȓgà ƙwallō; ~ a tent kafà laimà.

**pitch³** *adv*: ~ black baƙī ƙirin = baƙī wuluk; ~ dark duhù ƙirin.

**pitcher** *n* (*ewer*) tùlū *m* ⟨una⟩.

**pith** *n* (*of plant*) tōtùwā *f*.

**pitiful** *adj* (*mài*) ban tàusàyī *m*.

**pitiless** *adj* maràs tàusàyī *m*, maràs īmānì *m*.

**pity** 1. *n* tàusàyī *m;* have ~ for so., take ~ on so. ji tàusàyin w.: we should take ~ on the handicapped yā kàmātà mù ji tàusàyin nàƙàsàssū.
2. *excl*: what a ~! kaico! *excl*, kash! *excl*: what a ~ you live so far away kash! gidankà dà nīsā; (*showing compassion*) àsshā! *excl*.

**place¹** *n* a. wurì *m* ⟨aCe⟩, wajē *m*: this is the ~ where it happened nân nē wurìn dà ya fàru; they are at Audu's ~ sunà wajen Audù; take ~ (*happen*) fàru *v7*, àuku *v7*; wander about from ~ to ~ yi ràgaità *f*, yi gàntàlì *m*; lose one's ~ rasà indà akè. b. (*where sth. belongs*) màhàllī / mùhàllī *m*: everything has its ~ kōmē yanà dà màhàllinsà; put the book back in its ~ mai dà littāfì màhàllinsà. c. (*position*) matsayī *m*: our ~ in the modern world matsayinmù à dūniyaȓ yâu; win first ~ yi làmbàwân *m*; in the first ~...in the second ~... dà farko dai...na biyu kuma.... d. (*stead*) madàdì *m*, màimakō *m*: he sent Sule in his ~ yā àiki Sulè à madàdinsà; take so.'s ~ mayè *v4*, zaunà à matsayin w.; take so.'s ~ temporarily yi wà wucin gādì *m*.

**place²** *v* sā *v1*, ajè / ajìyē *v4*: she ~d the thread in the box tā sā zàrē cikin àkwàtì; ~ sth. on top of ɗōrà wà *v1*: they ~ed the sack on his head an ɗōrà masà bùhū à ka.

**placenta** *n* mahaifā *f*, mabiyìyā *f;* uwaȓ cībìyā *f*.

**plagiarism** *n* hankākancì *m*.

**plague** *n* ànnòbā / àllòbā *f*.

**plain¹** *n* (*open area*) fīlì *m* ⟨aye⟩; on the open ~s à sararin ƙasà.

**plain²** *adj* (*unmarked*) maràs àlāmà *f*.

**plainly** *adv* (*openly*) à fīlì *m*, ɓarō-ɓarò *idph*.

**plaintiff** *n* mài ƙārā *n*, mài kai ƙārā *n*, mài dà'àwā *n*.

**plait** 1. *v* (*hair*) kitsà *v1*, yi kitsò *m*.
2. *n* (*small ~s at one's temple*) taurā *f* ⟨aye⟩.

**plan** 1. *n* a. (*idea*) dàbārā *f* ⟨u⟩: a ~ of escape dàbāȓaȓ gudù. b. (*course of action*)

shirĭ *m*: what are your future ~s? mḕ
kakḕ shirìn yî nân gàba? c. (*arrange-*
*ment*) tsárĭ *m*, shirĭ *m*; draw up a ~
shiryā̀ *v1*, tsārā̀ *v1*. d. (*of a building*)
shācĭ *m*. e. (*design*) fasàlĭ *m*.
2. *v* a. (*prepare*) shiryā̀ *v1*, yi shirĭ
*m*: we are ~ning to leave tomorrow munā̀
shirĭ zā mù tāshì gòbe. b. (*arrange*)
tsārā̀ *v1*: how shall we ~ our work? yā̀yā̀
zā à tsārà aikìnmù? c. ~ ahead (*for the*
*future*) yi tānàdĭ *m*.

plane *n, see* airplane.

planet *n* tàurārò *m*, tàurārùwā *f* ⟨i⟩; (*esp.*
*bright,e.g.* Venus) zā̀ra *f*.

plank *n* kàtākò *m*, filankĭ *m* ⟨ai⟩.

planning *n* tsárĭ *m*, tānàdĭ *m*: due to poor
~, he didn't have enough money sabòdà
rashìn tānàdī, bâ shi dà ìsasshen
kuɗī.

plant[1] *n* (*factory*) masanā'antā *f*, ma'aikatā *f*.

plant[2] 1. *v* shūkà̀ *v1*: they ~ in the rainy
season dà dāminā akàn shūkà̀; ~ out
(*transplant*) dasà̀ *v1*, yi dàshē *m*.
2. *n* shūkà̀ *f* ⟨e²⟩, (*esp. newly sprouted*)
tsirò *m* ⟨e²⟩, tūshĕ *m*.

plantain *n* kàtūwaⓡ àyàbà *f*, àgàdè *f*.

plantation *n* gandū *m* ⟨aye⟩.

plaster 1. *n* a. (*bandaid*) filastā̀ *f*, [F]
ìspāⓡàdàⓡā *f*. b. (*for setting a fracture*)
filastā̀ *f*, [F] hùlātìⓡ *m*: encase a leg
in ~ yi wà kafā̀ shāfen filastā̀. c. (*of*
*building, wall*) yā̀ɓē *m*, shāfē *m*.
2. *v* (*a wall*) yāɓà̀ *v1*, shāfà̀ *v1*.

plasterer *n* mài yā̀ɓē *m*, mài shā̀fē *m*.

plastic *n* (*pliable*) lēdā̀ *f*; (*stiff*) ⓡōbā̀ *f*.

plate[1] *n* fàⓡantĭ *m* ⟨ai⟩.

plate[2] *v* (*a metal*) ɗaurāyē *v4*.

plateau *n* tudù *m* ⟨Cai⟩.

plating *n* (*metal*) ɗaurayĕ *m*.

platform *n* (*esp. in theatre*) dandamàlĭ *m*;
(*built against outer wall of house for sit-*
*ting*) dàkàlĭ *m*.

platter *n* (*mat of coiled basketry*) faifai *m*
⟨a..ai⟩.

play 1. *n* a. (*playing*) wā̀sā *m* ⟨anni⟩. b. (*of*
*theater*) wā̀san kwaikwayō *m*.
2. *v* a. yi wā̀sā *m*; ~ against so. (*Sport*)
karà dà *v1*: our team will ~ against theirs
next week ƙunglyaⓡmù zā tà karà dà
tāsù mākò mài zuwā̀. b. (*an instrument;*
*use v which goes with type of instrument*):
~ a flute būsà sàrēwā *m*; ~ a drum yi
kiɗà̀ *m*.

player *n* a. (*Sport*) ɗan wā̀sā *m*: football ~
ɗan wā̀san ƙwallon kafā̀. b. (*of a musi-*

cal *instrument, use* mài + *name of instru-*
*ment*): the *garaya* ~ mài gàrāyā.

playground *n* fīlin wā̀sā *m*.

playmate *n* àbōkin wā̀sā *m*.

plea *n* rṑkō *m*.

plead *v* (*beg*) rṑkā *v2* ⟨rṑkō⟩; ~ guilty to
the murder yi ìƙìⓡāⓡìn kisàn kâi.

pleasant *adj* (*to the senses*) (mài) dādĭ *m*;
(*esp. of an activity*) (mài) aⓡmashĭ *m*: the
music was ~ kiɗàn yā yi aⓡmashī; (*of*
*personality*) mài fàⓡa'à *n*, mài wàlwàlā
*n*; be ~ to so. bā̀ w. fuskā̀.

please[1] *v* a. ƙāyataⓡ/ƙāwataⓡ (dà) *v5*,
dādàdā wà *v1*, faràntā wà râi: children are eager to ~ their teachers yârā
nā̀ allà-allà sù dādàdā wà màlàmansù;
take whichever one ~s you ɗaùki duk
wandà kakḕ sô; just as you ~ yàddà ka
ga dāmā; he does as he ~s yakàn yi àbîn
dà ya ga dāmā. b. be ~d ji dādĭ *m*, yi
muⓡnā̀ *f*: I'm ~d that they came nā ji
dādin zuwànsù; I am very ~d with your
work nā yi muⓡnā̀ ƙwaⓡai dà aikìnkà.

please[2] *adv* a. (*most polite*) don Allàh (dà
Ànnabìnsà) (+ *subjunct.*): ~ help me
don Allàh kà tàimàkē nì; would you
~ do it at once don Allàh kù yī shì
yànzu-yànzun nàn. b. (*polite request*) sai
(+ *subjunct.*): ~ shut the door sai kà
rufè ƙōfā̀. c. (*inviting so. to do sth.*)
bìsìmillà̀ *excl*: ~ take a seat bìsìmillà̀
gà kujèrā. d. (*showing impatience*) mànà
(*following the v*) : ~ come in and we'll
have a talk shìgō mànà mù yi hīⓡa.

pleasure *n* jîn dādĭ *m*, muⓡnā̀ *f*, nìshādĭ
*m*: feel ~ ji dādī = yi muⓡnā̀; I felt
the greatest ~ when I saw them nā yi
matuƙaⓡ muⓡnā̀ dà na gan sù; give ~
to so. ƙāyataⓡ/ƙāwataⓡ (dà) *v5*: his visit
gave us great ~ zìyāⓡàⓡsà tā ƙāyataⓡ dà
mū.

pleat *n* ninkĭ *m*.

plebiscite *n* ƙùⓡi'àⓡ nēman ⓡa'àyī *f*.

pledge 1. *n* àlkawàⓡĭ *m* ⟨u-a⟩; (*esp. to one-*
*self*) àlwāshĭ *m*.
2. *v* yi àlkawàⓡĭ *m*.

plenary session *n* tàrō mài cìkakken īkò
*m*.

plenty *adj & adv* dà yawà̀, bìⓡjik *idph*,
jìngim *idph*: ~ of people mutànē dà
yawà̀; there's ~ of corn there hatsī yanà
can bìⓡjik; a land of ~ ƙasā mài yàlwā.

pleurisy *n* màɗaukai *m*, masōkìyā *f*.

pliable *adj* (mài) lànƙwàsuwā̀ *f*.

pliers *n* fìlāyà̀ *f* ⟨oCi⟩; [F] pâns *f*; (*of black-*
*smith*) àwāⓡtakĭ / àⓡàutakĭ *m* ⟨ai⟩.

plot[1] 1. n (conspiracy) ƙùllalliyā f, maƙaīƙashìyā f, mākiīcĩ m, jàmhūr̃ũ m, [F] kwàmbîn m: they uncovered a ~ against the governor sun gānō wata maƙaīƙashìyāī̃ dà akè yi wà gwamnà.
2. v haɗa bàkī, gama bàkī, ƙullā v1, yi maƙaīƙashìyā f: they ~ted to swindle him sun ƙullā sù yi masà zàmba; ~ against so. yi wà ƙùllalliyā f, shiryà cùtaī̃ w.; he's ~ting with them bàkinsù à haɗe yakè.

plot[2] n a. (of land) fulōtì m ⟨oCi⟩, fīlī m ⟨aye⟩, fēgì m ⟨una⟩, [F] kàr̃ê m, (small ~ of farmland) gàyaunā f ⟨i⟩. b. (of a story) ƙashī m.

plough, plow 1. n (large hoe) gàr̃mā f ⟨gar̃emanī⟩: ox ~ gàr̃maī̃ shānū.
2. v kaftā v1, yi kàftū m: ~ a farm yi kàftū à gōnā.

pluck[1] v a. (feathers) fīgè v1 ⟨fīgā⟩, cirè v4; ~ out (from a mass) tsāmō v6: he was ~ed out of the water an tsāmō shì dàgà cikin ruwa. b. (an instrument) bugā v1.

pluck[2] n (courage) ƙarfin zūcìyā m.

plug n a. (stopper) murfī m ⟨ai⟩. b. (sparkplug) fulōgì m, [F] bùjî m. c. (electric) kàn làntar̃kì m, [F] fîsh f.

plum n (with black fruit) dinyā f, (with yellow fruit) tsādā f.

plumber n mài aikìn famfò m.

plumbing n aikìn famfò m.

plump adj (mài) ƙibà f.

plunder v wāshè v4.

plunge v: he ~d a knife into her yā sōkà matà wuƙā; ~ into the water yi dàkē à ruwa.

plural adj jam'ì m.

plus prep dà prep: how much is 13 ~ 5? shà ukù dà bìyaī̃ nawà kè nan? 3 ~ 4 equals 7 ukù à tārà dà huɗu bakwài kè nan = in an tārà ukù dà huɗu bakwài kè nan; ~ sign àlāmaī̃ tāràwā f.

ply n (of string, rope) tùfkā f: 2-~ rope igiyà mài tùfkā biyu; 2-~ thread murjì m.

plywood n fale-falen kātākō m.

pneumonia n nàmōnìyā f, (bovine) ràngazā f.

pocket n àljīhū m ⟨una⟩.

pocketbook n (purse) jàkā f ⟨una[2]⟩.

pocketknife n askā f ⟨a-e⟩.

pocket money n gùzurī m.

pockmarks n (from smallpox) zanzanā f; her face is covered with ~ fuskàr̃tà tā yi caka-caka dà zanzanā.

pod n kwànsō m, kwàfsā / kwàsfā f: bean ~s kwàfsaī̃ wākē.

poem n wāƙā f ⟨oCi⟩,

poet n mawāƙī m, shā'ìr̃ī m ⟨ai⟩.

poetry n wāƙā f ⟨oCi⟩; oral ~ wāƙāī̃ bakà; written ~ r̃ubùtacciyaī̃ wāƙā.

point[1] n a. (sharp end) tsìnī m: ~ of a pencil tsìnin fensìī̃. b. (dot on map, in geometry) digò m. c. (significance) manufà f: what is the ~ of that? mēnē nè manufaī̃ wànnan? I didn't get the ~ of what he was saying bàn gānè àbin dà yakè nufì ba. d. (usefulness) fā'idà f: what is the ~ of writing him? he won't reply inā fā'idaī̃ r̃ubùtā masà? bà zâi amsà ba; it is ~ to keep on complaining about it bā fā'idà à dingà kūkansà. e. (of a matter): stick to the ~ tsayà kân bàkā; you should get to the ~ kadà kà yi kwàne-kwàne; from X's ~ of view à ganin X: from my ~ of view, what he did was wrong à ganìnā, àbin dà ya yi kurè nē. f. (in time): reach a ~ kai munzàlī, ìsa munzàlī: they've reached the ~ of not talking to each other sun kai munzàlin bā sà màganà dà jūnā; on the ~ of g̃oshin prep, gàbànnin prep, gab dà prep: he's on the ~ of leaving yanà g̃oshin tāshì = yanà gab dà tāshì; (esp. spontaneous) nà shirì m: he is on the ~ of getting angry yanà shirìn hàsalà. g. (Sport) cî m: they scored 2 ~s sun sàmi cî biyu. h. (mark on a test) mākì m.

point[2] v a. (at so., sth.) nūnà v1: he ~ed his finger at him yā nūnà shi dà yàtsà; ~ out the way nūnà hanyà; ~ out sth. to so. nūsaī̃ (dà) v5: I ~ed out his mistake to him nā nūsaī̃ dà shī kuskurènsà. b. (aim at so.) aunà v1: the hunter ~ed the gun at the warthog mahàr̃bī yā aunà gàdū dà bindigā. c. (at so., sth. with one's lips) yi wà zùndē m.

pointed adj (mài) tsìnī m: a ~ stick sàndā mài tsìnī; a man with a ~ nose mài tsìnin hancì.

pointless adj a. (meaningless) maràs mà'ànā f. b. (useless) maràs àmfànī m.

poise n hankàlī kwànce m.

poison 1. n gubā f; (venom) dafì m; take ~ shā gubā; (fig.) one man's meat is another man's ~ àbincin wani gubàī̃ wani.
2. v a. (so.) bā w. gubā. b. (contaminate) gur̃ɓàtā v1, sâ wà gubā.

poisonous adj (mài) gubā f, (mài) dafì m.

poke v a. (so.) tsōkanā v2, tsòkànē v4: he ~d me in the eye yā tsòkànē nì à ido = yā tsòkànē minì idò; ~ so. hard dàddagà v2. b. (at sth.) tsōkànā v1, ɗōsànā v1: he's poking at the ashes with a stick yanà tsōkànà garwashī dà sàndā; ~ a stick into (*small area, enclosure*) zungùrā *v1*: ~ a stick into a hole zungùrā sàndā à rāmī; ~ a fire (*to make it burn more*) izà wutā.

poker *n* matōnī *m*, matsōkanī *m*.

pole *n* dōguwar̃ sàndā *f*; (*for propelling canoe forward*) gwangwalā *f*; (*forked* ~ *used as support for stall, shed*) dir̃kà *f* ⟨oCi⟩; (*for a shadoof*) jīgò *m*; electric, telegraph ~ tangàr̃āhù *m*, fàlwayà *f*.

pole vault *n* tsallen gwangwalā *m*.

police *n* (*gen'l*) 'yan sàndā *p*, [F] fàlîs *f*; (*municipal*) 'yan dòkā *p*; (*gendarmerie*) [F] jandar̃mà *n*; military ~ kùrfau *n*, [F] fàlîs mìlìtâr̃ *f*; secret ~ 'yan sàndan ciki *p*, sī'aidî *m*; ~ compound bār̃ikì *m*; ~ force kungìyar̃ 'yan sàndā; ~ inspector sùfētò *m*, [F] ànspàktâr̃ *m*.

policeman *n* ɗan sàndā *m*, ɗan dòkā *m*, [F] fàlîs *m* ⟨ai⟩.

police officer *n* (*divisional level*) dīfî'ò *m*.

police station *n* ōfìshin 'yan sàndā *m*, cājì ōfìs *m*, [F] fas dà fàlîs *m*; (*headquarters*) [F] kwàmsàr̃iyà *f*; (*gendarmerie*) [F] jàndàr̃màr̃î *f*.

policy *n* a. (*Pol.*) manufā *f*. b. (*insurance*) takàr̃dar̃ ìnshōr̃à *f*.

polio *n* shān Innà *m*, shânyêwar̃ jìkī *f*.

polish 1. *v* a. (*with oil*) gōgà mâi ⟨gūgà⟩ *f*: ~ a car gōgà mâi à jìkin mōtà. b. (*a metal tool*) wāsà *v1*.
2. mâi *m*: shoe ~ mân tàkàlmī *m*, [F] sìr̃ājì *m*.

polite *adj* (mài) ladàbī *m*, (mài) bìyayyà *f*: be ~ to so. yi wà ladàbī; pretend to be ~ (*fig.*) yi ladàbin kūrā.

political *adj* na sìyāsà *f*: ~ asylum mafakar̃ sìyāsà.

political science *n* ilìmin sìyāsà *m*.

politician *n* ɗan sìyāsà *m*.

politics *n* sìyāsà *f*; cutthroat ~ sìyāsàr̃ kàwō-wuƙà.

poll 1. *v* bincìkè r̃a'àyin jàma'à.
2. *n* (*of opinion*) bìncìken r̃a'àyin jàma'à *m*; (*election place*) wurin jēfà ƙùr̃i'à *m*.

pollen *n* (*of grain, corn*) bunùnī *m*.

pollute *v* gur̃6àtà *v1*, ƙazantar̃ (dà) *v5*: ~ the enviroment gur̃6àtà yanàyin ƙasā; be(come) ~d gur̃6àcè *v4*.

polo *n* ƙwallon dawākī *m*, hōlò *m*.

polyester *n* fōlìyestà *f*.

polygamy *n* auren màcè fìye dà gùdā.

polytechnical college *n* kwalējìn fàsāhà dà sànà'à *m*, [F] lìsê tàknîk *f*.

polytheism *n* shir̃kù *m*.

pomegranate *n* r̃ùmân *m*.

pompous *adj* (mài) fàɗin râi *m*, (mài) girman râi *m*.

pond *n* ɗan tafkī *m* ⟨una, u-a⟩; (*borrowpit*) kùduddufī *m* ⟨ai⟩.

ponder *v* yi tùnànī *m*, yi tsōkàcī *m*, yi zùlùmī *m*.

pony *n* ƙūrù *m* ⟨una⟩.

pool[1] *n* (*body of water*): there are ~s of water everywhere ruwā yanà kwànce kō'ìnā.

pool[2] *n* (*of money*) àdàshi / àdàshe *m*: he paid his contribution to the ~ yā zubà àdàshi.

poor 1. *adj* a. (*psn.*) matàlàucī *m*, (*fig.*) matsìyàcī *m*, (*penniless*) mìskīnī *m* ⟨ai⟩: ~ farmers, countries matàlàutan manòmā, ƙasàshē; the rich and the ~ mawàdàtā da matàlàutā; become ~ zama matàlàucī, talàucē *v4*. b. (*not good*): the soil is ~ ƙasā bâ ta dà àlbar̃kà; the food is ~ ƙasā bâ yå dà kyâu = àbincîn bà na kir̃kì ba nè; his sight is ~ bâ yå ganī sòsai. c. (*unfortunate*): ~ you! kaico! that ~ girl! kaicon yàrinyàr̃ nan!
2. *n* talàkà *n* ⟨awa⟩, matàlàucī *m*, (*pejor.*) matsìyàcī *m*; (*euphem.*) gàjìyayyē *m*.

popcorn *n* guggur̃u *m*.

Pope *n* Pàpàr̃ōmà *m*.

pope's nose *n* (*rump of chicken*) zùmɓūtù *m*.

poplin *n* kòfìlîn *m*: shirts and robes are made from ~ anà taguwōyī dà rīgunà dà kòfìlîn.

popular *adj* (mài) farin jinī *m*, (mài) jinin mutànē: she is ~ with everyone tanà dà farin jinī = tanà dà jinin mutànē; blue is more ~ among Hausas than red wajen Hàusàwā shūdì yā fi jā farin jinī; that singer is ~ and well-liked in Hausaland mawàƙîn nan yanà tàshē wajen Hàusàwā.

popularity *n* farin jinī *m*; (*having* ~, *of psn.*) tàshē *m*: he's at the height of his popularity yanà cikin gàniyàr̃ tàshensà.

population *n* (*human*) yawàn jàma'à *m*: the country with the largest ~ is China ƙasar̃ dà ta fi yawàn jàma'à ita cè ƙasar̃ Sin; the human ~ yawàn bìl-Adamà; ~ control yāƙìn hanà yàɗuwar̃ àl'ummà; ~ explosion ambàliyàr̃ jàma'à.

porcelain *n* (*dishes*) tangar̃an *m* ⟨tangar̃àyē⟩, fàɗi-kà-mutù *m*, [F] kāyan kwabà *m*.

porch *n* rùmfā *f* ⟨una⟩.

porcupine *n* bēguwā *f* ⟨oCi⟩.

pork *n* nāmàn àladè *m*: eating ~ is forbidden in Islam cîn nāmàn àladè hàr̃âm nē à Musuluncî.

**pornography** n bātsa f.

**porridge** n, see mush.

**port** n (harbor) tashàr̃ jirgin ruwa f.

**portable** adj (mài) ɗaukuwā f.

**porter** n ɗan dakō m, ɗan alār̃ò m.

**portion** n (part) kashî m; (share) r̃àbō m.

**portrait** n hòtō m ⟨una⟩.

**pose** v a. (for photograph) shiryà kâi; (disguise oneself) yi sōjàn gōnā: he ~d as a policeman yā yi sōjàn gōnā ya cè shī ɗan sàndā nē. b. ~ a question yi tàmbayà f.

**position** n a. (place) wurī m ⟨aCe⟩: put it back in ~ kà mai dà shī à wurinsà. b. (situation) hālī / hālì m ⟨aye⟩: I am not in a ~ to do that bâ ni dà hālin yîn hakà; in our present ~ à hālìn dà mukè ciki yànzu; an awkward ~ wani irin hālî. c. (job) matsayī m, mùr̃āmî m: he has a low-ranking ~ yanà dà r̃àramin mùr̃āmî; I have a ~ as an accountant matsayīnā àkantà; he has taken over my ~ (temporarily) yā zaunà à matsayīnā, (permanently) yā ɗauki mùr̃āmînā. d. (job opening) gurbìn aikì m. e. (opinion) r̃a'àyī m: what is your ~ on this? mènē nè r̃a'àyinkà gàme dà wannàn?

**positive** adj a. (definite) tàbbàtaccē adj; I am ~ that I saw him nā tabbàtā nā gan shì.

**positively** adv bâ shakkà: it's ~ true gaskiyā nè bâ shakkà.

**possess** v màllakà v2.

**possessions** n dūkìyā f, sāmù m: he has a lot of ~ yanà dà sāmù; lose one's ~ yi hàsār̃àr̃ dūkìyā.

**possessive** adj (Gram.) na màllakà f: ~ pronoun làmīr̃ìn màllakà.

**possible** adj (mài) yìwuwā; be ~ yìwu v7: it is ~ that... mài yìwuwā nè (+ subjunct.)..., yā yìwu...: it is ~ that they will come mài yìwuwā nè sù zō = yanà yìwuwā sù zō = yā yìwu sù zō; I think it is ~ inà tsàmmānî zâi yìwu; it is not ~ bâ yà yìwuwā; come as early, soon as ~ zō dà wurwuri; do it as fast as ~ kà yī shì da sauri-sauri; do as much as you ~ can yi iyā yâddà zā kà iyà.

**possibly** adv I can't ~ go bà zâi yìwu ba ìn tàfi; it may ~ rain wàtàkīlà zā à yi ruwā.

**post¹** 1. v a. (a letter) aikà dà v1, jēfà v1. b. (so. to a job) kai v*: he's been ~ed to Sokoto to teach an kai shì Sakkwato yà yi aikìn màlàntā.
2. n (job, position) mùr̃āmî m, matsayī m.

**post²** 1. n (for tethering) turkè m ⟨a-a⟩; (for fence) tsàr̃nū m/p; (with forked end) dìr̃kà f ⟨oCi⟩.
2. v (put sth. on ~, wall) kafà v1: he ~ed a notice on the wall yā kafà sanâr̃wā à bangō.

**postage** n kuɗin sufùr̃in wàsîr̃ū p.

**postage stamp** n kân-sarkī m, sìtâm m, [F] tambùr̃ m.

**postcard** n kātìn gaisuwā m.

**post mail bag** n (P.M.B.) jàkar̃ gidan wayà f.

**postman** n māsinjàn gidan wayà m.

**postmark** n tambàrin gidan wayà m.

**postmaster** n bàbban àkàwun gidan wayà m.

**post office** n gidan wayà m, [F] fâs f.

**post office box** n (P.O.B.) àkwàtìn gidan wayà m.

**postal order** n fâs-ōdà f, [F] màndâ f.

**postpone** v (esp. meeting, event) ɗagà v1, fàsà v1: the meeting has been ~d for 2 days an ɗagà rānar̃ tàr̃ôn zuwà jìbi; (a matter temporarily) sâ à mālà: let's ~ it for another day mù sâ shi à mālà sai wata rānā.

**postponement** n ɗagàwā f, fāshì m.

**posture** n dirì m: he has good ~ yanà dà kyân dirî.

**pot** n (gen'l, for cooking) tukunyā f ⟨tukwànē⟩; (var. types of clay ~s): (medium, with narrow neck & handle, for water) kulà f; (large, for storing water) r̃àndā f ⟨una⟩; (spherical with narrow neck, for carrying water) tùlū m ⟨una⟩; (large, wide-mouthed) kwàtar̃niyà f ⟨kwàtàr̃nî⟩.

**potash** n kanwā f; (var. types): (used in cooking or for animals) farar̃ kanwā f; (used medicinally) jar̃ kanwā f; (natron) ùngùr̃nu m.

**potassium** n kanwā f.

**potato** n (local, sweet ~) dànkalî m; (Irish) dànkalìn Tùr̃àwā m, [F] kwambitàr̃ m; mashed ~es màrkàɗaɗɗen dànkalî.

**potsherd** n (small) tsìngàr̃ò m, kaskon tukunyā m; (large) kàtangà f ⟨u⟩.

**potter** n mài (ginìn) tukwànē n.

**pottery** n ginìn tukwànē m, kāyan yumɓū m.

**potty** n pô m.

**pouch** n (leather bag of barbers) zàbīr̃à f ⟨u⟩; tobacco ~ 'yar̃ jàkar̃ tābà f.

**pouf** n (stuffed leather cushion) tùntùn / tìntìn m, kushìn m.

**poultice** n shāfî m.

**poultry** *n* (*no gen'l term*); (*chickens*) kàjī *p*: ~ farming kīwòn kàjī.

**pounce on** *v* dirař wà *vdat*: the lion ~d on the gazelle zākī yā dirař wà bàrēwà; (~ & *seize*) faucè / fyaucè *v4*: the cat ~d on the mouse kyânwā tā faucè ɓeřā.

**pound¹** *n* a. (*unit of weight*) wayā *f* ⟨oCi⟩, lābā *f* ⟨oCi⟩: it weighs 3 ~s nauyin wannàn lābā ukù cē. b. (*currency unit*) fâm *m* ⟨Cai⟩.

**pound²** *v* (*to remove*) surfā *v1* ⟨sùrfē⟩, cāsā *v2*; (*final pounding of grain into flour*) dakā *v1* ⟨dakā⟩; (*sth. moist in mortar*) kirɓā *v1*: yams are ~ed to make pounded yams anā kirɓā dōyā tà zama sàkwàrā; ~ corn for pay yi dàkau *m*; ~ing in rotation (*at same mortar or anvil*) lùgùdē *m*.

**pour** *v* zubā *v1*, zùba *v3*; (*a lot of*) kwaràrā *v1*, mākā *v1*: the rain was ~ing down yesterday an mākà ruwā jiyà; the water is ~ing out in quantity ruwā nà kwaràrôwā = ruwā nà zubôwā shā; (*into small opening*) dūrā *v1*; (*in thin stream*) tsìyāyā *v2*: he ~ed a little water from the pot yā tsìyàyi ruwā dàga tùlū; (*quickly out of small opening so it gurgles*) bulbùlā *v1*; ~ out (*any liquid, grain*) zub dà / zubař (dà) *v5*; ~ out (*in drops, e.g. oil*) darsā *v1*, tarfā *v1*.

**pout** *v* zumɓùrà bākī.

**poverty** *n* talaucì *m*, (*pejor.*) tsìyā *f*: in a state of great ~ cikin matuƙař talaucì.

**poverty-stricken** *adj* matàlàucī *adj*.

**powder** 1. *n* a. (*esp. scented*) hōdā *f*; face ~ (*pancake make-up*) fankèkè *m*. b. (*insecticide*) hōdař ƙwārī *f*, [F] hūdìř *m*. c. (*medicinal*) gārī *m*: take the ~ 3 times a day shā wannàn gārin māgànîn sàu ukù à rānā.

2. *v* shāfā wà hōdā.

**power** *n* a. (*control*) īkò *m*: executive ~ īkòn aiwatářwā; he seeks ~ yanà dà sôn īkò; the ones in ~ màsu īkò; have, get ~ over so. màllakà *v2*. b. (*Pol.*) mulkì *m*: come to ~ hau kàřagař mulkì = riƙè ragàmař mulkì. c. (*force, strength*) ƙarfī *m*: be beyond one's ~ fi ƙarfin w., gàgarà *v2*, bùwàyā *v2*. d. (*Relig., of saints*) kàřāmā *f*; miraculous ~ (*of prophets*) mù'ùjizā *f*. e. (*source of energy*) ƙarfī *m*: electrical ~ ƙarfin wutař làntařkì; nuclear ~ ƙarfin nūkìlliyā; there was a ~ cut yesterday jiyà an kashè wutā = jiyà an daukè wutā; ~ plant gidan wutā, [F] (gidan) ìnàřjî.

**powerful** *adj* (mài) īkò *m*, (mài) ƙarfī *m*.

**powerless** *adj* maràs īkò, maràs ƙarfī.

**pox** *n*, see smallpox, chicken pox.

**practical** *adj* (mài) àmfānī *m*.

**practically** *adv* (*nearly*) kusan: we are ~ finished kusan ·mun gamà = mun kusa gamàwā.

**practice** 1. *v* a. (*try*) gwadā *v1*, jařřàbā *v1*. b. (*put into* ~) aikàtā *v1*: ~ the tenets of one's religion aikàtà duk àbîn dà àddīnìn ya umàřtā; they do not ~ what they preach sunà fàdà nè àmmā bā sà aikàtàwā; in ~ à àikàce *adv*. 2. *n* (*Sport*) fařātìs *m*; ~ makes perfect (*fig.*) yâu dà gòbe kā iyà.

**praise** 1. *v* yàbā *v2* ⟨yàbō⟩, yabà wà *v1*: I ~d him nā yàbè shì = nā yabà masà = nā yabà dà shī; I ~d them for their work nā yabà musù aikìnsù = nā yàbē sù sabôdà aikìnsù; God be ~d! àlhamdù lillāhī! 2. *n* yàbō *m*: deserve ~ ìsa yàbō; neither ~ nor blame bâ yàbō bâ fàllasā; self-~ yàbon kâi; ~ be to God! àlhamdù lillāhī!

**praise-epithet** *n* kirārì *m*.

**praise-singer** *n* marõƙī *m*.

**prance** *v* yi tàƙamā *f*.

**prank** *n* bařkwancì *m*, wāsā *m*.

**prattling** *n* (*petty talk*) ɓaɓātū *m*.

**prawn** *n* jàtan landè *m*.

**pray** *v* (*perform one's daily prayers*) yi sallā *f*; (*make a prayer*) yi àddu'à *f*; (*to God*) rōƙā *v2* ⟨rōƙō⟩: he ~ed to God for forgiveness yā rōƙi gāfařā gà Allàh.

**prayer** *n* a. (*obligatory, daily* ~s) sallā *f* ⟨oCi⟩: they are saying their ~s sunà sallā; he has performed the afternoon ~ yā yi sallař là'asàř; say congregational ~s yi sallař jam'ì; Friday congregational ~s sallař Jumma'à; the call for ~ kiràn sallā. b. (*the five* ~s of the day): (*dawn*) àsùbâ *f*; (*ca. 2 pm*) àzahàř *f*; (*ca. 4-5 pm*) là'asàř *f*; (*dusk*) màgàribà / màngàribà *f*, àlmūřù *f*; (*nightfall*) lìshā *f*. c. (*invocation*) àddu'à *f* ⟨oCi⟩: she said a ~ for their safety tā yi musù àddu'à 'Allàh yà kiyàyē'; my ~s have been answered an kàrɓi àddu'àtā.

**prayer beads** *n* càzbī / càřbī *m* ⟨una⟩, (*esp. black wooden beads*) kàřambā *f*.

**prayer grounds** *n* fīlin īdì *m*.

**prayer mat** *n* sùjadā *f*, dàřdūmā *f*, (*of goat or sheep skin, esp. used by Islamic scholars*) būzū *m* ⟨aye⟩.

**praying mantis** *n* ƙōƙì-ƙōƙì *m*, (*term used esp. by children*) dōkìn Allàh *m*.

**preach** *v* yi wa'àzī *m*.

preacher *n* mài wa'àzī *m*; (*Christian*) fàdā *m*.

precaution *n* rìgàkafì *m*: it is best to take ~s (*fig.*) rìgàkafì yā fi māgànī.

precede 1. *vt* (*in time*) a. rìgāyà *v2*, gàbātà *v2*: who ~d the present emir? wà ya rìgàyi sarkī na yànzu hawan sàrautà? 2. *vi* (*of time*) wucè *v4*, shigè *v4*, gàbātà *v3*, gushè *v4*: the months which ~d, the preceding months wàtànnin dà sukà gàbātà = wàtànnin dà sukà wucè.

precedence *n* fīfīkò *m*.

precious *adj* a. (*valuable*) (mài) dařajà *f*. b. (*beloved*) sòyayyē *adj*.

precise *adj* a. (*exact*) daidai *adv*: what are the ~ measurements of the room? nawà nē awòn dākìn daidai? b. (*real, actual*) ainihī *m*, tàkàmaimai *adv*: the ~ cause of the accident ainihin sanàdin hadàřīn = sanàdin tàkàmaimai na hadàřīn.

precisely *adv* tàkàmaimai *adv*: I don't know ~ what his work is bàn san aikìnsà tàkàmaimai ba; how many words ~ are there in this dictionary? kalmōmī nawà nē tàkàmaimai à cikin wannàn kāmùs dîn?

predecessor *n*: he is better than his ~s yā fi wadàndà sukà rìgàyē shì.

predestination *n* kàddarà *f*.

predicament *n* jìdālì *m*, alàkakài *m*: I'm in a ~ inà cikin jìdālì = yā zamè minì alàkakài.

predict *v* tsìnkāyà *v2* ⟨tsìnkāyā⟩ *f*, hangō *v6*: the economists ~ed the inflation masànā tattalin ařzìkîn sun hangō hàuhawàř fàřāshìn kāyā.

prediction *n* tsìnkāyā *f*, hàngē *m*.

predominant *adj*: be ~ fi rìnjāyà: groundnuts are the ~ crop in this region gyàdā tā fi rìnjāyà à yankìn nân.

preface *n* gabātàřwā *f*, mùkaddamà *f*.

prefect *n* (*administrator*) [F] pàřepē *m*; sub~ [F] sūpàřepē *m*.

prefer *v* fi sò: I ~ kolanuts to cigarettes nā fi sòn gōřò dà tābà; Hausas ~ indigo-dyed cloth Hàusàwā sun fi sòn shūnī; would have ~red gwammàcè *v4*: he would have ~red death to prison yā gwammàcè mutuwà dà à daurè shi.

preferable *adj*: it would be ~ to... zâi fi dācèwā ìdan....

preference *n* fīfīkò *m*: show, give ~ to nūnà wà fīfīkò, fīfìtā *v1*: they give ~ to people with experience sunà fīfìtā màsu kwarèwā; have a ~ for fi sò.

prefix *n* zankō *m*, dòriyar-farkō *m*.

pregnant *adj* (mài) cikì *m*: he made her ~ yā yi matà cikì; she is ~ tanà dà cikì = tā dau cikì = mài cikì cē = (*euphem.*) tanà dà jūnā biyu = tanà dà nauyī = (*pejor.*) tā yi cikì.

prejudice *n* nūnà bambancì *m*: there is still a lot of ~ in the world hař yànzu anà nūnà bambancì dà yawà à dūniyà; be ~d against nūnà wà bambancì; race ~ bambancìn launìn fātà.

premature *adj*: ~ baby bàkwàinī *m*.

premier *n* fìřīmiyà *m*, [F] pìřìmař *m*.

preoccupy *v* cī wà râi: the wedding plans are ~ing them these days kwānan nàn shirìn bìkin aurē nà cī musù râi; be preoccupied with sth. shàgalà dà *v3*, shàgàltu dà *v7*: everyone is preoccupied with his own affairs kōwā yā shàgalà dà àbîn dà kè gàbansà.

preparation *n* shirì *m* ⟨shìrye-shìrye⟩.

preparatory school *n*, *see* school.

prepare *v* a. (*make ready*) shiryà *v1*, yi shirì *m*: I am ~d to go nā shiryà = à shìrye nakè; ~ food yi girkì, dafà àbinci; ~ for war jà dàmaràř yākì; ~ for a journey kintsà *v1*: they ~d quickly for the trip nan dà nan sukà kintsà don tàfiyà. b. ~ for the future yi tànàdī *m*. c. (*be alert*): be ~d! look out! kà yi hattařà!

preposition *n* hařàfin bìgirè *m*.

prescribe *v* kayyàdē *v4*: within the ~d time cikin kàyyàdadden lōkàcī.

prescription *n* takàřdař sàyen māgànī *m*.

presence *n* a. (*being at a place*) hàllařà *f*: the ~ of the commissioner at the meeting hàllařař kwàmishinà à tàrōn; in the ~ of gàban *adv*: he was admitted in the ~ of the emir an shigō dà shī gàban sarkī. b. (*of mind*): lose one's ~ of mind dìmàucē *v4*, kìdìmē *v4*. c. (*bearing, charisma*) kwàrjinī *m*.

present[1] *adj & adv* a. (*attending*): be ~ hàllařà *v3*: how many boys were ~? yârā nawà sukà hàllařà? we were all ~ dukànmù mun hàllařà = duk munà wurîn; be ~ at (*esp. a meeting*) hàlařtà *v2*. b. (*of now*) na yànzu, mài cî: the ~ government gwamnatìn yànzu = gwamnatì mài cî; at the ~ time, at ~ kwānan nàn. c. (*Gram.*) mài cî *m*: the ~ tense lōkàcī mài cî.

present[2] 1. *n* (*gift*) kyàutā *f* ⟨uka[2]⟩, (*small*) hasàfī *m*: he gave me a watch as a ~ yā bā nì kyàutař àgōgo; (*souvenir or food brought back from journey*) tsàrabà *f* ⟨oci⟩; (*tip given to bearer of gift*) tukwīcì *m*, cì-gōřò *m*; (*given to street beggars*) dāshì *m*, [F] kàdô *m*.

2. *v* a. bā dà kyàutā: they ~ed a watch to me sun bā nì kyàutaȓ àgōgo. b. (*introduce formally*) gabātaȓ (dà) *v5*, ƙaddamaȓ (dà) *v5*: ~ a paper at a conference ƙaddamaȓ dà takàȓdā à bàbban tāȓō.

**presently** *adv* à yànzu *adv*: he is ~ living in Niamey yanà zàune à Yàmài yànzu.

**preserve** 1. *v* a. (*look after, maintain*) ādànā *v1*, yi ādànī *m*: he knows how to ~ his things yanà dà ādànī. b. (*save from future destruction*) tànadà *v2* ⟨tānàdī⟩: ways to ~ food hanyōyin tànadàȓ àbinci. 2. *n*: game ~ gandun dājì *m*.

**preside** *v* shùgàbantà *v2*.

**president** *n* shùgàbā *m* ⟨anni⟩, [F] gwamnà *m*, [F] fìȓjìdân *m*: ~ of a country shùgàban ƙasā; ~ for life shùgàban dindìndin; ~-elect shùgàba mài jiràn gàdŏ.

**press**[1] *v* a. (*iron clothes*) gōgè *v4*, yi gūgà *f*. b. (*compress*): ~ down, on dannà *v1*: ~ on a handle dannà mariƙī; don't ~ on my wound kadà kì dannà minì ràunī; ~ down gently tausà *v1*; ~ closely together matsà *v1*, matsè *v4*: ~ together to give him room kù matsè kù bā shì wurī; he ~d me against the wall yā matsè ni à bangŏ; (*fig.*) he's ~ed for money yanà cikin matsî = yanà cikin màtsuwā.

**press**[2] *n* a. (*news media*) 'yan jàȓìdū *p*. b. (*for printing*) madàba'ā *f*.

**pressing** *adj* (*urgent*) na gaggāwā *f*: there are some ~ matters àkwai wasu sha'anŏnin gaggāwā.

**pressure** *n* a. (*force*) ƙarfī *m*: air, gas ~ ƙarfin iskà, gâs; check the air ~ of a tire yi wà tāyà gèjî. b. (*influence*) matsî *m*: put ~ on so. matsà wà *v1*, yi wà matsî *m*: he put ~ on us so that we had to finish the work yā matsà manà sai dà mukà gamà aikìn. c. (*tension*) dàmuwā *f*: he is under a lot of ~ yanà cikin dàmuwā; financial ~ matsî *m*: he is under financial ~ yanà cikin matsî.

**pressure lamp** *n* fìtilàȓ ruwā *f*, [F] lampèdâ *f*.

**prestige** *n* (*esp. of psn.*) maȓtabà *f*, daȓajà *f*; (*esp. inspiring respect*) girmā *m*, kwàrjinī *m*.

**prestigious** *adj* (mài) kwàrjinī *m*: the Mercedes is the most prestigious car in Nigeria Maȓsandî ita cè mōtà mafî kwàrjinī à Nìjēȓiyà.

**presume** *v* ɗaukà cêwā: I ~ that he left nā ɗaukà cêwā yā tàshì.

**pretend** *v* nūnà kàmaȓ, yi kàmaȓ, yi w.a. dà gàngan *m*: he ~ed to be sick yā nūnà kàmaȓ bâ shi dà lāfiyà = wai, bâ shi dà lāfiyà; ~ not to hear (*fig.*) yi kûnnen uwaȓ shègū.

**pretentious** *adj* (mài) iyà yî *m*, (mài) sôn nūnà gwànintà; be ~ nūnà iyà yî = yi iyà yî.

**pretext** *n* uzùȓî *m*, hujjà *f* ⟨oCi⟩.

**pretty** *adj* kyàkkyāwā *adj*, (mài) kyâu *m*.

**prevail** *v* (*exist*) sàmu *v7*: peace ~ed over the country zaman lāfiyà yā sàmu à ƙasaȓ.

**prevailing** *adj*: the ~ wind iskà wâddà ta fi sàmuwā.

**prevalent** *adj*: bribery has become ~ bā dà ȓashawā yā zama ruwan dare = ȓashawā yā zaunà dà gìndinsà.

**prevent** *v* hanà *v1*: the wind ~ed us from going out iskà tā hanà mu fìtā.

**prevention** *n* (*precaution*) rìgàkafì *m*; (*fig.*) an ounce of ~ is worth a pound of cure rìgàkafì yā fi māgànî.

**previous** *adj* a. (*preceding*) wàndà ya gàbātà, wàndà ya shigè, wàndà ya wucè: the ~ week mākòn dà ya gàbātà. b. (*former*) na dâ: the ~ president shùgàbā na dâ.

**previously** *adv* (*earlier*) dâ *adv*.

**prey** 1. *n* kāmù *m*. 2. *v* (*by hovering*) yi jēwā *f*.

**price** *n* a. kuɗī *m/p*, fàȓāshì *m*: the ~ is too high kuɗîn sun yi yawà; name a ~! (*in bargaining*) kà tayà! please reduce the ~ for me don Allàh kà yi minì rangwamè; name me a good ~ and I'll sell it to you kà sàyā dà daȓajà ìn sayaȓ makà; the ~ seems reasonable gà àlāmà fàȓāshìnsà yā yi; that is a good ~ for it ai wannàn kuɗinsà nè; agree on a ~ (*by seller*) sallàmā *v1*; set the ~ of sth. yankà wà w.a. kuɗī; sell it at a reduced ~ sai dà shī dà ȓahamà. b. (*fig.*): you will pay the ~ for your dissolute ways zā kà yi nàdāmā sabòdà fāsiƙancìn dà kakè yî.

**prick** *v* sōkè *v4*: I ~ed myself with a needle nā sōkè dà àllūȓà.

**prickly** *adj* (mài) ƙayà *f*: the hedgehog's coat is ~ fātaȓ būshiyā nà dà ƙayà.

**pride** *n* a. (*arrogance*) jî-jî dà kâi *m*, girman kâi *m*, dàgāwā *f*. b. (*satisfaction*) àlfahàȓî / fahàȓî *m*, jîn kâi *m*.

**priest** *n* (*Christian*) fàdā *m*; [F] àlmàsīhù *n*.

**primarily** *adv* yawancī *m*: he deals ~ in printed cotton goods yawancī cìnikinsà na atamfōfī nè.

primary *adj* bàbba *adj* ⟨mânyà⟩: the ~ reason is... bàbban dàlīlī shī nè....

primary school *n, see* school.

prime *n* (*acme*) gāniyà *f*: he is in the ~ of his youth yanà gāniyàř ƙùrùciyařsà; be in one's ~ nà shā biyu: they are in their ~ sunà shā biyunsù.

prime minister *n* fiřāyìm ministà *m*, [F] pařam ministà *m*.

primer *n* (*school*) littāfìn kòyō na farkō *m*.

primitive *adj* (*psn.*) (mài) duhùn kâi *m*.

prince *n* ɗan sarkī *m*; (*trad. title*) yàřīmà *m*, ciřòmà *m*, mainà *m*.

princess *n* gimbìyā *f*, (*trad. title*) mairàmā *f*.

principal 1. *n* (*school*) shùgàban makařantà *m*, hèdìmastà *m*, [F] dìřàktàř *m*; (*of girls' school*) shùgàbař makařantař 'yammātà *f*, [F] dìřàktìřîs *f*.
2. *adj* bàbba *adj* ⟨mânyà⟩: my ~ reason bàbban dàlīlīnā.

principle *n* a. (*law*) ƙā'idà *f* ⟨oCi⟩. b. (*moral belief, value*) àƙīdà *f*: he is a man of high ~s mùtûm nē mài àƙīdà. c. (*philosophical ~ in life*) manufā *f* ⟨oCi⟩, àlƙiblà *f*.

print 1. *v* (*a book, newspaper, photo*) bugà *v1*; (*a photo from a negative*) wankè *v4*.
2. *n* a. (*writing done by machine*) řùbùtun bugùn ƙūsà *m*. b. (*of a photograph*) hòtō *m* ⟨una⟩, kātì *m*: I want 2 ~s of this à wankè minì kātì biyu ɗin wannàn.

printer *n* (*of books*) mài bugà lìttàttàfai *n*; (*of stationery*) mài bugà tàkàřdū *n*.

printing press *n* madāba'à *f*.

prior to *prep* gàbànnin *prep*, kàfìn *prep*, gòshin *prep*: ~ to my trip gàbànnin tàfiyàtā.

priority *n* fīfīkò *m*: give ~ to bā dà fīfīkò gà.

prison *n* kûřkukù *m*, gidan yārì *m*, gidan sarƙā *m*, jàřun *m*, [F] kasò *m*: he spent 6 months in ~ yā yi watà shidà à kûřkukù.

prisoner *n* fuřsùnà *m* ⟨oCi⟩, [F] ɗan kasò *m*, ɗan jàřun *m*, (*esp. in pl*) 'yan kûřkukù *p*; take so. ~ kai w. kûřkukù; an escaped ~ gùdajjen fuřsùnà; ~ of war fuřsùnàn yāƙì.

private[1] *adj* a. (*non-govermental*) mài zaman kânsà: a ~ hospital asìbitì mài zaman kânsà; the ~ sector kamfanōnī màsu zaman kânsù. b. (*personal*) in ~, ~ly à kêɓe *adv*, à kàɗaice *adv*, à àsìřce *adv*.

private[2] *n* (*Mil.*) fařābitì *m*, [F] fařmankalāshì *m*.

privilege *n* gātancì *m*.

prize 1. *n* lambàř girmā *f*: the Nobel prize lambàř girmā ta Nobel; win, get first ~ ci, yi làmbàwân, [F] ci fařmâl: his cattle took first ~ shānunsà sun yi làmbàwân; win ~ money (*in a contest*) ci kuɗin gàsā.
2. *v* dařajàntā *v1*.

probable *adj* (mài) yìwuwā; be ~ yìwu *v7*: it is ~ mài yìwuwā nè = yā yìwu.

probably *adv* wàtàƙīlà / wàtàkīlà / kīlà, hàlà mā *adv*: he'll ~ come hàlà mā zâi zō.

problem *n* a. màtsalà *f* ⟨oCi⟩, àbin dàmuwā *m*: a ~ problem bàbbař màtsalà; it's a ~ of money màtsalàř ta kuɗī cè; there is a ~ with your plan àkwai màtsalà à dàbāřàřkà; no ~! bâ dàmuwā! = bâ kōmē! b. (*fuss, uproar*) rìgimà *f*: what's the ~? mènè nè asalin rìgimà? c. (*in school*) aikì *m* ⟨ayyukà⟩.

procedure *n* hanyà *f* ⟨oCi⟩.

proceed *v* a. (*continue on*) ci gàba: the work is ~ing as planned aikìn yanà cî gàba kàmař yàddà ya kàmātà. b. (*begin & continue*) yi ta: they egged me on so I ~ed to beat him up sun zugà ni hař ìn yi ta dūkànsà.

process[1] *n* hanyà *f* ⟨oCi⟩: we have a new ~ for making it munà dà sābuwař hanyàř yînsà; in the ~ of gàrin (+ *vbl. n*): in the ~ of cooking, her dress caught on fire gàrin girkì, rìgařtà tā kāmà wutā.

process[2] *v* (*raw materials*) sařřàfā *v1*.

procession *n* tàwagà *f*, jērìn gwànō *m*; Sallah ~ hawan Sallà *m*.

proclaim *v* a. (*announce*) yi shèlà *f*, shèlàntā *v1*, ayyànā *v1*: ~ a holiday ayyànà rānař hūtū.

proclamation *n* shèlà *f*, yēkùwā *f*.

procrastinate *v* yi shìrīrìtā *f*, (*by dawdling*) shantàkē *v4*: stop procrastinating and finish up your work kà bař shantàkêwā, kà ƙàràsà aikìnkà.

procrastination *n* shìrīrìtā *f*.

procurer *n* (*pimp*) kàwālì *m* ⟨ai⟩.

prod *v* (*so.*) tsòkanà *v2*, tsòkànē *v4*, tsōnè *v4*; (*sth.*) tsòkànā *v1*, zungùrā *v1*; *see* poke.

prodigal *adj* àlmùbazzàřī / mùbazzàřī *m* ⟨ai⟩.

produce[1] *v* a. (*make*) yi *v0*: kerosene is ~d from petroleum anà yîn kànànzîř dà ɗanyen mâi. b. (*cause*) haifař (dà) *v5*: drought ~s hunger and disease fařī nà haifař dà yunwà dà cūtā. c. (*grow*) shūkà *v1*: they ~ cotton sunà shūkà

audùgā. d. (*manufacture*) ƙērā v1 ⟨ƙīrā⟩
f.

produce[2] n (*farm*) kāyan làmbū m.

product n (*manufactured*) samfùr̃ m ⟨oCi⟩:
a new ∼ sābon samfùr̃ = sābuwar̃ fitôwā
= sābuwar̃ shìgā.

productive adj (mài) àlbar̃kà f.

profanity n àshār̃ m, àshār̃iyà f: use ∼ yi
àshār̃.

profession n sànā'à f ⟨oCi⟩.

professor n (*term of addr. or ref.*) fàr̃fēsà
/ fùr̃ōfēsà n, [F] fàr̃fàsâr̃ n, shēhùn
mālàmī m.

proficiency n gwànintà f, ƙwarèwā f,
nàƙaltà f.

proficient adj (*psn.*) gwànī m ⟨aye⟩; be ∼
in a language iyà harshè.

profit 1. n r̃ībà f ⟨oCi⟩: he's only interested
in ∼ yā fi dàmuwā dà r̃ībà; make a ∼
from the sale of sth. ci r̃ībà ta wajen sai
dà w.a.
2. v a. (*make money*) ci r̃ībà f. b. (*benefit*) àmfānà v3; ∼ from, by àmfānà v2:
I ∼ed from your advice shāwar̃àr̃kà tā
àmfānē nì.

profitable adj (mài) r̃ībà f, (mài) àmfànī
m.

profiteer n mài cîn r̃ībà n.

profligacy n māshā'à f.

profligate adj fāsìƙī m ⟨u⟩.

profound adj (mài) zurfī m: he has ∼
knowledge zurfin ilìmī gàrē shì.

profusely adv (*often expr. by pluract. verbs
or specialized verbs which indicate 'doing a
lot of sth.'*): he insulted us ∼ yā ɗuɗɗùr̃ā
manà zāgì; he thanked us ∼ yā yi manà
gòdiyā sòsai.

profusion n: in ∼ caka-caka idph: the pimples came out in ∼ ƙuràjē sun fitō caka-
caka.

program 1. n a. (*of events*) shìrye-shìrye
p: radio, TV ∼ shìrye-shìryen r̃ēdiyò,
talàbijìn; (*printed ∼*) takàr̃dar̃ shirì
f. b. (*plan*) shirì m, tsārì m.
2. v shiryà v1, tsārà v1.

progress 1. n cî-gàba m: the country has
made a lot of ∼ ƙasar̃ tā sàmi cî-gàba
sòsai; ∼ is only possible with hard work
cî-gàba sai dà aikì tuƙùru; has he
made good ∼? yā ci gàba nè? make little
or no ∼ yi kwàn-gàba kwàn-bāya; in ∼
cikin yî.
2. v ci gàba; ∼ slowly (*fig.*) yi tàfiyàr̃
kūrā, yi tàfiyàr̃ hàwainìyā.

progressive n & adj (*Pol.*) (mài) r̃a'ayin
à-ci-gàba m, (mài) nēman sauyì m.

prohibit v hanà v1; (*Relig.*) har̃àmtā v1:
usury is ∼ed in Islam an har̃àmtà r̃ība
à Musuluncì.

prohibition n hanì m, hàr̃ām m.

project[1] n aikì m ⟨ayyukà⟩, shirì
m ⟨shìrye-shìrye⟩; research ∼ aikìn
bìncìkè m; (*plan*) tsārì m.

project[2] v (*protrude*) gōtà v1: the gutter ∼s
out over the wall ìndar̃ar̃ō yā gōtà gàr̃ū.

projectionist n (*movie*) àfàr̃ētà n, [F] mài
bugà sìlìmā n.

proleteriat n talakāwā p.

proliferate v yàɗu v7, bàzu v7, yàwaità v3;
nuclear proliferation yàɗuwar̃ nūkìliyà;
(*of germs*) hàyàyyafà v3.

prolong v tsawàità v1: he ∼ed his stay yā
tsawàità zamansà; may God ∼ their lives
Allàh yà tsawàità musù râi.

prominent adj (*psn.*) màshàhūr̃ì m, shàhà-
r̃àr̃r̃ē adj, sànannē adj.

promise 1. n a. àlkawàr̃ī m ⟨u-a⟩:
make, keep, break a ∼ yi, cikà, sāɓà
àlkawàr̃ī; (*esp. to self to accomplish sth.*)
àlwāshì m: I ∼d myself I would do it today nā ci àlwāshī zân yī shì yâu. b.
(*involving time, deadline*) wa'àdī m.
2. v yi àlkawàr̃ī m, yi wa'àdī m: he ∼d
me he would pay me by next week yā yi
minì wa'àdī zāi biyā nì màkō mài zuwà.

promote v a. (*so. in job*) ƙārà wà girmā,
ciyar̃ dà w. gàba. b. (*develop*) bunƙàsā
v1, kyautàtā v1, ciyar̃ dà w.a. gàba:
∼ the use of Hausa kyautàtā àmfànī dà
harshèn Hausa. c. (*Econ., a product*) yi
kiràn kàsuwā.

promotion n (*in a job*) ƙārìn girmā m, cî-
gàba m.

prompt adj (mài) saurī m.

promptly adv dà saurī.

pronoun n wàkīlìn sūnā m, làmīr̃ì m.

pronounce v fàɗā / faɗì v2*: please tell
me how to ∼ this word sai kà gayà
minì yàddà akè fàɗar̃ wannàn kalmà;
he doesn't ∼ it correctly lafàzinsà bà
daidai ba.

pronunciation n a. lafàzī m, nuɗùr̃ī m.
b. (*accent, dialectal*) karìn harshè m.

proof n a. (*Law*) shaidà f, hujjà f: establish
∼ kafà hujjà; burden of ∼ nauyin wankè
kâi; the burden of ∼ is on you nauyin
wankè kânkà yanà wajenkà. b. (*experiment*) gwajì m.

prop 1. n madōgarì m, madōgarà f, matōkarī
m.
2. v tōkàrā v1, tōkàrē v4, jingìnā v1: I
∼ped the stick against the wall nā tōkàrà

sàndā à jìkin bangō; she ~ped the window open with a stick tā tōkàrè tāgà dà sàndā.

**propaganda** n fùřòfàgandà / fàřfàgandà f, [F] fàřfàgandì f.

**propel** v tafiyař dà w.a. gàba.

**propeller** n fàřfēlà f ⟨oCi⟩, [F] fâlfēlà f.

**proper** adj a. (correct) daidai adv: that is not the ~ way to do it wannàn bà hanyàř daidai ba nè. b. (appropriate): do the ~ thing yi àbîn dà ya dācè; you didn't do the ~ thing àbin dà ka yi bài càncantà ba; wait for the ~ time dàkàtā hař lōkàcîn dà ya dācè.

**property** n (total wealth) dūkìyā f, (excluding money) kadařà f; (one's possessions) mallàkī m.

**prophecy** n dūbā m.

**prophet** n ànnabì m ⟨awa⟩; the P. Mohammed, may the peace and blessings of God be upon him Ànnabì Mùhammadù, Tsīrā dà Amincìn Allàh sù tàbbatà à gàrē shì; traditions about the P. Mohammed hàdīsì m.

**propitious** adj: at the ~ moment à kân karì.

**proportion** n a. gwařgwadō m; in ~ to gwařgwadon: they are taxed in ~ to their wealth anà sà musù hařājì gwařgwadon ařzìkinsù; you will be paid ~ately zā à biyā kù gwařgwadō. b. (ratio) ràbo m: the ~ of men to women ràbon mazā dà na mātā.

**proposal** n shāwařà f ⟨shāwàřwařī⟩, bàtū m ⟨uwa²⟩: present, put forth a ~ ḳaddamař dà shāwařà.

**propose** v shāwàřtā v1.

**proposition** n shāwařà f ⟨shāwàřwařī⟩.

**proprietor** n mài (+ n): ~ of the store mài kàntī.

**propriety** n: sense of ~ kunyà f, dà'à f, sanìn yā kàmātà m; go beyond the bounds of ~ (fig.) wucè gōnā dà irì = shigè makàdī dà rawā.

**prose** n zùbē m.

**prosecute** v yi wà shàri'à f; prosecuting attorney lauyàn gwamnatì.

**prosody** n ilìmin karì m.

**prosper** v yi àlbařkà f, nì'imtà v3; (in commerce) yi būdì m: may God let us ~ Allàh yà yi manà būdì!

**prosperity** n àlbařkà f, ni'imà f, ařzìkī m.

**prostitute** n kářùwà f ⟨ai⟩, (euphem.) magājìyā f, màcè mài zaman kàntà f, kilākì f ⟨ai⟩.

**prostitution** n kářuwancì m.

**prostration** n (Relig.) sùjadà f.

**protect** v a. (shield) kārè v4, kiyàyē v4: the country prepared to ~ itself from attack ḳasář tā shiryà kārè kàntà dàgà harì; may God ~ us from danger Allàh yà kiyàyè hadàrì. b. (defend) tsarè v4: ~ national boundaries tsarè iyàkař ḳasā. c. (save against future destruction) tànadà v2 ⟨tānàdī⟩: rare animals are ~ed in game parks anà tānàdin nàdìřan dabbōbī à gandun dājì.

**protection** n tsàrō m, kāriyā f.

**protectorate** n ḳasař riḳòn àmānà f: that country is a British ~ ḳasář nan tanà ḳàřḳashin riḳòn àmānař Ingìlà.

**protein** n fuřōtìn m.

**pro tem** adj (Pol.) na wucìn gàdì: president ~ shùgàban wucìn gàdì.

**protest** 1. n ḳārā f, rashìn yàřdā m; (organized) zàngà-zangà f. 2. v. yi ḳārā f, nūnà rashìn yàřdā.

**Protestant** n ɗan dàřīḳař fùřōtestàn m.

**protrude** v tūrō v6: his stomach ~d cikìnsà yā tūrō.

**proud** adj a. (arrogant) (mài) girman kâi m, (mài) jī-jī dà kâi m, (mài) dàgàwà f. b. (positive) (mài) àlfahàřī / fahàřī m, kīshì m; be ~ of yi àlfahàřī dà, jī dà: he is ~ of his country yanà àlfahàřī dà ḳasařsù; he is ~ of his son, his strength yanà jî dà ɗansà, ḳarfinsà; they are very ~ of their newspaper sunà matuḳař kīshìn jàřidàřsù; a ~ nation àl'ummà mài fahàřī dà kàntà. c. (important) (mài) àlfařmà f: it was a ~ day for us rānā cè mài àlfařmā gàrē mù.

**prove** v (verify) tabbatař (dà) v5, haḳīḳàntà v1: they didn't give him a chance to ~ his innocence bà sù bā shì dāmař haḳīḳàntà rashìn lâifinsà ba; be ~d true tàbbatà v3: the crime of which he has been accused has ~d to be false lâifin dà akè tùhumàřsà dà shī bài tàbbatà ba; ~ oneself innocent wankè kâi.

**proverb** n karìn màganà m ⟨karìn màgàngànū⟩.

**provide** v a. (supply sth.) sāmař (dà) v5: ~ equipment sāmař dà kāyan aikì; (supply so.) sāmà wà v1: ~ the village with electricity sāmař wà ḳauyèn wutà = sāmař dà wutā à ḳauyèn; ~ for the future yi tànàdī m; ~ for one's family riḳè ìyālì. b. ~d that ìdan conj, muddìn / muddař conj: you will get some ~ that you come early zā kù sāmù muddìn kā zō dà wuri; matsawař conj (+ neg.): ~ that he doesn't return late, we'll wait for him matsawař bài dāwō à màkàre ba, zā mù jirā shì.

providence n (Relig.) ƙaddařàř Allàh f, ìkòn Allàh m.

province n lařdì m ⟨una⟩.

provisional adj (Pol.): ~ government gwamnatìn wucìn gādì.

provisions n (for a journey) gùzurī m.

proviso n shařàdī m ⟨u-a⟩.

provocation n tsòkanà f.

provoke v a. (make angry) tsòkanà v2: if you ~ him, he'll bite ìdan kā tsòkànē shì, zâi cìjē kà. b. (cause) tàkalà v2: he ~d a fight yā tākalō fadà.

prudence n hankàlī m.

prune v ƙundùmē v4.

pry off v tāɓè v4.

psalms n zàbūřà f.

pseudonym n sūnan iskà m, sūnan ƙaryā m.

psychiatrist n likitàn tàɓàɓɓū m.

psychiatry n ilìmin hālin tàɓàɓɓū m.

psychologist n masànin hālin ɗan Adàm m.

psychology n ilìmin hālin ɗan Adàm m.

puberty n bàlagà f; reach ~ bàlagà v3; the girl has reached ~ (fig.) yārinyà tā ƙōsà.

pubic hair n zāzā f, (euphem.) gāshìn gàbā m.

public 1. n jàma'à f/p: in ~ à idòn jàma'à, à bainàl jàma'à, gàban mutànē: you shouldn't do that in ~ kadà kà yi hakà gàban mutànē.
2. adj na jàma'à f, na mutànē dukà; ~ opinion idòn jàma'à = řa'àyin jàma'à; for the ~ good don àmfànin jàma'à; a ~ servant ma'àikàcin hùkūmà = ma'àikàcin gwamnatì; ~ holiday rānař hūtū f; mold ~ opinion wāyař dà kân jàma'à; have ~ relations ƙullà zumuncìn jàma'à = yi huldà dà jàma'à; make sth. ~ (e.g. news) bayyànà v1: news of his death was not made ~ until 3 days later bà à bayyànà làbāřin ràsuwařsà sai bāyan kwānā ukù.

publication n ɗab'ì m.

publicity n (advertising) tàllà m.

publicize v ruwàità làbāřì.

publicly adv à idòn jàma'à, à bainàl jàma'à: he was ~ humiliated an ci mutuncinsà à bainàl jàma'à.

publish v (by publisher) bugà v1: the newspaper is ~ed 3 times a week anà bugà jàřìdà sàu ukù à sātī; (by author) wallàfā v1: he has ~ed many stories yā wallàfà làbàřai dà yawà.

publisher n maɗàba'à f, kamfànin bugà lìttàttàfai.

puddle n: there were many ~s ruwā yā kwàntā kō'ìnā.

puff adder n kāsā f.

pull v a. jā v0: ~ a cart, plow ja kūrā, gàřmā; ~ the rope some more kù ƙārà jàn igiyà. b. (var. v + adv/prep uses): ~ back (yank) fizgè v4: he caught hold of her hand but she ~ed it back yā kāmà hannuntà àmmā tā fizgè; ~ down (demolish) rūshè v4; ~ off to side of road rātsè dàgà hanyà; ~ off (leaves, feathers) tsìgè v4; ~ sth. off, out of (an enclosed place) zārō v6: ~ a book off the shelf zārō littàfì dàgà kantà; ~ a sword out (of its sheath) zārō takòbī; ~ sth. out (of narrow opening) sàkatà v2: he ~ed out the trouser string yā sākatō mazāgī; ~ out cirè v4: she ~ed the thorn out of my finger tā cirè minì ƙayà à yātsà; ~ up (grass) tūgè v4: they are ~ing up the weeds sunà tūgè cìyàyī.

pullet n sàgarà f, zàkarà m ⟨u⟩.

pulley n kūrā f.

pullover n rìgař sanyī f, sùwaità f.

pulp n tōtùwā f.

pulpit n mumbàřì m.

pulse n bugùn jinī m: take so.'s ~ aunà bugùn jinī.

pulverize v muřtsùkē v4.

pump 1. n famfò m ⟨una⟩.
2. v bā dà iskà.

pumpkin n (vegetable) kàbēwà f ⟨i⟩; (gourd) dumā m ⟨aCe⟩.

punch[1] 1. v (pierce with instrument) hūdà v1, yi hūjì m.
2. n mahūjī m, madōshì m.

punch[2] 1. v (hit with fist) nàusā v2.
2. n naushì m: I gave him a ~ in the nose nā kai masà naushì à hancì.

punctuation n alāmōmin řùbùtū p.

puncture 1. n (of tire) fācì m, fancà f: the tire has a ~ tāyà tā yi fancà.
2. v hūdà v1; (of tire) yi fancà f.

punish v hòrā v2, yi wà hòrō m: be ~ed for sth. evil yi wà hòrō sabòdà mūgùn aikì; (Law) hukùntā v1: he was ~ed for his crime an hukùntā shi sabòdà làifìn dà ya yi.

punishment n hòrō m; (Law) hukuncì m: capital ~ hukuncìn kisà; (as prescribed in the Koran) haddì m.

pupil[1] n ɗan makařantà m ⟨'yan makařantà⟩; (of Koranic school) àlmājìřī m ⟨ai⟩.

pupil[2] (of eye) ƙwàyař idò f.

puppet n a. (doll) 'yař tsana f. b. (Pol., fig.) ɗan bařàndà m; a ~ government mulkìn jě-ka-nā-yī-kà.

**puppy** *n* kwīkwiyŏ *m*.

**purchase** 1. *v* sàyā *v2* ⟨sàyē⟩.
2. *n*: ∼s sàye-sàye *p*, sàyayyà *f*.

**purdah** *n* kùllē *m*, tsarī *m*: women are kept in ∼ mātā sunā kùllē; she is kept in ∼ màtař kùllē cě = màtař tsarī cē; he doesn't keep his wife in ∼ bā yà kùllē.

**pure** *adj & adv* a. (*genuine, unalloyed*) tsantsā *adv*, zallā *adv*, gangàriyà *f*: it is of ∼ gold na zīnāřîyà cě zallā = na zīnāřîyà cě gangàriyàřtà; he speaks ∼ Hausa yanà màganà dà Hausa gangàriyà. b. (*clean*) (mài) tsabtà *f*, tsàbtàtaccē *adj*: is this water ∼? wannàn ruwā mài tsabtà nē? a ∼ person sālìhī *m*. c. (*Relig.*) (mài) tsarkī *m*, tsàrkàkakkē *adj*.

**puree** 1. *v* màrkàɗē *v1*.
2. *n* màrkàɗē *m*; ∼d potatoes màrkàɗaɗɗen dànkalì; tomato ∼ tùmātìřin gwang-wanī.

**purely** *adv* zallā *adv*.

**purgative** *n* māgànin wankè cikī *m*.

**purify** *v* tsabtàcē *v4*, tsarkàkē *v4*.

**purity** *n* tsarkī *m*.

**purple** *n* (*reddish, plum-like*) algàshī *m*.

**purpose** *n* a. (*basic objective*) màɍàsūdī *m*: his ∼ is to continue his studies màɍàsūdìnsà shī ně yà ci gàba dà kàřātū. b. (*meaning*) nufī *m*, niyyà *f*: what is the ∼ of his visit? měnē ně niyyař zìyāřàřsà? on ∼ dà gàngan, dà niyyà: she didn't do it on ∼ bà dà gàngan ta yī shì ba; for no other ∼ than... bà don wani àbù ba sai...; for the sole ∼ of tàkàmaimai *adv*: I've come to this place for the sole ∼ of seeing him nā zō nân wajēn tàkàmaimai sabŏdà ìn gan shì; to no ∼ à karìn banzā. c. (*underlying significance*) manufà *f*: the ∼ of life man-ufař ràyuwā.

**purposely** *adv* dà gàngan *adv*, à sàne *adv*: he ∼ made it look like a accident dà gàngan ya mai dà shī yà zama kàmař haɗàřī.

**purr** *v* yi gùřnànī *m*.

**purse**¹ *n* (*women's*) jàkā *f* ⟨una²⟩; (*small, for change*) cìkā-kà-yař *f*.

**purse**² *v*: ∼ one's lips tsūkè bàkī.

**pursue** *v* (*chase*) fàfarà *v2*.

**pus** *n* mūgunyà *f*; (*with blood*) sùrkāmī *m*.

**push** 1. *v* (*sth.*) tūrà *v1*; (*so.*) tūrè *v4*; ∼ one's way through a crowd kūtsà cikin mutànē; ∼ sth. aside, over tunkùɗà *v1*: he ∼ed the chair aside yā tunkùɗà kujèrā; ∼ sth. away bangàjē *v4*: I ∼ed the door open with my foot nā bangàjè ƙōfà dà

ƙafā; ∼ sth., so. forward hankàɗā *v1*; ∼ sth. over tunkùɗē *v4*; ∼ up (*one's sleeves, trousers*) naɗè *v4*; ∼ up (*of plants through ground*) bunƙùsā *v1*.
2. *n* tūrà *f*. (*fig.*) when ∼ comes to shove tūrā tā kai bangō.

**pushy** *adj*: be ∼ ( *esp. by children*) yi gîggīwà *f*, nūnà iyà yî *m*.

**put** *v* a. sâ / sakà / sânyā *v1*: ∼ the chair near the window sâ kujèrā kusa dà tāgà; ∼ salt in the sauce sâ gishirī cikin miyà; ∼ a child in school sâ yārŏ makařantā; we ∼ our trust in God mun dŏgarà dà Allàh. b. (*var. v + adv/prep uses*): ∼ sth. aside (*to one side*) ajìyē *v4*; ∼ aside sth. for the moment (*postpone*) sâ à mālà: let's ∼ aside these questions for the moment mù sâ waɗannàn tambayōyī à mālà; ∼ sth. around so.'s shoulder yàfā *v1*: she ∼ a wrap around his shoulders tà yàfà masà mayāfī; ∼ sth. away (*store in safe place*) ādànā *v1*; ∼ sth. back (*return*) mai dà / mayař (dà) *v5*; ∼ sth. down ajìyē *v4*; ∼ so. down (*belittle*) ci wà zařàfī, ci zařàfin w.: he ∼ her down because of her mistake yā ci zařàfintà sabŏdà kuskurèn dà ta yi; he is always ∼ting other people down cîn zařàfī gàre shì; ∼ down a riot kwantař dà tàřzŏmā; ∼ an end to a matter mântā dà màganà; ∼ so. in prison ɗaurè *v4*; ∼ off sth. (*postpone event*) fāsà *v1*: I shall ∼ off my journey till next week zân fāsà tàfiyàtā sai màkŏ mài zuwà; don't ∼ off till tomorrow what you can do today (*fig.*) fāshì ɓařnař aikì; ∼ on clothes sâ/sânyà tufāfī; ∼ on a necklace ɗaurà sarƙà à wuyà; ∼ sth. on top of sth. ɗŏrà à kân: she ∼ the box on top of the bed tā ɗŏrà àkwàtì à kân gadō; ∼ out the light kashè fìtilà; ∼ sth. with sth. haɗà *v1*: ∼ this box with the others kà haɗà àkwàtìn nân dà saurân.

**putrefy** *v* ruɓař (dà) *v5*; become putrefied rùɓa *v3*.

**putty** *n* fŏtî *m*.

**puzzle** 1. *n* ɗaurìn gwařmai *m*.
2. *v* rūɗè *v4*, rūɗař (dà) *v5*, rikitař (dà) *v5*, ɗaurè wà kâi: his action ∼d me àbîn dà ya yi yā ɗaurè minì kâi.

**puzzling** *adj* mài rūɗàřwā, mài rikitàřwā, mài ɗaurè kâi.

**pygmy** *n* wàdā *n*.

**pyjamas** *n* kāyan barcī *m*.

**pyramid** *n*: the groundnut ∼s in Kano were famous dà dàlař gyàɗā à Kanŏ shàhàřařřiyà cè.

**python** *n* mēsà *f* ⟨oCi⟩.

# Q

quack[1] n kūkan àgwàgwā m.

quack[2] n (doctor) likitàn ƙaryā m.

quadruple v riɓà sàu huɗu.

quail n (bird) ɓarɓar̃wā f.

quaint adj bàƙauyè adj: a ~ custom bàƙauyìyar̃ àl'ādà.

quake 1. v gir̃gìzā v1.
2. n (earthquake) gir̃gizàr̃ ƙasā f.

qualification n (experience) ƙwarèwā f: he doesn't have the ~s for the job bâ shi dà cìkakkiyar̃ ƙwarèwā à sàmi aikìn ba.

qualified adj ƙwàrarrē adj.

qualify v càncantà v2, dācè v4: she didn't ~ for the scholarship bà tà càncànci tà sàmi sùkōlàshîf ba.

quality n (good) amincì m, ingancì m, ƙwārī m: Holland wax prints are the best ~ cloth 'yar̃ Hōlàn tā fi kōwàcè àtàmfā amincì; this cloth is of poor ~ yādìn nân bâ shi dà ƙwārī; the highest ~ gangàriyà f: this cap is of the finest ~ hùlar̃ nàn gangàriyà cē.

quandary n shìga ukù m; I'm in a ~ nā shìga ukù.

quantity n yawà m: a large ~ of rice shìnkāfā mài yawà; in great quantities mài tārìn yawà, hamì / himì adv: goods were brought in great quantities an kāwō kāyā hamì; a moderate ~ kīmā adv: a moderate ~ of rice àbinci kīmā; a small ~ kàɗan adv: a small ~ of food àbinci ɗan kàɗan.

quarrel 1. n faɗà m ⟨fàɗàce-fàɗàce⟩, gar̃damā / gaddamā f ⟨gar̃dàndamī⟩; (loud) hàtsàniyā f, (bitter) hùsūmà f; they had a ~ over money sun yi faɗà à kân kuɗī; the ~ became serious faɗà yā tsànantà; stop this ~ing! kù bar̃ wannàn gar̃damà! pick a ~ jā faɗà = jā bàkī = jā màganà; who started the ~? wà ya fàrà jân faɗà? he likes to pick ~s with everyone yā fayè jân bàkī; settle a ~ rabà faɗà.
2. v yi faɗà m, ɓātà dà w.: I ~ed with him mun yi faɗà dà shī = mun ɓātà dà shī.

quarrelsome adj (psn.) mafàɗàcī m,

màsìfaffē adj, (mài) tsìyā f, (mài) jìdālì m: she is ~ mafaɗàcìyā cè = màsìfaffiyā cè = màsīfā̀ gàrē tà.

quarter[1] n (of an hour) kwatà f: a ~ to 5 ƙarfè bìyar̃ saurā kwatà; one ~ r̃ubù'ī m, see fourth: one ~ of his salary r̃ubù'in àlbâshinsà.

quarter[2] n (residential area) ùnguwā f ⟨oCi⟩, [F] kàr̃cê m.

quarterly adv: the magazine is published ~ anā bugà mùjallar̃ sàu huɗu à shèkarà.

quartermaster n kwàtàmastà m.

quarters n a. (of soldiers) bār̃ikìn sōjà m; (of servants) bâs kwatà f, [F] ɗākìn yārā m. b. in close ~s kusa-kusa, bàkī dà hancì: the people live together in close ~s mutànē nà̀ zàune bàkī dà hancì.

quay n kwàtà f.

queen n sàraunìyā f ⟨oCi⟩: Amina, Queen of Zaria Mài Girmā Sàraunìyar̃ Zazzàu; a beauty ~ sàraunìyar̃ kyâu; (in cards) ɗan ukù m.

quell v kashè v4.

quench v kashè v4: the water wasn't enough to ~ his thirst ruwā bài ìsa yà kashè masà ƙishirwā ba.

query n tàmbayà f ⟨oCi⟩.

quest n bìdā f: ~ for knowledge bìdar̃ ilìmī.

question 1. n a. tàmbayà f ⟨oCi⟩: he asked me a ~ yā yi mini tàmbayà. b. (matter, problem) màganà f ⟨u²⟩, màtsalà f ⟨oCi⟩: it's a ~ of money màganar̃ ta kuɗī cè; the thing in ~ àbîn dà akè màganà à kânsà; the ~ is... màtsalàr̃ ita cè.... c. (doubt) shakkà f, tantamā f: there's no ~ about it bâ shakkà gàme dà wannàn; it is out of the ~ wannàn bà zâi yìwu ba.
2. v a. (interrogate) tùhumtà v2: the police ~ed the witnesses about the accident 'yan sàndā sun tùhùmci shàidū gàme dà haɗar̃ī. b. (doubt) yi shakkà f, yi tantamā f: I don't ~ his honesty bā nà shakkàr̃ gàskiyar̃sà.

questionable adj: his character is ~ anà shakkàr̃ hālinsà; his story is ~ àkwai shakkà cikin làbār̃insà.

question mark n àlāmàr̃ tàmbayà f.

questionnaire n tsārìn tambayōyī m.

queue up v yi lāyì m, yi jērìn gwànō m.

quick adj a. (mài) saurī m, (mài) hanzarī m: be ~ about it! yi saurī mànà! b. (of wits) (mài) kaifin bàsīr̃à m.

quicken v ƙārà saurī.

quickly adv a. dà saurī, dà hanzarī, cikin hanzarī, maza-maza / mar̃maza adv, (usu. in commands) maza adv: bring

some water ~! kằwō ruwā maza-maza! =
yi maza kà kāwō ruwā! go ~ yi saurī
m, yi maza adv, gaggaùtā v1: go ~ and
call him! yi maza kà kirāwō shì! b.
(hastily, carelessly) (dà) gàrằjē m: don't
do your work so ~ kadà kà yi gàrằjē dà
aikìnkà. c. (suddenly) nan dà nan: he
became sick very ~ cīwồ yā kāmằ shi nan
dà nan. d. (in good time) dà wuri: his
health improved ~ yā warkề dà wuri.

quicksilver n zaibằ f.

quick-tempered adj (mài) saurin fushī
m, (mài) zāfin râi m: she is ~ tanằ dà
zāfin râi.

quid n: ~ of tobacco bǔzūzùn tābằ m.

quiet 1. adj (mài) shirū m: he's a very ~
person shirū-shirū nề; be, keep ~ yi
shirū = kāmề bằkī; tell the children to be
~ cē wà yârā sù yi shirū; and then everything was ~ sai shirū; be absolutely
~ yi tsit idph: the streets were empty
and everything was ~ tītunằ bā kōwā,
gàrī yā yi tsit; live in peace and ~
zaunằ cikin lùmānằ.
2. v: make so. ~ down (calm so.) làllāsằ
v2 ⟨lallāshī⟩, sanyàyā wà zūcìyā:
please make the children ~ down don
Allàh kì sanyàyā wà yârā zūcìyā.

quietly adv à hankàlī: shut the door ~ kì
rufè ƙōfằ à hankàlī.

quill n (of porcupine, hedgehog) ƙayằ f
⟨oCi⟩; (feather) gāshì m ⟨gāsū⟩.

quilt n (padding for horses) lifìdī m.

quinine n kùnî / kìnî m.

quit v a. (stop) dainằ v1: ~ doing that! kà
dainà yîn wannàn! b. (leave) barī v*:
I've ~ my job nā baƙ aikìnā.

quite adv a. (really) sồsai adv, ƙwaƙai adv:
it's ~ hot today yâu anằ zāfī ƙwarai. b.
(entirely, completely) saƙai adv: I don't
~ understand bàn gānề saƙai ba; I'm
~ well now nā warkề saƙai. c. (fairly,
somewhat): ~ a lot of people support him
mutằnē dà dāmā sunằ gōyon bāyansà; the
book is ~ good littāfìn bā lâifī =
littāfìn dà dāma-dāma yakề.

quiver n kwàrī m ⟨uka²⟩: put an arrow back
into the ~ mài dà kibiyằ cikin kwàrī.

quivering n ɓarì m, tsìmā f, kaƙkaƙwằ f:
she was ~ with fear jìkintà nằ ɓarì
sabồdà tsồrō.

quiz show n wằsan kà-cīci-kà-cīci m,
wằsà wāsằ ƙwaƙwalwā m.

quorum n yawàn ìsa shāwaƙằ m.

quotation n (esp. from Koran or relig. text)
nassì m.

quotation mark n àlāmàƙ zàncen wani f.

quote v (from any text, esp. relig.) jā nassì
m: he is always quoting from the Koran
kullum yanằ jàn nassì dàgà Àlƙùƙ'ānì;
he said, and I ~... yā cề wai....

# R

rabbit *n* zōmō *m* ⟨aye⟩; ~ hutch gidan zōmō *m.*

rabies *n* hàukan kàrē *m*: a rabid dog mahàukàcin kàrē.

race[1] *n* a. (*contest*) tsēre *m*, gàsā *f*: the children were running ~s yārân nà tsēre; the arms ~ gàsaŕ ƙīràŕ màkàmai. b. (*a running* ~) gudù *m*: relay ~ gudùn bā dà sàndā. c. (*esp. horse* ~) sukùwā *f*, [F] kùŕûs *f*; ~ course fīlin sukùwā.

race[2] *n* a. (*human*) jinsī *m*: the human ~ jinsìn ɗan Adàm = bìl Adamà; the black ~ baƙaŕ fātā; the white ~ jaŕ fātā = faraŕ fātā. b. (*group descent*) jinī *m*: they are of the same ~ jininsù ɗaya; the Chinese ~ jinin Sin; he is of mixed ~ shī ruwā biyu nè; ~ relations dàngàntakàŕ al'ummōmī; racial prejudice bambancìn launìn fātā.

race[3] *v* (*rush*) gaŕzàyā *v1*: I jumped into the car and ~d to the hospital nā fāɗà mōtà nà gaŕzàyā asìbitì; (*on foot*) rūgà dà gudù, rūgà à gùje: he ~d to get to the bus yā rūgà dà gudù don yà cim mà bâs.

racism *n* bambancìn launìn fātā *m*, (*esp. Pol.*) wāriyaŕ àl'ummà *f.*

racist *n* ɗan wāriyaŕ àl'ummà *m*: be a ~ nūnà wāriyaŕ àl'ummà.

rack *n* (*of bicycle*) kàriyà *f.*

racket[1] *n* (*noise e.g. banging*) kwàràmniyā *f*, (*e.g. talking, shouting*) hàyàniyā *f*, (*of an engine, motor*) ƙārā *f.*

racket[2] *n* (*tennis*) ŕākèt *m.*

racket[3], racketeering *n* (*swindle*) cùkù-cukū *m*: there's a ~ involved dà cùkù-cukū à ciki fa.

radar *n* ŕādā *f*, [F] ŕàdâŕ *m.*

radiator *n* (*of car*) làgìŕētò *m*, [F] gidan ruwā *m.*

radical 1. *n* (*Pol.*) mài tsaurin ŕa'àyī *n.* 2. *adj* (mài) tsaurī *m*: ~ changes cànje-cànje màsu tsaurī.

radio *n* ŕēdiyò *m*, [F] ŕàdiyô *m*: listen to the ~ sàuràri ŕēdiyò; a shortwave ~ ŕēdiyò mài gàjēren zango.

radio station *n* (*frequency*) tashàŕ ŕēdiyò *f*; (*broadcasting house*) gidan ŕēdiyò *m.*

raffia *n* (*from young dum palm*) kabà *f.*

raffle *n* ŕēhùl *m*, tàmbōlà *f*, [F] tàmbōlâ *f*: participate in a ~ yi ŕēhùl; win a watch in the ~ ci àgōgo à ŕēhùl.

raft *n* gadon fitò *m.*

rag *n* tsûmmā *m* ⟨tsummōkarà⟩: be dressed in ~s yi tigijin cikin tsûmmā.

ragball *n* (*children's game*) tamaula *f.*

rage *n* hàsalà *f*; fly into a ~ hàŕzuƙà *v3*, ƙulè *v4*, hàsalà *v3.*

raid *v* kai wà harì, màmayà *v2*: the police ~ his house 'yan sàndā sun màmàyi gidansà.

rail *n* (*of railroad*) dōgō *m*, kwàngìrì *m*: jump the ~s gōcè dàgà kân dōgō; send sth. by ~ aikà ta jirgin ƙasà.

railing *n* hannū *m* ⟨aye⟩: ~ of a staircase, bridge hannun matattākalà, gadà.

railroad *n* ŕēlùwè *f*: there's no ~ in Niger bābù ŕēlùwè à Nìjâŕ; ~ line hanyàŕ jirgin ƙasà; ~ signal sìmfô *m*; ~ tracks dōgō *m*, kwàngìrì *m.*

railway station *n* tashàŕ jirgin ƙasà *f*, ŕēlùwè *f.*

rain 1. *n* ruwā *m*, ruwan samà *m*: the first ~s ruwan farkō = ruwan fārì; we got caught in the ~ ruwā yā tsarè mu; the crops need ~ hatsī yanà dà ƙishirwā; we got soaking wet from the ~ (*fig.*) ruwā yā bā mù kāshī = mun shā kāshin ruwā; (*fig.*) it is ~ing cats and dogs anà ruwā kàmaŕ dà bàkin ƙwaryā; ~clouds hadarì *m*; ~ shower yayyafī *m*, tsattsafī *m.* 2. *v* yi ruwā *m*: it is ~ing anà ruwā; it started ~ing an sakō ruwā = ruwā yā sàuka; it ~ed heavily an mākà ruwā = an shēƙà ruwā = an gōcè dà ruwā; it was ~ing continuously throughout the day anà ta ruwā rānā gàba ɗayantà; what heavy ~! tsūgì! *excl*; it stopped ~ing ruwā yā ɗaukè.

rainbow *n* bàkan gizò *m.*

rainboots *n* tàkàlmin ruwā *m.*

raincoat *n* rìgaŕ ruwā *f.*

raindrop *n* digòn ruwā *m* ⟨e²⟩.

rainfall *n* yawàn ruwan samà *m*: measure ~ aunà yawàn ruwan samà.

rainstorm *n* ruwā dà iskà *m.*

rainy *adj*: yesterday was a ~ day jiyà an yi ta ruwā; the ~ season dàminà *f*; (*fig.*) save for a ~ day wankè tukunyā don gòbe = sabòdà gòbe akè wankan dare.

rainy season *n* dàminà *f*, (*height of the* ~) màŕƙā *f*: the ~ has set in dàminà tā fāɗì; the ~ is usually from June through August yawancī anà dàminà tun dàgà watàn

Yūnì haȓ zuwā watàn Àgustā; a good ~ dàminā mài àlbaȓkā.

raise 1. *v* a. (*lift up*) ɗagā *v1*: ~ one's head, hand, voice ɗagā kâi, hannū, muryà. b. (*cause to rise*) tā dà / tāyaȓ (dà) *v5*: the wind ~d a great deal of dust iskā tā tā dà kūra mài yawā. c. (*increase*) kārā *v1*: ~ so.'s salary, height of a shelf kārā wā àlbâshī, tsawon kantā. d. (*an issue, a matter*) tā dà / tāyaȓ (dà) *v5*: they ~d the question of their salaries sun tā dà màganàȓ àlbâshinsù. e. (*livestock*) yi kīwò *m*: he ~s horses and cattle yanā kīwòn dawākī dà shānū. f. (*bring up one's children*) gòyā *v2*: she ~d him until he was grown up tā gòyē shì haȓ yā girma; (*brin up others' children*) rikē *v1*: their grandmother ~d them kàkaȓsù tā rikē su; I was ~d by my grandmother wajen kàkātā na tāshì.
2. *n* (*in salary*) kārìn àlbâshī *m*.

rake 1. *n* (*esp. metal*) manjàgarā *f* ⟨u⟩, [F] ȓàtô *m*, (*wooden, bamboo*) mashārī *m*.
2. *v* sharē *v4*.

ram *n* rāgō *m* ⟨una⟩; slaughter a ~ at Sallah yankà rāgō à Bàbbaȓ Sallā.

Ramadan *n* watàn azùmī *m;* ~ Holiday Kàramaȓ Sallā = Sallàȓ Azùmī.

ramp *n* gangarē *m*.

rampart *n* gānuwā *f*.

ranch *n* (*for cattle*) gōnaȓ kīwòn shānū *f*.

rancid *adj* (mài) yāmī *m*.

random *adj*: at ~ dà ka: he chose 5 at ~ yā zàɓi gùdā bìyaȓ dà ka.

randomly *adv* bā kâi bā gìndī.

range[1] *n* a. (*trajectory*) zangò *m*: long-~ nuclear weapons màkàman nūkìliyā màsu dōgon zangò; (*Mil., shooting*) ȓanjī *m*. b. (*of mountains*) jērī *m*: Djado mountain ~ jērìn duwàtsun Jādō. c. (*choice*): a ~ of foodstuffs àbinci irì-irì.

range[2] *n* (*stove for cooking*) kūkā *m*, [F] kìzìnyâȓ *f*; (*esp. gas*) gâs kūkā *m*, ȓashô *m*, [F] ȓeshô *m*.

rank[1] 1. *n* a. (*position*) mùkāmì *m* ⟨ai⟩. b. (*Mil., professional*) mùkāmì *m*, ȓankì *m*, [F] gàȓad *m*: what is his ~? mēnē nè ȓankìnsà? we are equal in ~ mùkāmìnmù ɗaya; he has the ~ of colonel, a professor mùkāmìnsà kanàȓ, fùȓòfēsā nē; he has the ~ of corporal yanā dà igiyā biyu; reduce so. in ~ cirē wā igiyàȓsà; a high-~ing officer bàbban sōjà. c. (*stature*) maȓtabā *f*, ìsā *f*; person of high ~ mài maȓtabā = mài ìsā; he is of noble ~ bàsarākè nē; he is in the top ~ of his class

yanā dàgà na farkō cikin ajìnsà.
2. *v*: he was ~ed 3rd yā zō na ukù.

rank[2] *adj* (*smell*) (mài) wārī *m*, (mài) dòyī *m*.

ransom *n* kuɗin fansā *m*, kāmuwaȓ kuɗī *f*.

rap *v* (*on sth.*) kwankwàsā *v1*; (*so. on head with knuckles*) ȓankwasā / dànkwasā *v2*.

rape *v* yi wà fyàɗē *m*, (*esp. young girl*) ɓātā *v1*: he ~d her yā yi matà fyàɗē = (*euphem.*) yā yi àmfānī dà ita dà kaȓfin tsìyā.

rapid *adj* (mài) saurī *m*.

rapidly *adv* a. dà saurī: speak ~ yi màganà dà saurī. b. (*suddenly*) nan dà nan: his health deteriorated ~ cīwònsà yā tsànantà nan dà nan. c. (*in good time*) dà wuri: his health improved ~ yā warkè dà wuri.

rare *adj* a. (*one of a kind*) nādìȓī *m* ⟨ai⟩: this ring is ~ zōbèn nân nādìȓī nè; (*difficult to get*) (mài) wùyaȓ sàmuwā, (mài) wùyaȓ sāmū. b. (*in occurrence*): it is a ~ event bài cikà àukuwā ba.

rarely *adv* bā sàfài ba, nādìȓàn *adv*, dà wùyā (+ *subjunct.*), cikà *v1* (+ *neg.*): he ~ comes here bā sàfài yakè zuwā nân ba; nowadays, elephants are ~ seen in the bush à zāmànin yâu, dà wùyā à ga gīwā à dājì; it is found only ~ bā à sāmùnsà sai nādìȓàn = bà à cikà sāmùnsà ba; it ~ happens bài cikà àukuwā ba = dà wùya yà fàru.

rascal *n* shàiɗànī *m* ⟨u⟩, (*esp. child*) shàkìyyì *m* ⟨ai⟩.

rash[1] *n* kuràrrajī / kuràjē *p*: he broke out in a ~ kuràrrajī sun fitō masà à jìki.

rash[2] *adj* (*foolhardy*): do sth. ~ yi kàsadā *f*.

rat *n* ɓēȓā *m* ⟨aye⟩, kūsū *m;* (*giant bandicoot*) gafiyā *f* ⟨oCi⟩; (*male bandicoot*) buȓgū *m*.

rate[1] *n* a. (*cost*) kuɗī *m*: the water ~ is cheap kuɗin ruwā àȓàhā nè. b. (*amount*) yawā *m*: the birth ~ is increasing yawàn haihùwā nà kāruwā. c. (*other uses*): ~ of exchange of the dollar kaȓfin dalàȓ Amìȓkà; first-~ gangàriyā *f*; at a great ~ of speed dà saurī kwaȓai; at the ~ we're going dà yàddà mukè tàfiyà; at any ~ kō ta yàyà: at any ~, we'll meet next month kō ta yàyà zā mù hàɗu watàn gòbe.

rate[2] *v* (*esteem*) kīmàntā *v1*: he is highly ~d as a poet an kīmàntā wākōkinsà = an ɗauki wākōkinsà dà daȓajā.

rather *adv* a. (*be more willingly*): would ~ fi sô: I would ~ live in the country than in the town nā fi sôn zaman kauyè dà ìn

zaunà à gàrī; they'd ~ sleep than work
sun fi sô sù yi barcī dà sù yi aikī.
b. (somewhat) ɗan (+ sensory n), kàɗan
adv: this is ~ sweet wannàn yanà dà ɗan
zāƙī = yanà dà zāƙī kàɗan.

ratio n ràbō m: the ~ of men to women
ràbon mazā dà na mātā.

rational adj a. (sensible) (mài) hankàlī m,
(mài) nazàřī m: what you said was ~ kā
yi nazàřī à zàncenkà. b. (calm) (mài)
nìtsuwā f.

rattle 1. n (small gourd ~) cakī m, kacau-
kacau m.
2. v (make noise) yi càccakà f: the motor
is rattling injìn mōtā nà càccakà.

rave v (talk incoherently) yi sàmbàtū m; be
raving mad haukàcē v4; a raving madman
mahàukàcī tuburàn.

ravine n kwàzazzabò m ⟨ai⟩.

raw adj ɗanyē adj ⟨u⟩: some people eat ~
fish wasu sukàn ci kīfinsù ɗanyē; (fig.)
he got a ~ deal an ƙwàrē shì.

rawhide n ƙirgì m ⟨a-a⟩.

rayon n lilìn m.

razor n (straight ~) askā f ⟨a-e⟩; (safety ~)
řēzà f, [F] řàzùwâř m; ~ blade řēzà f, [F]
lâm f.

re- (prefix for v) sākè v4 (+ vbl. n), ƙarà
v4 (+ vbl. n): retie a package sākè ɗaurè
fàkitì; refuel ƙārà shân mâi; rejoin the
army sākè shìgā sōjà.

reach 1. v a. (arrive at) ìsa v3: when will
the train ~ the border? yàushè jirgîn
zâi ìsa iyàkàř? ~ an agreement yankè
shāwařà = tsai dà màganà; ~ maturity
bàlabà v3. b. (extend) kai v*: the ladder doesn't ~ the window tsānìn bài kai
tàgà ba; when we ~ed the bridge dà mukà
kai gadà; ~ out (stretch) mīƙà v1: he
~ed out his hand and took the bananas
yà mīƙà hannunsà yà ɗaukō àyàbà.
2. n: keep the medicine out of the ~ of
children kì ɓòyè màganī kadà yârà sù
ganī; it is within easy ~ kuřkusa nè.

react v ɗaukà v2*, ganī v*: how did she ~
to the news? yàyà ta ɗauki làbārìn?

reactionary n & adj (Pol.) ɗan kòmà-bāya
m, (mài) řa'àyin rìƙau m.

read v a. (sth.) kařàntā v1 ⟨kàřàtū⟩: ~
aloud kařàntā dà ƙarfī = kařàntā à
fīlī; ~ to oneself kařàntā à zūci; ~
silently kařàntā à ɓòye; can you ~ and
write? kā iyà řùbùtū dà kàřàtū? b. (as
an activity) yi kàřàtū m: I was ~ing
while she slept inà kàřàtū tanà barcī;
I like to ~ inà sôn kàřàtū. c. (study
an academic subject) yi kàřàtū m: he

is ~ing history at the university yanà
kàřàtun tāřīhī à jāmi'à; he is well-read
yā kàřàntu.

reader n (primer) littāfìn kòyon kàřàtū
m.

readily adv nan dà nan: he ~ agreed nan
dà nan ya yàřda.

reading n kàřàtū m: a ~ room dākìn
kàřàtū.

ready adv (à) shìrye adv: I'm always ~
to help you kullum à shìrye nakè ìn
tàimàkē kà; be ~ (of people) shiryà v1:
are you ~? kin shiryà? = à shìrye kikè?
get oneself ~ yi shirī m: have you got everything ~? kin yi shirī? = kin shiryà?
get ~ for a trip kintsà v1; be ~ (of a
thing, event) gamà v1: when will it be ~?
yàushè zā à gamà? the food is ~ an gamà
àbinci = àbinci yā yi; be almost ~ to
gab dà prep, bàkin, kusan, shirìn: we
were nearly ~ to leave when he came munà
gab dà tàshī sai ya zō = munà shirìn
tàshī sai ya zō.

ready reckoner n řaskwanà f, [F] řafkanà
f.

real adj a. (true, actual) na gàskiyā f,
na hàƙīƙà f, hàƙīƙànin: it is a ~ fact
àl'amàřīn gàskiyā nè; that is the ~
truth wannàn hàƙīƙànin gàskiyā cè;
what are the ~ facts? mènē nè hàƙīƙànin
màganà? b. (essential nature of sth.)
tàkàmaimai adv: he has no ~ reason for
refusing to come bâ shi dà wani dàlīlì
tàkàmaimai na ƙìn zuwà. c. (genuine)
na ainihī m: this is made of ~ gold
wannàn zīnàřìyā ta ainihī cè; what is
his ~ name? mènē nè ainihin sūnansà?
d. (pure, unadulterated) zallà adv: that
is the ~ truth wannàn gaskiyā cè zallà.
e. (serious) bàbba adj ⟨mânya-mânya⟩: it
is a ~ problem bàbbař màtsalà cē.

real estate n ƙasā f, fīlī m ⟨aye⟩: he has
a lot of ~ yā màllàki ƙasā dà yawà.

reality n hàƙīƙà f, hàƙīƙànī m: in ~ à
hàƙīƙà, à bisà gàskiyā: in ~, I don't
like it à bisà gàskiyā bā nà sônsà; become a ~ tàbbatà v3: his dream of getting rich became a ~ mafařkinsà na zama
àttàjìřī yā tàbbatà.

realize v a. ànkarà dà v3, fařga v3a: I
didn't ~ what had happened bàn ànkarà
dà àbîn dà ya fàru ba; I didn't ~ it bàn
fařga ba. b. (make sth. become true) cim
mà vdat: he ~d his goal of getting a degree
yā cim mà būrìnsà na sāmùn dìgìřī.

really 1. adv a. (truly) hàƙīƙànin: he
doesn't ~ know what happened bài san

hàƙīƙànin àbîn dà ya fàru ba; did he ~ say that? yā fàɗi hakà kùwa? did that ~ happen? dà gàske an yi hakà? is it ~ true? shin gaskiyā nè kùwa? b.(*essential nature of sth.*) tàkàmaimai *m*: I don't ~ know what it is about bàn san tàkàmaimansà ba; I don't ~ know what he is thinking bàn san tàkàmaiman àbîn dà yakè zàtō ba. c. (*purely, totally*) zallā *adv*: he's ~ crazy mahàukàcī nè zallā. d. (*very much*) ainùn *adv*, sòsai *adv*, ƙwaƙai *adv*: he ~ knows Hausa yā iyà Hausa ƙwaƙai.
2. *excl* a. (*for emphasis*) wàllāhì (tàl-lāhì)! *excl*. b. (*expressing doubt*) anyà? *excl*. c. (*in contradicting*) habà *excl*: ~, who is going to believe that? habà! wà zâi yàƙda dà wànnan? c. (*seeking confirmation*) àshē? *excl*, Allàh? (*to which reply is*: Allàh kùwa!).

**reap** *v* a. gìrbā *v2* ⟨girbì⟩, *see* harvest: they are ~ing the millet sunà girbìn gērō; (*fig.*) you ~ what you sow irìn dà akà shūkà shī yakàn tsirō; ~ a reward (*fig.*) yi gyàɗaƙ Dōgo.

**rear**[1] 1. *n* bāyā *m*: in the ~ à bāya; in the ~ of the building, bus à bāyan ginì, bâs.
2. *adj & adv* na bāya *m*: the ~ tire tāyà ta bāya; ~ light (*of car*) danjà *f*.

**rear**[2] *v* (*a child*) rēnā *v2* ⟨rēnō⟩.

**rear**[3] *v* (*by horse*) yi taɓaryā *f*.

**reason** *n* a. (*motive*) dàlīlì *m* ⟨ai⟩: I have a good ~ for doing it inà dà ƙwàƙƙwaran dàlīlìn yînsà; for no apparent ~ bâ kâi bâ gìndī; for that ~ à dàlīlìn hakà = sabòdà hakà; the ~ why it is so is... dàlīlìn dà ya sâ hakà nē k'uwa shī nè... = àbîn dà ya sâ hakà nē shī nè...; the real ~ is... ainihin dàlīlìn shī nè...; if for no other ~ than... bà don wani dàlīlì ba sai dai...; without rhyme or ~ bâ gaiƙà bâ dàlīlì. b. (*cause*) sanàdī *m*: Audu is the ~ why I am here Audù nē sanàdin zuwānā nân. c. (*evidence, excuse*) hujjà *f* ⟨oCi⟩: what ~ do you have for saying that? mēcē cè hujjàƙkà ta fàɗaƙ hakà? d. (*senses, mental faculty*) hankàlī *m*: he has lost his ~ hankàlinsà yā tàɓu = yā fìta hankàlinsà; he doesn't listen to ~ bà yà kàrɓaƙ shāwaƙà.

**reasonable** *adj* a. (*sensible*) (mài) hankàlī *m*: a ~ discussion tattàunâwā mài hankàlī. b. (*good*) (mài) kyâu *m*: it is a ~ plan shirì nē mài kyâu; the price seems ~ gà àlāmà fàƙashìnsà yā yi =

kuɗinsà bâ lâifī; a ~ amount (*moderate*) (mài) ɗan dāmā, kīmà *adv*: a ~ amount of water ruwā kīmà.

**rebel** 1. *n* a. (*Pol.*) ɗan tāwāyè *m*: crush the ~s murƙushè 'yan tāwāyè. b. (*unmanageable psn.*) kàngàrarrē *adj*.
2. *v* a. (*Pol.*) yi tāwāyè *m*, yi bōƙè *m*: ~ against a government yi wà gwamnatì tāwāyè. b. (*become difficult to control*) kàngarà *v3*: the children ~led and refused to go to school yârā sun kàngarà sun ƙi zuwà makaƙantā; ~ against kangàrē wà *v4*: he ~led against his parents yā kangàrē wà iyàyensà.

**rebellion** *n* (*Pol.*) tāwāyè *m*, bōƙè *m*.

**rebuff** *v* gwalè *v4*.

**recall** *v* a. (*remember*) tunà dà *v1*: I can't ~ seeing him bà zân iyà tunàwā dà nā gan shì ba; unable to ~ shà'afà dà *v3*: I can't ~ her name nā shà'afà dà sūnantà = sūnantà yā ɓacè minì. b. (*call back*) kōmā dà *v1*: the ambassador was ~ed an kōmā dà jàkādàn ƙasaƙsù.

**recede** *v* jànyē *v4*: the floodwaters have ~d ambàliyàƙ ruwā tā jànyē.

**receipt** *n* ƙasît / ƙasīdì *m*, shaidàƙ biyà *f*, [F] ƙēsî *m*: here is the ~ for ₦50 gà ƙasît dîn na naiƙà hàmsin; ask him for a ~ kà tàmbàyē shì ƙasīdì.

**receive** *v* a. (*accept*) kàrɓā *v2*, àmsā *v2*: I ~d some money from him nā kàrɓi kuɗi à hannunsà. b. (*get*) sāmù *v2*\*: I didn't ~ a letter from him bàn sàmi wàsīƙàƙsà ba. c. (*a guest*) kàrɓā *v2*: he ~d the guests warmly yā kàrɓi bàƙī dà hannū bībiyu. d. (*radio, television signal*) kāmā tashà.

**receiver** *n* (*of telephone*) kân tàƙhō *m*; (*radio*) ƙēdiyò *m* ⟨oCi⟩.

**recent** *adj* na kwànan nàn; a ~ visit zìyāƙà ta kwànan nàn; in ~ years à shèkàrun nàn.

**recently** *adv* a. (*these days*) kwānan nàn: we've seen a lot of him ~ kwānan nàn mun cikà ganinsà. b. (*a while ago*) kwànan bāya: I talked to him ~ about that mun yi màganà dà shī kân wànnan kwànan bāya.

**reception** *n* a. (*party*) lìyāfà *f*, [F] àmbìtē *m*: hold a ~ gàyyàci mutànē lìyāfà; hold a ~ in honor of yi wà lìyāfàƙ ban girmā. b. (*of equipment*): does your radio get good ~? ƙēdiyònkà yanà kāmà tashà sòsai?

**recess**[1] *n* ɗan hūtū *m*, (*at school*) taƙà *m*, [F] lìkìƙāsò *f*.

**recess**[2] *n* (*dark or inaccessible area*) sāƙò *m*, lungù *m*.

recession *n* gurgùncêwaɍ tattalin aɍzìkī *f.*

recipe *n* gìrke-gìrke *p.*

reciprocate *v* sākã wà *v1*: I did him a good turn and he ~d nā yi masà àlhēɍī yā sākã minì dà àlhēɍī.

recitation *n* (*Relig.*) tīlāwã *f.*

reckless *adj* (*careless*) maràs kùlā *f*; (*deliberately*) (mài) gangancī *m*: he is ~ yanã gangancī; a ~ driver matùƙī mài gangancī; ~ driving gangancin tūƙī = tūƙī na gangancī = mūgùn gudũ; show ~ courage yi ƙùru *m*, (*fig.*) yi ƙūnaɍ baƙin wākē *m*.

recklessness *n* rashìn kùlā *m*, (*deliberate*) gangancī *m.*

reckon *v* (*estimate*) kìntātã *v2*: he ~ed that it would cost ₦100 yā kìntàci kuɗinsà naiɍã dàrī; day of reckoning rānaɍ hìsābī.

recline *v* (*on one's elbow*) kìshìngidã *v3*, yi kìshìngìɗe *m*; in a reclining position à kìshìngìɗe.

recluse *n* mài ƙìn dūniyã *n.*

recognition *n* shâidàwā *f*; he was honored in ~ of his service an girmàmā shi don shâidà aikìn dà ya yi.

recognize *v* a. (*see & know*) gānè *v4*, shâidā *v1*: I don't ~ any of these people bàn gānè kōwā ba; I saw someone in the distance, but didn't ~ him nā hàngi wani àmmā bàn shâidà shi ba. b. (*acknowledge*) shâidā *v1*. c. (*Pol.*) amìncē dà *v4*: ~ a new government amìncē dà sābuwaɍ gwamnatì.

recoil *v* jā dà bāya.

recollect *v* tunã dà *v1.*

recommend *v* a. (*praise so.*) yabã wà *v1*: Audu has been ~ed as a cook an yabã wà Àudù aikìnsà na kūkù. b. (*support sth.*) gòyi bāyā, bā dà gōyon bāyā: the council ~ed that the school be built here hùkūmã tā bā dà gōyon bāya à ginà makaɍantaɍ à nân.

recommendation *n* yàbō *m*: a written ~ takàɍdaɍ yàbō.

recompense *n* (*reward*) lādā *m*; (*compensation for damages*) diyyã *f.*

reconcile *v* daidàitā *v1*, sāsàntā *v1*, sulhùntā *v1*, yi sulhũ tsàkānin, shiryà tsàkānin *v1*: the judge ~d them àlƙālī yā sāsàntā su = àlƙālī yā sulhùntā su = àlƙālī yā yi sulhũ tsàkāninsù; be(come) ~d dàidàitu *v7*, sàsàntu *v7*, shiryã *v1.*

reconciliation *n* sulhũ *m*, shirì *m*, sādàɍwā *f*; (*attempted ~ of so. run away*)

bīkò *m*: the husband attempted a ~ with his wife mijìn yā yi bīkòn màtaɍsà.

record[1] 1. *n* a. (*Law*) làbāɍin shàɍi'ã *m*. b. (*office* ~) fāyìl *m*, [F] dòsê *m*; put sth. on ~ ɍubùtā *v1*. c. (*official* ~ *of births, deaths*) ɍajistã *f*, [F] gìɍgam *m*. 2. *v* ɍubùtā *v1.*

record[2] 1. *n* (*music*) faifai *m* ⟨a..ai⟩, faifan gàɍmàhō *m*: play a ~ sā faifai; there's a ~ing of that poem àkwai faifan wannàn wāƙã. 2. *v* ɗaukã *v2\**, nàdā *v2* ⟨nadì⟩: they are ~ing all his poems anã nadìn duk wāƙōƙinsà.

record player, changer *n* canjã *f*, [F] êlêk *m*; (*manually wound*) gàɍmàhō *m.*

recorder *n* (*tape or cassette*) ɍàkōdã *f* ⟨oCi⟩.

recording *n* (*tape or record*) nadì *m* ⟨e[2]⟩.

recover[1] *v* a. (*from illness*) sàmi sauƙī; (*completely from illness*) warkè *v4*. b. (*from unconsciousness*) faffaɗō *v6*. c. (*sth. lost*) gānè *v4*: his goods were stolen but the police ~ed them an sācè masà kāyā, àmmā 'yan sàndā sun gānè su.

recover[2] *v* (*cover again*) sākè rufèwā.

recreation *n* (*sports*) wàsànnī *p.*

recrimination *n* (*mutual*) tsiyā-tsìyã *f.*

recruit *n* (*Mil.*) kuɍtù *m* ⟨a-a⟩, [F] làkuɍù *m.*

rectangle *n* mùkā'àbī *m.*

rectum *n* (*euphem.*) dubùɍā *f*, (*pejor.*) takāshì *f*, tsūlìyã *f.*

recuperate *v* ji sauƙī *m*, warkè *v4.*

recur *v* sākè àukuwã; (*esp. of illness, season*) kōmã *v1*, dāwō *v6*: my fever ~s often zàzzàɓīnā yanã yawàn kōmōwā; ~ regularly kōmã à kâi à kâi.

red *adj* jā *adj* ⟨jàjàyē⟩; bright ~ jā jà-wuɍ; ~-hot zāfī jà-ziɍ, mài tsananin zāfī: the iron was ~-hot dūtsèn gùgã yā yi zāfī jà-ziɍ; a ~ light (*traffic*) danjã *f.*

reddish *adv* jāja-jāja *adv*; ~-brown kōyã *f.*

red-handed *adv* ƙirī-ƙirì *idph*: they caught him ~ an kāmã shi ƙirī-ƙìrì.

redeem *v* (*slave*) fànsā *v2.*

redemption *n* (*Relig.*) cètō *m.*

reduce 1. *vt* a. (*decrease*) ragè *v4*, yi rangwamè *m*: ~ the national debt ragè bāshìn ƙasā; please ~ your price for me ai sai kà ragè minì kudī = ai sai kà yi minì rangwamè; buy at a ~d price sàyā dà ɍahamã; the judge ~d his sentence àlƙālī yā yi masà rangwamè. b. (*downgrade*) ƙasƙàntā *v1*: the corporal was ~d in rank

an ƙasƙàntà kōfùr̃ = an cirẽ wà kōfùr̃
igiyàr̃sà.
2. vi (lose weight, slim down) saɓẽ v4, zub
dà jìkī.

reduction n (in amount) ragĩ m: a ~ in
speed ragìn gudũ; (of a sentence, price)
rangwamẽ m: a 10 percent ~ rangwamèn
gōmà dàgà cikin dàrī.

reduplication n (Gram.) ninkĩ m.

reed n (var. types): (for making screen) ĩwā
f; (for making large mat, pen) gambã f; (for
making small ~ mat) tsaurē m; (for arrow shaft) kyaurō m; (for making broom)
tsintsiyā f.

redbuck n kwàntà-r̃àfi m.

reek v yi wārī m: he ~s of beer yanã wārin
giyã.

reel n (magnetic tape or film) faifai m
⟨a..ai⟩.

refer to v a. (mention, speak of) yi màganã
f: don't ever ~ to that again kadà kà
sākè màganàr̃ wannàn àbù. b. (concern)
shãfā v2: this letter ~s to the accident
wàsīƙàr̃ nân tā shãfi hadàr̃în; ~ring
to gàme dà, dàngàne/danganẽ dà: ~ring
to your recent letter gàme dà wàsīƙàr̃kà
ta kwānan bāya. c. (direct so. somewhere
for information): the emir ~red the matter to the council sarkī yā mīƙà màganã
gà màjàlisàr̃; they ~red us to you sun
tūr̃ō mù wajenkà; you should ~ to a dictionary sai kà dūbà cikin ƙāmùs.

referee 1. n àlƙālin wāsā m, r̃àfàlî /
làfàr̃î n, [F] àlbītìr̃ n.
2. v yi hukuncĩ m, hukùntā v1.

reference n a. (mention): he made no ~
to them bài cē kōmē ba gàme dà sū;
with ~ to gàme dà, dàngàne/danganẽ dà:
with ~ to your recent letter dàngàne dà
wàsīƙàr̃kà ta kwānan bāya. b. (written
recommendation) takàr̃daf̃ yàbō f.

referendum n ƙùr̃i'àr̃ nēman r̃a'àyī f.

refine v tācẽ v4.

refinery n matātā f: oil ~ matātar̃ mân
fētùr̃.

reflect v a. (of light) yi ƙyàllī m: a
mirror ~s light madūbī yanã ƙyàllī. b.
(think over) yi tùnãnī m, yi tsōkàcī m,
yi zulùmī m.

reflection n a. (of light) haskē m. b. (of
image) inuwã f: he saw his ~ in the water
yā ga inuwàr̃sà cikin ruwa. c. (thought)
tùnãnī m, tsōkàcī m, nìtsuwā f.

reform 1. v gyār̃ã v1; be(come) ~ed gyãru
v7; (Relig.) jaddàdā v1.
2. n gyārā m ⟨e²⟩: the government
has introduced many ~s gwamnatì tā

ɓullō dà gyàre-gyàre dà yawã; (Relig.)
tàjàdīdì m.

reformer n (Relig.) mùjaddàdī m ⟨ai⟩.

refrain n (Mus.) amshĩ m.

refrain from v ƙauràcē wà v4: I ~ed from
smoking in front of him nā ƙauràcē wà
shân tābā à gàbansà.

refresh v (oneself) shãƙàtā v1.

refresher course n bītã f, [F] ìstājì m.

refreshments n làshe-làshe dà tànɗe-
tànɗe p, cìye-cìye dà shãye-shãye p.

refrigerator n, see fridge.

refuge n mafakā m; take ~ fakẽ v4.

refugee n ɗan gudùn hijir̃ã m; political ~
ɗan mafakar̃ sìyāsã.

refund 1. v rāmà kudĩ v1, mai dà kudĩ:
if it doesn't fit, I'll ~ you the money ìdan
bài dācẽ ba, zân rāmã makà kudĩn.
2. n rāmuwã f: he refused to give me a ~
yā ƙi bā nì rāmuwã.

refuse[1] v ƙi v0: they ~d to come sun ƙi
zuwã; I ~ to see him ever again nā ƙi ìn
sākè ganinsà sam; ~ absolutely ƙi sam-
sam; ~ point-blank ƙi ƙēmēmē, ƙi ƙìrī
dà mùzū: he ~d me point-blank yā ƙī nì
ƙìrī dà mùzū.

refuse[2] n (trash) shãrā f; ~ dump, heap
jūjī m.

refute v musàntā v1: he ~d their arguments
yā musàntā màganàr̃sù.

regard 1. v a. (look at) dùbā v2: he ~ed me
with a smile yā dùbẽ nì yā yi mùr̃mùshī.
b. (consider) ɗaukā v2*: I ~ him as my
brother nā ɗaukẽ shì kàmar̃ ɗan'uwānā.
2. n a. (respect) girmā m: I have a
high ~ for Hamza inã ganin girman
Hamzã. b. (reference): with ~ to gàme
dà, dàngàne/danganẽ dà: he has no say
with ~ to what I do bâ shi dà ta cêwā
gàme dà sha'ànīnā.

regards n (wish, greeting): please give him
my ~ kà gayar̃ minì dà shī.

regarding prep kân zàncen, kân bàtun,
gàme dà, dàngàne/danganẽ dà: ~ the
money you owe me danganẽ dà bāshìn dà
nakẽ bînkà; I spoke to him ~ your request mun yi màganã dà shī kân bàtun
r̃ōƙonkà; what are the arrangements ~
the trip? yàyà shìrye-shìryẽn gàme dà
tàfiyàr̃?

regiment n r̃ajìmantĩ m, [F] bàtāliyã f.

region n yankĩ m ⟨una⟩, sāshẽ / sāshì m
⟨Ca⟩, shiyyã f ⟨oCi⟩: the ~ of Maradi à
shiyyàr̃ Marādi = à ƙasar̃ Marādi; the
cold ~s of the world sàssan dūniyã màsu
sanyī; the former Northern R. Jihàr̃
Arẽwa ta dâ.

register 1. n (for keeping records) r̃ajistā f; (for keeping accounts) lajā f, daftār̃ī m, [F] kundin lìssāfī m: tax ~ daftār̃in hār̃ajī.
2. v a. (mail at post office) yi r̃ajistā f, [F] yi r̃ìkùmàndê m: ~ a letter yi r̃ajistar̃ wàsīk̃ā; a ~ed letter wàsīk̃ā ta r̃ajistā = [F] lētìr̃ r̃ìkùmàndê. b. (a vehicle) yi wà mōtā lambā. c. (at hotel) sàuka v3.

registrar n r̃ajistar̃ā n.

registration n: ~ number (of car) lambàr̃ mōtā.

regress v kōmā dà bāya, jā dà bāya.

regret v yi bak̃in cikī m: I ~ that I can't come inā bak̃in cikī dà bà zân iyà zuwā ba; (esp. one's actions after the fact) yi dā-nā-sanī, yi nàdāmā f: if you do go, you may ~ it ìdan kin tàfi fa kyā yi dā-nā-sanī; I ~ted the argument that we had nā yi nàdāmār̃ fad̃àn dà mukà yi.

regretfully adv dà bak̃in cikī.

regular adj (normal) na yâu dà kullum: this is my ~ work wannàn aikìnā nè na yâu dà kullum.

regularly adv à kâi à kâi adv: he goes there ~ yanā zuwā cân à kâi à kâi; brush your teeth ~ kà gōgè hak̃ōrī à kâi à kâi; (~ but at no fixed time) kōyàushè adv: he comes here ~ yakàn zō nān kōyàushè.

regulate v (control) k̃ayyàdē v4; (adjust) daidàitā v1.

regulation n, see rule.

rehabilitation center n (esp. for handicapped) gidan gàjìyàyyū m.

rehearse v gwadā v1.

reign 1. n sàrautā f: during the ~ of Jan Gwarzo lōkàcin sàrautàr̃ Jan Gwar̃zo.
2. v yi sàrautā f.

reimburse v mai dà / mayar̃ (dà) kudī, rāmà kudī.

rein v jā kāmāzūr̃ū; ~ in a horse to a sliding stop zāmè dōkì.

reinforce v k̃arfàfā v1, ingàntā v1.

reinforcements n (Mil.) gudùmmawā f: troop ~s were sent in an yi musù gudùmmawā dà sōjà.

reins n kāmāzūr̃ū m: pull on the ~s jā kāmāzūr̃ū; (fig.) the ~ of government ragàmar̃ mulkì.

reiterate v nānàtā v1, sākè fàdā.

reject v (refuse) k̃i kàrbā: he ~ed my advice yā k̃i kàrbar̃ shāawàr̃ātā; (totally, scornfully) wancakalar̃ (dà) v5, wur̃gar̃ (dà) v5.

rejoice v yi mur̃nā f.

relate v a. (a narrative, news) ruwàitā v1, fàdā / fad̃ì v2*. b. (concern): ~ to dàngantā v2, shāfā v2: these words ~ to different branches of knowledge kalmōmin nàn sun dàngànci fannōnin ilìmī ìr̃ì-ir̃ì; this word is ~d to that one wannàn kalmā dangìn waccàn cē. c. (through kinship): be ~d to gamà dangì dà, jìbìntā v2: she is ~d to me mun gamà dangì dà ita = tā jìbìncē nì; I am ~d to him on my mother's side nā jìbìncē shì wajen mahaifìyātā; we are ~d mun jìbìntu; is he ~d to you? shī d̃an'uwankà nē? = shī dangìnkà nē? they are more or less ~d sun kusa dangancì dà jūnā.

relation n a. (kin), see relative. b. (relationship): be in ~ to, bear a ~ to shāfā v2: this bears no ~ to that wannàn bài shāfi waccàn ba. c. (concerning): in ~ to gàme dà, dàngàne/dangànè dà: this is in ~ to what you said earlier wannàn yanā dàngàne dà àbin ka cè dâ. d. (according to) gwàr̃gwadon prep: in ~ to their size gwàr̃gwadon girmansù.

relations n huld̃ā f ⟨oCi⟩: diplomatic ~ huld̃àr̃ jakādancì; establish diplomatic ~ k̃ullà huld̃àr̃ jakādancì; international ~s huld̃ōdin k̃asàshen dūniyā; break off ~ yankè huld̃ā.

relationship n a. dàngàntakā f. b. (friendship) k̃awàncē m.

relative n dangì m ⟨oCi⟩, d̃an'uwā m: he is not a ~ of mine bà mù gamà dangì dà shī ba.

relax v a. (rest) hūtā v1, shāk̃àtā v1, wālā v1: I don't have any time to ~ bâ ni dà sùkūnìn hūtāwā; (one's body) sakē v4, sākā v2: he is ~ed yā sakē = yā sàki jìkī = à sàke yakè; his face ~ed yā sàki fuskà. b. (lessen, ease) sassàutā v1: ~ the rules for imports sassàutā màtàkan shigō dà kāyā.

relaxation n wàlwàlā f.

relaxed adj (easy-going) (mài) sauk̃in kâi m; (in a good mood) (mài) wàlwàlā f.

relay race n gudùn bā-dà-sàndā m.

release 1. v (let free) sàkā v2: the judge ordered them to ~ him àlk̃ālī yā ùmàr̃cē sù dà sù sàkē shì; ~ me! sàkàn ni! (make sth. free) sakar̃ (dà) v5, saukar̃ (dà) v5: ~ the handbrake sakar̃ dà bir̃kìn hannu; (from above) sakā v1: the plane ~d its bombs jirgîn yā sakà bâm.
2. n (from prison) sakì m: Audu's ~ was granted an sāmi sakìn Audù.

relent v ji tàusàyī m, yi īmānī m.

relentlessly adv bâ jî bâ ganī, wur̃jànjàn

*idph*: he beat the donkey ~ yā bùgi jàkī bā jî bā ganī; they attacked their work ~ sun kāmà aikī wuřjànjàn.

**relevant** *adj*: be ~ to shāfā *v2*: your evidence isn't ~ to our case shaidàřkà bà tà shāfi màganàřmù ba.

**reliability** *n* ingancī *m*, amincī *m*.

**reliable** *adj* a. (*trustworthy*) matàbbàcī *adj*, tàbbàtaccē *adj*: a ~ source tàbbàtacciyař majiyā = majiyā mài makāmā. b. (*honest, dependable*) (mài) amincī *m*, àmìntaccē *adj*.

**relief** *n* a. sauřī *m*: get ~ from pain sàmi sauřin cīwò; a sigh of ~ àjiyàř zūcìyā. b. (*aid*) āgàjī *m*, tàimakō *m*: a ~ fund asūsùn āgàjī.

**relieve** *v* a. (*esp. pain*) sauřàřā *v1*: the medicine ~d his pain màganìn yā sauřàřā masà cīwò. b. (*so. of burden*): let me ~ you of that heavy box bàri ìn sàukè kà dà àkwàtìn nân mài nauyī; I ~d him of his obligation to pay the loan nā yāfè masà bāshìn. c. (*from worry*) kwantař dà hankàlī: I was ~d to hear the news jìn làbārìn yā kwantař dà hankàlīnā; I felt ~d nā ji sayau.

**religion** *n* àddīnī *m* ⟨ai⟩: the main ~s of the country are... mânya-mânyan àddīnan ƙasàř sū nè...; the ~ of Islam àddīnìn Musuluncī; the Christian ~ àddīnìn Kiřistà.

**religious** *adj* na àddīnī: a ~ matter màtsalàř àddīnī; (*having faith*) (mài) ìbādà *m*: he is a deeply ~ man mùtûm nē mài ìbādà sòsai.

**reluctance** *n* (*unwillingness, esp. re. one's duties*) nàwā *f*.

**reluctant** *adj* (mài) nàwā *f*: I am ~ to help him inà nàwā ìn tàimàkē shì; one must not be ~ to perform one's prayers bā à nàwā zuwà sallà; be ~ (*out of deference*) ji nauyī *m*: I was ~ to tell him the bad news nā ji nauyī ìn fadà masà làbārìn maràs dādī.

**rely on** *v* a. (*depend on*) dògarà dà *v3*: I ~ on him for help inà dògarà dà shī don tàimakō. b. (*trust*) amìncē dà *v4*.

**remain** *v* a. (*be left over*) saura *v3a*, ragè *v4*: whatever ~s is yours duk àbìn dà ya saura yā zama nākà; is there any ~ing? dà saurā? = dà ràgōwā? the ~ing ₦5 sauran naiřà bìyar; the children ate up the ~ing food yârā sun cînyē àbincìn dà ya ragè. b. (*stay behind*) zaunà *v1*, kasàncē *v4*: I left the village, but he ~ed there nā barō ƙauyèn àmmā shī yā zaunà nan = nā barō ƙauyèn àmmā shī

yā kasàncē à nan.

**remainder** *n* saurā *m*, ràgōwā *f*: the ~ of the money will be used for repairs zā à yi àmfànī dà sauran kudī wajen gyāregyāre.

**remains** *n* a. (*of sth.*) kufai *m*: ~ of a house, tree kufan gidā, bishiyà. b. (*corpse*) gāwā *f* ⟨aki²⟩, mamàcī *m*.

**remand** *v*: ~ so. to custody sâ w. à gidan waƙàfī.

**remark** 1. *n* màganà *f* ⟨u²⟩, furùcī *m*, kàlāmì *m*: kind ~ kàlāmì mài kiřkì; rude ~ màganà mài rashìn kunyà. 2. *v* furtà *v1*, cê *v*\*: he ~ed that it was getting late yā furtà cêwā darē yā yi.

**remarkable** *adj* gàgārùmī *adj* ⟨ai⟩, mùhimmì *adj* ⟨ai⟩.

**remedy** *n* māganī *m* ⟨u-a²⟩.

**remember** *v* tunà (dà) *v1*: I cannot ~ him bà zân iyà tunàwā dà shī ba; do you ~ what I told you? kā tunà dà àbìn dà na gayà makà? I ~ her as a little girl nā tunà lōkàcîn dà takè yārinyà; I ~ quite well nā tunà sařai; as far as I can ~ à iyà sanìnā dai; ~ so. to so. gayař wà dà w.: please ~ me to your family kà gayař minì dà ìyālìnkà.

**remembrance** *n* tunàwā *f*: in ~ of the dead don tunàwā dà wadàndà sukà cika.

**remind** *v* tunà wà *v1*, yi wà tunì *m*, yi wà matāshìyā *f*: ~ him to lock the door kà tunà masà yà kullè ƙōfàř; let me ~ you of it bàri ìn tunà makà = bàri in yi makà matāshìyā; his looks ~ me of my father kàmànninsà sun tunà minì dà mahàifīnā; ~ so. of past favors (*to embarrass*) yi wà gōřì *m*.

**reminder** *n* matāshìyā *f*, (wàsīƙàř) tunì *f*: I sent him a ~ nā aikà masà dà matāshìyā.

**remit** *v* biyā *v0*.

**remnant** *n* guntū *m* ⟨aye⟩, saurā *m*; (*of cloth*) ƙyallē *m* ⟨aye⟩, guntun yādì *m*.

**remorse** *n* nàdāmà *f*, dà-nā-sanì *m*.

**remote** *adj*: he lives in a ~ village way out there yanà zàune à wani ƙauyè can.

**remove** *v* a. (*esp. clothes*) cirè *v4*, tūɓè *v4*: you must ~ your shoes on entering the mosque wājìbī nè à cirè tàkalmì in zā à shìga masallācī. b. (*psn.*) fid dà / fitař (dà) *v5*: he's been ~d from his job an fid dà shi dàgà aikìn. c. (*to ano. place*) kau dà / kawař (dà) *v5*: these chairs have to be ~d dōlè à kau dà kùjèrun nàn.

**rendezvous** *n* (*meeting place*) magamà *f*: they arranged a ~ at a deserted building sun yi magamā à wani kangō.

**renew** v (sth., a structure) sābùntā v1; (a permit) sākè v4: ~ one's license, passport sākè lāsìn, fàsfô.

**renounce** v wātsar̃ (dà) v5: ~ one's faith wātsar̃ dà àddīnìnsà.

**renovate** n gyārā v1, sābùntā v1.

**renown** n shàhar̃ā f, sūnā m, màshàhūr̃àntakā f.

**renowned** adj shàhar̃ar̃r̃ē adj, màshàhūr̃ī m ⟨ai⟩; be ~ for yi sūnā m, shàhar̃à v3: he was ~ for his bravery yā shàhar̃à wajen jàr̃ùntakà.

**rent** 1. v (sth.) yi hayàr̃ w.a., kàr6i hayàr̃ w.a.: ~ a house, bicycle yi hayàr̃ gidā, kèkè; we've ~ed this house for the year mun kàr6i hayàr̃ gidân shèkar̃à ɗaya; ~ sth. out bā dà w.a. hayà: he has ~ed out his house yā bā dà gidansà hayà; ~ to so. bā w. hayàr̃ w.a.: he ~ed some bicycles to us for 3 days yā bā mù hayàr̃ kēkunā kwānā ukù; that house is not for ~ gidan nàn bà na hayà ba nè; a ~ed house, apartment gidan hayà.
2. n (kuɗin) hayà m: the landlord collects the ~ màigidan hayà yakàn kàr6i kuɗin hayà; I'm 2 months behind in my ~ watànā biyu kè nan bàn biyā kuɗin hayà ba; he hasn't paid his ~ yet bài biyā hayànsà ba tùkuna.

**reorganization** n gar̃ambāwùl m.

**repair** v gyārā v1 ⟨gyārā⟩, gyàrtā v1: ~ road, clock gyārà hanyà, àgōgo; (by sealing) līkè v4: ~ tire, pipe, roof līkè tāyà, būtūtū, rufī.

**reparations** n diyyà f.

**repay** v a. (refund) mai dà / mayar̃ (dà) v5. b. (so. for an action) rāmā wà v1: he repaid me for my kindness yā rāmā minì àlhēr̃ìn dà na yi masà.

**repeal** v sōkè v4: ~ a curfew sōkè ɗōkar̃ hanà fìta dà dare.

**repeat** v a. (an action) maimàita v1, sākè v1 (+ action n), k̃ar̃à v1 (+ action n): ~ what you said kà maimàita = kà sākè fàdā = kà sākè màganà; they ~ed the 3rd grade sun maimàità ajī na ukù. b. (a lesson, chapter in school) tusà / tisà v1, yi tushī/tishī m: let's ~ yesterday's lesson mù tusà dar̃àsin jiyà.

**repeatedly** adv bà sàu ɗaya bà sàu biyu ba: he beat the donkey ~ yā bùgi jākī bà sàu ɗaya bà sàu biyu ba; do sth. ~ yi ta: he told us ~ to get ready yā yi ta gayà manà mù shiryà.

**repent** v tūba v3a: when he realized that death was near, he ~ed dà ya ga ajàlinsà

yā kusa matsôwā, sai ya tūba.

**repentance** n tūbā m.

**repetition** n maimàitâwā f; (of lessons in school) tushī / tishī m.

**replace** v a. (take so.'s place, esp. temporarily) mayè gurbìn w., zaunà à matsayin w.: he ~d me for one week yā mayè gurbìnā mākò ɗaya = yā zaunà à matsayīnā mākò ɗaya; ~ so. by so. mai dà w. à matsayin w.: Audu has been ~ by Sani an mai dà Sāni à matsayin Audù. b. (take so.'s job) cikà gurbī, mayè w. à matsayī: Sani ~d Audu as secretary Sāni ya cikà gurbìn Audù na sakatar̃è; he ~d me as the mathematics teacher yā mayè ni à matsayīnā na kōyar̃ dà lìssāfī. c. (change to ano.) sākè v4: ~ a lightbulb sākè k̃wan làntar̃kì.

**replacement** n matsayī m, màimakō m, (for a position) mayèwā f: he is my ~ shī nè à matsayīnā na dâ; I need a ~ for this inà bùkātar̃ màimakonsà.

**replete** adj: be ~ k̃ōshi v3*.

**reply** 1. v bā dà amsà, mai/mayar̃ dà amsà: he hasn't replied yet bài bā da amsà ba tùkùna; have you replied to his letter? kā mayar̃ masà amsàr̃ wàsīk̃àr̃sà?
2. n amsà f ⟨oCi⟩: I am waiting for his ~ inà jiràn amsàr̃sà.

**report** 1. n a. (of news) làbār̃ī m ⟨u, ai⟩; an unconfirmed ~ wai (+ sent.): there has been a unconfirmed ~ that he was killed an kāwō làbār̃ìn cêwā wai an kashè shi. b. (esp. admin.) r̃ahōtò m ⟨anni⟩; submit a ~ mīk̃à r̃ahōtò.
2. v a. (make known): they are going to ~ the news zā à bā dà làbār̃ī. b. (submit a ~) kai r̃ahōtò: I've come to ~ a theft nā zō kāwō r̃ahōtòn sātā; we ~ed the boy to the principal mun kai k̃ārar̃ yār̃ò gàban shùgàban makar̃antā; ~ to so. (inform) shâidā wà v1; ~ for work zō aikì.

**reporter** n manèmin làbàr̃ai n; (newspaper) ɗan jar̃īdà m, (radio, TV) mài bā dà làbàr̃ai n.

**repossess** v k̃wācè wà v4: his car has been ~ed an k̃wācè masà mōtàr̃sà.

**represent** v a. wàkiltà v2, yi wà wakilcī m: he ~s Bauchi yā wàkìlci Bauci = yā yi wà Bauci wakilcī = wàkīlìn Bauci nè. b. (be symbol of) alàmtā v1, nūnà v1: the star and the crescent ~ peace watà dà tàurār̃ò nà nūnà zaman lāfiyà; this idol ~s their god gunkìn nân à zaman allànsù yakè.

**representation** n wakilcī m.

**representative** 1. n wàkīlī m ⟨ai⟩: ap-

point so. as ~ wakìltā v1: he appointed
me as his ~ in the matter yā wakìltā ni à
kân sha'ànîn; (in U.S. government) ɗan
Màjàlisàř Wàkìlai; (for sales) dìllālì
m ⟨ai⟩.

**2.** adj (mài) wakilcì m: a ~ government
gwamnatì mài wakilcì.

**repress** v: ~ an uprising kashè tàřzòmā.

**reprieve** v sōkè wà hukuncì.

**reprimand** v tsāwàtā wà v1, dakà wà
tsāwā, jā wà kûnnē.

**reproach** **1.** v (blame, censure) zàrgā v2;
(find fault with) kūshè wà v4.
 **2.** n: his manners are beyond ~ bâ shi
dà makūsā.

**reproduce** v hàifā v2.

**reptile** n jà-jìki m, jà-cikì m.

**republic** n jàmhūřiyà f.

**reputation** n sūnā m, shaidà f; (honor, self-
respect) iřìlì m; make a ~ for oneself yi
sūnā m, shàhařà v3; they ruined his ~ sun
ɓātà masà sūnā; he has a bad ~ bā yà
dà shaidà mài kyâu; give oneself a bad
~ ɓātà kâi.

**request** **1.** v nèmā v2 ⟨nēmā⟩, (esp. personal)
rôƙā v2 ⟨rôƙō⟩: ~ permission nèmi izìnī
= tàmbàyi izìnī; ~ relief aid, an investigation nèmi àgàjī, bìncìkē; ~ forgiveness rôƙi gāfařà.
 **2.** n rôƙō m, bùkātà f: grant so.'s ~ amsà
rôƙon w. = biyā bùkātàř w.; my ~ has
been granted bùkātàtā tā biyā.

**require** v (law) cê v*: do as the law ~s yi
daidai yàddà dōkà ta cè; the law ~s you
to have a visa dōkà tā cê kà yi bīzà;
be ~d to tīlàs ta sâ, yā kāmà tīlàs,
wàjìbī m: we were ~d to attend the meeting tīlàs ta sâ mukà hàlàřci tàrôn =
yā kāmà tīlàs mù hàlàřci tàrôn; everyone is ~d to pay taxes wàjìbī nè gà kōwā
yà biyā hařàjì.

**requirement** n a. (need) bùkātà f ⟨u⟩. b.
(condition) ƙā'idà f ⟨oCi⟩.

**rescind** v sōkè v4.

**rescue** **1.** v a. (save) cètā v2 ⟨cètō⟩, tsēřař
(dà) v5: he ~d her from drowning yā cècē
tà dàgà hàlakàř nitsèwā. b. (provide
aid, help) àgazà v2.
 **2.** n a. (act of saving) cètō m. b. (help)
àgàjī m; come to the ~ of àgazà v2.

**research** n bìncìkē m, nazàřī m.

**researcher** n mài bìncìkē n, mài nazàřī n.

**resemblance** n kàmā f ⟨anni⟩.

**resemble** v yi kàmā dà: he ~s my father
yanà kàmā dà bàbānā.

**reservation** n a. (doubt) tantamà f, shakkà
f: I have some ~s about that inà tan-

tamař wannàn. b. (e.g. at hotel): make a
hotel ~ rìƙè dākì à hòtâl; I've already
made a ~ for a place nā rigā nā kāmà
wurī.

**reserve** **1.** v a. (put aside) ajìyē v4, àdànà
v1: ~ this for later use ajìyè wannàn don
gàba; ~ a book ajìyè littāfì; ~ a room
ajìyè dākì = kāmà dākì. b. (restrict, set
apart) wārè v4, kēɓè v4: this section is ~d
for dignitaries an kēɓè wannàn wurī don
mânyan ƙūsōshì.
 **2.** n & adj: a forest ~ gandun dājì;
~ funds àjiyàř kudī; ~ troops sōjōjin
wucìn gādì.

**reserved** adj (secretive) (mài) zurfin cikì
m; (isolated from others) (mài) kawaicì
m: he is a ~ person yanà dà kawaicì =
bā yà shìga mutànē.

**reshuffle** n (in an organization) gařambāwùl
m.

**residence** n (home) gidā m ⟨aCe⟩, mazaunī
m.

**resident** n mazàunī m: city ~s mazàunā
bìřnī.

**resign** v a. (from work) barì v*; (from committee, position) sàuka dàgà v3; (from
high office) yi mùřābùs m. b. (acquiesce):
be ~ed to one's lot dànganà v3, hàƙurà
v3: even though I don't like living here,
I'm ~ed to it kō dà bā nà sôn zamānā
nân nā dànganà; he is ~ed to not finding a job here yā hàƙurà dà rashìn sāmùn
aikì à nân; be ~ed to God's will dànganà
gà Allàh; be ~ed to one's fate rùngùmi
ƙaddařà.

**resignation** n a. (from position, work)
barìn aikì m, sàukà f: hand in one's ~
mīƙà takàřdā ta sàukà dàga mùƙāmì. b.
(to one's fate) dànganà f, hàƙurì m.

**resin** n ƙārō m.

**resist** v a. (oppose) ƙi v0: I ~ed his suggestion nā ƙi shāwařàřsà; he ~ed arrest
yā ƙi à kāmà shi. b. (take firm stand
against) daddàgē wà v4: ~ the enemy
daddàgē wà àɓōkan gàba. c. (control oneself) daurè v4: we couldn't ~ flaughing at
him mun kāsà daurè yi masà dàriyā.

**resolution** n a. (decision) shāwařà f: reach
a ~ tsai dà shāwařà. b. (Pol.) zařtâřwā
f: adopt, pass a ~ kàrɓi zařtâřwā. c.
(determination) ƙarfin zūcìyā m.

**resolve** **1.** v a. (reconcile) shiryà v1,
daidàitā v1: he ~d their differences yā
shiryà tsàkāninsù = yā daidàitā su.
b. (be firm about) dàgē v4, tsayà tsayìn
dakà: they ~d to keep on fighting sun
dàgē kân sù ci gàba dà yāƙìn; he ~d

to finish the work by evening yā tsayà tsayìn dakà sai yā gamà aikìn kàfìn darē yà yi.

2. n (determination) ƙarfin zūcìyā m.

resourceful adj (mài) dàbār̃à f, (mài) kân gadō m.

resources n: national ~s ar̃zìkin ƙasā; natural ~s àlbar̃kàtun ƙasā.

respect 1. n a. (politeness toward so.) ladàbī m, bìyayyà f: show ~ to one's elders yi wà tsòfàffī ladàbī. b. (honor for one's superior) girmàmâwā f, ban girmā m, dar̃ajà f: he treated them with ~ yā girmàmā su = yā yi musù ban girmā = yā bā sù dar̃ajà; have ~ for so. mutùntā v1, ga girman w.; I have the greatest ~ for him inà ganin girmansà ƙwar̃ai; self-~ mutuncì m, ir̃llī m: never lose your self-~ kà kāre mutuncìnkà = kà san rìƙè mutuncìnkà = kadà kà zub dà mutuncì. c. (reference): with ~ to, see regard. d. (way) fuskà f, hanyà f: in what ~ are you better than him? ta wàcè fuskà cē kā fī shì?

2. v girmàmā v1, bā w. dar̃ajà, dar̃àttā v1, mutùntā v1, ga girman w.: I ~ed him for his knowledge inà girmàmā shi don illminsà; he is ~ed yanà dà girmā; ~ another's religion dar̃àttā àddīnìn w.; ~ the law bi dōkā; ~ another's rights ga hakkìn wani.

respectable adj (of psn.) (mài) hālin dattìjò m, (mài) dàttìjàntakà f: he is a ~ man yanà dà hālin dattìjò = yā rìƙè mutuncìnsà.

respectful adj (mài) ladàbī m, (mài) kunyà f; in a ~ way cikin girmā dà ar̃zìkī.

respects n (greetings): please pay my ~ to your family don Allàh dà Ànnabì kà isar̃ mini dà gaisuwātā gà ìyālìnkà.

respiration n numfāshī m.

respond v amsà v1: I called out to him and he ~ed nā kirā shì sai ya amsà minì.

response n a. (answer) amsà f ⟨oCi⟩: I am waiting for his ~ inà jiran amsàr̃sà; in ~ to gàme dà. b. (Lit.) amshì m.

responsibility n a. (moral ~ for so., sth.) àlhakī m. b. (duty, obligation) nauyī m: I take ~ for this work nā dauki nauyin wannàn aikì; place ~on so. azà wà nauyī; put a ~ on so. dōrà wà nauyī. c. (duty, esp. at work) aikì m: that's not my ~ wannàn bà aikìnā ba nè. d. (Law) hukuncì m: any person who is of age has legal ~ (for his actions) in mùtûm yā bàlagà duk wani hukuncì yā hau kânsà.

responsible adj a. (morally for others): you

will be held morally ~ for them if you don't help them in bà kà taimàkē sù ba, kā dauki àlhakinsù; you are ~ for this àlhakin wannàn yanà wuyànkà. b. (having a duty) (mài) nauyī m: a ~ position mùƙāmì mài nauyī; he is not ~ for this, I am wannàn bà nauyinsà ba nè, nāwa nè; make so. ~ for sth. dōrà wà nauyin w.a.

rest[1] 1. n hūtū m, (short) shāƙàtâwā f: let's take a little ~ mù dan shāƙàtā; Sunday is a day of ~ Lahàdì rānar̃ hūtū cè.

2. v a. (relax) hūtā v1, shāƙàtā v1: we let the horses ~ mun bar̃ dàwàkai sukà hūtà; I trust you have ~ed from your troubles inà fātā kā hūtà dà wàhalà; (fig.) put one's mind to ~ kwantar̃ dà hankàlī; ~ one's head on one's hand yi tàgumī m. b. (in condolences): may he ~ in peace Allàh yà ji ƙansà.

rest[2] n (remainder) saurā m, ràgōwà f: keep the ~ for me kà ajìyē mini saurān; the ~ have gone sauransù sun tàfi; where is the ~? inà ràgōwà? I'll pay the ~ next month zân cikà ràgōwà watà mài zuwà.

restaurant n hôtâl m, gidan àbinci m.

resthouse n gidan bàƙī m, masaukin bàƙī m, [F] kanfamā f.

restlessness n (going in & out) shìgi dà fìci m; (fidgeting) kùsùnniyà f, mùtsùniyà f, mùtsù-mutsū idph.

restore v a. (renovate) gyārà v1, sābùntā v1: the old Kano city gates have been ~d an sābùntà tsòfàffin ƙōfōfin bir̃nin Kanò. b. (revive) rāyà v1: ~ the old city rāyà tsōhon bir̃nī. c. (return) mai dà / mayar̃ (dà) v5.

restrain v a. (hold back) tsarè v4: ~ a madman tsarè mahàukàcī. b. (hinder) tauyè v4.

restrict (put a limit on) ƙayyàdè v4: ~ the sale of cigarettes ƙayyàdè tàllàn tābà.

restricted adj ƙàyyàdaddē adj, kèɓaɓɓē adj.

restroom n, see toilet.

result 1. n a. (outcome) sàkamakō m: ~s of the examination sàkamakon jar̃r̃àbâwā; his failure was a ~ of his laziness kāsàwar̃sà sàkamakon ragwancìnsà nē. b. (causal) sànàdiyyà f; as a ~ of à sànàdiyyar̃, sabōdà: they crashed as a ~ of his reckless driving à sànàdiyyar̃ gangancin tūƙìnsà sukà yi karò.

2. v (cause): ~ in zama sanàdī m: the fall ~ed in his death fādôwar̃ dà ya yi tā zama sanàdin mutuwàr̃sà.

resume v ci gàba: after a short rest, we ~d our journey bāyan 'yar̃ shāƙàtâwā, mun ci gàba dà tàfiyàr̃mù.

resurrection *n*: day of ~ rānaȓ kìyāmā̀ *f*.

resuscitate *v* faȓfaɗō dà. *v6*.

retail *n* (*trade*) kirī *m*; ~ dealer ɗan kirī *m*.

retain *v* riƙè *v4*.

retaliate *v* rāmā̀ *v1*, faȓkè *v4*: after the attack, they waited a week and then ~d bāyan harìn sun kwāna bakwài sai sukà rāmā̀.

retaliation *n* rāmuwā *f*, sā̀kayyā̀ *f*.

retard *v* (*slow down*) tauyè *v4*.

retarded *adj* (*psn.*) gaulā̀ *n* ⟨aye⟩.

retch *v*: he is ~ing amai yanā̀ tūƙā̀ masà.

reticence *n* zurfin cikì *m*.

retire *v* a. (*from work*) yi ȓìtāyà̀ *f*, [F] yi antaȓē *m*, yi mùȓābùs *m*; ~d workers tsòfàffin ma'àikàtā̀. b. (*pull back, out*) jā dà bāya.

retirement *n* ȓìtāyà̀ *f*, mùȓābùs *m*: forced ~ ȓìtāyà̀ ta dōlè; voluntary ~ ȓìtāyà̀ ta ganin dāmā̀.

retrace *v* bi asalī, bi diddigī.

retract *v* a. (*draw back into*) nōƙè *v4*, kuɗè *v4*: the tortoise ~ed its head kùnkurū yā nōƙè kânsà. b. (*take back*) jânyè *v4*: he ~ed his criticism yā jânyè sūkàȓsà.

retreat[1] *n* (*Relig.*) halwā̀ *f*.

retreat[2] *v* jā (dà) bāya, kōmā̀ dà bāya; the army ~ed sōjōjìn sun jā dà bāya.

retribution *n*: just ~ sā̀kàmakō *m*: the just ~ for good is good sā̀kàmakon àlhēȓì, àlhēȓì; bitter ~ rāmuwaȓ gayyā̀ *f*.

retrieve *v* ɗaukō *v6*.

return 1. *vi* (*go back*) kōmā̀ *v1*: he has ~ed to his country yā kōmā̀ ƙasaȓsù; (*come back*) dāwō *v6*, kōmō *v6*: he ~ed home yā dāwō gidā; I found it when I ~ed dà na kōmō nā taraȓ dà shī.

2. *vt* a. (*give sth. back*) mai dà / mayaȓ (dà) *v5*, kōmā̀ dà *v1*: he ~ed my book yā mai dà littāfìnā. b. (*repay*) sākā̀ wà *v1*: I did him a good deed but he ~ed it with evil nā yi masà àlhēȓì yā sākā̀ minì dà shaȓȓì.

3. *n* dāwôwā *f*, kōmôwā *f*: I found it on my ~ dà kōmôwātā sai na taraȓ dà shī; in ~ for à màimakon, sabōɗà: I filled his tank in ~ for the help he gave me nā cikà masà tankìn mōtà sabōɗà tàimakôn dà ya yi minì.

4. *adj*: ~ trip, ticket tàfiyàȓ, tikitìn zuwā̀ dà dāwôwā.

returns *n*: I wished him 'many happy ~!' nā yi masà 'Allàh yà maimàità (manà)'!

reunion *n*: have a ~ yi tàron sādà-zùmùntā *m*, sādà zùmùntā.

reveal *v* bayyànā *v1*: ~ one's true self bayyànà kânsà; ~ so.'s mistakes bayyànà kuskurèn w.; ~ so.'s secrets tōnā̀ wà àsīȓī, yi wà kwàrmatò *m*.

revelation *n* (*Relig.*) wahàyī *m*: a ~ came to the prophet an saukō wà ànnabì wahàyī = an yi wà ànnabì wahàyī.

revenge 1. *n* rāmuwā̀ *f*: get, take ~ rāmā̀ *v1*, ɗaukō fansā̀, faȓkè *v4*: they took ~ for last year's defeat sun rāmā̀ cîn dà akà yi musù bā̀ra; get real ~ yi rāmuwaȓ gayyā̀.

2. *v* rāmā̀ *v1*.

revenue *n* kuɗin shìgā / kuɗin shigôwā *m*.

reversal *n* (*esp. Pol.*) jūyìn wàinā *m*.

reverse 1. *v* a. (*revoke*) ɗanyàtā *v1*, sōkè *v4*: ~ a ruling, plan ɗanyàtā ƙa'idā̀, shirì. b. (*make opposite*): the sitiation has been ~d an yi jūyìn wàinā. c. (*a vehicle*) yi ȓìbâs *f*, [F] yi bāya-bāya.

2. *n* a. (*gear of car*) ȓìbâs *f*: put the car in ~ yi ȓìbâs dà mōtā̀. b. (*opposite*) akàsī *m*: the ~ of what I said akàsin màganātā; count in ~ order ƙidàyā ta bāya-bāya.

review *v* a. (*look over*) dūbà *v1*: ~ troops dūbà fàȓētìn sōjà. b. (*write a critique*) ȓubùtà shaȓhì: ~ a book ȓubùtà shaȓhìn littāfì. c. (*a lesson, chapter*) tusā̀ / tisā̀ *v1*, yi tushì/tishì *m*, (*esp. prior to an exam*) yi bītā̀ *f*.

revile *v* zàzzāgā̀ *v2*, rainà *v1* ⟨rainì⟩.

revive 1. *vt* rāyà *v1*: ~ the economy rāyà tattalin aȓzìkin ƙasā̀; the new market has ~d the town sābuwaȓ kàsuwâȓ tā rāyà gàrîn.

2. *vi* (*become refreshed*) faȓfaɗō *v6*: after he drank some water, he ~d bāyan yā shā ruwā̀, yā faȓfaɗō = hankàlinsà yā kōmō.

revoke *v* a. (*a law*) sōkè *v4*, ɗanyàtā *v1*. b. (*seize, take away*) ƙwācè *v4*: ~ so.'s licence ƙwācè wà lāsìsì.

revolt 1. *n* tāwàyè *m*, bōȓe *m*.

2. *v* yi tāwàyè *m*, tā dà bōȓe.

revolution *n* a. (*Pol.*) jūyìn mulkì *m*. b. (*complete change*) jūyìn jùyà-hālì *m*.

revolutionary *n* & *adj* (*Pol.*) (mài) nēman sauyì *m*.

revolve *v* kēwàyà *v1*: the moon ~s around the earth watā yanā̀ kēwàyà dūniyà̀.

revolver *n* lìbaȓbā̀ *f*, [F] pìstōlê *f*.

reward 1. *n* a. lādā *m*: offer a ~ for lost and found bā dà lādan tsintuwā = bā dà gōȓòn tsintuwā. b. (*Relig.*) sā̀kayyā̀ *f*.

2. *v* a. bā dà lādā. b. (*esp. by God*) sākā̀

wà *v1*: may God ~ us! Allàh yà sākà manà! = Allàh yà bā mù sàkayyà! may God ~ you for your good deed Allàh yà sākà dà àlhērì.

**rhetoric** *n* zàlāƙà *f*, fàsāhà à màganà.

**rheumatism** *n* àmōsànin ƙashī *m*, sanyin ƙashī *m*.

**rhinoceros** *n* kaƙkàndà *f*.

**rhyme** *n* 'yaƙ wāƙà *f*; (*of last syllable*) ƙāfiyā *f*; (*fig.*) without ~ or reason bā gaiƙà bā dàlīlì.

**rhythm** *n* karì *m* ⟨e²⟩, launìn wāƙà *m*: every song has its own ~ kōwàcè wāƙà nà dà karìntà; change the ~ canzà launìn wāƙà.

**rib(s)** *n* haƙàrƙarī *m/p*.

**ribbon** *n* kìƙtānì *m*; (*for typewriter*) zàrē *m*.

**rice** *n* shìnkāfà *f*; long-grained ~ shìnkāfà 'yaƙ kilākì; clean ~ (*remove sand with water*) rēgè *v4*.

**rich** *adj* a. (*wealthy*) (mài) aƙzìkī *m*, (mài) dūkìyā *f*, (mài) kuɗī *m*; a ~ man àttàjìrī *m* ⟨ai⟩; the ~ and powerful mànya-mànya, màsu hannū dà shūnī; the gap between the ~ and the poor rātā dà kè tsàkānin mawàdātā dà matàlàutā; make so. ~ aƙzùta *v1*; become, get ~ aƙzutà *v3*, wàdātà *v3*, aƙzùtu *v7*: they became ~ from oil sun aƙzùtu dà mân fētūƙ. b. (*fertile in natural resources*) (mài) àlbaƙkà *f*, (mài) aƙzìkī *m*: ~ soil ƙasā mài àlbaƙkà; that country is ~ in natural resources ƙasàƙ nan nà dà aƙzìkin ƙasā.

**riches** *n* dūkìyā *f*, aƙzìkī *m*.

**rid, get rid** *v* a. (*free oneself of*) ràbu dà *v7*: I don't know how to get ~ of my cold bàn san yàddà zân ràbu dà muƙà ba. b. (*eliminate*) kashè *v4*: how can we ~ ourselves of these cockroaches? yàyà zā mù iyà kashè kyànkyasòn nân? c. (*throw out*) yā dà / yaƙ (dà) *v5*: let's get ~ of these rags mù yaƙ dà tsummōkaràn nân.

**riddle, riddling** *n* kà-cīci-kà-cīci / kà-cinci-kà-cinci *m*.

**ride** 1. *v* a. (*an animal, vehicle*) hau *v\** ⟨hawā⟩: he rode a camel yā hau ràƙumī; she has never ridden a horse, bicycle bà tà taɓà hawan dōkì, kèkè ba; know how to ~ iyà *v1*: he knows how to ~ a horse, bicycle yā iyà dōkì, kèkè. b. (*in a vehicle*) shìga *v3*, hau *v\** ⟨hawā⟩: he rode the train to Maiduguri yā shìga jirgī zuwà Màidugùri.

2. *n* a. hawā *m*, tàfiyà *f*; horseback riding kìlīsà *f*, hawan dōkì *m*; we've been

spoiled from riding in cars hawan mōtà yā sangàƙtā mu. b. (*helping convey so. somewhere*) dànì *m*: he gave me a ~ into town yā bā nì dànì zuwà gàrī = yā ɗaukē nì zuwà gàrī; he gave me a ~ on his bicycle yā kai nì à kèkènsà.

**rider** *n* mahàyī *m*, ɗan (+ *name of specific animal, vehicle*): camel ~ ɗan ràƙumī; bicycle ~ ɗan kèkè.

**ridge** *n* a. (*row for planting*) kunyā *f* ⟨oCi⟩: bank up the ground to form ~s hūɗà don à tā dà kunyōyī. b. (*of hill, mountain*) kân dūtsè *m*.

**ridicule** 1. *n* (*mockery*) ba'à *f*; (*esp. through song*) zàmbō *m*.
2. *v* (*mock*) yi wà ba'à *f*; (*humiliate*) ci fuskàƙ w., wulāƙantaƙ (dà) *v5*, wulāƙantà *v1*: he was ~d in public an ci fuskàƙsà gàban jàma'à.

**ridiculous** *adj* a. (*laughable*) (mài) ban dàriyā. b. (*nonsensical*) na banzā *f*: it was a ~ suggestion zàncen banzā nè.

**riding** *n* hawā *m*; horseback ~ hawan dōkì *m*, kìlīsà *f*.

**rifle** *n* bindigà *f* ⟨oCi⟩; automatic ~ bindigà mài jìgìdā = bindigà mài hàƙsāshì; fire a ~ haƙbà bindigà.

**rift** *n* (*between people*) ɓarakà *f*: cause, mend a ~ kāwō, ɗinkè ɓarakà.

**rig¹** *n* (*oil*) injìn haƙaƙ mâi *m*.

**rig²** *v* (*defraud*): ~ an election yi zāluncì à zàɓē = yi màguɗī à zàɓē.

**right¹** 1. *adj & adv* a. (*correct*) daidai *adv*: there is a ~ way to do it and a wrong way àkwai hanyàƙ yînsà ta daidai, àkwai kuma wàddà bà daidai ba; is that clock ~ or not? àgōgôn yanà tàfiyà daidai kō kùwa? everything will come out all ~ kōmē zâi yi daidai; this is the ~ one ~ for you wannàn yā yi makà daidai; this is the ~ way to do it hakà akè yînsà; all ~ shì kè nan; is everything all ~? kōmē lāfiyà dai? b. (*true*) na gàskiyā *f*; you're ~ gàskiyaƙkà; I do not know which of them is ~ bàn san wàƙ gàskiyā cikinsù ba; is he in his ~ mind? yanà cikin hankàlìnsà kùwa? c. (*good, moral*) na hàlāl *m*: it is not ~ to steal sātā bà àbin hàlâl ba cè; teach children the difference between ~ and wrong kōyà wà yârā sanìn bambancì tsàkānin hàlâl dà hàƙâm. d. (*suitable*): you've made the ~ decision kā yi àbîn dà ya kàmātà; pay what you think is ~ kì biyā àbîn dà kikà ga yā dācè = kì sàyā dà daƙajà. e. ~ away kâi tsàye, yànzu-yànzu; ~ now yànzun nàn.
2. *v* a. (*correct sth. wrong*) daidàitā *v1*.

b. (*make stand up*) tsai dà / tsayař (dà) v5.

**right**[2] *n* a. (*power, authority*) īkò *m*, izìnī *m*: you don't have the ~ to do it bā kằ dà īkòn yînsà; by what ~ did you do that? wằ ya bā kà izìnin yîn hakà? b. (*priv- ilege*) hakkì *m* ⟨oCi⟩: I demand my ~s inằ nēman hakkìnā; I have the ~ to see the judge inằ dà hakkìn ganin àlƙālī; deprive so. of his ~s tauyè hakkìn w. = ɗauki hakkìn w.; human ~s hakkìn ɗan Adàm; oil ~s hakkìn hằƙař mâi; violate so.'s ~s kētà hakkìn w. = dannè hakkìn w. c. (*constitutional*) 'yancì *m*: the ~ of free speech 'yancìn fàɗař řa'àyī.

**right**[3] *n & adv* (*direction*) dāma *f*: his ~ hand hannunsà na dāma; it is on the ~- hand side yanà hannun dāma; to the ~ of us is the police station à dāmařmù gằ cājì-ōfìs; the road to the ~ hanyàř dāma; to the ~ of dāma dà: his house is to the ~ of mine gidansà nằ dāma dà nằwā; keep to the ~ bi (hannun) dāma; follow, turn ~ yi, jūyằ dāma.

**righteousness** *n* sanìn gàskiyà *m*.

**right-wing** *adj* (mài) řa'àyin rìƙau *m*.

**rigid** *adj* a. (*of thing or psn.*) ƙàndàrarrē *adj*; become ~ sandàrē v4, ƙandàrē v4. b. (*doctrinaire*) (mài) tsàttsauran řa'àyī *m*.

**rigorous** *adj* (mài) tsananī *m*.

**rigor mortis** *n* sanƙàmēwař jìkī *f*.

**rim** *n* (*of pot, wheel*) bằkī *m*; (*of bicycle wheel*) kangařwā *f*; (*of bicycle wheel used as toy*) gaře *m*.

**rind** *n* (*of melon, lemon*) ɓāwō *m*, fātà *f*.

**rinderpest** *n* cīwòn būshiyā *m*, cīwòn baurừ *m*.

**ring**[1] *n* (*esp. for finger*) zōbè *m* ⟨Ca⟩, (*smaller type*) zōbanyằ *f*: a gold ~ zōbèn zīnāřì; (*any metal ~*) ƙawanyằ *f* ⟨u⟩.

**ring**[2] 1. *vt* kaɗà v1: ~ a bell kaɗà ƙàrarrawā; (*esp. telephone, cash register*) bugà v1: I'll ~ you up tomorrow zân bugō mā wayằ gòbe; ~ up ₦10 on the cash reg- ister kì bugà naiřằ gōmà à màshìn. 2. *vi* (*of bell*) yi ƙārā *f*; (*of telephone*) bugà v1: the telephone is ~ing wayằ nằ bugàwā.

**ringworm** *n* màkērò *m*, (*tinea*) ƙyàsfī / ƙyàzbī *m*.

**rinse** *v* (*clothes, hair, dishes*) ɗauràyè v4 ⟨ɗaurayằ⟩ *f*; (*one's mouth*) kurkùrē v1 ⟨kùrkurằ⟩ *f*.

**riot** *n* tařzòmā *f*, bòře *m*: put down a ~ kashè tàřzòmā = tsai dà bòře.

**rioter** *n* ɗan bòře *m*.

**rip** 1. *v* (*cloth, paper*) ɓarkằ v1, kētà v1, fařkè v4; my dress is ~ped rìgātā tā kēcè.
2. *n* ɓàrakằ *f*, kètā *f*: the gown has a ~ in it rìgā tanằ dà ɓàrakằ.

**ripe** *adj* nùnannē *adj*; be(come) ~ (*of fruits*) nùna v3: the oranges are not quite ~ lèmôn bài nùna ba sòsai; it is nearly ~ yanằ bằkin nùnā; (*be ready for eating*) ƙōsà v1.

**ripen** *v* a. (*naturally*) nūnař (dà) v5, nùna v3: it won't ~ unless you put it in the sun bà zā tà nùna ba in bà à sâ ta à rāna ba; the sun has ~ed the bananas rānā tā nūnař dà àyàbà. b. (*by human action*) nukà v1: if you want to ~ bananas, put them in a covered pot ìdan anằ sôn à nukà àyàbà, sai à sâ ta cikin tukunyằ à rufè.

**rise** 1. *v* a. (*go up*) tāshì v3b: smoke ~s hayāƙī kàn tāshì; she always ~s at dawn takàn tāshì dà àsùbā; the bread has ~n buřōdì yā tāshì; ~ to one's feet mīƙè v4: the crowd rose to honor him jàma'ằ tā mīƙè don girmàmà shi. b. (*of sun*) fitō v6: when does the sun ~? yàushè rānā kè fitōwằ? c. (*of prices*) hàuhawà v3, haurà v1: prices have ~n kuɗin kāyā sun hàuhawà. d. (*of river, water*) cikō v6: the river is rising kōgī yanằ ta cikōwằ. d. (*other uses*): give ~ to jāwō v6: what has given ~ to such talk? mề ya jāwō wannàn irìn zàncè? ~ to power ƙàsaità v3; the land ~s here nân dà tudừ; rising and falling ground tudừ dà gàngarằ.
2. *n* a. (*in price, blood pressure*) hàuhawằ *f*: the ~ of prices hàuhawằř fàřàshì; the ~ and fall of prices hawā dà sàukař fàřàshì. b. (*high ground*) tudừ *m* ⟨Cai⟩.

**risk** 1. *n* a. (*chance*) kàsadà *f*: it's a ~ to drive without insurance kàsadằ cē à tūƙà mōtà bâ ìnshōřằ; take a ~ yi kàsadà. b. (*danger*) haɗàřī *m*: there's no ~ in it bâ wani haɗàřī à ciki; it's a ~y business hařƙà cē mài haɗàřī; you do it at your own ~ kōmē ya sằmē kà, kai kā jā; take a needless ~ (*fig.*) yi kằřàmbằnin àkuyằ.
2. *v*: ~ one's health yi wàsā dà lāfiyà; ~ one's life (*esp. by courageous action*) yi ƙùru *m*, (*fig.*) yi ƙūnař baƙin wākē: he ~ed his life going into the fire to save the child yā yi ƙùru dà ya shìga gòbařàř don yà tsērař dà yāròn; ~ one's wealth yi cācà dà dūkìyā.

**rite** *n* (*custom*) àl'ādà *f* ⟨u⟩; ~s enjoined by Islam sunnà *f* ⟨oCi⟩.

**ritual** *adj* na àl'ādà *f*.

**rival** *n* (*in competition*) àbōkin gàsā *m*,

àbōkin karāwā *m;* (*Pol.*) àbōkin hàmayyà *m,* ɗan tākaɍā *m;* (*esp. among co-wives*) kīshìyā *f* ⟨oCi⟩; he is without ~ bâ mài kàmaɍsà.

rivalry *n* a. (*jealousy*) kīshì *m,* ɗan'ubancì *m:* there's a ~ between them dà kīshì tsàkāninsù. b. (*competition*) gāsā *f,* tākaɍā *f;* (*Pol.*) hàmayyà *f.*

river *n* kŏgī *m* ⟨una⟩, (*small*) gulbī *m* ⟨a- e⟩: ~ bank bàkin kŏgī; ~ basin mak- waɍāraɍ kŏgī; ~ bed ƙwaryaɍ kŏgī; on the opposite side of the ~ à hayìn kŏgī = à gāɓaɍ kŏgī; source of a ~ idòn kŏgī; the Niger ~ Kŏgin Kwāɍā.

rivet *n* ɍîbô *m.*

road *n* hanyà *f* ⟨oCi⟩, *see* street; ~ bed zubìn hanyà *m;* tarred ~ (hanyà) kwàltâ *f,* [F] gùdàɍô *m;* secondary ~ gwadabè *m;* country ~ kaɍaukà *f;* an all-season ~ hanyàɍ rānī dà dāminā; is this the right ~? wannàn cē hanyàɍmù? where does this ~ lead to? ìnā wannàn hanyàɍ ta nùfā? = ìnā hanyàɍ takè zuwā? by ~ à mōtà: 4 hours by ~ awā huɗu à mōtà; did you go by ~ or by train? à mōtà ka jē kō à jirgī? tar a ~ yi wà hanyà kwàltâ; get off, leave a ~ rātsè *v4.*

road sign *n* àlāmàɍ hanyà *f,* [F] fànô *m.*

roam *v* yi gàntàlī *m,* (*esp. aimlessly*) yi yāwòn banzā *m,* yi gàràrī *m,* yi ràgaità *f,* yi gīlô *m.*

roan antelope *n* gwankī *m* ⟨aye⟩.

roar 1. *v* (*of fire*) rūrā *v1:* the fire is ~ing wutā tanā ta rūràwā; (*of lion, fire, en- gine*) yi rūrì *m;* (*of lion, wind*) yi ƙūgì *m.*
2. *n* rūrī *m,* ƙūgì *m.*

roast *v* gasā *v1:* ~ed meat gàsasshen nāmā; ~ed corn gàsasshiyaɍ masàɍā; (*in hot sand, e.g. peanuts*) sōyà *v1:* ~ed peanuts sòyayyiyaɍ gyàɗā.

rob *v* yi satà *f:* my house was ~bed an yi minì satà à gidā; (*by force, with arms*) yi fashì *m:* they ~bed him of all his money an yi masà fashìn duk kuɗinsà; (*fig.*) they ~bed me blind ɓàràyī sun baɍ nì huntū = ɓàràyī sun yi minì kakaf.

robber *n* ɓàrāwò *m,* ɓàraunìyā *f* ⟨i⟩, (*esp. armed*) ɗan fashì *m;* a gang of ~s 'yan fashì; the ~s left me without a shred of clothing ɓàràyī sun yi minì kakaf.

robbery *n* satà *f;* commit ~ yi satà; armed ~ fashì dà màkàmai.

robe *n* (*men's or women's*) rìgā *f* ⟨una⟩: a man's large ~ bàbbaɍ rìgā; he bought 3 ~s yā sàyi rìgā wuyà ukù; (*var. types of men's ~s*): (*small full ~*) shàkwàrā

*f;* (*for royalty*) rìgaɍ sàrautà; (*large*) gàɍè *f;* (*caftan*) kàftānī *m;* (*esp. ceremo- nial, often with hood*) àlkyabbà *f;* (*caftan style without embroidery*) hàɍtûm *f;* (*long & narrow*) jàllàbiyà *f.*

rock[1] *n* dūtsè *m* ⟨duwàtsū⟩.

rock[2] *v* (*to & fro*) yi rawā *f;* (*of boat*) tangàdā *v1;* (*a baby to sleep*) rurrùgā *v1.*

rocket *n* ɍōkà *f* ⟨oCi⟩: ~ engine injìn ɍōkà; launch a ~ haɍbà ɍōkà.

rod *n* sàndā *m* ⟨una⟩; (*used as whip*) tsumāgìyā / tsumangìyā *f* ⟨oCi⟩, tsabgà *f* ⟨oCi⟩.

rogue *n* (*swindler*) mazàmbàcī *m,* ɗan dàmfarà *m.*

role *n* (*function*) aikì *m.*

roll 1. *n* naɗì *m;* (*of cloth, yardage*) bandìɍ *m,* turmī *m* ⟨a-e⟩; ~ of film fîm *m.*
2. *vt* (*knead sth. soft*) lailàyā *v1,* mulmùlā *v1:* if you ~ the dough into thin strands, you'll get spaghetti in kin mulmùlā alkamā tà zama sīɍīɍìyā zā kì sàmi tàliyà; ~ sth. in (*coat with flour, liquid*) birkìdā *v1:* ~ the fish around in flour be- fore frying it kì birkìdà kīfī à cikin gàrī kàfìn à sōyà shi; ~ sth. round along the ground garà *v1,* mirgìnā *v1;* ~ food into a ball cūrà *v1,* mulmùlā *v1;* ~ up (*cloth, paper*) naɗè *v4:* he ~ed up the mat, his sleeves yā naɗè tàbarmā, hannun rìgaɍsà.
3. *vi:* ~ around on the ground (*of chil- dren*) mìrginà *v3,* (*of animal*) yi bir- gimā *f,* bìrkidà *v3;* ~ down, into gangàrā *v1:* the ball ~ed into the hole bâl tà gangàrā cikin rāmì; ~ over (*on one's back*) birkìcē *v4,* mirgìnē *v4.*

roll-call *n* kiràn sūnā *m.*

roof *n* rufī *m:* the houses are covered with corrugated iron ~s an yi wà dàkunàn rufìn kwānò; (*of thatch*) jinkā *f* ⟨aye⟩; (*flat, of clay*) sōrō *m* ⟨aye⟩.

room *n* a. ɗākì *m* ⟨una⟩: how many ~s are there in this compound? dàkunà nawà kè cikin wannàn gidân? inside a ~ à dakà *adv;* put it in the ~ kà sà shi à dakà; private ~ (*of head of household*) tùrākā *f.* b. (*space*) wurī *m:* is there ~ in the car? àkwai wurī à mōtàɍ? make ~ for so. bâ w. wurī: please squeeze together to make ~ for me to sit don Allàh kù matsà kù bā nì wurī ìn zaunà.

roommate *n* àbōkin hayà *m,* àbōkin zamā *m;* he is my ~ dàkìnmù ɗaya.

roomy *adj* (*of a container*) (mài) cikì *m;* (*of a structure, place*) (mài) fādī *m.*

rooster *n* zàkarà *m* ⟨u⟩.

root n a. (*of plant*) sâiwā f ⟨oCi⟩; ~ crops mabùnƙùsā ƙasā p; aerial ~ sâiwař bisà; tap ~ uwař saiwōyī = bàbbař sâiwā. b. (*origin*) asalī m, tūshè m: my ~s are in Africa asalīnā yanā Afiřkà. c. (*of a matter*) tūshè m, lōgā f: I discovered the ~ of the problem nā sāmō lōgař màganā; (*fig.*) love of money is the ~ of all evil sôn àbin dūniyā shī nè tūshèn yawancin mūgùn àbù. d. (*Gram.*) tūshè m.

rope n igiyà f ⟨oCi⟩: braid ~ tufkà igiyà.

rosary n, see prayer beads.

rosewater n tùrāren wàřdi m.

rot v ruɓè v4: eat it now or else it will ~ kà cī shì yànzu kadà yà ruɓè.

rotate v (*turn*) jūyā v1; (*alternate, e.g. crops*) sauyà v1.

rough adj a. (*not smooth*) (mài) kaushī m: ~ bark, skin ɓāwō, fātā mài kaushī. b. (*not gentle*): don't be ~ on the child kadà kì yi wà yārò ƙètā; he pushed me aside ~ly yā bangàjē ni dà ƙarfī; use ~ language yi baƙař màganā; ~ winds iskā mài ƙarfī; (*fig.*) he had a ~ time yā ɗanɗànà kūɗàřsà.

roughly adv a. (*approximately*) wajen, kàmař, kusan: there were ~ 200 people àkwai wajen mutānē ɗàrī biyu. b. (*not gently*) speak ~ to so. yi wà màganā gantsi-gantsi.

round 1. adj kèwàyayyē adj, (mài) kèwayà f, (mài) dā'iřā f: the world is ~ like a ball dūniyā kèwàyayyiyā cè kàmař ƙwallō; make me a ~ table kà ƙērā mini tēbùř mài dā'iřā; all the huts are ~ ɗākunā duk màsu kèwayà nē; big and ~ danƙwalēlè adj.
2. adv, see around.
3. n (*of a tournament*) karāwā f.

roundabout 1. n (*traffic circle*) řāwùl m, [F] řampùwân m.
2. adj (*not direct*): this is a ~ route hanyàř nân kèwàyē cè.

round-shouldered adj (mài) dōrō m: he is ~ yanā dà dōrō.

round-trip adj tàfiyà-dà-dāwôwā: a ~ ticket tikitìn tàfiyà-dà-dāwôwā.

roundworm n macìjin cikì m, tsūtsàř cikì m.

route n hanyà f ⟨oCi⟩: this is the best ~ to Sokoto wannàn hanyà tā fi sauƙī zuwà Sakkwato; a bus, train ~ hanyàř bâs, jirgī.

routine adj na yâu dà kullum: this is ~ work aikìn nân na yâu dà kullum.

rove v yi gàntàlī m, yi gīlò m.

row[1] v (*a boat*) tūƙā v1.

row[2] n a. (*of individual items*) jērī m: a ~ of books, people, mountains jērìn lìttàttàfai, mutānē, duwàtsū. b. (*forming a continuous line*) lāyī m ⟨uka⟩: we sat in the sixth ~ mun zaunā à lāyì na shidà; put them in a ~ kà sā waɗannân à lāyì; a horizontal or vertical ~ lāyìn kwànce kō na tsàye. c. (*esp. group of similar people, things*) sahū m: the soldiers were in the first ~, followed by policemen, and then the veterans sōjōjī sunā sahū na ɗaya, bìye dà sahun 'yan sàndā dà kuma na tsòfàffin sōjōjī; in a ~ à jère adv; in ~s jērì-jērì adv, lāyì-lāyì adv, sahū-sahū v: the books are arranged in ~s an jērà lìttàttàfai lāyì-lāyì. d. (*ridge for plants*) kunyā f ⟨oCi⟩: on the farms, you see ~s and ~s of maize à gōnàkī anā ganin masàřā kunyā-kunyā.

row[3] n (*argument*) gařdamā / gaddamā f ⟨gařdàndamī⟩, jā-ìn-jā f: have a ~ over the money yi gařdamā gàme dà kuɗī; (*verbal or physical*) faɗà m: he got into a ~ an yi masà faɗà.

rowboat n kwàlekwàle m.

royal adj (mài) sàrautā f; His R. Highness, the Emir of Kano Mài Girmā Sarkin Kanò.

royalties n (*of book*) kàmashò m.

royalty n sàrautā f; member of ~ bàsarākè m, sàràkī m ⟨ai⟩.

rub v a. (*sth. onto sth.*) gōgā v1 ⟨gūgā⟩ f, shāfā v1: ~ oil on the body shāfà mâi à jìki. b. (*sth.*) gōgè v4: he ~bed his face with a cloth yā gōgè fuskàřsà dà ƙyallē; he ~bed the mark out yā gōgè àlāmà sai tā fìta. c. (*with, between hands*) muřzā v1.

rubber n (*raw material*) danƙò m; (*manufactured*) řōbà m, [F] kàushû m.

rubber band n maɗaurin řōbà m.

rubber solution (*for patching tire*) shòli-shò m, [F] shàlìshô / shàlashà m/f.

rubber stamp n sìtâm m, [F] tàmpô m.

rubbish n shārā f, dàtti m: ~ container bōlà f, garwař shārā f; ~ heap jūjī m, bōlà f; (*fig.*) talk ~ yi màganàř banzā = yi màganàř wòfī; what ~! ji wata màganàř banzā!

rude adj a. (*impolite*) maràs ladàbī m, maràs dā'à f. b. (*disrespectful*) maràs kunyà f, (mài) rashìn kunyà m; (*esp. women*) (mài) tsīwà f, see insolent: he is ~ yanā dà rashìn kunyà = rashìn kunyà gàrē shì = bâ shi dà kunyà.

rudeness *n* rashìn ladàbī *m*, rashìn kunyà *m*; (*esp. of women*) tsīwà *f*.

rug *n* (*esp. Oriental*) dàr̃dūmā̀ *f*; ornamental ~ kìlīshī *m* ⟨ai⟩; (*tradit. round ~ of pieced leather*) kìlàgò *m* ⟨ai⟩.

rugby *n* k̃wallon zàri-r̃ùgā *m*, [F] r̃ùgùbī *m*.

ruin 1. *v* a. (*spoil*) rūsā̀ *v1*, 6ātā̀ *v1*, lālātā̀ *v1*: he ~ed our plans yā rūsà manà sha'ànī; the stain has ~ed my dress jìrwàyē yā 6ātà minì rìgā. b. (*make sth. deteriorate*) ta6ar6àrā *v1*, ta6ar6àrē *v4*: ~ the economy ta6ar6àrà tattalin ar̃zìkin k̃asā. c. (*of psn.*): be ~ed lālàcē *v4*, 6àcē *v5*, 6al6àlcē *v4*; he is a ~ed man (*unfortunate*) yā zama àbin tàusàyī.
2. *n* (*of building*) kangō *m* ⟨aye⟩: the building fell into ~s ginìn yā zama kangō; old ~s kangàyē na dâ; (*remains of a settlement, town*) kufai *m*: ~s of a house, village kufan gidā, k̃auyè; Roman ~s kufan Rûm.

rule 1. *n* a. (*Pol.*) mulkī̀ *m*, (*esp. traditional*) sàrautā̀ *f*: British ~ mulkìn Ingìlà; colonial ~ mulkìn màllakā̀. b. (*regulation, ruling*) dòkā *f* ⟨oCi⟩, k̃a'idā *f* ⟨oCi⟩: lay down a ~ kafà k̃a'idā; obey the school ~s bi dōkōkin makar̃antā; the ~s of grammar k̃a'idōjin nahawù; traffic ~s dōkōkin hanyà; break a ~ karyà dòkā = kētà k̃a'idā; it's against the ~s to hold the ball more than 30 seconds dòkā tā hanà à rik̃è k̃wallò samà dà sàkàn tàlàtin. ~s and regulations dōkōkī dà k̃a'idōjī. c. as a ~ gālìbàn *adv*: as a ~, he eats dinner at eight p.m. gālìbàn yakàn ci àbinci dà k̃arfè takwàs na yâmma.
2. *v* yi mulkī̀ *m*, yi sàrautā̀ *f*, rik̃è sàrautā̀: he ~d for 40 years yā yi shèkar̃à àr̃bà'in yanà rik̃è dà sàrautā; ~ over a group màllakā̀ *v2*.

ruler[1] *n* (*psn.*) mài īkò *n*, mài mulkī̀ *n*; (*tradit.*) sarkī *m* ⟨saràkunā̀⟩, mài sàrautā̀ *n*; (*other types of tradit. ~s*): (*district head*) hākìmī *m* ⟨ai⟩; (*village head*) mài gàrī *m*, dagacī̀ *m* ⟨ai⟩.

ruler[2] *n* (*for measuring*) r̃ūlà̀ / lūr̃à̀ *f* ⟨oCi⟩, [F] r̃ēgìl *f*: draw a straight line with a ~ jā lāyì dà lūr̃à̀.

rumbling *n* (*of far-off thunder*) cidà *f*; (*of stomach, thunder*) rùgùgī *m*.

rumor *n* jìta-jìta *f*, (*esp. malicious*) tsègùmī *m*; unfounded ~ (*fig.*) làbār̃ìn k̃anzon kùregē *m*; spread a ~ bazà jìta-jìta; get to source of a ~ bi ba'àsin jìta-jìta = nèmi tūshèn jìta-jìta; it

is ~ed that... an cê wai... = nā ji à wai....

rumormonger *n* mài bazà jìta-jìta *n*, mài tsègùmī *n*.

rump *n* (*of animal*) kutùr̃ī *m*.

run 1. *vi* a. gudù *v3b*, yi gudù *m*: he ran 2 miles yā yi gudùn mîl biyu; ~ quickly r̃ùgā̀ dà gudù *v1*, shēk̃à dà gudù; they ran towards their father sun rūgō wajen bàbansù; (*fig.*) turn tail and ~ r̃àntā cikin na kàrē. b. (*var. v + adv/prep uses*): ~ across (*a place*) k̃ētàrē à gùje; ~ after so. bi w. dà gudù; ~ for one's life (*fig.*) r̃àntā cikin na kàrē, yi ta k̃ai: we ran for our lives mun yi ta kânmù; ~ into (*collide with*) yi karò dà: the car ran into a tree mōtà tā yi karò dà bishiyà; ~ over an animal tàkē dabbā̀, hau dabbā̀. c. (*be quick*) yi saurī *m*: ~ for help! yi saurī à yiwō gudùmmawā! d. (*flow, of liquid*) gùdānà *v3*: there is water ~ning through the pipes ruwā nà gùdānà à famfò; ~ dry (*of river, well*) k̃afè *v4*; ~ over (*overflow*) bàtsē *v4*: she filled the bucket until it ran over tā cikà bōkitì har̃ yā bàtsē. e. (*of nose*) tàrārà *v3*, zubar̃ dà mājinā: my nose is ~ning hancìnā nà tàrārà. f. (*of tears*) zùba *v3*; tears were ~ning down her cheeks hawàyē nà zubō matà. g. (*of colors*) zùba *v3*: does this cloth ~? yādìn nân nà zùbā? h. (*of machinery*) yi aikī̀ *m*: the car is ~ning well mōtàr̃ tanà aikī̀ dà kyâu; it ~s on electricity yanà aikī̀ dà làntar̃kī̀; my car is expensive to ~ mōtàtà tanà cîn kudī dà yawà. i. (*other uses*): ~ for office shìga tàkar̃ar̃ zà6ē; ~ short (*have shortage*) gab̃cē *v4*; ~ out (*of sth.*) k̃àrē *v4*: we have ~ out of nails k̃ūsōshī sun k̃àrē manà; ~ out (*of time*) k̃urè *v4*: time has ~ out lōkàcī yā k̃urè = lōkàcī yā yi; we have ~ out of time lōkàcī yā k̃urè manà.
2. *vt* a. (*administer*) tafiyar̃ (dà) *v5*, gudānar̃ (dà) *v5*: ~ a business tafiyar̃ dà har̃kōkin cìnikī; ~ a meeting gudānar̃ dà tàrō. b. (*smuggle*) yi sùmōgà *f*: ~ drugs, guns across border yi sùmōgàr̃ k̃wàyā, màkàmai. c. (*make collide*) karà *v1*: he ran his bicycle into a fence yā karà kèkènsà à shingē.

rung *n* (*of ladder*) matākalar̃ tsānī *f*.

runner *n* magùjī *m*.

runner-up *n* na-biyu *m*.

running *adj & adv* a. ~ water ruwan famfò: our house has ~ water àkwai famfò à gidā. b. (*in succession*) à jèrē: two days

~ kwānā biyu à jère.

**rupture** 1. *v* ɓarkḕ *v4*, fashḕ *v4*: the tank
~d tānkì yā fashḕ.

2. *n* (*break, tear*) ɓàrakā̀ *f*, kītā̀ *f*; (*fig., in
a relationship*) ɓātā̀wā *f*.

**rural** *adj* na kàrkarā *f*: ~ area kàrkarā *f*;
~ development rāyà kàrkarā.

**rush** 1. *n* gaggāwā *f*: don't be in such a ~
kadà kà yi gaggāwā.

2. *v* gaggàutā *v1*; ~ away, ~ off (*esp. by
running*) rūgā̀ *v1*, shēɗā̀ *v1*: let me ~
home bàri in rūgā̀ gidā; the children
~ed up to me yârā sun shēɗō wajēnā;
~ into (*a place*) kūtsā̀ cikin; ~ to (*a
place*) gar̃zàyā *v1*: she ~ed to the market
tā gar̃zàyā (zuwā̀) kàsuwā.

**Russia** *n* Rāshā̀ *f*.

**rust** *v* yi tsātsā̀ *f*.

**rusty** *adj* (mài) tsātsā *f*: the nail is ~
tsātsā̀ tā ci ƙūsā̀.

**ruthless** *adj* maràs īmānì *m*, maràs tàusàyī
*m*.

**ruts** *n* (*in road*) gar̃gadā *f*, galàn *m*: the
road is full of ~ hanyā̀ tā cikà galàn.

# S

sabotage *n* maƙaＲƙashīyā *f.*

sack[1] *n* bùhū *m* ⟨una[2]⟩: ~ of cement bùhun
sùmuntī; (*paper*) jàkā *f* ⟨una[2]⟩; (*plastic*)
lēdā *f* ⟨oCi⟩; (*made from hide*) taikī *m*
⟨una⟩.

sack[2] *v* (*dismiss so.*) ƙòrā *v2.*

sacking, sackcloth *n* (*of hemp*) àlgàＲāＲā *f,*
(*used esp. to cover kolanuts*) àshāsha *f.*

sacred *adj* (mài) tsarkī *m.*

sacrifice 1. *n* (*Relig.*) hadāyā *f.*
　2. *v* a. (*slaughter animal*) yankā̀ *v1,* yi
yankā *m.* b. (*forfeit*) sadaukaＲ (dà) *v5,*
fansaＲ (dà) *v5:* they ~d their lives for
their country sun sadaukaＲ dà Ｒânsù don
ƙasaＲsù.

sacrilege *n* sā̀6ō *m.*

sad *adj* a. (*of psn.*) (mài) baƙin cikī *m,*
(mài) 6àcìn râi *m:* a ~ story lâbāＲìn
baƙin cikī; he is ~ yanā̀ baƙin cikī
= Ｒânsà yā 6àcì; why are you ~? mềnē
nề dàlīlìn 6àcìn rânkà? he looks ~
yā 6ātā̀ fuskā̀; make so. ~ 6ātā̀ wà
râi. b. (*invoking one's sympathy*) (mài)
ban tàusàyī: ~ news lâbāＲī̀ mài ban
tàusàyī; how ~! (*expressing sympathy*)
àyyā! *excl.*

sadden *v* 6ātā̀ wà râi, 6ātā̀ wà zūcìyā:
his death ~ed us very much ràsuwaＲsà tā
6ātā̀ manà râi ƙwaＲai.

sadness *n* 6àcìn râi *m.*

saddle 1. *n* siＲdī *m* ⟨a-a⟩.
　2. *v:* ~ a horse ɗaurā wà dōkī siＲdī.

saddle cloth *n* (*embroidered*) jàlālā̀ *f.*

safe[1] *adj* a. (*not dangerous*) (mài) lāfiyā̀
*f:* ~ and sound lāfiyā̀ ƙalau; have a ~
journey! kà sàuka lāfiyā̀! = Allàh yà
kiyāyè hanyà! b. (*good*) (mài) kyâu *m:*
is this water ~ to drink? ruwan nàn yanā̀
dà kyâu? c. (*reliable, strong*) àmìntaccē
*adj,* (mài) amincī *m:* the bridge isn't ~
gadàＲ bâ ta dà amincī = gadàＲ nân bằ
àmìntacciyā ba cḕ.

safe[2] *n* (*for valuables*) sêf *m,* [F] asūsù *m.*

safeguard *v* tsarè *v4:* ~ human rights
tsarè hakkìn ɗan Adàm.

safely *adv* lāfiyā̀ *adv:* they crossed the river
~ sun ƙētàrè kògīn lāfiyā̀; may you

arrive ~! kà sàuka lāfiyā̀! = Allàh yà
kiyāyē hanyā̀! get away ~ tsīra *v3a.*

safety *n:* ~ measure rìgākafì *m:* ~ first
rìgākafì yā fi māgànī; ~ regulations
dōkōkin kiyāyè hadāＲī.

safety pin *n* fîl *m,* [F] fangìl *m.*

safety razor *n* Ｒēzā̀ *f,* [F] ＲàzùwâＲ *m.*

sag *v* lōtsè *v4.*

sail *v* (*of boat*) tāshì *v3b.*

sailor *n* ma'àikàcin jirgin ruwa *m.*

saint *n* wàlī / wàliyyī *m* ⟨ai⟩.

saintliness *n* wàlìttakā̀ *f.*

sake *n* a. (*purpose*): for the ~ of dòmin /
don *conj:* he would never do that just for
the ~ of hurting us bà zâi ta6à yîn hakà
dòmin yà yi manà lâifī ba. b. (*benefit, advantage*) dòmin / don *prep,* sabòdà
*prep:* for their ~ dòminsù = sabòdà sū;
for goodness' ~, stop arguing don Allàh
kù baＲ gaＲdamā̀; (*for one's personal welfare*): he did it for his own ~ yā yī shì
don karìn kânsà = yā yī shì don ƙashin
kânsà.

salad *n* sàlâk *m,* latàs *m,* [F] sàlātī *m.*

salad dressing *n* mân sàlâk *m,* [F] ruwan
sàlātī *m.*

salary *n* (*weekly or monthly*) àlbâshī *m, see*
wages: he earns a good ~ yanā̀ sāmùn
àlbâshī mài tsōkā̀; a 10 percent ~ increase ƙarìn àlbâshin gōmà bisà dàrī.

sale *n* a. (*selling sth.*) sayâＲwā *f;* for
~ na sayâＲwā: is this for ~? wannàn
na sayâＲwā nề? b. (*reduction in price*)
gwànjō *m:* there is a ~ on soap today yâu
anā̀ gwànjon sàbulù.

salesclerk *n* mài jiràn kàntī *n,* [F] kwàmî
*m.*

salesman *n* (*one who gets a commission*)
ɗan kàmashò *m.*

saline *adj* na gishirī *m.*

saliva *n* miyau *m,* yāwū / yau *m:* spit out ~
tōfaＲ dà yau.

Sallah *n* (*Muslim holiday*) Sallā̀ *f.*

salt *n* gishirī *m;* (*var. types*): (*coarsely
ground*) bēzā̀ *f;* (*used medicinally*) mandā
*f;* (*in cakes, for animals*) màngûl *m;* (*from
Bilma*) balmā̀ *f;* a block of ~ kantùn
gishirī; put ~ on food sâ gishirī à
àbinci; use ~ shā gishirī.

salty *adj* (mài) gishirī *m:* be too ~ yi
gishirī = cikà gishirī.

salutations *n* gaisuwā *f.*

salute 1. *n* (*tradit., with raised fist*) jìnjinā̀
*f;* (*by horsemen during Sallah*) jāhì *m;*
(*military*) sārā *m;* give a gun ~ bugà
bindigā̀.
　2. *v* a. (*a psn.*) yi wà gaisuwā *f;* (*Mil.*)

sārǎ wǎ *v1* ⟨sārā⟩, [F] yi wǎ gàřdàbû: the soldiers ~d the president sōjōjī sun sārǎ wǎ shûgàban ƙasǎ. b. (*a flag*) gai dà *v5*.

salvation *n* cêtō *m*, tsīrā *f*.

same *adj* a. (*identical*) daya: they come from the ~ town gàrinsù daya ně; we arrived on the ~ day mun isō rānā daya; at this ~ time (*past or fut.*) wǎř hakà: at the ~ time yesterday, next year jiyà, bàdi wǎř hakà; all the ~ (*nevertheless*) duk dà hakà; it's all the ~ to us duk daya gàrē mù; (*of a surface, e.g. coat of paint, hair*) bâi daya: their hair is the ~ (in color) gàshìnsù bâi daya; the paint came out the ~ color ƙentī yā tāshì bâi daya. b. (*equal*): the ~ as daidai dà: he did the ~ as we did yā yi daidai dà yàddà mukà yi; give me the ~ as you did before bǎ ni daidai yàddà ka bā nì à dâ.

sample *n* samfùř / samfùřī *m* ⟨oCi⟩.

sanctify *v* tsarkàkā *v1*.

sanction *n* (*Econ.*) tàkunkùmī *m*: impose economic ~s sâ tàkunkùmin tattalin ařzìkī.

sand[1] *n* yàshī *m*: the soil here is very ~y ƙasař nàn tā cikà yàshī; (*fine*) ràiràyī / ràirai *m*; (*soil which has been kicked up*) tùrɓāyā *f*.

sand[2] *v* gōgè dà sàmfēfǎ.

sandals *n* silīfǎ *m*; (*with strap around heel*) sandàl *m*, (*flip-flops or tradit. with leather thong*) fadè *m*, silīfǎ *m*.

sandpaper *n* sàmfēfǎ *f*.

sandstorm *n* iskā mài ƙūrā *f*.

sandwich *n* sanwicī *m*, [F] sànwîc *m*.

sanitary *adj* (mài) tsabtǎ *f*.

sanitation *n* aikìn tsabtǎ *m*: ~ day rānař tsabtàcè mùhàllī; department of ~ ma'aikatař tsabtǎ.

sanitation inspector *n* dùbà-gàri *n*, [F] dan lařwai *n*.

sap *n* (*of tree*) ruwan bishiyǎ *m*.

sarcasm *n* gàtsē *m*.

sarcastic *adj* (mài) gàtsē *m*: be ~ to so. yi wà gàtsē.

sardines *n* kīfin gwangwanī *m*, sàdîn *m*, [F] sàřdîn *m*.

sash *m* (*for tying baby on back*) majanyī *m*, gyàlè *m*.

Satan *n* Shàidân *m*, Ìbìlîs *m*.

satchel *n* (*used esp. by Koranic scholars*) gafakǎ *f*.

satellite *n* (*in space*) kumbō *m*, watàn dan Adàm *m*; communications ~ kumbòn sǎƙō.

satin *n* lilìn *m*.

satire *n* zàmbō *m*, gàtsē *m*: a satirical play wǎsan kwaikwayō na zàmbō.

satisfaction *n* a. (*fulfillment*) biyàn bùkātǎ *m*, biyàn mùřàdī *m*: I'm getting ~ from my work inà biyàn bùkātǎ dàgà aikìnā. b. (*pride of one's achievement*) àlfahǎřī *m*. c. (*enjoyment*) gàmsuwā *f*.

satisfactory *adj* (mài) gamsǎřwā: his explanation wasn't ~ bàyānìnsà bǎ mài gamsǎřwā ba ně = bàyānìnsà bài gamsař ba; his work is ~ aikìnsà bâ lâifī.

satisfy *v* a. (*please*) gamsař (dà) *v5*: his excuse satisfied everyone uzùřinsà yā gamsař dà kōwā; be satisfied gàmsu *v7*: I'm satisfied with his work nā gàmsu dà aikìnsà. b. (*be enough, esp. food*) ƙosař (dà) *v5*; be satisfied (*replete*) ƙòshi *v3\**: would you like some more? no thanks, I'm satisfied ìn ƙārà makà? màdàllā, nā ƙòshi.

satisfying *adj* (mài) gàmsuwā *f*.

saturate *v* jiƙè jagab *v4*.

Saturday *n* Àsabàř *f*, Sātī *f*, [F] Subdû *f*, [F] Sàmdî *f*; ~ night daren Lahàdì.

sauce *n* miyà *f*, see stew; (*thin, like broth*) rōmō *m*.

saucer *n* falè *m*, fàřantī *m* ⟨ai⟩: cup and ~ kōfī dà falè.

saucepan *n* tukunyā *f* ⟨tukwànē⟩, tukunyař ƙarfè *f*.

savannah *n* dājì / jèjì *m*.

save *v* a. (*rescue*) tsērař (dà) *v5*, kuɓutař (dà) *v5*: they ~d him from drowning sun tsērař dà shī dàgà ruwa; lives can be ~d through vaccination anā iyà tsērař dà rāyukà ta hanyàř àllūřǎ; ~ me! wâyyō à tàimàkē nì! (*fig.*) ~ one's own neck yi ta kânsà. b. (*esp. from sin*) cētā *v2*. c. (*protect, preserve*) kiyàyē *v4*: ~ wildlife kiyàyè nāmun dājì; God ~ the King! rân sarkī yà dadè! d. (*store for future use*) tànadā *v2*, yi tānàdī *m*: the water is going to be cut off, so let's ~ some zā à rufè famfò, sabòdà hakà mù yi tānàdin ruwā. e. (*put money away*) ajìyè kudī: most people are unable to ~ money yawancin mutànē sun kàsà ajìyè kudìnsù. f. (*make unnnecessary*): ~ so. trouble hūtař dà w.; ~ so. work ragè wà aikī; in order to ~ time don kadà à ɓàtā lōkàcī.

savings *n* kudin àjiyà *m*, àjiyǎ *f*: someone has stolen all his ~ wani yā sācè masà àjiyàřsà kaf.

savior *n* macècī *m*, mài cētō *m*.

savory *adj* (mài) dādin dandanō *m*.

saw 1. *n* zařtồ *m* ⟨a-a⟩.
2. *v* yankà dà zařtồ.

sawdust *n* gằrin kātākō *m*.

sawmill *n* ma'aikatař kātākō *f*.

say 1. *v a*. (*state, relate*) cê *v**(*changes to* cê *after the subj pro* na/ka/ya/ta), fuřtà *v1*, fàdā / fàdì *v2**: he said that he didn't agree yā cê bài yàřda ba = yā fuřtà cêwā bài yàřda ba; that is what he said yā fàdi hakà = hakà ya fàdā; ~ it again sàkè fàdā = kà sàkè màganà; people ~..., it is said that... an cê wai... = an ruwaitō cêwā...; furthermore, he said... yā ƙārà dà cêwā...; I have nothing to ~ (on the matter) bâ ni dà ta cêwā; I didn't know what to ~ nā rasà ta cêwā; don't ~ a word! kà kāmè bàkinkà! who said so? Audu said so ìn ji wằ? ìn ji Audù; that is to ~ wằtồ / wằtàu: I'll pay you the day after tomorrow, that is to ~, Wednesday zân biyā kà jībi, wằtàu ran Lằřàbā. *b*. (*tell so*.) cê wà *v**, fadà wà *v1*: what did he ~ to you? mè ya cê makà? I said to him that I would come nā cê masà zân zō he said to himself... yā cê à rânsà....
2. *n*: he has no ~ in the matter bâ shi dà ta cêwā cikin màganà = bâ shi dà hannū à màganař.

saying *n*: there's a ~ in Hausa... Hàusàwā sunà cêwā....

scab *n* ɓamɓarōkī *m*.

scabbard *n* gidā *m* ⟨aCe⟩, kùbē *m* ⟨anni⟩.

scabies *n* (*on joints, buttocks*) ƙazwā *f*.

scaffold *n* tsānì *m* ⟨uka⟩.

scald *v* ƙōnè *v4*.

scale¹ *n a*. (*for weighing, measuring*) ma'aunì *m*, sìkēlì *m* ⟨oCi⟩; ~ on a map ma'aunin tàswīřà. *b*. (*for comparing, arranging*) tsārì *m*: salary ~ tsārìn àlbâshī.

scale² *v* (*a mountain*) hau *v** ⟨hawā⟩.

scales *n* (*of fish*) kamɓōrin kīfī *m*.

scalp *n* fātař kâi *f*; ~ disease (*favus*) kōřā *f*.

scalpel *n* askā *f* ⟨a-e⟩.

scan *v a*. (*read quickly*) ɗan lēƙà *v1*. *b*. (*in poetry*) yankà *v1*.

scansion *n* (*in poetry*) yankàn wāƙà *m*.

scandal *n* àbin kunyà *m*, àbin fàllasà *m*.

scandalize *v* kunyàtā *v1*.

scapegoat *n* kàřkàtacciyař kūkà mài dādin hawā *f*.

scar *v* tabō *m* ⟨Cai, Cuna⟩, [F] balshē *m*; (*tribal marks, scarification*) shâsshāwā *f*, tsāgā *f*, tsāgař gādồ *f*.

scarify *v* shasshàutā *v1*.

scarce *adj*: be ~ yi wùyā *f*, nằ dà wùyā, wùyātà *v3*: water is ~ these days ruwā yā yi wùyā yànzu.

scarcely *adv a*. (*with difficulty*) dà kyař / ƙyař: I could ~ understand him dà kyař na fàhìmcē shì. *b*. (*barely, hardly*): ~ had X than Y X kè nan sai Y, X kề dà wu'yā sai Y: ~ had he left than we returned tāshìnsà kè nan (sai) mukà dāwō = tāshìnsà kề dà wùyā sai gằ mu mun dāwō.

scarcity *n* ƙarancī *m*, rashì *m*: a ~ of rain ƙarancin ruwā; (*esp. of food*) ƙamfā *f*: a ~ of grain ƙamfař hatsī.

scare *v* tsōràtā *v1*, tsōratař (dà) *v5*; be ~d ji tsồrō *m*.

scarecrow *n* mùtum-mùtumī *m*.

scarf *n*, *see* kerchief.

scarlet *adj* jāwà *f*.

scatter 1. *vt* wātsā *v1*: ~ seeds on a field wātsā irì à gōnā; ~ sth. about wařgàzā *v1*, yi fàtàlī dà *m*: the wind ~ed the papers about everywhere iskà tā wařgàzà tàkàřdū kō'ìnā; all ~ed about yàshe à bàřkàtai *adv*: pieces of paper were ~ed about everwhere guntàyen tàkàřdū sunà yàshe à bàřkàtai kō'ìnā.
2. *vi* (*of a crowd, people*) wàtsu *v7*, wàřwàtsu *v7*: the crowd ~ed tàron mutànē sun wàřwàtsu.

scatterbrained *adj* bìji-bìji *idph*.

scent 1. *n* ƙanshī *m*; (*esp. perfume*) tùřàrē *m*.
2. *v* sansànā / shinshìnā *v1* ⟨sànsanà⟩ *f*: the dog ~s a hare kàrên nà sànsanař zōmō.

sceptical *adj*, *see* skeptical.

sceptre *n* kàndīřì *m* ⟨ai⟩.

schedule *n a*. takàřdař tsārì *f*; (*in tabular form*) jadawàlī *m* ⟨ai⟩: ~ of classes jadawàlin azūzuwà. *b*. (*regular time for doing sth*.) ƙā'idà *f*: according to ~ à kân ƙā'idà; everyone has a work ~ kōwa nà dà ƙā'idà ta yîn aikìnsà.

scheme 1. *n* tsārì *m* ⟨e²⟩, fasàlī *m* ⟨ai⟩; (*plan*) dàbāřà *f* ⟨u⟩.
2. *v* gamà bàkī, hadà kâi: they are scheming against me sunà hadà kâi sù jūyà minì bāyā; (*by women against men*) yi kissà *f*.

schistosomiasis *n* tsagiyā *f*.

scholar *n* masànì *m*, (*esp. Islamic*) shēhùn màlàmì *m*; Koranic ~ (*one who has memorized it*) hāfìzī *m* ⟨ai⟩.

scholarship *n* (*monetary*) sùkōlàshîf *m*, [F] bùřûs *f*.

school n a. makaɽantā f ⟨u⟩; (Koranic) makaɽantaɽ àllō = makaɽantaɽ Mùhàmmàdiyyà; (West. education) makaɽantaɽ bōkō; day ~ makaɽantaɽ jě-ka-kà-dāwō; boarding ~ makaɽantaɽ kwānà; girls' ~ makaɽantaɽ 'yammātā; boys' ~ makaɽantaɽ sàmàrī; ~ board hùkūmàɽ makaɽantā; ~ work aikìn makaɽantā; ~ begins at 9 o'clock anā fārà kàɽàtū dà ɽarfè taɽà; go to ~ shìga makaɽantā. b. (var. levels of ~): (primary, elementary) fiɽāmàɽè f, [F] làkkwâl f, [F] fiɽìmâɽ f; (lower secondary) midîl f, [F] sě'èjè f; (upper secondary) sakandàɽè f, [F] lîsê f; (preparatory, pre-university) makaɽantaɽ gàba dà sakandàɽè f. c. (group of alike beings) guɽguzū m: a ~ of fish guɽguzun kīfàyē.

science n kìmiyyà f: ~ and technology kìmiyyà dà fàsāhā.

scientific adj na kìmiyyà f.

scientist n masànin kìmiyyà m.

scissors n àlmakàshī m ⟨ai⟩: I need a pair of ~ inā bùkātàɽ àlmakàshī.

scoff at v wulàɽantā v1, wulàɽantaɽ (dà) v5.

scold v kyàrā v2, tsāwàtā wà v1, (fig.) jā kùnnen w.: his mother ~ed him for hitting his sister dà ya dàki ɽanwàɽsà sai uwaɽsù ta kyàrē shì; (abusively) zàgā v2 ⟨zāgì⟩: she ~ed the child thoroughly tā yi ta zāgìn yārò sôsai.

scoop out v kàmfatā v2, dībā v2*: she ~ed out some rice with a dipper tā kamfatō shìnkāfā dà mōdā.

scooter n (motor) bàbûɽ m, basfà m, sùkūtà f, [F] bàspâ m, [F] mòbìlât m.

scorch v ɽōnā v1.

score 1. n a. (Sport) yawàn cî m; what was the final ~? yàyà wàsân ya tāshì? what is the ~ now? nawà dà nawà akè yànzu? b. (on a test) mākì m: what was his ~ on the test? 70 points nawà ya sāmù à jaɽɽàbâwàɽ? mākì sàbà'in. 2. v (a victory, goal) ci v0, ci nasaɽā: Kano ~d 3 and Zaria 2 Kanò tā ci ukù, Zāriyà tā ci biyu; our team ~d again tîm dinmù yā sākè cî.

scorn 1. v rainà / rēnà v1. 2. n rainì / rēnì m.

scorpion n kùnāmà f ⟨u⟩: the ~ aimed its stinger kùnāmà tā danà ɽarì.

Scotch tape n salàtîf m, [F] ìskwâc m.

scoundrel n mazàmbàcī m, ɗan banzā m.

scout n: boy ~ ɗan sìkāwùt m, [F] sùkût m.

scowl v 6ātà fuskà, muɽtùkè fuskà, dur6ùnà fuskà.

scramble 1. v (for sth.) yi wàsōsò / yi wàwāsō m; ~ over (a place) hayè bàɽkàtài; ~d eggs daɽàshin ɽwai.
2. n wàsōsò / wàwāsō m, ɽibìbī m: the ~ for Africa wàsōsòn Afiɽkà = ɽibìbin Afiɽkà.

scrap n ràgōwà f.

scrape 1. v a. (abrade) kūjè / ɽūjè v4, daujè v4: I ~d my knee during the game nā kūjè gwīwā gàrin wàsân; (one's skin) sālù6ē v4, sālè v4, ɗāyè 4: my hand got ~d hannunā yā sālù6ē. b. (clean sth.) kankàrē v4; ~ insides of gourd, pumpkin fāfè v4. ~ food off kàtsè v4: I ~d the saucepan with my finger and licked it nā kàtsè tukunyaɽ miyā nā suɗè; ~ sth. with fingernail ɽwantàlā v1: I ~d the sauce off the gown nā ɽwantàlà miyà dàgà rìgā; ~ out (from narrow opening) ɽwāɽùlē v4 ⟨ɽwàɽulà⟩ f: he ~d out (wax from) his ear yā ɽwāɽùlè kùnnensà.
2. n (abrasion) kūjèwā / ɽūjèwā f.

scraper n makankarī m.

scratch 1. v a. (an itch) sōsà v1 ⟨sūsà⟩ f; don't ~ the pimples kadà ka sōsà ɽuràjē. b. (with sth. sharp) kaɽcè v4, ɽwaɽzanā v2: he ~ed his arm, the wall yā kaɽcè hannunsà, bangō; (with claw, fingernail) yàkusà v2, yàgā v2: the cat ~ed the child màgên tā yàkùshi yāròn. c. ~ out (to remove) kankàrē v4: he ~ed out my name from the list yā kankàrè sūnānā dàgà tsārìn; (fig.) ~ my back and I'll ~ yours cùɗàn ni ìn cùɗē kà.
2. n ɽwaɽzanè m, kaɽcèwā f: the car hasn't a ~ on it mōtà bābù kō ɽwarzanè à jìkintà.

scream v yi ɽārā f, yi kùrūruwà f.

screech n (of bird) kūkan tsuntsū m.

screen 1. v kangè v4; (temporarily) kārè v4: the latrine has been ~ed off with matting an kangè makèwayī dà zānā.
2. n kāriyā f.

screw 1. n ɽūsà f ⟨oCi⟩, [F] bîs f, [F] ěkuɽû m.
2. v ɗaurà ɽūsà: he ~ed the screw into the wood yā ɗaurà ɽūsà a jìkin kātākō; ~ up one's eyes kannè idò; (fig.) ~ up one's courage yi ɽùru m, (fig.) yi ɽūnan baɽin wākē m.

screwdriver n sùkùddìɽebà f, [F] tùɽnàbîs m.

scribe n maɽùbùcī m; court ~ mālàmin àlɽālī.

scrimp *v* yi tattalī *m; (esp. on food so it lasts longer)* yi jànjānī *m.*

script *n* r̃ùbūtū *m:* cursive ~ r̃ùbūtun tàfiyar̃ tsūtsà; printed ~ r̃ùbūtun k̃ek̃e; Hausa in Roman ~ bōk̃ò *m;* Hausa in Arabic ~ àjàmi *m.*

scriptures *n* littāfĩn àddīnī *m;* Holy S. Littāfĩn Àlmàsīhù *m.*

scrotal hernia *n* gwaiwā *f.*

scrotum *n* jàkar̃ k̃wàlàtai *f.*

scrub *v* gōg̃e *v4:* ~ a floor gōg̃e dàɓē dà bùr̃ōshī; *(oneself in bathing)* cūɗà jìkī.

scrubbing brush *n* bùr̃ōshī *m.*

scrupulous *adj* (mài) ādalcī *m.*

sculpt *v (wood)* sassàk̃ā *v1.*

sculptor *n* masàssàk̃ī *m.*

sculpture *n (wood)* sàssàk̃ā *f.*

scum *n (film)* yānā *f; (esp. from soap)* kumfā *f.*

scurry about *v (to do sth. neg.)* kai gwaurō kai màrī: he's ~ing about to break up their marriage yā kai gwaurō yā kai màrī don yà rabà aurēn.

scythe *n* làujē *m* ⟨una⟩.

sea *n* tēku *f;* travel by ~ yi tàfiyà ta jirgin ruwa. *(in geographical names)* bahà *f:* the Red Sea Bàhàr̃ Māliyà.

seal 1. *n (official)* hātĩmī *m* ⟨ai⟩, tambàrī *m* ⟨u-a⟩.
2. *v (with glue)* līk̃e *v4:* he ~ed the envelope yā līk̃e ambùlàn; ~ up *(an opening)* tōsh̃e *v4;* ~ off *(an area)* kàr̃e *v4.*

seam *n* ɗinkī *m,* (at selvedges) kàr̃bū *m,* (an undone ~) ɓarakà *f:* the ~ has come apart ɗinkī yā ɓark̃e.

search 1. *v* a. *(look for)* nēmā *v2* ⟨nēmà⟩, bìɗā *v2:* they are ~ing for a way out sunà nēman mafitā; *(for sth. needed or lost)* cigĩta *v1,* yi cigiyà *f.* b. *(try to discover)* gānō *v6:* ~ for a cure for the disease gānō màgànin cĩwòn. c. *(by an official)* cāj̃e *v4:* the policemen ~ed all his luggage 'yan sàndā sun cāj̃e kāyansà dukà; a ~ing look dūban tsabtà.
2. *n* nēmā *m,* bìɗā *f; (for sth. lost or needed)* cigiyà *f:* a job ~ cigiyàr̃ aikì.

search warrant *n* war̃antī *m,* [F] màndā *f,* [F] kwàmbùk̃àsô *f.*

season[1] *n* lōkàcin shēkarà *m; (names of ~al periods):* cold ~ *(Dec.-Jan.)* hùntūr̃ù *m,* lōkàcin dārī *m;* dry ~ *(Oct.-May)* rānī *m;* hot ~ *(just preceding rainy ~)* bazarà *f;* rainy, wet ~ *(June-Sept.)* dàminā *f;* harvest ~ *(Sept.-Oct.)* kàkā *f.*

season[2] *v (food)* sā kāyan yājì.

seasonings *n* kāyan yājì *m.*

seat 1. *n* a. àbin zamā *m:* the ~ is broken àbin zamā yā lālàc̃e; *(place to sit)* wurin zamā *m:* the bus has 60 ~s bâs nā dà wurin zamā sìttin; shall we change ~s? mù yi mùsàyar̃ wurin zamā? please take a ~ bismillà kù zaunà; front, back ~ kuj̃erar̃ gàba, bāya; bicycle ~ sìr̃dì *m* ⟨a-a⟩; *(fig.)* he's not on ~ bā yà nân.
b. *(center)* mazaunī *m:* ~ of government, learning mazaunin gwamnatì, ilìmī.
2. *v* zaunar̃ (dà) *v5:* he ~ed the children first and then sat down yā zaunar̃ dà yârā tùkùna sàn nan ya zaunà; this room can ~ 100 people dākìn nân yā ìsa mùtûm dàrī sù zaunà; being ~ed à zàune *adv:* they are ~ed by the door sunà zàune à bàkin k̃ōfà.

seatbelt *n* bêl *m,* maɗaurī *m:* fasten your ~ kù jā bêl.

secede *v* ɓall̃e *v4.*

secession *n* ɓallèwā *f.*

second[1] *quant* na biyu: this is the ~ time I've come here zuwànā nân na biyu k̃e nan; the ~ (day) of the month (rānar̃) biyu gà watà.

second[2] *n (of time)* dàk̃īk̃à *f* ⟨oCi⟩, sakàn *m;* please wait a ~ kà dākàtà kàdan; in a split ~ *(fig.)* k̃àfìn kyaftàwā dà bismillà.

second[3] *v (a motion)* g̃oyi bāyā: our representative ~ed the motion wàkīlinmù yā g̃oyi bāyan bàtū.

second[4] *v:* he has been ~ed to the Teachers' College an bā dà aronsà gà makar̃antar̃ hōron màlàmai.

secondary school *n, see* school.

second-class *n (ticket)* tikitìn sikin-kìlà, tikitìn gàma-gàri *m.*

second-hand *n* kwànc̃e *m,* jàc̃e *m:* a ~ car mōtà kwànc̃e; was it new when you bought it or ~? sābō ka sàyē tà kō kwànc̃e? ~ clothing gwànjō *m,* akir̃ka *f,* [F] ɓōshō *m:* I bought a ~ gown nā sàyi rìgā gwànjō = nā sàyi rìgà gwànjon rìgā.

second-rate *adj* maràs ingancì *m,* maràs nàgàr̃tā *f.*

secrecy *n* àsīrī *m.*

secret *n* a. àsīr̃ī *m* ⟨ai⟩: disclose so.'s ~ tōnà wà àsīr̃ī; keep so.'s ~ rìk̃e àsīr̃ī, rufà wà àsīr̃ī; tell so.'s ~ *(blab)* kwarmàtà wà *v1,* yi wà kwàrmatō *m;* in ~ à àsīr̃ce, à ɓōye. b. *(sth. held in confidence)* sìr̃r̃ī *m:* he and I have a ~ between us àkwai sìr̃r̃ī tsàkāninmù dà shī = inà sìr̃r̃ī dà shī. c. *(formula for doing, using sth. well)* nak̃àlī *m:* the ~ to learning a language is to practise speaking it naƙàlin iyà harshè màganà dà shī; she knows the ~ for (cooking) beans tanà dà naƙàlin wākē.

secretariat n sàkàtēr̃iyà f, [F] sàkàtàr̃ìyà f.

secretary n (of organization) magàtakàr̃dā m; (at office) sakatar̃è m; (Pol.) permanent ~ bàbban sakatar̃è.

secretive adj: he is a ~ person yanà dà zurfin cik̀ì.

secretly adv à àsīr̃ce adv: he left town ~ yā bar̃ gàrîn à àsīr̃ce.

sect n dàr̃īƙà f ⟨oCi⟩; member of a ~ ɗan dàr̃īƙà; the Tijjaniyya ~ Tījjàniyyà; the Qadariyya ~ Ƙàdĭr̃iyyà.

section n a. (of orange, kolanut) ƙwaryā f, ƙwàr̃ (+ numeral): most kolanuts have 2 ~s yawancin gōr̃ò ƙwàr̃ biyu nè. b. (geographical area) yankì m ⟨una⟩, ɓangarè m ⟨oCi⟩, sāshè / sāshì m ⟨Ca⟩: in the northern ~ of the state à ɓangarèn ar̃ēwacin jihàr̃; South Fage is the ~ of Kano where printed cloth is sold Fage ta kudù sāshèn Kanò nē indà akè sai dà atamfōfī. c. (admin. unit) sāshè / sāshì m ⟨Ca⟩: the Hausa ~ of the BBC sāshèn Hausa à gidan r̃ēdiyò na Bībīsì. d. (of town) ùnguwà f ⟨oCi⟩.

sectionalism n ɓangarancī m.

sector n shiyyà f ⟨oCi⟩: the eastern ~ of Berlin shiyyàr̃ Berlin ta gabàs.

secular adj: ~ education kàr̃àtun bōkò.

securely adv (of sth. closed, covered) kam idph: is the door shut ~? an kullè ƙōfàr̃ kam? (of sth. tied, fastened) kankan idph, tam idph; it is ~ fastened yā ɗauru tam.

security n a. (safety) tsàrō m: internal ~ tsàron gidā; national ~ tsàron ƙasā; ~ forces sōjōjin tsàron ƙasā; S. Council (of U.N.) Ƙwàmìtîn Sulhù. b. (surety for loan) àbin jìnginà m.

sedative n māgànin sà barcī m.

sediment n (in river) lākā f; (in dye-pit) dagwalò m.

sedition n bòr̃ē m.

see v a. ganī v*: do you ~ them? kin gan sù? let me ~ your papers bàri ìn ga tàkàr̃dunkà; I ~ no reason for doing that bàn ga dàlīlìn yîn hakà ba; (on) seeing that (dà) ganin (cêwa): ~ing that he was gone, I left dà ganin bā yà nan nā tāshì; ~ each other, ~ one another yi ar̃bà dà: Musa and I saw one another yesterday mun yi ar̃bà dà Mūsā jiyà; it has been 2 years since I've ~n him ràbuwar̃mù dà shī tun shèkarà biyu; ~ so. off rakà v1; ~ from a distance hàngā v2, (hàngē), tsìnkāyà v2;

~ into the future yi dūbā m; ~ you later! sai an jimà! (fig.) we don't ~ eye to eye bā mà shir̃ì; (fig.) ~ing is believing ganī yā ƙòri jî. b. (understand) gànè v4: do you ~ what I mean? kā gànè àbîn dà nakè nufì? you ~...? (as pause) kā ga?

seed n a. ir̃ì m ⟨e²⟩; (fig.) bad ~ mūgùn ir̃ì. b. (fruit pits) 'yā'yā p.

seedling n dàshē m: plant out ~s yi dàshē; the ~s have taken dàshē yā kāmà.

seek v nèmā v2 ⟨nēmā⟩, bìɗā v2: ~ advice, office, the truth nèmi shāwar̃à, zàɓē, gàskiyà; ~ sth. desperately (fig.) nèmi w.a. id̀ò rùfe = nèmi w.a. ruwā à jàllō.

seem v nūnà àlāmà: he ~ed to feel no shame bài kō nūnà àlāmar̃ jîn kunyà ba; it ~s as if, like gà àlāmà: it ~s like it's going to rain gà àlāmà zā à yi ruwā; he ~s to be a nice person gà àlāmà mùtumîn kir̃kì nē; ~ only like (contrastive) sai kà cê although it happened last year, it ~s only like yesterday kō dà yakè bàra akà yī shì, sai kà cê jiyà-jiyà nē.

segregate v wārè v4, kēɓè v4: the women have been ~d from the men an kēɓè mātā dàgà mazā.

segregration n wāriyā f: racial ~ wāriyar̃ àl'ummà.

seep v (of moisture) yi nàsō m.

seize v ƙwàcè v4: ~ power ƙwàcè mulkì.

seizure n a. (of goods, people) kāmuwā f. b. (epileptic) far̃fāɗiyā f.

seldom adv bà kàsàfài / sàfài / kàsài ba: he ~ comes here bà sàfài yakàn zō nân ba; it ~ rains in January bà kàsàfài akè ruwā à watàn Jànair̃ù ba.

select v zàɓā v2, yi zàɓē m: ~ what you want zàɓi àbîn dà kakè sô.

selection n (making a choice) zàɓē m ⟨e²⟩: you made a poor ~ zàɓenkì bà shi dà kyâu; a good ~ of cloth atamfōfī ir̃ì-ir̃ì.

self n a. (in reflexives) kâi n (+ poss. pro): I my~ know what to do nī kâinā nā san àbîn yî; he is angry with him~ yā yi fushī dà kânsà; the baby can't sit up by it~ yet jàr̃īr̃ìyā bà tà iyà zaunàwa ita kântà ba tùkùna; they went by themselves sun tàfi dà kânsù. b. (var. compounds): ~-awareness sanìn cīwòn kâi: he has no ~-awareness bài san cīwòn kânsà ba; ~-confidence jî dà kâi m: they have confidence in themselves sunà jî dà kânsù = sunà jîn kânsù; ~-control màllakàr̃ kâi; ~-government mulkìn kâi; ~-interest sôn zūcìyā: ev-

erything he does is purely out of ~-interest
duk àbîn dà yakè yî sabòdà sôn zūcìyā
nè kawài; ~-importance sôn girmā; ~-
pity tàusàyin kâi; ~-reliance n dōgarà
dà kâi: he has a lot of ~-reliance shī
mùtûm nē dà ya dōgarà dà kânsà; ~-
respect (dignity) mutuncî m: never lose
your ~-respect kà san rìfè mutuncìnkà
= kà kārè mutuncìnkà.

selfish adj (mài) sôn kâi m, (mài) sôn
zūcìyā m: he is a very ~ man shī mùtûm
nē mài sôn kâi; because of his ~ behavior sabòdà hālinsà na sôn kâi.

selfishness n sôn kâi m, sôn zūcìyā m:
show ~ in a matter nūnà sôn zūcìyā
cikin màganà.

sell v sai dà / sayař (dà) v5: I sold my
car to Audu na sayař wà Audù mōtàtā;
if you agree to ~ (at that price), I'll buy it
in zā kà sayař zān sàyā; people are buying and ~ing things at the market mutànē
nà sàyē dà sayâřwā à kàsuwā; this cloth
~s well yādìn nân yanà dà kàsuwā; sold!
(said by seller) nā sallàmā! ~ at a loss
(through necessity) karyař (dà) v5.

seller n mài sayârwā n.

sellotape n, see Scotch tape.

selvedge n kàřbū m.

semantics n fannìn mà'ànā m.

semaphor n (railroad signal) sìmfô m.

semen n màniyyî / mànî m.

semi-annually adv sàu biyu à shèkarà.

semicolon n wakàfī mài ruwā m.

Semitic adj bàsimitè adj: Arabic is a ~ language Lařabcī bàsimitèn harshè nē.

semi-trailer n, see truck.

semolina, semovita n sàmòbītā f, [F]
sàmàmbītā f.

senate n màjàlisař dàttîjai.

senator n dattîjò m ⟨ai⟩, ɗan màjàlisař
dàttîjai, [F] dìpìtê m.

send v a. (sth.) aikà dà v1: I have sent them
several letters nā aikà musù dà wàsīkū
dà yawà; I should ~ these shoes to be repaired lallè ìn aikà dà tàkalmàn nân
à gyārō minì. b. (so. to place) àikà
v2: he sent his son to the city yā àiki
ɗansà bìřnì; ~ a child to school sâ
yārò makařantā; ~ for a doctor kìrāwō
likìtà; (direct so. to a place or to so.)
tūrà v1: he sent me here to see you yā
tūrō nì wajenkà; ~ away (chase) kòrā
v2; ~ back sth. mai dà / mayař (dà) v5.

senility n rūɗèwař tsūfā f, gìgin-tsūfā m.

senior adj (in rank) na gàba m; one's ~ mài
gàba dà: he is ~ to me yanà gàba dà nī;
be ~ (in age) gìrmā v2: he is my ~ by

2 years yā gìrmē nì dà shèkarà biyu;
~ brother wâ, yàyā m ⟨yayyē, yāyū⟩; ~
sister yâ, yàyā f ⟨yayyē, yāyū⟩; ~ wife
uwařgidā f; ~ officer bàbban hafsà m; ~
service aikìn gwamnatì m.

senna n (used as laxative) filaskō m.

sensational adj (mài) bā dà màmākî.

sense 1. n a. (ability to reason) hankàlī m,
tùnànī m: he is a man of good ~ mùtûm
nè mài hankàlī; he's lost his ~s yā fìta
dàgà hankàlinsà; come back to one's ~s
(one's right mind) kōmō cikin hankàlī;
~ of right and wrong sanìn cīwòn kâi; ~
~ of pride àlfahàřī m; he has a good
~ of direction yā san hanyà; ~ of order lissāfì m (esp. in neg. sent.): he
has no ~ of order bā yà dà lissāfì. b.
(meaning) mà'ànā f ⟨oCi⟩: in what ~ are
you using the word? dà wàcè mà'ànā kakè
àmfànī dà kalmař? make ~ of gànē v4:
did you make any ~ of what he said? kā
gànē àbîn dà ya cè?
2. v: I ~d something was wrong (fig.)
jìkīnā yā bā nì wani àbù yā fàru.

senseless adj a. (lacking sense) (mài)
rashìn hankàlī m, maràs hankàlī m. b.
(lacking meaning) (mài) rashìn mà'ànā
m, maràs mà'ànā m. c. (esp. incoherent
talk) bā kâi bâi gìndī: what he said is
~ màganàřsà bā kâi bâ gìndī. his letter doesn't make any ~ wàsīkàřsà bâ ta
dà kâi bâ ta dà gìndī. d. (unconscious)
sùmammē adj.

senselessness n rashìn hankàlī m.

sensible adj (mài) hankàlī m, (mài) azancī
m, (mài) tùnànī m, (mài) kân gadō m.

sensitivity n a. (having humanity) īmànī
m. b. (respect for others' feelings) kàrā f.

sensual adj (sexual): he is very ~ yā fayè
jařabà.

sentence[1] n (Gram.) jimlà / jumlà f
⟨oCi⟩: a ~ usually contains a verb
yawancī àkwai fi'ìllī à jimlà; a simple
~ jimlà sàssaukà; a complex ~ jimlà
sàssarkà.

sentence[2] 1. n (Law) hukuncî m: the judge
gave him a 3 month ~ àlkālì yā yi masà
hukuncìn watà ukù; in some places, the
~ for theft is to sever the hand à wasu
wurārē hukuncìn sātà yankè hannū; the
death ~ hukuncìn kisà.
2. v hukùntà v1, yi wà hukuncî m, yankè
hukuncî, yankè shàři'à: he ~d the thief
yā yankè shàři'àř ɓàrāwò; he was ~d
to 2 years imprisonment an yankè masà
hukuncìn daurìn shèkarà biyu.

sentry n ɗan sintiřī m, mài řàngādì n, [F]

sàntìnâl *m;* ~ duty sintiřī *m,* řângādî *m.*

**separate** 1. *v* a. (*divide*) rabà *v1:* she ~d the potatoes into different piles tā rabà dànkalî kashî-kashî; I ~d them from arguing nā rabà su fadà. b. (*set apart*) wārè *v4:* ~ the good ones from the bad ones wārè màsu kyâu dàgà maràsā kyâu; the millet has been ~d from the sorghum an wārè gērō dà dāwà; ~ oneself wārè kâi.
2. *adj* dàbam: he kept them ~ yā ajìyē su dàbam; everyone went his ~ way kōwā yā bi hanyàřsà.

**separately** *adv* dai-dai, dàbam-dàbam: they came here ~ sun zō nân dai-dai; keep these things ~ kà wārè wadànnân abūbuwà dàbam-dàbam.

**separation** *n* ràbō *m,* ràbuwā *f.*

**separatism** *n* řa'àyin ɓallèwā *m.*

**September** *n* Sàtumbà *m.*

**sequence** *n* jērì *m* ⟨e²⟩.

**sequential** *adj:* in ~ arrangement à jère *adv;* in ~ order bî dà bî *adv.*

**sergeant** *n* sājà *m,* [F] sařjân *m:* S. Musa Sàjà Mūsā.

**sergeant-major** *n* sàmanjà *m* ⟨oCi⟩, [F] sařjan-màjâř *m.*

**series** *n:* a book ~ jērìn lìttàttàfai.

**serious** *adj* a. (*grave*) (mài) tsananī *m:* ~ illness cīwò mài tsananī; become ~ (*severe*) tsànantà *v3,* shàddadà *v3,* tà'àzzařà *v3,* yi tsāmārī *m:* the situation has become ~ àl'amàřīn yā tsànantà; have a ~ look, look ~ (*on face*) gamà fuskà; (*esp. quantitatively*) (mài) yawà *m:* ~ damage ɓařnā mài yawà. b. (*important*) bàbba *adj* ⟨manya-manya⟩, mùhimmì *adj* ⟨ai⟩, gàgārùmī *adj* ⟨ai⟩: a ~ matter mùhimmìn àl'amàřī; a ~ problem bàbbař màtsalà. c. (*of a psn.'s character*) (mài) nìtsuwā *f,* maràs gàràjē *m:* he is a ~ person mùtûm nē mài nìtsuwā.

**seriously** *adv:* take sth. ~ dauki w.a. dà zāfī; not take sth. ~ yi gàràjē dà w.a.

**sermon** *n* wa'àzī *m:* deliver a ~ yi wa'àzī; (*esp. at Friday mosque*) hudubà *f.*

**serpent** *n, see* snake.

**serrated** *adj* (mài) hakòrā *p:* a ~ knife wukā mài hakòrā.

**serval** *n* kàwun dàmisà *m.*

**servant** *n* barà *m,* baranyà *f* ⟨oCi⟩; (*domestic*) yārò *m* ⟨yârā⟩, bòyi *m* ⟨x²⟩, [F] bòyì *m:* they have 2 ~s, a cook-steward and a gardener sunà dà yâran gidā biyu, kūkù dà gādìnà; civil ~ ma'àikàcin gwamnatì *m.*

**serve** *v* a. (*give service to*) bâutā wà *v1:* ~ God, one's country bâutā wà Allàh, Kasā. b. (*work for*) yi aikì *m:* ~ in the army yi aikìn sōjà; he ~d as an accountant in the company yā yi wà kamfànīn aikìn àkantà = yā yi aikī à kamfànī à matsayin àkantà; (*fig.*) it ~s you right! bā ka dà kaico!

**service** *n* a. aikì *m:* government, civil ~ aikìn gwamnatì, [F] aikìn sàřūshì; the armed ~s aikìn sōjà; restaurant ~ aikìn sābìs, [F] aikìn sařbìs; National Youth S. Corps 'Yan Bâutā wà Kasā. b. (*to God*) ìbādà *f.*

**service station** *n* gidan mâi *m.*

**servility** *n* fādancì *m.*

**servitude** *n* bàutā *f,* bàràntakà *f.*

**sesame** *n* rīdī *m;* (*with red flowers*) nōmè *m;* (*nōmè leaves used for seasoning stews*) kařkashī *m.*

**session** *n:* a joint ~ hàdadden zamā; be in ~ nà cikin shāwařà: the legislature is now in ~ màjàlisà tanà cikin shāwařà yànzu.

**set**¹ *n* a. (*arrangement, group*) tsàrī *m,* zubì *m:* ~ of rules tsàrīn dōkōkī. b. (*of dishes*) saitì *m:* a new ~ of dishes sābon saitìn tangařan.

**set**² *v* a. (*var. v + obj uses*): ~ a clock daidàità àgōgo = yi saitìn àgōgo; ~ a date, time sâ rānā; ~ a dog on so. cūnà wà kàrē; ~ a good example nūnà hālī mài kyâu; ~ fire to sth. sâ wà w.a. wutā, cinnà wà w.a. wutā, dōsànà wutā à w.a.; ~ one's heart on kwallàfà râi à kân; ~ a limb dōrà *v1:* the doctor ~ my leg likità yā dorà minì kafà; ~ a load down saukè kāyà; ~ a trap, bomb danà tarkò, bâm; ~ so. free 'yantař dà w.; ~ so. up (*trick so.*) yi wà shirì. b. (*var. v + adv/prep uses*): ~ apart kēɓè *v4:* a special area has been ~ apart for important visitors an kēɓè wà mânyan bàkī wurin zamā; ~ aside, to one side ajìyē *v4;* ~ out for (*a place*) nùfà *v2,* dòsà *v2;* ~ to work kāmà aikì, tāsam mà aikì; ~ up a ruling, committee, tent kafà kà'idà, kwàmìtì, tantì *m.* c. (*of sun*) fādì *v3b* ⟨fādùwā⟩ *f:* the sun ~s in the west rānā nà fādùwā yâmma. d. be ~ as a way of life (*fig.*) zaunà dà gìndinsà.

**settle** 1. *vt* (*arbitrate*) sulhùntā *v1,* rabà *v1,* sāsàntā *v1:* he ~d the dispute between them yā sulhùntà rìkicin dà kè tsàkāninsù; ~ a debt biyā bashì; ~ a matter kashè màganà.
2. *vi* a. (*live permanently in a place*) zaunà

*v1.* b. (*die down*) kwântā *v1,* lafâ *v1:* the
dust ~d ƙūrā tā lafâ. c. (*resign oneself
to*) ~ for sth. dànganà dà *v3:* they'll ~ for
anything they can get zā sù dànganà dà
duk àbîn dà zā à iyà bā sù.

**settlement** *n* a. (*agreement*) yàr̃jējēnìyā
*f.* b. (*residence*) mazaunī *m;* nomadic ~
(*in dry season*) cîn rānī *m,* (*in wet season*) mashēkarī *m.*

**settler** *n* ɗan kàkà-gidā *m.*

**seven** *quant* bakwài *f:* there are 7 days in a
week àkwai kwānā bakwài à mākò.

**seventeen** *quant* (gōmà) shâ-bakwài *f.*

**seventh** *quant* na bakwài.

**seventy** *quant* sàbà'in *f.*

**sever** *v* yankè *v4:* the machine ~ed his hand
injìn yā yankè masà hannū; ~ diplo-
matic ties yankè huldàr̃ jakādancî.

**several** *quant* a. (*a few*) waɗansu/wasu *det:*
~ people were hurt wasu mutànē sun
ji ràunī; ~ of the pilgrims were hurt
waɗansu dàgà cikin manìyyàtā sun ji
ràunī. b. (*quite a few*) dà dāmā *adv:*
there have been ~ accidents on this road
an yi haɗar̃ur̃r̃ukà dà dāmā à hanyàr̃
nân.

**severe** *adj* (mài) tsananī *m,* matsànàncī
*adj:* a ~ windstorm demolished his
house iskà mài tsananī tā sâ gidansà
yā rūshè; ~ heat, cold zāfī, sanyī
mài tsananī; ~ hunger matsanancìyar̃
yunwà; become ~ tsànantà *v3,* shàddadà
*v3;* under ~ conditions à tsànànce: they
are living under ~ conditions sunà zamā a
tsànànce; treat so. ~ly tsanàntā *v1.*

**severity** *n* tsananī *m.*

**sew** *v* ɗinkà *v1;* ~ a button sâ maɓallī:
the tailor ~ed the button on the blouse
maɗinkī yā sâ maɓallī à rìgâr̃.

**sewer** *n* (*open*) làmbàtû *m, see* ditch.

**sewing machine** *n* kèkèn ɗinkì *m.*

**sex** *n* a. (*gender*) jinsî *m;* what ~ is it?
namijì nē kō màcè? b. (*sexual intercourse*) jìmā'ì *m;* have ~ with yi jìmā'ì
dà, (*euphem.*) tārà dà *v1,* sàdu dà *v7;*
(*vulg.*) ci *v0.*

**sex education** *n* ilìmin jìmā'ì *m.*

**sexism** *n* wāriyar̃ jinsî *f.*

**sexual intercourse** (*marital*) jìmā'ì *m;*
(*euphem.*) tāràwa *f,* sàduwā *f;* (*extra-
marital*) zìnā *f,* làlàtā *f;* (*vulg.*) cî *m.*

**shackles** *n* màrī *m.*

**shade** 1. *n* a. (*of tree*) inuwà *f:* in the ~
of a tree à inuwàr̃ bishiyà; give ~ bā
dà inuwà; this ~d area is perfect for rest-
ing wannàn inuwà tā dācè dà hūtàwā. b.
(*hue, color*) shigē *m,* ruwā *m:* it is a ~ of

blue yanā dà shigen shūdì.
2. *v* kārè *v4:* ~ one's eyes from the sun
kārè idò dàgà rānā.

**shadoof** *n* (*irrigation system*) jīgò *m.*

**shadow** *n* inuwà *f:* Musa's ~ inuwàr̃ Mūsā.

**shady** *adj* (mài) inuwà *f:* it is ~ here
àkwai inuwà nân; a ~ tree bishiyà mài
bā dà inuwà; it is getting ~ rānā tanà
dushēwā.

**shaft** *n* (*of axe*) ƙōtà *f* 〈oCi〉; (*of arrow*)
kyaurō *m* 〈aye〉.

**shaggy** *adj* (*psn.*) gàr̃gāsā *adj,* buzū-bùzū
*idph.*

**shake** 1. *vt* a. kaɗà *v1,* kaɗè *v4:* the wind
shook the trees iskà tā kaɗà itātuwà;
he answered by shaking his head (in agreement) yā amsà dà kaɗà kâi; ~ a finger
at so. (*as warning*) nūnà wà yàtsà; ~ a
fist, spear in salute yi jìnjinà *f;* ~ hands
yi mùsāfahà *f,* bā dà hannū, gaisà *v1.* b.
(*sideways*) gìr̃gīzà *v1,* yi gìr̃gīzà *f:* he
shook his head and said no yā gìr̃gīzà kâi
ya cè ā'à; the dog came out of the water
and shook itself kàrên yā fitō dàgà ruwa
yā yi gìr̃gīzà. c. (*up and down*) jijjìgà
*v1:* the car shook them up and down mōtà
tā jijjìgà su. d. (*a garment*) kaɓè *v4,*
gìr̃gīzà *v1;* ~ sth. off, out kakkàɓē *v4,*
kar̃kàɗè *v4:* he shook the dust off his robe
yā kakkàɓè ƙūrā dàgà rìgar̃sà; don't ~
the dust on me kaɗà kà kakkàɓā minì
ƙūrā; ~ sth. loose (*out of socket*) gìr̃gìɗē
*v4:* I shook the tooth loose nā gìr̃gìɗè
haƙōrī; ~ so. up (*startle*) gīgītā *v1.*
2. *vi* (*from cold, fear*) yi ɓarī *m,* yi
tsìmā *f,* yi màkyar̃kyatā *f;* (*esp. from illness*) yi rawā *f:* he is shaking jìkinsà nà
rawā.

**shake-up** *n* (*in an organization*) tànkàɗē dà
ràirayā *m.*

**shaky** *adj* (*unstable*) (mài) rawā *f,* maràs
ƙwārī *m:* the table is ~ tēbùr̃īn bā yà
dà ƙwārī.

**shall** *v aux, see* will[2].

**shallow** *adj* maràs zurfī *m.*

**shambles** *n* kaca-kaca *idph:* the room is in
~ dākì kaca-kaca yakè.

**shame** 1. *n* kunyà *f:* she has no ~ bâ ta dà
kunyà = bâ ta dà ta ido; with absolutely
no ~ bâ kunyà bâ tsòron Allàh; sense
of ~ jîn kunyà *m;* bring ~ on so. kunyàtā
*v1;* ~ on you! (*reprimand*) kā ji kunyà!
what a ~! (*pity*) àsshā!, kaico! *excl.*
2. *v* sâ w. jîn kunyà; (*by disclosing so.'s
secrets*) fàllasà *v2.*

**shameful** *adj* àbin kunyà *m,* (mài) bā dà
kunyà: he behaved ~ly yā yi àbin kunyà

= yā yi wani mūgùn àbù.

**shameless** *adj* maràs kunyà *f*: he is ~ bâ
shi dà kunyà = rashìn kunyà gàrē shì
= bâ shi dà ta ido; (*esp. insolent child*)
tsagèrā *n* ⟨u⟩.

**shampoo** *n* shàmfû *m*.

**shape** 1. *n* siffà / sifà *f* ⟨oCi⟩, (*structure*) sīgà *f* ⟨oCi⟩: what ~ is it? yàyà
siffàr̃sà? it has the ~ of a ball siffàr̃sà
kàmar̃ kwallō; (*fig.*) things are in bad ~
gàrī yā ci wutā.
2. *v* sīgàntā *v1*; ~ sth. into a ball (*with
hands*) cūrā *v1*, dunkùlā *v1*.

**shard** *n*, *see* potsherd.

**share** 1. *n* a. ràbō *m*: he didn't give me
my ~ bài bā nì ràbōnā ba; a fair ~
ràbon Allàh = ràbon gàskiyā. b. (*stock
in a company*) hannun jār̃ì *m*: the government owns a majority of ~s in the
banks gwamnatì nā̀ dà hannun jār̃ì mafî
rinjāyè à bankunā̀.
2. *v* rabā̀ *v1*: ~ profits rabà r̃ībà̀; I ~ a
house with him munā̀ zàune gidā ɗaya.

**shareholder** *n* mài hannun jār̃ì *n*.

**sharp** *adj* a. (*with a keen edge*) (mài) kaifī
*m*: you should cut it with a ~ knife
yā kàmātà kà yankè shi dà wukā̀ mài
kaifī; a ~ mind mài kaifin bàsīr̃à̀. b.
(*pointed*) (mài) tsìnī *m*: a ~ bone k̃ashī
mài tsìnī. c. (*other uses*): a ~ corner
k̃ùrarriyar̃ kwanā̀; a ~ pain (*esp. in side
of body*) masōkìyā *f*; a ~ voice muryà̀ mài
k̃wārī; speak ~ly to so. dakà̀ wà tsāwā.

**sharpen** *v* a. (*with whetstone*) wāsā̀ *v1*
⟨wāshì⟩: this knife needs ~ing wukàr̃ nàn
nā̀ bùkātàr̃ à wāsā̀ ta; (*fig.*) ~ one's
wits kaifàfà tùnānī. b. (*by beating the
edge*) kōɗā *v1* ⟨kūɗà⟩ *f*: they are ~ing their
swords sunā̀ kūɗar̃ takubbànsù. c. (*to a
point*) fēr̃è *v4* ⟨fīr̃à⟩ *f*: please ~ this pencil for me kà̀ fēr̃è mìnì fensìr̃ ɗîn.

**sharpness** *n* a. (*of an edge*) kaifī *m*; (*of
a point*) tsìnī *m*. b. (*of taste*) yājì *m*.
c. (*of intelligence*) hāzik̃ancì *m*, kaifin
bàsīr̃à̀ *m*.

**shatter** *v* far̃r̃àshē *v4*, r̃agar̃gàzā /
r̃ugur̃gùzā *v1*; r̃agar̃gàjē / r̃ugur̃gùjē
*v4*: the bottle ~ed into pieces kwalabà̀ tā
far̃r̃àshē r̃ugu-r̃ugu.

**shave** *v* (*head & face*) yi askì *m*; (*face only*)
gyārā fuskà̀: I haven't ~d yet bàn gyàrà
fuskà̀ ba tùkùna; he was freshly ~n yā
yi sābon gyāran fuskà̀.

**shaving** *n* askì *m*; ~ knife askā̀ *f*.

**shawl** *n* mayāfì *m*, lullu6ì *m*.

**shawm** *n*, *see* oboe.

**she** *pro*, *see* Appendix A.

**shea-nut** *n* (*tree*) kaɗanyā̀ *f*; (*nut*) k̃wār̃à̀ *f*;
~ butter mân kaɗē.

**sheaf** *n* damì *m* ⟨Ca, Cai⟩: ~ of millet stalks
damìn gērō.

**shear** *v* (*sheep*) yankè wà tumākī gāshì.

**shears** *n* bàbban àlmakàshī *m*.

**sheath** *n* gidā *m* ⟨aCe⟩, kùbē *m* ⟨anni⟩: put
a knife back into its ~ mai dà wuk̃ā à gidantà.

**shed**[1] *n* (*stall*) rùmfā *f* ⟨una⟩; (*for railroad cars*) shēdì *m*; (*for repairing railroad
cars*) lōkō *m*.

**shed**[2] *v* a. (*pour forth*) zub dà / zubar̃ (dà)
*v5*: ~ blood, hair zub dà jinī, gāshì; ~
tears yi hawāyē *p*. b. (*other v + n uses*):
~ one's clothes tū6e kāyā; ~ leaves kaɗè
ganyē = kakka6è ganyē; ~ light on sth.
haskàkā *v1*, jēfà haskē: he was able to
~ light on the matter yā jēfà haskē gàme
dà àl'amàr̃ī; ~ skin (*by snake*) yi sā6ā
*f*.

**sheep** *n* (*esp. ewe*) tunkìyā *f* ⟨tumākī⟩; a
flock of ~ garkèn tumākī; (*virgin ewe*)
kazganyà̀ *f*; (*ram*) rāgō *m* ⟨una⟩; (*long-
haired*) buzurwā *f* ⟨oCi⟩.

**sheepskin** *n* būzū *m* ⟨aye⟩, agalàmī *m* ⟨u-
a⟩.

**sheet** *n* a. (*for bed*) zanèn gadō *m*. b. (*single thickness of sth.*) fallē *m*. c. (*of paper*) war̃k̃ā *f* ⟨oCi⟩: a ~ of paper war̃k̃ar̃
takàr̃dā = fallen takàr̃dā.

**sheikh** *n* shēhǔ *m* ⟨shēhùnnai⟩.

**shelf** *n* kantà̀ *f* ⟨oCi⟩.

**shell** 1. *n* (*pod of cotton boll, kolanut*)
k̃wànsō *m*; (*of egg, peanuts*) 6āwō *m*,
kwàfsā / kwàsfā *f*; (*of mussel*) k̃ùmbā
*f*; (*of snail*) kàtantanwā *f*; (*of tortoise*)
k̃waryā *f*.
2. *v* 6ārè *v4*: ~ peanuts 6ārè 6āwon
gyàɗā.

**shelter** 1. *n* a. (*hut, shed*) rùmfā *f* ⟨una⟩.
b. (*housing*) màhâllī / mùhâllī *m*, wurin
zamā *m*: food, clothing, and ~ dà àbinci
dà tufā̀ dà màhâllī; ~ for the home-
less gidan gàjìyàyyū. c. (*place of refuge*)
mafakā *f*; take ~ fakè *v4*: we took ~ from
the rain mun fakè dàgà ruwā.
2. *v* (*protect, shield*) kārè *v4* : the tree
~ed us from the storm itàcēn yā kārè
manà iskà̀.

**shepherd** *n* mài kīwō *m*, makìyàyin tumākī
*m*: the Lord is my S. Allàh nē
makìyàyīnā.

**shield** 1. *n* gàrkuwā *f* ⟨oCi⟩.
2. *v* kārè *v4*, yi gàrkuwā *f*: ~ oneself from
a blow kārè dūkā̀; I used him to ~ me nā̀
yi gàrkuwā dà shī.

**shift** *v* a. (*position*) kau dà / kawař (dà) *v5*. b. (*gears of vehicle*) canjã *v1*.

**shiftless** *adj* (*lazy, aimless psn.*) ragō *m* ⟨aye⟩, sākařai *n* ⟨sākářkařī⟩.

**shifty** *adj* (*evasive, deceitful*): be ~ yi zūɓe-zūɓe *m*, yi wùnì-wunī *idph*, yi ɓumbìyà-ɓumbiyà *idph*: he's a ~ type yā fayè ɓumbìyà-ɓumbiyà.

**shilling** *n* (*old Nigerian unit of currency, but used informally for the 10 kobo piece, see Appendix F*) sulè *m* ⟨uka²⟩.

**shin** *n* ɓwàurī *m* ⟨uka⟩.

**shinbone** *n* sangalī / sangalalī *m*.

**shine 1.** *vi* a. (*give light*) yi haskē *m*: the moon was shining watà nà haskē; the light is shining in my eyes haskē yanà ɗaukař idònā = haskē nà kashè minì idò. b. (*reflect light*) yi ɓyàllī *m*, yi wàlɓiyà *f*: their swords shone brightly in the sun takubbànsù nà ɓyàllī wàl à rāna. c. (*esp. of skin, glossy hair, cloth*) yi shēɓī *m*: their faces were shining with happiness fuskàřsù nà shēɓī don farin cikì.
**2.** *vt* haskà *v1*: he shone a light into the room yā haskà fìtilà à ɗakì; ~ a light, flashlight on so. dallarō wà fìtilà, tōcìlàn.

**shingles** *n* (*Med.*) būlālìyà *f*.

**shiny** *adj* (mài) ɓyàllī *m*, (mài) shēɓī *m*, (mài) wàlɓiyà *f*, (mài) ɗaukàř idò.

**ship 1.** *n* jirgin ruwa *m* ⟨a-e⟩: the ~ has sailed jirgîn yā tāshì.
**2.** *v*: ~ one's goods by sea, by air aikà dà kāyā ta jirgin ruwa, ta jirgin samà.

**shirk** *v*: there's no ~ing it, it must be done bâ makawã sai an yī shì.

**shirt** *n* taguwà *f* ⟨oCi⟩; (*var. types*): (*short sleeved under~, round neck*) 'yař ciki *f*; (*3/4 length with embroidered neck & sleeves*) kuftà *f*; (*men's long-sleeved shirt worn under robe*) jamfã *f*; (*West. style*) shât *f*: he was dressed in a ~ and shorts yanà sànye dà taguwà dà gàjēren wàndō.

**shirting** *n* (*material*) zàwwàtì *m*.

**shiver** *v* yi ɓarì *m*, yi tsìmā *f*, yi màkyařkyatã *f*, yi rawã *f*: ~ from cold yi màkyařkyataf dārī = yi rawàf dārī.

**shock 1.** *n* a. (*force*) mōtsī *m*: feel the ~ of an earthquake ji mòtsin gìřgizàř ɓasà. b. (*electrical*) (wutař) làntařkì *f*, [F] (cīzòn) kùřân *m*: I got an electrical ~ làntařkì yā kāmà ni = [F] kùřân yā cìjē nì. c. (*surprise, fright*) fìrgità *f*; suffer from ~ gīgìcē *v4*: she's in a state of ~ tanà cikin fìrgità; the accident

put her in a state of ~ hadàřîn yā sâ tà gīgìcē.
**2.** *v* a. (*startle, frighten*) gīgìtā *v1*, firgitař (dà) *v5*: the news of the accident ~ed him làbàřîn hadàřîn yā gīgìtā shi. b. (*upset emotionally*) dāgùlā wà râi.

**shock absorber** *n* cakàsōbã *m*, [F] àmářtìsâř *m*.

**shocking** *adj* mài gīgìtářwā, mài firgitářwā: ~ news làbàřì mài gīgìtářwā.

**shoe** *n* tàkàlmi *m* ⟨tākalmã⟩: ~ repairman mài gyāran tàkàlmī; (*var. types*): (*West. style*) [F] sùlê *m*; (*with pointed toe*) bàlkã *m*; (*backless*) kùfùtai *p*, see sandals; (*football*) bōtì *m*, [F] kàřàmfô *m*; (*tennis*) kambàs *m*, [F] kìřâf *f*.

**shoelaces** *n* maɗaurin tàkàlmī *m*.

**shoemaker** *n* bàdūkù *m*; (*for modern shoes*) shùmēkà *m*.

**shoe polish** *n* mân tàkàlmī *m*.

**shoe shine boy** *n* shûshainã *m*, shûshāyè *m*.

**shoot¹** *v* a. (*so., sth.*) hàřbā *v2* ⟨hařbì⟩: he was shot with a poisoned arrow an hàřbē shì dà kibiyà mài gubà; ~ so. dead hařbè *v4*; ~ sth. down hařbō *v6*. b. (*a weapon*) hàřbã *v1* ⟨hařbì⟩, (*esp. a firearm*) bugà *v1*.

**shoot²** *n* (*of plant*) tsirò *m* ⟨e²⟩, tūshè *m*.

**shooting star** *n* mashì *m*.

**shop 1.** *n* a. (*store*) kàntī *m* ⟨una⟩. b. (*atelier, workshop*) shāgò *m*: barber, tailor ~ shāgòn mài askìn bābà, tēlà.
**2.** *v*: go ~ping yi sàyayyã *f*; (*esp. for groceries*) yi cèfànē *m*; do a lot of ~ping ci kàsuwā.

**shopkeeper** *n* mài kàntī *n*.

**shore** *n* (*of river*) gāɓã *f*; (*opposite to where one is*) gacī *m*; (*of lake, sea*) bàkī *m*.

**short** *adj* a. (*in size*) gàjērē *adj*, gàjērìyā *f* ⟨u⟩, (*dimin.*) duɓus *idph*: a ~ boy gàjēren yārò; she is really ~ gàjērìyā cè duɓus dà ita; I came by the ~ road nā biyō ta gàjērìyař hanyã. b. (*in quantity*): be, get ~ taɓàicē *v4*: time is getting ~ lōkàcī yā taɓàicē; a ~ while ago jìm kàɗan; after a ~ time bāyan gàjēren lōkàcī = jìm kàɗan; be ~ of sth. (*esp. money*) kāsà *v1*, gazà *v1*, yi shôt *m*, ragè *v4*: I am ~ of money kudī sun kāsà minì = kuɗīnā sun gazà; I am ₦2 ~ kuɗīnā sun yi shôt dà naiřã biyu; there is one ~ (*missing*) ɗaya yā ragè; in ~ (*briefly*) à taɓàice, à gàjàrce.

**shortage** *n* ɓarancī *m*, rashì *m*: a ~ of rain ɓarancin ruwā = rashìn ruwā; (*esp. of* *food*) ƙamfā *f*: there is a ~ of grain anà ƙamfaɍ hatsī = anà ƙarancin hatsī.

**short-change** *v* ƙwàrā *v2*.

**short-circuit** *n* ƙônêwā *f*.

**shortcoming** *n* a. (*weakness*) aibì *m* ⟨una⟩, illà *f* ⟨oCi⟩: his ~ is his impatience illàɍsà rashìn hàƙurī. b. (*deficiency*) cīkàs *m*: his major ~ is that he lacks education rashìn ilìminsà shī nè bàbban cīkàs gàre shì.

**short-cut** *n* (*road, way*) yànkē *m*, (*esp. one not known by others*) ɓàraunìyaɍ hanyà *f*.

**shorten** *v* a. (*lessen*) gajàrtā *v1*, taƙàità *v1*, ragè *v4*: ~ the length of a dress ragè tsawon rìgā; ~ a report by 2 pages taƙàità ɍàhōtò dà shāfì biyu. b. (*by cutting off*) dātsè *v4*: ~ the sleeves of a gown dātsè hannun rìgā.

**shortly** *adv* in an jimà, bà dà dadèwā ba: I shall see him ~ zân gan shì in an jimà; ~ afterwards... an jimà kàdan, sai... = jìm kàdan sai....

**shorts** *n* gàjēren wàndō *m*; (*underwear*) dùɍôs *m*, kamfai *m*, [F] kampē *m*.

**short-sighted** *adj*: he is ~ (*lit.*) bā yà ganin nēsà; (*fig.*) bâ shi dà tsìnkàyē.

**short-tempered** *adj* (mài) saurin fushī *m*, (mài) zāfin zūcìyā *m*.

**shortwave** *adj*: a ~ radio ɍēdiyò mài gàjēren zangò.

**shot** *n* a. (*sound of weapon*) bugù *m*: he heard the ~ of a gun yā ji bugùn bindigà. b. (*bullet*) hàɍsāshì *m*: he fired 3 ~s yā haɍbà hàɍsāshì ukù; (*fig.*) a ~ in the dark làlùbē cikin duhù. c. (*injection*) àllūɍà *f*: she went to the clinic to get a ~ tā jē asìbitì don à yi matà àllūɍà.

**shotgun** *n* bindigà *f* ⟨oCi⟩.

**shot putt** *n* jīfàn daɍmà *m*.

**should** *v* a. (*expressing mild request, suggestion*) sai (+ *subjunct.*): you ~ take a break sai kà hūtà; you ~ not work so hard bà sai kà yi aikì dà yawà hakà ba. b. (*for stronger suggestion, intent*) yā kàmātā (+ *subjunct.*): we ~ hurry yā kàmātā mù yi saurī; ~ have done kàmātà ya yi (+ *subjunct.*): why did he quarrel with her? she ~ have asked his permission first don mè ya yi matà fadà? kàmātà ya yi tà tàmbàyē shì izìnī tùkùn.

**shoulder** 1. *n* kàfadà *f* ⟨u⟩; (*of meat*) karfàtà *f* ⟨u⟩.
2. *v* (*a weapon, tool*) saɓà *v1*.

**shoulder blade** *n* àllon kàfadà *m*.

**shout** 1. *v* yi īhù *m* yi ƙārā *f*; (*for help*) yi kùrūruwà *f*: (*esp. joyfully*) yi kuwwà

*f*; the people ~ed for joy jàma'àɍ tā yi kuwwà don muɍnà; ~ at (*scold, command*) dakà wà tsāwā *v1*.
2. *n* īhù *m*, kuwwà *f*; (*esp. for help*) kùrūruwà *f*.

**shove** *v* bangàjē *v4*, tūrā *v1*.

**shovel** *n* shēbùɍ / tēbùɍ *m* ⟨oCi⟩, [F] fēlù *m*.

**show** 1. *v* a. (*display, demonstrate*) nūnà *v1*, gwadà *v1* ⟨gwajì⟩: his words ~ed that he didn't understand màganàɍsà tā nūnà cêwā bài gānè ba; ~ how to kwàtàntā *v1*, gwadà *v1* ⟨gwajì⟩: ~ me how it is done gwàdā minì yâddà akè yînsà; he ~ed us how to use the equipment yā kwàtàntā manà yâddà akè àmfànī dà nā'ūɍàɍ; ~ so. kindness yi wà àlhērì. b. (*reveal, explain*) bayyànā *v1*: that ~s that he is not kind wannàn yā bayyànā bâ shi dà kiɍkì. c. (*v + adv/prep uses*): ~ so. around town zāgàyā dà w. cikin gàrī; ~ off dagà hancì, yi tàƙamà *f*, yi tìnƙāhò *m*, yi bùɍgā *f*. (*esp. one's wealth*) yi gàdāɍà *f*; ~ up (*attend*) hàllafà *v3*.
2. *n* a. (*exhibit*) bìkī nūnà w.a. *m*: agricultural ~ bìkin nūnà àmfànin gōnā; film ~ (*outdoors*) mājìgī *m*. b. good ~! yâwwà! *excl.*

**shower** 1. *n* a. (*rain*) yayyafī *m*, tsattsafī *m*. b. (*bath*) shāwà *f*.
2. *v* a. (*rain*) yayyàfā *v1*. b. (*bathe*) yi wankā à shāwà.

**shreds** *n*: be torn to ~ fatattàkē *v4*.

**shrew** *n* (*musk* ~) jāɓà *f*.

**shrewd** *adj* (mài) wàyō *m*.

**shriek** *n* ƙārā *f*.

**shrike** *n* (*bird*) sùdā *f*.

**shrilling** *n* (*ululating*) gūdà *f* ⟨e²⟩: it is women who do ~ mātā nè kè yîn gūdà.

**shrimp** *n* jàtan landè *m*.

**shrink** *v* a. (*of garment, cloth*) dagè *v4*, shānyē *v4*, tauyè *v4*: wool ~s wūl nà dagèwā. b. (*get small*) ƙanƙàncē *v4*; (*fig., of distance*): because of the fast means of transport, the world has shrunk sabòdà saurin abūbuwàn sufùɍī, dūniyà kàmaɍ tā tsūkè.

**shrivel up** *v* yanƙwànē / yāƙwànē *v4*; (*esp. of whole body*) ƙanjàmē *v4*.

**shroud** *n* lìkkafànī *m*, lìfāfà *f*: ~s are made from white calico anà lìkkafànī dà alawayyò.

**shrubs** *n* tsìre-tsìre *p*.

**shrug** *v* dagà kàfadà.

**shuck** *v* (*e.g. maize*) ɓàrè ganyē.

**shudder** *v* yi rawā *f*.

**shuffle** *v* (*cards*) lālè *v4*.

shun v ƙauràcē wà *v4*, ƙi *v0*: ~ people ƙauràcē wà mutằnē = ƙi mutằnē.

shush *excl* shirū! *excl.*

shut 1. *v* rufè *v4*: I was ~ out of the room an rufè minì ƙōfằ; the door will not ~ ƙōfằ bā tằ rùfuwā; ~ electricity off kashè làntařƙ; ~ water off ƙullè famfò; ~ up! yi minì shirū! = rùfē mîn bằkī!
2. *adv* à rùfe *adv*: the door is always ~ kōyàushè ƙōfằ à rùfe takè.

shutter *n* (*of window*) ƙyauren tāgằ *m*.

shuttle *n* a. (*for weaving*) ƙōshiyằ *f*, ɗan jīfằ *m*. b. space ~ kumbò *m* 〈una〉.

shy[1] *adj*: be ~ ji kunyằ *f*, yi filātancī *m*: don't be ~ kadà kì yi filātancī; she is ~ about speaking Hausa tanà jîn kunyằ tà yi màganằ dà Hausa.

shy[2] *v* (*by horse*) waskè wà *v4*: the horse shied away from the light dōkìn yā waskè wà haskè.

shyness *n* jîn kunyằ *f*; (*out of respect to others' feelings*) kằrā *f*.

sibling *n* (*any ~*) ɗan'uwā *m*, 'yař'uwā *f* 〈'yan'uwā〉; full ~ (*same mother, same father*) shàƙīƙì *m* 〈ai〉; half-~ (*same father, diff. mother*) ɗan'ùbā *m*, 'yař'ùbā *f*, 〈'yan'ùbā〉; ~ rivalry (*esp. between half-~s*) 'yan'ubancì *m*.

sick *adj* maràs lāfiyằ *f*, (mài) cīwò *m*: she is ~ tanà cīwò = bâ ta dà lāfiyằ = tanà rashìn lāfiyằ = jìkintà yā yi nauyī; he has been ~ for a long time yā daɗè yanà rashìn lāfiyằ; a ~ animal dabbà maràs lāfiyằ; I got up feeling ~ nā tāshì dà rashìn lāfiyằ; feel ~ ji cīwò; feeling ~ to one's stomach tāshìn zūcìyā; make so. ~ sâ w. rashìn lāfiyằ.

sickle *n* làujē *m* 〈una〉.

sickle cell anemia *n* nàƙasằř ƙwāyōyin jinī *f*.

sickly *adj* (*psn.*) kùmāmā *n* 〈ai〉.

sickness *n* cīwò *m*, cùtā *f* 〈cìwàce-cìwàce〉, rashìn lāfiyằ *m*, [F] màlātì *m*: there has been a lot of ~ lately àkwai cìwàce-cìwàce dà yawà kwànan nàn; home ~ kēwař gida *f*; morning ~ laulàyin cikì *m*; motion ~ tāshìn zūcìyā *m*.

side *n* a. (*of sth.*) gēfè *m* 〈Ca〉: the box has 3 ~s àkwàtìn nà dà gēfè ukù; ~ by ~ kusa dà kusa; on the right, left ~ à (hannun) dāma, hagu. b. (*of one's body*) kwìɓì *m* 〈kwiyằɓà〉. c. (*area within a whole*) ɓangarè *m*: on this ~ of town à wannàn ɓangarèn gàrīn; on the other ~ of the mountain à ɗaya ɓangarèn dūtsèn.

d. (*edge of*): at the ~ of the road à bằkin hanyằ; at the ~ of the river à hayìn kòḡī.
e. (*opposite ~*): on the other ~ of the street à ƙētarèn hanyằ; opposite ~ of a river gacī *m*; on both ~s of the paper cikì dà bâi. f. (*point of view*): see both ~s of a question dūbà màtsalằř cikì dà bântà; take so.'s ~ gòyi bāyan w., bi ƙa'àyin w., gamà kâi dà w.: he's on our ~ yā gamà kâi dà mū = yanà gàme dà mū. g. (*Sports*) ƙungìyā *f* 〈oCi〉, tîm *m*, ɓangarè *m*: he's not on our ~ bā yà ɓangarènmù. h. (*a place apart*) wajē *m*: put sth. to one ~ ajìyè w.a. wajē ɗaya. i. (*kinship*) na wajen: I am related to them on my father's ~ sū dangìnā nè na wajen ùbā.

sideburns, sidewhiskers *n* sằjē *m*.

sideswipe *v* yi gūgằ *f*: someone ~d my new car wani yā yi gūgằ dà sābuwař mōtằtā.

sidewalk *n* gēfen hanyằ *m*.

sideways *adv* à kàikàice: he looked at me ~ yā kàllàcē nì à kàikàice.

siesta *n* ƙailūlā *f*, barcin rāna *m*.

sieve *n* rāriyā *f*, [F] tằmē *m*; (*of coarse mesh*) marāraƙī *m*.

sift *v* (*with sieve or small mat*) tankàɗā *v1* 〈tànkàɗē〉; (*esp. fine ground food*) rairàyē *v4* 〈ràirayằ〉 *f*.

sifter *n* rāriyā *f*, marāraƙī *m*.

sigh *v* yi àjiyằř zūcìyā *f*.

sight 1. *n* ganī *m*: at first ~ it seemed easy dà ganī dai sai kà cê bà wùyā; I know him by ~ nā taɓà ganinsà; there is nobody in ~ bā à ganin kōwā; his ~ is failing ganinsà yā ràgu; he has poor ~ bā yằ ganì sòsai; he has very poor ~ yanà ganì garma-garma; lose one's ~ makàncē *v4*; catch ~ of (*from a distance*) hàngā *v2* 〈hàngē〉, tsìnkāyằ *v2*; get out of my ~! ɓàce minì dà ganī.
2. *v* (*so. from a distance*) hàngā *v2* 〈hàngē〉; tsìnkāyằ *v2*.

sightseeing *n* yāwòn shāƙàtâwā *m*.

sign 1. *n* a. (*indication*) àlāmằ *f* 〈u〉: there are ~s of rain àkwai àlằmun ruwā; a ~ of old age, happiness, kindness àlāmằř tsūfā, farin cikì, kiřƙì. b. (*esp. sth. concrete*) lambằ *f* 〈oCi〉, àlāmằ *f* 〈oCi〉: street ~ lambằř tītì = àlāmằř tītì; road ~ (*showing directions*) àlāmằř hanyằ *f*, [F] fànō *m*. c. (*notice, announcement*) sanằřwā *f*.
2. *v* (*put signature*) sâ hannū: I haven't ~ed it yet bàn sâ hannūnā ba tùkùna.

signal 1. *n* àlāmằ *f* 〈u〉, sigìnà *f*: when I give you a ~, close the door in nā nūnà makà àlāmằ, kà rufè ƙōfằ; turn ~ (*in *car*) sigìnà *f*, [F] kìlìyòtân *m*: the turn ~ is blinking sigìnà tanã cî.

2. *v* kwatântā *v1*, yi sigìnà *f*, [F] yi kìlìyòtân *m*.

**signature** *n* sā hannū *m*, [F] sinyē *m*: is this your ~? wannàn sā hannunkà nē?

**significance** *n* a. (*semantic meaning*) mà'ànā *f* ⟨oCi⟩. b. (*importance*) muhimmancî *m*, fā'idã *f*: the ~ of prayers fā'idàȓ sallōlī. c. (*underlying purpose*) manufā *f*: what was the ~ of that war? mēnē nè manufaȓ wannàn yāƙì?

**significant** *adj* (*impressive*) gàgārùmī *adj* ⟨ai⟩, mùhimmì *adj* ⟨ai⟩: a ~ victory mùhimmìyaȓ nasarã.

**signify** *v* (*mean*) nùfā *v2* ⟨nufì⟩.

**silence** 1. *n* shirū *m*: we listened to him in ~ mun yi shirū mun sàurārē shì; a dead ~ tsit *idph*: there was complete ~ when he entered an yi tsit dà ya shigō; (*fig.*) ~ is golden kōmē dāɗin màganà shirū yā fī tà.

2. *v* sâ w. yà yi shirū.

**silencer** *n* (*of car*), *see* muffler.

**silent** *adj* (mài) shirū *m*; be ~ yi shirū, kāmè bàkī: he knows when to speak and when to be ~ yā san lōkàcin màganà yā kuma san lōkàcin shirū; be utterly ~ yi tsit *idph*: the streets were empty, the place was absolutely ~ tītunã bâ kōwā, gàrī yā yi tsit.

**silk** *n* (*fabric, imported*) sìlikì *m*; raw ~ (*from tamarind-fed worms*) tsāmiyā *f*; ~ thread (*imported*) àlhàȓīnī *m*.

**silk cotton tree** *n* (*kapok*) rīmī *m* ⟨aye⟩.

**silkworm** *n* tsūtsàȓ tsāmiyā *f*.

**silliness** *n* a. (*of psn.*) wâutā *f*, wāwancì *m*, shāshancì *m*. b. (*nonsense*) shìrmē *m*. that's the first time I've ever heard of such ~ tun dà nakè bàn taɓà jîn shìrmē irìn wannàn ba.

**silly** *adj* (*of psn. or his actions*) na wâutā *f*; be ~ yi wâutā = zama wāwā; ~ talk shìrmē *m*.

**silver** *n* azùȓfā *f*: he wore a ~ ring yā sâ zōbèn azùȓfā; ~ coins kuɗī *p*.

**silversmith** *n* maƙèrin farfarū, maƙèrin azùȓfā *m*.

**similar** *adj* (mài) kàmā *f*: they are ~ sun yi kàmā (dà jūnā); this one is ~ to that wannàn yā yi kàmaȓ wancàn = wannàn yā yi kàmā dà wancàn.

**similarity** *n* kàmā *f* ⟨anni⟩: what are their similarities and their differences? mēnē nè kàmànninsù dà bàmbànce-bàmbàncensù?

**simile** *n* tàmkā *f*.

**simple** *adj* a. (*easy*) (mài) sauƙī *m*, sàssauƙā *adj*: a ~ person mài sauƙin kâi; a ~ question tàmbayã mài sauƙī; please explain it to me in ~ language kà bayyànā minì cikin sàssauƙan harshè. b. (*pure, natural*) kawài *adv*: it's the ~ truth gàskiyā cè kawài; a ~ life zaman almājìȓcî.

**simpleton** *n* gàɓō *m*, gàɓùwā *f* ⟨oCi⟩, (*esp. naive*) bàƙauyè *m*, bàgidàjè *m*, kìdāhùmī *m* ⟨ai⟩.

**simplicity** *n* a. (*ease*) sauƙī *m*. b. (*naiveté*) gidādancī *m*, ƙauyancī *m*, kidāhumancī *m*.

**simplify** *v* sauƙàƙā *v1*.

**simply** *adv* a. (*easily*): speak ~ yi màganàȓ dà zā à gānè. b. (*only*) kawài *adv*: I did it ~ to spite him nā yī shì don ìn ɓātà masà kawài.

**simultaneously** *adv* à lōkàcī gùdā.

**sin** *n* zùnubì *m* ⟨ai⟩, sàɓō *m*: commit a ~ yi zùnubì = yi sàɓō; forgive so. for a ~ yàfè wà zùnubì; (*in Islam, ~s assumable from ano. psn.*) àlhakì *m*: when a boy refuses to listen to his parents, he commits a ~ against them ìdan yārò yā ƙi màganàȓ màhàifansù, yā ɗauki àlhakinsù.

**since** *prep & conj* a. (*subsequent to*) tun *prep & conj*: ~ that time tun lōkàcîn nan; ~ when? tun yàushè? I have not seen him ~ last week bàn gan shì ba tun mākòn dà ya wucè; he has been in Kano ever ~ tun lōkàcîn yanà Kanò; it's been 3 months ~ he left Nigeria watànsà ukù dà barìn Nìjēȓiyà; it has been a long time ~ I've seen you ràbonmù dà ganinkà yā daɗè. b. (*because*) tun dà (yakè): ~ we have no time now, let's leave it until tomorrow tun dà (yakè) bâ mu dà lōkàcī, mù barì sai gòbe.

**sincere** *adj* (*psn.*) sàhīhì *m* ⟨ai⟩, (mài) gàskiyā *f*.

**sincerely** *adv*: ~ yours (*in signing a letter*) hāzā wassàlàm, nākà àmìntaccē.

**sincerity** *n* gàskiyā *f*; with ~ dà cikì ɗaya.

**sinful** *adj* (mài) zùnubì *m*.

**sing** *v* yi wāƙā *f*, rērà wāƙā.

**singe** *v* babbàkē *v4*.

**singer** *n* mawàƙī *m*.

**single** 1. *quant* ɗaya *f*, gùdā *pro*: there wasn't even a ~ one left bâ saurà kō ɗaya tak.

2. *adj* (*unmarried*): he is ~ bâ shi dà aurē = shī maràs aurē nè; *see* unmarried.

**singlet** *n* singìlētì *f* ⟨oCi⟩, sōcì *f*.

**singly** *adv* dà ɗai-ɗai.

**singular** *adj* (*Gram.*) mufuřàdī *m*.

**sinister** *adj* mūgù *adj* ⟨miyàgū⟩.

**sink** 1. *vi* nitsè *v4*, dùlmuyà *v3*: the ship sank jirgī yā nitsè cikin ruwa; a ball can't ∼ bàl bā tà nìtsuwā; ∼ into lumè *v4*: his teeth sank into my arm haƙòransà sun lumè à hannūnā.
2. *vt* a. nitsař (dà) *v5*: the bomb sank the ship bâm yā nitsař dà jirgin ruwa. b. (*a well*) haƙà *v1*, [F] ginà *v1*.

**sinner** *n* mài zùnubī *n*, mài sàɓō *n*.

**sip** *v* kùrɓā *v2*.

**siphon** *v* zùƙā ta mēsà, [F] janyō ta tìyyô *m*.

**Sir** *hon* alàgàfàttà Màlàm, (*in addr. important psn.*) rànkà-yà-daɗè; (*esp. in addr. psn. of high rank*) yallàɓai *hon*.

**siren** *n* jìniyà *f*, [F] pīpà *f*.

**sister** *n* 'yař'uwā *f* ⟨'yan'uwā⟩; full ∼ shàƙīƙìyā *f* ⟨ai⟩; elder ∼ yâ *f*, yàyā *f* ⟨yayyē, yāyū⟩; younger ∼ ƙanwà *f* ⟨ƙànnē⟩.

**sister-in-law** *n* (*younger sister of wife or husband, younger brother's wife*) ƙanwà *f* ⟨ƙànnē⟩; (*older sister of wife or husband, older brother's wife*) yâ *f*, yàyā *f* ⟨yayyē, yāyū⟩.

**sit** *v* zaunà *v1*: please ∼ down à zaunà mànà; I asked him to ∼ down nā sà shi yà zaunà; ∼ properly! gyàrà zamankà! the baby can't ∼ up by itself yet jàrīrī bài iyà zaunàwā shī kànsà ba tùkùna; ∼ting on à kân: the book is ∼ting on the shelf littàfī yanà kân kantà; make so. ∼ up zaunař (dà) *v5*: I made the baby sit up nā zaunař dà jàrīrī.

**site** *n* wurī *m* ⟨aCe⟩.

**situation** *n* a. (*circumstances*) hàlī / hālī *m* ⟨aye⟩: a difficult ∼ mawùyàcin hàlī; an unexpected ∼ hàlīn bà-zàta; look at the ∼ we are in now gà hàlīn dà mukè ciki yànzu. b. (*state of affairs*) àl'amàřī / lamàřī *m* ⟨u-a⟩: the international ∼ àl'amàřin dūniyà; the ∼ has become serious àl'amàřīn yā tsànantà.

**six** *quant* shidà *f*.

**sixpence** *n* (*old Nigerian unit of currency, but used informally for the 5 kobo piece, see* Appendix F) sīsì *m*.

**sixteen** *quant* (gōmà) shà-shidà *f*.

**sixth** *quant* na shidà.

**sixty** *quant* sìttin *f*.

**size** *n* a. (*dimension*) girmā *m*: what is the ∼ of this room? mènē nè girman wannàn ɗākì? they are the same ∼ girmansù ɗaya nè. b. (*of clothing, shoes*) lambà *f*, sāyì *m*: do you have any in my ∼? kanà dà lambàtà? = kanà dà sāyīnā? what ∼ do you need? lambà nawà akè sô? they are arranged according to ∼ an shiryà su lambà-lambà nē.

**skein** *n* (*of cotton thread*) sūlū *m* ⟨aye⟩, wadàrī *m* ⟨u-a⟩.

**skeleton** *n* ƙwàřàngwal *m*.

**skeptical** *adj* (mài) shakkà *f*; be ∼ yi kòkwantō *m*, yi shakkà *f*: we were ∼ of its authenticity munà shakkàř ingancìnsà; I am a bit ∼ of what he says inà dai kòkwanton màganàřsà.

**sketch** 1. *v* zānà *v1*. 2. *n* zànē *m*, shàcì *m*.

**skewer** 1. *n* tsinkē *m*; barbecued meat on ∼s tsìrē *m*, tsinkà *f*. 2. *v* tsīrà *v1*: he ∼ed the meat for the barbecue yā tsīrà nāmà don yà yi tsìrē = yā sōkà nāmà dà tsinkē don yà yi tsìrē.

**skid** *v* zāmè *v4*, yi zāmiyà *f*: the car ∼ded into a tree mōtà tā zāmè tā yi karò dà itàcē = santsī yā kwāshè mōtà tā yi karò dà itàcē.

**skill** *n* a. (*ability*) iyàwā *f*; (*esp. learned*) gwànintà *f*: he has great ∼ in carpentry yanà dà gwànintà wajen aikìn sàssaƙà = shī gwànī nè wajen aikìn sàssaƙà. b. (*craftsmanship*) fàsāhà *f*: it was made with great ∼ an yī shi dà fàsāhà.

**skilled** *adj* (*psn.*) gwànī *adj* ⟨aye⟩, gògaggē *adj*: he is a ∼ carpenter shī gwànin masàssàƙī nè; ∼ labor gwanàyen 'yan ƙwādagō.

**skillet** *n* kwānòn sūyà *m*, kwānòn tūyà *m*.

**skillful** *adj* (mài) gwànintà *f*.

**skim** *v* yàɗā *v2*, yàɗè *v4*: she ∼med off the oil tā yàɗè mâi.

**skin** 1. *n* a. fàtà *f* ⟨fātū⟩, *see* hide[1]; (*of fruit, tubers*) ɓāwō *m*; cracked, dried ∼ (*on feet*) fàsō *m*; cracked ∼ (*on cheeks, due to dryness*) wàskànè *m*; ∼ disease (*tinea*) ƙyàzbī / ƙyàsfī *m*; ∼ cream mân shàfàwā *m*. b. (∼ *coloring*): light-∼ned farī *adj* ⟨aCe⟩, jàtau *m*; medium light-∼ned mài wankan tařwaɗà *n*; dark-∼ned baƙī *adj* ⟨aCe⟩; very dark-∼ned akawàlī *m*. 2. *v* (*an animal*) fēɗè *v4*.

**skinny** *adj* ràmammè *adj*, bùsasshè *adj*.

**skink** *n* kulɓà *f*: the ∼ has the appearance of a snake jìkin kulɓà shigē na macìjī nē.

**skip** *v* (*jump lightly*) yi ɗan tsallē *m*; ∼ rope yi wàsan igiyà; ∼ over (*omit*) tsallàkē *v4*; (*miss*) yi fāshì *m*: ∼ class yi fāshìn zuwà ajì.

**skirt** *n* (*West. style*) sìkềt *m*, [F] jîp *f*; (*with slit*) sìlît *m*; (*tradit. Hausa under-skirt*) fàtàrī *m*, ɗan tòfi *m*.

**skull** *n* ƙòƙon kâi *m*, kwanyā *f*; ~ and cross-bones ƙwàřàngwal *m*.

**skunk** *n*, *see* zorilla.

**sky** *n* samà *f*: there are no clouds in the ~ bâbù gìzãgìzai à samà; the skies sararī *m*, sararin samà *m*, sàmāniyầ *f*: we slept under the open skies mun kwàna à sararī; (*in talking of weather*) gàrī *m*: the ~ is overcast gàrī yā lumshề = rānā tā lumshề; the ~ has cleared up gàrī yā wãshề.

**slack** *adj* a. (*lethargic*) (mài) kàsālā *f*. b. (*esp. about work*) (mài) nàwā *f*: he is very ~ about his work yā cikà nàwā. c. (*not tight*) sako-sako *idph;* become ~ sassàucē *v*, sakwařkwàcē *v4*.

**slacken** *v* sassàutā *v1*.

**slag** *n* kāshin maƙềrā *m*.

**slander** *v* yĩ dà w. *v0*, yi raɗàř w., yi sūkàn w., ɓãtà sūnan w., yi wà tsègùmī *m*; (*esp. behind so.'s back*) ci nāmàn w., sãrā *v2*.

**slang** *n* sằrā *f*.

**slant** 1. *n* (*incline*) gàngarā *f*.
2. *v* kařkàtā *v1*, kaikàitā *v1*: he ~ed the angle of his cap yā kařkàtà hũlā; be ~ed à kàikàice *adv*, à kàřkàce *adv*.

**slap** 1. *v* màrā *v2;* ~ so. hard fallè w. dà màrī, ƙwàɗà wà màrī
2. *n* màrī *m*, tầfī *m*; (*~ping so.'s hand in greeting*) tàfàwā *f;* give so. a resounding ~ kwàɗà wà màrī = shàrà wà màrī = shềƙề w. dà màrī.

**slash** *v* yankề *v4*: he ~ed his arm yā yankè à hannu; ~ so. with sth. (*knife, sword, whip*) sharɓà wà *v1*, cãɓà wà *v1*: he ~ed them with his sword yā sharɓà musù takòbī.

**slate** *n* (*writing board*) àllō *m* ⟨una⟩.

**slaughter** *v* a. (*an animal*) yankā *v1*, yi yankā *m*. b. (*massacre people*) yi wà kisàn gillầ, yi wà àikà-aikà *f*.

**slaughterhouse** *n* mahautā *f*, mayankā *f*.

**slave** *n* bāwầ *m*, bâiwā *f* ⟨bāyī⟩: the ~ trade cìnikin bāyī; (*female*) kùyangā *f* ⟨i⟩.

**slavery** *n* bàutā *f*.

**sledgehammer** *n* ƙātùwař gùdumā *f* ⟨oCi⟩, [F] mâs *f*.

**sleep** 1. *n* barcī *m*; (*nap, siesta*) ƙàilũlā *f*, *see* nap; a deep ~, a good night's ~ dōgon barcī; get a little ~ rintsà *v1*.
2. *v* a. yi barcī *m*: I didn't ~ the whole night bàn yi barcī ba gàbã ɗayan darên; ~ heavily shãrè barcī; ~ lightly yi barcin zõmō; go to ~ quickly yi saurin

barcī; (*fig.*) ~ like a log yi wãwan barcī; go to ~ (*of limb*) sagề *v4*, mutù *v3b;* ~ with (*have sex with*) yi jìmã'ì dà *m*, tārā dà *v1;* ~ around with lãlàtā dà *v1*. b. (*spend the night*) kwàna *v3a*: where did you ~ last night? ìnā ka kwàna jiyà?

**sleeping pill** *n* māgànin barcī *m*.

**sleeping sickness** *n* cīwòn barcī *m*.

**sleeplessness** *n* rashìn rintsì *m*.

**sleepy** *adj*: be, feel ~ ji barcī *m*.

**sleeve** *n* (*of clothes*) hannū *m* ⟨aye⟩: roll up one's ~s naɗè hannun rĩgā.

**sleight-of-hand** *n* dabồ *m*, sìddabařù *m*.

**slender** *adj* (*psn.*) sìřĩřì *adj* ⟨sìřầřā⟩, (mài) ɗan jìkī *m*.

**slice** 1. *v* (*e.g. meat*) yankầ *v1*; (*e.g. meat into thin strips*) řềɗề *v4*; (*sth. hard in half*) sārề *v4*.
2. *n* yankì *m* ⟨e²⟩: a ~ of bread yankìn burồdì.

**slick** *adj* (mài) santsī *m*, (mài) sulɓī *m*.

**slide** 1. *v* zāmề *v4*, yi zāmiyā *f*: ~ down a hill zāmề dàgà kân tudù; ~ down from a tree zāmō dàgà bishiyầ; ~ on the ground yi zāmiyā *f;* ~ to a halt (*e.g. of horse*) tirjè *v4*, zāmề *v4*.
2. *n* (*in a playground*) wajen zāmiyā *m*.

**slides** *n* (*transparencies or slide show*) mājìgī *m*.

**slight**[1] *adj* a. (*in quantity*) kàɗan *adv*: a ~ mistake kuskurề kàɗan; I haven't the ~est idea kō kàɗan bàn sanì ba. b. (*of physique*): Bello has a ~ build Bellò mài ɗan jìkī nề.

**slight**[2] *v* (*treat so. discourteously*) ƙanƙàntā *v1*.

**slightly** *adv* kàɗan ⟨kàɗan⟩, ɗan kàɗan *adv*: I speak Hausa ~ nā iyà Hausa kàɗan-kàɗan; I know him ~ (*fig.*) nā san shì sanìn shānū = nā san shì kàɗan; ~ more dà dāma-dāma: his work has improved ~ aikìnsà dà dāma-dāma.

**slim down** *v* saɓề *v4*: she has ~med down tā saɓề = jìkintà yā saɓề.

**slime** *n* (*green algae*) gànsàkūkà *f*.

**slimy** *adj* (*viscous*) (mài) yauƙī *m*.

**sling** 1. *n* a. (*for hanging sth.*) ràtayā *f*. b. (*for sword*) hàmīlà *f* ⟨u⟩. c. (*weapon, toy*) màjajjawā *f*: he swung the ~ round and round and then let go of it yā jujjùyà màjajjawā sàn nan ya sakì.
2. *v* jēfầ *v1*; (*sth. over one's shoulder*) saɓā *v1*: he slung the rifle over his shoulder yā saɓā bindigầ.

**slingshot** *n* gwãfař dankồ *f*, [F] kàushû *m*.

**slink away** *v* yi làɓe-làɓe *m*.

slip¹ 1. *v* a. (*slide*) zāmě *v4*: he ~ped on a banana peel ƙafàr̃sà tā zāmě à kân 6āwon àyàbà; I ~ped on the steps and fell down nā zāmě dàgà kân matākalā nā fāɗì. b. (*fall on slippery surface*) yi santsī *m*: she ~ped santsī yā kwāshě ta = santsī yā ɗaukē tà. c. (*become loose, of sth. held*) sullù6ē *v4*, su6ùcē *v4*: it ~ped from my hand yā sullù6ē dàgà hannūnā; ~ one's mind shà'afà *v3*: his name has ~ped my mind nā shà'afà dà sūnansà = sūnansà yā kwântā minì. d. (*leave*): ~ away (*leave quietly*) sulàlē *v4*; ~ out (*of a place, escape*) kù6utà *v3*, ku6ùcē *v4*; the rat managed to ~ out of the trap 6ēr̃ā yā sàmi kù6utà dàgà cikin tarkò. e. (*give surreptitiously*) sunnà *v1*: he ~ped the official ₦20 yā sunnō wà ma'àikàcī nair̃ā àshir̃in.
2. *n* (*mistake*): make a ~ of the pen yi tuntu6èn àlƙalàmī; make a ~ of the tongue yi sù6utàr̃ bàkī *f*, yi sù6ùl-dà-bakà *f*.

slip² *n* (*small piece of sth.*): a ~ of paper 'yar̃ guntuwar̃ takàr̃dā *f*; a sales ~ shaidàr̃ biyà *f*, r̃àsît / r̃àsīdì *m*, [F] r̃ēsî *m*.

slip³ *n* (*tradit. woman's garment*) shìmî *f*; (*half-~*) fàtàr̃ī *m*, [F] ɗan tòfi *m*.

slipknot *n* zàr̃gē *m*.

slippers *n* silîfà *m*.

slippery *adj* (mài) santsī *m*: the road is very ~ because of the rain hanyàr̃ nà dà santsī sabòdà ruwā; (*esp. of sth. that can be held*) (mài) sul6ī *m*, *see* smooth.

slipperiness *n* santsī *m*, sul6ī *m*.

slit *v* tsāgà *v1*; (*the belly of animal or sth. bulky*) far̃dě *v4*; ~ open a seam 6arkà ɗinkì.

slither along *v* yi sùlùlù *idph*, yi sùmùmù *idph*.

slob *n* kùcākī *m*, kùcākā *f* ⟨ai⟩.

slogan *n* tākē *m*.

slope 1. *n* gàngarà *f*; the bottom of a ~ gangarě *m*: his farm is at the bottom of a ~ gōnar̃sà tanà gangarèn tudù.
2. *v* gangàrà *v1*.

sloppy *adj*: be ~ (*through haste*) yi gàràjē *m*: don't be ~ with your work kadà kà yi gàràjē dà aikìnkà = kadà kà yi aikì cikin gàràjē.

sloth *n* lālācì *m*, ragwancì *m*, sākar̃cì *m*.

slow *adj* a. (*not fast*) maràs saurī *m*: why are you so ~? mě ya sā ka rashìn saurī hakà? b. (*of a psn., sluggish by nature*) (mài) sanyin jìkī *m*: he has always been a ~-moving person yā tāshì

dà sanyin jìkī; he is a ~ learner bâ shi dà hāziƙancì. c. (*of clock*) yi lattì *m*: my watch is usually 3 minutes ~ àgōgōnā yakàn yi lattìn mintì ukù; (*fig.*) ~ but sure sànnu-sànnu kwānā nēsà = sànnu bâ tà hanà zuwà.

slow down *v* (*one's speed*) ragè gudù.

slowly *adv* a. (*not fast*) sànnu-sànnu *adv*: they are walking ~ sunà tàfiyà sànnu-sànnu; please speak ~ don Allàh kadà kà yi màganà dà saurī. b. (*carefully*) à hankàlī: we drove ~ through the village mun rātsà ƙauyèn à hankàlī.

sluggish *adj* (*by nature*) (mài) sanyin jìkī *m*; (*about doing one's work*) (mài) nàwā *f*.

slump *n* (*Econ.*): revive the economic ~ tā dà kōmaɗàr̃ tattalin ar̃zìkī.

slurp *v* sùr6ā *v2*; ~ up (*all at once*) zūƙě *v4*.

slush *n* (*mud*) cà6ī *m*; make a road ~y cā6à hanyà.

sly *adj* (*cunning*) (mài) mūgùn wàyō *m*.

smack 1. *v* a. (*slap*) mārā *v2*. b. ~ one's lips (*in pleasure*) yi ɗàɗar̃ bàkī *f*.
2. *n* (*slap*) mārì *m*.

small *adj* a. (*in size*) ƙaramī *adj* ⟨ƙanānà⟩, ƙanƙaně *m*, ƙànƙanùwā *f* ⟨ƙanānà⟩: ~ boys ƙanānàn yârā; the shirt is too ~ for me tagùwar̃ tā yi minì kàɗan. b. (*as dimin.*) ɗan *m*, 'yar̃ *f* ⟨'yan⟩: a ~ village ɗan ƙauyè; a ~ chair 'yar̃ kujèrā. c. (*in compar. constr. with* fi *v0*) ƙanƙantà *f*: these are ~er than mine waɗànnân sun fi nàwa ƙanƙantà = waɗànnân sun fi nàwa ƙanānà. d. (*in quantity*): a ~ amount, number kàɗan *adv*: he has a ~ amount of money yanà dà kuɗī kàɗan; only a ~ number of people came jàma'à kàɗan sukà zō.

small fry *n* ƙàramin àlhakī *m*, mài ƙàramin ƙarfī: he is just a ~ in the organization shī ƙàramin àlhakī nè à ƙunglìyar̃; a ~ like you ƙanƙanènkà dà kai.

smallness *n* ƙanƙantà *f*.

smallpox *n* agānā *f*, 'yar̃ rānī *f*; ~ marks zanzanā *f*.

smart¹ *adj* a. (*intelligent*) (mài) ƙwalwā *f*, (mài) kâi *m*: he's ~ ɗan ƙwalwā nè = yanà dà kâi. b. (*resourceful, clever*) (mài) azancī *m*, (mài) dàbàr̃à *f*, (mài) kân gadō *m*: he's not very ~ bâ shi dà kân gadō. c. (*fashionable*) (mài) iyà adō *m*; she is ~ly dressed tā ci adō.

smart² *v* (*sting*) yi r̃àɗàɗī *m*: his hand was ~ing hannunsà nà r̃àɗàɗī.

**smash** v fashḕ v4, faffàsā v1, řagařgàzā / řugufgùzā v1: he hit a tree and ~ed up his car yā yi karð dà itằcē yā řagařgàzà mōtằřsà; the bottle got ~ed to pieces kwalabā tā řagařgàjē = kwalabā tā faffàshē fugu-fugu.

**smear** v shāfà v1: she ~ed some cream on her body tā shāfà mân shāfàwā à jìkintà; ~ed with mud shằfe dà cằ6ī; (fig.) ~ so.'s reputation shāfà wà kāshin kầjī = 6ātà wà sūnā.

**smell** 1. n sànsanằ f: a good sense of ~ ḵarfin sànsanā: dogs have a good sense of ~ kàrē nằ dà ḵarfin sànsanằ; (var. types): (pleasant, savory) ḵanshī m: the ~ of cooking ḵanshin girkì; (strong, unpleasant) wārī m: ~ of garlic wārin tàfařnuwằ; (of urine or sth. moldy) zafnī m, ḵārī m: the ~ of urine zařnin fitsārī; (fetid, foul, rotten) dōyī m; (of sth. burnt) ḵaurī m: the ~ of burnt rubber ḵaurin fōbầ; (of sth. sour) tsāmī m; (of blood, fresh meat) ḵafnī / ḵannī m; (of rotten meat, fish) bāshī m. 2. vt a. sansànā / shinshìnā v1: she ~ed the flowers tā sansànà fùrannī. b. (~ sth. partic.) ji v0 (+ sensory n denoting partic. smell): I ~ smoke inằ jîn ḵaurin hayāḵī; we ~ed perfume in the room mun ji ḵanshin tùrằrē à dākì; it ~s like perfume ḵanshin tùrằrē yakḕ. 3. vi (of sth. pleasant) yi ḵanshī m: the food ~s good àbincîn nằ ḵanshī; (of sth. unpleasant, strong) yi wārī m, yi ḵafnī m: this fish ~s wannàn kīfī nằ ḵafnī; his breath ~s yanằ dà wārin bằkī.

**smelt** v narkař (dà) v5.

**smile** v yi mùřmùshī m: what made you ~ just now? mḕ ya sâ ka mùřmùshī dằzu? what are you smiling at? mḕ kakḕ yi wà mùřmùshī?

**smith** n maḵērī m.

**smithy** n maḵērā f.

**smoke** 1. n hayāḵī m: I smell ~ inằ jîn ḵaurin hayāḵī; the room was smoky àkwai hayāḵī cikin dākì; (fig.) where there's ~ there's fire ruwā bā yằ tsāmī banzā. 2. v a. (tobacco) shā tābằ, shā sìgārì: do you ~? kanằ shân tābằ? he usually ~s a pipe yakàn shā tābầř lōfḕ. b. (meat) ḵyāfḕ v4.

**smoker** n mài shân tābằ n; a chain ~ kābūsù m.

**smooth** adj a. sumul idph: the cloth is ~ yādìn sumul dà shī. b. (slick, slippery) (mài) santsī m, (esp. to hold on to) (mài)

sul6ī m: a ~ rock dūtsḕ mài santsī; this paper is not very ~ wannàn takằřdā bâ ta dà sul6ī; be worn ~ (of tires, shoes) sudḕ v4. c. (soft) (mài) laushī m, (mài) taushī m: ~ skin fātà mài laushī.

**smoothly** adv: I hope everything is proceeding ~ inằ fātā kōmē yanằ tằfiyằ daidai.

**smother** v bicḕ v4: ~ the fire with sand kù bicḕ wutā dà yằshī.

**smuggle** v yi fàsà-ḵwàuri m, yi sùmōgà / sùmōgàl m: ~ goods into a country shigō dà kāyā ta hanyàř fàsà-ḵwàuri; ~d goods kāyan sùmōgà.

**smuggler** n ɗan sùmōgà m, ɗan fàsà-ḵwàuri m.

**smut** n (soot) kùnkunnìyā f.

**snacks** n (esp. at a party) làshe-làshe dà tànɗe-tànɗe p.

**snag** v sarḵàfē v4: his gown got ~ged on a nail rìgařsà tā sarḵàfē à ḵūsà.

**snail** n dōdon kōɗì m.

**snake** n a. macìjī m ⟨ai⟩, (euphem.) àbin ḵasà m, majà-cikì m, igiyàř ḵasà f; poisonous ~ macìjī mài dafì. b. (var. types): (black-hooded cobra) gàmshēḵā f, kùmurcī m; (small green poisonous) dằmàtsīrī m; (puff adder) kāsà f; (python) mēsằ f ⟨oCi⟩; (viper) kùbūbuwầ f, (dark-colored) bidằ f.

**snakebite** n sāran macìjī m.

**snake charmer** n gařdì m ⟨gầřdàwā⟩.

**snakeskin** n fātàř macìjī f.

**snap** 1. v (of sth. stiff) karyḕ v4: the branch ~ped rēshḕn yā karyḕ; ~ in two (e.g. of string, chain) tsinkḕ v4, katsḕ v4: the thread ~ped in two zàrē yā tsinkḕ; ~ one's fingers kaɗà hannū; ~ a whip shauɗà būlālằ; the dog ~ped at him kàrē yā kāwō masà wằwarầ. 2. n (fastener) ma6allī m.

**snapshot** n hồtō m ⟨una⟩.

**snare** v (with rope, string) zargḕ v4.

**snarl**[1] v (by animal) yi gùřnànī m: the dog ~ed at me kàrē yā yi minì gùřnànī.

**snarl**[2] v (entangle) cukwīkwìyā v1; be(come) ~ cukwīkwìyē v4, hařɗè v4: the thread became ~ zàrē yā cukwīkwìyē.

**snatch** v fìgā v2, wằwurà v2: he ~ed the bag out of my hand yā fìgi jàkâř à hannūnā; (in violent manner) fīgḕ v4, fizgḕ v4; ~ up (by swooping down) sùrà v2: the hawk swooped down and ~ed up the mouse shāhồ yā sùri 6ḗřầ.

sneak v laɓàɓà *v1*: ~ up from behind laɓàɓà dàgà bāya; ~ out (*leave quietly*) sulàlē *v4*.

sneaky *adj* (*devious, evasive*): he's a ~ type ɗan cùkù-cukū nè = yā fayè wùnĩ-wunĩ; behave in a ~ manner yi ƙumbìyà-ƙumbiyā *idph*, yi wùnĩ-wunĩ *idph*, yi kwàne-kwàne *m*, yi zùƙe-zùƙe *m*.

sneakers *n* kambàs *m*, [F] kìɍàf *f*.

sneer *v* gàtsìnè hancî, yi gàtsìnē *m*.

sneeze *v* yi atìshāwà *f*; (*fig.*) it's nothing to ~ at bà àbin rainì ba nè.

sniff *v* sansànā / shinshìnā *v1*.

sniper *n* ɗan bindigà-dādī *m*.

snob *n* mài hūrà hancî *n*, mài ɗagāwà *n*.

snore *v* yi minshārī *m*, (*esp. loud*) kākārī *m*.

snot *n* màjinā *f*, (*dried*) tàsōnō *m*.

snow *n* ƙanƙarā *f*.

snow-white *adj* farī fat.

snub *v* gwalè *v4*, kwàɓā *v2*.

snuff *n* anwùɍù/angùɍù *m*.

so 1. *adv* a. (*thus, in that way*) (kàmaɍ) hakà *adv*: that is ~ hakà nē = hakànan nè; to drive ~ recklessly is dangerous tūƙì dà ganganci hakà haɗàɍī nè; even ~ duk dà hakà; ~ far as I know... à sanìnā dai...; is that ~? yes, it is ~ (*in confirming sth.*) Allàh? Allàh kùwa. b. (*similarly*): and ~ did X X mā hakànan, X mā kàzālikà: Musa climbed over the wall and ~ did Sule Mūsā ya haurà katangā Sulè mā kàzālikà; she wants some tea and ~ do I tanà sôn shāyì nī mā hakànan; and ~ forth and ~ on dà kàzā dà kàzā; or ~ kàmaɍ: it costs ₦5 or ~ kuɗinsà kàmaɍ naiɍà bìyaɍ. c. (*extremely*) ƙwarai *adv*, matuƙā *adv*, lallē *adv*: it was ~ kind of you kā kyâutā ƙwarai; I am ~ glad you came nā yi muɍnà matuƙā dà ka zō; he is ~ tall lallē yanà dà tsayì = yanà da tsayì ƙwarai; it is ~ hot today lallē yâu dà zāfī = yâu dà zāfī kàm; I am ~ tired that I can't go on any further nā gàji dà yawà haɍ nā kāsà cî gàba. d. ~ long! sai an jimà!
2. *conj*: a. (*in order that*): ~ that don *conj*: he stepped aside ~ that we could pass yā kaucè don mù shigè; ~ as not to don gudùn kada: he went around the car ~ as not to step in the mud yā kēwàyà mōtà don gudùn kada yà tākà tàɓō. b. (*with the result that*): ~ that don hakà, sabòdà hakà: I had a headache ~ I went to bed inà cīwòn kâi sabòdà hakà nā kwàntā; ~ long as (*provided that*) muddìn / muddàɍ *conj*: ~ long as you work hard,

you'll get ahead muddìn kanà aikì tuƙùru zā kà sàmi cî-gàba.

soak *v* (*sth.*) jiƙè *v4* ⟨jiƙò⟩: she is ~ing the laundry tanà jiƙòn kāyan wankì; be ~ing wet jiƙè shaɍaf = jiƙè shàɍkaf; we got ~ing wet from the rain (*fig.*) ruwā yā bā mù kāshī = mun shā kāshin ruwā.

so-and-so *n* wānè *m*, wāncè *f*, su wānè *p*: I saw ~ at the market nā ga wāncè à kàsuwā.

soap *n* sàbulù *m*, [F] sàbulì / sàbunì *m*: wash with ~ yi wankì dà sàbulù; a long bar of ~ sàndaɍ sàbulù; a bar of ~ (*laundry* ~ *cut from long bar*) sàbulùn yankan ƙūsà, (*facial* ~, *usu. wrapped*) ƙwàyaɍ sàbulù.

soap powder *n* ōmò *m*, [F] ōmô *m*.

sob *v* yi kūkā dà shàsshèƙā.

sober *adj* (*thoughtful*) nìtsattsē *adj*.

so-called *adj* wai: he's a ~ expert wai shì gwànī nè.

soccer *n* wàsan ƙwallō *m*, wàsan ƙwallon ƙafà *m*; ~ ball ƙwallon ƙafà *f*, [F] bàlô *f*; ~ player ɗan wàsan ƙwallō.

sociable *adj* (mài) sôn mutànē, (mài) faɍat-faɍat dà mutànē, (mài) habà-habā dà mutànē, (mài) shìgā jàma'à: Audu is really ~ kâi, Audù yanà habà-habā dà mutànē sòsai.

social *adj* na zaman jàma'à; ~ welfare jîn dādin jàma'à; ~ welfare officer jàmì'in lùɍa dà jîn dādin jàma'à.

socialism *n* guɍguzancì *m*, ɍa'àyin guɍguzù *m*.

socialist 1. *n* ɗan guɍguzū *m*, mài ɍa'àyin guɍguzū *n*.
2. *adj* na guɍguzū *m*.

socialize *v* (*be sociable*) yi huldà dà jàma'à.

society *n* a. (*social system*) zaman jàma'à *m*. b. (*organization*) ƙungìyā *f* ⟨oCi⟩.

sociology *n* ilìmin hàlayyàɍ zaman jàma'à *m*.

socket *n* a. (*electrical*) sōkèt *m*, [F] pìɍìs *f*: put a plug into a ~ sà kân làntaɍkì à sōkèt. b. (*of eye*) gurbì *m* ⟨a-u⟩.

socks *n* sàfā *f*, [F] sùsētì *m*.

sod *n* (*turf*) hōgè *m*, dàmbà *f*.

soda water *n* sōdà *f*, [F] bùlbît *m*.

sodium *n* gishirī *m*.

sodomy *n* lùwāɗī *m*.

soft *adj* a. (*to the touch, by pressure*) (mài) taushī *m*; (*by feeling*) (mài) laushī *m*: a ~ pillow matāshin kâi mài taushī; the ground is not very ~ now ƙasā bâ ta dà taushī sòsai yànzu. b. (*to the ear*)

(mài) taushī *m* tàttausā *adj*: ~ drumming kàɗe-kàɗe mài taushī; make sth.
~ tausàsā *v1*, mai dà w.a. tàttausā;
speak in a ~ voice yi màganā cikin
muryā mài sanyī; speak more ~ly! ràgè
muryā! c. (*gentle, of personality*) (mài)
jīn tàusàyī *m*.

**soft drink** *n* lềmō / lềmū *m*: I'll take a ~
zân shā lềmō.

**soften** *v* tausàsā *v1*.

**soggy** *adj* (*esp. of food*) làngàɓaɓɓē *adj*; be
~ langàɓē *v4*.

**soil** 1. *n* ƙasā *f* ⟨aCe⟩; rich ~ ƙasā mài
àlbařkà; (*sandy*) jìgāwā *f*; (*clay*) lākā
*f*; (*poor*) faƙō *m*.
2. *v* sā w.a. daudā, ɓātà (dà daudā),
lālàtā *v1*, dāgùlā *v1*.

**solar** *adj* na rānā *f*: ~ eclipse hùsūfin
rānā; ~ energy makāmashin zāfin rānā.

**solder** *v* yi sōdā *f*, [F] yi sùɗē *m*.

**soldier** *n* sōjà *m* ⟨oCi⟩, [F] sōjì *m/p*.

**sole**[1] *n* (*of foot*) tàfin ƙafà *m*, (~ *of foot
at the heel*) dundūnìyā *f* ⟨oCi⟩; (*of shoe*)
ƙasàn tàkàlmī *m*: the ~s of my shoes are
worn out ƙasàn tàkàlmīnā yā cînyē.

**sole**[2] *adj* (*only*) tīlō: his ~ heir magājinsà
tīlō.

**solicitor** *n* lauyà *m* ⟨oCi⟩, [F] àbōkà *m*.

**solid** *adj* (*of construction*) (mài) ƙwārī *m*,
ƙwàƙƙwārā *adj*: ~ foundation ƙwàƙƙwāran
hařsāshī; he is on ~ ground (*lit. or fig.*)
yā kāmà ƙasā.

**solidarity** *n* zùmùntā *f*, zumuncī *m*: affirm
~ with sādà zumuncī dà.

**solidify** *v* daskàrā *v1*, daskàrē *v4*.

**solitary** *adj* (mài) kaɗaicī *m*.

**solitude** *n* kaɗaicī *m*, hālin kawaicī *m*;
(*Relig.*) halwā *f*.

**solution** *n* māganī *m*: the only ~ to the
problem is patience māganin àl'amàřīn
shī nề hàƙurī; (*answer in arithmetic*)
amsā *f* ⟨oCi⟩.

**solve** *v* shāwō kân w.a., warwàrē *v4*: we
~d the problem mun shāwō kân màtsalàř;
be ~d wàrwaru *v7*: the problem cannot be
~d easily màtsalàř bà zā tà wàrwaru dà
saukī ba.

**some** 1. *quant* a. (*an unspecified amount,
not usu. translated*): give me ~ bread bā
ni buřōdì; we drank ~ water mun shā
ruwā; ~ days ago kwànàkin bāya. b. (*a
certain number, specific amount*) wani *m*,
wata *f*, waɗansu/wasu *p*: ~ workers went
on strike wasu ma'àikàtā sun yi yàjī.
c. (*as dimin.*) (wani) ɗan *m*, (wata) 'yař
*f*, (wasu) 'yan *p*: I had ~ difficulty finding
it nā shā wata 'yař wàhalà sāmùnsà; ~

belongings wasu 'yan kāyā.
2. *pro* wani *m*, wata *f*, waɗansu/wasu *p*:
~ like coffee, ~ like tea wani nā sôn kòfī
wani kuma nā sôn shāyī; he gave me ~
yā bā ni wasu.
3. *det* (*some*) wani *m*, wata *f*: ~ day
they'll return wata rānā sâ dāwō. ~ day
he'll return zâi dāwō wata rānā. until ~
other time sai wani lōkàcī = sai wata
rānā.

**somebody** *pro*, see someone.

**someday** *adv* nân gàba.

**somehow** *adv* kō ta yàyā, ta kōyàyā: you
must finish it up ~ dōlè kà kammàlā shi
ta kōyàyā.

**someone** *pro* a. (*indefinite*) wani *m*, wata *f*:
~ came to see you wani yā zō nēmankà;
~ else wani kuma = wani dàbam. b. (*definite*) wani mùtûm: did you see ~ at the
office? kā ga wani mùtûm à ôfîs?

**someplace** *adv*, see somewhere.

**somersault** *n* àlkāhùřā *f*.

**something** *pro* a. (*indefinite*) wani àbù *m*:
~ has happened to him wani àbù yā sàmē
shi; there was ~ else I wanted to tell you
àkwai dai wani àbîn kuma dà na kề sô
in faɗà makà. b. (*definite*) àbù *m*, àbā
*f* ⟨uwa[2]⟩: it is ~ that happens frequently
àbù nē dà yakàn fàru sàu dà yawà.

**sometime** *adv*: see you around ~! sai wani
lōkàcī! = sai wani jiƙō!

**sometimes** *adv* wani lōkàcī, wani jiƙō:
~ we see her at the market munā ganintà
wani lōkàcī à kàsuwā; (*from time to
time*) lōkàcī-lōkàcī *adv*, sā'ī-sā'ī *adv*,
lōtò-lōtò *adv*, jiƙò-jiƙò: ~ I go to see
a movie lōkàcī-lōkàcī nakàn jē kallon
sìlimà.

**somewhat** *adv* dà dāma-dāma *adv*.

**somewhere** *adv* wani wurī: I've met you ~
before nā dai taɓà gàmuwā dà kai wani
wurī; ~ else à wani wurī dàbam.

**son** *n* (*any male child*) dā (namijì) *m* (*one's
own*) ɗā *m* ⟨'yā'yā⟩: she gave birth to a
~ tā hàifi ɗā namijì; he is Yusufu's ~
shī ɗan Yūsufù nē; the eldest ~ ɗan fārì
*m*; step~ agòlà *m* ⟨ai⟩; ~-of-a-gun! (*mild
explet.*) ɗan banzā! = ɗan wōfī! you ~-
of-a-bitch! (*vulg. explet.*) uwàkà! = ùbākà!

**song** *n* wāƙā *f* ⟨oCi, e[2]⟩; (*of birds*) kūkā *m*;
theme ~ tākē *m*.

**son-in-law** *n* sùrukī *m* ⟨ai⟩, (*term of
addr.*) ɗā *m*.

**soon** *adv* (*in a short while*) an jimā *adv*,
dà wuri *adv*, jìm kàɗan: I shall be back
~ zân kōmō an jimā; come back again
~ kà sākè dāwôwā dà wuri; as ~ as dà

zārař, dà cêwā (+ complet.): as ~ as he returned... dà zārař yā dāwō... = dà cêwā yā dāwō...; as ~ as possible dà saurī, nan dà nan; as ~ as possible (in the fut.) nân gàba.

**sooner** adv: ~ or later kō bàdadè kō bàjimà, yâu dà gòbe: he will come back ~ or later zâi dai dāwō kō bàdadè kō bàjimà; ~ or later, you'll be able to do it yâu dà gòbe, kâ iyà; no ~ had X happened than Y X kè dà wùyā sai Y, X kè nan sai Y: no ~ had they left than it started to rain tāshìnsù kè dà wùyā sai akà fārà ruwā; no ~ had I arrived than he started to argue with me isôwātā kè nan sai ya fàdà ni dà fadà.

**soot** n kùnkunnìyā f.

**soothe** v sanyàyā wà zūcìyā, kwantař dà hankàlin w.: her singing ~d the child wāƙařtà tā sanyàyā wà yārò zūcìyā.

**soothsayer** n dan dūbā m.

**sophisticated** adj (worldly psn.) dan dūniyà m: just by looking at him you would know he's a ~ man dà ganinsà sai kà cê dan dūniyà nē.

**sorcerer** n māyè m, māyyā f ⟨māyū⟩.

**sorcery** n (animism) tsāfī m, sammù m.

**sordid** adj maràs dādī m, ƙazāmī adj.

**sore** 1. n (infection) mīkì m, gyàmbō m ⟨una⟩; open up a ~ fasà gyàmbō = yankà gyàmbō.
2. adj (mài) zāfī m, (mài) cīwò m: my finger is ~ yātsànā nà cīwò; feel ~ ji zāfī, ji cīwò; (aching of muscles) tsāmī m, zògī m: my leg is ~ because of the sprain ƙafàtā nà tsāmī sabòdà targadè.

**sorrel** n yākùwā f.

**sorrow** n baƙin cikì m, ɓācìn râi m; sth. ~ful àbin tàusàyī.

**sorry** 1. adj a. (being sad) baƙin cikì m: I'm ~ to inform you... inà baƙin cikì ìn shaidà makà...; feel ~ for so. ji tàusàyin w.: I feel ~ for them inà jîn tàusàyinsù = tàusàyinsù yā kāmà ni. b. (regretful) dà-na-sanì m: now he is ~ that he did it yànzu yanà dà-na-sanì; I'm very ~ (asking forgiveness) à gàfařcē nì.
2. excl: so ~! (expressing concern) sànnu! = kaico! = àyyà! excl; I'm so ~ to hear that! Allàh yà bā dà hàƙurī!

**sort**[1] n irì m ⟨x²⟩: what ~ of man would do that? wànè irìn mùtûm zâi yi hakà? all ~s irì-irì, kalà-kalà: they sell all ~s of things sunà sai dà abūbuwà irì-irì; any ~ of kōwànè irìn: I like any ~ of weaving inà sôn kōwàcè irìn sāƙà.

**sort**[2] v (arrange) kasà v1: tomatoes are ~ed according to size anà kasà tùmātìř gwařgwadon girmansù; I ~ed them into various piles nā kasà su kashì-kashì; ~ out warwàrē v4: ~ out a matter warwàrè màtsalàř.

**so-so** adv hakà-hakà adv: how's the work progressing? it's just ~ yàyà aikìn? hakà-hakà yakè.

**soul** n râi m: his ~ has gone to heaven rânsà yanà Àljannà.

**sound**[1] n a. (of sth. pleasant) amō m: the ~ of drumming amon gàngā = amon kidà. b. (of noise or sth. loud) ƙārā f: the ~ of a plane, car ƙārař jirgī, mōtà; what was that ~? wàcè irìn ƙārā cè wànnan? I heard the ~ of a crash nā ji wata ƙārā kwatsàm. c. (in language) sautì m ⟨uka²⟩, (vocal, esp. human) muryà f ⟨oCi⟩, the ~s of Hausa sauttuttukàn Hausa; the ~ of the vowel sautìn wasàlī; the ~ of voices muryàř mutànē; the ~ of footsteps mòtsin tàfiyà.

**sound**[2] adj (solid, strong) (mài) ƙwārī m, ƙwàƙƙwārā adj: a ~ reason ƙwàƙƙwāran dàlīlì.

**soup** n (broth) rōmō m; (thick, like a stew) miyà f, see stew; pepper ~ fàřfèsu m.

**sour** adj (esp. taste) (mài) tsāmī m; (smell or taste) (mài) yāmī m; go ~ (of food) lālàcē v4; ~ milk (with full curd & cream) kìndìřmō m.

**source** n a. (origin) mafārī m: the ~ of the River Niger mafārin Kògin Kwārà; ~ of the trouble mafārin rìkicī. b. (basis, foundation) tūshè m: here is the ~ of the trouble gà tūshèn rìgimàř. c. (means of obtaining sth.) hanyàř sāmùn w.a.: ~ of water, income hanyàř sāmùn ruwā, kudī. d. (of information) majiyā f: government ~s majiyař gwamnatì; reliable, informed ~s majiyā tagàri. e. (spring of water) idòn ruwā m, maɓuɓɓugā f.

**south** n & adv kudù m, [F] gusùm m: the river is ~ of the town kògìn yanà kudù dà gàrī; a wind was blowing from the ~ iskà tanà kadàwa dàga kudù; S. Africa Afiřkà ta Kudù; it is ~ of town yanà kudancin gàrī = yanà kudù dà gàrī.

**southeast** adv kudù masò gabàs: the village lies ~ of town ƙauyèn yanà kudù masò gabàs dà gàrīn.

**southern** adj na kudù, kudancin prep: the ~ states jihōhin kudù; the ~ African countries ƙasàshen kudancin Afiřkà; the ~ part of the country kudancin ƙasā.

**southerner** n bàkudù m.

**southward** *adv* kudù *adv*: it is facing ~ yanà fuskàr̃ kudù.

**southwest** *adv* kudù masò yâmma.

**souvenir** *n* àbin tunàwā *m*, tsàrabà *f* ⟨oCi⟩; (*from the Hajj*) màkàbūlì *m* ⟨ai⟩.

**sow**[1] *n* (*swine*) ta-màcèn àladè *f*.

**sow**[2] *v* (*seeds*) shūkà *v1*: ~ a field with wheat shūkà alkamà à gōnā; (*esp. before rains*) yi bìnnē *m;* (*in transverse direction*) gicclyā *v1*: millet has been ~n transversely an giccìyà maiwā.

**sovereignty** *n* zaman kâi *m*.

**soybeans** *n* wāken sōyà *m*.

**space** *n* a. (*area*) wurī *m* ⟨aCe⟩: there's no more ~ here bâbù sauran wurī à nân; it will occupy too much ~ zâi tsarè wurī dà yawà. b. (*any open area esp. outdoors*) fīlī *m* ⟨aye⟩: leave a ~ of about 2 feet between the rows kù bar̃ ɗan fīlī kàmar̃ ƙafà biyu tsàkānin kunyōyī. c. (*cleared, open area esp. in town*) fagē *m* ⟨aCe⟩. d. (*outer* ~) sararin sàmāniyà *m*.

**spacecraft** *n* kumbò *m* ⟨una⟩.

**spacious** *adj* (*expr. by var. ideophonic adj*) mākēkè *adj*, fankamēmè *adj*: the rooms are ~ dākunà mākā-màkà dà sū.

**spade** *n* shēbùr̃ / tēbùr̃ *m* ⟨u-a⟩, [F] fēlù *m*.

**spades** *n* (*in cards*) dūsà *m*, sùffà *f*.

**spaghetti** *n* tàliyà *f*.

**span** *n* (*of hand*) ɗanì *m*, takì *m; ~* of life ajàlin mùtûm *m*.

**spanner** *n*, *see* wrench.

**spare** 1. *v*: ~ so.'s life yi wà râi; ~ so. trouble hūtar̃ dà w.
  2. *adj*: ~ part kāyan gyārā *m*, sàfiyà *f; ~* tire sàfiyà *f*, [F] fìnē sèkûr̃ *m*.

**sparkle** *v* (*be shiny, glitter*) yi ƙyàlƙyàlī *m*.

**sparkling** *adj* a. (*gleaming*) (mài) ƙyàl-ƙyàlī *m*, (mài) wàlƙiyà *f*; they are ~ clean sun wànku tas sunà ƙyàlƙyàlī. b. (*clear*) garai-garai *idph*: ~ water ruwā garai-garai.

**spark plug** *n* fulōgì *m* ⟨oCi⟩, [F] bùjî *f*.

**sparks** *n* (*of fire*) tàr̃tsàtsin wutā *m*, 6àr̃6àshin wutā *m;* give off ~ yi tàr̃tsàtsī.

**sparrow** *n* (*grey*) gwarā *f*.

**spasm** *n* sūkà *m;* (*esp. in side of body*) masōkìyà *f;* (*abdominal*) tùƙā *f*, tsànkī *m*.

**spate** *n*: the river is in ~ kōgìn yā kāwō.

**spattered** *adj*: be completely ~ yi faca-faca *idph*.

**speak** *v* a. yi màganà *f*, fàɗā / fàɗì *v2\**: the child is not able to ~ yet yārò bài iyà màganà ba tùkùna; he's always quick to ~

yanà dà saurin màganà; ~ to so. yi wà màganà *f*: he spoke to me about her yā yi minì màganàr̃tà; if you are going to ~, ~ the truth in zā kà faɗì, fàɗi gàskiyā; ~ bluntly fitō 6arō-6àrò; ~ favorably about so. yi wà shaidàr̃ kir̃kì; ~ inappropriately, ~ out of context cā6à màganà, yi ɗanyar̃ màganà; ~ louder, ~ up ɗagà muryà; ~ softly ragè muryà; ~ out, openly fitō à fīlī. b. (*a language*) yi màganà dà, ji *v0*, iyà *v1*: they are ~ing Fulfulde sunà màganà dà Filātancī; he ~s several languages yanà jîn harsunà dà yawà; he ~s Hausa, Fulfulde, and English yā iyà Hausa dà Filātancī dà Tūr̃ancī. c. (*give a lecture, talk*) yi laccà *f*, yi jàwābì *m*.

**speaker** *n* a. (*psn.*) mài màganà *n*: how many Hausa ~s are there? nawà nē màsu màganà dà Hausa? he's a native Hausa ~ bàhaushè nē. b. (*lecturer*) mài bā dà jàwābì *n*. c. (*Pol., in legislature*) shùgàban tàron màjàlisà *m*. d. (*loudspeaker*) lāsìfīkà *f* ⟨oCi⟩, [F] ōpàr̃lar̃ *m*.

**spear** *n* māshì *m* ⟨māsū⟩.

**special** *adj* na mùsammàn: a ~ organization wata ƙungìyā ta mùsammàn.

**specialist** *n* gwànī *m* ⟨aye⟩, mài ƙwarèwā *n*: he's a ~ on political ideology gwànin r̃a'àyin sìyāsà nē.

**specialize** *v* ƙwarè *v4*: he ~s in fixing bicycles yā ƙwarè à kân gyāran kèkè.

**specialized** *adj* a. (*skilled*) ƙwàrarrè *adj*. b. (*restricted*) kè6a66è *adj*.

**specially** *adv*, *see* especially.

**species** *n* jinsì *m*, nau'ìn hàlittà *m*: the human ~ jinsìn ɗan Adàm.

**specific** *n & adv* (*precise, real*) tàkàmaimai *adj*: there's no ~ evidence confirming this bâbù wata hujjà tàkàmaimai dà ta tab-batar̃ dà wannàn; I don't know ~ally what he wants bân san tàkàmaiman àbin dà yakè sô ba; I went to that place ~ally to see him nā jē cân wajèn tàkàmaimai don ìn gan shì.

**specify** *v* ƙayyàdè *v4*: the agreement specifies payment on the first of the month jìnginà tā ƙayyàdè biyà à farkon kōwànè watà.

**specimen** *n* samfùr̃ *m* ⟨oCi⟩, mìsālì *m* ⟨ai⟩.

**speck** *n*: there wasn't a ~ of dust on the table bâbù ƙūrā kō ɗis kân tēbùr̃.

**speckled** *adj* dabbar̃è-dabbar̃è *adj*, wāke-wāke *adj*: ~ eggs ƙwai dabbar̃è-dabbar̃è.

**spectacle** *n* (*celebration*) bìkī *m* ⟨uwa²⟩.

spectacles *n, see* eyeglasses.

spectator *n* ɗan kallō *m*, mài kallō *n*.

speculate *v* yi hàsàshē *m*: he was speculating about the outcome of the election yanà hàsàshen sàkàmakon zāɓên.

speculation *n* hàsàshē *m*, kìntàcē *m*: what he said was mere ~ àbîn dà ya cè kìntàcē nē kawài; sheer ~ shàci-fàɗi *m*: disregard that, it's mere ~ kà ràbu dà wànnan, shàci-fàɗi nē.

speculative *adj*: ~ buying (*esp. of crops*) bafàndà *f*.

speculator *n* ɗan bafàndà *m*.

speech *n* a. màganà *f*, zàncē *m*: ~ is unique to man màganà kēɓaɓɓiyā cè gà ɗan Adàm; ~ disorder, error tsāmin bàkī *m*; inappropriate, impolite ~ ɗanyaf màganà *f*. b. (*esp. manner of speaking*) lafàzī *m*: his ~ is rough lafàzinsà bâ dādī. c. (*formal, public address*) jàwābī *m* ⟨ai⟩: deliver a ~ yi jàwābī.

speechless *adj*: be ~ kāsà (yīn) màganà, (*esp. from anger, impatience*) sikè *v4*: he was ~ from anger fushī yā sâ yā sikè.

speed 1. *n* a. saurī *m*, gaggàwā *f*. b. (*esp. of sth. moving*) gudù *m*: travel at a ~ of 60 miles an hour yi gudùn mîl sìttin; what is our ~? nawà nē yawàn gudùnmù? ~ limit kàyyàdadden yawàn gudù *m*; at full, top ~ dà gudùn gàske.
2. *v* yi gudù *m*; don't ~ kadà kà kārà gudù; ~ sth. up gaggàutā *v1*: they sped up the investigation, work sun gaggàutà bìncìkē, aikì; he ~ed up (in the car) yā tàkà mōtà.

speeding *n* mūgùn gudù *m*.

speedometer *n* mālējì *m*, [F] kwàntâf *m*.

spell[1] *v* fubūtà *v1*: how do you ~ this word? yàyà akè fubūtà wannàn kalmà?

spell[2] *n* (*magic*) māgànī *m* ⟨u-a[2]⟩, sihìfī *m*: the ~ has worked on him māgànī yā cī shì; break a ~ karyà māgànī; (*for causing neg. effect*) sammù *m*, jīfà *m*; cast, put a ~ on so. sammàcē *v4*, yi wà māgànī, yi wà sammù, yi wà sihìfī.

spend *v* a. (*money*) kashè *v4*, ɓad dà / ɓataf (dà) *v5*: how much have you spent? nawà ka ɓataf? don't ~ more than ₦10 kadà kà kashè fìye dà naifà gōmà. b. (*time doing sth.*) yi (+ *time expres.* + *contin.*): she spent 3 hours preparing the meal tā yi awà ukù tanà girkì; ~ the day yinì / wunì *v3b, see* day; ~ the night kwāna *v3a*.

spendthrift *n* àlmùbazzàfī *m* ⟨ai⟩, bùshāshà *n*.

sperm *n* màniyyì / mànî *m*.

sphere *n* kwallō *m* ⟨aye⟩.

spices *n* yājì *m*, kāyan kanshī *m/p*: so-and-so likes lots of ~ wancè tā cikà shân yājì.

spider *n* gizò-gizò *m*, tautàu *m*; (*small, bright red*) kàrammiskì *m*.

spiderweb *n* sākāf gizò-gizò *f*, yānaf gizò-gizò *f*, gidan tautàu *m*.

spike *n* tsìnī *m*.

spill 1. *vi* zubè *v4*, zùba *v3*: don't let the oil ~ kadà mâi yà zubè; (*in splotches*) fàntsamà *v3*: the oil ~ed on her dress mâi yā fàntsamà à rìgaftà.
2. *vt* zub dà / zubaf (dà) *v5*; (*by dropping*) ɓaf dà / ɓaraf (dà) *v5*: she ~ed the flour (from the sack) tā ɓaf dà gàrī.
3. *n*: an oil ~ zubèwaf mân fētùf.

spin *v* a. (*thread, a top*) kaɗà *v1*: the top is ~ning kàtantanwā tanà kaɗàwā; ~ a web yi sākāf gizò-gizò. b. (*go round & round*) jūyà *v1*: the wheel is ~ning wīlì nà ta jūyàwā.

spinach *n* àlayyàhō *m*.

spinal *adj* na kàshin bāyā.

spinal cord *n* lakà *f*.

spinal meningitis *n* sànkàrau *m*.

spindle *n* mazarī *m*.

spine *n* a. (*vertebrate*) kàshin bāya *m*. b. (*quill*) kayà *f*.

spinning *n* (*thread*) kaɗī *m*.

spinster *n* gwauruwā *f, see* unmarried.

spiny *adj* (mài) tsìnī *m*, (mài) kayà *f*.

spirit *n* a. (*of psn.*) kùrwā *f*: the sorcerer has trapped her ~ māyè yā kāmà kùrwaftà. b. (*abstr. entity*) fūhì *m*: the ~ of friendship fūhìn àbòkàntakà; the Holy S. Rūhì Mài Tsarkī *m*. c. (*supernatural being*) iskà *f* ⟨oCi⟩, àljanī *m* ⟨u⟩: evil ~ mūgùn àljanī; good ~ àljanī na kìfkì; ~ possession (*cult*) bòrī *m*. d. a ~ed person mài zūcìyā, mài kùzārī; he's in good ~s yanà jîn walwàlà.

spirits *n* (*alcoholic drinks*) bàfàsà *f*.

spiritual *adj* na ìbādà *f*; a ~ leader shēhù *m* ⟨shēhùnnai⟩.

spit 1. *n* (*saliva*) miyau / yau *m*; (*phlegm*) kàkī *m*; (*of infants*) tùmbudī *m*.
2. *v* tōfà *v1*, tsaftà *v1*, tōfaf dà yau *v5*, tsaftaf dà yau *v5*; ~ on so. tōfà wà yau; ~ out (*food*) furzà *v1*; ~ out (*in long thin stream*) yi tsaftuwā *f*: the snake is ~ting macìjī nà tsaftuwā.

spite[1] 1. *n* (*envy*) hassadà *f*.
2. *v* ɓātà wà *v1*: he did it to ~ me yā yi hakà don ɓātà minì.

spite[2] *n*: in ~ of duk dà, kō dà *conj*: in ~ of all our troubles, we succeeded duk dà

wahalōlîn dà mukà shā, mun ci nasařà;
in ~ of the fact that he was late to work,
he finished on time kō dà yā màkarà zuwà
aikî, àmmā yā gamã cikin lōkàcî.

**splash** v a. fantsàmā *v1*, fàntsamà *v3*: the
driver ~ed mud on us difēbà yā fantsàmā
manà cã6î; when the rock fell into the water, we got ~ed dà dūtsèn ya fādà ruwa,
sai ruwà ya fantsamō manà. b. (of rain)
yi fēshī *m*. c. (play in water): ~ around
noisily yi bùndùm-bundum *idph*.

**splattered** adj faca-faca *idph*: we were ~
with mud faca-faca mukè dà cã6î.

**spleen** n saifà *f* ⟨oCi⟩.

**splendid** 1. adj kyàkkyāwā *adj*.
2. excl māshā'àllāhù!, tùbařkallà!,
mādàllā!

**splint** n karan dōřî *m*.

**splinter** n sartsĕ *m*: take out a ~ cirè
sartsĕ.

**split** 1. vt a. (open up): ~ wood faskàrà
itàcē; ~ a kolanut 6ārà gōřò; ~ open a
calabash rabà ƙwaryā = fāfà ƙwaryā; ~
a coconut, an atom fasà kwākwà, ƙwàyař
zařřà. b. (divide) rabà *v1*: let's ~ the expenses 3 ways mù rabà kuɗin kashî ukù.
2. vi tsāgè *v4*: calabashes ~ easily at
the edges bàkin ƙwaryā yanà tsāgèwā dà
saurī; (of a seam) yāgè *v4*.
3. n tsāgā *f*: there's a ~ in the wood dà
tsāgā à kātākō.

**splotchy** adj dabbařè-dabbařè *adj*.

**spoil** 1. vt a. (ruin sth.) 6ātà *v1*, lālàtà *v1*:
he ~ed our plans yā 6ātà manà shirî.
b. (indulge a psn.) shagwa6ař (dà) *v5*,
sangàřtà *v1*: she really ~s her children
tā cikà shagwa6ař dà yârā; a ~ed child
shàgwà6a66ē *adj*, tà6àrarrē *adj*.
2. vi a. (of organic matter) ru6è *v4*, 6àcì
*v3b*, lālàcē *v4*: the meat has ~ed nāmà
yā 6àcì = nāmà yā ru6è. b. (deteriorate)
lālàcē *v4*, ta6ar6àrè *v4*.

**spoils** n (of war) gànīmà *f*.

**spoke** n (of wheel) wayà *f* ⟨oCi⟩, [F] sùpô
*m*.

**spokesman** n kàkàkī *m*: a government ~
kàkàkin gwamnatî.

**sponge** n sōsō *m*: cellulose ~ sōson řō6à.

**sponger** n (parasite) cî-mà-zàune *m*.

**spool** n (of thread) kwařkwařō *m*.

**spoon** n cōkàlī *m* ⟨u-a⟩, cibī *m*: one ~ful
cōkàlī ɗaya.

**sport** n wàsā *m* ⟨annī⟩: ~s play an important role in contemporary life matsayin
wàsànnī à řàyuwâř yâu mài muhimmancî
nē; he is a good ~ shī mài hālin kiřkì
nē.

**sportsman** n ɗan wàsā *m*.

**spot**[1] n a. (of any liquid) ɗigò *m* ⟨e²⟩: a ~
of oil ɗigòn mâi. b. ~s (markings on animals) dabbařè-dabbařè *p*: leopards have
~s dàmisà nà dà dabbařè-dabbařè. c.
(var. uses): on the ~ nan tàke, bâ wata-
wata: he died on the ~ nan tàke ya ràsu;
one's weak ~ lagò *m*; (fig.) he got himself
into a tight ~ wurī yā ƙurè masà.

**spot**[2] v (see from afar) hàngā *v1* ⟨hàngē⟩.

**spouse** n (husband) mijî *m* ⟨mazā, mazàjē⟩;
(wife) mātā *f* ⟨mātā⟩.

**spout** n a. (of kettle) bàkin būtà *m*. b. (on
roof gutter) indařařō *m*.

**sprain** v (twist, esp. a limb) guřɗè *v4*: I
have ~ed my knee nā guřɗè à gwīwà =
gwīwàtā tā guřɗè; (a joint) targàɗē *v4*,
yi targaɗè *m*: he ~ed his toe yā yi
targaɗè à bàbban yātsà.

**spray** 1. v (esp. from mouth) fēsà *v1*: ~ can
gwangwanin fēsàwā.
2. n fēshī *m*.

**spread** v a. (extend) yàɗà *v1*: ~ knowledge yàɗà ilìmī; flies ~ disease ƙuɗàjē
sunà yàɗà cūtuttukà; the disease, fire is
~ing cūtâř, gòbařâř tanà yàɗuwà; (of
weeds) baibàyē *v4*; (of water on a surface)
màlàlà *v3*. b. (information, news) yàɗà
*v1*, wàtsà *v1*. c. (esp. sth. neg.) bazà *v1*:
the rumors are ~ing anà bazà jìta-jìta
= jìta-jìta tanà bàzuwà; ~ manure on
the farm bazà tàkì à gōnà. d. (smear)
shàfà *v1*: ~ peanut butter on bread shàfà
tùnkūzà kân buřōdì. e. (clothing, flat
things) shimfìɗà *v1*: ~ a rug on the floor
shimfìɗà dàřdūmà à dà6ē; ~ out (display) bazà *v1*: the trader ~ out his wares
ɗan tīřēdà yā bazà kōlìnsà; ~ out
(esp. in sun, wind) shānyà *v1*: she ~ the
clothes out to dry tā shānyà tufàfī wàje
sù būshè; the birds are ~ing out their
wings (in the sun) tsuntsàyē nà shānyà
fìkàfìkai.

**spring**[1] v yi tsallē *m*, dakà tsallē: the
lion sprang at them zākī yā yiwō tsallē
wajensù = zākī yā zābuřam musù; ~
across, over tsallàkē *v4*: he sprang
over the wall and escaped yā tsallàkē
katangā yā tsīra; ~ up, forward zàbuřà
*v3*.

**spring**[2] n (of water) idòn ruwā *m*,
ma6u66ugà *f*: they drank from a nearby ~
sun shā ruwā dàgà ma6u66ugà nân kusa.

**spring**[3] n (coil) sìfìřîn *m*, [F] řēsuwâř *m*.

**spring**[4] n, see season.

**sprinkle** v (water, liquid) yayyàfā *v1*,
yi yayyafī *m*; (a powdery substance)

baṛbàɗā *v1*: she ~d spices on the meat
tā baṛbàɗā wà nāmā̀ yājì̃.

sprinkling *n (of water)* yayyafī *m*: it
is ~ outside anā̀ yayyafī à wàje; *(of
sth. sprinkled)* bàṛbadī *m*: a ~ of sugar
bàṛbaɗin sukàṛī.

sprinkling can *n* būtūtun gādìnà *m*.

sprout *v (new shoots)* tsirṑ *m* ⟨e²⟩, tūshè
*m*.

spur 1. *n* ƙaimī *m*.
2. *v* tsàburā *v2*, yi wà ƙaimī *m*: I ~red
the horse on nā tsàbùri dōkì dà ƙaimī.

spurn *v* ƙi *v0*.

spurt out *v* tsaṛtṑ *v6*: water is ~ing out of
the pipe ruwā nā̀ tsaṛtōwā dàgà famfò;
~ onto so. tsaṛtam/taṛtsam mà *vdat*: the
blood ~ed out onto Musa's gown jinī yā
taṛtsam mà Mūsā à rìgā.

sputum *n* kàkī *m*.

spy 1. *n* ɗan lḕƙen àsīrī *m*, ɗan ṛàhōtò
*m*; ~ movie fîm ɗin sī'aidî *m*, [F] àjân
*m*; secret ~ [F] àjan sèkìrê.
2. *v* lēƙà àsīrī: ~ on the enemy lēƙà
àsīrin àbòkan gàba.

spying *n* lḕƙen àsīrī *m*.

squalid *adj* ƙàzāmī *adj*: live in ~ conditions
zaunā à ƙàzāmin wurī.

squalor *n* ƙàzàntā *f*.

squander *v* ɓātaṛ (dà) *v5*, ɓaṛnataṛ (dà)
*v5*, banzaṛtaṛ (dà) *v5*, yi fàcàkā dà:
he has ~ed his wealth yā ɓātaṛ dà
dūkìyaṛsà dukà.

square *n* mùṛabbà'ī *m*, mùka'àbī *m*: fold
the paper into a ~ kà ninkà takàṛdā
tà zama mùṛabbà'ī; a ~ foot ƙafā
mùṛabbà'ī; it has an area of 50 ~
miles fàɗinsà in an riɓā dà tsawō mîl
mùṛabbà'ī hàmsin nè.

squash¹ *n (yellow ~)* kàbēwā *f* ⟨i⟩; *(marrow)* kàbūshì̃ / kàbûs *m*.

squash² *v (crush)* lātsà *v1*, lātsè *v4*: ~ a
cockroach lātsà kyànkyasò; *(esp. pulverize)* muṛtsùkē *v4*.

squat *v (on heels)* tsugùnà *v1*.

squeeze 1. *v* a. *(wring out liquid)* mātsà
*v1*: ~ a lemon, a wet sponge mātsà
lḕmō, sòsō; *(e.g. fruit to make it soft)*
lugwīgwìtà *v1*. b. *(constrict, press together)* matsà *v1*: he ~d me between
the wall and the door yā matsà ni
tsàkānin ƙōfà dà bangō; ~ together and
make room for them kù matsà musù sù
sāmi wurī; ~ through, into *(narrow or
crowded area)* kuṛɗà *v1*, ƙwāfà *v1*, ƙūƙùtā
*v1*: he ~d in between them yā ƙwāfà
tsàkāninsù.
2. *n (difficulty)* matsì̃ *m*, màtsuwā *f*: he's

in a tight ~ (for money) yanà cikin matsī̃
= yanà cikin màtsuwā.

squint *v* rintsà idò.

squirm *v* yi wàtsàl-watsal *idph*, yi
wàtsàlniyā *f*.

squirrel *n* kùrēgē *m* ⟨u⟩: tree ~ kùrēgen
bisà *m*.

squirt *v* tsaṛtā̀ *v1*.

stab *v (so.)* sòkā *v2* ⟨sūkà⟩ *f*: he ~bed her
in the heart yā sòkē tà à zūci; *(so.
with sth.)* sōkà wà *v1*: she ~bed him with
a needle tā sōkà masà àlluṛā̀; *(with a
knife)* lumà *v1*, mākà *v1*; *(excessively, with
a weapon)* cakà *v1*, zabgà *v1*, daɓà *v1*:
he ~bed the animal deeply yā zabgà wà
dabbā̀ wuƙā.

stability *n (of society)* zaman lāfiyā̀ *m*:
peace and ~ lùmānà dà zaman lāfiyā̀.

stable¹ *adj* a. *(durable)* (mài) ƙarkō *m*. b.
*(having stability)* (mài) zaman lāfiyā̀ *m*.

stable² *n (for animals)* bàṛgā *f*.

stack *n* tārì̃ *m*: a ~ of books tārìn
lìttàttàfai; *(of cut grain)* būshiyā *f*: a
~ of millet būshiyaṛ gērō.

stadium *n* fīlin wāsā *m*.

staff¹ *n* sàndā *f* ⟨una⟩: the royal ~ sàndaṛ
sàrautà; *(of a leader, ruler)* kàndīṛì̃ *m*
⟨ai⟩.

staff² *n (employees)* ma'àikàtā *p*.

stag beetle *n* bùzūzù *m*.

stage¹ *n (step in development)* matsayī *m*:
at this ~ à matsayin yànzu; before it
reaches that ~ kàfin à kai gà wànnan
matsayī̃; complete the final ~ kammàlā *v1*.

stage² *(platform in theatre)* dandamàlī *m*.

stagger *v* yi tàngadī *m*.

stagnant *adj*: the water in the borrow-pit is
~ ruwan kùduddufī bā yà gudù.

stagnate *v* guṛɓàcē *v4*; *(Econ.)* taɓaṛɓàrē
*v4*, jā dà bāya.

stain 1. *n (splotch)* tabṑ *m* ⟨Ca⟩, *(esp. of
liquid)* jìrwàyē *m*; *(fig.)* it is a ~ on his
character yā zama tabṑ à hālinsà.
2. *v* a. *(make a mark on)* ɓātà *v1*: the ink
has ~ed the gown tàwadā tā ɓātà rìgā.
b. *(wood)* shāfà *v1*. c. *(hands, feet with
henna)* yi ƙunshì̃ (dà lallè): she is ~ing
her hands tanà ƙunshì̃ à hannu.

staircase, stairs *n* matākalā / matattākalà *f*.

stake *n (peg)* fēgì̃ *m* ⟨una⟩.

stale *adj (e.g. smell of cigarettes)* (mài) wārī
*m*; my mouth tastes ~ bā nà jîn dāɗin
bàkīnā.

stalk *n (of corn, sugar cane)* karā *m* ⟨aCe⟩;
*(of a flower, leaf)* jìkī *m*.

stall¹ *n (e.g. at a market)* rùmfā *f* ⟨una⟩.

stall² v (procrastinate) yi shìrīrītā f, shantàkē v4.

stallion n ìngařmā̀ m.

stammer v yi ì'ìnā/ìn'ìnā f.

stamina n kùzārī m, zāfin nāmā̀ m.

stamp 1. n a. (official seal) hātìmī m ⟨ai⟩, tambàrī m ⟨u-a⟩; rubber ∼ sìtâm m, [F] tàmpô m. b. (postage) kân sarkī m, sìtâm m, [F] tambùř m: I want 5 stamps of 50k each inā̀ sôn kân sarkī bìyař na kwabò hàmsin hàmsin.
2. v (a document) bugà tambàrī, bugà hātìmī: they ∼ed my passport an bugā̀ minì tambàrī à fàsfô.

stamp on v (trample) tattàkā v1.

stand¹ 1. v a. tsayā̀ v1: there are no seats left, we shall have to ∼ bâ sauran wurin zamā, dōlè mù tsayā̀; I prefer ∼ing to sitting nā fi sôn tsàyuwā dà zamā; ∼ stiffly, stock-still tsayā̀ ƙìƙàm, ƙamḕ v4: the soldier stood stiffly at attention sōjà yanà tsàye ƙìƙàm = sōjà yā ƙamḕ. b. (var. v + adv/prep uses): ∼ apart, aloof tōgè v4: he stood aloof at the door yā tōgè à bàkin ƙōfā̀; ∼ up tāshì (tsàye) v3b, mīƙè v4; help so. ∼ up tā dà / tāsař (dà) v5: she helped the child who had fallen ∼ up tā tā dà yāròn dà ya fādì. b. (withstand) jūrè v4, daurè v4, yi jìmirī m: I cannot ∼ the cold nā kāsà daurè sanyī = bā nā̀ jìmirin sanyī; he can't ∼ dogs bā yā̀ jìmirin kàrē. c. (fig. uses): how do things ∼ now? yàyā̀ àl'àmùřàn sukè yànzu? ∼ by so. (be a guarantor) tsayā̀ wà v1: Sule will ∼ by me Sulè zâi tsayā̀ minì; ∼ for nūnà v1: this symbol ∼s for unity wannàn àlāmà̀ tanà̀ nūnà̀ haɗìn kâi; ∼ up for so. ƙarfàfā wà gwīwā̀.
2. n a. (for bicycle) jâk m, [F] kìřîk m. b. (position, opinion) řa'àyī m: take a ∼ on fàɗi řa'àyī gàme dà.

stand² n (stall) rùmfā̀ f ⟨una⟩.

standard 1. n a. (ideal) ƙā'idā̀ f ⟨oCi⟩: a person with high ∼s mùtûm mài bîn ƙā'idā̀. b. (measure of worth) mìzānī m: the gold ∼ mìzānìn zīnāřìyā; ∼ of living hālin rầyuwā.
2. adj (correct) dàidàitaccè adj: S. Hausa dàidàitacciyař Hausa.

standardize v daidàità v1: one of the functions of a dictionary is to ∼ orthography ɗaya dàgà cikin ayyukàn ƙāmùs shī nè daidàità hanyàř řùbūtū.

standstill n: the train came to a ∼ jirgī yā tsayā̀ cak; the work came to a ∼ aikìn yā cījè.

stanza n baitì m ⟨oCi⟩: a ∼ of 5 lines baitì mài ƙwàyā/ƙwàř bìyař.

staple¹ 1. v maƙàlē v4.
2. n (for a stapler) fîl m: there are no more ∼s fîl ɗin sìtēfilā̀ yā ƙàrè.

staple² n (basic commodity) kāyan màsàřūfì p: tuwo is one of the ∼s of the Hausa tuwō shī nè ɗaya dàgà cikin kāyan màsàřūfì na Hàusāwā.

stapler n sìtēfilā̀ f.

star n (in heavens or famous psn.) tàuràrò m, tàurārùwā f ⟨i⟩; (any bright ∼ or planet) zāřa f; morning ∼ gàmzākì m.

starch 1. n a. (of cassava) kwākī m. b. (for clothes) sìtācì / sìtātì m.
2. v sâ sìtātì.

stare 1. v (at psn.) zurà idò, ƙurà idò, yi zūrū dà idò: he ∼d at her yā zurà matà idò; (in anger) zārè idò; (rudely) yi mùzūřai m; (from shame, fear, hunger) yi zurū-zùrù dà idò; ∼ vacantly yi kallō gàlau.
2. n dūbā m: a rude ∼ dūban wùlāƙài.

stark adj: be ∼-naked yi tik idph, yi zigìdiř idph; he is ∼ raving mad mahàukàcī nè tubuřàn.

starling n càkwaikwaiwā f, zāřa f, shāyā̀ f.

start¹ 1. v a. (begin) fārā v1, sōmā v1: who ∼ed the war? wā̀ ya fārà yāƙìn? he has just ∼ed to learn Hausa kwānan nàn yā fārà kòyon Hausa; ∼ by saying fārà dà cêwā; ∼ a career kāmà aikì; ∼ a rumor bazà jìta-jìta = ƙirƙìrà jìta-jìta; ∼ a business kafà kamfànī; ∼ doing sth. fārà v1, shìga v3: she ∼ed to pack her clothes tā shìga kimsà kāyantà; ∼ negotiations shìga tattàunâwā; ∼ing from X (a specified time) dàgà X nân gàba: ∼ from tomorrow dàgà gòbe nân gàba; a ∼ing point mafārī m. b. (be the cause of) tā dà / tāyař (dà) v5, haddàsà v1: his remark ∼ed the trouble màganařsà tā tā dà rìkicī; a cigarette ∼ed the fire wutař tābā̀ tā haddàsà gòbařā. c. (a machine) tā dà / tāyař (dà) v5: she couldn't ∼ the car bà tā iyà tā dà mōtā̀ ba; the car won't ∼ mōtā̀ bā tā̀ tāshì.
2. n farkō m: from the ∼ tun (dàgà) farkō; from ∼ to finish tun farkō hař ƙàrshē; make an early ∼ (in the morning) yi sàmmakō m; a head ∼ rātā f.

start² v (be frightened, startled) fìrgità v3: the noise made me ∼ ƙāřář tā sâ ni fìrgità; jump with a ∼ yi firgigit idph: I woke up with a ∼ nā tāshì firgigit.

starter (of car engine) sìtātā̀ f.

startle v fìrgitař (dà) v5, tā dà hankàlin
w.: the news ~d us làbāřìn yā fìrgitař
dà mū = làbāřìn yā tā dà hankàlinmù;
be ~d fìrgità v3.

starvation n (matsanancìyař) yunwā f.

starve v ji matsanancìyař yunwā; they are
starving to death yunwā tanā ta kashè
su.

state[1] n (situation, circumstances) hālī /
hālì m ⟨aye⟩, matsayī m: his ~ of health
hālìn jìkinsà = matsayin lāfiyàřsà;
what ~ did you find him in? à wànè hālī
kukà sāmē shì? they are in a constant ~
of war kullum sunā hālin yāƙì; she's in
a ~ of anger, shock tanā cikin fushī,
fìrgità; things are in a bad ~ matsayin
al'amuřā bā kyâu.

state[2] n a. (country) ƙasā f ⟨aCe⟩: a
modern ~ ƙasā ta zāmànī; front-line
~s ƙasàshen bàkin dāgā. b. (government) gwamnatì f ⟨oCi⟩: the ~ provides
hospitals and schools gwamnatì takàn
ginà asibitōcī dà màkàřàntū; ~ house
gidan gwamnatì; ~ property kadařāř
gwamnatì; ~ reception lìyāfàř àlfařmā;
~ visit zìyāřàř aikì; secretary of ~ (of
U.S.) sakatařèn harkōkin wàje; minister of ~ (in Nigeria) ƙàramin ministà. c.
(division within a country) jihā f ⟨oCi⟩:
Kano S. Jihàř Kanò.

state[3] v a. fuřtà v1: he ~d that... yā fuřtà
cêwā.... b. (bring forth) bayyànà v1: ~
your complaint kà bayyànà ƙarařkà.

statement n bàyānì m: make a ~ to the
press yi wà 'yan jàřīdū bàyānì.

state of emergency n dòkař-tā-6ācì f:
declare a ~ kafà dòkař-tā-6ācì.

statesman n tsōhon ɗan sìyāsà m.

station n a. (for communication, transport) tashà f ⟨oCi⟩: railway ~ tashàř
jirgī; radio, television ~ (on dial)
tashàř řēdiyò, talàbijìn; (broadcasting offices) gidan řēdiyò, talàbijìn. b.
(for public services) gidā m ⟨aCe⟩: gas
~ gidan mâi; fire ~ gidan 'yan kwàna-
kwāna; police ~ ōfìshin 'yan sàndā,
cājì ōfìs m; buying ~ (for groundnuts,
cotton) fulōtì m.

stationary adj à tsàye adv: the target is
completely ~ àbin bàrā yanà tsàye cak;
the car was ~ at the time of the accident
mōtā bā tà mòtsī à lōkàcîn haɗàřîn.

stationery n takàřdā f.

stationmaster n ēshàm m.

statistics n ilìmin ƙìdìddigà m.

statue n mùtum-mùtumī m.

stature n girmā m, kwàrjinī m, ìsā f.

status n a. (state, position) matsayī m: the
~ of blacks in America matsayin baƙař
fātā à Amìřkà. b. (high rank) mùƙāmì m:
he has ~ shī wani mài mùƙāmì nē.

statute n dòkā f ⟨oCi⟩.

stay 1. v a. (remain in a place) tsayà v1,
zaunà v1: it is better for you to ~ here
gāra kà zaunà nân; ~ where you are!
tsàyā indà kukè! be unable to ~ put
yi wàlàgìgī m; ~ indoors yi zamā à
ɗakà; the door won't ~ closed ƙōfař bā
tā rùfuwā. b. (remain a while) jimà v1,
daɗè v4: don't ~ too long kadà kà jimà
dà yawà = kadà kà daɗè; don't ~ up too
late kadà kà cikà darē. c. (~ a specified period of time) yi (+ time expr.): ~ 2
hours yi àwā biyu; ~ 5 years yi shèkarà
bìyař; ~ up all night yi kwānan zàune.
d. (lodge) sàuka v3: which hotel are you
~ing at? à wànè hòtâl ka sàuka?
2. n zamā m: during his ~ in England
à zamansà dà ya yi à Ingìlà; (visit)
zìyāřā f: I have enjoyed my ~ here nā
ji dāɗin zìyāřàtā à nân.

steadfast adj tsàyayyē adj; be ~ tsayà
tsayìn dakà; ~ly à tsàitsàye adv.

steady adj (mài) ƙwārī m: this table is ~
tēbùřin nàn yanā dà ƙwārī.

steal v a. sàta v2, yi sātā f: he stole the
documents yā sàci tàkàřdûn; ~ from
sācè wà v4: he stole my goat yā sācè
minì àkuyā; ~ all of sācè kaf. b. (go
stealthily) yi sandā f, la6à6ē v4, sadàdā
v1: he stole out of the house yā yi sandā
yā ficè gidân; he stole into the room yā
la6à6ē yā shìga ɗākìn.

stealing n sātā f: he was sent to prison for
~ an ɗaurè shi don sātā.

stealth n sandā f: move ~ily yi sandā,
(like a snake) yi sùlùlù idph.

steam 1. n tùrùrī m; ~ treatment (for
medicinal purposes) sùrācè m.
2. v turàrā v1; (cook by ~) dambàtà v1.

steamer n (for cooking, made of clay)
madambacī m.

steel n baƙin ƙarfè m; ~-rolling mill
ma'aikatař mulmùlà ƙarfè f.

steep[1] adj (mài) tsawō m.

steep[2] v (infuse) tsimā v1, jiƙà v1.

steer[1] n dungurī m.

steer[2] v tūƙà v1 ⟨tūƙì⟩.

steering committee n kwàmìtîn shiryà
aikì m.

steering wheel n sìtìyāřì m, [F] bòlân m.

stem n a. (of plant) gàngař jìkī f. b.
(of watch) hannun wainì m. c. (Gram.)
tūshèn kalmā m.

stench n wārī m; (fetid, rotten) ɗòyī m.

step 1. n a. (pace) tākī m: he took a few ~s yā yi tākī kàɗan; march in ~ yi mācī daidai wà daidà; (fig., used as warning) watch your ~! yi tākā tsantsan dūniyā! = bi hannunkà mài sàndā! b. (stairs) matākalā / matattākalā f: slip on the ~s zāmē dàgà kân matākalā. c. (action, measure) matākī m: take ~s to combat smuggling ɗauki màtākan yāƙī dà sùmōgà; (fig.) take two ~s forward, one ~ backward yi kwàn-gàba kwàn-bāya; ~ by ~ dakī-dakī adv, fillā-fillā idph: he explained it to us ~ by ~ yā yi manà bàyānī fillā-fillā; the final ~ (toward completion of sth.) cìkàmakō m : writing a thesis is the final ~ in getting a degree ƙubūtà kundī shī nè cìkàmakon sāmùn dìgìřī.
2. v: ~ aside for so. kaucè wà v4, bā w. hanyà; ~ to the side kōmà wajē ɗaya: he ~ped to the side to clear his throat and spit yā kōmà wajē ɗaya yà yi kàkī yà tōfař; ~ forward matsà gàba, yi gàba; ~ on tākà v1: don't ~ on the flowers kadà kà tākà fùrē; ~ on the gas! kà tākà mōtà!

stepbrother n, see brother.

stepchild n agòlà m, agōlìyā f ⟨ai⟩.

stepmother n, see mother; (term of ref., esp. in tales) kīshìyař uwā f.

stepsister n, see sister.

sterile adj (woman) jūyà f ⟨oCi⟩.

sterling n a. (silver) azùřfā f. b. (British currency) kuɗin Ingìlà p.

stethoscope n nā'ūřař aunà sautìn jìkī f.

stew n miyà f; (var. types with diff. main ingredients): (without meat) miyàř lāmī; (okra) miyàř kuɓēwā; (spinach, other herbs) miyàř tàushē; (crushed baobab leaves) miyàř kūkà; (tomatoes & chillies) dage-dage m; (groundnuts) miyàř gyàɗā; (special herbs to make sauce viscous, slippery) miyàř kařkashī; (melon seeds) miyàř àgūsi; (head of goat, sheep) dàbgē m.

steward n (houseboy) bòyi m ⟨x²⟩, [F] bōyì m ⟨x²⟩.

stick¹ n a. sàndā m/f ⟨una⟩, (small piece of wood) icè m: he walks with the help of a ~ yanà dògarà dà sàndā; a forked ~ gwàfā f ⟨anni, oCi⟩. b. (flexible switch for hitting) tsabgà f ⟨oCi⟩, tsumangìyā f ⟨oCi⟩.

stick² 1. vt a. (pierce by sth. sharp) sōkà v2: tsìřā v2: a thorn got stuck in my foot ƙayà tā tsìřē nì à ƙafà; ~ sth. sharp into sōkà v1: the nurse stuck a needle into my arm nâs tā sōkà minì àllurà à hannu. b. (attach, fix to a place) maƙala v1: he stuck a pen in his pocket, behind his ear yā maƙàlà bīřò à àljīhū, à kûnnensà. c. (attach with glue or sth. sticky) līƙà v1, (esp. by pressing together) mannà v1: he stuck a stamp, some Scotch tape on the envelope yā mannà kân sarkī, salàtîf à jìkin ambùlàn. d. (make sth. adhere onto sth.) līƙà v1: someone stuck an announcement on the wall wani yā līƙà sanàřwā à jìkin bangō; be stuck ɗamfàrè v4: a shred of paper stuck to his sleeve guntun takàřdā yā ɗamfàrē à hannun rìgařsà. e. (embed) kafà v1: he stuck a peg in the ground, nail into the wall yā kafà fēgì à ƙasà, ƙūsà à bangō. f. (put, fix sth. in a place) maƙala v1: he stuck a pen in his pocket yā maƙàlà àlƙalàmī à àljīhū. g. (var. v + prep uses): ~ out one's tongue at so. yi wà gwālō = dallarō wà harshè; ~ to sth. (be firm about) kafè v4, tsayà (à) kân, dāgè (à) kân: we stuck firm to our decision mun tsayà kân shāwařàřmù.
2. vi a. (adhere, of sth. sticky) līƙè v4, līƙu v7, mànnu v7: the stamp won't ~ kân sarkī bā yà līƙuwā. b. (become embedded) kafè v4: the car got stuck in the mud mōtà tā kafè à càɓī. c. (become lodged, fixed in a place) maƙàlē v4, kākàrē v4: the key stuck in the lock makullī yā maƙàlē à kwàɗō; a bone got stuck in his throat ƙāshī yā kākàrē masà à màƙōgwàro. d. (var. v + adv/prep uses): ~ out ɓullō v6, tūrō v6: his feet were ~ing out from under the blanket ƙàfàfunsà nà ɓullōwā dàgà ƙařƙashin bàřgō; his stomach stuck out cikìnsà yā tūrō; ~ together, to one another kāmè v4: the stamps are stuck together kân sarkī sun kāmè.

sticky adj a. (mài) danƙò m: his hands are ~ hannunsà nà dà danƙò. b. (of weather) (mài) gùmī m: it is ~ today yâu àkwai gùmī.

stiff adj a. (of body, muscles): be ~ ƙagè v4, sagè v4: my arm is ~ hannūnā yā sagè. b. (from fear or being at attention): be ~ ƙamè v4: he was scared ~ tsòřō kāmà shi hař yā ƙamè. c. (from cold): be ~ kangàrē v4, sandàrē v4: his fingers are ~ from the cold yātsunsà sun kangàrē sabōdà sanyī. d. (from drying out): be(come) ~ ƙandàrē v4: the snakeskin has become ~ fātař macìjī tā ƙandàrē. e. (*of a corpse*): go, get ~ sanƙàmē *v4*: the corpse has gone ~ gàwā tā sanƙàmē.

**stiffly** *adv*: stand ~ (*e.g. at attention*) tsayà ƙìƙàm.

**still**[1] **1.** *adv* haƙ yànzu *adv*: he is ~ busy yanà cikin aikì haƙ yànzu; he ~ doesn't believe me haƙ yànzu bài yàƙda dà màganàtā ba. **2.** *conj* àmmā duk dà hakà: perhaps what he did was wrong but ~ he is my friend kīlà àbîn dà ya yi bà daidai ba àmmā duk dà hakà shī àbōkīnā nè.

**still**[2] *adj* **a.** (*without noise*) (mài) shirū *m*: be ~! yi shirū! **b.** (*without motion*) tsit *idph*: the town was ~ gàrī yā yi tsit; stay ~! yi tsit!

**stillborn** *adj*: the baby was ~ mài cikì tā yi ɓarī.

**stilts** *n* kwàrā-kwàrā *f*.

**stimulant** *n* àbù mài ƙàrà kùzārī *m*.

**stimulate** *v* **a.** (*encourage*) tsimà *v1*, zugà *v1*. **b.** (*increase energy*) ƙàrà kùzārī.

**sting 1.** *vt* (*by insect*) hàƙbà *v2*: a scorpion stung her kùnāmà tā hàƙbē tà. **2.** *vi* **a.** (*of body*) yi ƙàɗàɗī *m*: our eyes were ~ing from the smoke idànunmù nà ƙàɗàɗī saɓõda hayāƙī. **b.** (*of a substance*) sâ ƙàɗàɗī, sâ cīwò: iodine ~s aìdîn yanà sâ ƙàɗàɗī. **3.** *n* (*of scorpion, bee*) haƙbì *m*: a bee ~ haƙbìn zumà.

**stinger** *n* (*of scorpion, bee*) ƙarì *m*: the scorpion aimed its ~ kùnāmà tā ɗanà ƙarì.

**stinginess** *n* rōwà *f*, tsumulmulā *f*, maƙõ *m*.

**stingy** *adj* marõwàcī *adj*, mài rōwà *n*, mài tsumulmulā *n*, màtsōlò *m*; she is ~ mài rōwà cē = maƙõ gàrē tà.

**stinky** *adj* (mài) wārī *m*, (mài) dõyī *m*.

**stir** *v* jūyà *v1*: ~ sugar into tea jūyà sukàƙī à shāyì; (*whisk*) buƙgà *v1*; (*wet foods like furā*) dāmà *v1*; (*stiff foods like tuwō*) tūƙà *v1* ⟨tūƙì⟩; ~ up (*incite*) hanzùgà *v1*; ~ up (*sediment in liquid*) guƙɓàtà *v1*.

**stirring stick** *n* (*for food, esp. tuwō*) mūciyā *f*; (*for liquids*) mabuƙgī *m*.

**stirrup** *n* lìkkāfā *f* ⟨u⟩.

**stitch** *v* ɗinkè *v4*; (*bind edge of sth.*) dājè *v4*: ~ the edge of a mat dājè tàbarmā.

**stock**[1] **1.** *v* (*accumulate*) tārà *v1*. **2.** *n* (*inventory*) baƙaƙ hājà *f*; take ~ ƙidàyà kāyā.

**stock**[2] *n* (*geneology*) asalī *m*, zùƙiyà *f*: he comes from Tuareg ~ zùƙiyàƙsà būzū nè.

**stock**[3] *n* (*Econ.*) hannun jàƙì *m*: ~ exchange kàsuwaƙ jàƙì *f*.

**stockade** *n* kafì *m*.

**stockbroker** *n* dìllālìn jàƙì *m*.

**stockholder** *n* mài hannun jàƙì *m*.

**stock cube** *n, see* bouillon.

**stockings** *n* sàfā *f*.

**stockroom** *n, see* storeroom.

**stocky** *adj* (& *short*) dàɓaƙɓashī *adj* ⟨ai⟩.

**stoic** *adj*: be ~ daurè *v4*, jūrè *v4*, yi tamazā.

**stoke** *v*: ~ a fire izà wutā.

**stomach** *n* **a.** cikì *m* ⟨Cuna⟩: my ~ hurts cikì nà minì cīwò; lie on one's ~ kwàntā ƙub dà cikì; (*esp. organ*) tùmbī *m* ⟨una⟩: he bought a ~ and some liver at the market yā sàyi tùmbī dà hantà à kàsuwā. **b.** (*adverbial uses*): in the ~ à cikì *adv*, à tùmbi *adv*: they punched me in the ~ sun nàushē nì à cikì.

**stomach-ache** *n* cīwòn cikì *m*: I have a ~ inà cīwòn cikì.

**stone 1.** *n* **a.** (*rock*) dūtsè *m* ⟨duwàtsū⟩, (*esp. from laterite soil*) marmarā *f*; (*small pebble*) tsakuwā *f* ⟨oCi⟩: a ~ building ginìn dūtsè; the children were throwing little ~s at a dog yârā sunà jīfàn kàrē dà tsakuwõyī; (*fig.*) within a ~'s throw, a ~'s throw away bàkī dà hancì *adv*: the stores are within a ~'s throw away kantunà sunà nan bàkī dà hancì. **b.** (*as instrument*): ~ for ginning cotton maguƙjī *m*; grinding ~ dūtsèn niƙà; whet~ dūtsèn washì. **c.** (*of fruit*) ƙwallō *m* ⟨aye⟩. **2.** *v* jēfè *v4*: she was ~d for committing adultery an jēfè ta saɓõda zìnā.

**stooge** *n* ɗan baƙàndà *m*: an imperialist ~ ɗan baƙàndàn mulkìn màllakà.

**stool**[1] *n* kujèrā *f* ⟨u⟩; (*low, used by women*) kujèraƙ mātā.

**stool**[2] *n* (*feces*) bāyan gidā *m*, nàjasà *f*.

**stoop**[1] *n* dandamàlī *m*.

**stoop**[2] *v* dūƙà *v1*, sunkùyà *v1*, sunkùyà kâi: she ~ed down to pick up the child tā dūƙà tà ɗaukō yārõ.

**stop 1.** *vi* **a.** (*halt*) tsayà *v1*, dākàtà *v1*: the train ~ped jirgī yā tsayà; let's ~ and have a little rest bàri mù tsayà mù ɗan hūtà; without ~ping bâ tsayàwā = (*fig.*) bâ àyà bâ waƙàfī; we went (by car) without ~ping mun yi tàfiyà bâ biƙkì; ~ dead tsayà cak = tsayà cik. **b.** (*of rain*) ɗaukè *v4*: it has ~ped raining completely ruwā yā ɗaukē cak. **2.** *vt* **a.** (*halt sth.*) tsai dà / tsayaƙ (dà) *v5*, dākataƙ dà *v5*: the soldiers are ~ping all cars sōjōjī sunà tsai dà duk mōtōcī. **b.** (*cease an activity*) dainà *v1*, barì *v*\*:

he has ~ped coming to see us yā dainà zuwā gidanmù; my watch has ~ped working àgōgōnā yā dainà aikì; ~ all that chattering! kù bař sùřūtùn nan! c. (prevent) hanà v1: he ~ped me from going yā hanā ni tàfiyà; ~ a rumor from circulating hanà bàzuwař jìta-jìta. d. (block, obstruct) tarè v4: stop him! ~ that thief! kù tarè! kù tarè 6àrāwòn! the police ~ped us from passing 'yan sàndā sun tarè manà hanyà; ~ sth. up (seal an opening) līƙè v4; be ~ped up (e.g. of a channel) tōshè v4: the pipe is ~ped up būtūtū yā tōshè.
3. n: come to a dead ~ tsayà cak, tsayà cik; put a ~ to hanà v1.

**stop light** n danjà f.

**stopper** n murfī m ⟨ai⟩, matōshī m; (esp. of cork) [F] bùshô m.

**stopover** n zangò m: make a ~ yā dà zangò.

**storage drum** n tànô m, dùřô m.

**store** 1. n a. (shop) kàntī m ⟨una⟩. b. (storeroom) sìtô m, [F] màngàzā f, dākìn àjiyà m.
2. v (put away in a safe place) ādànà v1: this is how they ~ their crops gà yàddà akè ādànà àmfànin gōnařsù; (save for future use) tànadà v2, yi tānàdī m.

**storeroom** n sìtô m, [F] màngàzā f; private ~ (of head of house) taskà f.

**storey** n hawā m, (esp. of residential building) kwàtashì m: a building with 8 ~s bēnē mài hawā takwàs.

**stork** n (white billed) shāmuwā f; (saddle billed, marabou) bàbbā-dà-jàkā m, bòrin-tinkè m.

**storm** n ruwā dà iskā m: there was a big ~ yesterday ruwā dà iskā yā yi yawà jiyà; dust ~ (esp. before harvest) hadarìn kàkā m; hail~ iskā mài ƙanƙarā f; sand~ iskā mài ƙūrā f, ~y conditions hadarì m.

**stormclouds** n hadarì m: ~ are gathering, perhaps we'll get some rain hadarì nà hàɗuwā, kīlà zā mù sàmi ruwā.

**story** n làbārì m ⟨ai, u⟩; (fable) hìkāyà f; (legend) àlmàřā f; (folktale) tàtsūnìyā f ⟨oCi⟩; is it a true ~? làbārìn gàskiyā nè? detective, love ~ làbārìn sī'aidî, sòyayyà.

**stout** adj (mài) jìkī m, (mài) gwā6ī m, (mài) ƙibà f.

**stove** n (tradit.) murhù m ⟨a-u⟩, (modern) kūkà m, [F] kìzìnyêř f; (esp. gas) gâs kūkà m, řashô m, [F] řeshô m.

**straight** 1. adv a. (of a direction) sak idph, ciř idph: the road is very ~ hanyà tā tsayà ciř; be, go ~ mīƙè v4: go ~ to the end of the road kù mīƙè sōsai hař ƙarshen lāyìn; stand up very ~ mīƙè ciř. b. (of an action) kâi tsàye: he came ~ into the room yā shigō dākì kâi tsàye; keep ~ on this road bi hanyàř nân kâi tsàye = bi hanyàř nân sak; he went ~ to Kano yā nùfi Kanò kâi tsàye. c. (on the spot) nan tàke: I told him ~ out that he was a fool nā gayà masà nan tàke cêwā shī sākařai nè; ~ away nan dà nan. d. (correctly): put your cap on ~ kà gyārà hùlařkà daidai.
2. adj mīƙaƙƙē adj: ~ hair mīƙaƙƙen gāshì = gāshì mài tsawō; a ~ line is the shortest distance between two points lāyì mīƙaƙƙē shī nè mafì gajařtā tsàkānin wuřārē biyu; (fig.) he kept a ~ face bài sākè fuskàřsà ba.

**straighten** v a. (make straight) mīƙař (dà) v5: ~ out a wire, hair mīƙař dà wayà, gāshì; it is ~ed out yā mīƙè. b. (adjust) daidàità v1; ~ up (a place) gyārà v1: this room is a mess, let's ~ it up dākìn nân yā yi kaca-kaca, mù gyārà shi.

**strain**[1] n (burden) nauyī m, dàmuwā f: the ~ of work nauyin aikì; he is working under a ~ yanà aikì cikin dàmuwā.
2. v a. (make an effort) yunƙurā v1, yi yùnƙurī m, tāshì tsàye; ~ every nerve yi fàfìtìkà f. b. (a muscle) targàdē v4, guřdè v4: he ~ed his back while lifting the load yàyin ɗagà kāyā bāyansà yā guřdè.

**strain**[2] v (liquids) tācè v4.

**strainer** n rāriyā f, matācī m, matsàmī m.

**strand** n (ply) tùfkā f.

**strange** adj a. (alien, unknown) bāƙō adj ⟨i⟩: this is a ~ word wannàn kalmà bàƙuwā cè; a ~ custom, voice bàƙuwař dàbī'à, muryà. b. (new, not familiar) sābō adj ⟨sàbàbbī⟩: there is nothing ~ about it bàbù wani sābon àbù à ciki; what a ~ idea! ji wata sābuwà! c. (different) dàbam adv: I thought it ~ nā ga àbìn yā yi dàbam. d. (odd, puzzling, unexpected): he is a very ~ man shī wani irìn mùtûm nē; he behaved ~ly to us yā sākè manà = yi manà bà-zàta. e. (surprising): a ~ thing wani àbin màmākì.

**stranger** n bāƙō m ⟨i⟩: I'm a ~ in town nī bāƙō nè à gàrin nàn; he is a ~ to me bàn san shì ba.

**strangle** v māƙurè v4, shāƙè v4.

**strap** n (for hanging sth.) marātayī m; (for sandals) maɗaukī m.

**strategy** n dàbāřā f ⟨u⟩; come up with a new ~ (fig.) yi sābon lāle.

stratosphere *n* sararin samà *m*.

straw *n* hakì *m; (a piece of ~, a ~ for drinking)* tsinkē *m* ⟨aye⟩; *(crushed cornstalk used for animal bedding)* tattakā *f.*

stray *v (get lost)* yi makuwā *f,* 6atà *v3b:* the child ~ed from home yāròn yā yi makuwā bài san indà gidansà yakè ba; ~ from a road, path rātsè *v4;* ~ from one's path, ideals fandàrē *v4,* baudè̀ wà *v4:* he has ~ed from the right path yā fandàrē dàgà tafarkì madàidàicī.

stream[1] *n* ƙòramā̀ *f* ⟨u⟩; *(small)* rà̀fī *m* ⟨uka⟩.

stream[2] *v* a. *(of tears):* tears ~ed down her face hawàyē sun zubō matà. b. *(go toward a place in large numbers)* yi jērìn gwànō *m:* the people were ~ing toward the prayer grounds mutànē nà̀ jērìn gwànō zuwà fīlin ìdī.

street *n* hanyà *f* ⟨oCi⟩, *(smaller)* lāyì *m* ⟨uka⟩, *(esp. paved)* tītì *m* ⟨una⟩: he lives on this ~ yanā̀ zàune à wannàn lāyì; the main ~ of town bàbban lāyìn gàrī; a one-way ~ wanwē *f,* [F] hanyà̀ mài kâi daya.

street light *n* fìtilà̀r tītì *f.*

street sign *n* à̀lāmàr̃ tītì *f,* lambàr̃ tītì *f.*

strength *n* a. ƙarfī *m:* a man of great ~ mùtûm mài ƙarfī sòsai; the ~ of one's beliefs ƙarfin àƙīdà̀. b. *(of sth. built, constructed)* ƙwārī *m,* ƙarkō *m.*

strengthen *v* ƙarfàfā *v1.*

stress *n* a. *(tension)* dàmuwā *f:* ~ can cause headaches dàmuwā nà̀ iyà sâ cīwòn kâi. b. *(Gram.)* ƙarfin wasàlī *m,* jaddàdāwar̃ wasàlī *f.*

stretch 1. *vt* a. mīƙà̀ *v1:* he ~ ed out his hand to take the package yā mīƙà hannunsà yà daukō ƙunshì. b. *(straighten out sth.)* mīƙar̃ (dà) *v5:* ~ a rope mīƙar̃ dà igiyà̀. c. *(~ by tightening)* dāmè̀ *v4:* after the sheepskin is ~ed and dried, it can be used as a prayer mat bāyan an dāmè fātàr̃ rāgō an shānyā zā tà zama būzū. 2. *vi* mīƙè̀ *v4:* the lake ~es for miles tabkìn yā mīƙè̀ sòsai; *(oneself)* yi mìƙà *f,* mīƙè *v4:* he got up and ~ed himself yā tāshì yā yi mìƙà.

stretcher *n* gadon daukàr̃ maràs lāfiyà̀ *m.*

strict *adj* a. *(demanding)* (mài) tsananī *m:* a ~ teacher mālàmī mài tsananī; be ~ tsanàntā *v1:* they are not ~ about enforcing the law bā à̀ tsanàntāwā wajen zar̃taf dà dòkàr̃. b. *(inflexible)* maràs lànƙwàsuwā.

strike[1] 1. *n* yàjì *m,* yājìn aikì *m:* they

are on ~ again sun sākè yàjì; hunger ~ yàjìn cîn àbinci. 2. *v* yi yājìn aikì.

strike[2] 1. *v* a. *(hit)* dòkā *v2* ⟨dūkà̀⟩, bùgā *v2* ⟨bugù̀⟩, dàkā *v2:* why did you ~ him? mè̀ ya sâ ka dòkē shì? b. *(attack)* kai harì. c. *(var. uses):* ~ a bargain sallàmā *v1;* ~ a match ƙyastà/ƙyattà àshānā; ~ a name off a list kashè sūnā dàgà jērìn sūnāyē; the clock struck àgōgo yā yi ƙàrarrawā; he was struck by lightning àr̃ādù tā kashè shi; an idea struck him wata dàbār̃à̀ tā fàdō masà; *(fig.)* they struck up a friendship àbòtā tā ƙullu tsàkāninsù. 2. *n (Mil.)* harì *m:* pre-emptive ~ harìn shàmmà̀cē.

striker *n* mài yājìn aikì *m.*

string *n* a. kìr̃tānì *m:* a ball of ~ ƙullìn kìr̃tānì; trouser ~ mazāgī *m,* zārìyā *f,* là̀wùr̃jē *m.* b. *(of a bow or musical instrument)* tsirkìyā *f.*

stringent *adj* tsàttsaurā *adj.*

strip[1] *n* a. *(of handwoven cloth)* ƙwaryā *f* ⟨ƙòr̃ē⟩. b. *(of food):* cut meat into long ~s yanyànā *v1,* r̃ēdè *v4.* c. *(narrow area of land)* tsīrī *m:* the Gaza ~ tsīrin Gāzà.

strip[2] *v* a. *(a place)* tsiràitā *v1:* the room was ~ped clean an tsiraìtà dākìn; *(esp. by robbers)* wāshè *v4:* the robbers ~ped his house bare 6àrāyī sun wāshè gidansà. b. *(take clothing off)* tū6è̀ *v4,* tsìraità *v3,* yi tsìrārā̀ *f:* he ~ped off his clothes yā tū6è̀ kāyansà; ~ a bed dàukè shìmfidàr̃ gadō. c. *(bark or covering)* daidàyē *v4,* sassàƙē *v4,* tàyā *v2; (sth. joined, stuck onto sth.)* 6am6àrē *v4,* cirè *v4:* the wind ~ped the leaves off the trees iskà̀ tā cirè ganyàyen bishiyōyì. d. *(so. from a position)* tū6è̀ *v4:* he was ~ped of his title an tū6è̀ shi dàgà sàrautà; ~ so. of his dignity cī dà mutuncìn w. = *(fig.)* kētà wà r̃ìgar̃ mutuncì.

stripe *n* a. *(band of color)* rātsì *m.* b. *(Mil., chevron)* igiyà̀ *f* ⟨oCi⟩, [F] gàlô *m.*

striped *adj* (mài) rātsì-rātsì.

strive *v* dāgè̀ *v4,* hìmmàtu / hìmmàntu *v7,* nūnà ƙwàzō, yi fāmā *f:* he strove to finish on time yā dāgè̀ kàn gamà aikìnsà cikin lōkàcī.

stroke[1] *n (blow)* bugù *m,* dūkà̀ *m; (by any sharp weapon)* sārā *m:* a ~ of the sword sāran takōbì; *(fig.)* have a ~ of luck yi gàm dà Kàtar̃.

stroke[2] *v* shāfà̀ *v1:* he ~d the cat ya shāfà kyânwā.

**stroke**³ *n* (*Med., believed to be caused by a spirit*) shân Innà *m;* he suffered a ~ Innà tā kāmā shi.

**stroll** *n* yāwò *m*: go for a ~ yi yāwò = mīƙè ƙafā = shā iskā.

**strong** *adj* a. (*of psn., animal*) (mài) ƙarfī *m*, ƙàƙƙarfā *adj*: the boy is not ~ enough yāròn bā shi dà ƙarfī ìsasshē; he is as ~ as an lion ƙarfī gàrē shì kàmař zākì; she is ~er than you think ita ƙàƙƙarfā cē fìye dà yâddà kakè zàtō; it is as ~ as can be ƙàƙƙarfā nè na ƙìn ƙāràwā. b. (*of sth. built, constructed*) (mài) ƙwārī *m*, (mài) ƙarkō *m*, (mài) amincī *m*: the box was built very ~ly an yi àkwātìn dà ƙwārī.

**structure** *n* sīgā *f* ⟨oCi⟩.

**struggle** 1. *n* a. (*difficulty*) fāmā *f*, gwagwàřmayā *f*: they're having a ~ to get ahead sunā gwagwàřmayā sù sāmi cî-gàba. b. (*life's daily tasks, cares*) dàwàiniyā *f*: the ~ to support oneself dàwàiniyař nēman àbinci. c. (*strife*) dāgā *f*, jìdālì *m*, gwagwàřmayā *f*: class ~ (*Pol.*) gwagwàřmayař àl'ummā. 2. *v* a. (*with a problem, difficulty*) yi gwagwàřmayā *f*, yi fāmā *f*, yi jìdālì *m*, shā fāmā dà: he is struggling to feed his family yanā gwagwàřmayař cī dà ìyālìnsà. b. (*physical*) yi kòkawā *f*.

**strut** *v* yi tāƙamā *f*.

**stub** *n* guntū *m*, guntuwā *f* ⟨aye⟩: a cigarette ~ guntuwař sìgāřì; check ~ gìndin cāk.

**stubborn** *adj* (mài) taurin kâi *m*, (mài) kafiyā *f*, (mài) tsàyayyā *f;* be ~ yi taurin kâi, yi kafiyā *f*, dāgè *v4*.

**stuck, be(come)** *v, see* stick².

**student** *n* (*post-primary*) dālìbī *m* ⟨ai⟩; (*primary*) dan makařantā *m* ⟨'yan makařantā⟩; (*of Koranic school*) àmājìřī *m* ⟨ai⟩.

**study** 1. *v* a. (*learn*) kòyā *v2*, (*esp. academic subject*) yi kàřātū *m*: what do you ~ at the university? dà mè dà mè kakè kàřātū à jāmi'ā? b. (*analyze, do research on*) yi nazàřī *m*: he is studying the history of the kolanut trade yanā nazàřin tāřīhìn cìnikin gōřò. 2. *n* a. (*academic work*) kàřātū *m*: complete one's studies, education saukè kàřātū. b. (*analysis*) nazàřī *m*. c. (*a room*) dākìn kàřātū *m*.

**stuff**¹ *n* kāyā *p*, abūbuwā *p;* (*esp. odds and ends*) tàrkàcē *p*.

**stuff**² *v* cunkùsā / cinkùsā *v1*, cūsā *v1*: ~ a pillow cunkùsā matāshin kâi; ~ a

rag into a hole cūsā tsūmmā à rāmì; ~ one's mouth shāƙè bàkī; (*esp. in packing*) kimsā *v1*.

**stumble** *v* yi tuntuɓè *m*: she ~d over a rock tā yi tuntuɓè dà dūtsè.

**stump** *n* a. (*of tree*) kùtutturè *m* ⟨ai⟩, (*of cornstalk after reaping*) tūshìyā *f*. b. (*maimed limb*) dùngū *m*: a leper with a ~ of an arm kuturū mài dùngun hannū.

**stunt** *v* tsumburař (dà) *v5;* be ~ed tsumbùrē *v4*.

**stupid** *adj* a. (*foolish psn.*) wāwā *n* ⟨aye⟩, shāshāshā *n*, sūsùsū *n*, dōlō *m* ⟨aye⟩. b. (*lacking intellingence*) dàƙīƙì *m* ⟨ai⟩: I have never seen such a ~ person bàn taɓà ganin dàƙīƙì kàmař hakà ba. c. (*retarded*) gaulā *n* ⟨aye⟩. d. (*useless*) na banzā *f*, na wòfī *m*: a ~ answer amsàř banzā = amsàř wòfī.

**stupidity** *n* a. (*foolishness*) wāwancì *m*, wāutā *f*. b. (*lacking intelligence*) daƙīƙancì *m*. c. (*uselessness*) aikìn banzā *m*.

**sturdy** *adj* a. (*thick-set psn.*) (mài) gwāɓī *m*, kàkkaurā *adj*. b. (*strong, of things*) (mài) ƙwārī *m*.

**stutter** *v* yi ì'ìnā/ìn'ìnā *f*.

**stye** *n* hazbiyā *f*, kùmbulùgā *f*.

**style** *n* a. (*fashion*) salō *m*, (*esp. of dress*) yàyī *m*: it's out of ~ now bā à yàyinsà yànzu = tsōhon yàyī nè; she always wears the latest ~ kullum tanā sâ sābon yàyī; different ~s salō-salō = salō irì-irì. b. (*in self-expression, writing, speaking*) fàsāhā *f*, salon màganā *m*.

**styrofoam** *n* řōɓā *f*.

**subdue** *v* a. (*overcome*) rìnjāyā *v2*: he ~d his opponent yā rìnjàyi àbōkin karāwā. b. (*so. hysterical*) làllāsā *v2* ⟨lallāshī⟩.

**subject**¹ *n* a. (*topic*) bàtū *m* ⟨uwa²⟩: what is the ~ of the conversation? bàtun mè akè yî? change the ~ sākè bàtū; touch on the ~ of dan yi màganā à kân. b. (*academic*) fannī *m* ⟨oCi⟩: what ~s are you studying? wàdànnè fannōnī kakè kařātū? c. (*Gram.*) mìƙau *m*, fā'ìlì *m* ⟨ai⟩. d. (*Pol.*) mabìyī *m*, mài bî *n*: ~s of the Emir of Kano màsu bîn Sarkin Kanò; a British ~ talàkàn Ingìlà, dan Ingìlà.

**subject**² *v* gānā wà *v1*: they ~ed him to torture sun gānā masà àzābà.

**subjugate** *v* bī dà / biyař (dà) *v5*.

**submerge** *v* nitsè *v4*, nitsař (dà) *v5*.

**submissive** *adj*: be ~ (*fig.*) mīƙà wuyā.

**submit** *v* a. (*present*) gabātař (dà) *v5*, mīƙà *v1*: ~ a report mīƙà řahōtò; ~ your request through the proper channels kà gabātař dà bùkātàřkà ta hanyàř dà ta dācè. b. (*be resigned*) ~ to hàƙurà dà *v3*, dànganà dà *v3*: ~ to the will of God dànganà dà ƙaddaràƙ Allàh.

**subsequently** *adv* dàgà bāya, dàgà bì-sānī.

**subservient** *adj* (mài) fādancī *m*; speak in a ~ manner yi fādancī = yi bàfādìyaƙ màganà.

**subside** *v* (*of rains*) tsagàitā *v1;* let's leave now that the rain has ~ed a bit mù tāshì yànzu tun dà ruwân yā ɗan tsagàitā; (*of wind*) kwântā *v1*, sacè *v4;* (*of fire, heat, dispute*) lafà *v1;* (*of anger, heat*) hūcè *v4;* (*of floods*) jânyē *v4;* (*of swelling*) sacè *v4*, saɓè *v4*.

**subsidy** *n* rangwamè *m*: gasoline ~ rang-wamèn kuɗin mâi.

**subsistence** *n*: the farmers are living at a ~ level manòmā sunà ràyuwaƙ hannū bakà hannū ƙwaryā.

**substance** *n* a. (*thing*) àbù *m*, àbā *f* ⟨uwa²⟩ (*in the genitive, use* àbin): salt is a useful ~ gishirī àbù nē mài àmfànī. b. (*gist of sth.*) gundārī *m*: this is the ~ of what he said gà gundārin àbin dà ya fàɗā.

**substitute** 1. *n* madàdī *m*: bring a ~ for the one that's broken kàwō madàdin wândà ya fashè.
2. *v* canjà / canzà *v1*: ~ a pencil for a pen canjà fensìƙ dà bīƙò; ~ for so. cànjà *v2* ⟨canjì⟩: Audu ~d for Garba Audù yā cànji Gaƙbà.

**subtract** *v* ɗēbè *v4*: 8 ~ed from 17 is 9 shā bakwài à ɗēbè takwàs taƙà kè nan.

**subtraction** *n* ɗēbèwā *f*.

**subversive** *n* ɗan hūrà-wutā *m*.

**subvert** *v* yi yankan bāyā *m*: a plot to ~ the government shirìn yankan bāyan gwamnatì.

**succeed** *v* a. (*have success*) yi nasaƙà *f*, ci nasaƙà *f*, yi mùwāfakà *f*, dācè *v4*, yi dācè *m*: he always ~s in getting what he wants kullum yanà mùwāfakàƙ àbin dà yakè sô; may God help you ~ Allàh yà sà à dācè = Allàh yà yi makà mùwāfakà; who knows whether he will ~ or not kō yā ci kō yā fàɗì wà ya sanì; my plan did not ~ dàbàƙàtā bà tà ci ba. b. (*be a successor*) mayè *v4*, gàdā *v2*: he ~ed his father as head of the company yā mayè mahàifinsà à shūgabancìn kamfànī; he ~ed me as the English teacher yā gàjē nì wajen kōyaƙ dà Tūƙancī; he has no one to ~ him bâ shi dà magàjī.

**success** *n* a. (*victory*) nasaƙà *f* ⟨oCi⟩: may God grant us ~ Allàh yà bā mù nasaƙà = Allàh yà sà mù dācè; all his efforts

met with no ~ duk ƙòƙarinsà bài ci nasaƙà ba; he is at the height of his ~ yanà gāniyaƙ cîn dūniyàƙsà = yanà shā biyunsà. b. (*financial*) yi kàsuwā *f*: his book was not a ~ littāfìn dà ya wallàfà bài yi kàsuwā ba. c. (*advancement*) cî-gàba *m*.

**successful** *adj*: be ~ ci nasaƙà *f*, dācè *v4*: I tried to find it but wasn't ~ nā yi ƙòƙarin sāmùnsà àmmā bàn dācè ba; he is ~ Allàh yā bā shì.

**succession** *n*: one in the line of ~ to the throne mài jiràn gadon sàrautà; in ~ bì dà bî.

**successive** *adj* (*one after the other*): he made 3 ~ tries yā gwadà sàu ukù à jère; he had ~ losses (*fig.*) hàsaƙà tā zō masà gōmà dà gōmà.

**successor** *n* magàjī *m*.

**such** *adj* irìn wannàn: ~ joy farin cikì irin wannàn; don't talk ~ nonsense kadà kà yi irìn wannàn zàncen banzā; we have never had ~ cold weather bà mù taɓà jîn irìn wannàn sanyī ba; ~ as kàmaƙ, mìsālìn: ~ as what? kàmaƙ mè? countries ~ as Ghana ƙasàshē kàmaƙ Gānà = ƙasàshē mìsālìn Gānà; some ~ thing àbù kàzā; we bought many ~ things mun sàyi abūbuwà kàzā dà kàzā.

**suck** *v* tsōtsà *v1* ⟨tsōtsā⟩ *f*: ~ one's thumb, candy tsōtsà hannū, àlēwà; ~ in (*force-fully*) zūƙà *v2*.

**suckle** *v* shā dà / shāyaƙ (dà) *v5*.

**sudden** *adj & adv* a. (*without warning*) bà-zàta *adv*: he gave a ~ cry yā yi kūkā bà-zàta; all of a ~ bà zàtō bà tsàmmānì, faƙat ɗaya: all of a ~ the lights went out faƙat ɗaya fìtìlun nàn sukà mutù; a ~ death mutuwàƙ fuji'à. b. (*esp. of noise, appearance of sth.*) kwaràm *idph*: we heard a ~ noise mun ji mòtsī kwaràm.

**suddenly** *adv* (*unexpectedly*) bà zàtō bà tsàmmānì; (*of noise, appearance*) kwaràm *idph*, kwatsàm *idph*: a hyena ~ appeared kūrā tā ɓullō kwaràm; move ~ yi wuf *idph*: he ~ leaped up on the horse yā yi wuf yā hau dōkìn; get up ~ yi faƙat *idph*.

**suds** *n* kumfā *m*.

**sue** *v* kai ƙāraƙ w.

**suet** *n* kitsè *m*.

**suffer** 1. *vi* wàhalà *v3*, shā wàhalà *f;* make so. ~ bā w. wùyā, wuyātaƙ (dà) *v5*.
2. *vt* shā *v0*: ~ a defeat shā kāshì; ~ a loss (*financial*) yi hàsaƙà; ~ misfortune shā màsīfà; ~ a setback ji jìkī, wàhalà *v3;* ~ from the heat shā fāmā dà zāfī

*subtle*

= yi fāmā dà zāfī; ~ from hunger and thirst shā yunwā dà ƙishirwā; ~ from an illness yi fāmā dà cīwò = shā cīwò; he ~ed a great deal of pain due to the illness yā shā àzābàŕ cīwò.

**suffering** n wàhalà f ⟨oCi⟩; (great hardship, deprivation) tàgàyyaŕà f: inflict ~ on, cause ~ tagayyàŕà v1: famine causes great ~ yunwà tanà tagayyàŕà mutànē.

**suffice** v wàdātā v2, wadātaŕ (dà) v5, ìsā v2: shall I bring food and water? no, water will ~ ìn kāwō àbinci dà ruwā? ā'ā, ruwā zâi wadātaŕ; ~ it to say that... à tàƙàice....

**sufficient** adj mayàlwàcī adj, ìsasshē adj, wàdàtaccē adj: be ~ wàdātu v7, ìsa v3: there is ~ water ruwā yā ìsa; be ~ for wàdātā v2: ₦200 should be ~ for our trip naiŕà dàrī biyu zā sù wàdàcē mù wajen tàfiyà.

**sufism** n sūfàntakà f.

**suffix** n dòriyaŕ ƙarshē f.

**suffocate** v shāƙē v4.

**suffocation** n shāƙēwā f.

**sugar** n sukàŕī m: granulated ~ gàrin sukàŕī; cube of ~ ƙwàyaŕ sukàŕī; use ~ shā sukàŕī: I don't use ~ bā nà shân sukàŕī; brown ~ màzàrƙwailà f.

**sugar cane** n ràkē m, (guinea-corn type) tàkànɗa f: chew ~ shā ràkē.

**suggest** v bā dà shāwaŕà: have you anything new to ~? kō kanà dà wata sābuwaŕ shāwaŕà?

**suggestion** n shāwaŕà f ⟨shāwàŕwaŕī⟩: he accepted my ~s yā kàrɓi shāwàŕwaŕīnā.

**suicide** n kisàn kâi m: he committed ~ yā yi kisàn kânsà.

**suit**[1] n a. (clothing) kwât dà wàndō f. b. (Law) ƙārā f.

**suit**[2] v a. (be appropriate to) càncantà v2, dācè dà v4: this work does not ~ him wannàn aikì bài càncàncē shì ba; Musa is not ~ed to teaching Mūsā bài dācè dà aikìn kōyàŕwā ba. b. (esp. re. clothing, ornaments) kàrɓā v2, dācè dà a v4: that necklace ~s you sarƙàŕ nân tā kàrɓē kì.

**suitable** adj a. (appropriate, of sth.): be ~ dācè v4: this book is ~ for children littāfìn nân yā dācè dà yârā; his plan was the ~ suitable dàbāŕàŕsà tā fi dācèwā. b. (befitting so.) kàmātà v2: this is not a ~ place for you (to be in) wurin nàn bài kàmàcē kì ba.

**suitcase** n jàkā f ⟨una[2]⟩, fàntìmōtì m, [F] bàlîs f.

**suitor** n (of a prev. married woman) bàzawàrī m.

**sulk** v yi zùgum / jùgum idph.

**sullen** adj (mài) fushī m.

**sulfur, sulphur** n faraŕ wutā f.

**sultan** n sarkī m ⟨sarākunà⟩: the S. of Sokoto Sarkin Mùsùlmī.

**sum** 1. n adàdī m, jimlà f ⟨oCi⟩: their ~ is ten adàdinsù gōmà nē; a large ~ of money jimlàŕ kuɗī mài yawà.
2. v: ~ up taƙaitā v1; to ~ it up... à taƙaice....

**summarize** v taƙaitā v1: he ~d what had happened yā taƙaitā yâddà àbîn ya fàru.

**summary** n taƙaitāwā f.

**summer** n, see season.

**summit** n (of mountain) ƙōlōluwā f, tulluwā f; ~ meeting tàron ƙoli m.

**summon** v kirāwō v6.

**summons** n (police) sammācì m, takàŕdaŕ ƙārā f, takàŕdaŕ kirà f, [F] kwàmbùkàsô f: serve a ~ bā dà takàŕdaŕ ƙārā.

**sun** n rānā f: the ~ rises in the east and sets in the west rānā tanà fitôwā à gabàs tà fāɗì à yâmma; suffer from the blazing ~ shā ƙūnàŕ rānā; in the ~ à rāna adv.

**sunbathe** v shânyà kâi à rāna.

**sunbird** n shà-kaucì m.

**sunburnt** adj: she is ~ fātàŕtà tā yi jā.

**Sunday** n Lahàdì f, [F] Dìmāshì f.

**sundown** n fāɗùwaŕ rānā f.

**sun-glasses** n tàbàrau m.

**sunlight** n hasken rānā m.

**sunny** adj: it is ~ today yâu anà rānā; it is too ~ an cikà rānā.

**sunrise** n fitôwaŕ rānā f.

**sunset** n fāɗùwaŕ rānā f.

**sunshine** n hasken rānā m.

**superficial** adj samà-samà adv: a ~ wound ràunī samà-samà.

**superficially** adv samà-samà adv; (of acquaintance) sanìn shānū: I know him ~ nā san shì sanìn shānū.

**superior** 1. adj mafìfīcī adj: Sony makes ~ cassette recorders kamfànin Sony nà yîn mafìfītan ŕakōdōdī; be ~ to fi v0: these are ~ to those wàɗannân sun fi wàɗancân dukà.
2. n (in rank) magàbàcī m: he is our ~ magàbàcinmù nē.

**superiority** n fīfīkò m: show ~ over so. nūnà wà fīfīkò; sense of ~ sôn girmà m, (of older people) mànyàncē m; assert one's ~ fiffīƙē v4: he's always trying to assert his ~ kullum yanà fiffīƙēwā = yā cikà fiffīƙēwā.

**supernatural** adj na gaibù/gaibì m.

**superphosphate** n (fertilizer) sūfà m.

superpowers n mânyan ƙasàshē p.

supersede v: the laws of the constitution ~ all other laws dòkar̃ tsārìn mulkì tā ɗarà kōwàcè dòkā.

superstition n camfì m: I don't believe in ~s bàn yàr̃da dà camfì ba; he is super-stitious yā cikà camfì.

supervise v dūbà v1.

supervision n dūbàwā f.

supplement 1. n ƙārì m.
2. v ƙàrà v1.

supplies n (goods) kāyā m ⟨aki²⟩.

supply v a. (give) bā dà / bāyar̃ (dà) v5. b. (provide) sāmar̃ (dà) v5: the government will ~ all the equipment gwamnatì zā tà sāmar̃ dà duk kāyan aikì.

support 1. v a. (sustain weight) tōkàrē v4: these beams ~ the roof gìnshìkan nàn nà tōkàrè rufìn. b. (provide backing, material ~) gòyi bāyan w., tàllafà v2, tsayà wà v1: we didn't ~ the proposal bà mù gòyi bāyan shāwar̃ar̃; (~ sth. bad, a bad cause) ɗaurè wà gìndī: ~ an oppres-sive government ɗaurè wà mulkìn dan-niyà gìndī. c. (maintain a family, one-self) cī dà / ciyar̃ (dà) v5, riƙè v4: she ~s herself tanà cī dà kântà = tanà cîn gashìn kântà = tanà riƙè kântà.
2. n a. (for weight) madōgarà f, matōkarā f. b. (backing) gōyon bāyā m, tàimakō m: he didn't get the kind of ~ he needed bài sàmi irìn gōyon bāyân dà yakè bùkātà ba. c. (so. on whom one relies) gātā m: a father is the ~ of his children ùbā gātan 'yā'yansà; her youngest son was her sole ~ àutantà shī nè gātantà.

supporter n mài gòyon bāyā n: he has no ~s bâ shi dà màsu gòyon bāyansà; (ad-herent of a group) ɗan X: an NNPC ~ ɗan NNPC.

suppose v a. (presume) zàtā v2, yi tsàmmānì m, yi zàtō m, ji v0: I ~ you know the way? inà zàtō kā san hanyàr̃? = ìn ji kā san hanyàr̃? he is ~d to come inà jî zâi zō. b. (imagine) kàmar̃ à cê: ~ I went instead of you, what could they do? kàmar̃ à cê nā tàfi à màimakonkà, mề zā sù iyà yî? c. (be expected to) kàmātà à cê: he was ~d to have fixed my car for me by now yā kàmātà à cê yā gyārà minì mōtà yànzu; you are ~d to know the answer yā kàmātà à cê kā san amsà.

suppress v a. (quell) kashè v4: ~ a riot kashè tàr̃zōmā. b. (hide) dannè v4, taushè v4: they ~ed the truth sun dannè gàskiyā.

supremacy n fīfīkò m: this law has ~ over that one wannàn dòkā tanà dà fīfīkò kân wancàn.

supreme adj (of God only) maɗaukàkī adj; ~ court kōtùn ƙōli.

sure 1. adv haƙīƙà / hàkīƙà adv: he is ~ to come haƙīƙà zâi zō; be ~ tabbàtà v1: are you ~ about that? kā tabbàtà hakà? be really ~ haƙīƙàncē v4: I am really ~ I saw him at the market nā haƙīƙàncē nā gan shì à kàsuwā; make ~ of sth. tabbatar̃ (dà) v5: please make ~ that it gets done don Allàh kà tabbatar̃ an yī shì; you should make ~ that you have locked the door kà tabbatar̃ dà cêwā kā kullè ƙōfà; for ~ tabbàs adv, bâ shakkà, na haƙīƙà/hàkīƙà: he is com-ing for ~ zuwànsà tabbàs nē = zâi zō bâ shakkà = zuwànsà na haƙīƙà nē.
2. adj tàbbàtaccē adj: a ~ victory tàbbàtacciyar̃ nasar̃à.

surely adv haƙīƙà / hàkīƙà, tabbàs adv, lallē adv, bâ shakkà: it will ~ rain to-morrow bâ shakkà zā à yi ruwā gòbe; the train will ~ be late jirgîn lallē zâi màkarà.

surface n (of sth. solid) kâi m: ~ of the table kân tēbùr̃; (of sth. smooth) samà m: ~ of the water samàn ruwā; near the ~ samà-samà.

surgeon n likità n ⟨oCi⟩.

surgery n aikì m, tìyātà f, [F] òper̃ê m: perform ~ on yi wà aikì = yi wà tìyātà.

surmount v shāwō kân w.a., ci dùngumin w.a.

surname n sūnan mahàifī m.

surplus n rārà f.

surprise 1. n a. màmākì m: it gave me a ~ yā bā nì màmākī = nā yi màmākìnsà; (sth. amazing, wondrous) àbin àl'ajàbī m. b. (secret): take so. by ~ fàki numfāshin w., shàmmātà v2; carry out a ~ attack yi fàr̃makìn bā-zàta, màmayà v2.
2. v a. yi wà màmākì m, bā dà màmākì: she ~d us tā yi manà màmākì = tā bā mù màmākì = mun yi màmākìntà; I'm ~d that you don't know that inà màmākì dà bà kà san hakà ba. b. (an enemy) yi wà fàr̃makì m.

surprising adj (mài) ban màmākì, na màmākì m: a ~ story làbār̃ì mài ban màmākì; how ~! àbin màmākì! = ìkòn Allàh!

surrender v (sth.) sallàmà v1: they ~ed the town to us sun sallàmà manà gàrī; (oneself) bā dà kâi / bāyar̃ dà kâi; (in games) bā dà gàrī.

surround v a. (go around) gēwàyā / kēwàyā
v1: a wall ~s the town an kēwàyà gàrī
dà gānuwā; a town ~ed by hills gàrī mài
kēwàye dà tsaunukà. b. (hem in) ritsà
v1: the enemy has been ~ed an ritsà
àɓòkan gàɓā.

surroundings n kēwàyè m: Kano and its ~
Kanō dà kēwàyèntà.

survey v (geographical) yi sàfiyò m.

survive v ràyu v7: did any of them ~? kō
àkwai wândà ya ràyu à cikinsù? he ~d
his brother wànsà yā rigà shì mutuwà.

suspect 1. v a. (voice suspicion) zàrgā v2,
yi wà zàrgī m: he ~ed me of having
lost his book yā zàrgē nì à kân ɓad dà
littāfìnsà. b. (esp. Law) tùhumà v2, yi
tùhumàř w.: he is ~ed of the murder an
tùhumcē shì dà kisàn kân. c. (doubt) yi
shakkà f: I ~ he is not telling the truth inà
shakkàř màganàřsà. d. (think) yi zàtō
m.
2. n wândà akè tùhumà.

suspend v a. (hang) rātàyā v1. b. (a law,
ruling) sōkè v4. c. (a student) fid dà /
fitař (dà) v5.

suspicion n zàrgī m, (esp. Law) tùhumà
f, he is under ~ anà zàrginsà = anà
tùhumàřsà; he is under ~ of theft anà yi
masà tùhumàř sātà.

suspicious adj àbin zàrgī m: there is something ~ about the matter àkwai àbin
zàrgī cikin màganà; the entire affair is ~
àl'amàřīn duk àbin zàrgī nè; be ~ yi
mùmmūnan zàtō m; be ~ of so. yi shakkàř
w.

suture n ɗinkì m.

swaggering n tàƙamà f, ràngwaɗà f; (esp. of
women) yàngā f.

swallow[1] n (bird) alallakā f.

swallow[2] v hàɗiyà v2, haɗìyē v4: it's difficult to ~ when you have a sore throat in
anà cīwòn màƙōgwàrō, dà wùya a hàɗìyi
wani àbù.

swamp n fàdamà f ⟨u, oCi⟩.

swarm n (of bees) tàron zumà m.

sway 1. vi a. (of sth. in the wind) rau dà /
rawař (dà) v5: the branches are ~ing in
the wind iskā nà rau dà ràssā. b. (of so.
drunk) yi tàngaɗī m. c. (esp. of women
walking) ràngwaɗà v3, (pejor.) buntsùrà
ɗuwàiwai. d. (swing) yi līlò m.
2. vt (persuade) jāwō hankàlin w., shāwō
kân w.

swayback n gàntsarà f: he is ~ed yanà dà
gàntsàrà = gàntsàrarrē nè.

swear v a. (take an oath) rantsè v4, yi
rantsuwā f: I ~ to tell the truth nā rantsè

zân fàɗi gàskiyā; ~ by God rantsè dà
Allàh; ~ in so. (to office) rantsař (dà)
v5; ~ on the Koran, Bible saɓà lāyà;
I ~ to God! tsàkānī dà Allàh! = (fig.)
nā rantsè dà gàjīmàřē! b. (curse so.,
mildly) zàgā v2, yi wà zāgì m, yi tiř dà;
(strongly) là'antà v2. c. (use ~ words, obscene language) yi àshāř m, yi àshāřiyà
f: he swore at us profusely yā ɗuɗɗùrā
manà àshāř; a ~ word (obscene) ɗanyen
bàkī m, mūgùn bàkī m: that is a ~ word,
don't say it kalmàř nân mūgùn bàkī cè,
kadà kà fàɗe tà.

swearing n àshāř m, àshāřiyà f.

sweat 1. n gùmī m, zufà / zuffà f, jìɓī
m: on hearing about the accident, I broke
out into a ~ dà jìn làbàřìn hadàřī sai
gùmī ya karyō minì.
2. v yi gùmī m, yi zufà/zuffà f, yi jìɓī
m: heat makes us ~ zāfī nà sâ mu gùmī;
he ~s easily yanà dà sauƙin jìɓī; he ~ed
profusely yā yi gùmī shàřkaf.

sweater n rīgař sanyī f, sùwaità f ⟨oCi⟩.

sweaty adj: be ~ yi nàsō m: the gown is
all ~ rīgà duk tā yi nàsō = rīgà duk
tā jiƙè dà zufà.

sweep 1. v shārè v4: they ~ the floor daily
sunà shārè dàɓè kōwàcè rānā; ~ up the
dirt yi shārā f.
2. (fig.): he made a clean ~ of the prizes
yā kwāshè kyautukà dukà.

sweepings n shārā f.

sweet adj (mài) zāƙī m, (mài) dāɗī m: she
likes ~ things tanà sôn kāyan zāƙī; this
is too ~ for me zāƙinsà yā yi minì yawà;
really ~ dà zāƙī càřkwai.

sweeten v zāƙàƙā v1.

sweet potato n dànkalì m.

sweet-talk v yi wà rōmon bakà.

sweets n kāyan zāƙī m; (locally made
candy) àlēwà / àlāwà f, see candy.

swell up v kùmburà v3 , yi fushì m.

swelling n kùmburī m; (esp. from bite, sting)
ƙùllūtū / ƙùlūlù m.

swerve v a. gōcè v4, kaucè v4: the car ~d to
avoid hitting the goat mōtà tā gōcè don
kadà tà bankè àkuyà = mōtàř tā kaucè
wà àkuyà don kadà tà bankè ta; ~ off
from (a place) rātsè v1: the truck ~ed off
the road bàbbař mōtà tā rātsè hanyà. b.
(of a line, road) kařkàtā v1: the road ~s
to the right hanyà tā kařkàtā dāma.

swift[1] n (bird) tsàttsēwà f.

swift[2] adj (mài) saurī m.

swim v yi iyò m, yi nìnƙāyà f; know how
to ~ iyà ruwà; (underwater) yi nitsò m.

suspense

swindle 1. *v* zàmbatà *v2*, dàmfarà *v2*, yi wà
cùtā *f*.
2. *n* zàmba *f*, cùtā *f*.
swindler *n* mazàmbàcī *m*, ɗan dàmfarà *m*.
swine *n* àladè *m* ⟨ai, u⟩.
swing 1. *v* yi lïlò *m*, yi shillò *m*: monkeys like to ~ in trees birì nà sô yà yi
lïlò à bishiyà; ~ one's arms about rau
dà hannū = wuřgà hannū; (*fig.*) the market is in full ~ kàsuwā tā cìka màkil;
(*fig.*) the conversation is in full ~ hīřa tā
ci shūnī.
2. *n* lïlò *m*: there are ~s in the market-
place àkwai lïlò à kàsuwā.
switch¹ *n* (*flexible stick for hitting*) tsabgà
*f* ⟨oCi⟩, tsumāgìyā / tsumangìyā *f*.
switch² 1. *v* a. (*change*) sauyà *v1*: he ~ed
languages, seats yā sauyà bàkī, wurin
zamā; he ~ed from Hausa to English yā
sauyà dàgà Hausa zuwà Ingìlīshī. b.
(*turn on*) kunnà *v1*: he ~ed on the light
yā kunnà wutā.
2. *n* a. (*of apparatus, light*) makunnī *m*.
swizzle stick *n* mabuřgī *m*.
swollen *adj* (*from bites, boils*) řudū-řùdù
*idph*; be(come) ~ kùmburà *v3*, yi fushī
*m*.
swoop down *v* dìra *v3*; ~ down on diřař wà
*vdat*: the hawk ~ed down on the rat shāhò
yā diřař wà ɓēřā; (~ & seize) faucè /
fyaucè *v4*, sùřā *v2*.
sword *n* takòbī *m* ⟨u-a⟩, kansakàlī *m* ⟨u-
a⟩: unsheath a ~ zāřō takòbī; ~ sling
hàmīlà *f* ⟨u⟩.
sycophant *n* ɗan fādancī *m*, ɗan bam-
baɗancī *m*.
syllable *n* gaɓà *f* ⟨oCi, Cai⟩: closed ~ gaɓà
mài ɗaurì; open ~ gaɓà maràs ɗaurì.
syllabus *n* manhajà *f*.
symbol *n* àlāmà *f* ⟨u⟩: the crescent is one of
the ~s of Islam hìlālì ɗaya dàgà cikin
àlāmun àddīnìn Musuluncì.
symmetrical *adj* a. (*ordered, balanced*)
(mài) fasàlī *m*: a ~ building ginì mài
fasàlī. b. (*equal*) (mài) hannun rìgā *m*.
symmetry *n* a. (*balance*) fasàlī *m*. b.
(*equality*) dàidaitō *m*.
sympathetic *adj* (mài) jùyàyī *m*, (mài)
jìn tàusàyī *m*: they feel ~ towards us
sunà jùyàyinmù = sunà jìn tàusàyinmù
= tàusàyinmù yā kàmà su.
sympathize *v* yi jùyàyī *m*; (*take pity on*)
ji tàusàyin w., nūnà wà tàusàyī; (*commiserate over loss of belongings*) yi wà
jājē *m*.
sympathy *n* a. jìn tàusàyī *m*, jùyàyī *m*;
(*esp. for sth. lost*) jājē *m*: I expressed my

~ to him for his loss nā yi masà jājē. b.
(*condolences*) tà'àziyyà *f*: we expressed
our sympathies to his family mun yi wà
ìyālìnsà tà'àziyyà.
symptom *n* a. (*sign*) àlāmà *f* ⟨u, oCi⟩. b.
(*of disease*) bàyyanàř cùtā *f*.
syntax *n* ginìn jimlà *m*.
syphilis *n* tùnjērē *m*, (*euphem.*) ƙàbbā *f*.
syringe *n* àllūřà *f* ⟨ai⟩, sìřinjì *m*.
syrup (*medicinal*) māgànī na ruwā *m*, [F]
sìřô *m*.
system *n* a. (*way, method*) hanyà *f* ⟨oCi⟩.
b. (*arrangement*) tsārì *m*: a ~ of government tsārìn gwamnatì.
systematic *adj* (mài) tsārì *m*.

# T

T-shirt n singìlētī f ⟨oCi⟩, tî-shât f, [F] hŏlŏ f.

table n a. tēbùr̃ m ⟨u-a⟩, [F] tābùl m.
b. (of figures) jadawàlī m ⟨ai⟩: multiplication ~ jadawàlin sàu; ~ of contents abūbuwàn dà k̀ē ciki.

tablecloth n zanèn tēbùr̃ m.

tablespoon n bàbban cōkàlī m.

tablet¹ n, see pill.

tablet² n (notebook) littāfìn r̃ùbùtū m, [F] kàyē m.

table tennis n, see ping-pong.

taboo n: it is considered ~ to wear shoes in the presence of your superiors sāɓà wà àl'ādà nē zuwà gàban mânyā dà tàkàlmī.

taciturn adj (mài) shiru-shiru: he is ~ yanà shiru-shiru = shî shiru-shiru nè.

tack 1. v makàlā dà k̀ūsà.
2. n k̀àramar̃ k̀ūsà f.

tactful adj: be ~ yi kaffà-kaffà idph: I am ~ with him inà kaffà-kaffà dà shī.

tactic n dàbār̃à f ⟨u⟩.

tactless adj: be ~ yi kàtōɓarā f.

tadpole n tàlìbambam m.

tag n: price ~ guntuwar̃ takàr̃dar̃ fàr̃āshī.

tail n wutsiyà f ⟨oCi⟩, jèlā f, bindì m: his ~ is wagging wutsiyàr̃sà nà kaɗàwā; heads or ~s kân sarkī kō ɗamarà; (fig.) turn ~ and run ràntā cikin na kàrē.

taillight n danjà f.

tailor n maɗinkī m, tēlà m ⟨oCi⟩.

take v a. ɗaukà v2* (optionally shortens to ɗau when followed by n obj): ~ the book and hold it kà ɗauki littāfìn kà rìk̀ē; he took the responsibility for that yā ɗau nauyin wànnan; ~ steps to combat... ɗauki màtàkan yāk̀ī dà...; ~ (for granted) that ɗaukà cêwā: I ~ it that you've returned home for good nā ɗaukà cêwā kā dāwō gidā k̀ē nan; they took him for a fool sun ɗaukē shì wāwā. b. (get, accept) kàr̃ɓa v2: I took the bundle which was handed to me nā kàr̃ɓi k̀unshìn dà akà mīk̀à minì. c. (convey, carry to a place) kai v*: she was ~n to the hospital an kai tà asìbitì; the boy took the book to school yār̃ò yā kai littāfì makar̃antà; ~ me to the station! kài ni tashà! d. (remove, go off with) tàfi dà v3*, kau dà / kawar̃ (dà) v5: someone has ~n my bag an tàfi dà jàkātā. e. (enter a vehicle) shìga v3, hau v*: we took the train to Kaduna mun hau jirgin k̀asà zuwà K̀àdūna. f. (var. v + obj uses): ~ care (be careful) yi hankàlì m; ~ care of (be responsible for) kùla dà v3: he ~s care of the accounts yanà kùlā dà lìssāfìn kuɗī; ~ good care of sth. àdànā v1, yi àdànī m: he ~s care of his things yanà àdànà kāyansà = yanà dà àdànī; ~ charge of sth. ɗauki nauyin w.a.; ~ to one's heels shēk̀à dà gudù = rūgà à gùje; ~ ill yi rashìn lāfiyà, k̀àmu dà rashìn lāfiyà; ~ leave of so. yi wà ban kwānā; ~ medicine, sugar, a beating shā māgànī, sukàr̃ī, dūk̀à; ~ notice of (pay attention to) kulà dà v1, lùr̃a dà v3: I took no notice of him bàn kulà dà shī ba; ~ place fàru v7, àuku v7, gùdānā v3, wàkànā v3; ~ a photograph ɗauki hŏtō; ~ a prize yi làmbàwân m; ~ a road kāmà hanyà, bi hanyà; ~ time ɗau lōkàcī, ci lōkàcī: studying ~s a lot of time kàr̃àtū nà cîn lōkàcī dà yawà. g. ~ away (confiscate) k̀wāc̀ē v4: they've ~n away his driver's license an k̀wāc̀ē masà lāsìn; ~ away (move, remove) kau dà / kawar̃ (dà) v5: take this chair away kà kau dà kujèr̃ar̃ nàn; this medicine will ~ away the pain māgànin nàn zâi kau dà zāfin jìkī; ~ away all of (remove completely) kwāshè v4: the robbers took away all his belongings ɓàr̃āyī sun kwāshè masà kāyā dukà; ~ away (in subtraction) ɗēbè v4: 10 ~ away 3 is how much? gōmà à ɗēbè ukù nawà k̀ē nan? h. (other v + adv/prep uses): ~ sth. apart cirè v4; ~ after so. (resemble) gàdā v2: he ~s after his father yā gàji (hālin) ùbansà; ~ sth. back (return) kōmà dà v1, mai dà / mayar̃ (dà) v5: he took the damaged goods back to the store yā mai dà kāyā dāmējì à kàntī; ~ off (a garment) tūɓè v4, yāyè v4: she took off her wrap tā yāyè mayāfī; ~ off (flee) shēk̀à dà gudù; ~ out fitar̃ (dà) v5, fitō dà v6: she took the gown out of the trunk tā fitō dà r̃ìgā dàgà cikin àdakà; ~ over a government k̀wāc̀è mulkì; ~ up to (of time) kai v* ((+ time expr.): the work will ~ up to 2 days to do aikìn zâi kai har̃ kwānā biyu; ~ up space tsarè wurī:

this box ~s up too much space àkwàtìn nân yanà tsarè wurī dà yawà.

**talcum powder** n hōdà f.

**tale** n (folktale) tàtsūnìyā f ⟨oCi⟩: tell a ~ yi tàtsūnìyā; (fable, fantasy) hìkāyà f; fairy ~ làbāřìn àljanā m; (legend) àlmàřā f; dilemma ~ àlmàřař hālin ƙaƙà-nikà-yi; a tall ~ (fig.) zūƙì-ta-Màlle m; tell ~s (lie) yi ƙaryā f.

**talent** n hikimà f ⟨oCi⟩; (God-given, natural ability) baiwā f; (skill) iyàwā f, gwànintà f.

**talk** 1. v yi màganà f, yi zàncē m, (converse) yi hīřa f: ~ at length yi dōguwař màganà; we ~ed about him mun yi màganà à kânsà = mun yi hīřařsà; ~ a lot shā màganà; they spent the afternoon ~ing sun yinì sunà hīřa; don't ~ like that kadà kà yi irìn wannàn màganà; ~ privately with so. gànà dà v1: I would like to ~ to you in private inà sôn in gànà dà kai; ~ about so. behind his back yī dà w.: we were ~ing about them at Ladi's mun yī dà sū à gidan Làdì; ~ incoherently yi sàmbàtū m; ~ things over dūbà àbîn dà kè ciki.
2. n a. màganà f, zàncē m: that's mere ~ wannàn zàncē nè kawài = màganàř waiwai cè = zàncēn waiwai nè. b. (conversation) hīřa f. c. (idle, useless) sùřūtù m, hùlūlù m. d. (narrative) làbāřì m ⟨u⟩: give a ~ about bā dà làbāřì à kân = yi màganà à kân: he gave a ~ about his trip to Africa yā bā dà làbāřì à kân tàfiyàřsà Afiřkà. e. (lecture) laccà f: present a ~ gabātař dà laccà.

**talkative** adj (mài) sùřūtù m, (esp. verbose) (mài) kaudī m: children are very ~ yârā sun cikà sùřūtù.

**tall** adj dōgō adj ⟨aye⟩, (mài) tsawō m, (mài) tsayì m: it's a ~ animal dōguwař dabbà cē; the building is ~ ginìn yanà dà tsawō = ginìn dōgō nè; giraffes are ~ řàƙumin dawà nà dà tsayì; how ~ is he? mènē nè tsawonsà? he is ~er than his brother yā fi ɗan'uwansà tsawō; he is 5 feet 10 inches ~ tsayìnsà ƙafà bìyař dà incì gōmà.

**talon** n ƙàmbòrì m, akaifā f.

**tamarind** n (tree or fruit) tsāmiyā f ⟨oCi⟩.

**tame** 1. adj: a ~ animal dabbàř gidā.
2. v (an animal) hōrař (dà) v5; (psn. or animal) bī dà / biyař (dà) v5: she has ~d her husband tā biyař dà mijìntà.

**tan** 1. v (leather) jēmè v4 ⟨jīmà⟩ f.
2. n: he has a ~ fātàřsà tā yi duhù.

**tangerine** n tànjàřîn m.

**tangle** v cukwīkwìyā v1; be(come) ~d cukwīkwìyē v4, hařɗè v4: the thread was all ~d up zàrên yā cukwīkwìyē; (by rope, net) zargè wà v4: his legs got ~d in the net rāgà tā zargè masà à ƙafà.

**tank**[1] n (for storage) tankì m ⟨una⟩: gas, petrol ~ tankìn mâi; (drum for storing water) tànô m, dùřô m, [F] bàsân m.

**tank**[2] n (Mil.) tankà f, ìgwā mài ruwā f, [F] shař dà kwàmbà m.

**tanker** n (for petroleum) mōtàř mâi f, [F] sìtâř f.

**tanner** n majèmī m.

**tannery** n majēmā f.

**tanning** n jīmà f.

**tap**[1] v (knock lightly) ƙyanƙàsà v1, dàddaɓà v2: she ~ped the pot to see if it was strong tā ƙyanƙàsà tukunyā tà ga kō tanà dà ƙwārī; I felt so. ~ping me on the shoulder nā ji wani yanà dàddaɓàtā à kàfaɗà; (on door) ƙwanƙwàsā v1; (esp. edge of a pile, stack) kwakkwàfā v1: I ~ped the stack of papers (to make them even) nā kwakkwàfà tàkàřdū tsaf.

**tap**[2] n (for water) kân famfò m: turn off, turn on the ~ rufè, būdè famfò.

**tape** 1. n a. (magnetic or packing) tēf m: play a ~ sâ tēf. b. (cassette) kàsêt / kàsèt m: blank ~ kàsêt emtì; Scotch ~ salàtîf m.
2. v a. (a recording) ɗaukà à řàkōdà, nàdā v2 ⟨nadì⟩: they ~d the interview sun ɗauki hīřař à řàkōdà. b. (a package) naɗè dà tēf.

**tape measure** n tēf m, [F] mētìř m.

**tape recorder** n řàkōdà f, [F] mànyètô m.

**tapeworm** n tsīla f, farař tsūtsà f.

**tar** 1. n kwàltà f: a ~red road hanyàř kwàltà f.
2. v yi wà kwàltà f.

**tardy** adj: be ~ màkarà v3, yi lattì m.

**target** n a. (thing aimed at) àbin bàřā m: aim at a ~ yi bàřā; hit a ~ sàmi àbin bàřā. b. (goal) būrì / gūrì m.

**tariff** n kudin fitō p.

**tarnish** v dusàshē v4.

**tarpaulin** n tàmfâl m, tantì m.

**task** n a. (duty) dàwàiniyā f: he assigned me the ~ of feeding the animals yā azà minì dàwàiniyař cī dà dabbōbī. b. (errand) hidimà f ⟨oCi⟩: today I have a lot of little ~s to do yâu inà dà hidimōmī dà yawà.

**tassel** n tuntū m ⟨aye⟩.

**taste** 1. n ɗanɗanō m: a sharp ~ mài kaifin ɗanɗanō; the ~ of honey ɗanɗanon zumà; (var. types): (of sth. pleasant, savory) dādī m: it has an unpleasant ~ bā shi dà tasteless 272 tee-shirt

dāɗī = bâ shi dà dāɗin ɗanɗanō; (of sth. sour, going bad) yāmī m: this meat has a bad ~ nāmàn nân nằ dà yāmī; I have a bad ~ in my mouth bā nằ jîn dāɗin bằkîn; (astringent taste of sth. raw) gāfī m, bařcī m.
2. v ɗanɗanà v1, taɓà v1: ~ and see tàɓà kà ji; ~ this to see whether you like it ɗànɗànà wannàn kà ji kō kanā sô; (followed by adj) yi v0 (+ n denoting type of ~): it ~s sweet, sour yā yi zāƙī, tsāmī; it ~s spicy yanā dà yājī; it ~s salty to me inā jîn yā yi gishirī; what does it ~ like? yàyā ɗanɗanontà yakè? it ~s like ginger ɗanɗanon cìtta yakè.
tasteless adj (esp. having no salt or meat) (mài) lāmī m; (of other foods, liquids) salaf idph: this coffee is ~ wannàn kòfī salaf yakè.
tasty adj (mài) dāɗī m. how ~! ɗanɗàni! excl.
tatters n: be dressed in ~ yi tigijin cikin tsûmmā.
tattle on v (gossip about) sārà v2, yi sāran w., yi tsēgùmin w.: he was tattling on you to us yā yi sārankà à wajenmù; (blab) yi wà kwàrmatō m.
tattoo n shâsshāwà f, jàřfā f.
taut adj (mài) tsaurī m: the rope is ~ igiyà tā yi tsaurī; make ~ dāmê v4.
tax 1. n hàřājì m, [F] lanhù m; cattle ~ jangàlī m; market ~ kuɗin kàsuwā p, [F] fàtantī m; collect ~es tārà hàřājì = kàrɓi hàřājì; exempt so. from ~es ɗaukè wà biyàn hàřājì; impose a new ~ on so. dōrà wà sābon hàřājì; raise ~es ƙārà hàřājì.
2. v sâ hàřājì.
tax collector n mài tārà hàřājì n, mài kàrɓař hàřājì n.
taxi n tàsî f, [F] tàkàsî f: take a ~ shìga tàsî; charter a ~ yi shatàř tàsî; ~ driver ɗan tàsî.
tea n shāyì m, tî m: would you prefer ~ or coffee? shāyì ka fi sô kō kòfī?
teabag n jàkař shāyì f.
teach v (so.) kōyà wà v1: he taught us English yā kōyà manà Tūřancī; (a subject) kōyař (dà) v5: what does he ~? mè yakè kōyařwā? he ~es geography yanà kōyař dà làbāřin ƙasā.
teacher n (tradit. Koranic scholar) mālàm m; (in modern schools) mālāmī m ⟨ai⟩, mālàmin makařantā m: he's a history ~ shī mālàmin tārīhì nē; T. Training College makařantař hòron mālàmai f, tītīsî f, [F] kuř nòmâl f.

teaching n aikìn màlàntā / mālàntā m, aikìn kōyâřwā m; ~s of the Prophet Mohammed (complete rites, customs) sunnā f ⟨oCi⟩.
teakettle n būtàř shāyì f.
team n (Sport) ƙungìyā f ⟨oCi⟩, tîm m: the soccer ~ tîm ɗin ƙwallon ƙafà.
teammate n ɗan ƙungìyā m.
teamwork n aikìn gàyyā m.
teapot n būtàř shāyì f.
tear 1. vt a. yāgà v1, kētà v1: he has torn his gown yā yāgà rìgařsà; this cloth is easy to ~ yādìn nân nằ dà sauƙin yāgāwā; (esp. into two) tsāgà v1: I tore the cloth in two nā tsāgà zanè biyu; (rip) ɓarkà v1, ɓarkè v4: the thorn tore my gown ƙayā tā ɓarkà minì rìgā. b. (v + adv/prep uses): ~ sth. apart, to pieces ciccìrà v1: the lion tore the carcass to pieces zākìn yā ciccìrà gāwàř; ~ down (demolish) rūsà v1, rūshè v4; ~ off (remove) cirè v4, kēcè v4: she tore off the paper from the package tā cirè takàřdā dàgà ƙunshì; ~ out, up yāgè v4, tsāgè v4: ~ a page out of a book yāgè shāfì dàgà littāfì; ~ up completely yayyāgà v1, tsattsāgà v1: ~ up into shreds yayyāgà guntū-guntū.
2. vi kēcè v4, yāgè v4, tsāgè v4.
3. n ɓarakā f, karantsàyē m: there's a ~ in the gown àkwai ɓarakà à rìgàř.
tears n hawāyē p: the ~ ran down his cheeks hawāyè sun zubō masà; wipe one's ~ shārè hawāyē; shed ~ yi kūkā m, yi hawāyè: shed ~ of joy yi kūkan muřnà; burst into ~ fashè dà kūkā, ɓarkè dà kūkā; be on the verge of ~ yi ƙwāllā f.
tearful adj: be ~ yi ƙwāllā f: thinking of him made her ~ tùnāninsà yā sâ ta ƙwāllā.
tear gas n bàřkònon tsōhuwā m, tiyàgàs m.
tease v a. (provoke) tsòkanà v2: don't ~ the animals kadà kà tsòkàni dabbōbī. b. (mock, make fun of) zòlayà v2, càccakà v2. c. (cotton) shiɓà v1.
teasing n (joking) bařkwancī m.
teaspoon n ƙàramin cōkàlì m.
technical adj na sànā'à f: ~ college kwalējìn sànā'à f; ~ vocabulary kèɓàɓɓun kalmōmī.
technician n mài gyārā n: a television ~ mài gyāran talàbijìn.
technique n dàbārà f ⟨u⟩: farming ~s dàbāřun nōmā.
technology n fàsāhà f.
tee-shirt n, see T-shirt.

**teething** *n*: the baby is ~ jàrīrì nà haƙōrī.

**telegram** *n* talgìr̃am *m*, [F] tàlgàr̃âm *m*: send a ~ aikà dà talgìr̃am.

**telegraph** *v* aikà dà talgìr̃am *v1*.

**telegraph pole** *n* tangàr̃ăhù *m*.

**telephone** 1. *n* wayà *f*, (*instrument only*) tar̃hō *m*, [F] tàlhō *m*: answer the ~ ɗauki wayà; call so. on the ~ bugà wà wayà; connect a ~ haɗà wayà; disconnect a ~ yankè, cirè wayà; hang up the ~ ajìyè wayà; talk to so. on the ~ yi wà màganà ta wayà; the ~ is ringing wayà, tar̃hō nà bugàwā; what is your ~ number? mēnē nè lambàr̃ wayàr̃kà?
2. *v* bugà wà wayà *v1*, yi wà wayà *f*, yi wà tar̃hō *m*, kirà w. à wayà.

**telescope** *n* madūbin hàngen-nēsà *m*.

**television** *n* talàbijìn *f*; ~ channel tashà *f*; watch ~ yi kallon talàbijìn = kàlli talàbijìn; the ~ set is broken talàbijìn dîn bā tà aikì.

**tell** *v* a. (*sth.*) fàɗā / faɗì *v2**: always ~ the truth kōyàushè kà fàɗi gàskiyā; ~ a lie yi ƙaryā *f*; ~ a folktale yi tàtsūnìyā *f*; ~ time san lōkàcī: we use clocks to ~ time dà àgōgo mukàn san lōkàcī; let's ~ it like it is (*fig.*) bàri mù fēɗè birì har̃ wutsi. b. (~ *sth. to so.*) fàɗà wà *v1*, gayà wà *v1*: I told him what I wanted nā faɗà masà àbîn dà nakè bùkātà; I've told you many times nā shā gayà makà; that's just what I told you! àbîn dà na gayà makà kè nan! ~ me an interesting story bà ni làbār̃ì mài ban shà'awà; ~ so. how to kōyà wà *v1*: ~ me how to do it kōyà minì yâddà akè yînsà; ~ so. off kyār̃ā *v2*, jā ƙùnnen w.: ~ on so. sàr̃à *v2*, yi wà kwàrmatò *m*: he told on me to the teacher yā sàr̃ē nì wajen màlàmī. c. (*say to so.*) cê wà *v**, cê dà w.: they told me to come sun cê minì ìn zō = sun cê dà nī ìn zō; ~ him to wait kà cê masà yà dàkàtā = kà cê dà shī yà dākàtā; do as you are told yi kàmar̃ yâddà akà cê makà; I told you so! (it happened just as I told you!) (*fig.*) bà gà irìntà ba! d. (*inform*) shâidà wà *v1*, sanar̃ (dà) *v5*: someone has already told him about the accident an rigā an sanar̃ dà shī gàme da haɗàr̃în. e. (*differentiate*) rabè *v4*: I can't ~ them apart nā kāsà rabèwā tsàkāninsù.

**teller** *n* (*bank*) kàshiyà *n*, [F] kyàsiyê *m*.

**temper** *n* fushī *m*, zāfin râi *m*; bad-~ed (mài) zāfin râi, (mài) kùfulà; quick-~ed (mài) saurin fushī: treat him gently, he is quick-~ed kì lallàɓā

shi, saurin fushī gàrē shì; even-~ed (mài) sanyin zūcìyā, (mài) lāfiyà: she is an even-~ed person màcè cē mài sanyin zūcìyā; evil-~ed (mài) baƙar̃ zūcìyā; good-~ed mài lāfiyà; ill-~ed (mài) baƙin râi, tsagèr̃a *n*; lose one's ~ hàr̃zuƙà *v3*, hàsalà *v3*, kùfulà *v3*, fùsātà *v3*, yi fushī *m*; make so. lose his ~ har̃zùƙà *v1*, fusātà *v1*.

**temperament** *n* hālī *m* (aye): that's his ~ hālinsà kè nan.

**temperate** *adj*: a ~ climate madàidàicin yanàyī.

**temperature** *n* a. (*of climate*) yanàyī *m*: what is the ~ today? yàyà yanàyī yakè yâu? b. (*of body*) zāfin jìkī *m*; take so.'s ~ aunà zāfin jìkin w. c. (*fever*) zàzzàɓī *m*: he has a ~ yanà zàzzàɓī.

**temple** *n* (*of worship*) dākìn ìbādà *m*.

**temporary** *adj* bà na dindìndin ba; ~ job aikì na ɗan lōkàcī.

**tempt** *v* rayà / riyà wà *v1*: sometimes I was ~ed to steal the money wani lōkàcī zūcìyātā tā rayà minì ìn sàci kuɗin; I don't drink but I'm sometimes ~ed bà nà shân giyà àmmā wani lōkàcī inà shà'awà; (*esp. by the Devil*) r̃ùɗā *v2*, gwadà *v1*: he was ~ed by the Devil Shàiɗàn yā r̃ùɗē shì.

**temptation** *n* (*esp. sexual desire*) jàr̃abà *f* (u).

**ten** *quant* gōmà *f* (oCi); count by ~s ƙirgà da gōmà-gōmà= ƙirgà dà gōmōmī; ~ times ~ gōmà sàu gōmà.

**tenacious** *adj* tsàyayyē *adj*.

**tenacity** *n* taurin kâi *m*, tsàyayyà *f*.

**tenant** *n* ɗan hayà *m*.

**tend**[1] *v* (*animals*) yi kīwò *m*.

**tend**[2] *v* fayè / fiyè *v4*: she ~s to get angry easily tā fayè saurin fushī.

**tender**[1] *adj* (*e.g. of meat*) (mài) taushī *m*, (mài) laushī *m*: this meat is really ~ nāmàn nân dà taushī yakè.

**tender**[2] *n* (*bid on a contract*) tandà *f*.

**tendon** *n* (*Achilles*) agàrā *f*.

**tennis** *n* wàsan tanìs *m*, [F] tênîs *m*: ~ ball bâl dîn wàsan tanìs *f*; ~ net r̃āgar̃ tanìs *f*; ~ shoes kambàs *m*, [F] kìr̃âf *f*.

**tense** *n* (*Gram.*) lōkàcī *m*: future ~ lōkàcī na gàba; past ~ lōkàcîn dà ya wucè; the present ~ lōkàcī mài cî.

**tension** *n* a. (*stress*) dàmuwā *f*: he is under a lot of ~ yanà cikin dàmuwā = yanà cikin wani hālì. b. (*tautness*) tsaurī *m*, dāmēwà *f*: increase the ~ of sth. dāmè *v4*, dāmar̃ (dà) *v5*.

*[handwritten margin note:] à kân wucin-gàdi **

*[handwritten footnote:]* * Telephone message saying a line is temporarily out of service: Wannan lambar da aka buga a`oar tsai da ita na wucin-gadi. 'The number you have dialed is temporarily out of service.'

tent *n* laimã *f* ⟨oCi⟩, tantì *m*: set up, dismantle a ~ kafà, cirè tantì.

tenth *quant* na gōmà; one-~ ushìrī *m*.

tepid *adj* ⟨mài⟩ ɗan ɗùmī *m*.

term *n* a. (*predetermined period of time*) ajàlī *m*: his ~ has been extended an ƙārã masà ajàlī. b. (*school session*) fataɽàɽ kàɽātū *f*. c. (*in prison*) ōdã *f*: he's been given a ~ of 2 years an yi masà ōdã shèkarã biyu.

terminal[1] *n* tashã *f* ⟨oCi⟩: bus ~ tashàɽ mōtã.

terminal[2] *adj*: ~ illness cīwòn ajàlī.

terminology *n*: glossary of technical ~ jērìn kèɓaɓɓun kalmōmī.

termite(s) *n* (*white*) gàrã *f*; (*flying*) gìnã *f*; (*large*) zagō *m*; ~ hill sūrì / shūrì *m*.

terms *n* a. (*conditions*) shaɽuɗɗã *p*: what are your ~? mēnē nè shaɽuɗɗànkà? set ~s azà shaɽuɗɗã; come to ~ daidàitā *v1*, shiryà *v1*: they've come to ~ with each other sun shiryà dà jūnā. b. (*relations*): be on good ~ ɗāsà *v1*, jìtu *v7*, shàƙu *v7*: they are on good ~ sunà ɗāsàwā = sun jìtu; be on equal ~ zama ɗaya; in ~ of (*regarding*) gàme dà.

terrible *adj* (*bad, severe*) (mài) tsananī *m*, ƙàzāmī *adj* ⟨ai⟩, mūgù *adj* ⟨miyàgū⟩: a ~ accident ƙàzāmin haɗàrī = mūgùn haɗàrī; there is a ~ war going on there anà yàƙì mài tsananī can; how ~! àyyà! *excl.*

terrific *excl* tùbaɽkallã! *excl*, bâ dāmā! *excl*: the race was ~! sukùwaɽ nàn bâ dāmā!

terrify *v* firgìtā *v1*, tsōrataɽ (dà) *v5*, rāzànā *v1*; become terrified fìrgità *v3*, ràzanà *v3*, tùnzurà *v3*: she became terrified as the hyena approached tā ràzanà dà kūrā ta ƙaɽātō.

terrifying *adj* mài firgìtâwā, (mài) ban tsòrō *m*: the storm was ~ iskà tanà dà ban tsòrō.

territory *n* a. (*area*) yankì *m* ⟨una⟩: we are now in enemy ~ yànzu mun ìsa yankìn àbòkan gàbā. b. (*country*) ƙasā *f* ⟨aCe⟩.

terror *n* tsòrō *m*, ràzanà *f*.

terrorism *n* ta'addancì *m*; act of ~ ta'àdda *f*; commit ~ yi ta'àdda.

terrorist *n* ɗan ta'àdda *m*.

test 1. *v* a. jaɽɽàbā *v1*, gwadà *v1*. b. (*examine critically, weigh alternatives*) jinjìnā *v1*: you should ~ his words to find out his real intentions sai kà jinjìnà màganàɽsà don kà gànè nufìnsà. 2. *n* jaɽɽàbâwā *f*, gwajì *m*: pass a ~ ci jaɽɽàbâwā = yi fāsìn.

testament *n*: Old T. Àttauɽā *f*, Tsōhon Àlkawàɽī *m*; New T. Lìnjīlā *f*, Sābon Àlkawàɽī *m*.

testicles *n* gōlō *m* ⟨aye⟩, (*euphem.*) maràinā *f*, ƙwàlàtai *p*, tsuwãwū / tsuwai *m*; (*esp. enlarged from hernia*) gwaiwā *f*.

testify *v* yi shaidã *f*, bā dà shaidã: I will ~ to his honesty zān bā dà shaidàɽ gàskiyaɽsà; ~ at a trial yi shaidã à shàɽi'ã; ~ for so. yi wà shàidū.

testimonial *n* shaidàɽ halī *f*.

testimony *n* shaidã *f* ⟨u⟩.

tête-à-tête *n* gānàwā *f*.

tether 1. *n* gindī *m* ⟨aye⟩, tālālā *f*; I'm at the end of my ~ nā yi duk àbin da zân iyã; ~ing post turkè *m* ⟨a-a⟩. 2. *v* yi wà turkè *m*, yi wà tālālā *f*.

textbook *n* littāfì *m* ⟨littàttàfai⟩.

textile mill *n* masāƙā *f*.

textiles *n* yādì *m* ⟨uka[2]⟩.

than *conj* a. (*in comparisons, use vbl. constr. with* fi *v0*): this is larger ~ that wannàn yā fi wancàn girmā; he can't be more ~ 10 years old bà zâi fi shèkarà gōmà dà haihùwā ba; his house is smaller ~ yours gidansà yā fi nakà ƙanƙantà; less ~ ƙasà dà; be less ~ gazà *v1*, yi ƙasà dà: there are no less ~ 50 people there yawàn mutànè bài gazà hàmsin ba; more ~ fìye dà: it will take a little more ~ one hour zâi ɗau fìye dà awà gùdā; other ~ ban dà, sai: no one else saw her other ~ Musa bâ wândà ya gan tà sai Mūsā. b. (*in contrasting clauses*): had better do X ~ Y gāra X dà Y (+ *subjunct.*): you'd better go now ~ to wait any longer gāra kà tàfi yànzu dà kà ƙārà dākàtâwā; no sooner X ~ Y X kè̀ nan (sai) Y, X kè̀ dà wùyā (sai) Y: no sooner had he left ~ you returned tàfiyaɽsà kè̀ dà wùyā kukà dāwō.

thank *v* gōdè̀ wà *v4*, yi wà gòdiyā *f*: he ~ed his listeners for their support yā gōdè̀ wà màsu sàurāronsà don gōyon bāyansù; I ~ed him for his help nā yi masà gòdiyā don tàimakonsà; ~ you very much! (*esp. on receiving gift*) nā gōdè̀, Allàh yà amfānā! ~ God! àlhamdù lillàhì! *excl.*

thanks 1. *n* a. gòdiyā *f*: I give my heartfelt ~ to… inà matuƙaɽ gòdiyā gà…; special ~s gòdiyā ta mùsammàn; extend one's ~ isaɽ dà gòdiyā: please extend my ~s to them kà isaɽ minì dà gòdiyātā = kà mīƙà musù gòdiyātā; many ~s for your efforts! sànnu dà ƙōƙarī! many ~s for kindness! sànnu dà wàhalà! we give ~s to God mun gōdè̀ wà Allàh = mun

gōdè Allàh. b. (*so.'s influence*): ∼ to
àlbařkàcin *prep*: ∼s to you, they have
become successful àlbařkàcinkà sukà yi
nasařà; they succeeded ∼s to my influence sun sàmi àlbařkàcīnā.
**2.** *excl* (*said by superior*) mādàllā! (*said
by inferior*) nā gōdè! no ∼ I've already
eaten ā'à nā gōdè nā àmfānà = ā'à,
àlhamdù lillāhì! no ∼! (*said by seller
refusing buyer's offer*) àlbařkà! *excl.*

**that 1.** *det & pro* **a.** (*there*) wancàn *m*,
waccàn *f*, waɗàncân *p*; cân (*changes to*
càn *if prec. tone is H*): what is ∼?
mēnē nè wancàn? those are his waɗàncân
nāsà nē; ∼ date-palm tree wancàn
dabīnò = dabīnòn cân; ∼ tamarind
tree waccàn tsāmiyā = tsāmiyař càn;
those deleb-palms waɗàncân gìgìnyū =
gìgìnyun càn. **b.** (*distant*) wàncan *m*,
wàccan *f*, waɗàncan; can (*if prec. tone
is H, that tone changes to F*): ∼ building (way over there) wàncan ginì =
ginìn can; ∼ school wàccan makařantā
= makařantář can; those are granaries
wàɗàncan rumbunà nē. **c.** (*specific, the
one in question*) wànnan *m/f*, waɗànnan
*p*; nan (*if the prec. tone is H, that tone
changes to F*): ∼ (*specific*) tree wànnan
itàcē = itàcēn nan; do you remember
∼ house that we were talking about? kā
tunà dà gidân nan dà mukè màganà à
kâi? in ∼ year, there was a terrible famine
à cikin shèkarář nan, an yi wata yunwà
mài tsananī.
**2.** *det* (*to emphasize possession, use full
poss. pro before n + specific def art*): ∼
horse of yours nākà dōkìn; ∼ wife of
his tāsà màtář; ∼ house of theirs nāsù
gidân.
**3.** *rel pro* dà; wândà *m*, wâddà *f*, waɗàndà
*p*: the cap ∼ he sewed hùlâř dà ya ɗinkà
= hùlā wâddà ya ɗinkà; the people ∼
were working yesterday mutànên dà sukè
aikì jiyà = mutànē waɗàndà sukè aikì
jiyà.
**4.** *conj* **a.** (*to introduce clauses*) cêwā
/ cêwař: I think ∼... inà tsàmmānìn
cêwā...; she told me ∼ she would come tā
gayà minì cêwā zā tà zō; I know ∼ they
have already left nā san cêwař sun rigā
sun tāshì. **b.** so ∼, in order ∼ don *conj*:
I told him so ∼ he would be informed nā
gayà masà don yà sanì.
**5.** *adv* (*in that way, manner*) hakà *adv*:
don't do ∼ kadà kà yi hakà; ∼ is right
hakà daidai nè; ∼ is to say wàtàu: the
robe was in shreds, ∼ is to say, it's worn

out rìgā tā fatattàkē, wàtàu tā mutù
kè nan.
**thatch 1.** *n* jinkā *f*; (*old, used*) būnū *m*; lay
∼ on roof frame bàibayà *v2*.
**2.** *v* yi wà ɗākì jinkā, jinkè *v4*.
**thaw** *v* narkè *v4*.
**the** *def art* **a.** (*usu. not translated but
implied by context*): ∼ horse ran away
dōkì yā gudù; what is ∼ problem? ìnā
màtsalà? ∼ rich and ∼ poor mawàdàtā dà
matàlàutā; ∼ lion is a very strong animal zākì dabbà cē mài ƙarfī sōsai. **b.**
(*specific, the one in question*) -n *m/p*, -ř
*f* (*when suffixed to a syllable with H tone,
that tone changes to F*): I saw ∼ horse,
car, teachers (that we were talking about)
nā ga dōkìn, mōtář, màlàmân; ∼ robe
(in question) has been washed an wankè
rìgâř; he didn't come with ∼ money (in
question) bài zō dà kuɗìn ba.
**theater** *n* **a.** (*for plays*) gidan wàsan kwaikwayō *m*, [F] tìyātìř *m*; (*for movies*) (gidan) sìlìmâ / sìlìmân *m*. **b.** (*operating
room*) ɗākìn tìyātà *m*, [F] ɗākìn òpèřê
*m*.
**theft** *n* sātā *f* ⟨e²⟩: there have been several
cases of ∼ an shā yin sàce-sàce.
**their, theirs** *pro*, see Appendix A.
**them** *pro*, see Appendix A.
**theme** *n* (*literary*) jīgò *m*: ∼ of the story
jīgòn làbāřì; ∼ song tākè *m*.
**themselves** *pro*, see self, Appendix A.
**then** *adv* **a.** (*next in time*) sā'àn nan / sàn
nan *conj*: we went to the market and ∼ returned home mun tàfi kàsuwā sā'àn nan
mukà kōmō gidā; drink some water first,
∼ give him the rest sai kā shā tùkùna
sàn nan kà bā shì saurā; I will see you
tomorrow and ∼ I'll tell you zân gan kì
gòbe, sàn nan ìn gayà mikì. **b.** (*at that
time*) à lōkàcîn: we were children ∼ munà
yârā à lōkàcîn; since ∼ tun lōkàcîn,
tun rân nan; I haven't seen him since ∼
bàn gan shì ba tun lōkàcîn; before ∼
kàfìn lōkàcîn nan; now and ∼ lōkàcī-
lōkàcī, lōtò-lōtò *adv*; right there and ∼
nan tàke, nan dà nan. **c.** (∼ *and only* ∼)
kànà *conj*: eat first ∼ you may go kù ci
tùkùna kànà kù tàfi. **d.** (*in that case*)
in hakà nē: ∼ you ought not to tell him
in hakà nē, bài kyàutu kà gayà masà
ba.
**theology** *n* ilìmin sanìn Allàh *m*.
**theory** *n* nàzàřiyyà *f*, řa'ì *m*: a scientific ∼ nàzàřiyyař kìmiyyà; a sound ∼
nàzàřiyyà mài mà'ànā; in ∼ à nàzàřce:
in ∼ that's right, but in practice it is not

so à nàzàřce daidai nĕ àmmā à àikàce
bā hakà ba.

therapy n (esp. physical ~) gashĭ m.

there[1] adv a. cân adv: I saw it ~ on that
table nā gan shì cân kân wancàn tēbừ.
b. (distant or previously mentioned) nan
adv: she is over ~ by that tree tanā nan
kusa dà wàccan bishiyā̀; I think he is
still ~ (where we were talking about before) jì nakĕ yanā nan hař yànzu. c.
(far away, not visible) can adv: he lives
~ in that village far away yanā̀ zàune à
wani ƙauyè can mài nīsā. d. (in that
place) à wurîn: I saw him ~ nā gan shì
à wurîn; here and ~ (interspersed, scattered sparsely about) jēfì-jēfì adv: in
the desert, trees are found here and ~
cikin hàmādā, anā̀ sāmùn itàtuwā̀ jēfì-
jēfì. e. (in pointing at sth., so.): ~ X
is gā̀ X nan, gā̀ X can: where is Dan-
tata Road? ~ it is over ~ by that building
īnā tītīn Dantātā? gā̀ ta can kusa dà
wàncan ginì.

there[2] pro a. (stating existence of sth.): ~
is, ~ are (in affirm.) àkwai, dà (+ n); (in
neg.) bābù, bâ (+ n): ~ are many kinds of
foods àkwai àbinci irì-irì; are ~ any
left? àkwai saurā? = dà saurā? yes, ~
are ī, àkwai sù = ī, dà sū; ~ aren't
any peanuts left bābù sauran gyàɗā = bâ
sauran gyàɗā; (in folktales): once upon a
time ~ was a... wata rānā an yi wani....
b. (being available) nan adv: are ~ any
batteries? yes, ~ are, on that shelf àkwai
bātuřā? ī sunā nan à kân kantàř cân.

therefore adv don wannàn, don hakà,
sabồdà hakà.

thermometer n tsinken awòn zāfin jìkī
m.

thermos bottle n fìlâs m, tàřmâs m.

these det & pro, see this.

thesis n a. (fundamental proposition)
manufā f ⟨oCi⟩: the ~ of his book is... man-
ufař littāfìnsà ita cĕ.... b. (dissertation) kundī m ⟨aye⟩.

they pro, see Appendix A.

thick adj (mài) kaurī m: how ~ is that
board? mēnē nĕ kaurin kātākon càn? it
has a ~ skin yanā̀ dà fātā mài kaurī; a
~ blanket bàřgō mài kaurī = bàřgō mài
nauyī; a ~ forest kurmī mài duhū; be ~
with (smoke, dust, etc.) tuřnìƙē v4: the
room is ~ with smoke ɗākì yā tuřnìƙē dà
hayāƙī; (fig.) he's in ~ with them kânsù
à hàɗe yakè.

thicket n sàrƙaƙƙiyā f.

thickset adj (psn.) (mài) gwā6ī m, (mài)
kaurī m.

thief n 6àrāwò m, 6àraunìyā f ⟨i⟩; a ~ who
receives stolen goods 6àrāwòn zàune.

thigh n cinyā̀ f ⟨oCi⟩, (outside part of ~)
katarā̀ f ⟨oCi⟩.

thimble n sāfī m.

thin 1. adj a. (psn.) sīřīřī m ⟨sīřàřā⟩; get
~ rāmè v4, yi rāmā f, būshè v4; (esp. from
illness) ƙanjàmē v4. b. (of texture) maràs
kaurī m: this paper is ~ takàřdař nàn
bā ta dà kaurī.
2. v (dilute) surkā̀ v1.

thing n a. àbù m (in the genitive, use àbin),
àbā f ⟨uwa[2]⟩: a saw is a very useful ~
zařtồ àbù nē mài àmfānī; the ~ to do
àbîn dà zā à yi; he always says the
wrong ~ kullum yanā̀ fàɗař àbîn dà
bài dācĕ ba; the first, last ~ àbù na
farkō, na ƙàrshē; for one ~, they had no
time, and for another no money na farkō
dai bā su dà hālī, na biyu kuma bâ
su dà kuɗī; (fig.) everyone is doing his
own ~ kōwā yanā̀ kasàfinsà = kōwā yanā̀
kasàfin kânsà. b. (in neg. sent.) kōmē m:
don't worry about a ~ kadà kà ɗàmu dà
kōmē; he doesn't know a ~ (about it) bài
san kōmē ba.

thingamajig n àbin nàn m.

things n a. (belongings) kāyā m/p: pack all
my ~ at once kà tattàrà duk kāyānā
yànzun nàn. b. (matters, state of affairs) sha'ànī m ⟨oCi⟩, àl'amàřī m ⟨u-
a⟩, hařkā̀ f ⟨oCi⟩: how are ~? (greeting) yàyà hařkōkī? ~ are very bad
al'amuřā̀ sun lālàcè; make ~ worse
rikìtà sha'ànī; as ~ are now yâddà
al'amuřā̀ sukè yànzu; take ~ seriously
ɗauki w.a. dà muhimmancī; think ~ over
yi dōgon tùnānī kân w.a.

think v a. yi tsàmmānī m, zàtā v2, yi zàtō
m, ji v0: do you ~ that it will rain? kanā̀
zàtō zā à yi ruwā? I thought so nā yi
tsàmmānìn hakà = nā zàci hakà; that's
what I ~ hakà nakè zàtō = hakà nakè
jì; I don't ~ I'll come tomorrow bā nà
jîn zân zō gòbe; ~ of, about sth. yi
tùnānin w.a.: what are you ~ing about?
tùnānin mè kakè? = mè kakè tùnānī?
he ~s only about himself bā yā tùnānin
kōwā sai kânsà; ~ sth. over carefully yi
tùnānī à kân w.a., yi tsōkàcī à kân
w.a.: all right, I'll ~ it over carefully tô,
zân yi zurfin tùnānī à kâi; ~ to oneself yi zàncen zūcì; ~ twice about doing sth. (due to fear) yi tàřaddàdī m: I
thought twice about telling him the truth

nā yi tằɍaddằdin faɗằ masà gàskiyā.
b. *(have a feeling, hunch)* kyautằtà zàtō
cêwā: I ~ he'll come nā kyautằtà zàtō
cêwā zài zō. c. *(have opinion of)* ganī
*v*\*, jī *v0*: what did you ~ of his speech? mề
ka ganī gàme dà jàwābìnsà? = yằyằ kakề
jī dà jàwābìnsà? I thought it very interesting nā ji àbìn yanằ dà ban shà'awằ;
~ highly of so. yabằ wà *v1*: we ~ highly
of her mun yabằ matà; ~ highly of sth.
yabằ dà *v1*: I don't ~ much of that book
bàn yabằ dà wannàn littāfì sòsai ba.
d. *(interpret, assume)* ɗaukằ *v2*\*: what
will your father ~ of this? yằyằ bàbankà
zài ɗaùki wannàn? he thought we would
support his proposal yā ɗaukằ cêwā munằ
gòyon bāyansà. e. *(remember)* tunằ dà
*v1*: I can't ~ of his name nā kāsằ tunằwā
dà sūnansà; I didn't ~ of it bàn tunằ dà
shī ba = bài fàɗō minì à râi ba.
**third** *quant* na ukù: he came in ~ in the
race yā zō na ukù à tsēre; the T. World
ƙasàshē màsu tāsōwā; one-~ sulùsī *m*.
**thirst** *n* ƙishirwā *f*, ƙishī *m*: they died of
~ ƙishirwā tā kashè su.
**thirsty** *adj*: be ~ ji ƙishirwā *f*, yi ƙishī
*m*: I'm very ~ inằ jîn ƙishirwā sòsai
= ƙishirwā tā kāmằ ni sòsai.
**thirteen** *quant* (gōmà) shà ukù *f*.
**thirty** *quant* tàlàtin *f*.
**this** *det & pro* wannàn *m/f*, waɗànnân *p*; nàn
*(changes to* nàn *if prec. tone is H)*: what
is ~? mềnē nề wannàn? ~ one is better
wannàn tā fi kyâu; these are new pots
waɗànnân sàbàbbin tukwằnē nề; ~ horse
wannàn dōkì = dōkìn nàn; ~ cap wannàn
hùlā = hùlaɍ nàn; these shirts waɗànnân
taguwōyī = taguwōyin nàn.
**thither** *adv, see* hither.
**thorn** *n* ƙayằ *f* (oCi): a hedge of ~s shin-
gen ƙayằ; the stalk of the plant is ~y
jìkin itàcēn nằ dà ƙayằ; ~y thicket
sàrƙaƙƙiyā *f*.
**thorn tree** *n* kuɍnằ *f*.
**thorough** *adj* (mài) zurfī *m*, zùzzurfā *adj*:
a ~ investigation zùzzurfan bìncìkē.
**thoroughly** *adv* sòsai *adv*: she scolded the
child ~ tā dakà wà yārṓ tsāwā sòsai;
*(may be expressed by specialized verbs de-
noting thorough action)*: I caned him ~
nā dìɍkà masà sàndā; he whipped the
donkey ~ yā tsàlà wà jàkī būlālằ; he's
been ~ beaten yā shā zabgằ.
**those** *det & pro, see* that.
**though** *adv* kō dà yakè, *see* although.
**thought** *n* tùnằnī *m*, zàtō *m*, tsàmmānī *m*:
give the matter a great deal of ~ yi dōgon

tùnằnī kân àl'amàɍîn; be deep in ~ yi
zùgum/jùgum *idph;* have second ~s sākè
shāwaɍằ.
**thoughtful** *adj (considerate)* (mài) sanìn
yā kàmātà *m*, (mài) kùlā *f*: she is very
~ of others tanằ dà sanìn yā kàmātà gà
mutằnē; be ~ (to so.) kyâutā (wà) *v1*: you
were very ~ to send that to us kun kyâutā
ƙwaɍai dà kukà aikō manà wannàn.
**thoughtfully** *adv* dà hankàlī *m*: he spoke
~ yā yi màganằ dà hankàlī.
**thoughtless** *adj* maràs kùlā *f*, maràs
hankàlī *m*.
**thousand** *quant* a. dubū *f* (Cai): 6 ~
dubū shidà; ~s of people dùbban mutằnē;
*(in multiples only)* zambàɍ *m*: 10 ~
zambàɍ gōmà. b. *(in dates)* alìf *m*: 1989
à shēkarằ ta alìf dà ɗàrī taɍà dà
tàmằnin dà taɍà.
**thrash** *v*: ~ so. with a stick ƙwālằ wà
sàndā; ~ so. with a whip tsàlằ wà
būlālằ; ~ so. in a game bâ w. kāshī;
they ~ed us 5 to 0 mun shā kāshī an
cînyē mu bìyaɍ bâ kō ɗaya.
**thread** 1. *n* a. zàrē *m* (uka²); *(fine, manufactured)* aɍàfiyā *f*; *(coarse, hand-spun)*
abàwā *f*; tinsel ~ sìlikì *m*. b. *(on screw)*
tiɍēdì *m*.
2. *v* zurằ *v1*: he ~ed the needle yā zurà
zàrē à àllūɍằ; *(beads)* dūrằ *v1* (dūrì):
she is ~ing a coral necklace tanằ dūrìn
mùɍjānì.
**threadbare** *adj*: be ~ tattàkē *v4*.
**threadworm** *n* kwaɍba *f*.
**threat** *n* bàrằzanā *f*; *(empty)* kūrī *m*.
**threaten** *v* a. yi wà bàrằzanā *f*, ràzānà *v1*;
*(with evil intent)* bā dà tsòrō, yi wà ban
tsòrō *m*: he ~ed to shoot us yā bā mù
tsòrō cêwaɍ zâi hàɍbē mù. b. *(by bluster, intimidation)* yi wà bùɍgā *f*, ci w. dà
bùɍgā, yi wà kūrī *m*.
**three** *quant* ukù *f*.
**thresh** *v* sussùkā *v1* (sùssukằ) *f*: ~ grain
from the chaff by pounding sussùkè hatsī
ta hanyàɍ cāsà.
**threshold** *n* bàkin ƙōfà *m*.
**thrifty** *adj* (mài) tsimī *m*, (mài) tattalī
*m*: be ~ with the grain kù yi tsimin
hatsī; she is ~ and doesn't waste anything tanằ dà tattalī bà tà ɓaɍnataɍ
dà kōmē.
**thrill** *v* buɍgè *v4*: the dance ~ed the spectators rawā tā buɍgè 'yan kallō.
**throat** *n* *(windpipe)* màƙōgwàrō *m*; *(esophagus)* maƙōshī *m*: my ~ is full of dust
màƙōgwàrō yā cìka dà ƙūra; a sore ~

cīwòn màƙōgwàrō; clear one's ~ gyārà muryà.

throb v yi zōgī m: his head ~bed kânsà nà zōgī.

throne n gadon sàrautà m; the ~ of God Àl'ařshì f.

throttle¹ n (of car) tōtùř m, [F] àskìlàtàř m.

throttle² v (choke) māƙùrē v4, shāƙè v4.

through prep a. (via) ta prep: get a job ~ a friend sàmi gurbì ta hanyàř wani àbōkī; enter ~ a window shìga ta tāgà; peep ~ a keyhole lēƙà ta kafař makullī; go, cross ~ (a place) kētà v1, rātsà v1: we crossed through Sule's farm mun rātsà gōnař Sulè. b. (up until) hař prep: from Monday ~ Friday dàgà Lìttìnîn hař Jumma'à.

throughout adv (à) kō'ìnā, (à) duk adv: ~ the world kō'ìnā cikin dūniyà; the same language is spoken ~ the country harshè gùdà akè maganà dà shī à duk ƙasař; ~ all of yesterday I slept and slept gàbā ɗayan jiyà barcī na yi ta yî.

throw v a. (sth.) jēfà v1, wuřgà v1: he threw the ball 50 yards ya jēfà ƙwallō yādì hàmsin; (sth. to so.) jēfà wà v1: I threw the bone to the dog nà jēfà wà kàrē ƙashîn. b. (sth. at so.) jèfā v2 ⟨jīfà⟩: they threw a stone at the dog to chase him away sun jèfi kàrē dà dūtsè don sù ƙòrē shì; c. (var. v + adv uses): ~ away, ~ out jēfař (dà) v5, yā dà / yař (dà) v5: she threw out the empty match-box tā jēfař dà fànkō; ~ out (things which flow) zub dà / zubař (dà) v5: she threw out the water, the sand tā zubař dà ruwā, yàshī; ~ off (knock down) kā dà/ kāyař (dà) v5: the horse threw off its rider dōkìn yā kā dà mahàyinsà; ~ over one's shoulders (garment) yāfà v1: he threw a small blanket over his shoulders yā yāfà gwàdò; ~ up (vomit) yi amai m. d. (other uses): ~ so. into jail sâ w. à kûřkukù; ~ light on sth. haskàkà v1; ~ one's arms around so. rùngumà v2.

thrust v: ~ into diřkà v1: he ~ his hands into his pockets yā diřkà hannàyē à àljīhū; ~ a dagger into so. diřkà wà wuƙā.

thud n: with a ~ řîm idph: the sack fell out of the car with a ~ bùhū ya fādō dàgà mōtà řîm.

thug n ɗan dabà m, ɗan iskà m.

thumb n bàbban ɗan yātsà m.

thump v (so. on back) yi wà dùndū m.

thunder n tsāwā f, (euphem.) àbař samà f;

(far-off rumbling of ~) cidà f: if you hear the clap of ~, then lightning has struck in kā ji tsāwā, tô, àřādù tā fàdì; I swear by ~! àřādù! excl, tařnatsa! excl.

thunderbolt n gàtarin àřādù m.

thunderclap n tsāwā f, kwàřankwatsa f, tařnatsa f.

thunderhead(s) n hadarì m.

Thursday n Àlhàmîs f.

thus adv a. (in this way) hakà adv: if you hold it ~ it won't fall in kā riƙè shi hakà bài zâi fàdì ba. b. (therefore) sabōdà hakà: he didn't study and ~ failed the test bài yi kàřàtū ba sabōdà hakà yā fàdì à jařřàbâwā; ~ far hař yànzu.

tibia n sangalī / sangalalī m.

tick¹ n (insect) kaskà f.

tick² v: the clock is ~ing àgōgo nà aikì = àgōgo nà gudù.

ticket n tikitì m ⟨oCi⟩, [F] tìkê m, [F] řēsî m: first-class ~ tikitìn faskìlà; second-class ~ tikitìn gàmà-gàri = tikitìn sikinkìlà; round-trip ~ tikitìn zuwà dà dāwôwā; buy a ~ yànki tikitì.

tickle 1. v (under armpit) yi càkulkulī m, (on the side) tsìkara v2: she's tickling the baby tanà wà jàrīrī càkulkulī.

2. n (in throat) màƙaƙī m: I have a ~ in my throat màƙōgwàrō nà màƙaƙī.

tidy 1. adj tsaf idph: the place is ~ wurī yā yi tsaf.

2. v kintsà v1: don't leave until you've tidied up your things kadà kà tāshì sai kā kintsà kāyā tùkùna.

tie 1. v a. (bind together) ɗaurà v1 ⟨ɗaurì⟩: they ~d the bundles of corn sun ɗaurà damìn hatsī; ~ up ɗaurè v4: he ~d his horse (up) to a post yā ɗaurè dōkìnsà à turkè. b. (make a knot) ƙullà v1, yi ƙullì m: ~ one's shoelaces ƙullà maɗaurī; ~ the rope tightly kà ƙullà igiyà kankan; ~ a noose around so. zargà wà v1. c. (end evenly in a contest) yi kûnnen dōkì m, yi canjàřas m, yi dùřô m, yi tāyì m.

2. n (in a contest) kûnnen dōkì m, dùřô m, canjàřas m, tāyì m; the game ended in a ~ an yi kûnnen dōkì à wàsân.

tie-dye n: (star-like pattern) àdìře m; (stripe-like pattern) kàmfàlà f; (running stitch pattern) làllàftū m.

tiger-fish n tsagè m.

tiger-nut n ayà f.

tight adj & adv a. (taut) (mài) tsaurī m; (tightly) kankan idph, tam / tamau idph: a ~ knot ƙullì mài tsaurī; he tied the rope ~(ly) yā k̃ullà igiyà kankan. b. (*restricted*) màtsattsē *adj;* be ~ màtsā *v2:* this coat is too ~ for me in the shoulders wannàn kwât tā màtsē nì à k̃àfad̃à; his shoes are too ~ for him tākalmàn sun cī masà k̃afà.

**tighten** *v* (*by taking up slack, increasing tension*) d̃āmè *v4:* ~ a bowstring, rope d̃āmè bàkā, igiyà; (*by pulling together*) tsūk̃è *v4:* ~ drawstrings tsūk̃è mazāgī; ~ one's belt (*lit.*) tsūk̃è bêl = (*fig.*) tsūk̃è àljīhū; ~ a saddle jā sir̃d̃ì; ~ a screw d̃aurà k̃ūsà.

**tightly** *adv* a. (*of sth. tied, fastened*) kankan *idph*, tam / tamau *idph:* it is ~ fastened yā d̃auru tam. b. (*of sth. being held*) kaf *idph*, kankan *idph*, d̃ad̃af *idph:* hold it ~ kà kāmà shi kaf = kà rik̃è shi kankan; cling ~ to mak̃àlē d̃ad̃af. c. (*of sth. woven, braided*) dà tsaurī *m.*

**till**[1] *v* (*a farm*) yi nōmā *m.*

**till**[2] *prep & conj, see* until.

**tilt** *v* (*not be straight*) kar̃kàtā *v1*, kar̃kàcē *v4;* (*lean in certain direction*) tangàd̃ā *v1:* it ~ed to the left yā tangàd̃ā hagu; ~ over (*on side*) jirkìcē *v4.*

**timber** *n* (*beams for construction*) timbà *f*, (*beam from split deleb palm*) azàr̃à *f* ⟨u⟩.

**time** *n* a. lōkàcī *m* ⟨ai⟩, lōtò *m:* the ~ has gone by quickly lōkàcîn yā yi saurin yî; the ~ is up, it's ~ lōkàcī yā yi; the ~ is passing (*getting shorter*) lōkàcī nà k̃urēwā; there is not enough ~ (*to finish up*) lōkàcī yā k̃urè; at the same ~ (*together*) gàbā d̃aya, gà bàk̃ī d̃aya; at the same ~ as daidai lōkàcîn: he came at the same ~ as I yā zō daidai lōkàcîn dà na zō; at this same ~ (*in the fut.*) wàr̃ hakà: come at this ~ tomorrow kà zō gòbe wàr̃ hakà; by this ~ next year, he will have grown a lot bàd̃i wàr̃ hakà, yà girma sòsai; from ~ to ~ lōkàcī-lōkàcī *adv*, lōtò-lōtò *adv*, jik̃ò-jik̃ò *adv;* the present ~ yànzu *adv;* after a very long ~ à kwāna à tāshì; ~ after ~ kullum-kullum *adv;* on ~ à kân lōkàcī, cikin lōkàcī; right on ~ à daidai lōkàcîn; one at a ~ d̃ai-d̃ai dà d̃ai-d̃ai; until some other ~! sai wani lōkàcī! = sai wani jik̃ò! = sai wani karò! = sai an kwan biyu! b. (*var. v + ~ uses*): arrive on ~ ìsa cikin lōkàcī; run out of ~ k̃urè *v4:* I've run out of ~ lōkàcī yā k̃urè minì; take, consume ~ d̃au lōkàcī, ci lōkàcī: ~-consuming work aikì mài cîn lōkàcī; this machine will save us ~ injìn nân zâi ragè manà aikì; take a

lot of so.'s ~ cī wà lōkàcī, cī wà râi: the wedding arrangements took a lot of our ~ shirìn bìkin aurē yā cī manà râi; waste ~ 6ātā lōkàcī: stop wasting my ~ kà dainà 6ātà minì lōkàcī; be, take a long ~ dad̃è *v4:* it's been a long ~ since I saw you nā dad̃è bàn gan kà ba; it will take a long ~ to finish zā à dad̃è kàfìn à gamà. c. (*clock ~*) k̃arfè *m:* what ~ is it now? it is 3 o'clock k̃arfè nawà nē yànzu? ukù ta yi; tell ~ san lōkàcī; a ~ zone àgōgo *m:* Greenwich Mean T. àgōgon Ingìlà. d. (*opportunity*) dāmā *f*, hālī *m:* I haven't ~ to do it bâ ni dà dāmar̃ yînsà; free, spare ~ sùkūnī *m:* I never have ~ to watch television bâ ni dà sùkūnìn kallon talàbijìn. e. (*a specific occasion*) karò *m:* I'll forgive you this ~ zân yāfè makà wannàn karòn; have a good ~ yi ànnàshùwā *f*, yi nìshād̃ì *m*, (*fig.*) shèk̃à ayà: they were playing cards and having a good ~ sunà ta kar̃tà sunà nìshād̃ì; they're having a good ~ time telling folktales sunà shèk̃à ayar̃sù dà tàtsūnìyā. f. (*fixed, agreed upon ~*) wa'àdī *m:* we set a ~ to meet on every Tuesday mun yi wa'àdī zā mù gàmu kōwàcè ran Tàlātà. g. (*specific epoch, era*) zāmànī *m:* in the ~ of Muhammadu Bello à zāmànin Mùhammadù Bellò; a long long ~ ago tun shèkar̃à àr̃u-àr̃u = tun dâ can; in these ~s à zāmànin nàn, à yâu; one must move with the ~s (*fig.*) in kid̃à ya sàk̃è rawā sai tà sàk̃è; once upon a ~ there was a... wata rānā an yi wani.... h. (*preordained, esp. ref. to death*) ajàlī *m:* his ~ has come, was up yā kai ajàlī = ajàlinsà yā yi.

**timekeeper** *n* (*psn.*) tànkif̃à *n.*

**times** *prep* (*as a multiple of*) sàu *m:* 3 ~ 2 equals 6 ukù sàu biyu shidà kè nan; I want one 3 ~ as large inà sôn wândà ya kai ukùn wannàn; take this medicine 3 ~ a day kà shā māgànin nàn sàu ukù à rānā.

**timetable** *n* jadawàlī *m* ⟨ai⟩.

**timid** *adj* a. (*intimidated*): be ~ with yi d̃àri-d̃àri dà. b. (*reserved*) (mài) kawaicì *m.*

**tin** *n* a. (*ore*) kùzà *m;* a ~ roof rufìn kwānò *m.* b. (*can, for food*) gwangwanī *m* ⟨aye⟩, [F] kwankwanī / kwankò *m* ⟨aye⟩. c. (*4-gallon container for kerosene, water*) garwā *f*, [F] galàn *m.*

**tinder** *n* (*of dried leaves, grass, odds & ends*) būyāgī *m.*

**tiny** *adj* a. (*of sth.*) d̃an k̃àramī *adj* ⟨'yan

ƙanānằ); (of psn.) mìtsītsì adj ⟨mitsil-mitsil⟩, tsigil idph ⟨tsigil-tsigil⟩: she is a ~ girl mìtsītsìyar̃ yārinyằ cē = yārinyằ tsigil dà ita. b. (in quantity) ƙyas idph, ƙiris idph, ƙil idph: pour me a ~ bit of water zùbā minì ruwā ƙyas; there's a ~ bit left dà saurā ƙiris.

tip[1] n ƙàrshē m: the ~ of the arrow is very sharp ƙàrshen kibiyằ yanằ dà tsìnī sōsai; his name is on the ~ of my tongue gằ sūnansà àmmā nā kāsà fàɗā.

tip[2] n (gratuity) kyàutā f, cì-gōr̃ò m; (given by receiver of gift to its bearer) tukwīcì m.

tip over v kifề v4, kifar̃ (dà) v5: she ~ped the wastebasket over tā kifar̃ dà kwàndon shằrā.

tiptoe v yi sanɗā f: she ~d past so she wouldn't wake him tā shigề tanằ ta sanɗā kadà tà tā dà shī; stand on ~ yi ɗage m: she stood on ~ to reach the bottle tā yi ɗage tà ɗaukō kwalabā.

tire[1], tyre n (of vehicle) tāyằ f ⟨oCi⟩, [F] fìnê m, [F] ƙafàr̃ mōtā f; put air in a ~ yi wà tāyằ gējì.

tire[2] v gajī dà / gajiyar̃ (dà) v5, bā dà gàjiyằ: this work will ~ you wannàn aikì zāi gajiyar̃ dà kū.

tired, be v a. (fatigued): be ~d gàji v3* ⟨gàjiyằ⟩ f: I am ~d of telling you that nā gàji dà gayằ makà hakà; he never gets ~d of the work bā yằ gàjiyằ dà aikìn; without getting ~d bằ tàre dà gàjiyằ ba; I am extremely ~d nā gàji matuƙā; be dead ~d gàji tiƙis = tiɓis = liƙis idph. b. (weak, lethargic): feel ~d ji kàsālằ f: the heat makes you feel ~d zāfī kàn sâ ka jîn kàsālằ. c. (bored, fed up): be ~d ƙōsằ v1, gùndurà v3: they were ~d of eating the same food every day sun ƙōsằ dà cîn àbinci gùdā kullum; the peasants were ~ of the government and wanted a change manōmā sun gùndurà dà gwamnatìnsù sunā nēman sauyì.

tiresome adj (boring) (mài) cîn râi m, (mài) gùndurà f: this job is ~ aikìn nân nà dà cîn râi; find so. ~ gùndurà v2: I find her ~ tā gùndùrē nì.

tithe n zàkkā f.

title n a. (royal, tradit.) sàrautā f: ~ holder mài sàrautà; what is his ~? mènē nề sàrautar̃sà? b. (e.g. of book) sūnā m ⟨aye⟩.

to prep a. (toward) zuwằ prep: the road ~ Kano hanyằ zuwằ Kanồ; from here ~ there dàgà nân zuwằ cân. b. (often not translated with verbs indicating mo-

tion): they went ~ the market sun tàfi kàsuwā; they returned ~ school sun kōmằ makar̃antā; I took her ~ the hospital nā kai tà asìbitì. c. (up to, until) yà/wà/ì prep: the water came ~ his knees ruwā yā kai yà gwīwā. d. (up to the limit of) iyā prep: ~ the best of his ability iyā ƙōƙarinsà. e. (ind. obj) wà/mà (+ n), ma-(+ pro, see Appendix A): he sent a letter ~ me yā aikō minì takàr̃dā; I threw a ball to Musa nā jēfằ wà Mūsā bâl. f. (to expr. infinitive, use subjunct. cl. or vbl. n): they want ~ go, ~ help me sunằ sô sù tàfi, sù tàimàkē nì; he forgot ~ tell us yā mântā yà gayằ manà; it would be better for us ~ go than ~ stay gāra mù tàfi dà mù zaunā; he likes ~ run, quarrel yanằ sôn gudù, fadằ; this car is easy ~ drive mōtằr̃ nân nằ dà saurin tūƙàwā. g. (in order ~) dōmin / don conj: he did it ~ help his people yā yi hakà dōmin yà tàimàki jàma'àr̃sà; he's saying that only ~ get your attention yanằ màganằ hakà kawài don yà jāwō hankàlinkà.

toad n kwàɗō m ⟨i⟩; (diff. types): bùdiddìgī m ⟨ai⟩, ƙōzō m.

toast 1. v gasà bur̃ōdì v1.
2. n gàsasshen bur̃ōdì m.

tobacco n tābằ f: chewing ~ tābằ gàrī; cigarette ~ tābằ sìgār̃ì; pipe ~ tābàr̃ lōfề.

today adv (this day) yâu adv: a week ago ~ rānā yà/wà ta yâu; (of the present time) na yâu, na zāmànī m: people of ~ mutằnen yâu.

toe n yātsằ / yātsàn ƙafà m: big ~ bàbban ɗan yātsằ.

toenail n farcè m ⟨a-a⟩.

toffee n cākùlàn f, [F] tôfî m.

together adv tàre adv: they went ~ sun tàfi tàre; they live ~ in peace with their neighbors sunằ zamā cikin lùmanằ tàre dà maƙwàbtansù; ~ with gàme dà; all ~ gà bàkī ɗaya, gàbā ɗaya: they left all ~ sun tāshì gà bàkī ɗaya = sun tāshì gàbā ɗayansù.

toilet n bāyan gidā m, (euphem.) bàbban ɗākì m, bàn-ɗākì m, bā hayà m, kēwayè m, makēwayì m: where is the ~? ìnā makēwayì? = ìnā bàbban ɗākì? public ~s gidan wankā dà bā hayà; go to the ~ zāgằ v1, kēwàyà v1, tsugùnà v1: I need to go to the ~ inằ sô zân zāgằ = inằ jîn bāyan gidā.

tolerance n a. (respect) girmàmāwằ f: have ~ for another's religious beliefs, customs girmàmà àddīnìn, àl'àdun wani. b. (en-

*durance*) jìmirī *m*: he has a low ~ for pain bā yà jìmirin zāfī.

**tolerant** *adj* (mài) haƙurī *m*, (mài) sauƙin kâi *m*, mài lāfiyà *n*.

**tolerate** *v* a. (*respect*) girmàmā *v1*: ~ so.'s religious beliefs girmàmā wà w. àddīninsù; b. (*endure*) jūrè wà *v4*, yi jìmirī *m*: he can't ~ cold weather bā yà jìmirin sanyī.

**toll** *n* kuɗin fitŏ *m*, kuɗin hanyà *m*.

**tomato** *n* tùmātìr̃ *m*: ~ paste, puree tùmātìr̃in gwangwanī; a can of ~ gwangwanin tùmātìr̃; bitter ~ (*local var.*) yālō *m*.

**tomb** *n* (*esp. of important psn.*) kùshēwā *f* ⟨i⟩.

**tomcat** *n* mùzūrū *m* ⟨ai⟩.

**tomorrow** *adv* gŏbe *adv*: don't put it off till ~ kadà kà dākatar̃ dà àbîn zuwà gŏbe; the day after ~ jībi *adv*.

**ton** *n* tân *m*: it weighs 2 ~s nauyinsà tân biyu.

**tone** *n* a. (*sound*) amō *m*: the fiddle has a pleasant ~ kūkūmā tanà dà amō mài taushī; I knew from his ~ of voice that he was angry dà jîn amon màganàr̃sà nā gānè yā yi fushī. b. (*in language*) karìn sautī *m*: high, low, falling ~ karìn sautī mài hawā, mài sàukā, mài fāɗùwā; ~ mark àlāmàr̃ karìn sautī.

**tongs** *n* hàntsakī *m* ⟨ai, u-a⟩.

**tongue** *n* a. (*organ*) harshè *m* ⟨una⟩; tip of the ~ ƙàrshen harshè; his name is on the ~ of my tongue gà sūnansà àmmā nā kāsà fàdā; make a slip of the ~ yi sùɓùl dà bakà *m*, yi sùɓutàr̃ bàkī *f*, yi fāɗùwar̃ màganà *f*; stick one's ~ out at so. yi wà gwālō *m*. b. (*any language*) harshè *m* ⟨una⟩: mother ~ harshèn haihùwā = harshèn gidā; (*vernacular of an ethnic minority*) yàr̃ē *m*: he speaks Hausa but his mother ~ is Tera yā iyà Hausa àmmā yàr̃ensù Tèrancī; his mother ~ is Hausa bàhaushè nē.

**tongue twister** *n* wàsan karyà harshè *m*.

**tonic water** *n* tōnìk *m*, [F] tònîk *m*.

**tonight** *adv* yâu dà dare *adv*.

**too**[1] *adv* (*also*) mā *adv*, kuma *adv*: take this one ~ dàuki wannàn mā = dàuki wannàn kuma; should I come ~? nī mā ìn zō?

**too**[2] *adv*: be ~ X (*more than enough*) yi *v0* (+ *adj or quant*): it was ~ dark duhù yā yi yawà; there is ~ much water in it ruwā yā yi yawà à cikinsà; the robe is ~ expensive rīgā tā yi tsàdā; the sauce is ~ salty miyà tā yi gishirī; the pants are too small for him wàndôn yā yi masà

kàɗan; there are ~ many to count sun fi à ƙirgà; do ~ much of sth. cikà *v1* (+ *obj*): Kande speaks ~ quickly Kànde tā cikà màganà dà saurī; he smokes ~ yā cikà shân tābà; the children are talking ~ much yârā sun cikà sùr̃ūtù.

**tool(s)** *n* (*gen'l*) kāyan aikì *m*; (*a specific* ~) àbin aikì *m*: a hammer is a useful ~ hamà àbar̃ aikì cē mài àmfànī; any worn-out ~ dumɓu *m* ⟨aye⟩.

**tooth** *n* (*in mouth or of saw*) haƙōrī *m* ⟨haƙōrā⟩: her teeth are stained from tobacco flowers haƙōrantà sun yi jā saɓôdà fùr̃e; canine ~ fīƙà *f* ⟨oCi⟩; molar ~ mataunī *m*, turmī *m*; brush one's teeth gŏgè haƙōrā; pick one's teeth yi sàkàcē *m*; shed milk teeth yi fàmfar̃à *f*.

**toothache** *n* cīwòn haƙōrī *m*: I have a ~ haƙōrī nà minì cīwò.

**toothbrush** *n* bùr̃ōshì *m*, bùr̃ōshìn gŏgè bàkī *m* [F] magōgin haƙōr̃ā *m*.

**toothless** *adj*: he, she is ~ wāwilō nè, wāwilō cè.

**toothpaste** *n* mân gŏgè haƙōrā *m*, màkìlîn *m*, [F] kwàlgât *m*; tube of ~ gidan mân gŏgè haƙōrā.

**toothpick** *n* tsinken sàkàcē *m*, masākacī *m*: use a ~ to pick your teeth kà sâ masākacī kà sàkàcè haƙōrā.

**top**[1] 1. *n* a. (*cover*) murfī *m* ⟨ai⟩. b. (~ *side of sth.*) samà *m*: the ~ of the box is dusty samàn àkwàtìn nà dà ƙūr̃ā; on ~ (*above*) à samà. c. (*upper part of*) kâi *m*: from the ~ of the hill dàgà kân tsaunìn; on ~ of (à) kân: put it on ~ of the table kà sâ shi à kân tēbùr̃. d. (*highest point of*) ƙōlōluwā *f*, ƙōƙuwā *f*: the ~ of the mountain ƙōlōluwar̃ dūtsè; the ~ of the thatched roof ƙōƙuwar̃ jinkà; e. (*acme, apogee*) gāniyà *f*, hayyàcī *m*: he's at the ~ of his form yanà cikin gāniyàr̃ ƙarfinsà.

2. *adj* na samà: the ~ shelf kantàr̃ samà.

**top**[2] *n* (*toy*) kàtantanwà *f*: spin a ~ kaɗà kàtantanwà.

**topic** *n* bàtū *m* ⟨uwa[2]⟩: concerning the ~ of smoking gàme dà bàtun shân tābà.

**topple** 1. *vt* (*a government*) tumɓùkē *v4*.

2. *vi*: ~ over (*of psn.*) ɓingìrē *v4*, (*of thing*) tuntsùrē *v4*.

**Torah** *n* (*Old Testament*) Àttaur̃ā *f*.

**torch** *n* (*flashlight*) tōcìlàn / cōcìlàn *f*, [F] cōcìlà *f*.

**torment** 1. *n* azàbā *f*.

2. *v* azàbtā *v1*, tsanàntā wà *v1*, matsà wà *v1*.

torn *adj* kềtaccē *adj*, yằgaggē *adj*, tsằgaggē *adj; see* tear.

tornado *n* gừguwằ mằi ƙarfii *f.*

tortoise *n* kừnkurū *m* ⟨ai⟩.

torture 1. *n* àzābằ *f*: they subjected him to ~ sun gānằ masằ àzābằ.
2. *v* yi wà àzābằ, gānằ wà àzābằ, azabtař (dà) *v5*: he was ~d by the secret police 'yan sàndan ciki sun azabtař dà shī.

toss *v* a. (*small snacks into one's mouth*) afằ *v1*: he took a handful of peanuts and was ~ing them into his mouth yā dànƙi gyàdā yanằ ta afằwā. b. (*a ball*) jēfằ *v1*: he was ~ing a ball around yanằ jēfằ bâl yanằ cafèwā; ~ a coin (for heads or tails) yi kân sarkī kō d̃amarằ.

total 1. *n* jimlằ / jumlằ *f* ⟨oCi⟩, adàdī *m*: what is the ~? nawằ nē jimlằř? it comes to a ~ of ₦30 jimlằřsà naiřằ tàlàtin; the ~ doesn't add up to 100 adàdîn bài kai d̃arī ba.
2. *v* yi jimlằ *f*, jimlàtā *v1*: when I ~ed up the money, it came to ₦100 dà na jimlàtà kud̃în, sun kai naiřằ d̃arī.

totalitarianism *n* mulkìn danniyằ *m*, mulkìn kằmā-kàryằ *m.*

totem *n* (*of clan, family*) kân gidā *m.*

touch 1. *v* a. taɓằ *v1*: don't ~ the wire kadà kà taɓà wayằř. b. (*be emotionally affected*) ji tàusàyī *m*; a ~ing story làbằřì mài ban tàusàyī; we were ~ed to hear his story dà mukà ji làbằřìnsà sai tàusàyī yā kằmā mu; I was ~ed by their kindness nā yi yàbon kiřkìnsù.
2. *n* a. taɓằwā *f*, taɓì *m*: it is soft to the ~ yanằ dà laushin taɓằwā. b. (*fig.*): are you in ~ with him? kanằ dà làbằřìnsà?

tough *adj* a. (*strong, of things*) (mài) ƙarfī *m*; (*durable, esp. of cloth*) (mài) ƙwārī *m.* b. (*of food, meat*) (mài) taurī *m.* c. (*of psn. able to endure hardship*) (mài) ƙarfin hālī *m.*

tour 1. *n* a. (*by official*) řàngādì *m.* b. (*sightseeing*) yāwòn shằƙàtâwā *m.*
2. *v* zāgằ *v1*: they ~ed the city sun zāgà cikin gàrī.

tourism *n* yāwòn shằƙàtâwā *m.*

tourist *n* d̃an yāwòn shằƙàtâwā *m.*

tow *v* jā *v0*: they ~ed the wrecked car away an jānyē wàřgàzajjiyař mōtằ.

toward(s) *prep* a. zuwằ *prep*, wajen *prep*: he took the road ~ the south ya bi hanyằ zuwằ kudù; he arrived ~ evening yā isō wajen màràicē. b. (*close to*) gab dà *prep*: ~ the end of the rainy season gab dà ƙàrshen d̃aminā. c. (*for use with verbs,*

*see partic. verb entries; v6 verbs usu. indicate action ~ the speaker or beneficiary*): he ran ~ us (in our direction) yā gudō; he appeared unexpectedly coming ~ us yā ɓullō wajenmù.

towel *n* tāwùl *m*, [F] sằřbētì *m;* face ~ hankicì *m.*

tower *n* (*minaret, turret*) hàsūmiyằ *f;* transmission ~ ēřiyằř gidan řēdiyồ *f.*

town *n* gàrī *m* ⟨uwa²⟩, àlkaryằ *f* ⟨u⟩; leave ~ on a short trip yi bàlàguřō *m.*

town crier *n* mài shềlà *m*, (*esp. for festivities*) san ƙīrằ *m.*

town hall *n* ma'aikatař magàjin gàrī, [F] mềřì *f*, ōfīshin ƙàramař hùkūmằ *m.*

toxic *adj* (mài) gubằ *f*: ~ gas, waste hayāƙī, shằrā mài gubằ.

toy *n* àbin wāsằ *m;* a ~ soldier sōjàn wāsā.

trace 1. *n* (*sign*) ɓùřɓushī *m*, bùřbud̃ī *m*: we haven't found even a ~ of them bà mù gānō kō ɓùřɓushinsù ba; vanish without a ~ (*fig.*) yi lāyằř zānā.
2. *v* (*find origin of sth.*) bi diddigī.

trachea *n* màƙōgwàrō *m.*

track *n* a. (*path*) turbằ *f*, tafarkì *m*, hanyằ *f* ⟨oCi⟩; (*fig.*) be, get on the wrong ~ bi mūgùwař hanyằ. b. (*of railroad*) dōgō *m*, kwàngìrì *m.* c. (*made by animal, vehicle*) san/sāwun ƙafằ *m;* cover up one's ~s yi ɓàd-dà-sāwu *m.* d. (*trace*): keep ~ of so. sà wà id̃ồ; lose ~ of ɓacề wà *v4*: we have lost ~ of Kande Kànde tā ɓacề manà.

track and field *n* wằsànnin gùje-gùje *p.*

tractor *n* tằřaktằ *f* ⟨oCi⟩, [F] jirgin danƙarō *m;* (*caterpillar*) kàtàfīlằ *f* ⟨oCi⟩, [F] kàtàřfīlằ *f.*

trade 1. *n* a. (*commerce*) cìnikī *m*: ~ agreement yàřjējènìyař cìnikī; ~ deficit gìɓìn cìnikī; ~ preference fīfīkòn cìnikī; ~ relations cìnìkayyằ *f*; international ~ cìnìkayyằř ƙasằshen dūniyằ; ~ surplus rārař cìnikī; ~ sanctions, embargo tằkunkùmin tattalin ařzìkī; balance of ~ rārař cìnikī; retail ~ kirī *m;* wholesale ~ sàrì *m;* the kolanut trade kằsuwař gōřò; tourist ~ tiřēdằ *f*: develop the tourist ~ bunƙàsà tiřēdằ. b. (*profession*) sànā'ằ *f* ⟨oCi⟩: he is a mechanic by ~ sànā'ařsà makằnikancì nē; ~ school makařantař ƙōyon sànā'ằ.
2. *v* yi cìnikī *m*: he ~s in cattle yanằ cìnikin shānū.

trademark *n* tambằřī / tambằřin kamfànī *m.*

trader *n* d̃an kằsuwā *n*, mài sàyē dà sayářwā *n;* (*itinerant*) falkē / fařkē *m*

⟨fatākē⟩; petty ∼ (at outdoor table) ɗan
tēbùr̃ m, mài tēbùr̃ m, ɗan kōlì m; (esp.
of tourist goods) ɗan tir̃ēdā̀ m.
trade union n ƙungìyar̃ ma'àikàtā f, [F]
sàndìkâ f.
trading n cìnikī m, tà'ammàlī m; itinerant
∼ safàrà f; (esp. tourist goods) tir̃ēdā̀ f.
tradition n àl'ādàr̃ gar̃gājiyā f ⟨u⟩; ∼s
about the Prophet Mohammed hàdīsī m.
traditional adj na gar̃gājiyā f: a ∼ name
sūnan gar̃gājiyā; a ∼ custom àl'ādàr̃
gar̃gājiyā.
traffic n: there's a lot of ∼ today yâu àkwai
mōtōcī dà yawà = yâu mōtōcī sun yi
yawà.
traffic jam n cùnƙōson mōtōcī m, gô-sùlô
m, [F] lāyìn mōtōcī m: there's a ∼ today
yâu àkwai gô-sùlô.
traffic light n danjà f.
traffic officer n mài bā dà hannū n,
tar̃āfìs n.
tragedy n a. (disaster) bàlā'ì m. b. (Lit.)
wàsan kwaikwaiyō mài ban tàusàyī m.
tragic adj (mài) ban tàusàyī m: it was a ∼
accident haɗàr̃ī nḕ mài ban tàusàyī.
trailer n (of truck) tir̃ēlà f; ∼ truck n, see
truck.
train¹ n jirgin ƙasā m ⟨a-e⟩: board a
∼ shìga jirgī; get off a ∼ sàuka dàgà
jirgī; the ∼ to Kaduna has left jirgī
zuwà Kàdūna yā tāshì.
train² v a. (discipline so.) hōrā v2 ⟨hōrō⟩;
(an animal, bird) hōrar̃ (dà) v5: the dog
is ∼ed not to bite people an hōrar̃ dà kàrē
don kadà yà cìji jàma'à; he is well-∼ed
yā hōrḕ sōsai. b. (teach so. a job) kōyar̃
(dà) v5.
training n a. hōrō m. b. (moral, esp. for
children) tàr̃biyyà f.
trait n (of character) àbin hālī m.
traitor n macì àmānàr̃ ƙasā m.
trample v tattàkā v1; (fig.) dannḕ v4: ∼
on so.'s rights dannè hakkìn w.
tranquility n lùmānā̀ f: peace and ∼ zaman
lāfiyà dà lùmānā̀.
transaction n mà'āmalā̀ f ⟨oCi⟩, huldā̀ f.
transfer n a. (send so. to a new place)
mai dà / mayar̃ (dà) v5: I was ∼red to
Kano an mai dà nī Kanò. b. (send so.
out of a place) tā dà v5: I was ∼red
out of Kano an tā dà nī dàgà Kanò. c.
(move sth. elsewhere) sauyḕ v4: ∼ the water from the bucket to the water pot sauyè
ruwā dàgà bōkitì zuwà ràndā. d. (move
money, funds) fitar̃ (dà) v5, tūrā̀ v1.
transform vt mai dà / mayar̃ (dà) v5: the
witch ∼ed him into a tree mâyyā tā mai

dà shī bishiyà; ∼ oneself rìkiɗà v3: he
∼ed himself into a frog yā rìkiɗà yā zama
kwàɗō.
transformation n rìkìr̃kiɗā̀ f, sàwayā̀ f:
we are in a period of rapid ∼s munà cikin
zāmànī mài saurin rìkìr̃kiɗā̀.
transfusion n ƙārìn jinī m: give so. a
blood ∼ ɗūrā̀ wà (ƙārìn) jinī.
transgress v ƙētà dōkā.
transitive adj (Gram.): a ∼ verb àikàtau
sò-kàr̃6au m.
translate v (sth.) juyā̀ v1, fassàr̃ā v1, mai
dà v5: ∼ this into English kà juyā̀ shi
dà Tūr̃ancī = kà fassàr̃à wannàn zuwà
Tūr̃ancī = kà mai dà shī Tūr̃ancī; it
is difficult to ∼ from English into Hausa
fassàr̃ā dàgà Ingìlīshì zuwà Hausa dà
wùyā nḕ; please ∼ this paragraph for
me don Allàh kà fassàr̃ā minì wannàn
sakìn lāyī.
translation n fassàr̃ā f ⟨oCi⟩: a fairly literal ∼ fassàr̃àr̃ kâi tsàye; a free ∼
fassàr̃àr̃ mà'ànā; this is a good ∼ wannàn
fassàr̃ā tā dācḕ sōsai; this is the best
∼ for that word wannàn fassàr̃ā tā fi
dācēwā dà mà'ànar̃ wancàn kalmà.
translator n mài aikìn fassàr̃ā n, tàfintà
n ⟨oCi⟩.
transmit v aikà dà v1.
transmission tower n ēr̃iyar̃ gidan
r̃ēdiyò f.
transparency n (film) fîm m, [F] kìlìshē
m.
transplant v dasā̀ v1, yi dàshḕ m.
transport 1. v kai v*: goods are ∼ed by
rail anà kai kāyā ta jirgin ƙasà; (many
things in several trips) jìdā v2: tomorrow
they will start ∼ing the pilgrims to Mecca
gòbe zā à fàrà jìdar̃ manìyyàtā zuwà
Makà.
2. n (of people, goods) jigilà f; (of
freight) sufùrī m.
transportation n sufùrī m; means of ∼
àbin sufùrī = àbin hawā.
transversely adv à gìcciye adv: the rows
of beans are sown ∼ to those of corn
kunyar̃ wākē a gìcciye takè dà ta
hatsī.
transvestite n ɗan daudù m.
trap 1. n (any kind) tarkò m ⟨una⟩; (for
mice) almìnjīr̃ m; (box-∼ for rats) 6urmā
f; (pit ∼ to ambush animals) haƙò m; set
a ∼ (for an animal) haƙà tarkò, 6urmā;
fall into a ∼ fāɗà tarkò, haƙò; set a ∼
(for psn.) yi fàkon w., yi haƙòn w.
2. v a. (catch so.) kāmà dà tarkò; (with
rope, net) zargḕ v4: I ∼ped the hare with

a net nā zargè zōmō dà rāgā; the hare was ~ped in the net rāgā tā zargè wà zōmō. b. (*outwit so.*) yi wà shirì *m*, yi wà dàbāřà *f*, ƙullà wà dàbāřà.

**trash** *n* (*rubbish*) shầrā *f*; (*junk*) tàrkàcen banzā *m*.

**trash can** *n* bōlầ *f*, garwař shầrā *f*.

**trashy** *adj* ƙazāmī *adj* ⟨ai⟩.

**travel** 1. *n* tàfiyầ *f* ⟨e²⟩: he returned safely from his ~s yā dāwō lāfiyầ dầgà tàfìye-tàfìyensầ.
2. *v* a. yi tàfiyầ *f*: ~ by air, by car, on foot yi tàfiyầ ta jirgin samầ, à mōtầ, à ƙasầ; ~ on business yi safàřà *f*. b. (*for pleasure, tourism*) shā yāwòn dūniyầ, yi yāwòn shầƙàtāwā: they like to ~ sunầ sô sù shā yāwòn dūniyầ. c. (*of vehicle moving at certain speed*) yi tàfiyầ *f*, yi gudù *m*: the car was ~ing at 80 mph mōtầ tanầ gudù dà tầmằnin.

**traveller** *n* matàfìyī *m*, mài tàfiyầ *n*.

**traverse** *v* ƙētàrē *v4*, rātsầ *v1*.

**tray** *n* tìřê *m*, bầbban fầřantì *m*.

**treachery** *n* cìn àmānầ *m*, hầ'incì *m*, munāfuncì *m*.

**tread** *n* (*of tire*) zằnen tāyầ *m*: the ~ is worn down zằnen tāyầ yā sudè.

**treadle** *n* matākī *m*.

**treason** *n* cìn àmānầř ƙasā *m*.

**treasure** *n* dūkìyā *f* ⟨oCi⟩.

**treasurer** *n* ma'àjī *m*, mài àjiyầ *n*.

**treasury** *n* bàitùlmālì *m*.

**treat**¹ *n* (*of food*) àbin marmarī *m*: during the Id festival, there are many special ~s to eat ran Sallầh anầ cìn àbin marmarī irì-irì.

**treat**² *v* a. (*behave towards*) gānầ wà *v1*: he ~ed me badly, well yā gānầ minì wùyā, dầdī; ~ so. gently lallầɓầ *v1*. b. (~ *so. well, usu. said of God*) ɗaukàkā *m*: God has ~ed him well (in life) Allầh yā ɗaukàkā shi. c. (*Med.*) yi jiyyầ *f*, yi wà māgằnī *m*: the wounded are being ~ed anầ jiyyầř màsu ràunī.

**treatment** *n* (*Med.*) jiyyầ *f*.

**treaty** *n* yàřjējēnìyā *f*: sign a ~ ƙullà yàřjējēnìyā.

**tree** *n* itầcē *m* ⟨uwa⟩, icè *m*, bishiyầ *f* ⟨oCi⟩; dead ~ (*but still standing*) kwaurè *m* ⟨uka⟩.

**tremble** *v* (*of body*) yi ɓarì *m*, yi màkyařkyatầ *f*, yi kařkařwầ *f*, yi tsìmầ *f*: she was trembling jìkintà nầ ɓarì.

**tremendous** *adj* (*in size*) ƙātồ *adj* ⟨Ca⟩; (*in scope*) gầgārùmī *adj* ⟨ai⟩: a ~ crowd gầgārùmin tàrō; (*often expr. by ideo-*

*phonic adjs which go with specific nouns, see* huge, massive).

**trespass** *v* shìga ta lâifī, kētà haddìn w.; no ~ing here bā à shìga nân.

**trial** *n* a. (*Law*) shầři'ầ *f*: bring so. to ~ kai w. gàban shầři'ầ; he is on ~ for embezzlement yanầ gàban shầři'ầ sabồdà zàmba; this ~ has been going on for 10 days kwānā gōmà anầ shầři'ầř nân. b. (*test*) gwajì *m*, jařřàbâwā *f*.

**triangle** *n* àlwàtīkầ *f*.

**tribal** *adj* na kàbīlầ *f*.

**tribalism** *n* kabīlancì *m*.

**tribal marks** *n* (*on face*) shầsshāwầ *f*, jầřfā *f*, askā *f*, wutā *f*: these are Kurfa ~ wannàn askař Kùrfầwā cè.

**tribe** *n* kàbīlầ / ƙàbīlầ *f* ⟨u⟩.

**trick** 1. *n* a. (*sth. clever*) dàbāřầ *f* ⟨u⟩, àbin wầyō *m*, shirì *m*: pull a ~ on so. yi wà dàbāřầ; set so. up for a ~ yi wà shirì *m*. b. (*deception*) àbin zàmba *m*; play a dirty ~ on so. yi wà zàmba *f*. c. (*hoax*) girì *m*, (*esp. to embarrass so.*) gayyầ *f*. d. (*practical, friendly joke*) (àbin) wầyō *m*, àbin wầsā *m*: they played a ~ on me wầsā sukà yi dà nī. e. (*done by magician*) dabồ *m*, rùfầ-idồ *m*.
2. *v* (*deceive*) zàmbatā *v2*, yàudarầ *v2*; (*play a trick on*) yi wà shirì *m*, yi wà wầyō *m*: they realized immediately that they had been ~ed nan dà nan sukà fầhimtà dà cêwā an yàudàrē sù; they ~ed the enemy sun yi wà àbồkan gầɓā shirì.

**trickery** *n* a. (*deceit*) zàmba *f*, yàudarầ *f*. b. (*magic*) dabồ *m*, rùfầ-idồ *m*; (*sleight-of-hand*) sìddabařù *m*.

**trickle** *v* tàrārà *v3*, tsìyāyà *v3*, zùrārà *v3*: water was trickling out a hole in the bowl ruwā nầ zurārôwā dầgà hūjìn kwānồ.

**trickster** *n* mayàudàrī *m*; (*in Hausa folktales*) Gizồ *m*.

**tricky** *adj* (*mài*) wầyō *m* (*mài*) dàbāřầ *f*.

**trigger** *n* (*of gun*) kùnāmầ *f*: cock the ~ ɗanà kùnāmầ; ~-happy (*psn.*) ɗan bindigầ-dầdī *m*.

**trim** *v* (*cut a little off*) dātsầ *v1*.

**trip**¹ *n* tàfiyầ *f* ⟨e²⟩, (*esp. short*) bàlāguřồ *m*; a round ~ tàfiyầ zuwầ dà dāwôwā; go on a ~ yi bàlāguřồ *m*.

**trip**² 1. *vt* (*so. by extending foot out*) tầɗè *v4*, yi wà tầdiyā *f*.
2. *vi* (*stumble*) yi tuntuɓè *m*.

**triple** *v* riɓầ sầu ukù.

**triplets** *n* (*children*) ùkùnnī *p*.

**triplicate** *n*: type it in ~ kà bugầ shi kwafì ukù.

tripod *n* ƙafà *f.*

triumph *v* ci nasařà *f; ~* over difficulties shāwō kân wahalōlī.

troops *n* sōjà *m/p*, rùndunař sōjà *f.*

trophy *n* (*cup*) kwâf / kōfî *m* (una); (*plaque*) gàrkuwā *f* (oCi); (*medal*) lambà *f* (oCi): win a *~* ci kwâf.

tropical forest *n* kurmî *m* (a-u).

trot *v* yi kwàkkwàfā *f.*

trouble 1. *n* a. (*difficulty*) wùyā *f*, wàhalà *f*: I had a great deal of *~* nā shā wùyā ƙwařai; it gave me a lot of *~* yā bā nì wùyā ƙwařai; life is full of *~*s zaman dūniyà dà wàhalà; I had a lot of *~* reading his handwriting nā shā wùyā wajen kařàntà řùbùtunsà; his life was one of *~* yā yi zaman wàhalà; deep, serious *~* baƙar wàhalà = jar wàhalà; get into *~* shìga cikin wàhalà = shìga ukù; have *~* doing sth. wàhalà *v3*: I really had a lot of *~* before I found them lallē nā wàhalà kàfìn ìn sàmē sù; cause *~* wahalař (dà) *v5*; get so. into *~* jāwō wà sabàbī. b. (*crisis*) rìkicī *m*; the country is having economic *~*s ƙasâř tanà cikin rìkicin tattalin ařzìkin ƙasā; start *~* azà rìkicī. c. (*effort*) dàwàiniyā *f*, hidimā *f* (oCi): he took the *~* to provide us with lodging yā dàuki dàwàiniyař saukař dà mū; thank you for all the *~* you have taken nā gōdè mikì sabòdà duk hidimōmin dà kika shā. d. (*misbehavior, esp. in children*) rìkicī *m*; get into *~* shìga rìkicī; keep out of *~* kaucè wà rìkicī. e. (*fuss, uproar*) rìgimà *f*: what's all the *~* about? mènē nè asalin rìgimà? = mè ya kāwō rìgimàř? 2. *v* a. (*bother*) dàmā *v2* (dāmù): what is troubling her? mè kè dāmùntà? his leg *~*d him ƙafàřsà tā dàmē shì dà cīwò; be *~*d dàmu *v7*. b. (*cause difficulty*) wahalař (dà) *v5*. c. (*annoy, pester*) matsà wà *v1*: I am sorry to *~* you bā nà sôn ìn matsà makà.

trouble-maker *n* ɗan rìgimà *m*, mài fìtinà *n*, mài jāwō sabàbī *n*, mài rìkicī *n*.

troublesome *adj* a. (*esp. of children*) (mài) ƙìrìniyā *f*, (mài) fìtinà *f*, (mài) rìgimà *f*; this child is *~* yāròn nân yā cikà rìgimà = yā cikà fìtinà. b. (*worrisome*) (mài) dàmuwā *f*: a *~* matter àbin dàmuwā.

trough *n* kōmī *m* (aye), àkalà *f.*

trousers *n* wàndō *m* (una); (*West. style*) tùřōzà *m*, [F] zāzû *m*; (*tradit., loose, with drawstring*) ɗan ìtòři *m*, fànjāmà *m*,

[F] fìjàmà *m*; (*tradit., extremely wide & loose*) būjè *m*; (*Arab style, narrow at leg*) tsalà *m.*

trouser string *n* mazāgī *m*, zārìyā *f*, làwùřjè *m.*

trowel *n* wuƙař sìmintì *f*, [F] ƙōshiyàř sìmintì *f.*

truck *n* bàbbař mōtà *f* (mânyan mōtōcī); (*var. types*): (*pickup*) à-kòri-kūrà *f*; (*mammy wagon*) mōtà mal bōdìn kātākō *f*, tâlbōdì *f*, gingimāri *f*; (*semi-trailer*) tantēbùř *f*, gingimāri *f*, [F] řamâřk *f*, [F] sàmî *f*; (*flat-bed*) [F] tèlàm / tàlàm *f*; (*tipper*) tīfà *f* (oCi), ɗàgà-bōdì *f*; (*tanker*) mōtàř mâi *f*, [F] sìtâř *f.*

true *adj* na gàskiyā/gaskiyā *f*, na gàske, na hàƙīƙà: he was a *~* warrior jàřùmī nè na gàske; did you think that the story was *~*? kin ɗauki làbārìn gàskiyā nè? that is not *~* bà gaskiyā ba nè = bà hakà ba nè; come *~*, prove to be *~* gàskatà *v3*, tàbbatà *v3*: all their prophecies came *~* duk abūbuwàn dà sukà tsìnkāyà sun tàbbatà.

truly *adv* dà gàske, dà gàskiyā/gaskiyā: a *~* difficult situation hālī mài wùyař gàske; (*in signing a letter*) yours *~* hāzā wassàlàm, nī nè nākà.

trump *n* (*in cards*) kwâs *m.*

trumpet *n* (*very long metal ~ blown only for chiefs*) kàkàkī *m.*

trumpeter *n* mài būsà kàkàkī *m.*

trunk[1] *n* a. (*of tree, body*) gàngař jìkī *f.* b. (*of elephant*) hannū *m* (aye).

trunk[2] *n* a. (*of car*) bût *m*, [F] kyâs *f.* b. (*box*) àdakà *f*, bàbban àkwàtì *m.*

trust 1. *v* a. amìncē dà / amìncē wà *v4*, yàřda dà *v3*, bâ w. jìkī, bâ w. àmanà: I *~*ed him nā amìncē dà shī = nā bā shì jìkī; don't *~* what he says kâř kù amìncē wà màganàřsà; I wouldn't *~* him with my car bà zân bā shì àmānàř mōtàtà ba. b. (*depend on*) dògarà dà/gà *v3*: in God we *~* mun dògarà gà Allàh. 2. *n* a. (*relationship of ~*) amìncì *m*, amìncêwā *f*: they have *~* in each other àkwai amìncì tsàkāninsù; my *~* in him was shaken amìncêwàř dà na yi masà tā ràunanà. b. (*sth. entrusted*) àmānà *f*: a *~* territory ƙasař riƙon àmānà; give sth. to so. in *~* bâ w. àmānàř w.a.: the money has been put in *~* for them an bā dà àmānàř kuɗinsù = an sâ kuɗinsù à àmānà; betray a *~* ci àmānà; breach so.'s *~* yi wà zàmba cikin amìncì; keep a *~* riƙè àmānà. c. (*Law*): put sth. in *~* waƙàftā *v1*: his estate has been put in *~*

an waƙàftà dūkìyàr̃sà.

**trustworthy** *adj* àmìntaccē *adj*, (mài) riƙòn àmānà *m*, (mài) àlkawàr̃ī *m*: he is ~ yanà dà (riƙòn) àmānà = yanà dà àlkawàr̃ī; he is not ~ shī bà àmìntaccē ba nè.

**truth** *n* a. gàskiyā / gaskiyā *f* (*H tone variant used for emphasis*): I've already told you the ~, but you refuse to believe me nā fa shā gayà makà gàskiyā àmmā kā ƙi yàr̃dā; there is an element of ~ in it àkwai ƙanshin gàskiyā à ciki; the real ~ of the matter is... hàƙīƙanin gàskiyar̃ màganàr̃ ita cè...; it's the ~! gàskiyā cè/nè! tell the ~, is it really so? tsàkāninkà dà Allàh wannàn gaskiyā nè? it's the real ~! hàƙīƙanin gàskiyā nè! = ainihin gaskiyā nè! = gàskiyā cè tsàkānī dà Allàh! = ƙashin gaskiyā nè! there's not a single grain of ~ in it! kō àlāmàr̃ gaskiyā bābù à màganàr̃! (*fig.*) the ~ is bitter dā mā gaskiyā dācī gàrē tà; (*fig.*) the ~ will out gaskiyā tanà dà rānar̃tà.

**truthful** *adj* (mài) gàskiyā *f*, na gàskiyā *f*.

**truthfully** *adv*: to speak ~... bisà gàskiyā...; ~ speaking, what happened? tsàkānī dà Allàh, mè ya fàru?

**try** *v* a. (*make an effort*) yi ƙòƙarī *m*, tàɓūkà *v1*: I tried but failed nā yi ƙòƙarī àmmā nā kāsà; he tried his best yā yi yà ƙòƙarīnsà = yā yi yà yīnsà = yā ci yà cînsà. b. (*experiment*) gwadà *v1*, jar̃r̃àbā *v1*: here's my pen, ~ it gà àlƙalàmīnā kà jar̃r̃àbā; you won't know until you ~ sai an gwadà akàn san na ƙwar̃ai; let's ~ our luck mù jar̃r̃àbà hannunmù = mù gwadà sā'àr̃mù; ~ it and see it you like it (*esp. foods*) tàɓā kà ji. c. (*Law*) yi wà shàr̃i'à *f*: he was tried for murder an yi masà shàr̃i'àr̃ kisàn kâi.

**trypanosomiasis** *n* sammōr̃è *m*.

**tsetse fly** *n* ƙudan tsandō *m*.

**Tuareg** *n* a. (*member of ethnic group*) būzū *m*, būzuwā *f* ⟨aye⟩. b. (*language*) būzancī *m*.

**tub** *n* (*large metal*) kwānò *m* ⟨uka, oCi⟩; (*modern bathtub*) bāhò *m*.

**tube** *n* būtūtū *m*, tìyō *m*, [F] tìyyò *m*; inner ~ tîf *m*, [F] shambûr̃ *m*; ~ of toothpaste gidan mân gōgè haƙòrā.

**tuberculosis** *n* tībì *m*, cīwòn fùkā *m*.

**tuck** *v*: ~ in one's shirt yi zànzarō *m*.

**Tuesday** *n* Tàlātà *f*.

**tuft** *n* (*of hair*) zankò *m* ⟨aye⟩.

**tumble** *v* fāɗì *v3b*.

**tumbler** *n* (*drinking glass*) tambùlàn *m* ⟨tambulōlī, tambulà⟩, gìlāshì *m*, [F] fìnjālì *m* ⟨ai⟩.

**tumor** *n* (*malignant*) cīwòn dājì *m*, (*non-malignant*) ƙarì *m*.

**tumult** *n* hàyà-hàyà *f*, hàyàniyà *f*, r̃ūr̃ūmā *f*.

**tune** 1. *n* karìn waƙà *m*: be out of ~ karyà karìn waƙà. 2. *v*: ~ an engine daidàità tàfiyàr̃ injì.

**tunnel** *n* (*burrow*) rāmì *m* ⟨uka⟩.

**turban** *n* rawànī *m* ⟨u-a⟩: wind a ~ around naɗà rawànī.

**turbid** *adj* gùr̃ɓàtaccē *adj*.

**turkey** *n* tàlotàlo *m*.

**Turkish coffee** *n* gahawà *f*.

**turmeric** *n* gàngàmau *m*.

**turmoil** *n* hàrgitsī *m*, hàrgōwà *f*; (*esp. Pol.*) rìkicī *m*: the country is in ~ ƙasā tā rikìcē; his mind is in ~ hankàlinsà yā rūɗè.

**turn** 1. *v* a. (*rotate*) jūyà *v1*: ~ a key in a lock jūyà mabūɗī cikin kwàɗò; ~ sth. around jirkìtā *v1*: they ~ed the table around sun jirkìtā tēbùr̃. b. (*change direction*) kar̃kàtā *v1*, kar̃kàcē *v4*: the road ~s to the south hanyà tā kar̃kàtā kudù; ~ one's head around waiwàyà *v1*, yi wàiwàyē *m*: he ~ed his head around and looked at them yā waiwàyà yā dùbē sù; ~ to the right, left yi dāma, hagu = jūyà dāma, hagu; (*fig.*) he didn't know which way to ~ yā rasà indà zâi sà kânsà. c. (*var. v + adv/prep uses*): ~ against so. jūyà wà bāyā; he ~ed his back on me yā bā nì bāyā; ~ so. against so. haɗà w. dà w.: they ~ed Musa against me sun haɗà ni dà Mūsā; ~ aside, away (*put to one side*) kau dà / kawar̃ (dà) *v5*: he ~ed his eyes away yā kau dà ganī; ~ back (*return*) kōmō *v6*; ~ sth. inside out birkìtā *v1*: he ~ed his shirt inside out yā birkìtā tagùwā; ~ into (*become*) zama *v\**: the water ~ed into ice ruwā yā zama ƙanƙarā; ~ into sth. (*be transformed*) rìkiɗà *v3*: she was ~ed into a tree tā rìkiɗà tā zama bishiyà; ~ sth. into sth. (*change*) mai dà / mayar̃ (dà) *v5*: he ~ed his house into an office yā mai dà gidansà ōfìs; she ~ed the dress into a skirt tā mai dà rìgā fàtàrī; ~ off the road rātsè dàgà hanyà; ~ off the tap rufè kân famfò; ~ out the light kashè fìtilà; ~ out to be zamantō *v6*: everything ~ed out to be nonsense kōmē yā zamantō shìrmē; it ~s out that he has no money yā zamantō bâ shi

dà kuɗī; ~ over sth. birkìtā *v1;* be ~ed
over birkìcē *v4;* ~ toward fùskàntā *v2:*
he ~ed towards Mecca yā fùskànci Makà;
~ sth. upside down kifā *v1.*
2. *n* a. *(change in direction)* kwanā *m*
⟨e²⟩: a sudden, sharp ~ in the road wata
ƙùrarriyaɼ kwanā à hanyā. b. *(chance
to do sth.)* kāmū *m:* whose ~ is it? kāmùn
wānē nḕ? wait for your ~ kà dākàtā haɼ
kāmùnkà yā zō = kà dākàtā haɼ tà zō
kânkà; take ~s sauyà hannū: they took
~s driving sun sauyà hannū wajen tūƙī;
in ~ *(in sequence)* bî dà bî. c. *(favor):* a
good ~ àlhēɼī *m:* she did me a good ~ tā
yi minì wani ɗan àlhēɼī; one good ~ de-
serves another *(fig.)* àlhēɼī bā yā̀ fāɗùwā
ƙasà banzā.

**turn signal** *n* sigìnà *f,* [F] kìlìyòtân *m:*
the ~ is blinking sigìnà tanā cî.

**turtle** *n* ƙìfīfiyā *f.*

**tusk** *n* haurḕ *m,* haƙōrin gīwā *m.*

**tutor** *n* mālàmī *m* ⟨ai⟩.

**tweezers** *n* màtsēfatā *f* ⟨ai⟩.

**twelfth** *adj* na gōmà shà biyu.

**twelve** *quant* (gōmà) shà biyu *f.*

**twenty** *quant* àshìrin *f.*

**twice** *adv* sàu biyu: he is ~ as strong as
I am yā fi ƙarfīnā sàu biyu; *(multiple)* ninkì biyu: I want ~ as much
as that inā sôn ninkì biyun wannàn;
think ~ about it before you agree kà yi
tàɼaddàdin màganā kàfìn kà yàɼda.

**twigs** *n (for firewood)* ƙirārḕ *p.*

**twilight** *n* màgàɼibā / màngàɼibā *f,* àlmūɼū
*f.*

**twin(s)** *n* ɗan tagwai *m,* 'yaɼ tagwai *f,*
'yan biyu *p,* tagwāyē *p:* he is a ~ ɗan
tagwai nḕ; he is my ~ brother shī
àbōkin haihùwātā nḕ = tàre akà hàifē
mù dà shī; if they are born at the same
time, they are ~ in an hàifē sù à lōkàcī
gùdā, ('yan) tagwāyē nḕ.

**twine** *n* kìɼtānī *m.*

**twinkle** *v* yi ƙyàllī *m,* yi ƙyàlƙyàlī *m.*

**twist** *v* a. muɼɗā *v1:* ~ the key to the left
kà muɼɗà makullī hagu. b. *(distort, bend
out of shape)* muɼɗḕ *v4,* muɼgùɗē *v4:* ~ the
meaning, facts muɼɗḕ màganā, gàskiyā;
she ~ed her mouth *(to make a face)*
tā muɼgùɗè bàkī. c. *(sth. into strands)*
tufkā *v1:* ~ palm fronds to make a rope
tufkà kabā à yi igiyā dà ita. d. *(a
joint out of place)* yi taɼgaɗḕ *m,* guɼɗḕ
*v4:* he ~ed his ankle yā yi taɼgaɗḕ à
idòn sau; be ~ed out of shape kaɼkàcē
*v4.*

**twitch** *v:* the ears of the horse ~ed dōkì nā̀
kaɗà kunnuwànsà; the rabbit ~ed its nose
zōmō yā mōtsà hancì.

**two** *quant* biyu *f:* cut it in ~ kà rabà
shi biyu; into ~s, ~ each biyu-biyu /
bībiyu *adv:* divide them into ~s kà rabà
su bībiyu; they are ~ of a kind *(fig.)*
àbōkin damō guzā.

**type**[1] *n (kind)* irì *m* ⟨x²⟩, nau'ì *m* ⟨oCi⟩:
what ~ of bicycle do you have? wànè irìn
bāsukùɼ gàrē kà? what ~ of apparatus
is it? it's a recorder wànè nau'ìn nā'ūɼā
yakè? ɼàkōdā cē.

**type**[2] *v (on typewriter)* bugā *v1.*

**typewriter** *n* tàfìɼētā *m,* [F] màshîn *f.*

**typhoid fever** *n* zàzzàɓī *m.*

**typical** *adj:* that is ~ of Audu ai wannàn
hālin Audù nē; she is a ~ Hausa woman
ita bàhaushìyā cḕ sak.

**typically** *adv (usually)* yawancī *m:* the men
~ wear caps yawancī mazā sunā̀ sànye dà
hūlā.

**typist** *n* mài bugùn tàfìɼētā *n,* tàifîs *n,*
[F] dàktìlô *n.*

**tyrannize** *v* zàluntā *v2,* yi wà zālūncì *m.*

**tyranny** *n* zālūncì *m.*

**tyrant** *n* àzzàlùmī *m* ⟨ai⟩, mazàlùncī *m.*

**tyre** *n, see* tire.

# U

udder *n* hantsằ *f*.

ugliness *n* mūnî *m*.

ugly *adj* a. (*physically*) mùmmūnā *adj*, (mài) mūnî *m*: an ~ girl mùmmūnař yārinyằ = yārinyằ mài mūnî. b. (*fig.*) ƙàzāmī *adj* 〈ai〉: an ~ matter ƙàzāmař hařƙằ; turn, become ~ ƙàzantà *v3*, ƙazàncē *v4*: the situation has turned ~ àl'amàřîn yā ƙazàncē.

ulcer *n* (*external sore*) gyàmbō *m* 〈una〉, mīkî *m*.

ultimate *adj* na ƙàrshē *m*: that is our ~ goal shī nề būrînmù na ƙàrshē.

ultimatum *n* wa'àdī *m*: they were given an ~ to return to work or be fired an bā sù wa'àdī sù kōmà aikî kō à kòrē sù.

ululate *v* (*by women*) yi gūdằ *f* 〈e²〉.

umbilical cord *n* cībìyā *f*.

umbilical hernia *n* cībî *m*.

umbrella *n* laimằ *f* 〈oCi〉.

umpire *n* àlƙālin wằsā *m*, řàfàlî *m*, [F] àlbìtìř *m*.

un- (*neg. prefix for n & adj, see* in-) a. (*for nouns, usu. use* rashìn + *n*): unkindness rashìn kiřƙî; unhappiness rashìn jîn dādī. b. (*for attrib. adj, usu. use* maràs + *n*): an unkind man mùtûm maràs kiřƙî; an unpopular woman màtā maràs farin jinī. c. (*for pred. adj including deverbal adj, usu. use neg. sent. or a neg. v*): he is unable to work bài iyà yîn aikî ba = yā ƙāsà yîn aikî; he was unfit for the job bài dācề dà gurbî ba; she was unhappy bà ta ji dādī ba; the river is uncrossable kồgī bā yằ ƙềtàruwā.

unable *adj*: be ~ ƙāsà (+ *vbl. or action n*) *v1*, iyà *v1* (*in neg.*): he is ~ to make up his mind yā ƙāsà tsai dà shāwařằ = bài iyà tsai dà shāwařằ ba; he is ~ to tell a lie bā yằ iyà yîn ƙaryā.

unanimous *adj*: they are ~ about doing it kànsù ɗaya nề gà yînsà.

unanimously *adv* (gà) bằkī ɗaya, gằbā ɗaya: they supported him ~ sun gồyi bāyansà gà bằkī ɗaya.

unappealing *adj* (mài) baƙin jinī *m*.

unavoidable *adj* bâ makawā: it's ~, it must be done bâ makawā, sai an yī shì; an ~

matter, circumstance làřūřằ *f*: something ~ must have prevented him from coming hàƙīƙằ wata làřūřằ tā hanằ shi zuwằ.

unaware *adj*: we were ~ of the danger we were in bà mù fařga dà haɗàřîn dà mukề ciki ba; catch, take so. ~s fàki numfāshin w., shàmmātằ *v2*.

unbearable *adj*: this heat is ~ zāfin nàn yā shàddadằ.

unbelievable 1. *adj* (mài) ban màmākî: it was an ~ story làbářî nē mài ban màmākî; be ~ (*be impressive*) wucề mìsālî, zařcè mìsālî, wucề kīmằ: his story was ~ làbāřìnsà yā wucè mìsālî. 2. *excl* àbin màmākî!

unbeliever *n* (*infidel*) kāfìřī *m* 〈ai〉.

unbutton *v* ɓallề *v4*: he ~ed his coat yā ɓallề maɓallin kwât ɗinsà.

uncertain *adj* maràs tabbàs: the results are ~ sằkàmakôn bâ shi dà tabbàs.

uncertainty *n* rashìn tabbàcī *m*.

uncle *n* (*gen'l term of ref.*) kàwu / kāwù *m* 〈una〉; (*maternal*) řàfànī *m* 〈ai〉, bàba *m*; (*paternal*) kàwu, baffà / bàffa *m* 〈anni〉; (*terms of addr.*) bàba, baffà.

uncomfortable *adj*: my shoes are ~ bà nằ jîn dāɗin tākalmằ = tākalmàn sun cī minì ƙafằ; this chair is ~ kujềrař nàn bâ ta dà dāɗin zamā; make so. ~ ƙuntàtā wà *v1*: Audu makes life ~ for me Audù yā ƙuntàtā minì.

uncommon *adj* nādiřàn *adv*: it's an ~ sight bâ à ganinsà sai nādiřàn.

unconscious *adj* a. (*fainted*): become ~ sūma *v3a*, sômề *v4*, (*as in a coma*) fìta dàgà hayyàcī; make so. ~ sômař/sūmař (dà) *v5*: the blow knocked him ~ dūkàn yā sūmař dà shī; he remained ~ for 2 days yā kwāna biyu à sùme. b. (*not aware*): he is ~ of his actions bài san cīwòn kânsà ba.

unconsciously *adv* (*not on purpose*) bằ dà gàngan ba.

uncontrollable *adj* (*unruly*) kàngàrarrē *adj*, gàgàrarrē *adj*; be ~ kangàrē *v4*, gàgarà *v3*, fàskarà *v3*, *see* control: the children are ~ today yâu yârā sun gàgarà; her children are ~ 'yā'yantà sun gàgàrē tà.

uncooperative *adj* (*esp. about one's duties*) (mài) ƙyûyā / ƙîwā *f*.

uncover *v* a. (*a container*) būɗề *v4*. b. (*expose, make known*) tōnà *v1*, gānō *v6*: ~ a secret tōnà àsīřī; ~ a plot gānō maƙařƙashìyā; ~ oneself (*take off outer garment*) yāyè lulluɓī.

undecided *adj*: be ~ yi wàswāsĩ m: I'm ~ whether to go or not inà wàswāsĩ kō ìn tàfi kō ìn zaunā.

undefeated *adj*: the team is ~ bà à taɓà cînsù ba.

undeniable *adj* bâ shakkā: he knows how to work, that's ~ yā iyà aikĩ bâ shakkā.

under *prep* a. à ƙàrƙashin *prep*: it is ~ the table yanā ƙàrƙashin tēbùr̃; ~ a tree à ƙàrƙashin itàcē = à gìndin itàcē; ~ his reign à zāmànin mulkìnsà; the matter is ~ consideration anā dūbà màganàr̃. b. (*lower than*) ƙasà dà *prep*: she is ~ 13 years old tanā ƙasà dà shēkarā shâ ukù = shēkàruntà bà sù kai shâ ukù ba.

underbrush *n* (*thick undergrowth*) sàr̃ƙaƙ-ƙiyā *f*.

undercut *v* (*in business*) kashè wà kàsuwā.

underestimate *v* rainà / rēnà *v1*: I ~ed its cost, his strength nā rainà kuɗinsà, ƙarfinsà.

undergo *v*: ~ difficulties shā wàhalā; she underwent an operation an yi matà tìyātā.

underground *adv* (à) ƙàrƙashin ƙasā.

undergrowth *n* sàr̃ƙaƙƙiyā *f*.

underhanded *adj*: through ~ means ta hanyàr̃ cùkù-cukū.

underline *v* jā lāyì à ƙàrƙashī.

undermine *v* yi wà yankan bāyā.

underneath 1. *adv* à ƙàrƙashī *adv*: there is room ~ àkwai wurī à ƙàrƙashī; I want the one ~ inà sôn na ƙàrƙashī. 2. *prep* à ƙàrƙashin, see under.

underpants *n* (*women's*) kamfai *m*, dùr̃ôs na mātā *m*; (*men's*) kamfai *m*, dùr̃ôs *m*, bàntē *m* (una), fētō *m*, [F] kàlìsô *m*.

undershirt *n* (*short-sleeved*) 'yar̃ ciki *f*, 'yar̃ shārā *f*; (*sleeveless*) singìlētì *f* (oCi), sōcì *f*.

undershorts *n*, *see* underpants.

underskirt *n* fàtàrī *m*, ɗan tōfi *m*, mùƙurū *m*.

underside *n* ƙàrƙashī *m*.

understand *v* a. (*comprehend*) fàhimtà *v2*, fàhimtà *v3*, gānè *v4*: do you ~ what you are supposed to do? kā gānè àbin dà zā kà yi? he understood what I meant yā fàhìmci nufìnā = yā gānè hausātā; we ~d that we were not welcomed mun fàhimtà cêwā bà à sônmù; children ~ quickly yârā nà dà saurin fàhimtà; make oneself understood bayyànà kâi: I couldn't make myself understood nā kāsà bayyànà kâinā. b. (*hear*) ji *v0*: I didn't ~ what he said bàn ji àbin dà ya fàɗa

ba. c. (*a language*) ji *v0*: do you ~ English? kanā jîn Tūr̃ancī?

understanding 1. *n* a. (*intellect*) fahàmī *m*. b. (*comprehension*) fàhimtā *f*. c. (*accord, agreement*) fàhimtā *f*: mutual ~ fàhimtàr̃ jūnā; reach, come to an ~ shiryà *v1*; on the ~ that... dà shar̃àɗin cêwā.... 2. *adj* (*sympathetic*): he is a very ~ person mùtûm nē mài jîn tàusàyī.

undertake *v*: ~ a project yi aikĩ; ~ responsibility ɗauki nauyī.

underwear *n*, *see* underpants.

undo *v* a. (*reverse sth. done*): there's no way to ~ the damage bâ yâddà zā à yi gà ɓar̃nâr̃. b. (*untie*) kwancè *v4*; (*sth. wound around*) warwàrē *v4*. c. (*come apart*) ɓarkè *v4*: the stitches have come undone ɗinkì yā ɓarkè.

undoubtedly *adv* bàbù shakkà, tabbàs, à hàƙīƙà.

undress *v* tūɓè *v4*.

uneasy *adj*: I am ~ about this business wannàn sha'ànîn bài kwântā minì à râi ba.

unemployed *n* & *adj* maràs aikĩ *m*, mài zaman kashè-wàndō *m*, zàunā-gàrī-banzā *n*: be ~ yi zaman kashè-wàndō; the workers were ~ for 3 months ma'àikàtā sun yi watà ukù sunà zaman kashè-wàndō; there are a lot of ~ in the city àkwai maràsà aikĩ dà yawà à bir̃nîn.

unemployment *n* rashìn aikìn yî *m*, zaman kashè-wàndō *m*: the government is combatting ~ gwamnatì tanā yāƙì dà zaman kashè-wàndō.

unequivocally *adv* ɓarō-ɓàrò *idph*, à fìlī: he told them ~ that he wouldn't agree to their plan yā fitō musù ɓarō-ɓàrò bà zâi yàr̃da dà shirìnsù ba.

unexpected *adj* bâ-zàta *f*: an ~ gift, visit kyàutar̃, zìyār̃àr̃ bâ-zàta; his ~ behavior caused us some difficulties bâ-zàtàr̃ dà ya yi manà tā bā mù wàhalā.

unexpectedly *adv* (*suddenly*) bâ-zàta, bâ zàtō bâ tsàmmānì: I saw her quite ~ nā gan tà bâ zàtō bâ tsàmmānì; appear ~ ɓullō *v6*; meet so. ~ yi kìcìɓìs dà.

unfair *adj* a. (*unjust*) maràs àdalcì *m*: he is ~ to his students bà yà wà ɗàlìbansà àdalcì. b. (*dishonest*): be ~ to so. ƙwārà *v2*. c. (*inappropriate*): an ~ question tàmbayàr̃ dà bà tà dācè ba.

unfairly *adv* a. (*unjustly*): treat so. ~ zàluntà *v2*. b. (*dishonestly*) ƙwārà *v2*: he played ~ with us yā ƙwàrē mù.

unfasten *v* (*sth. tied*) kwancè *v4*, suncè *v4*; (*sth. not tied*) ɓallè *v4*: ~ a button, buckle ɓallè maɓallī, bōkùl; ~ a zipper jā zîk.

unfit *adj*: this water is ~ to drink ruwan nàn bài dācè dà shâ ba.

unfold *v* būɗè *v4*.

unfortunate *adj* a. (*unlucky*) maràs sā'à̃ *f*: it was ~ that you didn't find her at home kin yi rashìn sā'à̃ dà bà kì sāmē tà à gidā ba. b. (*annoying, vexing*): sth. ~ àbin tàkàicī *m*.

unfriendly *adj*: he is ~ bā yà̃ sôn mutà̃nē.

unglued *adj*: become ~ ɓallè *v4*: the picture has become ~ hòtôn yā ɓallè.

ungrammatical *adj* làhàntaccē *adj*: this is an ~ sentence wannàn jimlà̃ làhàntacciyā cè.

ungrateful *adj* (*psn.*) bùtùlu *m* ⟨ai⟩, (mài) rashìn gòdiyā *m; don't be ~ (for what you have) kadà kà yi butulcì; be ~ to so. (*fig.*) yi wà bàkin kàzā.

unhappiness *n* baƙin cikì *m*, rashìn jîn dàdī *m*, ɓàcìn râi *m*.

unhappy *adj* (mài) baƙin cikì *m*: I'm ~ today yâu inà baƙin cikì = yâu bā nà̃ jîn dàdī = yâu râinà yā ɓàcì; we were ~ about the situation bà mù ji dàdin àl'amàrîn ba; she looks ~ tā ɓàtà rântà; make so. ~ ɓàtà wà râi.

unhealthy *adj* a. (*psn.*) maràs lāfiyà *f*: this child is ~ yàròn nân bā shi dà lāfiyà = yanà̃ rashìn lāfiyà. b. (*of food, drink*) maràs kyâu *m*: this food is ~ àbincin nàn bā shi dà kyâu. c. (*of thing, state*) mùmmūnā *adj*: it is an ~ situation mùmmūnan hālì nē.

uniform[1] *n* kāyan aikì *m*, rìgar aikì *f*, inìfàm *f*; army ~ kāyan sōjà; nurse's ~ kāyan nâs; police ~ rìgar sarkī; school ~ kāyan makaɽantā.

uniform[2] *adj* (mài) bâi ɗaya *adv*: boxes of a ~ size akwàtunà̃ màsu bâi ɗaya; make sth. ~ daidàità *v1*.

uniformity *n* (*equality*) dàidaitō *m*: they are working toward ~ in wages anà̃ nēman sāmùn dàidaitō wajen àlbâshī.

unify *v* a. (*unite*) haɗè *v4*: they want to ~ the country sunà̃ sô sù haɗè sù zama ƙasā ɗaya. b. (*standardize*) daidàità *v1*: ~ a system daidàità tsārì.

unimportant *adj* maràs muhimmancì *m*: the matter is ~ màganàr bà ta dà muhimmancì = màganàr bà mùhimmìyar àbā ba cè.

uninhabited *adj*: an ~ house gidân dà bâ kōwā; an ~ building (*deserted*) kangō *m* ⟨aye⟩; a wild, ~ area ƙungurmin dājì.

unintelligibly *adv*: speak ~ yi gwàlàngwalan *idph*.

unintentionally *adv* bà dà gàngan ba.

uninteresting *adj* (mài) cîn râi *m*, maràs shà'awà̃ *f*: this work is ~ aikìn nân nà̃ dà cîn râi = aikìn nân bâ shi dà shà'awà̃.

union *n* ƙungìyā *f* ⟨oCi⟩ : labor ~ ƙungìyar ƙwādagō; trade ~ ƙungìyar ma'àikàtā.

Union Jack *n* tūtàr Ingìlà *f*.

unit *n* (*section, part, division*) sāshè / sāshì *m* ⟨Ca⟩.

unite *v* a. (*combine into one*) haɗè *v4*, hàɗu *v7*: they are ~d through marriage sun hàɗu ta aurē. b. (*join together against*) haɗà kâi: they ~d to fight the enemy sun haɗà kâi don sù yàƙi àbōkin gàbā; a ~d government gwamnatìn haɗìn kâi; ~ for the common good haɗà kâi sabòdà àmfã̀nin kōwā; ~ forces haɗà ƙarfī = gamà ƙarfī = haɗà gwīwà̃.

united *adj* hàɗaɗɗē *adj*.

United States of America *n* Amìrkà / Àmērikà *f*, [F] Àmìrîk *f*.

unity *n* a. (*cooperation*) haɗìn kâi *m* : live in ~ zaunà̃ cikin haɗìn kâi; ~ is strength haɗà kâi shī nè̃ ƙarfī. b. (*Relig., doctrine of the ~ of God*) tàuhīdì *m*.

universal *n & adj* ruwan dare *m*, gàmà-gàri *m*, na dūniyà̃ *f*: it has become ~ yā zama ruwan dare = yā zama gàmà-gàri; love is ~ sô gàmà-gàrin àbù nē = sô àbù nē na dūniyà̃.

universally *adv* a kō'ìnā *adv*: this is ~ true wannàn gàskiyā cè à kō'ìnā.

universe *n* dūniyà̃ *f* ⟨oCi⟩.

university *n* jàmi'à̃ *f* ⟨oCi⟩: go to ~ shìga jàmi'à̃; graduate from ~ saukè kàɽàtū dàgà jàmi'à̃.

unjust *adj* maràs ādalcì *m*.

unkind *adj* maràs kiřkì *m*; (*mean psn.*) mài baƙin cikì *m*; be ~ to so. cùtā *v2*, ƙwàrā *v2*: he treated me ~ly yā cùcē nì.

unknown 1. *adj* bàƙō *adj* ⟨i⟩: an ~ disease suddenly appeared wata bàƙuwar cùtā tā ɓullō.
2. *n* sanìn gaibù/gaibì *m*: only God knows the ~ sanìn gaibì sai Allàh.

unlawful *adj* (*esp. in Islam*) hàřâm *m*, hàřàmtaccē *adj*; it is ~ to do that yîn hakà hàřâm nē; declare, make sth. ~ hařàmtā *v1*.

unless *conj* a. ìdan/in (+ *neg. cl.*), sai (fa) ìdan/in (+ *complet.*): I will go ~ it rains zân tàfi ìdan bà à yi ruwā ba; don't go ~ it becomes necessary kadà kà tàfi sai fa ìdan yā zama dōlè; ~ I hear from you, I'll go ahead with it in bàn ji kōmē ba zân ci gàba dà shì. b. (*following a neg. cl.*) sai (dai) (+ *complet.*): he won't do it ~ you pay him first bà zâi yi ba sai kā biyā shì tùkùna; I won't give it to him ~ he comes for it himself bà zân bā shì ba sai yā zō dà kânsà.

unlikely *adv*: it is ~ that... dà ƙyaƙ nè ìdan (+ *fut.*), bā yà yìwuwā (+ *subjunct.*): it is ~ that he will stay dà ƙyaƙ nè ìdan zâi zaunā; it is ~ that he will finish on time bā yà yìwuwā yà gamā cikin lōkàcī.

unlimited *adj* (*for countable things*) bìlā haddìn *adv*: there are an ~ number of tickets àkwai tikitì bìlā haddìn; (*for mass nouns*) maràs iyākā *f*: the king has ~ power sarkī yanā dà ìkò maràs iyākā; the possibilities are ~ abūbuwàn dà zā à iyà yî bâ su dà iyākā.

unload *v* saukè kāyā, saukaƙ dà kāyā: ~ a donkey saukè kāyā dàgà kàn jàkī; ~ a truck saukè wà mōtā lōdì.

unlock *v* būdè dà makullì.

unlucky *adj* maràs sā'à *f*.

unmanageable *adj* kàngàrarrē *adj*, gàgàrarrē *adj*.

unmarried *adj* (*prev. married*) gwaurō *m*, gwauruwā *f* ⟨aye⟩; (*man, never married*) tùzūrū *m* ⟨ai⟩; (*girl, of marriageable age*) bùdurwā *f* ⟨oCi⟩; (*woman, prev. married*) bàzawàrā / zawàrā *f* ⟨zawarāwā⟩; she is still ~ haƙ yànzu bâ ta dà aurē.

unnecessary *adj*: it is ~ to do that bâ dōlè ba à yi hakà = bâ wājìbī nè à yi hakà ba.

unpack *v* kwancè kāyā.

unpleasant *adj* (*of sth.*) maràs dādī *m*; (*of psn.*) maràs wàlwàlā *f*, maràs faƙa'à *f*, (mài) dācin râi *m*.

unpopular *adj* (mài) baƙin jinī *m*, maràs farin jinī *m*: he is an ~ teacher mālàmī nè mài baƙin jinī; he is an ~ leader shūgàbā nè wàndà bā shi dà farin jinī.

unpredictable *adj* (*psn.*) miskìlī *m* ⟨ai⟩: he is ~ miskìlī nè = bā yà dà tabbàs; in an ~ way bà yàddà akè zàtō ba.

unprincipled *adj* maràs àƙīdā *f*.

unravel *v* warwàrē *v4*.

unrelated *adj* a. (*having no kinship*): they look alike but they are ~ sun yi kàmā àmmā bà sù gamà dangì dà jūnā ba. b. (*not connected with*): this is ~ to that wannàn bài shàfi wancàn ba.

unrest *n* tāshìn hankàlī *m*, hàrgitsī *m*, yāmùtsī *m*: there is widespread ~ àkwai tāshìn hankàlī dà yawā.

unripe *adj* ɗanyē *adj* ⟨u⟩.

unroll *v* warwàrē *v4*, būdè *v4*; (*of mat*) shimfìɗā *v1*.

unruly *adj* kàngàrarrē *adj*, gàgàrarrē *adj*.

unsafe *adj*: this bridge is ~ gadàƙ nân bâ ta dà amincì = bâ ta dà ƙwārī.

unscrew *v* kwancè ƙūsā.

unscrupulous *adj* maràs ādalcì *m*, maràs tàusàyī *m*.

unselfish *adj* (mài) kyàutā *f*: he is an ~ person mùtûm mài kyàutā nè.

unsophisticated *adj* (*psn.*) bàgidàjè *adj*, bàƙauyè *adj*.

unsuccessful *adj*: he was ~ bài ci nasaƙā ba = bài dācè ba.

unsuitable *adj* a. (*inappropriate*): this dress is ~ for you to wear rìgaƙ nàn bà tā dācè dà kē ba = bài càncantà kì sâ rìgaƙ nàn ba. b. (*unfit for so.*) kàmātā *v2* (+ *neg.*): this kind of work is ~ for women irìn wannàn aikì bài kàmàci mātā ba.

untidy *adj* ƙàzāmī *adj* ⟨ai⟩, maràs tsàrī *m*.

untie *v* kwancè *v4*, suncè *v4*; (*unravel*) warwàrē *v4*.

until 1. *prep* a. sai *prep & conj*: ~ tomorrow, next week sai gòbe, mākò mài zuwā; I didn't get to sleep ~ dawn bàn yi barcī ba sai gàrī yā wāyè; (*in greetings*): ~ you return! sai kā dāwō! ~ the next time! sai yâddà ta yìwu! b. (*up to spec. point in time*) haƙ (zuwā) *prep*: from Monday ~ Friday dàgà Lìttìnîn haƙ zuwā Jumma'à; it's been raining since yesterday up ~ this morning tun jiyà akè ruwā haƙ yâu dà sāfe.

2. *conj* a. (*ref. to fut. event*) (haƙ) sai (+ *complet.*), haƙ (+ *subjunct.*): wait ~ they come dākàtā sai sun zō = dākàtā haƙ sù zō; keep going ~ you get to the village kù ci gàba haƙ kù kai ƙauyèn; I won't know ~ I have tried it first bà zân iyà sanì ba sai nā gwadà tùkùna. b. (*ref. to past event*) haƙ (+ *complet.*): he lived there ~ he died yā zaunā can haƙ yā mutù; we waited ~ the rain stopped mun dākàtā haƙ ruwā yā ɗáukè; ~ after sai (dai) bāyan: I didn't find it ~ after they had left bàn sàmē shì ba sai dai bāyan sun tāshì. c. it was not ~ X that Y: sai dà X sā'àn nan Y (+ *rel. complet.*): it was not ~ they told us that we noticed it sai dà sukà gayà manà sā'àn nan mukà lùƙa.

untrue *adj* maràs gàskiyā *f*: the report was ~ ƙàhōtòn bâ na gàskiyā ba nè.

unusual *adv* a. (*seldom*) bâ sàfài...ba: it is ~ to see them bâ sàfài akàn gan sù ba. b. (*not normal*): it's ~ to have this kind of cold weather bà à sābà yîn irìn sanyin nàn ba.

unwillingness *n* nàwā *f*.

unwind *v* warwàrē *v4.*

unwise *adj*: it would be ~ to do that wāutā cě à yi hakà.

unworthy *adj*: he was ~ of the medal they gave him bài càncantà à bā shì lambàr̃ ba; make oneself ~ wulāk̃antar̃ dà kâi, wātsar̃ dà kâi.

up *adv* a. (*above, upstairs*) samā *adv*: he lifted it ~ yā d̃agà shi samà; he has gone ~ (*upstairs*) yā hau samà; prices are ~ today yâu fàr̃āshìn yā hau. b. (*for use as particle with verbs, see relevant verb entries; v4 verbs often convey total effect of an action*): he ate it all ~ yā cînyē shi; the well has dried ~ completely rījìyā tā k̃afè k̃af. c. (*a point in time*): ~ to har̃ *prep*: ~ to now har̃ yànzu; ~ to then, he had never left his village har̃ wànnan lōkàcī, bài tab̃à barìn k̃auyènsù ba; the time is ~ lōkàcī yā yi; the vacation is ~ hūtū yā k̃arè. d. (*a point in space*): ~ to har̃ yà *prep*, iyā *prep*: I accompanied him ~ to here nā rakà shi har̃ yà nân; the water came ~ to my knees ruwā yā kai har̃ yà gwīwà = ruwā yā kai iyā gwīwà. e. (*fig. uses*): what's ~? yàyà dai? = mè akè ciki? what are they ~ to? mè sukè yî? = mè sukè shiryàwā? he's ~ to no good bâ shi dà niyyàr̃ àlhēr̃ī; I've had it ~ to here with him yā kai nì iyā wuyà; the matter is ~ to you àl'amàr̃ìn sai yâddà ka ganī.

upbringing *n* (*re. moral training*) tàr̃biyyà *f*: his ~ is poor bâ shi dà tàr̃biyyà; (*re. behavior towards others*) ladàbì *m*.

uphill *adv*: the road goes ~ hanyà tanà hawā; walk ~ hau tudù.

upon *prep* a. (*on*) bisà, bisà kân, à kân; see on. b. (*to intro. cl.*) dà: ~ our return, we went to greet him dà dāwôwar̃mù mun jē mù gai dà shî; once ~ a time wata rānā: once ~ a time there was a king... wata rānā an yi wani sarkī....

upper *adj* na samà *m*: that book is on the ~ shelf littāfìn nan yanà kantà ta samà.

upright 1. *adj* (*just psn.*) nagàri *m*, tagàri *f* ⟨nagàrgàrū⟩, ādàlī *n* ⟨ai⟩.
2. *adv* (*standing up*) à tsàye; put sth. ~ tsai dà *v5*: stand the box ~ kà tsai dà àkwàtìn.

uprising *n* tāwāyè *m*, b̃ōr̃e *m*, tàr̃zōmā *f*: put down an ~ kashè tāwāyè = kwantar̃ dà tāwāyè.

uproar *n* hàrgàgī *m*, hàrgōwā *f*, hàrgitsī *m*: cause an ~ kāwō hàrgàgī = (*fig.*) tā dà zàune tsàye.

uproot *v* tumb̃ùkē *v4*; (~ *by shaking*)

gir̃gìd̃ē *v4.*

ups and downs *n*: life has its ~ (*fig.*) wata rānā à shā zumà, wata rānā madàcī.

upset *v* a. (*knock sth. over*) kifè *v4.* b. (*defeat*) kā dà / kāyar̃ (dà) *v5.* c. (*annoy so.*) bâ w. haushī, ji haushin w.: I was very ~ with Kande yesterday jiyà Kànde tā bā nì haushī k̃war̃ai = jiyà nā ji haushin Kànde k̃war̃ai; be ~ about, by sth. ji dācin w.a.: we were ~ by what Kande said mun ji dācin màganàr̃ Kànde. d. (*disturb emotionally*) gìgìtā *v1*: news of his death ~ everyone làbār̃ìn ràsuwar̃sà yā gìgìtā kōwā; become ~ gìgìcē *v4.* e. (*spoil*) b̃ātà *v1*: he ~ my plans yā b̃ātà minì shir̃ì.

upside-down *adv* à kìfe, à bìrkìce, à kàb̃ance; turn sth. ~ kifè *v4*, birkìtā *v1*, kab̃ancē *v4.*

upstairs *adv* samā *adv*, (à) bēnē *m*: bring him ~ hàwō dà shī bēnē; he came down from ~ yā saukō dàgà bēnē.

up-to-date *adj* na yànzu, na zāmànī *m*: ~ methods hanyōyin zāmànī.

upwards *adv* samā *adv*: it moved ~ yā yi gàba samā.

uranium *n* yùr̃ēniyàm *m*, [F] ìr̃ànìyân *m*.

urban *adj* na bir̃nī *m*: ~ development r̃āyà bir̃ānē.

urge *v* a. (*encourage*) k̃arfàfā wà *v1*, sâ wà k̃aimī: he ~d me to do it yā k̃arfàfā minì ìn yi. b. (*put pressure on*) matsà wà *v1*, tsanàntā wà *v1*: they ~d me to marry her sun matsà minì ìn àurē tà.

urgent *adj* na gaggāwā *f*: it is an ~ matter sha'ànin gaggāwā nè.

urgently *adv* dà gaggāwā *f*: you must look into this matter ~ dōlè kà dūbà màganàr̃ nân dà gaggāwā.

urgency *n* gaggāwā *f.*

urine *n* fitsārī *m*, (*euphem.*) bawàlī *m*: ~ has a sour smell bawàlī yanà zar̃nī.

urinate *v* yi fitsārī *m.*

us *pro, see* Appendix A; let ~/let's... (+ *v*) bàri mù... (+ *subjunct.*): let's give them a hand with that bàri mù tayà su dà wannàn.

use 1. *n* a. (*utility*) àmfànī *m*, fā'idà *f*: what is its ~? ìnā fā'idàr̃sà? it's of no ~ to me bâ shi dà wani àmfànī gàrē nì; this tool has many ~s àmfànin kāyan aikìn nân yanà dà yawà; the ~ of guns is prohibited an hanà àmfànī dà bindigōgī. b. (*benefit*) mamōr̃ā *f*: is there any ~ for this thing? ìnā mamōr̃ar̃ wannàn? get some ~ out of sth. mōrā *v2*: you can still get some ~ out of this old

bicycle hař yànzu kâ iyà m̀rař tsōhon k̀kèn nàn.
**2.** *v* a. (*utilize*) yi àmfànī dà: are you using this hammer? kanà àmfànī dà hamàř nân? which word should I ~ here? wàcè kalmà zân yi àmfànī dà ita à nân? ~ it in good health! Allàh yà amfànā! ~ sth. up ƙàrasař (dà) *v5;* be ~d up ƙàrè *v4:* the firewood is all ~d up itàcē yā ƙàrè. **b.** (*work by means of*) yi aikì dà: some typewriters ~ electricity wasu tāfiřētōcī nà aikì dà làntařkì. **c.** (*was formerly done*): ~d to dâ *adv*: I ~d to live there dâ can nakè dà zamā; he ~d to be a generous man but now he's a miser dâ mài kařimcī nē àmmā yànzu yā zama bàhīlì; they ~d to hunt with spears dâ anà fàrautà dà màsū.

**used**[1] *adj* (*second-hand*) kwàncē *m*: a ~ car mōtà kwàncē.

**used**[2] *adj* (*accustomed*): be, get ~ to sàbà dà *v1*: I'm getting ~ to this machine nā fàrà sàbàwā dà wannàn nā'ūřà; he is ~ to getting up early yā sàbà dà tàshì dà wuri.

**useful** *adj* **a.** (*utilizable*) (mài) àmfànī *m*, (mài) bā dà tàimakō: some ~ advice shāwařà mài àmfànī; it is very ~ yanà dà àmfànī ainùn = àmfàninsà yanà dà yawà; it is no longer ~ bâ shi dà sauran àmfànī; be ~ for yi àmfànī wajen; be ~ to àmfànà *v2*, yi wà àmfànī: this will be extremely ~ to students wannàn zâi àmfàni dàlìbai matuƙā = zâi yi wà dàlìbai àmfànī matuƙā. **b.** (*of benefit, value*): it is not at all ~ bâ shi dà mamōrā kō kàɗan = bâ shi dà wata mamōrā.

**usefulness** *n* **a.** (*utility*) àmfànī *m*, fā-'idà *f*: I question its ~ inà shakkàř fā-'idàřsà. **b.** (*benefit*) mamōrā *f*.

**useless** *adj* **a.** (*not useful*) maràs àmfànī *m*, maràs fā'idà *f*: it is ~ bâ shi dà àmfànī; I think such people are ~ bàn ga àmfànin irìn waɗànnân mutànē ba. **b.** (*senseless, worthless*) na banzā *f*: ~ work aikìn banzā; shouting is ~, there's no one around īhù banzā nè, bâ kōwā à nân; the car is ~ because of the accident haɗàřìn yā mai dà mōtà àbin banzā; a ~ person mùtumìn banzā *m*, wòfī *n*, ɗan banzā *m*, sākařai *n* ⟨sākàřkařī⟩.

**uselessness** *n* rashìn àmfànī *m*, rashìn fā'idà *m*, banzā *f*, sākařcì *m*.

**usual** *adj* **a.** (*common*): it is not ~ to do that bà sàfài akàn yi hakà ba. **b.** (*customary*): he is late as ~ yā màkarà kàmař yâddà ya sàbà; that's his ~ habit ai

dàbī'àřsà cē.

**usually** *adv* (*mostly*) yawancī *adv*, gālìbī *m*, gālibàn *adv*: ~ you see them at dusk yawancī dà màgàřibà akè ganinsù; I ~ get up at 6 o'clock gālibàn nakàn tāshì dàgà barcī dà ƙarfè shidà.

**usury** *n* (*Law*) řìba *f*.

**uterus** *n* mahaifà *f*.

**utmost** *n* iyàkà / iyākà *f*: do your ~ kà yi iyākař ƙòƙarinkà = kà ciccìjē = kà yi yà yînkà; we did our ~ to help mun yi iyàkař iyàwařmù mù bā dà tàimakō.

**utter**[1] *v*: he didn't ~ a word bài cê ƙàlà ba = bài cê uffàn ba.

**utter**[2] *adj* (*extreme*) na innānàhā *f*, na ƙìn ƙàrǎwā: he's an ~ fool wòfī nè na ƙìn ƙàrǎwā; that is ~ nonsense sùřūtù nē na innānàhā.

**utterance** *n* kàlāmì *m*, furùcī *m*.

**uvula** *n* b̀li / b̀lu *m*, hakìn wuyà *m*.

# V

vacancy *n* a. (*lodging*) wurī *m* ⟨aCe⟩: no ~ bābù wurī. b. (*job opening*) gurbìn aikī *m*.

vacant *adj*: that house is ~ gidan nàn bâ kōwā à cikinsà.

vacantly *adv*: stare ~ yi kallō gàlau.

vacation *n* a. (*official*) hūtū *m*, hūtun shāƙàtâwā *m*, lifī *m*, [F] kwànjê *m*: get, take a ~ sàmi lifī = yi hūtū = ɗauki hūtū; he is on ~ yanà cikin hūtū; I took my ~ last month nā ɗauki lifīnā watàn jiyà. b. (*esp. for students*) hūtū *m*, [F] bàkâns *f*; (*in Koranic schools*) tàshē *m*.

vaccinate *v* yi wà àllūrā *f*, yi wà lambà *f*, [F] yi wà shàsshāwā *f*: ~ so. against smallpox yi wà lambàr agànā; (*animals*) yi wà hūjī *m*.

vaccination *n* àllūrā *f*, lambà *f*, [F] shàsshāwā *f*; (*for animals, cattle*) hūjī *m*.

vacuum flask *n, see* thermos bottle.

vagabond *n* gàntàlallē *m* ⟨u⟩, mài wàlàgīgī *n*, mài ràgaitā *n*: he is a ~ shī gàntàlallē nè = mài ràgaitā nē; live like a ~ yi gàntàlī *m*; yi wàlàgīgī *m*, yi ràgaitā *f*.

vagina *n* farjī *m*; (*euphem.*) mātūcī / mātuncī *m*, gìndī *m*, gàbā *m*; (*vulg.*) dūrī *m*, gatô *m*, gùtsū *m*.

vagrancy *n* zaman banzā *m*, iskancī *m*.

vain *adj* a. (*conceited*) (mài) girman kâi *m*, (mài) jī-jī dà kâi *m*. b. (*useless*): in ~ à banzā, à wōfī: all their efforts were in ~ duk ƙōƙarinsù à banzā; it ended in ~ yā zama à wōfī.

valid *adj* a. (*defensible*) (mài) ƙarfī *m*, (mài) inganci *m*, ìngàntaccē *adj*: a ~ excuse hujjà mài ƙarfī. b. (*legal*): is your licence ~? shin lāsìn ɗinkà yanà aikī? = kanà dà lāsìn wàndà bài ƙarè ba? his passport is not ~ fàsfô ɗinsà yā ƙarè.

validity *n* inganci *m*.

valley *n* kwarī *m* ⟨uka²⟩.

valor *n* jàrùntakà *f*, màzàkutà *f*.

valuable *adj* a. (*of importance, value*) (mài) darajà *f*, (mài) kīmà/ƙīmà *f*; a ~ scholar masànī mài darajà. b. (*having economic worth*) (mài) kīmà/ƙīmà *f*: a ~ ring zōbè

mài ƙīmà. c. (*of use*) (mài) àmfànī *m*: a ~ lesson daràsī mài àmfànī.

value 1. *n* a. (*importance, worth*) darajà *f*, kīmà / ƙīmà *f*: for some people, knowledge is of little ~ ilìmī bā yà dà darajà wajen waɗansu mutànē. b. (*assessable, calculable worth*) kīmà / ƙīmà *f*: what is the ~ of your sheep? nawà nē kīmàr awākinkà? c. (*Econ.*) kadàrī *m*: the ~ of petroleum has decreased because of the glut kadàrin mâi yā karyè sabòdà yawànsà = an karyà kadàrin mâi sabòdà yawànsà; gold has a greater ~ than silver zīnārī yā fi azùrfā kadàrī. d. (*benefit*) àmfànī *m*, fā'idà *f*. 2. *v* (*consider important*) ɗauki w.a. dà darajà: I ~ my friendship with him nā ɗauki àbòtarmù dà shī dà darajà.

valve *n* (*in car*) bāwùl *m*, [F] sùfâf *m*.

van *n* (*passenger*) hayìs *f*, [F] hìyâs *f*; (*pickup type for delivering goods*) à-ƙòri-kūrā *f*.

vandal *n* ɗan iskà *m*, ɗan dabā *m*.

vandalism *n* iskancī *m*, dabancī *m*.

vanish *v* ɓacè *v4*: he ~ed into the crowd yā ɓacè cikin mutànē; ~ into water nitsè cikin ruwa; ~ into thin air (*fig.*) yi lāyàr zānā = yi lāyà.

vanity *n* girman kâi *m*, jī-jī dà kâi *m*, ɗàgāwā *f*.

vapor *n* tùrùrī *m*; ~ treatment (*for medicinal purposes*) sùràcē *m*.

vaporize *v* yi tùrùrī *m*.

variable *adj*: the weather is ~ yanàyī yā zama cànjau; the price is ~ fàrāshìnsà yanà hawā yanà sàukā.

variance *n*: be at ~ with yi sàɓānī *m*, sàɓà dà *v1*: your story is at ~ with theirs làbārìnkà yā sàɓà dà nāsù.

variation *n* bambancī *m*: ~ in price bambancìn fàrāshī.

varicose veins *n* nankarwā *f*.

variegated *adj* irī-irī *adv*; (*esp. having colors*) kalà-kalà *adv*, launī-launī *adv*.

variety *n* irī *m* ⟨e²⟩: this is not the ~ that I want wannàn bà irìn dà nakè sô ba; a ~ of (*lots of*) irī-irī: a ~ of hats hūlunà irī-irī.

various *adj* irī-irī *adv*, dàbam (dàbam) *adv*: ~ kinds of gifts kyàutā irī-irī; at ~ places à wasu wurārē dàbam; ~ ways of cooking hanyōyī dàbam-dàbam na dafà àbinci = hanyōyin girkī dàbam-dàbam; (*esp. of things having color*) kalà-kalà *adv*, launī-launī *adv*: : ~ kinds of cloth yādī kalà-kalà.

varnish *v* shāfà mân kātākō.

vary *v* a. (*change*) sauyà *v1*, canzà / canjà *v1*: the amount of rain varies according to the region yawàn ruwā yakàn sauyà gwàr̃gwadon shiyyà. b. (*differ*) yi dàbam: their opinions ~ r̃a'ayōyinsù sun yi dàbam.

vaseline *n* bàsîlîn *m*.

vast *adj* (*expr. by var. ideophonic adjs*) mākēkè *adj*, fankamēmè *adj*: a ~ field fîlī mākēkè.

vault *v* yi tsallē *m*; pole ~ (*Sport*) tsallen gwangwalā.

veal *n* nāmàn màrak̃ī *m*.

veer *v* a. kaucè *v4*: the car ~ed to the left mōtā tā kaucè hagu. b. (*of road*) kar̃kàtā *v1*: the road ~s south hanyà tā kar̃kàtā zuwà kudù.

vegetable(s) *n* kāyan làmbū *p*, [F] kāyan garkā *p*: spinach is a kind of ~ àlayyàhō yanà dàgà cikin kāyan làmbū.

vehicle *n* mōtā *f* ⟨oCi⟩; commercial ~s mōtōcin sufùr̃ī; ~ bureau ōfìshin lāsîsî.

veil *n* hìjābì *m*.

vein *n* jījìyā *f* ⟨oCi⟩, jè-zūci *m*.

velvet *n* kàrammiskì *m*.

vendor *n* (*street hawker*) mài tàllà *n*, ɗan kōlì *m*; (*at outdoor table*) ɗan tēbùr̃ *m*.

venereal disease *n* cīwòn sanyī *m*.

vengeance *n* rāmuwā *f*, sàkayyà *f*; take ~ for sth. rāmà *v1*.

venom *n* dafî *n*.

veranda *n* bàr̃andà *f*, fàfàr̃andà *f*.

verb *n* fi'ìlì *m* ⟨oCi⟩, àikàtau *m*; a ~ phrase yankìn àikàtau.

verbal *adj* a. (*oral*) dà bàki *m*: he gave me a ~ promise yā yi minì àlkawàr̃ī dà bàki. b. (*Gram.*) na àikàtau *m*.

verbose *adj* (*to the point of indiscretion*) (mài) kaudī *m*.

verdict *n* hukuncì *m* ⟨e²⟩: pronounce a ~ yankè hukuncì; abide by the ~ of the court yàr̃da dà hukuncìn kōtù.

verge *n*: on the ~ of gab dà *prep*, nā̀ har̃amà *f*, nā̀ shir̃ì *m*: she was on the ~ of going to sleep tanà gab dà yîn barcī = tanà har̃amàr̃ yîn barcī; be on the ~ of tears yi k̃wàllà *f*.

verify *v* gaskàtā *v1*, tabbàtā *v1*, tabbatar̃ (dà) *v5*, hak̃īk̃àntā *v1*: the report has been verified an gaskàtà r̃àhōtòn.

veritable *adj* na hàk̃īk̃à, na ainihī *m*.

vernacular *n* (*language of ethnic minority group*) yàr̃ē *m*: he speaks one of the ~s of the country yanà màganà dà ɗaya dàgà cikin yàr̃en k̃asàr̃.

verse *n* (*poetry*) wāk̃à *f* ⟨oCi⟩; (*section of a poem*) baitì *m* ⟨oCi⟩, (*from the Koran*) āyà *f* ⟨oCi⟩.

version *n* sīgà *f* ⟨oCi⟩: there are several ~s of this folktale tàtsūnìyar̃ nàn tanā̀ dà sīgōgī dà dāmā; each one had his own ~ of the accident kōwā yā fàɗi nāsà yàddà haɗàr̃īn ya àuku.

versus *prep* (*Sport*) dà: Niger vs. Russia Nìjâr̃ dà Rāshà.

vertical *adj* à tsàye *adv*: a ~ line lāyìn tsàye.

vertigo *n* jùwā *f*, jìrī *m*.

very *adv* a. (*extremely*) k̃warai *adv*, sòsai *adv*, ainùn *adv*: ~ difficult work aikì mài wùyā sòsai; I don't have ~ much money bâ ni dà kuɗī sòsai; a ~ important meeting tàrō mài muhimmancì k̃warai; it is ~ cold today yâu anà sanyī k̃warai; a ~ interesting book littāfì mài ban shà'awà ainùn; ~ ~ much k̃warai dà gàske: I like them ~ ~ much inà sôn sù k̃warai dà gàske. b. (*a lot*): ~ much dà yawà: he does not work ~ much bā yà aikì dà yawà. c. (*to emphasize certain sensory adjs, including colors, use specialized ideophones*): ~ black bak̃ī k̃irin; ~ red jā jà-wur̃; ~ old tsōhō tukuf; ~ sweet dà zāk̃ī càr̃kwai; ~ well lāfiyà k̃alau = lāfiyà lau. d. (*to emphasize certain sensory quality adjs, use 'intensive' forms*): ~ deep zùzzurfā *adj*; ~ hot zàzzāfā *adj*; ~ strong k̃àk̃k̃arfā *adj*. e. (*to emphasize certain personal qualities, actions*) cikà *v1* (+ *obj*), fayè / fiyè *v4* (+ *obj*): she is ~ talkative, argumentative tā cikà sùr̃ūtù, faɗà; he smokes ~ much yā fayè shân tābà. f. (*emphat. used with specific def art*): these ~ buildings wàɗannan gìne-gìnên; that ~ girl wàccan yārinyàr̃; that ~ man is the thief wànnan mùtumìn shī nè ɓàr̃àwòn. g. (*actual, real*) na gàske *adv*, na ainihī *m*: the ~ thing we need ainihin àbìn dà mukè bùkātā. h. (*mere*): the ~ sight of him annoys me kō ganinsà yanà bā nì haushī.

vessel *n* a. (*boat*) jirgin ruwa *m*. b. blood ~ jījìyā *f* ⟨oCi⟩.

vest *n* falmàr̃àn / far̃màlàn *f*.

veteran *n* tsōhon sōjà *m*, [F] tsōhon sōjì *m*: ~s' association k̃ungìyar̃ tsòfàffin sōjōjī.

veterinarian *n* likitàn dabbōbī *n*, bàtū-r̃èn shānū *m*.

veterinary *adj* na dabbōbī *p*; ~ clinic bìtìnàr̃iyà *f*.

veto 1. *n* hawan kujèrar̃-nā-k̃i *m*.

2. *v* hau kujèrař-nā-ƙi: he ~ed the bill yā hau kujèrař-nā-ƙi gàme dà shirìn.

**vex** *v* bâ w. haushī, bâ w. tàkâicī; be ~ed ji haushī = ji tàkâicī.

**via** *prep* ta *prep*: the way to go to Maradi is ~ Katsina akàn yi tàfiyà zuwà Marādi ta Kàtsinà.

**vice** *n* (*evil*) mùgùntā *f*.

**vice-chancellor** *n* matàimàkin shŭgàban jāmi'à *m*.

**vice-president** *n* matàimàkin shŭgàbā *m*.

**vicinity** *n* kusancì *m*: in the ~ of Zaria à kusancìn Zāriyà.

**vicious** *adj* mūgù *adj* ⟨miyàgū⟩; a ~ person mamùgùncī *m*, maƙètàcī *m*.

**victim** *n*: it is she who is the ~ ita akà yi wà lâifī.

**victor** *n* mài nasarà *n*.

**victory** *n* nasarà *f*: win a ~ ci nasarà.

**view** *n* a. (*sight*) ganī *m*: my ~ was blocked an tarè minì ganī = an kārè ni; it was hidden from ~ an ɓōyè shi; come into ~ ɓullō *v6*; disappear from ~ ɓacè *v4*. b. (*viewpoint, opinion*) řa'àyī *m* ⟨oCi⟩: an exchange of ~s mùsāyař řa'àyī; from my point of ~ à řa'àyīnā dai = à ganīnā dai; in ~ of sabōdà.

**vigor** *n* ƙwàzō *m*, himmà *f*, (*vitality*) kùzārī *m*: you must work with ~ kù mai dà ƙwàzō gà aikìnkù.

**vigorous** *adj* (mài) ƙwàzō *m*, (mài) himmà *f*, (mài) kùzārī *m*.

**village** *n* ƙauyè *m* ⟨uka⟩.

**villager** *n* ɗan ƙauyè *m*.

**village head** *n* (*admin.*) dagacì *m* ⟨ai⟩, mài gàrī *m*.

**villain** *n* mūgù *adj* ⟨miyàgū⟩, mamùgùncī *m*, maƙètàcī *m*.

**vinegar** *n* bìningà *f*, [F] bìnēgìř *m*.

**violate** *v* (*Law*) ƙētàrē *v4*, kētà *v1*; (*so.'s rights*) kētà *v1*: ~ human rights kētà hakkìn ɗan Adàm.

**violence** *n* a. (*cruelty*) rashìn īmānì *m*: there is a lot of ~ in today's movies àkwai rashìn īmānì mài yawà cikin sìlìmàn zāmānì. b. (*intentional physical harm*) àikà-aikà *f*. c. (*Pol.*) tāshìn hankàlī *m*, rìkicī *m*: some ~ has broken out in town wani rìkicī yā ɓarkè cikin gàrī. d. (*terrorism*) ta'àdda *f*.

**viper** *n* kùbūbuwà *f*; (*dark-colored*) bidà *f*.

**virgin** *n* bùdurwā *f* ⟨oCi⟩.

**virginity** *n* budurcì *m*.

**virility** *n* màzàkutà *f*.

**virtue** *n* kiřƙì *m*, nàgàřtā *f*.

**virtuous** *adj* (*psn.*) nagàri *m*, tagàri *f* ⟨nagàrgàrū⟩, na kiřƙì *m*: he is a ~ man mùtumìn kiřƙì nē = shī nagàri nè.

**visa** *n* bīzà *f*, [F] bìzâ *m*: obtain a ~ yi bīzà.

**viscous** *adj* (mài) yauƙī *m*.

**vision** *n* a. (*sight*) ganī *m*: he has poor ~ bā yà ganī sōsai = yanà ganī garma-garma = ganinsà garma-garma nè; he has sharp ~ yanà dà kaifin ganī; lose one's ~ makàncē *v4*. b. (*foresight*) hàngen nēsà *m*. c. (*mystical revelation*) wahàyī *m*.

**visit** 1. *n* zìyāřà *f* ⟨zìyàřce-zìyàřce⟩: an official ~ zìyāřàř aikì; pay so. a ~ kai wà zìyāřà; I'm only on a ~ nā zō zìyāřà nē kawài; pay a ~ to one's family jē ganin gidà. 2. *v* a. (*pay a ~*) zìyàřtà *v2*, bàƙuntà *v2*: when are we going to ~ them? yàushè zā mù zìyàřcē sù? we were pleased that he ~ed us mun yi muřnà dà ya bàƙùncē mù. b. (*go to a place*) zō *v0* ⟨zuwà⟩: I've never ~ed Katsina bàn taɓà zuwà Kàtsinà ba.

**visitor** *n* bàƙō *m* ⟨i⟩.

**vital** *adj* (*important*) (mài) muhimmancì *m*; one's ~ spot (*on body*) makasā *f*.

**vitality** *n* kùzārī *m*.

**vitamin** *n* bitāmîn *m*, [F] bìtāmîn *m*.

**viz.** *abbr* wàtàu.

**vizier** *n* (*chief advisor to emir*) wàzīřì *m* ⟨ai⟩.

**vocabulary** *n* kalmōmī *p*: the child has a big ~ yāròn yā san kalmōmī dà yawà; (*glossary*) tsārìn kalmōmī *m*.

**vocal** *adj* na muryà *f*.

**vocation** *n* sànā'à *f* ⟨oCi⟩: ~al school makařantař kōyon sànā'à.

**voice** *n* muryà *f* ⟨oCi⟩: I hear the sound of ~s nā ji sautìn muryōyī; lower one's ~ sassàutà muryà = kashè muryà; raise one's ~ ɗagà muryà; speak in a loud ~ yi màganà dà ƙarfī; V. of America Muryàř Amìřkà.

**volcano** *n* dūtsè mài aman wutā *m*; the ~ exploded dūtsèn yā yi aman wutā.

**volleyball** *n* (*game*) wàsan ƙwallon rāgā *m*.

**volume**[1] *n* a. (*size*) girmā *m*: the ~ of the container is 4 gallons girman garwā galàn huɗu = garwā tanà cìn galàn huɗu. b. (*loudness of sth.*) ƙarfin muryà *m*.

**volume**[2] *n* (*book*) juzù'ī *m*: the dictionary is in 2 ~s ƙāmùs yanà dà juzù'ī biyu.

**voluntarily** *adv* dà sôn râi, dà ganin dāmā: I came here ~ nā zō nân dà ganin dāmātà.

**voluntary** *adj* na ganin dāmā: ~ contribution kàřō-kàřō na ganin dāmā; ~ or-

ganization ƙungìyař sâ kâi = ƙungìyař
tàimakon kâi dà kâi.

**volunteer** 1. *n* mài tàimakō *n*, ɗan sâ kâi
*m;* ~ work aikìn tàimakon kâi dà kâi.
2. *v* sâ kâi: the people ~ed to protect the
neighborhood mutằnē sun sâ kâi sù yi
tsằron ùnguwā.

**vomit** *v* yi amai *m*, (*euphem.*) mayař (dà)
*v5;* feel like ~ing yi tũƙā *f*, ji amai: I
feel like ~ing cikìnā nằ tũƙā = inằ jîn
amai; the smell of the blood makes me
want to ~ wārin jinī nằ sâ ni jîn amai.

**vote** 1. *n* ƙùři'ằ *f* ⟨oCi⟩: take a ~ on yi
ƙùři'ằ à kân.
2. *v* jēfà ƙùři'ằ, yi zằɓē *m*: everyone
should have the right to ~ yā kàmātà à cê
kōwā yanằ dà haƙƙìn zằɓē; ~ for zằɓā
*v2:* whom did you ~ for? wằ ka zằɓā? how
did you ~? mề ka zằɓā?

**voter** *n* mài jēfà ƙùři'ằ *n*.

**vouch for** *v* tabbàtā dà *v1:* I will ~ for
his honesty zân tabbàtā dà gàskiyařsà
= zân bā dà shaidằř gàskiyařsà.

**voucher** *n* bōcằ *f*.

**vow** *v* ƙudùrā à zūci, (*fig.*) lằshi takồbī:
the government ~ed to combat the drug
trade gwamnatì tā lằshi takồbin yằƙař
fataucìn ƙwāyōyī.

**vowel** *n* wasàlī *m* ⟨u-a⟩; ~ length tsawon
wasàlī = jan wasàlī.

**vulcanize** *v* (*a tire*) yi wằ bàkànēzằ / yi
màkànēzằ *f*, [F] yi lìƙì *m*.

**vulgar** *n* a. (*rude, crude*) maràs dā'ằ *f*.
b. (*obscene*) ~ language bātsa *f*, ɗanyen
bằkì *m*: that is a ~ word wannàn kalmằ
ɗanyen bằkì cề.

**vulture** *n* ùngùlu *f* ⟨aye⟩, (*Ruppell's grif-
fon*) maikì / mīkì *m* ⟨oCi⟩.

# W

**waddle** *v* yi tàfiyàř àgwàgwā *f.*

**wag** *v* kaɗà *v1*: the dog is ~ging its tail kàrē nà kaɗà wutsiyà; his tail is ~ging wutsiyàřsà nà kaɗàwā.

**wage(s)** *n* (*esp. monthly, semi-monthly*) àlbâshī *m;* (*weekly*) kuɗin sātī *m;* (*hourly, piecework*) kuɗin ƙwādagō *m,* lādan aikì *m;* fix, negotiate ~ yi jìngā *f*: we fixed his ~ at ₦300 per month mun yi jìngař naiřà ɗàrī ukù dà shī kōwànè watà; a ~ freeze tàkunkùmin ƙarìn àlbâshī.

**wagon** *n* (*railroad car*) wāgùnù *m* ⟨oCi⟩, tàřagù *m* ⟨ai⟩.

**wail** *v* yi kūgù *m.*

**waist** *n* ƙūgù *m;* (*esp. of clothes*) gìndī *m.*

**waistband** *n* (*for drawstring of trousers*) ƙùbakà *f.*

**wait** 1. *v* dākàtā *v1*: ~ just a minute kà dākàtā kàdan = kà ɗan dākàtā; I can't ~ any longer bà zân iyà ƙàrà dākàtàwā ba; make so. ~ dākatař (dà) *v5;* ~ for a while jimā *v1;* ~ for so., sth. jirā *v0,* sàurārà *v2* ⟨sàurārē, sàurārō⟩: we're ~ing for him to come munà jìràn zuwànsà = munà sàurāren zuwànsà = munà sàurārō yà zō; ~ on so. (*serve food*) rabà wà àbinci.
2. *n*: lie in ~ for so. yi wà kwantō *m,* yi fàkon w.: they lay in ~ for the enemy sun yi wà àbòkan gàbā kwantō = sun 6ūya sunà fàkon àbòkan gàbā.

**waiter, waitress** *n* sābìs *n,* [F] sàřbîs *n.*

**waive** *v* ɗaukè *v4*: ~ a condition, requirement ɗaukè shaɽàdī, ƙā'idà.

**wake up** 1. *vi* faɽkà *v1,* tāshì *v3b*: I usually ~ up at 6 o'clock gālìbàn nakàn tāshì dàgà barcī dà ƙarfè shidà.
2. *vt* tàsà *v2,* tā dà / tāsař (dà) *v5*: ~ us up just before dawn à tàshē mù dà àssàlātù; (*by sth.*) faɽkař (dà) *v5*: the wind, alarm clock woke me up gùguwà, ƙàrarrawā tā faɽkař dà nī.

**walk** 1. *n* yāwò *m,* (*esp. for relaxation*) shân iskà *m*: I enjoyed that ~ nā ji dāɗin yāwòn; he's gone out for a ~ yā fìta yāwò = yā fìta shân iskà.
2. *v* a. yi yāwò *m,* yi tàfiyà *f*: they

~ed for about 2 hours sun yi yāwò kàmař awà biyu; they ~ed on until they reached the station sun yi ta tàfiyà hař sukà kai tashà; he ~s very quickly yanà dà saurin tàfiyà; (*go somewhere on foot*) tàfi à ƙasà: he ~s to the office but I go by bicycle yanà tàfiyà ōfìs à ƙasà àmmā nī dai inà tàfiyà à kèkè. b. (*var. v + adv/prep uses*): ~ across (*a street*) ƙētàrē *v4;* ~ around (*a place*) zāgà *v1;* ~ out of (*a meeting, place*) fìta dàgà *v3;* ~ out on the job yi yàjì *m;* the workers ~ed out on the job ma'àikàtā sun yi yajì; his wife ~ed out on him màtařsà tā yi yàjì; ~ over (*a bridge*) hau *v*\* ⟨hawā⟩; ~ up and down (*pace*) yi kai-dà-kàwō.

**wall** *n* (*interior, of room*) bangō *m* ⟨aye⟩; (*around a compound*) gàřū *m* ⟨uka⟩, katangà *f* ⟨u⟩; (*surrounding a town*) gānuwà *f.*

**wallet** *n* (*West. style*) walàt *f,* [F] fařtamāmì *m;* (*Tuareg style, hung around neck*) àlabè *m.*

**wallow** *v* tuřbùɗā *v1,* yi tùřbuɗā *f*: ~ in mud tuřbùɗā cikin càɓī.

**wander** *v* a. (*esp. aimlessly*) yi gàntàlī *m,* yi yāwòn banzā *m,* yi gàràrī *m,* yi ràgaità *f,* yi gīlò *m.* b. (*of the mind*) gàlàbaità *v3.*

**wanderer** *n* gàntàlallē *m* ⟨u⟩, mài ràgaità *n, see* vagabond.

**wane** *v* dusàshē *v4*: the moon, his reputation is waning watà, farin jininsà nà dusàshēwā.

**want** 1. *v* a. (*desire*) sō *v0*: what do you ~? mè kakè sô? I ~ to ask you something inà sô ìn tàmbàyē kà wani àbù; Audu really ~s to help Audù nà matuƙař sôn bā dà tàimakō; that is what he truly ~s àbîn dà yakè sô à rànsà kè nan; ~ sth. badly (*crave*) yi kwàɗayī *m,* yi ƙàwā/ƙwāwā *f.* b. (*seek*) nēmā *v2* ⟨nēmā⟩: he is ~ed anà nēmànsà.
2. *n* a. (*need*) bùkātà / bùƙātà *f* ⟨u⟩: my ~s are simple bùkātàtā mài sauƙī cè. b. (*lack*) rashì *m*: the trees died for ~ of water itàtuwà sun mutù don rashìn ruwā.

**war** *n* yāƙì *m* ⟨e²⟩: ~ has broken out yāƙì yā ɓarkè = yāƙì yā tāshì; he was killed in the ~ yā mutù à wurin yāƙì; make ~ on yi yāƙì dà: they are continually making ~ on each other sunà ta yāƙì tsàkāninsù kōyàushè; prepare for ~ (*fig.*) jā ɗamaràř yāƙì; a full-scale ~ kàsàitaccen yāƙì; the cold ~ (*fig.*) yāƙìn cācař bàkī; a holy ~ jìhādì *m.*

warbler n (bird) tsīgī m.

ward n (of town) ùnguwā f ⟨oCi⟩, [F] kàřcê m; ~ head mài ùnguwā m.

warden, warder n gàndufōbà m, ma'àikàcin gidan yārì m; chief ~ yārì m.

ward off v kārè v4, tarè v4: I ~ed off his blows nā kārè bugùn dà ya kāwō minì; we ~ed off the enemy mun tarè àbòkan gàbā.

warehouse n sìtô m, daffô m, [F] màngàzâ f.

wares n kāyan cìnikī p, hàjà f ⟨oCi⟩; (esp. of petty trader) kōlì m: the trader displayed his ~ ɗan kōlì yā bazà kōlìnsà.

warfare n yāƙì m: chemical ~ yāƙìn àmfānī dà gubà; guerilla ~ yāƙìn sùnƙūrū.

warm 1. adj (mài) ɗùmī m: ~ water ruwā mài ɗùmī; somewhat ~ mài ɗùmi-ɗumi; feel ~ ji ɗùmī; (fig.) they gave the governor a ~ reception sun yi mafàba dà gwamnà sòsai.
2. v: they lit a fire to ~ themselves sun hūrà wutā don sù ji ɗùmī; ~ up sth. ɗumāmā v1, sulàlā v1; be ~ed up ɗùmāmà v3, sùlālà v3.

warmth n ɗùmī m: ~ of a fire ɗùmin wutā = zāfin wutā.

warn v a. (esp. of danger) gàfgadà v2; (of public emergency) yi gangamī m, fadakař (dà) v5. b. (admonish) jā wà kùnnē, jā kùnnen w.

warning n (of danger) gàfgàdī m, (esp. public ~) gangamī m: without ~ bà dà an yi gàfgàdī ba; he was given a ~ yā sàmi gàfgàdī; a friendly ~ kàshēdī m; (mild) jān kùnnē m.

warp¹ n (in weaving) abàwā f.

warp² v bankàrā v1, kōmàɗā v1; be(come) ~ed (of wood) bankàrē v4, tanƙwàrē v4; (of metal, plastic) kōmàɗē / mōkàɗē v4: the saucepan is ~ed tukunyā tā mōkàɗē.

warrant n (for arrest) takàfdař kāmù f, [F] màndā dàhô m.

warranty n wafantî m, gàfàntî m.

warrior n gwařzō m ⟨aye⟩, jàfùmī ⟨ai⟩, mayàƙī m; mounted ~ bařdē m ⟨a-e⟩.

wart n tūsař jàkī f.

warthog n gàdū m, mūgùn dawà m; (red riverhog) àlhànzîr m.

wash 1. v a. (sth.) wankè v4: she ~ed her hands, her clothes tā wankè hannū, tufāfìntà; be well ~ed wànku v7: it has been ~ed spanking clean yā wànku tas = yā wànku tsaf; the rains have ~ed away the road ruwā yā yankè hanyà; the bridge has been ~ed out ruwā yā kā dà gadà;

(fig.) ~ one's hands of a matter kakkàɓè hannū dàgà àl'amàrîn. b. (bathe oneself) yi wankā m.
2. n (laundry) (kāyan) wankì m: hang out the ~ on the line shànyà wankì kân igiyà; ~ing up (of dishes, pots) wànkewànke m.

washcloth n (facecloth) hankicì m.

washer n (rubber or metal) wāshà f ⟨oCi⟩.

washerman n mài wankì m, wàshìmân m.

washing powder n ōmò m.

wasp n (dauber, mason) zànzarō m; see hornet.

waste 1. v a. (esp. water, time) ɓātà v1, (esp. money) ɓad dà / ɓataf (dà) v5: he ~d my time yā ɓātà minì lōkàcī; without wasting time bà tàre dà ɓātà lōkàcī ba; don't ~ your money, save it kadà kà ɓad dà kuɗinkà, kà ajìyē su. b. (excessively) ɓafnataf (dà) v5: ~ national resources ɓafnataf dà afzìkin ƙasā; be ~d (needlessly, for no gain) sàlwantà v3: many lives were needlessly ~d in the war rāyukà dà yawà sun sàlwantà à yāƙìn.
2. n ɓafnā f: it was a ~ of money ɓafnař kuɗī cè; she is ~ful tā cikà ɓafnā.

wastebasket n kwàndon shàrā m: I crumpled the letter and threw it in the ~ nā dunƙùlè wàsīƙà nā jēfà kwàndon shàrā.

watch¹ n àgōgo m ⟨una⟩, àgōgon hannu m: a Seiko ~ àgōgon Seiko.

watch² v a. (look) dūbà v1 ⟨dūbà⟩: ~ carefully how I do it kà dūbà dà kyâu yàddà nakè yînsà. b. (look at) kàllà v2 ⟨kallō⟩, kàllatà v2: ~ television kàlli talàbijìn; he stayed there ~ing the animals yā zaunà yanà kallon dabbōbîn. c. (be careful of, take care of) kùla dà v3: ~ your luggage (so no one takes it) kù kùla dà kāyankù; please ~ my bicycle for me don Allàh kà kulà minì dà kèkēnā = kà jirà minì kèkēnā; ~ out yi hankàlī m; ~ over (protect) kiyàyē v4: may God ~ over you! Allàh yà kiyàyē!

watchman n (night) mài gādì m, [F] gàfdìnyê m.

water 1. n a. ruwā m ⟨aye⟩: is this ~ fit to drink? ruwan nàn yanà dà kyâu? fetch ~ from a well ɗēbō ruwā dàgà rījìyā; this ~ is dirty ruwan nàn bà shi dà tsabtà; drinking ~ ruwan shâ; clear ~ baƙin ruwā; cold ~ ruwā mài sanyī = ruwan sanyī; hot ~ ruwā mài zāfī = ruwan zāfī; bath ~ ruwan wankā; distilled ~ ruwan bātìř. b. (adverbial uses): in(to) the ~ (à) (cikin) ruwa adv: first soak the beans in ~ kì jiƙà wākē cikin ruwa

tùkùna; he fell into the ~ yā fāɗā ruwa;
he was plucked out of the ~ an tsāmō shì
dàgà ruwa.
2. *v* a. (*an animal, plant*) bā dà ruwā, yi
wà ban ruwā: you should ~ the plants sai
kà yi wà shùke-shùke ban ruwā; (*an animal*) shā dà / shāyař (dà) *v5*: he ~ed
the horses yā shāyař dà dawākī (ruwā).
b. make one's eyes ~ sā idồ ruwā: the
smoke made my eyes ~ hayāƙīn yā sā
idồnā ruwā = hayāƙīn yā sā ni hawằyē.
**water bottle** *n* (*of gourd or clay*) būtā *f*
⟨oCi⟩; (*tradit., made of goatskin*) sàlkā *f*
⟨salềkanī⟩.
**waterbuck** *n* gwambāzā *f*.
**watering** *n* (*e.g. a garden*) ban ruwā *m*:
the garden needs ~ làmbûn yanằ bùkātàř
ban ruwā; ~ can būtūtun gādìnà *m*, [F]
àřèzùwâř *m*; ~ hole wurin ban ruwā *m*.
**waterlily** *n* badồ *m*.
**watermelon** *n* kankanā *f*.
**waterproof** *adj*: raincoats are ~ ruwā bā yằ
rātsà rìgař ruwā; the watch is ~ ruwā
bā yằ wà àgōgōn lahànī.
**waterway** *n* magudānař ruwā *f*.
**watery** *adj* (mài) ruwa-ruwa: this is too ~
wannàn yā yi ruwa-ruwa dà yawằ.
**wave**[1] *v* a. (*with hand*) ɗagà hannū: when I
saw him I ~d to him dà na hangō shì sai
na ɗagà masà hannū; ~ one's arms about
wuřgà hannū; ~ goodbye yi wà adàbồ *m*.
b. (*sth.*) kaɗà *v1*: ~ a flag kaɗà tūtā;
flags are waving (in the wind) tūtōcī sunà
kaɗằwā.
**wave**[2] *n* a. (*in water*) igiyàř ruwā *f*. b.
(*wavelength*) zangồ *m*, [F] gâm *f*: short,
medium, long ~ meterband mītằ mài
gàjēren, mài matsàkàicin, mài dōgon
zangồ.
**wax** *n* kākì *m*; bees~ kākìn zumằ *m*; (*inside
ear*) daudàř kunne *f*.
**waxbill** *n* (*bird*) cì-gōřồ *m*.
**way** *n* a. (*road, route*) hanyằ *f* ⟨oCi⟩: the ~
to Kano hanyàř zuwằ Kanồ; it is on our
~ yanằ (kân) hanyàřmù; I'll go a different
~ next time zân sākè hanyằ nân gàba;
it is a long ~ to go there zuwằ can yanằ
dà nīsā; everyone has gone his separate
~ kōwā yā kāmà hanyàřsà dàbam; be in
the ~ (*block*) tsarè hanyằ *v4*: this box
is in my ~ àkwātìn nân yā tsarè minì
hanyằ; by ~ of ta *prep*: you can reach
the market by ~ of this shortcut zā kà
kai kàsuwā ta wannàn yànkè; go by ~
of bi ta *v0*: he went by ~ of Wudil yā bi
ta hanyàř Wùdil; which ~ did he go? ta
ìnā ya bi? lose one's ~ yi dīmuwā *f*, yi

ɓatàn kâi; on the ~ à tàfe: here I come,
I'm on my ~ gằ ni nân tàfe; be on your
~! kù tàfi àbinkù! b. (*entry, exit*): the
~ in ƙōfàř shìgā = mashìgā; the ~ out
ƙōfàř fìtā = mafìtā; (*fig.*) he's looking
for a ~ out yanà nēman mafìtā. c. (*room,
space*) wurī *m*: make ~ for bā dà wurī:
we moved to one side to make ~ for the
chief mun kaucè don mù bā sarkī wurī;
get out of my ~! bằ ni wurī! d. (*method,
manner*) hanyằ *f* ⟨oCi⟩: the best ~ hanyằ
mafì kyâu; I know a better ~ than this
of doing it nā san wata hanyàř dà ta fi
wannàn ta yīn hakà; in whatever ~ possible ta kōwàcè hanyằ = ta kōyằyằ; everyone has his own ~ of doing it kōwā yanằ
dà yâddà yakè yînsà; there is no ~ to get
out of this difficulty bā yâddà zā à kuɓucè
wà wannàn wàhalà; there's no ~ to do it
bā dāmằ! this ~ (ta) hakà *adv*: do it in
this ~ kà yi shì ta hakà; this is the ~ to
do it hakà akè yînsà. e. (*habit, custom*) dàbī'ằ *f* ⟨u⟩, àl'ādằ *f* ⟨u⟩: that's
just the ~ he is! dàbī'àřsà kè nan! =
hālinsà kè nan! f. (*lifestyle of a group*)
zamā *m*, ràyuwā *f*: the Hausa ~ of life zaman Hàusàwā = ràyuwař Hàusàwā; that's
their ~ of life hakà zamansù yakè; corruption has become a ~ of life (*fig.*) cîn
hancì yā zaunằ dà gìndinsà. g. by the
~... (*incidentally*) af...: by the ~, have
you heard the latest gossip? af, kin ji
wata jìta-jìta mài dùmi-dùmintà?
**we** *pro, see* Appendix A.
**weak** *adj* a. (*psn.*) (mài) raunī *m*, ràrraunā
*adj*, maràs ƙarfī *m*, (*feeble*) kùmāmā *n*
⟨ai⟩: he is a ~ man ràrraunan mùtûm nề
= bā shi dà ƙarfī; he is too ~ to walk
yā kàsà tàfiyà sabồdà raunī; be(come),
get ~ ràunanà *v3*, karề *v4*: she has gotten ~ ƙarfintà yā ràunanà = tā karề;
their economy is ~ ařzìkin ƙasařsù yā
ràunanà; feel ~ (*temporarily*): I feel ~
jìkīnā yā mutù = jìkīnā yā yi sanyī;
this medicine makes me feel ~ wannàn
māgànī yakàn kashề minì jìkī; one's ~
spot (*of character*) lagồ *m*: I know his ~
spot nā san lagồnsà; give a ~ excuse yi
kùskùndā *f*. b. (*poorly constructed*) maràs
ƙwārī *m*, maràs ƙarkō *m*: the box is ~
and won't hold all these things àkwātìn
bā shi dà ƙwārī, bà zâi ɗau duk kāyan
nàn ba.
**weaken** 1. *v* a. raunànā *v1*: the illness has
~ed him cīwòn yā raunằnà shi. b. (*of
currency*) fādì *v3b*: the dollar has ~ed
against the pound dalàř Amìřkà tā fādì

in an kwatàntā dà fām.

**weakness** n a. (*physical, moral*) raunī m. b. (*physical*) rashìn ƙarfī m. c. (*fault, blemish*) illā f ⟨oCi⟩, lâifī m ⟨uka²⟩: his ~ is his lack of patience illàrsà bâ shi dà hàƙurī. d. (*weak spot*) lagò m: he has a ~ for sweets lagònsà kāyan zāƙī.

**wealth** n dūkìyā f, arzìkī m, wàdātā f, sāmù m: he lost all his ~ yā yi hàsārar dūkìyarsà dukà; (*fig.*) health is ~ lāfiyà uwar jìkī.

**wealthy** adj (mài) arzìkī m, (mài) sāmù m; a ~ person àttàjìrī m ⟨ai⟩, the ~ màsu hannū dà shūnī; become ~ wàdātà v3, arzùtā ƙai.

**wean** v (*by mother*) yāyè v4: she has ~ed her son tā yāyè ɗantà; (*an animal from its mother*) ɗaukē wà v4: within 2 months, the calf will be ~ed from its mother nân dà watà biyu, zā à ɗaukē wà sānìyā màraƙintà.

**weapon** n makāmī m ⟨ai⟩, kāyan yāƙī m: nuclear ~s màkàman nūkìliyà = màkàman ƙàrè-dangì.

**wear** v a. (*put on*) sā/sakā/sânyā v1: ~ clothes, glasses, shoes sā tufāfī, tàbàrau, tākalmà; be ~ing sth. sànye dà: she is ~ing a beautiful dress tanà sànye dà rīgā mài kyāu; ~ a wrapper, head-tie ɗaurà zanè, kallàbī; she is ~ing a new wrapper, head-tie tanà ɗaure dà sābon zanè, kallàbī. b. (*reduce by continued use*): I've worn a hole in my shoe ƙasàn tàkàlmīnā yā hūjè; ~ sth. down (*by erosion*) zāgè v4: the rain has worn down the wall ruwā yā sā katangā tā zāgè; ~ so. out gajiyar (dà) v5; be worn out (*of psn.*) gàji tiƙis; be worn down, smooth (*from friction*) ci v0, cînyē v4, sudè v4: the screw is worn ƙūsà tā ci; the soles of my shoes are worn down ƙasàn tàkàlmīnā yā cînyē; the tread of the tire is worn smooth zànen tāyà yā sudè; ~ off (*fade*) kōɗè v4: the paint has worn off fentìn yā kōɗè; be worn out (*of sth.*) mutù v3b, gàji v3*, tsūfa v3a, (*esp. of clothes*) shā jìkī: the chair is worn out kujèrā tā mutù; these trousers are really worn out lallē wàndon nàn yā shā jìkī.

**weary** adj (*psn.*) gàjìyayyē adj.

**weasel** n (*zorilla*) bòdarī m ⟨ai⟩.

**weather** n yanàyī m: the ~ is good today yâu yanàyī mài kyāu nē; what is the ~ like there? yàyà yanàyin ƙasā yakè à can?

**weave** v sāƙà v1, yi sāƙà f: he's weaving a cloth, mat yanà sāƙar zanè, tàbarmà; a

woven basket sàƙaƙƙen kwàndō.

**weaver** n masāƙī m ⟨ai⟩.

**weaverbird** n gàdō m ⟨una⟩, ɗan mārâi m; (*spotted backed*) kābarē m ⟨ai⟩; (*black-headed*) shaidà f.

**weaving** n sāƙà f.

**web** n, *see* spiderweb.

**wed** v àurā v2.

**wedding** n bìkin aurē m.

**wedge** 1. n wējì / waigì m, [F] kâl f. 2. v ƙwafà v1: I ~d a piece of wood under the door nā ƙwafà guntun itàcē ƙàrƙashin ƙyaurē.

**Wednesday** n Làrābā f.

**weed(s)** 1. n cìyāwà f ⟨i⟩; cut down ~ (*with a crude cutlass*) yi fìtikì m: they are cutting down the ~ around the school sunà fìtikì à kēwayèn makaranttà. 2. v yi nōmā m, nòmè cìyāwà.

**weeding** n nōmā m; first ~ (*after planting*) nōman fārì: if you don't do the first ~, weeds will spread ìdan bà à yin nōman fārì, cìyāwà zā tà baibàyē; second ~ maimai m.

**week** n mākò m ⟨anni⟩, sātī m, kwānā bakwài: every ~ kōwànè mākò; last ~ mākòn jiyà = mākòn dà ya wucè; next ~ mākò mài zuwà; at the end of this ~ à ƙàrshen mākòn nân; in three ~s' time bāyan mākò ukù = nân dà sātī ukù; he is paid by the ~ anà biyànsà mākò-mākò; day of the ~ rānā f: what day of the ~ is it today? yâu wàcè rānā cè? a ~ from today rānā yà/wà ta yâu; at this same time next ~ rānā yà ta yâu wàr hakà.

**weekend** n ƙàrshen mākò m.

**weekly** adj mākò-mākò adv, sātī-sātī adv: it is a ~ newspaper jàrīdàr mākò-mākò cē.

**weep** v yi kūkā m, yi hawàyē p; ~ for joy yi kūkan murnà.

**weevil** n màyā m.

**weft** n (*in weaving*) zàrē m.

**weigh** v a. aunà v1 ⟨awò⟩: a scale is used for ~ing things anà àmfànī dà sìkēlì don aunà nauyin abūbuwà; how much does this package ~? nawà nē nauyin wannàn fākitì? approximately how much does it ~? mènē nè kīmàr nauyinsà? b. (*where an alternative is possible*) jinjìnā v1: I ~ed his words carefully nā jinjìnà màganàrsà sòsai; here's another chicken; see if it ~s enough gà wata kàzā dàbam, kà jinjìnā kō tanà dà nauyī.

**weight** n a. nauyī m: these are sold by ~ anà sai dà sū gwàrgwadon nauyinsù; I was surprised at the ~ of the box nā yi màmākìn nauyin àkwàtìn; estimate the ~ of sth. ƙaddàřà kīmàř nauyin w.a. b. (of psn.'s body) lose ~ (slim down) saɓè v4, zub dà jìkī; lose ~ (due to illness, worry) rāmè v4, ƙanjàmē v4, yanƙwànē v4; put on ~ yi jìkī m, yi ƙibà f; put ~ back on (after illness) mai dà jìkī.

**weird** adj (peculiar): he is a ~ person shī wani irìn mùtûm nè.

**welcome** 1. v yi wà mařàba f, yi mařàba dà: wherever he went, he was ~d duk indà ya jē akàn yi mařàba dà shī; ~ so. on his arrival yi wà bařƙà dà sàukā; ~ with open arms kàrɓà dà hannū bībiyu. 2. n mařàba f: he was not given a warm ~ bà à yi masà kyàkkyāwař mařàba ba. 3. excl a. bařƙà dà zuwà! = mařàba! (esp. used by women) màřhabùn! = làlê! (esp. after long journey) bařƙà dà sàukā! ~ back! bařƙà dà dāwôwā! b. (reply to thanks) you're ~! tô mādàllā! = habà!

**weld** n yi wà waldà f, hadà v1, [F] yi wà sùdê m.

**welder** n mài waldà m.

**welfare** n (of society) zaman lāfiyà m; social ~ jìn dāɗin jàma'à.

**well**[1] 1. n rījìyā f (oCi), (with concrete rim) kankare m: clean out a ~ yāshè rījìyā; the ~ has dried up rījìyā tā ƙafè; lower a bucket in a ~ to draw water zurà gūgà à rījìyā don à jāwō ruwā; oil ~ rījìyař hàƙař mâi = mahaƙař mâi; dig a ~ haƙà rījìyā = [F] ginà rījìyā. 2. v: ~ up out of the ground ɓulɓulō dàgà ƙasà.

**well**[2] adj lāfiyà f: the children are all ~ yârā duk sunà lāfiyà; I am not ~ inà rashìn lāfiyà = bà ni dà lāfiyà; feel ~ ji dāɗin jìkī; get ~ warkè v4; I hope you get ~ soon! Allàh yà sâ kà sàmi sauƙī!

**well**[3] adv a. (carefully, thoroughly) dà kyâu m, sòsai adv, ƙwařai adv: read the instructions ~ kà kařàntà ùmàřnī dà kyâu; he speaks English ~ yā iyà Tūřancī sòsai; I know him very ~ nā san shì ƙwařai; extremely ~ ƙwařai dà gàske. b. (of quality): do, make sth. ~ amìntā v1: this chair was made ~ an amìntā kujèrař nàn = kujèrař nàn àmìntacciyā cè. c. (favorably): speak ~ of so. yàbà v2 (yàbō): everyone speaks ~ of him kōwā nà yàbonsà; get along ~ (with so.) yi shirì (dà), jìtu v7, shàƙu v7: Ladi and Kande get along ~ dà Làdì dà Kànde sunà shirì; he and I don't get along ~ at all bā mà jìtuwā kō kàɗan. d. (as adv

to denote completeness of an action, may use v7 verbs): the meat is ~ cooked nāmà yā dàfu; the robe has been ~ washed rìgā tā wànku; the book is ~ written littāfìn yā řùbùtu. e. as ~ as (and likewise) kàzālikà adv: Musa went as ~ as Sule Mūsā yā jē Sulè mà kàzālikà; as ~ as (in addition to) hař (dà): bring the red one as ~ as the white kàwō jân hař dà farìn.

**well**[4] excl a. (in pausing): ~ then,... tô,...: ~, how do you like Zaria? tô, yàyà zaman Zāriyà dai? b. (expr. of finality) very ~! tô shī kè nan! ~ done! mādàllā! c. (in confirming sth.): ~, it turned out to be true àshē, àbìn yā zama gàskiyā; ~, she saw that it was a blind man tā ga àshē màkàhõ nè.

**well-being** n (of psn.) hālin zamā m: I'm concerned about his ~ nā dàmu dà hālin zamansà.

**well-bred** adj (psn.) (mài) ladàbī m, (mài) dā'à f, hàifaffē adj: he is ~ yanà dà ladàbī = hàifaffē nè.

**well-fed** adj ƙōsasshē adj.

**well-known** adj sànannē adj, (esp. psn.) shàhàřařřē adj.

**well-made** adj (mài) amincì m, àmìntaccē adj, (mài) ƙwārī m.

**well-read** adj (of psn. who knows the Koran) makàřàncī m.

**well-to-do** adj (mài) sāmù m, (mài) sùkūnì m, (mài) hannū dà shūnì, (mài) àbin dūniyà.

**welt** n kùmburī m.

**west** n & adv yâmma f: the sun sets in the ~ rānā kàn fāɗì à yâmma; a wind was blowing from the ~ iskà nà kaɗàwā dàgà yâmma; W. Africa Afiřkà ta yâmma; it is ~ of town yanà yammacin gàrī = yanà yâmma dà gàrī.

**western** adj na yâmma, yammacin prep: the ~ states jihōhin yâmma; the ~ states of Nigeria jihōhin yammacin Nìjēřiyà; ~ bloc countries ƙasàshen yammacin Tūřai.

**westerner** n bàyâmmī m.

**wet** 1. v jiƙà v1; ~ the bed (at night) yi fitsārin kwànce. 2. adj jìƙaƙƙē adj: be(come), get ~ jìƙa v3, jiƙè v4: did you get ~? kā jiƙè? be soaking ~ jiƙè shàřkaf; we got soaking ~ from the rain (fig.) ruwā yā bā mù kāshī = ruwā yā yi manà dūkà; be dripping ~ yi tsamō-tsamõ idph; ~ paint sābon fentì.

**wet season** n dàminā f, see season.

**wharf** n kwàtā f.

**what 1.** *interrog pro* a. mè / mēnē nè *m*, mēcē cē *f*: ～ is this? mēnē nè wannàn? ～ are you looking at? mè kakè kallō? ～ is the matter with him? mè ya sāmē shì? ～ is this made of? dà mè akà yi wannàn? ～ for? don mè? = sabŏdà mè? b. (*in asking name of so., sth.*) yàyà, ìnā: ～ is your name? yàyà sūnankà? = ìnā sūnankà? ～ is the English word for this? yàyà sūnan wannàn dà Ingìlīshì? c. (*specialized uses*) ìnā: ～'s new? (*in greeting*) ìnā làbārì? ～'s up? (*in greeting*) yàyà hařkōkī? = yàyà dai? ～ is this used for? ìnā àmfānin wannàn? = mēnē nè àmfānin wannàn? ～ is to be done? ìnā dàbāřāř?

**2.** *interrog det* (*which*) wànè *m*, wàcè *f*, wàdànnè *p*: ～ kind of car do you have? wàcè irìn mōtà kakè dà ita? ～ kinds of things did you buy? wàdànnè ìre-ìren abūbuwà kikà sàyā? ～ color is this? wànè launī nē wannàn? ～ time is it? ƙarfè nawà nē?

**3.** *rel pro* àbìn dà: I didn't hear ～ they said bàn ji àbìn dà sukà cē ba; he knows ～ I mean yā san àbìn dà nakè nufì; I didn't know ～ to say nā rasà ta cêwā; do ～ you like kà yi àbìn dà ka ga dāmā; that's ～ I told him! àbìn dà na gayà masà kè nan!

**4.** *excl* (*var. uses*): ～ a pity! kaico! *excl*, kash! *excl*: ～ a pity you couldn't come kash! bà kà sāmi dāmař zuwà ba; ～ a great bicycle! wannàn kèkè bâ dāmā! ～ a gorgeous girl! yārinyař nân tùbařkallà!

**whatever 1.** *rel pro* duk àbìn dà, kōmē / kōmēnē nè (+ *rel. complet.*): buy ～ you like kà sàyi duk àbìn dà kakè sô; you must buy one, ～ its cost dōlè kà sàyi gùdā kōmē tsàdařsà; ～ we get, it is our lot kōmē mukà sāmũ, ràbonmù nē.

**2.** *det* kōwànè *m*, kōwàcè *f*, kōwàdànnè *p*: I agree with ～ plan you choose nā yàrda dà kōwànè shirìn dà kakè zāɓè; in ～ way possible ta kōwàcè hanyà = ta hanyà kōyàyà = ta hālin kōyàyà.

**whatsoever** *rel adv* kō kàdan: I have nothing ～ to do with the matter bâ ruwānā kō kàdan dà àl'amàřìn; none ～ kō ƙyas *idph*: we've had no news, none ～ kō ƙyas bâ mu dà làbārì.

**wheat** *n* alkamā *f*; whole ～ flour (*locally grown*) gàrin alkamā; refined ～ flour (*white, imported*) fulāwā *f*.

**wheel** *n* wīlì *m* ⟨oCi⟩, [F] ƙafař mōtà *f*; steering ～ sìtiyārì *m*, [F] bôlân *m*.

**wheelbarrow** *n* kūrā *f* ⟨aye⟩, bāřŏ *m*, [F]

bùřwētì *f*.

**when 1.** *interrog adv* yàushè / yàushē: ～ will it be ready? yàushè zā à gamà? since ～ have you known that? tun yàushè ka san hakà?

**2.** *rel adv* (*to intro. subord. cl.*) dà, lōkàcîn dà, sā'àn dà / sā'àd dà: ～ they returned we told them the news dà sukà dāwō sai mukà gayà musù làbārì; I don't know ～ he arrived bàn san lōkàcîn dà ya isō ba; ～ we were young sā'àn dà mukè yārā; we were in Zaria ～ that happened munà Zāriyà àbîn ya fàru.

**3.** *conj* a. (*if*) ìdan / in (+ *complet. or rel. complet.*) ～ you see him please greet him for me ìdan kin gan shì, don Allàh kà cē masà ìnā gaisuwā. b. (*after*) bāyan: ～ you finish this, you may leave bāyan kin gamà wannàn, sai kì tàshì.

**whenever** *rel adv* (*no matter when*) duk lōkàcîn dà, duk sā'àn dà, kōyàushè: come ～ you like kì zō duk lōkàcîn dà kikà ga dāmā = kì zō kōyàushè kikà ga dāmā; ～ I see him, I greet him kōyàushè na gan shì, sai nā gaishē shì; ～ I go to Kaduna, it rains duk lōkàcîn dà nakè Kàdūna anà ruwā.

**where 1.** *interrog adv* ìnā: ～ does he live? ìnā yakè dà zamā? ～ do they come from? dàgà ìnā sukà fitō? ～ are you off to? ìnā zā ka?

**2.** *rel pro* indà, wurîn dà: I don't remember ～ I put it bàn tunà dà indà na ajìyē shi ba; do you know ～ my cap is? kā san indà hūlātà takè? be careful ～ you walk, it is muddy kà kùla dà indà kakè sâ ƙafàřkà, àkwai tàɓō; the store ～ I buy canned goods kàntì indà nakè sàyen àbincin gwangwanī; (*fig.*) ～ there is life, there is hope in dà râi dà ràbō.

**whereas** *conj* kùwa (*follows n being contrasted*): an elephant is large ～ a mouse is small gīwā bàbba cē ɓērā kùwa ƙàramī nè; she is friendly ～ he mistrusts people tanà sôn jàma'à shī kùwa bâ yà amìncêwā dà mutānē.

**whereupon** *adv* sai (+ *rel. complet.*) *conj*: he gave the troops a signal ～ they opened fire yā nūnà wà sōjōjī àlāmà sai sukà būɗè wutā.

**wherever** *rel adv* duk indà, kō'ìnā: ～ we saw him, he was with her duk indà mukà gan shì, sunà tàre dà ita = kō'ìnā mukà gan shì...; sit ～ you like zàunā duk indà kakè sô.

**whether** *conj* kō: do you know ～ there is

any left? kā san kō dà saurā? ask him
~ he has found it kà tàmbàyē shì kō yā
ganō shì; it doesn't matter ~ he comes or
not kō yà zō kō kadà yà zō, duk daya
nè; I don't care ~ you like it or not kō
kanà sô kō bā kà sô, ôho.

**whetstone** n dūtsèn wāshì m.

**which 1.** interrog det wànè m, wàcè f,
wàdànnè p: ~ way did they go? wàcè
hanyà sukà bi?
**2.** interrog pro: ~ one? wànnē m, wàccè f,
wàdànnē p: ~ ones do you prefer? wàdànnē
kikà fi sô?
**3.** rel det dà: the meat ~ I bought nāmàn
dà na sàyā; the bag ~ she lost jàkàr̃ dà
ta yar̃.

**whichever 1.** det kōwànè m, kōwàcè f,
kōwàdànnè p: ~ road we take, it will take
us there kōwàcè hanyà mukà bi, zā tà
kai mù can.
**2.** pro: ~ one kōwànnē m, kōwàccē f,
kōwàdànnē p: ~ one you choose, make certain that it is good kōwànnē ka zàɓā, kà
tabbatar̃ dà mài kyâu nē.

**whiff** n ƙanshī m: a ~ of perfume, the truth
ƙanshin tùr̃àr̃ē, gàskiyā.

**while 1.** n ɗan lōkàcī m, 'yar̃ jimàwā f;
after a ~, a ~ later (in past) bāyan ɗan
lōkàcī, jimàwā kàɗan, jìm kàɗan; after a short ~ they arrived jimàwā kàɗan
sukà isō; please wait a ~ kù ɗan dākàtā
= kù dākàtā kàɗan = kù ɗan jimà; in a
~ (in fut.) (in) an jimà: he'll return in
a ~ zâi dāwō in an jimà; see you in a
~ sai an jimà; in a little ~ more we'll
be finished saurā kàɗan mù gamà = saurā
ƙiris mù gamà; once in a ~ (from time to
time) lōkàcī-lōkàcī adv, sā'ì-sā'ì adv,
lōtò-lōtò adv.
**2.** rel adv a. lōkàcîn dà, yàyîn dà: the
whole time ~ I was in Kaduna it was raining gàbā ɗayan lōkàcîn dà nakè Kàdūna
anà ta ruwā. b. (to express 2 actions
occurring closely together, use contin.):
~ I was working, he was sleeping inà
aikì, yanà barcī; ~ she was cooking, the
children were playing outside tanà girkì
yàrā nà wàsā wàje; ~ we were walking,
we saw a snake munà tàfiyà sai mukà ga
macìjī.
**3.** conj a. (in the process of) gàrin (+ action n): ~ cooking, her dress caught on
fire gàrin girkì, r̃īgar̃tà tā kāmà wutā.
b. (whereas) kùwa: he was given two, ~ I
got only one shī biyu akà bā shì, nī
kùwa daya tak na sāmù.

**whine** v (by psn.) yi shàgwaɓà f; (by animal)

yi kūkā m.

**whip 1.** n (of leather) būlālà f, (flexible
stick) tsumāgìyā / tsumangìyā f ⟨oCi⟩,
tsabgà f ⟨oCi⟩.
**2.** v shaudà wà būlālà, tsālà wà
būlālà.

**whirl** v (turn around) jujjùyā v1; (fig.) his
mind is in a ~ hankàlinsà yā gushè.

**whirligig** n (toy) filfilwà f, filfilò m.

**whirlwind** n gùguwà f.

**whisk**[1] **1.** v (liquid foods) bur̃gà v1, kaɗà v1.
**2.** n (for food) mabur̃gì m; (of horsehair,
for swatting flies) izgà f.

**whisk**[2] (take so. away quickly) yi awòn gàba
dà: the police ~ed him away 'yan sàndā
sun yi awòn gàba dà shī.

**whiskers** n (side) sàjē m.

**whiskey** n bàr̃àsā f, wuskì f, [F] wùskî f.

**whisper 1.** v raɗà v1: the imam ~ed the
child's name lìmâm yā raɗà sūnan yār̃òn;
~ to so. raɗà wà, yi wà raɗà; ~ about
so. yi raɗar̃ w.
**2.** n raɗà f; talk in ~s yi r̃àɗe-r̃àɗe.

**whistle 1.** n usùr̃ m, [F] sīhulē m: blow a
~ būsà usùr̃.
**2.** v yi fītò m: he ~d to his dog yā kirà
kàrensà dà fītò.

**white 1.** adj farī adj ⟨aCe⟩: they were
dressed all in ~ sunà sànye dà farār̃en
kāyā; black and ~ farī dà baƙī; snow
~ farī fat = farī sal.
**2.** n (psn. of ~ race) jar̃ fātà n, farar̃
fātà n.

**whiten** v faràntā v1.

**whitewash 1.** n farar̃ ƙasà f.
**2.** v yi wà farar̃ ƙasà: the hut has been
~ed an yi wà ɗākì farar̃ ƙasà.

**whitlow** n (finger disease) kàkkar̃ai m.

**whittle** v sàssaƙà v2.

**who 1.** interrog pro wà / wànē nè m, wàcē
cè f, su wà p: ~ is she? ita wàcē cè? ~
is there? wànē nè nan? ~ came? (pl.) su
wà sukà zō? ~ gave it to you? wà ya bā
kì? ~ did you show this to? wà kikà nūnà
wà wannàn? (fig.) ~ do you think you are
(to do such a thing)? wànē kai?
**2.** rel pro a. wàndà m, wàddà / wàccè
f, waɗàndà p; they were the ones ~ told
me sū nè waɗàndà sukà gayà minì; he
doesn't know ~ (f.) came bài san wàddà
ta zō ba; the one ~ is wearing the blue
robe wàndà kè sànye dà r̃īgā shūɗìyā.
b. dà (prec. by n + specific def art); wàndà
/ wandà m, wàddà / wàccè f, waɗàndà p:
the man ~ is talking mùtumìn wàndà dà
kè màganà; the woman ~ left màtar̃ dà
ta tàshì = màtā wàccè ta tàshì; the

men ~ attended the meeting mutànên dà sukà hàlàr̃ci tàr̃ôn.

**whoever** *pro* duk wândà *m*, duk wâddà *f*, duk wad̃andà *p*; kōwā *m*, kōwànē nè *m*, kōwằcē cè *f*, kōwàd̃annē nè *p*: ~ wants to go may do so duk wândà yakè sô yà tàfi, sai yà tàfi; ~ agrees to that is a fool kōwā ya yàr̃da dà hakà wāwā nè; give it to ~ comes kōwằnē nè ya zō, kà bā shì.

**whole** *adj* a. (*all*) dukà / duk: the ~ village was in flames ƙauyèn duk yā kāmà dà wutā. b. (*in its entirety, re. to time*) gàbā d̃aya: the ~ week mākō gàbā d̃ayansà = gàbā d̃ayan mākòn; he slept the ~ day yā yi barcī gàbā d̃ayan rānâr̃; (*in its entirety, re. to things*) sùkùtum *idph*: he didn't give me 50k but a ~ naira bài bā nì kwabò hàmsin ba, yā bā dà naìr̃à sùkùtum. c. (*complete*) cìkakkē *adj*: the ~ truth cìkakkiyar̃ gaskiyā.

**whole-heartedly** *adv* dà zūcìyā d̃aya: I ~ agree with you nā yàr̃da dà kai dà zūcìyā d̃aya.

**wholesale** *adv*: buy ~ sàr̃ā *v2*: he bought the cloth ~ from the factory yā sàri àtàmfā dàgà ma'aikatà; ~ trade sār̃ì *m*; sell ~ sārar̃ (dà) *v5*; ~ dealer d̃an sār̃ì *m*.

**wholly** *adv*: I ~ agree nā yàr̃da sòsai; he is not ~ to blame lâifīn bā nàsà kad̃ai ba nè.

**whom** *rel pro*, *see* who: the boy ~ you saw yāròn dà kukà ganī; the girl to ~ I told the news yārinyar̃ dà na gayà matà làbārìn; to ~ did you tell the news? wà ka gayà wà làbārìn? the one to ~ the letter was sent wândà akà aikà wà dà wàsīƙà.

**whooping cough** *n* tārin shīƙà *m*.

**whore** *n* mazinācìyā *f*, ƙar̃ùwà *f* ⟨ai⟩.

**whose 1.** *interrog det* na wằ/wằnē nè: ~ horse won the race? dōkìn wà ya ci sukùwā? ~ house is that? gidan wằnē nè wancàn?

**2.** *rel det*, *see* who: the man ~ gown is torn mùtûm wândà r̃ìgar̃sà ta yāgè; the man ~ horse Audu stole mùtumìn dà Audù ya sācè masà dōkì; a word ~ meaning he knew wata kalmà wâddà ya san mà'ànar̃tà.

**why 1.** *interrog adv* don mè, mè ya sâ, sabòdà mè: ~ did you do it? don mè ka yī shì? ~ did she come so early? mè ya sâ tā zō dà wuri hakà?

**2.** *rel adv* àbîn dà ya sâ, dàlīlìn dà ya sâ: we don't know ~ he died bà mù san àbîn dà ya sâ yā ràsu ba; that is ~ they

did it shī ya sâ sukà yi hakà; the reason ~ I am late is... dàlīlìn dà ya sâ nā màkarà shī nè...; ~ not? mè zâi hanà?

**whydah** *n* (*white-breasted*) zàlaidù *m*.

**wick** *n* (*of candle, lamp*) làgwànī *m*: trim a ~ dātsè làgwànī.

**wicked** *adj* (*psn.*) mamùgùncī *m*, mūgù *adj* ⟨miyàgū⟩: the ~ king mamùgùncin sarkī; ~ people miyàgun mutànē; sth. ~ mùgùntā *f*: a ~ thing has happened an yi mùgùntā = an aikàtà shar̃r̃ì.

**wide 1.** *adj* (*mài*) fād̃ī *m*: the road is ten meters ~ fād̃in hanyàr̃ mītà gōmà nē; how ~ is it? yàyà fād̃insà yakè? it isn't ~ enough fād̃insà bài kai ba; very ~ fàffād̃à *adj*; travel far and ~ shā tàfiyà.

**2.** *adv*: the door is ~ open an būd̃è ƙōfà sòsai; his ears are ~ apart kunnuwànsà fatō-fàtò; they are ~ awake idònsù biyu; open your mouth ~! (*usu. said to children*) hā!

**widen** *v* fād̃àd̃à *v1*: the bridge is too narrow, it needs to be ~ed gadàr̃ tā cikà màtsuwā, kàmātà ya yi à fād̃àd̃à ta.

**widespread** *adj*: be ~ bàzu *v7*: the illness is ~ cīwòn yā bàzu.

**widow, widower** *n* (*no gen'l terms*), *see* unmarried; live as a ~ yi zaman gwaurancī.

**width** *n* a. fād̃ī *m*: what is the ~ of the road here? nawà nē fād̃in hanyàr̃ à nân? b. (*esp. of cloth*) dar̃a'à *f*: the ~ of the cloth is 45 inches dar̃a'àr̃ ƙyallên incì àr̃bà'in dà bìyar̃; (*of handwoven cloth*) ƙwaryā *f*.

**wife** *n* màtā *f* ⟨màtā⟩; (*euphem., used esp. by man for his own ~*) uwar̃gidā *f*, mài dākì *f*: my ~ has gone on a trip mài dākīnà tā yi bàlàgur̃ò; his ~ walked out on him màtar̃sà tā yi yājì; favorite ~ mōwà *f*; non-favorite ~ bōr̃à *f*; senior ~ uwar̃gidā *f*; youngest ~ amaryā *f*; co-~ kīshìyā *f*.

**wiggle** *v* yi wàtsàl-watsal *idph*, yi wàtsàlniyā *f*.

**wild** *adj* na dājì *m*: ~ animal nāmàn dājì.

**wilderness** *n* ƙungurmin dājì *m*, dòkar̃ dājì *f*.

**wilful** *adj* (*mài*) ƙarfin halī *m*.

**will**[1] *n* a. (*wish*) sô *m*: against his ~ bà dà sònsà ba; good ~ fātan àlhēr̃ì *m*, farar̃ zūcìyā *f*; ill ~ baƙar̃ àniyà *f*; where there's a ~ there's a way (*fig.*) àbîn dà zūcìyā ta d̃aukà gàngar̃ jìkī bāwà nè. b. (*volition*) sôn râi *m*, ganin dāmā: I did it of my own free ~ nā yī shì don ganin dāmātà; strong ~, ~power ƙarfin halī *m.* **c.** (*pertaining to God*) k̃addar̃ã *f*, īkòn Allàh *m*: God's ~ prevails k̃addar̃ã tā rigā fātā; I leave it to God's ~ nā dangànā dà Allàh; free ~ (*Relig.*) zā6ĩ *m.* **d.** (*legacy*) wàsiyyà *f* ⟨oCi⟩: he left a ~ stating he should be buried in his compound yā bar̃ wàsiyyà cêwà à ruf̃e shi cikin gidansà.

**will**[2] *v aux* (*to indicate future aspect*) see Appendix A: she ~ help us, won't she? zā tà tàimàkē mù, kō bà hakà ba?

**willing** *adj*: be ~ yàr̃da *v3*: are you ~ to do it? kā yàr̃da kà yī shì?

**willpower** *n* k̃arfin halī *m.*

**wilt** *v* yi yaushī *m.*

**wily** *adj* (mài) wàyō *m*, (mài) dàbàr̃ã *f.*

**win** *v* ci *v0*, yi nasar̃ã *f*: who won? wà ya ci? (*sth.*) ci nasar̃àr̃ w.a.: who won the war? wà ya ci nasar̃àr̃ yàk̃ìn? (*in games*) kasà *v1*: I won the game nā kasà; ~ first prize yi làmbàwân *m*, [F] ci faf̃mâl *m;* ~ a cup (*Sport*) ci kòfĩ; ~ over rìnjàyā *v2*: his words won us over màganàr̃sà tā rìnjàyē mù.

**wind**[1] *n* iskà *f*, (*strong, esp. whirling*) gùguwà *f;* a dry ~ iskà maràs laimà; a high ~ gàwùr̃tacciyar̃ iskà; the ~ is coming from the south iskà tanà tāsôwā dàgà kudù; (*fig.*) he got his second ~ yā shà jinī. **b.** (*gas in stomach*) tūsà *f;* break, pass ~ yi tūsà, (*euphem.*) hūtà *v1.*

**wind**[2] *v* **a.** (*roll around*) naɗà *v1*: he wound on his turban yā naɗà rawànī; I wound the string around the box nā naɗà wà àkwàtì kìr̃tànī. **b.** (*turn, esp. a handle*) yi wà wànī *m*: ~ one's watch yi wà àgōgo wànī; ~ up sth. wànà *v1*: he wound up the toy yā wànà àbin wàsà.

**wind instrument** *n* àbin būsà *m*: a flute is a ~ sàrēwà àbar̃ būsà cē; ~s kàyan bùshe-bùshe *p.*

**window** *n* tāgà *f* ⟨oCi⟩, (*esp. one with glass*) wundò *m* ⟨una⟩.

**windowpane** *n* gìlāshìn wundò *m.*

**windpipe** *n* màk̃ōgwàrō *m.*

**windshield, windscreen** *n* gìlāshìn mōtà *m.*

**windshield wiper** *n* waifà *f* ⟨oCi⟩.

**windy**[1] *adj* (mài) iskà *f*: a ~ place wurī mài iskà; today it is very ~ yâu àkwai iskà dà yawà.

**windy**[2] *adj* (*of road*) (mài) kwàne-kwàne *p*: the road to Jos is very ~ hanyàr̃ Jàs tā cikà kwàne-kwàne.

**wine** *n* giyà *f*, [F] dùbân *m;* palm ~ bàmmī *m.*

**wing** *n* fiffikè *m* ⟨a..ai⟩.

**wink** **1.** *v* k̃iftà idò, yi k̃ìfcē *m*, kannè idò: he ~ed at her yā k̃iftà matà idò = yā yi matà k̃ìfcē. **2.** *n* k̃iftàwā *f*, k̃ìfcē *m*: in the ~ of an eye kàfìn k̃iftàwar̃ idò.

**winner** *n* mài nasar̃ã *n.*

**winnow** *v* (*with round mat & calabash*) shēk̃à *v1;* (*with flat woven tray*) tankàɗē *v4.*

**winter** *n* lōkàcin dārī *m*, see season: it is very cold in ~ àkwai sanyī k̃war̃ai lōkàcin dārī.

**wipe** *v* gōgè *v4*: he ~d the car with a rag yā gōgè mōtà dà tsùmmà; he ~d off the dust yā gōgè k̃ùrà; please ~ up the water on the table sai kà gōgè tēbùr̃ dà àbin tsanè ruwà; ~ one's feet at the doorstep gōgè k̃af̃à à dandamàlī; ~ away tears shàrē hawàyē; ~ one's nose gōgè hancī, (*with back of hand*) yi dàjìnē = yi shàɓùnē.

**wiper** *n* (*windshield*) waifà *f* ⟨oCi⟩.

**wire** *n* wàyà *f* ⟨oCi⟩, [F] fîl *m*: a ~ fence shingē na wàyà; barbed ~ wàyà (mài k̃ayà).

**wisdom** *n* hikimà *f*: old people have ~ tsòfàffī hikimà gàrē sù; the fear of God is the beginning of ~ tsòron Allàh shī nè masōmin hikimà.

**wisdom tooth** *n* hak̃ōrin hankàlī *m.*

**wise** *adj* **a.** (*of older psn.*) dattìjò *m* ⟨ai⟩: she is a ~ woman dattìjùwā cè. **b.** (*smart, resourceful*) (mài) hikimà *f*, (mài) dàbàr̃ã *f*: you were ~ not to go kā yi dàbàr̃ã dà bà kà jē ba; a ~ decision shàwar̃à mài kyâu.

**wish** **1.** *v* **a.** (*want, need*) sô *v0*: I ~ I could go with you inà sô ìn tàfi tàre dà kai; he had everything he could ~ for Allàh yā bā shì duk àbîn dà yakè sô; as you ~ kàmar̃ yàddà kakè sô = kàmar̃ yàddà ka cè. **b.** (*hope*) yi fātà *m*: I ~ to continue my studies inà fātà zân iyà cî gàba dà kàr̃àtūnā; I ~ed him well nā yi masà fātan àlhēr̃ī. **c.** (*for sth. contrary to fact*): I ~ I were rich! inà mā nī mài àr̃zìkī nè! he ~ed he were dead inà mā yā mutù = dà mā yā mutù.
**2.** *n* **a.** (*hope*) fātà *m*: his ~ was not granted fātansà bài sàmi kàr6à ba; with best ~es dà fātan àlhēr̃ī. **b.** (*ultimate need*) bùkātà / bùk̃àtà *f*, mùr̃àdī *m*, būrī / gūrī *m*: my ~ has been granted, fulfilled bùkātàtā tā biyā = būrīnā yā

cìka = nā cim mà būrĩnā; may God grant
your ~ Allàh yà biyā bùkātã = Allàh yà
biyā muřādĩ.

**wisp** n fìřkãkĩ m: ~s of cotton, straw
fìřkãkin audùga, cìyāwã.

**wit** n a. (humor) bařkwancĩ m. b. (intelligence) azancĩ m. c. (fig.): he went out of
his ~s yā fìta dàgà hankàlinsà; (fig.)
he is at his ~s' end bài san àbîn dà zāi
yi ba.

**witch** n māyyā f ⟨māyū⟩.

**witchcraft** n māitā f.

**witch doctor** n māyè m ⟨māyū⟩.

**with** prep a. dà prep: what should I do
~ this? mè zān yi dà wannàn? we get
along ~ them munà shirī dà sū; I cut it
down ~ an axe nā sārē shì dà gātarī;
he did it ~ our help yā yī shì dà
tàimakonmù; go on ~ your work kù ci
gàba dà aikinkù; I have nothing to do
~ them bâ ruwānā dà sū. b. (together
~) tàre dà, hàɗe dà: they are ~ their
mother sunà tàre dà mahaifìyařsù; he
came together ~ his family yā zō tàre
dà ìyālìnsà she was wearing a wrapper together ~ a head-tie tanà sànye
dà zanè hàɗe dà wani àdīkò. c. (characterized by, having) mài (+ n): the man
~ the horse mùtûm mài dōkì; an old man
~ gray hair wani tsōhō mài furfurā; the
building ~ the tower ginī mài hàsūmiyà.
d. (at so.'s place) (à) wurin / gurin /
gûn, (à) wajen: I am staying ~ friends
nā sàuka gûn wasu àbòkai; the book is
~ me littàfìn yanà wajēnā.

**withdraw** 1. vt jânyē v4: ~ one's hand,
one's support, a job application jânyè
hannū, gōyon bāyā, takàřdā nēman
aikī; ~ money karɓō kudī, [F] yi
řètìřè m; ~ troops ɗàukè sōjōjī.
2. vi (one's body) nōřè v4; (back up into
small opening) kuɗè v4: the mouse withdrew into its hole ɓēřā yā kuɗè cikin
rāmìnsà; ~ from a competition fìta dàgà
tākařā.

**withdrawn** adj: be ~ (shy, quiet) yi
kawaicì m.

**wither** v yāřwànē / yankwànē v4, yàusasà
v3; (esp. of plants) yi yaushī m; (esp. of
limb) shânyē v4: a ~ed arm shànyayyen
hannū.

**withhold** v řìřè v4: ~ information, taxes
řìřè làbārì, hařajì; ~ consent ƙi bā
dà izìnī; (esp. secretively) tōgè v4: they
withheld the truth sun tōgè gàskiyā.

**within** adv ciki adv: from ~ dàgà ciki;
(+ time expr.) cikin: he got well ~ 2

weeks yā warkè cikin mākò biyu; (expr.
fut. time) nân dà: it will be finished ~ 3
months zā à gamà nân dà watà ukù.

**without** prep a. (not having) bâ tàre dà X
ba: ~ any trouble at all bâ tàre dà wata
màtsalā ba; he left ~ my knowledge yā
tāshì bâ tàre dà sanìnā ba. b. (lacking in) ban dà, bābù / bâ: it isn't enjoyable to eat food ~ salt ci àbinci ban
dà gishirī bâ dāɗī; he is ~ a home,
money, or friends bâ shi dà gidā, bâ
kudī, bâ àbòkai; he was resigned to being ~ a job yā hàƙurà dà rashìn aikī;
~ a doubt bābù shakkà; come ~ fail kà
zō bâ makawā.

**witness** 1. n (mài) shaidà n ⟨u⟩; bear ~
shâidā v1; as God is my ~ Allàh yanà
ganī.
2. v ganī v*: he ~ed the crime yā ga
làifìn.

**witty** adj a. (clever with words) (mài) iyà
zàncē; he is very ~ yanà dà salon
màganà. b. (humorous) (mài) bařkwancĩ
m.

**wizard** n māyè m ⟨māyū⟩.

**wobble** v yi rawā m: the wheel of the car,
foot of the table is wobbling wīlìn mōtà,
ƙafàř tēbùř nà rawā.

**woe** n: a tale of ~ làbārì mài ban tàusàyī;
~ is me! kaicōnā!

**woman** n màcè f ⟨mātā⟩ (in the genitive, use
màtař), mùtūnìyā f: (young, of marriageable age) bùdurwā f ⟨oCi⟩; (widow or divorcee of marriageable age) bàzawàrā /
zawàrā f ⟨awa⟩.

**womanizer** n manèmin mātā m.

**womb** n mahaifā f, cikì m.

**wonder** 1. n a. àbin màmākì m: it is a ~
that you were not hurt àbin màmākì nē
dà bà kà ji ràunī ba; it's no ~ that he
didn't come bâ màmākì dà bài zō ba; ~s
never cease àbin màmākì bā yà ƙārèwā à
dūniyà. b. (sth. wondrous, inexplicable)
àbin àl'ajàbī m.
2. v: I ~ whether... kō (+ question): I ~
whether he is coming kō zâi zō kùwa? I ~
why he did that kō mè ya sâ ya yi hakà?
what he did made us ~ àbîn dà ya yi yā
bā mù màmākì.

**wonderful** 1. adj (mài) ban màmākì m: this
is a very ~ thing wannàn àbù gwànin ban
màmākì nē; we had a ~ trip tàfiyàř tā
bā mù màmākì; sth. ~ (wondrous, inexplicable) àbin àl'ajàbī.
2. excl how ~! ìkòn Allàh!
māshā'àllāhù!

**won't** v aux (use neg. fut. pro, see Ap-

pendix A): they ~ return today bà zā
sù dāwō yâu ba.

**woo** *v* nèmi w. dà aurē.

**wood** *n* (*raw* ~, *firewood*) itācē / icè
*m* (itātuwà): go buy some ~ (*for the
fire*) kà jē kà sayō itācē; (*finished* ~)
kātākō *m*: a bookcase made of ~ kantà
ta kātākō; is it made of ~ or metal? dà
kātākō akà yī shi kō dà ƙarfè?

**wood carver** *n* masàssaƙī *m*.

**woodcarving** *n* sàssaƙà *f*.

**wooden** *adj* na itācē *m*, na kātākō *m*: two
~ boxes akwātunà biyu na kātākō.

**woodpecker** *n* maƙwaƙƙwafī *m* (ai),
makōdìyā *f* (ai).

**woods** *n* dājì / jējì *m* (dāzuzzukà): walk
through the ~ kētà dājì.

**woodwork** *n* aikìn kātākō *m*.

**woof** *n* (*in weaving*) zàrē *m*.

**wool** *n* (*thread, yarn*) ūlù *m*, (*fabric, material*) wūl *m*: sweaters are made of ~ anà
sùwaità dà ūlù.

**woolen** *adj* na wūl *m*.

**word** *n* a. kalmà *f* (oCi): what is the meaning of this ~? mènē nè mà'ànaɍ kalmàɍ
nân? it is better to use simple ~s yā
fi kyâu à yi àmfànī dà kalmōmī màsu
sauƙī; that ~ is crude so don't use it
wannàn kalmà ɗanyen bàkī cè, bā à
fàdā; in other ~s wàtàu / wàtō: I've paid
half the cost, in other ~s, ₦50 nā biyā
rabìn kuɗinsà, wàtàu nairà hàmsin. b.
(*sth. said*): I was at a loss for ~s nā rasà
ta cêwā; he has a way with ~s yanà dà
salon màganà; I don't believe a ~ of his
story bàn yàɍda dà kōmē ba à zàncensà;
have a ~ with so. gānà dà *v1*: he spoke
a few ~s to me yesterday mun ɗan gānà
dà shī jiyà = yā yi minì 'yaɍ màganà
jiyà; not say, utter even a ~ cè ƙàlà,
cè kō uffàn (+ *neg. sent.*): he left without saying a ~ to us yā tàfi bài cè dà
mū ƙàlà ba; they didn't utter a ~ to each
other bà sù cè dà jūnā kō uffàn ba. c.
(*promise*) one's ~ àlkawàɍī *m*: she always
keeps her ~ ita mài cikà àlkawàɍī nè;
is he a man of his ~? yanà dà àlkawàɍī?
go back on one's ~ karyà àlkawàɍī; he
doesn't keep his ~ shī mài bàkī biyu nè.

**work 1.** *n* a. aikì *m* (ayyukà): he does good
~ aikìnsà yā yi kyâu; he found ~ at the
factory yā kāmà aikì à ma'aikatà; he is
out of ~ (*unemployed*) bâ shi dà aikì =
yanà zaman kashè-wàndō; start, set to ~
kāmà aikì = tāsam mà aikì; hard ~ jan
aikì; he is hard at ~ yanà aikì tuƙuru =
yanà cîn aikì; manual ~ lēbuɍancì *m*.

b. (*occupation, trade*) aikì *m* (ayyukà),
sànā'à *f* (oCi): what kind of ~ do you
do? wàcè sànā'à kakè yî? = wànè irìn
aikì kakè yî? c. (*of any artist, writer*)
ayyukà *p*, (*of a writer*) tālīfī *m*: the
~s of Shehu Usman Dan Fodio ayyukàn
Shēhù = tālīfìn Shēhù; the ~s of Shata
waƙōkin Shātā.

**2.** *v* a. (*be employed, have work*) yi aikì
*m*: he doesn't ~ at all bâ yā aikìn kōmē;
he ~s for the government yanà aikìn
gwamnatì; ~ hard yi aikì tuƙuru; ~ excessively shā aikì; (*fig.*) ~ like a dog yi
aikì kàmaɍ jàkī; ~ on yi aikì à kân;
~ off a debt ragè bāshì; ~ out a plan
tsārà shirì. b. (*be effective*) yi àmfànī
*m*: the medicine didn't ~ māgànîn bài yi
àmfànī ba. c. (*function, of a machine*)
yi aikì *m*: this machine ~s by (means
of) electricity injìn din nàn yanà aikì
dà wutaɍ làntaɍkì.

**worker** *n* ma'àikàcī *m*.

**workmanship** *n* fàsāhà *f*.

**workshop** *n* a. (*atelier*) shāgò *m* (una). b.
(*training course*) bītà *f*, [F] ìstājì *m*.

**world** *n* dūniyā *f* (oCi): he has travelled all
over the ~ yā shā yāwòn dūniyā; from
everywhere in the ~ dàgà duk wuràren
dūniyà; it is the same all over the ~ hakà
àbîn yakè duk fàɗin dūniyà; that's the
way the ~ is hālìn dūniyà kè nan; its
the best of all possible ~s dūniyà tā yi
dādī; the animal ~ dūniyàɍ dabbōbì =
zaman dabbōbī; the next ~ lāhiɍà *f*, gidan gàskiyā *m*; the Third W. ƙasàshē
màsu tāsôwā.

**worldly** *adj* (*psn.*) bàdūniyè *m*, ɗan dūniyà
*m*: he's very ~ bàdùniyī nè.

**worm** *n* tsūtsà *f* (oCi); earth~ tānā *f*;
round~ macìjin cikì *m*, tsūtsàɍ cikì
*m*; tape~ tsīlà *f*, daudàɍ cikì *f*.

**worn out, be** *v, see* wear.

**worry 1.** *n* a. (àbin) dàmuwā *f*, màtsalà *f*,
rashìn kwànciyaɍ râi *m*: you needn't
have the slightest ~ kadà kì yi wata
dàmuwā; it has become a ~ to me yā zamè
minì àbin dàmuwā; I don't have any worries bâ ni dà màtsalà = hankàlīnā yā
kwàntā = bâ ni dà àbîn dà kè dāmūnā;
she hasn't a ~ in the world bâ àbîn dà
ya dàmē tà zāfī; life is full of worries
dūniyà gidan wàhalà. b. (*esp. financial*)
màtsuwā *f*, matsì *m*: he has financial worries yanà cikin màtsuwā = yanà cikin
matsì = yā màtsu.

**2.** *v* dàmā *v2* (dāmù), tā dà hankàlin w.:
don't let that ~ you kadà wannàn yà dàmē

kà; the news worried her làbāřìn yā tā
dà hankàlìntà; get, become worried dằmu
*v7*: she is worried tā dằmu = hankàlìntà
yā tāshì; I'm always worried kullum inằ
cikin rashìn kwànciyař râi = kullum
hankàlīnā à tằshe yakè.

**worse** *adj*, *see* **bad**, **worst**: this one is
~ than the other wannàn yā fi wancàn
rashìn kyâu; his illness is getting ~
cīwònsà yanằ tsànantằ; it is ~ than
before yā fi na dà tsànantằ; ~ than
ever mài tsananī flye dà na dâ; things
are going from bad to ~ àbîn yā kàrà
lālàcêwā; why should I make matters ~?
(*fig.*) ìn yi màganà cībì yà zama kařī?

**worsen** *v* tsànantà *v3*, tà'àzzařà *v3*.

**worship** 1. *v* a. (*God, esp. in Islam*) bâutā
wà *v1*: to ~ God bâutā wà Allàh. b.
(*non-Islamic*) yi bàutā *f*: they ~ fetishes,
money sunà bàutař gumằkā, kudī.
2. *n* ìbādà *f*: a place of ~ wurin ìbādà;
Christians have their own form of ~
Kiřistà sunà dà nāsù àddīnìn.

**worst** *adj* mafì (+ *n of quality*), *see* **bad**,
**worse**: this road is the ~ one hanyář
nàn tā fi kōwàccè 6àcī; (*emphat.*) na
innànàhà *f*, na kìn kàràwā: he is my ~
enemy àbōkin gàbātā nè na kìn kàràwā;
the ~ accident hadàřī mafì tsananī =
hadàřī na kìn kàrêwā; be the ~ among
(+ *abstr. n*) fi saurā rashìn (+ *n*): this
student is the ~ one in the class dàlìbin
nàn yā fi saurân rashìn kōkarī; at ~ à
lālàce: at ~, you'll fail the examination
à lālàce, bà zā kà ci jařřàbâwā ba.

**worth** 1. *n* a. (*value*) dařajà *f*, kīmằ / kīmằ
*f*: its ~ has gone up, gone down dařajàřsà
tā tāshì, fādì; how would you estimate
its ~? yằyằ zā à kīmàntà dařajàřsà?
a person of ~ mùtûm mài dařajà =
mùtûm mài kīmà. b. (*esp. of merchandise*)
kadàřī / àlkadàřī *m*: these goods have
fallen in ~ kadàřin kāyan nàn yā karyè.
c. (*quantifiable amount*) kīmà / kīmà *f*:
I want about 2 kilos ~ of grain inà sôn
kīmař hatsī ta kilō biyu; about how
much is it ~? nawà nē kīmàřsà?
2. *adj* a. (*worthwhile*) (mài) àmfằnī *m*;
be ~ ci *v0*: it is ~ doing yā ci à yī
shì = yanà dà àmfằnī à yī shì; this
book is ~ reading littàfìn nàn yā ci à
kařàntà shi. b. (*in bargaining, offering
to buy sth.*): what is it ~ to you? nawà zā
kà tayà? it's ~ more than that ai, yā fi
hakà.

**worthless** *adj* a. (*useless*) na banzā *f*, na
wōfī *m*: the thing has become ~ àbîn yā

zama na wōfī; a ~ person mùtumìn banzā
*m*, wōfī *n*, sākařai *n* ⟨sākàřkařī⟩. b.
(*useless, of sth.*) maràs àmfằnī *m*. c. (*of
no value*) maràs dařajà *f*, maràs kīmà *f*:
their currency is ~ kudin kasařsù bā sằ
dà dařajà; this ring is ~ zōbèn nân bā
yằ dà kīmà.

**worthwhile** *adj* (*important*) (mài) àmfằnī
*m*, (mài) muhimmancì *m*: it is a ~ cause
àbù nē mài muhimmancì = àbù nē mài
mà'ànā.

**worthy** *adj* (mài) dařajà *f*, (mài) kīmà/kīmà
*f*.

**would** *v aux* a. (*in polite question*) kō (+
*fut.*): ~ you like a cold drink? kō zā kà
shā wani àbù mài sanyī? ~ like to sō *v0*:
I ~ like to go with them inà sô mù tàfi
tàre dà sū; ~ rather fi sô: I ~ rather
go for a walk nā fi sôn shân iskằ. b.
(*in past constr.*): he told me he ~ come
yā cê minì zâi zō. c. (*in past contrary-
to-fact statement*) (in) dà (+ *complet.*): if
we hadn't arrived on time the plane ~ have
left us behind in dà bà mù ìsa kân lōkàcī
ba dà jirgī yā bař mù; if I were you, I ~
not have gone dà nī nè kai, dà bà zân
tàfi ba. d. (*expr. habit. past action*) dà
(+ *contin.*): we ~ often eat together dà
munà cîn àbinci tàre.

**wound** 1. *n* ràunī *m* ⟨uka⟩; (*ulcerated*)
gyàmbō *m* ⟨una⟩, mīkì *m*: a serious ~
ràunī mài tsananī; this ~ is not heal-
ing well wannàn ràunī bā yằ warkèwā dà
wuri; have a ~ yi ràunī.
2. *v* yi wà ràunī *m*, jī wà cīwò *m*: he ~ed
me in the leg yā yi minì ràunī à kafà; ~
one another seriously (*fig.*) yi kàrē jinī
birī jinī.

**wow** *excl* kâi! *excl*, bâ dāmā! *excl*: ~,
what a beautiful girl! kâi, yārinyàř nân
tùbařkallà! = yārinyàř nân bâ dāmā!

**wrangle** *v* yi gařdamằ / gaddamằ *f*
⟨gařdàndamī⟩, yi hàtsàniyā *f*; (*arguing
back & forth without resolution*) yi cācař
bàkī *f*.

**wrap** 1. *v* a. (*a package, thing*) kunshè *v4*: ~
a gift in paper kunshè kyàutā à takàřdā;
~ sth. around sth. nadà wà *v1*: you must
first ~ paper around the package sai kà
nadà wà fākitì takàřdā tùkùna; ~ sth.
with sth. nadè *v4*: I ~ped the package with
paper nā nadè fākitì dà takàřdā. b.
(*garment around body*) yāfà *v1*, lullù6à
*v1*: she ~ped herself up with a shawl tā
yāfà mayāfī à kântà = tā yāfà wà kântà
mayāfī; (*fig.*) he was ~ped in his work
aikì yā dabaibàyē shi.

**2.** n (*woman's covering worn over head & shoulders*) mayāfī m; (*man's cotton blanket worn over shoulders*) gwàdò m ⟨Cuna⟩.

**wrapper** n (*woman's body cloth*) zanè m ⟨Cuwa⟩: wear, put on a ~ ɗaurà zanè.

**wreck 1.** n (*totally ~ed car*) màtacciyař mōtā f, (*of a vehicle still working*) akwalā f, kwàràrràɓaɓɓiyař mōtā f: I'm driving a ~ (of a car) inā tūƙìn akwalař mōtā. **2.** v: be ~ed (*esp. of metal objects*) kwararràɓē v4.

**wrench**[1] n (*spanner*) sùfānā f ⟨oCi⟩, [F] kìlē àmùlât m; (*adjustable*) [F] kìlē àmìřkân m.

**wrench**[2] v fizgè v4: he took hold of her hand but she ~ed it away yā kāmà hannuntà àmmā tā fizgè.

**wrestling** n a. (*Sport*) kòkawā f. b. (*struggling with problem*) gwagwàřmayā f, jìdālī m.

**wretched** adj (*psn.*) mìskīnī m ⟨ai⟩.

**wriggle** v yi wàtsàl-watsal idph, yi wàtsàlniyā f.

**wring out** v mātsā v1, muřɗè v4, mātsè v4: she wrung out the wrapper and laid it out to dry tā mātsè zanè tā shânyā.

**wrinkle** v yāmùtsā v1; be ~d yāmùtsē v4: her face is ~d fuskàřtà tā yāmùtsē; be ~d (*crumpled*) cukwīkwìyē v4.

**wrist** n wuyàř hannu f, tsintsìyař hannu f.

**wristbone** n mahaɗař hannu f.

**write** v a. řubùtā v1 ⟨řùbùtū⟩: he is writing her a letter yanà řubùtā matà wàsīƙā; please ~ to me don Allàh kì aikō minì dà wàsīƙà; ~ your name and address here kà řubùtà sūnankà dà àdìřēshìnkà nân; can you read and ~? kā iyà řubùtū dà kàřātū? the book is well written littāfìn yā řùbùtu dà kyâu. b. (*a published work*) wallàfā v1: who wrote this poem? wà ya wallàfà wāƙař nân? c. ~ off a debt sōkè bāshì.

**writer** n marùbùcī m, mawàllàfī m.

**writing** n (*handwriting or activity*) řùbùtū m: he is busy ~ yanà tsakiyàř řùbùtū; cursive ~ řùbùtun tàfiyàř tsūtsā.

**writing board** n àllō m ⟨una⟩.

**writings** n (*of a partic. writer*) tālīfī m: the ~ of Sa'adu Zungur tālīfìn Sà'àdu Zungùř.

**written** adj řùbùtaccē adj.

**wrong 1.** adj & adv a. (*not correct*) bà daidai ba: your answer is ~ amsàřkà bà daidai ba; I spelled it ~ bàn řubùtā shi daidai ba; you guessed ~ cìntařkà bà tà yi daidai ba; he did me ~ yā yi minì bà daidai ba; you are quite ~ in thinking that àbîn dà kakè tsàmmānī bà shī ba nè; that is the ~ road wannàn bà hanyàř ba cè; we took the ~ road mun kuskùrè hanyàř = hanyàř tā ɓacè manà. b. (*bad, immoral*) na hàřâm/hàřāmùn m, mūgù adj ⟨miyàgū⟩: it is ~ to lie yîn ƙaryā mūgùn àbù nē; it is ~ to steal hàřāmùn nē à yi sātā. c. (*not suitable*): do the ~ thing yi àbîn dà bài kàmātà ba. d. (*not as expected*): I'm afraid something went ~ inā tsòron wani àbù maràs kyâu yā fàru; is there sth. ~ with you? kō wani àbù ya sàmē kà? the plan went ~ shirìn bài yi ba.

**2.** n a. (*gen'l*) lâifī m ⟨uka[2]⟩, sàɓō m: he admitted he was in the ~ yā yàrda yanà dà lâifī = yā yàrda yā yi sàɓō; people who do ~ màsu sàɓō; do ~ to so. yi wà lâifī, sàɓā wà v1. b. (*as specified in Islam*) hàřâm / hàřāmùn m: children must be taught the difference between right and ~ yā kàmātà à kōyà wà yârā bambancī tsàkānin hàlâl dà hàřâm.

**3.** v (*a psn.*) sàɓā wà v1: I ~ed him when I said he was lazy nā sàɓà masà dà na cè shī ragō nè.

**wrongdoing** n sàɓō m.

# X Y Z

**X-ray** *n* hŏtō *m* ⟨una⟩, [F] ɍådìyô *m*: take an ~ of so. dàuki hŏton w. = yi wå hŏtō; chest ~ hŏton ƙìrjī; ~ room dākìn hŏtō.

**xerox** *v* yi hŏtō *m*.

**xylophone** *n* [F] bàlånhô *m*.

**yam** *n* dōyå *f*: aerial ~ dōyåɍ bisà; (*boiled but unpounded*) dōyå bùsà; (*boiled and pounded*) sàkwårā *f*.

**yank** *v*: ~ back, out fizgè *v4*.

**yard**[1] *n* (*in front of compound, house*) fàɍfåjìyå *f*.

**yard**[2] *n* (*unit of measurement*) yādì *m*: sell shirting material by the ~ sai dà zàwwātì yādì-yādì.

**yardstick** *n* sàndaɍ awô *f*.

**yarn** *n* zàrē *m*; (*woolen*) ūlù *m*.

**yawn** *v* yi hammå *f*: when you ~, cover your mouth with your hand in kanå hammå, kà kārè båkinkà dà hannū; stifle a ~ haɗìyè hammå.

**year** *n* shèkarå *f* ⟨u⟩: the ~ has almost gone shèkarå tā kusa cìkā; 3 ~s ago bāyan shèkarå ukù dà sukà wucè; within 2 ~s' time bāyan shèkarå biyu; he has lived here for ~s yā yi shèkarū dà dāmā à nân; a few ~s ago 'yan shèkàrun bāya; in recent ~s cikin 'yan shèkàrun nàn; ~ after ~, ~ in and ~ out, for ~s and ~s shèkarå dà shèkàrū; ~ by ~, each ~ kōwàcè shèkarå; many ~s ago shèkàrun dà sukà wucè; many many ~s ago shèkàrū àɍu-àɍu = tun dâ dâ; spend a ~, have a ~ pass shèkarà *v3*: I didn't see them again until after 5 ~s had passed bàn sākè ganinsù ba sai dà akà shèkarà bìyaɍ; this ~ bana *adv*; last ~ båra *adv*; the ~ before last båra wàccan; next ~ bàdi *adv*; the ~ after next bàdi wàccan; many ~s hence bàdin bàdådà; all ~ round rānī dà dāminā; Happy New Y.! Baɍkà dà Sàbuwaɍ Shèkarå!

**yearly** *adj* na shèkarå-shèkarå.

**yearn** *v* yi bègē *m*: they are ~ing to be free sunå bègen 'yancì.

**yeast** *n* yîs *m*.

**yell** *v* yi kuwwå *f*, yi īhù *m*; (*esp. for help*) yi kùrūruwå *f*; ~ at, scold so. dakå wà tsāwā.

**yellow** *adj* råwayå *f* ⟨u⟩, ruwan dòrawå *m*; light ~ dòrawå-dòrawå.

**yellow fever** *n* shāwaɍå *f*.

**yes** *excl* ī / ē *excl*; (*in reply to being called*) nà'am *excl*, ìyē *excl*; (*showing that one is listening to so. telling or narrating*) na'àm *excl*.

**yes-man** *n* ɗan 'amshìn Shātā *m*.

**yesterday** *adv* jiyà *adv*; the day before ~ shèkaranjiyà *adv*.

**yet** *adv* a. (*in neg. sent.*): not ~ tùkùna/ tùkùn *adv*, haɍ yànzu: he hasn't come ~ bài zō ba tùkùna; haven't you finished it ~? haɍ yànzu bà kà gamå ba? he has ~ to do what I requested haɍ yànzu bài yi àbìn dà nakè tàmbayå ba. b. (*still ano.*) haɍ ìlā yâu: there is ~ another reason haɍ ìlā yâu àkwai wani dàlīlì dàbam. c. (*nevertheless*) duk dà hakà: we may finish ~ duk dà hakà zā mù gamå; and ~ (*contrastive*) àmmā dai, àmmā duk dà hakà: he has everything that he needs, and ~ he is not happy yanå dà duk àbìn dā' yakè bùkātå àmmā duk dà hakà bà yå jin dādī.

**yield**[1] *v* sakaɍ wà *vdat*: we ~ed to him under pressure yā yi ta matså manå sai dà mukà sakam masà.

**yield**[2] *n* yawå *m*: last year's crop ~ was better than this year's yawàn àmfånin gōnā båra yā fi na bana.

**yoghurt** *n* kìndìɍmō *m*.

**yolk** *n* ƙwandùwā *f*, gwaidùwā *f*.

**Yoruba** *n* a. (*member of ethnic group*) bàyaɍàbè *m*. b. (*language*) Yaɍabancī *m*.

**you** *pro*, see Appendix A.

**young** 1. *adj* a. (*small*) ƙaramì *adj* ⟨ƙanƙanè⟩; (*of age*) yārô *m*, yārinyå *f* ⟨yârā⟩: she was ~ at the time; tanå ƙaramā à lōkàcīn = yārinyå cē a lōkàcīn; when I was ~ lōkàcīn dà nakè yārô = tun inå yārô; I haven't seen him since we were very ~ ràbonmù tun munå 'yan yârā; he is ~er than I am nā gìrmē shì; he is the ~est in our family shī àutanmù nē; he is not as ~ as he looks shèkàrunsà bà sù kai yåddà akè zàtō ba; ~er brother, sister ƙanè *m*, ƙanwå *f* ⟨ƙannē⟩; a ~ man sauràyī *m* ⟨sàmårī⟩; a ~ woman bùdurwå *f* ⟨oCi⟩. b. (*youthful*): she is ~ in spite of her age duk dà tsūfantà, haɍ yànzu tanå dà ƙarfintà; she is ~ at heart tanå dà bùdurwaɍ zūcìyā.

2. *n* (*pre-teen*) yârā *p,* (*teen-age*) matā̀sā
*p:* the ~ and the old tsòfàffī dà matā̀sā;
the ~ should help the old yā kàmātà yârā
sù tàimàki tsòfàffī.

**your, yours** *pro, see* Appendix A.

**yourself, yourselves** *pro, see* self, Appendix A.

**youth** *n* a. (*period in life*) ƙùrùciyā *f,*
yàrìntā *f;* (*of girls*) 'yammātancì *m:*
she spent her ~ in the village tā
yi 'yammātancìntà à ƙauyè; in his
~ à cikin ƙùrùciyaŕsà = à cikin
yàrìntaŕsà; in the prime of his ~ à cikin
gāniyàŕ ƙùrùciyaŕsà. b. (*young psn.*)
sauràyī *m* ⟨sàmā̀rī⟩, matā̀shī *m:* they
are mere ~s, they don't know anything sū
sàmā̀rī nè, bà sù san kōmē ba; today's ~
sàmā̀rin zāmànī; correctional facility for
~ makaŕantaŕ hòron matā̀sā.

**youthfulness** *n* (*state, quality of being
young, a child*) yà̀ràntakā̀ *f,* sàmā̀ŕtakā̀ *f.*

**Zarma** *n* a. (*member of ethnic group*)
bàzabaŕmè̀ *m.* b. (*language*) zabaŕmancī
*m.*

**zeal** *n* ƙwā̀zō *m,* himmā̀ *f;* attack, do sth. with
~ dìŕkākà *v2:* they worked with ~ sun
dìŕkàki aikì̄ = sun mai dà himmā̀ gà
aikì̄.

**zealot** *n* mài tsàttsauran ŕa'àyī *n.*

**zebra** *n* jàkin dawà *m.*

**zenith** *n* gāniyà̀ *f.*

**zero** *quant* sifìŕī *m:* the number is 506
lambàŕsà bìyaŕ sifìŕī shidà; the final
score of the game was 0 to 3 wā̀sân yā
tāshì sifìŕī dà ukù; we were beaten 5
to 0 an cī mù bìyaŕ bâ kō ɗaya.

**zigzag** *adj & v* a. (*esp. of a road*) (mài)
wàndàŕ-wandaŕ *idph,* (mài) kwàne-kwàne
*p:* the road ~s a lot hanyà̀ cè mài yawàn
kwàne-kwàne. b. (*type of stitch*) zīzà̀ *f:*
he sewed the hem with a ~ stitch yā yi
wà kàlmasà̀ zīzà̀.

**zinc** *n* (*corrugated roofing material*) kwānò̀
*m.*

**zip** *v* (*open or shut*) jā zîk.

**zipper** *n* zîk/ zîf *m,* [F] zî *m:* open, close
a ~ jā zîk.

**zodiac** *n:* sign of the ~ bùŕūjì̀ ⟨ai⟩:

**zone** *n* shiyyà̀ *f* ⟨oCi⟩, ɓangarè̀ *m.*

**zoo** *n* gidan zû *m,* gidan dabbōbī *m.*

**zoology** *n* ilìmin sanìn dabbōbī *m.*

**zorilla** *n* bò̀darī *m* ⟨ai⟩.

# APPENDIX A

# Hausa Pronoun Paradigms

Hausa distinguishes eight pronouns in non-subject uses and nine as subjects. The ninth is an "impersonal" pronoun, usually corresponding to English "one does" or "they do". Gender is distinctive in the second and third persons singular only. The pronominal categories refer to the following persons and are coded accordingly:

| | | |
|---|---|---|
| *first person singular* | 1s | "I, me, my, mine" |
| *second person masculine singular* | 2m | "you, your, yours" |
| *second person feminine singular* | 2f | "you, your, yours" |
| *third person masculine singular* | 3m | "he, him, his, it, its" |
| *third person feminine singular* | 3f | "she, her, hers, it, its" |
| *first person plural* | 1p | "we, us, our, ours" |
| *second person plural* | 2p | "you, your, yours" |
| *third person plural* | 3p | "they, them, their, theirs" |
| *impersonal* | 4p | "one" or "they" |

Each pronoun belongs to a grammatically determined paradigm. These paradigms reflect syntactic functions (e.g. direct object, indirect object) and, in the case of the subject pronouns, the tense/aspect/mood employed. Each paradigm below is illustrated by short examples.

## I. Non-Tense/Aspect Pronouns

### Independent

| | | | | |
|---|---|---|---|---|
| *1s* | nī | | *1p* | mū |
| *2m* | kai | | | |
| *2f* | kē | | *2p* | kū |
| *3m* | shī | | | |
| *3f* | ita | | *3p* | sū |

*Examples:*

| | |
|---|---|
| he is the chief | shī sarkī nḕ |
| it was you (f) we saw | kē cḕ mukà ganī |
| Ladi returned with it | Lādì tā dāwō dà shī |

### Direct Object

| | A. of Grade 1 & 4 verbs | B. of all other verbs |
|---|---|---|
| *1s* | ni | nì |
| *2m* | ka | kà |
| *2f* | ki | kì |
| *3m* | shi | shì |
| *3f* | ta | tà |
| *1p* | mu | mù |
| *2p* | ku | kù |
| *3p* | su | sù |

*Examples:*

| the police caught them | 'yan sàndā sun kāmà̃ su |
|---|---|
| they investigated it | sun bincìkē shi |
| she asked them | tā tàmbàyē sù |
| Ladi saw her yesterday | Lādì tā gan tà jiyà |

## Indirect Object

| | | | |
|---|---|---|---|
| *1s* | minì (= mîn) | *1p* | manà̃ |
| *2m* | makà (= mā, mâ) | | |
| *2f* | mikì | *2p* | mukù |
| *3m* | masà (= mishì) | | |
| *3f* | matà | *3p* | musù |

*Examples:*

| don't tell her the news | kadà kà gayà̃ matà là̃bāřì |
| --- | --- |
| I bought it for you | nā sayō makà |

## Free Possessive

| | A. Referring to *m/p* noun | B. Referring to *f* noun |
|---|---|---|
| *1s* | nà̃wa | tà̃wa |
| *2m* | nākà | tākà |
| *2f* | nākì | tākì |
| *3m* | nāsà | tāsà |
| *3f* | nātà | tātà |
| *1p* | nāmù | tāmù |
| *2p* | nākù | tākù |
| *3p* | nāsù | tāsù |

*Examples:*

| these pencils are mine | fensiřōřin nàn nà̃wa nè̃ |
| --- | --- |
| yours is better | tākà tā fi kyâu |
| that robe of his | tāsà rìgâř |

## Suffixed Possessive

| | A. Referring to *m/p* noun | B. Referring to *f* noun |
|---|---|---|
| *1s* | -nā | -tā |
| *2m* | -nkà | -řkà (=-kkà) |
| *2f* | -nkì | -řkì (=-kkì) |
| *3m* | -nsà | -řsà (=-ssà) |
| *3f* | -ntà | -řtà (=-ttà) |
| *1p* | -nmù | -řmù (=-mmù) |
| *2p* | -nkù | -řkù (=-kkù) |
| *3p* | -nsù | -řsù (=-ssù) |

*Examples:*

| | |
|---|---|
| is that your cap? | waccàn hũlar̃kà cē? |
| I hid the money in it | nā ɓōyè kuɗîn à cikinsà |
| we are waiting for them | munà jirànsù |
| on his arrival, we told him | dà isôwar̃sà, mun gayà masà |

## Reflexive

| | | | |
|---|---|---|---|
| *1s* | kâinā | *1p* | kânmù |
| *2m* | kânkà | | |
| *2f* | kânkì | *2p* | kânkù |
| *3m* | kânsà | | |
| *3f* | kântà | *3p* | kânsù |

*Examples:*

| | |
|---|---|
| they cheated themselves | sun cǔci kânsù |
| I fixed the car myself | nā gyārà mōtà dà kâinā |

# II. Tense/Aspect Pronouns

## Subjunctive

| | | | |
|---|---|---|---|
| *1s* | ìn | *1p* | mù |
| *2m* | kà | *2p* | kù |
| *2f* | kì | | |
| *3m* | yà | *3p* | sù |
| *3f* | tà | *4p* | à |

*Examples:*

| | |
|---|---|
| I want them to stay | inà sô sù zaunà |
| you'd better go now | gwàmmà kì tàfi yànzu |
| tell them I'm coming | kà gayà musù inà zuwà |

## Negative Subjunctive

The negative of the subjunctive is formed by using the prohibitive particle
**kadà/kâr̃** "don't" with a subjunctive pronoun.

*Examples:*

| | |
|---|---|
| don't do that again! | kâr̃ kù sākè yîn wànnan! |
| I told him not to run | nā gayà masà kadà yà gudù |

## Completive

| 1s | nā | | 1p | mun |
|----|----|----|----|-----|
| 2m | kā | | 2p | kun |
| 2f | kin | | | |
| 3m | yā | | 3p | sun |
| 3f | tā | | 4p | an |

*Examples:*

| we pounded the corn | mun dakà hatsī |
|---|---|
| they ran to school | sun gudù zuwā̀ makař̃antā |
| they (*impers*) praised him | an yi masà yàbō̄ |

## Negative Completive

| 1s | bàn...ba | | 1p | bà mù...ba |
|----|----------|----|----|------------|
| 2m | bà kà...ba | | 2p | bà kù...ba |
| 2f | bà kì...ba | | | |
| 3m | bài...ba | | 3p | bà sù...ba |
| 3f | bà tà...ba | | 4p | bà à...ba |

*Examples:*

| we didn't pound corn | bà mù dakà hatsī ba |
|---|---|
| they didn't run to school | bà sù gudù zuwā̀ makař̃antā ba |
| he wasn't praised | bà à yi masà yàbō̄ ba |

## Relative Completive[1]

| 1s | na | | 1p | mukà |
|----|----|----|----|------|
| 2m | ka | | 2p | kukà |
| 2f | kikà | | | |
| 3m | ya | | 3p | sukà |
| 3f | ta | | 4p | akà |

*Examples:*

| here is the corn we pounded | gā̀ hatsîn dà mukà dakā̀ |
|---|---|
| who (*pl*) ran to school? | su wā̀ sukà gudù zuwā̀ makař̃antā? |
| how did they praise him? | yā̀yā̀ akà yi masà yàbō̄? |

## Continuous

| 1s | inā̀ | | 1p | munā̀ |
|----|------|----|----|-------|
| 2m | kanā̀ | | 2p | kunā̀ |
| 2f | kinā̀ | | | |
| 3m | yanā̀ | | 3p | sunā̀ |
| 3f | tanā̀ | | 4p | anā̀ |

---

[1] Affirmative only.

*Examples:*

| | |
|---|---|
| she is pounding the corn | tanā̀ dakà hatsī |
| I am waiting for them | inā̀ jirànsù |
| he always helps his father[2] | kullum yanā̀ tàimakon mahàifinsà |
| Audu has a car | Audù (ya)nā̀ dà mōtā̀[3] |

## Negative Continuous

A. With verbal/stative/
   locative predicates

B. With "have" predicates

| | | |
|---|---|---|
| *1s* | bā̄ nā̀ | bâ ni |
| *2m* | bā̄ kā̀ | bâ ka |
| *2f* | bā̄ kyā̀ | bâ ki |
| *3m* | bā̄ yā̀ | bâ shi |
| *3f* | bā̄ tā̀ | bâ ta |
| *1p* | bā̄ mā̀ | bâ mu |
| *2p* | bā̄ kwā̀ | bâ ku |
| *3p* | bā̄ sā̀ | bâ su |
| *4p* | bā̄ ā̀ | bâ a |

*Examples:*

| | |
|---|---|
| she isn't pounding corn now | bā̄ tā̀ dakà hatsī yànzu |
| I am not waiting for her | bā̄ nā̀ jiràntà |
| Audu doesn't have a car | Audù bâ shi dà mōtā̀ |
| the boy isn't at school | yāròn bā̄ yā̀ makařantā |

## Relative Continuous[4]

A. With verbal predicates

B. With non-verbal predicates

| | | |
|---|---|---|
| *1s* | nakè̄ | nakè |
| *2m* | kakè̄ | kakè |
| *2f* | kikè̄ | kikè |
| *3m* | yakè̄ | yakè |
| *3f* | takè̄ | takè |
| *1p* | mukè̄ | mukè |
| *2p* | kukè̄ | kukè |
| *3p* | sukè̄ | sukè |
| *4p* | akè̄ | akè |

*Examples:*

| | |
|---|---|
| I don't know who is pounding corn | bàn san wâddà takè̄ dakà hatsī ba |
| he's not the one we're waiting for | bā̀ shī nè̄ wândà mukè̄ jirànsà ba |

---

[2] The continuous is often used to express habitual action.

[3] With noun subjects, the 3rd person pronouns **ya/ta/su** may be optionally deleted.

[4] Affirmative only.

where are the children now?       ìnā yârā sukè yànzu?

I don't know if the door is open    bàn san kō ƙōfȁ à bǔɗe takè ba

which student has a car?        wànè ɗālìbī kȅ dà mōtȁ?[5]


## Future

| | | | |
|---|---|---|---|
| *1s* | zân | *1p* | zā mù |
| *2m* | zā kà | *2p* | zā kù |
| *2f* | zā kì | | |
| *3m* | zâi | *3p* | zā sù |
| *3f* | zā tà | *4p* | zā à |

*Examples:*

she will pound corn tomorrow  zā tà dakà hatsī gȍbe

they (*impers*) will praise him   zā à yi masà yàbō


## Negative Future

| | | | |
|---|---|---|---|
| *1s* | bà zân...ba | *1p* | bà zā mù...ba |
| *2m* | bà zā kà...ba | *2p* | bà zā kù...ba |
| *2f* | bà zā kì...ba | | |
| *3m* | bà zâi...ba | *3p* | bà zā sù...ba |
| *3f* | bà zā tà...ba | *4p* | bà zā à...ba |

*Example:*

she won't pound corn tomorrow bà zā tà dakà hatsī gȍbe ba


## Potential/Indefinite Future

| | | | |
|---|---|---|---|
| *1s* | nâ | *1p* | mâ |
| *2m* | kâ | *2p* | kwâ |
| *2f* | kyâ | | |
| *3m* | tâ | *3p* | sâ |
| *3f* | yâ | *4p* | â |

*Examples:*

  you'll gradually be able to do it yâu dà gȍbe kâ iyȁ

  one day he will be praised     wata rānā â yi masà yàbō

---

[5]With noun subjects, the 3rd person pronouns ya/ta/su may be optionally deleted, in which case **kȅ** always has a long vowel.

## Negative Potential Future

| | | | |
|---|---|---|---|
| *1s* | bà nâ...ba | *1p* | bà mâ...ba |
| *2m* | bà kâ...ba | *2p* | bà kwâ...ba |
| *2f* | bà kyâ...ba | | |
| *3m* | bà yâ...ba | *3p* | bà sâ...ba |
| *3f* | bà tâ...ba | *4p* | bà â...ba |

*Example:*
you (*f*) might not pass the exam   bà kyâ ci jařřàbâwā ba


## Habitual

| | | | |
|---|---|---|---|
| *1s* | nakàn | *1p* | mukàn |
| *2m* | kakàn | *2p* | kukàn |
| *2f* | kikàn | | |
| *3m* | yakàn | *3p* | sukàn |
| *3f* | takàn | *4p* | akàn |

*Examples:*

we usually wake up at 7            mukàn tāshì dà ƙarfè bakwài

he goes to Wudil every Tuesday    yakàn jē Wùdil kōwàcè ran Tàlātà

NOTE: The negative of the habitual, bà̀...ba, is rarely used; instead, the negative continuous is employed to express negative customary action.

# APPENDIX B

# Pronunciation of Hausa Personal Names

The following is a selected list of commonly used Hausa personal names. It consists of three types of names: (a) Islamic proper names (known as **sūnan yankā** and considered a person's true name); (b) other traditional names or contracted forms of Islamic names (known as **sūnan rānā**); and (c) "nicknames" (known as **laƙabī**) or names that have traditional associations with other specific names. This list is intended primarily for pronunciation purposes. Thus there is no attempt to relate variants of the same name (apart from minor phonological alternations separated by a slash) nor to point out semantic or cultural relationships between specific names. The names are presented in alphabetical order, with men's names first followed by women's names.

## Masculine

Abbà, Abdù, Àbdùlƙādìr̃, Àbdùllāhì/Abdullāhì, Àbdùlmālìk, Àbdùlsàlâm, Àbdùr̃r̃àhàmân, Àbūbakàr̃, Àdàmu/Ādamù, Àdō, Ahmàd, Àr̃īlù, Àlhajì, Àli, Àliyù, Àmadù, Àmīnù, Āmir̃ù, Àtīkù, Àttā, Àttāhir̃ù, Audù, Àwwalù, Ayūbà.

Bàgàri, Bàgudù, Bàƙo, Bàlā, Bàlàr̃abè, Bàr̃ā'ù, Bashàr̃i, Bàshîr̃, Bàtūr̃è, Bāwà, Bellò, Bir̃aimà, Būbà, Bùhār̃i, Bukàr̃.

Cindò.

Dābò, Daudā̀, Dīnì, Dōgo, Dūnà.

Dāhir̃ù, Dàlhatù, Dan Àsàbe, Dan Àutā, Dan Azūmi, Dan Jūmà, Dan Kàka, Dan Lādì, Dan Làmî, Dan Lār̃ai, Dan Lìti, Dan Màrka, Dan Tàlā, Dan Yārò, Dàyyabù.

Fàr̃uƙù.

Gàmbo, Gar̃bà, Gwadabè.

Hàbîb, Hàbībù, Hàbū, Hāfizù, Haladù, Hàlīlù, Hamīdù, Hāmisù, Hāmu, Hamzà, Har̃ū, Har̃ūnà, Hasàn, Hāshìm, Hāshimù, Hùsainì.

Ibr̃ā, Ìbr̃āhìm, Ibr̃ō, Ìdī, Ìdìr̃îs, Igudà, Īlà, Iliyā, Iliyāsù, Īlù, Inūsà, Inuwà, Īr̃o, Īsā, Isihù, Isiyā, Isiyākù, Ìsmā'īlà, Ìsmā'īlù.

Jàfar̃ù, Jàlālù, Jàtau, Jìbìr̃în, Jibò̀, Jìlāni, Jūmà.

Kàbīr̃ù, Kàka, Kàllā, Kàllamù, Kyàuta.

Lawàl, Lawàn, Lìmâm.

Mà'āzù, Madù, Magàji, Màhammàn, Màì Kanò̀, Màì Kuɗi, Màì R̃īga, Màì Tàlātā̀, Màì Wàdā, Màlle, Mammadā, Mammàn, Màmūdà, Màmūdù, Mānī, Mānù, Mànzō, Màtī, Màude, Mijìnyawà, Mūdī, Mùhammadù, Mùntār̃i, Mūsā, Mustàfā, Mùtār̃i.

Na-Dābò, Na-Jùme, Na-Sīdì, Nāsir̃ù, Nuhù, Nūr̃à.

Rābi'ù, Rùfā'i.

Sà'ādù, Sābi'ù, Sadaukī, Sàdi, Sādī, SàdīƘù, Sādisù, Sà'Īdù, Sālè, Sālihù, Sālisù, Sàmā'Īlà, Sambò, Sāminù, Sàmmāni, Sandà, Sāni, Sarki, Saunà, Shēhù, Shù'aibù, Sīdì, Sulè, Sulèmānù.

Talle, Tallàfi, TànĪmù, Tankò, Tijjằ, Tìjjāni.

Tsàlhā.

Ùmmaɍù/Ūmaɍù, Ùsùmānù/Usumānù.

Wàdā, Wāli.

Yàhàyā, Yàhūzā, YàƘubù, Yārò, Yunūsà, Yūsī, Yūsufù.

Zàilāni, Zakaɍì.

# Feminine

NOTE: The feminine suffix -u/-tu in Islamic proper names derived from Arabic is being increasingly dropped in Hausa; it has generally been omitted from this list.

Ābù, Adamà, Ā'i, Ā'ishā, Àlti, AmĪnà/AmĪnā, Àsàbe, Àsmā'ù, Àtìne, Azùmi.

Bàtūɍìyā, Bìlki, BìlkĪsù, Bintà, Bìntu.

Dēlằ, Dēlu, Dìje, Dūdù(wā).

Fādìmatù, Fàtī, Fātimà.

Gimbìyā, Gōɗì, Gòshi, Gwāri.

Hàbī, Habībà, Hàdīzà, Hàfsatù, Hajìyā, Hàlīmà, Hànnatù, Hànne, Hasànā, Hàwwa, Husàinā.

Ìndō, Innà.

Jàɍu, Jummai.

Kằka, Kànde, Kyàllu, Kyàuta.

Lādì/Lādī, Lằdīdī, Lằmî, Lằɍàbā, Lēkò.

Màimunà, Mài Rìga, Màiɍo, Magājìyā, Mằɍī, Māɍìyā, Màrka, Maɍyàm, Munāɍi.

Rābi, Ràhīlā, RuƘàyya.

Sà'ā, Sà'ādatù, Sàlāmatù, Sāɍà, Sāɍatù, Shàtu/Shatù, Shēkàrā.

Tàlā, Tàlātù(wā), Talle, Tànî, Ta-Sallà, Ta-Sīdì, Tūɍai.

Uwāni.

Yàlwa.

'Yaɍ Àutā, 'Yaɍ KōƘì.

Zàhàɍā, Zàinabù, Zằɍa.

# APPENDIX C

# Pronouncing Gazetteer: Nigeria and Niger

The following is a selected list of place names in the Hausa-speaking parts of Nigeria and Niger. Also included are Hausa names for some non-Hausa towns from other areas of Nigeria and Niger. For Nigeria, the states and their abbreviations are also given.

## Nigeria Nìjḗřiyà/Nàjḗřiyà

### States

| | | | | | | |
|---|---|---|---|---|---|---|
| Akwa-Ibom | AK | Àkwā-Ibòm | Katsina | KT | Kàtsinà |
| Anambra | AN | Ànambařa | Kwara | KW | Kwārà |
| Bauchi | BC | Bauci | Lagos | LG | Lēgàs |
| Bendel | BD | Bendèl | Niger | NG | Nējà |
| Benue | BN | Binuwài | Ogun | OG | Ògun |
| Borno | BR | Bàřno | Ondo | OD | Òndo |
| Cross River | CR | — | Oyo | OY | Ŏyo |
| Gongola | GG | Gwàngōlà | Plateau | PL | Filàtô |
| Imo | IM | Imò | Rivers | RV | — |
| Kaduna | KD | Kàdūna | Sokoto | SK | Sakkwato |
| Kano | KN | Kanŏ | | | |

### Cities and Towns

| | | | | | | |
|---|---|---|---|---|---|---|
| Aba | IM | Aba | Dambatta | KN | Ɗambattà |
| Abeokuta | OG | Àbēkùta | Daura | KT | Dàurā |
| Abuja | Fed.C.T. | Àbūjā | Dikwa | BR | Dìkuwa |
| Akure | OD | Àkūřè | Dutsen Ma | KT | Dūtsèn Mā |
| Apapa | LG | Àfāřa | Dutsen Wai | KD | Dūtsèn Wài |
| Argungu | SK | Argungù(n) | Dutsi | KN | Dūtsè |
| Auchi | BD | Auci | Enugu | AN | Inugù |
| Azare | BC | Azàře | Fika | BR | Fìkà |
| Badagari | LG | Bàdāgàři | Funtua | KT | Fùntuwà |
| Bauchi | BC | Bauci | Garko | KN | Gařkò |
| Benin City | BD | Biřnin Bìni | Gashua | BR | Gashùwa |
| Bichi | KN | Bicì | Gboko | BN | Bŏkò |
| Bida | NG | Biddà | Geidam | BR | Gàidam |
| Birnin Gwari | KD | Biřnin Gwāri | Gobir | SK | Gŏbiř |
| Birnin Kebbi | SK | Biřnin Kabì | Gombe | BC | Gwàmbè |
| Birnin Kudu | KN | Biřnin Kudù | Gumel | KN | Gumàl |
| Birniwa | KN | Bìřnīwà | Gusau | SK | Gùsau |
| Biu | BR | Bìyû | Gwandu | SK | Gwandu |
| Calabar | CR | Kàlàba | Gwaram | KN | Gwàřam |
| Dala | KN | Dàla | Gwarzo | KN | Gwāřzo |
| Damaturu | BR | Damātuřu | Hadejia | KN | Haɗējà |

| | | | | | | |
|---|---|---|---|---|---|---|
| Ibadan | OY | Bǎdùn/Ìbǎdàn | Malumfashi | KT | Malumfāshi |
| Ife | OY | Ife | Minna | NG | Mìnà |
| Ijebu | OG | Ìjěbu | Misau | BC | Mìsàu |
| Ikara | KD | Ìkǎřà | Mubi | GG | Mūbì |
| Ikeja | LG | Ìkējà | Nasarawa | PL | Nasařāwā |
| Ilesha | OY | Ìlēshà | Nguru | BR | Guřu |
| Ilorin | KW | Ìlǒři/Ìlǒři | Nsukka | AN | Ìnsukà |
| Isa | SK | Īsà | Okene | KW | Òkēne |
| Jahun | KN | Jāhùn | Onitsha | AN | Ànàcà |
| Jalingo | GG | Jālingò | Owerri | IM | Ùwěři |
| Jamaare | BC | Jama'ārè | Owo | OD | Ŏwo |
| Jebba | KW | Jabà | Port Harcourt | RV | Fatākwàl |
| Jega | SK | Jěga | Potiskum | BR | Fatāskùm(à) |
| Jibiya | KT | Jibiyà | Rano | KN | Rano |
| Jos | PL | Jàs | Rigachikun | KD | Rìgǎcikun |
| Kabba | KW | Kabbà | Ringim | KN | Ringìm |
| Kachia | KD | Kàciya | Sabon Birni | SK | Sābon Biřni |
| Kaduna | KD | Kàdūna | Sardauna | BR | Sàrdauna |
| Kafanchan | KD | Kàfàncàn | Shendam | PL | Shàndam |
| Kaita | KD | Kaita | Soba | KD | Sōbǎ |
| Kano | KN | Kanǒ | Sokoto | SK | Sakkwato |
| Katagum | BC | Katāgùm | Takum | GG | Tākùm |
| Katsina | KT | Kàtsinà | Tureta | SK | Turētà |
| Kaura Namoda | SK | Kaurař Namōdà | Wudil | KN | Wùdil |
| Kazaure | KN | Kàzaure | Wukari | GG | Wùkāři |
| Keffi | PL | Kafì | Yankari | BC | Yànkàri |
| Kontagora | NJ | Kwàntàgǒra | Yashi | KD | Yǎshi |
| Lafia | PL | Lāřiyà | Yawuri | SK | Yāwùri |
| Lagos | LG | Ìkko/Lēgàs | Yelwa | SK | Yàlwa |
| Lokoja | KW | Lakwajà | Yola | GG | 'Yōlà |
| Mafuta | SK | Mahūta | Zamfara | KT | Zàmfàrà |
| Maiduguri | BR | Màidugùři | Zaria | KD | Zāriyà/Zazzàu |
| Makurdi | BN | Makuřdi | Zuru | SK | Zūřu |

## Niger Nìjâř

### Towns and Other Place Names

| | | | |
|---|---|---|---|
| Adar | Ādàř | Maradi | Marādi |
| Agades | Agadàs/Àgadàs | Matamaye | Mātāmâi |
| Azben | Azbìn/Abzìn | Mirria | Miryà |
| Birnin Konni | (Biřnin) Kwànni | Niamey | Yàmài/Yàmè |
| Damagaram | Dàmagàřam | Niger River | Kǒgin Īsà |
| Diffa | Dìfa | Sahara | Sàhàřā |
| Dogondoutchi | Dōgon Dūtsì | Tahoua | Tǎwa |
| Dosso | Dǒso | Tanout | Tānìt |
| Filingue | Hilinge | Tasawa | Tāsāwā |
| Kurfay | Kuřfai | Tenere | Taněře |
| Madawa | Mādāwā | Zinder | Zàndâř |

# APPENDIX D

# Pronouncing Gazetteer: Foreign Names

The following is a selected list of foreign geographical names (countries, continents, cities, and bodies of water) which have their own Hausa spelling and pronunciation.

| | | | |
|---|---|---|---|
| Accra | Ànkàřà | Lake Chad | Tafkìn Cādì |
| Africa | Afiřkà | Lebanon | Labanàn |
| Algeria | Àljēriyà | Liberia | Làbēřiyà |
| America | Amìřkà/Àmēřikà | Libya | Libiyà |
| Angola | Àngōlà | London | Landàn |
| Australia | Òstàřēliyà | Malawi | Màlāwì |
| Baghdad | Bàgàdāzà | Mali | Mālì |
| Beirut | Bàiřût/Bàiřûl | Mauritania | Mŏřìtāniyà |
| Benin | Bĩni | Mecca | Makà |
| Botswana | Bàswānà | Medina | Màdīnà |
| Britain | Biřìtāniyà | Mediterranean Sea | Bàhàř Rûm |
| Burkina Faso | Bùřkīnà Fāsò | Morocco | Màřōkò |
| Burundi | Bùřundì | Mozambique | Màzambìk |
| Cairo | Àlḵāhiřà/Kaiřò | Netherlands | (Kasař) Hōlàn |
| Cameroon | Kàmàřû | Niger River | Kŏgin Kwārà |
| Canada | Kyànàdā | Nile River | Kŏgin Nîl |
| Chad | Cādì | Pakistan | Pākistàn |
| China | Sin/Cainà | Palestine | Pàlàsďīnù |
| Congo Republic | Kwangò | Paris | Pāřìs |
| Damascus | Dàmaskàs | Red Sea | Bàhàř Māliyà |
| Egypt | Masàř/Misiřà | Rome | (Biřnin) Rûm |
| England | Ingìlà | Russia | Rāshà |
| Ethiopia | Habashà | Rwanda | Rùwandà |
| France | Fàřansà/Fàřanshì | Saudi Arabia | Kasař Makà |
| Gabon | Gàbôn | Senegal | Sinigàl |
| Gambia | Gambìyà | Sierra Leone | Sàlìyô |
| Ghana | Gānà | Somalia | Sŏmāliyà |
| Guinea | Ginì | South Africa | Afiřkà ta Kudù |
| Guinea-Bissau | Ginì Bìsau | Sudan | Sùdân |
| India | Indìyà | Syria | Shâm/Sĩřiyà |
| Indonesia | Ìndùnūsiyà | Tanzania | Tànzāniyà |
| Iran (Persia) | Ìřân (Fāřisà) | Timbuktu | Tàmbūtù |
| Iraq | Ìřàḵ | Togo | Tōgò |
| Istanbul | Sàntàmbûl | Tripoli | Tařābulùs |
| Italy | Ìtāliyà | Tunisia | Tùnūsiyà |
| Ivory Coast | Ābiřù Kwâs | Uganda | Yùgandà |
| Japan | Jàpân | W. Germany | Jāmùs ta Yâmma |
| Jerusalem | (Biřnin) Ḵudùs | Yemen | Yamàl |
| Kenya | Kenyà | Zaire | Zàyâř |
| Kuwait | Kwìyât | Zambia | Zambìyà |

# APPENDIX E

# Names of Organizations

## Nigerian Federal Ministries and Agencies

The following is a selected list of Nigerian federal government ministries and agencies and their equivalent names in Hausa. (In the list below, "M. of" = "Ministry of".)

| | |
|---|---|
| Bureau of Motor Vehicles | Ōfìshin Lāsīsìn Mōtà |
| Directorate for Social Mobilization (MAMSA) | Hùkūmàr̃ Wāyar̃ dà Kân Jàma'à |
| M. of Agriculture, Water Resources, & Rural Development | Ma'aikatar̃ Har̃kōkin Nōmā dà Sāmar̃ dà Ruwā dà Rāyà Kàrkarā |
| M. of Aviation | Ma'aikatar̃ Zìr̃gàr̃-Zìr̃gar̃ Jirãgen Samà |
| M. of Communications | Ma'aikatar̃ Sādâr̃wā |
| M. of Defense | Ma'aikatar̃ Tsàrō |
| M. of Economic Affairs | Ma'aikatar̃ Tsārà Tattalin Ar̃zìkin Kasā |
| M. of Education | Ma'aikatar̃ Ilìmī |
| M. of Employment, Labor, & Productivity | Ma'aikatar̃ Sāmar̃ dà Aikìn Yî dà Kwādagō dà Ingàntà Nàgàr̃tar̃ Aikì |
| M. of External Affairs | Ma'aikatar̃ Har̃kōkin Wàje |
| M. of Federal Capital Territory | Ma'aikatar̃ Kùlā dà Sābon Bàbban Birnin Tàrayyà Àbūjā |
| M. of Finance & Economic Development | Ma'aikatar̃ Kuɗī dà Rāyà Kasā |
| M. of Health | Ma'aikatar̃ Kīwòn Lāfiyà |
| M. of Industry | Ma'aikatar̃ Màsànã'àntū |
| M. of Information & Culture | Ma'aikatar̃ Làbàr̃ai dà Àl'àdū |
| M. of Internal Affairs | Ma'aikatar̃ Har̃kōkin Cikin Gidā |
| M. of Justice | Ma'aikatar̃ Shàr̃i'à |
| M. of Mines, Power, & Steel | Ma'aikatar̃ Mà'àdìnai dà Làntar̃kì dà Kar̃àr̃ā |
| M. of Petroleum Resources | Ma'aikatar̃ Mâi |
| M. of Science & Technology | Ma'aikatar̃ Kìmiyyà dà Fàsāhà |
| M. of Social Development, Youth, & Sports | Ma'aikatar̃ Kyautàtà Rãyuwar̃ Jàma'à dà Matàsā dà Wàsànnī |
| M. of Trade | Ma'aikatar̃ Cìnikī |
| M. of Transport | Ma'aikatar̃ Sufùr̃ī |
| M. of Works & Housing | Ma'aikatar̃ Ayyukà dà Gidàjē |
| National Electric Corp. (NEPA) | Hùkūmàr̃ Bā dà Wutar̃ Làntar̃kì |
| Water Resources & Energy Construction Agency (WRECA) | Hùkūmàr̃ Gìne-Gìne dà Bā dà Ruwan Shâ |

## Foreign and International Organizations

The following is a selected list of international organizations and their equivalent names in Hausa. (In the list below, "Int'l" = "International" and "MDD" = Màjàlisàřˍ Ďinkìn Dūniyà̀.)

| | |
|---|---|
| Amnesty Int'l | Kungìyař Ahuwà̄ ta Dūniyà̀ |
| Arab League | Kungìyař Kasà̄shen Lā̄řabā̄wā |
| Atomic Energy Agency | Hùkūmàř Al'amuřàn Nūkìliyà̀ ta Kasà̄shen Dūniyà̀ |
| Council of Europe | Kungìyař Kasà̄shen Tūřai |
| ECOWAS | Kungìyař Tattalin Ařzìkin Kasà̄shen Afiřkà ta Yâmma |
| EEC | Hùkūmàř Kà̀suwař Tà̀rayyà̀ř Tūřai |
| Int'l Labor Organization (ILO) | Kungìyař Kwādagō ta Dūniyà̀ |
| Int'l Monetary Fund (IMF) | Asūsùn Fasàltà Kuɗà̀ɗē dà Bā dà Ràncē na Dūniyà̀ |
| League of Nations | Tsōhuwař Màjàlisà̀ř Ďinkìn Dūniyà̀ |
| NASA | Ma'aikatař Bìncìken Sararin Sàmāniyà̀ |
| NATO | Kungìyař Kà̀wàncē ta Kasà̄shen Yammacī |
| OAU | Kungìyař Haɗà Kân Afìřkà |
| OPEC | Kungìyař Kasà̄shē Màsu Ařzìkin Mân Fētùř |
| Red Cross | Kungìyař Ā̄gàjī ta Red Cross |
| United Nations (UN) | Màjàlisà̀ř Ďinkìn Dūniyà̀ (MDD) |
| UN Development Program | Kungìyař Rāyà Kasà̄shen Màsu Tāsōwā ta MDD |
| UN FAO | Kungìyař Àbinci dà Aikìn Nōmā ta MDD |
| UN General Assembly | Bàbban Tà̄ron MDD |
| UN Int'l Court of Justice | Kōtùn MDD |
| UN Office on Refugee Matters | Ō̄fìshin Kùlā dà 'Yan Gudùn Hijiřā na MDD |
| UN Security Council | Kwàmìtîn Sulhù na MDD |
| UNESCO | Kungìyař Kyautàtà Ilìmī dà Kĭmiyyà̀ dà Àl'ādū ta MDD |
| UNICEF | Asūsùn Tàimakon Yârā na MDD |
| UN WHO | Kungìyař Lāfiyà̀ ta MDD |
| USAID | Hùkūmàř Rāyà Kasà̄shen Màsu Tāsōwā ta Amìřkà |
| World Bank | Bankìn Dūniyà̀ |

# APPENDIX F

# Currency Systems of Nigeria and Niger

## Nigeria

The basic unit of currency in Nigeria is the **naira** (abbreviated as "₦"), which consists of 100 **kobo** (abbreviated as "k"). Some of the coins and currency notes have popular names by which they are known.

*Coins:*

| | |
|---|---|
| lk | kwabõ |
| 5k | k. bìyař = sīsì |
| 10k | k. gõmà = sulè |
| 25k | k. àshìřin dà bìyař = dalà |
| 50k | k. hàmsin = sulè bìyař |

*Notes:*

| | |
|---|---|
| 50k | k. hàmsin = sulè bìyař |
| ₦1 | naiřà |
| ₦5 | n. bìyař = mài Tafāwà Bàlēwà |
| ₦10 | n. gõmà = bàlamā |
| ₦20 | n. àshìřin = 'yař Muřtàlà |

## Niger

The basic unit of currency in Niger is the CFA **franc**. The 1 franc coin, called **tammā** *f*, is rare, as is the 2 franc coin, called **kwabõ** *m*. The smallest functional unit is 5 francs or **dalà** *f*. For 1,000 francs and above, the basic unit is **jìkā** *f*.

*Coins:*

| | |
|---|---|
| CFA5 | dalà |
| CFA10 | d. biyu |
| CFA25 | d. bìyař |
| CFA50 | d. gõmà |
| CFA100 | d. àshìřin |

*Notes:*

| | |
|---|---|
| CFA500 | 'yař ɗàrī |
| CFA1,000 | 'yař jìkā |
| CFA5,000 | 'yař jìkā bìyař |
| CFA10,000 | 'yař jìkā gõmà |
| CFA1,000,000 | 'yař jìkā dubū |

The following terms are provided to help the learner count in CFA francs using bases of 5 and 1,000.

| | |
|---|---|
| 5 | dalà |
| 50 | d. gõmà |
| 100 | d. àshìřin |
| 200 | d. àřbà'in |
| 250 | d. hàmsin |
| 375 | d. sàbà'in dà bìyař |
| 500 | d. ɗàrī |
| 700 | d. ɗàrī dà àřbà'in |

| | |
|---|---|
| 1,000 | jìkā |
| 1,500 | j. dà dalà ɗàrī = j. dà rabì |
| 2,000 | j. biyu |
| 5,000 | j. bìyař |
| 7,500 | j. bakwài dà dalà ɗàrī |
| 10,000 | j. gõmà |
| 100,000 | j. ɗàrī |
| 200,000 | j. mètan = j. ɗàrī biyu |